Annual Review of Food Science and Technology

Production Editor: Absolom J. Hagg
Bibliographic Quality Control: Mary A. Glass
Electronic Content Coordinator: Suzanne K. Moses

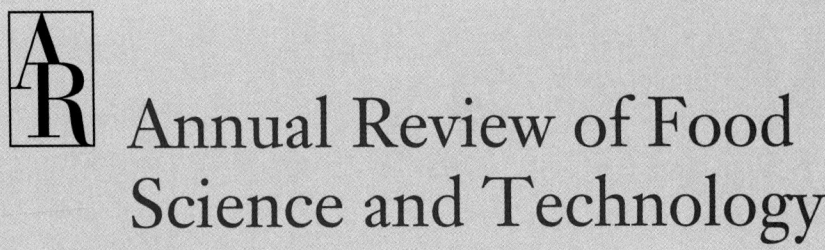

Annual Review of Food Science and Technology

Volume 2, 2011

Michael P. Doyle, *Co-Editor*
University of Georgia

Todd R. Klaenhammer, *Co-Editor*
North Carolina State University

www.annualreviews.org • science@annualreviews.org • 650-493-4400

Annual Reviews
4139 El Camino Way • P.O. Box 10139 • Palo Alto, California 94303-0139

Annual Reviews
Palo Alto, California, USA

International Standard Serial Number: 1941-1413
International Standard Book Number: 978-0-8243-4902-8

∞ The paper used in this publication meets the minimum requirements of American National Standards for Information Sciences—Permanence of Paper for Printed Library Materials, ANSI Z39.48-1992.

TYPESET BY APTARA
PRINTED AND BOUND BY EDWARDS BROTHERS, ANN ARBOR, MICHIGAN

Annual Review of Food Science and Technology

Volume 2, 2011

Contents

Errata

An online log of corrections to *Annual Review of Food Science and Technology* articles may be found at http://food.annualreviews.org

Related Articles

From the ***Annual Review of Microbiology***, Volume 64 (2010)

Viruses, microRNAs, and Host Interactions
Rebecca L. Skalsky and Bryan R. Cullen

Basis of Virulence in Community-Associated Methicillin-Resistant *Staphylococcus aureus*
Michael Otto

Genetic Diversity among Offspring from Archived *Salmonella enterica* ssp. *enterica* Serovar Typhimurium (Demerec Collection): In Search of Survival Strategies
Abraham Eisenstark

From the ***Annual Review of Nutrition***, Volume 30 (2010)

The Effect of Exercise and Nutrition on Intramuscular Fat Metabolism and Insulin Sensitivity
Christopher S. Shaw, Juliette Clark, and Anton J.M. Wagenmakers

Iron Homeostasis and the Inflammatory Response
Marianne Wessling-Resnick

Iron, Lead, and Children's Behavior and Cognition
Katarzyna Kordas

Between Death and Survival: Retinoic Acid in Regulation of Apoptosis
Noa Noy

Evolutionary Adaptations to Dietary Changes
F. Luca, G.H. Perry, and A. Di Rienzo

Physiological Insights Gained from Gene Expression Analysis in Obesity and Diabetes
Mark P. Keller and Alan D. Attie

The Effect of Nutrition on Blood Pressure
Vincenzo Savica, Guido Bellinghieri, and Joel D. Kopple

From the ***Annual Review of Phytopathology***, Volume 48 (2010)

Ecology of Plant and Free-Living Nematodes in Natural and Agricultural Soil
Deborah A. Neher

Engineering Pathogen Resistance in Crop Plants: Current Trends and Future Prospects
David B. Collinge, Hans J.L. Jørgensen, Ole S. Lund, and Michael F. Lyngkjær

Go Where the Science Leads You
Richard S. Hussey

Induced Systemic Resistance and Plant Responses to Fungal Biocontrol Agents
Michal Shoresh, Gary E. Harman, and Fatemeh Mastouri

Managing Nematodes Without Methyl Bromide
Inga A. Zasada, John M. Halbrendt, Nancy Kokalis-Burelle, James LaMondia, Michael V. McKenry, and Joe W. Noling

Pathogen Refuge: A Key to Understanding Biological Control
Kenneth B. Johnson

Annual Reviews is a nonprofit scientific publisher established to promote the advancement of the sciences. Beginning in 1932 with the *Annual Review of Biochemistry*, the Company has pursued as its principal function the publication of high-quality, reasonably priced *Annual Review* volumes. The volumes are organized by Editors and Editorial Committees who invite qualified authors to contribute critical articles reviewing significant developments within each major discipline. The Editor-in-Chief invites those interested in serving as future Editorial Committee members to communicate directly with him. Annual Reviews is administered by a Board of Directors, whose members serve without compensation.

Annual Reviews of

Analytical Chemistry
Anthropology
Astronomy and Astrophysics
Biochemistry
Biomedical Engineering
Biophysics
Cell and Developmental Biology
Chemical and Biomolecular Engineering
Clinical Psychology
Condensed Matter Physics
Earth and Planetary Sciences
Ecology, Evolution, and Systematics
Economics
Entomology
Environment and Resources
Financial Economics
Fluid Mechanics
Food Science and Technology
Genetics
Genomics and Human Genetics
Immunology
Law and Social Science
Marine Science
Materials Research
Medicine
Microbiology
Neuroscience
Nuclear and Particle Science
Nutrition
Pathology: Mechanisms of Disease
Pharmacology and Toxicology
Physical Chemistry
Physiology
Phytopathology
Plant Biology
Political Science
Psychology
Public Health
Resource Economics
Sociology

SPECIAL PUBLICATIONS
Excitement and Fascination of Science, Vols. 1, 2, 3, and 4

P F Fox

Mammals, Milk, Molecules, and Micelles

P.F. Fox

School of Food & Nutritional Sciences, University College Cork, Ireland; email: pff@ucc.ie

Annu. Rev. Food Sci. Technol. 2011. 2:1–19

First published online as a Review in Advance on November 17, 2010

The *Annual Review of Food Science and Technology* is online at food.annualreviews.org

This article's doi:
10.1146/annurev-food-072910-094544

1941-1413/11/0410-0001$20.00

Keywords

milk proteins, cheese, heat stability, enzymology

Abstract

After a brief description of my family background and school days, my professional career as a dairy scientist is described under three headings: research, teaching, and writing. My research activities fall into four areas: biochemistry of cheese, fractionation and characterization of milk proteins, heat stability of milk, and dairy enzymology. Finally, I offer some advice to young scientists.

SCHOOL YEARS

I was born on November 20, 1937 and reared on a dairy farm near Mitchelstown, County Cork, Ireland; my ancestors had farmed there for more than 200 years. Although Ireland was not involved in World War II, it did suffer shortages, especially of manufactured goods and foods not produced in Ireland, which were rationed until the early 1950s. As with most Irish farmers at that time, my family was self sufficient in the principal foods, so although we lacked luxury foods, we did not suffer from malnutrition. Because coal was not available, peat was used as a substitute. However, there are no peat bogs in the Mitchelstown area, forcing us to harvest poor-quality peat from the local low hill. We depended on oil lamps and candles for light (electricity was not available in rural Ireland until the early 1950s). Although the 1940s were not a nice period in Ireland, life there was often better than in most of Europe at that time.

I attended a small (approximately 80 students and 2 teachers) local primary school (Knockadea) from 1943 to 1950. Like my schoolmates, I was not very studious and preferred outdoor pursuits to reading; however, my grandmother ensured that I did my homework. I helped on the farm from an early age and did work such as hand-milking cows, feeding calves, and tending to pigs and hens.

In 1950, I transferred to a secondary school at Mitchelstown, to which I cycled approximately eight kilometers on a poor-quality road in all sorts of weather. The transition to secondary school involved larger classes, new subjects, and specialized teachers (some of whom were not very stimulating). At my first Christmas tests, I came out at the top of the class, a position I maintained throughout my five years in secondary school. The school was relatively small and at that time had a high attrition rate (not unique to this school). From a class of approximately 45 in my first year, only six completed the five-year course. Students dropped out for various reasons, especially on reaching the school-leaving age (14 years at that time), and took up trivial jobs or eventually emigrated to the United Kingdom or the United States. Our school was not very distinguished academically, athletically, or socially, and some students transferred to more prestigious schools. It was an all-boys school (as most Irish secondary schools still are), but we managed to meet the girls from the neighboring all-girls school.

During the course of my secondary schooling, I would have taken up farming as a career, and my father would have been happy for me to do so, but my mother, and especially my grandmother, did not approve of me going into farming, which was reasonable, considering that I had performed reasonably well at school and was the oldest of eight children, including two younger brothers, who did take up farming. At the National (School) Leaving Certificate Examinations at the end of secondary school, I achieved good results and could have chosen any university or other program I wished.

UNIVERSITY DAYS

At that time, there was little advice on careers; I do not recall any in-depth discussions on careers, but I registered at University College, Cork (UCC) in October 1959 to study for a Bachelor of Science (BSc) degree in Dairy Science. Ireland has a long history of dairying, especially in the production of butter, most of which was exported through the Cork Butter Market, established in 1760 to coordinate the export of butter. Starting around 1860, buttermaking technology underwent a series of improvements, and schools were established throughout northern Europe to train farm buttermakers. Such schools were established at Cork and Dublin in 1880. Buttermaking worldwide changed suddenly from a farm-based to a creamery-based industry following the development of the centrifugal separator by Gustav de Laval in 1878. Industrialization of buttermaking created the need for suitably qualified personnel to manage creameries. A six-month course for creamery managers was introduced at Cork and Dublin in 1893. This course was extended and improved progressively and moved to the Royal College of Science for Ireland (RCScI; a technological university), Dublin in 1915. In 1924, the RCScI was transferred to University College, Dublin, but the Creamery Managers' Course was transferred to UCC, where a Faculty of Dairy Science was established in 1924. The Creamery Managers' course was designed to train managers for cream-separating stations and small central creameries where butter was manufactured. To meet the need for more in-depth trained personnel, a four-year course was established at the RCScI in 1915, and this course, leading to a BSc in Dairying, was also transferred to UCC.

The first year of this course consisted of mathematics, applied mathematics, physics, chemistry, and a language; surprisingly, biology was not included. At the end-of-year examinations, I obtained good results and placed third in my class. A component of the BSc in Dairying course was 20 weeks work placement, spread over the summer vacations. I obtained a placement at a small local cooperative creamery, Garryspillane. On my first day on the job, the manager gave sledge hammers to me and another student, and set us to break up a concrete floor in preparation for the installation of a new pasteurizer—this was valuable experience for a budding dairy scientist! Things improved thereafter, and I learned the basics of the Irish dairy industry.

The second year of the course consisted of chemistry, electrical engineering, and civil engineering (still no biology); presumably, the engineering elements reflected the need that a small creamery should be as self sufficient as possible. Practicals in engineering included free-hand drawing and metalwork. I retained third place in the class at the summer examinations in 1957. During summer 1957, I spent a few weeks at a factory in Coleford, Gloucestershire, England, which produced the blackcurrant juice product Ribena. This was my first overseas travel, and it included new experiences [living in a POW camp, drinking crude cider (scrumpy), and visiting Tintern Abbey (the ruins of a magnificent abbey razed by Henry VIII)]. However, I spent most of that summer in Ireland, managing a traveling creamery, a small cream-separating station mounted on a truck, serving small, widely dispersed milk suppliers in southwest Ireland.

Our third year at UCC consisted of courses in dairy technology, dairy bacteriology, dairy engineering, physical chemistry, accounting, economics, and dairy husbandry. I spent the summer of 1958 at various dairy factories: Wall's ice cream factory in Acton, London, the branch creamery of Garryspillane, the cheese (natural and processed) factory of Mitchelstown Co-op, and the Condensed Milk Company in Limerick, which produced concentrated and powdered milk.

The fourth year of the course consisted of dairy chemistry, dairy bacteriology, dairy technology, economics, and accounting. These courses included long, and not very efficient, practicals. At the summer examinations in June 1959, I placed at the top of the class. In Ireland, a professor from a foreign university is involved in each subject as an extern examiner. In Dairy Technology, the extern examiner gave each student a very thorough oral examination, and I believe that I scored very well at that examination, which I attribute to my wide-ranging work placements.

Following the results of my final examination, I decided to undertake postgraduate studies in microbiology. I approached Professor Michael Grimes. However, he was about to retire and was not accepting new postgraduate students. He suggested that I speak to Frank Kosikowski, Cornell University, Ithaca, NY, who was a Fulbright Fellow at UCC in 1958–1959. Professor Kosikowski (Kosi) arranged for me to start on a PhD program at Cornell in August 1959. During that summer, I did relief work at Mitchelstown Creameries; one day, the general manager told me that the manager of their largest branch was about to leave and asked if I was interested in the position. I told him about my plans to go to the United States, and he said, "Go West, young man," which I did.

POSTGRADUATE STUDIES

In August 1959, I left for the United States. My parents probably would have preferred that I took the job at Mitchelstown Creameries, but they raised no objections. At that time I had done very little foreign travel, just two brief periods in England and in both cases with friends; I had never been on a plane. My parents and 82-year-old grandmother accompanied me to Shannon airport to see me off (I presume that they felt like millions of Irish parents during the previous century who saw their children emigrate). In this, the prejet era, the flight from Shannon to New York took about 20 hours, with a fueling stop at Gander, Newfoundland. Idlewild (now JFK) airport is an intimidating place even for an experienced traveler, but I passed through immigration and customs and took a shuttle bus to the Port Authority Bus Terminal, where I boarded a Greyhound bus to Ithaca, NY. I remember being very impressed by the road system in New York and New Jersey and the skyline of Manhattan. At that time there were approximately 20 Irish postgraduate students at Cornell [mainly in Agriculture], one of whom, Tony O'Sullivan, a Dairy Science graduate from UCC, offered me temporary accommodation in an apartment shared by five Irish students at 208 William Street. One of the occupants returned to Ireland shortly after I arrived, and I replaced him. I spent the next five years in that appartment, with a series of housemates.

The day after my arrival, following a quick tour of the campus with Tony O'Sullivan, I met Professor Kosikowski at the Department of Dairy Industries (changed to the Department of Food Science a few years later). Cornell is a very picturesque campus situated on a hill between two deep gorges and overlooking one of the Finger Lakes, Cayuga (the college anthem goes: Far above Cayuga's water, there's an awful smell, some say it's Cayuga's water, we know it's Cornell). Cornell is mainly a private university (Ivy League) founded in 1865, with four state colleges (at that time called Agriculture and Life Sciences, Veterinary Science, Home Economics, and Industrial and Labor Relations) attached. Its College of Agriculture is regarded as one of the best in the United States, especially in Animal Sciences. The Head of the Department of Dairy Industries, which was established in 1902, was D.F. Holland; other staff were F.V. Kosikowski, B.L. Herrington, F.W. Shipe, V. Krukowski, W.K. Jordon, Jim White, and Dick Marsh. Two well-known retired members, A.C. Dahlberg and E.S. Guthrie, frequented the Department.

At an early meeting, Kosi outlined my academic program. I was to concentrate on coursework for the first year. Kosi, who was familiar with my background, advised that I should major in Dairy Science (later Food Science), with minors in Biochemistry and Microbiology. He felt that I had an adequate knowledge of dairy science and technology and recommended that I take only his own course on cheese, for which I was also a teaching assistant (TA). I also took a postgraduate-level course on dairy chemistry by B.L. Herrington, which involved reading and discussing *Principles of Dairy Chemistry* by R. Jenness and S. Patton, published in 1959. I served as a TA for eight of the ten semesters I was at Cornell, three times for Kosi's cheese course and five for B.L. Herrington's Analytical Methods course.

I had no problem achieving the required grades in coursework and was happy to take a range of undergraduate and postgraduate courses in microbiology and biochemistry. As I progressed, my preferences shifted from microbiology to chemistry, and I took courses in organic, analytical, and physical chemistry.

Although research was a minor part of my program during the first two years, I was associated with and assisted senior postgraduate students and became familiar with a range of analytical techniques. My first publication (Fox 1963) arose from such work. For various reasons, I had to determine the salt (NaCl) content of cheese frequently, using a modification of the Volhard titration, which is laborious and smelly. In the Analytical Methods course, for which I was TA, we studied various potentiometric titrations, including for halides. It occurred to me that it might be possible to use a potentiometric titration for the determination of NaCl in cheese. I investigated this principle, and it proved to be very satisfactory. The potentiometric method is now a standard International Dairy Federation (IDF)/AOAC method for determining the salt content of cheese. I think that I have always been good at recognizing opportunities for research, of which this is an early example.

Around 1960, Kosi's group was involved in two main areas: cheese flavor and a bioassay for antibiotics in milk. Kosi had been studying cheese flavor for several years, especially proteolysis and amino acid catabolism. By 1959, with Dick Scarpillino and Bob Hall, he was using gas chromatography (GC) to study the volatiles in cheese. I became fairly adept with GC and considered developing a research project using GC to study cheese ripening, but Kosi discontinued this work.

In approximately 1960, the United States Department of Agriculture (USDA) permitted the treatment of cheesemilk with H_2O_2 as an alternative to heat treatment. Kosi disapproved of this and was interested in developing a method to detect milk that had been treated with H_2O_2/catalase (when present, H_2O_2 could be detected using any of several redox indicators, but this approach was not applicable when the H_2O_2 had been reduced by catalase). He asked me to take on this project. Essentially, the project became a study of the effects of H_2O_2 on various chemical and physicochemical properties of milk. Although we did not develop a method for the detection of H_2O_2/catalase-treated milk, I did learn a number of useful techniques and worked for the first time on milk proteins, which have been the focus of most of my research for the past 45 years. The results of my work were published in Fox & Kosikowski (1967). I have often thought that it would be interesting to repeat this work, using the better techniques now available, but I never did.

In early 1964, I decided that I had done sufficient work for a PhD thesis, and I started writing. When I presented a draft of my thesis to Kosi, he was not impressed; he said, "You come from a country that has produced many famous writers, now go and emulate them"—I have been trying to do so since, with some success. Eventually, I got my thesis into an acceptable form and arranged for my PhD examination, which went well. κ-Casein was discovered in 1956 by von Hipple & Waugh, who proceeded to explain the colloidal stability of milk and to develop a model of the casein micelle. I have always been fairly conscientious about reading the literature (and still impress on my students the need to do so) and had recently read Waugh's publications on the casein micelle—at the viva voce, I spoke eloquently on the casein micelle, which, I believe, impressed my examiners. The structure and properties of the casein micelle are still active areas for research. I have kept abreast of this work and have written occasionally on the subject (e.g., Fox & Brodkorb 2008).

In early 1964, Kosi received a Public Health Service grant to investigate the effectiveness of bactofugation to reduce the bacterial population in cheesemilk; he asked me to undertake the study as a research assistant. I spent about four months on the project, which showed that bactofugation is very effective (Kosikowski & Fox 1968). This was the first publication on the use of bactofugation to decontaminate milk, a technique which is now widely used, especially for Swiss-type cheese, to remove *Clostridium tyrobutyricum*, which causes gas blowing, as an alternative to nitrate.

In addition to being professionally fruitful, the five years I spent at Cornell were very enjoyable. Notable events included drinking beer at the Palms bar in Collegetown, parties at 208 William Street (and elsewhere), dating girls from Cornell, Wells College, and Cortland Teachers College, occasional visits to the Irish club (AOH) at Syracuse and to New York City, Boston, the Gettysburg battlefield, and Washington DC, as well as dinner at Thanksgiving, Christmas, and other times with staff members or married postgraduate students. I attended annual meetings of the American Dairy Science Association (ADSA) at the University of Maryland and at the University of Arizona, Tucson, where I gave my first public oral presentation [I made a very interesting journey by car from Ithaca to Tucson with a Professor of Dairy Husbandry and his wife; I returned from Tucson to East Lansing with three graduate students from Michigan State University (MSU), in about 30 hours of continuous driving].

GOING FURTHER WEST

In early 1964, I successfully applied for a postdoctoral position with Dr. Hans Lillevik, Biochemistry Department, MSU, East Lansing, scheduled to commence in September 1964. After completing my PhD, I returned to Ireland in May 1964 for a vacation and to assess job prospects. I took interviews with the Irish Dairy Board (no offer) and with the (State) Agricultural Institute [An Foras Taluntas (AFT)]. I worked on the bactofugation project from May to August and planned to go to MSU early in September. Shortly before I was due to go to MSU, I received an offer from AFT for a research position at their Dairy Research Center at Moorepark; I requested a postponement (which I received) and went to MSU, which was a good move. [During my postdoc at MSU and subsequent postdoc at the University of California-Davis (UC Davis), I got hands-on experience of several valuable research techniques, became familiar with other aspects of dairy chemistry and became generally more confident as a result of a successful outcome to my research.]

The Department of Biochemistry at MSU had recently been formed; Dr. Lillevik had been a member of the chemistry department, where I was based for a few months, awaiting completion of a new biochemistry building. Lillevik was basically a physical chemist who had worked with Leroy Palmer at the University of Minnesota, St. Paul, and done a postdoc with K. Linderstrom-Lang at the Carlsberg Laboratories, Copenhagen. He was a very interesting, philosophical character, with a very disciplined approach to research. My project was to improve methods for the isolation of individual caseins. Lillevik collaborated with Bob Brunner in the Department of Food Science, whose students were working on the isolation and characterization of several minor milk proteins. I had many interesting and stimulating conversations with Lillevik and Brunner, and learned to do starch gel electrophoresis (recently developed), free boundary electrophoresis, anion exchange chromatography, and analytical ultracentrifugation.

I attended the 1965 annual meeting of the ADSA in Lexington, Kentucky and made an oral presentation. I believe I impressed a group of professors from UC Davis who were recruiting a young dairy chemist to replace the recently retired Dr. Gene Jack. I had a number of discussions with them, as a result of which they encouraged me to apply for the position at Davis. I declined to do so immediately but accepted a postdoctoral position with Dr. Nick Tarassuk at UC Davis on the isolation of lipase from milk and agreed to discuss the matter again after six months.

I returned to Ireland in late August 1965 and was married on September 11 to an Irish girl, Olive Lenihan, whom I had first met in New Jersey and later in Chicago, where she was a nurse. We returned to the United States on September 12 and set off by car from Chicago to Davis, stopping off at various places along the way.

Tarassuk had been working on milk lipase for many years. In 1965, he had a postdoc, M. Yaguchi, who had done a PhD on lipase with Tarassuk and was convinced that κ-casein had lipase activity because they coeluted from DEAE-cellulose. Yaguchi was about to leave Davis to take up a position at the National Research Council, Ottawa, Canada, and I was to replace him. Basically, my job was to confirm or refute the κ-casein hypothesis. I had a fortunate break, as A.G. Mackinlay and R.G. Wake of the University of Sydney had just published a paper describing a new method for the isolation of κ-casein, using the mild dissociating agent, dimethylformamide, in DEAE chromatography. Using this chromatography system, I succeeded in separating lipase from κ-casein and eventually isolated a homogeneous preparation of lipase, which we characterized (Fox et al. 1967, Fox & Tarassuk 1968, Patel et al. 1968). I failed to recognize that milk lipase is the lipoprotein lipase (LPL) of blood serum (in 1962, E.D. Korn showed that milk contains a LPL which was studied in detail by T. Olivecrona and collaborators in the 1970s).

After six months at UC Davis, the search committee asked if I had reached a decision; I replied that, for better or worse, I had decided to return to Ireland, which I did on January 1, 1967. I often wonder if I made the best decision—certainly, I would have had better facilities at UC Davis, not just in my own laboratory but also elsewhere in the department and in the university generally. A university like UC Davis has many major advantages over Moorepark or UCC, including great libraries and experts on various topics, not just at UC Davis but even more so at its sister university at Berkeley. However, I have no regrets.

ESTABLISHING A RESEARCH CAREER IN IRELAND

AFT was established in 1958 by the Irish government, which transferred some research facilities from the Department of Agriculture to AFT and established some new centers. One of the latter was the National Dairy Research Center (NDRC) at Moorepark, which was established on a large estate about 40 km from Cork that had been a British Cavalry base from 1890 to 1922. The NDRC comprised five departments: Dairy Husbandry, Dairy Chemistry, Dairy Microbiology, Dairy Technology, and Pig Husbandry. I was assigned to the Dairy Technology Department, of which Tony O'Sullivan was head. Moorepark was established on a greenfield site and by 1967, the facilities were still very rudimentary; when I joined, the Dairy Technology Department was housed in a Nissen/Quonset hut, but we moved into new laboratories in September 1967.

Although the lack of equipment and a very poorly stocked library were major problems, there was a very good pioneering spirit at Moorepark, and I managed to get some research projects started, including a search for rennet substitutes, factors that affect the proteolysis of caseins by rennet, and the dissociation of casein micelles by urea and their reformation on removal of the urea by dialysis (Fox 1969a,b, 1970; Fox & Walley 1971a,b; McGann & Fox 1974). This work showed that bovine pepsin is a very good rennet substitute and was used widely, alone or mixed with chymosin, until the introduction of fermentation chymosin in approximately 1990 [which I also assessed (O'Sullivan & Fox 1991)]. The reformation of casein micelles from urea-treated milk was quite a clever idea that I regret not pursuing. Much later, we investigated the dissociation and reformation of casein micelles from ethanol-treated milk (O'Connell et al. 2001, 2003) or by pH adjustment.

As the mission of AFT, including the NDRC, was to improve Irish agriculture, we were expected to do some applied work. I got involved with cheese factories, in whey utilization and especially in the manufacture and use of casein. After attending an IDF symposium on casein and caseinates in Paris in 1967, I decided that I would try to develop these products in Ireland, where at that time there was only one small factory making rennet casein for the manufacture of plastics. I wrote a monograph on casein and caseinates (published by AFT) and discussed casein production with several dairy companies, including those that became Glanbia and Kerry Foods. I like to think that I had some influence on the development of the modern casein industry in Ireland, which is now one of the principal global manufacturers of functional protein products.

PROFESSOR OF FOOD CHEMISTRY

In 1969, Professor G.T. Pyne in the Dairy Chemistry department at UCC retired. He had joined the Faculty of Dairy Science, UCC, upon its foundation in 1924 and served as lecturer and later as Professor of Dairy Chemistry. He did excellent research on milk proteins and milk salts (his work on milk salts is still cited), but he never built up a significant research group and never invested much in equipment—he relied on ideas rather than on equipment. For his work on the heat stability of milk, he used a saucepan with an oscillating device made from the motor of an old record player, heated by a micro-Bunsen burner controlled by a technician and heat-sealed glass vials prepared by his technician from glass tubing; he was a good example of quality over quantity. He was quite active in university politics and frequently served as Deputy President.

Starting in 1960, UCC changed from Dairy Science to Food Science and following Pyne's retirement, the Professorship of Dairy Chemistry was changed to Professor of Dairy and Food Chemistry [and in 1987 to Food Chemistry]. There were six applicants for the Professorship, two others of whom had also worked on milk lipase but failed to isolate it due to its strong association properties. I was appointed and took up office on October 1, 1969 at the age of 32 (one of the youngest Professors appointed by UCC).

The department I inherited had two technicians, no postgraduate students, limited laboratory space, very little equipment, and two lecturers, one of whom, D.T. McSweeney, also served as Supervisor of Examinations; the other was Patrick Morrissey (also appointed on October 1, 1969), who had recently been awarded the PhD degree for work on the rennet-induced coagulation of milk under Pyne's supervision. Classes commenced a few days after my appointment, and my primary initial task was to keep ahead of lectures and practicals. This task was made more challenging, as I included lectures on the structure and biochemistry of muscle and meat, which required much reading.

Three postgraduate students registered in 1970 and commenced work on (*a*) the isolation and characterization of pepsins (O'Leary & Fox 1973, 1974, 1975; Fox et al. 1977), (*b*) proteolysis in cheese (Fox & Guiney 1973, Phelan et al. 1973), (*c*) fractionation of caseins (Fox & Guiney 1972), and (*d*) heat stability of milk (Frank O'Mahoney, supervised by Pat Morrissey). In subsequent years, Pat took over the meat area, which he developed to a high level, and I took over work on the heat stability of milk.

Gradually, the situation regarding equipment improved. Laboratory space was very restricted until 1979 when the Food Science faculty moved into a new building, which permitted the intake of increased numbers of undergraduate and postgraduate students and an increase in research activity. Laboratory facilities were increased again in 1993, resulting in another surge in student numbers.

In comparison with the United States and many European countries, money for research at Irish universities was very limited. We piggybacked on grants made available by the university for teaching, and by carefully selecting projects, we survived. European Union (EU) funds became available after approximately 1980, and in 1995 the Irish Department of Agriculture and Food, for the first time, earmarked substantial grants for food research, but by then it was too late for me!!!

Throughout my career, I worked on four main areas: cheese biochemistry, milk proteins, heat stability of milk, and food enzymology; summaries of my contributions in these areas, with selected references, are given below.

Cheese

Arising from my association with Dr. Kosikowski, because of the potential of cheese as a research subject, the importance of cheese to the dairy industry (about 35% of all milk), and its desirable organoleptic, convenience, and nutritional properties, cheese has been the principal subject of my research since the 1960s. I have published about 180 research papers, 70 reviews (e.g., Fox et al. 1996a,b; Hayaloglu et al. 2002) and seven books [*Fundamentals of Cheese Science* and *Cheese: Chemistry, Physics and Microbiology* (a two-volume book in its third edition)] on the science and technology of cheese. The principal aspects on which I have worked, with selected references, are:

1. Rennet substitutes were one of my early projects, on which work continued for several years (Fox 1969b; Fox et al. 1977; O'Leary & Fox 1973, 1974, 1975; O'Sullivan & Fox 1991; Bansal et al. 2009).
2. Methods for quantifying proteolysis in cheese. Some of the methods developed are widely used and have attained almost standard methods status (Kuchroo & Fox 1983, Kuchroo et al. 1983, Shalabi & Fox 1987, Folkertsma & Fox 1992, O'Shea et al. 1996, Pripp et al. 2000).
3. The contribution of various agents to cheese ripening: rennet, indigenous milk enzymes, starter lactic acid bacteria (LAB), nonstarter LAB (NSLAB), and secondary microorganisms. To study the contribution of each of these, we developed or modified methods for producing NSLAB-free cheese, starter-free cheese using gluconic acid-δ-lactone to acidify the curd or rennet-free curd by inactivating the residual rennet in the curd by increasing the pH or using specific inhibitors [pepstatin or α_2-macroglobulin (in blood serum)] (O'Keeffe et al. 1978; Farkye & Fox 1991; Shakeel-ur-Rehman et al. 1998a,b; Bansal et al. 2010).
4. Cheese-related microorganisms (Mullan et al. 1981; Farkye et al. 1990; Law et al. 1992, 1993; Wilkinson et al. 1994, McGarry et al. 1994; O'Donovan et al. 1996; Fernandez-Espla & Fox 1998; Lynch et al. 1999; Brennan et al. 2001, 2002)
5. NaCl is critical for cheese ripening and quality; we studied the following aspects: variations in the concentration and distribution of NaCl in cheese, correlation between salt concentration and cheese quality, factors (physical and compositional) that affect the diffusion of salt in cheese curd, and the influence of NaCl on the growth of *Penicillium roqueforti*, *Penicillium camemberti*, and *Lactococcus* spp. in cheese and on the quality of Cheddar, Blue, and Camembert cheese (Godinho & Fox 1982; Guinee & Fox 1984, 1986, 2004; Morris et al. 1985).
6. Specificity of chymosins, pepsins, plasmin, and microbial rennet substitutes on individual caseins (Mulvihill & Fox 1979b, McSweeney et al. 1993).
7. Identification of the large water-insoluble and small water-soluble peptides in Cheddar cheese; about 200 peptides were identified (Singh et al. 1995, Mooney et al. 1998, Fernandez et al. 1998).
8. Intervarietal comparison of cheese (Hewedi & Fox 1984; Madkor et al. 1987; Zarmpoutis et al. 1997; Gobbetti et al. 1997b, 2002; McGoldrick & Fox, 1999; Hayaloglu et al. 2005; Di Cagno et al. 2007; Vernile et al. 2009; Bansal et al. 2009).
9. Acceleration of cheese ripening by elevating the ripening temperature or adding exogenous enzymes; production of enzyme-modified cheese (Folkertsma et al. 1996; Wallace & Fox 1997; Shakeel-ur-Rehman & Fox 2002; Kilcawley et al. 1998, 2006).
10. Rennet-induced coagulation of milk (Huppertz et al. 2005, O'Connell et al. 2006, Bansal et al. 2007).
11. Factors that affect the quality of cheese (Gobbetti et al. 1999; Shakeel-ur-Rehman et al. 2000, 2004; Guinee et al. 2002).

Heat Stability of Milk

In comparison with other biological systems, milk is very heat-stable, which allows heat sterilization without major physical changes. Unconcentrated milk withstands all commercial heat treatments, but the stability of concentrated ($>2\times$) milk is marginal, as a result of which sterilized concentrated (evaporated) milk was not commercialized until 1884 (by Thomas Myenberger); attempts to do so by Nicolas Appert in 1809 and by Gail Borden in 1856 were unsuccessful. The variability and unpredictability of the heat stability of milk were of concern to the dairy industry in the nineteenth century, but the first published work on the subject was by Sommer & Hart in 1919. In the early twentieth century, evaporated milk was an important product in Ireland and was one of the research areas of G.T. Pyne; I continued these investigations. The study of heat stability was attractive because, in addition to being commercially important, it is fundamentally interesting and challenging but because few laboratories have been involved, progress is slow and simple equipment is sufficient (progress depends more on ideas than on equipment).

Aspects investigated included variability, correlation with compositional factors, interspecies (bovine, ovine, caprine, equine, porcine, and human milk) comparison, each of which has a distinctive HCT-pH profile (Fox & Hoynes 1975, 1976), effect of various additives (phosphates, polyvalent organic acids and their salts, amides, including urea, and carbonyls, including sugars and polyphenols) on heat stability (Shalabi & Fox 1982; Tan-Kinita & Fox 1996; O'Connell & Fox 1999, 2001b; O'Sullivan et al. 2002) and the mechanism of the maximum-minimum in the HCT-pH profile (Fox 1981, Mohammed & Fox 1987, Singh & Fox 1987, O'Connell & Fox 2001a). I published 60 research papers on the heat stability of milk and reviewed the literature three times (Fox & Morrissey 1977, Fox 1982, O'Connell & Fox 2003). Singh & Fox (1987) and O'Connell & Fox (2001a) proposed that the pH dependency of the heat stability of milk is due to the effect of β-lactoglobulin on the dissociation of κ-casein from the surface of the casein micelles; κ-casein-depleted micelles are sensitive to calcium-induced coagulation. In the pH range 6.5 to 6.9, β-lactoglobulin reduces the dissociation of κ-casein but increases pH to >6.9, thereby creating a maximum-minimum in the HCT-pH profile, and this hypothesis has been widely supported.

Milk Proteins

Most of my research has been on properties of milk proteins. In addition to work on cheese and the heat stability of milk, I have worked on the fractionation, isolation, interspecies comparison, and functional properties of milk proteins, the structure and properties of casein micelles, and the effect of high pressure on milk proteins. I have published approximately 60 research papers (e.g., see Fox & Morrissey 1972; Fox & Guiney 1972; O'Connor & Fox 1973; McGann & Fox 1974; Mulvihill & Fox 1979a; Murphy & Fox 1991; Lucey et al. 1996; O'Connell et al. 2003, 2006; Malin et al. 2001; Zobrist et al. 2005; Huppertz et al. 2006b) and 25 reviews (e.g., see Fox 2003, Huppertz et al. 2006a, Fox & Brodkorb 2008, Uniacke-Lowe et al. 2010) on milk proteins. Volume 1 of *Advanced Dairy Chemistry* is devoted to milk proteins.

I started the work on functional milk proteins (casein and caseinates) during the 1960s, when the transition from industrial to food-grade products occurred, and this area later became a major theme for our department, especially for Professor D.M. Mulvihill.

Although the lactoproteins of all species that have been studied are generally similar, there are large interspecies differences with respect to concentration, types, and properties. Sporatically, I have worked on the proteins of bovine, ovine, caprine, human, porcine, equine, asinine, canine, elephant, eland, wildebeest, and monkey milk. The proteins of equine and asinine milk are more like those of human milk than are ruminant milks and are attracting attention for the nutrition of human infants who are allergenic to bovine milk proteins (see Uniacke-Lowe et al. 2010). There are approximately 4500 species of mammal, but the milk of only about 50 species has been studied sufficiently for the data to be considered reliable. There is great opportunity for research on the milk proteins of various species, which is important from evolutionary and classification viewpoints, the nutrition of orphaned infants, the preservation of endangered species and, at least in some cases, the elucidation of commercially important properties.

Food Enzymology

Milk contains about 70 indigenous enzymes, which are important from the spoilage, stability, protection, or digestion viewpoints (see Fox & Kelly 2006). I became involved in enzymology when I worked on milk lipoprotein lipase at UC Davis; I have published 57 research papers and 31 reviews on various aspects of food enzymology and edited a two-volume book, *Food Enzymology*. I have worked on indigenous lipoprotein lipase, plasmin, cathepsin D, and the acid phosphatase of milk (Fox et al. 1967; Fox & Tarassuk 1968; Patel et al. 1968; Grufferty & Fox 1988a,b; Akuzawa & Fox 1998).

Microbial enzymes are important in several dairy products, and I have worked on the extracellular proteinases, peptidases, and lipases of *Pseudomonas fluorescens*, *Arthrobacter nicotianae*, *Brevibacterium linens*, *Corynebacterium variabilis*, *Lactococcus* spp., *Lactobacillus* spp., *Propionibacterium shermani*, and *Micrococcus* spp. (Stepaniak et al. 1982; Fox et al. 1989; Garcia de Fernandez & Fox 1991; Requena et al. 1993; Gobbetti et al. 1995, 1997a, 2001; Baral et al. 1995; Stepaniak & Fox 1995; Rattray et al. 1996, 1997; Rattray & Fox 1997; Fernandez-Espla & Fox 1997; Fernandez-Espla et al. 1997; Smacchi et al. 1999).

Exogenous enzymes are used widely in the processing of foods, including milk (see Fox 2002). The principal exogenous enzymes I have worked on are rennet substitutes, proteinases, and lipases for the acceleration of cheese ripening, and proteinases and transglutaminase to modify the functional properties of milk proteins.

TEACHING

Teaching is an integral part of the work of a university professor, and when I joined UCC, teaching (lectures and practicals) was the principal part of the job. During my career as Professor of Food Chemistry, I taught courses such as Introductory (General) Chemistry, Analytical Methods in Chemistry, Chemistry of Food Constituents, Food Analysis, Dairy Chemistry, and Food Enzymology. My lecturing style varied with the level of the course. I tried to introduce a tutorial system, but the students disliked it, perhaps because they had too many courses to cope with. For students taking Food Chemistry in their final year, I introduced a library project on an assigned topic and a minor research project instead of set practicals. These projects are now integral parts of food science and technology courses at UCC. I enjoyed formal teaching, and I believe the students appreciated my style and effort.

I regarded research as an aspect of teaching (if my research generated some commercially useful results, that was a bonus, but it was not the primary objective). I supervised about 65 MSc theses, most of which were published. Most of these graduates work for Irish food industries, but some are spread around the world. I supervised the research of 35 PhD candidates (some jointly with colleagues) and about 15 postdoctoral fellows. A high proportion of my PhD students and postdocs have entered academic life at universities or research institutes in Ireland, the United States, Australia, New Zealand, Netherlands, Norway, Spain, Italy, Greece, Egypt, South Africa, Japan, and Iraq; some of these have been very successful and are highly ranked by the ISI. It is very gratifying to me that many of my students are in academic positions—they are my academic progeny who continue my research and teaching work.

WRITING AND EDITING

In the course of my academic career, I have written extensively. In addition to approximately 350 research papers, I have written 170 reviews, coauthored two textbooks, and edited or coedited

30 books, some of which are in the third edition. I was one of the founding editors and served as one of the editors for eight years of the *International Dairy Journal*, one of the leading journals for dairy science and technology.

I became involved in the publication of textbooks by accident in 1980, when I met George Olley of Applied Science Publishers at a symposium. In the course of our discussions, George asked if I thought that there was a need for a textbook on dairy chemistry, to which I replied yes. He asked if I would edit it, and I agreed, thus beginning 30 years in book preparation. The principal themes have been: *Advanced Dairy Chemistry* (three volumes, three editions); *Cheese: Chemistry, Physics and Microbiology* (two volumes, three editions); *Food Enzymology* (two volumes), written for postgraduate students, lecturers, and researchers and the leading books in the field; and the *Encyclopedia of Dairy Sciences* (four volumes, two editions), intended for undergraduates and anybody interested in reading around their area of specialization in the general area of dairy science and technology. I have also coauthored two undergraduate textbooks, *Dairy Chemistry and Biochemistry* and *Fundamentals of Cheese Science*, based on my lecture courses at UCC.

OTHER ACADEMIC ACTIVITIES

As a visiting professor, I have given lectures on Dairy Chemistry at the University of California, Davis; Agricultural University, Uppsala, Sweden; Massey University, Palmerston North, New Zealand; the University of Minnesota, St. Paul; University of the Orange Free State, Bloemfontein, South Africa; the University of Wisconsin, Madison; Escola Superior Biotecnologia, Porto, Portugal; Northeast Agricultural College, Harbin, China; National Agricultural University, Vicosa, Brazil; University of Campinas, Brazil; University Complutensa, Madrid, Spain; Universidad Nacional del Litoral, Santa Fe, Argentina; California Polytechnic State University, San Luis Obispo, California; the University of Melbourne, Australia; University della Basilicata, Potenza, Italy; South Dakota State University, Brookings.

I have served as Extern Examiner for PhD candidates at the Universities of Glasgow, Edinburgh, Strathclyde, Bradford, Reading, and Leeds; Agricultural University, Uppsala; Aarhus; Agricultural University, Wageningen; the University of the Orange Free State, Bloemfontein, South Africa; Massey University, Palmerston North, New Zealand; Agricultural University of Norway (Aas); and the University of Bourgogne, Dijon, France.

I was a member of the Permanent Committee of Commission F (Dairy Science, Nutrition, Education) of the IDF, 1977–1979 and President of IDF Commission F, 1979–1983. I served as a member of the Irish Council for Educational Awards, 1972–1980.

AWARDS

- Research and Innovation Award. (Irish) National Board for Science & Technology (1983)
- Miles Marschall Award of the American Dairy Science Association (1987)
- Medal of Honor, University of Helsinki (1991)
- Senior Medal, Agricultural & Food Chemistry Division, Royal Society of Chemistry, London (2000)
- Highly Cited Award of the Institute of Scientific Information; *In recognition of Prof Fox being the most highly cited researcher in Agricultural Science during the period, 1995–2002* (2002)
- International Dairy Federation Distinguished Service Award; *In recognition of an outstanding contribution to dairying, worldwide* (2003)
- Gold Medal, (UK) Society of Dairy Technology; only three such awards are made per decade (2007)

COMMENTS AND ADVICE

I am approaching the end of a fairly productive career in dairy science and technology as a teacher, researcher, and author. Several factors have made this possible; I would highlight the following and have the audacity to offer my experience as advice to young scientists.

- I have a reasonable level of intelligence, but at all stages I had classmates or colleagues who were brighter than me. I believe that the principal reason for my success has been that when I got an opportunity to improve my situation, I was in a position to avail of it and did so.
- At all stages of my career I had options; I believe that I made the correct choices and have no regrets.
- I have been an empirical scientist who relied on experimentation rather than on theory. In retrospect, I could, and perhaps should, have been more rigorous and quantitative. However, had I done so, my approach would have been narrower, and I would probably have overlooked or ignored many of the areas I did explore.
- I have had a long career, 47 years since my first publication. I did not suffer from burn-out; I still find research as exciting as when I started. I regard my research, and especially my writing, as a hobby. I like to work steadily and consistently and if possible to avoid pressure.
- I avoided administration as far as possible. As head of a small university department, a certain amount of administration was inevitable, but I did not make it my raison d'être. I did serve on some university and national committees, but I never found committee work attractive—too much discussion and compromise.
- During most of my career, facilities and resources available to me for research were very limited, yet we managed to operate a productive research program. An objective measure of this is that I was the most highly cited researcher in Agricultural Science, worldwide, during the period 1995–2002. Thirteen years after retiring, I am still ranked 67th in the ISI Highly Cited list of Agricultural Scientists.
- I believe that reading widely and keeping up to date with the relevant literature are essential. When I read a paper or attend a lecture, several ideas for research evolve. Kosi used to tell me that when one had a research idea, it was best to do the research first and then read the literature, presumably to guarantee originality. I do not know how Kosi's ideas evolved but I prefer to read the literature first—there is not much point in reinventing the wheel!
- I keep a fairly broad research base—if one's research area is too narrow, it will soon become essentially exhausted; also, students can be offered a choice.
- Endeavor to attract good postgraduate students, they will keep you young and fresh! A poor student requires more input for less output than a good student. Of course, this is a chicken-and-egg situation, good students look for well-established and active professors. I interacted closely with both undergraduate and postgraduate students and operated an open door policy.
- One of the more effective ways of attracting recognition is via the development of good/novel analytical methods—they are usually the most highly cited papers. Another route is via good critical reviews, which many researchers, especially young scientists, use as an introduction to a subject. At least some universities do not recognize reviews as publications for the purpose of promotion, which I find strange—it requires much more effort to write a good review than a research paper.
- Not everybody is equally good at writing but everybody can improve; work at improving your writing skills.
- Discuss science with colleagues within and outside your immediate environment.
- Avail of facilities and equipment in other departments/laboratories in your university or institute.

- If possible, work at interfaces; even work at interfaces between relatively closely related areas can be rewarding. Take up and apply new equipment and methods.
- Research is expensive in terms of personnel, facilities, and financial resources. It is a continuous struggle to find funding for university research. In comparison with other areas, e.g., military and medical, agriculture and food science are low-priority areas. Most research on agricultural and food science is done by national institutes and to a lesser extent by universities. The large international food companies, e.g., Nestle, Unilever, and Kraft-General Foods, have excellent research facilities, but these represent only a small proportion of the global food industry—most food is processed by small or very small companies that have little or no R & D facilities. In my experience, public funding for food research is becoming more industrially orientated. Obviously, this approach has certain benefits, which are probably short term. It seems desirable that some funds should be ring-fenced for more basic research in food science and technology, i.e., research that has no immediate application. Such basic research is best undertaken by universities.

DISCLOSURE STATEMENT

The author is not aware of any affiliations, memberships, funding, or financial holdings that might be perceived as affecting the objectivity of this review.

ACKNOWLEDGMENTS

During my 41 years at UCC, I have interacted in various ways with many colleagues, without whose support my work would not have been possible. I wish to acknowledge, in particular, the comraderie and professional help of my academic colleagues: Declan McSweeney*, Pat Morrissey, Donie Mulvihill, Paul McSweeney, Eileen O'Neill, Tom O'Connor, John O'Brien, Charlie Daly, Albert Flynn, and Alan Kelly; technicians Pat Buckley*, John Lyons*, Jim Holland, Matt Healy, Therese Uniacke, Therese Dennehy, Linda Linehan, and Avril McCord; our secretaries, Mary Ronan, Anna O'Neill, and Anne Cahalane. In regard to the approximately 220 postgraduate students, postdocs, and visiting personnel, they were the lifeblood of the department and kept the atmosphere young and vibrant, and introduced new professional and cultural ideas. I also acknowledge colleagues at Teagasc, Moorepark, especially Tim Cogan and Tim Guinee, with whom I have interacted in various ways over a long period. I think that the atmosphere of the department was always friendly and supportive; we have had, and still do have, many enjoyable discussions on wide-ranging topics at morning and afternoon tea or coffee breaks.

LITERATURE CITED

Akuzawa R, Fox PF. 1998. Purification and characterization of an acid phosphatase from *Lactococcus lactis* ssp. *lactis* 303. *Food Res. Int.* 31:157–65

Bansal N, Fox PF, McSweeney PLH. 2007. Aggregation of rennet-altered casein micelles at low temperatures. *J. Agric. Food Chem.* 55:3120–26

Bansal N, Fox PF, McSweeney PLH. 2009. Comparison of the level of residual coagulant activity in different cheese varieties. *J. Dairy Res.* 76:290–93

Bansal N, Fox PF, McSweeney PLH. 2010. Inhibition of rennet activity in cheese using equine blood serum. *Dairy Sci. Technol.* 90:1–13

---

*Deceased.

Bansal N, Drake MA, Piraino P, Broe ML, Harboe M, et al. 2009. Suitability of recombinant camel (*Camelus dromedarius*) chymosin as a coagulant for Cheddar cheese. *Int. Dairy J.* 19:510–17

Baral A, Fox PF, O'Connor TP. 1995. Isolation and general characterization of an extracellular proteinase from *Pseudomonas tolassii* LMG 234T. *Phytochemistry* 39:757–62

Brennan NM, Brown R, Goodfellow M, Ward AC, Bersford TP, et al. 2001. *Corynebacterium mooreparkense* sp. Nov., and *Corynebacterium casei* sp. Nov., isolated from surface smear-ripened cheese. *Int. J. Syst. Evol. Microbiol.* 51:843–52

Brennan NM, Ward AC, Beresford TP, Fox PF, Goodfellow M, Cogan TP. 2002. Biodiversity of the bacterial flora on the surface of a smear cheese. *Appl. Environ. Microbiol.* 68:820–30

Di Cagno R, Miracle RE, De Angelis M, Minervini F, Rizzelo CG, et al. 2007. Comparison of the compositional, microbiological, volatile profile and sensory characteristics of four Italian semi-hard goats' milk cheese. *J. Dairy Res.* 74:468–79

Farkye NY, Fox PF. 1991. Preliminary study on the contribution of plasmin to Cheddar cheese ripening: cheese containing plasmin inhibitor, 6-aminohexanoic acid. *J. Agric. Food Chem.* 39:786–88

Farkye NY, Fox PF, Fitzgerald GF, Daly C. 1990. Proteolysis and flavour development in Cheddar cheese made exclusively with single strain Prt^{+} or Prt^{-} strains. *J. Dairy Sci.* 73:874–80

Fernandez M, Singh TK, Fox PF. 1998. Isolation and characterization of peptides from the diafiltration permeate of the water-soluble fraction of Cheddar cheese. *J. Agric. Food Chem.* 46:4512–17

Fernandez-Espla MD, Fox PF. 1997. Purification and characterization of a X-prolyl dipeptidyl aminopeptidase from *Propionibacterium shermanii* NCDO 853. *Int. Dairy J.* 7:23–29

Fernandez-Espla MD, Fox PF. 1998. Effect of adding *Propionibacterium shermanii* NCDO 853 or *Lactobacillus casei* ssp. *casein* IFPL 731 on proteolysis and flavour development in Cheddar cheese. *J. Agric. Food Chem.* 46:1224–34

Fernandez-Espla MD, Fox PF, Martin-Hernandez MC. 1997. Purification and characterization of a novel serine-aminopeptidase from *Lactobacillus casei* ssp. *casei* IFPL 736. *J. Agric. Food Chem.* 45:1624–28

Folkertsma B, Fox PF. 1992. Use of the Cd-ninhydrin reagent to assess proteolysis in cheese during ripening. *J. Dairy Res.* 59:217–24

Folkertsma B, Fox PF, McSweeney PLH. 1996. Accelerated ripening of Cheddar cheese at elevated temperatures. *Int. Dairy J.* 6:1117–34

Fox PF. 1963. Potentiometric determination of salt in cheese. *J. Dairy Sci.* 46:744–45

Fox PF. 1969a. Influence of temperature and pH on the proteolytic activity of rennet extract. *J. Dairy Sci.* 54:1214–18

Fox PF. 1969b. Milk-coagulating and proteolytic activities of rennet, bovine pepsin and porcine pepsin. *J. Dairy Res.* 36:427–33

Fox PF. 1970. Influence of aggregation on the susceptibility of casein to proteolysis. *J. Dairy Res.* 37:173–80

Fox PF. 1981. Heat-induced changes in milk proceeding coagulation. *J. Dairy Sci.* 64:2127–37

Fox PF. 1982. Heat-induced coagulation of milk. In *Developments in Dairy Chemistry*, Vol. 1: *Proteins*, ed. PF Fox, pp. 189–228. London: Applied Science Publ.

Fox PF. 2002. Exogenous enzymes in dairy technology. In *Handbook of Food Enzymology*, ed. JR Whitaker, AGJ Voragen, D Wong, G Beldman, pp. 279–301. New York: Marcel Dekker

Fox PF. 2003. Milk proteins: general and historical aspects. See Fox & McSweeney 2003, pp. 1–48

Fox PF, Brodkorb A. 2008. The casein micelle: historical aspects, current concepts and significance. *Int. Dairy J.* 18:677–84

Fox PF, Guiney J. 1972. A procedure for the partial fractionation of the α_s-casein complex. *J. Dairy Res.* 39:49–53

Fox PF, Guiney J. 1973. Casein micelle structure: susceptibility of various casein systems to proteolysis. *J. Dairy Res.* 40:229–34

Fox PF, Hoynes MCT. 1975. Heat stability of milk: influence of colloidal calcium phosphate and β-lactoglobulin. *J. Dairy Res.* 42:427–35

Fox PF, Hoynes MCT. 1976. Heat stability characteristics of ovine, caprine and equine milks. *J. Dairy Res.* 43:433–42

Fox PF, Kelly AL. 2006. Indigenous enzymes in milk: overview and historical aspects—Parts 1 & 2. *Int. Dairy J.* 16:500–16, 517–32

Fox PF, Kosikowski FV. 1967. Some effects of hydrogen peroxide on casein and its implications in cheese-making. *J. Dairy Sci.* 50:1183–88

Fox PF, McSweeney PLH, eds. 2003. *Advanced Dairy Chemistry*, Vol. 1: *Proteins*. New York: Kluwer Acad. -Plenum. 3rd ed.

Fox PF, Morrissey PA. 1972. Casein micelle structure: location of κ-casein. *J. Dairy Res.* 39:387–94

Fox PF, Morrissey PA. 1977. Reviews in the progress of dairy science: the heat stability of milk. *J. Dairy Res.* 44:627–46

Fox PF, O'Connor TP, McSweeney PLH, Guinee TP, O'Brien NM. 1996a. Cheese: physical, biochemical and nutritional aspects. *Adv. Food Nutr. Res.* 39:163–328

Fox PF, Power P, Cogan TM. 1989. Physical and biochemical properties. In *Enzymes of Psychrotrophs in Raw Foods*, ed. RC McKellar, pp. 58–120. Boca Raton, FL: CRC Press

Fox PF, Tarassuk NP. 1968. Bovine milk lipase. I. Isolation from skim milk. *J. Dairy Sci.* 51:826–33

Fox PF, Walley BF. 1971a. Influence of sodium chloride on the proteolysis of casein by rennin and pepsin. *J. Dairy Res.* 38:165–70

Fox PF, Walley BF. 1971b. Bovine pepsin: preliminary cheese-making experiments. Irish. *J. Agric. Res.* 10:358–60

Fox PF, Whitaker JR, O'Leary PA. 1977. Isolation and characterization of sheep pepsin. *Biochem. J.* 161:389–98

Fox PF, Yaguchi M, Tarassuk NP. 1967. Distribution of lipase in milk proteins. II. Dissociation from κ-casein with dimethylformamide. *J. Dairy Sci.* 50:307–12

Fox PF, Wallace JM, Morgan S, Lynch CM, Niland EJ, Tobin J. 1996b. Acceleration of cheese ripening. *Antonie van Leeuwenhoek* 70:271–97

Garcia de Fernando GD, Fox PF. 1991. Extracellular proteinases from *Micrococcus* GF. II. Isolation and characterization. *Lait* 71:371–82

Gobbetti M, Corsetti A, Fox PF. 1995. Purification and characterization of an aminopeptidase from *Pseudomonas fluorescens*. *J. Dairy Sci.* 78:44–54

Gobbetti M, Fox PF, Stepaniak L. 1997a. Esterases from *Lactobacillus*: isolation and characterization of an esterase from *Lactobacillus plantarum* 2739. *J. Dairy Sci.* 80:3099–106

Gobbetti M, Lanciotti R, Di Angelis M, Carbo MA, Massini R, Fox PF. 1999. Study of the effects of temperature, pH, NaCl and a_w on the proteolytic and lipolytic activities of cheese-related lactic acid bacteria (NSLAB) by quadratic response surface methodology. *Enzyme Microbiol. Technol.* 25:795–809

Gobbetti M, Lowney S, Smacchi E, Battistotti B, Damiani P, Fox PF. 1997b. Microbiology and biochemistry of Taleggio cheese during ripening. *Int. Dairy J.* 7:509–17

Gobbetti M, Morea M, Baruzzi F, Carbo MR, Matarante A, et al. 2002. Microbiological, compositional, biochemical and textural characterisation of Caciocavallo Pugliese cheese during ripening. *Int. Dairy J.* 12:511–23

Gobbetti M, Smacchi E, Semeraro M, Fox PF, Lanciotti R, Cogan TM. 2001. Purification and characterization of an extracellular proline iminopeptidase from *Corynebacterium variabilis* NCDO 2101. *J. Appl. Microbiol.* 90:449–56

Godinho M, Fox PF. 1982. Ripening of Blue cheese: influence of salting rates on proteolysis. *Milchwissenschaft* 37:72–75

Grufferty MB, Fox PF. 1988a. Factors affecting the release of plasmin from casein micelles. *NZ. J. Dairy Sci. Technol.* 23:153–63

Grufferty MB, Fox PF. 1988b. Milk alkaline proteinase: a review. *J. Dairy Res.* 55:609–30

Guinee TP, Auty MAE, Feeney EP, Fox PF. 2002. Effect of pH and calcium concentration on the textural and functional properties of low-moisture Mozzarella cheese. *J. Dairy Sci.* 85:1655–69

Guinee TP, Feeney EP, Auty MAE, Fox PF. 2002. Effect of pH and calcium concentration on some textural and functional properties of Mozzarella cheese. *J. Dairy Sci.* 85:1655–69

Guinee T, Fox PF. 1984. Studies on Romano-type cheese: general proteolysis. *Irish J. Food Sci. Technol.* 8:105–14

Guinee TP, Fox PF. 1986. Influence of cheese geometry on the movement of sodium chloride and water during ripening. *Irish J. Food Sci. Technol.* 10:97–118

Guinee TP, Fox PF. 2004. Salt in cheese: physical, chemical and biological aspects. In *Cheese: Chemistry, Physics and Microbiology*, ed. PF Fox, PLH McSweeney, TM Cogan, TP Guinee, 1:207–59. London: Elsevier Acad. 3rd ed.

Hayaloglu AA, Guven M, Fox PF. 2002. Microbiological, biochemical and technological properties of Turkish White cheese, "Beyaz Peynir": a review. *Int. Dairy J.* 12:635–48

Hayaloglu AA, Guven M, Fox PF, McSweeney PLH. 2005. Influence of starters on chemical, biochemical and sensory changes in Turkish white-brined cheese during ripening. *J. Dairy Sci.* 88:3460–74. Erratum. 2005. *J. Dairy Sci.* 89:2353

Hewedi MM, Fox PF. 1984. Blue cheese: characterization of proteolysis. *Milchwissenschaft* 39:198–201

Huppertz T, Fox PF, de Kruif CG, Kelly AL. 2006a. High pressure–induced changes in bovine milk: a review. *Biochim. Biophys. Acta* 1764:593–98

Huppertz T, Hennebel J-B, Considine T, Shakeel-ur-Rehman, Kelly AL, Fox PF. 2006b. A method for the large-scale isolation of β-casein. *Food Chem.* 99:45–50

Huppertz T, Hinz K, Zobrist MR, Uniacke T, Kelly AL, Fox PF. 2005. Effects of high pressure treatment on the rennet coagulation and cheese-making properties of heated milk. *Innovative Food Sci. Emerg. Technol.* 6:279–85

Kilcawley KN, Wilkinson MG, Fox PF. 1998. Enzyme-modified cheese: a review. *Int. Dairy J.* 8:1–10

Kilcawley KN, Wilkinson MG, Fox PF. 2006. A novel two-stage process for the production of enzyme-modified cheese. *Food Res. Int.* 39:619–27

Kosikowski FV, Fox PF. 1968. Low heat, hydrogen peroxide and bactofugation treatments of milk to control coliforms in Cheddar cheese. *J. Dairy Sci.* 51:1018–22

Kuchroo CN, Fox PF. 1983. A fractionation scheme for the water soluble nitrogen in Cheddar cheese. *Milchwissenschaft* 38:389–91

Kuchroo CN, Rahilly J, Fox PF. 1983. Assessment of proteolysis in cheese by reaction with trinitrobenzene sulfonic acid. *Ir. J. Food Sci. Technol.* 7:129–33

Law JM, Fitzgerald GF, Daly C, Fox PF, Farkye NY. 1992. Proteolysis and flavour development in Cheddar cheese made with single starter strain *L. lactis* subsp. *lactis* 317 or *L. lactis* subsp. *cremoris* HP. *J. Dairy Sci.* 75:1173–85

Law JM, Fitzgerald GF, Uniacke-Lowe T, Daly C, Fox PF. 1993. Contribution of lactococcal starter proteinases to proteolysis in Cheddar cheese. *J. Dairy Sci.* 72:2455–67

Lucey JA, Gorry C, O'Kennedy B, Kalab M, Tan-Kinita R, Fox PF. 1996. Effect of acidification and neutralization of milk on some physico-chemical properties of casein micelles. *Int. Dairy J.* 6:257–72

Lynch CM, Muir DD, Banks JM, McSweeney PLH, Fox PF. 1999. Influence of adjunct cultures of *Lactobacillus paracasei* ssp. *paracasei* or *Lactobacillus plantarum* on Cheddar cheese ripening. *J. Dairy Sci.* 82:1618–28

Madkor S. Fox PF, Shalabi S. Metwalli NH. 1987. Studies on the ripening of Stilton cheese: lipolysis. *Food Chem.* 25:93–109

Malin EL, Alaimo MH, Brown EM, Aramini JM, Germann MW, et al. 2001. Solution structures of casein peptides: NMR, FTIR, CD, and molecular modelling of α_{s1}-casein 1–23. *J. Prot. Chem.* 20:391–404

McGann TCA, Fox PF. 1974. Physico-chemical properties of casein micelles reformed from urea-treated milk. *J. Dairy Res.* 41:45–53

McGarry A, Law J, Coffey A, Daly C, Fox PF, Fitzgerald GF. 1994. Effect of genetically modifying the lactococcal proteolytic system on ripening and flavour development in Cheddar cheese. *Appl. Environ. Microbiol.* 60:4226–33

McGoldrick MA, Fox PF. 1999. Intervarietal comparison of proteolysis in cheese. *Z. Lebensm. Forsch. A* 208:90–99

McSweeney PLH, Olson NF, Fox PF, Healy A, Hojrup P. 1993. Proteolytic specificity of chymosin on bovine α_{s1}-casein. *J. Dairy Res.* 60:401–12

Mohammed KS, Fox PF. 1987. Heat-induced association-dissociation of casein micelles preceeding coagulation. *J. Dairy Res.* 54:377–87

Mooney JS, Fox PF, Healy A, Leaver J. 1998. Identification of principal water-insoluble peptides in Cheddar cheese. *Int. Dairy J.* 8:813–18

Morris HA, Guinee TP, Fox PF. 1985. Salt diffusion in Cheddar cheese. *J. Dairy Sci.* 68:1851–58

Mullan WMA, Daly C, Fox PF. 1981. Effects of cheese-making temperature on the interactions of lactic streptococci and their phages. *J. Dairy Res.* 48:465–71
Mulvihill DM, Fox PF. 1979a. Isolation and characterization of porcine β-casein. *Biochim. Biophys. Acta* 578:317–24
Mulvihill DM, Fox PF. 1979b. Proteolytic specificity of chymosin on bovine α_{s1}-casein. *J. Dairy Res.* 46:641–51
Murphy JM, Fox PF. 1991. Functional properties of α_s-/κ- or β-rich casein fractions. *Food Chem.* 39:211–28
O'Connell JE, Fox PF. 1999. Proposed mechanism for the effect of polyphenols on the heat stability of milk. *Int. Dairy J.* 9:523–36
O'Connell JE, Fox PF. 2001a. Effect of β-lactoglobulin and precipitation of calcium phosphate on the thermal coagulation of milk. *J. Dairy Res.* 68:81–94
O'Connell JE, Fox PF. 2001b. Significance and application of phenolic compounds in the production and quality of milk and dairy products. *Int. Dairy J.* 11:103–20
O'Connell JE, Fox PF. 2003. Heat-induced coagulation of milk. In *Advanced Dairy Chemistry*, Vol. 1: *Proteins*, 3rd ed, ed. PF Fox, PLH McSweeney, pp. 879–945. New York: Kluwer Academic-Plenum Publishers
O'Connell JE, Kelly AL, Fox PF, de Kruif C. 2001. Mechanism for the ethanol-dependent, temperature dissociation of casein micelles. *J. Agr. Food Chem.* 49:4424–28
O'Connell JE, Saracino P, Huppertz T, Uniacke T, de Kruif CG, et al. 2006. Influence of ethanol on the rennet-induced coagulation of milk. *J. Dairy Res.* 73:312–17
O'Connell JM, Steinle S, Reiter F, Auty MAE, Kelly AL, Fox PF. 2003. Properties of casein micelles reformed from heated mixtures of milk and ethanol. *Colloid Interfac. Sci. A: Physicochem. Eng. Aspects* 213:265–73
O'Connor P, Fox PF. 1973. Temperature-dependent dissociation of casein micelles from the milk of various species. *Neth. Milk Dairy J.* 27:199–217
O'Donovan CM, Wilkinson MG, Guinee TP, Fox PF. 1996. An investigation of the autolytic properties of different strains of lactococci during cheese ripening. *Int. Dairy J.* 6:1149–65
O'Keeffe AM, Fox PF, Daly C. 1978. Proteolysis in Cheddar cheese: role of coagulant and starter bacteria. *J. Dairy Res.* 45:465–77
O'Leary PA, Fox PF. 1973. Ovine pepsin: suitability as a rennet substitute. *Ir. J. Agric. Res.* 12:267–73
O'Leary PA, Fox PF. 1974. A method for the quantitative analysis of the enzyme complement in commercial rennets. *J. Dairy Res.* 41:381–87
O'Leary PA, Fox PF. 1975. A procedure for the isolation of gastric enzymes. *J. Dairy Res.* 42:445–51
O'Shea BA, Uniacke-Lowe T, Fox PF. 1996. Objective assessment of Cheddar cheese quality. *Int. Dairy J.* 6:1135–47
O'Sullivan M, Fox PF. 1991. Evaluation of microbial chymosin from genetically engineered *Kluyveromyces lactis*. *Food Biotechnol.* 5:19–32
O'Sullivan MM, Kelly AL, Fox PF. 2002. Effect of transglutaminase on the heat stability of milk: a possible mechanism. *J. Dairy Sci.* 85:1–7
Patel CV, Fox PF, Tarassuk NP. 1968. Bovine milk lipase. II. Characterization. *J. Dairy Sci.* 51:1879–86
Phelan JA, Guiney J, Fox PF. 1973. Proteolysis of β-casein in Cheddar cheese. *J. Dairy Res.* 40:105–12
Pripp AH, Shakeel-ur-Rehman, McSweeney PLH, Sorhaug T, Fox PF. 2000. Comparative study by multivariate statistical analysis of proteolysis in a sodium caseinate solution under cheese-like conditions caused by strains of *Lactococcus*. *Int. Dairy J.* 10:25–31
Rattray FP, Fox PF. 1997. Purification and characterization of an intracellular esterase from *Brevibacterium linens* ATCC 9174. *Int. Dairy J.* 7:273–78
Rattray FP, Fox PF, Healy A. 1996. Specificity of an extracellular proteinase from *Brevibacterium linens* ATCC 9174 on bovine α_{s1}-casein. *Appl. Environ. Microbiol.* 62:501–506
Rattray FP, Fox PF, Healy A. 1997. Specificity of an extracellular proteinase from *Brevibacterium linens* ATCC 9174 on bovine β-casein. *Appl. Environ. Microbiol.* 63:2468–71
Requena T, Piallez C, Fox PF. 1993. Peptidases and proteinase activity on *Lactococcus lactis*, *Lactobacillus casei* and *Lactobacillus plantarum*. *Z. Lebensm. Forsch.* 196:351–55
Shakeel-ur-Rehman, Banks JM, Muir DD, Brechney E, McSweeney PLH, Fox PF. 2000. Influence of ripening temperature on the volatiles profile and flavour of Cheddar cheese made raw or pasteurised milk. *Int. Dairy J.* 10:55–65

Shakeel-ur-Rehman, Fox PF. 2002. Effect of added α-ketoglutaric acid, pyruvic acid or pyridoxal phosphate on proteolysis and quality of Cheddar cheese. *Food Chem.* 76:21–26

Shakeel-ur-Rehman, McSweeney PLH, Fox PF. 1998a. Protocol for the manufacture of minature cheeses. *Le Lait* 78:607–20

Shakeel-ur-Rehman, Feeney EP, McSweeney PLH, Fox PF. 1998b. Inhibition of residual coagulant in cheese using pepstatin. *Int. Dairy J.* 8:987–92

Shakeel-ur-Rehman, Waldron DS, Fox PF. 2004. Effect of modifying lactose concentration in cheese curd on proteolysis and quality of Cheddar cheese. *Int. Dairy J.* 14:591–97

Shalabi SI, Fox PF. 1982. Heat stability of milk: influence of modification of lysine and arginine on the heat stability–pH profile. *J. Dairy Res.* 49:607–17

Shalabi SI, Fox PF. 1987. Electrophoretic analysis of cheese: comparison of methods. *Ir. J. Food Sci. Technol.* 11:135–51

Singh H, Fox PF. 1987. Heat stability of milk: role of β-lactoglobulin in the pH-dependent dissociation of micellar κ-casein. *J. Dairy Res.* 54:509–21

Singh TK, Fox PF, Healy A. 1995. Water-soluble peptides in Cheddar cheese: isolation and identification of peptides in the diafiltration retentate of the water-soluble fraction. *J. Dairy Res.* 62:629–40

Smacchi E, Gobbetti M, Lanciotti R, Fox PF. 1999. Purification and characterization of an extracellular proline iminopeptidase from *Arthrobacter nicotianae* 9458. *FEMS Microbiol. Lett.* 178:191–97

Stepaniak L, Fox PF. 1995. Characterization of the principal intracellular endopeptidase from *Lc. lactis* ssp. *lactis* MG 1363. *Int. Dairy J.* 5:699–713

Stepaniak L, Fox PF, Daly C. 1982. Isolation and general characterization of a heat-stable proteinase from *Pseudomonas fluorescens* AFT 36. *Biochim. Biophys. Acta* 717:376–83

Tan-Kinitia RH, Fox PF. 1996. Effect of enzymatic hydrolysis of lactose on the heat stability of milk or concentrated milk. *Neth. Milk Dairy J.* 50:267–77

Uniacke-Lowe T, Huppertz T, Fox PF. 2010. Equine milk proteins: chemistry, structure and nutritional significance. *Int. Dairy J.* 20:609–20

Vernile A, Spano G, Beresford TP, Fox PF, Massa M. 2009. Biodiversity of *Staphylococcus* species in Pecorino Siciliano cheese. *Milchwissenschaft* 64:67–70

Wallace JM, Fox PF. 1997. Effect of adding free amino acids to Cheddar cheese curd on proteolysis, flavour and texture development. *Int. Dairy J.* 7:157–67

Wilkinson MG, Guinee TP, Fox PF. 1994. Autolysis of and proteolysis by different strains of starter bacteria during Cheddar cheese ripening. *J. Dairy Res.* 61:249–62

Zarmpoutis IV, McSweeney PLH, Fox PF. 1997. Proteolysis in blue-veined cheese: an intervarietal study. *Ir. J. Agric. Food Res.* 36:219–29

Zobrist MR, Huppurtz T, Uniacke T, Fox PF, Kelly AL. 2005. High pressure–induced changes in the rennet coagulation properties of bovine milk. *Int. Dairy J.* 15:655–62

Dairy Products in the Food Chain: Their Impact on Health

Kirsty E. Kliem and D.I. Givens

University of Reading, Reading RG6 6AR, United Kingdom; email: k.e.kliem@reading.ac.uk, d.i.givens@reading.ac.uk

Annu. Rev. Food Sci. Technol. 2011. 2:21–36

First published online as a Review in Advance on September 14, 2010

The *Annual Review of Food Science and Technology* is online at food.annualreviews.org

This article's doi:
10.1146/annurev-food-022510-133734

1941-1413/11/0410-0021$20.00

Keywords

milk, dairy, cardiovascular disease, cancer, fatty acids

Abstract

Milk is a complex and complete food containing an array of essential nutrients that contribute toward a healthy, balanced diet. Numerous epidemiological studies have revealed that high consumption of milk and dairy products may have protective effects against coronary heart disease (CHD), stroke, diabetes, certain cancers (such as colorectal and bladder cancers), and dementia, although the mechanisms of action are unclear. Despite this epidemiological evidence, milk fatty acid profiles often lead to a negative perception of milk and dairy products. However, altering the fatty acid profile of milk by changing the dairy cow diet is a successful strategy, and intervention studies have shown that this approach may lead to further benefits of milk/dairy consumption. Overall, evidence suggests individuals who consume a greater amount of milk and dairy products have a slightly better health advantage than those who do not consume milk and dairy products.

THE CONTRIBUTION OF MILK AND DAIRY PRODUCTS TO THE HUMAN DIET

SFA: saturated fatty acid(s)

Introduction

Milk is a unique and complex food of great interest, intended to be a complete food for young mammals. The important role of cow's milk in the human diet as a supplier of energy, protein, and other key nutrients, including calcium, is well known. Milk is essentially a complex colloidal system comprising globules of milk fat suspended in an aqueous medium containing lactose, a range of proteins, mineral salts, and water soluble vitamins. Milk from modern Holstein/Friesian cows will typically contain about 40, 36, and 45 g kg^{-1} of fat, protein, and lactose, respectively, and have an energy content of approximately 2.8 MJ kg^{-1}. The fat and protein contents of milk vary considerably due to the breed and nutrition of the cow. The effect of breed is particularly noticeable in milk from Channel Island breeds, which typically have a fat content of approximately 65 g kg^{-1}. Although milk is widely consumed, there has recently been increased concern that a high proportion (>50%) of the energy in milk is derived from fat, approximately 70% of which is made up of saturated fatty acids (SFA).

Trends in Milk and Dairy Product Consumption

Globally, the demand for animal-derived foods in general is growing rapidly, driven by a combination of population growth, urbanization, and rising income. **Table 1** shows the trends in milk consumption over the past 40 years for various regions of the world. Although the historical and projected trend is upward, in the United Kingdom and other Western countries consumption has shown considerable change over recent decades. The decline in whole milk consumption in the United Kingdom and the increase in lower-fat milk consumption (Givens & Kliem 2009) reflects a general trend in a number of other developed countries (**Figure 1**, see color insert). Denmark, France, the United States, and Canada also show similar trends since the 1970s. Germany, however, has shown a less-marked decline in whole milk consumption, and there has been little change in consumption of lower-fat milk up to 1993, although data for recent years were not available. The consumption of liquid milk in Italy has always been much lower than in northern Europe, but between 1977 and 1990 this remained relatively constant for both whole and lower-fat milk (**Figures 1** and **2**, see color insert).

Figure 3 (see color insert) illustrates the changes in cheese consumption. Of the selected countries, France has the highest consumption followed by Italy. The United Kingdom has always had the lowest. Most countries show a gradual increase in cheese consumption, although that of Canada and Denmark did fluctuate during the 1990s, and that of the United Kingdom post-1980s remained relatively constant. Butter consumption appears to have followed several different trends (**Figure 4**, see color insert). Consumption in Germany, Italy, and the United States appears to

Table 1 Trends in consumption of milk (from WHO/FAO 2003)

	Milk (kg/person/year)		
Region	**1964–66**	**1977–99**	**2030**[a]
World	73.9	78.1	89.5
Developing countries	28.0	44.6	65.8
Transition countries	156.7	159.1	178.7
Industrialized countries	185.5	212.2	221.0

[a]projected.

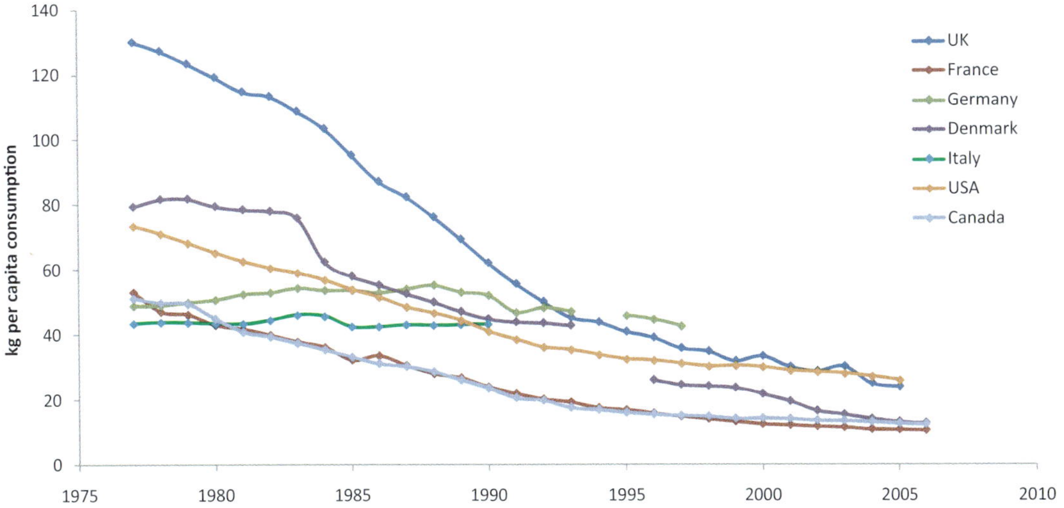

Figure 1

Consumption of whole milk in selected countries, 1977–2006. Sources: IDF, personal communication; DEFRA (2001, 2005); CNIEL (2007); ZMP (2007); USDA (2007); Agriculture and Agri-Food Canada (2007); Danish Dairy Board (2007).

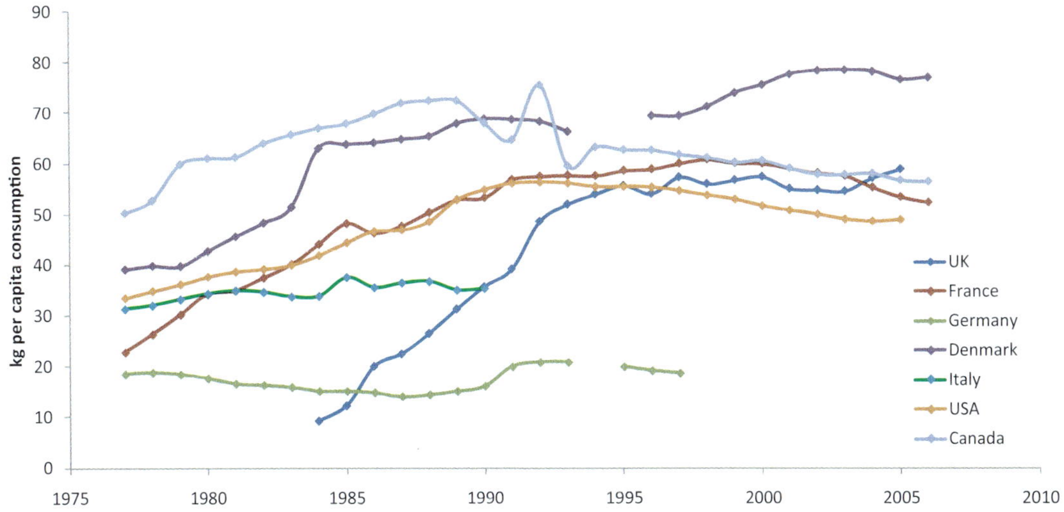

Figure 2

Consumption of lower fat milk in selected countries, 1977–2006. Sources: IDF, personal communication; DEFRA (2001, 2005); CNIEL (2007); ZMP (2007); USDA (2007); Agriculture and Agri-Food Canada (2007); Danish Dairy Board (2007).

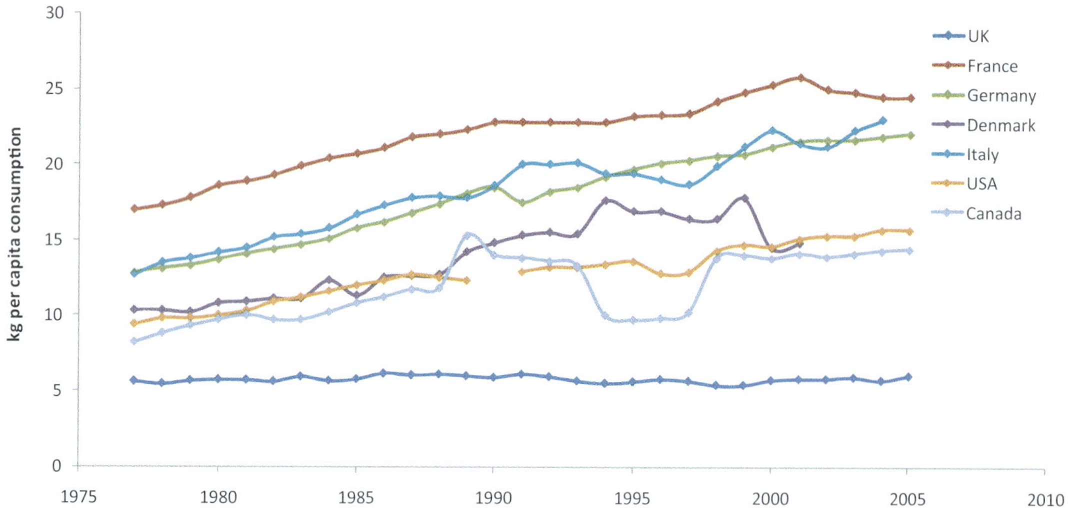

Figure 3

Consumption of cheese in selected countries, 1977–2006. Sources: IDF, personal communication; DEFRA (2001 & 2005); CNIEL (2007); ZMP (2007); USDA (2007); Agriculture and Agri-Food Canada (2007); Danish Dairy Board (2007).

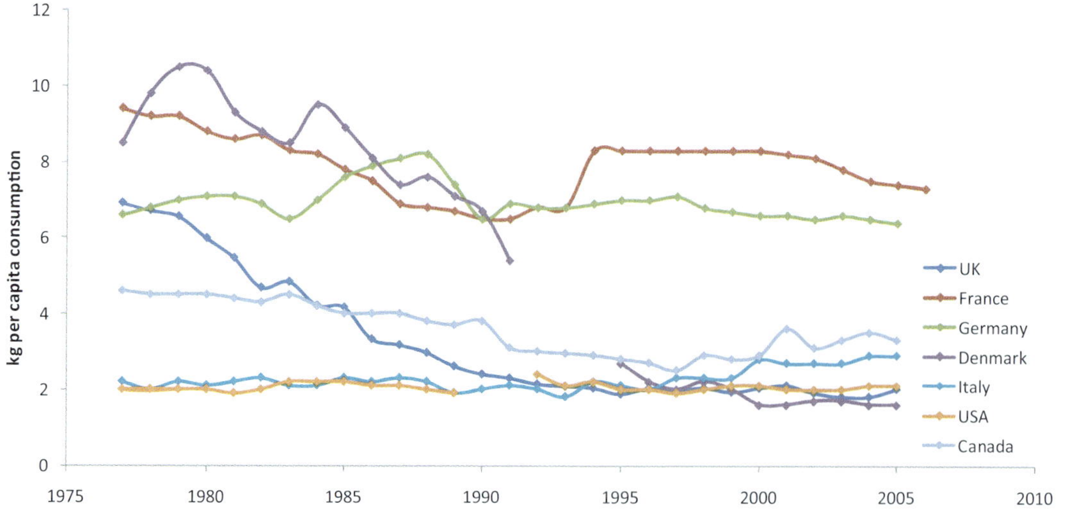

Figure 4

Consumption of butter in selected countries, 1977–2006. Sources: IDF, personal communication; DEFRA (2001 & 2005); CNIEL (2007); ZMP (2007); USDA (2007); Agriculture and Agri-Food Canada (2007); Danish Dairy Board (2007).

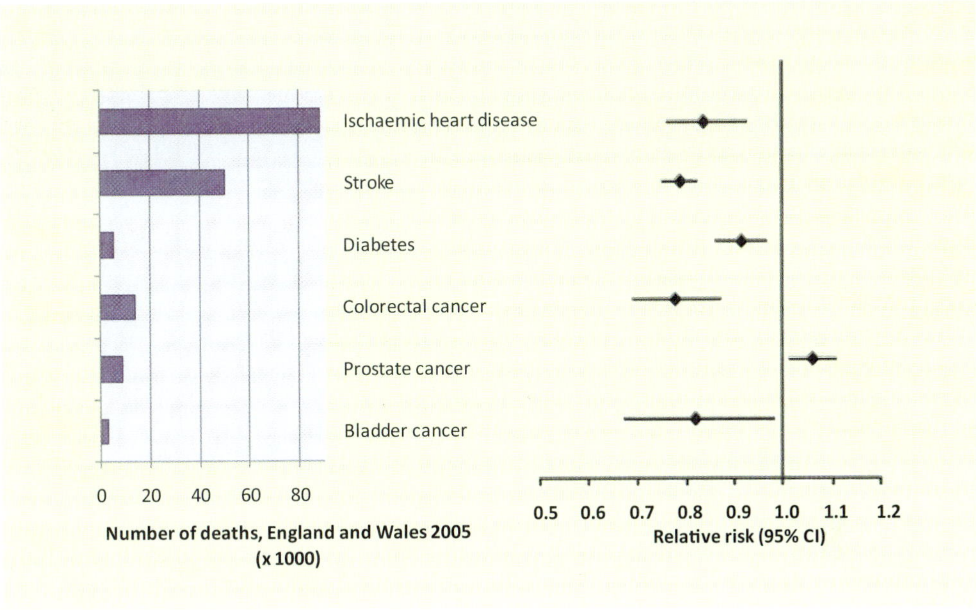

Figure 5

Deaths in England and Wales (2005) from various causes verses relative risk for these causes in subjects with highest dairy consumption relative to subjects with lowest dairy consumption (adapted from Elwood et al. 2008).

have remained constant, whereas that in the United Kingdom and Denmark has declined, and that of France and Canada has fluctuated.

Nutrients Provided by Milk and Dairy Products

Milk and dairy-derived foods are available in the retail market in many forms. Based on food intakes assessed by the U.K. National Diet and Nutrition Survey (Henderson et al. 2003a,b) over the period July 2000 to June 2001, the contribution of the major dairy-derived food types to energy and nutrient intakes of the United Kingdom male population (aged 19 to 64 years) is shown in **Table 2**.

Milk and dairy food products are clearly important sources of protein, calcium, phosphorus, iodine, riboflavin, and vitamins A and B_{12}. Indeed, milk and dairy products alone usually provide

Table 2 Energy and selected nutrients provided by milk and dairy products to men's diets in the UK (derived from Henderson et al. 2003a,b)

Energy/ nutrient	Contribution from milk and dairy products	Liquid whole milk	Semi- and skimmed milk	Cheese	Other dairy products	Butter	Total dairy
Energy	Intake (MJ/d)	0.49	nas[a]	0.29	0.10	0.10	0.97
	% of EAR[b]	5	nas	3	1	1	9
Protein	Intake (g/d)	1.8	5.3	4.4	1.8	0	13.2
	% of RNI[c]	3	10	8	3	0	24
Fat	Intake (g/d)	1.7	2.6	5.2	2.6	2.6	14.7
	% of ADI[d]	2	3	6	3	3	17
Calcium	Intake (mg/d)	61	203	112	41	nas	417
	% of RNI	9	29	16	5	nas	60
Phosphorus	Intake (mg/d)	45	165	90	30	nas	330
	% of RNI	8	30	16	6	nas	60
Magnesium	Intake (mg/d)	6.2	19	nas	6.2	nas	31
	% of RNI	2	6	nas	2	nas	10
Zinc	Intake (mg/d)	0.21	0.60	0.64	0.21	nas	1.7
	% of RNI	2	7	7	2	nas	18
Iodine	Intake (μg/d)	15	46	4.4	11	nas	77
	% of RNI	11	33	3	8	nas	55
Vitamin A[e]	Intake (μg/d)	20	31	61	31	41	183
	% of RNI	3	4	9	4	6	26
Riboflavin	Intake (mg/d)	0.12	0.40	0.07	0.09	nas	0.68
	% of RNI	9	31	5	7	nas	52
Vitamin B_{12}	Intake (μg/d)	0.41	1.4	0.34	0.14	nas	2.2
	% of RNI	27	91	23	9	nas	150
Folate	Intake (μg/d)	25	nas	nas	nas	nas	25
	% of RNI	13	nas	nas	nas	nas	13

[a]nas, not available separately, included in total.
[b]EAR, estimated average requirement.
[c]RNI, reference nutrient intake.
[d]ADI, average daily intake.
[e]Retinol equivalents.

more than the daily recommended intake of vitamin B_{12}. The current importance of semi-skimmed and skimmed milk in the diet is clear and notably, some 70% of liquid milk is consumed as semi-skimmed (Milk Development Council 2004). Although milk and dairy products only provide about 13% of the recommended folate intake of 200 μg day^{-1} (Henderson et al. 2003b), there is evidence that the presence of milk in the diet can increase overall folate bioavailability compared with diets containing no milk (Wigertz et al. 1997). Also, Smith et al. (1985) proposed that folate present in milk is more available than folates from other foods, at least for infants. It is probable that these properties of milk are due to the fact that it uniquely contains folate-binding proteins. Although their exact role is not fully understood (de Jong et al. 2005), it is possible that these proteins increase the availability of folate in other foods consumed and make milk a good candidate for fortification with folate.

MUFA: monounsaturated fatty acid

PUFA: polyunsaturated fatty acid

Prospective cohort study: follows a group of individuals over a length of time, to detect how factors being studied affect health outcome

Case-control study: compares individuals with a defined condition with individuals who do not have the condition but are otherwise similar

CHD: coronary heart disease

RR: relative risk

Milk and dairy products, including butter, contribute almost 20% of the total fat consumed, but because the lipids in these products are rich in SFA they make a major contribution to SFA intake. In the United Kingdom, the National Diet and Nutrition Survey (Henderson et al. 2003a) estimated the contribution as 30% of total SFA intake, although this excluded milk fats in manufactured foods such as cakes, biscuits, etc. A study on fatty acid intake across Europe (Hulshof et al. 1999) suggested a higher figure of 40% for the United Kingdom, and milk and dairy foods were consistently the largest source of SFA, with the greatest contribution being observed in Germany and France, where some 60% of SFA were from these foods (Hulshof et al. 1999). Contribution of milk and dairy products to *cis*-monounsaturated fatty acid (MUFA) consumption averaged 18% across the 13 European countries included in the study of Hulshof et al. (1999). However, milk and dairy products are not a major contributor to *cis*-polyunsaturated fatty acid (PUFA) consumption (Hulshof et al. 1999).

Milk and milk-derived foods contribute to most of the *trans* fatty acids consumed (Hulshof et al. 1999). The contribution in Germany, Italy, and France is particularly high at approximately 72%, 62%, and 61%, respectively, although in the United Kingdom this is lower (25%). The high contributions in Germany arise mainly from butter consumption, whereas in Italy cheese is probably the main source. In addition, milk and dairy products are major contributors to the consumption of conjugated linoleic acid isomers (67% total consumption) (Lawson et al. 2001), which are mainly found in ruminant products.

EFFECTS OF MILK AND DAIRY PRODUCT CONSUMPTION ON CHRONIC DISEASE RISK

Epidemiological studies presenting outcomes in terms of disease incidence have major advantages over the use of risk factors as predictors of disease. Disadvantages of such studies include the long periods of time required to measure disease outcomes and the large numbers of participants required. Nonetheless, there are many published prospective cohort and case-control studies that have attempted to investigate relationships between dairy product consumption and risk of chronic disease. In general, prospective cohort studies provide stronger evidence than case-control studies (Elwood et al. 2010).

Coronary Heart Disease

Coronary heart disease (CHD) refers to the failure of the coronary circulation to supply adequate blood flow to cardiac and surrounding tissue. Risk factors for CHD include hypertension, diabetes, and hyperlipidemia. Several case-control studies have demonstrated an overall reduced relative risk (RR) (0.83) of myocardial infarction in patients consuming higher amounts of milk and/or dairy products (Elwood et al. 2008). A number of prospective cohort studies (with follow-up periods of between 8 and 28 years) reported differences in RR of CHD related to milk and dairy consumption. For example, Mann et al. (1997) reported an increase in RR (1.50) of CHD events in high milk consumers (n = 10,802), whereas a significant risk reduction (0.88) of CHD events was observed by Shaper et al. (1991) in high milk consumers (n = 7,735). The Nurses' Health Study specified variations in response to milk of different fat levels in terms of RR of CHD events, with high whole milk consumers having increased RR (1.67) compared with high low-fat milk consumers (0.78) (Hu et al. 1999). A meta-analysis of fifteen prospective cohort studies (Elwood et al. 2008) revealed that overall, high milk consumption did not result in an increase of RR of CHD (0.91 when including whole milk consumption reported by Hu et al. 1999; 0.84 when including low-fat milk consumption reported by Hu et al. 1999). More recent, large meta-analyses of both prospective cohort and clinical studies concluded that milk consumption displayed weak evidence (RR = 0.94) of being the cause of CHD (Mente et al. 2009), and the study of Elwood et al. (2010) involving 4.3 million person-years and 16,212 CHD events concluded that high intakes of milk are suggestive of a reduced risk of CHD [RR = 0.92, 95% confidence interval (CI) 0.80–0.99].

Meta-analysis: combines the results of several studies that address a set of related research hypotheses

CI: confidence interval

LDL: low density lipoprotein

HDL: high density lipoprotein

The mechanism of action of milk and dairy products on risk of CHD is complicated. Some studies have reported that increased dairy consumption increases circulating total lipoprotein concentrations and low density lipoprotein (LDL) concentrations (Thompson et al. 1982, Steinmetz et al. 1994). However, there is limited evidence of effect of dairy product consumption on circulating high density lipoprotein (HDL) cholesterol levels, increases in which are known to exert a protective effect against CHD. A prospective case-control study that used plasma phospholipid 15:0 and 17:0 concentrations as markers of milk fat intake found there was an inverse relationship between the sum of 15:0 and 17:0 in phospholipids and total cholesterol and plasma triacylglycerols (Warensjö et al. 2004). Interestingly, different dairy products may exert varying effects on plasma lipoprotein levels. Plasma total and LDL cholesterol were significantly higher in volunteers consuming 40 g of dairy fat as butter per day compared with the same amount of cheese (Nestel et al. 2005). It was suggested that fermentation products in cheese or the physical state of cheese fat globules compared with butter may explain differences between the two dairy fat types.

Stroke

A meta-analysis of eleven cohort studies (with follow-up periods ranging from 12.9 to 68 years) with ischemic stroke as an outcome reported that overall, the risk of stroke in subjects with the highest dairy intake compared to that of subjects with the lowest intake was reduced (RR = 0.79, 95% CI 0.68–0.91), although there was significant heterogeneity between studies (Elwood et al. 2010). The same authors attempted to differentiate between cohort studies reporting hemorrhagic strokes and subarachnoid bleeds (Elwood et al. 2010), although there were fewer published data with these events as an outcome and again significant heterogeneity. The maximum follow-up period was 16 years. Overall, high dairy consumers displayed a lower RR for hemorrhagic (0.75) and subarachnoid (0.65) strokes. However, this meta-analysis should be considered with caution due to the low number of studies included.

Individual cohort studies have suggested possible mechanisms behind the apparent protective effect of high dairy intake against stroke incidence. The Honolulu study (a cohort of initially 8,006 men) reported that over 22 years, men who did not drink milk were twice as likely to experience a stroke event as those who regularly consumed two glasses or more of milk per day (Abbott et al. 1996). More detailed analysis of intake data revealed that calcium intake from nondairy sources was not related to stroke incidence, suggesting that other constituents of milk may also have an effect, which will be discussed later.

Hypertension is itself a risk factor for stroke (and CHD). A prospective cohort of 28,886 women (with a 10-year follow up) reported that a high intake of low fat dairy products was associated with an 11% reduced RR of hypertension (Wang et al. 2008). A smaller study involving 2,245 older participants (≥55 years) demonstrated an inverse relationship between dairy product consumption and hypertension (Engberink et al. 2009). When analyzed in greater detail, it was apparent that this reduced risk of hypertension was specific to milk consumption and not that of cheese or fermented dairy products. The effect of dairy products on hypertension is thought to be mainly related to calcium intake because dietary calcium suppresses 1,25 dihydroxyvitamin D production, which among other things reduces the cellular influx of calcium into smooth muscle cells, thus reducing contraction and vascular resistance of smooth muscle cells (Zemel 2001). Comparisons of dairy and nondairy sources of calcium have shown that dairy calcium may exert a greater effect on hypertension (Griffith et al. 1999), which may reflect the balanced composition of milk in terms of calcium, potassium, and magnesium content. The review of Álvarez-León et al. (2006) concluded that a diet balanced in these minerals is recommended to prevent hypertension. Also, the presence of bioactive peptides within the casein and whey fractions of milk may also contribute to reduced vascular resistance in high dairy product consumers. These have been found to inhibit angiotensin-I-converting enzyme, thus modulating endothelial function and leading to vasodilation (Fitzgerald & Meisel 2000).

Diabetes

Type II diabetes incidence is increasing worldwide, and the combination of diabetic characteristics such as dysfunctional glucose-insulin homeostasis, dyslipidaemia, and proinflammatory states leads to diabetes increasing the risk of cardiovascular disease. There are relatively few cohort studies analyzing the relationship between milk and dairy consumption and diabetes incidence. The longest cohort study to date was followed up over 25 years and showed that a higher milk intake resulted in a reduced RR (0.57) of diabetes than low milk intakes in 640 males (Elwood et al. 2007). Four other cohort studies (with follow-up periods ranging from 6.9 to 12 years) resulted in similar outcomes for high dairy consumers. A meta-analysis concluded that overall, the RR of diabetes incidence from high versus low milk and dairy consumption was 0.85 (95% CI, 0.75–0.96) (Elwood et al. 2010). Another recent review and meta-analysis reached the same conclusion (Pittas et al. 2007) and suggested that incidence of type II diabetes was inversely related to total vitamin D and calcium status.

Selected Cancers

Table 3 presents relevant information from the recent report of the World Cancer Research Fund (2007). These data suggest that increased milk consumption appears to reduce the RR of colorectal cancers, and possibly bladder cancer, although data from both the cohort and case-control studies displayed moderate to high heterogeniety. However, the data also suggest a high milk and dairy intake may increase risk of prostate cancer.

Colorectal cancer. Cho et al. (2004) conducted a pooled analysis of ten prospective cohort studies, which involved detailed investigation into different types of foods consumed. The follow-up periods ranged from 6 to 16 years, and over 500,000 subjects (men and women) were included. The authors showed that milk consumption (>250 g day^{-1} compared with <70 g day^{-1}) was

Table 3 Relationship between milk and dairy product consumption and cancer (data taken from the World Cancer Research Fund (2007)

Cancer	Predictor	Number of studies	Pooled relative risk	Heterogeneity
Colorectal	Milk	4 cohorts	0.94 (0.85–1.03)	Low
	Milk	10 cohorts	0.78 (0.69–0.88)	Not reported
Prostate	Milk	8 cohorts	1.05 (0.98–1.14)	Low
	Milk	6 case-control	1.08 (0.98–1.19)	Moderate
	Milk and dairy	8 cohorts	1.06 (1.01–1.11)	Moderate
	Milk and dairy	5 case-control	1.03 (0.99–1.07)	Low
Bladder	Milk	4 cohorts	0.82 (0.67–0.99)	Moderate
	Milk	3 case-control	1.00 (0.87–1.14)	High

inversely related to colorectal cancer incidence (RR 0.85). The same authors also reported that there was no significant evidence that cheese or yogurt affected RR. It was concluded that both milk and calcium intake were associated with a reduction in risk of colorectal cancer.

Prostate cancer. A meta-analysis of case-control studies revealed that high milk consumers tended to show an increased risk (as measured by an odds ratio of 1.68) of prostate cancer compared with low milk consumers (Qin et al. 2004). However, these authors pointed out that eight of the eleven studies involved hospital-based controls, which are more prone to bias. A larger study (whereby thirty-seven prospective cohort and four intervention studies were reviewed) reported that consumption of milk and dairy products was either positively associated or had no effect on prostate cancer risk (Dagnelie et al. 2004). Further investigation revealed that calcium intakes of between 1330 mg day^{-1} and 1840 mg day^{-1} showed no association with prostate cancer risk (Shuurman et al. 1999 and Chan et al. 2000, respectively), and yet calcium intakes of greater than 2000 mg day^{-1} were associated with increased risk (Giovannucci et al. 1997, Rodriguez et al. 2003). Elwood et al. (2008) calculated from the results of pooled cohort studies that overall, milk and dairy products increased RR to prostate cancer (RR 1.06). However, Huncharek et al. (2008) carried out a meta-analysis of pooled data from 45 observational studies and concluded that cohort studies showed no evidence of a relationship between dairy products (RR 1.06; 95% CI 0.92, 1.02) or milk consumption (RR 1.06; 95% CI 0.91, 1.23) and risk of prostate cancer, and this conclusion was supported by data from case-control studies. Similarly, Parodi (2009) concluded that there was not any plausible biological explanation for an association between dairy product consumption and prostate cancer; however, he conditioned this by saying that a combination of factors, as yet undetermined, cannot be excluded. Overall, the current evidence indicates very little, if any, evidence that high consumers of milk have greater risk of prostate cancer than low consumers.

Bladder cancer. The results from the World Cancer Research Fund (2007) (**Table 3**) highlight the heterogeneity of data from cohort studies measuring the effects of dairy consumption on risk of bladder cancer. Results of a more recent cohort study involving 120,852 men and women, and with a follow-up period of 16.3 years, demonstrated little effect of dairy intake on bladder cancer risk (Keszei et al. 2010). However, when individual dairy products were analyzed it was reported that fermented dairy product intake appeared to have an inverse relationship with bladder cancer risk (hazard ratio 0.71), whereas butter intake by women was positively associated with bladder cancer (hazard ratio 1.61). A similar effect with fermented dairy products was observed by Larsson et al. (2008) over a 9.4 year follow up, with no effect of total dairy consumption or milk and cheese.

Figure 5 (see color insert) illustrates the number of deaths in England and Wales in 2005 from various causes, together with pooled RRs for these diseases in subjects with the highest milk/dairy consumption relative to risk in subjects with the lowest consumption. RR estimates for all cancers are those listed in **Table 3**. These data suggest that consumers of high intakes of dairy products appear to have a survival advantage compared with consumers of low intakes of dairy products (Elwood et al. 2008).

Dementia

Partly because of the increased life expectancy, there is growing concern about the trend in the prevalence of dementia, with the numbers in the United Kingdom projected to double between 2001 and 2040 (Jagger et al. 2009). There are few studies that have examined any relationship between milk consumption and risk of dementia. One study that did look at this was the Adult Health Study, a prospective cohort of 1,774 subjects in Hiroshima, Japan born before September 1932 (Yamada et al. 2003). Between 1992 and 1997, 1,660 were shown to have no dementia and 114 had dementia (51 with Alzheimer's disease, 38 with vascular dementia). Vascular dementia prevalence increased significantly with age, with higher systolic blood pressure and, crucially, with lower milk intake. The odds ratios of vascular dementia for age (in five-year increments), systolic blood pressure (10 mm Hg increments), and milk intake (almost daily versus less than four times a week) were 1.29, 1.33, and 0.35, respectively. Yamada et al. (2003) concluded that increased blood pressure and low milk intake in midlife were associated with vascular dementia detected 25 to 30 years later. The mechanism whereby milk provided protection cannot be stated with certainty but given other evidence linking milk consumption with lowered blood pressure, it would seem probable that this mechanism was involved. Clearly, much further research is needed in this area.

IMPROVING THE NUTRITIONAL QUALITY OF MILK USING ANIMAL NUTRITION

Manipulating milk constituent content is a difficult task, not least due to the complex nature of milk and its production by lactating mammals. The majority of milk consumed in Western diets is of bovine origin, so the following discussions relate to experimental studies involving dairy cows. The previous sections of this chapter have suggested that the apparent protective or detrimental effects of milk and dairy products against certain chronic diseases can be partially attributed to the high calcium content of milk or the presence of a high concentration of SFA (as a proportion of total fatty acids). Calcium excretion in milk is highly complex with calcium taking a variety of forms, including casein-bound calcium, colloidal calcium phosphate, calcium citrate, and free ionized calcium, with the majority being within casein micelles (Neville et al. 1995). Casein content of milk is independent of nutrition (Coulon et al. 1998), so changing milk calcium content indirectly by manipulating casein content by nutrition is unrealistic. However, a recent study has shown a moderate heritability for milk calcium concentration, which would lead to good prospects for selective breeding (van Hulzen et al. 2009).

Including a wide range of lipid-rich supplements in the diet of the dairy cow has been the most common means for manipulating milk fatty acid composition. However, both the type and source of the lipid and basal diet influences the extent of changes that can be achieved. Attempts to increase the concentration of one or more fatty acids may cause changes in other fatty acids, which may reduce potential beneficial effects. For example, feeding diets to enrich milk fat with *cis*-9 C18:1, C20:5 *n-3* or C22:6 *n-3* content will usually also result in an increase in *trans* C18:1

concentrations. Although likely to have few negative effects on health, such changes are generally perceived negatively by consumers and some health professionals.

The following sections summarize the possibilities of using animal nutrition to alter the fatty acid profile of milk, which, if adopted on a wide scale, may offer a potential means of reducing cardiovascular disease at a population level.

Reducing the Saturated Fatty Acid Content of Bovine Milk

Supplements of plant oils or oilseeds rich in unsaturated C18 fatty acids can be used to reduce the proportion of short- and medium-chain fatty acids (C6:0-C16:0) and increase the concentrations of long-chain fatty acids in milk (Grummer 1991, Doreau et al. 1999). These changes are primarily due to long-chain fatty acids (C16 and above) inhibiting de novo fatty acid synthesis in the mammary gland and because lipid supplements increase the amount of circulating long-chain fatty acids available for incorporation into milk fat. In general, feeding plant lipids to cows (other than palm oil rich in C16:0) has no effect on milk fat content of C4:0 or long-chain saturates (C16 and above), but consistently increases C18:0 concentrations at the expense of C16:0 (Palmquist et al. 1993, Chilliard et al. 2000). Furthermore, comparison of milk fatty acid responses when oils are fed in the diet compared with rumen-protected sources or duodenal infusions of these lipids indicates that the proportion of C6 and C8 fatty acids are lowered when dietary fats are exposed to ruminal metabolism, whereas the increase in milk C18 content during early lactation or in response to duodenal infusion is associated with a reduction in C10-C16 content (Chilliard et al. 2000). In all cases, inclusion of plant oils and oilseeds in the diet results in an unavoidable increase in milk *trans* C18:1 content in milk due to extensive lipolysis and biohydrogenation of C18 PUFA in the rumen. A number of studies on the effects of plant lipids on milk SFA were summarized by Givens & Kliem (2009).

An example of the effects of reducing the degree of saturation of fatty acids in dairy products was shown by the human dietary intervention study of Noakes et al. (1996) who studied 33 men and women for eight weeks, comparing the effects of fatty acid modified (51% SFA, 39% *cis*-MUFA) dairy products with normal dairy (70% SFA, 28% *cis*-MUFA). The modified products resulted in a significant reduction in total (0.28 mmol/l) and LDL cholesterol (0.24 mmol/l), with HDL cholesterol being unaffected. The authors suggest that if these changes were applied to Western populations, they would represent a potential strategy to lower the risk of CHD by about 10% without the need to change normal eating patterns.

Increasing the *cis* Monounsaturated Fatty Acid Content of Milk

Although C18:0 is the predominant long-chain fatty acid available for incorporation into milk fat, secretion of *cis*-9 C18:1 in milk exceeds mammary C18:0 uptake due to the activity of stearoyl CoA (Δ-9) desaturase activity in mammary secretory cells. Conversion of C18:0 to *cis*-9 C18:1 is the predominant precursor:product of the Δ-9 desaturase, transforming about 40% of C18:0 uptake by the mammary gland (Chilliard et al. 2000). It is therefore theoretically possible to exploit the ability of the mammary gland to enhance milk fat *cis*-9 C18:1 by supplementing diets with lipids rich in C18:0, such as tallow or hydrogenated oils. However, this approach does not change the *cis*-9 C18:1:C18:0 ratio in milk fat, and the feeding of tallow to dairy cows is not permitted within the European Union (Chilliard et al. 2000). Feeding plant oils or oilseeds rich in *cis*-9 C18:1 can be used to enhance milk fat *cis*-9 C18:1 content, but unless these sources are effectively protected from ruminal metabolism, this strategy will also increase the concentrations of *trans* C18:1 in milk. Supplements of *cis*-9 C18:1 acyl amides (Jenkins 1998, Loor et al. 2002) or high levels of rapeseeds or rapeseed oil in the diet (Murphy et al. 1987, Givens et al. 2003, Ryhänen et al. 2005) have been shown to substantially increase milk fat *cis*-9 C18:1 content (Givens & Kliem 2009), but both approaches can cause significant reductions in feed intake that can result in lowered milk production. Recent studies in our laboratory have however shown that rapeseed prepared by careful milling with wheat has substantial potential to be used in dairy cow diets to produce milk with lower saturates and higher *cis*-MUFA in a sustainable way (Givens et al. 2009, Kliem et al. 2009).

Effect of Increasing Monounsaturated Fatty Acids in Milk on *Trans* Fatty Acids

Including plant oils rich in C18:2 *n-6* and C18:3 *n-3* and fish oils in dairy cow diets causes *trans*-11 C18:1 to accumulate in the rumen, and this subsequently leads to increased concentrations in milk. While *trans*-11 C18:1 normally represents the major *trans* fatty acid, increases in it are usually accompanied by increases in other *trans* fatty acids.

There has been concern for many years about the negative health effects of dietary *trans* fatty acids because high intakes have been associated with a substantially increased risk of CHD (Willett et al. 1993, Kromhout et al. 1995, Ascherio et al. 1999), and the more recent meta-analysis of Mensink et al. (2003) indicated that *trans* fatty acids represented a greater risk to CHD than SFA. Early studies in the United Kingdom identified an association between consumption of hydrogenated vegetable and marine oils and deaths from ischemic heart disease (Thomas et al. 1983, Thomas 1992), and by the mid 1990s it was clear that not only did epidemiological data highlight the increased CHD risk, but unique adverse effects on blood lipids were also evident (Ascherio et al. 1999).

Despite the concern about dietary *trans* fatty acids, it seems that the metabolic response to different *trans* fatty acids can be variable, and it is of note that the profile of *trans* fatty acids in milk fat is quite different to that in industrially hydrogenated foods (Shingfield et al. 2008). Four prospective epidemiological studies have examined the relationship between the intake of *trans* fatty acids from ruminant derived foods and the risk of CHD (Willet et al. 1993, Pietinen et al. 1997, Oomen et al. 2001, Jakobsen et al. 2006). None of these studies found a significant positive relationship, and indeed in three of the studies there was a nonsignificant trend toward a negative relationship. These findings are supported by the overarching evidence discussed earlier, that increased milk consumption is associated with a reduction in the risk of ischemic heart disease (Elwood et al. 2004). Mozaffarian et al. (2006) proposed that lack of an increased risk of CHD associated with the intake of *trans* fatty acids from ruminant-derived foods relative to the substantially increased risk from industrially produced *trans* fatty acids may be a result of lower intakes, different bioactivities, or the fact that dairy and meat products contain some other factors that negate any negative effects that the *trans* fatty acids present cause. It is noteworthy, however, that because comparisons of ruminant and industrial *trans* fatty acids have been based on few studies using relative intake data (e.g., quintiles of intakes), the review of Weggemans et al. (2004) examined the relationship between absolute intake (i.e., g consumed per day) of ruminant and industrial *trans* fatty acids and risk of CHD. They reported that where direct comparison was possible, there was no difference in risk between total, ruminant, and industrial *trans* fatty acids for daily intakes up to 2.5 g. At higher daily intakes (>3 g) total and industrial *trans* fatty acids are associated with an increased risk of CHD, but there were insufficient data available on ruminant *trans* fatty acids at this level of intake. Weggemans et al. (2004) therefore concluded that based on the small amount of data available there was no case to discriminate between ruminant and industrial *trans* fatty acids in dietary recommendations or legislation, although subsequently Lock et al. (2005) challenged this interpretation.

Because of the small amount of data available and given that most human intervention studies have evaluated monounsaturated *trans* fatty acids from industrial sources, a study (TRANSFACT) was designed to directly compare the effects of *trans* fatty acids from milk and industrial sources on risk factors for cardiovascular disease in healthy humans (Chardigny et al. 2006). The first output from the TRANSFACT study showed that industrial and ruminant *trans* fatty acids have different effects on CHD risk factors. Only industrial *trans* fatty acids lowered HDL cholesterol, although the responses were greater in women than in men (Chardigny et al. 2008). Another clinical comparison at two intake levels revealed that both sources increased total:HDL cholesterol similarly at a higher intake level (3.7% EI), but at a lower intake level (1.5% EI) there was little difference between a diet containing ruminant-derived *trans* fatty acids and the control diet (Motard-Bélanger et al. 2008). A recent review of 39 clinical studies concluded that all fatty acids with a double bond in the *trans* configuration can raise the ratio of LDL:HDL cholesterol (Brouwer et al. 2010). However, it should be remembered that clinical studies tend to be quite short in duration, and many involve higher intakes in *trans* fatty acids than that which is normally observed. Overall, there appears to be little if any increased risk of CHD from consumption of ruminant *trans* fatty acids, at least at current intakes.

CONCLUSIONS

Although it is generally accepted that milk and dairy products are foods that provide the diet with important amounts of key nutrients, there has been concern that high levels of consumption would increase the risk of cardiovascular disease and other chronic health problems. This concern has mainly been the result of the fact that milk-derived foods are often the largest single source of dietary SFA. Epidemiological evidence does not support this view, and indeed there are indications that milk may provide some protective effects against vascular disease and other conditions. Despite this, there is intervention evidence that further benefits may be had from consumption of milk/dairy products that have had some of the SFA replaced by *cis*-monounsaturates. This, however, needs further evaluation in more powerful intervention studies.

SUMMARY POINTS

1. Consumption of whole milk is on the decline in many Western countries; however, since the early 1980s consumption of lower fat milk appears to be increasing. Cheese and butter consumption trends have varied depending on country.
2. Milk and dairy products are important sources of many essential nutrients (such as vitamin B_{12} and riboflavin) and have been shown to contribute toward around 60% of the recommended adult calcium and phosphorus intakes.
3. Prospective cohort and clinical studies have revealed that, overall, consumers of greater amounts of milk and dairy products appear not to have an increased risk of coronary heart disease, stroke, or hypertension compared with individuals with lower dairy consumption. Some studies have reported a possible protective effect of dairy products against cardiovascular disease risk.
4. The relative risk of type II diabetes incidence has been reported to be reduced for consumers of high amounts of dairy products compared with low dairy consumption.

5. A high milk and dairy intake may reduce the relative risk of colorectal and, possibly, bladder cancers. However, a meta-analysis of prospective cohort and case-control studies has reported inconclusive results for risk of prostate cancer.
6. Many of the protective effects of milk and dairy consumption are thought to be related to milk calcium content. However, milk also contains other essential nutrients, such as bioactive peptides, that may contribute.
7. Despite epidemiological evidence suggesting protective effects of milk on coronary heart disease, the saturated fat content of milk fat has led to recommendations to reduce milk and dairy product consumption. Studies have shown that changing the fatty acid profile of milk by reducing saturates and increasing *cis*-monounsaturates by altering the dairy cow diet is one strategy for further improving the beneficial effects of milk consumption.

FUTURE ISSUES

1. Epidemiological evidence relates mainly to full fat milk, and there are few data relating to fat-reduced milk, cheese, butter, cream, etc. Given the trends in dairy product consumption, this needs attention, such that any differential effects can be confirmed.
2. Epidemiology does not ascribe causes or mechanisms. There is a need to follow up the key epidemiological outcomes with well-powered intervention and mechanistic studies.
3. Attention should focus on the effects of milk/dairy foods on vascular health. Newer functional measures, such as endothelial function, should be explored.
4. Intervention evidence is needed to confirm the benefits from consumption of milk/dairy products that have had some of the saturated fatty acids replaced by *cis*-monounsaturates.

DISCLOSURE STATEMENT

The authors are not aware of any affiliations, memberships, funding, or financial holdings that might be perceived as affecting the objectivity of this review.

LITERATURE CITED

Abbott RD, Curb JD, Rodriguez BL, Sharp DS, Burchfiel CM, Yano K. 1996. Effect of dietary calcium and milk consumption on risk of thromboembolic stroke in older middle-aged men. *Stroke* 27:813–18

Agric. Agri-Food Can. 2007. *Canadian Dairy Information Center*. **http://www.dairyinfo.gc.ca/index_e.php?s1=dff-fcil&s2=cons&s3=cons**

Álvarez-León E-E, Roman-Vinas B, Serra-Majem LS. 2006. Dairy products and health: a review of the epidemiological evidence. *Br. J. Nutr.* 96:594–99

Ascherio A, Katan MB, Stampfer MJ, Willett WC. 1999. *Trans* fatty acids and coronary heart disease. *N. Engl. J. Med.* 340:1994–98

Brouwer IA, Wanders AJ, Katan MB. 2010. Effect of animal and industrial *trans* fatty acids on HDL and LDL cholesterol levels in humans—a quantitative review. *PLoS ONE* 5:1–10

Chan JM, Pietinen P, Virtanen M, Malila N, Tangrea J, et al. 2000. Diet and prostate cancer risk in a cohort of smokers, with a specific focus on calcium and phosphorus (Finland). *Cancer Causes Control* 11:859–67

Chardigny J-M, Destaillats F, Malpuech-Brugère C, Moulin J, Bauman DE, et al. 2008. Do *trans* fatty acids from industrially produced sources and from natural sources have the same effect on cardiovascular disease risk factors in healthy subjects? Results of the *trans* Fatty Acids Collaboration (TRANSFACT) study. *Am. J. Clin. Nutr.* 87:558–66

Chardigny J-M, Malpuech-Brugère C, Dionisi F, Bauman DE, German B, et al. 2006. Rationale and design of the TRANSFACT project phase I: A study to assess the effect of the two different dietary sources of *trans* fatty acids on cardiovascular risk factors in humans. *Contemp. Clin. Trials* 27:364–73

Chilliard Y, Ferlay A, Mansbridge RM, Doreau M. 2000. Ruminant milk fat plasticity: nutritional control of saturated, polyunsaturated, *trans* and conjugated fatty acids. *Ann. Zootech.* 49:181–205

Cho E, Smith-Warner SA, Spiegelman D, Beeson WL, van den Brandt PA, et al. 2004. Dairy foods, calcium, and colorectal cancer: a pooled analysis of 10 cohort studies. *J. Natl. Cancer Inst.* 96:1015–122

CNIEL. 2007. **http://www.maison-du-lait.com/scripts/public/stat.asp?Language=GB**

Coulon JB, Hurtaud C, Remond B, Vérité R. 1998. Factors contributing to variation in the proportion of casein in cows' milk true protein: a review of recent INRA experiments. *J. Dairy Res.* 65:375–87

Dagnelie PC, Schuurman AG, Goldbohm RA, Van Den Brandt PA. 2004. Diet, anthropometric measures and prostate cancer risk. *BJU Int.* 98:1939–50

Danish Dairy Board. 2007. **http://www.mejeri.dk**

DEFRA. 2001. *The National Food Survey.* **http://www.statistics.defra.gov.uk/esg/**

DEFRA. 2005. *Expenditure and Food Survey.* **http://www.statistics.defra.gov.uk/esg/**

De Jong RJ, Verwei M, West CE, Van Vliet T, Sieberlink E. 2005. Bioavailability of folic acid from fortified pasteurised and UHT-treated milk in humans. *Eur. J. Clin. Nutr.* 59:906–913

Doreau M, Chillard Y, Rulquin H, Demeyer DL. 1999. Manipulation of milk fat in dairy cows. In *Recent Advances in Animal Nutrition*, ed. PC Garnsworthy, J Wiseman, pp. 81–109. Nottingham, UK: Nottingham Univ. Press

Elwood PC, Givens DI, Beswick AD, Fehily AM, Pickering JE, Gallacher J. 2008. The survival advantage of milk and dairy consumption: an overview of evidence from cohort studies of vascular diseases, diabetes and cancer. *J. Am. Coll. Nutr.* 27:S723–34

Elwood PC, Pickering JE, Fehily AM. 2007. Milk and dairy consumption, diabetes and the metabolic syndrome: the Caerphilly Prospective study. *J. Epidemiol. Commun. Health* 61:695–98

Elwood PC, Pickering JE, Givens DI, Gallacher JE. 2010. The consumption of milk and dairy foods and the incidence of vascular disease and diabetes: An overview of the evidence. *Lipids.* doi: 10.1007/s11745-010-3412-5

Elwood PC, Pickering JE, Hughes J, Fehily AM, Ness AR. 2004. Milk drinking, ischaemic heart disease and ischaemic stroke II. Evidence from cohort studies. *Eur. J. Clin. Nutr.* 58:718–24

Engberink MF, Hendriksen MA, Schouten EG, van Rooij FJA, Hofman A, et al. 2009. Inverse association between dairy intake and hypertension: the Rotterdam Study. *Am. J. Clin. Nutr.* 89:1877–83

Fitzgerald RJ, Meisel H. 2000. Milk protein-derived peptide inhibitors of angiotensin-1-converting enzyme. *Br. J. Nutr.* 84(Suppl. 1):S33–37

Giovannucci E, Rimm EB, Wolk A, Ascherio A, Stampfer MJ, et al. 1997. Calcium and fructose intake in relation to risk of prostate cancer. *Cancer Res.* 58:442–47

Givens DI, Allison R, Blake JS. 2003. Enhancement of oleic acid and vitamin E concentrations of bovine milk using dietary supplements of whole rapeseed and vitamin E. *Anim. Res.* 52:531–42

Givens DI, Kliem KE. 2009. Improving the nutritional quality of milk. In *Functional and Speciality Beverage Technology*, ed. P Paquin, pp. 135–69. Cambridge, UK: Woodhead

Givens DI, Kliem KE, Humphries DJ, Shingfield KJ, Morgan R. 2009. Effect of replacing calcium salts of palm oil distillate with rapeseed oil, milled or whole rapeseeds on milk fatty acid composition in cows fed maize silage-based diets. *Animal* 3:1067–74

Griffith LE, Guyatt GH, Cook RJ, Bucher HC, Cook DJ. 1999. The influence of dietary and nondietary calcium supplementation on blood pressure: an updated metaanalysis of randomized controlled trials. *Am. J. Hypertens.* 12:84–92

Grummer RR. 1991. Effect of feed on the composition of milk fat. *J. Dairy Sci.* 74:3244–57

Henderson L, Gregory J, Irving K, Swan G. 2003a. *The National Diet and Nutrition Survey: Adults Aged 19–64 Years. Volume 2: Energy, Protein, Carbohydrate, Fat and Alcohol Intake*. London: The Station. Off.

Henderson L, Irving K, Gregory J, Bates CJ, Prentice A, et al. 2003b. *The National Diet and Nutrition Survey: Adults Aged 19–64 Years. Volume 3: Vitamin and Mineral Intake and Urinary Analytes*, London: The Station. Off.

Hu FB, Stampfer MJ, Mandon JE, Ascherio A, Colditz GA, et al. 1999. Dietary saturated fats and their food sources in relation to the risk of coronary heart disease in women. *Am. J. Clin. Nutr.* 70:1001–8

Hulshof KFAM, van Erp-Baart MA, Anttolainen M, Becker W, Church SM, et al. 1999. Intake of fatty acids in Western Europe with emphasis on trans fatty acids: The TRANSFAIR study. *Eur. J. Clin. Nutr.* 53:143–57

Huncharek M, Muscat J, Kupelnick B. 2008. Dairy products, dietary calcium and vitamin D intake as risk factors for prostate cancer: A meta-analysis of 26,769 cases from 45 observational studies. *Nutr. Cancer* 60:421–41

Jagger C, Matthews R, Lindesay J, Robinson T, Croft P, Brayne C. 2009. The effect of dementia trends and treatments on longevity and disability: a simulation model based on the MRC Cognitive Function and Ageing Study (MRC CFAS). *Age Ageing* 38:319–25

Jakobsen MU, Bysted A, Andersen NL, Heitmann BL, Hartkopp HB, et al. 2006. Intake of ruminant *trans* fatty acids and risk of coronary heart disease. *Atheroscler. Suppl.* 7:9–11

Jenkins TC. 1998. Fatty acid composition of milk from Holstein cows fed oleamide or canola oil. *J. Dairy Sci.* 81:794–800

Keszei AP, Schouten LJ, Goldbohm RA, van den Brandt PA. 2010. Dairy intake and the risk of bladder cancer in the Netherlands Cohort Study on diet and cancer. *Am. J. Epidemiol.* 171:436–46

Kliem KE, Humphries DJ, Givens DI. 2009. Effects of normal and high oleic acid rapeseed in the dairy cow diet on milk fatty acid composition. *Proc. Br. Soc. An. Sci.* 87

Kromhout D, Menotti A, Bloemberg B, Aravanis C, Blackburn H, et al. 1995. Dietary saturated and *trans* fatty acids and cholesterol and 25-year mortality from coronary heart disease: the Seven Countries Study. *Prev. Med.* 24:308–15

Larsson SC, Andersson SO, Johansson JE, Wolk A. 2008. Cultured milk, yoghurt and dairy intake in relation to bladder cancer risk in a prospective study of Swedish women and men. *Am. J. Clin. Nutr.* 88:1083–87

Lawson RE, Moss AR, Givens DI. 2001. The role of dairy products in supplying conjugated linoleic acid to man's diet: a review. *Nutr. Res. Rev.* 14:153–72

Lock AL, Parodi PW, Bauman DE. 2005. The biology of *trans* fatty acids: implications for human health and the dairy industry. *Aust. J. Dairy Technol.* 60:134–42

Loor JJ, Herbein JH, Jenkins TC. 2002. Nutrient digestion, biohydrogenation, and fatty acid profiles in blood plasma and milk fat from lactating Holstein cows fed canola oil or canolamide. *Anim. Feed Sci. Technol.* 97:65–82

Mann JI, Appleby PN, Key TI, Thorogood M. 1997. Dietary determinants of ischaemic heart disease in health conscious individuals. *Heart* 78:450–55

Mensink RP, Zock PL, Kester AD, Katan MB. 2003. Effects of dietary fatty acids and carbohydrates on the ratio of serum total to HDL cholesterol and on serum lipids and apolipoproteins: a meta-analysis of 60 controlled trials. *Am. J. Clin. Nutr.* 77:1146–55

Mente A, de Koning L, Shannon HS, Anand SS. 2009. A systematic review of the evidence supporting a causal link between dietary factors and coronary heart disease. *Arch. Int. Med.* 169:659–69

Milk Dev. Counc. 2004. *Dairy Facts and Figures 2003*. Cirencester, UK: Milk Dev. Counc.

Motard-Bélanger A, Charest A, Grenier G, Paquin P, Chouinard Y, et al. 2008. Study of the effect of *trans* fatty acids from ruminants on blood lipids and other risk factors for cardiovascular disease. *Am. J. Clin. Nutr.* 87:593–99

Mozaffarian D, Katan MB, Ascherio A, Stampfer MJ, Willett WC. 2006. *Trans* fatty acids and cardiovascular disease. *N. Engl. J. Med.* 354:1601–13

Murphy M, Udén P, Palmquist DL, Wiktorsson H. 1987. Rumen and total diet digestibilities in lactating cows fed diets containing full-fat rapeseed. *J. Dairy Sci.* 70:1572–82

Nestel PJ, Chronopulos A, Cehun M. 2005. Dairy fat in cheese raises LDL cholesterol less than that in butter in mildly hypercholesterolaemic subjects. *Eur. J. Clin. Nutr.* 59:1059–63

Neville MC, Zhang P, Allen JC. 1995. Minerals, ions and trace elements in milk. In *Handbook of Milk Composition*, ed. RG Jensen, pp. 577–92. San Diego, CA: Academic

Noakes M, Nestel PJ, Clifton PM. 1996. Modifying the fatty acid profile of dairy products through feedlot technology lowers plasma cholesterol of humans consuming the products. *Am. J. Clin. Nutr.* 63:42–46

Oomen CM, Ocke MC, Feskens EJ, van Erp-Baart MA, Kok FJ, Kromhout D. 2001. Association between *trans* fatty acid intake and 10-year risk of coronary heart disease in the Zutphen Elderly Study: a prospective population-based study. *Lancet* 357:746–51

Palmquist DL, Beaulieu DA, Barbano DM. 1993. Feed and animal factors influencing milk fat composition. *J. Dairy Sci.* 76:1753–71

Parodi PW. 2009. Dairy product consumption and the risk of prostate cancer. *Int. Dairy J.* 19:551–65

Pietinen P, Ascherio A, Korhonen P, Hartman AM, Willett WC, et al. 1997. Intake of fatty acids and risk of coronary heart disease in a cohort of Finnish men: the Alpha-Tocopherol, Beta-Carotene Cancer Prevention Study. *Am. J. Epidemiol.* 145:876–87

Pittas AG, Lau J, Hu FB, Dawson-Hughes B. 2007. The role of vitamin D and calcium in type 2 diabetes. A systematic review and meta-analysis. *J. Clin. Endocrinol. Metab.* 92:2017–29

Qin LQ, Xu JY, Wang PY, Kaneko T, Hoshi K, Sato A. 2004. Milk consumption is a risk factor for prostate cancer: meta-analysis of case-control studies. *Nutr. Cancer* 48:22–27

Rodriguez C, McCullough ML, Mondul AM, Jacobs EJ, Fakhrabadi-Shokoohi D, et al. 2003. Calcium, dairy products and risk of prostate cancer in a prospective cohort of United States men. *Cancer Epidemiol. Biomark. Prev.* 12:597–603

Ryhänen E-L, Tallavaara K, Griinari JM, Jaakkola S, Mantere-Alhonen S, Shingfield KJ. 2005. Production of conjugated linoleic acid enriched milk and dairy products from cows receiving grass silage supplemented with a cereal-based concentrate containing rapeseed oil. *Int. Dairy J.* 15:207–17

Shaper AG, Wannamethee G, Walker M. 1991. Milk, butter, and heart disease. *Br. Med. J.* 302:785–86

Shingfield KJ, Chilliard Y, Toivonen V, Kairenius P, Givens DI. 2008. *Trans* fatty acids and bioactive lipids in ruminant milk. *Adv. Exp. Med. Biol.* 606:3–65

Shuurman AF, van den Brandt PA, Dorant E, Goldbohm RA. 1999. Animal products, calcium and protein and prostate cancer risk in The Netherlands Cohort Study. *Br. J. Cancer* 80:1107–13

Smith AM, Picciano MF, Deering RH. 1985. Folate intake and blood concentrations of term infants. *Am. J. Clin. Nutr.* 41:590–98

Steinmetz KA, Childs MT, Stimson C. 1994. Effect of consumption of whole milk and skim milk on blood lipid profiles in healthy men. *Am. J. Clin. Nutr.* 59:612–18

Thomas LH. 1992. Ischaemic heart disease and consumption of hydrogenated marine oils in England and Wales. *J. Epidemiol. Commun. Health* 46:78–82

Thomas LH, Winter JA, Scott RG. 1983. Concentration of 18:1 and 16:1 *trans* unsaturated fatty acids in the adipose body tissue of decedents dying of ischaemic heart disease compared with controls: analysis by gas liquid chromatography. *J. Epidemiol. Commun. Health* 37:16–21

Thompson LU, Jenkins DJA, Amer MAV, Reichert R, Jenkins A, Kamulsky J. 1982. The effect of fermented and unfermented milks on serum cholesterol. *Am. J. Clin. Nutr.* 36:1106–11

USDA. 2007. *Food Availability (per capita) System.* **http://www.ers.usda.gov/data/foodconsumption/**

van Hulzen KJE, Sprong RC, ven der Meer R, van Arendonk JAM. 2009. Genetic and nongenetic variation in concentration of selenium, calcium, potassium, zinc, magnesium and phosphorus in milk of Dutch Holstein-Friesian cows. *J. Dairy Sci.* 92:5754–59

Wang L, Manson JE, Buring JE, Lee IM, Sesso HD. 2008. Dietary intake of dairy products, calcium and vitamin D and the risk of hypertension in middle-aged and older women. *Hypertension* 51:1073–79

Warensjö E, Jansson J-H, Berglund L, Boman K, Ahrén B, et al. 2004. Estimated intake of milk fat is negatively associated with cardiovascular risk factors and does not increase the risk of a first acute myocardial infarction. A prospective case-control study. *Br. J. Nutr.* 91:635–42

Weggemans RM, Rudrum M, Trautwein EA. 2004. Intake of ruminant versus industrial *trans* fatty acids and risk of coronary heart disease—what is the evidence? *Eur. J. Lipid Sci. Technol.* 106:390–97

Wigertz K, Hallmans G, Sandberg A-S, Tidehag P, Jägerstad MI. 1997. *Improved apparent dietary folate absorption in ileostomy subjects with the incorporation of milk into a mixed diet.* Milk Folates. Characterization and availability. PhD thesis. Lund Univ.

Willett WC, Stampfer MJ, Manson JE, Colditz GA, Speizer FE, et al. 1993. Intake of trans fatty acids and risk of coronary heart disease among women. *Lancet* 341:581–85

WHO/FAO. 2003. *Diet, Nutrition and the Prevention of Chronic Diseases. Report of a Joint WHO/FAO Expert Consultation*. Geneva: WHO

World Cancer Res. Fund. 2007. *World Cancer Research Fund/American Institute for Cancer Research: Food, Nutrition, Physical Activity and the Prevention of Cancer: A Global Perspective*, pp. 129–32. Washington, DC: Am. Inst. Cancer Res.

Yamada M, Kasagi F, Sasaki H, Masunari N, Mimori Y, Suzuki G. 2003. Association between dementia and midlife risk factors: the radiation effects research foundation Adult Health Study. *J. Am. Geriatr. Soc.* 51:410–14

Zemel MB. 2001. Calcium modulation of hypertension and obesity: mechanisms and implications. *J. Am. Coll. Nutr.* 20:S428–35

ZMP. 2007. *Evaluation of the School Milk Measure*. **http://ec.europa.eu/agriculture/eval/reports/schoolmilk/index_en.htm**

Avian Influenza: Public Health and Food Safety Concerns*

Revis Chmielewski and David E. Swayne

Southeast Poultry Research Laboratory, Agricultural Research Service, U.S. Department of Agriculture, Athens, Georgia 30605; email: David.Swayne@ars.usda.gov

Annu. Rev. Food Sci. Technol. 2011. 2:37–57

First published online as a Review in Advance on September 14, 2010

The *Annual Review of Food Science and Technology* is online at food.annualreviews.org

This article's doi:
10.1146/annurev-food-022510-133710

1941-1413/11/0410-0037$20.00

Keywords

bird flu, high pathogenicity avian influenza (HPAI), low pathogenicity avian influenza (LPAI), H5N1, H7N7

Abstract

Avian influenza (AI) is a disease or asymptomatic infection caused by *Influenzavirus* A. AI viruses are species specific and rarely cross the species barrier. However, subtypes H5, H7, and H9 have caused sporadic infections in humans, mostly as a result of direct contact with infected birds. H5N1 high pathogenicity avian influenza (HPAI) virus causes a rapid onset of severe viral pneumonia and is highly fatal (60% mortality). Outbreaks of AI could have a severe economic and social impact on the poultry industry, trade, and public health. Surveillance data revealed that H5N1 HPAI has been detected in imported frozen duck meat from Asia, and on the surface and in contaminated eggs. However, there is no direct evidence that AI viruses can be transmitted to humans via the consumption of contaminated poultry products. Implementing management practices that incorporate biosecurity principles, personal hygiene, and cleaning and disinfection protocols, as well as cooking and processing standards, are effective means of controlling the spread of the AI viruses.

INTRODUCTION

What is the Bird Flu?

Avian influenza (AI) is a disease or asymptomatic infection caused by viruses in the family *Orthomyxoviridae*, genus *Influenzavirus* A, which contains a genome composed of eight segments of single-stranded negative-sense RNA (Swayne & Halvorson 2008). The virus surface contains spikes of hemagglutinin and neuraminidase glycoproteins. The segmented RNA allows for the easy reassortment of the viral genome. The viral genome encodes for ten proteins: one nucleocapsid (NP), three transcriptase proteins (PB-1, PB-2, and PA), the hemagglutinin and neuraminidase surface glycoproteins (HA and NA), two matrix proteins (M1 and M2), and two nonstructural proteins (NS1 and NS2) (Alexander 2000, Lee & Saif 2009). Nucleocapsid and the three transcriptases (PB-1, PB-2, and PA) form the ribonucleoprotein complex that is responsible for mRNA transcription. AI viruses are characterized by their subtypes, pathotypes, genetic lineages, and clades. AI viruses are subtyped by their surface HA and NA glycoproteins, which are major determinants of the pathogenicity, transmission, and adaptation of the AI virus to other species, but these three traits plus infectivity are multigenic. However, the major determinant of pathogenicity is the HA. The HA is important for attachment and entrance into cells to replicate, whereas the function of neuraminidase is to release newly formed viruses (Swayne & Halvorson 2008). There are 16 different hemagglutinin (H1–16) and nine different neuraminidase (N1–9) subtypes. Such viruses have been detected in more than 100 species of wild birds, mostly from the orders *Anseriformes* (ducks, geese, and swans) and *Charadriiormes* (gulls, terns, and shorebirds), but usually without causing clinical signs and are thus of low pathogenicity (LP) (Stallknecht & Brown 2007). Mammals such as humans, pigs, horses, seals, whales, and cats have been sporadically infected with AI viruses (Swayne & Halvorson 2008). In the cases involving carnivores, infection occurred mainly through the consumption of H5N1 HPAI virus–infected birds or their products. Only H5 and H7 have been seen in nature in the high pathogenicity (HP) form, but most H5 and H7 AI viruses are of LP. Most commercially reared poultry in developed countries are free of AI viruses and such infections are rare (Swayne 2008b). When AI is present, it is usually as low pathogenicity avian influenza (LPAI) virus, but if infected by high pathogenicity avian influenza (HPAI) virus, the outcome can be devastating with near 100% mortality in chickens and turkeys. Commonly used vernacular for Eurasian H5N1 HPAI is bird flu, but technically, any AI virus could be termed bird flu.

Human Infection

AI viruses are considered species specific and rarely cross the species barrier (Cox & Uyeki 2008). However, since 1959, some AI virus isolates of subtypes H5, H7, and H9 have caused sporadic infections in humans (INFOSAN IFSAN- 2004). H5N1 HPAI virus was isolated from a domestic goose in Guangdong, China in 1996, and the following year was isolated from an outbreak in the live bird markets in Hong Kong. During the live bird market outbreaks of 1997, the first human case of H5N1 occurred in May, and by the end of 1997, there were 18 hospitalized cases with six fatalities. Other incidences of human infections associated with H5N1 HPAI outbreaks in poultry were reported in China in 2003 and throughout Southeast Asia from 2004 to the present. Human infections were mostly due to direct contact with infected birds (CDC 2006, WHO 2006). Unlike the human H1N1 and H3N2 seasonal flu as upper respiratory infection and low mortality, the H5N1 HPAI virus causes a rapid onset of severe viral pneumonia and has a high fatality rate (60% mortality). There are many cultural practices that increase the risk of exposure of human to HPAI virus. In many Southeast Asian and Middle Eastern countries, poultry flocks are reared in the backyard, rooftops, or in close proximity to human dwellings with close interaction with humans.

The close proximity of birds to humans increases the risk of transmission to humans via aerosol or large airborne droplets, fecal contamination with dispersion via fomites, and direct contact with infected birds. Also, sick birds may be slaughtered for consumption in the developing world, leading to increased risk of exposure (WHO 2005a). H5N1 HPAI virus has expanded its host range, as it has infected dogs and other mammals through the consumption of uncooked infected poultry, wild birds, or their products (Thanawongnuwech et al. 2005, CDC 2007, WHO 2007). This has raised concern that dogs and other pets have the potential to be intermediate carriers that can transfer the H5N1 influenza virus to humans. Although rare, evidence of direct human-to-human transmission of H5N1 associated with a poultry outbreak occurred in Southeast Asia. Sustained human-to-human transmissibility of H5N1 HPAI would require genetic adaption of AI PB2 internal protein (Hatta et al. 2001, WHO 2008, Gao et al. 2009). In addition, because the human population lacks immunity to H5, H7, and H9 viruses, emergence of a pandemic virus that is adapted to humans could be devastating. To date, there have been 493 human infections with 293 fatalities due to H5N1, 114 infections due to H7N7 HPAI with one death, and four infections of young children from H9N2 LPAI viruses (Cox & Uyeki 2008, WHO 2010). Currently, these AI viruses are not adapted to humans and a pandemic has not developed.

Economic Consequence to Poultry Producers

The Food and Agriculture Organization (FAO) estimated the global poultry production in 2007 at 83.7 million metric tons with 8.1 million metric tons in global trade (FAO 2007). The United States, China, the European Union (EU), and Brazil were the largest producers of poultry, with Brazil, the United States, and the EU being the largest exporters. The United States exported 2.3 million metric tons of poultry meat in 2005. Outbreaks of AI since the 1990s have had severe economic and social effects on the poultry industry, international agricultural trade, and public health (Burns et al. 2008). Reductions in consumer sales both domestically and internationally owing to fear and loss of confidence, additional costs for implementing control and prevention measures such as culling, block eradication, and compensation to producers, and other costs (restocking costs, biosecurity, surveillance, vaccinations) are some of the economic consequences of an outbreak (Yalcin 2006). There is also the loss in the export market due to international embargoes and the loss of market share due to competition from other poultry-producing nations. Importing nations also bear the economic impact of increased cost for importing product because of a lack of international competition (Lokuge 2005, McLeod et al. 2005). In regions of the world where there have been HPAI outbreaks, changes in the consumption pattern have been evident, with temporary decreases in poultry consumption. For example, the domestic impact in Turkey in 2006, where 2.5 million birds were culled due to an outbreak of H5N1 HPAI, had a cost of $226 million. In the capital city, Ankara, there was a 54% decrease in sales of poultry products, with a 32% decrease in poultry meat prices, and prices of eggs and other poultry products also decreased (WHO 2005a, Oner et al. 2006, Yalcin 2006).

At least 62 countries reported outbreaks of H5N1 HPAI in either domesticated or wild birds between 1996 and 2010 (OIE 2009). The HPAI virus has caused devastating economic losses to poultry growers and rural households in Asia, Europe, and Africa (McLeod et al. 2005, Otte et al. 2008, FAO 2010). In developing countries, most poultry production occurs in small backyard flocks in rural and periurban areas, so outbreaks economically impacted these small farmers more than commercial industries. Between 1996 and 2003, there were 1,645 H5N1 HPAI outbreaks worldwide that resulted in 43 million birds dead or destroyed, and between 2004 and 2007 more than 250 million birds died or were destroyed (McLeod et al. 2005). The economic consequence of HPAI outbreaks in Southeast Asia for 2003–2005 was between 0.5% and 2% of the area's GDP, or about $10 billion. More than 50% of the Southeast Asian population derived its income from poultry. For example, in Indonesia 20% of the commercial farm workers lost their jobs as a result of the outbreak. In Vietnam, 44 million birds, or 17% of the bird population, were culled at a cost of $120 million (World Bank 2010). HPAI outbreaks have had a major impact on the livelihood of small and large farmers and have negatively impacted the nutritional stature of millions of people in the developing world.

Effect on International Trade

AI is a notifiable disease and is defined by the World Organization for Animal Health [Office Internationale des Epizooties (OIE)] Terrestrial Animal Health Codes as a poultry disease caused by influenza A viruses of subtypes H5 and H7 or AI virus with an intravenous pathogenicity index of 1.2 or higher. The worldwide monitoring of notifiable diseases is the responsibility of the OIE. Although H5N1 HPAI is primarily an animal health issue, the increasing frequency of human infection has raised concerns about its pandemic potential. The world human and animal health organizations [FAO, OIE, and World Health Organization (WHO)] are collaborating with and aiding countries in the development of risk management strategies to reduce the circulation of AI viruses in the poultry population, to assess the risk of human exposure from production-to-consumption, and to implement mitigation measures. The OIE is responsible for the phytosanitary safety standards (SPS) for the international trade of terrestrial animals and animal products, including poultry. These standards are implemented by national veterinary agencies of the importing and exporting countries. The World Trade Organization enforces the standards in an effort to prevent disease transmission and to ascertain fair trade (OIE 2009). The individual countries may implement trade embargoes on countries that have reported notifiable diseases, such as AI and virulent Newcastle disease, as nontariff trade barriers, but such embargoes must be science based and not political in scope.

International trade implications following an outbreak with HPAI could be economically severe. Gaining the confidence of importing nations require improvements in biosecurity systems, surveillance, vaccination, and other preventative measures (Lokuge 2005, McLeod et al. 2005) At least ten Southeast Asian countries have been impacted by H5N1 HPAI since 2003, although the countries most severely impacted have been China, Cambodia, Indonesia, Laos, and Thailand. Southeast Asian countries account for a quarter of the world's poultry production, and one third to one half of the population derives income from poultry, hence the consequence of HPAI outbreaks with the limitation of trade within and between countries has been devastating to their economies and worsened food security for rural communities. In 2004, Thailand was the fourth largest exporter of poultry and poultry products in the world. The country exported 40% of its poultry production, primarily to Europe and Japan, but following the HPAI outbreak and the ban on international trade of poultry, its poultry industry was economically devastated by losing 50% of its export market (Lokuge 2005). The Netherlands experienced a similar reduction in exports (30%) following its H7N7 HPAI outbreak in 2003. Exporting countries that did not have concurrent outbreaks of HPAI had the advantage of gaining export market share when such outbreaks occurred in Asia. Trade embargoes or bans imposed on a country due to animal disease outbreaks affect all poultry producers as well as importing countries.

Concerns Related to Food-Borne Transmission

Surveillance data revealed that H5N1 HPAI virus was detected in imported frozen duck meat and on the surface and in internal contents of contaminated eggs (Tumpey et al. 2002, Beato et al.

2009, Harder et al. 2009). Experimentally, HPAI virus was detected in breast and thigh meat, and blood and bones, as well as in eggs of HPAI virus–infected chickens (Swayne 2006). Although there is no direct evidence that AI has been transmitted to humans via the consumption of contaminated poultry products, there is anecdotal and experimental evidence that the consumption of uncooked poultry blood or meat has transmitted the H5N1 HPAI virus to carnivorous animals, including tigers, leopards, domestic cats, domestic dogs, and a stone martin (WHO 2005a, CDC 2007, Writ. Comm. Second WHO Consult. Clin. Aspects Hum. Infect. Avian Influenza A Virus 2008).

VIRUS ECOLOGY AND EPIDEMIOLOGY

Natural Reservoirs

Wild waterfowl and shorebirds are natural reservoirs for LPAI viruses, whose replication is primarily limited to the epithelial cells of the intestinal tract (Ito et al. 2000, Webster et al. 2007), and infected birds remain asymptomatic but shed the virus into the environment via feces, and less frequently saliva and nasal secretions (Hinshaw 1985). One of the primary routes of transmission is via the fecal-oral route. LPAI viruses can survive up to 20 days in chicken manure (−4°C) (CDC 2006), in water for at least 10 days (Guan et al. 2002a, Domanska-Blicharz et al. 2010), and on fomites for up to three weeks (Lu et al. 2003), and can replicate in feather follicles and survive on feathers for at least six days (Tiwari et al. 2006, Yamamoto et al. 2008). However, survival is highly temperature and moisture content dependent, i.e., survival is shortened by high environmental temperatures and dry conditions. LPAI viruses with antigenic subtypes H3 and H6, as well as N2, N6, and N8, were the most frequently isolated viruses from wild ducks, whereas H9, H11, and H13 were predominant HA subtypes in shorebirds and gulls (Suarez 2008, Swayne & Halvorson 2008). By contrast, HPAI viruses have not been maintained in wild bird reservoirs but have been derived from H5 and H7 LPAI viruses after circulation in poultry populations (Horimoto et al. 1995). The insertion of multiple basic amino acids, insertion of large amounts of extraneous RNA coding for additional amino acids, substitution of nonbasic with basic amino acids, or loss of shielding glycosylation sites in the cleavage site of HA motif can enable a H5 or H7 LP virus to become HP (Perdue et al. 1996, Suarez 2008).

H5 in Poultry

Many neuraminidase subtypes have been linked with H5 subtypes associated with poultry in both HP (N1–3 and N8–9) and LP (N1–9) forms. The largest outbreak of HPAI in the past 50 years has been the H5N1 HPAI epizootic in Asia, Africa, and Europe (1996–present). This epizootic has affected at least 62 countries and has been isolated from infected poultry flocks in Asia, the Middle East, Africa, and Europe, as well as, but less frequently, from waterfowl, shorebirds, passerine birds, pigeons, and falcons (Stallknecht & Brown 2007). H5N1 HPAI virus was first reported in 1996 in China (HPAI virus type strain A/goose/Guangdong/1/1996) followed by reports of outbreaks in live poultry markets (LPM) of Hong Kong and in humans in 1997, and spread in 2003–2004 through eastern and southeastern Asia, affecting poultry, captive birds, and the human population. Genetic characterization of the Hong Kong viruses revealed that these H5 viruses had the H5 HA gene from A/goose/Guangdong/1/96, NA gene from H6N1 LPAI virus related to A/teal/HK/W312/97, and the internal genes of H9N2 LPAI virus associated with Japanese quail or H6N1 viruses (Xu et al. 1999, Guan et al. 2002a, Kim et al. 2009). Surveillance and phylogenetic analysis revealed that in Hong Kong between 1999 and 2002 there was transmission of H5N1 HPAI virus from domestic poultry to domestic ducks. In general, the ducks were less susceptible to AI virus infection than chickens and remain asymptomatic when infected. However, in 2002 a H5N1 HPAI virus appeared in Hong Kong that infected and killed captive-reared ducks in a wildlife park.

LPAI viruses usually replicate in the intestines of the ducks. However, the H5N1 HPAI virus in ducks produces primary infection with higher titers in the respiratory tract than in the intestinal tract. Recent studies revealed that some species of ducks have high susceptibility to the H5N1 virus. Experimental evidence with wild-type mallard and Muscovy ducks indicates that mallards may be more resistant to the H5N1 virus than Muscovy ducks (Hulse-Post et al. 2005; Kim et al. 2009; C Cagle, J Wasilenko, E Spackman E, TL To, T Nguyen, M Pantin-Jackwood, unpublished results). However, when mallards become immunocompromised due to another infection, the birds have increased susceptibility to H5N1 infection (Ramirez-Nieto et al. 2010). Since appearing in 1996, the H5N1 HPAI virus has changed genetically, by drifting, to have 10 distinguishable clades (clade 0–9) with at least six subclades. A few of these subclades (2.1, 2.2, 2.3, 2.5) have been responsible for the human H5N1 infections and deaths, with clade 2.2 being the most frequently reported in humans in Asia, Europe, the Middle East, and Africa (CDC 2007, Webster et al. 2007). Other aspects of concern are the transmission of H5N1 from domestic birds to migratory aquatic birds, as occurred in Qinghai Lake, China in 2005 (Chen et al. 2006). Today, the H5N1 HPAI viruses have predominantly replicated in the respiratory tract and less so in the intestinal tract. Some wild waterfowls are more susceptible to H5N1 virus infection than others (Webster et al. 2007, WHO 2007).

The persistence of H5N2 LPAI virus in the poultry population of Mexico for over a year eventually led to critical mutations that resulted in the 1994 outbreak of H5N2 HPAI. Phylogenetic analysis indicated the H5N2 LPAI virus that circulated in the poultry population in Mexico in 1993 was derived from a North American lineage circulating in migratory aquatic birds, which was mutated by adding an insert of two basic amino acids and substitution of a nonbasic with basic amino acid in the HA cleavage site, and consequently caused an outbreak of HPAI in 1994–1995 (Horimoto et al. 1995, Perdue et al. 1996). Mexico initiated a vaccination program in January 1995, and the last HPAI virus was isolated in June 1995. However, H5N2 LPAI virus has continued to circulate.

H7 in Poultry

Several NA combinations with H7 HA subtypes have been reported for LPAI (N1–4, N7, and N9) and HPAI (N1, N3, N4, and N7) viruses in birds and/or humans. Since 1995, infection of poultry with H7 AI viruses has greatly increased, as well as its geographic spread. Outbreaks of H7N1 LPAI occurred in Italy (1999–2001) and in Canada (2000). H7N2 LPAI outbreaks occurred in the Unites States (1996–98, 2002, 2003, 2004) and the United Kingdom (2007). H7N3 LPAI outbreaks occurred in Italy (2002–2003), Chile (2002), Canada (2004), the United Kingdom (2006), and Pakistan (2001–2004), whereas H7N7 LPAI outbreaks occurred in Australia (1976, 1979), the United Kingdom (1996), Ireland (1995, 1998), and Germany (2001, 2003). Outbreaks of H7N1 HPAI have occurred in Italy (1999–2000), whereas outbreaks of H7N3 HPAI occurred in the United Kingdom (1963), Australia (1992 and 94), Pakistan (1995–2004), Chile (2002), and Canada (2004). In Australia, there were outbreaks of H7N4 HPAI (1997) and H7N7 HPAI (1976, 1985, and 1996), but the most severe outbreak of H7N7 HPAI occurred in The Netherlands (2003) (Capua & Alexander 2004, Belser et al. 2009). The H7N7 HPAI virus in the Netherlands resulted in the culling of 30 million birds. Since 1995, at least 75 million poultry (chicken/turkey) worldwide have been culled or depopulated because of H7 HPAI epizootics (Capua & Alexander 2004, Swayne 2008c, Belser et al. 2009). For LPAI viruses in the United States, the LPM system has various frequencies of poultry infected with various LPAI viruses. H7N2 LPAI viruses have been circulating in LPM from 1994 to 2006, whereas H5N2 LPAI viruses have been sporadically isolated from LPM in the northeast United States since 1983 (Senne et al. 2003, Suarez et al. 2002, Senne 2010). Phylogenetic analysis of H7N2 LPAI isolates from commercial poultry outbreaks in Pennsylvania (1997–98, and 2001–2002); Virginia, West Virginia, and North Carolina (2002); and in Connecticut (2003) were linked to H7N2 LPAI viruses circulating in the LPM in the northeastern United States (Spackman et al. 2003, Akey 2009). The fact that H5 and H7 LPAI viruses can mutate to HPAI viruses after circulating in the poultry population (Horimoto et al. 1995, Dusek et al. 2009) has prompted surveillance studies to track the genetic changes of the H5 and H7 subtypes circulating in LPM in the United States over a seven-year period (Horimoto et al. 1995, Spackman et al. 2003). These researchers noted specific substitution changes at the hemagglutinin cleavage site of H7 with the addition of basic amino acids.

Public Health Concerns

Outbreaks of HPAI viruses in wild and domestic birds are rare, but once infection occurs it can be serious from veterinary, medical, and public health perspectives. Since the outbreaks of H5N1 HPAI in poultry and humans in Hong Kong in 1997 and H7N7 HPAI in the Netherlands in 2003, there have been concerns that AI viruses could persist in some poultry populations and emerge as a pandemic virus for humans through multiple mutations or reassortment. For an AI virus to cause a pandemic requires the virus to develop the ability to be transmitted from human-to-human and cause high morbidity or mortality rates. During the twentieth century, the emerged viruses had been new hemagglutinin subtypes for which the human population has no exposure and thus no immunity (CDC 2007). The 2009 pandemic H1N1 was the result of a reintroduction of H1N1, which over time had mutated and reassorted influenza A genes from various avian, human, and swine influenza viruses (Dunham et al. 2009, Liu et al. 2009, Sinha et al. 2009). Today, AI viruses of concern as potential pandemic strains are some H5, H7, and H9 subtypes that have crossed the human species barrier multiple times to produce sporadic infections. This will be discussed in following sections (Li et al. 2003, WHO 2005, CDC 2007, Webster et al. 2007, Pappas et al. 2007).

H5 in Humans

Although very rare, subtype H5 AI viruses have crossed the species barrier to produce sporadic infections of humans (Gilsdorf et al. 2006, Cox & Uyeki 2008, Writ. Comm. Second WHO Consult. Clin. Aspects Hum. Infect. Avian Influenza A Virus 2008). The first case of transmission of H5 HPAI virus from birds to humans occurred in association with the LPM of Hong Kong in 1997, which caused 18 hospitalized cases and six fatalities. To date, 493 human cases of H5N1 illness have been reported, of which 292 died, for a case fatality rate of 60% (WHO 2005a, 2010; Kim et al. 2009). The vast majority of human infections occurred as a result of direct exposure to live or dead infected poultry, with one instance through the consumption of raw duck blood, and another in which individuals in Azerbaijan (2006) became infected while defeathering dead wild swans (Gilsdorf et al. 2006, WHO 2007, Writ. Comm. Second WHO Consult. Clin. Aspects Hum. Infect. Avian Influenza A Virus 2008). Although human-to-human transmission of AI virus is limited, reports of this type of transmission have occurred in Thailand (2004), Vietnam (2004), Azerbaijan (2006), Indonesia (2006), Pakistan (2007), and Egypt (2007), usually as a result of one of the family members having direct contact with infected poultry prior to infecting members of the household or one family member or health care worker becoming infected from an infected patient (CDC 2006, WHO 2008). These transmissions were mainly among family members and not communal. H5N1 HPAI viruses continued to evolve, although transmission from the avian to human host is relatively low. However, with increased exposure to a human host, the chance of the virus adapting for efficient human infectivity increases or reassorting with a human-adapted influenza virus may occur.

The symptoms of H5N1 HPAI virus infection in humans include fever, severe respiratory disease, dyspnea, multi-organ failure, and death, with an incubation period between five and ten days (Tam 2002, Ungchusak et al. 2005, Gilsdorf et al. 2006). The case fatality rate has been approximately 60%. In 2004, patients in Thailand infected with HPAI virus exhibited drastically different clinical symptoms than seasonal flu. Within two to eight days following exposure, patients symptoms progressed from flu-like to vomiting, diarrhea, and abdominal pain (Yuen et al. 1998, Ungchusak et al. 2005, WHO 2005a).

H7 in Humans

Humans have rarely been infected with H7 AI viruses, but when infected they usually had symptoms of mild respiratory disease and conjunctivitis. The North American H7 LPAI and HPAI viruses caused milder, self-limiting infection with no human-to-human transmission, as compared with the Eurasian 2003 H7N7 HPAI virus in which limited human-to-human transmission occurred. There have been sporadic reports of individual cases of mild respiratory disease due to H7N2, H7N3, and H7N7 virus infections. In the United Kingdom in 1996, a patient was infected with H7N7 LPAI virus after an eye abrasion, leading to conjunctivitis. In the United States (Virginia, 2002; New York, 2003) and the United Kingdom (2007), patients infected with H7N2 LPAI viruses developed mild respiratory symptoms. These infections were phylogenetically linked with the H7N2 circulating in the live bird market (Spackman et al. 2003, Suarez et al. 2009). Similarly, other sporadic cases of H7N3 LPAI and HPAI virus infections occurred in Canada (2004), resulting in two cases of conjunctivitis and mild respiratory symptoms. In Wales in 2007, an infection with H7N2 LPAI virus was associated with poultry obtained from a live bird market (Nguyen-Van-Tam et al. 2006, Editorial team 2007). The patients had symptoms of conjunctivitis, flu-like symptoms, and neurological and gastrointestinal symptoms (Capua & Alexander 2004, Editorial team 2007). However, the greatest numbers of H7 human cases were associated with the H7N7 HPAI epizootic in the Netherlands in 2003, which also spread to neighboring commercial farms in Belgium and Germany. Eighty-nine farm workers became infected; 78 with conjunctivitis, five with conjunctivitis and flu-like symptoms, two with flu-like symptoms, four with other symptoms, and one death from severe respiratory disease. Three of the cases were as a result of human-to-human transmission from a farm worker to his family (Fouchier et al. 2004, Koopmans et al. 2004). Phylogenetic analysis revealed the H7N7 virus from a patient and viruses from infected chickens were identical, indicating that the HA had nearest homology with A/mallard/Netherland/12/00 (H7N3) and the NA had nearest homology with A/mallard/NL/2/00 (H10N7) viruses isolated from mallards. All the internal genes (NP, PA, PB1 and 2, NS, MA) of the outbreak isolate were of the Eurasian lineage. The genomic analysis from the fatal case (A/NL/219/03) had a 26-nucleotide substitution, of which four were in the HA gene and eight in the PB2 gene (Fouchier et al. 2004). The Eurasian lineage of H7N7 HPAI virus maintained tropism toward α2-3 sialic acid cell membrane receptor, which preferentially binds to cells in avian species. HA of the North American H7N2 LPAI virus (A/turkey/Virginia/4529/02 and A/chicken /Connecticut/260413-2/03), and the H7N3 HPAI virus (A/chicken/Canada/504/04) had adapted to recognize and have increased affinity for α2-6 sialic acid cell receptors, which preferentially bind to some human cells, but neither virus changed sufficiently to be pandemic viruses. Nevertheless, the Eurasian lineage of the H7N7 HPAI virus (2003) caused one fatality, indicating greater virulence for humans and that other factors such as mutation in the PB2 (E627K) internal protein may have contributed to the human pathogenicity of the Eurasian lineage (Belser et al. 2009).

Other AI Subtypes: H9

There have been sporadic cases of humans infected with H9N2 LPAI viruses. Outbreaks of H9N2 have occurred throughout the world beginning in the 1990s in poultry flocks in China, Pakistan, and the Middle East. There were reported outbreaks in Europe, such as in domestic ducks, chickens, and turkeys in Germany (1995–1998), in ostriches in South Africa, and in turkeys in the United States, the Middle East, and Korea (Capua & Alexander 2004). However, these H9N2 viruses were not associated with human infections. By comparison, rare H9N2 human infections occurred in China in 1999 and again in 2003, producing self-limiting mild respiratory disease. These infections occurred in young children (Capua & Alexander 2004).

EVOLUTION AND PATHOGENICITY

Genetic Changes in the Virus: Antigenic Drift and Antigenic Shift

AI viruses are genetically unstable and are constantly evolving. The antigenic variation for some HA subtypes is large, with conserved regions being as little as 30% of the genome (Lee & Saif 2009). Genetic changes occur either by antigenic drift or by antigenic shift.

Antigenic Drift

AI viruses lack a proofreading and error correction mechanism during replication, therefore small, constant genetic changes occur due to point mutation, deletion, or substitution, which can result in new mutants (CDC 2005, Escorcia et al. 2008). The insertion of multiple basic amino acids in the cleavage site of the HA motif can enable an H5 or H7 LPAI virus to become an HPAI virus. An example of such a mutational event occurred with the H5N2 LPAI virus that appeared in Mexico in 1993, circulated in poultry for more than one year, and mutated into an HPAI virus in November 1994. By 1995, phylogenetic analysis revealed that the virus had acquired an insertion of two additional basic amino acids and a basic for nonbasic substitution at the hemagglutinin proteolytic cleavage site, which was responsible for the acquired HP phenotype. Genetic analysis also revealed the poultry LPAI virus originated from the LPAI virus of migrating waterfowls prior to introduction into the poultry population (Horimoto et al. 1995, Perdue et al. 1996). Since 1995, the H5N2 LPAI virus has continued to circulate among poultry in Mexico with continued antigenic drift in the protective epitopes of the HA protein as compared to the 1994 vaccine seed strain. Outbreaks as a result of the mutation of H5 and H7 LPAI to the HPAI viruses have also occurred in Pennsylvania (1983) and Italy (2000), respectively (Kawaoka et al. 1984, Donatelli et al. 2001, Spackman et al. 2003, Suarez et al. 2009)

Antigenic Shift

Reassortment of gene segments has occurred due to coinfection of a host with more than one subtype of influenza A virus. Such a mechanism was responsible for development of the human pandemic H1N1 (1918), H2N2 (1957), and H3N2 (1968) viruses that arose in the human population. This shift in gene segments has also occurred in birds, with H5N1 HPAI virus appearing in Hong Kong in 1997, following the reassortment of the H5 gene from H5N1 of Guangdong lineage virus, NA from an H6N1 virus, and internal genes (NS, PB2, M, and PA) from the H9N2 virus (Xu et al. 1999, Guan et al. 2002a). This suggests that poultry were infected with a reassortant virus of wild waterfowl origin that circulated in the poultry and adapted by optimizing AI virus gene segments through mutations and reassortment.

Host Restriction

The ability of the virus to infect a host depends on its affinity to bind with the host cell receptor and initiate the replication process. In general, receptor binding contributes to the infectivity of AI viruses. The virus HA binds to the host α-sialic acid cell receptors, so the receptor cell motif restricts the ability of viruses to bind and invade the host cell. The HA of most AI viruses has the affinity for α2-3 sialic acid receptors that are predominant on avian cells, whereas human influenza A viruses have the affinity for α2-6 sialic acid receptors that are predominant on human cells. Although α2-3 sialic acid is predominant in avian species, including chickens, turkeys, and ducks, some investigators have found that reduced numbers of α2-6 sialic acid receptors may be expressed in the epithelial tissue of many organs in various poultry species (Ito et al. 2000, Gambaryan et al. 2002, Matrosovich et al. 2004, Kuchipudi et al. 2009). Influenza viruses have found other means of circumventing host restrictions. For example, virus adaptation to its host after passage in that species can result in changes in viral molecular structure. Adaptation of virus from wild duck-to-chicken produces common adaptive changes such as the shortening of the NA stalk by deletion of 19 amino acids. Pathogenicity studies revealed that a deletion in the stalk of the NA of AI viruses resulted in increased viral replication and an increase in pathogenicity in chickens (Webster et al. 1992, Matrosovich et al. 2004, Munier et al. 2010, Ramirez-Nieto et al. 2010). Genetic adaptations are evident in H9N2 LPAI viruses in Asia that have acquired human virus-like specificity for binding to α2-6 sialic acid receptors and in H5N1 HPAI viruses that have selective tropism for α2-3 sialic acid receptors that are present in the alveoli of the lower human lungs (Matrosovich et al. 2004, Wan et al. 2008).

Adaptive Mutation to Infect Humans

Viral adaptation is an important factor in enabling human cell receptor binding and virus transmission. Influenza viruses alter the receptor-binding properties of HA to increase infectivity and transmission. The HA proteins in H5N1 HPAI viruses have low affinity for α2-6 sialic acid receptors (human), therefore adaptations are needed to efficiently infect and transmit between humans. Studies of the HA binding of AI viruses to sialic acid receptors of host cells revealed that mutation of amino acid residues 226leu and 228ser at the HA binding site increased the binding affinity for the human α2-6 sialic acid receptors. Mutation of the PB2 internal protein at amino acid residues 627K and 701N was also correlated with increased virus replication efficiency and host range, but did not increase virus transmission. These studies indicated that multiple genes may regulate virus replication and transmission. Genetic studies of the H5N1 HPAI virus clade 2.2 revealed changes both in the HA receptor site and PB2 genes. These changes imply that H5N1 (clade 2.2) is evolving its efficiency for transmission to humans, but additional undefined changes are necessary for the virus to become a pandemic virus (Gao et al. 2009).

Pathogenicity in Birds

AI viruses are also classified by pathotypes, i.e., LPAI and HPAI viruses. Birds infected with LPAI virus can exhibit mild signs such as ruffled feathers, a decrease in egg production, and mild respiratory disease that lasts for approximately 10 days. Birds infected with HPAI viruses exhibit severe respiratory and neurological signs, multiple organ failure, and death within 48–96 h. The peak mortality rate is between 90% and 100%. The H5 and H7 AI viruses have been introduced into the poultry population as LPAI viruses (WHO 2005a) and, with adaptation and sustained replication, this has led to the emergence of HPAI viruses. In addition to tissue tropism and adaptive mutation, protease activity of the host on the HA cleavage site of the virus is one of the major determinants for pathogenicity. The ability of the host proteases to cleave the HA is important for infectivity and viral spread (Hatta et al. 2001, Lee & Saif 2009), hence the conversion of LPAI to HPAI viruses is dependent on changing the cleavability of HA from trypsin-like enzymes to the host's furin-like proteases (Hatta et al. 2001, Lee & Saif 2009). LPAI viruses can replicate in localized tissues (respiratory and digestive) in which trypsin-like proteases are present, whereas HPAI viruses replicate systemically in most organs and cell types by using ubiquitous furin-like proteases or trypsin-like proteases. In LPAI viruses, there are two basic amino acids at the HA cleavage site motif (Walker & Kawaoka 1993). This restricts the cleavage of this site to extracellular trypsin-like enzymes present primarily in the respiratory and digestive tracts. In HPAI viruses, the multiple basic amino acids at the HA cleavage sites can be cleaved by a larger range of intracellular enzymes (furin and subtilisin) commonly found in many organs and tissues allowing the virus to infect and grow systemically, i.e., pantropic (Hulse-Post et al. 2005).

TRANSMISSION/DISTRIBUTION

The transmissibility of AI viruses to poultry or humans is dependent on the virus strain, environmental factors, and host species susceptibility.

Bird Transmission and Exposure

As the natural reservoir for AI, infected waterfowl are believed to pass the AI virus to domestic poultry by the fecal-oral route through contaminated water sources, feed, and housing facilities/shared environment, where infectious virus can be excreted by birds for up to 10 days. The virus can survive at 4°C in feces for at least 35 days (Brown et al. 2007, Stallknecht & Brown 2007). Transmission is possible via aerosols or airborne droplets, as well as by wind dispersion of fomites including contaminated dust. Indirect exposures occur through surface contamination of equipment, clothing, and shoes from dust, feces, secretions, and contaminated feathers (CDC 2006, Gilsdorf et al. 2006, Yamamoto et al. 2009).

In developing countries such as Vietnam, Indonesia, and Egypt, it is estimated that 80%–85% of poultry are reared in small flocks outdoors or on rooftops as village poultry (Branckaert & Guye 1997, Biswas et al. 2009). These flocks are a vital source for the LPM and are valuable commodities to these subsistence growers, whose cultural preference is to consume freshly slaughtered meat. The close living proximity of these small backyard or rooftop flocks to humans increases the chance for AI virus transmission through contact with contaminated feces or airborne virus. There are also exposures due to bird respiratory secretions, contaminated dust, and contaminated bodies of water such as ponds. Surveillance studies in the United States have traced H7N2 LPAI virus from the LPM system to poultry on commercial farms (turkeys; layer, breeder, and meat chickens) in the northeastern United States, resulting in millions of infected birds. Historically, the LPM system in Hong Kong also contributed to the interaction of domestic quail and domestic chickens, giving rise to the reassortant H5N1 HPAI viruses (Spackman et al. 2003, Duan et al. 2007, Suarez et al. 2009, WHO 2005a). However, interspecies transmissions of AI viruses have occurred in other species as well. H1N1 and H3N2 commonly circulate in swine in Europe and the United States, and have crossed species to infect turkeys, particularly breeder hens, which require a lower exposure dose of virus to produce a productive infection in turkeys than is needed to infect chickens (Pillai et al. 2010). H1N2 swine influenza virus has also infected turkeys. Recently, several flocks of breeder turkey hens in Canada, Chile, and the United States were infected with 2009 pandemic H1N1 virus, and the field syndrome was experimentally reproduced by reproductive tract insemination (Suarez et al. 2009, Pantin-Jackwood et al. 2010). Epidemiologic evidence in the Canadian case suggested that a poultry worker with respiratory illness may have transmitted the virus to the turkey flock (OIE 2009).

Human Transmission

Most reports indicate that human infection with H5N1 HPAI virus was the result of direct contact with live or dead infected birds. An exposure survey in Hong Kong in 1997 determined that 3%–10% of the poultry workers involved in the culling of birds in the live bird market were seropositive for H5N1 when surveyed after working in the depopulation program (Bridges et al. 2000, Katz et al. 2008). People at greatest risk for AI virus exposure and infection include farm workers, live bird market workers, butchers and home processors of poultry, hunters that slaughter, eviscerate, and defeather infected wild birds, and those preparing to cook contaminated meat getting viruses on their hands and transferring them by touching mucus membranes (WHO 2005b, 2007). Veterinarians are also at high risk when working with infected flocks. Other sources of exposure are due to cultural practices of slaughtering sick birds and close living conditions between human and infected birds (INFOSAN IFSAN- 2004). Direct human-to-human transmission mostly occurs in clusters as a result of family or health-care worker exposure (WHO 2004, 2008). There appears to be an undefined human genetic factor that is responsible for the familial association.

Food Transmission: Meat

In some countries, the cultural preference for the consumption of freshly slaughtered poultry meat supports village production systems and LPM, which increases the risk of transmission of AI virus (Katz et al. 2008). AI virus has survived in imported raw infected meat, such as frozen infected duck carcasses, in Korea (2001), Japan (2003), and Germany (2007), and was isolated from chicken thigh and breast meat from experimental studies with HPAI viruses (Tumpey et al. 2002, Swayne & Beck 2004, Mase et al. 2005, Beato et al. 2009, Harder et al. 2009). The titers of H5N1 HPAI virus recovered from experimentally infected chicken thigh meat were as high as 10^7 EID_{50} (median egg infectious dose) g^{-1} (Swayne & Beck 2004, Swayne 2006, Thomas & Swayne 2007). In Southeast Asia, one of the cultural practices is to slaughter sick poultry instead of accepting an economic loss. Butchering or home slaughtering of sick birds increases the risk of AI virus exposure through cross contamination from live and dead birds to human handlers or airborne virus generation during slaughter. Improper cooking, handling, and preparation may allow AI virus survival and increases the potential for productive exposure, therefore the consumption of raw or undercooked food is not advisable. Although there is no evidence of human infection due to food consumption, there is one anecdotal incident of infection through the consumption of raw duck blood, and natural and experimental infection in mammals occurred when infected meat was consumed by tigers, leopards, house cats, dogs, ferrets, and other mammals (Beato et al. 2009). Experimental studies in simulated LPM slaughter of H5N1 HPAI virus–infected chickens produced airborne viruses that were transmitted to chickens and ferrets, resulting in fatal infections (Swayne 2005, 2008a; D.E. Swayne, unpublished data). In commercially produced poultry, HPAI virus–infected poultry are destroyed and not used for human food consumption.

Eggs

HPAI virus has been found on egg shells and internally in albumen and yolk from eggs produced by experimentally infected chicken, but with LPAI viruses, only egg shells have been determined to be contaminated and not the internal contents (Cappucci et al. 1985, Promkuntod et al. 2006). When experimentally added to products, H5N2 LPAI virus survived in egg yolk and albumen for at least 17 days when held at 4°C–20°C (de Wit et al. 2004), but LPAI viruses have not been shown to contaminate eggs from the field (de Wit et al. 2004). Most birds infected with HPAI virus stop laying eggs, but the last few eggs produced may be infected. No human cases from consumption of infected eggs have been reported, but pigs were infected from consuming raw eggs with shell from H7N7 HPAI virus–infected flocks in the Netherlands (WHO 2007). In many developed countries, markets have developed for deshelled, liquid eggs because of a drop in demand for shelled eggs (Lokuge 2005). Early HPAI virus infection of a flock before clinical signs provides the possibility of AI virus–contaminated eggs being included in the liquid egg product. However, the egg pasteurization process inactivates HPAI and LPAI viruses (Swayne & Beck 2004).

Water

Fecal-contaminated water can be a source of infectious AI virus. AI virus can survive in water for at least 10 days and for up to a year (Brown et al. 2007, Domanska-Blicharz et al. 2010). The survival and infectivity of AI is influenced by temperature, pH, and salinity of the water. Survival increases as temperature decreases (Guan et al. 2002b, Brown et al. 2007, Domanska-Blicharz et al. 2010). Open bodies of water such as ponds and lakes may be a haven for AI virus–infected migratory ducks and birds, which may become AI virus contaminated and used as a water source for domesticated birds. When ducks were experimentally infected with AI virus, they shed as much as $10^{7.8}$EID g^{-1} in their feces, which in turn can contaminate the water source (Brown et al. 2007, Stallknecht & Brown 2007, Stallknecht et al. 2010). This reinforces the need for growers to implement proper biosecurity measures to ensure that potable water does not become contaminated with AI virus from wild bird sources.

Fomites

Equipment, surfaces, shoes, and clothes can be sources of contamination, as AI viruses can survive up to three weeks on some fomites (Lu et al. 2003, Tiwari et al. 2006).

PREVENTION/CONTROL

Farm to Table Risk Management

The control of AI in poultry, from village to commercial sectors, requires farm-to-table risk management. Some of the basic needs include implementation of good agricultural practices such as training of workers in good management and biosecurity practices, in particular poultry cullers, establishing a biosecure environment to isolate poultry from potential AI virus carriers, supplying a source of potable water, providing a feed supply that is secure and free of contaminants, disinfection and decontamination of the premises and equipment prior to the introduction of a new flock or after culling of poultry flocks, establishing routine composting of litter and carcasses for all flocks, and safe disposal of carcasses from known infected farms (Brglez & Hahn 2008, Swayne 2008b, Guan et al. 2009). Good risk communication with workers, veterinarians, and suppliers is essential to manage risk. Following an outbreak, disease surveillance and inspection, controlled depopulation, rapid culling, and potentially a vaccination program must be implemented. Although the vaccination program may be country specific, a delay in this control measure when rapid depopulation is not a viable option could result in enormous economic cost, whereas rapid intervention could dramatically reduce costs and the spread of infection. From a national level, effective risk communication with growers and producers is essential as affected countries must address improvements in biosecurity as a cost-effective investment (Koopmans & Duizer 2004, Lokuge 2005). In developed countries, commercially produced HPAI virus infected poultry and their products are prohibited from going into the food chain. In addition, LPAI and HPAI viruses are rare in commercial and noncommercial poultry in developed countries.

In developing countries with H5N1 HPAI virus infections, on a local level safe food handling such as keeping raw meat separate from cooked foods, cleaning of all work surfaces, cooking meat to the proper temperature (70°C), and maintaining proper storage temperatures must be practiced. It is essential to inform food preparers that AI can survive refrigeration and freezing. Low temperature increases its stability (INFOSAN IFSAN- 2004), so refrigeration is not a means of control. Therefore practicing good hygiene is essential to prevent cross contamination (INFOSAN IFSAN- 2004). Effective vaccination prevents systemic infection of poultry and mitigates the risk of H5N1 HPAI virus from being in meat and other poultry products (Swayne & Suarez 2007).

In 2004, WHO began contemplating whether H5N1 HPAI virus–infected poultry products (refrigerated or frozen carcass) or eggs may pose some risk to human health in developing countries. Deshelled liquid eggs are typically pasteurized to inactivate bacteria such as *Salmonella*. The pasteurization processes have been validated with established critical limits in the HACCP

Table 1 Thermal death times (D_T) for low pathogenicity avian influenza A/Ck/NY/13142-5/1994 and high pathogenicity avian influenza A/Ck/PA/1370/1983 in egg products (imitation egg, whole homogenized egg, liquid egg white, 10% salted egg, dried egg white) heated at 55°C to 63°C

Temp °C	Imitation egg product (IEP)		Whole homogenized eggs (WHE)		Liquid egg white (LEW)		10% salted egg (SEW)	
	D_T							
	[1]LPAI-NY	[2]HPAI-PA	[1]LPAI-NY	[2]HPAI-PA	[1]LPAI-NY	[2]HPAI-PA	[1]LPAI-NY	[2]HPAI-PA
55	2.9 min	18.6 min	6.7 min	11 min	6.6 min	4.3 min	41 s	20.3 s
56.7	1.4 min	8.5 min	20 min	4.5 min	52 s	33 s	36 s	<20 s
57	0.8 min	3.8 min	1.6 min	3.2 min	21 s	23 s	22 s	<20 s
58	0.7 min	2.6 min	22 s	22 s	<19 s	<19 s	<20 s	<20 s
59	0.7 min	2 min	<20 s	<19 s	<19 s	<19 s	<20 s	<20 s
61	0.5 min	0.8 min	<20 s	<19 s	<19 s	<19 s	<20 s	<20 s
63	<0.1	<0.5	<20 s	<19 s	<19 s	<19 s	<20 s	<20 s

[1]low pathogenicity avian influenza A/Ck/NY/13142-5/1994.
[2] high pathogenicity avian influenza A/Ck/PA/1370/1983.
LPAI-IEP: Log $_{10}$D-value = 0.0239(Temp)^2 – 2.8927(Temp)x + 87.30.
HPAI-IEP: Log $_{10}$D-value = –0.3565(Temp) + 1.6407.
LPAI-HWE: Log $_{10}$D -value = 0.0305(Temp)^2 – 3.7702(Temp) + 116.
HPAI-HWE: Log $_{10}$D -value = 0.0324(Temp)^2 – 4.0265(Temp) + 124.75.
LPAI-LEW: Log $_{10}$D value = 0.0467(Temp)^2 – 5.6432(Temp) + 169.77.
HPAI-LEW: Log $_{10}$D -value = 0.057(Temp)^2 – 6.8432(Temp) + 204.5.
LPAI-SEW: Log $_{10}$D -value = 0.0115(Temp)^2 – 1.3848(Temp)+ 41.32.
HPAI-SEW: Log $_{10}$D-value = Undetectable after 20 s of heat exposure regardless to temperature.

Table 2 FSIS pasteurization standards for egg products with thermal death times (D_T) based on the thermal inactivation of *Salmonella*

	FSIS Standards	
	Temp °C	Inactivation time for 7 log10 of *Salmonella*
Whole egg	60	3.5 min
Whole blend	60	6.2 min
Whole blend	61.1	3.5 min
Liquid egg white	55.6	6.2 min
Liquid egg white	56.7	3.5 min
10% salted yolk	62.2	6.2 min
10% salted yolk	63.3	3.5 min
Imitation egg product	56.7	4.6 min
Dried egg white (pan dried)	51.7	5 d
Dried egg white (spray dried)	54.4	7 d

(Hazard Analysis Critical Control Point) process control and risk management scheme (Whiting & Buchanan 1997). Thermal inactivation data have been obtained to validate the United States pasteurization standards for egg products. AI viruses, HP and LP, were artificially inoculated in whole homogenized eggs, liquid egg whites, 10% salted egg, dried egg whites, and imitation egg products. The inoculated egg products were heat treated at various time and temperature combinations to obtain pasteurization inactivation curves. Heat inactivation data were generated for poultry eggs products (**Table 1**) showing the time required to inactivate AI viruses by one log at a specific temperature (D_T-value). The heat inactivation data for AI virus inoculated in the egg products (whole homogenized eggs, liquid egg whites, 10% salted egg, and dried egg whites) revealed that the USDA pasteurization standards were adequate to inactivate HPAI (A/Ck/PA/1370/1983) virus (**Tables 1** and **2**) and that a standard cooking temperature of 70°C for poultry meat would adequately inactivate HPAI viruses in chicken meat at levels produced in experimental studies (**Table 3**) (Swayne & Beck 2004, Thomas & Swayne 2007, Thomas et al. 2008, Chmielewski & Swayne 2010).

Table 3 Thermal death times (D_T) for highly pathogenic avian influenza A/Ck/PA/1370/1983 in chicken meat heated at 57.8°C to 73.9°C and the FSIS pasteurization standard for cooking meat

	[1]HPAI-PA/83	[1]HPAI- PA/83	FSIS standards based on 1% fat level
Temp °C	[2]D-value	log10 (EID50) reduction of HPAI virus titer using FSIS time to inactivate 7log10 *Salmonella*	Time to inactivate 7log10 *Salmonella*
57.8	4 min	15.8	63.3 min
58.9	2.2 min	18	39.7 min
60	1.2 min	21	25.2 min
61.1	37.6 s	25.6	16.1 min
70	0.24 s	91.3	21.9 s
73.9	0.03 s	33/s	<10 s

[1]high pathogenicity avian influenza A/Ck/PA/1370/1983.

[2]$\text{Log}_{10}\text{D-value} = [(-0.2157)(\text{temperature}) + 14.677]$.

CONCLUSIONS

AI outbreaks have caused severe economic losses and agricultural trade restrictions. Migratory aquatic birds cannot be controlled, but biosecurity measures can be established to prevent interaction of wild birds and domestic poultry, thereby reducing the risk of AI virus introduction into domestic poultry. The LPM system may be a reservoir for some AI viruses, so risk management strategies have to be implemented, including AI testing and restriction of infected birds from sale, implementing appropriate cleaning, disinfection, and hygiene practices, and enforcing movement restrictions and one-directional movement of poultry from farm to market. H5N1 HPAI viruses have caused sporadic infection of humans, primarily from direct contact with infected birds, producing a high case fatality rate (60%) for human infections, but with limited human-to-human spread and rare transmission through raw food products. AI viruses are a minor food safety issue, as cooking and pasteurization are effective in inactivating the virus, and poultry meat is seldom consumed without undergoing heat treatment or cooking sufficient to inactivate the virus.

SUMMARY POINTS

1. AI is caused by type A influenza viruses, and infections in humans can range from asymptomatic to mild respiratory disease, and in chickens symptoms range from decreased egg production to fatal systemic disease. On the rare occasions when humans were infected with H5N1 HPAI virus, the disease was serious and had a high case fatality rate of 60%. Most other human infections with AI viruses have been mild and self limiting.
2. Wild ducks and other aquatic birds are the natural host of LPAI viruses and exhibit no signs of illness when infected.
3. Transmission of AI viruses among wild birds and poultry usually results from exposure to contaminated feces, respiratory secretions, and feathers, and occasionally from cannibalization of carcasses. Between farms, spread is through airborne viruses, viruses adherent to dust, and contaminated equipment, shoes, and clothing. Poultry in LPM systems and village flocks are a high risk for being infected and spreading AI viruses.
4. The economic consequence of HPAI outbreaks is severe due to the cost of culling and bird replacement, loss of customer confidence, local and international trade losses, the cost of biosecurity, and the cost for veterinary and infrastructure improvement. All segments of the poultry industry within a country lose as a result of international trade embargoes.
5. There is concern for public health from the H5N1 HPAI viruses because of human infections and fatalities.
   a. Most infections have resulted from direct exposure to live or dead infected poultry.
   b. There is limited evidence of human-to-human transmission.
   c. There are rare cases of human AI virus infections obtained through consumption of raw or undercooked contaminated poultry products.
6. Various components are needed for successful control and mitigation strategies.
   a. Most countries prohibit HPAI virus–infected poultry from entering the food chain, but in developing countries, asymptomatic or sick HPAI virus–infected village poultry may enter the food chain.

b. Management practices that incorporate biosecurity principles are the key to preventing infection of poultry flocks by AI viruses.
c. Essential components for control include quarantine of infected flocks with depopulation and environmentally sound disposal, cleaning and disinfection of facilities, and composting of manure.
d. Education and risk communication are essential for all persons involved in poultry production to know how they can prevent the spread of the virus.
e. Standard cooking and pasteurization processes are effective at inactivating both LPAI and HPAI viruses in food products.

DISCLOSURE STATEMENT

Funding for avian influenza virus inactivation research reported in this paper was provided by Current Research Information System Project 6612-32000-048-00D, Foreign Agricultural Service of United States Department of Agriculture, and the American Egg Board.

LITERATURE CITED

Akey ŠBL. 2009. Low-pathogenicity H7N2 avian influenza outbreak in Virginia during 2002. *Avian Dis.* 47:1099–103
Alexander DJ. 2000. A review of avian influenza in different bird species. *Vet. Microbiol.* 74:3–13
Beato MS, Capua I, Alexander DJ. 2009. Avian influenza viruses in poultry products: a review. *Avian Pathol.* 38:193–200
Belser JA, Bridges CB, Katz JM, Tumpey TM. 2009. Past, present, and possible future human infection with influenza virus A subtype H7. *Emerg. Infect. Dis.* 15:860–65
Biswas PK, Christensen JP, Ahmed SSU, Das A, Rahman MH, et al. 2009. Risk for infection with highly pathogenic avian influenza virus (H5N1) in backyard chickens, Bangladesh. *Emerg. Infect. Dis.* 15:1931–36
Branckaert RDS, Guèye EF. 1997. Poultry as a tool in poverty eradication and promotion of gender equality. In *FAO's Programme for Support to Family Poultry Production, Proc. Workshop*, pp. 1–9. Rome: FAO
Brglez B, Hahn J. 2008. Methods for disposal of poultry carcasses. See Swayne 2008a, pp. 333–52
Bridges CB, Katz JM, Seto WH, Chan PKS, Tsang D, et al. 2000. Risk of influenza A (H5N1) infection among health care workers exposed to patients with influenza A (H5N1), Hong Kong. *J. Infect. Dis.* 181:344–48
Brown JD, Swayne DE, Cooper RJ, Burns RE, Stallknecht DE. 2007. Persistence of H5 and H7 avian influenza viruses in water. *Avian Dis.* 51:285–89
Burns A, van der Mensbrugghe D, Timmer H. 2008. Evaluating the economic consequences of avian influenza. In *Global Development Finance*, pp. 1–6. **http://siteresources.worldbank.org/EXTAVIANFLU/Resources/EvaluatingAHIeconomics_2008.pdf**
Cappucci DT, Johnson DC, Brugh M, Smith TM, Jackson CF, et al. 1985. Isolation of avian influenza virus (subtype H5N2) from chicken eggs during a natural outbreak. *Avian Dis.* 29:1195–2000
Capua I, Alexander DJ. 2004. Avian influenza: recent developments. *Avian Pathol.* 33:393–404
CDC. 2005. Avian influenza (bird flu). In *Influenza Viruses*, pp. 1–3. **http://www.cdc.gov/flu/avian/gen-info/pdf/flu_viruses.pdf**
CDC. 2006. Avian influenza (flu). In *Avian Influenza A Virus Infections of Humans*, pp. 1–3. **http://www.cdc.gov/flu/avian/gen-info/avian-flu-humans.htm**
CDC. 2007. Avian influenza: current H5N1 situation. In *Avian Influenza (Bird Flu)*, pp. 1–4. **http://www.cdc.gov/flu/avian/outbreaks/current.htm**
Chen H, Smith GJD, Li KS, Wang J, Fan XH, et al. 2006. Establishment of multiple sublineages of H5N1 influenza virus in Asia: implications for pandemic control. *Proc. Natl. Acad. Sci. USA* 103:2845–50

Chmielewski R, Swayne DE. 2010. Thermal inactivation of Newcastle virus in imitation egg product. *Res. Prog. Rep. Am. Egg Board.* 3 June 2010:1–9

Cox N, Uyeki TM. 2008. Public health implications of avian influenza viruses. See Swayne 2008a, pp. 453–84

de Wit JJ, Fabri THF, Hoogkamer A. 2004. *Survival of Avian Influenza Virus on Eggs*, Gezondheidsdienst voor Dieren, Res. Dev. Poult. Health, Deventer, the Netherlands

Domanska-Blicharz K, Minta Z, Smietanka K, March S, van den Berg T. 2010. H5N1 high pathogenicity avian influenza virus survival in different types of water. *Avian Dis.* 54:734–37

Donatelli I, Campitelli L, Trani LD, Puzelli S, Selli L, et al. 2001. Characterization of H5N2 influenza viruses from Italian poultry. *J. Gen. Virol.* 82:623–30

Duan L, Campitelli L, Fan XH, Leung YH, Vijaykrishna D, et al. 2007. Characterization of low-pathogenic H5 subtype influenza viruses from Eurasia: implications for the origin of highly pathogenic H5N1 viruses. *J. Virol.* 81:7529–39

Dunham EJ, Dugan VG, Kaser EK, Perkins SE, Brown IH, et al. 2009. Different evolutionary trajectories of European avian-like and classical swine H1N1 influenza A viruses. *J. Virol.* 83:5485–94

Dusek RJ, BortnerbJB, DeLibertocTJ, HoskinsbJ, FransonaJC, et al. 2009. Surveillance for high pathogenicity avian influenza virus in wild birds in the pacific flyway of the United States, 2006–2007. *Avian Dis.* 53:222–30

Influenza team (ECDC). 2007. Low Pathogenicity Avian Influenzas and human health. *Euro. Surveill.* 12(5):E070531.3. **http://www.eurosurveillance.org/ew/2007/070531.asp#3**

Escorcia M, Vázquez L, Méndez ST, Rodríguez-Ropón A, Lucio E, Nava GM. 2008. Avian influenza: genetic evolution under vaccination pressure. *Virology* 5:1–5

FAO. 2007. Food Outlook Global Market Analysis. In *Meat and Meat Product Prices*, pp. 30–31. Rome: FAO. **http://www.fao.org/giews/english/fo/index.htm#2007**

FAO. 2010. Despite many successes, avian influenza still threatens: FAO calls for sustained action on H5N1 and emerging infections. In *FAO Media Centre*, Rome. **http://www.fao.org/news/story/en/item/41276(icode/FAO)**

Fouchier RAM, Schneeberger PM, Rozendaal FW, Broekman JM, Kemin SAG, et al. 2004. Avian influenza A virus (H7N7) associated with human conjunctivitis and a fatal case of acute respiratory distress syndrome. *Proc. Natl. Acad. Sci. USA* 101:1356–61

Gambaryan A, Webster R, Matrosovich M. 2002. Differences between influenza virus receptors on target cells of duck and chicken. *Arch. Virol.* 147:1197–208

Gao Y, Zhang Y, Shinya K, Deng G, Jiang Y, et al. 2009. Identification of amino acids in HA and PB2 critical for the transmission of H5N1 avian influenza viruses in a mammalian host. *PLoS Pathog.* 5:e1000709

Gilsdorf A, Boxall N, Gasimov V, Agayev I, Mammadzade F, et al. 2006. Two clusters of human infection with influenza A/H5N1 virus in the Republic of Azerbaijan, February–March. *Eurosurveillance* 11:122–26

Guan J, Chan M, Grenier C, Wilkie DC, Brooks BW, Spencer JL. 2009. Survival of avian influenza and Newcastle disease viruses in compost and at ambient temperatures based on virus isolation and real-time reverse transcriptase PCR. *Avian Dis.* 53:26–33

Guan Y, Peiris JSM, Lipatov AS, Ellis TM, Dyrting KC, et al. 2002a. Emergence of multiple genotypes of H5N1 avian influenza viruses in Hong Kong SAR. *Proc. Natl. Acad. Sci. USA* 99:8950–55

Guan Y, Peiris M, Kong KF, Dyrting KC, Ellis TM, et al. 2002b. H5N1 influenza viruses isolated from geese in Southeastern China: evidence for genetic reassortment and interspecies transmission to ducks. *Virology* 292:16–23

Harder TC, Teuffert J, Starick E, Gethmann J, Grund C, et al. 2009. Highly pathogenic avian influenza virus (H5N1) in frozen duck carcasses, Germany, 2007. *Emerg. Infect. Dis.* 15:1–8

Hatta M, Gao P, Halfmann P, Kawaoka Y. 2001. Molecular basis for high virulence of Hong Kong H5N1 influenza A viruses. *Science* 293:1840–42

Hinshaw VS. 1985. The nature of avian influenza in migratory waterfowl, including interspecies transmission. In *1986 Proc. 2nd Int. Symp. Avian Influenza*, pp. 133–41. Athens, GA: Am. Assoc. Avian Pathol.

Horimoto T, Rivera E, Pearson J, Senne D, Krauss S, et al. 1995. Origin and molecular changes associated with emergence of a highly pathogenic H5N2 influenza virus in Mexico. *Virology* 213:223–30

Hulse-Post DJ, Sturm-Ramirez KM, Humberd J, Seiler P, Govorkova EA, et al. 2005. Role of domestic ducks in the propagation and biological evolution of highly pathogenic H5N1 influenza viruses in Asia. *Proc. Natl. Acad. Sci. USA* 102:10682–87

INFOSAN IFSAN-. 2004. Avian influenza. In *INFOSAN Inf. Note No. 2/04*. 3 pp.

Ito T, Suzuki Y, Suzuki T, Takada A, Horimoto T, et al. 2000. Recognition of N-glycolylneuraminic acid linked to galactose by the alpha 2,3 linkage is associated with intestinal replication of influenza A virus in ducks. *J. Virol.* 74:9300–5

Katz JM, Veguilla V, Belser JA, Maines TR, Hoeven NV, et al. 2008. The public health impact of avian influenza viruses. *Poult. Sci.* 88:872–79

Kawaoka Y, Naeve CW, Webster RG. 1984. Is virulence of H5N2 influenza viruses in chickens associated with loss of carbohydrate from the hemagglutinin? *Virology* 139:303–16

Kim J-K, Negovetich NJ, Forrest HL, Webster RG. 2009. Ducks: the "Trojan horses" of H5N1 influenza. *Influenza Respir. Viruses* 3:121–28

Koopmans M, Duizer E. 2004. Foodborne viruses: an emerging problem. *Int. J. Food Microbiol.* 90:23–41

Koopmans M, Wilbrink B, Conyn M, Natrop G, van der Nat H, et al. 2004. Transmission of H7N7 avian influenza A virus to human beings during a large outbreak in commercial poultry farms in the Netherlands. *Lancet* 363:587–93

Kuchipudi SV, Nelli R, White GA, Bain M, Chang KC, Dunham S. 2009. Differences in influenza virus receptors in chickens and ducks: Implications for interspecies transmission. *J. Mol. Genet. Med.* 3:143–51

Lee C-W, Saif YM. 2009. Avian influenza virus. *Comp. Immunol. Microbiol. Infect. Dis.* 32:301–10

Li KS, Xu KM, Peiris JSM, Poon LLM, Yu KZ, et al. 2003. Characterization of H9 subtype influenza viruses from the ducks of Southern China: a candidate for the next influenza pandemic in humans? *J. Virol.* 77:6988–94

Liu J, Bi Y, Qin K, Fu G, Yang J, et al. 2009. Emergence of European avian influenza virus-like H1N1 swine influenza A viruses in China. *J. Clin. Microbiol.* 48:2643–46

Lokuge B. 2005. *Avian influenza, world food trade and WTO rules: The economics of transboundary disease control. Rep.* Work. Pap. Jan., The Aust. Natl. Univ., Canberra

Lu H, Castro AE, Pennick K, Liu J, Yang Q, et al. 2003. Survival of avian influenza virus H7N2 in SPF chickens and their environment. *Avian Dis.* 47:1015–21

Mase M, Eto M, Tanimura N, Imai K, Tsukamoto K, et al. 2005. Isolation of a genotypically unique H5N1 influenza virus from duck meat imported into Japan from China. *Virology* 339:101–9

Matrosovich MN, Matrosovich TY, Gray T, Roberts NA, Klenk H-D. 2004. Human and avian influenza viruses target different cell types in cultures of human airway epithelium. *Proc. Natl. Acad. Sci. USA* 101:4620–24

McLeod A, Morgan N, Prakash A, Hinrichs J. 2005. *Economic and Social Impact of Avian Influenza*. Rome: FAO Emerg. Cent. Transbound. Anim. Dis. Oper. (ECTAD)

Munier S, Larcher T, Cormier-Aline F, Soubieux D, Su B, et al. 2010. A genetically engineered waterfowl influenza virus with a deletion in the stalk of the neuraminidase has increased virulence for chickens. *J. Virol.* 84:940–52

Nguyen-Van-Tam JSN, Nair P, Acheson P, Baker A, Barker M, et al. 2006. Outbreak of low pathogenicity H7N3 avian influenza in UK, including associated case of human conjunctivitis. *Eurosurveillance* 11:1–2

OIE. 2009. OIE Terr. Anim. Health Code: Avian influenza, Article 10.4.1. In *Health Standards*. Paris, Fr.: OIE. **http://www.oie.int/eng/normes/mcode/en_chapitre_1.10.4.htm**

Oner AF, Bay A, Arslan S, Akdeniz H, Sahin HA, et al. 2006. Avian influenza A (H5N1) infection in eastern Turkey in 2006. *N. Engl. J. Med.* 355:2179–85

Otte J, Hinrichs J, Rushton J, Roland-Holst D, Zilberman D. 2008. Impacts of avian influenza virus on animal production in developing countries. *CAB Rev.: Perspect. Agric. Vet. Sci. Nutr. Nat. Resour.* 3:1–18

Pantin-Jackwood M, Wasilenko JL, Spackman E, Suarez DL, Swayne DE. 2010. Susceptibility of turkeys to pandemic-H1N1 virus by reproductive tract insemination. *Virol. J.* 7:27

Pappas C, Matsuoka Y, Swayne DE, Donis RO. 2007. Development and evaluation of an influenza virus subtype H7N2 vaccine candidate for pandemic preparedness. *Clin. Vaccine Immunol.* 14:1425–32

Perdue ML, Garcia M, Beck J, Brugh M, Swayne DE. 1996. An Arg-Lys insertion at the hemagglutinin cleavage site of an H5N2 avian influenza isolate. *Virus Genes* 12:77–84

Pillai SPS, Pantin-Jackwood M, Yassine HM, Saif YM, Lee CW. 2010. The high susceptibility of turkeys to influenza viruses of different origins implies their importance as potential intermediate hosts. *Avian Dis.* 54:522–26

Promkuntod N, Antarasena C, Prommuang P, Prommuang P. 2006. Isolation of avian influenza virus A subtype H5N1 from internal contents (albumen and allantoic fluid) of Japanese quail (*Coturnix coturnix japonica*) eggs and oviduct during a natural outbreak. *Ann. NY Acad. Sci.* 1081:171–73

Ramirez-Nieto G, Shivaprasad HL, Kim C-H, Lillehoj HS, Song H, et al. 2010. Adaptation of a mallard H5N2 low pathogenicity influenza virus in chickens with prior history of infection with infectious bursal disease virus. *Avian Dis.* 54:513–21

Senne DA. 2010. Avian influenza in North and South America, the Caribbean, and Australia, 2006–2008. *Avian Dis.* 54:179–86

Senne DA, Suarez DL, Pedersen JC, Panigrahy B. 2003. Molecular and biological characteristics of H5 and H7 avian influenza viruses found in live-bird markets of northeastern United States during 1994–2001. *Avian Dis.* 47:898–904

Sinha NK, Roy A, Das B, Das S, Basak S. 2009. Evolutionary complexities of swine flu H1N1 gene sequences of 2009. *Biochem. Biophys. Res. Commun.* 390:349–51

Spackman E, Senne DA, Davison S, Suarez DL. 2003. Sequence analysis of recent H7 avian influenza viruses associated with three different outbreaks in commercial poultry in the United States. *J. Virol.* 77:13399–402

Stallknecht DE, Brown JD. 2007. Wild birds and the epidemiology of avian influenza. *J. Wildl. Dis.* 43:S15–20

Stallknecht DE, Goekjian VH, Wilcox BR, Poulson RL, Brown JD. 2010. Avian influenza virus in aquatic habitats: What do we need to learn? *Avian Dis.* 54:461–65

Suarez D. 2008. Influenza A virus. See Swayne 2008a, pp. 3–22

Suarez DL, Spackman E, Senne DA. 2009. Update on molecular epidemiology of H1, H5, and H7 influenza virus infections in poultry in North America. *Avian Dis.* 47:888–97

Suarez DL, Woolcock PR, Bermudez AJ, Senne DA. 2002. Isolation from turkey breeder hens of a reassortant H1N2 influenza virus with swine, human, and avian lineage genes. *Avian Dis.* 46:111–21

Swayne DE. 2005. Occupational and consumer risks from avian influenza viruses. *Dev. Biol.* 124:85–90

Swayne DE. 2006. Microassay for measuring thermal inactivation of H5N1 high pathogenicity avian influenza virus in naturally infected chicken meat. *Int. J. Food Microbiol.* 108:268–71

Swayne DE, ed. 2008a. *Avian Influenza*. Ames, IA: Blackwell

Swayne DE. 2008b. Epidemiology of avian influenza in agricultural and other man-made systems. See Swayne 2008a, pp. 59–85

Swayne DE. 2008c. The global nature of avian influenza. See Swayne 2008a, pp. 123–43

Swayne DE, Beck JR. 2004. Heat inactivation of avian influenza and Newcastle disease viruses in egg products. *Avian Pathol.* 33:512–18

Swayne DE, Halvorson DA. 2008. Influenza. In *Diseases of Poultry*, ed. YM Saif, JR Glisson, AM Fadly, LR McDougald, L Nolan, pp. 153–84. Ames, IA: Blackwell

Swayne DE, Suarez DL. 2007. Current developments in avian influenza vaccines, including safety of vaccinated birds as food. *Dev. Biol.* 130:123–33

Tam JS. 2002. Influenza A (H5N1) in Hong Kong: an overview. *Vaccine* 20:S77–81

Thanawongnuwech R, Amonsin A, Tantilertcharoen R, Damrongwatanapokin S, Theamboonlers A, et al. 2005. Probable tiger-to-tiger transmission of avian influenza H5N1. *Emerg. Infect. Dis.* 11:699–701

Thomas C, King DJ, Swayne DE. 2008. Thermal inactivation of avian influenza and Newcastle disease viruses in chicken meat. *J. Food Prot.* 71:1214–22

Thomas C, Swayne DE. 2007. Thermal inactivation of H5N1 high pathogenicity avian influenza virus in naturally infected chicken meat. *J. Food Prot.* 70:674–80

Tiwari A, Patnayak DP, Chander Y, Parsad M, Goyal SM. 2006. Survival of two avian respiratory viruses on porous and nonporous surfaces. *Avian Dis.* 50:284–87

Tumpey TM, Suarez DL, Perkins LEL, Senne DA, Lee J-G, et al. 2002. Characterization of a highly pathogenic H5N1 avian influenza A virus isolated from duck meat. *J. Virol.* 76:6344–55

Ungchusak K, Auewarakul P, Dowell SF, Kitphati R, Auwanit W, et al. 2005. Probable person-to-person transmission of avian influenza A (H5N1). *N. Engl. J. Med.* 352:333–40

Walker JA, Kawaoka Y. 1993. Importance of conserved amino acids at the cleavage site of the haemagglutinin of a virulent avian influenza A virus. *J. Gen. Virol.* 74:311–14

Wan H, Sorrell EM, Song H, Hossain MJ, Ramirez-Nieto G, et al. 2008. Replication and transmission of H9N2 influenza viruses in ferrets: evaluation of pandemic potential. *PLoS ONE* 3:e2923

Webster RG, Bean WJ, Gorman OT, Chambers TM, Kawaoka Y. 1992. Evolution and ecology of influenza A viruses. *Microbiol. Rev.* 56:152–79

Webster RG, Krauss S, Hulse-Post D, Sturm-Ramirez K. 2007. Evolution of influenza A virus in wild birds. *J. Wildl. Dis.* 43:S1–6

Whiting RC, Buchanan RL. 1997. Development of a quantitative risk assessment model for *Salmonella enteritidis* in pasteurized liquid eggs. *Int. J. Food Microbiol.* 36:111–25

WHO. 2004. Avian influenza A(H5N1) in humans and in poultry in Asia: food safety considerations. In *Food Safety*, pp. 1–2. **http://www.who.int/foodsafety/micro/avian1/en/print.html**

WHO. 2005. Avian influenza frequently asked questions. In *Communicable Disease Surveillance and Response*, pp. 1–6. **http://www.who.int/csr/disease/avian_influenza/avian_faqs/en/print.html**

WHO. 2005a. Evolution of H5N1 avian influenza viruses in Asia. *Emerg. Infect. Dis.* 11:1515–21

WHO. 2005b. Highly pathogenic H5N1 avian influenza outbreaks in poultry and in humans: food safety implications. In *International Food Safety Authorities Network-Avian Influenza*, pp. 1–5. **www.who.int/foodsafety**

WHO. 2006. H5N1 avian influenza: timeline of major events. In *Global Alert and Response*, 10 pp. **http://www.who.int/csr/disease/avian_influenza/ai_timeline/en/index.html**

WHO. 2007. Questions and answers on avian influenza in relation to animal, food and water. In *Food Safety*, pp. 1–14. **http://www.who.int/foodsafety/micro/AI_QandA_Apr07_EN.pdf**

WHO. 2008. Update: WHO-confirmed human cases of avian influenza A(H5N1) infection, November 2003–May 2008. *Wkly Epidemiol. Rec.* 83:415–20

WHO. 2010. Avian influenza: cumulative number of confirmed human cases of avian influenza A/(H5N1) reported to WHO. In *Global Alert and Response*. **http://www.who.int/csr/disease/avian_influenza/country/cases_table_20WHO**

World Bank. 2010. Health, nutrition and population: economic impact of avian flu. In *Global Program for Avian Influenza and Human Pandemic*, pp. 1–4. Washington, DC: World Bank

Writ. Comm. Second WHO Consult. Clin. Aspects Hum. Infect. Avian Influenza A Virus. 2008. Update on avian influenza A (H5N1) virus infection in humans. *N. Engl. J. Med.* 358:261–73

Xu X, Subbarao K, Cox NJ, Guo Y. 1999. Genetic characterization of the pathogenic influenza A/Goose/Guangdong/1/96 (H5N1) virus: similarity of its hemagglutinin gene to those of H5N1 viruses from the 1997 outbreaks in Hong Kong. *Virology* 261:15–19

Yalcin C. 2006. Market impact of HPAI outbreaks: a rapid appraisal process-turkey. In *The Market and Trade Dimensions of Avian Influenza*, pp. 1–28. Rome: FAO

Yamamoto Y, Nakamura K, Okamatsu M, Yamada M, Mase M. 2008. Avian influenza virus (H5N1) replication in feathers of domestic waterfowl. *Emerg. Infect. Dis.* 14:149–51

Yamamoto Y, Nakamura K, Yamada M, Ito T. 2009. Zoonotic risk for influenza A (H5N1) infection in wild swan feathers. *J. Vet. Med. Sci.* 71:1549–51

Yuen KY, Chan PKS, Peiris M, Tsang DNC, Que TL, et al. 1998. Clinical features and rapid viral diagnosis of human disease associated with avian influenza A H5N1 virus. *Lancet* 351:467–71

Molecular Design of Seed Storage Proteins for Enhanced Food Physicochemical Properties

Mary Rose G. Tandang-Silvas,[1] Evelyn Mae Tecson-Mendoza,[2] Bunzo Mikami,[3] Shigeru Utsumi,[1] and Nobuyuki Maruyama[1,*]

[1] Laboratory of Food Quality Design and Development, Graduate School of Agriculture, Kyoto University, Uji, Kyoto 611-0011, Japan; email: marunobu@kais.kyoto-u.ac.jp

[2] Institute of Plant Breeding, Crop Science Cluster, College of Agriculture, University of the Philippines Los Baños, College 4031, Laguna, Philippines

[3] Laboratory of Basic and Applied Molecular Biotechnology, Graduate School of Agriculture, Kyoto University, Uji, Kyoto 611-0011, Japan

Annu. Rev. Food Sci. Technol. 2011. 2:59–73

First published online as a Review in Advance on October 4, 2010

The *Annual Review of Food Science and Technology* is online at food.annualreviews.org

This article's doi: 10.1146/annurev-food-022510-133718

1941-1413/11/0410-0059$20.00

*Corresponding author.

Keywords

structure-function, protein engineering, emulsion, gelation

Abstract

Seed storage proteins such as soybean globulins have been nutritionally and functionally valuable in the food industry. Protein structure-function studies are valuable in modifying proteins for enhanced functionality. Recombinant technology and protein engineering are two of the tools in biotechnology that have been used in producing soybean proteins with better gelling property, solubility, and emulsifying ability. This article reviews the molecular basis for the logical and precise protein designs that are important in obtaining the desired improved physicochemical properties.

This chapter is dedicated to the memory of Professor Shigeru Utsumi who passed away on 1 December 2008.

INTRODUCTION

Seed storage proteins have been nutritionally and functionally valuable in the food industry. In 2002, the world's soybean production was reported to be 180 million metric tons (MTs) (FAO 2003). Although 85% of the production is processed into animal feed and vegetable oil, approximately 2% of the soybean meal is processed into flour and protein isolate for use as a food ingredient, and 6% is consumed directly as human food, mostly in Asia (Soyatech 2010). Sales of soyfood products such as tofu, soymilk, soycheese, energy bars, and meat alternatives reached close to $4 billion in 2004 (Soyatech & SPINS 2005). Most of these soy protein products, except those used in nutritional applications, are utilized for their functional properties, such as solubility, water absorption and binding, viscosity, gel formation, elasticity, emulsification, binding, cohesion-adhesion, fat absorption, flavor binding, foaming, and color control (Kinsella 1979).

Presently, the variety of soy products and their different characteristics are brought about by formulation and various processing treatments that may involve the use of solvents, enzymes, heat, fractionation, and pH adjustment, or any combination of these treatments. To develop more and better products, the main ingredient, the seed, could be modified using conventional breeding and genetic engineering, specifically, protein engineering. Through conventional breeding, soybean with increased protein levels, especially those of the 7S and 11S globulins (Kwanyuen et al. 1998), low levels of lipoxygenase to reduce the production of beany off-flavors (Nielsen et al. 1992), and higher level of β-conglycinin (Heller 2005) have been developed. Soybean with low levels of the flatulence factors raffinose oligosaccharides and lipoxygenase, and associated off-flavors, has been developed using genetic engineering (Johnson 1999).

Since the early 1990s, the research team of Professor Shigeru Utsumi of Kyoto University has pioneered the molecular design of storage proteins and protein engineering to enhance their physicochemical, functional, and nutritional qualities (Kim et al. 1990, Utsumi et al. 1993). These studies consist of isolation and cloning of the storage protein gene and expression in *Escherichia coli*, characterization of the recombinant protein, protein structure determination using X-ray crystallography, gene modification to enhance the protein's properties, analysis of the physicochemical properties of the modified storage proteins, and gene transformation and expression in selected crops, such as rice, soybean, and potato. These studies have covered storage proteins from several crops: soybean, adzuki bean, mungbean, rapeseed, and French bean. Ultimately, the goal is to develop crops with these modified genes that will produce the enhanced storage proteins.

This chapter focuses on the molecular design of storage proteins specifically for enhanced physicochemical and functional properties and covers (*a*) an overview of seed storage proteins, (*b*) their physicochemical properties, (*c*) their three-dimensional structure, and (*d*) protein engineering to improve their physicochemical properties.

OVERVIEW OF SEED STORAGE PROTEINS

Classification

The grouping of seed storage proteins based on their solubility (Osborne 1924) is not absolute but is still used for convenience. Seed storage proteins are classified into (*a*) globulins or salt soluble fraction, (*b*) albumins or water soluble fraction, (*c*) glutelins or dilute acid/alkali fraction, and (*d*) prolamins or alcohol-soluble fraction. The globulins are subdivided based on their sedimentation coefficients into 7S or vicilins and 11S or legumins. Although prolamins and glutelins have different solubility, they are sometimes put in one group because of the relatedness in their amino acid sequence and content (Shewry et al. 1995). In addition, the subunits released by glutelins in a reduced condition are alcohol-soluble, as in the case of wheat glutenins (Weiser 2007). The prolamins were thus further classified into sulfur-poor, sulfur-rich, and high-molecular weight prolamins (Utsumi 1992). The 2S albumins are compact, globular, and cysteine-rich (Shewry et al. 1995, Moreno & Clemente 2008). The amount of these storage proteins in food crops varies. In general, legumes contain mostly globulins, whereas cereals contain mostly prolamins and glutelins (Utsumi 1992). Oats and rice are exceptions to most cereals because they have mostly 11S globulin-like storage proteins and only approximately 5% to 10% prolamins (Shewry et al. 1995).

7S and 11S Globulins

This review is primarily focused on 7S and 11S globulins, the most extensively studied seed storage proteins, perhaps because of their predominance in nature. The 7S globulins are trimer molecules with molecular weights of 150–200 kDa and have 40–70 kDa monomers. The 11S globulins, on the other hand, are hexamer molecules involving two trimers, have molecular weights of 300–400 kDa, and have 50–60 kDa monomers (Utsumi 1992). They are synthesized, sorted, processed and accumulated during seed development. Their monomers are translated into a single pre-propeptide in the rough endoplasmic reticulum (rER). After cotranslational cleavage of the signal peptide in the endoplasmic reticulum (ER), the propeptides accordingly assemble into trimers. The composition of the newly synthesized proteins in the ER was suggested to determine their transport pathway (Mori et al. 2004).

Unlike 11S globulins, 7S globulins are generally cotranslationally glycosylated at Asn residues of the consensus sequence Asn-X-Ser/Thr (Katsube et al. 1998). There are, however, rare reports of glycosylated 11S globulins such as lupin (Duranti et al. 1988) and cocosin (Garcia et al. 2005). Glycosylated (Derbyshire et al. 1976) and unglycosylated (Kimura et al. 2008) pea 7S globulins and unglycosylated coconut 7S globulins (Garcia et al. 2005) have been reported as well. The 7S globulins are usually lacking in cysteine residues, hence, they are devoid of disulfide bridges. The 11S globulins have two conserved disulfide bridges **(Figure 1)**. The cleavage of acidic and basic polypeptides by asparaginyl endopeptidase in the protein storage vacuoles (PSVs) was suggested to trigger hexamer formation to attain mature 11S globulins (Dickinson et al. 1989, Jung et al. 1998). The crystal structure of mature A3B4 revealed that the hydrophobic residues needed for the face to face association of the two trimers become exposed after the cleavage (Adachi et al. 2003a). Storage proteins are kept indefinitely in mature seeds in various organelles depending on the crop. Rice accumulates prolamins in protein bodies (Müntz 1998, Shewry & Halford 2002) whereas soybeans store 7S and 11S globulins in PSV (Mori et al. 2009). At the onset of germination, they are rapidly mobilized, used, and depleted.

The soybean 7S globulin called β-conglycinin has three types of subunits, namely, α (~67 kDa), α′ (~71 kDa), and β (~50 kDa) (Maruyama et al. 1998), as shown in **Figure 1**. All have a highly homologous core region but only α and α′ have a highly acidic extension region at the N-terminus. Both α and α′ have two N-glycans within their core regions, whereas β has only one (Maruyama et al. 2001). Soybean 11S globulin or glycinin has five types of subunits that are grouped into two based on their amino acid sequence. Group I consists of A1aB1b, A1bB2, and A2B1a, whereas group II consists of A3B4 and A5A4B3. A schematic representation of A1aB1b is shown in **Figure 1**. The sequence identity among the subunits is approximately 45%, whereas it is approximately 80% within the group (Maruyama et al. 2006). There are five variable regions among the 11S globulins.

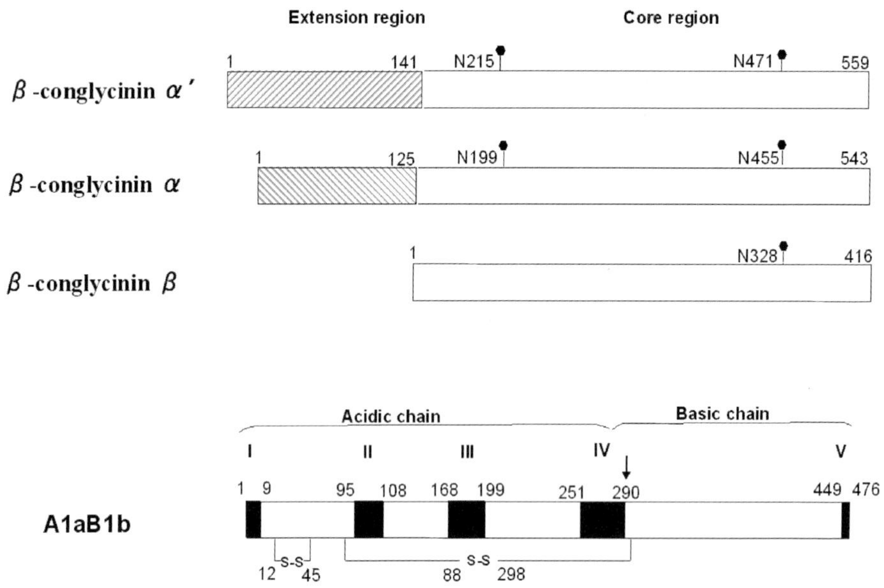

Figure 1

Schematic representation of β-conglycinin α′, α, β, and glycinin A1aB1b (*from top to bottom*). The small closed circles on β-conglycinin represent N-glycans. The five variable regions in 11S globulins are indicated by I, II, III, IV, and V, and the processing site is indicated by an arrow (Utsumi 1992, Maruyama et al. 1998).

Recombinant Technology

Recombinant technology has been used to rapidly obtain highly pure protein in an appreciable quantity. This technique takes advantage of the ability of hosts such as bacteria and yeasts to produce non-endogenous proteins with the aid of expression plasmids. One of the limitations of the usual expression host, *E. coli*, is its inability to carry out posttranslational modifications. Hence, the recombinant 7S globulins are unglycosylated, and the recombinant 11S globulins are uncleaved and unprocessed into mature forms. Both were, however, able to fold correctly and assemble into trimers (Kim et al. 1990, Maruyama et al. 1998, Lauer et al. 2004, Garcia et al. 2006). There is a good number of reports on purification and characterization of food plant proteins over the last three decades as a result of this technology. Soybean is one of the crops that has been intensively investigated (Utsumi et al. 1997, Maruyama et al. 2007). Most initial studies on plant proteins were primarily focused towards improving their nutritional properties, followed by functional and pharmacological studies. Recently, studies were prompted by the search for the molecular basis of their allergenicity and cross reactivity (Albillos et al. 2008; Jin et al. 2009a,b).

FOOD PHYSICOCHEMICAL PROPERTIES OF SEED STORAGE PROTEINS

Overview of Food Physicochemical Properties

Storage proteins are the predominant source of amino acids and peptides in seeds. Therefore, they mostly determine the seed's nutraceutical and functional values. Physicochemical properties such as thermal stability, surface hydrophobicity, solubility, and emulsifying and gelling ability are important in their application in the food industry. Protein structure affects physicochemical

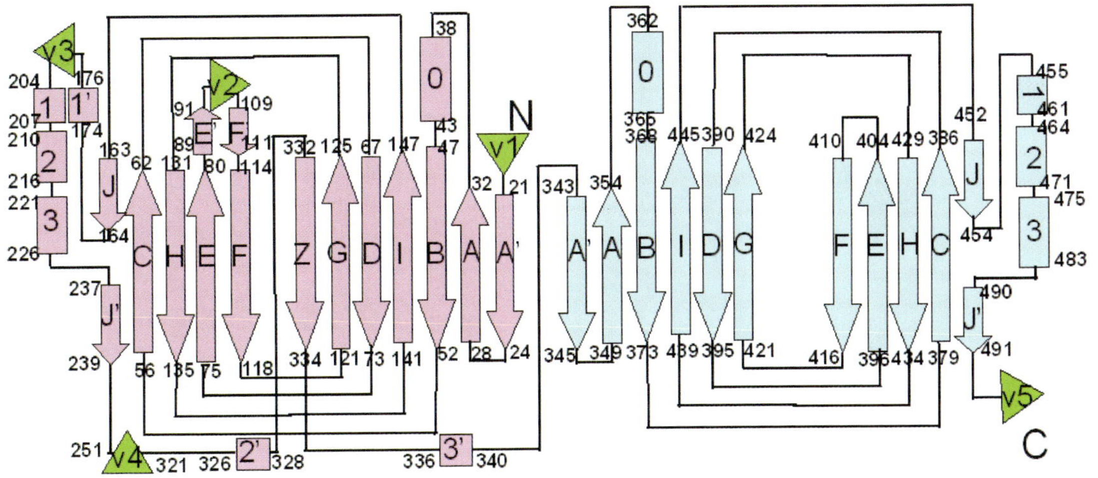

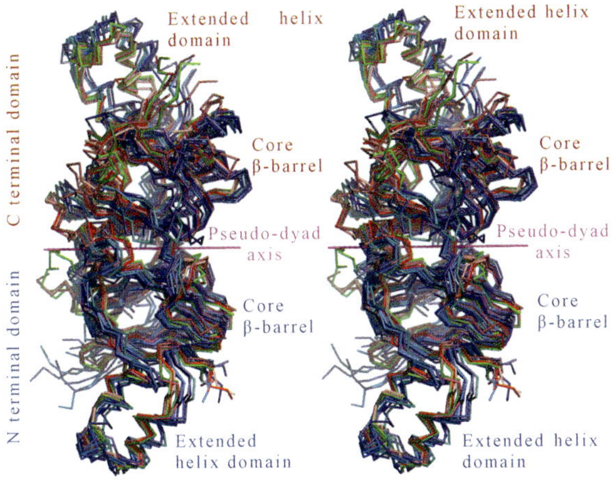

Figure 2

Schematic diagram of the secondary structures in mature glycinin A3B4 (PDB id: 2D5H) (*top*) (from Maruyama et al. 2010 with permission from the publisher). The N-terminal and C-terminal domains are in pink and cyan, except for the variable regions (v1–v5), which are represented by green triangles. N and C indicate the N- and C-terminal ends. 7S and 11S globulin monomers are superimposed (*bottom*) (from Tandang-Silvas et al. 2010 with permission from the publisher).

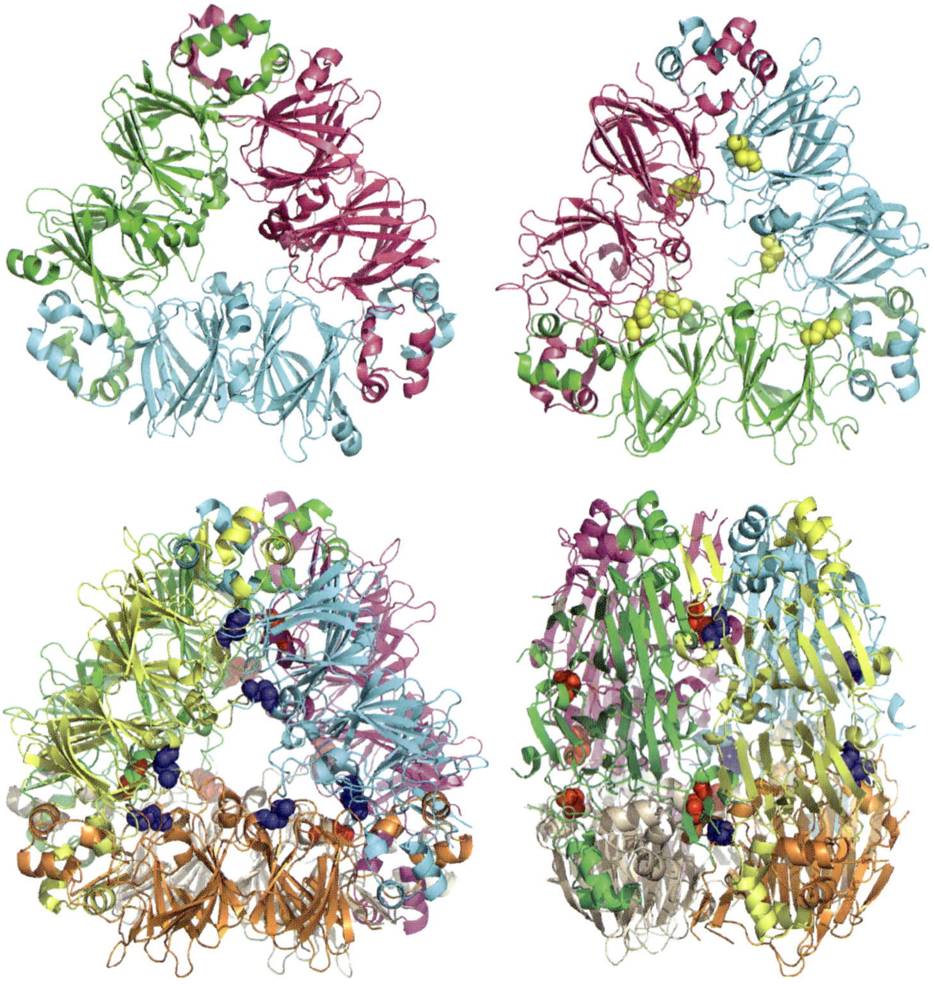

Figure 3

The cartoon models of β-conglycinin α′ core (*top left*, PDB id 1UIK), proA3B4 (*top right*, PDB id 2D5H), and mature A3B4 (PDB id 2D5F) at threefold axis (*bottom left*) and side view (*bottom right*). The disulfide bridges are designated by spheres. Images were generated using the program Pymol.

properties, and it imparts characteristic texture, hardness, viscosity, and water and fat absorption, among other properties, in foods such as sausages, mayonnaise, salad dressing, gravies, bread, cake, and beverages.

Solubility is perhaps an initial intrinsic property that should be considered in determining the potential use of food proteins because other properties depend highly on this. Fukuda et al. (2005) correlated the emulsifying ability of 7S and 11S globulins in wild-type and cultivated soybeans to solubility. The emulsion formation was found to be most favored by the variety with the most soluble globulins. Consumer acceptability of food products is highly influenced by appearance, which is also dictated by solubility. Furthermore, surface hydrophobicity is correlated with solubility, thermal stability, and foaming and emulsifying abilities. Gelling property is highly influenced by thermal stability. These results established that these functional properties do not work independently of each other. Also, numerous studies have shown that factors like ionic strength and pH greatly affect these properties.

Food Physicochemical Properties of Soybean Seed Storage Proteins

Soybean has long been used in various food products like tofu gel. Protein gel is a three-dimensional random network of partially denatured proteins formed by heating and subsequent cooling. It can be composed of either random aggregates or polymers of strings of beads (Doi 1993). Both glycinin (Nakamura et al. 1984b) and β-conglycinin (Mohamed Salleh et al. 2004) gels are composed of strings of beads as verified by transmission and scanning electron microscopy. Glycinin is known to have better gelling property than β-conglycinin (Nakamura et al. 1986b, Kohyama et al. 1995). β-conglycinin α, α′, and β were earlier reported to participate uniformly in 7S soy protein gel (Utsumi & Kinsella 1985). A more recent study (Mohamed Salleh et al. 2004) clarified that although no secondary structural differences were observed in the three subunits, they formed gels with different density and strand thickness. The hardest gel was formed from an α′-lacking sample, followed by normal 7S and α-lacking sample. The different wild soybeans surveyed by Fukuda and coworkers (2005) did not have uniform distribution of globulins, and microheterogeneity in the subunits was also reported. Slight variations, such as the natural deletion of four amino acids in the hypervariable region of wild soybean glycinin, affected thermal stability that could in turn affect gelation. Some soybean cultivars were demonstrated to have better gelling property than the others (Nakamura et al. 1984a). Glycinin from the cultivars with the A5A4B3 subunit formed gels twice as fast as those without it, whereas the cultivars with higher A3B4 subunit formed harder gels. Apparently, the five glycinin subunits impart different gelling properties.

β-conglycinin and glycinin gels have different properties (Nakamura et al. 1986a). The gelation mechanism between the two are not the same because sulfhydryl (SH) and disulfide (SS) exchange reactions in β-conglycinin are unlikely. Gel formation of glycinin was described in two steps by Mori et al. (1981). The first step involves the formation of soluble aggregates. Further heating leads to the second step in which the soluble macroaggregates form gel. If protein concentration is low, the dissociation of acidic and basic polypeptides only results in soluble aggregates and no gelation proceeds. The forces involved in gel formation include hydrophobic interactions, hydrogen bonds, ionic interactions, and disulfide bonding (Catsimpoolas & Meyer 1970, Nakamura et al. 1984a, Mori et al. 1986). Two proposed mechanisms for the formation of crosslinked aggregates of proteins during heating are (*a*) inaccessible cysteine residues and disulfide bonds becoming available and reactive to form intermolecular crosslinks and (*b*) aggregation lowering the unfavorable exposure of hydrophobic patches (Visschers & de Jong 2005). Some factors that affect gel formation and quality include pH, ionic strength, protein concentration, heating time, and temperature (Doi 1993). A prerequisite for heat-induced gelation is partial protein denaturation such that the heating temperature should be above the thermal denaturation midpoint value (T_m) of the protein. Sufficient heating time for denaturation to occur is also important. Higher protein concentration forms harder gels.

Other physicochemical properties of α, α', and β have been studied individually (Maruyama et al. 1998, 1999). Versions of α and α' subunits without an extension region, α_c and α'_c, were also constructed and studied. Their T_m values were as follows: 78.6°C for α, 82.7°C for α', 90.8°C for β, 77.3°C for α_c, and 83.3°C for α'_c. Thermal stability, therefore, was dictated mostly by the core region, whereas the extension region showed very little influence. The T_m value of β-conglycinin heterotrimer was determined by the subunit having the lowest T_m value (Maruyama et al. 2002b), but glycinin heterotrimer did not follow this trend (Maruyama et al. 2004a). Surface hydrophobicity was determined by the core regions. Solubility of α and α' was similar to native proteins, but α_c and α'_c have lower solubility, as with β at $\mu = 0.08$. This showed that the highly acidic extension regions contribute to solubility. Glycan and extension regions prevented heat-induced association and improved the emulsifying ability of β-conglycinin subunits (Maruyama et al. 1999, 2002a).

Other physicochemical properties of glycinin were also studied individually, and their solubility profiles were found to be unique from each other at both $\mu = 0.08$ and $\mu = 0.5$. Prak et al. (2005) reported the following patterns: (*a*) for emulsifying ability, A1bB2 < A2B1a < A5A4B3 < A3B4 $\leq$ A1aB1b; (*b*) for surface hydrophobicity, A5A4B3 < A1aB1b $\leq$ A3B4 < A1bB2 < A2B1a; and (*c*) for thermal stability, A1bB2 < A2B1a $\leq$ A5A4B3 < A3B4 $\leq$ A1aB1b.

Food Physicochemical Properties of Seed Storage Proteins of Other Food Crops

Some recombinant 7S globulins and their native forms evaluated for physicochemical and functional properties were from adzuki bean (Fukuda et al. 2007, 2008), mungbean (Garcia et al. 2006), and French bean (Kimura et al. 2008, 2010). The native French bean 7S globulin, phaseolin, has T_m values of 88.3°C and 80.8°C at $\mu = 0.5$ and $\mu = 0.08$, respectively, which are relatively higher than the other 7S globulins from cowpea, fava bean, pea, and soybean. Soybean 7S globulin has the least T_m values of 78.5°C and 65.7°C at $\mu = 0.5$ and $\mu = 0.08$, respectively. The solubility of recombinant phaseolin was better than the recombinant β-conglycinin β, suggesting that phaseolin was inherently more soluble. Like in β-conglycinin, glycan improved the solubility of mungbean 8S globulin or 8Sα, and it had no effect on T_m values of adzuki 7S and mungbean 8Sα. Native adzuki 7S globulins have better emulsifying ability than β homotrimers even if both have no extension region. Glycan has minimal contribution to emulsifying ability of mungbean 8Sα, unlike in β-conglycinin. The remarkable emulsifying ability of native phaseolin was attributed to the glycans. Comparison of native and recombinant phaseolin revealed that N-glycans lower the molecule's surface hydrophobicity by possibly covering a hydrophobic patch on the surface, and they prevented protein aggregation at low ionic strength.

Pea prolegumin, rapeseed procruciferin, and pumpkin pro11S were among the 11S globulins studied (Tandang et al. 2004, Tandang-Silvas et al. 2010). Comparison between cruciferin and glycinin revealed that (*a*) glycinin is more thermally stable, (*b*) cruciferin has higher surface hydrophobicity, (*c*) cruciferin can form harder gels, (*d*) cruciferin has better solubility at $\mu = 0.08$ but was less soluble at $\mu = 0.5$, and (*e*) soybean proteins have better emulsifying ability (Mohamed Salleh et al. 2002). Like procruciferin, pumpkin pro11S has high surface hydrophobicity (Tandang-Silvas et al. 2010). The 11S globulin from sunflower meal, helianthinin, has a high T_m value of 105°C at pH 7.5 and $\mu = 0.54$ (Molina et al. 2004). Hence, it is not a very good candidate in producing gel. Furthermore, it has very low water solubility.

THREE DIMENSIONAL STRUCTURES OF SEED STORAGE PROTEINS

Overview

Figure 2 (see color insert) shows a schematic representation of the secondary structures present in mature glycinin A3B4 subunits and the superimposed structures of 7S and 11S globulins. The acidic N-terminal and the basic C-terminal domains are very similar and can be divided by a pseudo-dyad axis. Each terminal consists of a conservative beta barrel core domain and a divergent alpha helix domain (Itoh et al. 2006, Jin et al. 2009b, Tandang-Silvas et al. 2010). The variable regions among the 11S globulins roughly coincide with the disordered regions in their crystal structures. The 7S and 11S globulins, which both belong to the cupin superfamily, have similar tertiary structures such that their peptide backbones are highly superimposable with each other. Representative cartoon models showing the biological assembly of the 7S, pro11S, and mature 11S globulins are shown in **Figure 3** (see color insert).

A summary of the seed storage proteins with known crystal structures is presented in **Supplemental Table 1** (follow the Supplemental Material link from the Annual Reviews home page at **http://www.annualreviews.org**). The effects of some structural features on their physicochemical and functional properties have been reported, but some correlations are not clear and still cannot be explained. The deposited structures in protein data bank can be useful in understanding their currently known properties and in conceptualizing their future food applications.

Hydrophilic Domains

The hydrophilic domains in 7S globulins are extension regions, whereas in 11S globulins, they are the variable regions. Glycans of 7S globulins also affect a hydrophilicity. The presence or absence of a glycan had no influence on the crystal structures of recombinant and native β-conglycinin β homotrimers. The root mean square deviation (rmsd) for 343 common C_α atoms within 2.0 Å of the two structures was 0.43–0.51 Å (Maruyama et al. 2001). The extension region, on the other hand, apparently hampers the crystal formation of α' and α because none of their crystal structures have been determined until after it was removed in α' (Maruyama et al. 2004b). The crystal structures of 11S globulins generally do not include the five variable regions because they are often disordered. The modified proteins in which variable regions I–V were separately deleted from A1aB1b were still able to assemble into trimers (Kim et al. 1990). These regions are at the molecular surface and were suggested to be suitable targets for modification by protein engineering. Studies have shown that although the variable and extension regions are not important in the structure formation and maintenance of the seed globulins, they can greatly alter their physiochemical and functional properties.

Disulfide Bridges

Disulfide bridges are known to aid in correct folding and in maintaining the tertiary structure of proteins. The highly conserved intra- and interdisulfide bridges among 11S globulins were, however, found to be unimportant on these aspects. Previous mutations on proA1aB1b to disrupt the intra- (Cys12-Cys45) and interdisulfide (Cys88-Cys298) bridges **(Figure 1)** by creating C12G, C88S, and C12G/C88S **(Figure 4)** mutants did not hamper correct assembly (Utsumi et al. 1993). The crystal structures of C12G and C88S had C_α rmsd values of 0.207 Å and 0.325 Å against the unmodified A1aB1b (Adachi et al. 2003b).

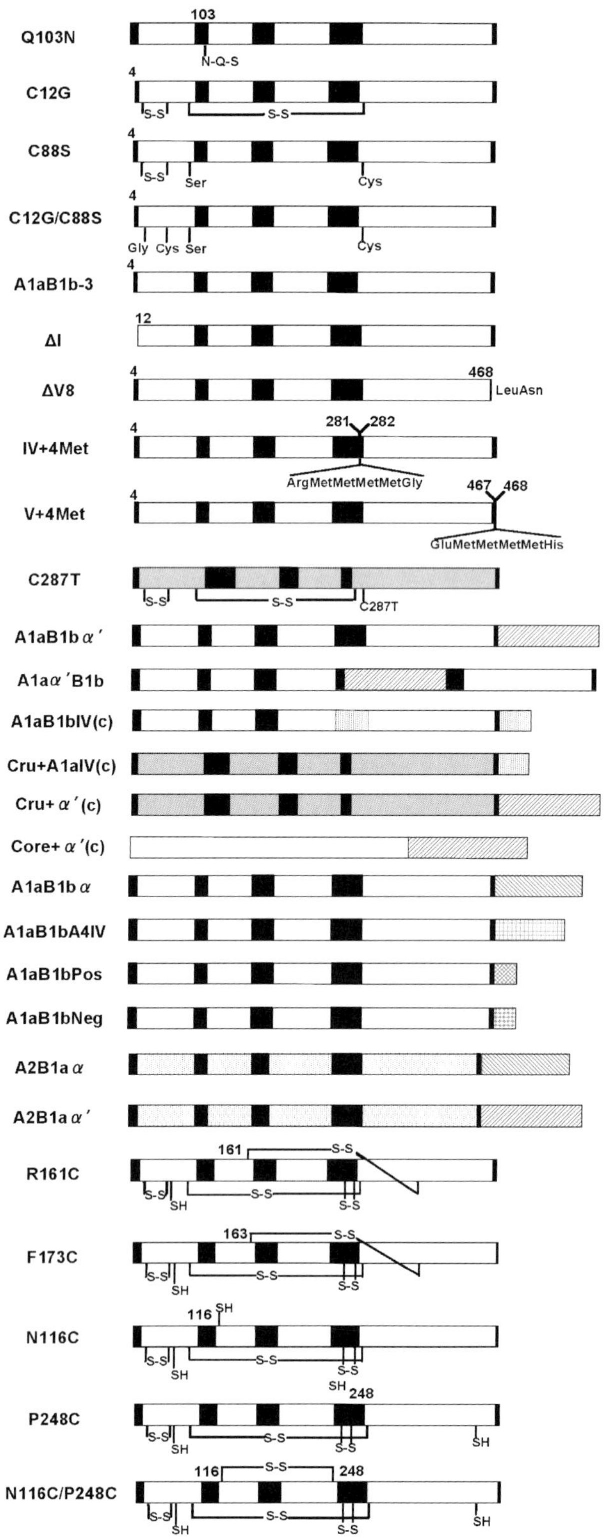
Q103N
103
N-Q-S
C12G
4
S-S
S-S
C88S
4
S-S
Ser
Cys
C12G/C88S
4
Gly
Cys
Ser
Cys
A1aB1b-3
4
ΔI
12
ΔV8
4
468
LeuAsn
IV+4Met
4
281
282
ArgMetMetMetMetGly
V+4Met
4
467
468
GluMetMetMetMetHis
C287T
S-S
S-S
C287T
A1aB1bα′
A1aα′B1b
A1aB1bIV(c)
Cru+A1aIV(c)
Cru+α′(c)
Core+α′(c)
A1aB1bα
A1aB1bA4IV
A1aB1bPos
A1aB1bNeg
A2B1aα
A2B1aα′
R161C
161
S-S
S-S
SH
S-S
S-S
F173C
163
S-S
S-S
SH
S-S
S-S
N116C
116
SH
S-S
SH
S-S
S-S
P248C
SH
248
S-S
SH
S-S
S-S
SH
N116C/P248C
116
S-S
248
S-S
SH
S-S
S-S
SH

Structural Factors for Thermal Stability

Structural basis for the higher thermal stability of β (T_m = 90.8°C) compared with α'_c (T_m = 83.3°C) (Maruyama et al. 1998) was addressed by looking at their crystal structures. Structural features of α'_c that could have caused this difference are its larger total cavity volume, its lack of the intermonomer salt bridge present in β, its smaller cluster of charged residues at intermonomer interface, its more hydrophobic solvent accessible surface, its lower percent of proline residues, and its longer loops (Maruyama et al. 2004b). Mungbean 8Sα has relatively lower T_m value (77.5°C) compared with other 7S globulins, mostly owing to its larger cavity size (Itoh et al. 2006). Fukuda et al. (2008) have emphasized that the T_m values of 7S globulins in soybean, mungbean, and adzuki are inversely correlated to cavity size. Adzuki 7S1 and 7S3 have T_m values of 92.4°C and 92.5°C because of their smaller cavity size.

Mature 11S globulins have been reported to be more thermally stable than their proform counterparts (Maruyama et al. 2004a, Tandang et al. 2004, Kimura et al. 2008). Structural analysis of proA3B4 and mature A3B4 revealed that the mature form has smaller cavity size, more number of H bonds, increased hydrophobic interactions, and shorter loops (Tandang-Silvas et al. 2010). Structural features of pro11S globulins from soybean, pea, pumpkin, and rapeseed that may influence thermal stability were also looked at, but no specific feature was singled out as being responsible (Tandang-Silvas et al. 2010). Collective factors such as smaller cavity size, shorter loop, higher aliphatic hydrophobic residues on molecular surface, and more proline residues were mentioned.

IMPROVEMENT OF PHYSICOCHEMICAL PROPERTIES OF SEED STORAGE PROTEINS BY PROTEIN ENGINEERING

Protein Engineering

Protein engineering is a systematic approach to alter the primary structure of a protein with the hope of attaining a desired specific effect. The cDNA that encodes the desired protein and the polymerase chain reaction (PCR) primers that will introduce precise nucleotide modifications are the basic requirements in protein engineering. Prior knowledge of the physicochemical and functional properties, and structural information, especially the three dimensional structure, are important tools in developing rational molecular designs for improved food functionality. An expression system for the cDNA and a suitable host are needed to produce the desired proteins. Not all designed modifications lead to successful protein expressions. Very low expression level, insolubility, and instability of the expressed proteins were some of the problems encountered (Utsumi et al. 2002, Tandang et al. 2005).

Safety evaluation and expression of the modified storage globulin genes in transgenic plants to obtain proteins with enhanced functional properties are the final aims of plant food protein engineering. Expression, accumulation, and safety assessments on the introduction of normal or modified soybean genes in crops such as rice and potato had been done to address these goals

Figure 4

Schematic representation of the modified proteins. Q103N (Katsube et al. 1998); Aa1B1b-3, C12G, C88S, and C12G-C88S (Utsumi et al. 1993); ΔI, ΔV8, IV+4Met, and V+4Met (Kim et al. 1990); C287T (Tandang et al. 2004); A1aB1bα′, A1aα′B1b, A1aB1bIV(c), Cru+A1aIV(c), Cru+α′(c), and Core+α′(c) (Tandang et al. 2005); A1aB1bα, A1aB1bA4IV, A1aB1bPos, A1aB1bNeg, A2B1aα, and A2B1aα′ (Prak et al. 2007); R161C, F163C, N116C, P248C, and N116C/P248C (Adachi et al. 2004).

(Utsumi et al. 1994, Hashimoto et al. 1999, Momma et al. 2000, Taikawa et al. 2008, Motoyama et al. 2010).

Over the past two decades, proA1aB1b with improved gelling property (Kim et al. 1990, Utsumi et al. 1993, Adachi et al. 2004) and several pro11S globulins with improved solubility and emulsifying property (Kim et al. 1990, Tandang et al. 2005, Prak et al. 2007) were designed successfully at a molecular level through the use of protein engineering. Schematic representations of the modified proteins are shown in **Figure 4,** and their acquired physicochemical and functional attributes discussed above are summarized in **Supplemental Table 2**. Introduction of these specific modified genes in transgenic crops, however, has not yet been done.

Modifications for Improved Emulsifying Ability

Balance between the molecule's hydrophobicity and hydrophilicity defines its surface behavior, which is manifested in functional properties like emulsifying activity. Amphipathic proteins that have polarized hydrophilic and hydrophobic regions can exhibit emulsifying ability (Utsumi 1992).

An earlier approach to improve the emulsifying ability of proA1aB1b was to increase its hydrophobicity by removing the hydrophilic variable regions. The modified proteins A1aB1b-3, ΔI, ΔV8, IV+4Met, and V+4Met exhibited better emulsifying ability than the native glycinin (Kim et al. 1990). The extent of improvement in ΔV8 and V+4Met was more than twice that of the native glycinin. A more recent and more pronounced improvement in solubility and emulsifying ability was achieved by attaching a hydrophilic domain. A1aB1bα′ exhibited a remarkable improvement in both emulsifying ability and emulsion stability (Tandang et al. 2005). A1aα′B1b, however, did not exhibit any improvement on emulsifying ability. These results indicated that the insertion of an α′ extension region was more effective at the C terminus than within variable region IV. One of the rationales behind this, as revealed by the proA1aB1b crystal structure (Adachi et al. 2001), is the higher molecular accessibility of the C terminus because it is situated at the periphery of the molecule. The C-terminal region of 11S globulins seems to be an ideal site of modification to improve emulsifying ability through increasing either its hydrophobicity or hydrophilicity.

Aside from the site where the hydrophilic region will be introduced, the nature of the insert was also found to be critical. For instance, A1aB1bIV(c) and cru+A1aIV(c) did not result in better emulsifying ability (Tandang et al. 2005). Variable region IV from proA1aB1b was not an effective insert for improving emulsion. Prak et al. (2007) correlated the hydrophilicity of the last 20–30 amino acids added to the C terminus with emulsifying ability. A1aB1bα exhibited the best emulsifying ability followed by A1aB1bα′ and A1aB1bA4IV. The α extension region was the most hydrophilic insert followed by the α′ extension region and A4IV polypeptide. A1aB1bPos and A1aB1bNeg exhibited less superior emulsion ability than A1aB1bα even if positive and negative peptides are more hydrophilic than the α extension region. Emulsions from A2B1aα′, cru+α′(c), and core+α′(c) were better than those from their original proteins. These results corroborated the beneficial effect of adding a hydrophilic domain at the C terminus on the emulsifying properties of 11S globulins.

Modifications for Improved Gelling Properties

Modified proA1aB1b with disrupted disulfide bonds, C12G and C88S, exhibited an improved gelling property (Utsumi et al. 1993). In contrast, the introduction of new disulfide bonds to the same molecule resulted in increased gel hardness (Adachi et al. 2004). Molecular designs to increase the sulfhydryl and disulfide bonds on proA1aB1b included N116C, P248C, R161C, F163C, and N116C · 248C. All of the mutants formed harder gels than proA1aB1b, particularly N116C · 248C.

Remarkable 3.7°C and 4.8°C increases in the T_m values of F163C and N116C · 248C, respectively, were observed. The introduced cysteine residues were designed so that they are far from any inherent cysteine residues. Based on this study, gel hardness increased with the number of cysteine residues. Heat-induced gelation was suggested to be favored by the topology and number of sulfhydryl groups.

In procruciferin, there is a free Cys287 that is very close to Cys283 that forms an interchain disulfide link with Cys83. Modified procruciferin C287T has similar thermal stability with the original protein but heating for 5 min at 80°C and 90°C resulted in more soluble aggregates in C287T (Tandang et al. 2004). The SH/SS exchange reaction with Cys287 was suggested to cause unfavorable association.

The effect of glycosylation in proA1aB1b was investigated by introducing glycosylation consensus sequence Asn-X-Ser/Thr at its variable regions II, III, IV, and V (Katsube et al. 1998). Signal peptide processing, trimer assembly, and targeting of proA1aB1b in the yeast vacuoles were not disturbed by the introduced glycans. Q103N is a glycosylated proA1aB1b at residue 103 due to mutation of Gln103 to Asn, thereby creating Asn-Gln-Ser glycosylation site. Q103N did not acquire thermal stability, but beyond the onset of its T_m value, less coagulation was observed such that it has higher percent of soluble fraction than normal proA1aB1b. The glycan was suggested to inhibit protein-protein interaction. Glycosylated proteins should therefore be avoided in food products that involve thermal gelation. Instead, proteins that easily destabilize and readily coagulate are desirable for food gel products.

CONCLUSION

Genetic crop improvement of seed storage proteins in legumes, cereals, and other edible plants is important in addressing food quality- and processing-related issues. Recombinant DNA technology and protein engineering have led to expansive and direct studies on the individual subunits of seed storage proteins. Knowledge derived from this research can provide baseline data for crop breeders to produce superior or enhanced genetic lines of industrially important crops. Public awareness on the studies on quality evaluation and safety assessment of genetically modified foods are important to make this powerful approach more acceptable.

DISCLOSURE STATEMENT

The authors are not aware of any affiliations, memberships, funding, or financial holdings that might be perceived as affecting the objectivity of this review.

ACKNOWLEDGMENTS

We apologize to all colleagues whose relevant work we couldn't cite because of space limitations. Research in our laboratories was supported in part by grants from Ministry of Education, Culture, Sports, Science, and Technology (S.U. and N.M.), from the Program for Promotion of Basic Research Activities for Innovative Biosciences (S.U. and B.M.) and from the Development of Fundamental Technologies for Production of High-Value Materials Using Transgenic Plants project from the Ministry of Economy, Trade, and Industry (S.U. and N.M.).

LITERATURE CITED

Adachi M, Chunying H, Utsumi S. 2004. Effects of designed sulfhydryl groups and disulfide bonds into soybean proglycinin on its structural stability and heat-induced gelation. *J. Agric. Food Chem.* 52:5717–23

Adachi M, Kanamori J, Masuda T, Yagasaki K, Kitamura K, et al. 2003a. Crystal structure of soybean 11S globulin: glycinin A3B4 homohexamer. *Proc. Natl. Acad. Sci. USA* 100:7395–400

Adachi M, Okuda M, Kaneda Y, Hashimoto A, Shutov AD, et al. 2003b. Crystal structures and structural stabilities of the disulfide bond–deficient soybean proglycinin mutants C12G and C88S. *J. Agric. Food Chem.* 51:4633–39

Adachi M, Takenaka Y, Gidamis AB, Mikami B, Utsumi S. 2001. Crystal structure of soybean proglycinin A1aB1b homotrimer. *J. Mol. Biol.* 305:291–305

Albillos SM, Jin T, Howard A, Zhang Y, Kothary MH, Fu TJ. 2008. Purification, crystallization and preliminary X-ray characterization of prunin-1, a major component of the almond (*Prunus dulcis*) allergen amandin. *J. Agric. Food Chem.* 56:5352–58

Catsimpoolas N, Meyer EW. 1970. Gelation phenomena of soybean globulins. I. Protein-protein interactions. *Cereal Chem.* 47:559–70

Derbyshire E, Wright DJ, Boulter D. 1976. Legumin and vicilin, storage proteins of legume seeds. *Phytochem.* 15:3–24

Dickinson CD, Hussen EHA, Nielsen NC. 1989. Role of posttranslational cleavage in glycinin assembly. *Plant Cell* 1:459–69

Doi E. 1993. Gels and gelling of globular proteins. *Trends Food Sci. Technol.* 4:1–5

Duranti M, Guerrieri N, Takahashi T, Cerletti P. 1988. The legumin-like storage protein of *Lupinus albus* seeds. *Phytochem.* 27:15–23

FAO (Food and Agriculture Organization of the United Nations). 2003. *Selected indicators of food and agriculture development in Asia-Pacific region 1992–2002.* **http://www.fao.org/docrep/004/ad452e/ad452e1i.htm**

Fukuda T, Maruyama N, Kanazawa A, Abe J, Shimamoto Y, et al. 2005. Molecular analysis and physicochemical properties of electrophoretic variants of wild soybean *Glycine soja* storage proteins. *J. Agric. Food Chem.* 53:3658–65

Fukuda T, Maruyama N, Mohamed Salleh MR, Mikami B, Utsumi S. 2008. Characterization and crystallography of recombinant 7S globulins of adzuki bean and structure-function relationships with 7S globulins of various crops. *J. Agric. Food Chem.* 56:4145–53

Fukuda T, Prak K, Fujioka M, Maruyama N, Utsumi S. 2007. Physicochemical properties of native adzuki bean (*Vigna angularis*) 7S globulin and the molecular cloning of its cDNA isoforms. *J. Agric. Food Chem.* 55:3667–74

Garcia RN, Adachi M, Tecson-Mendoza EM, Bernardo AEN, Utsumi S. 2006. Physicochemical properties of native and recombinant mungbean (*Vigna radiata* L. Wilczek) 8S globulins and the effects of the N-linked glycans. *J. Agric. Food Chem.* 54:6005–10

Garcia RN, Arocena RV, Laurena AC, Tecson-Mendoza EM. 2005. 11S and 7S globulins of coconut (*Cocos nucifera* L.): purification and characterization. *J. Agric. Food Chem.* 53:1734–39

Hashimoto W, Momma K, Katsube T, Ohkawa Y, Ishige T, et al. 1999. Safety assessment of genetically engineered potatoes with designed soybean glycinin: compositional analyses of the potato tubers and digestibility of the newly expressed protein in transgenic potatoes. *J. Sci.Food Agric.* 79:1607–12

Heller L. 2005. *Monsanto, Solae to create new soy protein line.* **http://www.foodnavigator-usa.com/content/view/print/172486**

Itoh T, Garcia RN, Adachi M, Maruyama Y, Tecson-Mendoza EM, et al. 2006. Structure of 8Sα globulin, the major seed storage protein of mung bean. *Acta Cryst.* D62:824–32

Jin T, Albillos SM, Guo F, Howard A, Fu T-J, et al. 2009a. Crystal structure of prunin-1, a major component of the almond (*Prunus dulcis*) allergen amandin. *J. Agric. Food Chem.* 57:8643–51

Jin T, Guo F, Chen Y, Howard A, Zhang Y. 2009b. Crystal structure of Ara h 3, a major allergen in peanut. *Mol. Immunol.* 46:1796–804

Johnson LA. 1999. Process for producing improved soy protein concentrate from genetically-modified soybeans. *U.S. Patent No.* 5936069

Jung R, Scott MP, Nam Y-W, Beaman TW, Bassüner R, et al. 1998. The role of proteolysis in the processing and assembly of 11S seed globulins. *Plant Cell* 10:343–57

Katsube T, Kang IJ, Takenaka Y, Adachi M, Maruyama N, et al. 1998. N-glycosylation does not affect assembly and targeting of proglycinin in yeast. *Biochim. Biophys. Acta* 1379:107–17

Kim C-S, Kamiya S, Sato T, Utsumi S, Kito M. 1990. Improvement of nutritional value and functional properties of soybean glycinin. *Protein Eng.* 3:725–31

Kimura A, Fukuda T, Zhang M, Motoyama S, Maruyama N, Utsumi S. 2008. Comparison of physicochemical properties of 7S and 11S globulins from pea, fava bean, cowpea, and French bean with those of soybean–French bean 7S globulin exhibits excellent properties. *J. Agric. Food Chem.* 56:10273–79

Kimura A, Tandang-Silvas MR, Fukuda T, Cabanos C, Takegawa Y, et al. 2010. Carbohydrate moieties contribute significantly to the physicochemical properties of French bean 7S globulin phaseolin. *J. Agric. Food Chem.* 58:2923–30

Kinsella JE. 1979. Functional properties of soy proteins. *J. Am. Oil Chem. Soc.* 56:242–58

Kohyama K, Murata M, Tani F, Sano Y, Doi E. 1995. Effects of protein composition on gelation of mixtures containing soybean 7S and 11S globulins. *Biosci. Biotech.Biochim.* 59:240–45

Kwanyuen P, Wilson RF, Burton JW. 1998. Soybean protein quality. In *Emerging Technologies, Current Practices, Quality Control, Technology Transfer and Environmental Issues*, ed. SS Koseoglu, KC Rhee, RF Wilson, p. 285. Champaign, IL: AOCS Press

Lauer I, Foetisch K, Kolarich D, Ballmer-Weber BK, Conti A, et al. 2004. Hazelnut (*Corylus avellana*) vicilin Cor a 11: molecular characterization of a glycoprotein and its allergenic activity. *Biochem. J.* 383:327–34

Maruyama N, Adachi M, Takahashi K, Yagasaki K, Kohno M, et al. 2001. Crystal structures of recombinant and native soybean β-conglycinin β homotrimers. *Eur. J. Biochem.* 268:3595–604

Maruyama N, Katsube T, Wada Y, Oh MH, Barba dela Rosa AP, et al. 1998. The roles of the N-glycans and extension regions of soybean β-conglycinin in folding, assembly and structural features. *Eur. J. Biochem.* 258:854–62

Maruyama N, Mikami B, Utsumi S. 2010. Globulin tanpakushitsu. In *Daitsu no Subete*, ed. K Kitamura, pp. 115–121. Tokyo, Jpn. Sci. Forum

Maruyama N, Mohamed Salleh MR, Takahashi K, Yagasaki K, Goto H, et al. 2002a. The effect of the N-linked glycans on structural features and physicochemical functions of soybean β-conglycinin homotrimers. *JAOCS* 79:139–44

Maruyama N, Mohamed Salleh MR, Takahashi K, Yagasaki K, Goto H, et al. 2002b. Structure-physicochemical function relationships of soybean β-conglycinin heterotrimers. *J. Agric. Food Chem.* 50:4323–26

Maruyama N, Mun LC, Tatsuhara M, Sawada M, Ishimoto M, Utsumi S. 2006. Multiple vacuolar sorting determinants exist in soybean 11S globulin. *Plant Cell* 18:1253–73

Maruyama N, Prak K, Motoyama S, Choi S-K, Yagasaki K, et al. 2004a. Structure-physicochemical function relationships of soybean glycinin at subunit levels assessed by using mutant lines. *J. Agric. Food Chem.* 52:8197–201

Maruyama N, Sato R, Wada Y, Matsumura Y, Goto H, et al. 1999. Structure-physicochemical function relationships of soybean β-conglycinin constituent subunits. *J. Agric. Food Chem.* 47:5278–84

Maruyama N, Tecson-Mendoza EM, Maruyama Y, Adachi M, Utsumi S. 2007. Molecular design of soybean proteins for enhanced food quality. In *Functional Foods and Biotechnology*, ed. K Shetty, G Paliyath, AL Pometto, RE Levin, pp. 25–50. New York: Taylor & Francis

Maruyama Y, Maruyama N, Mikami B, Utsumi S. 2004b. Structure of the core region of the soybean β-conglycinin α′ subunit. *Acta Cryst.* D60:289–97

Mohamed Salleh MR, Maruyama N, Adachi M, Hontani N, Saka S, et al. 2002. Comparison of protein chemical and physicochemical properties of rapeseed cruciferin with those of soybean glycinin. *J. Agric. Food Chem.* 50:7380–85

Mohamed Salleh MR, Maruyama N, Takahashi K, Yagasaki K, Higasa T, et al. 2004. Gelling properties of soybean β-conglycinin having different subunit compositions. *Biosci. Biotechnol. Biochem.* 68:1091–96

Molina MI, Petruccelli S, Añon MC. 2004. Effect of pH and ionic strength modifications on thermal denaturation of the 11S globulin of sunflower (*Helianthus annuus*). *J. Agric. Food Chem.* 52:6023–29

Momma K, Hashimoto W, Yoon H-J, Ozawa S, Fukuda Y, et al. 2000. Safety assessment of rice genetically modified with soybean glycinin by feeding studies on rats. *Biosci. Biotechnol. Biochem.* 64:1881–86

Moreno FJ, Clemente A. 2008. 2S albumin storage proteins: What makes them food allergens? *Open Biochem. J.* 2:16–28

Mori T, Maruyama N, Nishizawa K, Higasa T, Yagasaki K, et al. 2004. The composition of newly synthesized proteins in the endoplasmic reticulum determines the transport pathways of soybean seed storage proteins. *Plant J.* 40:238–49

Mori T, Nakamura T, Utsumi S. 1981. Gelation mechanism of soybean 11S globulin: formation of soluble aggregates as transient intermediates. *J. Food Sci.* 47:26–30

Mori T, Nakamura T, Utsumi S. 1986. Behavior of intermolecular bond formation in the late stage of heat-induced gelation of glycinin. *J. Agric. Food Chem.* 34:33–36

Mori T, Saruta Y, Fukuda T, Prak K, Ishimoto M, et al. 2009. Vacuolar sorting behaviors of 11S globulins in plant cells. *Biosci. Biotechnol. Biochem.* 73:53–60

Motoyama T, Amari Y, Tandang-Silvas MR, Cabanos C, Kimura A, et al. 2010. Development of transgenic rice containing a mutated β subunit of soybean β-conglycinin for enhanced phagocytosis-stimulating activity. *Peptides* 31:1245–50

Müntz K. 1998. Deposition of storage proteins. *Plant Mol. Biol.* 38:77–99

Nakamura T, Utsumi S, Kitamura K, Harada K, Mori T. 1984a. Cultivar differences in gelling characteristics of soybean glycinin. *J. Agric. Food Chem.* 32:647–51

Nakamura T, Utsumi S, Mori T. 1984b. Network structure formation in thermally induced gelation of glycinin. *J. Agric. Food Chem.* 32:349–52

Nakamura T, Utsumi S, Mori T. 1986a. Mechanism of heat-induced gelation and gel properties of soybean 7S globulins. *Agric. Biol. Chem.* 50:1287–93

Nakamura T, Utsumi S, Mori T. 1986b. Interactions during heat-induced gelation in a mixed system of soybean 7S and 11S globulins. *Agric. Biol. Chem.* 50:2429–35

Nielsen NC, Evans DE, Wilcox JR. 1992. Special purpose soybean varieties. *New Crop News.* **http://www.hort.purdue.edu/newcrop/newcropsnews/92-2-1/soybean.html**

Osborne TB. 1924. *The Vegetable Proteins.* London: Longmans

Prak K, Nakatani K, Katsube-Tanaka T, Adachi M, Maruyama N, Utsumi S. 2005. Structure-function relationships of soybean proglycinins at subunit levels. *J. Agric. Food Chem.* 53:3650–57

Prak K, Nakatani K, Maruyama N, Utsumi S. 2007. C-terminus engineering of soybean proglycinin: improvement of emulsifying properties. *Protein Eng. Design Selection* 20:433–42

Shewry PR, Halford NG. 2002. Cereal seed storage proteins: structures, properties and role in grain utilization. *J. Experimental Bot.* 53:947–58

Shewry PR, Napier JA, Tatham AS. 1995. Seed storage proteins: structures and biosynthesis. *Plant Cell* 7:945–56

Soyatech, LLC. 2010. *Soy facts.* **http://72.32.142.180/soy_facts.htm**

Soyatech, LLC, SPINS Inc. 2005. *Soyfoods: The U.S. Market 2005.* **http://www.soyatech.com/pdf/soyfoods05.pdf**

Taikawa F, Sakuta C, Choi S-K, Tada Y, Motoyama T, Utsumi S. 2008. Co-expression of soybean glycinins A1aB1b and A3B4 enhances their accumulation levels in transgenic rice seed. *Plant Cell Physiol.* 49:1589–99

Tandang MR, Adachi M, Inui N, Maruyama N, Utsumi S. 2004. Effects of protein engineering of canola procruciferin on its physicochemical and functional properties. *J. Agric. Food Chem.* 52:6810–17

Tandang MR, Atsuta N, Maruyama N, Adachi M, Utsumi S. 2005. Evaluation of the solubility and emulsifying property of soybean proglycinin and rapeseed procruciferin in relation to structure modified by protein engineering. *J. Agric. Food Chem.* 53:8736–44

Tandang-Silvas MR, Fukuda T, Fukuda C, Prak K, Cabanos C, et al. 2010. Conservation and divergence on plant seed 11S globulins based on crystal structures. *Biochim. Biophys. Acta* 1804:1432–42

Utsumi S. 1992. Plant food protein engineering. *Adv. Food Nutr. Res.* 36:89–208

Utsumi S, Gidamis AB, Kanamori J, Kang IJ, Kito M. 1993. Effects of deletion of disulfide bonds by protein engineering on the conformation and functional properties of soybean proglycinin. *J. Agric. Food Chem.* 41:687–91

Utsumi S, Kinsella JE. 1985. Structure-function relationships in food proteins: subunit interactions in heat-induced gelation of 7S, 11S and soy isolate proteins. *J. Agric. Food Chem.* 33:297–303

Utsumi S, Kitagawa S, Katsube T, Higasa T, Kito M, et al. 1994. Expression and accumulation of normal and molecular designed soybean glycinins in potato tubers. *Plant Sci.* 102:181–88

Utsumi S, Maruyama N, Satoh R, Adachi M. 2002. Structure-function relationships of soybean proteins revealed by using recombinant systems. *Enzyme Microbial Technol.* 30:284–88

Utsumi S, Matsumura Y, Mori T. 1997. Structure-function relationships of soy proteins. In *Food Proteins and Their Applications*, ed. D Damodaran, A Paraf, pp. 257–91. New York: Marcel Dekker

Visschers RW, de Jongh HHJ. 2005. Disulphide bond formation in food protein aggregation and gelation. *Biotech. Adv.* 23:75–80

Wieser H. 2007. Chemistry of gluten proteins. *Food Microbiol.* 24:115–19

Minimization of *Salmonella* Contamination on Raw Poultry*

N.A. Cox, J.A. Cason, and L.J. Richardson[1]

USDA/Agricultural Research Service, Russell Research Center, Athens, Georgia 30605; email: nelson.cox@ars.usda.gov; john.cason@ars.usda.gov

[1]Current address: The Coca Cola Company, Atlanta, Georgia 30313; email: jasonrichardson31@gmail.com

Annu. Rev. Food Sci. Technol. 2011. 2:75–95

First published online as a Review in Advance on September 27, 2010

The *Annual Review of Food Science and Technology* is online at food.annualreviews.org

This article's doi:
10.1146/annurev-food-022510-133715

1941-1413/11/0410-0075$20.00

Keywords

sampling, cultural methodology, prevalence, enumeration, serotype, risk

Abstract

Many reviews have discussed *Salmonella* in poultry and suggested best practices to minimize this organism on raw poultry meat. Despite years of research and conscientious control efforts by industry and regulatory agencies, human salmonellosis rates have declined only modestly and *Salmonella* is still found on raw poultry. Expert committees have repeatedly emphasized the importance of controlling risk, but information about *Salmonella* in poultry is often limited to prevalence, with inadequate information about testing methods or strains of *Salmonella* that are detected by these methods and no information about any impact on the degree of risk. This review examines some assumptions behind the discussion of *Salmonella* in poultry: the relationships between sampling and cultural methodology, prevalence and numbers of cells, and the implications of serotype and subtype issues. Minimizing *Salmonella* contamination of poultry is not likely to reduce human salmonellosis acquired from exposure to contaminated chicken until these issues are confronted more systematically.

INTRODUCTION

Many reviews on the topic of minimizing *Salmonella* on raw poultry are not much more than exhortatory lists of best practices in which greater levels of effort and vigilance are urged in the application of remarkably similar recommendations. Such papers have been available for 40 years, with presentations on this topic a regular feature of poultry meetings during that time. Many of these reviews have been useful for thinking about the *Salmonella* problem and possible interventions, but we doubt that we can do a significantly better job of writing such a review than has already been done by many of our colleagues.

The drawback of best practices lists is that they address *Salmonella* contamination in a general way that may be more effective over the long-term, but they do not assure consistent *Salmonella* control for every flock that is produced. In particular, continued *Salmonella* problems are seen in parent and grandparent flocks, which are more valuable and thus receive more conscientious and consistent levels of best-practice care than do flocks of production birds. If five years from now, control efforts in production flocks are at the same level as those devoted to breeder flocks today, there will still be *Salmonella*-positive flocks, even though all of them will have received an improved standard of care. It is also likely that public and regulatory standards will be more demanding, whatever degree of success the worldwide poultry industry may have in reducing *Salmonella* contamination in its products relative to today. The purpose of this review is to examine some of the assumptions behind efforts to reduce *Salmonella* contamination of raw poultry, with the ultimate goal of reducing the risk of human salmonellosis. Reduced incidence of human salmonellosis will be only an accidental product of more demanding standards for *Salmonella* on raw poultry unless those standards are scientifically linked to reduced risk.

ATTRIBUTION OF HUMAN SALMONELLOSIS FROM EXPOSURE TO RAW POULTRY MEAT

> It is widely known that *Salmonella* is associated with poultry products, but we do not know what proportion of human salmonellosis cases are caused by chicken, turkey, eggs, or non-poultry sources, so we do not know how much disease FSIS actions could theoretically prevent. Similarly, we do not know what proportion of cases are associated with undercooking, cross-contamination, or other means of transmission. Without such information, it is difficult to design the most effective strategies to control *Salmonella* contamination in poultry to reduce the pathogen level in the end product or to evaluate the efficacy of FSIS control strategies after they have been implemented.
>
> National Research Council 2009

The possibility of reducing human salmonellosis by targeting raw poultry meat is limited to the amount of illness associated with exposure to *Salmonella* on poultry meat and any related cross-contamination during food preparation. Many studies and expert reports have concluded, however, that only a small amount of data is available for attributing illness to specific foods or for developing effective intervention strategies (Batz et al. 2005, Hald et al. 2004, NRC 2009). Human salmonellosis will not decrease until the risk of acquiring the illness is reduced, and any scientific approach to controlling risk will be constrained by the quality of available information. A science-based food safety policy requires a scientific link between microbiological criteria that are being established and the public health problem that justifies the policy (ICMSF 2006, IOM/NRC 2003, Todd 2004).

Estimates of the percentage of salmonellosis caused by exposure to contaminated food vary from 55% to 96% in different countries (Havelaar et al. 2008, Mead et al. 1999, Sumner et al. 2003).

People in different parts of the world have characteristic ways of producing and preparing foods, so it is unlikely that all parts of the world have similar proportions of foodborne salmonellosis. Moreover, food systems and consumer practices change over time and attribution percentages change and need periodic reexamination (Greig & Ravel 2009).

Methods for attributing illness to specific food sources can be classified into four main approaches: epidemiology, microbiology, risk assessment, and expert elicitation, with all methods having advantages and disadvantages (Batz et al. 2005, EFSA 2008, NRC 2009, Pires et al. 2009, USDA/FSIS 2008). Elicitation of expert opinion tends to produce the highest estimates for human cases of salmonellosis associated with exposure to poultry meat (such as 35% in Hoffman et al. 2007); although, international outbreak data can also yield estimates in the same range (Greig & Ravel 2009). Whether outbreak data can be extrapolated to all cases of salmonellosis is not certain.

Over the past 40 years, rates of human salmonellosis have declined in most developed countries, even as consumption of poultry meat has increased considerably. Current estimates of the percentage of human cases of salmonellosis attributed to exposure to poultry meat generally range from 10% to 22% in developed countries (Dalton et al. 2004, EFSA 2008, Havelaar et al. 2008, Karns et al. 2007, Kirk et al. 2008, Mullner et al. 2009, Pires et al. 2010, Ravel et al. 2009, USDA/FSIS 2008, Van Asselt et al. 2009). According to some authorities, however, the rate of nonfoodborne transmission is underestimated (Barber et al. 2003, Mead et al. 2010).

In the United States, the source of *Salmonella* is identified in only about 0.13% of the estimated 1,400,000 annual human cases of salmonellosis (Barber et al. 2003), leaving considerable uncertainty regarding sources of exposure. If there are more than a million cases annually, then at any moment there are tens of thousands of human carriers (Barber et al. 2003). Several reviews have emphasized the carrier role of humans and the need to isolate poultry from humans (Aho 1992, Barber et al. 2003). Kinde et al. (1996) identified sewage effluent as the likely source of a *Salmonella* infection in a California layer flock, and several surveys have isolated *Salmonella* from human sewage sludge or effluent, including 54 serotypes from 11 sewage treatment plants in the United States (Kinde et al. 1997) and 49 serotypes from eight plants in Sweden (Sahlstrom et al. 2004, 2006).

In the Netherlands, the major risk for Typhimurium infections in children from ages 4 to 12 was playing in a sandbox (Doorduyn et al. 2006). Working in a garden was one of the leading risk factors in Canada for the months of June and July (Ravel et al. 2010). Despite the widespread perception of poultry meat and eggs as the predominant sources of *Salmonella*, recent outbreaks in the United States have been caused by contaminated jalapeno peppers (the largest outbreak in a decade), peanut butter, tomatoes, ground beef, puffed vegetable snacks, and pets such as turtles and African dwarf frogs (CDC 2005, 2008a, 2010). The wide variation in numbers of cases coming from nonfood and nonpoultry sources makes it extremely difficult to attribute a specific amount of human salmonellosis to raw poultry meat, even though we know that poultry meat is a source of *Salmonella*.

RELATIONSHIP BETWEEN *SALMONELLA* ON RAW POULTRY AND ACQUISITION OF HUMAN SALMONELLOSIS

> There exist only limited data that provide evidence for the success (or failure) of national and international control programs in terms of reducing human salmonellosis.
>
> Hald et al. 2004

If the amount of salmonellosis caused by exposure to raw poultry meat cannot be determined with a reasonable degree of certainty, is it possible to estimate how much of a reduction in

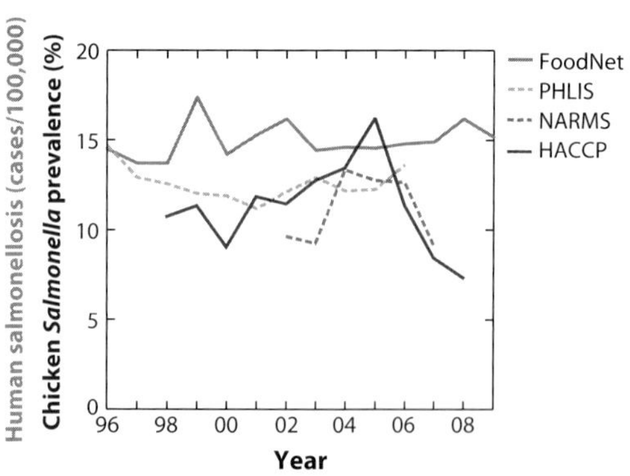

Figure 1

Human salmonellosis data (cases per 100,000) from FoodNet and the Public Health Laboratory Information System (PHLIS), *Salmonella* prevalence data (%) from retail chicken breasts [National Antimicrobial Resistance Monitoring System (NARMS)], and chilled chicken carcasses [Hazard Analysis Critical Control Point (HACCP)] from 1996 to 2009.

Salmonella contamination of raw poultry is needed to observe an associated decrease in the rate of human illness? Can the contribution of nonfood and nonpoultry-related sources be adequately determined to enable an accurate determination of the number of human cases of salmonellosis associated with raw poultry exposure? The ability to correlate reductions in *Salmonella* contamination of raw poultry meat with human salmonellosis is limited by the imprecision of the data collected and the large annual, seasonal, and geographic variation in rates of illness.

Examples of various national and international surveillance systems have been reported by Doyle & Erickson (2006). In the United States, the Public Health Laboratory Information System (PHLIS) and FoodNet are the primary sources of national data regarding the incidence of human salmonellosis. Information about *Salmonella* on raw chicken is available from Hazard Analysis Critical Control Point (HACCP) data collected by the Food Safety and Inspection Service (FSIS) of the United States Department of Agriculture (USDA) and the National Antimicrobial Resistance Monitoring System (NARMS) program, which samples retail chicken breasts in areas that provide FoodNet human data. **Figure 1** provides HACCP data for the prevalence of *Salmonella* on chilled chicken carcasses (USDA/FSIS 2010), NARMS data for the prevalence of *Salmonella* on retail chicken breasts (US FDA 2010), and Public Health Laboratory Information System (CDC 2008b) and FoodNet data (CDC 2009) of the incidence of human salmonellosis (cases per 100,000).

Analysis of the data in **Figure 1** reveals why attribution of human illness to a specific food commodity is problematic. There is no significant correlation (J.A. Cason, N.A. Cox, and L.J. Richardson, unpublished data) between the two measures of *Salmonella* prevalence on raw chicken, between the two measures of incidence of human salmonellosis, or between any combination of the chicken and human data. Perhaps there are too many other sources of *Salmonella* contributing to human salmonellosis that mask the relationship between human illness and prevalence on chicken, or prevalence of *Salmonella* on raw chicken is not the best measure of risk of human salmonellosis from chicken, or *Salmonella* prevalence on chicken is not measured in a way that relates to risk of human illness, e.g., many *Salmonella* serotypes from poultry, such as Kentucky strains, rarely cause human illness.

Data from studies using different sampling methods are available from some European countries. Human salmonellosis rates from 2008 (EFSA 2010a) can be compared to processing plant data of *Salmonella* prevalence on chickens that were sampled in the same year (EFSA 2010b). Data are not available for all member countries of the European Union (EU), but illustrative results

Table 1 Prevalence of *Salmonella*-positive chickens at slaughter, human cases of salmonellosis, and imported cases of human salmonellosis in countries of the European Union and the United States, for 2008

Country	Neck skin % *Salmonella*-positive[1]	Human cases per 100,000[2]	Percentage of imported human cases of salmonellosis[2]
Austria	2.4	27.7	19.4
Belgium	16.3	35.9	NR
Bulgaria	22.5	19.8	NR
Czech Republic	5.5	103.1	2.2
Denmark	0	67.0	19.0
Estonia	0	48.2	6.5
Finland	0	59.0	59.0
Germany	15.0	52.2	5.8
Italy	13.5	5.4	0.5
Netherlands	9.5	15.5	10.6
Slovenia	1.7	51.0	NR
Spain	14.9	8.5	0
Sweden	0.2	45.6	82.1
	Whole carcass rinse: % *Salmonella*-positive	Human cases per 100,000	
United States	7.3[3]	16.2[4]	NR

NR = not reported.
[1]EFSA 2010b.
[2]EFSA 2010a.
[3]USDA/FSIS 2009.
[4]CDC 2009.

are shown in **Table 1**, along with the 2008 results from the United States. **Table 1** also includes estimates of the percentage of salmonellosis cases attributed to international travel (not acquired domestically) (EFSA 2010a).

The correlation between *Salmonella* prevalence on raw chicken and salmonellosis in humans in **Table 1** is not significant, whether calculated for all reported human cases or only for cases attributed to domestic origin, nor are there significant correlations if the three countries with a prevalence of zero *Salmonella* in neck skin samples are left out of the calculations (J.A. Cason, N.A. Cox, and L.J. Richardson, unpublished data). Problems similar to those mentioned in the analysis of the United States data may exist for the European data set as well. The lack of correlation between the prevalence of *Salmonella* in poultry and the incidence of human salmonellosis in both the United States and Europe illustrates the difficulty of attributing human salmonellosis to specific foods, as discussed above.

In addition to the nonfood and nonpoultry sources of human exposure that complicate efforts to define the relationship between *Salmonella* contamination of poultry and associated human illness, there is a strong seasonal component to human salmonellosis. In recent FoodNet data for the United States, the peak-to-trough ratio is more than two, with the peak in cases occurring in the summer months (CDC 2007), a pattern reported by many other countries as well (Ravel et al. 2010). *Salmonella* prevalence data from broiler chicken HACCP samples analyzed by FSIS show a lower peak-to-trough ratio, with peak prevalence occurring between August and November (Lange 2006). *Salmonella* prevalence on broiler chicken farms in the Netherlands also peaks during the months of July to December (van der Fels-Klerx et al. 2008), although seasonal differences for on-farm *Salmonella* were not so apparent in another study (van de Giessen et al. 2006), and there was no seasonal effect seen in processing plants (van der Fels-Klerx et al. 2008). A study conducted in Canada found little seasonality in *Salmonella* prevalence on retail chicken and no correlation with the seasonal pattern in human illness (Ravel et al. 2010). Less seasonal variation has been reported for the more serious cases of human salmonellosis (Gradel et al. 2007), with further complicating factors such as increased likelihood of antibiotic use in the weeks before human illness (Gradel et al. 2008).

SAMPLING ISSUES

> Much of the research efforts, however, involve only the final portion of the procedure, i.e., the detection or identification of the microorganisms. The upstream portions that deal with sampling and sample preparation are often overlooked.
>
> Brehm-Stecher et al. 2009

After more than a half century of sampling poultry carcasses and environments for *Salmonella*, sampling and experimental design issues still exist. Recent reviews have addressed sample preparation (Brehm-Stetcher et al. 2009), the quality of experimental design and reporting (Sargeant et al. 2009), the quality of statistical analysis (Gardner 2004, Ogliari et al. 2007), and the best practices for investigating and reporting the relationship between food animals and food safety (O'Connor et al. 2010). Many reviews are available for microbiological sampling of poultry (Aho 1992, Capita et al. 2004, Carrique-Mas et al. 2008, Davies 2005, Mead 2007). A recent review of measurement uncertainty in sampling of food for bacteria reports that bias can be introduced by the choice of sampling method, in the way that the original sample is collected, transported, and stored, in subsampling methods, or by the accuracy of all of these procedures (Corry et al. 2007).

An expert consensus on the most appropriate sampling sites and methods for determining the *Salmonella* status of poultry flocks and poultry meat has never been reached, because comparing results between different methods is not a simple matter (Mead et al. 2010). The lack of uniformity in pre- and postharvest sampling methods can lead to misinterpretation of results when comparing *Salmonella* prevalence across different studies. In a recent compilation of data on the prevalence of *Salmonella* on poultry meat, for example, a summary table revealed that reporting countries used either 1, 25, 50, or 60 gram samples of meat (EFSA 2010b). The likelihood of isolating *Salmonella* increases with a larger sample weight and with increasing amounts of skin included in the sample (Jorgenson et al. 2002).

In general, sampling methods were developed based largely on ease of performance and cost, and the relationship of results to human illness was not an important consideration. There are many potential sampling sites and types of sampling methods used in feed mills, hatcheries, farms, processing plants, and distribution channels. Some typical sample types are discussed in Mead et al. 2010 and other previously cited reviews. On farms in Europe, sampling of fecally contaminated litter is done using boot swabs (Davies 2005). Several reports indicate that intestinal tract samples from birds identify more *Salmonella*-positive flocks (Rasschaert et al. 2007, Van Hoorebeke et al. 2009), but it has never been shown whether flocks identified as *Salmonella*-positive by more intensive sampling approaches are more likely to cause human illness.

During processing, several different carcass and meat sampling methods are frequently used. Neck skin sampling and meat samples of 10 or 25 grams are commonly used in Europe. Whole carcass rinsing with 400 or 500 milliliters of rinse liquid per carcass is used in countries such as the United States and Australia with 7.5% or 20% of the rinse liquid cultured for *Salmonella* (USDA/FSIS 1996b, FSANZ 2010). Chilling carcasses in air, as is a common practice in the EU, or in water, which is commonly done in the United States, may affect the results if drying of the skin enables *Salmonella* cells to better attach to the carcass.

The European Food Safety Authority's Panel on Biohazards has recently suggested that more data are needed from additional studies on the "possible correlation between *Salmonella* targets in broiler flocks and expected contamination levels in the resulting poultry meat," indicating that such a correlation needs further refinement (EFSA 2010b). The panel also stated that it is not possible to establish a quantitative link between the *Salmonella* criteria for poultry meat and any risk or implication for public health.

If rearing and processing modifications aimed at reducing *Salmonella* are not tested using appropriate sampling methods, apparent reductions may be misleading and may not reduce human salmonellosis. If conditions experienced by bacteria in the sample during transport to the laboratory are not equivalent to those conditions experienced by the chicken meat destined for the consumer, results from the sample might not be relevant to public health. Currently, there is no validated method for detecting *Salmonella*-contaminated carcasses or flocks that are the greatest risk to human health because risk assessment has not reached that level of sophistication.

CULTURE METHODOLOGY ISSUES

> This survey found major differences in isolation methods. In fact, no two [of 74] laboratories isolated *Salmonella* the same way.
>
> Waltman & Mallinson 1995

No studies have been reported that correlate laboratory culture methods for detecting *Salmonella* in foods with the risk of acquiring human salmonellosis. Current methods were developed to obtain the greatest number of *Salmonella*-positive samples with an acceptable cost and ease of performance, and no consideration was given to determining the relationship of results to the risk of acquiring human salmonellosis. Different types of samples can contain different microbial competitors, nutrients, and antimicrobial inhibitors, and there is a different response regarding *Salmonella* growth, depending on the degree of stress or sublethal injury that the bacteria may have experienced; hence, sample characteristics and history must be considered when selecting a cultural methodology for *Salmonella* detection or isolation. Even for a relatively well-understood sample type such as a chilled poultry carcass, there is no internationally recognized standard methodology for *Salmonella* detection, either for sample size or microbiological methods. Use of different cultural media is not simply a matter of laboratory choice, with some methods delineated by regional, national, or international organizations.

Classical cultural techniques for *Salmonella* detection generally follow a standard sequence, including a nonselective preenrichment (which may be used depending on whether cells are stressed or are present in low numbers), a selective enrichment, isolation on selective agar media, biochemical screening with triple sugar and lysine iron agars, and serological confirmation with poly-O and poly-H antisera. Many different media formulations have been developed for the preenrichment, enrichment, and selective isolation steps in the detection sequence. A survey of diagnostic veterinary laboratories in the United States revealed that 17 different selective enrichment media were being used (Waltman & Mallinson 1995). There were also differences in incubation temperatures, whether samples were incubated for 24 h or 48 h or both, or whether samples were subjected to delayed secondary enrichment conditions (e.g., samples held at room temperature for up to five additional days). Selective enrichment cultures were inoculated onto 14 different plating media, with most labs using two or more different types of media to increase the likelihood of recovering

Salmonella. Finally, the survey revealed considerable variation in numbers of colonies selected for further testing by the different laboratories, with many selecting and identifying only one colony.

Several collaborative studies have been done in 16 national reference laboratories in Europe comparing the efficacy of procedures for *Salmonella* isolation and identification from feces (Voogt et al. 2002a,b). When standard samples were provided to all participating labs, the results revealed significant differences among the labs and within different subsections of the study in the ability to detect *Salmonella* and identify the serotypes that were isolated. Several modified methods were used as the studies progressed, and new methods were developed in the absence of an official reference method for isolating *Salmonella* from fecal samples. Discussions of *Salmonella* detection in control or regulatory samples often assume accurate and reproducible results, but the reality of results of laboratory assays is that considerable variability can occur (Waltman & Mallinson 1995; Voogt et al. 2002a,b).

The commonly used liquid and solid media utilized for isolation of *Salmonella* in food laboratories have changed over time. Lactose broth, Gram negative broth, Rappaport (Vassiliadis) broth, selenite cystine broth, and tetrathionate broth were used years ago. All of these broths are still used to some degree, but the last three have been significantly modified to increase their effectiveness. Plating media used over the years for *Salmonella* isolation included brilliant green, bismuth sulfite, Hektoen enteric, *Salmonella-Shigella*, and XLD agars. Some of these are rarely used today and others have been modified to increase isolation efficiency from different types of samples. Brilliant green with sulfapyridine added is now called BGS. XLD has had many modifications, including addition of sodium thiosulfate and Tergitol 4 to make XLT4 agar. These additions have improved overall performance of these media. Food microbiology laboratories usually use two or more plating media to reduce the occurrence of false-negative results (Cox & Berrang 2000). Rappaport's enrichment medium was modified to become the widely used Rappaport-Vassiliadis (RV) broth (Vassiliadis 1983) and was then further modified with the development of modified semisolid RV (MSRV) for selection of motile *Salmonella* (De Smedt et al. 1986).

The main reason for development and adoption of different media has always been isolation of the maximum number of colonies of *Salmonella* serotypes other than Typhi. The widespread use of MSRV in Europe during the past 20 years, as opposed to less use in the United States and some other parts of world, may have influenced the reported differences in isolation rates and prevalence of different serotypes in various parts of the world.

Polymerase chain reaction (PCR)-based, immunological, and other nontraditional methods skip some of the steps in classical microbiology and are used in many laboratories, but presumptive positives still must be confirmed by traditional cultural methods. In addition to confirmation, this provides an isolate that can be used for serotyping. Even with the development of more rapid methods, such assays usually require the presence of 10^3 or 10^4 cells for detection; hence, enrichment is still required for most food samples, which generally have less than 10^3 salmonellae per 25 g. PCR was determined to be better than traditional culture methods for detecting *Salmonella* in neck skin samples, but both methods together detected more positives than either method individually (Whyte et al. 2002), also a common observation for any two conventional cultural methods. Additional sampling and methodology issues are discussed in a recent publication by the National Advisory Committee on Microbiological Criteria for Foods (NACMCF 2010).

SALMONELLA PREVALENCE ISSUES

> As generally used, enrichment culture effectively erases valuable information about initial microbial numbers within a sample, downgrading a potentially quantitative test into a qualitative one.
>
> Brehm-Stecher et al. 2009

What is the true prevalence of *Salmonella* on poultry? *Salmonella* prevalence rates on chicken carcasses can be increased or decreased depending on the sampling methods used, such as changing the portion cultured after whole carcass rinsing or changing the sample weight in neck skin or meat sampling (Cox & Blankenship 1975; King et al. 2008; Simmons et al. 2003a,b; Surkiewicz et al. 1969). Culturing a smaller sample size can reduce the prevalence of *Salmonella* on poultry, whereas larger-than-typical size samples can increase the prevalence. Sampling methods for determining *Salmonella* prevalence are often based on convenience or previous experience, and prevalence data are often presented and compared with insufficient information regarding testing methods.

Studies at the retail level have revealed that there has been less change in prevalence of *Salmonella* on chicken meat than anticipated (Fletcher 2006). Remarkably, data reported in 81 publications between 1961 and 2004 revealed average *Salmonella* prevalence on chicken meat was similar in different parts of the world, in different decades, and as determined by several different methods. Despite many programs to control *Salmonella* in chickens, not much changed in broad averages of data from supermarkets and shops at the point nearest the consumer, with a mean retail prevalence of about 31%. Fletcher concluded that regulatory pressure to reduce *Salmonella* in processing plant samples would not improve public health unless *Salmonella* prevalence was also reduced at the point of distribution and sale. The location at which prevalence samples are obtained may also be an important factor in determining the relationship between prevalence of *Salmonella* on raw poultry and the risk of acquisition of human salmonellosis.

Compared to other sampling methods, neck skin samples have less variation in indicator bacteria that are present in relatively high numbers (Hutchison et al. 2006). *Salmonella* prevalence results from neck skin samples are sometimes similar to results from whole carcass rinse sampling (Cox et al. 2010c, Sarlin et al. 1998); although, higher prevalence in neck skin samples has been reported in cutting plants (Burfoot et al. 2009) and with retail chicken (Jorgenson et al. 2002). A study in which only one to four grams of neck skin were assayed compared to the 25 grams usually tested today revealed that whole carcass rinses had a significantly higher *Salmonella* prevalence (Cox et al. 1978). The neck skin–whole carcass rinse comparison may be affected by the number of *Salmonella* cells that are present on the carcasses and the extent to which they are attached to the carcass, so that different flocks and different processing methods may affect the results. Three of the cited studies were done with immersion-chilled carcasses (Cox et al. 1978, 2010c; Sarlin et al. 1998), one with air-chilled carcasses (Burfoot et al. 2009), and the chilling method was not apparent in the other paper (Jorgenson et al. 2002).

In whole carcass rinse sampling, the rinse liquid comes in contact with the entire surface of the carcass if the rinse procedure is properly conducted. A neck skin sample of approximately 25 grams is a relatively small percentage of the total skin or surface area of the whole carcass, so the approximate equivalence observed in several studies may imply that there are more than a few *Salmonella* cells that are attached or associated with the skin and carcass and are about as likely to be isolated from macerating the neck skin as from a rinse of the entire carcass. Finding a higher *Salmonella* prevalence in neck skin than in whole carcass rinse samples may indicate that many of the cells are attached or associated to some degree with the skin and are not being recovered by rinsing the carcass. In whole carcass rinse sampling, the first *Salmonella*-positive rinse is found sometimes only after multiple negative rinses of the same carcass (Izat et al. 1991, Lillard 1989).

As indicated by Brehm-Stecher and colleagues (2009), prevalence reports the proportion of samples that are positive without reference to the number and strains of bacteria that are present. This review points out many examples in which prevalence information alone is inadequate for a human health risk assessment.

SALMONELLA ENUMERATION ISSUES

> Most studies that have investigated foodborne pathogen contamination on meat have focused on the prevalence of samples that are positive for the organism. These prevalence measures are largely irrelevant for predicting risks that depend on the quantity of pathogens ingested, as most foodborne illnesses are expected to come from the right tail (i.e., exceptionally high region) of the frequency distribution of microbial loads on meats.
>
> Singer et al. 2007

Enumeration of *Salmonella* is difficult and expensive compared to estimating counts of many common bacteria. As a result of the cost of most-probable-number (MPN) procedures that are largely used to estimate numbers of *Salmonella* in samples, *Salmonella* cell numbers are rarely reported in the scientific literature compared with the number of papers that report *Salmonella* prevalence. A three-tube MPN inoculated at three dilutions will be about nine times more expensive than a prevalence test and will have confidence intervals that are considerably larger than those from counting bacteria on plates.

Enumeration of salmonellae on carcasses or parts of carcasses is done by removing bacteria from the sample and suspending them in liquid. The resulting estimates have an uncertain relationship with the number of salmonellae that remain on the carcass (as in whole carcass rinsing for which the carcass is not incubated) or were not included in the partial sample (as in neck skin sampling for which salmonellae on the remainder of the carcass are not included in the sample). Salmonellae that are not included in the suspension tested in the laboratory may remain on the carcass and reach the consumer. For aerobic bacteria and *Enterobacteriaceae* that are present on poultry carcasses in large numbers, a single whole carcass rinse removes only about 10% of the total bacteria that can be removed with repeated, multiple rinses (Lillard 1988, 1989). The numerical relationship between bacterial cells removed and cells remaining on the carcass is much less certain for bacteria that are present in relatively low numbers. For broiler chickens, the mean MPN value for *Salmonella*-positive whole carcass rinses is often cited as approximately 30, a much lower and more variable number than that of aerobic bacteria or *Enterobacteriaceae* in chicken carcass rinses.

Some information is available, however, concerning the relatively few chicken carcasses or chicken parts carrying high numbers of *Salmonella*. MPN values of 2,071 immersion-chilled chicken carcasses were reported using the same methods (USDA/FSIS 1996a, CFIA 2000). Of the 2,071 carcasses sampled in the two baselines, there were four carcasses that had MPN values greater than 12,000 per carcass (MPN per milliliter multiplied by the number of milliliters of rinse), with the most contaminated sample containing 112,000. In the most recent baseline study of 3,275 carcasses sampled at the rehang point between the kill and evisceration sections of processing plants, the most contaminated carcass had a total *Salmonella* MPN of 1,100 per ml or 440,000 for the entire carcass (USDA/FSIS 2009). A study in England in which 241 whole chickens at retail were sampled revealed two carcasses with approximately 10^4 salmonellae each, as determined by direct plating (Jorgenson et al. 2002). Results of other studies have revealed large numbers in a few samples when *Salmonella* cells on chicken carcasses, chicken breasts, or meat were enumerated (Cason et al. 2007, DuFrenne et al. 2001, Straver et al. 2007, Uyttendaele et al. 2009). If the single-rinse to total-carcass bacteria ratios reported for aerobic bacteria counts and *Enterobacteriaceae* cell numbers hold true for carcasses contaminated with large numbers of *Salmonella*, there are likely many more *Salmonella* cells present on those carcasses that are not recovered in any type of nondestructive sampling.

The importance of enumerating *Salmonella* has been emphasized in an expert report by the American Society for Microbiology (ASM 2006) and the National Advisory Committee on

Microbiological Criteria for Foods (NACMCF 2004). The ASM report indicated that enumeration of *Salmonella* would be "a major scientific step forward." Both organizations reported that the efficacy of pathogen reduction cannot be determined without enumeration, because control efforts could reduce pathogen cell numbers and risk to human health even if prevalence is not changing. Cell numbers are also important for conducting risk assessments, which have shown that risk can be reduced with no change in prevalence (Lammerding 2006, WHO 2002). Risk assessments have also revealed that most of the risk of acquiring human salmonellosis is from exposure to chicken carcasses and parts that are contaminated with large numbers of salmonellae (Straver et al. 2007, Uyttendaele et al. 2009, WHO 2002).

Many experts believe that most poultry-related cases of salmonellosis are caused by cross-contamination in the kitchen from raw poultry meat to other foods or back to cooked poultry, with cross-contamination studies revealing movement of bacteria from chicken skin to other surfaces with relative ease (Chen et al. 2001, Luber 2009, Zhao et al. 1998). Luber (2009) noted that the World Health Organization risk model for chicken meat (WHO 2002) does not include the risk of cross-contamination of *Salmonella* from meat to other surfaces. It is likely that a highly contaminated carcass or portion of meat has a greater probability of transferring *Salmonella* cells to other surfaces than a carcass contaminated with only a few cells of *Salmonella*.

Calculations can be done to relate *Salmonella* cell numbers present in a sample to the likelihood of a *Salmonella*-positive prevalence test result. For whole carcass rinse samples, for example, a portion of the total rinse is cultured for the presence of *Salmonella*, with aliquot volume varying in different testing plans (King et al. 2008, USDA/FSIS 1996a). Assuming that all cells recover and reproduce during enrichment, the probability of a *Salmonella*-positive test can be calculated as $P(+) = 1-(1-30/400)^n$ where n equals the number of suspended cells in 400 milliliters of rinse and a 30-ml aliquot is tested for the presence of *Salmonella*. **Figure 2** shows an approximate histogram of the relationship between cell numbers of *Salmonella* in a whole carcass rinse versus *Salmonella* prevalence based on an aliquot from that rinse, with the x-axis (total cell numbers recovered in a carcass rinse) on a log scale and with observed frequency on the y-axis. With nine cells suspended in the rinse, there is an approximately 50% chance of a *Salmonella*-positive test result, so at the low end of the x-axis there are many false-negative results even though the rinses contain cells of *Salmonella*. However, we believe that these *Salmonella*-negative results have little significance for human illness because risk models indicate that most human salmonellosis is caused by exposure

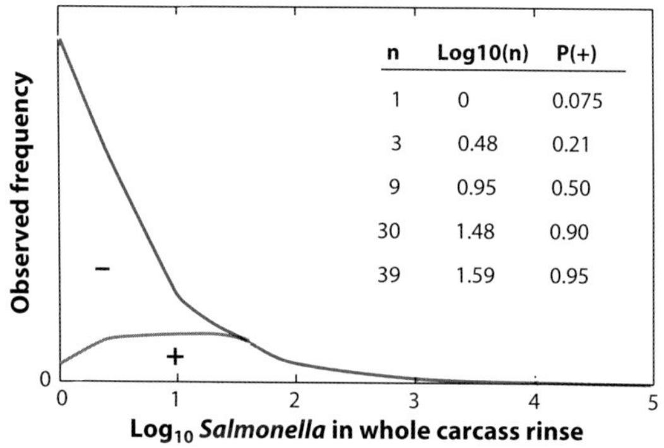

Figure 2

Histogram of log10 *Salmonella* cells in whole carcass rinses (*blue line*) showing the relationship between numbers of cells in 400 ml of rinse and the probability of a positive test when an aliquot of 30 ml is cultured, with the gray line separating test positive and test negative results.

to chicken carcasses and parts contaminated with more than 10^4 cells per carcass (Straver et al. 2007, WHO 2002). Hence, the most contaminated chicken meat products carry a higher risk of causing salmonellosis (Uyttendaele et al. 2009). Heavily contaminated carcasses should also be much more likely to cross-contaminate other foods.

SALMONELLA SEROTYPING ISSUES

> ...The probability of detecting a specific *Salmonella* strain had little to do with its starting concentration in the sample. The bias introduced by culture could be dramatically biasing *Salmonella* surveillance systems...
>
> Singer et al. 2009

Although the scientifically conservative position is to regard all *Salmonella* serotypes as human pathogens (all are considered pathogenic at some dose), there are known differences between serotypes in ability to survive stress, colonize animals, invade tissues, and cause disease with varying outcomes. Among the common *Salmonella* serotypes causing human illness, the percentage of cases of salmonellosis that are hospitalized varies from 14% to 67%, with the range of case fatality rates varying by more than 100-fold (Jones et al. 2008). Septecemia caused by different serotypes is strongly influenced by increasing age of the patient, but there are major serotype differences, with Virchow being more invasive in young children and Enteritidis in persons more than 60 years of age (Weinberger et al. 2004). *Salmonella* of different serotypes also differ in ability to survive food processing conditions, with Enteritidis surviving better than Typhimurium and Infantis, and much better than Dublin (Hald et al. 2004).

In a model that incorporated seven major *Salmonella* serotypes (not including Enteritidis) with all serotypes assumed to be equally capable of causing disease, in United States data, there was a mismatch between observed illnesses and expected outcomes (Sarwari et al. 2001). More illnesses than expected were caused by Typhimurium and Newport, with many fewer cases than expected caused by Kentucky and Derby. When a tenfold higher risk was assumed for each major food animal (cattle, swine, and poultry), there was little effect on the results, with each serotype's ability to cause disease having more impact on human illness than the type of serotypes in each animal. In Danish surveillance data, serotypes Newport, Virchow, and Thompson were more virulent than Enteritidis (Pires & Hald 2010).

In general, *Salmonella* methodology has been selected based on maximum recovery of positive colonies and not on finding specific *Salmonella* serotypes within a food sample. Many studies have demonstrated, however, that cultural techniques can influence the serotypes that are recovered from samples (Carrique-Mas & Davies 2008, Harvey & Price 1967, Kinde et al. 2004, Love & Rostagno 2008, Rostagno et al. 2005, Singer et al. 2009). Serotype bias has been documented since the 1950s, but the public health significance is still little known and poorly understood. Enteritidis, for instance, is a major serotype in human illness, but when mixed in equal proportions and incubated overnight, Enteritidis is outgrown by Newport (Singer et al. 2009) and by Heidelberg and Senftenberg (Kinde et al. 2004). Growth of Enteritidis in the presence of other serotypes in feces or hatchery fluff is also reduced by the stress of drying (Cox et al. 2010d). The unequal competition between serotypes may have implications for pooling of samples in monitoring of *Salmonella* in poultry. Some samples are routinely pooled in neck skin and farm sampling in Europe, possibly distorting the picture of what serotypes are present in multi-serotype samples.

Multiple serotypes have been isolated from the same samples in some reports. In a study that sampled retail chicken wings and turkey necks by two culture methods, multiple serotypes were recovered from a high proportion of *Salmonella*-positive samples (Temelli et al. 2010). In a recent study in our laboratory, 49 of 52 broiler chicken carcasses rinsed immediately after defeathering were *Salmonella*-positive, with one serotype isolated from seven carcasses, two from 19 carcasses, three from 18 carcasses, and four from five carcasses (Cox et al. 2010a). Other studies have revealed isolation of multiple *Salmonella* serotypes from individual samples (FSANZ 2010, Jorgenson et al. 2002). Using multiple isolation media and picking three to five suspect colonies from each plate can result in the isolation of multiple *Salmonella* serotypes from a large percentage of individual samples. Picking only one colony per plate may underestimate the number of *Salmonella* serotypes that are present in a sample.

Two recent research projects in our laboratory revealed different effects of plating media on serotype isolation from hatchery fluff and carcass rinses (Cox et al. 2010a,e). From the fluff samples, 455 presumptive *Salmonella* isolates were subtyped with antisera. Serogroup C1 (later identified as Lille) was isolated 34 times from BGS or Hektoen Enteric plates, but only once from XLT4 plates. In the broiler carcass rinse study, on the other hand, serotype Kiambu was detected 15 times on XLT4 and never on BGS. When the isolates were later restreaked, the Lille was determined to be a weak H_2S producer that did not appear as a typical *Salmonella* on XLT4, and the Kiambu was a strong H_2S producer that formed smaller-than-average colonies on BGS. All of the work was done by technicians well-experienced in isolating *Salmonella*, demonstrating that nontypical *Salmonella* colonies can be overlooked on plates that have many suspect colonies, even when multiple colonies are being selected.

Serotype differences may explain some of the difficulty in attributing human salmonellosis to different foods. Many studies have revealed a poor match between human and animal *Salmonella* serotypes (Heithoff et al. 2008, Jones et al. 2008, Kariuki et al. 2002, Pointon et al. 2008, Ravel et al. 2010, Sarwari et al. 2001, Schlosser et al. 2000, Stevens et al. 2009, Sumner et al. 2004, Todd 2004). One explanation may be that changes in serotype patterns have occurred between the hatchery and farm (Bailey et al. 2002), between the farm and processing plant (McCrea et al. 2006, van der Fels-Klerx et al. 2008, Rasschaert et al. 2008, Volkova et al. 2009), and between the processing plant and retail (Mellor et al. 2010, Van Asselt et al. 2009, Van de Giessen et al. 2006). New serotypes can be introduced into a flock because of contaminated transport cages and because of cross-contamination of serotypes between different flocks via processing equipment (Corry et al. 2002, Rasschaert et al. 2008). Differences in *Salmonella* isolation methods may be part of the reason for serotype changes from hatchery to farm to processing plant. Composition of samples is different (environment and fecal, carcass rinses or neck skin) and stresses experienced by the salmonellae can be different (dry versus wet, temperature changes, chemical stress in some countries). The differential response of *Salmonella* of various serotypes to different laboratory culture methods may also be a factor in the changing serotype patterns reported during rearing and processing of poultry.

Mismatches are observed frequently in serotypes of *Salmonella* isolates obtained from food animals and from infected humans. Isolations of Paratyphi B var. L(+) tartrate+ (formerly known as Java) increased explosively in poultry in recent years in the Netherlands and northern Europe (Van Pelt et al. 2003, Van de Giessen et al. 2006, Van Asselt et al. 2009), with few human illnesses caused by this serotype being reported. More isolations of this serotype occur in retail samples than in processing plant samples (Van de Giessen et al. 2006). Kentucky has been isolated from more than 50% of chicken HACCP samples and from NARMS retail chicken breast monitoring samples, but Kentucky typically causes only 0.3% of human cases in the United States (CDC 2008b). Serotype Sofia (now known by its antigenic formula II $\underline{1}$,4,12,$\underline{27}$:b:[e,n,x]) has been isolated from more than 90% of poultry isolates during some years in parts of Australia, but has been isolated from few human cases there (Harrington et al. 1991, Mellor et al. 2010, Pointon et al.

2008, Sumner et al. 2004). Sofia attaches to processing plant equipment surfaces more efficiently than other *Salmonella* serotypes (Chia et al. 2009), so it may have properties that make it more likely to be isolated from poultry samples.

SALMONELLA SUBTYPING ISSUES

> At present there is an urgent need for *Salmonella* fingerprinting to determine the true extent of genetic diversity among isolates of the same serotype, whether a limited number of clones are associated with human disease and the molecular basis for virulence of these strains.
>
> Manfreda & De Cesare 2005

Despite the importance of serotyping as a useful tool for understanding the contamination of raw poultry by *Salmonella*, serotype information alone is not sufficient for ecological and epidemiologic investigations to understand the movement of *Salmonella* through the different stages of poultry production or the relationship of those strains to human salmonellosis. Hald et al. (2004) reported that serotype distributions are not enough information and that "discriminatory epidemiological typing methods" are needed for intensive monitoring of animal and human serotypes. Strain differences in virulence in mice of animal and human Typhimurium isolates were the main reason why there was a weak correlation between these strains in animal and human isolations (Heithoff et al. 2008). Antibiotic resistance patterns in isolates from imported meat and returning international travelers were helpful in identifying specific sources of some strains of *Salmonella* (Hald et al. 2007).

Different *Salmonella* isolates of the same serotype found in environmental samples and in a chicken flock are not always the same subtype, with preharvest strains usually not predominant in neck skin samples from processed carcasses (Heyndrickx et al. 2007). There are also important differences in strains of *Salmonella* from different parts of the world, with relatively avirulent strains of Sofia in Australia compared with virulent strains of the same serotype causing substantial human illness in Israel (Harrington et al. 1991).

Enteritidis is a serotype that is responsible for a major percentage of human salmonellosis worldwide, but it is a somewhat unusual *Salmonella* in that it has relatively low genetic variability compared to other serotypes. Liebana et al. (2001) concluded that better methods such as phage typing or multiple molecular methods are needed to differentiate different strains of Enteritidis isolated from poultry. As with many subtyping methods, there is no definitive international agreement on the best molecular methods for subtyping *Salmonella* isolates.

Pulsed field gel electrophoresis (PFGE) and antibiogram patterns can also be used to evaluate the diversity within individual *Salmonella* serotypes. In another study in our laboratories, the PFGE and antimicrobial resistance patterns of *Salmonella* isolates were compared to 4,620 XbaI patterns originating from testing 17,597 isolates in USDA-VetNet (Cox et al. 2010b). The isolates for this study originated from 52 whole carcass rinses that were tested using culture method combinations that are not commonly used by regulatory agencies. Compared to patterns within the USDA-VetNet database, a total of 10 new *Salmonella* PFGE XbaI patterns were identified from only 49 positive samples. The identification of new patterns suggests that further work needs to be conducted on cultural influences that select certain *Salmonella* serotypes and subtypes.

Taking into account the distinctions between *Salmonella* serotypes and strains that have been recognized in recent years, many older publications may need to be reevaluated. Many assumptions concerning generic *Salmonella* at different stages of rearing and processing were likely confounded with different serotypes and strains involved. Serotypes of *Salmonella* isolates obtained from the farm and during processing may not have been the same strain. Sampling and cultural methods may have skewed the results that were obtained.

SUMMARY POINTS

1. There is a poor correlation between *Salmonella* prevalence in poultry meat and human salmonellosis, indicating that prevalence as measured is not closely related to risk.
2. In several parts of the world, as much as half of *Salmonella*-positive samples from poultry are serotypes that are rarely associated with human disease.
3. Programs to reduce *Salmonella* contamination in poultry meat are not likely to greatly affect the risk of acquiring human salmonellosis unless those serotypes that cause a large proportion of human illness are targeted and reduced.
4. Monitoring programs for *Salmonella* in poultry may not be adequate to detect reductions in the risk of acquiring human salmonellosis.
5. Methods for isolating *Salmonella* from poultry and other foods are not equally effective in obtaining all serotypes, thereby influencing the accurate identification of the *Salmonella* serotypes that are present.
6. Improved *Salmonella* enumeration methods are needed to develop more useful risk assessments.
7. A better understanding of the ecology of *Salmonella* in poultry and humans is needed to develop more strategies to reduce the risk of human salmonellosis.
8. Internationally agreed upon sampling and laboratory culture methods for *Salmonella* in poultry from the farm to retail are needed.

DISCLOSURE STATEMENT

The authors are not aware of any affiliations, memberships, funding, or financial holdings that might be perceived as affecting the objectivity of this review.

LITERATURE CITED

Aho M. 1992. Problems of *Salmonella* sampling. *Int. J. Food Microbiol.* 15:225–35

Am. Soc. Microbiol. (ASM). 2006. May 17, 2006—ASM submits comments on FSIS *Salmonella* verification reporting [Docket No. 04-026N]. **http://www.asm.org/index.php/policy/may-17-2006-asm-submits-comments-on-fsis-salmonella-verification-reporting.html**

Bailey JS, Cox NA, Craven SE, Cosby DE. 2002. Serotype tracking of *Salmonella* through integrated broiler chicken operations. *J. Food Prot.* 65:742–45

Barber DA, Miller GY, McNamara PE. 2003. Models of antimicrobial resistance and foodborne illness: examining assumptions and practical applications. *J. Food Prot.* 66:700–9

Batz MB, Doyle MP, Morris JG Jr, Painter J, Singh R, et al. 2005. Attributing illness to food. *Emerg. Infect Dis.* 11:993–99

Brehm-Stecher B, Young C, Jaykus LA, Tortorello ML. 2009. Sample preparation: the forgotten beginning. *J. Food Prot.* 72:1774–89

Burfoot D, Archer J, Horvath E, Hooper G, Allen V, et al. 2009. Technical report submitted to EFSA. Fate of *Salmonella* spp. on broiler carcasses before and after cutting and/or deboning. **http://www.efsa.europa.eu/en/scdocs/doc/45e.pdf**

Can. Food Insp. Agency. 2000. *Canadian microbiological baseline survey of chicken broiler and young turkey carcasses, June 1997–May 1998*. **http://dsp-psd.pwgsc.gc.ca/Collection/A62-53-2000E.pdf**

Capita R, Prieto M, Alonso-Calleja C. 2004. Sampling methods for microbiological analysis of red meat and poultry carcasses. *J. Food Prot.* 67:1303–8

Carrique-Mas JJ, Breslin M, Sayers AR, McLaren I, Arnold M, Davies R. 2008. Comparison of environmental sampling methods for detecting *Salmonella* in commercial laying flocks in the UK. *Lett. Appl. Microbiol.* 47:514–19

Carrique-Mas JJ, Davies RH. 2008. Sampling and bacteriological detection of *Salmonella* in poultry and poultry premises: a review. *Rev. Sci. Tech.* 27:665–77

Cason JA, Hinton A Jr, Northcutt JK, Buhr RJ, Ingram KD, et al. 2007. Partitioning of external and internal bacteria carried by broiler chickens before processing. *J. Food Prot.* 70:2056–62

Cent. Dis. Control Prev. (CDC). 2005. Preliminary FoodNet data on the incidence of infection with pathogens transmitted commonly through food—10 states, 2004. *Morb. Mortal. Wkly. Rep.* 54(14):352–56

Cent. Dis. Control Prev. (CDC). 2007. *Foodborne active disease surveillance network (FoodNet) surveillance report 2007, pp. 1–46*. **http://www.cdc.gov/foodnet/annual/2007/2007_annual_report_508.pdf**

Cent. Dis. Control Prev. (CDC). 2008a. Preliminary FoodNet data on the incidence of infection with pathogens transmitted commonly through food—10 states, 2007. *Morb. Mortal. Wkly. Rep.* 57:366–70

Cent. Dis. Control Prev. (CDC). 2008b. *Salmonella* Surveillance: Annual Summary, 2006. Atlanta, GA: U.S. Dep. Health Hum. Serv. **http://www.cdc.gov/ncidod/dbmd/phlisdata/salmtab/2006/SalmonellaAnnualSummary2006.pdf**

Cent. Dis. Control Prev. (CDC). 2009. Preliminary FoodNet data on the incidence of infection with pathogens transmitted commonly through food—10 states, 2008. *Morb. Mortal. Wkly. Rep.* 58:333–37

Cent. Dis. Control Prev. (CDC). 2010. Preliminary FoodNet data on the incidence of infection with pathogens transmitted commonly through food—10 states, 2009. *Morb. Mortal. Wkly. Rep.* 59:418–22

Chen Y, Jackson KM, Chea FP, Schaffner DW. 2001. Quantification and variability analysis of bacterial cross-contamination rates in common food service tasks. *J. Food Prot.* 64:72–80

Chia TWR, Goulter RM, McMeekin T, Dykes GA, Fegan N. 2009. Attachment of different *Salmonella* serovars to materials commonly used in a poultry processing plant. *Food Microbiol.* 26:853–59

Corry JEL, Allen VM, Hudson WR, Breslin MF, Davies RH. 2002. Sources of *Salmonella* on broiler carcasses during transportation and processing: modes of contamination and methods of control. *J. Appl. Microbiol.* 92:424–32

Corry JEL, Jarvis B, Passmore S, Hedges A. 2007. A critical review of measurement uncertainty in the enumeration of food micro-organisms. *Food Microbiol.* 24:230–53

Cox NA, Berrang ME. 2000. Inadequacy of selective plating media in field determination of *Salmonella*. *J. Appl. Poult. Res.* 9:403–6

Cox NA, Blankenship LC. 1975. Comparison of rinse sampling methods for detection of salmonellae on eviscerated broiler carcasses. *J. Food Prot.* 40:1333–34

Cox NA, Fedorka-Cray PJ, Richardson LJ, Buhr RJ, House SL. 2010a. *Salmonella* serotype diversity from broiler carcass rinsates evaluated by two secondary enrichments along with two plating media. *Int. Poultry Sci. Forum*, January 25–26, Atlanta, GA

Cox NA, Fedorka-Cray PJ, Richardson LJ, Buhr RJ, McGlinchey B, et al. 2010b. Pulsed field gel electrophoresis along with antimicrobial resistance pattern of *Salmonella* serotypes isolated from broiler external carcass rinses. *Int. Poult. Sci. Forum*, January 25–26, Atlanta, GA

Cox NA, Mercuri AJ, Tanner DA, Carson MO, Thomson JE, Bailey JS. 1978. Effectiveness of sampling methods for *Salmonella* detection on processed broilers. *J. Food Prot.* 41:341–43

Cox NA, Richardson LJ, Cason JA, Buhr RJ, Vizzier-Thaxton Y, et al. 2010c. Comparison of neck skin excision and whole carcass rinse sampling methods for microbiological evaluation of broiler carcasses before and after immersion chilling. *J. Food Prot.* 73:976–80

Cox NA, Richardson LJ, Fedorka-Cray PJ, Cason JA, Buhr RJ. 2010d. *Salmonella* growth characteristics utilizing different enrichment broths which contain other *Salmonella* serovars and extraneous microflora. *Int. Poult. Sci. Forum*, January 25–26, Atlanta, GA

Cox NA, Richardson LJ, Fedorka-Cray PJ, Cason JA, Mauldin JM, et al. 2010e. Sensitivity and selectivity of cultivation methods to recovery a specific *Salmonella* serogroup from hatchery plenum samples. *Int. Poult. Sci. Forum*, January 25–26, Atlanta, GA

Dalton CB, Gregory J, Kirk MD, Stafford RJ, Givney R, et al. 2004. Foodborne disease outbreaks in Australia, 1995 to 2000. *Commun. Dis. Intell.* 28:211–24

Davies RH. 2005. Pathogen populations on poultry farms. In *Food Safety Control in the Poultry Industry*, ed. GC Mead, pp. 101–52. Cambridge, UK: Woodhead

De Smedt JM, Bolderdijk R, Rappold H, Lautenschlaeger D. 1986. Rapid *Salmonella* detection in foods by motility enrichment on modified semisolid Rappaport-Vassiliadis medium. *J. Food Prot.* 49:510–14

Doorduyn Y, Van Den Brandhof WE, Van Duynhoven YTHP, Wannet WJB, Van Pelt W. 2006. Risk factors for *Salmonella* Enteritidis and Typhimurium (DT104 and non-DT104) infections in The Netherlands: predominant roles for raw eggs in Enteritidis and sandboxes in Typhimurium infections. *Epidemiol. Infect.* 134:617–26

Doyle MP, Erickson MC. 2006. Emerging microbiological food safety issues related to meat. *Meat Sci.* 74:98–112

Dufrenne J, Ritmeester W, Delfgou-van Asch E, van Leusden F, de Jonge R. 2001. Quantification of the contamination of chicken and chicken products in the Netherlands with *Salmonella* and *Campylobacter*. *J. Food Prot.* 64:538–41

Eur. Food Saf. Auth. (EFSA). 2008. A quantitative microbiological risk assessment on *Salmonella* in meat: source attribution for human salmonellosis from meat. *EFSA J.* 625:1–32

Eur. Food Saf. Auth. (EFSA). 2010a. The community summary report on trends and sources of zoonoses, zoonotic agents and food-borne outbreaks in the European Union in 2008. *EFSA J.* 8:1496

Eur. Food Saf. Auth. (EFSA). 2010b. Scientific opinion on the link between *Salmonella* criteria at different stages of the poultry production chain. *EFSA J.* 8:1545

Fletcher DL. 2006. Influence of sampling methodology on reported incidence of *Salmonella* in poultry. *J. AOAC Int.* 89:512–16

Food Stand. Aust. N.Z. (FSANZ), South Aust. Res. Dev. Inst. 2010. *Baseline survey on the prevalence and concentration of* Salmonella *and* Campylobacter *in chicken meat on-farm and at primary processing*. **http://www.foodstandards.gov.au/scienceandeducation/factsheets/factsheets2010/rawchickenmeatmicrob4764.cfm**

Gardner IA. 2004. An epidemiological critique of current microbial risk assessment practices: the importance of prevalence and test accuracy data. *J. Food Prot.* 67:2000–7

Gradel KO, Dethlefsen C, Ejlertsen T, Schonheyder HC, Nielsen H. 2008. Increased prescription rate of antibiotics prior to non-typhoid *Salmonella* infections: a one-year nested case-control study. *Scand. J. Infect. Dis.* 40:635–41

Gradel KO, Dethlefsen C, Schonheyder HC, Ejlertsen T, Sorensen HT, et al. 2007. Severity of infection and seasonal variation of non-typhoid *Salmonella* occurrence in humans. *Epidemiol. Infect.* 135:93–99

Greig JD, Ravel L. 2009. Analysis of foodborne outbreak data reported internationally for source attribution. *Int. J. Food Microbiol.* 130:77–87

Hald T, Vose D, Wegener HC, Koupeev T. 2004. A Bayesian approach to quantify the contribution of animal-food sources to human salmonellosis. *Risk Anal.* 24:255–69

Hald T, Wong DLF, Aarestrup FM. 2007. The attribution of human infections with antimicrobial resistant *Salmonella* bacteria in Denmark to sources of animal origin. *Foodborne Pathog. Dis.* 4:313–26

Harrington CS, Lanser JA, Manning PA, Murray CJ. 1991. Epidemiology of *Salmonella sofia* in Australia. *Appl. Environ. Microbiol.* 57:223–27

Harvey RW, Price TH. 1967. The examination of samples infected with multiple *Salmonella* serotypes. *J. Hyg.* 65:423–34

Havelaar AH, Galindo AV, Kurowicka D, Cooke RM. 2008. Attribution of foodborne pathogens using structured expert elicitation. *Foodborne Pathog. Dis.* 5:649–59

Heithoff DM, Shimp WR, Lau PW, Badie G, Enioutina EY, et al. 2008. Human *Salmonella* clinical isolates distinct from those of animal origin. *Appl. Environ. Microbiol.* 74:1757–66

Heyndrickx M, Herman L, Vlaes L, Butzler J-P, Wildemauwe C, et al. 2007. Multiple typing for the epidemiological study of the contamination of broilers with *Salmonella* from the hatchery to the slaughterhouse. *J. Food Prot.* 70:323–34

Hoffmann S, Fischbeck P, Krupnick A, McWilliams M. 2007. Using expert elicitation to link foodborne illnesses in the United States to foods. *J. Food Prot.* 70:1220–29

Hutchison ML, Walters LD, Mead GC, Howell M, Allen VN. 2006. An assessment of sampling methods and microbiological hygiene indicators for process verification in poultry slaughterhouses. *J. Food Prot.* 69:145–53

Int. Comm. Microbiol. Specif. Foods (ICMSF). 2006. Use of epidemiologic data to measure the impact of food safety control programs. *Food Control* 17:825–37

Inst. Med./Natl. Res. Counc. (IOM/NRC). 2003. *Scientific Criteria to Ensure Safe Food*. Washington, DC: Natl. Acad. Press

Izat AL, Yamaguchi W, Kaniawati S, McGinnis JP, Raymond SG, et al. 1991. Research note: use of consecutive carcass rinses and a most probable number procedure to estimate salmonellae contamination of inoculated broilers. *Poult. Sci.* 70:1448–51

Jones TF, Ingram LA, Cieslak PR, Vugia DJ, Tobin-D'Angelo M, et al. 2008. Salmonellosis outcomes differ substantially by serotype. *J. Infect. Dis.* 198:109–14

Jorgensen F, Bailey R, Williams S, Henderson P, Wareing DRA, et al. 2002. Prevalence and numbers of *Salmonella* and *Campylobacter* spp. on raw, whole chickens in relation to sampling methods. *Int. J. Food Microbiol.* 76:151–64

Kariuki S, Revathi G, Gakuya F, Yamo V, Muyodi J, Hart CA. 2002. Lack of clonal relationship between non-typhi *Salmonella* strain types from humans and those isolated from animals living in close contact. *FEMS Immunol. Med. Microbiol.* 33:165–71

Karns SA, Muth MK, Coglaiti MC. 2007. *Results of an additional expert elicitation on the relative risks of meat and poultry products. Final Rep.* Research Triangle Park, NC: Research Triangle Inst. **http://www.fsis.usda.gov/PDF/RBI_Elicitation_Report.pdf**

Kinde H, Adelson M, Ardans A, Little EH, Willoughby D, et al. 1997. Prevalence of *Salmonella* in municipal sewage treatment plant effluents in southern California. *Avian Dis.* 41:392–98

Kinde H, Castellan DM, Kass PH, Ardans A, Cutler G, et al. 2004. The occurrence and distribution of *Salmonella enteritidis* and other serovars on California egg laying premises: a comparison of two sampling methods and two culturing techniques. *Avian Dis.* 48:590–94

Kinde H, Read DH, Ardans A, Breitmeyer RE, Willoughby D, et al. 1996. Sewage effluent: likely source of *Salmonella enteritidis*, phage type 4 infection in a commercial chicken layer flock in southern California. *Avian Dis.* 40:672–76

King S, Galea F, Hornitzky M, Adams MC. 2008. A comparative evaluation of the sensitivity of *Salmonella* detection on processed chicken carcasses using Australian and US methodologies. *Lett. Appl. Microbiol.* 46:205–9

Kirk MD, McKay I, Hall GV, Dalton CB, Stafford R, et al. 2008. Foodborne disease in Australia: the OzFoodNet experience. *Clin. Infect. Dis.* 47:392–400

Lammerding AM. 2006. Modeling and risk assessment for *Salmonella* in meat and poultry. *J. AOAC Intl.* 89:543–52

Lange L. 2006. FSIS overview of the CY05 broiler and ground poultry *Salmonella* data. Food Safety and Inspection Service. Advances in Post-Harvest Interventions to Reduce *Salmonella* in Poultry, Atlanta, GA, Feb. 23. **http://www.fsis.usda.gov/PDF/Slides_022306_Lange.pdf**

Liebana E, Garcia-Migura L, Breslin MF, Davies RH, Woodward MJ. 2001. Diversity of strains of *Salmonella enterica* serotype Enteritidis from English poultry farms assessed by multiple genetic fingerprinting. *J. Clin. Microbiol.* 39:154–61

Lillard HS. 1988. Comparison of sampling methods and implications for bacterial decontamination of poultry carcasses by rinsing. *J. Food Prot.* 51:405–8

Lillard HS. 1989. Incidence and recovery of salmonellae and other bacteria from commercially processed poultry carcasses at selected pre- and post-evisceration sites. *J. Food Prot.* 52:88–91

Love BC, Rostagno MH. 2008. Comparison of five culture methods for *Salmonella* isolation from swine fecal samples of known infection status. *J. Vet. Diagn. Invest.* 20:620–24

Luber P. 2009. Cross-contamination versus undercooking of poultry meat or eggs—which risks need to be managed first? *Int. J. Food Microbiol.* 134:21–28

Manfreda G, De Cesare A. 2005. *Campylobacter* and *Salmonella* in poultry and poultry products: hows and whys of molecular typing. *World's Poult. Sci. J.* 61:185–97

McCrea BA, Macklin KS, Norton RA, Hess JB, Bilgili SF. 2006. A longitudinal study of *Salmonella* and *Campylobacter jejuni* isolates from day of hatch through processing by automated ribotyping. *J. Food Prot.* 69:2908–14

Mead GC. 2007. *Microbiological Analysis of Red Meat, Poultry and Eggs*. Cambridge, UK: Woodhead. 348 pp.

Mead GC, Lammerding AM, Cox NA, Doyle MP, Humbert F, et al. 2010. Scientific and technical factors affecting the setting of *Salmonella* criteria for raw poultry: a global perspective. *J. Food Prot.* 73:1566–90

Mead PS, Slutsker L, Dietz V, McCraig LF, Bresee HS, et al. 1999. Food-related illness and death in the United States. *Emerg. Infect. Dis.* 5:607–25

Mellor GE, Duffy LL, Dykes GA, Fegan N. 2010. Relative prevalence of *Salmonella* Sofia on broiler chickens pre- and postprocessing in Australia. *Poult. Sci.* 89:1544–48

Mullner P, Jones G, Noble A, Spencer SEF, Hathaway S, French NP. 2009. Source attribution of food-borne zoonoses in New Zealand: a modified Hald model. *Risk Anal.* 29:970–84

Natl. Advisory Committee on Microbiological Criteria for Foods (NACMCF). 2004. Response to questions posed by FSIS regarding performance standards with particular reference to broilers (young chickens). **http://www.fsis.usda.gov/OPHS/nacmcf/2004/NACMCF_broiler_4_13_04.pdf**

Natl. Advisory Committee on Microbiological Criteria for Foods (NACMCF). 2010. Response to questions posed by the Food Safety and Inspection Service regarding determination of the most appropriate technologies for the Food Safety and Inspection Service to adopt in performing routine and baseline microbiological analyses. *J. Food Prot.* 73:1160–200

Natl. Res. Counc. (NRC). 2009. *Letter report. Review of the Food Safety and Inspection Service proposed risk-based approach to and application of public-health attribution*. Washington, DC: Natl. Acad. Press. **http://www.nap.edu/catalog/12650.html**

O'Connor AM, Sargeant JM, Gardner IA, Dickson JS, Torrence ME, et al. 2010. The REFLECT statement: methods and processes of creating reporting guidelines for randomized controlled trials for livestock and food safety. *J. Food Prot.* 73:132–39

Ogliari PJ, Franciso D, De Andrade DF, Pacheco JA, Franchin PR, Batista CRV. 2007. Statistical methodology for pathogen detection. *J. Food Prot.* 70:1933–36

Pires SM, Evers EG, Van Pelt W, Ayers T, Scallan E, et al. 2009. Attributing the human disease burden of foodborne infections to specific sources. *Foodborne Pathog. Dis.* 6:417–24

Pires SM, Hald T. 2010. Assessing the differences in public health impact of *Salmonella* subtypes using a Bayesian microbial subtyping approach for source attribution. *Foodborne Pathog. Dis.* 7:143–51

Pires SM, Vigre H, Makela P, Hald T. 2010. Using outbreak data for source attribution of human salmonellosis and campylobacteriosis in Europe. *Foodborne Pathog. Dis.* **http://www.liebertonline.com/doi/pdf/10.1089/fpd.2010.0564**

Pointon A, Sexton M, Dowsett P, Saputra T, Kiermeier A, et al. 2008. A baseline survey of the microbiological quality of chicken portions and carcasses at retail in two Australian states (2005 to 2006). *J. Food Prot.* 71:1123–34

Rasschaert G, Houf K, De Zutter L. 2006. Impact of the slaughter line contamination on the presence of *Salmonella* on broiler carcasses. *J. Appl. Microbiol.* 103:333–41

Rasschaert G, Houf K, Godard C, Wildemauwe C, Pastuszczak-Frak M, De Zutter L. 2008. Contamination of carcasses with *Salmonella* during poultry slaughter. *J. Food Prot.* 71:146–52

Rasschaert G, Houf K, Van Hende A, De Zutter L. 2007. Investigation of the concurrent colonization with *Campylobacter* and *Salmonella* in poultry flocks and assessment of the sampling site for status determination at slaughter. *Vet. Microbiol.* 123:104–9

Ravel A, Greig J, Tinga C, Todd E, Campbell G, et al. 2009. Exploring historical Canadian foodborne outbreak data sets for human illness attribution. *J. Food Prot.* 72:1963–76

Ravel A, Smolina E, Sargeant JM, Cook A, Marshall B, et al. 2010. Seasonality in human salmonellosis: assessment of human activities and chicken contamination as driving factors. *Foodborne Pathog. Dis.* 7:785–94

Rostagno MH, Gailey JK, Hurd HS, McKean JD, Leite RC. 2005. Culture methods differ on the isolation of *Salmonella* enteric serotypes from naturally contaminated swine fecal samples. *J. Vet. Diagn. Invest.* 17:80–83

Sahlstrom L, Aspan A, Bagge E, Danielsson-Tham ML, Albihn A. 2004. Bacterial pathogen incidences in sludge from Swedish sewage treatment plants. *Water Res.* 38:1989–94

Sahlstrom L, De Jong B, Aspan A. 2006. *Salmonella* isolated in sewage sludge traced back to human cases of salmonellosis. *Lett. Appl. Microbiol.* 43:46–52

Sargeant JM, Saint-Onge J, Valcour J, Thompson A, Elgie R, et al. 2009. Quality of reporting in clinical trials of preharvest food safety interventions and associations with treatment effect. *Foodborne Pathog. Dis.* 6:989–99

Sarlin LL, Barnhart ET, Caldwell DJ, Moore RW, Byrd JA, et al. 1998. Evaluation of alternative sampling methods for *Salmonella* critical control point determination at broiler processing. *Poult. Sci.* 77:1253–57

Sarwari AR, Magder LS, Levine P, McNamara AM, Knower S, et al. 2001. Serotype distribution of *Salmonella* isolates from food animals after slaughter differs from that of isolates found in humans. *J. Infect. Dis.* 183:1295–99

SAS Inst. Inc. 1999. *SAS Procedures Guide, Version 8*. Cary, NC: SAS Inst. Inc.

Schlosser W, Hogue A, Ebel E, Rose B, Umholtz R, et al. 2000. Analysis of *Salmonella* serotypes from selected carcasses and raw ground products sampled prior to implementation of the pathogen reduction; hazard analysis and critical control point final rule in the US. *Int. J. Food Microbiol.* 58:107–11

Simmons M, Fletcher DL, Berrang ME, Cason JA. 2003a. Comparison of sampling methods for the detection of *Salmonella* on whole broiler carcasses purchased from retail outlets. *J. Food Prot.* 66:1768–70

Simmons M, Fletcher DL, Cason JA, Berrang ME. 2003b. Recovery of *Salmonella* from retail broilers by a whole-carcass enrichment procedure. *J. Food Prot.* 66:446–50

Singer RS, Cox LA Jr, Dickson JS, Hurd HS, Phillips I, Miller GY. 2007. Modeling the relationship between food animal health and human foodborne illness. *Prev. Vet. Med.* 79:186–203

Singer RS, Mayer AE, Hanson TE, Isaacson RE. 2009. Do microbial interactions and cultivation media decrease the accuracy of *Salmonella* surveillance systems and outbreak investigations? *J. Food Prot.* 72:707–13

Stevens MP, Humphrey TJ, Maskell DJ. 2009. Molecular insights into farm animal and zoonotic *Salmonella* infections. *Philos. Trans. R. Soc. B* 364:2709–23

Straver JM, Janssen AFW, Linnemann AR, van Boekel MAJS, Beumer RR, Zwietering MH. 2007. Number of *Salmonella* on chicken breast filet at retail level and its implications for public health risk. *J. Food Prot.* 70:2045–55

Sumner J, Raven G, Givney R. 2003. Which food categories cause salmonellosis in Australia? *Food Aust.* 55:597–601

Sumner J, Raven G, Givney R. 2004. Have changes to meat and poultry food safety regulation in Australia affected the prevalence of *Salmonella* or of salmonellosis? *Int. J. Food Microbiol.* 92:199–205

Surkiewicz BF, Johnston RW, Moran AB, Krumm GW. 1969. A bacteriological survey of chicken eviscerating plants. *Food Technol.* 23:80–85

Temelli S, Eyigor A, Carli KT. 2010. *Salmonella* serogroup detection in poultry meat samples by examining multiple colonies from selective plates of two standard culture methods. *Foodborne Pathog. Dis.* doi:10.1089/fpd.2010.0570. **http://www.liebertonline.com/doi/pdfplus/10.1089/fpd.2010.0570**

Todd ECD. 2004. Microbiological safety standards and public health goals to reduce foodborne disease. *Meat Sci.* 66:33–43

USDA/FSIS. 1996a. *Nationwide broiler chicken microbiological baseline data collection program, July 1994–June 1995*. Washington, DC. **http://www.fsis.usda.gov/OPHS/baseline/contents.htm**

USDA/FSIS. 1996b. Pathogen reduction; hazard analysis and critical control point (HACCP) systems; final rule. *Fed. Regist.* 61:38806–989

USDA/FSIS. 2008. *Improvements for poultry slaughter inspection. Appendix A—Public Health Attribution and Performance Measures Methods*. **http://www.fsis.usda.gov/OPPDE/NACMPI/Feb2008/Slaughter_Appendix_A.pdf**

USDA/FSIS. 2009. *Quarterly results for serotyping of salmonellae from meat and poultry products, January–December 2008*. **http://www.fsis.usda.gov/PDF/Q1-4_2008_*Salmonella*_Serotype_Results.pdf**

USDA/FSIS. 2010. *Progress report on Salmonella testing of raw meat and poultry products, 1998–2009.* **http://www.fsis.usda.gov/PDF/Progress_Report_*Salmonella*_Testing.pdf**

US FDA. 2010. *NARMS retail meat annual report, 2002–2007.* **http://www.fda.gov/AnimalVeterinary/SafetyHealth/AntimicrobialResistance/NationalAntimicrobialResistanceMonitoringSystem/ucm059103.htm**

Uyttendaele M, Baert K, Grijspeerdt K, De Zutter L, Horion B, et al. 2009. Comparing the effect of various contamination levels for *Salmonella* in chicken meat preparations on the probability of illness in Belgium. *J. Food Prot.* 72:2093–105

Van Asselt ED, Thissen JTNM, van der Fels-Klerx HJ. 2009. *Salmonella* serotype distribution in the Dutch broiler supply chain. *Poult. Sci.* 88:2695–701

Van de Giessen AW, Bouwknegt M, Dam-Deisz WDC, van Pelt W, Wannet WJB, Visser G. 2006. Surveillance of *Salmonella* spp. and *Campylobacter* spp. in poultry production flocks in The Netherlands. *Epidemiol. Infect.* 134:1266–75

van der Fels-Klerx HJ, Jacobs-Reitsma WF, van Brake R, van der Voet R, Van Asselt ED. 2008a. Prevalence of *Salmonella* in the broiler supply chain in The Netherlands. *J. Food Prot.* 71:1974–80

Van Hoorebeke S, Van Immerseel F, De Vylder J, Ducatelle R, Haesebrouck F, et al. 2009. Faecal sampling underestimates the actual prevalence of *Salmonella* in laying hen flocks. *Zoonoses Public Health* 56:471–76

Van Pelt W, van der Zee H, Wannet WJB, Van de Giessen AW, Mevius DJ, et al. 2003. Explosive increase of *Salmonella* Java in poultry in The Netherlands: consequences for public health. *Euro Surveill.* 8:31–35

Vassiliadis P. 1983. The Rappaport-Vassiliadis (RV) enrichment medium for the isolation of salmonellas: an overview. *J. Appl. Bacteriol.* 54:69–76

Volkova VV, Bailey RH, Rybolt ML, Dazo-Galarneau K, Hubbard SA, et al. 2009. Inter-relationships of *Salmonella* status of flock and grow-out environment at sequential segments in broiler production and processing. *Zoonoses Public Health.* **http://onlinelibrary.wiley.com/doi/10.1111/j.1863-2378.2009.01263.x/pdf**

Voogt N, Nagelkerke NJD, Van de Giessen AW, Henken AM. 2002a. Differences between reference laboratories of the European community in their ability to detect *Salmonella* species. *Eur. J. Clin. Microbiol. Infect. Dis.* 21:449–54

Voogt N, Wannet WJB, Nagelkerke NJD, Henken AM. 2002b. Differences between national reference laboratories of the European community in their ability to serotype *Salmonella* species. *Eur. J. Clin. Microbiol. Infect. Dis.* 21:204–8

Waltman WD, Mallinson ET. 1995. Isolation of *Salmonella* from poultry tissue and environmental samples: a nationwide survey. *Avian Dis.* 39:45–54

Weinberger M, Andorn N, Agmon V, Cohen D, Shohat T, Pitlik SD. 2004. Blood invasiveness of *Salmonella enterica* as a function of age and serotype. *Epidemiol. Infect.* 132:1023–28

Whyte P, McGill K, Collins JD, Gormley E. 2002. The prevalence and PCR detection of *Salmonella* contamination in raw poultry. *Vet. Microbiol.* 89:53–60

World Health Organ. (WHO). 2002. *Risk assessments of Salmonella in eggs and broiler chickens.* WHO/FAO/UN, Geneva, Switz. **http://www.fao.org/docrep/005/y4392e/y4392e00.htm**

Zhao P, Zhao T, Doyle MP, Rubino JR, Meng J. 1998. Development of a model for evaluation of microbial cross-contamination in the kitchen. *J. Food Prot.* 61:960–63

Nutrigenomics and Personalized Diets: What Will They Mean for Food?

J. Bruce German,[1,2,3] Angela M. Zivkovic,[1,2] David C. Dallas,[2] and Jennifer T. Smilowitz[1,2]

[1]Foods for Health Institute, University of California, Davis, California 95616; email: jensm@ucdavis.edu

[2]Department of Food Science & Technology, University of California, Davis, California 95616

[3]Nestle Research Center, Lausanne 1000 Switzerland

Annu. Rev. Food Sci. Technol. 2011. 2:97–123

First published online as a Review in Advance on October 16, 2010

The *Annual Review of Food Science and Technology* is online at food.annualreviews.org

This article's doi:
10.1146/annurev.food.102308.124147

1941-1413/11/0410-0097$20.00

Keywords

proteomics, metabolomics, health assessment, nutritional phenotype, personalized foods, functional foods

Abstract

The modern food system feeds six billion people with remarkable diversity, safety, and nutrition. Yet, the current rise in diet-related diseases is compromising health and devaluing many aspects of modern agriculture. Steps to increase the nutritional quality of individual foods will assist in personalizing health and in guiding individuals to achieve superior health. Nutrigenomics is the scientific field of the genetic basis for varying susceptibilities to disease and the diverse responses to foods. Although some of these genetic determinants will be simple and amenable to personal genotyping as the means to predict health, in practice most will not. As a result, genotyping will not be the secret to personalizing diet and health. Human assessment technologies from imaging to proteomics and metabolomics are providing tools to both understand and accurately assess the nutritional phenotype of individuals. The business models are also emerging to bring these assessment capabilities to industrial practice, in which consumers will know more about their personal health and seek personal solutions.

INTRODUCTION

The human genome initiative provides life science with a blueprint including goals of basic research and opportunities to translate this research to improvements in human health (Collins et al. 2003). Nutrigenomics, as a subset of the broader field of genomics, actively addresses the genetic basis of response to diet and, in parallel, the variations in dietary responsiveness among humans that are assignable to genotype. Much like pharmacogenomics views its logical translation—personalized medicine—the logical translation of nutrigenomics, both in principle and in detail, is the establishment of a more personalized approach to diet and health. However, diet has a much broader mandate than simply curative therapeutics of disease. Diet as a cornerstone of an individual's overall environment has a major influence on health in the widest sense, from the prevention of diseases to performance, enjoyment, and the overall quality of life. Foods will be the carriers of this value once science has related the various aspects of health to diet. Understanding both the role of diet in the varying expression of a genome and the role of genetics in the varying responses to diet are fundamental to understanding human health.

It is known that individuals respond differently to the same dietary intake. For example, it has been known for the past 20 years that dietary cholesterol can cause changes in plasma cholesterol (Miettinen & Kesaniemi 1989), but this is dependant upon the individual (Glatz et al. 1993). In fact, it has been shown that some variation in response to dietary cholesterol is genotype-dependent (Ordovas 2009). Nutrition's greatest opportunity and its most difficult challenge will be in establishing these basic relationships and applying them to improving the health of all individuals, at all ages, with the most obvious goal of actively preventing disease. Nonetheless, nutrigenomics can only provide part of the answer to personalizing diet. Other nongenetic factors are also intimately involved in an individual's phenotype, their health status, and their risks of and trajectories toward different disease states. Understanding the postgenomic and posttranscriptional events from single cells all the way to whole body behaviors will also take part in the scientific underpinning of personalizing diet and health. Once diet and health are understood, foods will need to be the central providers and value generators of this systems approach to personalizing diet and health.

Food research is going to have its hands full in moving to personalized health, yet this is not news. Food, as both a scientific field and a practical venture, has been changing continuously for the past 100 years. The twentieth century experienced a massive transformation in all aspects of the agricultural enterprise. Societies themselves changed from rural, farm-dominated lifestyles to urban, technology-driven lifestyles. Agriculture changed from many small family farms to a few corporate industries. Food as a business went from a commodity-focused model, in which processing was performed mostly by consumers in-house, to a product-focused model employing centralized, in-factory processing. The food marketplace went from a clearing house for raw commodities to a packaged, personal product showcase. The health challenges of diet went from solving nutrient deficiencies caused by inadequate food choices to caloric imbalances caused by inappropriate food choices. In turn, consumers' concerns of food changed from fear of acute safety to fear of long-term health deterioration.

It is fashionable today to view all of these major changes in agriculture and food as being a net failure simply because of the visibility of some of the health problems remaining. It is true that twentieth century agriculture and food did not solve all of life's problems. Nonetheless, the successes are undeniable and the epic challenge of feeding six billion largely urbanized people, most of whom will live to an unprecedented lifespan, is vivid proof of what is achievable. In fact, the knowledge gained during the past century of food research on the composition of commodities and food materials, the structure-function relationships of those biomaterials, and the technologies to disassemble and reformulate complex, stable foods are precisely the capabilities needed to move adroitly into a more personalized future. As health sciences identify the basis of human diversity and diagnostic sciences commercialize technologies to bring personalizing health assessment to practice, the dexterity available to food manufacturing is ready to develop equally personalized diets as health solutions. The first steps of functional foods, although clumsy, provide evidence of how rapidly, seamlessly, and eventually effectively those solutions will emerge.

The systemic response of metabolism to the combined effects of nutrient status, genetic background, epigenetic changes, lifestyle choices, and environmental fluctuations within an individual at a specific point in time (e.g., metabolic phenotype) is potentially a more sensitive and actionable reflection of nutritional and metabolic status. With such nutritional and metabolic status indicators in place, intelligent interventions, including foods, supplements, and lifestyle modifications, would be recommended to guide an individual's metabolic phenotype in a more beneficial or personally desired direction. Such a vision would bring a fundamentally different perspective to human diet management and empower a much more detailed, interactive, and ultimately valuable industrial engine to delivering health. At this point in time, it is appropriate to ask, where are we in the scientific development of the needed tools and knowledge?

In this review, nutrigenomics is defined as the combination of three complementary areas: (*a*) the direct relationship between nutrients and DNA to modify genetic expression, (*b*) epigenetic interactions in which nutrients modify the structure of DNA (DNA methylation and chromatin remodeling), affecting gene expression, and (*c*) genetic variations within humans that relate to the variations between humans in their response to diet (single nucleotide polymorphisms). The combination of these nutrient-gene mechanisms define an individual's metabolic phenotype—measurable physical and biochemical characteristics, including nutrient status and requirements (German et al. 2003).

NUTRIGENOMICS AND FOOD

The arrival of genomics is unquestionably altering our view of humans and informing the next generation of disease care. However, for food science as an integrative field of science, genomics will create an even wider range of opportunities. The same tools that probe genetic and metabolic diversity of humans in their health-related responses to food can be used to identify the diversity of personal sensory preferences to foods and sensitivities and intolerances to food materials, as well as apply the same toolsets to probe food materials themselves. Nutrigenomics will inform research into the nutritional requirements and responses of humans and the genetic basis of their diversity across a wide range of traits. Agricultural genomics of food commodities will in turn inform our understanding of the biology, chemistry, and functionality of all the biomaterials that make up food (Sequencing et al. 2009). The genomes of production animals will guide research into everything from the efficiency of absolute production yields to redesigning the composition of edible tissues to their protection from pathogens and toxins (Lemay et al. 2009, Sequencing et al. 2009). One final subset of genomics is becoming increasingly interesting to food: metagenomics or the genomics of microbial ecosystems. The genomes of microorganisms are already redefining all aspects of microbial food safety and are beginning to guide the science of food microbiology and its applications to professional microorganisms from enhanced bioprocessing of foods to the explicit inclusion of live microorganisms for their food health value (Sela et al. 2008).

Genomics is also the centerpiece of systems biology as the science of understanding living organisms and entire living ecosystems. Food is society's most important industrial system, and many of the principles being developed in other fields of systems biology will apply to food. One of the most obvious examples of a systems approach to food is lactation and milk. The Darwinian pressure to supply a complete system of nourishment for offspring has driven the development of an unparalleled bioreactor in mammals, the mammary gland (Lemay et al. 2009). The structures, functions, and benefits of the components of milk arising through evolution have guided nutrition research for over a century. The arrival of mammalian genomes and the insights into molecular evolution that they provide will drive a new era of research in which the biology of the mammary gland and lactation will guide a much broader view of food research from ingredient functionality to bioprocessing.

NUTRIGENOMICS: ESSENTIAL AND NONESSENTIAL NUTRIENTS

The task of discovering the essential nutrients for human health is scientifically complete. The public health mandate is now to ensure that everyone in the population chooses a diet replete with these nutrients. The food strategy of ensuring adequacy of all of the essential nutrients in a diverse population is to overdose everyone. This approach is based on an important biological advantage. Because individual humans normally regulate each essential nutrient relatively well across a wide range of intakes, it is possible to resolve the problem of essential nutrients by ostensibly slightly overdosing most of the population. In spite of this, subsets of the population still suffer from deficiencies or suboptimal intakes of essential nutrients. This continuing problem of nutrient deficiency is due to overt poverty, food choices, genetic polymorphisms that increase or modify needs, conditions or medications that alter nutrient utilization or metabolism, or malabsorption syndromes such as celiac disease. In some examples, such as vitamin D, unusual diets and lifestyle choices that minimize alternative sources (e.g., sun exposure) are the basis of isolated inadequacies and even deficiencies. In addition, using a one-size-fits-all model, population-based fortification of one nutrient can lead to detrimental consequences. For example, the fortification of folic acid in the food supply has not only concealed vitamin B12 deficient–anemia, but evidence is emerging that this may result in impaired cognitive functioning in subsets of the population (Refsum & Smith 2008, Winkels et al. 2008).

How will food recommendations deal with the biological reality that some individuals, even following normal dietary guidelines, do not achieve effective nutrient adequacy? The causes in many cases are genetic, and the field of nutrigenomics is actively tracking them down, from the effects of dietary fat composition on plasma lipids (Ferguson et al. 2010, Joffe et al. 2010) and risk for obesity (Joffe et al. 2010) to the effect of epigenetics on the widespread increased rates of food allergy (Allen & Martin 2010) (**Table 1**). The application of this science will almost invariably require a more personalized approach to delivering essential nutrients. Solving the problems of personalizing essential nutrient intakes will be simple because they can be delivered as supplements. Personalizing the overall diet will not be as simple.

Nutritional health depends on more than essential nutrient intake. In fact, the global epidemic of noncommunicative diseases is largely driven by diets in which essential nutrition is adequate, but chronic imbalances of diet in a background of varying lifestyles and genetics are causing metabolic diseases. In addition to the essential nutrients, nonessential nutrients and other environmental factors also interact with the genome and postgenomic products (**Table 2**). Such factors include diet composition, fiber, food structure, and antioxidant capacity (Domínguez et al. 2010, O'Sullivan et al. 2010, Papathanasopoulos & Camilleri 2009, Puchau et al. 2009), as well as environmental and metabolic regulation, including gut microbiota composition (Vijay-Kumar et al. 2010), prebiotics (Cani et al. 2009), metabolic phenotype (Peppa et al. 2010), and activity (Ilanne-Parikka et al. 2010). The goal of personalizing nutrition based on individuals' genotypic and metabolic variations will first require the identification of responders from nonresponders to diet. Individually and in concert, food commodities will be produced to meet the growing health, metabolism, performance, and cognitive demands of the consumer.

GENOTYPE AND PHENOTYPE

Humans are different in their needs for and responses to the various components of a diet. The active subject of research is exactly how and why. Identifying which of those differences are due to heritable genetic sequence variations is a key area of ongoing nutrigenomics research. The most complete picture emerging to date is the variation around the metabolism of folic acid (Zeisel 2007). The common polymorphism in the methylene tetrahydrofolate reductase (MTHFR) gene is associated with a functional difference in metabolism in carriers. This variation affects both the absolute requirement of individuals for the nutrient folate and has been recognized to be associated with an increasing number of phenotypic outcomes, including heart disease (Gohil et al. 2009) and cancer (Galván-Portillo et al. 2009). Most importantly for the success of applying the genetics to nutrition, evidence is emerging that folate supplementation in those carrying genetic risk due to MTHFR reduces the incidence of various health problems associated with low folic acid status (Galván-Portillo et al. 2009).

Genotyping determines individual (or species) genetic variation, ranging in nucleotide coverage from single allele and genome-wide determination of particular genetic differences [e.g., single nucleotide polymorphisms (SNPs)] to complete genomic sequencing (Venter et al. 2001). The tools used to conduct genotyping experiments include hybridization methods, allele-specific polymerase chain reaction (PCR) [e.g., fluorescence resonance energy transfer (FRET) primers], primer extensions (e.g., pyrosequencing), oligonucleotide ligation (e.g., microarray ligation), rolling circle amplification, and endonuclease cleavage (e.g., restriction site analysis) (Syvänen 2001). By mapping genetic differences among individuals and comparing them to phenotypic data, genome-wide association studies have led to the discovery of hypothesis-generating associations between genetic variation and phenotypes (Hindorff et al. 2009). Complete sequencing and mapping of all genetic variation in association with phenotypes are proceeding with projects like the Human Variome Project (Cotton 2007) and the 1,000 Genomes Project (Zhang & Dolan 2010). Variations in the genome are associated with susceptibility or resistance to disease, and metabolic responses to diet, pharmacology, and environment. Thus, metabolic phenotype is influenced in part by developmental plasticity, by imprinting early in life, and by the interactions of environmental factors over time. Both intrauterine signaling and early childhood environmental exposures influence full genotypic expression and ultimately metabolic phenotype (Montmayeur & le Coutre 2009). For example, a polymorphism in a fatty acid desaturase gene involved in long-chain polyunsaturated fatty acid (PUFA) synthesis is associated with higher IQ associated with breastfeeding, illustrating the crucial effects of early imprinting (Caspi et al. 2007). The epigenetic control of gene expression by dietary and environmental factors in utero determines lifelong health trajectories through DNA methylation (Kim et al. 2009). In addition, nutrigenomic imprinting early in life modulates gene expression during development and maturity, and enables an organism to respond to environmental cues and adjust its phenotypic development to match its environment (Gluckman et al. 2009). Such phenotypic plasticity demonstrates how natural selective pressures influence the metabolic outcomes resulting from the interactions between genetic variation and the environment. The high degree of developmental plasticity (Gluckman et al. 2009) and technology (Omenn 2010) has led to the widespread prevalence of positively selected traits. However, by sharing the same genes and epigenetic regulation but not the environment of our Paleolithic ancestors, contemporary humans are accosted with the epidemics of metabolic diseases (Eaton et al. 2010). The goal of nutrigenomics is not to persuade individuals to consume the diets and adopt the lifestyles of ancient hunter-gatherers, but to identify phenotypic responses in the population caused by the interaction between diet and genomic variation.

Table 1 Interactions between essential nutrients and gene polymorphisms on clinical outcomes

Nutrient	Gene polymorphism	Effects on nutrient status	Clinical manifestations	References
Calcium	Calcium sensing receptor (CASR) A986S	Loss of function for calcium, associated with higher serum calcium, and higher urinary calcium excretion	Association with bone mineral density	(Laaksonen et al. 2009)
Selenium	Missense mutation in selenium binding protein 2 (SBP2)	Causes defective selenocysteine insertion sequence (SECIS)-driven selenocysteine incorporation, downregulates expression of selenoproteins	Defective thyroid function	(Hesketh 2008)
Iron	Human hemochromatosis protein (HFE) 187C>G or 845G>A	Both187C>G or 845G>A associated with iron overload (hemochromatosis)	Iron overload, liver cirrhosis, and cardiomyopathy, especially in diets high in iron	(Hulgan et al. 2008)
Folate	5,10-methylenetetrahydrofolate reductase (MTHFR) 677C>T	Causes a 70% reduction in MTHFR activity, hyperhomocysteinemia and reduced plasma folate concentration	Hyperhomocysteinemia is associated with increased risk of coronary heart disease, neural tube defects, occlusive vascular disease and breast cancer. In carriers, sufficient folate dietary intake decreases risk of colorectal cancer, and deficiencies increase risk of colorectal cancer	(Ericson et al. 2009, Friso & Choi 2002, Hustad et al. 2004, Messika et al. 2010, Simopoulos 2010)
Sodium	Angiotensin gene (AGT) nucleotide −6 G>A,	The A substitution in AGT affects the interaction between at least one *trans*-acting nuclear factor and its promoter, resulting in increased gene transcription and increased angiotensin protein levels	Carriers of the A allele respond to low sodium diets with reductions in blood pressure; GG genotype is not salt-sensitive	(Simopoulos 2010)

Vitamin D	Vitamin D binding protein DBP-1 (rs7041, exon 11 T>G) and DBP-2 (rs4588, exon 11C>A)	SNPs for DBP-1 and DBP-2 are inversely related to levels of circulating 25(OH) vit D_3 in premenopausal women	Unclear whether carriers would benefit from dietary supplementation or sun exposure	(Sinotte et al. 2009)
Vitamin K	Vitamin K epoxide reductase complex subunit 1 (VKORC1)j – +2255T>C	Associated with vitamin K recycling, vitamin K–dependent clotting factors and Warfarin resistance	Increased risk of arterial vascular disease such as stroke, coronary heart disease, and aortic dissection	(Suh et al. 2009)
Vitamin A	β-carotene 15,15′-monoxygenase (BCMO1) R267S (rs12934922) and A379V (rs7501331)	Carriers of 267S or 267S + 379V have reduced activity in converting B-carotene to retinal	Increased risk for vitamin A deficiency, when B carotene is the major dietary source	(Leung et al. 2009)
Vitamin B12 (cobalamin)	Methionine synthase TCN2 776C>G and 67A>G	Causes hyperhomocysteinemia	Associated with birth defects	(Brouns et al. 2008)
Carbohydrates	Beta-2-adrenergic receptors Q27E	Unknown	Higher risk of obesity in female carriers with carbohydrate intake >49% of energy	(Martinez et al. 2003)
Omega 3 and 6 fatty acids	Fatty acid desaturase, FADS SNP rs174537	Lower plasma arachidonic and eicosapentaenoic acids and higher plasma alpha linolenic and linoleic acids in carriers of the minor allele versus noncarriers.	The minor allele homozygotes (TT) have lower plasma total cholesterol and LDL-C compared with noncarriers	(Tanaka et al. 2009)

Table 2 Interactions between nonessential nutrients and genomic and postgenomic products

Nutrient	Target	Outcome	References
Isothiocyanates	Glutathione S-transferase (GST) subtypes M, T, and P	Deletions in GSTM1 and GSTT1 result in defective enzymatic activities and decreased carcinogen detoxification capacities; high isothiocyanate intake by GSTM1 and T1 carriers had decreased colorectal cancer risk	(Seow et al. 2002)
Carotenoids	Manganese superoxide dismutase (MnSOD) Ala16Val	Reduced MnSOD activity and lower response to oxidative stress; dietary carotenoids increase risk of cancer for carriers	(Mikhak et al. 2008)
Lipoic acid	Gene expression for B cell receptor, T cell differentiation signaling pathway, and free radical scavengers	Supplementation reduces high fat diet–induced chronic oxidative stress and immuno-suppression in mice jejunum	(Cui et al. 2008)
Catechin	Gene expression for adhesion molecules, energy and lipid metabolism, lipid trafficking	Supplementation reduces atherosclerotic lesion development in apo E-deficient mice	(Auclair et al. 2009)
	Gene expression for mitochondrial activity	Supplementation with regular exercise ameliorates age-associated decline in physical performance in mice	(Murase et al. 2008)
Cholesterol	7-alpha hydroxylase (CYP7A1) A278C	Larger increase in plasma HDL-C in carriers in response to a cholesterol-rich diet; elevated LDL-C is found in homozygous carriers	(Hofman et al. 2004)
Fiber	Adiponectin (ADIPOQ) rs1501299	Lower plasma ADIPOQ levels in carriers when fiber intake was low; associated with increased risk of childhood obesity	(Ntalla et al. 2009)
Saturated fat (SFA)	Scavenger receptor class B type I (SRB-I) gene, −1 G->A	Higher plasma LDL-C in heterozygote carriers in response to an SFA-rich diet; carriers had greater reductions of plasma LDL-C after switching from a high SFA diet to high carbohydrate diet compared with noncarriers; possible increased risk for atherosclerosis when consuming a SFA-rich diet.	(Perez-Martinez et al. 2005)
	Apolipoprotein E (ApoE), E2 and E4 alleles	Larger increases in plasma LDL-C in response to SFA intake in E2 and E4 carriers; impact of SFA intake on incidence of myocardial infarction is more evident in the E2 and E4 allele carriers than noncarriers	(Minihane 2010)

Sesame seed lignans	Gene expression for hepatic genes involved in fatty acid oxidation and fatty acid transport	Unknown	(Puiggros et al. 2009)
Grape seed proanthocyanidins	Gene expression for hepatic genes related to lipogenesis and lipoprotein secretion	Normalized plasma triglycerides and LDL-C on a high fat diet	(Quesada et al. 2009)
Choline	Epigenetic modification	Reduction in methylation influences on neurogenesis, including increased neural tube closure defects in infants of mothers with choline deficiency; maternal choline intake during early pregnancy is associated with increased hippocampal progenitor cell proliferation, decreased apoptosis, and enhanced visual-spatial and auditory memory in rodents' lifetimes; prevents memory loss during aging	(Mehedint et al. 2010, Zeisel 2009)
Soy isoflavones	Gene expression for cell adhesion, apoptosis, autophagy, cell cycle, cell differentiation, DNA associated proteins, mRNA processing and splicing, transport, and inflammatory responses	Protection against oxidative stress and cancer	(Barve et al. 2008)

PROBING NUTRIGENOMIC DIVERSITY: THE TOOLS AT HAND

The tools of systems biology are being used to examine the genetic variations in humans that affect metabolic status and health, the variations in microbial pathogens that are threats to food safety, the variations in microbial communities within humans that affect their health, and the diversity of food and food commodities. In addition to identifying genotypic variation, a systems biology approach encompasses the use of highly sensitive, high-throughput and comprehensive postgenomic technologies—transcriptomics, proteomics, and metabolomics—combined with bioinformatics and multivariate statistics all directed to discover how human phenotypes vary in response to diet and how those phenotypes could be improved.

Gene Expression as an Output: Transcriptomics

Transcriptomics simultaneously measures thousands of transcripts from a tissue or biofluid (Nguyen et al. 2002). DNA microarray technology and quantitative real time PCR have successfully evaluated the interactions between diet and genes measured as changes in genetic expression. Compared with traditional biochemical methods, transcriptomics is a more sensitive and informative tool to assess nutrient status, including minor deficiencies (Harvey & McArdle 2008) and metabolic responses to diet (Fukasawa et al. 2010). For example, the upregulation of transcripts-related adverse changes in skeletal muscle function and structure suggested that the current recommended daily allowance (RDA) for protein is too low. This inadequacy of the RDA was not seen before with typical measurements of protein sufficiency, including nitrogen balance and isotope labeling studies (Thalacker-Mercer et al. 2010). Expression technology can also reveal the interactions between diet and metabolic outcomes. Energy balance (Kallio et al. 2007), dietary structure (Crujeiras et al. 2008, Fukasawa et al. 2010), and composition (Konstantinidou et al. 2010, Wang et al. 2008) have been shown to alter expression of genes involved in insulin sensitivity, lipid metabolism, oxidation, immunity, and inflammation.

The tools of genomics research are being used in identifying functional molecular markers in everything from human and animal health to accelerating crop improvement in efficiency, nutrient quality, disease resistance, and safety (EFSA 2008, Kogel et al. 2010, Polesani et al. 2010). The knowledge gained from identifying the alleles at all loci in a population allow breeders to design a genotype in silico based on the desired phenotype.

Protein as an Output: Proteomics

Proteomics is dedicated to describing the entire complement of proteins and their modifications of cells, tissues, and organisms (Mischak et al. 2007). Unlike the human genome, which is relatively fixed and steady throughout the human body, the human proteome is far more complex and dynamic, varying over time and among cells. It is the proteins themselves and their modifications that elicit their biochemical, physiological, and structural functions in tissues and cells. Mass spectrometry platforms are used to detect, identify, and quantify thousands of proteins in a sample (Cravatt et al. 2007). Still viewed as the most challenging of the 'omics fields, proteomics has struggled to reach a proof-of-principle success story, in part because scientists are still coming to grips with the analytical challenges posed by the true breadth and extent of protein diversity in biology. The use of proteomics for biomarker identification and validation was imagined to revolutionize clinical diagnostics. However, this most obvious application still faces several challenges ranging from appropriate platforms (Rifai et al. 2006) to study design (Mischak et al. 2007) to regulatory oversight (Regnier et al. 2010). Nonetheless, significant progress has been made, and diagnostic products based on the simultaneous measurement of multiple proteins are beginning to emerge (Kolberg et al. 2009). Notably, true proteomics is currently used as the means to identify a subset of proteins that are carried forward as diagnostics.

Although consensus has yet to be achieved for the standardization and application of proteomic technologies for use in the clinical setting, this field has revealed cutting-edge breakthroughs for the fields of nutrition and food science. Proteomics is capable of exposing many of the molecular mechanisms resulting from dietary interventions compared with traditional biochemical methods. Parallel proteomic analysis from the livers of grape seed extract–supplemented rats revealed 140 differentially expressed proteins, uncovering effects of grape seed extract on a variety of biochemical processes, including zinc transport, lipogenesis, G-protein signaling, and sulfur metabolism (Baiges et al. 2010).

For the fields of food science, biotechnology, and nutrition, proteomics is strategically positioned for discovering functional foods with metabolic effects. This is especially relevant in the research of plant- and animal-secreted proteins for breeding next generation crop plants (Agrawal et al. 2010), in identifying novel clinical biomarkers (Pavlou & Diamandis 2010), and in discovering therapeutic targets (Katz-Jaffe et al. 2009). The secretome describes the global study of proteins that are secreted by a cell, tissue, or organism at any given time or under certain conditions (Hathout 2007). During cellular posttranslational modification, proteins become chemically modified, which plays a key role in product secretion. Furthermore, posttranslational modification also influences protein biological and physiological functions such as cell signaling, cell recognition, and cell protection. Rather than simply providing amino acid substrates, the complex proteins in milk are secretory, which, as intact or partially digested products, exert bioactive functions (Affolter et al. 2010, Froehlich et al. 2010, Kanwar et al. 2009, Mok et al. 2007). Food science and biotechnology are beginning to exploit the health enhancing effects of bioactive proteins and peptides of milk.

Metabolism as an Output: Metabolomics

Metabolomics—the measurement of small molecules in biofluids, tissues, and cells using spectroscopic analytical platforms—has been included in the National Institutes of Health (NIH) roadmap as a core technology in the overall initiative to guide the development of diagnostics and assist in delivering the therapeutic solutions to human metabolic diseases (Zerhouni 2003). Metabolomics is more helpful in identifying the complexities of metabolic regulation than measurements of single biomarkers using traditional biochemical methods (Bakker et al. 2010). The metabolome, like the proteome, is not definable in the same sense as the genome. Unlike the genome, which remains static, metabolites change in every cell and body fluid, notably in response to food intake, for example (Zivkovic & German 2009). All of our cells and biofluids contain a finite number of key metabolites, and metabolic homeostasis is generally maintained so that the actual variations in any given metabolite pool are typically minor relative to the abundance of the metabolites. These basic molecules and their fluxes through human metabolism, i.e., those that all humans have in relatively constant amounts (Bernini et al. 2009), include substrates, intermediates, and products of endogenous metabolism (Holmes et al. 2008). Hence, the metabolome will remain a discussable biological construction in which pragmatic clinical utility will require that assumptions, protocols, and reference conditions are standardized. Nonetheless, metabolomics is already proving to be informative in revealing the complex metabolic effects to diet (Vinaixa et al. 2010), in predicting responders to drugs (Winnike et al. 2010) and changes in body composition during energy restriction (Smilowitz et al. 2009), and in identifying metabolic aberrations associated with disease (Yap et al. 2010).

Application of metabolomics specifically to the field of nutrition faces a number of challenges. The ongoing development of analytical platforms is beyond the scope of this review (Büscher et al. 2009, Dettmer et al. 2007, Issaq et al. 2009, Wikoff et al. 2009, Zhang et al. 2009), and the challenges of identification are being addressed in part through increasingly accurate libraries of metabolite spectra (mass, nuclear magnetic resonance, etc.) and chemical properties of diverse biological samples (Forsythe & Wishart 2009). Defining the molecules that constitute this core metabolite pool is an immediate priority. The Human Metabolome Project (Forsythe & Wishart 2009) has established the first draft of this endogenous metabolome. The problem of quantification is more daunting. Whether in early discovery research or in clinical applications, probing an individual's nutritional status will invariably require that the amount of metabolites, not their simple presence or absence, is accurately determined. Studies that take quantitative measures of metabolites are already revealing both the complexity of metabolism and the value of measuring it.

GENOMICS OF FOOD

The molecular tools used to elucidate the metabolic effects of genetic-nutrient interactions are proving to be valuable across the food and agricultural sciences. The genetic structure and expression of bovine genes identified numerous quantitative trait loci (QTL) affecting nutrient quality and quantity (Naslund et al. 2008, Roy et al. 2006). Additionally, recombinant technology has led to the production of food commodities with bioactive ingredients found in breast milk. Human genes for milk proteins with known bioactive functions expressed in rice (Tang et al. 2010, Zavaleta et al. 2007) are resistant to heat and acid/basic environments, thereby maintaining biological activities identical to their native counterparts (Lönnerdal 2006). Interestingly, molecules found in milk, such as the products of lactoferrin digestion, lactoferricin and lactoferrampin, exert their activities after exposure to physiological processing. Recently, microbial peptide fusion to crystalline proteins produced from genes cipA and cipB of *Photorhabdus luminescens* subsp. *akhurstii* led to high-level expression and purification of these two proteins (Tang et al. 2010). Together, the bioactive properties of milk, guided by natural selection and the applications of biotechnologies to isolate them, are increasingly being viewed as a first generation ingredient list for the production of functional and medical foods that address the targeted health needs of individuals from diarrheal to metabolic diseases.

COMMODITY GENOMES

Humans are not the only genomes of interest to food. The genomes of commodity plants, animals, yeast, molds, bacteria, and viruses are guiding scientists to understand nutrient contents, stability, processing strategies, and safety.

Plants

Plant genomes tend to be monstrous due to polyploidy. Hence, the sequencing of entire plant genomes lags somewhat behind other life forms simply because of the scale of the projects. Nonetheless, a variety of agriculturally important genomes are complete or nearing completion, and are forming the basis of a major knowledge resource for food research. From the perspective of production agriculture, these genomes have already shown value. Quantity traits for yield, pest resistance, and water stress are increasingly deliverable as genetic inserts (Cui et al. 2008, Deshmukh et al. 2010, Fu et al. 2010, Zhang et al. 2009). Similarly, there are striking examples of how specific crop plants can be manipulated to improve their basic nutritional value

(Hirschi 2009). However, nutritionists are still struggling with the basic strategies for moving beyond the identification of genes associated with essential nutrients to maximizing their agricultural suitability and nutrient bioavailability. The genome of an organism represents the culmination of its evolutionary history and the ensemble of genes emerging under the Darwinian selection pressures that guided the organism's development. For plants, this pressure was applied, in part, by the need to avoid the ubiquitous pathogens and aggressive predation by the other organisms in their environment. Understanding these predatory influences and the strategies that different plants have developed in the context of their overall genomes will be critical to appreciating the net nutritional value when plants and plant parts are consumed (Lagaert et al. 2009). It is also in this context of composition and protective strategies of plants that we need to understand the ingenuity of the vast array of food processing techniques that humans invented as they first gathered and subsequently grew and harvested plant commodities (Anastasio et al. 2010, Reale et al. 2007, Sieuwerts et al. 2008).

Animals

The anthropological history of humans is consistent with a carnivorous hunter-predator wed to an omnivorous gatherer. A diet rich in diverse animal products was clearly a part of our evolutionary history (Braun et al. 2010). Humans migrated to and succeeded in a remarkable breadth of environmental ecosystems literally from equator to pole (Wells & Stock 2007). One intriguing additional complexity on human diets and evolution was the tantalizing discovery of the confounding effects of cooking on the quality of diets (Carmody & Wrangham 2009). Unquestionably, whether raw or cooked, the rich nutrient quality of animal products was one of the enabling factors to the apparently healthy Paleolithic diet and the spread of humans around the globe (Jonsson et al. 2009).

The challenges for modern animal products as food is to understand productivity and bioactivity, and to defend their higher production cost using health and other value attributes. The genomes of the major domestic agricultural animals—fish, chicken, swine, beef, lamb, goat—are complete or in the final phases of assembly and annotation. Chicken and bovine emerged as production animals for good reasons, and their genomes encode for both the animals themselves and for the associated nourishing products, eggs and milk. Productivity of the chicken is already a remarkable achievement in feed conversion and egg production, and genomics is accelerating progress in research focused on minimizing disease for production costs and food safety (Cheng 2010).

The bovine genome has only recently been completed but already considerable information is emerging from genomics research on lactation and its various biological and nutritional qualities (Lemay et al. 2009, Sequencing et al. 2009). Companion research is taking advantage of sequence information to assemble the milk proteome (Affolter et al. 2010). Genetic analyses are beginning to describe the natural variability in bovine species, revealing the basis for differences in key nutrients in milk (van Hulzen et al. 2009). Expanding to a systems biology approach, the bioprocess of lactation offers researchers invaluable insight about the structures and functions of safe and effective bioactive ingredients. Expression arrays can monitor the effects of breeding and dietary manipulation (Carriquiry et al. 2009).

Microorganisms

Microbial fermentation is one of the mainstays of historic food processing (Poutanen et al. 2009), owing benefits to food stability, safety, and bioavailability, as well as myriad advantages to the organoleptic properties of foods (Gálvez et al. 2010). The concept that living microorganisms or their direct products are valuable constituents of human diets beyond the provision of specific vitamins is not new, yet it remains relatively unexplored both scientifically and technologically.

Variation in the gut microbiota within and between individuals is large (Turnbaugh & Gordon 2009). Modulation of gut microbiota could be a key component of personalized nutrition, as gut microbiota and their byproducts have been shown to alter host metabolome, genome, transcriptome, proteome, and health status (Lewis & Burton-Freeman 2010). The gut microbiome of individuals contributes to the variation in systemic energy balance. Plasma urinary metabolites reflect human gut microflora metabolism and the obesity phenotype (Calvani et al. 2010). The metabolism of indigestible carbohydrates by gut microbiota can alter energy extraction from the diet by the host (O'Keefe 2008). Short chain fatty acids produced by microflora represent 7% of the substrates that enter gluconeogenesis (Ford & Simmons 2008) and 5%–15% of the total human energy requirement (Neish 2009). However, it is unknown how different dietary components enhance the selective growth of one microbial population over another to produce desirable systemic metabolic consequences. The intimate link between gut microbiota composition and health is demonstrated by the prepathogenic state induced by the inoculation of germ-free mice with human bacteria (Martin et al. 2007, Rezzi et al. 2008), the priming of the innate immune system by microbiota-produced peptidoglycans (Clarke et al. 2010), and the association of specific bacterial populations with obesity (Lewis & Burton-Freeman 2010, Turnbaugh et al. 2008, Vrieze et al. 2010).

Diet can alter host microbial composition based on carbohydrate and fiber content, cruciferous vegetable and fat intake (Benus et al. 2010, Carroll et al. 2009, Hildebrandt et al. 2009), and through direct inoculation via fermented or functional foods (Sanders & Marco 2010). Prebiotics have been shown to alter host microbiota (Candela et al. 2010). For example, oligosaccharides in human milk selectively feed the beneficial gut bacteria *Bifidobacterium longum* subsp. *infantis* to the exclusion of other bacteria (Sela et al. 2008), and the prebiotic panose shows in vitro stimulation of *Bifidoba terium* growth and reduction in *Bacteroides* and *Clostridium* growth (Mäkeläinen et al. 2009). Modulation of gut bacteria with prebiotics has been shown to reduce intestinal barrier dysfunction, endotoxemia, and systemic and liver inflammation induced by a high-fat diet (Cani et al. 2009) and improve cholesterol homeostasis (Martinez et al. 2009). It is clear that human gut microbiota have profound effects on human metabolism, gene expression, and health. Identifying these microbial-food interactions has biological potential and holds innovative promise for developing new metabolically targeted foods, which will lead to improved health, metabolism, and protection.

INTESTINAL FUNCTION: FROM IMMUNITY TO MICROBIOLOGY

Dietary compounds and nutrients have widespread effects on gene expression in all tissues, including the intestine. Their effects can be either direct (e.g., as ligands for nuclear transcription factors) or indirect. The indirect effects of dietary compounds on intestinal function and gene expression can be manifested in a number of ways as whole compounds or as modified, metabolized, or hydrolyzed molecules (e.g., peptides). For example, consumption of human milk oligossaccharides, which are completely indigestible by the developing neonate, are actually consumed by specific strains of bifidobacteria that are posultated to maintain a healthy gut (Zivkovic et al. 2010). Although still in its infancy, the relationship between dietary components and the modulation of gut microflora has recently received a great deal of interest as a result of the Human Microbiome Project (Turnbaugh et al. 2007) as well as in research highlighting the importance of the interaction between diet and the intestinal microbiome as a new dimension of human health.

The modulation of the immune system in the gastrointestinal tract by food compounds is involved in the induction of oral tolerance or the suppression of immune response to food antigens. Food proteins (e.g., antigens) may have direct effects on intestinal immune cells, inducing phenotypic maturation and the secretion of specific cytokine profiles, which in turn have a net effect on T cell activation and immune response (MacDonald et al. 2009). It also appears that the timing of introduction of foods in early childhood can determine the risk of developing food allergies and autoimmune disease (Prescott et al. 2008), and that these effects are mediated in part by the host-microbe interactions.

Dietary compounds also play a key role in the establishment of infant gut microflora. Specific constituents in human milk guide the colonization of the infant gut by selectively promoting the growth of specific microbial populations. *B. longum* subsp. *infantis* found in the intestine of breast-fed infants is the first bacterial strain to be characterized as selectively supported by constituents in human milk (LoCascio et al. 2007). The genomic sequence and metabolic characterization of *B. infantis* revealed multiple genes in four discrete clusters that are required to digest, metabolize, and ferment the oligosaccharides in human milk and thus support its ecological niche in the infant.

ADIPOSE TISSUE: EFFICIENCY OR DYSFUNCTION?

Adipose tissue is not a new theme of nutrition-related research. The importance of this dynamic tissue to metabolic health and disease has brought adipose to modern celebrity status. The attention is warranted by the dramatic increase in the global prevalence of obesity (Balkau et al. 2007). The variations in the development and consequences of obesity are due in part to the complex interactions of genetic predisposition (Bochukova et al. 2010, Cauchi et al. 2009, Cheung et al. 2010, Walters et al. 2010) and genetic-nutrient interactions (Garaulet et al. 2009, Warodomwichit et al. 2009). The burgeoning field of nutrigenomics has taken on a tremendous feat to discover interactions between genetic variation and diet to produce measurable phenotypes ultimately stratified into subject cohorts as responders and nonresponders to various food-based solutions. For example, carriers of the ADIPOQ -11391 G>A SNP had both lower BMI and risk of obesity when monounsaturated fat (MUFA) was $\geq 13\%$ of total energy intake. However, the effect of genetic variation on disease risk was not found in -11391A carriers in which MUFA intake was $<13\%$ of total energy (Warodomwichit et al. 2009). Intake of MUFA $\geq 13\%$ of total energy was associated with higher fasting plasma concentrations and HOMA-IR (a measurement of insulin resistance) individuals carrying the major allele rs4850704 CLOCK gene (Garaulet et al. 2009).

As the field of nutrigenomics offers great insight in the interactions between genes and diet, many challenges remain. Research in the field of nutrigenomics does not only require large and long validation studies necessary to identify all of the nutrient-gene interactions and their phenotypic outcomes. The clinical relevance attributed to the genetic causes of obesity is quite small and are not translatable to all individuals in the population (Cauchi et al. 2009, Cheung et al. 2010, Han et al. 2010, Wen et al. 2010). Obesity is a complex multifactorial metabolic disease such that its causes, and approaches for its treatment and prevention, will vary within the population. Nutrigenomics alone cannot identify all of the variation that determines metabolic responses to food. Metabolic regulation is a result of the complex interactions between genomics, metabolic phenotype, and environment—largely diet.

Attempts to elucidate gene-diet interactions have largely focused on composition, yet food structure influences the rate at which dietary composition—substrates and intermediates of metabolic pathways—flux into circulation and influence hormones and enzymes that regulate metabolic pathways. For example, a low- versus high-glycemic index dietary challenge administered after a bout of exercise increased the gene expression and protein levels of the fatty acid transporter (FAT/CD36) of skeletal muscle (Cheng et al. 2009), partially explaining how low-glycemic meals enhance fatty acid oxidation (Stevenson et al. 2009). Using an integrated 'omics approach, carbohydrate structure alters the serum metabolic profile, involving lysophosphatidylcholine species, and mRNA expression of stress reactions-related and adipose tissue differentiation-related genes in adipose tissue, demonstrating that high glycemic carbohydrates elicit proinflammatory responses involved in adversely altering insulin and glucose metabolism (Lankinen et al. 2010). Manufacturing foods that will target metabolic pathways of interest requires understanding how food composition and structure interact with the dynamic complexity of all metabolic processes.

SKELETAL MUSCLE: ARE ATHLETES BORN OR MADE?

Epidemiologic data show profound benefits of exercise to health, protection from disease, even longevity (Sun et al. 2010), yet this would seem paradoxical. If you want to increase the longevity of your car, you keep it in the garage. Why does moving your muscles improve the health of not only your muscle but apparently everything else? Skeletal muscle has been studied for its impact on multiple aspects of metabolism, physiology, and immunology. These studies provide interesting roles for skeletal muscle in everything from glucose clearance and diabetes protection to fat oxidation and protection from obesity. However, these are all acute effects. It took studies on organelle-biogenesis to reveal the mechanism behind long-term, systemic protection. The understanding of cellular responses to exercise links genetic regulation of mitochondria biogenesis to tissue protection (Handschin & Spiegelman 2008, Narkar et al. 2008). In effect, stimulation of muscle via exercise signals the transcription coactivator PGC1-α, which simultaneously controls the complete system of mitochondrial biogenesis and a variety of muscle phenotypic features (Calvo et al. 2008). In parallel, PGC1-α stimulates the expression of a wide range of genes that protect against precisely the consequences of mitochondrial activity and reactive oxygen (Handschin & Spiegelman 2008). In turn, the activity of these genes facilitates protection from a wide range of cellular toxins. Demonstrating this molecular mechanism, the single insertion of PGC1-α in a murine genetic model produces the same exercise protection from sarcopenia during aging without the exercise (Wenz et al. 2009).

NUTRIGENOMICS AND THE LIVER

Probing the liver's status with measures of its metabolic products has been a hallmark of diagnostics for decades (e.g., the measurement of plasma lipoprotein cholesterol as a marker of heart disease risk). How much variation is genuinely genetic, and how much is postgenomic and diet dependent? Several recent articles characterized the general effects of high-fat diets as well as the specific effects of individual fatty acids and plant-derived compounds on hepatic gene expression, particularly those involved in lipid metabolism. Researchers found a multiphasic adaptation response to high-fat feeding in a mouse model of obesity and metabolic syndrome, which was characterized by an inflammatory, lipotoxic early phase and a steatotic, adipogenic late phase (Radonjic et al. 2009). The inflammatory effects associated with the early phase were largely regulated by NFkβ, whereas the steatotic phase was largely mediated by PPARγ, suggesting two distinct transcriptional programs at work in the acute response compared with the chronic response to high-fat feeding in mouse liver. In rats, a long-term, high-fat diet was associated with greater weight gain, a greater increase in adiposity, and increased expression of metabolic genes in adipose tissue and muscle of female rats compared with male rats (Priego et al. 2008). In male rats, the increased expressions of

PPARα and CPT1 in the liver were associated with higher liver triglyceride content and higher blood insulin compared with female rats, suggesting gender-related differences in fuel partitioning between the major metabolic organs in response to high-fat feeding in rats. Researchers also found that longer-chain, more unsaturated fatty acids had much stronger effects on gene expression in mouse liver than did shorter-chain, more saturated fatty acids, which were mostly mediated by PPARα (Sanderson et al. 2008).

A number of recent nutrigenomic studies have revealed important features of metabolic regulation mediated by PPARs. PPARα is known to be responsive to dietary fatty acids, but recent evidence points to its sister transcription factor, PPARβ/δ, as the sensor of plasma-free fatty acids in the liver. Researchers showed that transcriptional activation of PPARβ/δ genes Lpin2, a gene involved in lipid metabolism, followed plasma-free fatty acid concentrations, whereas this was not the case for PPARα (Sanderson et al. 2009). A more recent study by the same group further showed that PPARβ/δ deletion resulted in upregulation of pathways related to innate immunity and inflammation, and downregulation of pathways related to lipoprotein metabolism and glucose utilization, which was correlated with increased plasma glucose and triglycerides (Sanderson et al. 2010).

In contrast to the metabolic response of dietary fats alone, consumption of grape seed proanthocyanidins on the background of a high-fat diet attenuated the increased expression of hepatic genes related to lipogenesis and lipoprotein secretion, and normalized plasma triglycerides and LDL-cholesterol in rats (Quesada et al. 2009). Grape seed flavonoids were also found to regulate the expression of genes involved in oxidative stress (Puiggros et al. 2009). Sesame seed lignans, however, increased the expression of genes involved in fatty acid oxidation in male rats, as well as increasing the expression of other proteins involved in fatty acid transport (Ide et al. 2009).

PERSONALIZING HEALTH AND NUTRITION

The ultimate goal of personalizing nutrition is to enable each individual to be guided by predictive knowledge of their personal health to diets that prevent disease and maximize health potential. To achieve such a goal, the science needed will extend from new accurate and predictive measures of health based on molecular signatures of metabolites, proteins, transcripts, genes, and microbiota (Panagiotou & Nielsen 2009). The need for personalized nutrition is derived from the recognition that people are metabolically, physiologically, and genetically different and therefore have different responses to food compounds (Panagiotou & Nielsen 2009). These differences are not just genetic but also extend to age, current lifestyle, and prior lifestyle (Zivkovic et al. 2009). For example, it is clear that the diet of an elderly person should be different than the diet of an elite athlete, as these two groups have unique needs and requirements. The differences between individuals are not simply a reflection of acute needs for fuel and protection.

The increasing incidence of diet-related metabolic disorders such as obesity, being overweight, hypertension, and diabetes in Western populations, although considered epidemic, are affecting the population differently and indeed some populations appear unaffected (Alberti 2001, Watzke & German 2009). Hence, the health and economic cost of noncontagious disease has made the need for a more personalized approach to nutrition particularly apparent. Personalization of aspects of diet as simple as total caloric intake are needed, as research shows that for many, their diets today are unbalanced simply in terms of calories and macronutrients (Popkin 2006, Watzke & German 2009). Despite the visible effects of an unbalanced diet and individual awareness of the problem, people continue to struggle with changing their health trajectories (Petrovici & Ritson 2006, Watzke & German 2009). The question for the entire agriculture and health sector, however, from consumers to industries, from health regulators to educators, is how do you personalize this massive global enterprise?

THE COMMERCIALIZATION OF PERSONALIZED DIETS

Achieving personal health will require that entire diets are personal not just occasional foods. This means that at the most basic level nutritional needs are integrated in some way with all foods consumed in a day. Entire diet plans that deliver all foods in a day to each individual match this nutritional need, but such approaches destroy the traditional joy of the diversity in the open food marketplace and are unlikely to be sustainable for this reason alone. Knowledge-based foods systems that combine the ability to formulate dietary needs for each individual and yet allow for personal choices are needed. Once basic nutritional needs are met, opportunities to providing for the more personal aspirations for health will invariably arrive. Developing diets based on individual metabolic, performance, and even cognitive needs are first steps, and food products and devices are already reaching the marketplace. The substantial research accomplishments in genetic diversity of humans will be valuable, but likely only for a subset of consumers for whom genotype is particularly predictive. Food companies have created diets for such individuals based on genetic analysis of up to 30 gene polymorphisms (McCabe-Sellers et al. 2009). This technology allows individuals to make meal choices and produce this meal from basic ingredients.

Sensation is food's greatest asset. Food is critical to one's quality of life, and the freedom to choose foods that we each find delicious is synonymous with success at every socioeconomic level. The food marketplace is driven by personal choice. And, from a nutrition perspective, sensation drives compliance. Individuals, whose diets are imbalanced, still find that foods that make up the diet are attractive. How can these disparate forces be reconciled? How can the foods that are most personally healthy be most personally delicious? Is it even possible? From a biological perspective, only the sensation of taste is innate (Chandrashekar et al. 2006). That is, we are born liking the tastes of sweet, salty, and umami and born disliking bitter and sour. These taste preferences are thought to be the logical drivers of nutrition (essential fuel, salt, amino acids, and toxicity), secondary plant metabolites, and spoilage (Hevezi et al. 2009, Liman 2006). The balance of sensory preferences—olfaction, texture, and sound—are almost completely learned (Beauchamp & Mennella 2009). That is, however delightful or repulsive you find a particular aroma, you have personally acquired that preference within your lifetime. Scientific research is rapidly building a detailed mechanistic understanding of these innate and learned processes and how they differ and how different commodities interact with these sensations (Crowhurst et al. 2008). Understanding the sensation of foods and the variation in human responses is providing clues to how particular individuals self-select inappropriate diets (Garcia-Bailo et al. 2009). An obvious next step is to simultaneously match genetic health needs with sensory preferences into organoleptic-based, personalized foods.

CONCLUSION

The nutritional status of humans remains a major challenge for public health agencies, clinical practices, and the food industry, as people around the world are suffering diet-related illness due to inappropriate food choices and lifestyles. Routine assessment could provide the means to recognize individual variations in nutritional status, but a merging of scientific knowledge and commercial innovation will be needed to bring such assessment to practice. Technologies of assessment from genotyping to metabolomics and imaging to activity measurement are bringing diagnostic sciences to health practice. Engineering innovations are actively developing analytical platforms capable of providing these measures fast and cheap in accessible biological fluids. In parallel, the scientific community is beginning to apply these tools to annotating how these genetic, metabolic, and physiological profiles differ in individuals according to their health. Electronic databases are being designed to house the results of this initiative as public knowledge resources. The first generations of these innovations are likely to be in more acute health problems. For example, the dysregulations in hepatic lipid metabolism are at the center of a new diet-disease paradigm (metabolic syndrome, type 2 diabetes, obesity) and are amenable to a first generation of personalizing health through metabolic assessment. The first proofs of principle building the knowledge to bring actionable diagnostics to food and diet practice are now appearing. In time, personalizing diets to enable each individual to achieve their own aspirations for health will realize a major change in the human condition. We will look back and ask what took so long?

DISCLOSURE STATEMENT

The authors are not aware of any affiliations, memberships, funding, or financial holdings that might be perceived as affecting the objectivity of this review.

ACKNOWLEDGMENTS

This publication was made possible in part by support from the University of California Discovery Program (05GEB01NHB), the National Institute of Environmental Health Sciences (P42ES004699), the California Dairy Research Foundation, and the CHARGE study (P01 ES11269).

LITERATURE CITED

Affolter M, Grass L, Vanrobaeys F, Casado B, Kussmann M. 2010. Qualitative and quantitative profiling of the bovine milk fat globule membrane proteome. *J. Proteomics* 73:1079–88

Agrawal GK, Jwa N-S, Lebrun M-H, Job D, Rakwal R. 2010. Plant secretome: unlocking secrets of the secreted proteins. *Proteomics* 10:799–827

Alberti G. 2001. Noncommunicable diseases: tomorrow's pandemics. *Bull. WHO* 79:907

Allen KJ, Martin PE. 2010. Clinical aspects of pediatric food allergy and failed oral immune tolerance. *J. Clin. Gastroenterol.* 44:391–401

Anastasio M, Pepe O, Cirillo T, Palomba S, Blaiotta G, Villani F. 2010. Selection and use of phytate-degrading LAB to improve cereal-based products by mineral solubilization during dough fermentation. *J. Food Sci.* 75:M28–35

Auclair S, Milenkovic D, Besson C, Chauvet S, Gueux E, et al. 2009. Catechin reduces atherosclerotic lesion development in apo E-deficient mice: a transcriptomic study. *Atherosclerosis* 204(2):e21–27

Baiges I, Palmfeldt J, Bladé C, Gregersen N, Arola L. 2010. Lipogenesis is decreased by grape seed proanthocyanidins according to liver proteomics of rats fed a high fat diet. *Mol. Cell. Proteomics* 9:1499–513

Bakker G, van Erk M, Pellis L, Wopereis S, Rubingh C, et al. 2010. An antiinflammatory dietary mix modulates inflammation and oxidative and metabolic stress in overweight men: a nutrigenomics approach. *Am. J. Clin. Nutr.* 91:1044–59

Balkau B, Deanfield JE, Després J-P, Bassand J-P, Fox KA, et al. 2007. International Day for the Evaluation of Abdominal Obesity (IDEA): a study of waist circumference, cardiovascular disease, and diabetes mellitus in 168,000 primary care patients in 63 countries. *Circulation* 116:1942–51

Barve A, Khor T, Nair S, Lin W, Yu S, et al. 2008. Pharmacogenomic profile of soy isoflavone concentrate in the prostate of Nrf2 deficient and wild-type mice. *J. Pharm. Sci.* 97:4528–45

Beauchamp GK, Mennella JA. 2009. Early flavor learning and its impact on later feeding behavior. *J. Pediatr. Gastroenterol. Nutr.* 48(Suppl. 1):S25–30

Benus RFJ, van der Werf TS, Welling GW, Judd PA, Taylor MA, et al. 2010. Association between *Faecalibacterium prausnitzii* and dietary fibre in colonic fermentation in healthy human subjects. *Br. J. Nutr.* 29:1–8

Bernini P, Bertini I, Luchinat C, Nepi S, Saccenti E, et al. 2009. Individual human phenotypes in metabolic space and time. *J. Proteome Res* 8:4264–71

Bochukova EG, Huang N, Keogh J, Henning E, Purmann C, et al. 2010. Large, rare chromosomal deletions associated with severe early-onset obesity. *Nature* 463:666–70

Bovine Genome Seq. Anal. Consort., Elsik CG, Tellam RL, Worley KC, Gibbs RA, Muzny DM, et al. 2009. The genome sequence of taurine cattle: a window to ruminant biology and evolution. *Science* 324:522–28

Braun DR, Harris JWK, Levin NE, McCoy JT, Herries AIR, et al. 2010. Early hominin diet included diverse terrestrial and aquatic animals 1.95 Ma in East Turkana, Kenya. *Proc. Natl. Acad. Sci. USA* 107:10002–7

Brouns R, Ursem N, Lindemans J, Hop W, Pluijm S, et al. 2008. Polymorphisms in genes related to folate and cobalamin metabolism and the associations with complex birth defects. *Prenat. Diagn.* 28:485–93

Burdge G. 2004. α-Linolenic acid metabolism in men and women: nutritional and biological implications. *Curr. Opin. Clin. Nutr. Metab. Care* 7:137–44

Büscher J, Czernik D, Ewald J, Sauer U, Zamboni N. 2009. Cross-platform comparison of methods for quantitative metabolomics of primary metabolism. *Anal. Chem.* 81:2135–43

Calvani R, Miccheli A, Capuani G, Tomassini Miccheli A, Puccetti C, et al. 2010. Gut microbiome-derived metabolites characterize a peculiar obese urinary metabotype. *Int. J. Obes.* 34:1095–98

Calvo JA, Daniels TG, Wang X, Paul A, Lin J, et al. 2008. Muscle-specific expression of PPARγ coactivator-1 α improves exercise performance and increases peak oxygen uptake. *J. Appl. Physiol.* 104(5):1304–12

Candela M, Maccaferri S, Turroni S, Carnevali P, Brigidi P. 2010. Functional intestinal microbiome, new frontiers in prebiotic design. *Int. J. Food Microbiol.* 140:93–101

Cani PD, Lecourt E, Dewulf EM, Sohet FM, Pachikian BD, et al. 2009. Gut microbiota fermentation of prebiotics increases satietogenic and incretin gut peptide production with consequences for appetite sensation and glucose response after a meal. *Am. J. Clin. Nutr.* 90:1236–43

Carmody RN, Wrangham RW. 2009. Cooking and the human commitment to a high-quality diet. *Cold Spring Harb. Symp. Quant. Biol.* 74:427–34

Carriquiry M, Weber WJ, Fahrenkrug SC, Crooker BA. 2009. Hepatic gene expression in multiparous Holstein cows treated with bovine somatotropin and fed n-3 fatty acids in early lactation. *J. Dairy Sci.* 92:4889–900

Carroll IM, Threadgill DW, Threadgill DS. 2009. The gastrointestinal microbiome: a malleable, third genome of mammals. *Mamm. Genome* 20:395–403

Caspi A, Williams B, Kim-Cohen J, Craig IW, Milne BJ, et al. 2007. Moderation of breastfeeding effects on the IQ by genetic variation in fatty acid metabolism. *Proc. Natl. Acad. Sci. USA* 104:18860–65

Cauchi S, Stutzmann F, Cavalcanti-Proença C, Durand E, Pouta A, et al. 2009. Combined effects of MC4R and FTO common genetic variants on obesity in European general populations. *J. Mol. Med.* 87:537–46

Chandrashekar J, Hoon MA, Ryba NJP, Zuker CS. 2006. The receptors and cells for mammalian taste. *Nature* 444:288–94

Cheng H-W. 2010. Breeding of tomorrow's chickens to improve well-being. *Poult. Sci.* 89:805–13

Cheng IS, Liao SF, Liu KL, Liu HY, Wu CL, et al. 2009. Effect of dietary glycemic index on substrate transporter gene expression in human skeletal muscle after exercise. *Eur. J. Clin. Nutr.* 63:1404–10

Cheung CY, Tso AW, Cheung BM, Xu A, Ong KL, et al. 2010. Obesity susceptibility genetic variants identified from recent genome-wide association studies: implications in a Chinese population. *J. Clin. Endocrinol. Metab.* 95:1395–403

Clarke TB, Davis KM, Lysenko ES, Zhou AY, Yu Y, Weiser JN. 2010. Recognition of peptidoglycan from the microbiota by Nod1 enhances systemic innate immunity. *Nat. Med.* 16:228–31

Collins FS, Green ED, Guttmacher AE, Guyer MS. 2003. A vision for the future of genomics research. *Nature* 422:835–47

Cotton RGH. 2007. Recommendations of the 2006 Human Variome Project meeting. *Nat. Genet.* 39:433–36

Cravatt BF, Simon GM, Yates JR 3rd. 2007. The biological impact of mass-spectrometry-based proteomics. *Nature* 450:991–1000

Crowhurst RN, Gleave AP, MacRae EA, Ampomah-Dwamena C, Atkinson RG, et al. 2008. Analysis of expressed sequence tags from Actinidia: applications of a cross species EST database for gene discovery in the areas of flavor, health, color and ripening. *BMC Genomics* 9:351

Crujeiras AB, Parra D, Milagro FI, Goyenechea E, Larrarte E, et al. 2008. Differential expression of oxidative stress and inflammation related genes in peripheral blood mononuclear cells in response to a low-calorie diet: a nutrigenomics study. *OMICS: J. Integr. Biol.* 12:251–61

Cui K, Huang J, Xing Y, Yu S, Xu C, Peng S. 2008. Mapping QTLs for seedling characteristics under different water supply conditions in rice (*Oryza sativa*). *Physiol. Plant.* 132:53–68

Deshmukh R, Singh A, Jain N, Anand S, Gacche R, et al. 2010. Identification of candidate genes for grain number in rice (*Oryza sativa* L.). *Funct. Integr. Genomics* 10:339–47

Dettmer K, Aronov PA, Hammock BD. 2007. Mass spectrometry-based metabolomics. *Mass Spectrom. Rev.* 26:51–78

Domínguez C, Cabrera L, Rodríguez P, Borges Á, Carrillo F, et al. 2010. Association between glycemic index, glycemic load, and fructose with insulin resistance: the CDC of the Canary Islands study. *Eur. J. Nutr.* Online First: 1–8

Eaton SB, Konner MJ, Cordain L. 2010. Diet-dependent acid load, Paleolithic nutrition, and evolutionary health promotion. *Am. J. Clin. Nutr.* 91:295–97

EFSA (Eur. Food Saf. Auth.). 2008. Panel Working Group on Animal Feeding Trials (2008) Safety and nutritional assessment of GM plants and derived food and feed: the role of animal feeding trials. *Food Chem. Toxicol.* 46:2–70

Ericson UC, Ivarsson MI, Sonestedt E, Gullberg B, Carlson J, et al. 2009. Increased breast cancer risk at high plasma folate concentrations among women with the MTHFR 677T allele. *Am. J. Clin. Nutr.* 90:1380–89

Ferguson JF, Phillips CM, McMonagle J, Pérez-Martínez P, Shaw DI, et al. 2010. NOS3 gene polymorphisms are associated with risk markers of cardiovascular disease, and interact with omega-3 polyunsaturated fatty acids. *Atherosclerosis* 211:539–44

Ford E, Simmons H. 2008. Gluconeogenesis from caecal propionate in the horse. *Br. J. Nutr.* 53:55–60

Forsythe IJ, Wishart DS. 2009. Exploring human metabolites using the human metabolome database. *Curr. Protocols Bioinforma.* 25:14.8-1–45

Friso S, Choi SW. 2002. Gene-nutrient interactions and DNA methylation. *J. Nutr.* 132(Suppl. 8):S2382–87

Froehlich JW, Dodds EE, Barboza M, McJimpsey EL, Seipert RR, et al. 2010. Glycoprotein expression in human milk during lactation. *J. Agric. Food Chem.* 58:6440–48

Fu Q, Zhang P, Tan L, Zhu Z, Ma D, et al. 2010. Analysis of QTLs for yield-related traits in Yuanjiang common wild rice (*Oryza rufipogon Griff.*). *J. Genet. Genomics* 37:147–57

Fukasawa T, Kamei A, Watanabe Y, Koga J, Abe K. 2010. Short-chain fructooligosaccharide regulates hepatic peroxisome proliferator-activated receptor α and farnesoid X receptor target gene expression in rats. *J. Agric. Food Chem.* 58:7007–12

Galván-Portillo M, Oñate-Ocaña LF, Pérez-Pérez GI, Chen J, Herrera-Goepfert R, et al. 2009. Dietary folate and vitamin B12 intake before diagnosis decreases gastric cancer mortality risk among susceptible MTHFR 677TT carriers. *Nutrition* 26:201–8

Gálvez A, Abriouel H, Benomar N, Lucas R. 2010. Microbial antagonists to food-borne pathogens and biocontrol. *Curr. Opin. Biotechnol.* 21:142–48

Garaulet M, Lee YC, Shen J, Parnell LD, Arnett DK, et al. 2009. CLOCK genetic variation and metabolic syndrome risk: modulation by monounsaturated fatty acids. *Am. J. Clin. Nutr.* 90:1466–75

Garcia-Bailo B, Toguri C, Eny KM, El-Sohemy A. 2009. Genetic variation in taste and its influence on food selection. *OMICS: J. Integr. Biol.* 13:69–80

German JB, Roberts MA, Watkins SM. 2003. Personal metabolomics as a next generation nutritional assessment. *J. Nutr.* 133:4260–66

Glatz JF, Turner PR, Katan MB, Stalenhoef AF, Lewis B. 1993. Hypo- and hyperresponse of serum cholesterol level and low density lipoprotein production and degradation to dietary cholesterol in man. *Ann. N.Y. Acad. Sci.* 676:163–79

Gluckman P, Hanson M, Buklijas T, Low F, Beedle A. 2009. Epigenetic mechanisms that underpin metabolic and cardiovascular diseases. *Nat. Rev. Endocrinol.* 5:401–8

Gohil R, Peck G, Sharma P. 2009. The genetics of venous thromboembolism. A meta-analysis involving ~120,000 cases and 180,000 controls. *Thromb. Haemost.* 102:360–70

Han X, Luo Y, Ren Q, Zhang X, Wang F, et al. 2010. Implication of genetic variants near SLC30A8, HHEX, CDKAL1, CDKN2A/B, IGF2BP2, FTO, TCF2, KCNQ1, and WFS1 in type 2 diabetes in a Chinese population. *BMC Med. Genet.* 11:81

Handschin C, Spiegelman B. 2008. The role of exercise and PGC1 in inflammation and chronic disease. *Nature* 454:463–69

Harvey L, McArdle H. 2008. Biomarkers of copper status: a brief update. *Br. J. Nutr.* 99:10–13

Hathout Y. 2007. Approaches to the study of the cell secretome. *Expert Rev. Proteomics* 4:239–48

Hesketh J. 2008. Nutrigenomics and selenium: gene expression patterns, physiological targets, and genetics. *Annu. Rev. Nutr.* 28:157–77

Hevezi P, Moyer BD, Lu M, Gao N, White E, et al. 2009. Genome-wide analysis of gene expression in primate taste buds reveals links to diverse processes. *PLoS One* 4:e6395

Hildebrandt M, Hoffmann C, Sherrill-Mix S, Keilbaugh S, Hamady M, et al. 2009. High-fat diet determines the composition of the murine gut microbiome independently of obesity. *Gastroenterology* 137:1716–24

Hindorff LA, Sethupathy P, Junkins HA, Ramos EM, Mehta JP, et al. 2009. Potential etiologic and functional implications of genome-wide association loci for human diseases and traits. *Proc. Natl. Acad. Sci. USA* 106:9362–67

Hofman MK, Weggemans RM, Zock PL, Schouten EG, Katan MB, Princen HM. 2004. CYP7A1 A-278C polymorphism affects the response of plasma lipids after dietary cholesterol or cafestol interventions in humans. *J. Nutr.* 134:2200–4

Holmes E, Wilson ID, Nicholson JK. 2008. Metabolic phenotyping in health and disease. *Cell* 134:714–17

Hulgan T, Tebas P, Canter J, Mulligan K, Haas D, et al. 2008. Hemochromatosis gene polymorphisms, mitochondrial haplogroups, and peripheral lipoatrophy during antiretroviral therapy. *J. Infect. Dis.* 197:858–66

Hustad S, Nedrebø BG, Ueland PM, Schneede J, Vollset SE, et al. 2004. Phenotypic expression of the methylenetetrahydrofolate reductase 677C- > T polymorphism and flavin cofactor availability in thyroid dysfunction. *Am. J. Clin. Nutr.* 80:1050–57

Ide T, Nakashima Y, Iida H, Yasumoto S, Katsuta M. 2009. Lipid metabolism and nutrigenomics–impact of sesame lignans on gene expression profiles and fatty acid oxidation in rat liver. *Forum Nutr.* 61:10–24

Ilanne-Parikka P, Laaksonen DE, Eriksson JG, Lakka TA, Lindström J, et al. 2010. Leisure-time physical activity and the metabolic syndrome in the Finnish diabetes prevention study. *Diabetes Care* 33:1610–17

Issaq HJ, Van QN, Waybright TJ, Muschik GM, Veenstra TD. 2009. Analytical and statistical approaches to metabolomics research. *J. Sep. Sci.* 32:2183–99

Joffe Y, van der Merwe L, Carstens M, Collins M, Jennings C, et al. 2010. Tumor necrosis factor-alpha gene-308 G/A polymorphism modulates the relationship between dietary fat intake, serum lipids, and obesity risk in black South African women. *J. Nutr.* 140:901–7

Jönsson T, Granfeldt Y, Ahrén B, Branell U-C, Pålsson G, et al. 2009. Beneficial effects of a Paleolithic diet on cardiovascular risk factors in type 2 diabetes: a randomized cross-over pilot study. *Cardiovasc. Diabetol.* 8:35

Kallio P, Kolehmainen M, Laaksonen DE, Kekäläinen J, Salopuro T, et al. 2007. Dietary carbohydrate modification induces alterations in gene expression in abdominal subcutaneous adipose tissue in persons with the metabolic syndrome: the FUNGENUT Study. *Am. J. Clin. Nutr.* 85:1417–27

Kanwar J, Kanwar R, Sun X, Punj V, Matta H, et al. 2009. Molecular and biotechnological advances in milk proteins in relation to human health. *Curr. Protein Pept. Sci.* 10:308–38

Katz-Jaffe MG, McReynolds S, Gardner DK, Schoolcraft WB. 2009. The role of proteomics in defining the human embryonic secretome. *Mol. Hum. Reprod.* 15:271–77

Kim KC, Friso S, Choi SW. 2009. DNA methylation, an epigenetic mechanism connecting folate to healthy embryonic development and aging. *J. Nutr. Biochem.* 20:917–26

Kogel KH, Voll LM, Schäfer P, Jansen C, Wu Y, et al. 2010. Transcriptome and metabolome profiling of field-grown transgenic barley lack induced differences but show cultivar-specific variances. *Proc. Natl. Acad. Sci. USA* 107:6198–203

Kolberg JA, Jørgensen T, Gerwien RW, Hamren S, McKenna MP, et al. 2009. Development of a type 2 diabetes risk model from a panel of serum biomarkers from the Inter99 cohort. *Diabetes Care* 32:1207–12

Konstantinidou V, Covas MI, Muñoz-Aguayo D, Khymenets O, de la Torre R, et al. 2010. In vivo nutrigenomic effects of virgin olive oil polyphenols within the frame of the Mediterranean diet: a randomized controlled trial. *FASEB J.* 24:2546–57

Laaksonen MM, Outila TA, Kärkkäinen MU, Kemi VE, Rita HJ, et al. 2009. Associations of vitamin D receptor, calcium-sensing receptor and parathyroid hormone gene polymorphisms with calcium homeostasis and peripheral bone density in adult Finns. *J. Nutrigenet. Nutrigenomics* 2:55–63

Lagaert S, Beliën T, Volckaert G. 2009. Plant cell walls: protecting the barrier from degradation by microbial enzymes. *Semin. Cell Dev. Biol.* 20:1064–73

Lankinen M, Schwab U, Gopalacharyulu PV, Seppänen-Laakso T, Yetukuri L, et al. 2010. Dietary carbohydrate modification alters serum metabolic profiles in individuals with the metabolic syndrome. *Nutr. Metab. Cardiovasc. Dis.* 20:249–57

Lemay D, Lynn D, Martin W, Neville M, Casey T, et al. 2009. The bovine lactation genome: insights into the evolution of mammalian milk. *Genome Biol.* 10:R43

Leung WC, Hessel S, Meplan C, Flint J, Oberhauser V, et al. 2009. Two common single nucleotide polymorphisms in the gene encoding beta-carotene 15,15′-monoxygenase alter {beta}-carotene metabolism in female volunteers. *FASEB J.* 23:1041–53

Lewis KD, Burton-Freeman BM. 2010. The role of innovation and technology in meeting individual nutritional needs. *J. Nutr.* 140:S26–36

Liman ER. 2006. Use it or lose it: molecular evolution of sensory signaling in primates. *Pflügers Arch. Eur. J. Physiol.* 453:125–31

LoCascio RG, Ninonuevo MR, Freeman SL, Sela DA, Grimm R, et al. 2007. Glycoprofiling of bifidobacterial consumption of human milk oligosaccharides demonstrates strain specific, preferential consumption of small chain glycans secreted in early human lactation. *J. Agric. Food Chem.* 55:8914–19

Lönnerdal B. 2006. Recombinant human milk proteins. *Nestlé Nutr. Workshop Ser. Pediatr. Program* 58:207–15

MacDonald T, Voessenkamper A, Di Sabatino A. 2009. Antigen presenting cells and T cell interactions in the gastrointestinal tract. *Mol. Nutr. Food Res.* 53:947–51

Mäkeläinen H, Hasselwander O, Rautonen N, Ouwehand A. 2009. Panose, a new prebiotic candidate. *Lett. Appl. Microbiol.* 49:666–72

Martin FP, Dumas ME, Wang Y, Legido-Quigley C, Yap IK, et al. 2007. A top-down systems biology view of microbiome-mammalian metabolic interactions in a mouse model. *Mol. Syst. Biol.* 3:112

Martinez I, Wallace G, Zhang C, Legge R, Benson AK, et al. 2009. Diet-induced metabolic improvements in a hamster model of hypercholesterolemia are strongly linked to alterations of the gut microbiota. *Appl. Environ. Microbiol.* 75:4175–84

Martinez JA, Corbalán MS, Sánchez-Villegas A, Forga L, Marti A, Martínez-González MA. 2003. Obesity risk is associated with carbohydrate intake in women carrying the Gln27Glu beta2-adrenoceptor polymorphism. *J. Nutr.* 133:2549–54

McCabe-Sellers B, Chenard C, Lovera D, Champagne C, Bogle M, Kaput J. 2009. Readiness of food composition databases and food component analysis systems for nutrigenomics. *J. Food Compos. Anal.* 22:S57–62

Mehedint MG, Niculescu MD, Craciunescu CN, Zeisel SH. 2010. Choline deficiency alters global histone methylation and epigenetic marking at the Re1 site of the calbindin 1 gene. *FASEB J.* 24:184–95

Messika A, Kaluski D, Lev E, Iakobishvili Z, Shohat M, et al. 2010. Nutrigenetic impact of daily folate intake on plasma homocysteine and folate levels in patients with different methylenetetrahydrofolate reductase genotypes. *Eur. J. Cardiovasc. Prev. Rehabil.* Published Ahead of Print: 10.1097/HJR.1090b1013e32833a32831cb32835

Miettinen TA, Kesäniemi Y. 1989. Cholesterol absorption: regulation of cholesterol synthesis and elimination and within-population variations of serum cholesterol levels. *Am. J. Clin. Nutr.* 49:629–35

Mikhak B, Hunter D, Spiegelman D, Platz E, Wu K, et al. 2008. Manganese superoxide dismutase (MnSOD) gene polymorphism, interactions with carotenoid levels and prostate cancer risk. *Carcinogenesis* 29:2335–40

Minihane AM. 2010. Fatty acid–genotype interactions and cardiovascular risk. *Prostaglandins Leukot. Essent. Fat. Acids* 82:259–64

Mischak H, Apweiler R, Banks RE, Conaway M, Coon J, et al. 2007. Clinical proteomics: a need to define the field and to begin to set adequate standards. *Proteomics Clin. Appl.* 1:148–56

Mok K, Pettersson J, Orrenius S, Svanborg C. 2007. HAMLET, protein folding, and tumor cell death. *Biochem. Biophys. Res. Commun.* 354:1–7

Montmayeur J-P, le Coutre J, eds. 2009. *Fat Detection: Taste, Texture, and Post Ingestive Effects*. Boca Raton, FL: CRC

Murase T, Haramizu S, Ota N, Hase T. 2008. Tea catechin ingestion combined with habitual exercise suppresses the aging-associated decline in physical performance in senescence-accelerated mice. *Am. J. Physiol. Regul. Integr. Comp. Physiol.* 295:R281

Narkar VA, Downes M, Yu RT, Embler E, Wang YX, et al. 2008. AMPK and PPARdelta agonists are exercise mimetics. *Cell* 134:405–15

Näslund J, Fikse WF, Pielberg GR, Lundén A. 2008. Frequency and effect of the bovine acyl-CoA: diacylglycerol acyltransferase 1 (DGAT1) K232A polymorphism in Swedish dairy cattle. *J. Dairy Sci.* 91:2127–34

Navarro-Allende A, Khataan N, El-Sohemy A. 2008. Impact of genetic and environmental determinants of taste with food preferences in older adults. *J. Nutrit. Elder.* 27:267–76

Neish AS. 2009. Microbes in gastrointestinal health and disease. *Gastroenterology* 136:65–80

Nguyen D, Arpat A, Wang N, Carroll R. 2002. DNA microarray experiments: biological and technological aspects. *Biometrics* 58:701–17

Ntalla I, Dedoussis G, Yannakoulia M, Smart M, Louizou E, et al. 2009. ADIPOQ gene polymorphism rs1501299 interacts with fibre intake to affect adiponectin concentration in children: the GENe–Diet Attica Investigation on childhood obesity. *Eur. J. Nutr.* 48:493–97

O'Keefe SJ. 2008. Nutrition and colonic health: the critical role of the microbiota. *Curr. Opin. Gastroenterol.* 24:51–58

Omenn GS. 2010. Evolution in health and medicine Sackler colloquium: evolution and public health. *Proc. Natl. Acad. Sci. USA* 107(Suppl. 1):1702–9

Ordovas JM. 2009. Genetic influences on blood lipids and cardiovascular disease risk: tools for primary prevention. *Am. J. Clin. Nutr.* 89:S1509–17

O'Sullivan TA, Bremner AP, O'Neill S, Lyons-Wall P. 2010. Comparison of multiple and novel measures of dietary glycemic carbohydrate with insulin resistant status in older women. *Nutr. Metab.* 7:25

Panagiotou G, Nielsen J. 2009. Nutritional systems biology: definitions and approaches. *Annu. Rev. Nutr.* 29:329–39

Papathanasopoulos A, Camilleri M. 2009. Dietary fiber supplements: effects in obesity and metabolic syndrome and relationship to gastrointestinal functions. *Gastroenterology* 138:65–72

Pavlou M, Diamandis E. 2010. The cancer cell secretome: A good source for discovering biomarkers? *J. Proteomics* 73(10):1896–1906

Peppa M, Koliaki C, Nikolopoulos P, Raptis SA. 2010. Skeletal muscle insulin resistance in endocrine disease. *J. Biomed. Biotechnol.* 2010:527850

Pérez-Martínez P, Pérez-Jiménez F, Bellido C, Ordovas JM, Moreno JA, et al. 2005. A polymorphism exon 1 variant at the locus of the scavenger receptor class B type I (SCARB1) gene is associated with differences in insulin sensitivity in healthy people during the consumption of an olive oil-rich diet. *J. Clin. Endocrinol. Metab.* 90:2297–300

Petrovici D, Ritson C. 2006. Factors influencing consumer dietary health preventative behaviours. *BMC Public Health* 6:222

Polesani M, Bortesi L, Ferrarini A, Zamboni A, Fasoli M, et al. 2010. General and species-specific transcriptional responses to downy mildew infection in a susceptible (*Vitis vinifera*) and a resistant (*V. riparia*) grapevine species. *BMC Genomics* 11:117

Popkin BM. 2006. Global nutrition dynamics: The world is shifting rapidly toward a diet linked with noncommunicable diseases. *Am. J. Clin. Nutr.* 84:289–98

Poutanen K, Flander L, Katina K. 2009. Sourdough and cereal fermentation in a nutritional perspective. *Food Microbiol.* 26:693–99

Prescott S, Smith P, Tang M, Palmer D, Sinn J, et al. 2008. The importance of early complementary feeding in the development of oral tolerance: concerns and controversies. *Pediatr. Allergy Immunol.* 19:375–80

Priego T, Sánchez J, Picó C, Palou A. 2008. Sex-differential expression of metabolism-related genes in response to a high-fat diet. *Obesity* 16:819–26

Puchau B, Zulet MA, de Echávarri AG, Hermsdorff HH, Martinez JA. 2009. Dietary total antioxidant capacity: a novel indicator of diet quality in healthy young adults. *J. Am. Coll. Nutr.* 28:648–56

Puiggros F, Sala E, Vaqué M, Ardévol A, Blay M, et al. 2009. In vivo, in vitro, and in silico studies of Cu/Zn-superoxide dismutase regulation by molecules in grape seed procyanidin extract. *J. Agric. Food Chem.* 57:3934–42

Quesada H, Del Bas J, Pajuelo D, Díaz S, Fernandez-Larrea J, et al. 2009. Grape seed proanthocyanidins correct dyslipidemia associated with a high-fat diet in rats and repress genes controlling lipogenesis and VLDL assembling in liver. *Int. J. Obes.* 33:1007–12

Radonjic M, de Haan JR, van Erk MJ, van Dijk KW, van den Berg SA, et al. 2009. Genome-wide mRNA expression analysis of hepatic adaptation to high-fat diets reveals switch from an inflammatory to steatotic transcriptional program. *PLoS One* 4:e6646

Reale A, Konietzny U, Coppola R, Sorrentino E, Greiner R. 2007. The importance of lactic acid bacteria for phytate degradation during cereal dough fermentation. *J. Agric. Food Chem.* 55:2993–97

Refsum H, Smith AD. 2008. Are we ready for mandatory fortification with vitamin B-12? *Am. J. Clin. Nutr.* 88:253–54

Regnier FE, Skates SJ, Mesri M, Rodriguez H, Tezak Z, et al. 2010. Protein-based multiplex assays: mock presubmissions to the U.S. Food and Drug Administration. *Clin. Chem.* 56:165–71

Rezzi S, Martin FP, Kochhar S. 2008. Defining personal nutrition and metabolic health through metabonomics. *Ernst Schering Found. Symp. Proc.* 4:251–64

Rifai N, Gillette M, Carr S. 2006. Protein biomarker discovery and validation: the long and uncertain path to clinical utility. *Nat. Biotechnol.* 24:971–83

Roy R, Ordovas L, Zaragoza P, Romero A, Moreno C, et al. 2006. Association of polymorphisms in the bovine FASN gene with milk-fat content. *Anim. Genet.* 37:215–18

Sanders ME, Marco ML. 2010. Food formats for effective delivery of probiotics. *Annu. Rev. Food Sci. Technol.* 1:65–85

Sanderson LM, Degenhardt T, Koppen A, Kalkhoven E, Desvergne B, et al. 2009. Peroxisome proliferator-activated receptor beta/delta (PPAR beta/delta) but not PPARalpha serves as a plasma free fatty acid sensor in liver. *Mol. Cell. Biol.* 29:6257–67

Sanderson LM, de Groot PJ, Hooiveld GJ, Koppen A, Kalkhoven E, et al. 2008. Effect of synthetic dietary triglycerides: a novel research paradigm for nutrigenomics. *PLoS One* 3:e1681

Sela DA, Chapman J, Adeuya A, Kim JH, Chen F, et al. 2008. The genome sequence of *Bifidobacterium longum* subsp. *infantis* reveals adaptations for milk utilization within the infant microbiome. *Proc. Natl. Acad. Sci. USA* 105:18964–69

Seow A, Yuan JM, Sun CL, Van Den Berg D, Lee HP, Yu MC. 2002. Dietary isothiocyanates, glutathione S-transferase polymorphisms and colorectal cancer risk in the Singapore Chinese Health Study. *Carcinogenesis* 23:2055–61

Sieuwerts S, de Bok FA, Hugenholtz J, van Hylckama Vlieg JE. 2008. Unraveling microbial interactions in food fermentations: from classical to genomics approaches. *Appl. Environ. Microbiol.* 74:4997–5007

Simopoulos A. 2010. Nutrigenetics/nutrigenomics. *Annu. Rev. Public Health* 31:53–68

Sinotte M, Diorio C, Bérubé S, Pollak M, Brisson J. 2009. Genetic polymorphisms of the vitamin D binding protein and plasma concentrations of 25-hydroxyvitamin D in premenopausal women. *Am. J. Clin. Nutr.* 89:634–40

Smilowitz JT, Wiest MM, Watkins SM, Teegarden D, Zemel MB, et al. 2009. Lipid metabolism predicts changes in body composition during energy restriction in overweight humans. *J. Nutr.* 139:222–29

Stevenson EJ, Astbury NM, Simpson EJ, Taylor MA, Macdonald IA. 2009. Fat oxidation during exercise and satiety during recovery are increased following a low-glycemic index breakfast in sedentary women. *J. Nutr.* 139:890–97

Suh JW, Baek SH, Park JS, Kang HJ, Chae IH, et al. 2009. Vitamin K epoxide reductase complex subunit 1 gene polymorphism is associated with atherothrombotic complication after drug-eluting stent implantation: 2-center prospective cohort study. *Am. Heart J.* 157:908–12

Sun Q, Townsend MK, Okereke OI, Franco OH, Hu FB, Grodstein F. 2010. Physical activity at midlife in relation to successful survival in women at age 70 years or older. *Arch. Intern. Med.* 170:194–201

Syvänen A. 2001. Accessing genetic variation: genotyping single nucleotide polymorphisms. *Nat. Rev. Genet.* 2:930–42

Tanaka T, Shen J, Abecasis GR, Kisialiou A, Ordovas JM, et al. 2009. Genome-wide association study of plasma polyunsaturated fatty acids in the InCHIANTI Study. *PLoS Genet.* 5:e1000338

Tang L, Wu JJ, Ma Q, Cui T, Andreopoulos FM, et al. 2010. Human lactoferrin stimulates skin keratinocyte function and wound re-epithelialization. *Br. J. Dermatol.* 163:38–47

Tang Z, Zhang Y, Stewart AF, Geng M, Tang X, et al. 2010. High-level expression, purification and antibacterial activity of bovine lactoferricin and lactoferrampin in *Photorhabdus luminescens*. *Protein Expr. Purif.* 73:132–39

Thalacker-Mercer AE, Fleet JC, Craig BA, Campbell WW. 2010. The skeletal muscle transcript profile reflects accommodative responses to inadequate protein intake in younger and older males. *J. Nutr. Biochem.* Epub ahead of print

Turnbaugh PJ, Gordon JI. 2009. The core gut microbiome, energy balance and obesity. *J. Physiol.* 587:4153–58

Turnbaugh PJ, Hamady M, Yatsunenko T, Cantarel BL, Duncan A, et al. 2008. A core gut microbiome in obese and lean twins. *Nature* 457:480–84

Turnbaugh PJ, Ley R, Hamady M, Fraser-Liggett C, Knight R, Gordon J. 2007. The human microbiome project. *Nature* 449:804–10

van Hulzen KJE, Sprong RC, Van Der Meer R, van Arendonk JAM. 2009. Genetic and nongenetic variation in concentration of selenium, calcium, potassium, zinc, magnesium, and phosphorus in milk of Dutch Holstein-Friesian cows. *J. Dairy Sci.* 92:5754–59

Venter JC, Adams MD, Myers EW, Li PW, Mural RJ, et al. 2001. The sequence of the human genome. *Science* 291:1304–51

Vijay-Kumar M, Aitken JD, Carvalho FA, Cullender TC, Mwangi S, et al. 2010. Metabolic syndrome and altered gut microbiota in mice lacking toll-like receptor 5. *Science* 328:228–31

Vinaixa M, Rodríguez M, Rull A, Beltrán R, Bladé C, et al. 2010. Metabolomic assessment of the effect of dietary cholesterol in the progressive development of fatty liver disease. *J. Proteome Res.* 9:2527–38

Vrieze A, Holleman F, Zoetendal E, de Vos WM, Hoekstra JB, Nieuwdorp M. 2010. The environment within: how gut microbiota may influence metabolism and body composition. *Diabetologia* 53:606–13

Walters R, Jacquemont S, Valsesia A, de Smith A, Martinet D, et al. 2010. A new highly penetrant form of obesity due to deletions on chromosome 16p11. 2. *Nature* 463:671–75

Wang J, Chen L, Li P, Li X, Zhou H, et al. 2008. Gene expression is altered in piglet small intestine by weaning and dietary glutamine supplementation. *J. Nutr.* 138:1025–32

Warodomwichit D, Shen J, Arnett DK, Tsai MY, Kabagambe EK, et al. 2009. ADIPOQ polymorphisms, monounsaturated fatty acids, and obesity risk: the GOLDN study. *Obesity* 17:510–17

Watzke HJ, German JB. 2009. Personalizing foods. In *An Integrated Approach to New Food Product Development*, ed. HR Moskowitz, S Saguy, T Straus, Chapter 9, pp. 133–73. Boca Raton, FL: CRC

Wells JCK, Stock JT. 2007. The biology of the colonizing ape. *Yearb. Phys. Anthropol.* 50:191–222

Wen J, Rönn T, Olsson A, Yang Z, Lu B, et al. 2010. Investigation of type 2 diabetes risk alleles support *CDKN2A/B*, *CDKAL1*, and *TCF7L2* as susceptibility genes in a Han Chinese cohort. *PLoS One* 5(2):e9153

Wenz T, Rossi SG, Rotundo RL, Spiegelman BM, Moraes CT. 2009. Increased muscle PGC-1α expression protects from sarcopenia and metabolic disease during aging. *Proc. Natl. Acad. Sci. USA* 106:20405–10

Wikoff WR, Anfora AT, Liu J, Schultz PG, Lesley SA, et al. 2009. Metabolomics analysis reveals large effects of gut microflora on mammalian blood metabolites. *Proc. Natl. Acad. Sci. USA* 106:3698–703

Winkels RM, Brouwer IA, Clarke R, Katan MB, Verhoef P. 2008. Bread cofortified with folic acid and vitamin B-12 improves the folate and vitamin B-12 status of healthy older people: a randomized controlled trial. *Am. J. Clin. Nutr.* 88:348–55

Winnike JH, Li Z, Wright FA, Macdonald JM, O'Connell TM, Watkins PB. 2010. Use of pharmacometabonomics for early prediction of acetaminophen-induced hepatotoxicity in humans. *Clin. Pharmacol. Ther.* 88:45–51

Yap IKS, Angley M, Veselkov KA, Holmes E, Lindon JC, Nicholson JK. 2010. Urinary metabolic phenotyping differentiates children with autism from their unaffected siblings and age-matched controls. *J. Proteome Res.* 9:2996–3004

Zavaleta N, Figueroa D, Rivera J, Sánchez J, Alfaro S, Lönnerdal B. 2007. Efficacy of rice-based oral rehydration solution containing recombinant human lactoferrin and lysozyme in Peruvian children with acute diarrhea. *J. Pediatr. Gastroenterol. Nutr.* 44:258–64

Zeisel SH. 2007. Nutrigenomics and metabolomics will change clinical nutrition and public health practice: insights from studies on dietary requirements for choline. *Am. J. Clin. Nutr.* 86:542–48

Zeisel SH. 2009. Epigenetic mechanisms for nutrition determinants of later health outcomes. *Am. J. Clin. Nutr.* 89:S1488–93

Zerhouni E. 2003. The NIH roadmap. *Science* 302:63–72

Zhang G, Gu C, Wang D. 2009. Molecular mapping of soybean aphid resistance genes in PI 567541B. *Theor. Appl. Genet.* 118:473–82

Zhang N, Yu S, Tiller P, Yeh S, Mahan E, Emary W. 2009. Quantitation of small molecules using high-resolution accurate mass spectrometers-a different approach for analysis of biological samples. *Rapid Commun. Mass Spectrom.* 23:1085–94

Zhang W, Dolan M. 2010. Impact of the 1000 Genomes Project on the next wave of pharmacogenomic discovery. *Pharmacogenomics* 11:249–56

Zivkovic AM, German JB. 2009. Metabolomics for assessment of nutritional status. *Curr. Opin. Clin. Nutr. Metab. Care* 12:501–7

Zivkovic AM, German JB, Lebrilla CB, Mills DA. 2010. Human milk glycobiome and its impact on the infant gastrointestinal microbiota. *Proc. Natl. Acad. Sci. USA* Epub ahead of print

Zivkovic AM, Wiest MM, Nguyen U, Nording ML, Watkins SM, German JB. 2009. Assessing individual metabolic responsiveness to a lipid challenge using a targeted metabolomic approach. *Metabolomics* 5:209–18

Influence of Formulation and Processing on Absorption and Metabolism of Flavan-3-Ols from Tea and Cocoa

Andrew P. Neilson[1,2] and Mario G. Ferruzzi[3,4]

[1]Department of Family Medicine, University of Michigan, Ann Arbor, Michigan 48109

[2]Comprehensive Cancer Center, University of Michigan, Ann Arbor, Michigan 48109

[3]Department of Food Science, Purdue University, West Lafayette, Indiana 47907

[4]Department of Foods and Nutrition, Purdue University, West Lafayette, Indiana 47907; email: mferruzz@purdue.edu

Annu. Rev. Food Sci. Technol. 2011. 2:125–51

First published online as a Review in Advance on October 18, 2010

The *Annual Review of Food Science and Technology* is online at food.annualreviews.org

This article's doi:
10.1146/annurev-food-022510-133725

1941-1413/11/0410-0125$20.00

Keywords

catechins, bioavailability, bioaccessibility, digestion

Abstract

Flavan-3-ols are a major subclass of the class of plant phytochemicals known as flavonoids. Flavan-3-ols are commonly found in fruit, vegetable, and botanical products, including tea, cocoa, grapes, and apples. Both monomeric catechins and polymeric procyanidins are common in the diet, along with several derivatives produced by degradation of these species during processing. Both epidemiological and biological evidence suggests a health-protective role for dietary flavan-3-ols, leading to increased interest in the bioavailability of these compounds from foods. Flavan-3-ol bioavailability depends on numerous factors, including digestive release, absorption, metabolism, and elimination. In addition to these in vivo factors, the complexity of whole-food systems (physical form, flavan-3-ol form and dose, macronutrient and micronutrient profile, processing, etc.) influences the absorption efficiency and circulating profile of flavan-3-ols. An understanding of how food matrices may influence flavan-3-ol absorption will provide a framework to design and develop functional products that positively affect flavan-3-ol absorption and, by extension, potential bioactivity.

INTRODUCTION

Flavan-3-ols are polyphenols belonging to the broader class of plant phytochemicals known as flavonoids. Interest in flavonoids has intensified over the past decade due to the significant number of epidemiological associations linking flavonoid-rich diets with prevention of several chronic and degenerative diseases, including cancer (Neuhouser 2004), cardiovascular disorders (Ding et al. 2006), obesity, and diabetes (Nagao et al. 2009, Thielecke & Boschmann 2009), as well as neurodegenerative disorders (Mandel et al. 2005). Flavan-3-ols are a major subclass of flavonoids that includes monomeric catechins and polymeric procyanidins. This flavonoid subclass is believed to account for approximately 83.5% (~157 mg/d) of the total flavonoid consumption in the U.S. diet (estimated to be ~190 mg/day) (Chun et al. 2007), making flavan-3-ols a significant dietary flavonoid form. In addition to epidemiological associations and high dietary exposure, specific biological activities consistent with disease prevention have been reported for flavan-3-ols, including antioxidant activities (Fraga & Keen 2003), stimulation of endogenous antioxidant systems (Pietta & Simonetti 1998), stimulation of nitric oxide (NO) production and vasodilation (Grassi et al. 2006), regulation of xenobiotic-metabolizing enzymes (Moon et al. 2006), increased fatty acid oxidation and insulin sensitivity, and alteration of glucose absorption and utilization (Boschmann & Thielecke 2007).

With a growing body of epidemiological and biological evidence suggesting a protective role for dietary flavan-3-ols, interest in the bioavailability and metabolism of these compounds from foods and dietary supplements has expanded. Current knowledge of flavan-3-ol bioavailability from foods is variable (Manach et al. 2004, Williamson & Manach 2005) and dependent on numerous factors, including source and type of flavan-3-ol, interindividual variability in absorption, metabolism, and elimination (Feng 2006, Lambert et al. 2007). Although numerous studies have focused on flavan-3-ol absorption from pure compounds or refined extracts, knowledge of flavan-3-ol absorption from food remains limited. This is due, in part, to the complexity of whole-food systems and potential interactions between flavan-3-ols with specific macronutrients, micronutrients, or other food components that often complicate interpretations (Neilson et al. 2009, Peters et al. 2010, Roura et al. 2008, Schramm et al. 2003). A better understanding of flavan-3-ol absorption, metabolism, and tissue distribution from foods remains essential to understanding the role these flavonoids may play in prevention of chronic disease. Furthermore, understanding how the food matrix may influence flavan-3-ol absorption provides guidance in design and development of products to positively affect flavan-3-ol absorption.

In this context, the purpose of this review is to provide an overview of flavan-3-ol composition and bioavailability from tea and cocoa products, which are common dietary sources of these compounds. Key research describing the impact of processing on flavan-3-ol composition and bioavailability is described, including the impact of digestion, intestinal uptake, and metabolism on physiological flavan-3-ol profiles. Finally, the impact of specific food and beverage formulation factors on bioavailability of flavan-3-ols is discussed.

CLASSIFICATION OF FLAVAN-3-OLS

As a subclass of the flavonoid family, flavan-3-ols can be subdivided based upon degree of polymerization, oxidative state, and substitution pattern of the B- and C-rings (Beecher 2003, Heim et al. 2002). In this review, both monomeric and oligomeric flavan-3-ol forms are described.

Monomeric Flavan-3-ol (Catechins)

Five major monomeric flavan-3-ols, referred to as catechins, are found in the diet: (+)-catechin (C), (−)-epicatechin (EC), (−)-epigallocatechin (EGC), (−)-epicatechin gallate (ECG), and

(−)-epigallocatechin gallate (EGCG) (**Figure 1*a***) (Del Rio et al. 2004). Structurally, gallocatechins (EGC and EGCG) differ from catechins (C, EC, and ECG) by having a third B-ring hydroxyl group at C5′. Catechin gallates (EGCG and ECG) have a gallic acid residue esterified to the C3 hydroxyl. Due to the two chiral carbons in the C-ring (C2 and C3), multiple stereoisomers exist for each catechin. Oxidation of catechin monomers during processing results in formation of several products, including theaflavins (TFs) (**Figure 1*b***), theasinensins, and other polymers such as thearubigins and theabrownins (Menet et al. 2004, Tanaka et al. 2002).

Oligomeric Flavan-3-ols (Procyanidins and Proanthocyanidins)

In addition to monomers, more complex flavan-3-ols exist, including the procyanidins (PCs). The PCs are dimers (2 monomer residues), oligomers (3–7), and polymers (≥8) of flavan-3-ol monomers (Beecher 2003, Jeong & Kong 2004, Manach et al. 2004). Monomers are bonded by interflavan linkages between the C-ring of the first monomer and either the A- or C-ring of the next. B-type PCs have only one interflavan linkage (typically a C4→C8 or C4→C6 carbon-carbon bond) (**Figure 1*c***). A-type PCs have monomers joined by two interflavan linkages: the C4→C8 bond plus a C2→O→C7 ether bond (**Figure 1*d***) (Beecher 2003, Khanbabaee & van Ree 2001). C-type condensed tannins are trimeric B-type condensed tannins.

DIETARY SOURCES OF FLAVAN-3-OLS

Numerous reviews on flavonoid contents of foods have identified tea, cocoa, grapes, apples, and other fruits and vegetables as the predominant dietary sources of monomeric and complex flavan-3-ols (Manach et al. 2004, Scalbert & Williamson 2000).

Tea

Tea (brewed from leaves of *Camellia sinensis*) is one of the richest dietary sources of monomeric flavan-3-ols, accounting for up to 77% of flavonoid intake by adults in the United States (Chun et al. 2010). Various types of tea are consumed, which differ primarily in type and extent of leaf processing and, by extension, flavan-3-ol profiles. Green tea is a minimally processed (unfermented) tea product (Astill et al. 2001). In green tea leaf, catechins represent up to 85% of the total flavonoid content (Astill et al. 2001, Yao et al. 2005). On a wet-weight basis (wwb), total catechins levels in green tea have been reported between 4 and 140 mg g^{-1}. Extreme variability exists, arising from agroclimactic factors as well as between varieties, brands, and area of harvest (Friedman et al. 2005, Khokhar & Magnusdottir 2002). EGCG is most abundant (7–74 mg g^{-1} wwb), followed by EGC (0–55 mg g^{-1}), ECG (1–40.5 mg g^{-1}), EC (0.1–17 mg g^{-1}), and C (0–8 mg g^{-1}) (Friedman et al. 2005, Khokhar & Magnusdottir 2002, Lee et al. 2000). Traditional brewing of green tea with hot water generates infusions containing 50–540 mg per cup (approximately 8 oz or 236 mL) of total catechins (Bronner & Beecher 1998, Henning et al. 2003).

Black tea is produced from the same botanical material as green tea but differs in that the leaf is highly processed by natural oxidative enzymes present in the leaf, including polyphenol oxidase and peroxidase. Known as fermentation, this processing significantly alters the flavonoid profile (Astill et al. 2001). Specifically, oxidation of catechin monomers results in generation of complex products, including theaflavin (TF), TF-monogallate (TFMG), TF-digallate (TFDG), theasinensins, and thearubigins, which provide characteristic color and flavor to black tea (Bailey et al. 1992, Menet et al. 2004, Tanaka et al. 2002). Although the extent of fermentation varies significantly (between products and regions), generally, monomer oxidation (particularly EGCG

a

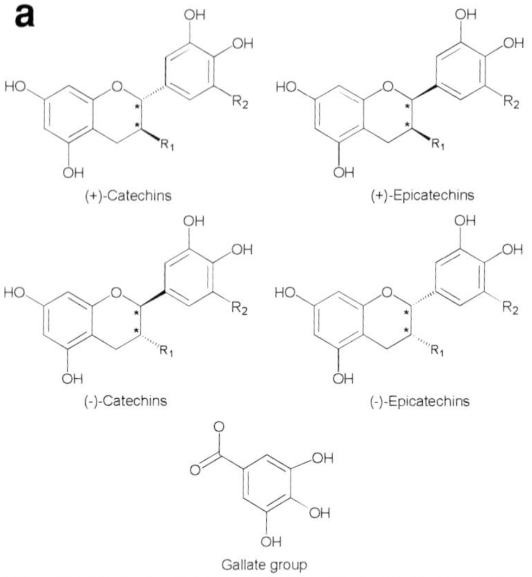

C3 Configuration	Compound	Abbreviation	R_1	R_2
(+) or (−)	Catechin	C	OH	H
(+) or (−)	Gallocatechin	GC	OH	OH
(+) or (−)	Catechin gallate	CG	Gallate	H
(+) or (−)	Gallocatechin gallate	GCG	Gallate	OH
(+) or (−)	Epicatechin	EC	OH	H
(+) or (−)	Epigallocatechin	EGC	OH	OH
(+) or (−)	Epicatechin gallate	ECG	Gallate	H
(+) or (−)	Epigalocatechin gallate	EGCG	Gallate	OH

b

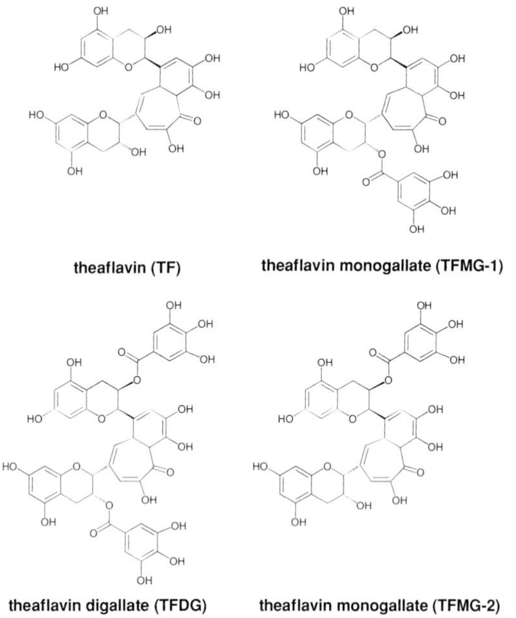

c

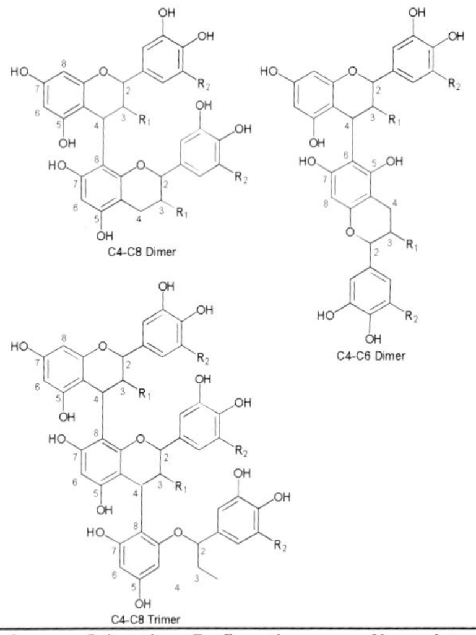

Bond	Orientation	Configuration	Nomenclature
C4-C8 (interflavan)		β	monomer$_1$-(4β→8)-monomer$_2$
		α	monomer$_1$-(4α→8)-monomer$_2$
C4-C6 (interflavan)		β	monomer$_1$-(4β→6)-monomer$_2$
		α	monomer$_1$-(4α→6)-monomer$_2$

d

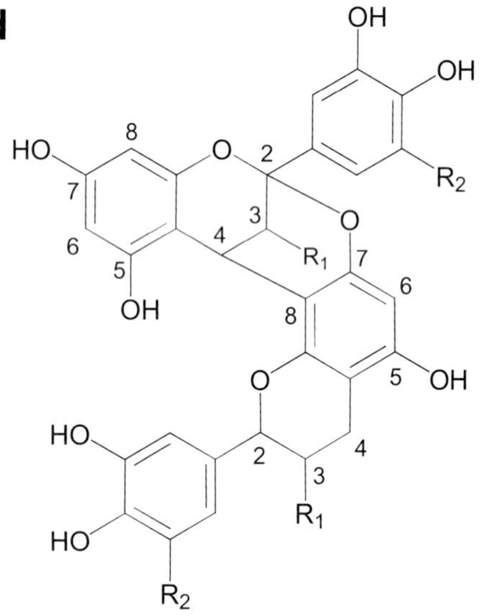

C4-C8, C2-O-C7 Dimer

Bond	Orientation	Configuration	Nomenclature
C2-C7 (interflavan)		β	monomer$_1$-(2β→O→7)-monomer$_2$
		α	monomer$_1$-(2α→O→7)-monomer$_2$

and EGC) reduces the levels of catechins relative to green tea. Levels of total catechins in black tea leaf range widely from 5–110 mg g^{-1} wwb, with theaflavins present at 5–21 mg g^{-1} wwb (Friedman et al. 2005, Wright et al. 2002). EGCG (0.5–47 mg g^{-1} wwb) and ECG (2–67 mg g^{-1} wwb) are the most abundant catechins in black tea, followed by EGC (0–10 mg g^{-1} wwb) and EC (0.4–7 mg g^{-1} wwb). Individual theaflavin species (TF, TFMG, and TFDG) are typically present at similar levels in black tea (Friedman et al. 2005, 2006). Brewing of black tea generates beverages containing between 50 and 370 mg per cup total catechins and 4–18 mg per cup theaflavins (Bronner & Beecher 1998, Henning et al. 2003).

Cocoa and Chocolate

Cocoa and chocolate products, made from beans of *Theobroma cacao* fruit, are another major source of flavan-3-ols (Cooper et al. 2007, Gu et al. 2002, Natsume et al. 2000). Significant variation exists in the qualitative and quantitative profiles of flavan-3-ols and PCs in cocoa owing to differences in geographical region, season, processing, and formulation. The predominant flavan-3-ol monomers in chocolate are (−)-EC, as well as two forms of C: (+)-C and (−)-C (referred to collectively as C) (Cooper et al. 2007). Cocoa also contains PCs with varying of degrees of polymerization (Nelson & Sharpless 2003, Sanchez-Rabaneda et al. 2003).

On a fat-free basis (ffb), cocoa powder contains 0.7–2 mg g^{-1} C, 2–15 mg g^{-1} EC, and 25–55 mg total PCs (Gu et al. 2006, Miller et al. 2006, Natsume et al. 2000). Dutched cocoa has considerably lower contents of C (0.3–0.4 mg g^{-1}), EC (0.2–0.5 mg g^{-1}), and PC (8–13 mg g^{-1}) than standard cocoa (Gu et al. 2006). Dark chocolate has relatively high levels of flavan-3-ols, with C at 0.15–0.5 mg g^{-1}, EC at 0.7–2 mg g^{-1}, and PCs at 0.5–31 mg g^{-1}. Milk chocolate contains less cocoa powder by weight than dark chocolate and therefore has proportionally lower levels of C (0.7–0.2 mg g^{-1}), EC (0.3–0.4 mg g^{-1}), and PCs (0.6–3.2 mg g^{-1}) (Adamson et al. 1999, Gu et al. 2006, Miller et al. 2006, Natsume et al. 2000). Major cocoa PCs have a degree of polymerization (DP) of 2–10 (Adamson et al. 1999, Hammerstone et al. 2000). The predominant PCs in cocoa products are dimers B2 and B5, trimer C1, and cinnamtannin A2 (Cooper et al. 2008).

The source, processing method, and finished form of cocoa products greatly influence the profile of monomers and PCs present. Processing of cocoa involves physical and chemical alterations to the raw beans. This typically involves fermentation, air drying, cleaning of the bean, roasting and winnowing, grinding of the nibs, separating cocoa butter from cocoa powder via pressing, alkalization of cocoa powder (also called Dutching, an optional step), refining, formulating, conching, and repeated cooling/heating (Wollgast & Anklam 2000).

Fermentation of raw cocoa beans results in oxidative degradation of monomers (C, EC) and PCs to form large, insoluble tannins (Hansen et al. 1998, Kealey et al. 1998). Roasting of the fermented beans induces epimerization, along with other reactions that impact flavan-3-ol profile.

Figure 1

Primary dietary flavan-3-ol derivatives present in cocoa and tea. (*a*) Structures and stereochemistry of the major monomeric flavan-3-ols (catechins). Chiral carbons are identified with asterisks. (*b*) Structures of derived tannins (theaflavins). (*c*) Structures of B-type condensed tannins (dimers are shown) and C-type (trimeric) condensed tannins. The identities of the R1 group (-H or -OH) and R2 group (-OH or -gallate), the configuration of C2 (+/−), and the configuration of the C2/C3 substituents relative to the C-ring plane (*cis*/*trans*) depend upon the identity of each constituent flavan-3-ol monomer residue (see **Figure 3**). The procyanidins are composed of (−)-EC and/or (+)-C residues, whereas the prodelphinidins are composed of (−)-EGC and/or (−)-EGCG residues. (*d*) Structures of A-type condensed tannins (a dimer is shown). The identities of the R1 group (-H or -OH) and R2 group (-OH or -gallate), the configuration of C2 (+/−), and the configuration of the C2/C3 substituents relative to the C-ring plane (*cis*/*trans*) depend upon the identity of each constituent flavan-3-ol monomer residue (see **Figure 3**). See **Figure 4** for the stereochemistry of the C4-C8 interflavan linkage.

Specifically, (+)-C in fermented beans appears to be highly degraded/epimerized, with losses of 67%–97% during roasting (Kofink et al. 2007, Oliviero et al. 2009).

Cocoa and cocoa products are a rare and significant dietary source of (−)-C. Although the majority of plant foods contain mostly (+)-C, as do the native *Theobroma cacao* beans (Gotti et al. 2006), (+)-C is largely epimerized during processing to (−)-C (Andres-Lacueva et al. 2008, Kofink et al. 2007), resulting in cocoa products that contain mixtures of (±)-C, with up to 90% (−)-C and 10% (+)-C (Donovan et al. 2006, Gotti et al. 2006). Additionally, the levels of PCs as well as total polyphenols decrease during roasting, with greater losses at higher temperatures (Kealey et al. 1998).

CHEMICAL PROPERTIES OF FLAVAN-3-OLS

With growing interest in bioavailability and biological activities of flavan-3-ols, it is critical to consider their susceptibility to heat and oxidative conditions typically encountered in food processing. These properties determine stability and the extent of chemical changes that occur between harvest of the raw plant and consumption (i.e., during holding, processing, packaging, self-storage, and digestion), thereby affecting the qualitative profiles and concentrations of flavan-3-ols available to influence human health.

Thermal Stability

Numerous foods containing flavan-3-ols are subjected to thermal processes, including fermentation, retorting, pasteurization, and in-home cooking/preparation, that influence qualitative and quantitative profiles of flavan-3-ols in finished products and make them available for absorption and utilization. Several studies have investigated the thermal stabilities for flavan-3-ols in aqueous solutions (Chen et al. 2001, Wang & Helliwell 2000, Xu et al. 2003). The predominant reactions of catechins during exposure to heat appear to be isomerization and autooxidation (Komatsu et al. 1993, Wang et al. 2006). Isomerization of epicatechins to their nonepi isomers is thermodynamically favorable (Okumura et al. 2008). The heats of formation (ΔH_f) of the nonepi isomers are 1–2 kcal mol^{-1} lower than those of epi forms, and this difference is sufficient to drive epimerization during typical thermal processes (Okumura et al. 2008). The significance of thermally induced isomerization is reflected in studies demonstrating that retorted green tea beverages contain (−)-GCG as their predominant catechin species, whereas (−)-EGCG is the predominant species present in unprocessed green tea (Chen et al. 2001, Zhu et al. 2003). Dutching and roasting of cocoa also facilitate epimerization of (−)-EC to (−)-C (Kofink et al. 2007).

The theoretical thermal stabilities of catechins are believed to be ECG > EGC > EC > EGCG (Okumura et al. 2008). However, stabilities in food systems are confounded by autooxidation reactions, which preferentially degrade EGCG and EGC (Komatsu et al. 1993). This was illustrated by a study demonstrating that brewing tea (100°C for 5 min) in tap water (containing metal ions and dissolved O_2 at 1.1 mg L^{-1}) resulted in infusions with more nonepi species (GCG and GC) and less epi species (EGCG and EGC) than brewing in purified water (Wang & Helliwell 2000).

Oxidative Stability of Flavan-3-ols

The oxidative stability of catechins in aqueous systems is highly dependent on pH (Zhu et al. 1997). The relative stabilities of catechins to elevated pH conditions (pH > 5.5) have been reported to be EC > ECG > EGCG ≥ EGC (Chen et al. 2001, Sang et al. 2005, Su et al. 2003, Zhu et al. 1997). Although Dutching, or alkaline processing of cocoa, is typically a desired process to enhance cocoa color, this treatment at high pH reduces levels of monomers C and EC and PCs by 3- to 8-fold in finished products (Andres-Lacueva et al. 2008, Gu et al. 2006). pH-driven degradation of EGCG and EGC is thought to proceed by oxidative mechanisms involving the donation of $H^{\bullet}$ to quench oxygen radicals (Hou et al. 2005, Miura et al. 1998, Sang et al. 2005). Catechins with the catechol B-ring structures (EC and ECG) are more stable, compared to those with the pyrogallol B-ring structures (EGCG and EGC) (Mochizuki et al. 2002). The half-life of EGCG at pH 7.2–7.4 is 30 min to 2 h (Chen et al. 1998, 2001; Hong et al. 2002; Sang et al. 2007). EGCG is highly unstable in cell culture media (pH 7.4), with a half-life of 30 min (Sang et al. 2005) and 95% loss in 4 h (Hou et al. 2005). Eighty-five percent of EGCG was degraded within 30 min in intestinal juice (pH 8.5), and 79% was degraded within 30 min in mouse plasma (Yoshino et al. 1999). Oxidation of EGCG by reactive oxygen species (ROS) at elevated pH results in the generation of several autooxidation products, including dimers. These dimers include the theasinensins (THSNs) A and D, and a more complex dimer referred to as P-2 (Hou et al. 2005; Sang et al. 2005,2007; Yoshino et al. 1999) (**Figure 2*a***).

Although the majority of research regarding pH-driven autooxidation has focused on EGCG, relatively little is known regarding the behavior of EGC, which is one of the most abundant flavan-3-ols in green tea. EGC appears to be highly labile to oxidative degradation and also generates oxidative dimers during tea processing (Matsuo et al. 2008) and in solution (Neilson et al. 2007, 2010b). Additionally, autooxidation of these flavan-3-ol mixtures (commonly present in foods, as opposed to individual compounds) results in heterodimerization between species. For example, autooxidation of EGCG and EGC mixtures in model systems forms EGC homodimers structurally analogous to the THSNs and P-2 as well as EGCG and EGC heterodimers (Neilson et al. 2007). Although the relevance of these species remains to be determined, conditions favoring autooxidation exist in select food and beverage systems, as well as in the small intestinal lumen (**Figure 2*b***). These conditions include elevated pH ($\geq$5.5), residual dissolved O_2, and presence of ROS (Parks 1989). More recently, the presence of several of these autooxidation dimers of EGC and EGCG have been identified in fermented black and oolong teas (Neilson et al. 2010b), indicating their presence in the diet and highlighting the need to better understand factors driving their formation and/or biological significance.

DIGESTION, ABSORPTION, AND METABOLISM OF FLAVAN-3-OLS FROM TEA AND COCOA

Absorption of flavan-3-ol is a multistep process, starting with the (*a*) digestive release of the flavan-3-ol from the food or beverage matrix, followed by (*b*) solubilization of stabile flavan-3-ols in the gut lumen, (*c*) uptake and transport by intestinal epithelial cells, and (*d*) metabolism (colonic, intestinal, and hepatic) of flavan-3-ols (**Figure 3**). Each step of this process can ultimately influence the circulating and/or tissue flavan-3-ol profiles. For the purpose of this review, bioavailability is defined as the fraction of flavan-3-ol compounds from a food absorbed and secreted into circulation (as native or metabolized forms) and made available for tissue uptake and metabolism. The term bioaccessibility is often utilized to describe the fraction of flavan-3-ols made available for absorption at the luminal surface of the intestinal epithelia during the initial stages of digestive release and solubilization/stability of flavan-3-ols in the intestine (Ferruzzi 2010).

Digestive Stability and Bioaccessibility

Several factors determine the bioaccessibility of flavan-3-ols. First, flavan-3-ols must be released from molecular interactions with other food components as well as bulk-phase interactions with

a

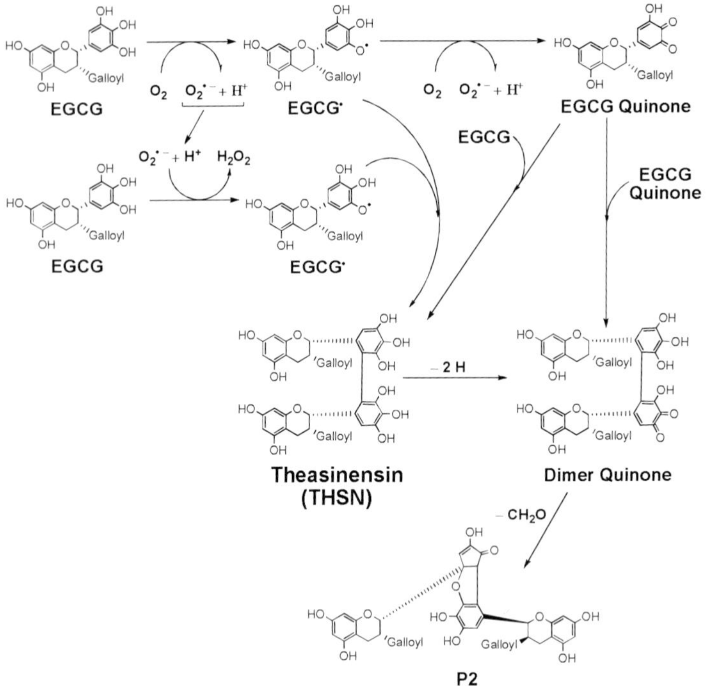

b

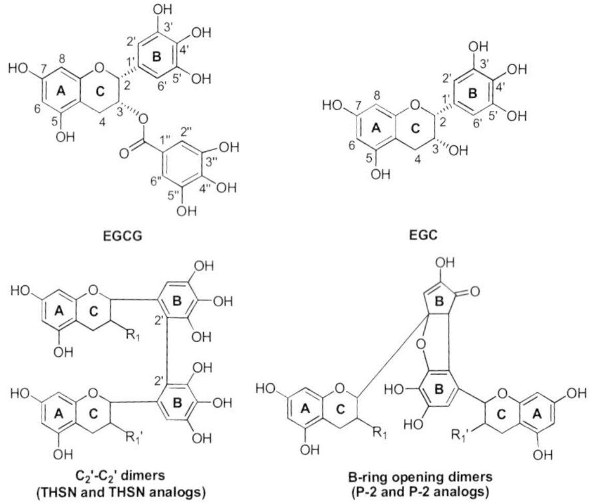

Linkage	Type	Compound	Precursors	MW[a] (g/mol)	Substitution[b] R_1	Substitution[b] $R_{1'}$
C2'-C2'	Homo	THSN A/D	2 EGCG	914	G	G
	Homo	THSN C/E	2 EGC	610	OH	OH
	Hetero	THSN B	EGCG + EGC	762	G	OH
B-ring opening	Homo	P-2	2 EGCG	884	G	G
	Homo	P-2 analog	2 EGC	580	OH	OH
	Hetero	P-2 analog	EGCG + EGC	732	G/OH	OH/G

[a]Nominal molecular weight
[b]G = galloyl residue

the physical food matrix. Second, flavan-3-ols must be soluble in the bulk aqueous phase in order to diffuse across the unstirred water layer that protects the enterocyte surface. Finally, flavan-3-ols must be stable to gastrointestinal conditions, including exposure to saliva, gastric juice, and intestinal secretions, as well as wide pH variations. Only the flavan-3-ol fraction that meets these criteria will be available for absorption (i.e., bioaccessible).

Both monomeric flavan-3-ols and PCs appear to be generally stable in both oral and gastric environments. Recovery of monomeric catechins and select PCs, following short incubations (10–60 min) with authentic or simulated saliva (pH 6.9, α-amylase), has been reported between 85% and 102% (Laurent et al. 2007, Tsuchiya et al. 1997). Simulated gastric recovery of C and EC, and PCs B2 and B3 is 97% to125% (some PCs were hydrolyzed to C and EC, resulting in >100% recovery for these compounds) (Laurent et al. 2007). This finding was similar to a report that found the gastric stability of flavan-3-ols from both green and black tea to be >80%, with the exception of EGCG, EGC, and GCG, which experienced gastric losses of roughly 50% for black tea only (Record & Lane 2001). GCG was found to increase by 30% for green tea, suggesting that acid-catalyzed epimerization of EGCG may occur under gastric conditions (Record & Lane 2001).

In contrast, individual flavan-3-ols appear to be less stable in intestinal conditions. Record & Lane (2001) reported that the recovery of flavan-3-ols during simulated intestinal digestion (pH 7.5, no enzymes) of green teas was 1% for EGCG, 8% for EGC, 38% for GCG, 59% for ECG, and 71% for EC. Separate studies confirmed the simulated digestive stability of catechol-containing EC, C, and ECG compared with pyrogallol-containing EGCG and EGC (Green et al. 2007, Neilson et al. 2007). These results suggest that flavan-3-ol degradation may be driven by autooxidation at near-neutral or greater pH common in the small intestine. In support of this hypothesis, autooxidation dimers of EGCG and EGC have been identified in simulated intestinal digesta containing monomeric flavan-3-ols (Neilson et al. 2007, 2010b).

In addition to instability, intestinal solubility of flavan-3-ols may be a factor that limits bioaccessibility. Laurent et al. (2007) reported that recoveries of EC and C and PCs B2 and B3 could be enhanced from <55% to >85% (with PCs improving from 0% to >85%) from simulated digesta by extraction with acetonitrile. This suggests that physical associations with food and intestinal secretions, as well as solubility, may be important factors limiting the bioaccessibility of flavan-3-ols, particularly the PCs.

In one of the few studies of actual intestinal stability and recovery in vivo, Auger et al. (2008) reported that recovery of flavan-3-ols in ileal fluid (i.e., unabsorbed and nondegraded) of humans consuming green tea extract (Polyphenon E) was 21%–36%, 47%–59%, 53%–74%, and 26%–34% for EC, EGCG, GCG, and ECG, respectively. Additionally, ileal recovery of total flavan-3-ols was 39% to 46%. Although these data should be taken in context due to the altered physiological state (lack of a colon) of the individuals included in the study, the higher ileal recoveries of flavan-3-ols observed compared to those predicated by in vitro experiments, particularly for EGCG and

Figure 2

Flavan-3-ol autooxidation leads to formation of complex products. (*a*) Proposed autooxidation reaction mechanism of (−)-epigallocatechin gallate (EGCG) at near-neutral or greater pH, leading to the formation of the homodimers theasinensin, and P-2 (Hou et al. 2005, Miura et al. 1998, Mochizuki et al. 2002, Sang et al. 2007). Two EGCG monomers form a C-C bond in the B-ring, resulting in the net loss of 2 H atoms, to generate the homodimers theasinensin (THSN A and THSN D). Two EGCG monomers also undergo B-ring opening and subsequent condensation, resulting in the net loss of 2 H atoms and formaldehyde (CH2O), to generate the homodimer P-2. (*b*) Structures of EGCG and (−)-epigallocatechin (EGC), as well as the known autooxidation dimers (THSNs and P-2 analogs) of EGCG and EGC formed though in vitro digestion, incubation in a variety of fluids at near-neutral pH (cell-culture media, authentic intestinal juices, plasma, etc.), and enzymatic oxidation both in vitro as well as in tea. Adapted from Neilson et al. 2010b with permission.

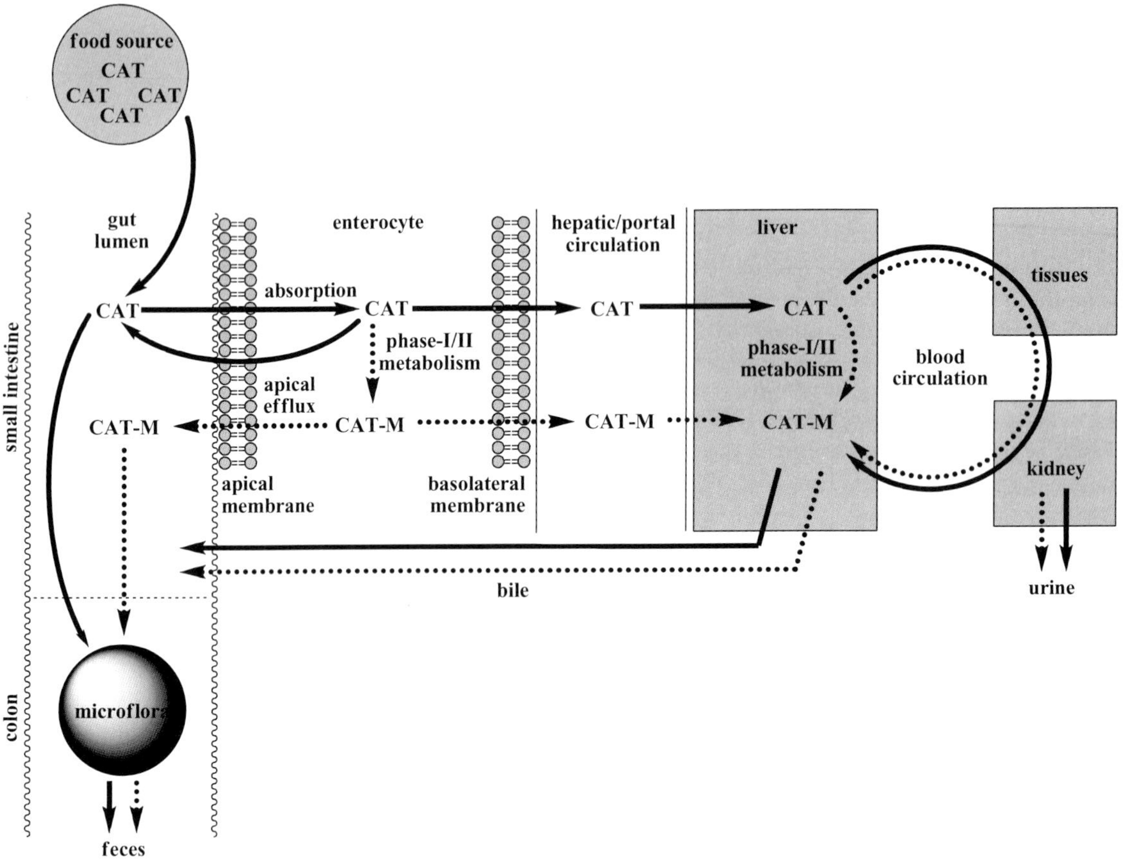

Figure 3

Schematic of the processes that affect systemic bioavailability and metabolism of flavan-3-ols. CAT, catechins; CAT-M, catechin phase-II metabolites; →, pathways of native catechins; ···→, pathways of catechin metabolites.

EGC, suggest that the extent to which intestinal degradation of flavan-3-ols occurs in vivo requires additional investigation.

Intestinal Absorption

Following digestive release and solubilization, flavan-3-ols are absorbed in the upper small intestine. Intestinal uptake of flavan-3-ols is believed to proceed principally through the monocarboxylic acid (MCT) transporter present in the brush border of intestinal epithelial cells. Additionally, but to a more limited extent, flavan-3-ol absorption may proceed by passive diffusion (Crespy et al. 2003, Lambert et al. 2007, Vaidyanathan & Walle 2003). Animal and Caco-2 cell models have been widely applied in the study of flavan-3-ol intestinal absorption. The relative apical → basolateral permeability of flavan-3-ols in Caco-2 monolayers has been reported to be EGC (1.5×10^{-7} cm s^{-1}) > EC (1.4) > ECG (1) > EGCG (0.8), suggesting that poor transepithelial transport efficiency for flavan-3-ol monomers limits overall bioavailability especially for gallated derivatives (EGCG and ECG) (Zhang et al. 2004).

A key factor limiting transepithelial intestinal transport is the affinity for flavan-3-ols of the ATP-binding cassette (ABC) trans-membrane transporters, specifically P-glycoprotein (Pgp) and multidrug resistant proteins (MRP) 1 and 2 (Feng 2006, Takano et al. 2006). These transporters actively remove xenobiotics from the cell interior to the lumen, interstitial space, or bloodstream surrounding the cells (Feng 2006). The affinity of flavan-3-ols for these transport systems significantly limits the ability of flavan-3-ol to cross into the bloodstream. Although 35% to 80% of a flavan-3-ol dose may be absorbed by the intestinal epithelia, 11% to 52% may be subsequently effluxed back into the lumen (Feng 2006, Vaidyanathan & Walle 2001). The effective efflux rate was found to be as high as 20% to 80% of the absorption rate for flavan-3-ols in a perfused rat intestine (Crespy et al. 2003), indicating that along with digestive instability, affinity for this transport system is a major barrier to the overall systemic bioavailability of flavan-3-ols from foods.

Flavan-3-ol Metabolism and Plasma Profiles

Following uptake by intestinal absorptive cells, flavan-3-ols are subject to xenobiotic metabolic transformation. Although flavan-3-ols are not typically substrates for phase-I metabolizing systems (Chan et al. 2004, Williamson et al. 2000), they serve as substrates for several phase-II conjugation systems, both in the intestine and the liver. Glucuronidation of C5, C7, and/or C3′ on a flavan-3-ol is carried out by uridine diphosphate glucuronyl-transferase (UDPGT). Sulfation of absorbed flavan-3-ols at various sites is carried out by sulfotransferase (SULT) or phenol-sulfotransferase (PST). O-methylation of flavan-3-ols may occur at C3′, C4′, C3″, and/or C4″ positions by catechol O-methyl transferase (COMT) (Feng 2006, Williamson et al. 2000).

The majority of flavan-3-ol metabolism is believed to occur in the small intestine. Flavan-3-ol phase-II conjugates formed in intestinal enterocytes are efficiently effluxed into the interstitial space and bloodstream by MRP1 and into the gut lumen by MRP2 (Feng 2006, Takano et al. 2006, Vaidyanathan & Walle 2001). Although reduced relative to intestinal metabolism (Cai et al. 2002, Lambert et al. 2003), first-pass hepatic metabolism does exert an effect on the profile of circulating phase-II metabolites in rats. COMT activity is highest in the liver, generating 3′ O-methyl, 4′ O-methyl, 4″ O-methyl, and 3′,4″ di-O-methyl flavan-3-ol metabolites (Piskula & Terao 1998, Zhu et al. 2001). Liver COMT appears to preferentially form 3′ O-methyl derivatives over 4′ O-methyl derivatives, with 3″ and 4″ O-methyl derivatives formed in small amounts (Feng 2006, Kohri et al. 2003, Silberberg et al. 2005, Zhu et al. 2001). Additionally, glucuronidation of the A-ring does not appear to prohibit methylation by liver COMT isoforms (Feng 2006). The liver also possesses strong UDPGT and SULT activity (Feng 2006). Liver microsomes glucuronidate EGC and EGCG (8% to 12%) more effectively than intestinal epithelial microsomal fractions (1% to 3%), suggesting that ECG and EGCG are predominantly glucuronidate in the liver (Crespy et al. 2003). EC and EGCG are sulfated in the liver, and the liver appears to be the predominant site of PST expression (Feng 2006).

Individual flavan-3-ols are metabolized differentially, generating a diverse plasma profile of metabolites and native forms. EGCG is metabolized to a lesser extent than other species. EGCG was predominantly in the native form in plasma, following consumption of EGCG-rich green tea or Polyphenon E by humans (Chow et al. 2004, Stalmach et al. 2009, Van Amelsvoort et al. 2001). Some studies have reported phase-II metabolites of EGCG, including sulfated forms (58% to 72% of circulating species) and glucuronide forms (8% to 19% of circulating species) (Feng 2006). ECG exhibits similar plasma profiles to EGCG and is found predominantly in the native form in plasma, following consumption by humans (Chow et al. 2004, Stalmach et al. 2009, Van Amelsvoort et al. 2001). Native ECG was eight times more abundant than its phase-II metabolites in plasma of rats fed pure ECG (Kohri et al. 2003). EGC exists in several metabolized forms in plasma (glucuronides, sulfates, O-methyl forms, O-methyl sulfates, and O-methyl glucuronides) (Chow et al. 2004, Stalmach et al. 2009, Yang et al. 1998). Following consumption of green tea, 14% of EGC was in methylated form (O-methyl or O-methyl conjugates) in plasma, whereas 10% was found as free form (Van Amelsvoort et al. 2001). C and EC appear to be the most extensively metabolized flavan-3-ols. C and EC predominantly exist as glucuronides, with some sulfates and O-methyl forms, in the plasma of rats fed C and EC (Harada et al. 1999, Piskula & Terao 1998, Silberberg et al. 2005). EC was almost exclusively phase-II metabolites in plasma following consumption of green tea and Polyphenon E in humans (Chow et al. 2001, 2004).

Metabolism by Intestinal Microflora

Small intestinal absorption and systemic (plasma/urine) bioavailability of intact catechins and their phase-II metabolites are poor (<25%), with most figures suggesting 0.1% to 10% (Donovan et al. 2002, Kohri et al. 2001a, Lee et al. 2002, Scalbert & Williamson 2000). These data suggest that a large portion of the ingested dose is not absorbed in the small intestine but rather reaches the colon and its microflora as native compounds (or phase-II metabolites that have been effluxed by enterocytes) (Kohri et al. 2001a, Scalbert & Williamson 2000). Additionally, native catechins and their phase-II metabolites may be excreted into the bile and reintroduced into the intestinal lumen via enterohepatic recycling (Donovan et al. 2001, Harada et al. 1999, Kohri et al. 2001b).

The colon harbors a complex bacterial ecology composed of more that 500 species and a bacterial load of approximately 10^9–10^{12} cells g^{-1} of luminal contents (O'Hara & Shanahan 2006, 2007). The metabolic capacity of colonic bacteria results in extensive fermentation of unabsorbed material, and colonic bacteria metabolize polyphenols to simpler metabolites (Bravo et al. 1994, Kohri et al. 2001a). In vitro fermentation studies using fecal inocula have demonstrated that fecal bacteria metabolize 5% to 100% of polyphenols (Justesen et al. 2000, Lin et al. 2003, Tzounis et al. 2008, Winter et al. 1989). Native polyphenols are extensively degraded in the colon by a variety of reactions to generate a wide array of 1,3-diphenylpropanes, γ-valerolactones, phenylalkyl carboxylic acids, benzoic acids, and other aromatic compounds (**Figure 4**) (Kohri et al. 2003, Lin et al. 2003, Simons et al. 2005, Tzounis et al. 2008). Following formation, colonic bacterial metabolites are absorbed into the bloodstream, providing another source of potentially bioactive compounds (Gonthier et al. 2003, Kohri et al. 2001b, Rios et al. 2003).

Excretion and Elimination

Circulating flavan-3-ols and their metabolite forms are largely extracted from the bloodstream by the kidneys and subsequently excreted in the urine. Glucuronide and sulfate conjugates appear to be more readily excreted into the urine than the native forms (Lambert et al. 2003, Yang et al. 2000). C, EC, and EGC appear to be readily excreted in the urine as glucuronides, sulfates, and O-methylated forms of these conjugates (Auger et al. 2008, Chow et al. 2004, Li et al. 2001, Stalmach et al. 2009, Van Amelsvoort et al. 2001, Yang et al. 2000). In spite of the high urinary excretion of the other flavan-3-ols, human studies have reported that virtually no EGCG is excreted in the urine in conjugated, O-methylated, or native forms; similarly, little ECG is believed to be excreted in the urine in any form (Auger et al. 2008, Chow et al. 2004, Stalmach et al. 2009, Yang et al. 1998, 2000). Free EGCG, ECG, and O-methylated forms of these and other flavan-3-ols are believed to be secreted from the liver into bile, either by first-pass or subsequent metabolism (Harada et al. 1999, Kohri et al. 2003, Yang et al. 1998).

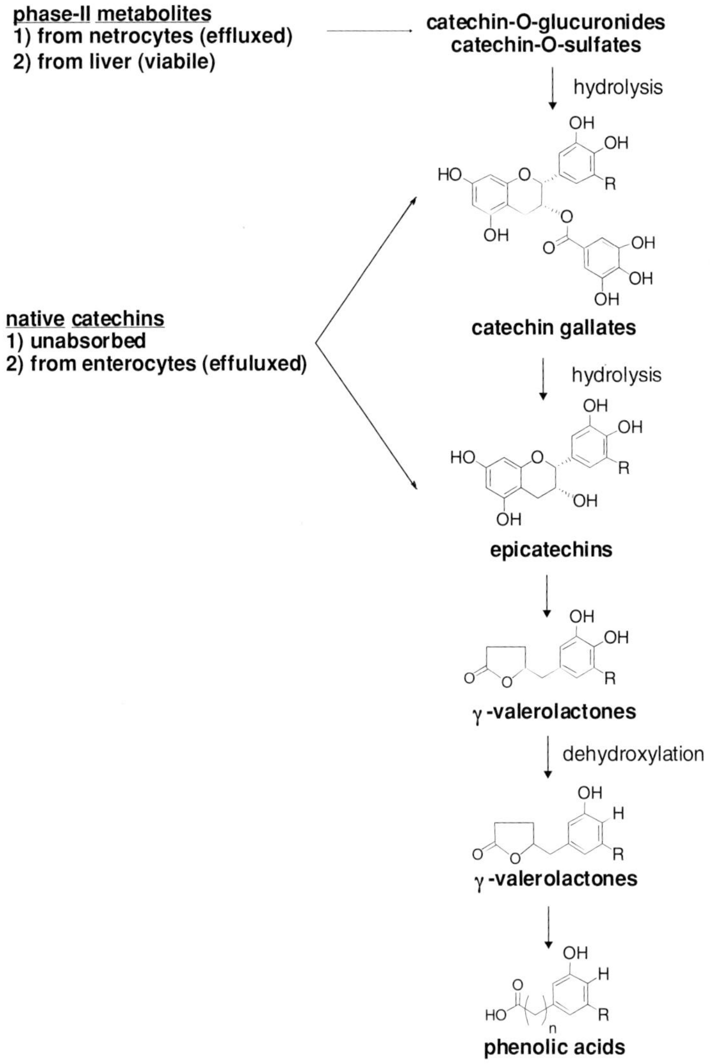

Figure 4

Colonic metabolism of dietary epicatechins.

FACTORS AFFECTING FLAVAN-3-OL BIOAVAILABILITY AND METABOLISM

The impact that food formulation and processing have on flavan-3-ol bioavailability is particularly critical for tea and cocoa, considering they are typically consumed as formulated products rather than purified extracts or supplements. Although cocoa is most commonly consumed as chocolate, tea may be formulated by consumers and food processors with specific adjuncts. In such complex food systems, both physical and chemical interactions between the flavan-3-ols and the food matrix may impact preabsorptive and absorptive events, ultimately influencing circulating flavan-3-ol profiles in humans.

Numerous pharmacokinetic investigations of flavan-3-ol absorption in humans are reported in the literature. Generally, these studies follow the appearance of individual flavan-3-ols and their metabolites in plasma and urine, following an acute dose of tea- or cocoa-containing foods/beverages. Several pharmacokinetic parameters are subsequently calculated and reported, including area under the plasma pharmacokinetic curve (AUC), maximum plasma flavan-3-ol concentration (C_{MAX}), and time of maximum plasmaflavan-3-ol concentration (T_{MAX}). The following discussion focuses on these parameters in describing the impact of food matrix and formulation on flavan-3-ol bioavailability.

Tea

As one of the most prominent dietary sources, the bioavailability of tea flavan-3-ols has been the subject of numerous clinical studies, some of which are summarized in **Table 1** (Chow et al. 2003; Henning et al. 2004; Kyle et al. 2007; Lee et al. 2002; Puch et al. 2008; Reddy et al. 2005; Stalmach et al. 2009, 2010; Van Amelsvoort et al. 2001; van het Hof et al. 1998; Warden et al. 2001; Yang et al. 1998). From plain green and black tea products, flavan-3-ols appear to be rapidly absorbed following consumption, with plasma C_{MAX} levels varying between 0.5 h and 2 h postadministration followed by rapid metabolism and clearance and a return to baseline levels within 8 h to 12 h postadministration. Interestingly, bioavailability of gallated catechins (EGCG and ECG) appears to be markedly lower than nongallated catechins (EGC and EC), making EGC and EC metabolites the most abundant circulating tea-derived flavan-3-ols in humans (Henning et al. 2004, Stalmach et al. 2009, 2010, Van Amelsvoort et al. 2001, Warden et al. 2001).

Impact of formulation to the bioavailability of flavan-3-ols from tea. Tea is commonly consumed with food and/or formulated with sweeteners (caloric and noncaloric) and creamers (dairy or nondairy). It appears that absorption of flavan-3-ols from tea may be influenced by consumption with or without a meal. Chow et al. (2005) reported overall bioavailability (measured as AUC) to be approximately fourfold higher in participants administered 400 mg EGCG as a green tea extract (Polyphenon E) in a fasted (127 ng*min ml^{-1}) compared to fed state (37 ng*min ml^{-1}). Additionally, average T_{MAX} values were lower in the fasted state (~1.5 h) relative to the fed state (~2 h), suggesting that coconsumption with food may slow the rate and extent of flavan-3-ol from tea.

In addition to consumption with food, tea is commonly prepared with milk. Several studies have assessed the influence of milk on the bioavailability of flavan-3-ols from black and more recently green tea. Van het Hof et al. (1998) reported that addition of skim milk did not impact any of the pharmacokinetic parameters (AUC, C_{MAX}, T_{MAX}, or $t_{1/2}$) of flavan-3-ols from black tea. However, Reddy et al. reported that the presence of milk with black tea did not negate increases in plasma antioxidant activity but did lower plasma AUC of total catechins over 3 h in subjects consuming milk with black tea compared to plain (0.95 versus 1.14 min*μM, respectively) (Reddy et al. 2005). These findings should be considered in the context of potential differences in kinetics of absorption and that plasma levels were only monitored for 3 h. Overall, these results suggest that formulation of tea with milk has a limited impact on absorption of flavan-3-ols from tea.

In addition to traditional in-home preparation, commercial ready-to-drink tea products have expanded in popularity in recent years. These products are often formulated with food additives such as ascorbic acid and EDTA (antioxidants and chelators), as well as citric acid or other acidulants and buffers to minimize loss of flavan-3-ols to autooxidative reactions in beverage systems (Chen et al. 1998). Additionally, tea beverages blended with other botanical extracts and fruit juices are increasingly common in the marketplace. Although these products are becoming a large portion of the tea market in the United States (Del Rio et al. 2010), limited information is currently available on the potential impact of these added ingredients on bioavailability of flavan-3-ols from tea.

As described previously, the primary flavan-3-ols in tea (EGC and EGCG) are sensitive to autooxidation reactions, and conditions of the small intestinal lumen may facilitate such reactions, leading to a diminished bioaccessibility (Green et al. 2007, Neilson et al. 2007, Record & Lane 2001). Similar to ascorbic acid's stabilizing effect in beverage systems (Chen et al. 1998), formulation of green tea with ascorbic acid has been reported to markedly enhance digestive stability (bioaccessibility) of EGCG and EGC in in vitro models (Green et al. 2007, Peters et al. 2010). Furthermore, formulation of green tea with sucrose or ascorbic acid–rich citrus juices enhanced in vitro digestive recovery, suggesting that these formulation factors may enhance bioavailability in vivo (Green et al. 2007). These data are in line with the observation that EGCG absorption from green tea extracts was enhanced 14% in humans by coformulation of tea with nutrient-rich mixtures including ascorbic acid (Gawande et al. 2008). Similarly, bioavailability of EGC and EGCG was enhanced by 2.5- to 3-fold in rats treated with green tea [50 mg kg^{-1} body weight (BW)] formulated with 1.25 g kg^{-1} BW sucrose and 10 mg kg^{-1} BW ascorbic acid compared to unformulated green tea (GT) (Peters et al. 2010). Combined, these data suggest that formulation of tea products with common food additives may alter absorption of bioactive flavan-3-ols. However, more research is required to determine the clinical relevance of these modifications to flavan-3-ol bioavailability and the extent to which metabolism of tea derived flavan-3-ols may be impacted by formulation.

Cocoa and Chocolate

Although C and EC are the predominant monomeric flavan-3-ols in chocolate, C is typically present at extremely low concentrations in blood, relative to EC, in the majority of studies. Therefore, the majority of published data regarding the bioavailability of monomeric flavan-3-ols from chocolate has focused exclusively on EC. This phenomenon is likely due to three primary factors: (*a*) the lower C content of most cocoa powders relative to EC (EC is typically present at 2- to 5-fold higher concentrations) (Cooper et al. 2007, Gu et al. 2006, Natsume et al. 2000), (*b*) the fact that, unlike most foods, C in cocoa is predominantly (−)-C as opposed to (+)-C (Cooper et al. 2007, Donovan et al. 2006), and (*c*) the reported lower bioavailability of (−)-C compared to (+)-C and (−)-EC (Baba et al. 2001, Donovan et al. 2006). It should be noted that the reverse-phase high performance liquid chromatography (HPLC) methods typically used to assess C and EC levels do not resolve (+)-C and (−)-C, and therefore both elute as one peak and are quantified together collectively as (±)-C in biological samples.

Bioavailability. Owing to its typical consumption in beverages and confections, the food matrix composition of chocolate has great potential to modulate the absorption and pharmacokinetics of flavan-3-ols. The main factors affecting the pharmacokinetics of flavan-3-ols from cocoa are the macronutrient composition [carbohydrates (typically sucrose), lipids, and proteins (typically milk or milk solids)] and physical state (liquid versus solid) of the product. Numerous studies have been performed on the bioavailability of EC, and these are summarized in **Table 2** (Engler et al. 2004, Heiss et al. 2005, Holt et al. 2002, Keogh et al. 2007, Mullen et al. 2009, Muniyappa et al. 2008, Rein et al. 2000, Richelle et al. 1999, Roura et al. 2005, Schramm et al. 2001, Schroeter et al. 2006, Serafini et al. 2003, Taubert et al. 2007, Wan et al. 2001, Wang et al. 2000, Wiswedel et al. 2004).

Carbohydrates, and particularly sucrose, have generally been reported to increase C_{MAX} of EC relative to control and other macronutrients (lipid, milk protein) for confections as well as

Table 1 Plasma bioavailability of catechins from tea

Study	Formulation	Time (h)	Compound	Dose (mg)	AUC (nM*h)	C_{MAX} (nM)	T_{MAX} (h)	AUC/dose (nM*h mg^{-1})	C_{MAX}/dose (nM mg^{-1})
Stalmach 2010	GT	24	EC+C[a]	18	1120	369	0.8–1.3	61.6	20.3
			EGC+GC[a]	73	1720	487	0.5–2.2	23.4	6.6
			ECG	28	50	17	1.0	1.8	0.6
			EGCG+GCG	111	90	35	0.6	0.8	0.3
Stalmach 2009	GT	24	C+EC[a]	19.4	~1020	~208	~1.7	52.6	10.7
			GC+EGC[a]	89.7	~1320	~251	~2.2	14.7	2.8
			ECG	21.7	120	25	1.6	5.5	1.3
			EGCG+GCG	109	170	55	1.9	1.6	0.5
Puch 2008[b]	GT, milk, w/ meal	0-6	Total catechins	47	248	98	2	5.3	2.1
	GT w/ meal				310	88	4.5	6.6	1.9
Kyle 2007[c,d]	BT	0-3	Total catechins	395 μmol	?	~350	1.3	?	?
	BT, 25% milk				?	~300	1.3	?	?
Reddy 2005	BT, sugar	0-3	Total catechins	~200	1140	670	2	~5.7	~3.4
	BT, sugar, 20% milk				950	420	2	~4.8	~2.1
Henning 2004	GT	0-8	EC	76.5	1010	330	1.2	13.2	4.3
			EGC	269.6	2590	740	1.3	9.6	2.7
			ECG	119.3	320	82	1.4	2.7	0.7
			EGCG	213.6	270	80	1.3	1.3	0.4
	BT		EC	39.8	270	80	1.4	6.8	2.0
			EGC	103.4	970	220	1.5	9.4	2.1
			ECG	122.5	290	70	1.5	2.4	0.6
			EGCG	230.8	370	100	1.4	1.6	0.4
Chow 2003	EGCG	24	EGCG	400	1707	301.3	3.1	4.3	0.8
	EGCG (after 4-week exposure)				1598	351.5	2.3	4.0	0.9
	EGCG			800	3479	513.1	3.7	4.3	0.6
	EGCG (after 4-week exposure)				5298	851.5	3.5	6.6	1.1

Lee 2002	GT	0-24	EC	? (20 mg GT solids/kg body weight)	1826	428	1.2	?	?
			EGC		3089	730	1.3	?	?
			EGCG		1110	170	1.6	?	?
	GT, decaffeinated		EC		533	112	1.0	?	?
			EGC		964	262	1.1	?	?
			EGCG		198	53	1.2	?	?
Warden 2001[c]	BT, co-consumed w/ sugar cookie (4 servings over 6 h)	0-24	EC	67	?	135	7	?	2.0
			EGC	61.9	?	72	5	?	1.2
			ECG	124.6	?	22	24	?	0.18
			EGCG	146.2	?	16	5	?	0.1
Van Amelsvoort 2001	Pure compounds in hot water w/ syrup	0-24	EGC[a]	459	65,500	13,600	1.4-2	142.7	29.6
			ECG	663	12,100	1300	4	18.3	2.0
			EGCG	687	39,900	3100	2.9	58.1	4.5
Yang 1998	GT, decaffeinated, 45 g sugar, 8 g coffee creamer	25	EC	37.5	963	190	1.4	25.7	5.1
				75	3654	652	1.8	48.7	8.7
				112.5	4137	656	1.8	36.8	5.8
			EGC	68	2018	484	1.4	29.7	7.1
				136	8152	1661	1.8	59.9	12.2
				204	10,729	1799	1.3	52.6	8.8
			EGCG	73	1955	259	1.6	26.8	3.5
				146	4846	711	2.4	33.2	4.9
				219	5367	700	2.7	24.5	3.2
van het Hof 1998	GT	0-8	Total catechins	930	2220	550	2.3	2.4	0.6
	BT			300	530	170	2.2	1.8	0.6
	BT, 17% milk			300	600	180	2	2.0	0.3

Abbreviations: GT, green tea; BT, black tea.

[a]Sum of reported metabolites.

[b]Units are as follows: AUC in $\mu g^{*}h\ L^{-1}$, C_{MAX} in $\mu g\ L^{-1}$, AUC/dose in $\mu g^{*}h/L\ mg^{-1}$, and C_{MAX}/dose in $\mu g/L\ mg^{-1}$. Easier to read?

[c]Baseline values subtracted.

[d]C_{MAX} is reported as nmol.

Table 2 Plasma bioavailability of cocoa catechins

Study	State	Formulation	Time (h)	Compound	Dose (mg)	AUC (nM*h)	C_{MAX} (nM)	T_{MAX} (h)	AUC/dose (nM*h mg^{-1})	C_{MAX}/dose (nM mg^{-1})
Mullen 2009[a]	L	Water, 1 g paracetamol, 5 g lactulose	0–8	C+EC	13.1	296	143	1-1.4	22.6	10.9
		Milk, 1 g paracetamol, 5 g lactulose				260	127	1.3	19.8	9.7
Neilson 2009	L	Water, 6 g milk solids	0–6	EC	27	143	42	1.1	5.3	1.6
		Water, 15 g sugar, 6 g milk solids				132	43	0.9	4.9	1.6
	S	20 g fat, 7 g sugar	0–6	EC	27	121	32	2.3	4.5	1.2
		12 g fat, 15 g sugar				128	34	1.8	4.7	1.3
		14 g fat, 7 g sugar, 6 g milk solids				101	25	2.3	3.7	0.9
Muniyappa 2008[b]	L	Water, 1g fat, 17g CHO, 9g protein	0–3	C+EC	118	1754	765	1.4	14.9	6.5
Roura 2007[b]	L	Water, 58 g CHO, 2 g fat, 6 g protein	2	EC	28	?	330	?	?	11.8
		Milk, 31 g CHO, 11 g fat, 14 g protein				?	274	?		9.8
Taubert 2007	S	2 g fat, 3 g CHO, 0.3 g protein	0–8	C	1.7	13	3.9	1.3	7.6	2.3
				EC	5.1	44	12.5	1.3	8.6	2.5
Keough 2007	L	Water, 7 g fat, 7 g sugar	0–8	C	? (2 g polyphenols	1100	210	~3.5	?	?
				EC		58,615	12,890	3		
		3 g fat, 8 g (sugar+ lactose), 3 g milk protein		C		1075	200	2		
				EC		58,340	12,420	3		
Schroeter 2006[a,c]	L	Water, ?	0–6	C+EC	?	8875	150	2.5	?	?
Heiss 2005	L	Water, 0.5 g fat, 6 g sugar, 1.5 g protein	0–2	C	?	?	9	?	?	?
				EC	~10.5		188			~17.9
		Water, 1 g fat, 12 g sugar, 3 g protein		C	?		19			?
				C	~21		289			~13.8
		Water, 2 g fat, 25 g sugar, 6 g protein		EC	?		18			?
					~42		386			~9.2
Roura 2005	L	Milk	2	EC	54	?	626	?	?	11.6
Engler 2004	S	15 g fat, 21 g sugar, 2 g protein	2	EC	46	?	~200	?	?	~4.3

Serafini 2004	S	Dark chocolate Dark chocolate + 200 mL milk Milk chocolate	4	EC	?	225 120 69	?	?	?	?
Wiswedel 2004	L		2	EC	? (187 mg favanol)	?	144	?	?	?
Schraam 2003	P	Control, water	0–8	EC	1.53 mg C+EC kg^{-1} body weight (~107 mg for 70 kg subject)	4230	1022	~1.5	?	?
		Sugar, water (69 g CHO)				5172	1209	~1.5		
		High sugar, water (138 g CHO)				6072	1436	~2		
		Control, water				4398	1185	~1.5		
		Bread, water (3 g fat, 45 g CHO, 7 g protein)				5748	1517	~1.5		
		Butter, water (29 g fat, 0 g CHO, 0 g protein)				4171	1177	~1.5		
		Steak, water (9 g fat, 0 g CHO, 48 g protein)				4966	1221	~1.5		
		Control, water				4930	1109	~1.5		
		Bread, water (3 g fat, 45 g CHO, 7 g protein)				6954	1514	~1.5		
		Milk (14 g fat, 20 g CHO, 14 g protein)				5769	1163	~1.5		
		Grapefruit juice (1 g fat, 61 g CHO, 3 g protein)				5944	1273	~1.5		
Holt 2002	L	Water, co-consumed w/ bread	0–6	C EC	? (323 mg C+EC)	?	160 5920	2 2	?	?
Wan 2001	P/S	?	0–24	EC	? (111mg C+EC)	?	36	2	?	?
Schraam 2001	S	12.2 g fat, 18.8 g CHO, consumed w/ bagel	0–6	EC	40.7	?	21	2	?	0.5
Rein 2000	S	27 g fat	0–6	EC	137	?	257	~2	?	1.9
Wang 2000	S	?, consumed w/ bread: 0.8 g fat, 25 g CHO, 4.5 g protein)	0–6	EC	27	500	133	2	18.5	4.9
					53	1000	258	2	18.9	4.9
					80	1500	355	2	18.8	4.4
Richelle 1999	S	?, consumed w/ bread, water	0–8	EC	82 164	1534 3686	355 676	2 2.6	18.7 22.5	4.3 4.1

[a]Sum of reported metabolites.
[b]EC, glucuronide.
[c]AUC estimated from the author's published data.
Abbreviations: S, solid; L, liquid; P, powder.

beverages (Neilson et al. 2009, Roura et al. 2007, Schramm et al. 2003). Although the mechanism by which sucrose enhances the absorption rate of catechins is unclear, similar studies with green tea have indicated that formulation with sucrose may improve catechin bioavailability by enhancing solubility and intestinal uptake (Peters et al. 2010).

The formulation factor that has been the most controversial for chocolate is the presence of milk and milk protein. Several studies have been performed regarding the influence of milk protein on the bioavailability of EC from cocoa beverages and chocolate. Serafini et al. (2003) reported that milk resulted in a reduced AUC for EC relative to control in chocolate confections, whereas other studies (Keogh et al. 2007, Roura et al. 2007, Schramm et al. 2003, Schroeter et al. 2003) reported no statistical difference between the AUC of EC from cocoa beverages consumed with water or milk. It is critical to note that Serafini examined confections, whereas the studies demonstrating no difference between milk and control were performed using cocoa beverages. Recently, we (Neilson et al. 2009) compared absorption of EC from beverages versus confections with differing macronutrient composition, finding that the AUC and C_{MAX} of EC from a milk chocolate confection were lower, though not significantly different, than control dark chocolate. However, the highest AUC and C_{MAX} values in this study were observed from milk-containing beverages of these chocolate formulations. Taken together, these studies suggest that milk protein may modulate the pharmacokinetics of flavan-3-ol absorption from confections, exerting a mild, but not always significant, suppressive effect on their bioavailability.

In addition to milk protein, the lipid content of cocoa and chocolate products has been associated with lower AUC and C_{MAX} of EC in confections (Neilson et al. 2009, 2010a, Roura et al. 2007, Schramm et al. 2003). However, this effect may be related to slower gastric emptying induced by lipid and digestive release of EC from the food matrix, as the lipid matrix must melt and be emulsified for EC to be solubilized in the intestine.

In addition to macronutrient composition of either beverages or confections, the physical form of the product may play a large role in determining the relative pharmacokinetic properties of cocoa-containing products, specifically the rate of absorption from the intestine and the subsequent plasma T_{MAX} and C_{MAX}. It is possible that the physical state of the food matrix may significantly modulate GI mobility (stomach-emptying time and transit through the intestine) and the rate of EC release and solubilization in the intestine, resulting in the observed distinct pharmacokinetic curve shapes and parameters between beverages and confections (Neilson et al. 2009). For example, milk does not appear to exert the same suppressive effects of EC bioavailability in beverages compared to confections. Milk-containing beverages produce generally higher serum AUC and C_{MAX} values than confections formulated with or without milk (Neilson et al. 2009). Rapid emptying of beverages from the stomach and rapid digestive release from beverages compared to confections may explain a more rapid appearance of EC (T_{MAX}) in the blood. Additionally, slower absorption from confections may result in pharmacokinetic curves that do not return to baseline as quickly as beverages. This may result in incomplete curves with apparently different AUC values that may in fact be similar if the entire curve were available (Neilson et al. 2009, 2010a; Serafini et al. 2003).Overall, these findings suggest that the absorption rate, but not the bioavailability of EC (AUC) from physiologically relevant doses of cocoa and chocolate, is more likely to be influenced by physical form rather than ingredient composition.

CONCLUSIONS

Interest in the bioavailability of flavan-3-ols from foods has grown because of the epidemiological and biological evidence of their health effects. Absorption of flavan-3-ols from food is a complex multistep process that appears to be influenced by several factors including (*a*) botanical source and flavan-3-ol profile, (*b*) type and extent of food processing, and (*c*) formulation and product formulation/composition. Bioavailability of flavan-3-ols from tea appears to be differentially affected by formulation with carbohydrate and ascorbic acid positively influencing absorption, whereas milk is believed to have minimal impact on overall bioavailability of these compounds from tea. Interestingly, for cocoa products, bioavailability of flavan-3-ols (C and EC, specifically) do not appear to differ greatly based on formulation, but the physical state of the product may influence pharmacokinetic parameters, including T_{MAX} and C_{MAX}, suggesting that beverages may be employed for more rapid absorption and higher peak plasma levels, whereas confections may provide more sustained plasma levels of flavan-3-ols.

Future efforts should consider these factors when designing experiments to assess the efficacy or bioavailability of flavan-3-ol from food products. Also, specific information on how food formulation factors influence metabolism and tissue distribution of flavan-3-ols remains limited and requires additional exploration. Finally, definition of target tissue profiles and identification of biologically active flavan-3-ol metabolites are also required to better define food matrix factors that favor delivery of physiologically relevant flavan-3-ol forms.

DISCLOSURE STATEMENT

Mario G. Ferruzzi has received grants and honoraria from, and has consulted for, food, beverage, and ingredient companies with interests in flavan-3-ols, including but not limited to Kraft Foods, Mead Johnson, Sensient Flavors, and Heinz.

LITERATURE CITED

Adamson GE, Lazarus SA, Mitchell AE, Prior RL, Cao GH, et al. 1999. HPLC method for the quantification of procyanidins in cocoa and chocolate samples and correlation to total antioxidant capacity. *J. Agric. Food Chem.* 47:4184–88

Andres-Lacueva C, Monagas M, Khan N, Izquierdo-Pulido M, Urpi-Sarda M, et al. 2008. Flavanol and flavonol contents of cocoa powder products: influence of the manufacturing process. *J. Agric. Food Chem.* 56:3111–17

Astill C, Birch MR, Dacombe C, Humphrey PG, Martin PT. 2001. Factors affecting the caffeine and polyphenol contents of black and green tea infusions. *J. Agric. Food Chem.* 49:5340–47

Auger C, Mullen W, Hara Y, Crozier A. 2008. Bioavailability of poluphenon E flavan-3-ols in humans with an ileostomy. *J. Nutr.* 138:1535–42

Baba S, Osakabe N, Natsume M, Muto Y, Takizawa T, Terao J. 2001. In vivo comparison of the bioavailability of (+)-catechin, (−)-epicatechin and their mixture in orally administered rats. *J. Nutr.* 131:2885–91

Bailey RG, Nursten HE, McDowell I. 1992. Isolation and analysis of a polymeric thearubigin fraction from tea. *J. Sci. Food Agric.* 59:365–75

Beecher GR. 2003. Overview of dietary flavonoids: nomenclature, occurrence and intake. *J. Nutr.* 133:S3248–54

Boschmann M, Thielecke F. 2007. The effects of epigallocatechin-3-gallate on thermogenesis and fat oxidation in obese men: a pilot study. *J. Am. Coll. Nutr.* 26:S389–95

Bravo L, Abia R, Eastwood MA, Saura-Calixto F. 1994. Degradation of polyphenols (catechin and tannic-acid) in the rat intestinal-tract—effect on colonic fermentation and fecal output. *Br. J. Nutr.* 71:933–46

Bronner WE, Beecher GR. 1998. Method for determining the content of catechins in tea infusions by high-performance liquid chromatography. *J. Chromatogr. A* 805:137–42

Cai Y, Anavy ND, Chow HHS. 2002. Contribution of presystemic hepatic extraction to the low oral bioavailability of green tea catechins in rats. *Drug Metab. Dispos.* 30:1246–49

Chan LMS, Lowes S, Hirst BH. 2004. The ABCs of drug transport in intestine and liver: efflux proteins limiting drug absorption and bioavailability. *Eur. J. Pharm. Sci.* 21:25–51

Chen ZY, Zhu QY, Tsang D, Huang Y. 2001. Degradation of green tea catechins in tea drinks. *J. Agric. Food Chem.* 49:477–82

Chen ZY, Zhu QY, Wong YF, Zhang ZS, Chung HY. 1998. Stabilizing effect of ascorbic acid on green tea catechins. *J. Agric. Food Chem.* 46:2512–16

Chow HHS, Cai Y, Alberts DS, Hakim I, Dorr R, et al. 2001. Phase I pharmacokinetic study of tea polyphenols following single-dose administration of epigallocatechin gallate and Polyphenon E. *Cancer Epidemiol. Biomark. Prev.* 10:53–58

Chow HHS, Cai Y, Hakim IA, Crowell JA, Shahi F, et al. 2003. Pharmacokinetics and safety of green tea polyphenols after multiple-dose administration of epigallocatechin gallate and Polyphenon E in healthy individuals. *Clin. Cancer Res.* 9:3312–19

Chow HHS, Hakim IA, Vining DR, Crowell JA, Ranger-Moore J, et al. 2005. Effects of dosing condition on the oral bioavailability of green tea catechins after single-dose administration of Polyphenon E in healthy individuals. *Clin. Cancer Res.* 11:4627–33

Chow HHS, Hakim IA, Vining DR, Crowell JA, Ranger-Moore J, et al. 2004. Effects of dosing condition on the oral bioavailability of green tea catechins after single-dose administration of Polyphenon E in healthy individuals. *Cancer Epidemiol. Biomark. Prev.* 13:S1885–85

Chun OK, Chung SJ, Song WO. 2007. Estimated dietary flavonoid intake and major food sources of US adults. *J. Nutr.* 137:1244–52

Chun OK, Floegel A, Chung SJ, Chung CE, Song WO, Koo SI. 2010. Estimation of antioxidant intakes from diet and supplements in U.S. adults. *J. Nutr.* 140:317–24

Cooper KA, Campos-Gimenez E, Alvarez DJ, Nagy K, Donovan JL, Williamson G. 2007. Rapid reversed phase ultra-performance liquid chromatography analysis of the major cocoa polyphenols and inter-relationships of their concentrations in chocolate. *J. Agric. Food Chem.* 55:2841–47

Cooper KA, Campos-Gimenez E, Alvarez DJ, Rytz A, Nagy K, Williamson G. 2008. Predictive relationship between polyphenol and nonfat cocoa solids content of chocolate. *J. Agric. Food Chem.* 56:260–65

Crespy V, Morand C, Besson C, Cotelle N, Vezin H, et al. 2003. The splanchnic metabolism of flavonoids highly differed according to the nature of the compound. *Am. J. Physiol. Gastrointest. Liver Physiol.* 284:G980–88

Del Rio D, Calani L, Scazzina F, Jechiu L, Cordero C, Brighenti F. 2010. Bioavailability of catechins from ready-to-drink tea. *Nutrition* 26:528–33

Del Rio D, Stewart AJ, Mullen W, Burns J, Lean MEJ, et al. 2004. HPLC-MSn analysis of phenolic compounds and purine alkaloids in green and black tea. *J. Agric. Food Chem.* 52:2807–15

Ding EL, Hutfless SM, Ding X, Girotra S. 2006. Chocolate and prevention of cardiovascular disease: a systematic review. *Nutr. Metab.* 3:2

Donovan JL, Crespy V, Manach C, Morand C, Besson C, et al. 2001. Catechin is metabolized by both the small intestine and liver of rats. *J. Nutr.* 131:1753–57

Donovan JL, Crespy V, Oliveria M, Cooper KA, Gibson BB, Williamson G. 2006. (+)-catechin is more bioavailable than (−)-catechin: relevance to the bioavailability of catechin from cocoa. *Free Radic. Res.* 40:1029–34

Donovan JL, Kasim-Karakas S, German JB, Waterhouse AL. 2002. Urinary excretion of catechin metabolites by human subjects after red wine consumption. *Br. J. Nutr.* 87:31–37

Engler MB, Engler MM, Chen CY, Malloy MJ, Browne A, et al. 2004. Flavonoid-rich dark chocolate improves endothelial function and increases plasma epicatechin concentrations in healthy adults. *J. Am. Coll. Nutr.* 23:197–204

Feng WY. 2006. Metabolism of green tea catechins: an overview. *Curr. Drug Metab.* 7:755–809

Ferruzzi MG. 2010. The influence of beverage composition on delivery of phenolic compounds from coffee and tea. *Physiol. Behav.* 100:33–41

Fraga CG, Keen CL. 2003. Flavanols and procyanidins as modulators of oxidation in vitro and in vivo. In *Free Radicals, Nitric Oxide, and Inflammation: Molecular, Biochemical, and Clinical Aspects*, ed. A Tomasi, T Ozben, VP Skulachev, NATO Sci. Ser. 344:2433. Netherlands: IOS Press

Friedman M, Kim SY, Lee SJ, Han GP, Han JS, et al. 2005. Distribution of catechins, theaflavins, caffeine, and theobromine in 77 teas consumed in the United States. *J. Food Sci.* 70:C550–59

Friedman M, Levin CE, Choi SH, Kozukue E, Kozukue N. 2006. HPLC analysis of catechins, theaflavins, and alkaloids in commercial teas and green tea dietary supplements: comparison of water and 80% ethanol/water extracts. *J. Food Sci.* 71:C328–37

Gawande S, Kale A, Kotwal S. 2008. Effect of nutrient mixture and black grapes on the pharmacokinetics of orally administered (−)epigallocatechin-3-gallate from green tea extract: a human study. *Phytother. Res.* 22:802–8

Gonthier MP, Cheynier V, Donovan JL, Manach C, Morand C, et al. 2003. Microbial aromatic acid metabolites formed in the gut account for a major fraction of the polyphenols excreted in urine of rats fed red wine polyphenols. *J. Nutr.* 133:461–67

Gotti R, Furlanetto S, Pinzauti S, Cavrini V. 2006. Analysis of catechins in *Theobroma* cacao beans by cyclodextrin-modified micellar electrokinetic chromatography. *J. Chromatogr. A* 1112:345–52

Grassi D, Desideri G, Croce G, Lippi C, Ferri C, Pasqualetti P. 2006. Cocoa and cardiovascular health: the sweet heart protection. *Agro Food Ind. Hi-Tech* 17:XIII–XVI

Green RJ, Murphy AS, Schulz B, Watkins BA, Ferruzzi MG. 2007. Common tea formulations modulate in vitro digestive recovery of green tea catechins. *Mol. Nutr. Food Res.* 51:1152–62

Gu LW, House SE, Wu XL, Ou BX, Prior RL. 2006. Procyanidin and catechin contents and antioxidant capacity of cocoa and chocolate products. *J. Agric. Food Chem.* 54:4057–61

Gu LW, Kelm M, Hammerstone JF, Beecher G, Cunningham D, et al. 2002. Fractionation of polymeric procyanidins from lowbush blueberry and quantification of procyanidins in selected foods with an optimized normal-phase HPLC-MS fluorescent detection method. *J. Agric. Food Chem.* 50:4852–60

Hammerstone JF, Lazarus SA, Schmitz HH. 2000. Procyanidin content and variation in some commonly consumed foods. *J. Nutr.* 130:S2086–92

Hansen CE, del Olmo M, Burri C. 1998. Enzyme activities in cocoa beans during fermentation. *J. Sci. Food Agric.* 77:273–81

Harada M, Kan Y, Naoki H, Fukui Y, Kageyama N, et al. 1999. Identification of the major antioxidative metabolites in biological fluids of the rat with ingested (+)-catechin and (−)-epicatechin. *Biosci. Biotechnol. Biochem.* 63:973–77

Heim KE, Tagliaferro AR, Bobilya DJ. 2002. Flavonoid antioxidants: chemistry, metabolism and structure-activity relationships. *J. Nutr. Biochem.* 13:572–84

Heiss C, Kleinbongard P, Dejam A, Perre S, Schroeter H, et al. 2005. Acute consumption of flavanol-rich cocoa and the reversal of endothelial dysfunction in smokers. *J. Am. Coll. Cardiol.* 46:1276–83

Henning SM, Fajardo-Lira C, Lee HW, Youssefian AA, Go VLW, Heber D. 2003. Catechin content of 18 teas and a green tea extract supplement correlates with the antioxidant capacity. *Nutr. Cancer* 45:226–35

Henning SM, Niu YT, Lee NH, Thames GD, Minutti RR, et al. 2004. Bioavailability and antioxidant activity of tea flavanols after consumption of green tea, black tea, or a green tea extract supplement. *Am. J. Clin. Nutr.* 80:1558–64

Holt RR, Lazarus SA, Sullards MC, Zhu QY, Schramm DD, et al. 2002. Procyanidin dimer B2 epicatechin-(4 beta-8)-epicatechin in human plasma after the consumption of a flavanol-rich cocoa. *Am. J. Clin. Nutr.* 76:798–804

Hong J, Lu H, Meng XF, Ryu JH, Hara Y, Yang CS. 2002. Stability, cellular uptake, biotransformation, and efflux of tea polyphenol (−)-epigallocatechin-3-gallate in HT-29 human colon adenocarcinoma cells. *Cancer Res.* 62:7241–46

Hou Z, Sang SM, You H, Lee MJ, Hong J, et al. 2005. Mechanism of action of (−)-epigallocatechin-3-gallate: auto-oxidation-dependent inactivation of epidermal growth factor receptor and direct effects on growth inhibition in human esophageal cancer KYSE 150 cells. *Cancer Res.* 65:8049–56

Jeong WS, Kong ANT. 2004. Biological properties of monomeric and polymeric catechins: green tea catechins and procyanidins. *Pharm. Biol.* 42:84–93

Justesen U, Arrigoni E, Larsen BR, Amado R. 2000. Degradation of flavonoid glycosides and aglycones during in vitro fermentation with human faecal flora. *Lebensm.-Wiss. Technol.* 33:424–30

Kealey KS, Snyder RM, Romanczyk LJ, Geyer HM, Myers ME, et al. 1998. Cocoa components, edible products having enhanced polyphenol content, methods of making same and medical uses. *Patent Coop. Treaty (PCT) WO 98/09533*, Mars Inc., McLean, VA

Keogh JB, McInerney J, Clifton PM. 2007. The effect of milk protein on the bioavailability of cocoa polyphenols. *J. Food Sci.* 72:S230–33

Khanbabaee K, van Ree T. 2001. Tannins: classification and definition. *Nat. Prod. Rep.* 18:641–49

Khokhar S, Magnusdottir SGM. 2002. Total phenol, catechin, and caffeine contents of teas commonly consumed in the United Kingdom. *J. Agric. Food Chem.* 50:565–70

Kofink M, Papagiannopoulos M, Galensa R. 2007. (−)-Catechin in cocoa and chocolate: occurence and analysis of an atypical flavan-3-ol enantiomer. *Molecules* 12:1274–88

Kohri T, Matsumoto N, Yamakawa M, Suzuki M, Nanjo F, et al. 2001a. Metabolic fate of (−)-[4-3H]epigallocatechin gallate in rats after oral administration. *J. Agric. Food Chem.* 49:4102–12

Kohri T, Nanjo F, Suziki M, Seto R, Matsumoto N, et al. 2001b. Synthesis of (−)-4-H-3 epigallocatechin gallate and its metabolic fate in rats after intravenous administration. *J. Agric. Food Chem.* 49:1042–48

Kohri T, Suzuki M, Nanjo F. 2003. Identification of metabolites of (−)-epicatechin gallate and their metabolic fate in the rat. *J. Agric. Food Chem.* 51:5561–66

Komatsu Y, Suematsu S, Hisanobu Y, Saigo H, Matsuda R, Hara K. 1993. Studies on preservation of constituents in canned drinks. Effects of ph and temperature on reaction-kinetics of catechins in green tea infusion. *Biosci. Biotechnol. Biochem.* 57:907–10

Kyle JAM, Morrice PC, McNeill G, Duthie GG. 2007. Effects of infusion time and addition of milk on content and absorption of polyphenols from black tea. *J. Agric. Food Chem.* 55:4889–94

Lambert JD, Lee MJ, Lu H, Meng XF, Ju J, et al. 2003. Epigallocatechin-3-gallate is absorbed but extensively glucuronidated following oral administration to mice. *J. Nutr.* 133:4172–77

Lambert JD, Sang SM, Yang CS. 2007. Biotransformation of green tea polyphenols and the biological activities of those metabolites. *Mol. Pharm.* 4:819–25

Laurent C, Besançon P, Caporiccio B. 2007. Flavonoids from a grape seed extract interact with digestive secretions and intestinal cells as assessed in an in vitro digestion/caco-2 cell culture model. *Food Chem.* 100:1704–12

Lee MJ, Maliakal P, Chen LS, Meng XF, Bondoc FY, et al. 2002. Pharmacokinetics of tea catechins after ingestion of green tea and (−)-epigallocatechin-3-gallate by humans: formation of different metabolites and individual variability. *Cancer Epidemiol. Biomark. Prev.* 11:1025–32

Lee MJ, Prabhu S, Meng XF, Li C, Yang CS. 2000. An improved method for the determination of green and black tea polyphenols in biomatrices by high-performance liquid chromatography with coulometric array detection. *Anal. Biochem.* 279:164–69

Li CA, Meng XF, Winnik B, Lee MJ, Lu H, et al. 2001. Analysis of urinary metabolites of tea catechins by liquid chromatography/electrospray ionization mass spectrometry. *Chem. Res. Toxicol.* 14:702–07

Lin Y-T, Hsiu S-L, Hou Y-C, Chen H-Y, Chao P-DL. 2003. Degradation of flavonoid aglycones by rabbit, rat and human fecal flora. *Biol. Pharm. Bull.* 26:747–51

Manach C, Scalbert A, Morand C, Remesy C, Jimenez L. 2004. Polyphenols: food sources and bioavailability. *Am. J. Clin. Nutr.* 79:727–47

Mandel SA, Avramovich-Tirosh Y, Reznichenko L, Zheng HL, Weinreb O, et al. 2005. Multifunctional activities of green tea catechins in neuroprotection: modulation of cell survival genes, iron-dependent oxidative stress and PKC signaling pathway. *Neurosignals* 14:46–60

Matsuo Y, Yamada Y, Tanaka T, Kouno I. 2008. Enzymatic oxidation of gallocatechin and epigallocatechin: effects of C-ring configuration on the reaction products. *Phytochemistry* 69:3054–61

Menet MC, Sang SM, Yang CS, Ho CT, Rosen RT. 2004. Analysis of theaflavins and thearubigins from black tea extract by MALDI-TOF mass spectrometry. *J. Agric. Food Chem.* 52:2455–61

Miller KB, Stuart DA, Smith NL, Lee CY, McHale NL, et al. 2006. Antioxidant activity and polyphenol and procyanidin contents of selected commercially available cocoa-containing and chocolate products in the United States. *J. Agric. Food Chem.* 54:4062–68

Miura YH, Tomita I, Watanabe T, Hirayama T, Fukui S. 1998. Active oxygens generation by flavonoids. *Biol. Pharm. Bull.* 21:93–96

Mochizuki M, Yamazaki S, Kano K, Ikeda T. 2002. Kinetic analysis and mechanistic aspects of autoxidation of catechins. *Biochim. Biophys. Acta* 1569:35–44

Moon YJ, Wang XD, Morris ME. 2006. Dietary flavonoids: effects on xenobiotic and carcinogen metabolism. *Toxicol. in Vitro* 20:187–210

Mullen W, Borges G, Donovan JL, Edwards CA, Serafini M, et al. 2009. Milk decreases urinary excretion but not plasma pharmacokinetics of cocoa flavan-3-ol metabolites in humans. *Am. J. Clin. Nutr.* 89:1784–91

Muniyappa R, Hall G, Kolodziej TL, Karne RJ, Crandon SK, Quon MJ. 2008. Cocoa consumption for 2 wk enhances insulin-mediated vasodilatation without improving blood pressure or insulin resistance in essential hypertension. *Am. J. Clin. Nutr.* 88:1685–96

Nagao T, Meguro S, Hase T, Otsuka K, Komikado M, et al. 2009. A catechin-rich beverage improves obesity and blood glucose control in patients with type 2 diabetes. *Obesity* 17: 310–17

Natsume M, Osakabe N, Yamagishi M, Takizawa T, Nakamura T, et al. 2000. Analyses of polyphenols in cacao liquor, cocoa, and chocolate by normal-phase and reversed-phase HPLC. *Biosci. Biotechnol. Biochem.* 64:2581–87

Neilson AP, George JC, Janle EM, Mattes RD, Rudolph R, et al. 2009. Influence of chocolate matrix composition on cocoa flavan-3-ol bioaccessibility in vitro and bioavailability in humans. *J. Agric. Food Chem.* 57:9418–26

Neilson AP, Hopf AS, Cooper BR, Pereira MA, Bomser JA, Ferruzzi MG. 2007. Catechin degradation with concurrent formation of homo- and heterocatechin dimers during in vitro digestion. *J. Agric. Food Chem.* 55:8941–49

Neilson AP, Sapper TN, Janle EM, Rudolph R, Matusheski NV, Ferruzzi MG. 2010a. Chocolate matrix factors modulate the pharmacokinetic behavior of cocoa flavan-3-ol phase II metabolites following oral consumption by Sprague–Dawley rats. *J. Agric. Food Chem.* 58:6685–91

Neilson AP, Song BJ, Sapper TN, Bomser JA, Ferruzzi MG. 2010b. Tea catechin auto-oxidation dimers are accumulated and retained by caco-2 human intestinal cells. *Nutr. Res.* 30:327–40

Nelson BC, Sharpless KE. 2003. Quantification of the predominant monomeric catechins in baking chocolate standard reference material by LC/APCI-MS. *J. Agric. Food Chem.* 51: 531–37

Neuhouser ML. 2004. Flavonoids and cancer prevention: What is the evidence in humans? *Pharm. Biol.* 42:36–45

O'Hara AM, Shanahan F. 2006. The gut flora as a forgotten organ. *EMBO Rep.* 7:688–93

O'Hara AM, Shanahan F. 2007. Gut microbiota: mining for therapeutic potential. *Clin. Gastroenterol. Hepatol.* 5:274–84

Okumura H, Ichitani M, Takhara T, Kunimoto KK. 2008. Effect of cyclodextrins on the thermal epimerization of tea catechins. *Food Sci. Technol. Res.* 14:83–88

Oliviero T, Capuano E, Cämmerer B, Fogliano V. 2009. Influence of roasting on the antioxidant activity and HMF formation of a cocoa bean model systems. *J. Agric. Food Chem.* 57:147–52

Parks DA. 1989. Oxygen radicals - mediators of gastrointestinal patho-physiology. *Gut* 30:293–98

Peters CM, Green RJ, Janle EM, Ferruzzi MG. 2010. Formulation with ascorbic acid and sucrose modulates catechin bioavailability from green tea. *Food Res. Int.* 43:95–102

Pietta P, Simonetti P. 1998. Dietary flavonoids and interaction with endogenous antioxidants. *Biochem. Mol. Biol. Int.* 44:1069–74

Piskula MK, Terao J. 1998. Accumulation of (−)-epicatechin metabolites in rat plasma after oral administration and distribution of conjugation enzymes in rat tissues. *J. Nutr.* 128:1172–78

Puch F, Samson-Villeger S, Guyonnet D, Blachon JL, Rawlings AV, Lassel T. 2008. Consumption of functional fermented milk containing borage oil, green tea and vitamin E enhances skin barrier function. *Exp. Dermatol.* 17:668–74

Record IR, Lane JM. 2001. Simulated intestinal digestion of green and black teas. *Food Chem.* 73:481–86

Reddy VC, Sagar GVV, Sreeramulu D, Venu L, Raghunath M. 2005. Addition of milk does not alter the antioxidant activity of black tea. *Ann. Nutr. Metab.* 49:189–95

Rein D, Lotito S, Holt RR, Keen CL, Schmitz HH, Fraga CG. 2000. Epicatechin in human plasma: in vivo determination and effect of chocolate consumption on plasma oxidation status. *J. Nutr.* 130:S2109–14

Richelle M, Tavazzi I, Enslen M, Offord EA. 1999. Plasma kinetics in man of epicatechin from black chocolate. *Eur. J. Clin. Nutr.* 53:22–26

Rios LY, Gonthier M-P, Remesy C, Mila I, Lapierre C, et al. 2003. Chocolate intake increases urinary excretion of polyphenol-derived phenolic acids in healthy human subjects. *Am. J. Clin. Nutr.* 77:912–18

Roura E, Andres-Lacueva C, Estruch R, Bilbao MLM, Izquierdo-Pulido M, Lamuela-Raventos RM. 2008. The effects of milk as a food matrix for polyphenols on the excretion profile of cocoa (−)-epicatechin metabolites in healthy human subjects. *Br. J. Nutr.* 100:846–51

Roura E, Andres-Lacueva C, Estruch R, Mata-Bilbao ML, Izquierdo-Pulido M, et al. 2007. Milk does not affect the bioavailability of cocoa powder flavonoid in healthy human. *Ann. Nutr. Metab.* 51:493–98

Roura E, Andres-Lacueva C, Jauregui O, Badia E, Estruch R, et al. 2005. Rapid liquid chromatography tandem mass spectrometry assay to quantify plasma (−)-epicatechin metabolites after ingestion of a standard portion of cocoa beverage in humans. *J. Agric. Food Chem.* 53:6190–94

Sanchez-Rabaneda F, Jauregui O, Casals I, Andres-Lacueva C, Izquierdo-Pulido M, Lamuela-Raventos RM. 2003. Liquid chromatographic/electrospray ionization tandem mass spectrometric study of the phenolic composition of cocoa (*Theobroma cacao*). *J. Mass Spectrom.* 38:35–42

Sang SM, Lee MJ, Hou Z, Ho CT, Yang CS. 2005. Stability of tea polyphenol (−)-epigallocatechin-3-gallate and formation of dimers and epimers under common experimental conditions. *J. Agric. Food Chem.* 53:9478–84

Sang SM, Yang I, Buckley B, Ho CT, Yang CS. 2007. Autoxidative quinone formation in vitro and metabolite formation in vivo from tea polyphenol (−)-epigallocatechin-3-gallate: studied by real-time mass spectrometry combined with tandem mass ion mapping. *Free Radic. Biol. Med.* 43:362–71

Scalbert A, Williamson G. 2000. Dietary intake and bioavailability of polyphenols. *J. Nutr.* 130:S2073–85

Schramm DD, Karim M, Schrader HR, Holt RR, Kirkpatrick NJ, et al. 2003. Food effects on the absorption and pharmacokinetics of cocoa flavanols. *Life Sci.* 73:857–69

Schramm DD, Wang JF, Holt RR, Ensunsa JL, Gonsalves JL, et al. 2001. Chocolate procyanidins decrease the leukotriene-prostacyclin ratio in humans and human aortic endothelial cells. *Am. J. Clin. Nutr.* 73:36–40

Schroeter H, Heiss C, Balzer J, Kleinbongard P, Keen CL, et al. 2006. (−)-Epicatechin mediates beneficial effects of flavanol-rich cocoa on vascular function in humans. *Proc. Natl. Acad. Sci. USA* 103:1024–29

Schroeter H, Holt RR, Orozoco TJ, Schmitz HH, Keen CL. 2003. Nutrition: milk and absorption of dietary flavanols. *Nature* 426:787–88

Serafini M, Bugianesi R, Maiani G, Valtuena S, De Santis S, Crozier A. 2003. Plasma antioxidants from chocolate: dark chocolate may offer its consumers health benefits the milk variety cannot match. *Nature* 424:1013

Silberberg M, Morand C, Manach C, Scalbert A, Remesy C. 2005. Co-administration of quercetin and catechin in rats alters their absorption but not their metabolism. *Life Sci.* 77:3156–67

Simons AL, Renouf M, Hendrich S, Murphy PA. 2005. Human gut microbial degradation of flavonoids: structure-function relationships. *J. Agric. Food Chem.* 53:4258–63

Stalmach A, Mullen W, Steiling H, Williamson G, Lean MEJ, Crozier A. 2010. Absorption, metabolism, and excretion of green tea flavan-3-ols in humans with an ileostomy. *Mol. Nutr. Food Res.* 54:323–34

Stalmach A, Troufflard S, Serafini M, Crozier A. 2009. Absorption, metabolism and excretion of choladi green tea flavan-3-ols by humans. *Mol. Nutr. Food Res.* 53:S44–53

Su YL, Leung LK, Huang Y, Chen ZY. 2003. Stability of tea theaflavins and catechins. *Food Chem.* 83:189–95

Takano M, Yumoto R, Murakami T. 2006. Expression and function of efflux drug transporters in the intestine. *Pharmacol. Ther.* 109:137–61

Tanaka T, Mine C, Watarumi S, Fujioka T, Mihashi K, et al. 2002. Accumulation of epigallocatechin quinone dimers during tea fermentation and formation of theasinensins. *J. Nat. Prod.* 65:1582–87

Taubert D, Roesen R, Lehmann C, Jung N, Schomig E. 2007. Effects of low habitual cocoa intake on blood pressure and bioactive nitric oxide: a randomized controlled trial. *JAMA* 298:49–60

Thielecke F, Boschmann M. 2009. The potential role of green tea catechins in the prevention of the metabolic syndrome - a review. *Phytochemistry* 70: 11–24

Tsuchiya H, Sato M, Kato H, Okubo T, Juneja LR, Kim M. 1997. Simultaneous determination of catechins in human saliva by high-performance liquid chromatography. *J. Chromatogr. B* 703:253–58

Tzounis X, Vulevic J, Kuhnle GGC, George T, Leonczak J, et al. 2008. Flavanol monomer-induced changes to the human faecal microflora. *Br. J. Nutr.* 99:782–92

Vaidyanathan JB, Walle T. 2001. Transport and metabolism of the tea flavonoid (−)-epicatechin by the human intestinal cell line Caco-2. *Pharm. Res.* 18:1420–25

Vaidyanathan JB, Walle T. 2003. Cellular uptake and efflux of the tea flavonoid (−)-epicatechin-3-gallate in the human intestinal cell line caco-2. *J. Pharmacol. Exp. Ther.* 307:745–52

Van Amelsvoort JMM, Hof KHV, Mathot J, Mulder TPJ, Wiersma A, Tijburg LBM. 2001. Plasma concentrations of individual tea catechins after a single oral dose in humans. *Xenobiotica* 31:891–901

van het Hof KH, Kivits GAA, Weststrate JA, Tijburg LBM. 1998. Bioavailability of catechins from tea: the effect of milk. *Eur. J. Clin. Nutr.* 52:356–59

Wan Y, Vinson JA, Etherton TD, Proch J, Lazarus SA, Kris-Etherton P. 2001. Effects of cocoa powder and dark chocolate on LDL oxidative susceptibility and prostaglandin concentrations in humans. *Am. J. Clin. Nutr.* 74:596–602

Wang HF, Helliwell K. 2000. Epimerisation of catechins in green tea infusions. *Food Chem.* 70:337–44

Wang JF, Schramm DD, Holt RR, Ensunsa JL, Fraga CG, et al. 2000. A dose-response effect from chocolate consumption on plasma epicatechin and oxidative damage. *J. Nutr.* 130:S2115–19

Wang R, Zhou WB, Wen RAH. 2006. Kinetic study of the thermal stability of tea catechins in aqueous systems using a microwave reactor. *J. Agric. Food Chem.* 54:5924–32

Warden BA, Smith LS, Beecher GR, Balentine DA, Clevidence BA. 2001. Catechins are bioavailable in men and women drinking black tea throughout the day. *J. Nutr.* 131:1731–37

Williamson G, Day AJ, Plumb GW, Couteau D. 2000. Human metabolic pathways of dietary flavonoids and cinnamates. *Biochem. Soc. Trans.* 28:16–22

Williamson G, Manach C. 2005. Bioavailability and bioefficacy of polyphenols in humans. II. Review of 93 intervention studies. *Am. J. Clin. Nutr.* 81:S243–55

Winter J, Moore LH, Dowell VR, Bokkenheuser VD. 1989. C-ring cleavage of flavonoids by human intestinal bacteria. *Appl. Environ. Microbiol.* 55:1203–8

Wiswedel I, Hirsch D, Kropf S, Gruening M, Pfister E, et al. 2004. Flavanol-rich cocoa drink lowers plasma F-2-isoprostane concentrations in humans. *Free Radic. Biol. Med.* 37:411–21

Wollgast J, Anklam E. 2000. Review on polyphenols in *Theobroma cacao*: changes in composition during the manufacture of chocolate and methodology for identification and quantification. *Food Res. Int.* 33:423–47

Wright LP, Mphangwe NIK, Nyirenda HE, Apostolides Z. 2002. Analysis of the theaflavin composition in black tea (*Camellia sinensis*) for predicting the quality of tea produced in central and southern Africa. *J. Sci. Food Agric.* 82:517–25

Xu JZ, Leung LK, Huang Y, Chen ZY. 2003. Epimerisation of tea polyphenols in tea drinks. *J. Sci. Food Agric.* 83:1617–21

Yang B, Arai K, Kusu F. 2000. Determination of catechins in human urine subsequent to tea ingestion by high-performance liquid chromatography with electrochemical detection. *Anal. Biochem.* 283:77–82

Yang CS, Chen LS, Lee MJ, Balentine D, Kuo MC, Schantz SP. 1998. Blood and urine levels of tea catechins after ingestion of different amounts of green tea by human volunteers. *Cancer Epidemiol. Biomark. Prev.* 7:351–54

Yao LH, Caffin N, D'Arcy B, Jiang YM, Shi J, et al. 2005. Seasonal variations of phenolic compounds in Australia-grown tea (*Camellia sinensis*). *J. Agric. Food Chem.* 53:6477–83

Yoshino K, Suzuki M, Sasaki K, Miyase T, Sano M. 1999. Formation of antioxidants from (−)-epigallocatechin gallate in mild alkaline fluids, such as authentic intestinal juice and mouse plasma. *J. Nutr. Biochem.* 10:223–29

Zhang L, Zheng Y, Chow MSS, Zuo Z. 2004. Investigation of intestinal absorption and disposition of green tea catechins by caco-2 monolayer model. *Int. J. Pharm.* 287:1–12

Zhu BT, Patel UK, Cai MX, Lee AJ, Conney AH. 2001. Rapid conversion of tea catechins to monomethylated products by rat liver cytosolic catechol-O-methyltransferase. *Xenobiotica* 31:879–90

Zhu QY, Hammerstone JF, Lazarus SA, Schmitz HH, Keen CL. 2003. Stabilizing effect of ascorbic acid on flavan-3-ols and dimeric procyanidins from cocoa. *J. Agric. Food Chem.* 51:828–33

Zhu QY, Zhang AQ, Tsang D, Huang Y, Chen ZY. 1997. Stability of green tea catechins. *J. Agric. Food Chem.* 45:4624–28

Rheological Innovations for Characterizing Food Material Properties

H.S. Melito and C.R. Daubert*

Department of Food, Bioprocessing, and Nutrition Sciences, North Carolina State University, Raleigh, North Carolina 27695; email: cdaubert@ncsu.edu

Annu. Rev. Food Sci. Technol. 2011. 2:153–79

First published online as a Review in Advance on October 28, 2010

The *Annual Review of Food Science and Technology* is online at food.annualreviews.org

This article's doi:
10.1146/annurev-food-022510-133626

1941-1413/11/0410-0153$20.00

*Corresponding author

Keywords

rheological testing, shear testing, rheo-NMR, microrheology, large amplitude oscillatory shear (LAOS) testing

Abstract

Rheological methods are continually evolving to encompass novel technologies and measurement methods. This review highlights novel techniques used to analyze the rheological properties of foods over the previous decade. Techniques reviewed include large amplitude oscillatory shear (LAOS) testing and rheological techniques coupled with other measurement methods, such as microscopy and nuclear magnetic resonance (NMR). Novel techniques are briefly overviewed and discussed in terms of advantages and disadvantages, previous use, and suggested future utilization.

INTRODUCTION

Linear viscoelastic region (LVR): the stress/strain region in which the sample exhibits a linear stress response to an applied strain; the complex, elastic, and viscous moduli are constant in this region

Small amplitude oscillatory shear (SAOS) testing: oscillatory shear testing within the linear viscoelastic region

Large amplitude oscillatory shear (LAOS) testing: oscillatory shear testing outside the linear viscoelastic region

Rheology is the study of the flow and deformation of matter. Rheological measurements are used in the food industry for scaleup and quality control as well as in the laboratory for scientific research. Although there are many possible tests, analyses of interest in food rheology may be grouped as either tensile, compressive, or shear testing. This review focuses on novel shear-testing techniques.

The validity and repeatability of the measurements gathered from shear testing depend on both instrumentation and methodology. For example, determination of rheological properties may be difficult when instrument sensitivity is below that needed to determine the property, or if the methodology used requires the sample to be altered (by mixing with a solvent, heating, cooling, shearing, etc.) or contains assumptions that may not hold true for the sample. Additionally, certain foods such as foams, foods with high lipid content, and foods containing hydrocolloids can be difficult to analyze, as these foods can be extremely shear sensitive and exhibit phenomena such as slip or problems associated with significant normal stress differences. Traditional rheological tests are inherently disruptive to the sample, applying sufficient force to the sample to induce a deformation. This force may damage sensitive structures, altering the rheological properties of the sample. It is often necessary to develop protocol that is minimally disruptive to the sample. Depending on the desired measurement, it may also be necessary to couple rheological equipment with other analytical tools such as microscopy or magnetic resonance equipment. In particular, methodology that couples microscopy with traditional rheological techniques, or microrheology, has evolved significantly over the past decade. Although microrheological measurements are not directly relatable to traditional rheological measurements, microrheology is able to overcome several limitations of traditional shear rheology. Additionally, methodology that can account for nonideal behavior or behavior beyond the linear viscoelastic region (LVR) may prove useful when measuring rheological properties of foods, given that foods are ultimately subjected to stresses outside the linear elastic domain. The objective of this paper is to highlight the rheological techniques that have been novel to food science over the past decade. Rather than providing in-depth explanations, a general overview of each technique is provided, and recent advances and potential applications in food science are discussed.

LARGE AMPLITUDE OSCILLATORY SHEAR

Oscillatory shear testing of materials may be broken down into small amplitude oscillatory shear (SAOS) and large amplitude oscillatory shear (LAOS). Both SAOS and LAOS testing may be performed on a standard stress- or strain-controlled rheometer, as both instruments involve a rheological tool (bob, cone, vane, etc.) imparting an oscillating stress or deformation to the sample. The major difference between the two testing methods is that SAOS testing is restricted to the LVR, whereas LAOS testing occurs beyond linearity. Although LAOS testing has been used to study various polymers and polymer melts for over 40 years (Debbaut & Burhin 2002), it is not widely used in the food industry. Most studies use SAOS testing as a means to quantify rheological properties of foods. Keeping the material tested in the LVR results in material responses independent of the magnitude of applied stress or strain, or the rate of strain application. However, many processes involving foods, such as chewing and swallowing, require very large deformations, occurring well outside the LVR (Steffe 1996). Using LAOS to quantify material responses under large deformations allows for the study of rheological properties during common food processes (Song et al. 2006, Brenner et al. 2009).

When a sample is sheared, it often undergoes microstructural changes such as polymer chain alignment with the flow field, increased chain interaction, and network formation or disruption

(Sim et al. 2003). Because of sensitivity to microstructural changes, LAOS is often used to determine rheological properties of polymers (Hyun et al. 2002, Carotenuto et al. 2008). This sensitivity is a useful analytical tool for classifying polymers based on general microstructural changes during large strain application (Hyun et al. 2002). Hyun et al. (2002) tested several polymer melts as well as a xanthan gum solution under LAOS at constant frequency (1 rad s^{-1}) and varied strain (3% to 1000%). The resulting data indicated that polymers could be divided into four categories based on their behavior during LAOS: strain softening (both G', the storage modulus, and G'', the shear loss modulus, decrease), strain hardening (both G' and G'' increase), weak strain overshoot (G' decreases and G'' initially increases, then decreases), and strong strain overshoot (both G' and G'' initially increase, then decrease). Strain hardening was defined as a decrease in deformation rate with increasing strain, whereas strain softening was defined as an increase in deformation rate with increasing strain (Hyun et al. 2002). Although calculation of G' and G'' requires a linear relationship between stress and calculations involving these parameters outside of the LVR should be invalid, Hyun et al. (2002) performed strain and measurements beyond the region of linearity and analyzed stress responses via Fourier transform, and concluded that the deviation from linearity was not significant. Sim et al. (2003) created a nonlinear network model of the stress tensor matrix created by application of LAOS on various types of polymers. Although simplistic, the model was found to have good agreement with the results of Hyun et al. (2002) (Sim et al. 2003). Sim et al. (2003) hypothesized that the model could be useful in explaining polymer behavior in terms of microstructural changes.

There has been an increased interest in Fourier analysis to examine LAOS data. Fourier analysis is more precise and modern computing technology can readily perform the necessary calculations (Debbaut & Burhin 2002, Sim et al. 2003). In oscillatory testing, strain is applied according to a sinusoidal function. The shear rate at any time may be found by differentiating the applied strain function with respect to time. Using Fourier analysis, the absolute value of the shear rate expression is converted to a sum of different harmonic contributions (Wilhelm 2002), enabling LAOS data to be analyzed for the contribution of different harmonics. Although the stress response from SAOS may be described by the first harmonic alone, stress responses from LAOS include higher-order harmonics (Debbaut & Burhin 2002). The contribution from the higher-order harmonics becomes significant in the nonlinear region due to the dependency of apparent viscosity on applied strain rate: Strain rate varies sinusoidally, so apparent viscosity will also vary sinusoidally. This sinusoidal variation in apparent viscosity can be used to explain differences among viscoelastic samples: Samples with the same apparent viscosity may have significantly different higher-order harmonic intensities and thus different flow behavior (Wilhelm 2002). Fourier transforms are also useful for increasing the signal-to-noise ratio, the measure of signal strength to random fluctuations for improved sensitivity (Wilhelm 2002). In addition to analysis of shear stress, strain, and phase angle data, Fourier transforms have also been used to examine normal stress during LAOS (Nam et al. 2008), linear to nonlinear material behavioral transitions (Wilhelm 2002), polymer morphology (Wilhelm 2002, Carotenuto et al. 2008), accuracy of predictive rheological models (Debbaut & Burhin 2002, Wilhelm 2002), and characterization of polymer dispersions (Wilhelm 2002).

A method to simultaneously quantify both viscous and elastic nonlinear behavior using LAOS was recently developed by Ewoldt et al. (2008). In this method, the general stress response is broken down into elastic (σ') and viscous stress (σ'') responses. The elastic and viscous stresses are plotted against the strain (γ) and strain rate ($\dot{\gamma}$) input functions, and Chebyshev polynomials (first kind) are fit to the plots

$$\sigma'\left(\frac{\gamma}{\gamma_o}\right) = \gamma_o \sum_{n:odd} e_n(\omega, \gamma_o) T_n \left(\frac{\gamma}{\gamma_o}\right) \tag{1}$$

and

$$\sigma''\left(\frac{\dot{\gamma}}{\dot{\gamma}_o}\right) = \dot{\gamma}_o \sum_{n:odd} \upsilon_n(\omega, \dot{\gamma}_o) T_n\left(\frac{\dot{\gamma}}{\dot{\gamma}_o}\right), \tag{2}$$

where γ_o is the strain amplitude, $\dot{\gamma}_o$ is the strain rate amplitude, $e_n(\omega, \gamma_o)$ and $\upsilon_n(\omega, \dot{\gamma}_o)$ are the elastic and viscous Chebyshev coefficients, respectively, and $T_n(\frac{\gamma}{\gamma_o})$ and $T_n(\frac{\dot{\gamma}}{\dot{\gamma}_o})$ are n^{th} order Chebyshev polynomials of the first kind. A general form of the Chebyshev polynomials of the first kind is given by

$$T_n(x) = 2xT_{n-1}(x) - T_{n-2}(x). \tag{3}$$

The Chebyshev polynomials were chosen for fitting the data because these polynomials consist of orthogonal terms, have odd symmetry around $\frac{\gamma}{\gamma_o} = 0$, and have a bounded range for higher-order coefficients. The third-order Chebyshev coefficients (e_3 and υ_3) may then be used to determine material behavior (Ewoldt et al. 2008). Ewoldt et al. (2008) grouped materials into four main categories: strain hardening ($e_3 > 0$), strain softening ($e_3 < 0$), shear thickening ($\upsilon_3 > 0$), and shear thinning ($\upsilon_3 < 0$). The third-order Chebyshev coefficients may also be calculated from the third-order Fourier coefficients,

$$e_3 = -|G_3^*| \cos \delta_3 \tag{4}$$

and

$$\upsilon_3 = \frac{|G_3^*|}{\omega} \sin \delta_3, \tag{5}$$

where δ_3 is the initial value of the third-order harmonic contribution and varies between 0 and 2π. These coefficients give a physical interpretation to the Fourier coefficients (Ewoldt et al. 2008).

Ewoldt et al. (2008) also developed a new interpretation of viscoelastic moduli in the nonlinear region. Previously, it was not possible to calculate storage or loss moduli in the nonlinear region, as the assumptions for the equations were violated, and the results had no physical meaning (Steffe 1996, Hyun et al. 2002, Cho et al. 2005). Many of the studies using LAOS to investigate the nonlinear region attempted to develop a method to extend the validity of the calculations for stress and shear rate used in the linear region to the nonlinear region rather than develop new interpretations of the data. However, Ewoldt et al. (2008) were able to derive viscous and elastic behavior from the first- and third-order Chebyshev coefficients. The elastic modulus was broken down into a minimum strain modulus, G'_M (the tangent modulus measured at zero strain), and large strain modulus, G''_L (the secant modulus measured at maximum strain), that took higher harmonic contributions into account. These two moduli may be seen in a Lissajous plot of shear stress versus applied strain (**Figure 1**, see color insert). The dynamic viscosity was broken down into the instantaneous viscosity at minimum shear rate, η'_M, and the instantaneous viscosity at maximum shear rate, η'_L. As with the newly defined elastic moduli, the instantaneous viscosities took higher harmonic contributions into account. These instantaneous viscosities may be seen in a Lissajous plot of shear stress versus applied strain rate (**Figure 1**). The elastic moduli and instantaneous viscosities were used to calculate the strain-hardening and shear-thickening ratios, respectively (Ewoldt et al. 2008). Ewoldt et al. (2008, 2009) used this method to determine the properties of gastropod pedal mucus, a 0.2% xanthan gum solution, and cetylpyridinium chloride and sodium salicylate in brine. The method may also be used for food and pharmaceutical products, yielding valuable information about nonlinear rheological behavior. LAOS testing has been used in many studies on suspension and polymer behavior (Debbaut & Burhin 2002, Joshi 2005, Narumi et al. 2005, Hyun et al. 2006, Sugimoto et al. 2006, Grosso & Maffettone 2007, Ravindranath & Wang 2008) to examine rheological behavior of various solutions exposed to large deformations. A few studies have examined food ingredients, including oil in water emulsions (Knudsen et al.

2008), gluten gels (Ng & McKinley 2008), fish protein isolate gels (Brenner et al. 2009), skim milk gels (Knudsen et al. 2006), and hydrocolloid solutions (Song et al. 2006, Klein et al. 2008). This technique shows great potential for application in the food industry: most food processing as well as oral processing occurs in a region well outside the LVR and a general means to characterize food behavior in such processes is not currently in use.

RHEOLOGY COUPLED WITH OTHER MEASUREMENT TECHNIQUES

Over the past decade, there has been growing interest in using rheology coupled with various other techniques such as microscopy, ultrasound, and magnetic resonance. These techniques allow for the observation of material structure on both a macroscopic and microscopic level (Nicolas et al. 2003b, Squires & Brady 2005), as well as material behavior under process conditions (Nicolas et al. 2003b, Barnes et al. 2006, Wiklund et al. 2007). Combining rheology with other measurement methods allows limitations of traditional shear rheometry, such as the need for relatively large sample sizes (Squires & Brady 2005, Cicuta & Donald 2007), sample disruption (Barnes et al. 2006), limitations on stress and frequency ranges tested (Cicuta & Donald 2007), and inability to precisely replicate process conditions (Wiklund et al. 2007).

Many of the methods that couple rheological techniques with other measurement techniques fall under the definition of microrheology (Nicolas et al. 2003b, Cicuta & Donald 2007). The term microrheology has several definitions, although the general definition is a method that links local properties to bulk rheological behavior (Nicolas et al. 2003b, Mizuno et al. 2008, Kimura 2009). Microrheology may also be defined as rheology from mutual interactions of microparticles or rheology using microliter sample sizes (Nicolas et al. 2003b, Mizuno et al. 2008). Rheology coupled with nuclear magnetic resonance (NMR) (Nicolas et al. 2003b), magnetic resonance imaging (MRI), confocal scanning laser microscopy (CSLM) (Nicolas et al. 2003b, Filip et al. 2006), atomic force microscopy (AFM) (Filip et al. 2006), and diffusing wave spectroscopy (DWS) (Harden & Viasnoff 2001) are all examples of microrheological techniques and are discussed further in the next sections.

Nuclear magnetic resonance (NMR): a spectroscopy technique that uses the spin properties of certain nuclei to determine the sample composition

Magnetic resonance imaging (MRI): a technique that uses multiple nuclear magnetic resonance images to create a three-dimensional map of the sample

Confocal scanning laser microscopy (CSLM): a microscopy technique that uses a scanning laser to create a three-dimensional image of the sample

Atomic force microscopy (AFM): a microscopy technique that uses a tip attached to a cantilever to scan and create a contour map of the sample surface

Diffusing wave spectroscopy (DWS): a spectroscopy technique that correlates the light scattering pattern to sample properties

Rheology and Ultrasound

Ultrasound is defined as mechanical wavelengths ranging from 0.001 to 1.0 mm in length. The methodology for using ultrasound to measure the rheological properties of materials was developed in the late 1990s (Ouriev et al. 2000) and has become widely used for characterizing rheological properties of foods during the past decade. Ultrasound has been used to characterize many different foods, including carrageenan gels (Wang et al. 2005), protein gels (Wang et al. 2007), dairy products (Dukhin et al. 2005, Eskelinen et al. 2007), chocolate (Ouriev et al. 2004), cake batter (Gómez et al. 2008), flour doughs (Ross et al. 2004, Garcia-Alvarez et al. 2006, Álava et al. 2007), honey (Kulmyrzaev & McClements 2000), tomato concentrate (Choi et al. 2006), and tofu (Ting et al. 2009). Ultrasound may be used to measure the rheological properties of either stationary samples or fluids flowing in a pipe. Both methodologies use frequencies ranging from 1 to 100 Hz (Ouriev et al. 2000, Dukhin et al. 2005).

The methodology of ultrasonic measurements in a stationary sample involves two transducers placed on either side of a sample chamber containing the material to be measured (**Figure 2**). One transducer (T_1) converts an input electrical impulse into a sonic pulse at a preset frequency and directs the pulse at the sample. The sound waves travel through the sample and are detected by the second transducer. The second transducer (T_2) converts the waves back to an electrical impulse and sends the electrical pulse to a computer for comparison to the input pulse for signal

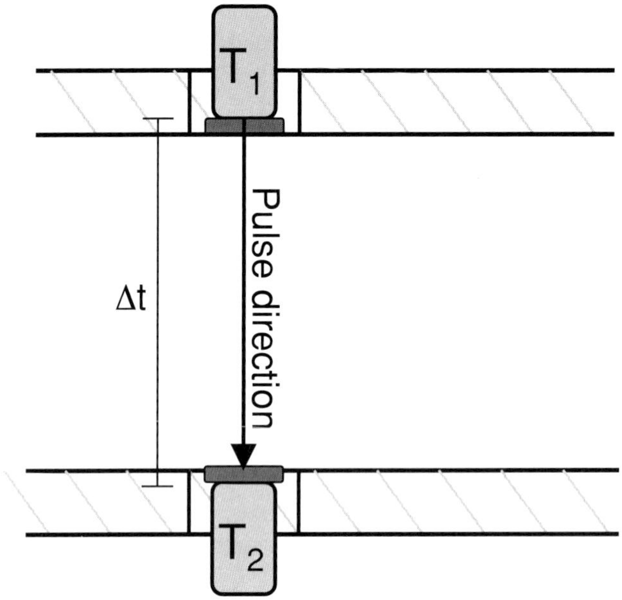

Figure 2

Two-transducer ultrasound instrumentation setup for static sample.

loss due to attenuation and time delay (Dukhin et al. 2005). Various properties of the material, such as storage and loss modulus, and size of suspended particles, can then be calculated from the velocity and time data (Dukhin et al. 2005). A second method using ultrasound to calculate shear properties of materials was developed by Kulmyrzaev & McClements (2000). This method uses an ultrasonic shear transducer with a delay line. The transducer fires an ultrasonic pulse along the delay line at the sample interface, which reflects the pulse, and the same transducer detects the reflected pulse. The phase and magnitude as a function of frequency are then analyzed by Fourier transform. Complex shear modulus, phase angle, and dynamic viscosity may be calculated from the Fourier transform of the data (Kulmyrzaev & McClements 2000). Ting et al. (2009) used a similar method to examine changes in viscoelasticity of tofu during gelation.

Although static measurements of materials using ultrasound yield valuable rheological information, there are several disadvantages to this method. Measurement rate is slow and generally provides data at a single shear rate (Dogan et al. 2005, Pfund et al. 2006, Wiklund et al. 2007). It is also difficult to properly replicate process conditions in a laboratory (Dogan et al. 2005, Wiklund et al. 2007), so the properties or the velocity profiles of the material measured in the lab may not be the same as those of the material in the process (Dogan et al. 2005, Young et al. 2008). In addition, calculating rheological properties from available process information (temperature, pressure, etc.) is extremely difficult (Ouriev et al. 2004). Therefore, it is necessary to measure rheological properties of the material during processing using an in-line technique. Many studies have been done over the past decade to develop such techniques that utilize ultrasound (Ouriev et al. 2000, Ouriev & Windhab 2002, Dogan et al. 2005, Wiklund et al. 2007).

Techniques using ultrasound to measure properties of fluids flowing in a pipe take advantage of the Doppler effect (Ouriev et al. 2000, Ouriev & Windhab 2002). A transducer is mounted at a set angle of inclination in a flow adapter cell in the pipe in which measurements will be taken (**Figure 3*a***). The transducer fires short pulses of ultrasonic waves into the fluid as it flows through the pipe. The pulses are separated by a set time period. The waves are reflected by the fluid

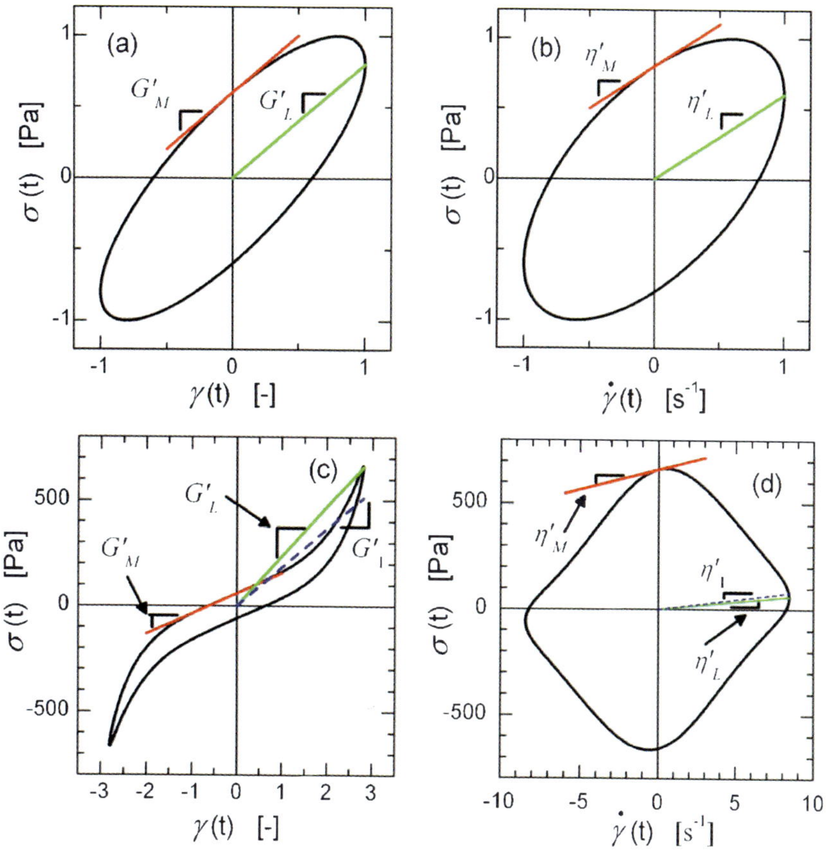

Figure 1

Lissajous plot showing minimum strain modulus (G'_M), large strain modulus (G'_L), instantaneous viscosity at minimum shear rate (η'_M), and instantaneous viscosity at maximum shear rate (η'_L). In *a* and *b*, elastic modulus and dynamic viscosity are shown, respectively, for a system under linear viscoelastic conditions, whereas *c* and *d* responses show elastic modulus and dynamic viscosity, respectively, for a system under nonlinear viscoelastic conditions. In *c* and *d*, the subscript "1" denotes the elastic modulus and dynamic viscosity, respectively, that is calculated based on the assumption that only the first harmonic contributes to these parameters.

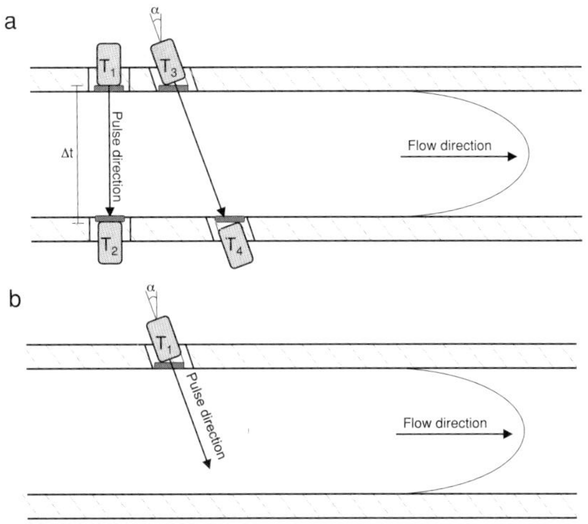

Figure 3

(*a*) Two pair transducer ultrasound instrumentation setup used for pipe flow. (*b*) Single transducer ultrasound instrumentation setup used for pipe flow.

and received either by the same transmitter, which is switched into receiving mode when not transmitting ultrasonic pulses, or a second transducer in receiving mode (Young et al. 2008, Wiklund et al. 2007). The returned pulses are shifted slightly in frequency owing to the Doppler effect (Wiklund et al. 2007). A Fourier transform of the received waves may be used to calculate the Doppler shift frequency spectrum at each radial position in the pipe (Dogan et al. 2005). Frequency shift and time interval between transmitted and received pulses are then used to calculate the velocity profile of the fluid (Wiklund et al. 2007). Wiklund et al. (2007) developed algorithms using fast Fourier transforms to improve the signal-to-noise ratio for estimating velocity profiles.

A second method of measuring properties of flowing fluids using ultrasound involves two pairs of transducers (**Figure 3*b***), one pair (T_1 and T_2) set perpendicular to the pipe wall and a second pair (T_3 and T_4) set at an angle (α) to the pipe wall. The first pair of transducers is used to measure the velocity of the fluid from time-of-flight measurements. The second pair of transducers is used to determine the velocity profile of the fluid. This setup allows simultaneous measurement of acoustic properties of the fluid and the flow profile of the fluid (Wiklund & Stading 2006).

Velocity profile measurements derived from the ultrasonic measurements are often combined with measurements of pressure drop in the fluid, resulting in a technique known as ultrasonic pulsed echo Doppler-pressure difference (UVP-PD) (Ouriev & Windhab 2002). UVP-PD may be used to measure flow profiles, viscosity over a range of shear rates, wall slip behavior, yield stress behavior, volumetric flow rate (Ouriev & Windhab 2002), and physical changes in process material (Ouriev et al. 2004, Dogan et al. 2005, Wiklund & Stading 2006).

Ultrasound may be used to measure various properties of foods such as gelling behavior (Wang et al. 2005, 2007; Ting et al. 2009), fat content (Dukhin et al. 2005), particle size (Dukhin et al. 2005), molecular relaxation (Wang et al. 2007), shear properties (Kulmyrzaev & McClements 2000, Dukhin et al. 2005, Ting et al. 2009), and viscosity (Wang et al. 2007). Ultrasound has also been used for quality control (Álava et al. 2007, Eskelinen et al. 2007). Advantages of ultrasound include nondestructive measurement of samples (Dukhin & Goetz 2002, Eskelinen et al. 2007), precise and rapid measurements (Dukhin & Goetz 2002, Eskelinen et al. 2007), propagation of waves through opaque materials and pipe walls (Ouriev & Windhab 2002), relatively low cost compared to other imaging techniques (Dogan et al. 2005, Eskelinen et al. 2007), and ability to characterize volumetric viscosity (Dukhin & Goetz 2002). However, the sensitivity and accuracy of ultrasound measurements depend upon the penetration depth of the sound waves. Too small a penetration depth decreases the signal-to-noise ratio of the measurements, decreasing measurement accuracy (Eskelinen et al. 2007). Penetration depth depends on the food and is highly frequency dependent (Dukhin et al. 2005). In addition, air bubbles in the sample can increase attenuation at low frequencies (Dukhin et al. 2005). Measurement sensitivity of in-line Doppler measurements is dependent on the spatial resolution of the ultrasound measurements, which is impacted by pulse width, beam width, and demodulation filter bandwidth (Pfund et al. 2006). Finally, velocity measurements are very temperature sensitive, requiring temperature control to 0.1°C for accurate measurement (Dukhin et al. 2005).

Rheology and Nuclear Magnetic Resonance

NMR, an analytical technique traditionally used to determine material components and molecular structure, has been used in food science since the 1970s to study the structure and dynamics of solid systems (Bertocchi & Paci 2008, Mariette 2009). Because NMR can differentiate between different structural orientations and arrangements, it is commonly used as a fingerprinting method for various foods and food components, such as carbohydrate, proteins, and lipids (Bertocchi & Paci 2008). Over the last decade, the use of NMR in food science has begun to shift from a fingerprinting tool to a rheological tool. Several advances in NMR technology have allowed rheological properties to be determined from NMR output. In particular, NMR velocity profiling, diffusometry, and relaxometry have been particularly useful in determining rheological properties of foods (Thybo et al. 2004, Callaghan 2006). NMR velocity profiling involves the use of MRI (Götz et al. 2001, Barnes et al. 2006, Callaghan 2006) and will be discussed in the next section.

NMR diffusometry examines the translational motion of molecules and particles (Nydén & Holmberg 2009) and has been widely used in the investigation of colloidal and emulsion behavior (Hollingsworth & Johns 2004, Gabriele et al. 2009, Nydén & Holmberg 2009, Voda & van Duynhoven 2009). Pulsed field gradient (PFG) NMR (**Figure 4**) is the most common type of NMR method used in this type of study, as it is most capable of quantitatively measuring droplet size distribution (Voda & van Duynhoven 2009). Knowing the droplet size distribution is critical to understanding emulsion rheology and functionality (Johns & Hollingsworth 2007, Johns 2009, Voda & van Duynhoven 2009). In PFG NMR, the sample is placed in a chamber surrounded by a radio frequency (RF) coil. Two sweep coils are located on either side of the sample. A transmitter fires two gradient pulses of the same magnitude and duration through the RF coil into the sample. Because PFG NMR works on the basis of spin echo, a 180° pulse is fired into the sample between the two gradient pulses. The first gradient pulse dephases proton precession frequency, whereas the second gradient pulse rephrases the frequencies. Particle diffusion causes a phase shift in proton frequency, leading to signal loss in the second pulse (Johns 2009, Voda & van Duynhoven 2009). The self-diffusion coefficient may be calculated from the phase shift and the gradient pulse parameters (Johns 2009). Droplet size distribution may also be calculated, as the phase shift is a distribution rather than a single value (Johns & Hollingsworth 2007, Voda & van Duynhoven 2009). This technique has been used by many researchers to study the behavior of various food and pharmaceutical colloids and emulsions (Hollingsworth & Johns 2004, Johns & Hollingsworth 2007, Gabriele et al. 2009, Johns 2009, Nydén & Holmberg 2009, Voda & van Duynhoven 2009), as well as gelatin (Brand et al. 2006).

NMR offers several advantages over other techniques used to study emulsions. Being noninvasive, it may be used for opaque emulsions, emulsions contaminated with gas or suspended solids, and highly concentrated emulsions (Gabriele et al. 2009, Johns 2009). NMR also allows the

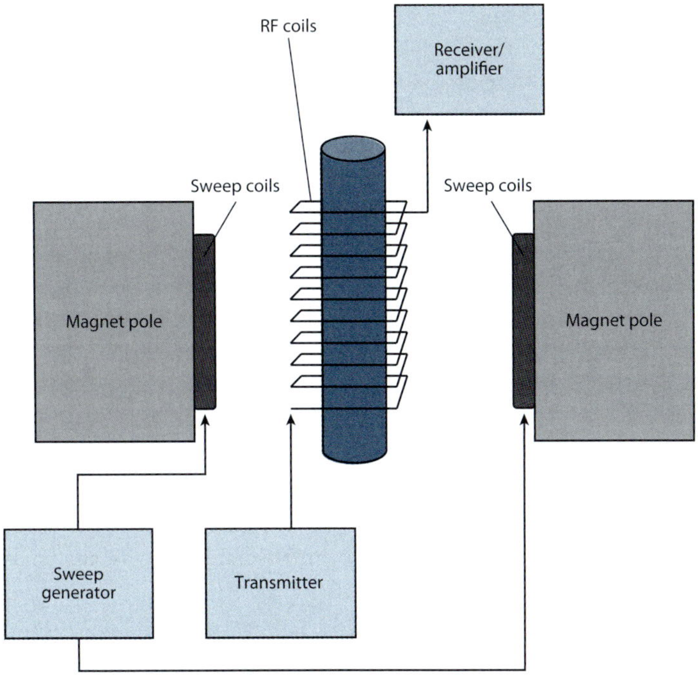

Figure 4

Nuclear magnetic resonance instrumentation setup.

identification and analysis of the behavior of each component in the sample from a single measurement (Occhipinti & Griffiths 2008). However, the sensitivity of NMR in this application is limited by the restricted molecular diffusion. A rule of thumb given by Johns (2009) for sufficient sensitivity is that the mean molecular diffusion length should be approximately equivalent to the droplet radius. Sensitivity is also limited by the instrument: Benchtop NMR instruments usually have relatively low magnetic field homogeneity and strength. The lower-quality magnetic field results in decreased measurement sensitivity reproducibility. However, recent technological advances, as discussed by Voda & van Duynhoven (2009), have been shown to improve measurement sensitivity. In addition, the sample must contain a spin-active nucleus (Occhipinti & Griffiths 2008). Hydrogen (^{1}H) is typically used when studying foods because it is the most sensitive probe for water (Zhou & Li 2007), which is generally present in large quantities in food products.

NMR relaxometry measures the spin-lattice and the spin-spin relaxation of particles in a material. Spin-lattice relaxation refers to the interaction of a spin and the environment, whereas spin-spin relaxation refers to the mobility of interacting spins (Baranowska et al. 2008). In relaxation, energy is exchanged between a spin and the environment (spin-lattice) and among spins (spin-spin) (Kim et al. 2008) to bring the material to an equilibrium state. It is possible to relate the spin-lattice and the spin-spin relaxation of a particle to the molecule containing the particle (Ahmad et al. 2005, Callaghan 2006, Baranowska et al. 2008). In food systems, the most common spin-active molecule used in this technique is ^{1}H. By measuring the spin-lattice and spin-spin relaxation time of a food component such as water, it is possible to determine the mobility of water in the food. It is also possible to determine the mobility of components (polymers, etc.) in the water by examining the chemical exchange of ^{1}H between the water and the second component (Ahmad et al. 2005). This information may be used to determine phase behavior, such as the transition from liquid to solid state (Goh et al. 2009). For these reasons, NMR relaxometry has been used to examine gelling behavior of egg white protein (Goh et al. 2009), fish proteins (Ahmed et al. 2005), gelatin (Zandi et al. 2007), starches (Karim et al. 2007), various hydrocolloids (Baranowska et al. 2008), and pectins (Dobies et al. 2008). Additionally, it has been used to study the gelatinization behavior of starch (Dona et al. 2007, Ritota et al. 2008), dough behavior (Assifaoui et al. 2006a,b; Lopez-da-Silva et al. 2007), addition of starch to imitation cheeses (Noronha et al. 2008), fat content and crystallization (Mariette 2009), and melting behavior of sugar solutions with added hydrocolloids (Herrera et al. 2007). Many of these studies showed good correlation between traditional rheometry and NMR data.

Rheology and Magnetic Resonance Imaging

MRI, an analytical technique that forms images from NMR data, is generally associated with the medical field as a diagnostic tool, but it can be used for many other purposes. Recently, it has been used to measure many different parameters in many branches of science (d'Avila et al. 2005, Bonn et al. 2008), including food science and rheology. An MRI apparatus generally consists of three parts: a magnet, an RF coil, and gradient coils (**Figure 5**). The magnet creates a constant, homogenous magnetic field in the sample, and the RF coil both sends out and detects pulses in the sample (d'Avila et al. 2005, Bonn et al. 2008). The gradient coils detect motion in the sample, allowing the motion to be resolved spatially (Deka et al. 2006, Bonn et al. 2008). This spatial resolution allows parameters such as proton density, spin-lattice relaxation, spin-spin relaxation, and diffusion properties, as well as a general profile of the sample, to be mapped (Thybo et al.

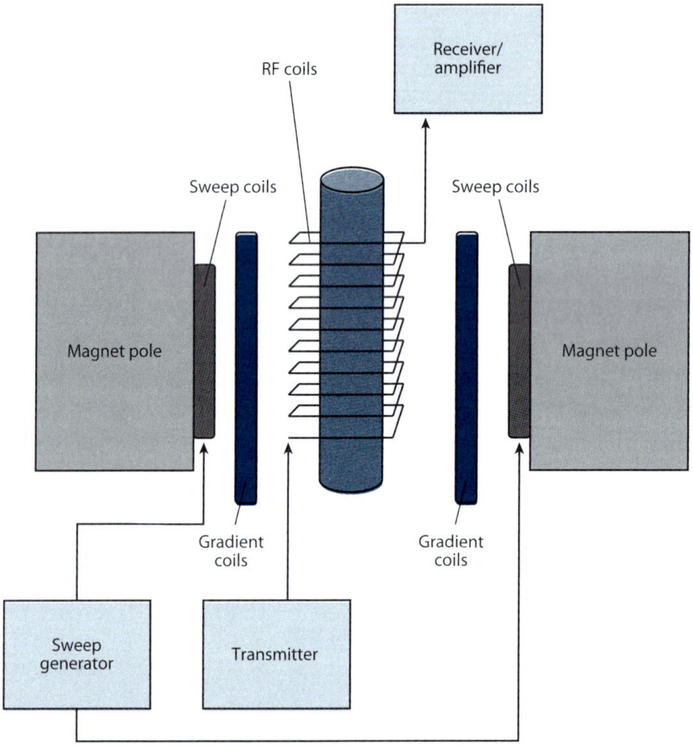

Figure 5

Magnetic resonance imaging instrumentation setup.

2004). A sequence of these mapped parameters over time yields valuable information on material behavior, e.g., the interaction of water with other compounds in the sample and the relative amounts of water and lipid present (Thybo et al. 2004). Studies examining foams (Stevenson et al. 2007), emulsions (Johns & Hollingsworth 2007), oil migration in confectionary products (Deka et al. 2006), pasta drying (Xing et al. 2007), structural changes in bread during baking (Wagner et al. 2008), changes in foods during storage (Zhou & Li 2007, Lodi et al. 2007), and gelation of meat systems (Herrero et al. 2009) have taken advantage of this ability, revealing new insights on these food processes. MRI has advantages and disadvantages similar to NMR: It is a nondestructive technique that can be used on opaque samples (Uludag et al. 2001, d'Avila et al. 2005, Elkins & Alley 2007), but its sensitivity is limited by the strength and homogeneity of the magnetic field (Metz & Mäder 2008).

Rheo-NMR: the use of MRI to map a material's velocity profile, allowing calculation of flow properties

One novel application of MRI that is of particular interest in rheology is MRI velocity profiling, also called rheo-NMR. This has been done in both a cup and bob apparatus and in pipe flow. The principle for either experiment remains the same. The velocity of the material in the apparatus is measured by using the time-of-flight, spin-tagging, or phase-shift method (Bonn et al. 2008), with time-of flight and phase-shift being the most common methods (Uludag et al. 2001, d'Avila et al. 2005). The time-of-flight method is the oldest method of velocity measurement and tracks the NMR excitation of a predetermined part of the sample. The displacement of that part of the sample is tracked over time, allowing calculation of the velocity. This technique is relatively simple to perform and gives accurate results at steady-state flow but cannot be used for multidirectional flow and is not sensitive enough to measure low velocities (less than 1 mm s^{-1}) (d'Avila et al. 2005). The spin-tagging method is similar to this method but looks at the magnetic pattern over the whole sample, allowing flow in the entire sample to be mapped (Bonn et al. 2008). The phase-shift method is more accurate than time-of-flight and spin-tagging. This technique maps the NMR signal in the sample and compares the measured phase of each pixel with the phase of that pixel in a flow-compensated reference map (Bonn et al. 2008).

Determination of the velocity profile of the material allows the calculation of flow properties such as viscosity (Uludag et al. 2001), yield stress behavior during flow (Raynaud et al. 2002, Barnes et al. 2006), thixotropic behavior (Raynaud et al. 2002), and shear stress and shear rate (Bonn et al. 2008). MRI velocity profiling can also be used to study complex flow (Elkins & Alley 2007, Bonn et al. 2008), shear banding phenomena (Callaghan 2006, Bonn et al. 2008), wall slip (Cullen et al. 2000, Yoon & McCarthy 2002), and crystallization behavior (Mazzanti et al. 2008). Because most foods are complex, viscoelastic, non-Newtonian, or a combination thereof, this technique is highly useful in studying flow behavior of foods, although few foods have been studied in this manner. Foods studied in a Coutette-type apparatus using MRI velocity imaging include lipids (Mazzanti et al. 2008) and food emulsions (Hollingsworth & Johns 2004, d'Avila et al. 2005, Gabriele et al. 2009). MRI velocity profiling data had similar results to traditional rheometry data (Hollingsworth & Johns 2004, Gabriele et al. 2009). MRI velocity imaging of foods has also been studied in pipe flow of hydrocolloids (Goloshevsky et al. 2005), yogurt (Yoon & McCarthy 2002, Henningsson et al. 2006), and biscuit dough (Barnes et al. 2006).

Advantages of MRI velocity imaging include the ability to measure opaque materials and to measure velocity without the need for flow markers or optical access, as well as noninvasive measurements (Cullen et al. 2000, Götz et al. 2001, Barnes et al. 2006, Elkins & Alley 2007). It also has the ability to measure materials during processing, yielding valuable information on food behavior under processing conditions (Uludag et al. 2001, Barnes et al. 2006). Disadvantages include possible image blurring at high velocities, the need for large sample sizes with time-of-flight methods to improve signal strength (Callaghan 2006), and the inability to use the Couette cell with certain materials such as pastes (Götz et al. 2001). However, these disadvantages are

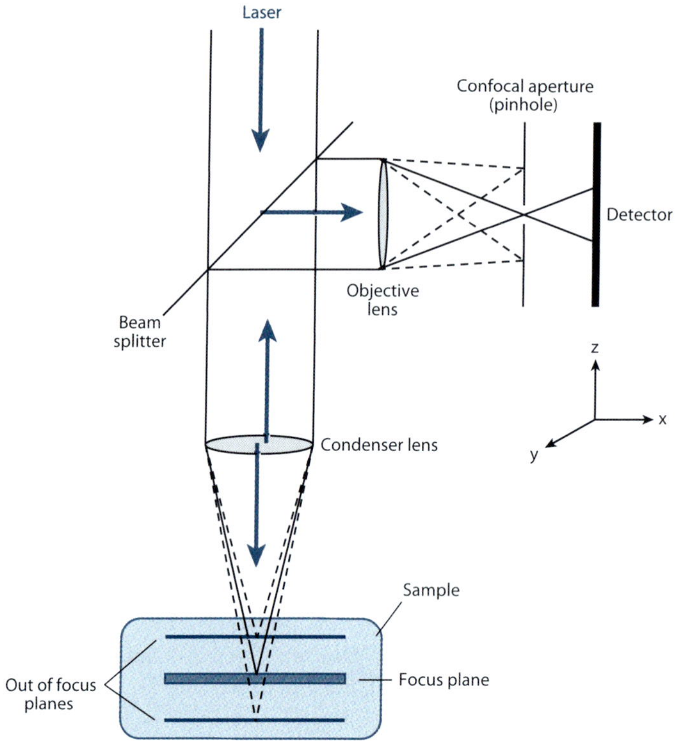

Figure 6

Confocal scanning laser microscopy instrumentation setup.

mitigated by several recent advances, such as rapid imaging techniques (Sederman et al. 2003, 2004; Callaghan 2006) and the use of Fourier transforms (Callaghan 2006).

Rheology and Confocal Scanning Laser Microscopy

CSLM has been used to investigate the microstructure of foods since the 1980s. CSLM works on the same principle as confocal microscopy (**Figure 6**). A point light source (a laser) is shone through an objective lens, which focuses the beam at a certain depth on a very small region of the sample. The optical system focuses the reflected, scattered, or fluoresced light from the sample at that point through a pinhole in front of a detector. The pinhole is situated in such a manner that only the light backscattered from the laser is in focus, enabling it to pass through, yielding one image point. Confocal scanning laser microscopes are able to scan along the *x* and *y* axes (perpendicular to the direction of the beam), forming a two-dimensional image of the sample at the focal depth. Scanning along the *z*-axis (parallel to the direction of the beam) forms a stack of two-dimensional images, allowing a three-dimensional image to be constructed (Branzan et al. 2007).

Advantages of using CSLM for imaging include viewing of several different compounds at one time by use of different stains (Nicolas et al. 2003b, Puppo et al. 2008), ability of three-dimensional imaging (Nicolas et al. 2003b), no image blurring (Nicolas et al. 2003b, Nicolas & Paques 2003), and relatively little sample preparation as compared to other microscopy techniques (Nagano et al. 2008, Guggisberg et al. 2009). CSLM has the disadvantage of the penetration depth of the beam ranging only from a few micrometers to a few millimeters. In addition, the optical spatial resolution is limited to the submicron level, the penetration depth is a property of the sample examined (Nicolas et al. 2003b), the acquisition rate of points is inversely proportional to the desired spatial resolution (Nicolas et al. 2003b, Nicolas & Paques 2003), and the images collected may become distorted under dynamic conditions (Ko & Gunasekaran 2007). However, recent developments in high-speed cameras have enabled collection of images with resolution in the millisecond range (Kimura 2009), and various algorithms have been developed to mitigate several errors in CSLM image collection and assembly (Ko & Gunasekaran 2007).

It is not often possible to validate a hypothesis about material behavior from rheological data alone. By using CSLM to view the microstrucure of foods, the rheological properties of the food under different conditions may be investigated in an in-depth manner. Over the past decade, CSLM has been used in conjunction with various rheological tests to investigate the properties of emulsions (Puppo et al. 2008), hydrocolloid gels (Nunes et al. 2006, Nagano et al. 2008, Savary et al. 2008, Firoozmand et al. 2009), dairy proteins (Dubert-Ferrandon et al. 2006, Bertrand & Turgeon 2007, Lutz et al. 2009, Ye & Hewitt 2009), yogurt (Guggisberg et al. 2009), starches (Noisuwan et al. 2008, Vallons & Aredt 2009), bread dough (Mariotti et al. 2009), meat products (Chattong et al. 2007), and bread (Renzetti & Arendt 2009, Renzetti et al. 2008). In general, the CSLM images in these studies supported and provided insights into rheological data. Common uses of CSLM in conjunction with rheology include determination of starch gelatinization behavior and gels under various conditions.

Recently, CSLM and rheology have been used to examine the properties of more specialized products, such as gluten-free dough and bread structure (Mariotti et al. 2009, Renzetti & Arendt 2009, Renzetti et al. 2008). There has also been some study on using CSLM and rheology in the nonlinear region using colloidal probes that were pulled through the sample with an optical tweezer, or a focused laser beam used to move particles via optical gradient forces (Dufresne & Grier 1998). The theory used ignored hydrodynamic interactions, so could only be used for shear-thinning fluids in dilute solutions. It was suggested that the addition of hydrodynamic effects would allow the method to be used for shear-thickening fluids as well (Squires & Brady 2005). Suggested further work included the use of multiple probes and the investigation of microstructural deformations in nonequilibrium conditions (Squires & Brady 2005). Another study by Nicolas & Paques (2003) used CSLM and rheology to study fish protein gels in compression. Nicolas & Paques (2003) noted that these techniques were useful for studying behavior of food structure during oral processing and manufacturing conditions.

Rheology and Atomic Force Microscopy

A second microscopy technique recently coupled with rheology is AFM. AFM enables study of both individual molecules and the interaction between molecules, such as network formation and aggregation (Funami et al. 2009), as well as film surface topography (Bonaccurso et al. 2008, Handojo et al. 2009). This technique enables a relationship between physical, chemical, and structural behavior to be formed (Noda et al. 2008). AFM provides a high-resolution image of the sample surface by scanning it with a pointed tip attached to a cantilever (**Figure 7**) (Bonaccurso et al. 2008, Handojo et al. 2009).

The sample is scanned in the x, y, and z directions. Depending on the instrumentation used, the sample may be placed on a platform that shifts the sample in the x, y, and z directions as it is scanned by a stationary cantilever (**Figure 7*a***), or the cantilever may be moved in the x, y, and z directions as it scans a stationary sample (**Figure 7*b***). There are two main operational modes in which AFM may be used: contact mode and tapping mode (Handojo et al. 2009). Contact mode is sometimes called scratching mode (Handojo et al. 2009). In this mode, the tip is in continuous contact with the sample surface, and the force placed on the sample by the tip may be changed by adjusting the cantilever parameters. As the sample is scanned in the x and y directions, the deflection of the

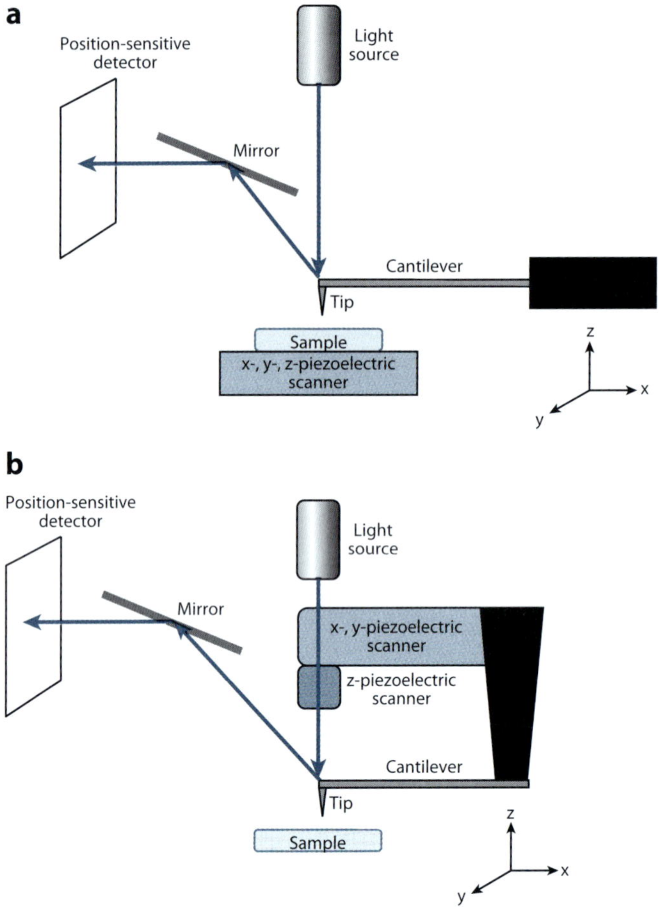

Figure 7

(*a*) Atomic force microscopy (AFM) instrumentation setup for a moving sample. (*b*) AFM instrumentation setup for a stationary sample.

cantilever in the z direction indicates the force between the tip and the sample. Plotting cantilever deflection versus tip position on the sample creates a topographic image of the sample surface (Bonaccurso et al. 2008). However, this method may damage the sample or tip when large loading forces are applied (Sahin et al. 2007). Because of this potential issue, tapping mode, which is much less likely to cause tip or sample damage, is generally used. In tapping mode, the cantilever vibrates at its resonance frequency as it is brought in contact with the sample. Contact with the sample changes the phase and amplitude with which the cantilever vibrates. Changes in the vibrations, used to create a topography map, are monitored by a feedback system (Sahin et al. 2007).

An issue with AFM in rheology is hydrodynamic drag on the cantilever due to friction between the tip and the sample, especially in soft samples (Alcaraz et al. 2002). This drag force may be estimated and taken into account during contact force measurement, although it is difficult to determine precisely and is often underestimated. A study by Alcaraz et al. (2002) investigated hydrodynamic drag in soft samples and developed correction factors for drag based on cantilever height, tip velocity, and oscillation frequency. Alcaraz et al. (2002) noted that drag force could be accurately estimated by the extrapolation of drag force data from measurements taken at varying heights above the sample, allowing an increase in scanning velocity and velocity range.

AFM may be used to examine heterogeneous samples, as it is able to differentiate between the length, diameter, and conformation of molecules in the sample. Because AFM scanning involves vertical movements of either the sample or the probe, the image generated also contains quantitative information on sample surface topography (Ikeda 2003). Other advantages of AFM include nanoscale resolution, small sample size requirements, little sample damage in preparation, ability to view molecular interactions (gel structures, aggregations, etc.), and ability to examine interfacial behavior (Sriamornsak et al. 2008, Funami et al. 2009). Although AFM is able to resolve individual molecules, it may not be able to resolve some subdomain structures. In these cases, spectroscopy is required for further study (Ikeda 2003). Furthermore, artifacts may be present in the sample after preparation of more fragile samples (Noda et al. 2008).

AFM is typically used in the study of surface structure and topography but can also be used to measure local viscoelasticity (Kimura 2009). AFM has been used in combinations with rheological techniques to examine various material properties such as gelling behavior under various conditions (Ikeda 2003; Funami et al. 2007, 2008, 2009; Noda et al. 2008), interfacial behavior (Patino et al. 2007, Gromer et al. 2009), behavior in aqueous solutions (Yang et al. 2008), and film behavior (León et al. 2009). Foods tested with this technique include hydrocolloid gels and solutions (Funami et al. 2008, 2009; Noda et al. 2008; Shimoni 2008; Yang et al. 2008; Gromer et al. 2009; León et al. 2009) and dairy proteins (Ikeda 2003, Shimoni 2008). As with CSLM, AFM has supported and provided insights into rheological data. A study by Boskovic et al. (2002) showed that AFM and AFM cantilevers may also be used to measure density and viscosity in liquids and gases, including turbid and opalescent samples. The method developed was also able to measure sample properties in situ (Boskovic et al. 2002).

One study by Filip et al. (2006) combined AFM and CSLM to study local rheological properties of gelled emulsions (**Figure 8**). Filip et al. (2006) showed that AFM was able to provide a

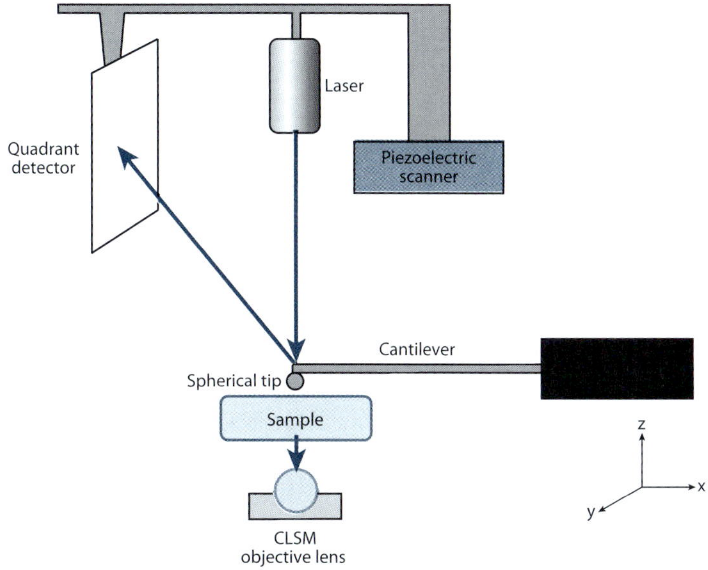

Figure 8

Combined atomic force microscopy–confocal scanning laser microscopy instrumentation setup.

mechanical fingerprint of the emulsion that gave information on stress relaxation, force hysteresis, and material stiffness, whereas CSLM showed how the emulsion was affected by the AFM probe. These measurements were taken simultaneously at several time points, allowing the effects of aging on the sample to be studied. It was found that the combined AFM-CSLM method was able to differentiate between elastic and plastic behavior of the sample and detail how the sample changed over time, as well as semiquantitatively provide surface deformation information. Filip et al. (2006) noted that multiple measurements on the same sample were possible, allowing more accurate measurements on materials that have behavior dependent on mechanical history. It should be noted, however, that the measurements of the AFM-CSLM technique were not directly relatable to traditional rheometry measurements. Samples with structures that are heterogeneous at length scales greater than that of the length of the AFM probe show different behavior based on where the sample is measured. These heterogeneous samples should either be measured with a larger probe (provided that the cantilever is able to operate properly with the larger probe) or be measured in several locations and the force curves averaged to give a general material response to the probe (Filip et al. 2006). Overall, this technique may be useful for the study of food emulsions, gels, and foams, but further work must be done to correlate the microrheological measurements to traditional rheometry measurements.

Rheology and Diffusing Wave Spectroscopy

DWS is a light-scattering technique with a frequency range of up to 1 MHz that uses particle movements to determine material viscoelastic properties (Nicolas et al. 2003a, Waigh 2005, Cicuta & Donald 2007, Kimura 2009). Unlike conventional light scattering techniques, which require transparent or nearly transparent samples, DWS requires highly turbid or opaque samples. When analyzing DWS data, the transmittance of light is considered to be a diffusion process, so it is necessary to use samples with strong multiple scattering, or with sufficient turbidity to provide a constant volume fraction and refractive index throughout the sample (Scheffold et al. 2004, Horne et al. 2005, Corredig & Alexander 2008). DWS has two operational modes: transmittance (forward scattering) and backscattering (**Figure 9**) (Corredig & Alexander 2008, Kimura 2009). The basic principle of DWS is as follows: A laser is shone through one side of the sample, resulting in an induced dipole moment in the particles. The light is scattered due to particle motion from resonance as a result of the dipole moment, causing fluctuations in light intensity. Photons from the laser that exit the sample strike a detector, which records the number and location of photons incident on its surface. Developing a correlation function for the pattern of photons on the detector allows the characteristics of the sample to be determined and examined (Corredig & Alexander 2008).

The main differences between transmittance and backscattering modes involve the placement of the detection system. In transmittance mode, the laser is shone into one side of the sample and the detector is placed on the opposite side. This mode requires a powerful laser, since the light intensity on the detection side of the sample must be sufficient for proper detection (Corredig & Alexander 2008). Backscattering mode, on the other hand, does not require as powerful a laser, since the laser and detection system are placed on the same side of the sample. However, data analysis in this mode is more difficult than in transmission mode due to the varying penetration depths of the detected photons (Corredig & Alexander 2008).

DWS may be used for opaque materials and is able to detect small changes in wavelength over short time periods (Cicuta & Donald 2007, Kimura 2009). It is also a nondestructive technique (Horne et al. 2005), requires very small sample volumes (Ubbink et al. 2008), and is sensitive to particle size changes (Hemar et al. 2004). In addition, DWS has been shown to correspond more

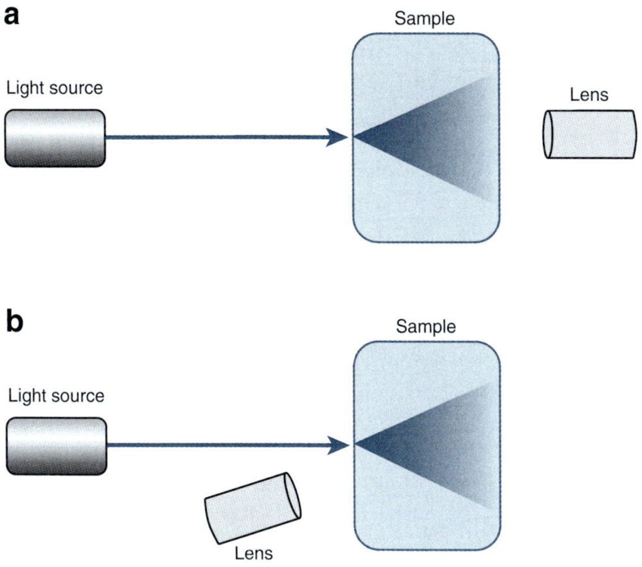

Figure 9

Diffusing wave sprectroscopy instrumentation setup in (*a*) forward scattering and (*b*) backscattering mode.

closely to traditional rheometry testing than other microscopy techniques (Ubbink et al. 2008). One major disadvantage of DWS is that samples need to be opaque or turbid, as the technique depends on multiple scattering events (Scheffold et al. 2004, Horne et al. 2005).

DWS has been used to study gelation of various substances (Cullen et al. 2000; Nicolas et al. 2003a,b; van der Linden et al. 2003; Hemar et al. 2004; Alexander & Dalgleish 2007; Corredig &

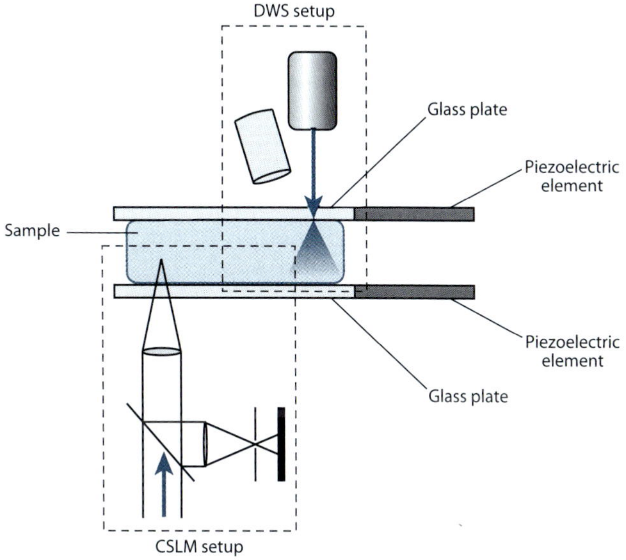

Figure 10

Combined diffusion wave spectroscopy–confocal scanning laser microscopy instrumentation setup.

Table 1 Comparison of rheological techniques

Method	Advantages	Disadvantages	Possible uses
Large amplitude oscillatory shear (LAOS)	Allows rheological properties outside of the linear viscoelastic region (LVR) to be determined	Not suitable for materials with shear-sensitive structure	Soft solids, viscous liquids, viscoelastic materials
	Gives physical meaning to storage and loss moduli calculated outside of the LVR	Computationally intensive	
	Accounts for higher oscillation harmonics		
Ultrasound	Nondestructive sample measurement	Velocity measurements are highly temperature dependent	Homogenous liquids and semisolid foods that are able to flow under measurement conditions
	Precise measurements	Slow measurement rate	
	May be used with opaque materials	Provides data at a single shear rate	
	Able to characterize volume viscosity	Measurement sensitivity depends on wave penetration depth (varies with food and frequency used)	
	Allows for measurement of rheological properties under process conditions	Inline measurements dependent on spatial resolution	
	Low cost imaging technique	Inline measurements require additional pressure drop measurements to calculate rheological properties	
Nulcear magnetic resonance (NMR)	Noninvasive technique	Measurement sensitivity limited by molecular diffusion	Gels and other foods with relatively few components
	May be used with opaque materials	Benchtop instruments have relatively low magnetic field strength and homogeneity	
	May be used with heterogeneous samples	Sample must contain a spin-active nucleus	
	Allows identification of multiple components with one measurement		
Magnetic resonance imaging (MRI)	Noninvasive technique	Benchtop instruments have relatively low magnetic field strength and homogeneity	Low-viscosity liquids, pumpable liquids, and semisolids
	May be used with opaque materials	Sample must contain a spin-active nucleus	
	May be used with heterogeneous samples	Possible image blurring at high velocities	
	Allows study of complex flow behavior	Large sample sizes required with time-of-flight methods	
	Enables velocity measurements without flow markers or optical access	Certain materials may not be used in a Couette cell	

(Continued)

Table 1 (*Continued*)

Method	Advantages	Disadvantages	Possible uses
	Allows for measurement of rheological properties under process conditions		
Confocal scanning laser spectroscopy (CSLM)	Several different compounds may be viewed at once by use of different stains	Beam penetration depth ranges from a few micrometers to a few millimeters	Foods with sensitive structures, foams, gels, semisolid, and solid foods
	Allows for three-dimensional imaging	Optical spatial resolution limited to the submicron level	
	No image blurring in static conditions	Penetration depth is a property of the sample examined	
	Relatively little sample preparation as compared to other microscopy techniques	Acquisition rate of points is inversely proportional to desired spatial resolution	
		Images may become distorted under dynamic conditions	
		Rheological measurements are not directly convertible to traditional measurements	
Atomic force microscopy (AFM)	Able to differentiate between length, diameter, and conformation of molecules in the sample	Hydrodynamic drag on the cantilever due to friction between the tip and the sample may affect measurements	Semisolid and solid foods
	Image generated contains quantitative information on sample surface	Certain subdomain structures are not resolvable	
	Nanoscale image resolution	Artifacts may be present in fragile samples	
	Small sample size requirements	Rheological measurements are not directly convertible to traditional measurements	
	Little sample damage in preparation		
	Allows observation of molecular interactions		
	Allows examination of interfacial behavior		
Diffusing wave spectroscopy (DWS)	May be used for opaque materials	Samples must be turbid or opaque	Semiopaque or opaque liquids, semisolids, and solids
	Able to detect small changes in wavelength over short time periods	Rheological measurements are not directly convertible to traditional measurements	
	Nondestructive technique		
	Small sample size requirements		
	Sensitive to particle size changes		
	Corresponds more closely to traditional rheometry testing than other microscopy techniques		

Alexander 2008), emulsion behavior (Blijdenstein et al. 2003; Nicolas et al. 2003a,b; Horne et al. 2005; Gancz et al. 2006; Alexander & Dalgleish 2007; Ruis et al. 2007; Corredig & Alexander 2008), and behavior of concentrated suspensions (Pinder et al. 2006). Other studies involving DWS and rheology include optical rheology at near-zero shear (Corredig & Alexander 2008) and the use of tracer particles to increase turbidity for solutions that do not have sufficient light-scattering properties (Alexander & Dalgleish 2007). Foods studied by DWS include milk and dairy proteins (Cullen et al. 2000; Nicolas et al. 2003a,b; Hemar et al. 2004; Alexander & Dalgleish 2007; Ruis et al. 2007) and various hydrocolloids (van der Linden et al. 2003, Gancz et al. 2006, Pinder et al. 2006, Corredig & Alexander 2008). The majority of the available studies focus on skim milk and milk-based systems, as they have properties ideal for study with DWS (Alexander & Dalgleish 2007). As with CSLM and AFM, DWS results have been generally in agreement with and provided insights into traditional rheological data. Several studies have remarked upon the versatility of DWS and its potential use in industry (Nicolas et al. 2003a,b; Hemar et al. 2004; Corredig & Alexander 2008).

Several studies have used DWS in combination with CSLM (**Figure 10**) to study structural changes in gels and emulsions under various conditions (Blijdenstein et al. 2003; Nicolas et al. 2003a,b; Corredig & Alexander 2008). This combined technique was able to determine network formation and strengthening, sample relaxation behavior, behavior during oscillatory shear (emulsion droplet mobility and network elasticity), surface properties, interfacial tension, and phase change behavior (Blijdenstein et al. 2003; Nicolas et al. 2003a,b; Corredig & Alexander 2008). Nicolas et al. (2003a,b) noted that this approach to studying rheological properties, and microrheology in general, was highly versatile, able to be used for both food and nonfood substances, and able to overcome the limitations of traditional rheological techniques. Microrheological techniques appear to have great potential for use in the food industry, provided that the data gathered from microrheological testing may be related to traditional rheometry results. However, more work remains to be done in the correlation of microrheology to traditional rheometry.

All of the techniques discussed in this paper have certain advantages and disadvantages, as well as applications to which they are suited. Advantages, disadvantages, and suggested applications are summarized in **Table 1**.

CONCLUSIONS

Novel rheological techniques have been developed to gain a deeper understanding of various properties of foods. Other techniques not usually associated with rheology, such as microscopy, magnetic resonance, and ultrasonics, have been coupled with traditional rheological measurements to provide valuable insight into material behavior. These coupled rheological techniques, particularly the microscopy techniques, have been used primarily on model food systems. It has been suggested that the use of these techniques be expanded to foods and food products, as the techniques may be used for an in-depth investigation of food behavior under various conditions. Additionally, many of the techniques discussed in this paper are novel to food science but not necessarily novel to rheology in general. The polymer industry in particular has developed a number of rheological techniques able to measure properties of materials that are viscoelastic, exhibit slip, undergo phase transitions during testing, or exhibit other phenomena that confound the measuring of rheological properties. The majority of these techniques may be adapted for measuring rheological properties of foods.

Over the past decade, the focus of rheological techniques has shifted from the macro scale to the micro scale, especially with the introduction of coupled rheological techniques. Microrheology is able to overcome several limitations of traditional shear rheology; however, microrheological measurements are not directly related to macrorheological measurements. Further study of microrheological measurements compared to macrorheological measurements is necessary to develop fundamental equations to relate the two sets of measurements. Developing these equations, however, will allow rheological behavior in materials and areas previously considered too difficult for accurate measurement to be explored, providing a deeper understanding of the rheological behavior of foods.

DISCLOSURE STATEMENT

The authors are not aware of any affiliations, memberships, funding, or financial holdings that might be perceived as affecting the objectivity of this review.

LITERATURE CITED

Ahmad MU, Tashiro Y, Matsukawa S, Ogawa H. 2005. Comparison of horse mackerel and tilapia surimi gel based on rheological and ^{1}H NMR relaxation properties. *Fish. Sci.* 71(3):655–61

Álava JM, Sahi SS, García-Álvarez J, Turó A, Chávez JA, et al. 2007. Use of ultrasound for the determination of flour quality. *Ultrasonics* 46(3):270–76

Alcaraz J, Buscemi L, Puig-de-Morales M, Colchero J, Baró A, Navajas D. 2002. Correction of microrheological measurements of soft samples with atomic force microscopy for the hydrodynamic drag on the cantilever. *Langmuir* 18(3):716–21

Alexander M, Dalgleish DG. 2007. Diffusing wave spectroscopy of aggregating and gelling systems. *Curr. Opin. Colloid Interface Sci.* 12(4–5):179–86

Assifaoui A, Champion D, Chiotelli E, Verel A. 2006a. Characterization of water mobility in biscuit dough using a low-field ^{1}H NMR technique. *Carbohydr. Polym.* 64(2):197–204

Assifaoui A, Champion D, Chiotelli E, Verel A. 2006b. Rheological behavior of biscuit dough in relation to water mobility. *Int. J. Food Sci. Technol.* 41(S2):124–28

Baranowska HM, Sikora M, Kowalski S, Tomasik P. 2008. Interactions of potato starch with selected polysaccharide hydrocolloids as measured by low-field NMR. *Food Hydrocoll.* 22(2):336–45

Barnes EC, Wilson DI, Johns ML. 2006. Velocity profiling inside a ram extruder using magnetic resonance (MR) techniques. *Chem. Eng. Sci.* 61(5):1357–67

Bertocchi F, Paci M. 2008. Applications of high-resolution solid-state NMR spectroscopy in food science. *J. Agric. Food Chem.* 56(20):9317–27

Bertrand M-E, Turgeon SL. 2007. Improved gelling properties of whey protein isolate by addition of xanthan gum. *Food Hydrocoll.* 159–66

Blijdenstein TBJ, Nicolas Y, van der Linden E, van Vliet T, Paques M, et al. 2003. Monitoring the structure of flocculated emulsions under shear by DWS and CSLM. In *Proc. 3rd Int. Symp. Food Rheol. Struct.*, ed. P Fischer, I Marti, EJ Windhab, pp. 343–46. Lappersdorf: Kerschensteiner Verlag

Bonaccurso E, Kappi M, Butt H-J. 2008. Thin liquid films studied by atomic force microscopy. *Curr. Opin. Colloid Interface Sci.* 13(3):107–19

Bonn D, Rodts S, Groenink M, Rafaï S, Shahidzadeh-Bonn N, Coussot P. 2008. Some applications of magnetic resonance imaging in fluid mechanics: complex flows and complex fluids. *Annu. Rev. Fluid Mech.* 40:209–33

Boskovic S, Chon JWM, Mulvaney P, Sader JE. 2002. Rheological measurements using microcantilevers. *J. Rheol.* 46(4):891–99

Brand T, Richter S, Berger S. 2006. Diffusion NMR as a new method for the determination of the gel point of gelatin. *J. Phys. Chem.* 110(32):15853–57

Branzan AL, Landthaler M, Szeimies R-L. 2007. In vivo confocal scanning laser microscopy in dermatology. *Lasers Med. Sci.* 22(2):73–82

Brenner T, Nicolai T, Johannsson R. 2009. Rheology of thermo-reversible fish protein isolate gels. *Food Res. Int.* 42(8):915–24

Callaghan PT. 2006. Rheo-NMR and velocity imaging. *Curr. Opin. Colloid Interface Sci.* 11(1):13–18

Carotenuto C, Grosso M, Maffettone PL. 2008. Fourier transform rheology of dilute immiscible polymer blends: a novel procedure to probe blend morphology. *Macromolecules* 41(12):4492–500

Chattong U, Apichartsrangkoon A, Bell AE. 2007. Effects of hydrocolloid addition and high pressure processing on the rheological properties and microstructure of a commercial ostrich meat product "Yor" (Thai sausage). *Meat Sci.* 76(3):548–54

Cho KS, Hyun K, Ahn KH, Lee SJ. 2005. A geometrical interpretation of large amplitude oscillatory shear response. *J. Rheol.* 49(3):747–58

Choi YJ, Milczarek RR, Fleck CE, Garvey TC, McCarthy KL, McCarthy MJ. 2006. In-line monitoring of tomato concentrate physical properties during evaporation. *J. Food Process Eng.* 29(6):615–32

Cicuta P, Donald AM. 2007. Microrheology: a review of the method and applications. *Soft Matter* 3:1449–55

Corredig M, Alexander M. 2008. Food emulsions studied by DWS: recent advances. *Trends Food Sci. Technol.* 19(2):67–75

Cullen PJ, Duffy AP, O'Donnel CP, O'Callaghan DJ. 2000. Process viscometry for the food industry. *Trends Food Sci. Technol.* 11(12):451–57

d'Avila MA, Rowell RL, Phillips RJ, Shapley NC, Walton JH, Dungan SR. 2005. Magnetic resonance imaging (MRI): a technique to study flow and microstructure of concentrated emulsions. *Braz. J. Chem. Eng.* 22(1):49–60

Debbaut B, Burhin H. 2002. Large amplitude oscillatory shear and Fourier-transform rheology for a high-density polyethylene: experiments and numerical simulation. *J. Rheol.* 46(5):1155–76

Deka K, MacMillan B, Ziegler GR, Marangoni AG, Newling B, Balcom BJ. 2006. Spatial mapping of solid and liquid lipid in confectionery products using a 1D centric SPRITE MRI technique. *Food Res. Int.* 39(3):365–71

Dobies M, Kempka M, Kusima S, Jurga S. 2008. Acid-induced gelation oflow-methoxyl pectins studied by 1H NMR and rheological methods. *Appl. Magn. Reson.* 34(1–2):71–84

Dogan N, McCarthy MJ, Powell RL. 2005. Application of an in-line rheological characterization method to chemically modified and native corn starch. *J. Texture Stud.* 36:237–54

Dona A, Yuen C-WW, Peate J, Gilbert RG, Castignolles P, Gaborieau M. 2007. A new NMR method for directly monitoring and quantifying the dissolution kinetics of starch in DMSO. *Carbohydr. Res.* 342(10):2604–10

Dubert-Ferrandon A, Niranjan K, Grandison AS. 2006. A novel technique for differentiation of proteins in the development of acid gel structure from control and heat treated milk using confocal scanning laser microscopy. *J. Dairy Res.* 73(4):423–30

Dufresne ER, Grier DG. 1998. Optical tweezer arrays and optical substrates created with diffractive optics. *Rev. Sci. Instrum.* 69(5):1974–77

Dukhin AS, Goetz PJ. 2002. *Ultrasound for Characterizing Colloids: Particle Sizing, Zeta Potential, Rheology*. Mount Kisco, NY: Dispers. Technol. 425 pp.

Dukhin AS, Goetz PJ, Travers B. 2005. Use of ultrasound for characterizing dairy products. *J. Dairy Sci.* 88:1320–34

Elkins CJ, Alley MT. 2007. Magnetic resonance velocimetry: applications of magnetic resonance imaging in the measurement of fluid motion. *Exp. Fluids* 43(6):823–58

Eskelinen JJ, Alavuotunki AP, Hæggström E, Alatossava T. 2007. Preliminary study of ultrasonic structural quality of Swiss-type cheese. *J. Dairy Sci.* 90:4071–77

Ewoldt RH, Hosoi AE, McKinley GH. 2008. New measures for characterizing nonlinear viscoelasticity in large amplitude oscillatory shear. *J. Rheol.* 52(6):1427–58

Ewoldt RH, Hosoi AE, McKinley GH. 2009. Nonlinear viscoelastic biomaterials: meaningful characterization and engineering inspiration. *Integr. Comp. Biol.* 49(1):40–50

Filip D, Duits MGH, Uricanu VI, Mellema J. 2006. Plastic-to-elastic transition in aggregated emulsion networks, studied with atomic force microscopy-confocal scanning laser microscopy microrheology. *Langmuir* 22(10):4558–66

Firoozmand H, Murray BS, Dickinson E. 2009. Microstructure and rheology of phase-separated gels of gelatin + oxidized starch. *Food Hydrocoll.* 23(4):1081–88

Funami T, Fang Y, Noda S, Ishihara S, Nakauma M, et al. 2009. Rheological properties of sodium alginate in an aqueous system during gelation in relation to supermolecular structures and Ca^{2+} binding. *Food Hydrocoll.* 23(7):1746–55

Funami T, Hiroe M, Noda S, Asai I, Ikeda S, Nishinari K. 2007. Influence of molecular structure imaged with atomic force microscopy on the rheological behavior of carrageenan aqueous systems in the presence or absence of cations. *Food Hydrocoll.* 21(4):617–29

Funami T, Noda S, Nakauma M, Ishihara S, Takahashi R, et al. 2008. Molecular structures of gellan gum imaged with atomic force microscopy in relation to the rheological behavior in aqueous systems in the presence or absence of various cations. *J. Agric. Food Chem.* 56(18):8609–18

Gabriele D, Migliori M, Di Sanzo R, Rossi CO, Ruffolo SA, de Cindio B. 2009. Characterisation of dairy emulsions by NMR and rheological techniques. *Food Hydrocoll.* 23:619–28

Gancz K, Alexander M, Corredig M. 2006. In situ study of flocculation of whey protein-stabilized emulsions caused by addition of high methoxyl pectin. *Food Hydrocoll.* 20(2–3):293–98

Garcia-Alvarez J, Alava JM, Chavez JA, Turo A, Garcia MJ, Salazar J. 2006. Ultrasonic characterisation of flour-water systems: a new approach to investigate dough properties. *Ultrasonics* 44(S1):e1051–55

Goh KS, Bhat R, Karim AA. 2009. Probing the sol-gel transition of egg white proteins by pulsed-NMR method. *Eur. Food Res. Technol.* 228(3):367–71

Goloshevsky AG, Walton JH, Shutov MV, de Ropp JS, Collins SD, McCarthy MJ. 2005. Nuclear magnetic resonance imaging for viscosity measurements of non-Newtonian fluids using a miniaturized RF coil. *Meas. Sci. Technol.* 16:513–18

Gómez M, Oliete B, García-Álvarez J, Ronda F, Salazar J. 2008. Characterization of cake batters by ultrasound measurements. *J. Food Eng.* 89(4):408–13

Götz J, Kreibich W, Peciar M, Buggisch H. 2001. MRI of Couette experiments in a newly developed shear device—suitable for pastes and concentrated suspensions? *J. Non-Newton. Fluid Mech.* 98(2–3):117–39

Gromer A, Kirby AR, Gunning AP, Morris VJ. 2009. Interfacial structure of sugar beet pectin studied by atomic force microscopy. *Langmuir* 25(14):8012–18

Grosso M, Maffettone PL. 2007. A new methodology for the estimation of drop size distributions of dilute polymer blends based on LAOS flows. *J. Non-Newton. Fluid Mech.* 143(1):48–58

Guggisberg D, Cuthbert-Steven J, Piccinali P, Bütikofer U, Eberhard P. 2009. Rheological, microstructural and sensory characterization of low-fat and whole milk set yoghurt as influenced by inulin addition. *Int. Dairy J.* 19(2):107–15

Handojo A, Zhai Y, Frankel G, Pascall MA. 2009. Measurement of adhesion strengths between various milk products on glass surfaces using contact angle measurement and atomic force microscopy. *J. Food Eng.* 92(3):305–11

Harden JL, Viasnoff V. 2001. Recent advances in DWS-based micro-rheology. *Curr. Opin. Colloid Interface Sci.* 6(5–6):438–45

Hemar Y, Singh H, Horne DS. 2004. Determination of early stages of rennet-induced aggregation of casein micelles by diffusing wave spectroscopy and rheological measurements. *Curr. Appl. Phys.* 4(2–4):362–65

Henningsson M, Östergren K, Dejmek P. 2006. Plug flow of yoghurt in piping as determined by cross-correlated dual-plane electrical resistance tomography. *J. Food Eng.* 76(2):163–68

Herrera ML, M'Cann JI, Ferrero C, Hagiwara T, Zaritzky NE, et al. 2007. Thermal, mechanical, and molecular relaxation properties of frozen sucrose and fructose solutions containing hydrocolloids. *Food Biophys.* 2(1):20–28

Herrero AM, de la Hoz L, Ordóñez JA, Castejón D, Romero de Avila MD, Cambero MI. 2009. Magnetic resonance imaging study of the cold-set gelation of meat systems containing plasma powder. *Food Res. Int.* 42(9):1362–72

Hollingsworth KG, Johns ML. 2004. Rheo-nuclear magnetic resonance of emulsion systems. *J. Rheol.* 48(4):787–803

Horne DS, Dickinson E, Eliot C, Hemar Y. 2005. Gels, particle mobility, and diffusing wave spectroscopy—a cautionary tale. In *Food Colloids: Interactions, Microstructure, and Processing*, ed. E Dickinson, pp. 432–42. Cambridge, UK: R. Soc. Chem. 497 pp.

Hyun K, Kim SH, Ahn KH, Lee SJ. 2002. Large amplitude oscillatory shear as a way to classify the complex fluids. *J. Non-Newton. Fluid Mech.* 107(1–3):51–65

Hyun K, Nam JG, Wilhellm M, Ahn KH, Lee SJ. 2006. Large amplitude oscillatory shear behavior of PEO-PPO-PEO triblock copolymer solutions. *Rheol. Acta* 45(3):239–49

Ikeda S. 2003. Heat-induced gelation of whey proteins observed by rheology, atomic force microscopy, and Raman scattering spectroscopy. *Food Hydrocoll.* 17(4):399–406

Johns ML. 2009. NMR studies of emulsions. *Curr. Opin. Colloid Interface Sci.* 14(3):178–83

Johns ML, Hollingsworth KG. 2007. Characterisation of emulsion systems using NMR and MRI. *Process Nucl. Magn. Res. Spectrosc.* 50(2–3):51–70

Joshi YM. 2005. Nonlinear dynamics of confined polymer melts with attractive walls. *Langmuir* 21(20):9013–16

Karim AA, Oo PS, Seow CC. 2007. Pulsed NMR measurements of freeze/thaw-induced retrogradation of corn and wheat starch gels: correlation with rheological measurements. *Food Hydrocoll.* 21(7):1041–45

Kim YR, Cornillon P, Campanella OH, Stroshine RL, Lee S, Shim J-Y. 2008. Small and large deformation rheology for hard wheat flour dough as influenced by mixing and resting. *J. Food Sci.* 73(1):E1–8

Kimura Y. 2009. Microrheology of soft matter. *J. Phys. Soc. Jpn.* 78(4):041005-1-8

Klein C, Venema P, Sagis L, van der Linden E. 2008. Rheological discrimination and characterization of carrageenans and strarches by Fourier transform-rheology in the non-linear viscous regime. *J. Non-Newton. Fluid Mech.* 151(1–3):145–50

Knudsen JC, Karlsson AO, Ipsen R, Skibsted LH. 2006. Rheology of stirred acidified skim milk gels with different particle interactions. *Colloids Surf. A* 274(1–3):56–61

Knudsen JC, Øgendal LH, Skibsted LH. 2008. Droplet surface properties and rheology of concentrated oil in water emulsions stabilized by heat-modified β-lactoglobulin B. *Langmuir* 24(6):2603–10

Ko S, Gunasekaran S. 2007. Error correction of confocal microscopy images for in situ food microstructure evaluation. *J. Food Eng.* 79(3):935–44

Kulmyrzaev A, McClements DJ. 2000. High frequency dynamic shear rheology of honey. *J. Food Eng.* 45(4):219–24

León PG, Chillo S, Conte A, Gerschenson LN, Nobile MAD, Rojas AM. 2009. Rheological characterization of deacylated/acylated gellan films carrying l-(+)-ascorbic acid. *Food Hydrocoll.* 23(7):1660–69

Lodi A, Abduljalil AM, Vodovotz Y. 2007. Characterization of water distribution in bread during storage using magnetic resonance imaging. *Magn. Reson. Imaging* 25(10):1449–58

Lopez-da-Silva JA, Santos DMJ, Freitas A, Brites C, Gil AM. 2007. Rheological and nuclear magnetic resonance (NMR) study of the hydration and heating of underdeveloped wheat doughs. *J. Agric. Food Chem.* 55(14):5636–44

Lutz R, Aserin A, Portnoy Y, Gottlieb M, Garti N. 2009. On the confocal images and the rheology of whey protein isolated and modified pectins associated complex. *Colloids Surf. B* 69(1):43–50

Mariette F. 2009. Investigations of food colloids by NMR and MRI. *Curr. Opin. Colloid Interface Sci.* 14(3):203–11

Mariotti M, Lucisano M, Pagani MA, Ng PKW. 2009. The role of corn starch, amaranth flour, pea isolate, and *Psyllium* flour on the rheological properties and the ultrastructure of gluten-free doughs. *Food Res. Int.* 42(8):963–75

Mazzanti G, Mudge EM, Anom EY. 2008. In situ rheo-NMR measurements of solid fat content. *J. Am. Oil Chem. Soc.* 85(5):405–12

Metz H, Mäder K. 2008. Benchtop-NMR and MRI—a new analytical tool in drug delivery research. *Int. J. Pharm.* 364(2):170–75

Mizuno D, Head DA, MacKintosh FC, Schmidt CF. 2008. Active and passive microrheology in equilibrium and nonequilibrium systems. *Macromolecules* 41(19):7194–202

Nagano T, Tamaki E, Funami T. 2008. Influence of guar gum on granule morphologies and rheological properties of maize starch. *Carbohydr. Polym.* 72(1):95–101

Nam JG, Hyun K, Ahn KH, Lee SJ. 2008. Prediction of normal stresses under large amplitude oscillatory shear flow. *J. Non-Newton. Fluid Mech.* 150(1):1–10

Narumi T, See H, Suzuki A, Hasegawa T. 2005. Response of concentrated suspensions under large amplitude oscillatory shear flow. *J. Rheol.* 49(1):71–85

Ng TSK, McKinley GH. 2008. Power law gels at finite strains: the nonlinear rheology of gluten gels. *J. Rheol.* 52(2):417–49

Nicolas Y, Paques M. 2003. Microrheology: an experimental technique to visualize food structure behavior under compression-extension deformation conditions. *J. Food Sci.* 68(6):1990–94

Nicolas Y, Paques M, Knaebel A, Steyer A, Munch J-P, et al. 2003a. Microrheology: structural evolution under static and dynamic conditions by simultaneous analysis of confocal microscopy and diffusing wave spectroscopy. *Rev. Sci. Instrum.* 74(8):3838–44

Nicolas Y, Paques M, Van Der Ende D, Dhont JKG, van Polanen RC, et al. 2003b. Microrheology: new methods to approach the functional properties of food. *Food Hydrocoll.* 17(6):907–13

Noda S, Funami T, Nakauma M, Asai I, Takahashi R, et al. 2008. Molecular structures of gellan gum imaged with atomic force microscopy in relation to the rheological behavior in aqueous systems. 1. Gellan gum with various acyl contents in the presence and absence of potassium. *Food Hydrocoll.* 22(6):1148–59

Noisuwan A, Bronlund J, Wilkinson B, Hemar Y. 2008. Effect of milk protein products on the rheological and thermal (DSC) properties of normal rice starch and waxy rice starch. *Food Hydrocoll.* 22(1):174–83

Noronha N, Duggan E, Ziegler GR, O'Riordan ED, O'Sullivan M. 2008. Inclusion of starch in imitation cheese: its influence on water mobility and cheese functionality. *Food Hydrocoll.* 22(8):1612–21

Nunes MC, Raymundo A, Sousa I. 2006. Rheological behaviour and microstructure of pea protein/κ-carrageenan/starch gels with different setting conditions. *Food Hydrocoll.* 20(1):106–13

Nydén M, Holmberg K. 2009. NMR for studying structure and dynamics in colloidal systems. *Curr. Opin. Colloid Interface Sci.* 14(3):169–70

Occhipinti P, Griffiths PC. 2008. Quantifying diffusion in mucosal systems by pulsed-gradient spin-echo NMR. *Adv. Drug Deliv. Rev.* 60(15):1570–82

Ouriev B, Breitschuh B, Windhab EJ. 2000. Rheological investigation of concentrated suspensions using a novel in-line Doppler ultrasound method. *Colloid J.* 62(2):234–37

Ouriev B, Windhab EJ. 2002. Rheological study of concentrated suspensions in pressure-driven shear flow using a novel in-line Doppler ultrasound method. *Exp. Fluids* 32:204–11

Ouriev B, Windhab EJ, Braun P, Birkhofer B. 2004. Industrial application of ultrasound based in-line rheometry: from stationary to pulsating pipe flow of chocolate suspension in precrystallization process. *Rev. Sci. Instrum.* 75(10):3164–68

Patino JMR, Caro AL, Niño MRR, Mackle AR, Gunning AP, Morris VJ. 2007. Some implications of nanoscience in food dispersion formulations containing phospholipids as emulsifiers. *Food Chem.* 102(2):532–41

Pfund DM, Greenwood MS, Bamberger JA, Pappas RA. 2006. Inline ultrasonic rheometry by pulsed Doppler. *Ultrasonics* 44(S1):e477–82

Pinder DN, Swanson AJ, Hebraud P, Hemar Y. 2006. Micro-rheological investigation of dextran solutions using diffusing wave spectroscopy. *Food Hydrocoll.* 20(2–3):240–44

Puppo MC, Beaumal V, Chapleau N, Speroni F, de Lamballerie M, et al. 2008. Physicochemical and rheological properties of soybean protein emulsions processed with a combined temperature/high-pressure treatment. *Food Hydrocoll.* 22(6):1079–89

Ravindranath S, Wang S-Q. 2008. Large amplitude oscillatory shear behavior of entangled polymer solutions: particle tracking velocimetric investigation. *J. Rheol.* 52(2):341–58

Raynaud JS, Moucheront P, Baudez JC, Bertrand F, Guilband JP, Coussot P. 2002. Direct determination by nuclear magnetic resonance of the thixotropic and yielding behavior of suspensions. *J. Rheol.* 46(3):709–32

Renzetti S, Arendt EK. 2009. Effect of protease treatment on the baking quality of brown rice bread: from textural and rheological properties to biochemistry and microstructure. *J. Cereal Sci.* 50(1):22–28

Renzetti S, Bello FD, Arendt EK. 2008. Microstructure, fundamental rheology and baking characteristics of batters and breads from different gluten-free flours treated with a microbial transglutaminase. *J. Cereal Sci.* 48(1):33–45

Ritota M, Gianferri R, Bucci R, Brosio E. 2008. Proton NMR relaxation study of swelling and gelatinisation process in rice starch–water samples. *Food Chem.* 110(1):14–22

Ross KA, Pyrak-Nolte LJ, Campanella OH. 2004. The use of ultrasound and shear oscillatory tests to characterize the effect of mixing time on the rheological properties of dough. *Food Res. Int.* 37(6):567–77

Ruis HGM, van Gruijthuijsen K, Venema P, van der Linden E. 2007. Transitions in structure in oil-in-water emulsions as studied by diffusing wave spectroscopy. *Langmuir* 23(3):1007–13

Sahin O, Magonov S, Su C, Quate CF, Solgaard O. 2007. An atomic force microscope tip designed to measure time-varying nonchemical forces. *Nat. Nanotechnol.* 2:507–14

Savary G, Handschin S, Conde-Petit B, Cayot N, Doublier J-L. 2008. Structure of polysaccharide-starch composite gels by rheology and confocal laser scanning microscopy: effect of the composition and of the preparation procedure. *Food Hydrocoll.* 22(4):520–30

Scheffold F, Romer S, Cardinaux F, Bissig H, Stradner A, et al. 2004. New trends in optical microrheology of complex fluids and gels. *Prog. Colloid Polym. Sci.* 123:141–46

Sederman AJ, Hollingsworth KG, Johns ML, Gladden LF. 2004. Development and application of rotationally compensated RARE. *J. Magn. Reson.* 171(1):118–23

Sederman AJ, Mantle MD, Gladden LF. 2003. Single excitation multiple image RARE (SEMI-RARE): ultra-fast imaging of static and flowing systems. *J. Magn. Reson.* 161(1):15–24

Shimoni E. 2008. Using AFM to explore food nanostructure. *Curr. Opin. Colloid Interface Sci.* 13(5):368–74

Sim HG, Ahn KH, Lee SJ. 2003. Large amplitude oscillatory shear behavior of complex fluids investigated by a network model: a guideline for classification. *J. Non-Newton. Mech.* 112(2–3):237–50

Song K-W, Kuk H-Y, Change G-S. 2006. Rheology of concentrated gum solutions: oscillatory shear flow behavior. *Korea-Aust. Rheol. J.* 18(2):67–81

Squires TM, Brady JF. 2005. A simple paradigm for active and nonlinear microrheology. *Phys. Fluids* 17(7):073101–21

Sriamornsak P, Thirawong N, Nunthanid J, Puttipipatkhachron S, Thongborisute J, Takeuchi H. 2008. Atomic force microscopy imaging of novel self-assembling pectin–liposome nanocomplexes. *Carbohydr. Polym.* 71(2):324–29

Steffe JF. 1996. *Rheological Methods in Food Process Engineering*. East Lansing, MI: Freeman. 418 pp. 2nd ed.

Stevenson P, Mantle MD, Hicks JM. 2007. NMRI studies of the free drainage of egg white and meringue mixture froths. *Food Hydrocoll.* 21(2):221–29

Sugimoto M, Suzuki Y, Hyun K, Ahn KH, Ushioda T, et al. 2006. Melt rheology of long chain-branched polypropylenes. *Rheol. Acta* 46(10):33–44

Thybo AK, Karlsson AH, Bertram HC, Andersen HJ. 2004. Nuclear magnetic resonance (NMR) and magnetic resonance imaging (MRI) in texture measurement. In *Texture in Food: Solid Foods*, ed. D Kilcast. Boca Raton, FL: CRC Press LLC. 537 pp.

Ting C-H, Kuo F-J, Lien C-C, Sheng C-T. 2009. Use of ultrasound for characterising the gelation process in heat induced $CaSO_4 \times 2H_2O$ tofu curd. *J. Food Eng.* 93(1):101–7

Ubbink J, Burbidge A, Mezzenga R. 2008. Food structure and functionality: a soft matter perspective. *Soft Matter* 4(8):1569–81

Uludag Y, McCarthy MJ, Barrall GA, Powell RL. 2001. Polymer melt rheology by magnetic resonance imaging. *Macromolecules* 34(6):5520–24

Vallons KJR, Arendt EK. 2009. Effects of high pressure and temperature on the structural and rheological properties of sorghum starch. *Innov. Food Sci. Emerg. Technol.* 10(4):449–56

van der Linden E, Sagis L, Venema P. 2003. Rheo-optics and food systems. *Curr. Opin. Colloid Interface Sci.* 8(4–5):349–58

Voda MA, van Duynhoven J. 2009. Characterization of food emulsions by PFG NMR. *Trends Food Sci. Technol.* 20(11–12):533–43

Wagner M, Quellec S, Trystram G, Lucas T. 2008. MRI evaluation of local expansion in bread crumb during baking. *J. Cereal Sci.* 48(1):213–23

Waigh TA. 2005. Microrheology of complex fluids. *Rep. Prog. Phys.* 68:685–742

Wang Q, Bulca S, Kulozik U. 2007. A comparison of low-intensity ultrasound and oscillating rheology to assess the renneting properties of casein solutions after UHT heat pre-treatment. *Int. Dairy J.* 17(1):50–58

Wang Q, Rademacher B, Sedlmeyer F, Kulozik U. 2005. Gelation behaviour of aqueous solutions of different types of carrageenan investigated by low-intensity-ultrasound measurements and comparison to rheological measurements. *Innov. Food Sci. Emerg. Technol.* 6(4):465–72

Wiklund J, Shahram I, Stading M. 2007. Methodology for in-line ultrasound Doppler velocity profiling and pressure difference techniques. *Chem. Eng. Sci.* 62:4277–93

Wiklund J, Stading M. 2006. *Rheology and velocity profiles of real food suspensions containing large solid particles investigated using UVP-PD method*. Presented at 4th Int. Symp. Food Rheol. Struct., 20–23 Febr., Zurich, Switz.

Wilhelm M. 2002. Fourier-transform rheology. *Macromol. Mater. Eng.* 287(2):83–105

Xing H, Takhar PS, Helms G, He B. 2007. NMR imaging of continuous and intermittent drying of pasta. *J. Food Eng.* 78(1):61–68

Yang L, Kuang J, Li Z, Zhang B, Cai X, Zhang L-M. 2008. Amphiphilic cholesteryl-bearing carboxymethylcellulose derivatives: self-assembly and rheological behaviour in aqueous solution. *Cellulose* 15(5):659–69

Ye A, Hewitt S. 2009. Phase structures impact the rheological properties of rennet-casein-based imitation cheese containing starch. *Food Hydrocoll.* 23(3):867–73

Yoon WB, McCarthy KL. 2002. Rheology of yogurt during pipe flow as characterized by magnetic resonance imaging. *J. Texture Stud.* 33(5):431–44

Young NWG, Wassell P, Wiklund J, Stading M. 2008. Monitoring structurants of fat blends with ultrasound based in-line rheometry (ultrasonic velocity profiling with pressure difference). *Int. J. Food Sci. Technol.* 43(11):2083–89

Zandi M, Mirzadeh H, Mayer C. 2007. Early stages of gelation in gelatin solution detected by dynamic oscillating rheology and nuclear magnetic spectroscopy. *Eur. Polym. J.* 43(4):1480–86

Zhou R, Li Y. 2007. Texture analysis of MR image for predicting the firmness of Huanghua pears (*Pyrus pyrifolia* Nakai, cv. Huanghua) during storage using an artificial neural network. *Magn. Reson. Imaging* 25(5):727–32

Pomegranate as a Functional Food and Nutraceutical Source

Suzanne D. Johanningsmeier[1,2] and G. Keith Harris[2,*]

[1]USDA-ARS Food Science Research Unit Raleigh, North Carolina 27695; email: sdjohann@ncsu.edu

[2]Department of Food, Bioprocessing and Nutrition Sciences at North Carolina State University, Raleigh, North Carolina 27695; email: gkharris@ncsu.edu

Annu. Rev. Food Sci. Technol. 2011. 2:181–201

First published online as a Review in Advance on November 15, 2010

The *Annual Review of Food Science and Technology* is online at food.annualreviews.org

This article's doi:
10.1146/annurev-food-030810-153709

1941-1413/11/0410-0181$20.00

*Corresponding author

Keywords

antioxidant, ellagitannin, urolithin, cancer, cardiovascular health, diabetes

Abstract

Pomegranate, a fruit native to the Middle East, has gained widespread popularity as a functional food and nutraceutical source. The health effects of the whole fruit, as well as its juices and extracts, have been studied in relation to a variety of chronic diseases. Promising results against cardiovascular disease, diabetes, and prostate cancer have been reported from human clinical trials. The in vitro antioxidant activity of pomegranate has been attributed to its high polyphenolic content, specifically punicalagins, punicalins, gallagic acid, and ellagic acid. These compounds are metabolized during digestion to ellagic acid and urolithins, suggesting that the bioactive compounds that provide in vivo antioxidant activity may not be the same as those present in the whole food. Anthocyanins and the unique fatty acid profile of the seed oil may also play a role in pomegranate's health effects. A more complete characterization of pomegranate components and their physiological fate may provide mechanistic insight into the potential health benefits observed in clinical trials.

INTRODUCTION

Polyphenolic: a diverse group of natural compounds that contain one or more phenol entities and may possess antioxidant and other potentially health-promoting properties

Pomegranate (*Punica granatum*) and its juices and extracts are currently being widely promoted, with or without scientific support, to consumers as one of the new superfoods, capable of addressing a variety of health ailments. This fruit, which has been consumed and used as a medicinal food in the Middle East for thousands of years, has recently gained popularity in the United States. The potential capabilities of pomegranate as listed on a number of Web sites selling pomegranate products include its use as an antioxidant, an antiinflammatory, an antiviral, an antibacterial, and an antifungal. Specific health benefits listed on these Web sites include anticancer properties, improvement in cardiovascular health, diabetes prevention and management, relief of menopausal symptoms, hormone balance, increased libido in both genders, improved male virility and erectile function, skin nourishment including antiwrinkle effects, and protection against Alzheimer's disease and rheumatoid arthritis. The high antioxidant activity of the fruit and juice as compared with other fruits and antioxidant beverages (Halvorsen et al. 2002, Gil et al. 2000, Stangeland et al. 2007, Wolfe et al. 2008, Seeram et al. 2008a, Chidambara Murthy et al. 2002, Guo et al. 2008) has been the basis for much of the purported health benefits and has stimulated interest in research on potential nutraceutical and functional food applications. Unfortunately, the number of popular press, pomegranate-promoting publications far outweighs the number of significantly supportive scientific studies, as evidenced by the approximately 5,700:1 ratio of internet Google™ hits for "pomegranate health" (2,240,000) as compared with a MEDLINE® search for peer-reviewed journal articles on pomegranate (388). Nonetheless, research on the health-promoting properties of pomegranate has advanced rapidly. In the past two years alone, the number of peer-reviewed journal articles has nearly doubled, and several human clinical trials are in progress. Results from these studies may shed more light on the putative health effects of pomegranate. Although the research on pomegranate as a functional food and nutraceutical source is in its infancy, recently published scientific studies suggest that these phytonutrient-rich products may be beneficial to health. The purpose of this review is to provide an overview of pomegranate chemistry and the potential health effects of pomegranate products.

FUNCTIONAL FOOD AND NUTRACEUTICAL PRODUCTS

In addition to the increased marketing of fresh pomegranate fruit, a number of pomegranate-containing products have recently been introduced into the U.S. market and are being heavily advertised for their health-promoting benefits (**Figure 1**, see color insert). These products include 100% juices, pomegranate-containing beverages, liquid and powdered polyphenolic extracts of pomegranate plant parts such as leaves, flowers, arils, and peel, pomegranate seed oil, and skin care products containing pomegranate extracts and/or pomegranate seed oil as ingredients. The sales of pomegranate juice alone increased from $84,507 in 2001 to $66 million in 2005 in the United States (AC Nielson, **http://www.factsfiguresfuture.com/archive/june_2005.htm**) illustrating the rapid growth in sales of these products. Recent publications evaluating commercial pomegranate juices and extracts for their phytochemical composition highlight the need for more comprehensive standardization criteria. Commercial juices from 23 manufacturers were tested for authenticity based on anthocyanin composition, the presence of pomegranate-specific ellagitannins, sugar, organic acid and amino acid profiles, and potassium content. Of these, a surprisingly low number (six) met the proposed requirements for authenticity, indicating that several of the juices had been supplemented with other ingredients or diluted (Zhang et al. 2009a). Similarly, 27 commercially available pomegranate extracts were analyzed for ellagitannin content and in vitro antioxidant capacity. Only five contained significant quantities of pomegranate-specific ellagitannins, the punicalins and

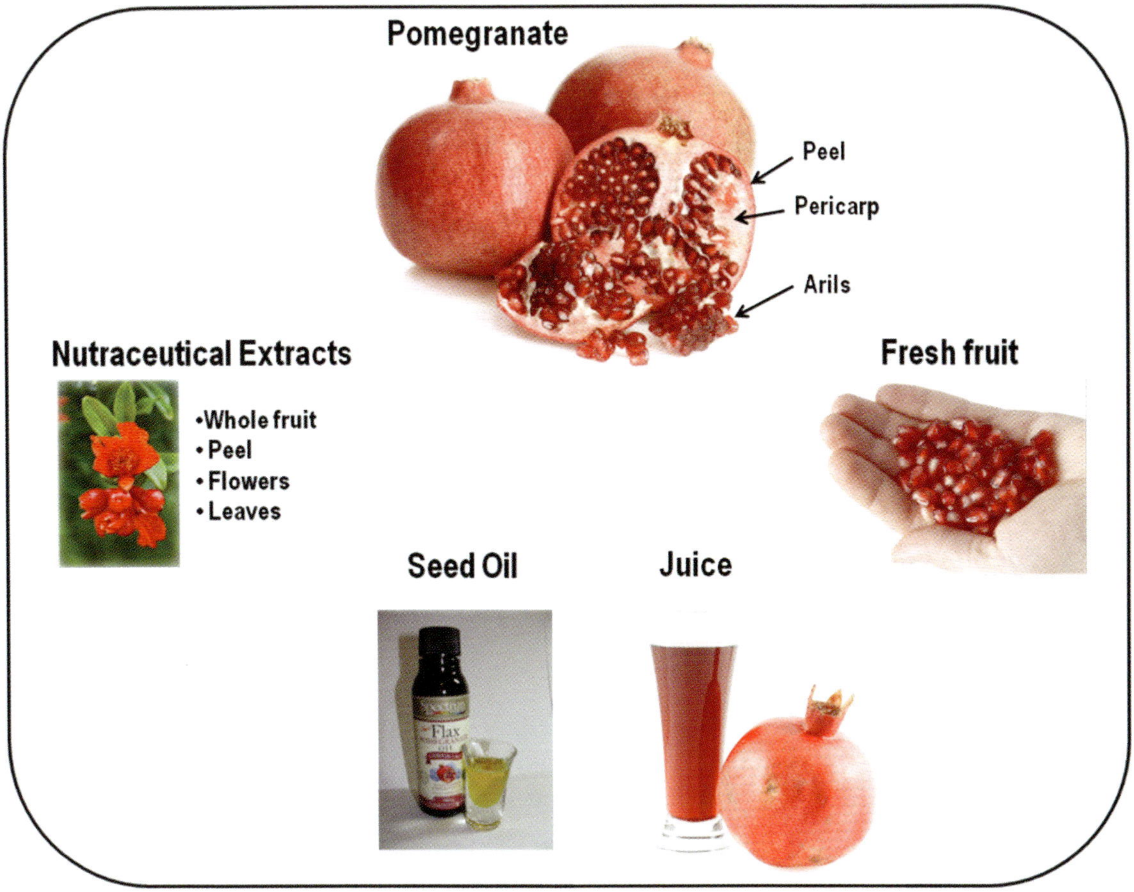

Figure 1

Pomegranate products studied for their health effects.

punicalagins. Seventeen commercial extracts contained primarily ellagic acid, the currently used standardization compound, and five extracts had very little ellagitannin or ellagic acid content and also exhibited low to no antioxidant activity (Zhang et al. 2009b). Interestingly, the only extracts that contained punicalagins were the ones that were labeled as such, indicating that some companies are taking extra measures to produce standardized pomegranate extracts. In the rapidly growing nutraceutical market, production and sales often preceed knowledge and standardization. However, these studies combined with continued research on the specific bioactive components of pomegranate hold promise for future products that can deliver the health benefits as specified.

Oxidative stress: an unusually high level of oxidation that may result in damage to vital biomolecules, including protein and DNA, thereby increasing disease risk

Trolox equivalent antioxidant capacity (TEAC): an in vitro estimate of antioxidant properties that uses trolox, a water-soluble vitamin E analog, as a standard

Ascorbic acid equivalent antioxidant capacity (AEAC): an in vitro estimate of antioxidant properties that uses vitamin C as a standard

Ex vivo: laboratory experiments using biological fluids, such as blood or saliva, in order to predict what might be observed if a compound was ingested or otherwise internalized

CHEMISTRY

The high in vitro antioxidant activity of pomegranate products has stimulated studies of its health effects pertaining to a number of chronic diseases thought to be related to oxidative stress. In several studies using multiple antioxidant activity assays, pomegranate fruit and juices have demonstrated antioxidant properties similar to or higher than other foods considered to have high antioxidant activity, including red wine and green tea. (Halvorsen et al. 2002, Gil et al. 2000, Stangeland et al. 2007, Wolfe et al. 2008, Seeram et al. 2008a). The major phytochemical component classes identified to date in pomegranate fruit are anthocyanins and hydrolyzable tannins, specifically ellagitannins, which release ellagic acid when hydrolyzed (**Figure 2**). Punicalagin, punicalin, gallagic acid, and ellagic acid were found to account for the majority of the ellagitannins in pomegranate juices and homogenates from 29 lines over two growing seasons (Tzulker et al. 2007). Research has shown that the antioxidant activity of pomegranate juices as measured by trolox equivalent antioxidant capacity (TEAC) and ascorbic acid equivalent antioxidant capacity (AEAC) methods was primarily attributable to the concentration of these hydrolyzable tannins, with anthocyanins contributing very little to in vitro antioxidant capacity (Gil et al. 2000). In whole fruit pomegranate homogenates, antioxidant activity was also correlated significantly with total polyphenols ($R^2 = 0.90$, $P < 0.01$), but not with total anthocyanin content ($R^2 = 0.05$, $P > 0.05$) (Tzulker et al. 2007). Nevertheless, anthocyanins have been associated with health effects, including prevention of cardiovascular disease, obesity, and diabetes (He & Giusti 2010) and should not be ignored as potentially bioactive components of pomegranate. The major anthocyanins in pomegranate juice across several Iranian cultivars were delphinidin 3,5-diglucoside, cyanidin 3,5-diglucoside, pelargonidin 3,5-diglucoside, delphinidin 3-glucoside, cyanidin 3-glucoside, and pelargonidin 3-glucoside (Alighourchi et al. 2008, Mousavinejad et al. 2009).

Pomegranate peel extracts have been shown to have higher antioxidant activity than the juice (Kelawala & Ananthanarayan 2004, Zhang et al. 2008) or seed extracts (Zhang et al. 2008, Singh et al. 2002), and were effective at preventing lipid peroxidation (Kelawala & Ananthanarayan 2004, Singh et al. 2002) and ex vivo low-density lipoprotein (LDL) oxidation at levels between 50 ppm and 100 ppm peel extract. Additionally, pomegranate peel extract was a more effective antioxidant than turmeric or ascorbic acid (vitamin C), two food-derived compounds that are known for their antioxidant properties (Kelawala & Ananthanarayan 2004).

Although the seeds have lower polyphenol content and in vitro antioxidant capacity (Zhang et al. 2008, Singh et al. 2002), the oils produced from them contain other components that may contribute health benefits. The seed oil has high phytosterol content and a unique fatty acid profile that includes punicic acid (**Figure 3**), a conjugated linolenic acid isomer (Kaufman & Wiesman 2007). Across 15 Turkish pomegranate cultivars, punicic acid constituted 70% to 76% of the pomegranate seed oil. The balance of the oil consisted of α-eleostearic, linoleic, oleic, catalpic, palmitic, stearic, β-eleostearic, gadoleic, arachidic, and behenic acids (Kýralan et al. 2009). Other researchers reported a similar fatty acid profile for a commercial cold-pressed pomegranate seed oil

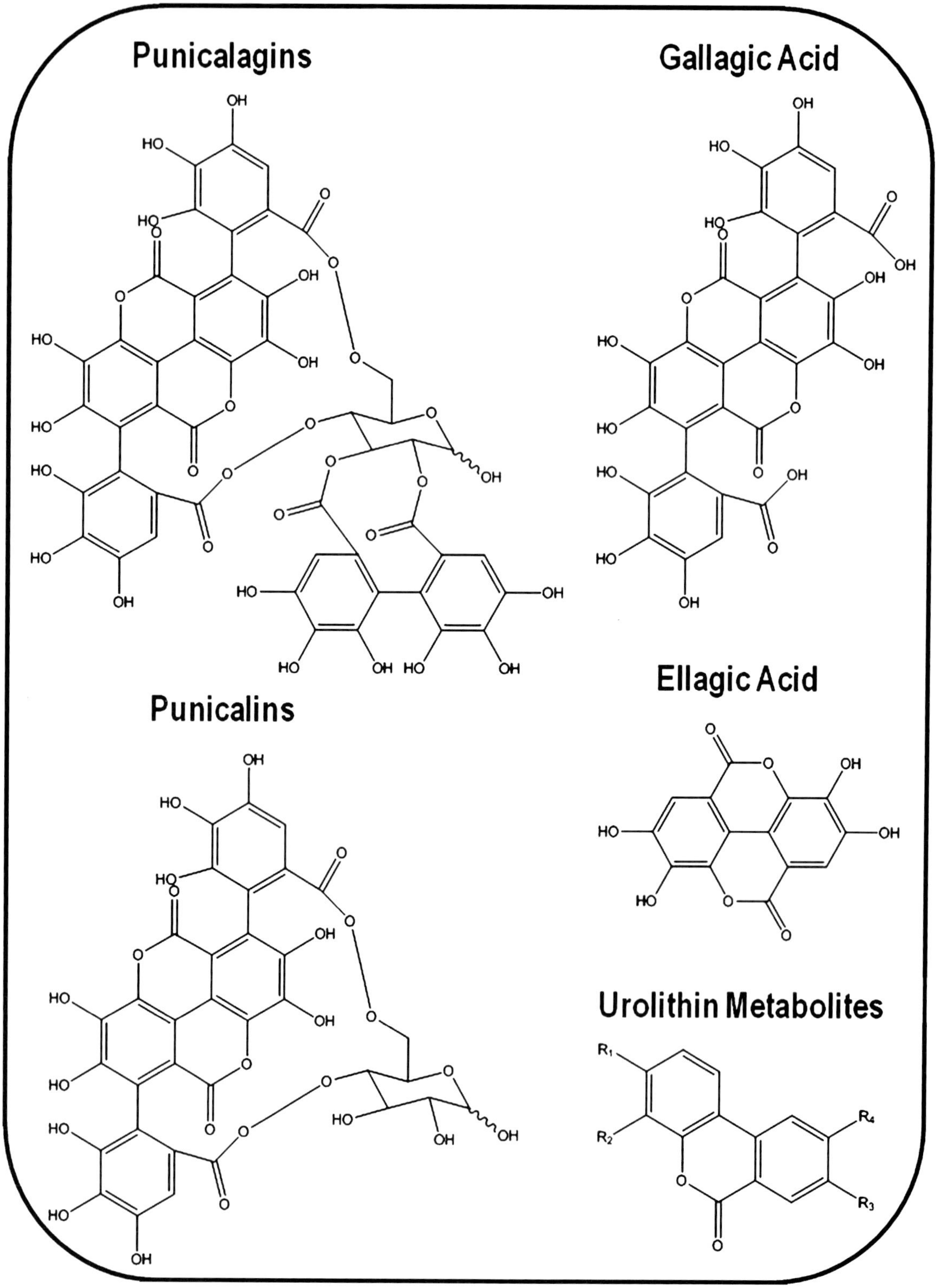
Punicalagins
Gallagic Acid
Punicalins
Ellagic Acid
Urolithin Metabolites

with the added detection of minor amounts of vaccenic (C18:1), lignoceric (C24:0), and nervonic (C24:1) acids (Sassano et al. 2009). This unique chemical composition of pomegranate seed oil has stimulated research specific to the healthful effects of the oil, including weight control, skin repair, and alteration of blood lipid profiles in hyperlipidemic individuals.

BIOAVAILABILITY

The high in vitro antioxidant capacity of pomegranate products has been attributed mostly to the high content of polyphenolic compounds, specifically the ellagitannins. However, the bioavailability of ellagitannins must be established in order to provide a link between these compounds and health effects related to in vivo antioxidant activity. In studies of ellagitannin bioavailability in human subjects, ellagic acid and its metabolites were detected in the plasma of individuals post-pomegranate juice consumption (Seeram et al. 2004, 2006). Furthermore, no difference in bioavailability as indicated by plasma ellagic acid or its metabolites was found among pomegranate juice, liquid extract, or powdered extract forms of treatment that contained similar levels of total polyphenols standardized as gallic acid equivalents (Seeram et al. 2008b). In contrast, a second study reported that no ellagic acid, punicalagin, anthocyanins, or their biological degradation products were found in plasma after pomegranate juice consumption (1 liter per day distributed in 5–200 mL bottles), even though the levels of ellagic acid and punicalagin in the juice were higher in this study. Urolithin metabolites were discovered, however, which the authors hypothesized were contributed by colonic microbial metabolism of the pomegranate juice polyphenols based on the timing of the appearance of the metabolites in plasma and urine samples (Cerdá et al. 2004) and their previous work on bioavailability of punicalagin in rats (Cerdá et al. 2003b). It is important to note that the timing of plasma sampling was different between these seemingly contrasting studies, and that since the half life of ellagic acid in the plasma was relatively short, between 0.65–1.79 h, (Seeram et al. 2008b), it may have been cleared from the blood prior to the first sampling in the other study (Cerdá et al. 2004). Thirty-one ellagitannin metabolites were detected using acorn-fed Iberian pigs as a model system, but only urolithin A, urolithin B, dimethyl ellagic acid and their glucuronide derivatives were found in plasma (Espín et al. 2007). Furthermore, urolithin metabolites have been shown to be readily absorbed in mouse models, with the highest levels accumulated in prostate, colon, and intestinal tissues (Seeram et al. 2007). Similarly, urolithin A glucuronide, urolithin B glucuronide, and dimethylellagic acid were the only ellagic acid metabolites detected in human prostate tissues after three days of supplementation with pomegranate juice (González-Sarrías et al. 2010a), indicating that the animal models may be suitable surrogates for studying the bioavailability and metabolism of ellagitannins. Overall, it appears that ellagitannins are hydrolyzed in the stomach where some portion of ellagic acid may be absorbed into circulation. The remaining ellagic acid is metabolized to urolithin derivatives by gut microflora. The less polar of these urolithin derivatives (A and B) are absorbed into circulation and metabolized further to glucuronides. Urolithins A, C, and D have been shown to possess antioxidant activity in a cell-based assay (Bialonska et al. 2009a), and urolithin A was found to have significant anti-inflammatory activity in an in vitro colon fibroblast model (González-Sarrías et al. 2010b). Therefore, it is possible that pomegranate polyphenolic compounds may act in multiple

Bioavailability: a concept that reflects the ability of dietary components to be both absorbed and utilized in the body

Glucuronide: a molecule to which glucuronic acid has been added by the liver or kidneys as a means of increasing its ability to be excreted from the body

Figure 2

Chemical structures of pomegranate ellagitannins and microbially derived urolithin metabolites (Urolithin A: R_1 = OH, R_2 = H, R_3 = OH, R_4 = H; Urolithin B: R_1 = H, R_2 = H, R_3 = OH, R_4 = H; Urolithin C: R_1 = OH, R_2 = H, R_3 = OH, R_4 = OH; Urolithin D: R_1 = OH, R_2 = OH, R_3 = OH, R_4 = OH).

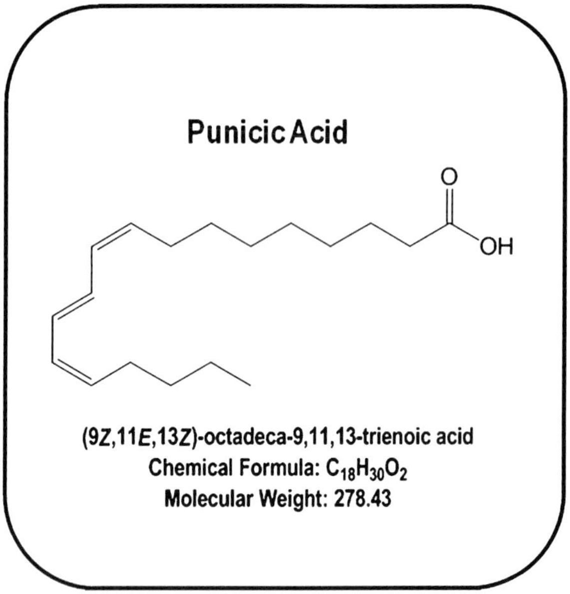

Punicic Acid
O
OH
(9Z,11E,13Z)-octadeca-9,11,13-trienoic acid
Chemical Formula: $C_{18}H_{30}O_2$
Molecular Weight: 278.43

Figure 3

Chemical structure of punicic acid, a conjugated linolenic acid isomer unique to pomegranate seed oil.

ways, with some being absorbed and entering the bloodstream to act directly as antioxidants, and the remainder being digested by the colonic microflora to provide other biologically active substances.

HEALTH EFFECTS

Pomegranate has reportedly been used medicinally by the peoples of many cultures for centuries to treat conditions such as diabetes and to combat malarial parasites (Xu et al. 2009, Dell'Agli et al. 2009). However, it is just within the past decade that scientific research related to the health effects of pomegranate has increased substantially. Because of the high in vitro antioxidant activity of pomegranate products, a wide variety of diseases and health conditions that appear to have some relationship to the body's ability to ward off oxidative stresses have been investigated (**Table 1**). Of note, many pomegranate products are being marketed for specific health effects, despite limited scientific data. Human clinical trials are relatively few in number but have shown positive effects of pomegranate juice consumption on prostate cancer prevention and cardiovascular health. Beneficial effects of pomegranate products have also been observed in animal models for prostate, colon, breast, and skin cancers, as well as for hyperlipidemia, atherosclerosis, and diabetes prevention and treatment. Although the weight of evidence is not sufficient for any one health claim, there is some preliminary evidence that shows promise.

Hyperlipidemia: excessively high cholesterol and/or triglycerides levels, associated with increased cardiovascular disease risk

Cancer

Inhibition of cancer by pomegranate products has been studied for prostate, breast, colon, skin, lung, and cervical cancers, as well as leukemia. Of these, prostate cancer has been the most well studied, and positive effects of pomegranate juice consumption have been demonstrated in humans. Less is known at this time about the beneficial effects of pomegranate toward other cancers.

Table 1 Scientific studies on the potential health effects of pomegranate products

Disease/health claim	Total studies	Human clinical trials (# study subjects)	Animal model studies	Cell culture studies
Cancer	32	1	11	20
-prostate	11	1 (46)		
-colon	6			
-breast	6			
-skin	3			
-lung	2			
-cervical	1			
-leukemia	1			
Cardiovascular disease	22	8 (10, 13, 22, 20, 45, 289, 30)	9	7
Diabetes	11	3 (22, 20, 30)	7	1
Arthritis	3	0	2	1
Antimicrobial	8	3 (60, 60, 32)	0	5
Skin care	14	2 (20, 13)	5	7
Weight control	3	0	3	0
Inflammatory bowel disease	2	0	2	0
Chronic obstructive pulmonary disease	1	1 (30)	0	0
Alzheimer's disease	1	0	1	0
Neonatal neuroprotectant	1	0	1	0
Male infertility	1	0	1	0
Erectile dysfunction	1	1 (53)	0	0
Immune function	1	0	1	0
Menopause	1	1 (351)	0	0

Prostate. In a study of 46 men with rising prostate-specific antigen (PSA) levels following treatment for prostate cancer, consumption of 8 oz per day of pomegranate juice significantly delayed the rise in PSA, increasing the PSA doubling time from 15 months to 54 months based on baseline versus post-treatment measurements. Plasma analysis before and after treatment with pomegranate juice showed the treated subjects' plasma to have higher antioxidant and antiproliferative activities (Pantuck et al. 2006). At the time of publication, these authors indicated that a placebo-controlled trial to study these effects in more detail was underway. Furthermore, several studies in cell culture and animal models have reported inhibition of prostate cancer by pomegranate juice and extracts (Seeram et al. 2005, 2007; Albrecht et al. 2004; Lansky et al. 2005a,b; Malik et al. 2005; Sartippour et al. 2008; Rettig et al. 2008; Hong et al. 2008), and a number of mechanisms have been proposed. In vitro, pomegranate ellagitannins and their urolithin metabolites were shown to inhibit CYP1B1, a cytochrome P450 (CYP450) enzyme associated with prostate cancer initiation and progression. However, only urolithins A and B at higher concentrations inhibited this enzyme in prostate cancer cell cultures (Kasimsetty et al. 2009). Furthermore, urolithin A glucuronide, urolithin B glucuronide, and dimethyl ellagic acid were the only ellagitannin metabolites detected in human prostate tissues after three days of pomegranate juice or walnut consumption prior to fasting for surgery (González-Sarrías et al. 2010a). Given that these ellagitannin entities have been

Prostate-specific antigen (PSA): a protein associated with prostate cancer progression

Cytochrome P450 (CYP450) enzymes: enzymes found primarily in the liver and kidneys that serve to metabolize, detoxify, and aid in the excretion of foreign compounds demonstrated to accumulate in prostate tissues in vivo, inhibition assays in cell cultures using these compounds may add to our knowledge of the underlying mechanisms.

Apoptosis: an orderly form of cell death often associated with reduced cancer risk

Antiangiogenic: able to prevent the formation of new blood vessels, often associated with reduced risk of the spread of cancer in the body

Nuclear factor-kappa-B (NF-κB): a transcription regulator, generally present in an inactive form, which, when activated, initiates processes associated with inflammation, immunity, and cell growth

UVB: one of three general types of ultraviolet rays that causes direct DNA damage and is most strongly associated with skin cancer

Colon. Prevention of colon cancer with pomegranate products is mostly theoretical, with only a few studies in animal models and cell cultures for support. The number of azoxymethane-induced aberrant crypt foci in rats, an animal model for colon cancer, was significantly decreased by consumption of pomegranate juice (Boateng et al. 2007) and punicic acid–rich pomegranate seed oil (Kohno et al. 2004). Additionally, in human colon cell cultures, pomegranate juice inhibited proliferation and induced apoptosis (Seeram et al. 2005), possibly via an inflammatory cell signaling mechanism (Adams et al. 2006). Punicalagin, the primary ellagitannin in pomegranate was shown to release ellagic acid in cell culture media, which actively induced apoptosis of colon cancer–derived Caco-2 cells (Larrosa et al. 2006). It has also been shown that specific ellagitannins from pomegranate and the corresponding urolithin metabolites inhibited proliferation and induced apoptosis of HT-29 human colon cancer cells (Kasimsetty et al. 2010).

Breast. In breast cancer cell cultures, growth was inhibited by pomegranate extracts via apoptosis (Jeune et al. 2005). Similarly, a breast cancer mouse model showed reduction in lesions when treated with fermented pomegranate juice polyphenols, a purified unknown compound from the fermented pomegranate, and pomegranate seed oil (Mehta & Lansky 2004). Further research with these pomegranate components indicated that the inhibition observed in breast cancer models may be due to an antiangiogenic mechanism of action (Toi et al. 2003) and inhibition of nuclear factor-kappa-B (NF-κB) (Khan et al. 2009). Additionally, differentiation-promoting ability was shown for fermented pomegranate juice and peel extracts in a leukemia cell model (Kawaii & Lansky 2004). Given the intestinal metabolism of pomegranate polyphenols, several ellagitannin metabolites were tested in vitro for their antiproliferative and antiaromatase activities. Urolithin B displayed the greatest inhibition of both aromatase (an enzyme that interconverts testosterone and estrogen hormones) activity and proliferation (Adams et al. 2010), indicating that the bioactive components of the polyphenolic pomegranate extracts may be the microbially derived metabolites. Punicic acid, a major component of pomegranate seed oil, also inhibited breast cancer cells, but this effect was dependent on lipid peroxidation (Grossmann et al. 2010). Taken together, there appears to be some evidence in animal and cell culture models that a variety of bioactive compounds may exist in pomegranate extracts and oil that could have anticarcinogenic properties.

Skin. Both pomegranate seed oil and pomegranate fruit extract applied topically to mouse models for skin cancer inhibited the incidence and multiplicity of tumors, as well as delayed their onset (Hora et al. 2003, Afaq et al. 2005b). Sunlight provides UVA, UVB, and UVC radiation, but UVB (290–320 nm) tends to be most carcinogenic. The negative cellular effects of UVB exposure were studied in normal human epidermal keratinocytes in cell culture, and pomegranate fruit extract treatment was found to inhibit changes in NF-κB and mitogen-activated protein kinase (MAPK) pathways that would normally be stimulated by UVB exposure (Afaq et al. 2005a). Pomegranate juice, extract, and oil applied to reconstituted human skin prior to UVB exposure were equally successful in preventing UVB-mediated damage related to both aging and skin cancer (Afaq et al. 2009). Similarly, pomegranate extract has been shown to inhibit markers for UVB-induced skin damage in cultured human skin fibroblasts (Park et al. 2010, Pacheco-Palencia et al. 2008), with the effects attributed to the content of catechin (Park et al. 2010) and ellagic acid (Bae et al. 2010). Thus, the protective effects of pomegranate extracts on skin cells may be beneficial for both cancer prevention and reduction of photoaging.

Other. Pomegranate fruit extract was demonstrated to have an inhibitory effect that was specific to lung cancer cells, having very little effect on normal bronchial cells in cell culture, and that reduced tumor growth and multiplicity in mouse models (Khan et al. 2007a,b). In contrast, pomegranate extract standardized to 50 $\mu g\ ml^{-1}$ gallic acid equivalents was only slightly cytotoxic to cervical cancer cells in vitro and one of the least effective among the fruits tested (McDougall et al. 2008).

Intima media thickness (IMT): artery wall thickness, associated with cardiovascular disease progression

Metabolic syndrome: simultaneous presence of several risk factors for cardiovascular disease and diabetes-related conditions, including glucose intolerance, large waist size, and hypertension

Cardiovascular Health

Research on effects of pomegranate products on cardiovascular health has been primarily focused on the prevention of atherosclerosis and the management of hyperlipidemia in diabetic individuals (see below). Several human studies have been conducted, most of which have shown benefits of pomegranate products on cardiovascular health in relation to blood pressure, cholesterol, intima media thickness, and endothelial function. Elderly, hypertensive subjects (n = 10) that consumed pomegranate juice containing 1.5 mmol total phenols per day for two weeks experienced a 36% decrease in serum angiotensin II converting enzyme activity and a 5% decrease in systolic blood pressure, both of which are markers for cardiovascular disease risk (Aviram & Dornfeld 2001). After consumption of 50 ml pomegranate juice per day for two weeks, plasma from 13 healthy nonsmoking young men had higher antioxidant activity, decreased lipid peroxides, increased arylesterase activity, and increased resistance to copper sulfate–induced high-density lipoprotein (HDL) oxidation (Aviram et al. 2000). In this same report, it was demonstrated that pomegranate juice consumption decreased the number of foam cells and the size of atherosclerotic lesions by 44% in apolipoprotein E–deficient mice, an animal model for atherosclerosis.

In other human studies, atherosclerotic patients with carotid artery stenosis (a narrowing of the arteries in the neck that supply blood to the brain) that consumed pomegranate juice (50 ml day^{-1}) in addition to their regular medication for one year (n = 10) had on average a 30% decrease in intima media thickness (IMT) compared with a 9% increase in IMT in control patients (n = 9) (Aviram et al. 2004). In a larger clinical trial (n = 289) conducted over an 18-month period, healthy individuals with moderate risk factors for coronary heart disease (CHD) were instructed to consume either a pomegranate juice or placebo beverage daily. There was no overall difference in carotid IMT progression found between placebo and pomegranate juice groups. However, subpopulations that were in the top third of participants for total triglycerides (TG), total cholesterol:HDL cholesterol ratio, TG:HDL ratio, and apolipoprotein B showed significant reduction in carotid IMT progression with pomegranate juice supplementation (Davidson et al. 2009). The authors concluded from these data that individuals at higher risk for CHD benefited from pomegranate juice consumption. Additionally, a placebo-controlled human clinical trial using 45 patients with ischemic CHD found that daily consumption of 240 ml pomegranate juice for three months significantly decreased stress-induced myocardial ischemia ($P < 0.05$), whereas it increased in the placebo group (Sumner et al. 2005). In another study, the short-term benefits of pomegranate juice consumption on cardiovascular health were demonstrated. Endothelial function was significantly improved in adolescents with metabolic syndrome (n = 30) after four weeks of supplementation with 240 ml per day of pomegranate juice or grape juice (Hashemi et al. 2010). Overall, it appears that pomegranate juice supplementation may contribute significantly to prevention of cardiovascular diseases, which is consistent with current dietary guidelines that encourage consumption of at least five servings per day of fruits and vegetables.

In a human clinical trial with hyperlipidaemic individuals (n = 45), consumption of 400 mg pomegranate seed oil twice daily for four weeks increased HDL cholesterol and decreased the total cholesterol:HDL cholesterol ratio as compared with a placebo (Mirmiran et al. 2010). These results indicate that there may be some long-term benefits of pomegranate seed oil consumption on plasma lipid profiles that are associated with cardiovascular health.

Studies in atherosclerotic mouse models have also shown that pomegranate juice consumption significantly reduced the development of atherosclerosis (de Nigris et al. 2005, Kaplan et al. 2001). The antiatherosclerotic activity of pomegranate juice was associated with increased serum paraoxonase activity, decreased macrophage lipid peroxides, and decreased uptake of oxidized low-density lipoprotein (LDL) in macrophage cells (Kaplan et al. 2001). A dose-dependent decrease in cellular oxidative stress and decreased uptake of oxidized LDL in macrophage cells treated with pomegranate juice has been demonstrated in vitro (Fuhrman et al. 2005), and it has been proposed that the decreased cellular oxidative stress observed with pomegranate juice treatment may be at least partially attributed to upregulation of paraoxonase 2 expression (Shiner et al. 2007). Furthermore, a decrease in oxidation-sensitive gene expression and an increase in nitric oxide synthase activity were found in response to pomegranate juice supplementation in both hypercholesterolemic mice and human coronary artery endothelial cells exposed to high shear stress (de Nigris et al. 2005). Pomegranate juice was also shown to increase the bioactivity of nitric oxide synthase in human coronary endothelial cells by inhibiting the oxidation of LDL (oxidized LDL inhibits nitric oxide synthase) and upregulating the expression of endothelial nitric oxide synthase (de Nigris et al. 2006). Therefore, it appears that oxidized cholesterol can contribute to the formation of atherosclerotic lesions (blocking of blood vessels) and also cause vasoconstriction due to a decrease in the vasodilating compound nitric oxide. These animal studies suggest that pomegranate supplementation could attenuate these effects by reducing the uptake of oxidized LDL in macrophages, and maintaining or increasing nitric oxide levels in endothelial cells, thus preventing both atherosclerosis progression and vasoconstriction in partly blocked vessels.

Extracts of pomegranate flowers, peels, arils, and pomegranate juice each decreased atherosclerotic lesions and lipid peroxides in mouse models and cell culture systems, but the seed extracts had no effect (Aviram et al. 2008). Similarly, an extract prepared from pomegranate juice production by-product (the remaining portion of the whole fruit after juicing) reduced atherosclerotic lesion size by up to 57% and decreased markers of oxidative stress in a mouse model (Rosenblat 2006b). Despite questions remaining on the bioavailability and metabolism of pomegranate ellagitannins, an unidentified hydrolyzable tannin isolated from pomegranate juice was also shown to significantly reduce atherosclerotic lesion size, decrease plasma lipid peroxidation, and inhibit macrophage uptake of oxidized LDL in apolipoprotein E-decificient mice (Kaplan et al. 2001). Based on human clinical trials and on animal data, the consumption of pomegranate juice and extracts appear to have promise for maintaining or improving cardiovascular health.

Diabetes

Pomegranate flower extract and pomegranate juices and concentrates have been studied for their roles in management of diabetes in both animal models (Zucker diabetic rats) and humans. Pomegranate flower extract consumed by Zucker diabetic rats, a type II diabetes model, decreased the expected glucose load–induced increase in plasma glucose levels but had no effect on Zucker lean rats (Li et al. 2005, Huang et al. 2005a). Authors hypothesized that this effect was due to increased insulin receptor sensitivity via pomegranate flower stimulation of the peroxisome proliferator-activated receptors (PPAR)-γ (Huang et al. 2005a) or inhibition of intestinal α-glucosidase (Li et al. 2005). In addition to glucose metabolism in diabetic states, pomegranate flower extract has also been shown to decrease triglycerides and total cholesterol (Huang et al. 2005b), decrease cardiac fibrosis (Huang et al. 2005c), and reduce fatty liver via upregulation of fatty acid oxidation (Xu et al. 2009) in Zucker diabetic rat model systems. Pomegranate flower extract was also shown to increase HDL cholesterol, glutathione, and antioxidant enzymes in streptozotocin-induced diabetic Wistar rats and decrease fasting blood glucose, TG, LDL cholesterol, VLDL cholesterol, and tissue lipid peroxidation (Bagri et al. 2009). This is in agreement with the previous animal studies and provides additional information on the improvement in oxidative state upon treatment with pomegranate flower extract, a traditional antidiabetic medicine. Similarly, pomegranate juice extract consumed for four weeks was able to ameliorate the biochemical and physiological effects of diabetes and hypertension induced in Wistar rats (Mohan et al. 2009).

Interleukin-6 (IL-6): a protein-based cellular signaling molecule involved in communication among immune cells and in the inflammation process

Hyperlipidemia and oxidative stress in diabetic patients puts them at increased risk for heart disease. Three human clinical trials have been conducted with diabetic patients to study the effect of pomegranate juice consumption on plasma lipid and oxidation profiles. Oxidative stress was decreased by 35% upon consumption of 50 ml per day of pomegranate juice for four weeks and was attributed to increased serum HDL-associated PON1 stability and activity (Rock et al. 2008). After eight weeks of pomegranate juice concentrate (40 g) consumption by 22 diabetic patients, plasma lipid profiles were improved, as evidenced by decreased total cholesterol, LDL cholesterol, and LDL/HDL ratio (Esmaillzadeh et al. 2004). Pomegranate juice consumption (50 ml day^{-1}) for three months by diabetic patients and their healthy subject controls decreased serum lipid peroxides by 23%, an indicator of an overall increased antioxidant activity in vivo (Rosenblat et al. 2006a). There were also no negative consequences of pomegranate juice consumption in terms of blood glucose parameters (Rock et al. 2008, Rosenblat et al. 2006a). These clinical results involved only a few patients, but were supported by the animal model work that had been done in this area (Rozenberg et al. 2006, de Nigris et al. 2007).

Arthritis

The effect of pomegranate fruit extract on arthritis has been studied to a limited degree in animal models. Pomegranate fruit extract fed to mice in their drinking water significantly delayed the onset and reduced the incidence and severity of arthritis in a collagen-induced arthritis model, and inflammatory cytokine interleukin 6 (IL-6) was reduced. (Shukla et al. 2008) Similarly, pomegranate juice prevented chondrocyte damage in a mouse model for osteoarthritis in a dose-dependent fashion (Hadipour-Jahromy & Mozaffari-Kermani 2010). Human osteoarthritis cartilage samples (chondrocyte cell cultures) pretreated with an anthocyanin-rich pomegranate fruit extract in vitro resisted interleukin 1-B-induced cytotoxicity, and cartilage degradation was inhibited as evidenced by decreased proteoglycan release (Ahmed et al. 2005) These studies suggest a positive effect of pomegranate consumption on arthritis, thus providing some basis for studying the effects in human clinical trials.

Antimicrobial Applications

Antiviral, antifungal, and antibacterial properties of pomegranate products have been studied to some extent in vitro, but to a very limited degree in animal models or human clinical trials. In screening of fruit juices for inhibition of infection by HIV-1 IIIB, pomegranate juice, even from different growing regions, was consistently the most inhibitory. These researchers further isolated the active antiviral component(s) by binding them to corn starch and tested for retention of HIV-specific antiviral activity through development of a potential topical microbicide. Authors proposed that this microbicide could be applied vaginally prior to intercourse to prevent the binding of HIV viral particles to their cell receptors, thus preventing infection (Neurath et al. 2005). Studies to test its efficacy in human populations where control of HIV is difficult may be warranted.

Pomegranate extract was shown to inhibit the influenza virus by blocking its replication, inhibiting agglutination of red blood cells, and possessing virucidal activity (Haidari et al. 2009). Further study of individual polyphenols present in the pomegranate extract showed that punicalagin was responsible for the antiviral activity. A clinical trial to study this effect in humans is currently underway. Given our current knowledge of the intestinal metabolism of punicalagin in animals, it will be of much interest whether the antiviral properties of pomegranate extract can be effectively delivered in humans.

Human clinical trials that investigated the use of pomegranate extracts for topical antibacterial and antifungal treatments in dental hygiene applications suggest some beneficial effects. Twenty-one of thirty patients with denture stomatitis responded to treatment with pomegranate gel extract compared with 27 of 30 patients that received the standard micronazole treatment (Vasconcelos et al. 2003). Although the pomegranate treatment had a lower success rate than the micronazole, a significant proportion of patients responded to this treatment, indicating that there is potential for development of this into a more effective product. Pomegranate extract was also found to be an effective antiplaque rinse, similar in efficacy to chlorhexidene (Menezes et al. 2006), and was suggested for use as a thrice-daily rinse for reduction of gingivitis risk (DiSilvestro et al. 2009).

Desirable antimicrobial activities of pomegranate fruit extracts have been demonstrated in a number of in vitro studies. These include direct antifungal, antibacterial, and antiplasmodial activities (Braga et al. 2005b; Vasconcelos et al. 2006; Dell'Agli et al. 2009; Johann et al. 2010; Bialonska et al. 2009b, 2010) and a synergistic effect with antibiotics for treating methicillin-resistant *Staphylococcus aureus* (Braga et al. 2005a). However, translation of these in vitro activities into therapeutic products for use in humans has yet to be proven.

Skin Care

Skin care products containing pomegranate extracts and seed oil are increasingly available and promise rejuvenation, youthfulness, and beauty. However, research on the ability of pomegranate to act as an effective cosmeceutical ingredient is in the early stages of development. In human cell cultures, pomegranate seed oil extract increased the number of keratinocytes resulting in an increase in thickness of the epidermis and pomegranate peel extract had no effect on keratinocytes, but increased the number of fibroblasts in a dose-response fashion, indicating stimulation of dermal repair mechanisms (Aslam et al. 2006). Whole fruit extracts of pomegranate used to pretreat keratinocyte cells prior to UVA or UVB radiation blocked the oxidative stresses normally observed under those conditions that are commonly associated with aging (Syed et al. 2006, Zaid et al. 2007). Oral supplementation with pomegranate extract provided protection against UV-induced pigmentation in human subjects that were prone to sunburn (Kasai et al. 2006). There was no overall effect of supplementation when the entire group of subjects ($n = 37$) was considered, indicating a need for a larger study to validate the specific effects in susceptible individuals. Pomegranate peel extract has also been studied in a guinea pig model for skin whitening and found to be effective (Yoshimura et al. 2005). Only one study of a pomegranate cosmeceutical product was evaluated in human subjects (Hsu et al. 2007). This study was composed of 20 females aged 35–65 who applied each cream (placebo or treatment) to half of their face twice a day for 60 days. A slight increase in skin smoothness was observed for the pomegranate treatment cream. However, the cream was a blend of pomegranate, green and white teas, and mangosteen, so the effect cannot be distinctly associated with pomegranate from these data. To date, there are limited scientific data to support the cosmeceutical claims for pomegranate. Still, the cell culture work in this area supports a potential protective effect of pomegranate extract on skin cell repair, providing a basis for investigation in human clinical trials.

Other Disease States and Health Claims

Studies related to chronic obstructive pulmonary disease (COPD) (Cerdá et al. 2006), Alzheimer's disease (Hartman et al. 2006), neonatal neuroprotection (Loren et al. 2005), male infertility (Turk et al. 2008), erectile dysfunction (Forest et al. 2007), menopause (Newton et al. 2006), and immune function (Yamasaki et al. 2006) are either limited to a single animal study or have not shown significant improvement in condition upon pomegranate product usage. Two of these, COPD and erectile dysfunction, have been studied in human clinical trials, but no positive effects were observed. Of special note is the fact that pomegranate supplements are currently being marketed on the guarantee to relieve menopausal symptoms, yet the only publication in the scientific literature on this purported health effect is a single human clinical trial that incorporated pomegranate into a multibotanical supplement that included black cohosh and eight other ingredients. Not only was pomegranate not tested independently, the pomegranate-containing multibotanical also had no effect on the vasomotor symptoms of menopause over a 12-month study (Newton et al. 2006). In contrast, there is some preliminary evidence in animal models for weight control using pomegranate extract (Lei et al. 2007) or pomegranate seed oil (Arao et al. 2004, McFarlin et al. 2009) and for anti-inflammatory effects of pomegranate extract against ulcerative colitis in animal models of inflammatory bowel disease (Larrosa et al. 2009, Singh et al. 2009). In summary, these studies represent the initial research on the effects of pomegranate on a variety of health issues. More research is needed in the areas where these preliminary animal models have shown positive effects of pomegranate treatment.

Lethal dose 50 (LD_{50}): the dose at which 50% of the animals given a test compound die

No observable adverse effect level (NOAEL): the dose of a compound at which no detrimental effects occur

TOXICITY AND POTENTIAL DRUG INTERACTIONS

The human clinical trials that have been conducted to date have mostly involved consumption of a moderate amount of pomegranate juice or a concentrated liquid or powder that is equivalent in polyphenolic content to an 8 oz serving of juice. No adverse side affects have been noted in these studies, and it is generally considered safe to consume the fresh fruit and juice of pomegranates. Owing to the development of concentrated extracts as dietary supplements, toxicity studies have been carried out in rat and mouse models. The lethal dose 50 (LD50) for pomegranate fruit extract standardized to 30% punicalagins was found to be greater than 5 g kg^{-1} body weight. This group also studied the effect of feeding the pomegranate fruit extract at levels between 0 mg kg^{-1} and 600 mg kg^{-1} body weight to Wistar rats for 90 days. At the end of the trial, there were no observed toxic effects even at the highest dose (Patel et al. 2008). In another toxicological study, rat diets were replaced with a 20% pomegranate powder:80% rat chow diet that resulted in 6% punicalagin (equilibrated concentration). This diet was fed for 37 days with no evidence of toxicity (Cerdá et al. 2003a). The safety of POMx brand pomegranate extract powder (1 or 2 capsules daily versus placebo) was demonstrated in a study of 64 overweight individuals who experienced no significant negative effects or changes in renal or liver function parameters over the course of a 28 day treatment period (Heber et al. 2007). The no observable adverse effect level (NOAEL) for pomegranate seed oil was found to be equivalent to 4.3 g kg^{-1} body weight per day (Meerts et al. 2009). While this evidence is limited in scope, it indicates that a healthy individual may safely consume pomegranate oil, juice, or even powdered extracts in moderation without great risk.

Although it seems that it would take some effort to ingest a toxic dose of pomegranate extract, there may be some effects on cytochrome P450 enzymes that could potentially influence the metabolism of other components in one's system (for example, prescription drugs). Research in rat models has shown that pomegranate juice inhibited cytochrome P450 enzymes CYP2C9

(Nagata et al. 2007) and CYP3A (Hidaka et al. 2005) in vitro and increased levels of absorbed tolbutamide and carbamazepine by increasing bioavailability. Interestingly, there was no effect on the clearance of these compounds by the corresponding liver enzymes (Nagata et al. 2007, Hidaka et al. 2005). Consumption of pomegranate juice for four weeks in a mouse model showed an overall decrease in liver CYP450 concentration and an increase in the sleep effect induced by pentobarbital. The decrease in total CYP450 was attributed to decreases in liver CYP1A2 and 3A, and the authors concluded that this may be a mechanism for cancer prevention or a possibility for drug interaction (Faria et al. 2007). One human study with a small number of subjects (n = 15) was conducted to test the interference of pomegranate juice consumption with CYP3A and midazolam, a sedative used for short-term treatment of insomnia, as compared with this known drug interaction with grapefruit juice. Although pomegranate juice inhibited CYP3A in vitro, there was no effect on midazolam metabolism post-pomegranate juice consumption (Farkas et al. 2007). More research is needed to fully understand the interaction of pomegranate products with CYP450 enzymes and the implications of those interactions for human health.

CONCLUSIONS AND FUTURE DIRECTIONS

To date, the majority of scientific research studies on the promising health effects of pomegranate have been carried out in cell culture or animal models. Many different potential functional food and nutraceutical applications have been studied, but sufficient depth of knowledge on the effectiveness of many of these proposed uses has not yet been attained. However, the positive results in vitro and in animal models indicate that further study in humans is warranted. Recent human clinical trials have shown significant positive effects of pomegranate juice consumption on lipid profiles in diabetic patients, atherosclerosis reduction, and on PSA levels in prostate cancer patients. Although these human studies are limited in number, they show evidence that regular consumption of pomegranate juice may aid in the prevention or management of chronic diseases.

There are currently 17 registered ongoing human clinical trials testing the potential health effects of pomegranate products (**http://clinicaltrials.gov**). The majority of these studies are related to prostate cancer, a few studies deal with the complications of diabetes, and single studies are listed for cardiomyopathy, lymphoma, intrauterine growth restriction, and influenza. As with previous human studies, the study designs employ a whole foods approach using pomegranate juices or whole fruit polyphenol extracts. A more complete characterization of the bioactive components of pomegranate products and their physiological actions will be required to study the underlying mechanisms for the potential health benefits that have been demonstrated in clinical trials.

SUMMARY POINTS

1. Pomegranates have been used for centuries by Middle Eastern cultures to treat health conditions such as diabetes and parasitic infections.
2. Clinical trials have been conducted examining a wide range of the potential health effects for pomegranate, but the total number of trials is small. The most promising data thus far come from the studies examining the effects of pomegranate on heart disease, diabetes, and prostate cancer.
3. A number of clinical trials are ongoing in the area of prostate cancer, and these could shed further light on the proposed anticancer effects of pomegranate.

4. Pomegranate contains a number of unique ellagitannin-based compounds, including punicalagins, punicalins, and gallagic acid, as well as anthocyanins and a distinct fatty acid profile, all of which may contribute to potential and reported health effects.
5. The high in vitro antioxidant activity of pomegranate has been largely attributed to its ellagitannin content, but the bioavailability of these compounds is very low.
6. Although the bioactive components of pomegranate responsible for its observed in vivo effects are yet to be fully elucidated, it is possible that the health effects of pomegranate are due to its metabolites (e.g., urolithins) rather than the components of the intact fruit per se.

DISCLOSURE STATEMENT

The authors are not aware of any affiliations, memberships, funding, or financial holdings that might be perceived as affecting the objectivity of this review.

LITERATURE CITED

Adams LS, Seeram NP, Aggarwal BB, Takada Y, Sand D, Heber D. 2006. Pomegranate juice, total pomegranate ellagitannins, and punicalagin suppress inflammatory cell signaling in colon cancer cells. *J. Agric. Food Chem.* 54:980–85

Adams LS, Zhang Y, Seeram NP, Heber D, Chen S. 2010. Pomegranate ellagitannin–derived compounds exhibit antiproliferative and antiaromatase activity in breast cancer cells in vitro. *Cancer Prev. Res.* 3:108–13

Afaq F, Malik A, Syed D, Maes D, Matsui MS, Mukhtar H. 2005a. Pomegranate fruit extract modulates UV-B-mediated phosphorylation of mitogen-activated protein kinases and activation of nuclear factor kappa B in normal human epidermal keratinocytes. *Photochem. Photobiol.* 81:38–45

Afaq F, Saleem M, Krueger CG, Reed JD, Mukhtar H. 2005b. Anthocyanin- and hydrolyzable tannin-rich pomegranate fruit extract modulates MAPK and NF-kappaB pathways and inhibits skin tumorigenesis in CD-1 mice. *Int. J. Cancer* 113:423–33

Afaq F, Zaid MA, Khan N, Dreher M, Mukhtar H. 2009. Protective effect of pomegranate-derived products on UVB-mediated damage in human reconstituted skin. *Exp. Dermatol.* 18:553–61

Ahmed S, Wang N, Hafeez BB, Cheruvu VK, Haqqi TM. 2005. *Punica granatum* L. extract inhibits IL-1beta-induced expression of matrix metalloproteinases by inhibiting the activation of MAP kinases and NF-kappaB in human chondrocytes in vitro. *J. Nutr.* 135:2096–102

Albrecht M, Jiang W, Kumi-Diaka J, Lansky EP, Gommersall LM, et al. 2004. Pomegranate extracts potently suppress proliferation, xenograft growth, and invasion of human prostate cancer cells. *J. Med. Food* 7:274–83

Alighourchi H, Barzegar M, Abbasi S. 2008. Anthocyanins characterization of 15 iranian pomegranate (*Punica granatum* L.) varieties and their variation after cold storage and pasteurization. *Eur. Food Res. Technol.* 227:881–87

Arao K, Wang YM, Inoue N, Hirata J, Cha JY, et al. 2004. Dietary effect of pomegranate seed oil rich in 9*cis*, 11*trans*, 13*cis* conjugated linolenic acid on lipid metabolism in obese, hyperlipidemic OLETF rats. *Lipids Health. Dis.* 3:24

Aslam MN, Lansky EP, Varani J. 2006. Pomegranate as a cosmeceutical source: Pomegranate fractions promote proliferation and procollagen synthesis and inhibit matrix metalloproteinase-1 production in human skin cells. *J. Ethnopharmacol.* 103:311–18

Aviram M, Dornfeld L. 2001. Pomegranate juice consumption inhibits serum angiotensin converting enzyme activity and reduces systolic blood pressure. *Atherosclerosis* 158:195

Aviram M, Dornfeld L, Rosenblat M, Volkova N, Kaplan M, et al. 2000. Pomegranate juice consumption reduces oxidative stress, atherogenic modifications to LDL, and platelet aggregation: studies in humans and in atherosclerotic apolipoprotein E-deficient mice. *Am. J. Clin. Nutr.* 71:1062–76

Aviram M, Rosenblat M, Gaitini D, Nitecki S, Hoffman A, et al. 2004. Pomegranate juice consumption for 3 years by patients with carotid artery stenosis reduces common carotid intima-media thickness, blood pressure and LDL oxidation. *Clin. Nutr.* 23:423–33

Aviram M, Volkova N, Coleman R, Dreher M, Reddy MK, et al. 2008. Pomegranate phenolics from the peels, arils, and flowers are antiatherogenic: Studies in vivo in atherosclerotic apolipoprotein e-deficient (E 0) mice and in vitro in cultured macrophages and lipoproteins. *J. Agric. Food Chem.* 56:1148–57

Bae JY, Choi JS, Kang SW, Lee YJ, Park J, Kang YH. 2010. Dietary compound ellagic acid alleviates skin wrinkle and inflammation induced by UV-B irradiation. *Exp. Dermatol.* 19:e182–90

Bagri P, Ali M, Aeri V, Bhowmik M, Sultana S. 2009. Antidiabetic effect of *Punica granatum* flowers: effect on hyperlipidemia, pancreatic cells lipid peroxidation and antioxidant enzymes in experimental diabetes. *Food Chem. Toxicol.* 47:50–54

Bialonska D, Kasimsetty SG, Khan SI, Ferreira D. 2009a. Urolithins, intestinal microbial metabolites of pomegranate ellagitannins, exhibit potent antioxidant activity in a cell-based assay. *J. Agric. Food Chem.* 57:10181–86

Bialonska D, Kasimsetty SG, Schrader KK, Ferreira D. 2009b. The effect of pomegranate (*Punica granatum* L.) byproducts and ellagitannins on the growth of human gut bacteria. *J. Agric. Food Chem.* 57:8344–49

Bialonska D, Ramnani P, Kasimsetty SG, Muntha KR, Gibson GR, Ferreira D. 2010. The influence of pomegranate by-product and punicalagins on selected groups of human intestinal microbiota. *Int. J. Food Microbiol.* 140:175–82

Boateng J, Verghese M, Shackelford L, Walker LT, Khatiwada J, et al. 2007. Selected fruits reduce azoxymethane (AOM)-induced aberrant crypt foci (ACF) in fisher 344 male rats. *Food Chem. Toxicol.* 45:725–32

Braga LC, Leite AA, Xavier KG, Takahashi JA, Bemquerer MP, et al. 2005a. Synergic interaction between pomegranate extract and antibiotics against *Staphylococcus aureus*. *Can. J. Microbiol.* 51:541–47

Braga LC, Shupp JW, Cummings C, Jett M, Takahashi JA, et al. 2005b. Pomegranate extract inhibits *Staphylococcus aureus* growth and subsequent enterotoxin production. *J. Ethnopharmacol.* 96:335–39

Cerdá B, Ceron JJ, Tomás-Barberán FA, Espín JC. 2003a. Repeated oral administration of high doses of the pomegranate ellagitannin punicalagin to rats for 37 days is not toxic. *J. Agric. Food Chem.* 51:3493–501

Cerdá B, Espín JC, Parra S, Martínez P, Tomás-Barberán FA. 2004. The potent in vitro antioxidant ellagitannins from pomegranate juice are metabolised into bioavailable but poor antioxidant hydroxy-6H-dibenzopyran-6-one derivatives by the colonic microflora of healthy humans. *Eur. J. Nutr.* 43:205–20

Cerdá B, Llorach R, Ceron JJ, Espín JC, Tomás-Barberán FA. 2003b. Evaluation of the bioavailability and metabolism in the rat of punicalagin, an antioxidant polyphenol from pomegranate juice. *Eur. J. Nutr.* 42:18–28

Cerdá B, Soto C, Albaladejo MD, Martínez P, Sánchez-Gascón F, et al. 2006. Pomegranate juice supplementation in chronic obstructive pulmonary disease: a 5-week randomized, double-blind, placebo-controlled trial. *Eur. J. Clin. Nutr.* 60:245–53

Chidambara Murthy KN, Jayaprakasha GK, Singh RP. 2002. Studies on antioxidant activity of pomegranate (*Punica granatum*) peel extract using in vivo models. *J. Agric. Food Chem.* 50:4791–95

Davidson MH, Maki KC, Dicklin MR, Feinstein SB, Witchger M, et al. 2009. Effects of consumption of pomegranate juice on carotid intima-media thickness in men and women at moderate risk for coronary heart disease. *Am. J. Cardiol.* 104:936–42

Dell'Agli M, Galli GV, Corbett Y, Taramelli D, Lucantoni L, et al. 2009. Antiplasmodial activity of *Punica granatum* L. fruit rind. *J. Ethnopharmacol.* 125:279–85

de Nigris F, Balestrieri ML, Williams-Ignarro S, D'Armiento FP, Fiorito C, et al. 2007. The influence of pomegranate fruit extract in comparison to regular pomegranate juice and seed oil on nitric oxide and arterial function in obese zucker rats. *Nitric Oxide* 17:50–54

de Nigris F, Williams-Ignarro S, Botti C, Sica V, Ignarro LJ, Napoli C. 2006. Pomegranate juice reduces oxidized low-density lipoprotein downregulation of endothelial nitric oxide synthase in human coronary endothelial cells. *Nitric Oxide* 15:259–63 de Nigris F, Williams-Ignarro S, Lerman LO, Crimi E, Botti C, et al. 2005. Beneficial effects of pomegranate juice on oxidation-sensitive genes and endothelial nitric oxide synthase activity at sites of perturbed shear stress. *Proc. Natl. Acad. Sci. USA* 102:4896–901

DiSilvestro RA, DiSilvestro DJ, DiSilvestro DJ. 2009. Pomegranate extract mouth rinsing effects on saliva measures relevant to gingivitis risk. *Phytother. Res.* 23:1123–27

Esmaillzadeh A, Tahbaz F, Gaieni I, Alavi-Majd H, Azadbakht L. 2004. Concentrated pomegranate juice improves lipid profiles in diabetic patients with hyperlipidemia. *J. Med. Food* 7:305–8

Espín JC, González-Barrio R, Cerdá B, López-Bote C, Rey AI, Tomás-Barberán FA. 2007. Iberian pig as a model to clarify obscure points in the bioavailability and metabolism of ellagitannins in humans. *J. Agric. Food Chem.* 55:10476–85

Faria A, Monteiro R, Azevedo I, Calhau C. 2007. Pomegranate juice effects on cytochrome P450S expression: in vivo studies. *J. Med. Food* 10:643–49

Farkas D, Oleson LE, Zhao Y, Harmatz JS, Zinny MA, et al. 2007. Pomegranate juice does not impair clearance of oral or intravenous midazolam, a probe for cytochrome P450-3A activity: comparison with grapefruit juice. *J. Clin. Pharmacol.* 47:286–94

Forest CP, Padma-Nathan H, Liker HR. 2007. Efficacy and safety of pomegranate juice on improvement of erectile dysfunction in male patients with mild to moderate erectile dysfunction: a randomized, placebo-controlled, double-blind, crossover study. *Int. J. Impot. Res.* 19:564–67

Fuhrman B, Volkova N, Aviram M. 2005. Pomegranate juice inhibits oxidized LDL uptake and cholesterol biosynthesis in macrophages. *J. Nutr. Biochem.* 16:570–76

Gil MI, Tomás-Barberán FA, Hess-Pierce B, Holcroft DM, Kader AA. 2000. Antioxidant activity of pomegranate juice and its relationship with phenolic composition and processing. *J. Agric. Food Chem.* 48:4581

González-Sarrías A, Giménez-Bastida JA, García-Conesa MT, Gómez-Sánchez MB, García-Talavera NV, et al. 2010a. Occurrence of urolithins, gut microbiota ellagic acid metabolites and proliferation markers expression response in the human prostate gland upon consumption of walnuts and pomegranate juice. *Mol. Nutr. Food Res.* 54:311–22

González-Sarrías A, Larrosa M, Tomás-Barberán FA, Dolara P, Espín JC. 2010b. NF-kappaB-dependent anti-inflammatory activity of urolithins, gut microbiota ellagic acid-derived metabolites, in human colonic fibroblasts. *Br. J. Nutr.* 26:1–10

Grossmann ME, Mizuno NK, Schuster T, Cleary MP. 2010. Punicic acid is an omega-5 fatty acid capable of inhibiting breast cancer proliferation. *Int. J. Oncol.* 36:421–26

Guo C, Wei J, Yang J, Xu J, Pang W, Jiang Y. 2008. Pomegranate juice is potentially better than apple juice in improving antioxidant function in elderly subjects. *Nutr. Res.* 28:72–77

Hadipour-Jahromy M, Mozaffari-Kermani R. 2010. Chondroprotective effects of pomegranate juice on monoiodoacetate-induced osteoarthritis of the knee joint of mice. *Phytother. Res.* 24:182–85

Haidari M, Ali M, Casscells SW III, Madjid M. 2009. Pomegranate (*Punica granatum*) purified polyphenol extract inhibits influenza virus and has a synergistic effect with oseltamivir. *Phytomedicine* 16:1127–36

Halvorsen BL, Holte K, Myhrstad MCW, Barikmo I, Hvattum E, et al. 2002. A systematic screening of total antioxidants in dietary plants. *J. Nutr.* 132:461–71

Hashemi M, Kelishadi R, Hashemipour M, Zakerameli A, Khavarian N, et al. 2010. Acute and long-term effects of grape and pomegranate juice consumption on vascular reactivity in paediatric metabolic syndrome. *Cardiol. Young.* 20:73–77

Hartman RE, Shah A, Fagan AM, Schwetye KE, Parsadanian M, et al. 2006. Pomegranate juice decreases amyloid load and improves behavior in a mouse model of alzheimer's disease. *Neurobiol. Dis.* 24:506–15

He J, Giusti MM. 2010. Anthocyanins: natural colorants with health-promoting properties. *Annu. Rev. Food Sci. Technol.* 1:163–87

Heber D, Seeram NP, Wyatt H, Henning SM, Zhang Y, et al. 2007. Safety and antioxidant activity of a pomegranate ellagitannin-enriched polyphenol dietary supplement in overweight individuals with increased waist size. *J. Agric. Food Chem.* 55:10050–54

Hidaka M, Okumura M, Fujita K, Ogikubo T, Yamasaki K, et al. 2005. Effects of pomegranate juice on human cytochrome p450 3A (CYP3A) and carbamazepine pharmacokinetics in rats. *Drug Metab. Dispos.* 33:644–48

Hong MY, Seeram NP, Heber D. 2008. Pomegranate polyphenols down-regulate expression of androgen-synthesizing genes in human prostate cancer cells overexpressing the androgen receptor. *J. Nutr. Biochem.* 19:848–55

Hora JJ, Maydew ER, Lansky EP, Dwivedi C. 2003. Chemopreventive effects of pomegranate seed oil on skin tumor development in CD1 mice. *J. Med. Food* 6:157–61

Hsu J, Skover G, Goldman MP. 2007. Evaluating the efficacy in improving facial photodamage with a mixture of topical antioxidants. *J. Drugs Dermatol.* 6:1141–48

Huang TH, Peng G, Kota BP, Li GQ, Yamahara J, et al. 2005a. Anti-diabetic action of *Punica granatum* flower extract: activation of PPAR-gamma and identification of an active component. *Toxicol. Appl. Pharmacol.* 207:160–69

Huang TH, Peng G, Kota BP, Li GQ, Yamahara J, et al. 2005b. Pomegranate flower improves cardiac lipid metabolism in a diabetic rat model: role of lowering circulating lipids. *Br. J. Pharmacol.* 145:767–74

Huang TH, Yang Q, Harada M, Li GQ, Yamahara J, et al. 2005c. Pomegranate flower extract diminishes cardiac fibrosis in zucker diabetic fatty rats: modulation of cardiac endothelin-1 and nuclear factor-kappaB pathways. *J. Cardiovasc. Pharmacol.* 46:856–62

Jeune MA, Kumi-Diaka J, Brown J. 2005. Anticancer activities of pomegranate extracts and genistein in human breast cancer cells. *J. Med. Food* 8:469–75

Johann S, Cisalpino PS, Watanabe GA, Cota BB, Siqueira EP, et al. 2010. Antifungal activity of extracts of some plants used in brazilian traditional medicine against the pathogenic fungus *Paracoccidioides brasiliensis*. *Pharm. Biol.* 48:388–96

Kaplan M, Hayek T, Raz A, Coleman R, Dornfeld L, et al. 2001. Pomegranate juice supplementation to atherosclerotic mice reduces macrophage lipid peroxidation, cellular cholesterol accumulation and development of atherosclerosis. *J. Nutr.* 131:2082–89

Kasai K, Yoshimura M, Koga T, Arii M, Kawasaki S. 2006. Effects of oral administration of ellagic acid-rich pomegranate extract on ultraviolet-induced pigmentation in the human skin. *J. Nutr. Sci. Vitaminol.* 52:383–88

Kasimsetty SG, Bialonska D, Reddy MK, Ma G, Khan SI, Ferreira D. 2010. Colon cancer chemopreventive activities of pomegranate ellagitannins and urolithins. *J. Agric. Food Chem.* 58:2180–87

Kasimsetty SG, Bialonska D, Reddy MK, Thornton C, Willett KL, Ferreira D. 2009. Effects of pomegranate chemical constituents/intestinal microbial metabolites on CYP1B1 in 22Rv1 prostate cancer cells. *J. Agric. Food Chem.* 57:10636–44

Kaufman M, Wiesman Z. 2007. Pomegranate oil analysis with emphasis on MALDI-TOF/MS triacylglycerol fingerprinting. *J. Agric. Food Chem.* 55:10405–13

Kawaii S, Lansky EP. 2004. Differentiation-promoting activity of pomegranate (*Punica granatum*) fruit extracts in HL-60 human promyelocytic leukemia cells. *J. Med. Food* 7:13–18

Kelawala NS, Ananthanarayan L. 2004. Antioxidant activity of selected foodstuffs. *Int. J. Food Sci. Nutr.* 55:511–16

Khan GN, Gorin MA, Rosenthal D, Pan Q, Bao LW, et al. 2009. Pomegranate fruit extract impairs invasion and motility in human breast cancer. *Integr. Cancer Ther.* 8:242–53

Khan N, Afaq F, Kweon MH, Kim K, Mukhtar H. 2007a. Oral consumption of pomegranate fruit extract inhibits growth and progression of primary lung tumors in mice. *Cancer Res.* 67:3475–82

Khan N, Hadi N, Afaq F, Syed DN, Kweon MH, Mukhtar H. 2007b. Pomegranate fruit extract inhibits prosurvival pathways in human A549 lung carcinoma cells and tumor growth in athymic nude mice. *Carcinogenesis* 28:163–73

Kohno H, Suzuki R, Yasui Y, Hosokawa M, Miyashita K, Tanaka T. 2004. Pomegranate seed oil rich in conjugated linolenic acid suppresses chemically induced colon carcinogenesis in rats. *Cancer Sci.* 95:481–86

Kýralan M, Gölükcü M, Tokgöz H. 2009. Oil and conjugated linolenic acid contents of seeds from important pomegranate cultivars (*Punica granatum* L.) grown in turkey. *J. Am. Oil Chem. Soc.* 86:985–90

Lansky EP, Harrison G, Froom P, Jiang WG. 2005a. Pomegranate (*Punica granatum*) pure chemicals show possible synergistic inhibition of human PC-3 prostate cancer cell invasion across matrigel. *Invest. New Drugs* 23:121–22

Lansky EP, Jiang W, Mo H, Bravo L, Froom P, et al. 2005b. Possible synergistic prostate cancer suppression by anatomically discrete pomegranate fractions. *Invest. New Drugs* 23:11–20

Larrosa M, González-Sarrías A, Yáñez-Gascón MJ, Selma MV, Azorín-Ortuño M, et al. 2009. Anti-inflammatory properties of a pomegranate extract and its metabolite urolithin-A in a colitis rat model and the effect of colon inflammation on phenolic metabolism. *J. Nutr. Biochem.* 21:717–25

Larrosa M, Tomás-Barberán FA, Espín JC. 2006. The dietary hydrolysable tannin punicalagin releases ellagic acid that induces apoptosis in human colon adenocarcinoma caco-2 cells by using the mitochondrial pathway. *J. Nutr. Biochem.* 17:611–25

Lei F, Zhang XN, Wang W, Xing DM, Xie WD, et al. 2007. Evidence of anti-obesity effects of the pomegranate leaf extract in high-fat diet induced obese mice. *Int. J. Obes.* 31:1023–29

Li Y, Wen S, Kota BP, Peng G, Li GQ, et al. 2005. *Punica granatum* flower extract, a potent alpha-glucosidase inhibitor, improves postprandial hyperglycemia in zucker diabetic fatty rats. *J. Ethnopharmacol.* 99:239–44

Loren DJ, Seeram NP, Schulman RN, Holtzman DM. 2005. Maternal dietary supplementation with pomegranate juice is neuroprotective in an animal model of neonatal hypoxic-ischemic brain injury. *Pediatr. Res.* 57:858–64

Malik A, Afaq F, Sarfaraz S, Adhami VM, Syed DN, Mukhtar H. 2005. Pomegranate fruit juice for chemoprevention and chemotherapy of prostate cancer. *Proc. Natl. Acad. Sci. USA* 102:14813–18

McDougall GJ, Ross HA, Ikeji M, Stewart D. 2008. Berry extracts exert different antiproliferative effects against cervical and colon cancer cells grown in vitro. *J. Agric. Food Chem.* 56:3016–23

McFarlin BK, Strohacker KA, Kueht ML. 2009. Pomegranate seed oil consumption during a period of high-fat feeding reduces weight gain and reduces type 2 diabetes risk in CD-1 mice. *Br. J. Nutr.* 102:54–59

Meerts IA, Verspeek-Rip CM, Buskens CA, Keizer HG, Bassaganya-Riera J, et al. 2009. Toxicological evaluation of pomegranate seed oil. *Food Chem. Toxicol.* 47:1085–92

Mehta R, Lansky EP. 2004. Breast cancer chemopreventive properties of pomegranate (*Punica granatum*) fruit extracts in a mouse mammary organ culture. *Eur. J. Cancer Prev.* 13:345–48

Menezes SM, Cordeiro LN, Viana GS. 2006. *Punica granatum* (pomegranate) extract is active against dental plaque. *J. Herb Pharmacother.* 6:79–92

Mirmiran P, Fazeli MR, Asghari G, Shafiee A, Azizi F. 2010. Effect of pomegranate seed oil on hyperlipidaemic subjects: a double-blind placebo-controlled clinical trial. *Br. J. Nutr.* 104:402–6

Mohan M, Waghulde H, Kasture S. 2009. Effect of pomegranate juice on angiotensin II-induced hypertension in diabetic wistar rats. *Phytother. Res.* 24(Suppl. 2):S196–203

Mousavinejad G, Emam-Djomeh Z, Rezaei K, Khodaparast MHH. 2009. Identification and quantification of phenolic compounds and their effects on antioxidant activity in pomegranate juices of eight Iranian cultivars. *Food Chem.* 115:1274–78

Nagata M, Hidaka M, Sekiya H, Kawano Y, Yamasaki K, et al. 2007. Effects of pomegranate juice on human cytochrome P450 2C9 and tolbutamide pharmacokinetics in rats. *Drug Metab. Dispos.* 35:302–5

Neurath AR, Strick N, Li YY, Debnath AK. 2005. *Punica granatum* (pomegranate) juice provides an HIV-1 entry inhibitor and candidate topical microbicide. *Ann. NY Acad. Sci.* 1056:311–27

Newton KM, Reed SD, LaCroix AZ, Grothaus LC, Ehrlich K, Guiltinan J. 2006. Treatment of vasomotor symptoms of menopause with black cohosh, multibotanicals, soy, hormone therapy, or placebo: a randomized trial. *Ann. Intern. Med.* 145:869–79

Pacheco-Palencia LA, Noratto G, Hingorani L, Talcott ST, Mertens-Talcott SU. 2008. Protective effects of standardized pomegranate (*Punica granatum* L.) polyphenolic extract in ultraviolet-irradiated human skin fibroblasts. *J. Agric. Food Chem.* 56:8434–41

Pantuck AJ, Leppert JT, Zomorodian N, Aronson W, Hong J, et al. 2006. Phase II study of pomegranate juice for men with rising prostate-specific antigen following surgery or radiation for prostate cancer. *Clin. Cancer Res.* 12:4018–26

Park HM, Moon E, Kim AJ, Kim MH, Lee S, et al. 2010. Extract of *Punica granatum* inhibits skin photoaging induced by UVB irradiation. *Int. J. Dermatol.* 49:276–82

Patel C, Dadhaniya P, Hingorani L, Soni MG. 2008. Safety assessment of pomegranate fruit extract: acute and subchronic toxicity studies. *Food Chem. Toxicol.* 46:2728–35

Rettig MB, Heber D, An J, Seeram NP, Rao JY, et al. 2008. Pomegranate extract inhibits androgen-independent prostate cancer growth through a nuclear factor-kappaB-dependent mechanism. *Mol. Cancer Ther.* 7:2662–71

Rock W, Rosenblat M, Miller-Lotan R, Levy AP, Elias M, Aviram M. 2008. Consumption of wonderful variety pomegranate juice and extract by diabetic patients increases paraoxonase 1 association with high-density lipoprotein and stimulates its catalytic activities. *J. Agric. Food Chem.* 56:8704–13

Rosenblat M, Hayek T, Aviram M. 2006a. Anti-oxidative effects of pomegranate juice (PJ) consumption by diabetic patients on serum and on macrophages. *Atherosclerosis* 187:363–71

Rosenblat M, Volkova N, Coleman R, Aviram M. 2006b. Pomegranate byproduct administration to apolipoprotein e-deficient mice attenuates atherosclerosis development as a result of decreased macrophage oxidative stress and reduced cellular uptake of oxidized low-density lipoprotein. *J. Agric. Food Chem.* 54:1928–35

Rozenberg O, Howell A, Aviram M. 2006. Pomegranate juice sugar fraction reduces macrophage oxidative state, whereas white grape juice sugar fraction increases it. *Atherosclerosis* 188:68–76

Sartippour MR, Seeram NP, Rao JY, Moro A, Harris DM, et al. 2008. Ellagitannin-rich pomegranate extract inhibits angiogenesis in prostate cancer in vitro and in vivo. *Int. J. Oncol.* 32:475–80

Sassano G, Sanderson P, Franx J, Groot P, Straalen J, Bassaganya-Riera J. 2009. Analysis of pomegranate seed oil for the presence of jacaric acid. *J. Sci. Food Agric.* 89:1046–52

Seeram NP, Adams LS, Henning SM, Niu Y, Zhang Y, et al. 2005. In vitro antiproliferative, apoptotic and antioxidant activities of punicalagin, ellagic acid and a total pomegranate tannin extract are enhanced in combination with other polyphenols as found in pomegranate juice. *J. Nutr. Biochem.* 16:360–67

Seeram NP, Aronson WJ, Zhang Y, Henning SM, Moro A, et al. 2007. Pomegranate ellagitannin-derived metabolites inhibit prostate cancer growth and localize to the mouse prostate gland. *J. Agric. Food Chem.* 55:7732–37

Seeram NP, Aviram M, Zhang Y, Henning SM, Feng L, et al. 2008a. Comparison of antioxidant potency of commonly consumed polyphenol-rich beverages in the United States. *J. Agric. Food Chem.* 56:1415–22

Seeram NP, Henning SM, Zhang Y, Suchard M, Li Z, Heber D. 2006. Pomegranate juice ellagitannin metabolites are present in human plasma and some persist in urine for up to 48 hours. *J. Nutr.* 136:2481–85

Seeram NP, Lee R, Heber D. 2004. Bioavailability of ellagic acid in human plasma after consumption of ellagitannins from pomegranate (*Punica granatum* L.) juice. *Clin. Chim. Acta* 348:63–68

Seeram NP, Zhang Y, McKeever R, Henning SM, Lee R, et al. 2008b. Pomegranate juice and extracts provide similar levels of plasma and urinary ellagitannin metabolites in human subjects. *J. Med. Food* 11:390–94

Shiner M, Fuhrman B, Aviram M. 2007. Macrophage paraoxonase 2 (PON2) expression is up-regulated by pomegranate juice phenolic antioxidants via PPAR gamma and AP-1 pathway activation. *Atherosclerosis* 195:313–21

Shukla M, Gupta K, Rasheed Z, Khan KA, Haqqi TM. 2008. Consumption of hydrolyzable tannins-rich pomegranate extract suppresses inflammation and joint damage in rheumatoid arthritis. *Nutrition* 24:733–43

Singh K, Jaggi AS, Singh N. 2009. Exploring the ameliorative potential of *Punica granatum* in dextran sulfate sodium induced ulcerative colitis in mice. *Phytother. Res.* 23:1565–74

Singh RP, Chidambara Murthy KN, Jayaprakasha GK. 2002. Studies on the antioxidant activity of pomegranate (*Punica granatum*) peel and seed extracts using in vitro models. *J. Agric. Food Chem.* 50:81–86

Stangeland T, Remberg SF, Lye KA. 2007. Antioxidants in some Ugandan fruits. *Afr. J. Ecol.* 45:29–30

Sumner MD, Elliott-Eller M, Weidner G, Daubenmier JJ, Chew MH, et al. 2005. Effects of pomegranate juice consumption on myocardial perfusion in patients with coronary heart disease. *Am. J. Cardiol.* 96:810–14

Syed DN, Malik A, Hadi N, Sarfaraz S, Afaq F, Mukhtar H. 2006. Photochemopreventive effect of pomegranate fruit extract on UVA-mediated activation of cellular pathways in normal human epidermal keratinocytes. *Photochem. Photobiol.* 82:398–405

Toi M, Bando H, Ramachandran C, Melnick SJ, Imai A, et al. 2003. Preliminary studies on the anti-angiogenic potential of pomegranate fractions in vitro and in vivo. *Angiogenesis* 6:121–28

Turk G, Sonmez M, Aydin M, Yuce A, Gur S, et al. 2008. Effects of pomegranate juice consumption on sperm quality, spermatogenic cell density, antioxidant activity and testosterone level in male rats. *Clin. Nutr.* 27:289–96

Tzulker R, Glazer I, Bar-Ilan I, Holland D, Aviram M, Amir R. 2007. Antioxidant activity, polyphenol content, and related compounds in different fruit juices and homogenates prepared from 29 different pomegranate accessions. *J. Agric. Food Chem.* 55:9559–70

Vasconcelos LC, Sampaio FC, Sampaio MC, Pereira Mdo S, Higino JS, Peixoto MH. 2006. Minimum inhibitory concentration of adherence of *Punica granatum* linn (pomegranate) gel against *S. mutans*, *S. mitis* and *C. albicans*. *Braz. Dent. J.* 17:223–27

Vasconcelos LC, Sampaio MC, Sampaio FC, Higino JS. 2003. Use of *Punica granatum* as an antifungal agent against candidosis associated with denture stomatitis. *Mycoses* 46:192–96

Wolfe KL, Kang X, He X, Dong M, Zhang Q, Liu RH. 2008. Cellular antioxidant activity of common fruits. *J. Agric. Food Chem.* 56:8418–26

Xu KZY, Zhu C, Kim MS, Yamahara J, Li Y. 2009. Pomegranate flower ameliorates fatty liver in an animal model of type 2 diabetes and obesity. *J. Ethnopharmacol.* 123:280–87

Yamasaki M, Kitagawa T, Koyanagi N, Chujo H, Maeda H, et al. 2006. Dietary effect of pomegranate seed oil on immune function and lipid metabolism in mice. *Nutrition* 22:54–59

Yoshimura M, Watanabe Y, Kasai K, Yamakoshi J, Koga T. 2005. Inhibitory effect of an ellagic acid–rich pomegranate extract on tyrosinase activity and ultraviolet-induced pigmentation. *Biosci. Biotechnol. Biochem.* 69:2368–73

Zaid MA, Afaq F, Syed DN, Dreher M, Mukhtar H. 2007. Inhibition of UVB-mediated oxidative stress and markers of photoaging in immortalized HaCaT keratinocytes by pomegranate polyphenol extract POMx. *Photochem. Photobiol.* 83:882–88

Zhang L-H, Li L-L, Li Y-X, Zhang Y-H. 2008. In vitro antioxidant activities of fruits and leaves of pomegranate. *Acta Hortic.* 765:31–34

Zhang Y, Krueger D, Durst R, Lee R, Wang D, et al. 2009a. International multidimensional authenticity specification (IMAS) algorithm for detection of commercial pomegranate juice adulteration. *J. Agric. Food Chem.* 57:2550–57

Zhang Y, Wang D, Lee RP, Henning SM, Heber D. 2009b. Absence of pomegranate ellagitannins in the majority of commercial pomegranate extracts: implications for standardization and quality control. *J. Agric. Food Chem.* 57:7395–400

Emerging Technologies in Food Processing

D. Knorr,*[,1] A. Froehling,[2] H. Jaeger,[1] K. Reineke,[1] O. Schlueter,[2] and K. Schoessler[1]

[1]Berlin University of Technology, Department of Food Biotechnology and Food Process Engineering, D-14195 Berlin, Germany; email: dietrich.knorr@tu-berlin.de

[2]Leibniz Institute for Agricultural Engineering Potsdam, Department of Horticultural Engineering, D-14469 Potsdam, Germany

Annu. Rev. Food Sci. Technol. 2011. 2:203–35

First published online as a Review in Advance on November 15, 2010

The *Annual Review of Food Science and Technology* is online at food.annualreviews.org

This article's doi:
10.1146/annurev.food.102308.124129

1941-1413/11/0410-0203$20.00

*Corresponding author

Keywords

nonthermal food processing, high pressure, pulsed electric fields, ultrasound, cold plasma

Abstract

High hydrostatic pressure (HHP), pulsed electric fields (PEFs), ultrasound (US), and cold plasma (CP) are emerging technologies that have already found application in the food industry or related sectors. This review aims to describe the basic principles of these nonthermal technologies as well as the state of the art concerning their impact on biological cells, enzymes, and food constituents. Current and potential applications will be discussed, focusing on process-structure-function relationships, as well as recent advances in the process development.

INTRODUCTION

The development of emerging technologies in food processing addresses specific consumer needs toward safe, healthy, and minimally processed foods. These innovative processes also lead to environmentally friendly and sustainable food manufacturing techniques with low energy requirements and reduced water use that overcome some limitations given by current food processing practices (Toepfl et al. 2006). Taking advantage of specific potentials and opportunities of these new processes, including the understanding and control of the complex process-structure-function relationships, offers the possibility for a science-based development of tailor-made foods. High hydrostatic pressure (HHP), pulsed electric fields (PEFs), ultrasound (US), and cold plasma (CP) are used to exemplify scalable and flexible food manufacturing techniques. In this review, we discuss the state of the art regarding the research and application of these emerging technologies and demonstrate the potential of establishing new routes of process and product development by interfacing food science and food manufacturing.

Significant, science-based achievements have been made to better understand the basic principles underlying HHP and PEF processing (Hendrickx & Knorr 2002, Raso & Heinz 2006). In addition, the collection of kinetic data, especially on microbial and enzyme inactivation by HHP treatment and on metabolite recovery and microbial inactivation treatment by PEFs, as well as the generation of data related to mechanisms including the use of plant cell cultures as model systems (Doona & Feeherry 2007, Dörnenburg & Knorr 1993, Wouters et al. 2001), has laid the groundwork for targeted processing.

The food and beverage industry offers many possibilities for the use of US. The basic phenomena, such as microstreaming and cavitation, and the resulting hydrodynamic shear-forces, make US an alternative technology for the realization of homogenization, dispersion, and emulsification, as well as for the disintegration of tissue to enhance mass transfer processes (Mason et al. 1996, Povey & Mason 1998).

CP-based surface treatments, such as ultrafine cleaning, etching, surface functionalization, and thin film deposition, and environmental applications, such as exhaust air cleaning, are proven techniques and already applied using industrial scale plasma systems (Foest et al. 2005, Roth 1995). A strong increase of plasma applications in medical device technology and therapeutic medicine is currently taking place, including applications such as plasma decontamination, and research is focusing on the interaction between plasma and biological cells and tissue as well as on the plasma diagnostics with regard to the understanding and control of the complex behavior of CP (Daeschlein et al. 2010, Weltmann et al. 2009). Similar research is undertaken in the field of food science to explore the potential for CP application in the food industry (Mastwijk & Nierop Groot 2010), which will be discussed below.

Understanding the impact and potential of such technologies on food systems at the cellular level will enable the design of tailor-made foods and to establish process-structure-function relationships. Based on this knowledge, completely new process design and the incorporation of HHP, PEFs, US, and CP in traditional processes, as well as the generation of improved equipment design, will be possible. Consequently, the use of such nonthermal processes for maintenance or even improvement of product quality via processing to fulfill the PAN (consumer preference, acceptance, and needs) concept of the European Technology Platform Food for Life (**http://etp.ciaa.eu**), and thus the reverse food engineering approach will be one major innovative concept within the food industry.

HIGH PRESSURE PROCESSING

The demand for high-quality food opens high pressure (HP) as the most developed emerging processing technology for gentle preservation of food, the possibility to move from the research and development environment into widespread industrial-scale applications. The pressure levels range from several tens of MPa in common homogenizers or supercritical fluid extractors to several hundreds of MPa in ultra-HP homogenizers or HP pasteurization units. In addition to the inactivation of microorganisms to enhance the shelf life of the treated food, there are numerous other interesting applications, such as food structure engineering (Diels & Michiels 2006, Knorr et al. 2006, Sharma & Yadav 2008).

Process Description

Without doubt, the inactivation of vegetative microorganisms to extend the shelf life of food is currently the largest commercial application of isostatic HP at an industrial scale by far. Typical industrial HP units consist of a horizontal HP vessel and an external pressure generating device. The simplest practical system of an intensifier is a single-acting, hydraulically driven pump. (Rovere 2002).

For the HP treatment, the packaged food is deposed in a carrier and automatically loaded into the HP vessel, and the vessel plugs are closed. The pressure-transmitting media, usually water, is pumped into the vessel from one or both sides. After reaching the desired maximum pressure the pumping is stopped, and in ideal cases no further energy input is needed to hold the pressure during dwell time. In contrast to thermal processing in which temperature gradients occur, all molecules in the HP vessel are subjected to the same amount of pressure at exactly the same time because of the isostatic principle of pressure transmission (Heinz et al. 2009, Rastogi et al. 2007).

Given that pressure and temperature are closely connected parameters, the thermodynamic effect of the adiabatic heat of compression, which occurs during the compression and decompression of the treated food and the pressure-transmitting media, has to be taken into account. Following the first and the second law of thermodynamics and by a rearrangement of the Maxwell equations, heating during compression and cooling during decompression can be described as a function of thermophysical properties of the compressible product (Perry 1984, Reineke et al. 2008). This quasi-adiabatic heating or cooling occurs instantly. Hence, pressure-induced temperature changes are predictable and homogeneous throughout the product, assuming it is homogeneous in composition. This ideal adiabatic process does not occur in practical applications, but the extent of temperature increase could be estimated with 3°C–9°C per 100 MPa dependence of the treated food or food composition, respectively (Ting et al. 2002).

Another possibility for the treatment of liquid unpacked products, such as fruit juices, is to fill the vessel with the liquid product, which also acts as the pressure transmitting media and realize the compression directly via a moving piston (Patterson et al. 2007, Rovere 2002).

A further HP process for the treatment of liquid food is the HP homogenization (150 MPa $< p <$ 400 MPa), which became more important during the last decade. It is used not only for the preparation or stabilization of emulsions and suspensions, or for creating physical changes such as viscosity changes in products (Pandolf 1998, Paquin 1999), but also for cell disruption of yeasts or bacteria to release intracellular products. It can be anticipated that HP homogenization for the production of emulsions or suspensions will also cause a partial inactivation of the microbial population (Diels & Michiels 2006).

History

The first HP treatment of food was reported in the late 1890s dealing with the inactivation of microorganisms in milk (Hite 1899), showing extended shelf life of bovine milk after HP treatment. Bridgman (1914) reported the coagulation of egg albumin by HP and determined different product properties as compared to gels obtained by heat coagulation. Furthermore, he presented an extensive data set for the phase diagram of pure water (Bridgman 1912). Since the early 1980s, HP treatment has been evaluated as a food processing alternative to classical heat treatment technologies (Knorr et al. 1998). Decisive for the emerging research effort in this field was the growing consumer demand for minimally processed, fresh-like, safe, high quality food products (Hendrickx & Knorr 2002).

The first industrial HP application for the commercial preservation of food was installed in 1991 in Japan (Yaldagard et al. 2008). The food industry and related research institutes have extensively explored this field and introduced the HP technology to a broad range of products. As a result, during the past 10 years the number of industrial HP systems increased steadily, and at present more than 150 industrial scale installations with a maximum volume of 687 liters and total annual production of more than 300,000 tons are in use worldwide (Tonello Samson C., personal communication).

Research State of the Art

In general, small molecules are only slightly affected by HPP because no covalent bonds are split at pressure below 2 GPa. However, the impact of HPP on macromolecules, microorganisms, and complex systems such as food are manifold and hence discussed separately.

Impact on biological cells. In order to find an alternative to conventional thermal processing while maintaining a maximum level of food safety, intensive research on the HP inactivation of vegetative microorganisms and bacterial spores has been carried out in the past. However, in HP applications, thermal effects cannot be fully ruled out because of the adiabatic heat of compression, and HP inactivation of vegetative microorganisms is almost always connected to a thermal treatment (Smelt et al. 2001). The specific effects and damages of pressure on vegetative microorganisms are complex and cannot be evaluated detached from these effects. Primarily, the lethal effects of HP on vegetative microorganisms are attributed to enzyme inactivation and cell membrane rupture (Ananta 2005, Ardia 2004). In the course of identifying inactivation mechanisms, flow cytometry was used as a potent tool to gain insights to the states and mechanisms of cell damage of pressure-treated microorganisms (Black et al. 2007, Mathys et al. 2007).

Pressure treatments do not necessarily weaken biological cells. At low pressure levels, increased resistance of microbial cells was observed, and pressure-induced thermo-tolerance of lactic acid bacteria occured after HP treatment between 100 and 200 MPa (Ananta & Knorr 2003). As a result of this phenomenon, pressure-induced stress response was found to offer promising processing options such as pretreatment of lactic acid bacteria before drying or freezing for the purpose of starter culture production (Ananta 2005).

Microbial inactivation of more than five-log cycles in food products is reported by several authors to occur at pressures between 300 and 800 MPa (Ananta et al. 2005, Hendrickx & Knorr 2002). The special shape of isokinetic lines at higher pressure (**Figure 1**, see color insert) for the inactivation of microorganisms shows the synergisms between pressure and temperature. This behavior is typical for vegetative cells but was also observed for bacterial spores (Ardia 2004, Margosch et al. 2006), viruses (Isbarn et al. 2007), and proteins (Heinz & Kortschack 2002, Smeller 2002). By increasing the process temperature, it is possible to decrease the applied pressure, but unwanted reactions (e.g., based on residual enzyme activity) that would lead to quality losses also have to be taken into account.

According to Smelt et al. (2001) the HP-induced effects resulting in vegetative cell death can be summarized as follows:

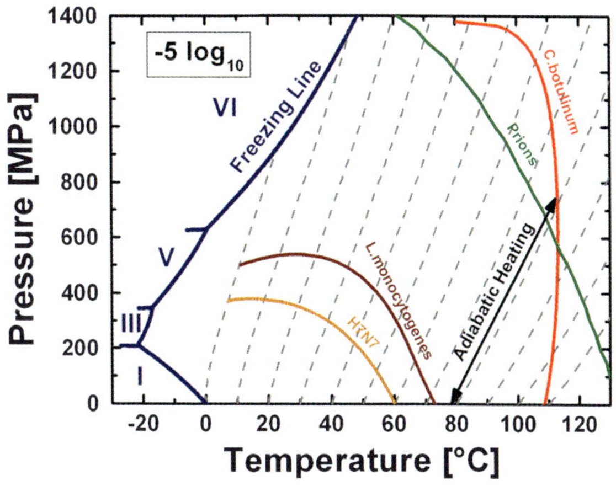

Figure 1

Isokinetic lines for a five-log10 reduction of H7N7, surrogate for bird flu virus H5N1 (chicken-meat suspension 15 s^{-1}) (Isbarn et al. 2007), with adiabatic lines due to compression (–) of water in comparison with significant sensory-rheological changes in raw turkey or chicken meat (Tintchev 2007).

1. Proteins and enzymes: HP induces unfolding of globular proteins. It is assumed that the combined, complete, or partial inactivation of numerous enzymes and metabolic pathways leads to the inability to proliferate and cell death (Bunthof 2002).
2. Membranes: Other than the inactivation of enzymes, membrane damage is considered as one of the key events related to microbial cell death. Membranes undergo phase transitions and solidify under pressure, and perturbations are promoted (Schlueter 2004, Winter 1996). In addition, pressure leads to the detachment and inactivation of membrane proteins (Ulmer et al. 2002).
3. Ribosomes: The disintegration of ribosomes in their subunits is promoted by pressure and may be related to cell death (Niven et al. 1999).
4. pH: The maintenance of intracellular pH is crucial for the survival of cells. Some authors related cell death predominantly to intracellular pH changes, which are related to inactivation of enzymes controlling the acidity and membrane damage (Molina-Gutierrez et al. 2002).

Bacterial spores have a higher barotolerance than vegetative bacteria and survive pressures above 1,200 MPa at ambient temperatures (Ananta et al. 2001, Margosch et al. 2006). Early approaches toward spore inactivation aimed at a pressure-induced germination at moderate pressure. However, combination processes with spore germination at pressures below 200 MPa and an additional moderate heat treatment could not guarantee sufficient inactivation because a small population of spores could not be germinated and remain in the dormant state (Heinz & Knorr 1996). The HP inactivation of bacterial spores is not yet fully understood and is still highly relevant in modern HP sterilization research activity. A detailed discussion of HP-related spore inactivation mechanisms is given by Mathys (2008).

Impact on Enzymes

HP is regarded as a mild process by which the primary structure of proteins is not affected. However, it could have an impact on hydrophobic interactions, which stabilize the quaternary and tertiary structure through reversible unfolding, and the secondary structure through irreversible unfolding. Generally, pressure-induced changes in proteins and enzymes between 100 and 300 MPa at ambient temperature are reversible, whereas an increase of pressure above 400 MPa could cause an irreversible unfolding, leading to inactivation of the enzyme. Pressure also favors an unfolding of protein chains as well as a dissociation of oligomeric proteins (Buckow 2006, Tauscher 1995).

Owing to conformational changes, unfolding of an enzyme can alter its functionality and result in a decreased or increased biological activity and could even change its substrate specificity (Buckow & Heinz 2008, Ludikhuyze et al. 2002). The pressure stability of enzymes can vary significantly ranging from pressure-sensitive enzymes such as phosphohexose isomerase from bovine milk ($p < 400$ MPa) (Rademacher & Hinrichs 2006) to extreme pressure resistant enzymes such as horseradish peroxidase ($p > 700$ MPa) (Smeller & Fidy 2002). However, a categorization of enzymes as a result of their pressure stability is not appropriate, because there is structural variability among enzymes catalyzing the same reaction (Buckow & Heinz 2008).

Figure 2 depicts the inactivation of 90% of different polyphenol oxidases (PPO) after 10 min in the pressure and temperature landscape. Furthermore, the pressure-temperature resistance of enzymes shows a significant dependence on matrix conditions such as the pH value (Riahi & Ramaswamy 2004, Zipp & Kauzmann 1973), whereas even isoforms of an enzyme from the same origin can vary in physical stability between several hundred MPa (Buckow et al. 2005, Rodrigoa et al. 2006).

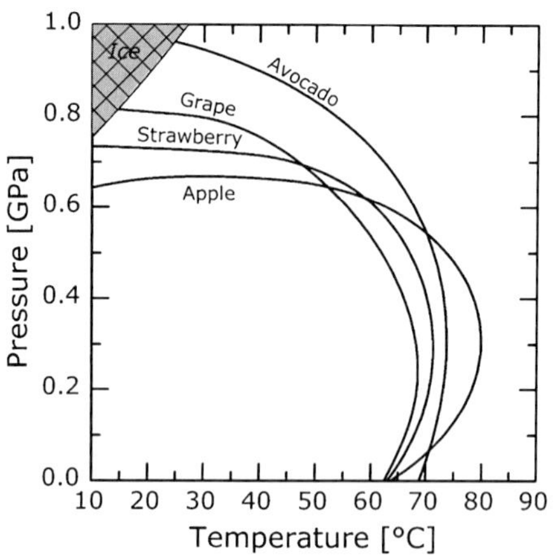

Figure 2

Pressure-temperature isorate diagram for 90% inactivation of polyphenol oxidase after 10 min under isobaric and isothermal conditions, from apple (Buckow et al. 2009), advocado (Weemaes et al. 1998), white grapes (Rapeanu et al. 2005), and strawberry (Dalmadi et al. 2006) (Figure taken from Buckow & Heinz 2008).

Moreover, owing to the fact that pressure and temperature often act antagonistically, this could further result in an enhanced thermostability of enzymes at specific pressures (Heremans & Smeller 1998). Such stabilization of enzymes could occur when the volume difference between the folded and unfolded state of the protein is positive, which might be caused by the promoted formation of noncovalent bonds under the applied pressure.

Impact on food constituents. HP could well be used for food texture engineering, owing to its influence on the properties of food ingredients. The primary structure of low molecular weight molecules such as peptides, lipids, vitamins, and saccharides is rarely affected by isostatic HP because of the very low compressibility of covalent bonds at pressures below 2 GPa (Cheftel & Culioli 1997, Oey et al. 2006, Van den Broeck et al. 1998). Conversely, HP can change the native structure of macromolecules such as starch similar to thermal-induced structure changes.

Several studies have investigated the gelatinization of different starches under HP. Potato starch was found to be less affected by pressure treatment than the other starches investigated, such as tapioca or wheat starches. Several studies revealed that the swelling of starch granules as measured by loss of birefringence depends on pressure treatment conditions as well as on the type of starch granules. Furthermore, damaged starch granules are less pressure resistant than intact starch granules (Bauer & Knorr 2005, Douzals et al. 1996, Michel & Autio 2002).

In consideration of the impact of pressure and dwell time on the pressure-induced starch gelatinization, suspensions of starch can also possibly act as a potential indicator for pressure, time, and temperature treatment of foods (Rumpold 2005). Another possible HP application is the modification of proteins. Dumay et al. (1998) observed gelatinization by HP treatment of solutions of a ß-lactoglobulin isolate. The pressure-induced gel matrix offered small particles in highly packed ß-lactoglobulin, unlike the gels after heating, which exhibit fine-stranded aggregates (Dumay et al. 1998). Furthermore, Zeece et al. (2008) reported that an HP treatment from 400 MPa to 800 MPa at 20°C improved considerably the digestibility of ß-lactoglobulin. Effects of HP on protein and polysaccharide mixtures have been studied extensively by Michel & Autio (2002) with the aim to establish and facilitate the creation and control of new textures.

Current Applications/Developments

HP pasteurization is currently the main application in industrial HP processing. The success of HP-treated products is primarily because HP-treated foods, in addition to their microbiological safety, retain more of their original fresh taste, texture, and nutritional content. These products are consequently products with superior quality compared to their thermally treated counterparts (Patterson et al. 2007).

At present, there is a wide range of HP-processed products available, from meat products, fruit juices, and seafood to dairy products and ready-to-eat meals. More than 30% of the total vessel volume is used to process meat products like sliced ham, turkey or chicken cuts, and ready-to-eat-meals, primarily to inactivate *Listeria* and to increase shelf life of the treated product. Thirty-four percent of the total vessel volume is utilized to inactivate enzymes (e.g., PPO in avocado-based products) and to modify the texture of vegetables and fruits and related products such as fruit desserts, smoothies, or ready-to-eat vegetable dishes. In 13% of the total vessel volume, fruit juices are processed to increase the shelf life by maintaining their sensory quality.

Another 14% of the total vessel volume is used for the pressure treatment of seafood, mainly oysters and shellfish. A further advantage, other than an increased shelf life (destruction of *Vibrio vulnificus*) during the treatment of oysters, is an easier opening of the oyster shell and improved meat extraction of lobsters and crabs (**www.nchyperbaric.com**).

Process-Structure-Function Interactions

The potential use of HP in food structure engineering implies diverse advantages when pressure is applied with moderate temperatures. Knorr et al. (2006) investigated HP applications for food biopolymers regarding protein stability, enzymatic activity, and starch gelatinization. The pressure-induced gelatinization differs from the thermally induced gelatinization of starches. For instance, HP-treated starches retain their granular structure and exhibit reduced swelling and can form weak gels. Therefore, they offer different functional properties than heat-treated starches do. Pressure, temperature, pressure dwell time, type of starches, and the content of free available water can influence the phase transition of various starches (Rumpold 2005).

Additionally, pressure-induced protein gels retain their original flavor and color. Furthermore, they are glossy, unlike heat-induced gels. Hence, HP treatment can be applied for the manufacturing of milk products to improve yogurt texture (Johnston et al. 1993) or increase cheese yield (López-Fandino et al. 1996).

Process Developments

HP offers several interesting applications for the food industry. For example, HP-treated starches have reduced digestibility and might be used to substitute fat in dietary foods (Sharma et al. 2008, Zhang et al. 2008). Furthermore, the inactivation behavior of enzymes under pressure could be used as an indicator for reaching HP pasteurization or sterilization conditions and to detect temperature differences in the pressure vessel during processing (Grauwet et al. 2010).

A further possible application of HP is its combination with temperatures below 0°C for subzero storage of food in the liquid state or a cold denaturation of proteins to form gels with unique properties. Moreover, HP could be used to reduce the thawing time for frozen products such as fish (LeBail et al. 2002, Schubring et al. 2003).

Research Needs and Challenges

The continuous increase of HP research over the past decades has already generated the basis for several commercially available HP-processed high quality products. Besides the cold pasteurization, isostatic HP can also be used to generate novel functional features, such as specific textures or health-promoting properties to develop tailor-made foods. A very promising field for further research is to use HP to modulate microbial fermentations or enzymatic conversations. Furthermore, HP might also influence the biosyntheses pathways and could lead to the formation of product variants with novel functional properties (Aertsen et al. 2009). A better understanding of the mechanisms underlying the pressure and temperature stability could also enable the possibility to construct HP-resistant enzymes. In spite of extensive research, there is still a lack of data about the behavior of nutrients, allergens, and food-spoiling viruses under the defined matrix (e.g., pressure stable buffer solutions) (Mathys & Knorr 2009) and treatment conditions (isothermal and isobaric conditions during dwell time), which could be used for modeling or the investigation of the underlying mechanisms.

Further research is needed on the process conditions that are necessary to inactivate pressure-resistant bacterial endospores. However, to successfully introduce the HP thermal sterilization in the food industry, a pressure-temperature resistant indicator microorganism has to be identified, and the microbial targets that lead to an inactivation have to be understood. It should also be noted that physicochemical properties of food constituents such as water vary under HP or high temperature conditions, making process development and understanding of mechanisms challenging (Mathys & Knorr 2009). To reduce the processing cost as well as to investigate the temperature distribution during the HP treatment, especially under sterilization conditions, modeling and simulation of the behavior of HP-treated biomaterials plus the temperatures distributions in the HP vessel will also present a challenge (Delgado et al. 2008).

PULSED ELECTRIC FIELDS

Process Description

When exposed to high electric field pulses, cell membranes develop pores that may be permanent or temporary, depending on the intensity and treatment conditions (Angersbach et al. 2000, Zimmermann et al. 1974). Pore formation increases the membrane permeability, resulting in the loss of cell content or intrusion of surrounding media (Vorobiev & Lebovka 2008). Low-intensity treatment has the potential to induce stress reactions in plant cells, resulting in the promotion of a defense mechanism by increased production of secondary metabolites (Dörnenburg & Knorr 1993, Galindo et al. 2009, Gomez Galindo et al. 2008). An irreversible perforation of the cell membrane reduces permanently its barrier effect, causing cell death, which can be applied for plant and animal raw material disintegration (Angersbach & Knorr 1998, Toepfl & Heinz 2007), as well as for the nonthermal inactivation of microorganisms (Lelieveld et al. 2007).

PEF processing consists of the application of very short electric pulses (1–100 μs) at electric field intensities in the range of 0.1–1 kV cm^{-1} (reversible permeabilization for stress induction in plant cells), 0.5–3 kV cm^{-1} (irreversible permeabilization of plant and animal tissue), and 15–40 kV cm^{-1} for the irreversible permeabilization of microbial cells. Depending on cell size and shape, the before-mentioned field intensities lead to the formation of a critical transmembrane potential, which is regarded to be the precondition for membrane breakdown (Tsong 1996).

Because the mechanism of electroporation is based mainly on a mechanical electrocompressive force affecting the cell membrane, the PEF technology is considered a nonthermal cell disintegration or preservation process. It provides an alternative to mechanical, thermal, or enzymatic cell disintegration of plant and animal raw materials, providing a short-time (milliseconds), low-energy treatment, as well as to the traditional thermal pasteurization of liquid food products (Barbosa-Cánovas et al. 1999, Raso & Heinz 2006).

Generally, high-intensity electric pulses can be generated by the switched discharge of a suitable capacitor bank. The characteristics of the discharge circuit determine the shape of the time-dependent potential at the treatment chamber where the product is exposed to the electric field (Barsotti et al. 1999). Depending on the product and application, parallel plate electrode treatment chamber configuration or colinear type treatment chambers are most commonly used. A comprehensive review on treatment chamber configurations can be found in Huang & Wang (2009).

History

A first commercial application of electrical energy for pasteurization was the Electropure process established in the 1920s for the extension of shelf life of milk, based on ohmic heating. Unlike the Electropure process, based on Joule heating, which involves the passage of an electrical current resulting in the generation of heat by the resistivity of the food material, a technology using high voltage electricity up to 32 kV for a pulsed discharge application across two electrodes has been investigated since the 1950s and resulted in a process called electrohydraulic treatment (Gilliland & Speck 1967).

Pioneering experimental work of the PEFs application for food processing was undertaken by Heinz Doevenspeck (Doevenspeck 1961). The first systematic studies on the nonthermal lethal effect of PEFs on microorganisms were conducted at Unilever Research Center in the United Kingdom (Sale & Hamilton 1967). Krupp Maschinentechnik was recognizing the technique's potential and developed the processes Elcrack® and Elsteril® (Krupp 1988). The first commercial PEF application was installed in 2005 in the United States for fruit juice preservation (Clark 2006). Food and Drug Administration (FDA) clearance had been available since 1996, indicating the technique's potential for safe and gentle preservation.

Research State of the Art

Effective inactivation for most of the spoilage and pathogenic microorganisms has been shown, and colony count reductions depending on treatment intensity, product properties, and type of microorganism in the range of 4–6-log cycles are comparable to traditional thermal pasteurization. Bacterial spores and viruses are not affected by the PEF treatment (Lelieveld et al. 2007). Reports on the effects of PEFs on enzymes are limited, and different experimental setups and processing parameters make them difficult to compare (Van Loey et al. 2002). Thermal effects were also found to contribute to enzyme inactivation during PEF treatment (Jaeger et al. 2009a, Jaeger et al. 2010). Industrial large-scale applications have been realized for the disintegration of plant raw materials such as sugar beet and fruit mashes (Bluhm & Sack 2009). Industrial equipment is available up to capacities of a single system of 2,200 liters h^{-1} for PEF processing of liquids for nonthermal pasteurization with total treatment costs of 0.6 cents kg^{-1} and 22 ton h^{-1} for cell disintegration applications with related total treatment costs of 0.5 Euro ton^{-1} (DIL 2009).

Impact on biological cells. Until now there has been no clear evidence on underlying mechanisms at a cellular level, but two main effects have been described to be triggered by the electric field: the ionic punch-through effect (Coster 1965) and the dielectric breakdown of the membrane (Zimmermann et al. 1974). The factors that affect microbial inactivation during PEF treatment are process factors such as electric field intensity, pulse width and shape, treatment time and temperature, microbial factors such as type, shape, size, concentration, and growth stage of microorganism, and media factors such as pH, antimicrobials, ionic compounds, electrical conductivity, and medium ionic strength.

Membrane damage and inactivation of microorganisms due to PEFs, first considered as an all-or-nothing event in some studies (Russel et al. 2000, Simpson et al. 1999), revealed a required differentiated approach, even if the critical parameters for the electrical breakdown of cell membranes are exceeded. Membrane damage and sublethal injury is repairable under certain conditions, and the extent to which cells repair their injuries was found to depend on treatment intensity and microorganism and treatment medium pH (Garcia et al. 2005, Somolinos et al. 2008a, Somolinos et al. 2008b).

Impact on enzymes. The evaluation of the effect of PEFs on enzymes is complex. Available reports on mechanisms are limited, and different experimental setups and processing parameters make them difficult to compare (Schuten et al. 2004, Van Loey et al. 2002, Yang et al. 2004). PEF side effects such as changes of pH at the electrode surface due to electrochemical reactions (Saulis et al. 2005), as well as the occurrence of temperature hot spots due to ohmic heating effects within a nonuniform electric field (Jaeger et al. 2009a), may contribute to the observed overall enzyme inactivation during PEF processing.

Although enzymes do not contain membrane structures, which are the target for an inactivation based on electroporation, the possible impact of PEF side effects indicates that process modifications toward the inactivation of microorganisms and enzyme structures are also possible (Aguiló-Aguayo et al. 2010, Martín-Belloso & Elez-Martínez 2005). A further discussion of PEF impact on proteins and enzymes is conducted in the following section.

Impact on food constituents. Only small amounts of data are available regarding PEFs effects on other food constituents, especially proteins (Barsotti et al. 2001). Perez & Pilosof (2004) reported a partial modification of the native structure of β-lactoglobulin when subjecting the concentrate to an electric field of 12.5 kV cm^{-1}, whereas bovine immunoglobulin G subjected to PEFs at 41 kV cm^{-1} for 54 μs did not show any detectable changes in the secondary structure or the thermal stability (Li et al. 2005). No effects of PEF treatment on the physicochemical properties of lactoferrin were found by Sui et al. (2010) for treatment intensities up to 35 kV cm^{-1} and a total specific energy input of 41 kJ kg^{-1} (treatment time 19 μs) with temperatures below 65°C.

Fernandez-Diaz et al. (2000) studied the effects of PEFs on ovalbumin solutions (2%; pH 7; 5 mS cm^{-1}) and dialyzed egg white (pH 9.2; 4–5 mS cm^{-1}), applying an electric field strength in the range of 27–33 kV cm^{-1}. Partial protein unfolding or enhanced sulfhydryl (SH) group ionization of ovalbumin was observed after PEF treatment and was found to increase with increasing the total specific energy input.

Recent investigations by Marco-Moles et al. (2009) focused on the PEF effect on protein and lipids in liquid whole egg and the microstructure of these components studied by low temperature scanning electron microscopy (Cryo-SEM). A partial denaturation and insolubilization of the protein was observed during conventional pasteurization and resulted in a thickening of the lipoprotein matrix as observed by Cryo-SEM. Microstructure of PEF-treated samples showed some discontinuities in the lipoprotein matrix.

Owing to the application of PEFs, changes in the conformational state of proteins might cause changes in enzyme structure and activity (Bendicho et al. 2003, Tsong 1990). In general, the mechanisms involved in the inactivation of enzymes by PEFs are not fully understood (Ohshima et al. 2006). Possible mechanisms are proposed (Castro et al. 2001, Perez & Pilosof 2004). If the duration of the pulse is long enough, the effects of PEFs on proteins could entail polarization of the protein molecule, dissociation of noncovalently linked protein subunits involved in quaternary structures, changes in the protein conformation so that hydrophobic amino acid or sulfhydryl groups are exposed, attraction of polarized structures by electrostatic forces, and hydrophobic interactions or noncovalent bonds forming aggregates.

The effect of a PEF treatment of suspensions of potato and corn starch was under investigation by Han et al. (2009a) and Han et al. (2009b). Physicochemical properties of potato and corn starch granules were found to be significantly affected because of the electric field exposure, with electric field strength intensities in the range of 30–50 kV cm^{-1} (no other PEF treatment parameters were reported). Treatment effects included an intragranular molecular rearrangement and a partial loss of the crystalline structure.

The same research group reported the effect of a PEF processing (electric field strength 20–50 kV cm^{-1}, no other PEF parameters reported) of peanut oil on fatty acid composition, acid value, and peroxide value after treatment and storage (Zeng et al. 2010). Although the applicability and feasibility of a PEF treatment of an electrically insulating media such as oil may be questionable, the authors found a significant increase of the peroxide value of the treated oil after 100 days of storage at 40°C, whereas the acid value decreased. No differences were found between the control and the PEF-treated sample immediately after treatment. Further research is required concerning the PEF effect on lipids and carbohydrates in order to confirm first results obtained in the above-mentioned studies. However, the electric field application and its effect on physicochemical material properties may have a potential for a targeted modification of functional food characteristics.

Current Applications

PEF technology is on the verge of industrial application with various pilot scale units available worldwide (Lelieveld et al. 2007, Raso & Heinz 2006). Controlled reversible permeabilization offers the potential for a sublethal stress induction on biological cells triggering a metabolic response (Bonnafous et al. 1999, Gomez Galindo et al. 2008) and an increased production of secondary metabolites such as phenols or phytosterols, leading to increased antimicrobial and antioxidative effects (Dörnenburg & Knorr 1995). It also offers the potential for the infusion of precursors or other desired constituents into cells as well as the recovery of metabolites from cells while maintaining their viability and productivity (Tryfona & Bustard 2008).

The irreversible rupture of plant membranes offers various applications to replace or support conventional thermal, as well as enzymatic, processes for cell disintegration (Vorobiev & Lebovka 2008). Irreversible permeabilization allows significant improvement of mass transfer especially for drying, expression, concentration, and extraction, resulting in higher product yields, shorter processing times, and consequently reduced energy consumption (Toepfl et al. 2006).

Microbial inactivation of vegetative cells via PEFs offers pasteurization with low energy input, selective inactivation of microorganisms depending on cell size or shape (Toepfl et al. 2007), and retention of bioactive heat-sensitive food compounds while inactivating pathogenic microorganisms and increasing product shelf live and safety (for a comprehensive overview on the various fields of application of PEFs in the food industry, follow the **Supplementary Material link** from the Annual Reviews home page at **http://www.annualreviews.org**) (Guerrero-Beltrán et al. 2010, Jaeger et al. 2009b, Sui et al. 2010).

Process-Structure-Function Interactions

The effect of PEFs on food constituents such as proteins and carbohydrates and the resulting changes of functional properties were discussed above. The following section focuses on the PEF effect on structured foods.

PEFs affect the cell membranes and thus can be expected to influence the texture of products in which the structure is largely dependent on the integrity of cells. The possible use of PEFs in food processing has now been investigated for a number of years. These studies have mainly focused on the effect of electric pulses on inactivation of different types of microorganisms in different states and also electric permeabilization of plant cells to increase the yield of different material, such as juices. Other than the changes occurring on a cellular level, there has been very little research on the effect of PEF treatment on microstructures of the raw material or the food, which continues developing during further processing of the PEF-treated raw material.

Fundamental research on the modification of textural properties of plant and animal raw materials represents the basis for further possible applications. Lebovka et al. (2004) studied the impact of PEFs on apple, carrot, and potato tissue. Stress deformation and relaxation tests were performed to analyze the changes in tissue texture. PEF treatment, in combination with a mild heat pretreatment, leads to complete elimination of the textural strength of tissue. It was shown that by proper selection of PEF treatment conditions, it was possible to obtain a controlled degree of tissue softening.

Suitable methods such as impedance measurement (Angersbach et al. 1999) and acoustic impulse response (Grimi et al. 2010) were developed and are in use as efficient tools to quantify structural modifications. Improved water binding during cooking of meat was found to occur after PEF pretreatment because of enhanced microdiffusion of brine and water-binding agents. Hydrocolloids will influence protein swelling and water-binding activity, and their microdiffusion into the meat tissue can be enhanced by PEF pretreatment (Toepfl 2006).

The impact of a PEF treatment on microstructure and texture of salmon was investigated by Gudmundsson & Hafsteinsson (2001). Fish muscle was found to be more susceptible for gaping due to PEF treatment in comparison with chicken meat, most likely due to the lower content of connective tissue (0.6% in comparison to 2% for chicken meat). No direct-effect PEF treatment on protein denaturation was found by electrophoresis, so the changes in microstructure were related to permeabilization of the cell membrane and leakage of cell fluids into extracellular space. The understanding of the impact and the potential of the PEF technology on food systems at the cellular level will allow the design of tailor-made foods, establishing process-structure-function relationships.

Process Developments

Application of PEF technology as a short-time (milliseconds) continuous operation will improve sustainability of food processing and/or reduce energy requirements while maintaining or improving food quality and safety. Even if PEFs require an additional input of electrical energy, it has beneficial effects on total energy consumption of mass transfer processes such as extraction, pressing, or drying. Processing times are reduced, utilization of production capacities is improved, and water, as well as raw material, consumption is decreased (Toepfl et al. 2006).

Application of PEFs in combination with mild heat seems to be a promising technique for a gentle, multihurdle preservation process. PEF treatment in combination with mild heat provides a potential to reduce the thermal load and retain native enzyme activity. A reduction of thermal load could be used to increase operating time of heat exchangers by reducing the amount of biofouling.

Another key aspect for the successful application of PEF pasteurization is its selective inactivation capability, given that the pore formation process and the required *trans*-membrane potential depend on the size of the treated cell. Larger cells such as yeasts require a smaller intensity of the external electric field, and thus they are more sensitive to electropermeabilization. Hence,

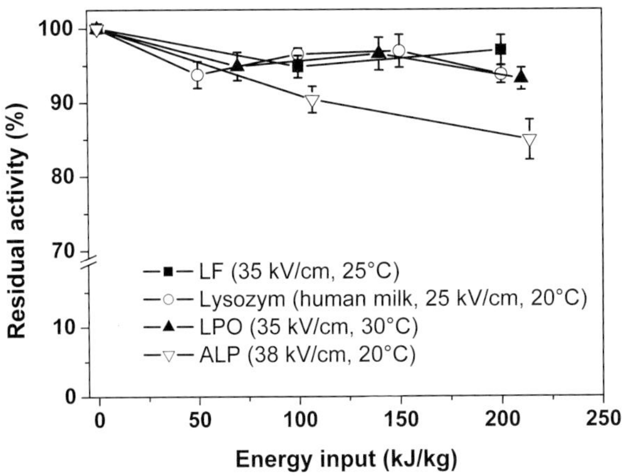

Figure 3

Impact of pulsed electric field treatment on enzymes and bioactive, antimicrobial components in milk (LF, lactoferrin; LPO, lactoperoxidase; ALP, alkaline phosphatase) according to Jaeger et al. (2009b).

inactivation of yeast in a product containing desirable probiotic bacteria can be realized without a loss of bacterial cell vitality.

Selectivity of PEF inactivation based on cell size and other factors that affect the electroporation mechanism are different from the susceptibility of microorganisms to thermal treatment. Thermotolerant microorganisms can be affected by PEFs, and inactivation of the more PEF-resistant species can be conducted by thermal effects; consequently, a combination of thermal and PEF treatment can improve the inactivation effectiveness in addition to the synergistic temperature effect on PEF inactivation below the thermal inactivation level.

As the PEF effect on proteins and enzymes, as well as on other food constituents, remains small, possible applications could include the pasteurization of bioactive antimicrobial milk fractions such as lactoperoxidase, lactoferrin, or immunoglobulins, as well as heat-sensitive vitamin solutions, which are destroyed during thermal pasteurization. **Figure 3** shows the retention of milk bioactives after pasteurization with PEFs. On the other hand, process improvements like treatment chamber design have offered the ability to selectively retain enzyme activity or to inactivate them via temperature effects caused by the electrodes and flow conditions in the treatment chamber.

Research Needs and Challenges

The application of PEFs to induce stress reactions in biological systems and the basic understanding of underlying mechanisms on a cellular and metabolic level will be the main focus of the research undertaken in the field of reversible permeabilization of plant cells. First attempts that have been described above are already showing the potential for the modification and the improvement of the production of valuable secondary metabolites.

The application of PEFs for the irreversible cell disintegration of plant and animal raw material was limited by the availability of large-scale pulse modulators, but a forward-looking technical development was already undertaken in the last years to overcome production scale limitations. In order to implement the cell disintegration processing step into existing processes, an integrative approach will be required that considers pre- and post-PEF processing unit operations, such as mechanical disintegration of solid-liquid separation in the case of extraction of juice recovery to successfully transfer the cell disintegration provided by PEFs into improved process results, such as higher juice yields.

For PEF-assisted pasteurization, the design and optimization of the PEF treatment chamber is the most challenging point with regard to different product properties, such as viscosity and electrical conductivity, as well as with regard to uniform treatment conditions in terms of electric field and temperature distribution. Many authors (Fiala et al. 2001, Gerlach et al. 2008, Jaeger et al. 2009a, Lindgren et al. 2002, van den Bosch et al. 2002) have described the temperature distribution in a PEF treatment chamber and reported the occurrence of high local temperatures due to the inhomogeneous distribution of the electrical field, limited flow velocity, and recirculation of the liquid. Numerical simulations using computational fluid dynamics gain interest for this purpose because experimental measurement of the related parameters is not possible in most cases, owing to small dimensions of the treatment chamber as well as the interference of the measuring device with the product flow and electric field. Treatment homogeneity and the avoidance of overprocessing of the product, including the occurrence of local high temperatures, are key aspects to guarantee predictable cell disintegration and microbial inactivation while maintaining heat-sensitive food constituents.

In PEF systems working at higher electric field intensities, electrochemical reactions can occur at the electrode surface (Morren et al. 2003). Related unwanted effects such as a partial electrolysis of the solution, the corrosion of the electrode material, and an introduction of small particles of electrode material in the liquid can be limited or avoided by suitable selection of electrode materials and by adaptation of the electrical pulse shape and duration (Roodenburg et al. 2005, Saulis et al. 2005). Its consideration is a crucial prerequisite during the study of inactivation kinetics to exclude other simultaneously occurring side effects.

Protective effects existing in real food systems may limit the process effectiveness of PEFs compared with inactivation studies conducted in model solutions, and the occurrence of sublethally injured cells has to be taken into account with regard to food safety aspects (Jaeger et al. 2009c). A comprehensive statement concerning food safety aspects of PEF treatment can be found in Knorr et al. (2008). Furthermore, in addition to the complexity of treatment media, the consideration of microbial growth state, adaptation to the treatment media, and the existence of inhomogeneous microbial populations with less sensitive subpopulations seem to be the most challenging aspects when transferring inactivation results to real products and industrial implementation.

ULTRASOUND

Process Description

During the past years US-assisted processing has attracted growing interest in the field of food science and technology. Positive effects have been reported for various applications such as the assistance of thermal treatments, the improvement of mass transfer processes, and food preservation, as well as for texture manipulation and analysis.

When sound energy is transferred into a medium, longitudinal waves are formed causing continuous compression and rarefaction of elastic materials (Povey & Mason 1998). The resulting physical, chemical, and biochemical effects strongly depend on the energy applied (Knorr et al. 2004). The application of US in food technology can be divided into two different approaches: low energy diagnostic US in the MHz range used for nondestructive testing and high power US in the kHz range applied for material alteration. At low treatment intensities and amplitudes, the pressure waves induce acoustic streaming, whereas high intensities and amplitudes result in local pressures below the vapor pressure of the liquid. This leads to a constant growth of gas bubbles in

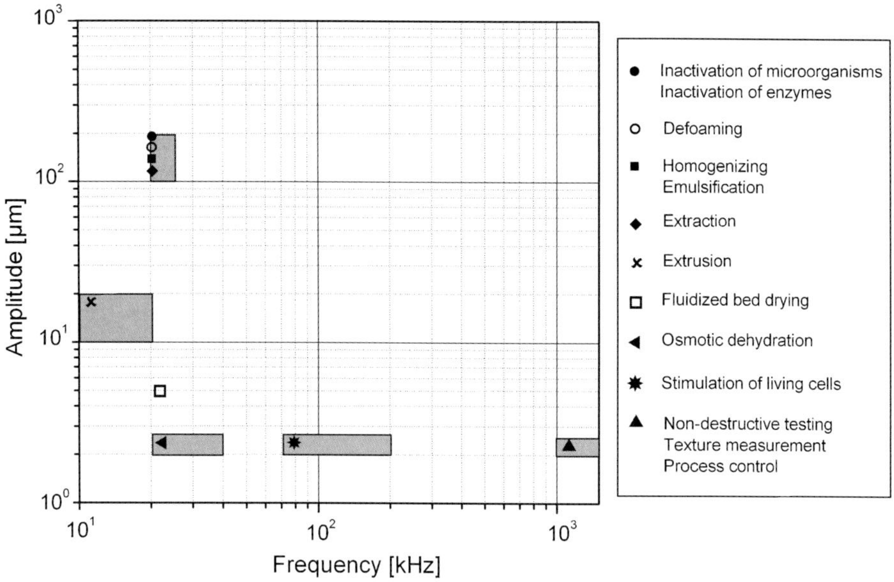

Figure 4

Comparison of treatment parameters (amplitude and frequency) of selected sonication processes in food science and technology (for references for the parameters used in the above-mentioned applications, see Supplemental Materials).

the medium, resulting in their violent collapse (cavitation) (Patist & Bates 2008). Cavitation and associated phenomena are responsible for the majority of the effects of high power US in food processing.

History

The first generation of ultrasonic waves goes back to the 1830s. Research for the potential of US in food processing started in the 1920s. Since the 1950s, US has been used on industrial equipment for cleaning and homogenization (Mawson & Knoerzer 2007). The initial ultrasonic tester at the industrial level in 1950 was followed by the commercial adoption of ultrasonic cutting in food processing. In the 1990s, the sealing of packaging materials and welding of plastic emerged. The development of piezoelectric transducers led to an increase in US research within the past decades and with the technical feasibility of higher treatment intensities, US was applied in disintegration of food materials, homogenization, and extraction (Mawson & Knoerzer 2007).

At present, US research is highly versatile, and US-assisted processes have been proposed for nearly every aspect of food production (**Figure 4**).

Research State of the Art

US research focuses mainly on three different aspects of food processing: the stimulation of fermentations and enzyme reactions at low treatment intensities; the application of high power US for preservation using synergistic effects of US, heat, and pressure; and the alteration of food consitutuents or structure leading to new product characteristics or improved mass and heat transfer during extraction or drying processes, where US can furthermore affect boundary layers.

Impact on biological cells. Biological cells are important raw materials and processing units for the food industry. Low-intensity US was reported to improve fermentation processes because of increased mass transfer through the cell wall and membrane and its influence on boundary layers (Sinisterra 1992). Increased fermentation rates could be observed because of the sonication-assisted removal of CO_2, which otherwise can inhibit fermentations (Matsuura et al. 1994).

A bactericidal effect of US was first reported in the 1920s (Harvey & Loomis 1929). The upcoming developments in ultrasonic equipment lead to higher acoustic densities and an increase in inactivation rates. US-induced cell damage is primarily explained by cavitation phenomena such as shear disruption (microstreaming), localized heating, and free radical formation (Hughes & Nyborg 1962). Cell wall and membrane of biological cells can be damaged by surface rubbing, leading to fracture and leakage (Kinsloe et al. 1954). Equally, separation of the cytoplasmic membrane due to ultrasonic treatments has been reported (Alliger 1975), and free radicals are assumed to cause DNA damage (Hughes & Nyborg 1962).

Several studies showed an additive or even synergistic effect when US was combined with other lethal effects such as elevated temperatures [thermosonication (TS)], pressure [manosonication (MS)], or both [manothermosonication (MTS)] (Knorr et al. 2004), which has been explained by the weakening of the cell wall, making it more susceptible to the effects of cavitation (Patist & Bates 2008). Ultrasonic pasteurization carried out at 50°C could present a high potential in preserving physicochemical properties, color, and flavor compared with conventional thermal pasteurization techniques (Patist & Bates 2008).

A comparative study on the inactivation of *Escherichia coli* by all four treatments (sonication, TS, MS, and MTS) showed significantly shortened treatment times to achieve a five-log reduction with combined treatments. In the case of sonicated samples, extensive cell damage and breakage could be shown by SEM analysis (Lee et al. 2009).

Although the overall results seem promising, the specific energy requirement of sonication-assisted processes was reported to surmount that of a comparable thermal process (Zenker et al. 2003) and has to be considered as the most important limitation for the application of US in food preservation processes today.

Impact on enzymes. Enzymes are valuable processing agents for the food industry. Positive effects on enzyme activity can be achieved by the application of low energy US. Substrates can be made available in large amounts, and the transport of substrate toward immobilized enzymes is increased by microstreaming (Mason et al. 1996).

The research in inactivation of enzymes for food preservation revealed increased effects for TS, MS, or MTS compared with sonication alone. Nevertheless, the sensitivity can be very different from one enzyme to another. Positive results have been reported for tomato pectic enzymes as well as for α-chymotrypsin and porcine lipase, whereas phospholipase A_2 was nearly insensitive to MTS, and the sensitivity of trypsin was found to be temperature dependent (Vercet et al. 2001, Vercet et al. 2002).

Impact on food constituents. The effects of sonication on food are various and range from compression and rarefaction to temperature peaks up to 5,000°C and local pressures up to 100 MPa (Suslick 2003). This leads to wide-ranging impact on food constituents with positive as well as critical results.

Sonication can modify proteins and product structure, improve flow behavior and increase heat transfer as it was exemplified with continuous formation of an edible coating of raw sausages (Knorr et al. 2004). A heated tubular sonotrode was used to form a skin of denatured proteins around the raw emulsion inside.

Critical results were obtained in the case of rabbiteye blueberries with reduction of product quality after an ultrasonic treatment (Stojanovic & Silva 2006). The application of US for the preservation of fruit juices was considered promising, as sonication resulted in only minor color changes and retention of 94% of the anthocyanins in blackberry juice (Tiwari et al. 2009). However, the application of US for food preservation could be limited because of a destruction of the physicochemical properties of the food, if parameters have to be designed with the objective to inactivate extremely heat-resistant microbial forms (Knorr et al. 2002).

Current Applications

Although US research in the field of food technology is versatile and shows a lot of promising effects, so far only a few treatments have reached industrial level. This discrepancy can be explained by the fact that ultrasonic equipment has to be custom designed for every single application and by a lack of appreciation of the food industry (Mawson & Knoerzer 2007), which has to be overcome by closer collaborations between research and industry in future.

One of the most common pieces of sonication equipment at the industrial level are ultrasonic filtration systems as add-ons to existing vibratory screens, while the combination of US and membrane filtration is still in the early phase of development (Patist & Bates 2008). Airborne US is used for defoaming of carbonated beverages and fermentation systems (Gallego-Juárez 1998).

Ultrasonic pulverization techniques are applied for the destruction of residual cell wall material and vegetable purees achieving significant modifications of textural and rheological properties, as by releasing pectin from cell walls, which contributes to the formation of continuous matrices (Bates et al. 2006, Mawson & Knoerzer 2007). In the case of the preparation of biomaterials for further processing by fermentation or enzyme digestion, US-assisted pulverization of cell matrices is used to facilitate the release of substrates or nutrients (Matsuura et al. 1994, Mawson & Knoerzer 2007, Wu et al. 2000).

Process-Structure-Function Interactions

Process-structure-function interactions are the basis for several processes in food technology. Consequently, the potential of US in assisting and influencing these processes has been widely studied.

Proteins are used for texturizing and thickening of sauces, dressings, dairy products, and gels. A study about the physical properties of US-treated soy proteins showed significant texture changes in model food systems (Jambrak et al. 2009). Soy protein isolate creamed during the treatment with an ultrasonic probe (20 kHz, 15 min) and soy protein concentrate showed changes in conductivity, increased solubility, and increased specific surface area, which is of importance for food texture and functionality. Contrarily, sonication did not improve emulsifying or foaming properties.

Extrusion processes can be improved by the ultrasonic excitation of a metal tube or extrusion dye and ultrasonic vibrations can lead to a reduction in drag resistance and improved flow characteristics (Knorr et al. 2004, Mousavi et al. 2007).

In meat processing, sonication has been successfully applied to improve binding strength, water holding capacity, product color, and yield of processed meat (Vimini et al. 1983), and was reported to be beneficial in the meat tenderization process (Roberts 1992).

Ultrasonic pretreatments of vegetables and fruits led to cavitation damage, an increased distortion of cells and the creation of microscopic channels (Fernandes et al. 2009, Jambrak et al. 2007). These changes in tissue structure were shown to have potential for increasing mass transfer processes.

Process Developments

Within the past few years, US research has covered nearly every aspect of food technology. Cavitation and associated phenomena such as microstreaming, pressure fluctuation, and local heating effects led to numerous improvements at laboratory scale.

Thermal processes can be improved by enhanced heat transfer, microstreaming at boundary layers, reduced fouling due to cavitation phenomena, and a faster formation of gas bubbles in evaporation processes. Airborne US was reported to have a positive impact on hot-air drying of carrots (García-Pérez et al. 2006). An influence on mass transfer rates has likewise been observed during the osmotic dehydration of apple cubes (Simal et al. 1998).

During extraction processes, cavitation can improve the penetration with the solvent and disrupt cell walls when high intensities are applied (Li et al. 2004). The mass transfer resistances during the extraction of vanillin from vanilla pods and of phospholipids from palm-pressed fiber could be reduced by the application of US (Chua et al. 2009, Jadhav et al. 2009). Positive results for sonication-assisted supercritical extraction of ginger indicate that cavitation, which will not occur in supercritical fluids due to the absence of liquid/gas boundaries, is not the only US effect having an important influence on the mass transfer rate (Balachandran et al. 2006). Acoustic streaming and the presence of gas pockets in the solid causing cavitational collapse have been discussed (Patist & Bates 2008).

Cavitation, shear forces, and an influence on boundary layers provide the opportunity to improve emulsification and homogenizing (Jafari et al. 2007, Villamiel & de Jong 2000). In the case of milk homogenization, subsequent yogurt fermentation led to a product with decreased syneresis, improved water-holding capacity, and increased viscosity (Wu et al. 2000).

A change in the sonication parameters can lead to the opposite effect and emulsions can be split into their components (Pangu & Feke 2004). Acoustic radiation force was reported to hold particles in position in a stationary field leading to coalescence, which has been presented as a novel principle for particle separation (Masudo & Okada 2006).

Sonication during freezing processes can promote ice nucleation and enhance heat and mass transfer processes (Zheng & Sun 2006). Crystal size distribution can be controlled, leading to reduced cell destruction and cavitation effects can minimize fouling in surface freezers (Acton & Morris 1992).

At lower treatment intensities US can be applied for the detection of foreign bodies in packaged and nonpackaged food (Knorr et al. 2004, Leemans & Destain 2009) and for nondestructive testing. Conventional methods such as microscopy, textural analysis, and rheology require laboratory practice and are unsuitable for real-time applications (Ting et al. 2009). Low-intensity US has been successfully tested for the monitoring of the gelation process in milk and tofu (Dwyer et al. 2005, Ting et al. 2009) and the measurement of the mechanical properties of cheese products (Benedito et al. 2000).

Research Needs and Challenges

The presented overview of ultrasonic research in the food industry underlines the versatility of sonication processes. One of the most important challenges for the industrial application of US is the definition of optimized parameters for every single process and product, which demands many research capacities and a close collaboration between researchers, equipment suppliers, and the food industry. In addition to the promising effects of sonication in food technology, detailed knowledge about quality aspects together with a thorough analysis of energy requirements are the basis for the successful scale-up from laboratory tests to industrial scale. Furthermore, technology transfer from other fields such as medical applications may prove beneficial.

PLASMA TREATMENT

Process Description

Plasmas can be described as quasineutral particle systems in the form of gaseous or fluid-like mixtures of free electrons and ions, frequently containing neutral particles (atoms, molecules), with a large mean kinetic energy of the electrons and/or all of the plasma components and a substantial influence on the charge carriers and their electromagnetic interaction on the system properties (Rutscher 2008).

In the field of plasma research, a complex nomenclature considering the temperature of the electrons and the bulk gas and/or the surrounding pressure can be found (Goldston & Rutherford 1997, Roth 1995). According to Fridman et al. (2005), all varieties of plasma-chemical systems are traditionally divided into two major categories: thermal and nonthermal plasmas, with specific advantages and disadvantages. Thermal plasmas [usually arcs or radiofrequency (RF) inductively coupled plasma discharges] are associated with Joule heating and thermal ionization, and enable the delivery of high power (to over 50 MW per unit) at high operating pressures. Besides other limitations, very high gas temperatures limit their applicability to food systems.

In nonthermal plasmas, the electron temperature is much higher than the bulk gas temperature. Whereas the electron temperature can reach several ten thousands K, the gas temperature remains at temperature levels below 40°C (Mastwijk & Nierop Groot 2010). Nonthermal plasmas may be produced by a variety of electrical discharges at different pressure levels. Working pressure below atmospheric conditions are mainly suitable for dried food materials or packaging materials, since a vacuum will support liquid to gaseous phase changes in high-moisture food products. The most suitable system for food processing is an atmospheric-pressure plasma device in which no extreme conditions are required and low temperatures can be realized. Atmospheric-pressure plasma is commonly generated by corona discharge, dielectric barrier discharge (DBD), or plasma jet (Keener 2008). For the treatment of nonuniformly shaped products, the application of plasma jets offers advantages due to various options regarding design and construction (Foest et al. 2005).

History

In the year 1808, Sir Humphry Davy developed the steady-state DC arc discharge, and in the 1830's, Michael Faraday and others developed the high-voltage DC electrical discharge tube. Rapid progress was made in electrical discharge physics during the nineteenth century, nearly all of it in a few laboratories in England and Germany. In 1857, Siemens designed an ozone generator that has evolved into the cylindrical dielectric type that covers most of the commercially available ozone generators in use. In 1840, Schönbein named the substance, which gave off this odor, ozone from the Greek word ozein, to smell (Rubin 2001), after van Marum already noticed in 1785 that air near his electrostatic machine acquired a characteristic odor when electric sparks were passed. In 1801, Cruickshank confirmed that a certain odor occurs at the anode during the electrolysis of water. In 1898, Sir William Crookes introduced the term ionization to describe the breakup of the neutral atom into an electron and a positive ion. Irving Langmuir introduced the term plasma in 1928, by which he meant an approximately electrically neutral collection of ions and electrons that may or may not contain a background neutral gas and that is capable of responding to electric and magnetic fields. More detailed information on the history of plasma research is given by Roth (Roth 1995).

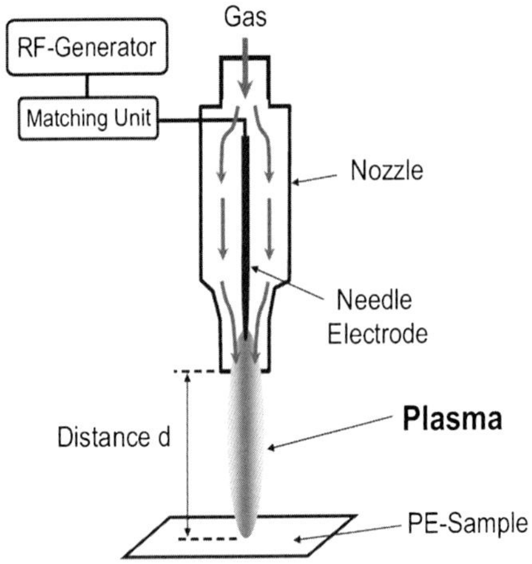

Figure 5

Experimental setup of a plasma jet according to Brandenburg et al. (2007).

Research State of the Art

Recent research activities in food-related application of plasma focus mainly on inactivation of microbes, but little is known about the effect of plasma on food matrices. Because emitted reactive species react with bacteria, they may also affect food components such as water, lipids, proteins, and carbohydrates (Deng et al. 2007b, Keener 2008). Owing to recent technical developments, plasma sources can operate at ambient conditions, keeping the processing temperature low. For example, RF-driven plasma jets can be used for studies on treatment of food-related materials. Such a plasma source consists of a needle electrode in the center of a ceramic nozzle and a grounded outer electrode. The RF voltage is coupled via a matching network to the needle electrode. The gas flowing between the electrodes is ionized and then ejected from the source (Brandenburg et al. 2007). Design principles of a plasma jet system are shown in **Figure 5**.

Impact on microorganisms. Inactivation of food-related microorganisms by plasma treatment is commonly conducted using model systems. An overview of microbial inactivation in model systems using nonthermal plasma published during the last three years is given by Wan et al. (2009).

The antimicrobial activity of nonthermal plasma against Gram-negative and Gram-positive bacteria, yeast and fungi, biofilm formers, and endospores was shown in various studies (Brandenburg et al. 2007, Kelly-Wintenberg et al. 1999, Laroussi 2005, Montie et al. 2000, Vleugels et al. 2005). Although several reviews focus on the inactivation mechanisms of plasma (Boudam et al. 2006, Gaunt et al. 2006, Moisan et al. 2001, Moreau et al. 2008), it is not yet fully understood. Moisan et al. (2001) stated that three basic mechanisms are involved in plasma inactivation: (*a*) ultraviolet (UV) irradiation of genetic material, (*b*) intrinsic photodesorption, and (*c*) etching. Most researchers claim that UV plays a minor role in the inactivation of microorganisms at atmospheric pressure, and the inactivation process is controlled by chemically reactive species. However, it was shown that in some cases UV photons can play a role in the inactivation process of microorganisms at atmospheric pressure (Boudam et al. 2006). Moreau et al. (2008) compared plasma inactivation effects to the effects of micropulses. Similar to the effects of micropulses, the cell membranes of microorganisms are perforated after plasma treatment. Besides the perforation of the cell membrane, the inactivation effect of plasma is induced by the bombardment of the cell membrane by radicals (OH or NO). These radicals are absorbed onto the bacteria surface, and volatile components are formed and eliminated from the cells (etching). Two mechanisms of plasma inactivation described by Gaunt et al. (2006) are the electrostatic disruption of cell membranes and lethal oxidation of cellular components.

Impact on enzymes. Information regarding the impact of plasma on enzymes is only given in a very few papers. Dudak et al. (2007) found a decrease of enzyme activity after treatment with plasma generated in RF-driven glow discharge with the highest decrease in activity within the first 10 minutes of treatment. They showed plasma-chemical oxidation as well as fragmentation of the proteins. Additionally, changes in the secondary protein structure due to the plasma treatment were detected. A fragmentation of proteins was also found by Deng et al. (2007b) after DBD treatment. In this process, atomic oxygen was shown to play a dominant role in destruction and degradation reactions. Oxygen plasma generated by RF discharge led to a reduction of C-H and N-H bonds in casein protein and to a modification of the secondary protein structure (Hayashi et al. 2009).

Impact on food constituents. Although much work has already been performed on the effects of nonthermal plasma on microorganisms, information of plasma interaction with food components is rare. This is mainly due to the fact that the application of plasma was long limited to heat- and vacuum-resistant materials. As mentioned before, today plasma can operate at ambient pressure and low processing temperature.

Applying CP to improve the shelf life of fresh or freshly prepared food is new, and little is currently known about the effect of plasma treatment on bioactive plant substances. The degradation of mycotoxins in microwave-induced atmospheric pressure argon plasma has recently been shown by Park et al. (2007). Plasma treatment resulted in a significant time-dependent decrease in aflatoxin B1, deoxynivalenol, and nivalenol, coming along with a dose-dependent reduced cytotoxity. A time- and dose-dependent degradation has also been observed for flavonoids, known for their high antioxidant activity, which protects cells against the damaging effects of reactive oxygen species. The degradation rate strongly depended on the polyphenolics substitution pattern. Although glycosidic flavonoids showed a rather inert behavior throughout plasma treatment, aglycosid derivates were quickly degraded (Grzegorzewski et al. 2010b).

The potential of nonthermal plasma surface treatment to decontaminate food surfaces is investigated in various studies, often neglecting the effects on quality parameters. However, organoleptic analysis of plasma-treated nut samples likewise showed no relation between treatment and perceptual sensory character (Basaran et al. 2008). On a molecular level, SEM analysis of different cabbage and lettuce species yet revealed that under certain conditions, plasma treatment may lead to changes of plant surface hydrophobic wax layers (Grzegorzewski et al. 2010a). On the other hand, Ragni et al. (2010) observed no negative effects of plasma treatment on egg quality.

Current Applications

Plasma technologies in food processing are not yet established, but investigations using complex food raw materials have been performed. Some studies focus on the plasma-related decontamination of bacteria at the surface of several fruit and vegetable samples like apples, cantaloupe, and lettuce without evaluating the obtained product quality (Niemira & Sites 2008). A five-log reduction of *E. coli* inoculated on almonds was found after 30 s nonthermal plasma treatment at 30 kV and 2000 Hz (Deng et al. 2007a). Basaran et al. (2008) treated various nut samples inoculated with

Aspergillus parasiticus and tested the antifungal efficiency of low pressure CP (LPCP). They used air gases and sulfur hexafluoride (SF_6) and found that SF_6 plasma application (five-log reduction) was more effective than air gas plasma treatment (one-log reduction). In contrast, the efficiency of air gas plasma against aflatoxin was greater than the efficiency of SF_6 plasma. Equally, seeds inoculated with *Aspergillus* spp. and *Penicillium* spp. were treated with LPCP using air gases and SF_6 (Selcuk et al. 2008). The fungal attachment was reduced below one percent by the treatment while the germination quality of the seeds was preserved (for additional examples on the inactivation of microorganisms on food surfaces, see **Supplemental Table 1**).

Process Developments

The industrial use of applied plasma technology in the nonfood sector is diverse (e.g., plasma switches for power networks, cost-effective light sources, high-definition large area flat panel displays, plasma-improved printability of foils, etc.). Recent research increasingly concentrates on plasma treatment of living vegetative or mammalian cells and tissues (Shashurin et al. 2008, Stoffels et al. 2008). Much work has already been done in the field of plasma medicine and related topics. Using CP jets, eradication of yeast grown on agar (Kolb et al. 2008), blood coagulation, and tissue sterilization (Fridman et al. 2006), as well as ablation of cultured liver cancer cells (Cho et al. 2008), have been shown.

In the past decade, concerted research efforts were expended to understand and to apply atmospheric pressure plasmas as a sterilization method. Modular and selective plasma sources were developed. These combine the technological advantages of atmospheric pressure plasmas (avoidance of vacuum devices and batch processing) with the flexibility and handling properties of modular devices (Ehlbeck et al. 2008). Along with the applications in food processing, progress in germ-reduction technologies is important for medical and biomedical application, biotechnology, the pharmaceutical industry, and the packaging industry. The treatment of components with complex geometry requires the development of plasma sources for surface treatment and of cavity-penetrating plasmas. Because energy transfer of a low-temperature plasma to a surface is small, the treatment of heat-sensitive materials is feasible. In environmental applications, plasma technologies can be applied to flue gas cleaning and can substitute wet-chemical processes that generate waste water by environmentally desirable dry processes (Weltmann et al. 2008).

Another possible application of nonthermal plasma is the treatment of packaged products. Schwabedissen et al. (2007) described the different application fields of the *PlasmaLabel*™, e.g., fresh food conservation or packaged goods. However, further investigations are required to characterize the plasma applied and to better understand the interactions of reactive species with organic surfaces as well as vital biosystems (Mastwijk & Nierop Groot 2010). This will allow for control of the effects of plasma and the ability to design highly specified and efficient plasma processes.

Research Needs and Challenges

Approaches to the study of the effects of plasmas in industrial plasma engineering often regard plasma as a black box with inputs and outputs. Also, studies focusing on plasma application to foods as the desired output of a plasma-related process are mainly achieved by adjusting inputs until the desired result is obtained. Within such approaches, no serious attempt is made to understand the plasma-physical, plasma-chemical, or plasma-biological processes occurring in this black box. Future research needs to involve more interdisciplinary studies to allow a better understanding of the complex interactions during plasma processing, thus resulting in the design of beneficial and controlled plasma applications for food processing, which may encompass microbial inactivation as well as the modification of functional food properties. Further, plasma processing has to be considered as a surface treatment, and the impact of potential toxicological effects resulting from chemical reactions based on plasma-air-food surface interactions have to be viewed in relation to the surface to volume ratio of the particular product.

CONCLUSION

HHP treatment has a high potential to produce microbiologically safe, high quality, tailor-made foods under gentle processes conditions. Process improvement can only be achieved by understanding and applying the different temperature, time, or pressure dependencies of wanted and unwanted reactions. Detailed studies regarding inactivation kinetics and mechanisms of pathogens should be performed in the respective food matrix and have to result in constant process parameters, and if not possible, in optimally controlled process parameters. Controlled and reproducible studies on pressure effect of HP on nutrients biopolymers, toxins, and allergens are also needed.

The interactions between products and PEF process and possible undesired changes during PEF treatment still remain uncertain and require further investigation. For example, high-value products such as enzyme or vitamin solutions or protein fractions isolated from milk, which are all heat sensitive, are potential products for a nonthermal pasteurization by PEFs. The combination of techniques that deliver effective preservation without the excessive use of any single conventional process parameter such as time or temperature allows the selective retention or inactivation of food constituents. The combination of PEFs with other stress factors like mild heat, antimicrobial compounds, pH, or organic acids, as well as the combination with other thermal or nonthermal decontamination techniques, will determine further development. The impact of PEFs on the structure of food matrices and on mass transfer within food matrices and the subsequent understanding of PEF-related process-structure-relationships will allow the development of unique tailor-made foods.

US-assisted processing offers advantages for a large variety of food production processes. The unique characteristics of sound waves provide opportunities to treat products with specifically adapted parameters. For instance, US with low maximum pressure amplitude will cause microstreaming in fluids, gently manipulating mass transfer, whereas high sound pressure amplitudes cause cavitation associated with high sound pressure and temperature peaks permitting changes in cell structure as well as homogenization of disperse systems. However, the large range of attainable effects is one of the most important obstacles for the transfer of laboratory scale results to industrial level. Equipment and parameters have to be directly adapted to every single product and objective. Furthermore, undesired changes in product structure and quality have to be known and minimized. A better understanding of basic mechanisms of ultrasonic treatments in dependency of product and process parameters is necessary to allow drawing general conclusions and to simplify the design of new processes and applications.

CP treatment at atmospheric pressures offers various opportunities in food processing, e.g., surface decontamination, modification of surface properties, and enhancement of mass transfer with respect for foods and food-related materials. Attempts to limit the heat transfer to sensitive materials such as food products resulted in the development of new atmospheric plasma jets and will allow efficient in-line integration in production lines; however, further research is required in light of the lack of data regarding the plasma-matrix-interactions and to ensure the development of safe and tailor-made processes for food application. Further investigations focusing on the spatial composition of plasma, physicochemical reaction kinetics, penetration depths, etc. should be supported by validated mathematical models and simulation approaches.

DISCLOSURE STATEMENT

The authors are not aware of any affiliations, memberships, funding, or financial holdings that might be perceived as affecting the objectivity of this review.

ACKNOWLEDGMENTS

This work was supported by the Federal Ministry of Economics and Technology (via AiF) and the FEI (Forschungskreis der Ernährungsindustrie e.V., Bonn), Project AiF 15610 N; by Federal Institute of Food, Agriculture and Consumer Protection (BMELV) and supported by the Federal Institute for Agriculture and Food (BLE), project FriPlas (FKZ 28-1-63.003-07) and Verbundprojekt Hochdrucktechnologie; by the Federal Ministry of Education and Research, project BioMed; by the Commission of the European Communities, Framework 6, Priority 5 Food Quality and Safety, Integrated Project NovelQ FP6-CT-2006-015710 and Framework 7 (FP7/2007-2013) under grant agreement n°222233.

LITERATURE CITED

Acton E, Morris GJ. 1992. *U.S. Patent No. W.O. 99/20420*

Aertsen A, Meersman F, Hendrickx M, Vogel R, Michiels CW. 2009. Biotechnology under high pressure: applications and implications. *Trends Biotechnol.* 27:434–41

Aguiló-Aguayo I, Soliva-Fortuny R, Martín-Belloso O. 2010. Impact of high-intensity pulsed electric field variables affecting peroxidase and lipoxygenase activities of watermelon juice. *LWT-Food Sci. Technol.* 43:897–902

Alliger H. 1975. Ultrasonic disruption. *Am. Lab.* 10:75–85

Ananta E. 2005. *Impact of Enviromental Factors on Vitality and Stability and High Pressure Pretreatment on Stress Tolerance of* Lactobacillus Rhamnosus *GG (ATCC 53103) During Spray Drying*. Berlin, Germany: Technische Universität Berlin

Ananta E, Heinz V, Knorr D. 2005. Assessment of high pressure induced damage on *Lactobacillus rhamnosus* GG by flow cytometry. *Food Microbiol.* 21:567–77

Ananta E, Heinz V, Schlüter O, Knorr D. 2001. Kinetic studies on high-pressure inactivation of *Bacillus stearothermophilus* spores suspended in food matrices. *Innov. Food Sci. Emerg. Technol.* 2:261–72

Ananta E, Knorr D. 2003. Pressure-induced thermotolerance of *Lactobacillus rhamnosus* GG. *Food Res. Int.* 36:991–97

Angersbach A, Heinz V, Knorr D. 1999. Electrophysiological model of intact and processed plant tissues: cell disintegration criteria. *Biotechnol. Prog.* 15:753–62

Angersbach A, Heinz V, Knorr D. 2000. Effects of pulsed electric fields on cell membranes in real food systems. *Innov. Food Sci. Emerg. Technol.* 1:135–49

Angersbach A, Knorr D. 1998. Impact of high-intensity electric field pulses on plant membrane permeabilization. *Trends Food Sci. Technol.* 9:185–91

Ardia A. 2004c. *Process considerations on the application of high pressure treatment at elevated temperature levels for food preservation*. Ph.D thesis. Berlin University of Technology, Berlin. 94 pp.

Balachandran S, Kentish SE, Mawson R, Ashokkumar M. 2006. Ultrasonic enhancement of the supercritical extraction from ginger. *Ultrason. Sonochem.* 13:471–79

Barbosa-Cánovas GV, Góngora-Nieto MM, Pothakamury UR, Swanson BG. 1999. *Preservation of Foods with Pulsed Electric Fields*. San Diego, CA: Academic

Barsotti L, Dumay E, Mu TH, Fernandez Diaz MD, Cheftel JC. 2001. Effects of high voltage electric pulses on protein-based food constituents and structures. *Food Sci. Technol.* 12:136–44

Barsotti L, Merle P, Cheftel JC. 1999. Food processing by pulsed electric fields: 1. Physical effects. *Food Rev. Int.* 15:163–80

Basaran P, Basaran-Akgul N, Oksuz L. 2008. Elimination of *Aspergillus parasiticus* from nut surface with low pressure cold plasma (LPCP) treatment. *Food Microbiol.* 25:626–32

Bates DM, Bagnall WA, Bridges MW. 2006. *U.S. Patent No. 20060110503*

Bauer BA, Knorr D. 2005. The impact of pressure, temperature and treatment time on starches: pressure-induced starch gelatinisation as pressure time temperature indicator for high hydrostatic pressure processing. *J. Food Eng.* 68:329–34

Bendicho S, Barbosa-Cánovas GV, Martín O. 2003. Reduction of protease activity in simulated milk ultrafiltrate by continuous flow high intensity pulsed electric field treatments. *J. Food Sci.* 68:952–57

Benedito J, Carcel JA, Sanjuan N, Mulet A. 2000. Use of ultrasound to assess Cheddar cheese characteristics. *Ultrasonics* 38:727–30

Black EP, Wei J, Atluri S, Cortezzo DE, Koziol-Dube K, et al. 2007. Analysis of factors influencing the rate of germination of spores of *Bacillus subtilis* by very high pressure. *J. Appl. Microbiol.* 102:65–76

Bluhm H, Sack M. 2009. Industrial-scale treatment of biological tissues with pulsed electric fields. In *Electrotechnologies for Extraction from Food Plants and Biomaterials*, ed. E Vorobiev, N Lebovka, pp. 237–69. New York: Springer

Bonnafous P, Vernhes M-C, Teissié J, Gabriel B. 1999. The generation of reactive-oxygen species associated with long-lasting pulse-induced electropermeabilisation of mammalian cells is based on a nondestructive alteration of the plasma membrane. *Biochim. Biophys. Acta* 1461:123–34

Boudam MK, Moisan M, Saoudi B, Popovici C, Gherardi N, Massines F. 2006. Bacterial spore inactivation by atmospheric-pressure plasmas in the presence or absence of UV photons as obtained with the same gas mixture. *J. Phys. D-Appl. Phys.* 39:3494–507

Brandenburg R, Ehlbeck J, Stieber M, von Woedtke T, Zeymer J, et al. 2007. Antimicrobial treatment of heat sensitive materials by means of atmospheric pressure rf-driven plasma jet. *Contrib. Plasma Phys.* 47:72–79

Bridgman PW. 1912. Water, in the liquid and five solid forms, under pressure. *Proc. Am. Acad. Arts Sci.* 47:441–558

Bridgman PW. 1914. The coagulation of albumen by pressure. *J. Biol. Chem.* 19:511–12

Buckow R. 2006. *Pressure and Temperature Effects on the Enzymatic Conversion of Biopolymers*. Berlin: Technsiche Universität Berlin

Buckow R, Heinz V. 2008. High pressure processing: a database of kinetic information. *Chem. Ingenieur Technik* 80:1081–95

Buckow R, Heinz V, Knorr D. 2005. Two fractional model for evaluating the activity of glucoamylase from *Aspergillus niger* under combined pressure and temperature conditions. *Food Bioprod. Process.* 83:220–28

Buckow R, Weiss U, Knorr D. 2008. Inactivation kinetics of apple polyphenol oxidase in different pressure-temperature domains. *Innov. Food Sci. Emerg. Technol.* 10(4):441–48

Bunthof CJ. 2002. *Flow cytometry, fluorescent probes, and flashing bacteria*. PhD thesis. Wageningen University, Wageningen, The Netherlands. 160 pp.

Castro AJ, Swanson BG, Barbosa-Cánovas GV, Zhang QH. 2001. Pulsed electric field modification of milk alkaline phosphatase activity. In *Electric Fields in Food Processing*, ed. GV Barbosa-Cánovas, QH Zhang, pp. 65–82. Lancaster, PA: Technomic

Cheftel JC, Culioli J. 1997. Effects of high pressure on meat: a review. *Meat Sci.* 46:211–36

Cho G, Kim JH, Jeong JM, Hong BH, Koo JH, et al. 2008. Electron plasma wave propagation in external-electrode fluorescent lamps. *Appl. Phys. Lett.* 92

Chua SC, Tan CP, Mirhosseini H, Lai OM, Long K, Baharin BS. 2009. Optimization of ultrasound extraction condition of phospholipids from palm-pressed fiber. *J. Food Eng.* 92:403–9

Clark P. 2006. Pulsed electric field processing. *Food Technol.* 60:66–67

Coster HGL. 1965. A quantitive analysis of the voltage-current relationships of fixed charge membranes and the associated property of "punch-through". *Biophys. J.* 5:669–86

Daeschlein G, Woedtke TV, Kindel E, Brandenburg R, Weltmann K-D, Jünger M. 2010. Antibacterial activity of an atmospheric pressure plasma jet against relevant wound pathogens in vitro on a simulated wound environment. *Plasma Process. Polym.* 7:224–30

Dalmadi I, Rapeanu G, Van Loey A, Smout C, Hendrickx M. 2006. Characterization and inactivation by thermal and pressure processing of strawberry (*Fragaria ananassa*) polyphenol oxidase: a kinetic study. *J. Food Biochem.* 30:56–76

Delgado A, Rauh C, Kowalczyk W, Baars A. 2008. Review of modelling and simulation of high pressure treatment of materials of biological origin. *Trends Food Sci. Technol.* 19:329–36

Deng SB, Ruan R, Mok CK, Huang GW, Lin XY, Chen P. 2007a. Inactivation of *Escherichia coli* on almonds using nonthermal plasma. *J. Food Sci.* 72:M62–M66

Deng XT, Shi JJ, Chen HL, Kong MG. 2007b. Protein destruction by atmospheric pressure glow discharges. *Appl. Phys. Lett.* 90:051504

Diels AMJ, Michiels CW. 2006. High-pressure homogenization as a non-thermal technique for the inactivation of microorganisms. *Crit. Rev. Microbiol.* 32:201–16

DIL. 2009. Elcrack generators and technology. In *Fact Sheet German Institute of Food Technologies (DIL)*, Quakenbrueck, Germany

Doevenspeck H. 1961. Influencing cells and cell walls by electrostatic impulses. *Fleischwirtschaft* 13:968–87

Doona CJ, Feeherry FE. 2007. *High Pressure Processing of Foods*. Hoboken, NJ: Wiley-Blackwell

Dörnenburg H, Knorr D. 1993. Cellular permeabilization of cultured plant cell tissues by high electric field pulses or ultra high pressure for recovery of secondary metabolites. *Food Biotechnol.* 7:35–38

Dörnenburg H, Knorr D. 1995. Strategies for the improvement of secondary metabolite production in plant cell cultures. *Enzyme Microb. Technol.* 17:674–84

Douzals JP, Marechal PA, Coquille JC, Gervais P. 1996. Microscopy study of starch gelatinization under high hydrostatic pressure. *J. Agric. Food Chem.* 44:1403–8

Dudak FC, Kousal J, Seker UÖS, Boyaci IH, Choukourov A, Biederman H. 2007. *Influence of the plasma treatment on enzyme structure and activity*. Presented at ICPIG, 28th, Prague, Czech Republic

Dumay EM, Kalichevsky MT, Cheftel JC. 1998. Characteristics of pressure-induced gel of beta-lactoglobulin at various times after pressure release. *Lebensmittel-Wiss. Technol.* 31:10–19

Dutreux N, Notermans S, Wijzes T, Góngora-Nieto MM, Barbosa-Canovas GV, Swanson BG. 2000. Pulsed electric fields inactivation of attached and free-living *Escherichia coli* and *Listeria innocua* under several conditions. *Int. J. Food Microbiol.* 54:91–98

Dwyer C, Donnelly L, Buckin V. 2005. Ultrasonic analysis of rennet-induced pregelation and gelation processes in milk. *J. Dairy Res.* 72:303–10

Ehlbeck J, Brandenburg R, von Woedtke T, Krohmann U, Stieber M, Weltmann KD. 2008. PLASMOSE: antimicrobial effects of modular atmospheric plasma sources. *GMS Krankenhaushygiene interdisziplinär* 3: Doc14

Fernandes FAN, Gallão MI, Rodrigues S. 2009. Effect of osmosis and ultrasound on pineapple cell tissue structure during dehydration. *J. Food Eng.* 90:186–90

Fernandez-Diaz MD, Barsotti L, Dumay EC. 2000. Effects of pulsed electric fields on ovalbumin solutions and dialyzed egg white. *J. Agric. Food Chem.* 48:2332–39

Fiala A, Wouters PC, van den Bosch E, Creyghton YLM. 2001. Coupled electrical-fluid model of pulsed electric field treatment in a model food system. *Innov. Food Sci. Emerg. Technol.* 2:229–38

Foest R, Kindel E, Ohl A, Stieber M, Weltmann KD. 2005. Non-thermal atmospheric pressure discharges for surface modification. *Plasma Phys. Control. Fusion* 47:B525–36

Fridman A, Chirokov A, Gutsol A. 2005. Non-thermal atmospheric pressure discharges. *J. Phys. D-Appl. Phys.* 38:R1–R24

Fridman G, Shereshevsky A, Peddinghaus M, Gutsol A, Vasilitis V, et al. 2006. *Bio-Medical Applications of Non-Thermal Atmospheric Pressure Plasma*. Presented at AIAA Plasma Dyn. Lasers Conf., 37th, San Francisco

Galindo F, Dejmek P, Lundgren K, Rasmusson A, Vicente An, Moritz T. 2009. Metabolomic evaluation of pulsed electric field-induced stress on potato tissue. *Planta* 230:469–79

Gallego-Juárez JA. 1998. Some applications of air-borne ultrasound to food processing. In *Ultrasound in Food Processing*, ed. MJW Povey, TJ Mason, pp. 127–43. London: Thomson Science

García-Pérez JV, Cárcel JA, de la Fuente-Blanco S, Riera-Franco de Sarabia E. 2006. Ultrasonic drying of foodstuff in a fluidized bed: parametric study. *Ultrasonics Proc. Ultrasonics Int. (UI'05) World Congr. Ultrasonics (WCU)* 44:e539–e43

Garcia D, Gómez N, Manas P, Condon S, Raso J, Pagan R. 2005. Occurence of sublethal injury after pulsed electric fields depending on the microorganism, the treatment medium pH and the intensity of the treatment investigated. *J. Appl. Microbiol.* 99:94–104

Gaunt LF, Beggs CB, Georghiou GE. 2006. Bactericidal action of the reactive species produced by gas-discharge nonthermal plasma at atmospheric pressure: a review. *IEEE Trans. Plasma Sci.* 34:1257–69

Gerlach D, Alleborn N, Baars A, Delgado A, Moritz J, Knorr D. 2008. Numerical simulations of pulsed electric fields for food preservation: a review. *Innov. Food Sci. Emerg. Technol.* 9:408–17
Gilliland SE, Speck ML. 1967. Inactivation of microorganisms by electrohydraulic shock. *Appl. Microbiol.* 15:1031–37
Goldston RJ, Rutherford PH. 1997. *Introduction to Plasma Physics*. Bristol, UK: Inst. Phys. Publ.
Gomez Galindo F, Wadsö L, Vicente A, Dejmek P. 2008. Exploring metabolic responses of potato tissue induced by electric pulses. *Food Biophys.* 3:352–60
Grahl T, Märkl H. 1996. Killing of microorganisms by pulsed electric fields. *Appl. Microbiol. Biotechnol.* 45:148–57
Grauwet T, Van der Plancken I, Vervoort L, Hendrickx M, Van Loey A. 2010. Solvent engineering as a tool in enzymatic indicator development for mild high pressure pasteurization processing. *J. Food Eng.* 97:301–10
Grimi N, Mamouni F, Lebovka N, Vorobiev E, Vaxelaire J. 2010. Acoustic impulse response in apple tissues treated by pulsed electric field. *Biosyst. Eng.* 105:266–72
Grzegorzewski F, Rohn S, Kroh LW, Geyer M, Schlüter O. 2010a. Surface morphology and chemical composition of lamb's lettuce (*Valerianella locusta*) after exposure to a low-pressure oxygen plasma. *Food Chem.* 122:1145–52
Grzegorzewski F, Rohn S, Quade A, Schröder K, Ehlbeck J, et al. 2010b. Reaction chemistry of 1,4-benzopyrone derivates in non-equilibrium low-temperature plasmas. *Plasma Process. Polym.* 7(6):466–73
Gudmundsson M, Hafsteinsson H. 2001. Effect of electric field pulses on microstructure of muscle foods and roes. *Food Sci. Technol.* 12:122–28
Guerrero-Beltrán J, Sepulveda DR, Góngora-Nieto MM, Swanson B, Barbosa-Cánovas GV. 2010. Milk thermization by pulsed electric fields (PEF) and electrically induced heat. *J. Food Eng.* 100:56–60
Han Z, Zeng X-A, Zhang B-S, Yu S-J. 2009a. Effects of pulsed electric fields (PEF) treatment on the properties of corn starch. *J. Food Eng.* 93:318–23
Han Z, Zeng XA, Yu SJ, Zhang BS, Chen XD. 2009b. Effects of pulsed electric fields (PEF) treatment on physicochemical properties of potato starch. *Innov. Food Sci. Emerg. Technol.* 10:481–85
Harvey EN, Loomis AL. 1929. The destruction of luminous bacteria by high frequency sound waves. *J. Bacteriol.* 17:373–76
Hayashi N, Kawaguchi R, Liu H. 2009. *Treatment of Protein Using Oxygen Plasma Produced by RF Discharge*. Presented at 14th Int. Congr. Plasma Phys. (ICPP2008), J. of Plasma Fusion Res. SERIES
Heinz V, Knoch A, Lickert T. 2009. Product innovation by high pressure processing. *New Food* 2:43–44
Heinz V, Knorr D. 1996. High pressure inactivation kinetics of *Bacillus subtilis* cells by a three-state-model considering distribution resistance mechanisms. *Food Biotechnol.* 10:149–61
Heinz V, Kortschack F. 2002. *Germany Patent No. WO 02/49460*
Hendrickx M, Knorr D. 2002. *Ultra High Pressure Treatment of Foods*. New York: Kluwer Acad./Plenum Publ.
Heremans R, Smeller L. 1998. Protein structure and dynamics at high pressure. *Biochim. Biophys. Acta* 1386:353–70
Hite BH. 1899. The effect of pressure in the preservation of milk: a preliminary report. *West Va. Agr. Exp. Stat. Bull.* 58:15–35
Ho SY, Mittal GS, Cross JD, Griffith MW. 1995. Inactivation of *Pseudomonas fluorescens* by high voltage electric pulses. *J. Food Sci.* 60:1337–40
Huang K, Wang J. 2009. Designs of pulsed electric fields treatment chambers for liquid foods pasteurization process: a review. *J. Food Eng.* 95:227–39
Hughes DE, Nyborg WL. 1962. Cell disruption by ultrasound: streaming and other activity around sonically induced bubbles is a cause of damage to living cells. *Science* 138:108–14
Isbarn S, Buckow R, Himmelreich A, Lehmacher A, Heinz V. 2007. Inactivation of avian influenza virus by heat and high hydrostatic pressure. *J. Food Prot.* 70:667–73
Jadhav D, Rekha BN, Gogate PR, Rathod VK. 2009. Extraction of vanillin from vanilla pods: a comparison study of conventional soxhlet and ultrasound assisted extraction. *J. Food Eng.* 93:421–26
Jaeger H, Meneses N, Knorr D. 2009a. Impact of PEF treatment inhomogeneity such as electric field distribution, flow characteristics and temperature effects on the inactivation of *E. coli* and milk alkaline phosphatase. *Innov. Food Sci. Emerg. Technol.* 10:470–80

Jaeger H, Meneses N, Knorr D. 2009b. *Pulsed Electric Field Preservation of Heat Sensitive Products—Food Safety and Qualtiy Aspects*. Presented at Int. Conf. on Bio- and Food Electrotechnol., Compiegne, France

Jaeger H, Meneses N, Moritz J, Knorr D. 2010. Model for the differentiation of temperature and electric field effects during thermal assisted PEF processing. *J. Food Eng.* 100:109–18

Jaeger H, Schulz A, Karapetkov N, Knorr D. 2009c. Protective effect of milk constituents and sublethal injuries limiting process effectiveness during PEF inactivation of *Lb. rhamnosus*. *Int. J. Food Microbiol.* 134:154–61

Jafari SM, He Y, Bhandari B. 2007. Production of submicron emulsions by ultrasound and microfluidization techniques. *J. Food Eng.* 82:478–88

Jambrak AR, Lelas V, Mason TJ, Kresic G, Badanjak M. 2009. Physical properties of ultrasound treated soy proteins. *J. Food Eng.* 93:386–93

Jambrak AR, Mason TJ, Paniwnyk L, Lelas V. 2007. Ultrasonic effect on pH, electric conductivity and tissue surface of button mushrooms, brussels sprouts and cauliflower. *Czech J. Food Sci.* 25:90–100

Johnston DE, Austin BA, Murphy RJ. 1993. Properties of acid-set gels prepared from high-pressure treated skim milk. *Milchwissenschaft* 48:206–9

Keener KM. 2008. Atmospheric non-equilibrium plasma. *Encycl. Agric. Food Biol. Eng.* 1:1–5

Kelly-Wintenberg K, Hodge A, Montie TC, Deleanu L, Sherman D, et al. 1999. Use of a one atmosphere uniform glow discharge plasma to kill a broad spectrum of microorganisms. *J. Vac. Sci. Technol. A: Vac. Surf. Films* 17(4):1539–44

Kinsloe H, Ackermann E, Reid JJ. 1954. Exposure of microorganisms to measured sound fields. *J. Bacteriol.* 68:373–80

Knorr D, Ade-Omowaye BIO, Heinz V. 2002. Nutritional improvement of plant foods by nonthermal processing. *Proc. Nutr. Soc.* 61:311–18

Knorr D, Engel K-H, Vogel R, Kochte-Clemens B, Eisenbrand G. 2008. Statement on the treatment of food using a pulsed electric field. *Mol. Nutr. Food Res.* 52:1539–42

Knorr D, Heinz V, Buckow R. 2006. High pressure application for food biopolymers. *Biochim. Biophys. Acta* 1764:619–31

Knorr D, Schlüter O, Heinz V. 1998. Impact of high hydrostatic pressure on phase transitions of foods. *Food Technol.* 52:42–45

Knorr D, Zenker M, Heinz V, Lee D-U. 2004. Applications and potential of ultrasonics in food processing. *Trends Food Sci. Technol.* 15:261–66

Kolb JF, Mohamed AAH, Price RO, Swanson RJ, Bowman A, et al. 2008. Cold atmospheric pressure air plasma jet for medical applications. *Appl. Phys. Lett.* 92

Krupp. 1988. Fish processing by the Elcrack process. *Brochure Krupp Maschinentechnik GmbH.* Hamburg, Germany

Laroussi M. 2005. Low temperature plasma-based sterilization: overview and state-of-the-art. *Plasma Process. Polym.* 2:391–400

LeBail A, Chevalier D, Mussa DM, Ghoul M. 2002. High pressure freezing and thawing of foods: a review. *Int. J. Refrigeration* 25:504–13

Lebovka NI, Praporscic I, Vorobiev E. 2004. Effect of moderate thermal and pulsed electric field treatments on textural properties of carrots, potatoes and apples. *Innov. Food Sci. Emerg. Technol.* 5:9–16

Lee H, Zhou B, Liang W, Feng H, Martin SE. 2009. Inactivation of *Escherichia coli* cells with sonication, manosonication, thermosonication, and manothermosonication: microbial responses and kinetics modeling. *J. Food Eng.* 93:354–64

Leemans V, Destain M-F. 2009. Ultrasonic internal defect detection in cheese. *J. Food Eng.* 90:333–40

Lelieveld HLM, Notermans S, de Haan SWH, eds. 2007. *Food Preservation by Pulsed Electric Fields*. Abington, UK: Woodhead Publ.

Li H, Pordesimo L, Weiss J. 2004. High intensity ultrasound-assisted extraction of oil from soybeans. *Food Res. Int.* 37:731–38

Li S-Q, Bomser JA, Zhang QH. 2005. Effects of pulsed electric fields and heat treatment on stability and secondary structure of bovine immunoglobulin G. *J. Agric. Food Chem.* 53:663–70

Lindgren M, Aronsson K, Galt S, Ohlsson T. 2002. Simulation of the temperature increase in pulsed electric field (PEF) continuous flow treatment chambers. *Innov. Food Sci. Emerg. Technol.* 3:233–45

López-Fandino R, Carrascosa AV, Olano A. 1996. The effects of high pressure on whey protein denaturation and cheese making properties of raw milk. *J. Dairy Sci.* 79:929–36

Ludikhuyze L, Van Loey A, Indrawati, Denys S, Hendrickx M. 2002. Effects of high pressure on enzymes related to food quality. In *Ultra High Pressure Treatments of Food*, ed. M Hendrickx, D Knorr, pp. 115–66. New York: Kluwer Acad./Plenum Publ.

Marco-Moles R, Perez-Munuera I, Quiles A, Hernando I. 2009. Effect of pulsed electric fields on the main chemical components of liquid egg and stability at 4°C. *Czech J. Food Sci.* 27:109–12

Margosch D, Ehrmann MA, Buckow R, Heinz V, Vogel RF, Gänzle MG. 2006. High-pressure-mediated survival of *Clostridium botulinum* and *Bacillus amyloliquefaciens* endospores at high temperature. *Appl. Environ. Microb.* 72(5):3476–81

Martín-Belloso O, Elez-Martínez P. 2005. *Enzymatic Inactivation by Pulsed Electric Fields Emerging Technologies for Food Processing*. ed. D-W Sun, pp. 155–81. London: Acad.

Mason TJ, Paniwnyk L, Lorimer JP. 1996. The uses of ultrasound in food technology. *Ultrasonics Sonochem. Proc. Symp. Chem. Eff. Ultrasound 1995 Int. Chem. Congr. Pac. Basin Soc.* 3:S253–S60

Mastwijk HC, Nierop Groot MN. 2010. Use of cold plasma in food processing. In *Encyclopedia of Biotechnology in Agriculture and Food*, ed. DR Heldman, A Bridges, DG Hoover, MB Wheeler. New York: Taylor & Francis

Masudo T, Okada T. 2006. Particle separation with ultrasound radiation force. *Curr. Anal. Chem.* 2:213–27

Mathys A. 2008. *Inactivation mechanisms of Geobacillus and Bacillus spores during high pressure thermal sterilization*. Ph.D. thesis. Technische Universität Berlin, Berlin. 162 pp.

Mathys A, Chapman B, Bull M, Heinz V, Knorr D. 2007. Flow cytometric assessment of *Bacillus* spore response to high pressure and heat. *Innov. Food Sci. Emerg. Technol.* 8:519–27

Mathys A, Knorr D. 2009. The properties of water in the pressure-temperature landscape. *Food Biophys.* 4:77–82

Matsuura K, Hirotsune M, Nunokawa Y, Satoh M, Honda K. 1994. Acceleration of cell growth and ester formation by ultrasonic wave irradiation. *J. Ferment. Bioeng.* 77:36–40

Mawson R, Knoerzer K. 2007. *A brief history of the application of ultrasonics in food processing*. Presented at Int. Congr. Acoust., 19th, Madrid

Michel M, Autio K. 2002. Effects of high pressure on protein- and polysaccharide-based structures. In *Ultra High Pressure Treatments of Foods*, ed. MEG Hendrickx, D Knorr, pp. 189–214. New York: Kluwer Acad.

Moisan M, Barbeau J, Moreau S, Pelletier J, Tabrizian M, Yahia LH. 2001. Low-temperature sterilization using gas plasmas: a review of the experiments and an analysis of the inactivation mechanisms. *Int. J. Pharmaceutics* 226:1–21

Molina-Gutierrez A, Stippl V, Delgado A, Gaenzle MG, Vogel RF. 2002. In situ determination of the intracellular pH of *Lactococcus lactis* and *Lactobacillus plantarum* during pressure treatment. *Appl. Environ. Microbiol.* 68:4399–406

Montie TC, Kelly-Wintenberg K, Roth JR. 2000. An overview of research using the one atmosphere uniform glowdischarge plasma (OAUGDP) for sterilization of surfaces and materials. *IEEE Trans. Plasma Sci.* 28:41–50

Moreau M, Orange N, Feuilloley MGJ. 2008. Non-thermal plasma technologies: new tools for biodecontamination. *Biotechnol. Adv.* 26:610–17

Morren J, Roodenburg B, de Haan SWH. 2003. Electrochemical reactions and electrode corrosion in pulsed electric field (PEF) treatment chambers. *Innov. Food Sci. Emerg. Technol.* 4:285–95

Mousavi SAAA, Feizi H, Madoliat R. 2007. Investigations on the effects of ultrasonic vibrations in the extrusion process. *J. Mater. Process. Technol.* 187–188:657–61

Niemira BA, Sites J. 2008. Cold plasma inactivates *Salmonella* stanley and *Escherichia coli* O157: H7 inoculated on Golden Delicious apples. *J. Food Prot.* 71:1357–65

Niven GW, Miles CA, Mackey BM. 1999. The effects of hydrostatic pressure on ribosome conformation in *Escherichia coli*: an in vivo study using differential scanning calorimetry. *Microbiology* 145:419–25

Oey I, Verlinde P, Hendrickx M, Van Loey A. 2006. Temperature and pressure stability of l -ascorbic acid and/or [6s] 5-methyltetrahydrofolic acid: a kinetic study. *Eur. Food Res. Technol.* 223:71–77

Ohshima T, Tamura T, Sato M. 2006. Influence of electric field on various enzyme activities. *J. Electrost.* 65:156–61

Pandolf WD. 1998. High-pressure homogenization: latest technology expands performance and product possibilities. *Chem. Process.* 61:39–43

Pangu GD, Feke DL. 2004. Acoustically aided separation of oil droplets from aqueous emulsions. *Chem. Eng. Sci.* 59:3183–93

Paquin P. 1999. Technological properties of high-pressure homogenizers: the effect of fat globules, milk proteins and polysaccharides. *Int. Dairy J.* 9:329–35

Park BJ, Takatori K, Sugita-Konishi Y, Kim IH, Lee MH, et al. 2007. Degradation of mycotoxins using microwave-induced argon plasma at atmospheric pressure. *Surf. Coatings Technol.* 201:5733–37

Patist A, Bates D. 2008. Ultrasonic innovations in the food industry: from the laboratory to commercial production. *Innov. Food Sci. Emerg. Technol. Food Innov.: Emerg. Sci., Technol. Appl. (FIESTA) Conf.* 9:147–54

Patterson MF, Linton M, Doona CJ. 2007. Introduction to high pressure processing of foods. In *High Pressure Processing of Foods*, ed. CJ Doona, FE Feeherry, pp. 1–15. New York: Wiley

Perez O, Pilosof AMR. 2004. Pulsed electric field effects on the molecular structure and gelation of ß-lactoglobulin concentrate and egg white. *Food Res. Int.* 37:102–10

Perry RH. 1984. *Perry's Chemical Engineers' Handbook*. Columbus, OH: McGraw-Hill Book Co.

Povey MJW, Mason TJ. 1998. *Ultrasound in Food Processing*. London: Blackie Acad. Prof.

Rademacher B, Hinrichs J. 2006. Effects of high pressure treatment on indigenous enzymes in bovine milk: reaction kinetics, inactivation and potential application. *Int. Dairy J.* 16:655–61

Ragni L, Berardinelli A, Vannini L, Montanari C, Sirri F, et al. 2010. Non-thermal atmospheric gas plasma device for surface decontamination of shell eggs. *J. Food Eng.* 100:125–32

Rapeanu G, Van Loey A, Smout C, Hendrickx M. 2005. Thermal and high-pressure inactivation kinetics of polyphenol oxidase in Victoria grape must. *J. Agric. Food Chem.* 58:2988–94

Raso J, Heinz V, eds. 2006. *Pulsed Electric Fields Technology for the Food Industry*. Heidelberg: Springer Verlag. 245 pp.

Rastogi NK, Raghavarao KSM, Balasubramaniam VM, Niranjan K, Knorr D. 2007. Opportunities and challenges in high pressure processing of foods. *Crit. Rev. Food Sci. Nutr.* 47:1–44

Reineke K, Mathys A, Heinz V, Knorr D. 2008. Temperature control for high pressure processes up to 1400 MPa. *J. Phys.: Conf. Series* 121:142012–16

Riahi E, Ramaswamy HS. 2004. High pressure inactivation kinetics of amylase in apple juice. *J. Food Eng.* 64:151–60

Roberts RT. 1992. High intensity ultrasonics. In *The Chemistry of Muscle-based Foods*, ed. DE Johnston, MK Knight, DA Ledward, pp. 287–97. Cambridge, UK: R. Soc. Chem.

Rodrigoa D, Cortésb C, Clynenc C, Schoofsc L, Van Loeya A, Hendrickx M. 2006. Thermal and high-pressure stability of purified polygalacturonase and pectinmethylesterase from four different tomato processing varieties. *Food Res. Int.* 39:440–48

Roodenburg B, Morren J, Berg HE, de Haan SWH. 2005. Metal release in a stainless steel pulsed electric field system. Part I. Effect of diferent pulse shapes; theory and experimental method. *Innov. Food Sci. Emerg. Technol.* 6:327–36

Roth JR. 1995. *Industrial Plasma Engineering, Volume 1: Principles*. Bristol and Philadelphia: Inst. Phys. Publ.

Rovere P. 2002. Industrial-scale high pressure processing of foods. In *Ultra High Pressure Treatments of Foods*, ed. MEG Hendrickx, D Knorr, pp. 251–68. New York: Kluwer Acad./Plenum Publ.

Rubin MB. 2001. The history of ozone. Theschönbein period, 1839–1868. *Bull. Hist. Chem.* 26(1):40–56

Rumpold BA. 2005. *Impact of High Hydrostatic Pressure on Wheat, Tapioca, and Potato Starches*. Berlin: Berlin Univ. Technol. pp. 1–120

Russel NJ, Colley M, Simpson RK, Trivett AJ, Evans RI. 2000. Mechanism of action of pulsed high electric field (PHEF) on the membranes of food-poisoning bacteria is an "all-or-nothing" effect. *Int. J. Food Microbiol.* 55:133–36

Rutscher A. 2008. Characteristics of low-temperature plasmas under nonthermal conditions: a short summary. In *Low Temperature Plasmas: Fundamentals, Technologies, and Techniques*, ed. R Hippler, H Kersten, M Schmidt, KH Schoenbach, pp. 1–14. Weinheim: Wiley-VCH Verlag GmbH & Co KGaA

Sale AJ, Hamilton WA. 1967. Effect of high electric fields on micro-organisms. I. Killing of bacteria and yeast. II. Mechanism of action of the lethal effect. *Biochim. Biophys. Acta* 148:781–800

Sampedro F, Rivas A, Rodrigo D, Martinez A, Rodrigo M. 2006. Effect of temperature and substrate on Pef inactivation of *Lactobacillus plantarum* in an orange juice-milk beverage. *Eur. Food Res. Technol.* 223:30–34

Saulis G, Lape R, Praneviciute R, Mickevicius D. 2005. Changes of the solution pH due to exposure by high-voltage electric pulses. *Bioelectrochemistry* 67:101–8

Schlueter O. 2004. *Impact of High Pressure: Low Temperature Processes on Cellular Materials Related to Foods*. Berlin: Technische Universität Berlin. 172 pp.

Schubring R, Meyer C, Schlüter O, Boguslawski S, Knorr D. 2003. Impact of high pressure assisted thawing on the quality of fillets from various fish species. *Innovative Food Sci. Emerg. Technol.* 4:257–67

Schuten H, Gulfo-van Beusekom K, Pol I, Mastwijk H, Bartels P. 2004. *Enzymatic stability of PEF processed orange juice*. Presented at Safe Consort. Semin.: Nov. Preserv. Technol. Relat. Food Saf., Brussels, Belgium

Schwabedissen A, Lacinski P, Chen X, Engemann J. 2007. PlasmaLabel: a new method to disinfect goods inside a closed package using dielectric barrier discharges. *Contrib. Plasma Phys.* 47:551–58

Selcuk M, Oksuz L, Basaran P. 2008. Decontamination of grains and legumes infected with *Aspergillus* spp. and *Penicillum* spp. by cold plasma treatment. *Bioresour. Technol.* 99:5104–09

Sharma A, Yadav BS. 2008. Resistant starch: physiological roles and food applications. *Food Rev. Int.* 24:193–234

Shashurin A, Keidar M, Bronnikov S, Jurjus RA, Stepp MA. 2008. Living tissue under treatment of cold plasma atmospheric jet. *Appl. Phys. Lett.* 93:18501

Simal S, Benedito J, Sánchez ES, Rosselló C. 1998. Use of ultrasound to increase mass transport rates during osmotic dehydration. *J. Food Eng.* 36:323–36

Simpson RK, Whittington R, Earnshaw RG, Russell NJ. 1999. Pulsed high electric field causes "all or nothing" membrane damage in *Listeria* monocytogenes and *Salmonella typhimurium*, but membrane H+-ATPase is not a primary target. *Int. J. Food Microbiol.* 48:1–10

Sinisterra JV. 1992. Application of ultrasound to biotechnology: an overview. *Ultrasonics* 30:180–85

Smeller L. 2002. Pressure-temperature phase diagram of biomolecules. *Biochim. Biophys. Acta* 1595:11–29

Smeller L, Fidy J. 2002. The enzyme horseradish peroxidase is less compressible at higher pressures. *Biophys. J.* 82:426–36

Smelt JP, Hellemons JC, Patterson M. 2001. Effects of high pressure on vegetative microorganisms. In *Ultra High Pressure Treatments of Foods*, ed. M Hendrickx, D Knorr, pp. 55–76. New York: Kluwer Acad.

Somolinos M, García D, Mañas P, Condón S, Pagán R. 2008a. Effect of environmental factors and cell physiological state on pulsed electric fields resistance and repair capacity of various strains of *Escherichia coli*. *Int. J. Food Microbiol.* 124:260–67

Somolinos M, Mañas P, Condón S, Pagán R, García D. 2008b. Recovery of *Saccharomyces cerevisiae* sublethally injured cells after pulsed electric fields. *Int. J. Food Microbiol.* 125:352–56

Stoffels E, Sakiyama Y, Graves DB. 2008. Cold atmospheric plasma: charged species and their interactions with cells and tissues. *IEEE Trans. Plasma Sci.* 36:1441–57

Stojanovic J, Silva JL. 2006. Influence of osmoconcentration, continuous high-frequency ultrasound and dehydration on properties and microstructure of rabbiteye blueberries. *Drying Technol.: Int. J.* 24:165–71

Sui Q, Roginski H, Williams RPW, Versteeg C, Wan J. 2010. Effect of pulsed electric field and thermal treatment on the physicochemical properties of lactoferrin with different iron saturation levels. *Int. Dairy J.* In press

Suslick KS. 2003. Sonochemistry. In *Comprehensive Coordination Chemistry* II. ed. JA McCleverty, TJ Meyer, pp. 731–39. Oxford: Pergamon

Tauscher B. 1995. Pasteurization of food by hydrostatic high pressure: chemical aspects. *Lebensm.-Unters. Forsch.* 200(1):3–13

Ting C-H, Kuo F-J, Lien C-C, Sheng C-T. 2009. Use of ultrasound for characterising the gelation process in heat induced $CaSO_4 \cdot 2H_2O$ tofu curd. *J. Food Eng.* 93:101–7

Ting E, Balasubramaniam VM, Raghubeer E. 2002. Determining thermal effects in high pressure processing. *J. Food Technol.* 56:31–35

Tintchev F. 2007. *Sensorische veränderungen von schweine und geflügelfleisch durch hochdruck und temperatur*. Diploma thesis. Berlin University of Technology, Berlin. 128 pp.

Tiwari BK, O'Donnell CP, Cullen PJ. 2009. Effect of sonication on retention of anthocyanins in blackberry juice. *J. Food Eng.* 93:166–71

Toepfl S. 2006. *Pulsed electric fields (PEF) for permeabilization of cell membranes in food and bioprocessing: applications, process and equipment design and cost analysis*. PhD thesis. University of Technology, Berlin. 180 pp.

Toepfl S, Heinz V. 2007. Application of pulsed electric fields to improve mass transfer in dry cured meat products. *Fleischwirtschaft Int.* 22:62–64

Toepfl S, Heinz V, Knorr D. 2007. High intensity pulsed electric fields applied for food preservation. *Chem. Eng. Process.* 46:537–46

Toepfl S, Mathys A, Heinz V, Knorr D. 2006. Review: potential of high hydrostatic pressure and pulsed electric fields for energy efficient and environmentally friendly food processing. *Food Rev. Int.* 22:405–23

Tryfona T, Bustard MT. 2008. Impact of pulsed electric fields on *Corynebacterium glutamicum* cell membrane permeabilization. *J. Biosci. Bioeng.* 105:375–82

Tsong TY. 1990. Electrical modulation of membrane-proteins: enforced conformational oscillations and biological energy and signal transductions. *Annu. Rev. Biophys. Biophys. Chem.* 19:83–106

Tsong TY. 1996. Electrically stimulated membrane breakdown. In *Electrical Manipulation of Cells*, ed. PT Lynch, MR Davey, pp. 15–36. New York: Chapman & Hall

Ulmer HM, Herberhold H, Fahsel S, Gänzle MG, Winter R, Vogel RF. 2002. Effects of pressure-induced membrane phase transitions on inactivation of HorA, an ATP-dependent multidrug resistance transporter, in *Lactobacillus plantarum*. *Appl. Environ. Microbiol.* 68:1088–95

van den Bosch HFM, Morshuis PHF, Smit JJ. 2002. *Temperature distribution in fluids treated by pulsed electric fields*. Presented at Int. Conf. on Dielectr. Liq., Graz, Austria

Van den Broeck I, Ludikhuyze L, Weemaes C, Van Loey A, Hendrickx M. 1998. Kinetics for isobaric-isothermal degradation of l-ascorbic acid. *J. Agric. Food Chem.* 46:2001–6

Van Loey A, Verachtert B, Hendrickx M. 2002. Effects of high electric field pulses on enzymes. *Trends Food Sci. Technol.* 12:94–102

Vercet A, Burgos J, Crelier S, Lopez-Buesa P. 2001. Inactivation of proteases and lipases by ultrasound. *Innovative Food Sci. Emerg. Technol.* 2:139–50

Vercet A, Sánchez C, Burgos J, Montañés L, Lopez Buesa P. 2002. The effects of manothermosonication on tomato pectic enzymes and tomato paste rheological properties. *J. Food Eng.* 53:273–78

Villamiel M, de Jong P. 2000. Influence of high-intensity ultrasound and heat treatment in continuous flow on fat, proteins, and native enzymes of milk. *J. Agric. Food Chem.* 48:472–78

Vimini RJ, Kemp JD, Fox JD. 1983. Effects of low frequency ultrasound on properties of restructured beef rolls. *J. Food Sci.* 48:1572–73

Vleugels M, Shama G, Deng XT, Greenacre E, Brocklehurst T, Kong MG. 2005. Atmospheric plasma inactivation of biofilm-forming bacteria for food safety control. *IEEE Trans. Plasma Sci.* 33:824–28

Vorobiev E, Lebovka N, eds. 2008. *Electrotechnologies for Extraction from Plant Foods and Biomaterials*. New York: Springer. 272 pp.

Walkling-Ribeiro M, Noci F, Cronin DA, Lyng JG, Morgan DJ. 2008. Inactivation of *Escherichia coli* in a tropical fruit smoothie by a combination of heat and pulsed electric fields. *J. Food Sci.* 73:M395–99

Wan J, Coventry J, Swiergon P, Sanguansri P, Versteeg C. 2009. Advances in innovative processing technologies for microbial inactivation and enhancement of food safety--pulsed electric field and low-temperature plasma. *Trends Food Sci. Technol.* 20:414–24

Weemaes CA, Ludikhuyze L, Van den Broeck I, Hendrickx M. 1998. Effect of pH on pressure and thermal inactivation of avocado polyphenol oxidase: a kinetic study. *J. Agric. Food Chem.* 46:2785–92

Weltmann K-D, Kindel E, Brandenburg R, Meyer C, Bussiahn R, et al. 2009. Atmospheric pressure plasma jet for medical therapy: plasma parameters and risk estimation. *Contrib. Plasma Phys.* 49:631–40

Weltmann KD, Brandenburg R, von Woedtke T, Ehlbeck J, Foest R, et al. 2008. Antimicrobial treatment of heat sensitive products by miniaturized atmospheric pressure plasma jets (APPJs). *J. Phys. D: Appl. Phys.* 41:194008

Winter R. 1996. High pressure effects on the structure and mesophase behaviour of supramolecular lipid aggregates and model membrane systems. *Prog. Biotechnol.* 13:21–28

Wouters PC, Alvarez I, Raso J. 2001. Critical factors determining inactivation kinetics by pulsed electric field food processing. *Trends Food Sci. Technol.* 12:112–21

Wu H, Hulbert GJ, Mount JR. 2000. Effects of ultrasound on milk homogenization and fermentation with yogurt starter. *Innovative Food Sci. Emerg. Technol.* 1:211–18

Yaldagard M, Mortazavi SA, Tabatabaie F. 2008. The principles of ultra high pressure technology and its application in food processing/preservation: a review of microbiological and quality aspects. *Afr. J. Biotechnol.* 7:2739–67

Yang RJ, Li SQ, Zhang QH. 2004. Effects of pulsed electric fields on the activity of enzymes in aqueous solution. *J. Food Sci.* 69:241–48

Zeece M, Huppertz T, Kelly A. 2008. Effect of high pressure treatment on in vitro digestibility of beta-lactoglobulin. *Innovative Food Sci. Emerg. Technol.* 9:62–69

Zeng X-A, Han Z, Zi Z-h. 2010. Effects of pulsed electric field treatments on quality of peanut oil. *Food Control* 21:611–14

Zenker M, Heinz V, Knorr D. 2003. Application of ultrasound-assisted thermal processing for preservation and quality retention of liquid foods. *J. Food Prot.* 66:1642–49

Zhang G, Sofyan M, Hamaker BR. 2008. Slowly digestible state of starch: mechanism of slow digestion property of gelatinized maize starch. *J. Agric. Food Chem.* 56:4695–702

Zheng L, Sun D-W. 2006. Innovative applications of power ultrasound during food freezing processes—a review. *Trends Food Sci. Technol.* 17:16–23

Zimmermann U, Pilwat G, Riemann F. 1974. Dielectric breakdown in cell membranes. *Biophys. J.* 14:881–99

Zipp A, Kauzmann W. 1973. Pressure denaturation of metmyoglobin. *Biochemistry* 12:4217–28

Food Components with Anti-Obesity Effect

Kee-Hong Kim[1] and Yeonhwa Park[2]

[1]Department of Food Science, Purdue University, West Lafayette, Indiana 47907; email: keehong@purdue.edu

[2]Department of Food Science, University of Massachusetts, Amherst, Massachusetts 01003; email: ypark@foodsci.umass.edu

Annu. Rev. Food Sci. Technol. 2011. 2:237–57

First published online as a Review in Advance on November 19, 2010

The *Annual Review of Food Science and Technology* is online at food.annualreviews.org

This article's doi: 10.1146/annurev-food-022510-133656

1941-1413/11/0410-0237$20.00

Keywords

energy balance, food intake, energy expenditure, thermogenesis, adipogenesis

Abstract

Although many food components are reportedly beneficial to body-weight management, lack of understanding of molecular mechanisms and their function in overall adiposity under physiological conditions hinders successful and safe development of antiobesity functional foods. A positive energy balance resulting from an increase in food intake, a reduced energy expenditure, and/or dysfunction of adipose biology is associated with the development of obesity. This article provides an overview of the components involved in energy balance and adipose development and function. There is evidence that numerous ingredients found in foods can modulate energy balance and adipose biology, thereby potentially lowering adiposity.

INTRODUCTION

BMI: body-mass index

Obesity confers an adverse effect on health and is recognized as a leading global health concern. It is a disease associated with accumulation of an excess amount of body fat. Body fat can be easily measured by a formula called body-mass index (BMI), which combines weight and height with an assumption of a cylindrical shape of the whole body with uniform density. According to guidelines from the World Health Organization (WHO), overweight in adults is defined as a BMI of 25.0 to 29.9, and obesity is defined as a BMI of 30.0 or higher (World Health Report 2002). Obesity in adults has dramatically increased in every continent. The National Health and Nutrition Examination Survey (NHANES) has shown a striking increase in the prevalence of obesity over time in the United States. The most recent data from the NHANES (2007–2008) show that approximately 32.2% of U.S. men and approximately 35.5% of U.S. women are obese (Ogden et al. 2010). Of these, African-American adults had the highest rates of obesity, followed by Mexican-Americans and Caucasians. In Europe, a recent epidemiological study revealed that the prevalence of obesity ranged from 4.0% to 28.3% and 6.2% to 36.5% in men and women, respectively, depending on geographic location, with higher prevalence in Central, Eastern, and Southern Europe (Berghofer et al. 2008). A dramatic increase in overweight and obesity prevalence was also observed in mainland China. In 2002, the prevalence of overweight and obesity in Chinese adults was 22.8% and 7.1%, respectively, which was an increase of 40.7% and 97.2%, respectively, over 1992 (Chen 2008).

The increasing prevalence of obesity is not confined only to adults. The most recent data from the NHANES show that childhood obesity in the United States has tripled since 1980. However, it seems to have remained steady with no decrease during the past 10 years. In 2007–2008, almost 12% of children in the United States were reported to be obese (Ogden et al. 2010). In Europe, in 2006, 31.8% of school-aged children were either overweight or obese, with 7.9% of children being obese (Fussenegger et al. 2008). Similarly, more than 29% of boys and 17% of girls in China were reported to be overweight or obese in 2000 (Chen 2008). A rapidly increasing population of overweight children has been observed in many countries, and the overweight children are likely to remain obese in their adulthood.

Obesity is associated with an increased risk of chronic diseases such as type 2 diabetes and coronary heart disease (Semenkovich 2006, Weyer et al. 2000), suggesting the importance of body fat as a contributor to these diseases. Previous studies demonstrated that specific nutrients in diets and foods might play an important role in body-weight management and controlling obesity-associated diabetes (Ludwig et al. 1999, Tuomilehto et al. 2001). These studies suggest that some bioactive food components are effective for prevention of obesity and its related health complications.

This review provides an overview of the biological function of the components involved in energy balance, as well as adipose development and function. This review also investigates evidence of the effect of bioactive food components and their mode of action in regulating body fat gain and obesity, and focuses on directions for future work toward dietary prevention of obesity.

ENERGY BALANCE AND OBESITY

Obesity is influenced by an interaction between genetic, environmental, and psychosocial factors, which together contribute to alteration of the energy balance equation (the balance between energy intake and expenditure) (Kopelman 2000). Although genetic factors certainly play an important role in determining genetic susceptibility to obesity within a population, the dramatic increase in the prevalence of obesity in recent years suggests the involvement of nongenetic factors, such as environmental and psychosocial factors, in changes in energy balance. Examples of these include an increase in energy density in diet by having refined foods with more simple sugars and less fiber, and/or increased fat content due to urbanization and economic development. This is usually accompanied by an altered eating behavior that includes consuming more processed foods and beverages, and consuming less whole grains, fruits, and vegetables (Gardner & Rhodes 2009).

CNS: central nervous system

CCK: cholecystokinin

GLP-1: glucagon-like peptide-1

PYY: peptide YY

The energy balance equation represents a balanced conversion of food and oxygen to carbon dioxide, water, heat, and work in the body. Obesity develops when energy intake, in the form of feeding, exceeds energy expenditure, which consists of physical activity, basal metabolism, and adaptive thermogenesis. The result is storage of excess energy in adipose tissue. Accordingly, prevention of obesity could be achieved through modulating energy balance by lowering energy intake or increasing energy expenditure. Moreover, inhibition of accumulation of excess energy storage in adipose tissue could also attribute to reducing the incidence of obesity. However, our understanding of the regulation of energy balance and adipose function by bioactive food components is poor. Thus, this review first focuses on the critical details about the molecular and biochemical basis of food intake, energy expenditure, and adipose function in obesity. The effects of some dietary components on energy balance and adipose function are discussed later in the review.

Regulation of Energy Intake by Peptides and Hormones

The regulation of energy intake through an appetite-mediated central network in the hypothalamus has been extensively reviewed (Schwartz et al. 2000, Woods & D'Alessio 2008). Briefly, signaling peptides produced from peripheral tissues such as adipose tissue, pancreas, and gut are known to link peripheral adiposity and energy homeostasis to central nervous system (CNS)-regulated food intake. The following are important signaling molecules affecting central control of energy intake and energy balance: leptin secreted from adipocytes; insulin secreted from the pancreas; and cholecystokinin (CCK), glucagon-like peptide-1 (GLP-1), peptide YY (PYY), and ghrelin secreted from the gastrointestinal tract (**Table 1**).

Leptin was the first hormone discovered that links energy storage in adipocytes to negative feedback regulation of food intake in brain, specifically the hypothalamus (Zhang et al. 1994). Given that leptin is largely produced from adipose tissue, its plasma level is proportional to total body fat content (Considine et al. 1996, Schwartz et al. 1996). The interaction between leptin and the hypothalamic leptin receptor is reported to facilitate leptin uptake and its food intake

Table 1 Peptides/hormones implicated in the regulation of energy balance

Molecule	Produced by	Function(s) in energy balance
CCK	Intestine (mucosa)	Lowering food intake
GLP-1	Pancreas, intestine, brainstem	Lowering food intake, appetite and body weight gain
PYY	Intestine	Lowering food intake
Ghrelin	Stomach	Stimulating appetite and food intake
Leptin	Adipose tissue	Lowering food intake
Insulin	Pancreatic β-cells	Lowering food intake and stimulating energy expenditure
NPY	Brain (hypothalamus)	Stimulating food intake and lowering energy expenditure
α-MSH	Pituitary gland	Lowering food intake
AgRP	Brain (hypothalamus)	Stimulating food intake and lowering energy expenditure
Adiponectin	Adipose tissue	Stimulating food intake and lowering energy expenditure (during fasting)

AgRP: agouti-related peptide

NPY: neuropeptide Y

POMC: prepropeptide proopiomelanocortin

regulation in the brain (Tartaglia et al. 1995). This is through leptin-induced cleavage of prepropeptide proopiomelanocortin (POMC) to form α-melanocyte-stimulating hormone (α-MSH), whose binding to melanocortin receptors is known to trigger the catabolic pathway and a decrease in food intake (Schwartz et al. 2000). Conversely, a reduced level of circulating leptin contributes to increasing hyperphagia and body fat by leptin deficiency–activated hypothalamic agouti-related peptide (AgRP)- and neuropeptide Y (NPY)-dependent anabolic pathways. Simultaneously, the leptin deficiency–induced release of AgRP protein in the hypothalamus suppresses the inhibitory function of POMC in food intake.

The body adiposity is sensed by the pancreatic hormone insulin. The generation and secretion of insulin from pancreatic β-cells are proportional to body fat content and whole body insulin sensitivity (Bagdade et al. 1967). Insulin entering the CNS is also involved in regulating food intake and energy homeostasis through its binding to the insulin receptor located in ARC neurons in the hypothalamus (Benoit et al. 2002, Grossman 1986). Similar to leptin, the catabolic and anabolic action of insulin in the hypothalamus relies upon insulin receptor–mediated activation of POMC neurons and NPY/AgRP neurons, respectively.

It should be noted that although both adiposity hormones leptin and insulin are involved in the central control of energy homeostasis, elevated levels of leptin and its receptor in the brain are likely required for effective regulation of central food intake and energy balance. Accordingly, both the administration of leptin or leptin receptor agonists and the activation of the leptin-sensing POMC pathway in the hypothalamus have been suggested to be useful therapeutic strategies for reduced food intake and obesity prevention. However, because of potential side effects (e.g., psychiatric concerns), few pharmacological treatments are successful in long-term use for body-weight management through central regulation of food intake (Bray 2009). Furthermore, central control of food intake by dietary bioactive components is associated with a number of limitations. These include poor stability and bioavailability during digestion and absorption, and poor blood-brain barrier–penetrating abilities.

The gut is an endocrine organ that synthesizes and releases many peptides that regulate various components, such as the size and the frequency of meals, of energy balance. Therefore, the gut peptides contribute to changes in body weight and ingestive behavior by transmitting endocrine and neural signals to the hypothalamus and brainstem to influence food intake, mainly short-term feelings of hunger and satiety. Among more than 20 well-documented gut hormones that control appetite are CCK, GLP-1, PYY, and ghrelin.

CCK is a satiety hormone released postprandially from the small intestine to inhibit food intake through its binding to the G protein–coupled CCK receptors in the hindbrain, which in turn transfers signals to the hypothalamus for appetite control (Moran 2000, Smith & Gibbs 1975). Beside its effect of lowering food intake, CCK also delays gastric emptying, stimulates secretion of pancreatic digestive enzymes, and contracts the gall bladder in response to nutrients in the gut. Thus, regulation of food intake by CCK and its binding to the CCK receptors might be an attractive idea. However, apparently it is likely to be effective only in short-term control of appetite because a study of continuous infusion of CCK showed little effect on food intake in animals (Crawley & Beinfeld 1983).

GLP-1 is a gene product of preproglucagon that is highly expressed in the pancreas, intestine, and brainstem. A series of proteolytic cleavages is known to facilitate the release of the active form of GLP-1 and other satiety-controlling peptides such as GLP-2 and oxyntomodulin from the preproglucagon (Holst 2004). Secretion of GLP-1 is sensed by nutrient presence, causing both short-term control of appetite and long-term control of body-weight gain through binding to its specific receptor in the pancreas (Drucker 2006). Animal and human studies suggest a potential role of GLP-1 in lowering food intake, appetite, and weight gain (Drucker 2006, Turton et al.

1996). Moreover, a negative correlation between circulating GLP-1 level and adiposity has been observed (Verdich et al. 2001).

PYY is another satiety gut hormone from the same peptide family as NPY (Larhammar 1996). There are two forms of PPY, $PPY_{1\text{-}36}$ and $PPY_{3\text{-}36}$, with the latter being the major form found in circulation (Eberlein et al. 1989). PPY secreted by the gut has been shown to influence gastrointestinal responses similar to CCK. Particularly, low-dose intravenous infusion of PYY is shown to reduce food intake in animals and humans (Batterham et al. 2002, Chelikani et al. 2006).

BMR: basal metabolic rate

UCPs: uncoupling proteins

BAT: brown adipose tissue

Ghrelin is a hormone released from the stomach, and its secretion is increased by fasting. It is known to stimulate appetite (Asakawa et al. 2001, Kojima et al. 1999). Acylation of secreted ghrelin plays a critical role in facilitating its binding to the growth-hormone-secretagogue receptor (GHS-R) in the brain (Kojima et al. 1999). Conversely, impairment of ghrelin gene expression results in reduced food intake and incidence of obesity in animals (Wortley et al. 2005). This hunger hormone might be a useful target for treating obesity because administration and central infusion of ghrelin promote adiposity in experimental animals (Theander-Carrillo et al. 2006, Tschop et al. 2000).

Taken together, any changes in the expression and function of these gut hormones, and in their binding abilities to their specific receptors in CNS, should be considered in developing dietary strategy for the control of appetite. Recent studies have provided evidence that consumption of coffee (Tunnicliffe & Shearer 2008), some isoflavones (Zhang et al. 2009), and fatty acids with various chain length (Poppitt et al. 2010) has a beneficial function in lowering satiety potentially through suppression of satiety hormone release.

Regulation of Energy Expenditure by Uncoupling Proteins

Excess energy entering the body as food should be expended as work or heat in order to maintain energy balance. Basal metabolic rate (BMR), physical exercise, and adaptive thermogenesis are known to contribute to energy expenditure. However, adaptive thermogenesis (i.e., facultative thermogenesis) is important in regulating energy expenditure in response to environmental temperature and food intake. Adaptive thermogenesis activated by cold and diet is believed to be responsible in the mitochondria for combusting stored or excess energy into heat as measured calories. One mechanism underlying mitochondrion-mediated thermogenesis is uncoupling of calorie burning and adenosine triphosphate (ATP) synthesis, resulting in loss of energy as heat. This is through a leakage of protons to the mitochondrial membrane, thereby bypassing ATP synthesis and activation of various mitochondrial inner membrane–bound uncoupling proteins (UCPs) UCP-1 to UCP-5 (Adams et al. 2001). These UCPs are members of the mitochondrial anion carrier superfamily. Although UCP-2 is expressed in various tissues, UCP-1 is expressed mainly in brown adipose tissue (BAT), which is a dark-colored, mitochondrion-rich adipose tissue with an enhanced ability for respiratory uncoupling and adaptive thermogenesis. UCP-3 is highly expressed in BAT and muscle, and UCP-4 and UCP-5 are largely expressed in the CNS (Adams et al. 2001). The role of UCPs in energy expenditure and thermoregulation is known from many studies. For example, mice overexpressing UCP-1 (Li et al. 2000) or UCP-3 (Clapham et al. 2000, Tiraby et al. 2007) were resistant to diet-induced obesity and showed improved insulin sensitivity. Although UCP-1, UCP-2, and UCP-3 knockout mice were not obese, these mice were sensitive to cold and had impaired thermogenesis and/or elevated levels of reactive oxygen species (ROS) (Arsenijevic et al. 2000, Gong et al. 2000). The amount of β-adrenergic receptor-dependent sympathetic nervous system–induced cyclic AMP and elevated levels of free fatty acids in BAT are known to mediate UCP-1-induced thermogenesis. It should be noted that UCP-regulated thermogenesis is also tightly linked to various energy metabolisms such as fatty acid oxidation, mitochondrial biogenesis, and glucose homeostasis (Kozak & Anunciado-Koza 2008, Lowell & Spiegelman 2000). Thus, these studies suggest that physiological activation of UCPs might be beneficial to achieving positive energy expenditure, thereby treating obesity and its related energy disorders.

AMPK: AMP-activated protein kinase

Role of Adipose Tissue in Obesity

Traditionally adipose tissue has been viewed as an energy storage organ. During the past decade, adipose tissue has been recognized as an endocrine tissue. Adipose tissue integrates various homeostatic processes, such as energy balance, through synthesis and secretion of adipose-specific peptide hormones such as leptin, adiponectin, and resistin. Besides its role in the central control of food intake, leptin secreted from adipose tissue also contributes to improving energy homeostasis in peripheral tissues such as the liver and muscle. This occurs by lowering intracellular lipids and improving insulin sensitivity through activation of AMP-activated protein kinase (AMPK)-dependent signaling pathways (Minokoshi et al. 2002). Adipose tissue secreted factor adiponectin, also referred to as ACRP30, adipoQ, and apM1 (**Table 1**) (Yamauchi et al. 2001), regulates both glucose and lipid metabolism. Adiponectin is known to target AMPK activity to decrease gluconeogenesis and increase glucose uptake and fatty acid oxidation in the liver and muscle, resulting in ameliorating insulin sensitivity (Yamauchi et al. 2002). Unlike other adipocyte-secreted peptides, the inverse correlation between circulating adiponectin level and adiposity suggests a possible strategy of stimulating adiponectin secretion in obese and/or diabetic patients. In the CNS, adiponectin and its receptors have been shown to stimulate food intake and decrease energy expenditure through activation of AMPK (Kubota et al. 2007). In addition to leptin and adiponectin, resistin, also referred to as FIZZ3 and adipose-specific secretory factor (ADSF) (Holcomb et al. 2000, Kim et al. 2001, Steppan et al. 2001), is an adipocyte-specific hormone regulated by hormonal and nutritional signals. An elevated level of resistin is associated with adiposity and type 2 diabetes. Although more studies are needed to understand the physiological function of resistin in human obesity, it is suggested that resistin has potential proinflammatory, antiadipogenic, and prodiabetic properties (Kim et al. 2001, Reilly et al. 2005, Steppan et al. 2001). Interestingly, a recent study implicates resistin in hypothalamic control of food intake through inhibiting the hyperphagic effect of NPY (Brown et al. 2009).

Adipose tissue grows by hypertrophy (cell size increase) and hyperplasia (cell number increase). When energy intake exceeds energy expenditure, energy continues to be stored in adipose tissue leading to hypertrophy and weight gain. Adipocyte hypertrophy in turn is known to affect the ability of adipocytes to secrete aforementioned adipose-specific hormones, proinflammatory cytokines, and free fatty acids. These secreted molecules contribute to various physiological processes such as appetite, energy expenditure, and immunity.

Although adipocyte hyperplasia is not necessary to directly promote adiposity, the adipocyte number set during childhood and adolescence is likely to have a dominant role in determining the lipid-storing capacity of adipose tissue and fat mass in adults (Spalding et al. 2008). To increase adipocyte number, mesodermal pluripotent stem cells must commit to the adipocyte lineage before differentiation. These preadipocytes are then subjected to a cellular differentiation process called adipogenesis under appropriate hormonal and nutritional signals. Adipogenesis consists of four major events: (*a*) cell confluence and growth arrest, (*b*) mitotic clonal expansion, (*c*) early transcriptional changes, and (*d*) terminal differentiation (Gregoire et al. 1998). Although it is beyond the scope of this review to discuss the details in each of these events, it should be noted that coordinated regulation of mitotic clonal expansion and early transcriptional changes are critical in determining the effectiveness of adipogenesis. Levels of cell-cycle regulators and cell proliferation–related proteins, and their phosphorylational modification, are known to contribute to cell proliferation, DNA replication, and cell division events that occur during the mitotic clonal expansion phase. Other factors such as insulin, growth hormone, growth factors [e.g., insulin-like growth factor-I (IGF-I), transforming growth factors (TGFs), and epidermal growth factor-I (EGF-I)], glucocorticoids, intracellular cyclic AMP, and related cellular signaling pathways are known to positively or negatively regulate the mitotic clonal expansion phase (Tang et al. 2003). Once mitotic clonal expansion is activated, it triggers a subsequent transcriptional activation of adipogenic transcription factors such as the CCAAT-enhancer-binding proteins (C/EBPs) family and peroxisome proliferator-activator receptor γ (PPARγ), which orchestrates transactivation of adipocyte genes involved in cell morphological change, lipid metabolism, and synthesis of adipocyte-specific peptides and cytokines during terminal differentiation. C/EBPβ and, to a lesser extent, C/EBPδ are known to be acutely expressed upon initiation of adipogenesis, which is required for subsequent expression of PPARγ and C/EBPα in differentiating adipocytes (Rosen & MacDougald 2006). Thus, C/EBPβ is considered to be the key transcription factor that initiates the transcriptional cascade of adipogenesis through stimulation of C/EBPα and PPARγ function during the terminal stage of adipogenesis.

C/EBPs: CCAAT-enhancer-binding proteins

PPARγ: peroxisome proliferator-activator receptor γ

It is believed that modulation of cellular and molecular events in adipogenesis could serve as an effective means to control body-weight gain and obesity. However, it should be recognized that inhibiting only adipogenesis without affecting whole body energy balance could possibly contribute to adipocyte hypertrophy and/or redistribution of body fat into nonadipose peripheral tissues in physiological conditions. This would be detrimental to control of obesity and its related diseases. Therefore, other approaches to increase energy expenditure in adipocytes, such as stimulation of thermogenesis and fatty acid oxidation together with blockage of adipogenesis, should be considered to control energy balance by modulating adipose biology.

REGULATION OF OBESITY BY FOOD COMPONENTS

A number of bioactive food components have been proposed to control energy balance, thereby improving body-weight loss. Here, we summarize recent findings on some of the potential antiobesity food components and their impact on the components in energy balance and adipose biology.

Components in Fruits and Vegetables

The health benefits of fruit and vegetable consumption are well recognized and include weight control. In addition to the fiber content of fruits and vegetables, other components are known to contribute to weight management, such as components from berries, soybeans, teas, spices, and citrus.

Fiber. According to the American Association of Cereal Chemists (AACC) International, dietary fiber is defined as "the edible parts of plants or analogous carbohydrates that are resistant to digestion and absorption in the human small intestine with complete or partial fermentation in the large intestine." Dietary fiber includes polysaccharides, oligosaccharides, lignin, and associated plant substances. Dietary fiber promotes beneficial physiological effects including laxation and/or blood cholesterol attenuation and/or blood glucose attenuation. Dietary fiber can be divided into soluble and insoluble fiber based on water solubility. Soluble fiber is known to be a good substrate for colonic fermentation. Soluble fiber has beneficial effects on glucose and lipid metabolism due to increased viscosity of gut contents. Insoluble fiber has a relatively low fermentability, but it also provides health benefit by its bulking capacity (Anderson et al. 2009, Papathanasopoulos & Camilleri 2010).

In addition to its well-known health benefits for cardiovascular diseases and diabetes, dietary fiber has been linked to lowering body-weight gain and reducing obesity. Suggested mechanisms of dietary fiber on prevention of obesity are increasing satiety, decreasing energy intake, and increasing fecal energy loss (Anderson et al. 2009, Astrup et al. 2010, Papathanasopoulos & Camilleri 2010, Sartorelli et al. 2008). Increased satiety of dietary fiber may come from the physical properties of dietary fiber that function to add bulk, form gels, delay gastric emptying, and reduce postprandial insulin responses (Astrup et al. 2010, Papathanasopoulos & Camilleri 2010, Salas-Salvado et al. 2008). High dietary fiber–containing meals also contribute to reduced total energy intake by lowering energy density of foods (Papathanasopoulos & Camilleri 2010). Lastly, it has been suggested that dietary fiber increases fecal energy and fat excretion (Astrup et al. 2010). There are no safety concerns associated with dietary fiber consumption. Knowledge about the influences of dietary fiber on hormonal modulation associated with food intake is seemingly inconsistent (Astrup et al. 2010, Papathanasopoulos & Camilleri 2010).

Blueberries and other berries. Consumption of berry fruits, such as blueberry, blackberry, raspberry, cranberry, and strawberry, has been associated with a number of positive impacts on human health. They are rich in antioxidants, such as anthocyanines, which are water-soluble pigments (Prior et al. 2008). Berries provide a good source of dietary fiber. Berry consumption, in particular, has been linked to reduced weight gain and appetite that are not associated with berry fiber content. Molan et al. (2008) reported that the consumption of water-soluble blueberry extracts reduced appetite in an animal model. This was not correlated with their antioxidant contents. Similar results of reduced weight gain were reported with blueberry juice in an obese animal model (Vuong et al. 2009). However, others reported no difference in body weight or body fat with whole blueberries (DeFuria et al. 2009). Purified anthocyanines from blueberries may contribute to reduced obesity in animal models (Prior et al. 2008, 2009). More studies with human trials are needed to draw any conclusions regarding consumption of berries and controlling obesity.

Soybeans. Soybeans (*Glycine max*) have been consumed for centuries in Asian countries, and serve as a good source of polyunsaturated fatty acids and protein. It is well recognized that soy consumption is associated with reduced risk of cardiovascular diseases and diabetes, prevention of certain types of cancer, and improved bone health (Cederroth & Nef 2009, Xiao 2008). Most of the health benefits of soybean consumption are linked particularly to soy protein and soy isoflavones, mainly diadzein and genistein, which are referred to as phytoestrogens because of their similarity to estrogen (Cederroth & Nef 2009, Xiao 2008). Diadzein and genistein in soy are present as glycosides, which are inactive. However, once ingested, these glycosides are hydrolyzed by intestinal bacteria, resulting in active aglycones. Diadzein can be metabolized to equol and *O*-demethyangolensin, and genistein metabolized to *p*-ethyl phenol and these metabolites are the major isoflavones observed from in vivo samples (Cederroth & Nef 2009).

There are reports linking soy consumption to reduced obesity. Suggested mechanisms involve increased energy expenditure and physical activity, and increased fatty acid oxidation (Aoyama et al. 2000, Cederroth & Nef 2009). These are supported by increased levels of AMPK and acetyl-CoA carboxylase (ACC), increased lipolysis through inhibition of cAMP phosphodiesterases by genestein, and activated PPARs. Other reports showed an inhibitory role of soy components in PPARγ and C/EBPα expression in 3T3-L1 adipocytes (Cederroth & Nef 2009, Orgaard & Jensen 2008). However, unlike a large number of studies that report health benefits of soy products on markers of cardiovascular diseases, there are relatively limited and inconsistent reports of soy protein or isoflavone effects on obesity prevention (Bhathena & Velasquez 2002, Cederroth & Nef 2009, Orgaard & Jensen 2008). It is also not conclusive whether any effects of soy products on obesity are due to soy protein or soy isoflavones (Bhathena & Velasquez 2002, Orgaard & Jensen 2008).

Use of soy or purified soy isoflavones may pose certain health concerns, such as stimulation and/or interference with tamoxifen used as breast cancer treatment and immune-related responses (Cederroth & Nef 2009, Orgaard & Jensen 2008).

EGCG: epigallocatechin gallate

Teas. Tea is made from the leaves of the *Camellia sinensis* L. plant of the Theaceae family (Hursel & Westerterp-Plantenga 2010). There are four main types of teas, green, oolong, black, and white, depending on the maturity of the leaves and the oxidative status. Although there are differences in active components and their effects, all tea types have been linked to well-known bioactive compounds (Hursel & Westerterp-Plantenga 2010, Westerterp-Plantenga et al. 2006). Most of the health benefits of tea have been investigated using green tea, thus this review focuses on green tea.

Most short-term human studies with consumption of green tea extract and caffeine have resulted in increased energy expenditure and fat oxidation. However, two studies reported either no difference or an insignificant increase in energy expenditure and fat oxidation (Hursel & Westerterp-Plantenga 2010). In contrast, a significant reduction in body weight and body fat was found in almost all human studies in which catechins were consumed for three months or more (Diepvens et al. 2007, Hursel & Westerterp-Plantenga 2010, Westerterp-Plantenga et al. 2006).

Tea has shown to increase energy expenditure, in part through a thermogenic effect and fat oxidation, and decrease body fat and body weight (Hursel & Westerterp-Plantenga 2010). Studies also have shown that green tea limits weight regain after weight loss. The suggested mechanism is by preventing reduced energy expenditure that usually occurs with a low-energy diet (Diepvens et al. 2007). Habitual caffeine consumption may influence the effects of tea in weight maintenance after weight loss. Subjects with a low habitual caffeine intake may have better outcome than those with a high caffeine intake (Hursel et al. 2009, Westerterp-Plantenga et al. 2006).

Tea exhibits a thermogenic effect due to its catechins, which include epicatechin, epicatechin gallate, epigallocatechin, and epigallocatechin gallate (EGCG), as well as caffeine (Westerterp-Plantenga et al. 2006). The thermogenic effect of green tea cannot be attributed solely to its caffeine content; there was a significant increase in energy expenditure and fat oxidation following consumption of green tea extract compared to placebo or to caffeine alone (Westerterp-Plantenga et al. 2006). Animal studies have shown that EGCG particularly is linked to reduced food intake and increased energy expenditure (Diepvens et al. 2007).

Suggested biochemical mechanisms for catechins and caffeine are well reviewed by Hursel & Westerterp-Plantenga (2010). Catechins stimulate nuclear factor-κB (NF-κB), which subsequently upregulates enzymes for fat oxidation. Catechins also increase norepinephrine and adenyl cyclase through the inhibition of catechol *O*-methyltransferase, resulting in increased lipolysis and decreased glucose uptake. Along with the upregulation of adenyl cyclase, caffeine increases cAMP by inhibiting phosphodiesterase, resulting in increased energy expenditure and fat oxidation via protein kinase A (Hursel & Westerterp-Plantenga 2010).

Green tea has been widely consumed in China and Japan for centuries and is regarded as safe. The major health concern over tea consumption is related to its caffeine content. One study reported a small, short-term increase in blood pressure as a result of green tea consumption, but the significance of this study needs validation because others found no effect on blood pressure or heart rate associated with tea consumption (Diepvens et al. 2007).

Capsaicin. One spice principle shown to be an effective weight management agent is capsaicin, which is the pungent component from red pepper (*Capsicum annuum*). Its analog, capsiate, from the nonpungent cultivar CH-19 Sweet (*Capsicum annuum* L.), has also been shown to be a good alternative to capsaicin because of its mild taste yet similar effects (Belza et al. 2007, Belza & Jessen 2005, Reinbach et al. 2009).

Consumption of capsaicin or capsiate is reportedly associated with reduced body weight and body fat (Kawabata et al. 2006, Kawada et al. 1986). Other reports show no effects on weight or fat mass (Lejeune et al. 2003, Snitker et al. 2009). Consumption of capsaicin has been associated with decreased energy intake only following consumption of capsaicin in food form but not capsules, indicating that sensory perception of capsaicin is significant (Westerterp-Plantenga et al. 2005, Yoshioka et al. 2004). It also has been shown that capsaicin taken with breakfast significantly reduced the desire to eat (and hunger for) lunch and mid-afternoon snack (Yoshioka et al. 1999). In contrast, others found no difference in satiety following capsaicin consumption. This may have been due to the fact that only a single exposure was tested in these reports (Smeets & Westerterp-Plantenga 2009).

The suggested mechanisms of capsaicin (or red pepper) are increased energy expenditure by way of stimulating thermogenesis and increased fat oxidation (Lejeune et al. 2003, Snitker et al. 2009, Yoshioka et al. 1999). Capsaicin has been found to stimulate adrenal medullary catecholamine secretion in rats via transient receptor potential vanilloid 1 (TRPV1) (Hursel & Westerterp-Plantenga 2010, Kawabata et al. 2009). Treatment with capsiate increased levels of UCP-1 and UCP-2 (Masuda et al. 2003), which may be the result of catecholamine's binding to β-adrenoceptors to increase thermogenesis (Hursel & Westerterp-Plantenga 2010). However, a single administration or a short-term study did not result in any significant changes in energy expenditure (Galgani et al. 2010, Smeets & Westerterp-Plantenga 2009).

Numerous human studies have shown that capsaicin is safe for human consumption (Hursel & Westerterp-Plantenga 2010, Snitker et al. 2009, Westerterp-Plantenga et al. 2005), with only a few mild and diverse gastrointestinal events reported (Snitker et al. 2009). One study has shown irreversible damage to chemosensitive primary sensory neurons in newborn rats, but damage was reversible in adult rats (Jancso et al. 1977).

Other spices. Turmeric (*Curcuma longa* L.) is a well-known food ingredient also used to treat inflammation (Maheshwari et al. 2006). Curcumin is the main bioactive polyphenol component from turmeric. Many studies have shown that curcumin lowers serum triglyceride and cholesterol levels (Srinivasan et al. 2004), but few studies have investigated its direct antiobesity effects. In mice, a high fat diet supplemented with curcumin did not affect food intake but reduced body-weight gain, adiposity, and microvessel density in adipose tissue (Ejaz et al. 2009). Others reported that curcuminoids, commercial grade curcumin [i.e., a mixture of curcumin (73.4%), demethoxycurcumin (16.1%), and bisdemethoxycurcumin (10.5%)] prevented high fat diet–induced lipid accumulation in the epididymal adipose tissue and the liver of rats (Asai & Miyazawa 2001). In both cell culture and in mice models, curcumin increased 5′AMPK phosphorylation, reduced glycerol-3-phosphate acyl transferase-1, and increased carnitine palmitoyltransferase-1 expression, leading to increased oxidation and decreased fatty acid esterification (Ejaz et al. 2009). Curcumin is also reported to decrease adipogenesis via decreasing expressions of PPARγ and C/EBPα, and/or via inhibiting mitogen-activated protein kinase (MAPK) [extracellular signal-regulated kinases (ERKs), c-Jun N-terminal kinase (JNK), and p38] phosphorylation in 3T3-L1 adipocytes (Ahn et al. 2010, Ejaz et al. 2009). Curcumin also has been shown to increase apoptosis in 3T3-L1 adipocytes (Ejaz et al. 2009).

Black pepper is from unripe berries of *Piper nigrum* Linn. The main pungent component in black paper is peperine, which is an alkaloid similar to capsaicin (Astrup et al. 2010, Srinivasan 2007). The effects of black pepper or piperine on thermogenesis are believed to be mediated by the sympathetic nervous system. However, it is not conclusive that black pepper or piperine has an effect on energy balance or thermogenesis (Astrup et al. 2010).

CLA: conjugated linoleic acid

Ginger is the rhizome from *Zingiber officinale* Roscoe. The pungent components of ginger are gingerols, shogaols, and zingerone. Ginerols are present in fresh ginger, and the other two are derived from gingerols during dehydration and degradation (Astrup et al. 2010). Similar to piperine and capsaicin, these bioactive components from ginger are known to induce sympathetic nervous system–mediated thermogenesis (Astrup et al. 2010). Others reported influence of ginger on appetite; however, the evidence is still very preliminary (Astrup et al. 2010).

Mustard comes from the seeds of different species of mustard plants, including *Sinapis alba*, *Brassica juncea*, and *Brassica nigra*. The pungent component in mustard is allyl isothiocyanate, which increases thermogenesis similar to capsaicin (Astrup et al. 2010). However, there are limited data available on the significance of mustard or allyl isothiocyanate on obesity.

Citrus extract. The interest in citrus regarding obesity is focused on *Citrus aurantium*, commonly named bitter orange, sour orange, or Seville orange (Haaz et al. 2006). The fruit is sometimes used as a food but the plant is more widely used as a dietary supplement for weight loss. The popularity for use of bitter orange is due to the ban on ephedra-containing products for weight loss. *C. aurantium* contains a compound that is similar to ephedra, called synephrine (Haaz et al. 2006). Synerphine is a sympathomimetic drug, which is primarily an α-adrenergic agonist, but also has some β-adrenergic agonist properties (Bent et al. 2004, Haaz et al. 2006).

Some limited human studies have suggested that consumption of bitter orange extract reduced body weight or body fat, and others reported no effects (Bent et al. 2004, Haaz et al. 2006). This is likely to be associated with enhancement of metabolism, suppression of appetite via reducing gut motility, and promotion of lipolysis in adipocytes (Haaz et al. 2006, Hess & Sullivan 2005). In addition, a polyphenolic mixture extract prepared from red orange, grapefruit, guarana, and bitter orange has been shown to reduce body fat. This is mediated through increasing lipolysis from adipocytes, which is stimulated by β-adrenergic agonists resulting in inhibition of cAMP-dependent phosphodiesterase (Dallas et al. 2008).

There are major health concerns over consumption of *C. aurantium*. Synerpherine is known to cause vasoconstriction, resulting in increased blood pressure and increased heart rate. *N*-methyltyramine increases blood pressure by increasing norephinephrine release, thus resulting in additive hypertensive effects. The other components from bitter orange, furocoumarins, can inhibit CYP3A4 isoenzyme, resulting in potential drug interactions, such as antifungals, glucocorticoids, or calcium-channel blockers (Bent et al. 2004, Haaz et al. 2006, Hess & Sullivan 2005). Thus, the use of bitter orange, particularly long-term, needs close evaluation.

Lipid-Based Components

Although it is generally recommended to limit the intake of dietary fat to maintain proper body weight, there are lipid-based components that can contribute to weight control, such as conjugated linoleic acid (CLA), modified glycerides, and fish oil.

Conjugated linoleic acid. One bioactive food component that has drawn significant attention for its antiobesity effect is CLA. It was originally found as an anticancer component from ground beef extract in 1985 (Pariza & Hargraves 1985). Since then a number of other biologically beneficial effects of CLA have been identified, including antiatherosclerosis, immune-modulation, antidiabetes, antiosteoporosis, and antiobesity effects (Park 2009, Park & Pariza 2007, Park & Pariza 2009).

The name CLA was given based on the fact that CLA is a mixture of geometric and positional isomers of linoleic acid. There are a number of CLA isomers reported. However, because of their biological functions, two main isomers are the focus of current research: *cis*-9, *trans*-11 and *trans*-10, *cis*-12 (Pariza 2004, Park & Pariza 2007). The *cis*-9, *trans*-11 isomer is the predominant isomer found in natural sources, such as beef, milk, and dairy products (Park 2009). The origins of this isomer are either from biohydrogenation of linoleic acid to stearic acid by rumen bacteria or from the delta-9 desaturation of *trans*-11 vaccenic acid in mammalian tissues (Park 2009). The other major isomer of CLA, *trans*-10, *cis*-12, is present at very low levels in food but primarily originates from synthetically prepared CLA (Park & Pariza 2007). Currently most studies on the bioactivities of CLA have used these two mixed isomers. It is known that the effects of CLA are the result of interaction between these two isomers (Pariza 2004, Park 2009).

It is well recognized that CLA, particularly the *trans*-10, *cis*-12 isomer, reduces body fat in animal models while improving lean mass and bone mass (Park et al. 1997, Park et al. 1999). Multiple mechanisms have been suggested for CLA's effect on body fat reduction: (*a*) increasing energy expenditure by enhancing thermogenesis and enhancing UCP expressions, (*b*) modulating lipid metabolism by decreasing lipogenesis and increasing lipolysis, (*c*) reducing adipocyte cell number and size by increasing apoptosis and inhibiting lipoprotein lipase from adipocytes, and (*d*) increasing fatty acid β-oxidation in skeletal muscle (Kennedy et al. 2010, Park & Pariza 2007). It has been suggested that CLA's effects on adipocytes are mediated by interaction with PPAR γ, NF-κB, AMPK, tumor necrosis factor-α (TNF-α), and/or inflammatory mediators (Jiang et al. 2009, Kennedy et al. 2010). However, at the moment it is unknown whether CLA has potential upstream targets for its activities on adipocytes.

The efficacy of CLA in human studies on body fat control was much less significant than that seen in animals (Park 2009). This is suggested to be due to: (*a*) lower doses used in human compared to animal studies, (*b*) differences in age, gender, duration used, and CLA preparations, and most importantly (*c*) differences in experimental design. Regarding the latter, animals were not restricted with regard to energy, whereas most human studies were restricted with regard to calorie intake (Park 2009, Park et al. 1999).

The main health concerns for CLA consumption are lipodystrophy, fatty liver, glucose intolerance, and increased oxidative stress (Pariza 2004, Park 2009, Park & Pariza 2007). Lipodystrophy, fatty liver, and glucose intolerance are mainly associated with animal models, whereas minimal effects were observed in human studies [for review of animal and human studies, see Park (2009)]. Increased oxidative stress by CLA supplementation has been reported in human studies, although the significance of this observation still needs further evaluation.

Modified glycerides. The majority of naturally occurring fats and oils are in the form of triacylglycerols (TAG), with minor components as forms of diacylglycerols (DAG) and monoacylglycerols (MAG). There was great interest on the effects of DAG in recent years as a tool to control obesity [for review, see Hibi et al. (2009) and Rudkowska et al. (2005)]. The suggested mechanism of DAG is mainly attributed to its unique structural and metabolic characteristics, rather than differences in fatty acid composition, digestibility, and energy values compared with DAG and TAG (38.9 kJ g^{-1} and 39.6 kJ g^{-1}, respectively) (Murase et al. 2001, Rudkowska et al. 2005). It is suggested that instead of 2-monoacylglycerol and free fatty acids, the digested products from TAG, the end products of DAG digestion are glycerol and free fatty acids, which may be less likely incorporated into chylomicrons (Tada 2004, Yang & Kuksis 1991). Thus, free fatty acids from digested DAG are moved into the liver directly.

DAG consumption is also associated with modulating blood lipid profiles, particularly triglyceride and cholesterol, and improving glucose metabolism (Saito et al. 2006, Takase et al. 2005, Yanai et al. 2008). Consumption of DAG also has been associated with increased fatty acid β-oxidation in the liver. It is suggested to be associated with influx of free fatty acids to the liver (Hibi et al. 2008, Jackman et al. 2006, Meng et al. 2004, Osaki et al. 2008).

The overall effects of DAG in weight loss or body fat are rather inconsistent. Some reported reduced body weight (Maki et al. 2002, Nagao et al. 2000), whereas others reported no changes in weight with DAG (Teramoto et al. 2004, Yamamoto et al. 2001, Yasunaga et al. 2004). DAG consumption is associated with increased energy expenditure as the major beneficial effect (Kawashima et al. 2008, Maki et al. 2002, Nagao et al. 2000, Saito et al. 2006). Increased energy expenditure mediated by DAG was suggested to be associated with increased resting metabolic rate (RMR), which may be due to diet-induced thermogenesis originating from the differences in metabolism between DAG and TAG (Hibi et al. 2008, Rudkowska et al. 2005). However, others reported no changes of energy expenditure in humans (Hibi et al. 2008, Kamphuis et al. 2003). Maki et al. (2002) suggested that the effects of DAG may not be substantial but could result in cumulative effects over time.

Overall, no adverse effects were reported from animals (Kasamatsu et al. 2005, Soni et al. 2001) or humans consuming DAG for up to one year [for review, see Morita & Soni (2009)].

Fish oils. In addition to its well-known effects of protection against cardiovascular diseases, consumption of long-chain ω-3 fatty acids, such as marine-originated fish oils, has been reported to be associated with obesity prevention (Al-Hasani & Joost 2005, Buckley & Howe 2009, Carpentier et al. 2006, Hill et al. 2007, Parra et al. 2008, Watts et al. 2006). A number of animal studies indicated that fish oil consumption lowered accumulation of adipose tissue mass, particularly in diet-induced obesity models (Buckley & Howe 2009). Human studies, however, were less consistent; beneficial effects were observed in some studies but not in others (Buckley & Howe 2009).

Reported antiobesity mechanisms of fish oil include increasing resting energy expenditure, increasing fat oxidation, and suppressing appetite, as suggested from human studies (Buckley & Howe 2009, Micallef et al. 2009, Perez-Matute et al. 2007). Additionally, feeding ω-3 fatty acids increased expression of genes and protein involved in fatty acid oxidation in liver, intestine, heart, and skeletal muscle, and decreased expression of genes involved in lipogenesis in adipose tissue from animal studies (Buckley & Howe 2009). These are supported by observations of increased skeletal and heart muscle CPT-1, increased skeletal muscle UPC-3, increased skeletal muscle, liver, and heart peroxisomal acyl-CoA oxidase (Acyl-CoA), and increased intestinal lipid oxidation in animal models, all of which can support increased resting energy expenditure and less effective fat oxidation by ω-3 fatty acids (Buckley & Howe 2009).

Potential concerns over fish or fish oil consumption include adverse responses in platelet function, as well as methylmercury and other environmental contaminants, particularly with fish consumption. However, its potential adverse effects must be weighed against the potential benefits, including cardiovascular disease prevention and brain development (Lien 2009, Oken & Bellinger 2008).

Others: Calcium

The consumption of calcium, particularly dairy calcium, has been linked to reduced body weight and/or body fat mass (Astrup et al. 2010, Van Loan 2009, Zemel et al. 2005). There are three suggested mechanisms associated with calcium and body fat control. First, high intake of dairy calcium increases fecal fat and energy excretion (Astrup et al. 2010, Van Loan 2009). This is due to the formation of insoluble calcium-fatty acid soaps as well as binding to bile acids, thus resulting in a decreased total energy uptake (Astrup et al. 2010). Recently, Christensen et al. (2009) reported metaanalysis of calcium studies, concluding that dairy calcium intake is significantly associated with increased fecal fat excretion. This difference is not dramatic but would result in an estimated 1–2.2 kg weight loss over a one-year period.

Secondly, calcium may modulate lipid metabolism in adipocytes by decreasing de novo lipogenesis and increasing lipolysis (Astrup et al. 2010, Zemel & Sun 2008). This effect has been suggested to be linked to circulating calcitrol, which controls intracellular calcium in adipocytes, resulting in stimulation of lipogenesis and lipolysis as well as suppressing UCP-2 (Zemel & Miller 2004, Zemel & Sun 2008). During a high-calcium diet, calcitrol is suppressed, thus controlling adiposity (Zemel & Miller 2004, Zemel & Sun 2008). Lastly, limited study reported an association between supplementation of calcium and appetite regulation, although this is inconclusive (Astrup et al. 2010).

CONCLUSION

The past decade has laid groundwork to understanding physiological and molecular mechanisms of central and peripheral control of energy balance and adipose biology. This will allow us to perform an efficient search for antiobesity bioactive food components that could specifically regulate central and/or peripheral cellular pathways for the control of food intake, thermogenesis, and adipose development and function. Recently, many exciting findings identified a number of food components with antiobesity properties. The examples presented in this review have highlighted the potential use of some food components in dietary prevention of obesity through targeting various cellular pathways. However, more studies are needed to elucidate the molecular basis underlying the antiobesity properties of these components. Furthermore, studies in improving bioavailability, safety, interaction with food matrix, and effective delivery of these components to the target tissues should also be addressed in order to be used as active food ingredients for the benefit of body-weight control.

SUMMARY POINTS

1. The CNS receives endocrine and nervous signals from adipose tissue, intestine, and other peripheral tissues to control the energy balance between food intake and energy expenditure.
2. Improvement of UCP-regulated thermogenesis and fatty acid oxidation in peripheral tissues contributes to positive energy expenditure and lowering the risk of the development of obesity.
3. Adipose tissue–secreted hormones participate in many aspects of energy balance, such as food intake, systemic energy metabolism, and thermogenesis. In addition, a transcriptional program of adipocyte hyperplasia is likely to be a promising target of dietary prevention of the development of obesity.
4. Energy intake, appetite, and satiety are likely to be targeted by some antiobesity food components (e.g., dietary fiber, berries, capsaicin, citrus extracts, and fish oils).

5. The potential antiobesity functions of soybean, tea, capsaicin, some spices (curcumin, black pepper, ginger, and mustard), CLA, and modified glycerides are largely mediated through stimulation of energy expenditure (e.g., thermogenesis and fatty acid oxidation).
6. Soybean components, curcumin, citrus extract, CLA, modified glycerides, fish oil, and calcium exert their potential antiobesity function through modulation of adipose biology (e.g., adipogenesis and lipolysis) and lipid metabolism in nutrient-sensing tissues such as liver, adipocytes, and intestine.

FUTURE ISSUES

1. In most cases, the in vivo relevance of the antiobesity functions of the food components described above still needs to be demonstrated.
2. It remains to be investigated whether there are any food components that could cross the blood-brain barrier for direct control of central food intake.
3. Dietary regulation of lipid and energy metabolism in the intestine remains unclear. Further study is required to resolve this.
4. Improving the stability and solubility of antiobesity food components in the gastrointestinal tract will provide great value to increase their beneficial effects on overall energy balance in vivo.

DISCLOSURE STATEMENT

Yeonhwa Park is one of the inventors of CLA use patents that are assigned to the Wisconsin Alumni Research Foundation.

ACKNOWLEDGMENTS

Authors thank Rengaswami Chandrasekaran, Jayne M. Storkson, and Julia Tomanio for their assistance and helpful comments. Kee-Hong Kim acknowledges research grant support from the Ralph W. and Grace M. Showalter Research Trust, and an Agriculture and Food Research Initiative (AFRI) grant 2009–65200-05994 from the USDA National Institute for Food and Agriculture.

LITERATURE CITED

Adams SH, Pan G, Yu XX. 2001. Perspectives on the biology of uncoupling protein (UCP) homologues. *Biochem. Soc. Trans.* 29:798–802

Ahn J, Lee H, Kim S, Ha T. 2010. Curcumin-induced suppression of adipogenic differentiation is accompanied by activation of Wnt/beta-catenin signaling. *Am. J. Physiol. Cell Physiol.* 298:C1510–16

Al-Hasani H, Joost HG. 2005. Nutrition-/diet-induced changes in gene expression in white adipose tissue. *Best Pract. Res. Clin. Endocrinol. Metab.* 19:589–603

Anderson JW, Baird P, Davis RH Jr, Ferreri S, Knudtson M, et al. 2009. Health benefits of dietary fiber. *Nutr. Rev.* 67:188–205

Aoyama T, Fukui K, Takamatsu K, Hashimoto Y, Yamamoto T. 2000. Soy protein isolate and its hydrolysate reduce body fat of dietary obese rats and genetically obese mice (yellow KK). *Nutrition* 16:349–54

Arsenijevic D, Onuma H, Pecqueur C, Raimbault S, Manning BS, et al. 2000. Disruption of the uncoupling protein-2 gene in mice reveals a role in immunity and reactive oxygen species production. *Nat. Genet.* 26:435–39

Asai A, Miyazawa T. 2001. Dietary curcuminoids prevent high-fat diet-induced lipid accumulation in rat liver and epididymal adipose tissue. *J. Nutr.* 131:2932–35

Asakawa A, Inui A, Kaga T, Yuzuriha H, Nagata T, et al. 2001. Ghrelin is an appetite-stimulatory signal from stomach with structural resemblance to motilin. *Gastroenterology* 120:337–45

Astrup A, Kristensen M, Gregersen NT, Belza A, Lorenzen JK, et al. 2010. Can bioactive foods affect obesity? *Ann. New York Acad. Sci.* 1190:25–41

Bagdade JD, Bierman EL, Porte D Jr. 1967. The significance of basal insulin levels in the evaluation of the insulin response to glucose in diabetic and nondiabetic subjects. *J. Clin. Investig.* 46:1549–57

Batterham RL, Cowley MA, Small CJ, Herzog H, Cohen MA, et al. 2002. Gut hormone PYY(3–36) physiologically inhibits food intake. *Nature* 418:650–54

Belza A, Frandsen E, Kondrup J. 2007. Body fat loss achieved by stimulation of thermogenesis by a combination of bioactive food ingredients: a placebo-controlled, double-blind 8-week intervention in obese subjects. *Int. J. Obes.* 31:121–30

Belza A, Jessen AB. 2005. Bioactive food stimulants of sympathetic activity: effect on 24-h energy expenditure and fat oxidation. *Eur. J. Clin. Nutr.* 59:733–41

Benoit SC, Air EL, Coolen LM, Strauss R, Jackman A, et al. 2002. The catabolic action of insulin in the brain is mediated by melanocortins. *J. Neurosci.* 22:9048–52

Bent S, Padula A, Neuhaus J. 2004. Safety and efficacy of citrus aurantium for weight loss. *Am. J. Cardiol.* 94:1359–61

Berghofer A, Pischon T, Reinhold T, Apovian CM, Sharma AM, Willich SN. 2008. Obesity prevalence from a European perspective: a systematic review. *BMC Public Health* 8:200

Bhathena SJ, Velasquez MT. 2002. Beneficial role of dietary phytoestrogens in obesity and diabetes. *Am. J. Clin. Nutr.* 76:1191–201

Bray GA. 2009. Medications for obesity: mechanisms and applications. *Clin. Chest Med.* 30:525–38

Brown RE, Wilkinson PM, Imran SA, Wilkinson M. 2009. Resistin differentially modulates neuropeptide gene expression and AMP-activated protein kinase activity in N-1 hypothalamic neurons. *Brain Res.* 1294:52–60

Buckley JD, Howe PR. 2009. Anti-obesity effects of long-chain omega-3 polyunsaturated fatty acids. *Obes. Rev.* 10:648–59

Carpentier YA, Portois L, Malaisse WJ. 2006. N-3 fatty acids and the metabolic syndrome. *Am. J. Clin. Nutr.* 83:1499S–504S

Cederroth CR, Nef S. 2009. Soy, phytoestrogens and metabolism: a review. *Mol. Cell. Endocrinol.* 304:30–42

Chelikani PK, Haver AC, Reidelberger RD. 2006. Dose-dependent effects of peptide YY(3–36) on conditioned taste aversion in rats. *Peptides* 27:3193–201

Chen CM. 2008. Overview of obesity in mainland China. *Obes. Rev.* 9(Suppl. 1):14–21

Christensen R, Lorenzen JK, Svith CR, Bartels EM, Melanson EL, et al. 2009. Effect of calcium from dairy and dietary supplements on faecal fat excretion: a meta-analysis of randomized controlled trials. *Obes. Rev.* 10:475–86

Clapham JC, Arch JR, Chapman H, Haynes A, Lister C, et al. 2000. Mice overexpressing human uncoupling protein-3 in skeletal muscle are hyperphagic and lean. *Nature* 406:415–18

Considine RV, Sinha MK, Heiman ML, Kriauciunas A, Stephens TW, et al. 1996. Serum immunoreactive-leptin concentrations in normal-weight and obese humans. *New Engl. J. Med.* 334:292–5

Crawley JN, Beinfeld MC. 1983. Rapid development of tolerance to the behavioural actions of cholecystokinin. *Nature* 302:703–6

Dallas C, Gerbi A, Tenca G, Juchaux F, Bernard FX. 2008. Lipolytic effect of a polyphenolic citrus dry extract of red orange, grapefruit, orange (SINETROL) in human body fat adipocytes. Mechanism of action by inhibition of cAMP-phosphodiesterase (PDE). *Phytomedicine* 15:783–92

DeFuria J, Bennett G, Strissel KJ, Perfield JW 2nd, Milbury PE, et al. 2009. Dietary blueberry attenuates whole-body insulin resistance in high fat–fed mice by reducing adipocyte death and its inflammatory sequelae. *J. Nutr.* 139:1510–16

Diepvens K, Westerterp KR, Westerterp-Plantenga MS. 2007. Obesity and thermogenesis related to the consumption of caffeine, ephedrine, capsaicin, and green tea. *Am. J. Physiol. Regul. Integr. Comp. Physiol.* 292:R77–85

Drucker DJ. 2006. The biology of incretin hormones. *Cell Metab.* 3:153–65

Eberlein GA, Eysselein VE, Schaeffer M, Layer P, Grandt D, et al. 1989. A new molecular form of PYY: structural characterization of human PYY(3–36) and PYY(1–36). *Peptides* 10:797–803

Ejaz A, Wu D, Kwan P, Meydani M. 2009. Curcumin inhibits adipogenesis in 3T3-L1 adipocytes and angiogenesis and obesity in C57/BL mice. *J. Nutr.* 139:919–25

Fussenegger D, Pietrobelli A, Widhalm K. 2008. Childhood obesity: political developments in Europe and related perspectives for future action on prevention. *Obes. Rev.* 9:76–82

Galgani JE, Ryan DH, Ravussin E. 2010. Effect of capsinoids on energy metabolism in human subjects. *Br. J. Nutr.* 103:38–42

Gardner DS, Rhodes P. 2009. Developmental origins of obesity: programming of food intake or physical activity? *Adv. Exp. Med. Biol.* 646:83–93

Gong DW, Monemdjou S, Gavrilova O, Leon LR, Marcus-Samuels B, et al. 2000. Lack of obesity and normal response to fasting and thyroid hormone in mice lacking uncoupling protein-3. *J. Biol. Chem.* 275:16251–57

Gregoire FM, Smas CM, Sul HS. 1998. Understanding adipocyte differentiation. *Physiol. Rev.* 78:783–809

Grossman SP. 1986. The role of glucose, insulin and glucagon in the regulation of food intake and body weight. *Neurosci. Biobehav. Rev.* 10:295–315

Haaz S, Fontaine KR, Cutter G, Limdi N, Perumean-Chaney S, Allison DB. 2006. Citrus aurantium and synephrine alkaloids in the treatment of overweight and obesity: an update. *Obes. Rev.* 7:79–88

Hess AM, Sullivan DL. 2005. Potential for toxicity with use of bitter orange extract and guarana for weight loss. *Ann. Pharmacother.* 39:574–75

Hibi M, Takase H, Meguro S, Tokimitsu I. 2009. The effects of diacylglycerol oil on fat oxidation and energy expenditure in humans and animals. *Biofactors* 35:175–77

Hibi M, Takase H, Yasunaga K, Yamaguchi T, Harada U, et al. 2008. Fat utilization in healthy subjects consuming diacylglycerol oil diet: dietary and whole body fat oxidation. *Lipids* 43:517–24

Hill AM, Buckley JD, Murphy KJ, Howe PR. 2007. Combining fish-oil supplements with regular aerobic exercise improves body composition and cardiovascular disease risk factors. *Am. J. Clin. Nutr.* 85:1267–74

Holcomb IN, Kabakoff RC, Chan B, Baker TW, Gurney A, et al. 2000. FIZZ1, a novel cysteine-rich secreted protein associated with pulmonary inflammation, defines a new gene family. *EMBO J.* 19:4046–55

Holst JJ. 2004. On the physiology of GIP and GLP-1. *Horm. Metab. Res.* 36:747–54

Hursel R, Viechtbauer W, Westerterp-Plantenga MS. 2009. The effects of green tea on weight loss and weight maintenance: a meta-analysis. *Int. J. Obes.* 33:956–61

Hursel R, Westerterp-Plantenga MS. 2010. Thermogenic ingredients and body weight regulation. *Int. J. Obes.* 34:659–69

Jackman MR, Kramer RE, MacLean PS, Bessesen DH. 2006. Trafficking of dietary fat in obesity-prone and obesity-resistant rats. *Am. J. Physiol. Endocrinol. Metab.* 291:E1083–91

Jancso G, Kiraly E, Jancso-Gabor A. 1977. Pharmacologically induced selective degeneration of chemosensitive primary sensory neurones. *Nature* 270:741–43

Jiang S, Wang Z, Riethoven JJ, Xia Y, Miner J, Fromm M. 2009. Conjugated linoleic acid activates AMP-activated protein kinase and reduces adiposity more effectively when used with metformin in mice. *J. Nutr.* 139:2244–51

Kamphuis MM, Mela DJ, Westerterp-Plantenga MS. 2003. Diacylglycerols affect substrate oxidation and appetite in humans. *Am. J. Clin. Nutr.* 77:1133–39

Kasamatsu T, Ogura R, Ikeda N, Morita O, Saigo K, et al. 2005. Genotoxicity studies on dietary diacylglycerol (DAG) oil. *Food Chem. Toxicol.* 43:253–60

Kawabata F, Inoue N, Masamoto Y, Matsumura S, Kimura W, et al. 2009. Non-pungent capsaicin analogs (capsinoids) increase metabolic rate and enhance thermogenesis via gastrointestinal TRPV1 in mice. *Biosci. Biotechnol. Biochem.* 73:2690–97

Kawabata F, Inoue N, Yazawa S, Kawada T, Inoue K, Fushiki T. 2006. Effects of CH-19 sweet, a non-pungent cultivar of red pepper, in decreasing the body weight and suppressing body fat accumulation by sympathetic nerve activation in humans. *Biosci. Biotechnol. Biochem.* 70:2824–35

Kawada T, Hagihara K, Iwai K. 1986. Effects of capsaicin on lipid metabolism in rats fed a high fat diet. *J. Nutr.* 116:1272–78

Kawashima H, Takase H, Yasunaga K, Wakaki Y, Katsuragi Y, et al. 2008. One-year ad libitum consumption of diacylglycerol oil as part of a regular diet results in modest weight loss in comparison with consumption of a triacylglycerol control oil in overweight Japanese subjects. *J. Am. Diet. Assoc.* 108:57–66

Kennedy A, Martinez K, Schmidt S, Mandrup S, LaPoint K, McIntosh M. 2010. Antiobesity mechanisms of action of conjugated linoleic acid. *J. Nutr. Biochem.* 21:171–79

Kim KH, Lee K, Moon YS, Sul HS. 2001. A cysteine-rich adipose tissue-specific secretory factor inhibits adipocyte differentiation. *J. Biol. Chem.* 276:11252–6

Kojima M, Hosoda H, Date Y, Nakazato M, Matsuo H, Kangawa K. 1999. Ghrelin is a growth-hormone-releasing acylated peptide from stomach. *Nature* 402:656–60

Kopelman PG. 2000. Obesity as a medical problem. *Nature* 404:635–43

Kozak LP, Anunciado-Koza R. 2008. UCP1: its involvement and utility in obesity. *Int. J. Obes.* 32(Suppl. 7):S32–38

Kubota N, Yano W, Kubota T, Yamauchi T, Itoh S, et al. 2007. Adiponectin stimulates AMP-activated protein kinase in the hypothalamus and increases food intake. *Cell Metab.* 6:55–68

Larhammar D. 1996. Structural diversity of receptors for neuropeptide Y, peptide YY and pancreatic polypeptide. *Regul. Pept.* 65:165–74

Lejeune MP, Kovacs EM, Westerterp-Plantenga MS. 2003. Effect of capsaicin on substrate oxidation and weight maintenance after modest body-weight loss in human subjects. *Br. J. Nutr.* 90:651–59

Li B, Nolte LA, Ju JS, Han DH, Coleman T, et al. 2000. Skeletal muscle respiratory uncoupling prevents diet-induced obesity and insulin resistance in mice. *Nat. Med.* 6:1115–20

Lien EL. 2009. Toxicology and safety of DHA. *Prostaglandins Leukot. Essent. Fatty Acids* 81:125–32

Lowell BB, Spiegelman BM. 2000. Towards a molecular understanding of adaptive thermogenesis. *Nature* 404:652–60

Ludwig DS, Pereira MA, Kroenke CH, Hilner JE, Van Horn L, et al. 1999. Dietary fiber, weight gain, and cardiovascular disease risk factors in young adults. *JAMA* 282:1539–46

Maheshwari RK, Singh AK, Gaddipati J, Srimal RC. 2006. Multiple biological activities of curcumin: a short review. *Life Sci.* 78:2081–87

Maki KC, Davidson MH, Tsushima R, Matsuo N, Tokimitsu I, et al. 2002. Consumption of diacylglycerol oil as part of a reduced-energy diet enhances loss of body weight and fat in comparison with consumption of a triacylglycerol control oil. *Am. J. Clin. Nutr.* 76:1230–36

Masuda Y, Haramizu S, Oki K, Ohnuki K, Watanabe T, et al. 2003. Upregulation of uncoupling proteins by oral administration of capsiate, a nonpungent capsaicin analog. *J. Appl. Physiol.* 95:2408–15

Meng X, Zou D, Shi Z, Duan Z, Mao Z. 2004. Dietary diacylglycerol prevents high-fat-diet-induced lipid accumulation in rat liver and abdominal adipose tissue. *Lipids* 39:37–41

Micallef M, Munro I, Phang M, Garg M. 2009. Plasma n-3 polyunsaturated fatty acids are negatively associated with obesity. *Br. J. Nutr.* 102:1370–74

Minokoshi Y, Kim YB, Peroni OD, Fryer LG, Muller C, et al. 2002. Leptin stimulates fatty-acid oxidation by activating AMP-activated protein kinase. *Nature* 415:339–43

Molan AL, Lila MA, Mawson J. 2008. Satiety in rats following blueberry extract consumption induced by appetite-suppressing mechanisms unrelated to in vitro or in vivo antioxidant capacity. *Food Chem.* 107:1039–44

Moran TH. 2000. Cholecystokinin and satiety: current perspectives. *Nutrition* 16:858–65

Morita O, Soni MG. 2009. Safety assessment of diacylglycerol oil as an edible oil: a review of the published literature. *Food Chem. Toxicol.* 47:9–21

Murase T, Mizuno T, Omachi T, Onizawa K, Komine Y, et al. 2001. Dietary diacylglycerol suppresses high fat and high sucrose diet-induced body fat accumulation in C57BL/6J mice. *J. Lipid Res.* 42:372–78

Nagao T, Watanabe H, Goto N, Onizawa K, Taguchi H, et al. 2000. Dietary diacylglycerol suppresses accumulation of body fat compared to triacylglycerol in men in a double-blind controlled trial. *J. Nutr.* 130:792–97

Ogden CL, Carroll MD, Curtin LR, Lamb MM, Flegal KM. 2010. Prevalence of high body mass index in US children and adolescents, 2007–2008. *JAMA* 303:242–49

Oken E, Bellinger DC. 2008. Fish consumption, methylmercury and child neurodevelopment. *Curr. Opin. Pediatr.* 20:178–83

Orgaard A, Jensen L. 2008. The effects of soy isoflavones on obesity. *Exp. Biol. Med.* 233:1066–80

Osaki N, Meguro S, Onizawa K, Mizuno T, Shimotoyodome A, et al. 2008. Effects of a single and short-term ingestion of diacylglycerol on fat oxidation in rats. *Lipids* 43:409–17

Papathanasopoulos A, Camilleri M. 2010. Dietary fiber supplements: effects in obesity and metabolic syndrome and relationship to gastrointestinal functions. *Gastroenterology* 138:65–72.e1–2

Pariza MW. 2004. Perspective on the safety and effectiveness of conjugated linoleic acid. *Am. J. Clin. Nutr.* 79:1132S–36S

Pariza MW, Hargraves WA. 1985. A beef-derived mutagenesis modulator inhibits initiation of mouse epidermal tumors by 7,12-dimethylbenz[a]anthracene. *Carcinogenesis* 6:591–93

Park Y. 2009. Conjugated linoleic acid (CLA): good or bad trans fat? *J. Food Compos. Anal.* 22S:4–12

Park Y, Albright KJ, Liu W, Storkson JM, Cook ME, Pariza MW. 1997. Effect of conjugated linoleic acid on body composition in mice. *Lipids* 32:853–58

Park Y, Pariza MW. 2007. Mechanisms of body fat modulation by conjugated linoleic acid (CLA). *Food Res. Int.* 40:311–23

Park Y, Pariza MW. 2009. Bioactivities and potential mechanisms of action for conjugated fatty acids. *Food Sci. Biotechnol.* 18:586–93

Park Y, Storkson JM, Albright KJ, Liu W, Pariza MW. 1999. Evidence that the trans-10,cis-12 isomer of conjugated linoleic acid induces body composition changes in mice. *Lipids* 34:235–41

Parra D, Ramel A, Bandarra N, Kiely M, Martinez JA, Thorsdottir I. 2008. A diet rich in long chain omega-3 fatty acids modulates satiety in overweight and obese volunteers during weight loss. *Appetite* 51:676–80

Perez-Matute P, Perez-Echarri N, Martinez JA, Marti A, Moreno-Aliaga MJ. 2007. Eicosapentaenoic acid actions on adiposity and insulin resistance in control and high-fat-fed rats: role of apoptosis, adiponectin and tumour necrosis factor-alpha. *Br. J. Nutr.* 97:389–98

Poppitt SD, Strik CM, MacGibbon AK, McArdle BH, Budgett SC, McGill AT. 2010. Fatty acid chain length, postprandial satiety and food intake in lean men. *Physiol. Behav.* 101:161–67

Prior RL, Wu X, Gu L, Hager TJ, Hager A, Howard LR. 2008. Whole berries versus berry anthocyanins: interactions with dietary fat levels in the C57BL/6J mouse model of obesity. *J. Agric. Food Chem.* 56:647–53

Prior RL, Wu XL, Gu LW, Hager T, Hager A, et al. 2009. Purified berry anthocyanins but not whole berries normalize lipid parameters in mice fed an obesogenic high fat diet. *Mol. Nutr. Food Res.* 53:1406–18

Reilly MP, Lehrke M, Wolfe ML, Rohatgi A, Lazar MA, Rader DJ. 2005. Resistin is an inflammatory marker of atherosclerosis in humans. *Circulation* 111:932–39

Reinbach HC, Smeets A, Martinussen T, Moller P, Westerterp-Plantenga MS. 2009. Effects of capsaicin, green tea and CH-19 sweet pepper on appetite and energy intake in humans in negative and positive energy balance. *Clin. Nutr.* 28:260–65

Rosen ED, MacDougald OA. 2006. Adipocyte differentiation from the inside out. *Nat. Rev. Mol. Cell Biol.* 7:885–96

Rudkowska I, Roynette CE, Demonty I, Vanstone CA, Jew S, Jones PJ. 2005. Diacylglycerol: efficacy and mechanism of action of an anti-obesity agent. *Obes. Res.* 13:1864–76

Saito S, Tomonobu K, Hase T, Tokimitsu I. 2006. Effects of diacylglycerol on postprandial energy expenditure and respiratory quotient in healthy subjects. *Nutrition* 22:30–35

Salas-Salvado J, Farres X, Luque X, Narejos S, Borrell M, et al. 2008. Effect of two doses of a mixture of soluble fibres on body weight and metabolic variables in overweight or obese patients: a randomised trial. *Br. J. Nutr.* 99:1380–87

Sartorelli DS, Franco LJ, Cardoso MA. 2008. High intake of fruits and vegetables predicts weight loss in Brazilian overweight adults. *Nutr. Res.* 28:233–38

Schwartz MW, Peskind E, Raskind M, Boyko EJ, Porte D Jr. 1996. Cerebrospinal fluid leptin levels: relationship to plasma levels and to adiposity in humans. *Nat. Med.* 2:589–93

Schwartz MW, Woods SC, Porte D Jr, Seeley RJ, Baskin DG. 2000. Central nervous system control of food intake. *Nature* 404:661–71

Semenkovich CF. 2006. Insulin resistance and atherosclerosis. *J. Clin. Investig.* 116:1813–22

Smeets AJ, Westerterp-Plantenga MS. 2009. The acute effects of a lunch containing capsaicin on energy and substrate utilisation, hormones, and satiety. *Eur. J. Nutr.* 48:229–34

Smith GP, Gibbs J. 1975. Cholecystokinin: a putative satiety signal. *Pharmacol. Biochem. Behav.* 3:135–38

Snitker S, Fujishima Y, Shen H, Ott S, Pi-Sunyer X, et al. 2009. Effects of novel capsinoid treatment on fatness and energy metabolism in humans: possible pharmacogenetic implications. *Am. J. Clin. Nutr.* 89:45–50

Soni MG, Kimura H, Burdock GA. 2001. Chronic study of diacylglycerol oil in rats. *Food Chem. Toxicol.* 39:317–29

Spalding KL, Arner E, Westermark PO, Bernard S, Buchholz BA, et al. 2008. Dynamics of fat cell turnover in humans. *Nature* 453:783–87

Srinivasan K. 2007. Black pepper and its pungent principle-piperine: a review of diverse physiological effects. *Crit. Rev. Food Sci. Nutr.* 47:735–48

Srinivasan K, Sambaiah K, Chandrasekhara N. 2004. Spices as beneficial hypolipidemic food adjuncts: a review. *Food Rev. Int.* 20:187–220

Steppan CM, Bailey ST, Bhat S, Brown EJ, Banerjee RR, et al. 2001. The hormone resistin links obesity to diabetes. *Nature* 409:307–12

Tada N. 2004. Physiological actions of diacylglycerol outcome. *Curr. Opin. Clin. Nutr. Metab. Care* 7:145–49

Takase H, Shoji K, Hase T, Tokimitsu I. 2005. Effect of diacylglycerol on postprandial lipid metabolism in non-diabetic subjects with and without insulin resistance. *Atherosclerosis* 180:197–204

Tang QQ, Otto TC, Lane MD. 2003. Mitotic clonal expansion: a synchronous process required for adipogenesis. *Proc. Natl. Acad. Sci. USA* 100:44–49

Tartaglia LA, Dembski M, Weng X, Deng N, Culpepper J, et al. 1995. Identification and expression cloning of a leptin receptor, OB-R. *Cell* 83:1263–71

Teramoto T, Watanabe H, Ito K, Omata Y, Furukawa T, et al. 2004. Significant effects of diacylglycerol on body fat and lipid metabolism in patients on hemodialysis. *Clin. Nutr.* 23:1122–26

The World Health Report. 2002. *Reducing Risks Promoting Healthy Life*. Geneva: World Health Organ.

Theander-Carrillo C, Wiedmer P, Cettour-Rose P, Nogueiras R, Perez-Tilve D, et al. 2006. Ghrelin action in the brain controls adipocyte metabolism. *J. Clin. Investig.* 116:1983–93

Tiraby C, Tavernier G, Capel F, Mairal A, Crampes F, et al. 2007. Resistance to high-fat-diet-induced obesity and sexual dimorphism in the metabolic responses of transgenic mice with moderate uncoupling protein 3 overexpression in glycolytic skeletal muscles. *Diabetologia* 50:2190–99

Tschop M, Smiley DL, Heiman ML. 2000. Ghrelin induces adiposity in rodents. *Nature* 407:908–13

Tunnicliffe JM, Shearer J. 2008. Coffee, glucose homeostasis, and insulin resistance: physiological mechanisms and mediators. *Appl. Physiol. Nutr. Metab.* 33:1290–300

Tuomilehto J, Lindstrom J, Eriksson JG, Valle TT, Hamalainen H, et al. 2001. Prevention of type 2 diabetes mellitus by changes in lifestyle among subjects with impaired glucose tolerance. *New Engl. J. Med.* 344:1343–50

Turton MD, O'Shea D, Gunn I, Beak SA, Edwards CM, et al. 1996. A role for glucagon-like peptide-1 in the central regulation of feeding. *Nature* 379:69–72

Van Loan M. 2009. The role of dairy foods and dietary calcium in weight management. *J. Am. Coll. Nutr.* 28(Suppl. 1):120–9

Verdich C, Toubro S, Buemann B, Lysgard Madsen J, Juul Holst J, Astrup A. 2001. The role of postprandial releases of insulin and incretin hormones in meal-induced satiety—effect of obesity and weight reduction. *Int. J. Obes. Relat. Metab. Disord.* 25:1206–14

Vuong T, Benhaddou-Andaloussi A, Brault A, Harbilas D, Martineau LC, et al. 2009. Antiobesity and antidiabetic effects of biotransformed blueberry juice in KKA(y) mice. *Int. J. Obes.* 33:1166–73

Watts GF, Chan DC, Ooi EM, Nestel PJ, Beilin LJ, Barrett PH. 2006. Fish oils, phytosterols and weight loss in the regulation of lipoprotein transport in the metabolic syndrome: lessons from stable isotope tracer studies. *Clin. Exp. Pharmacol. Physiol.* 33:877–82

Westerterp-Plantenga M, Diepvens K, Joosen AM, Berube-Parent S, Tremblay A. 2006. Metabolic effects of spices, teas, and caffeine. *Physiol. Behav.* 89:85–91

Westerterp-Plantenga MS, Smeets A, Lejeune MP. 2005. Sensory and gastrointestinal satiety effects of capsaicin on food intake. *Int. J. Obes.* 29:682–88

Weyer C, Foley JE, Bogardus C, Tataranni PA, Pratley RE. 2000. Enlarged subcutaneous abdominal adipocyte size, but not obesity itself, predicts type II diabetes independent of insulin resistance. *Diabetologia* 43:1498–506

Woods SC, D'Alessio DA. 2008. Central control of body weight and appetite. *J. Clin. Endocrinol. Metab.* 93:S37–50

Wortley KE, del Rincon JP, Murray JD, Garcia K, Iida K, et al. 2005. Absence of ghrelin protects against early-onset obesity. *J. Clin. Investig.* 115:3573–78

Xiao CW. 2008. Health effects of soy protein and isoflavones in humans. *J. Nutr.* 138:1244S–9S

Yamamoto K, Asakawa H, Tokunaga K, Watanabe H, Matsuo N, et al. 2001. Long-term ingestion of dietary diacylglycerol lowers serum triacylglycerol in type II diabetic patients with hypertriglyceridemia. *J. Nutr.* 131:3204–7

Yamauchi T, Kamon J, Minokoshi Y, Ito Y, Waki H, et al. 2002. Adiponectin stimulates glucose utilization and fatty-acid oxidation by activating AMP-activated protein kinase. *Nat. Med.* 8:1288–95

Yamauchi T, Kamon J, Waki H, Terauchi Y, Kubota N, et al. 2001. The fat-derived hormone adiponectin reverses insulin resistance associated with both lipoatrophy and obesity. *Nat. Med.* 7:941–46

Yanai H, Yoshida H, Tomono Y, Hirowatari Y, Kurosawa H, et al. 2008. Effects of diacylglycerol on glucose, lipid metabolism, and plasma serotonin levels in lean Japanese. *Obesity* 16:47–51

Yang LY, Kuksis A. 1991. Apparent convergence (at 2-monoacylglycerol level) of phosphatidic acid and 2-monoacylglycerol pathways of synthesis of chylomicron triacylglycerols. *J. Lipid Res.* 32:1173–86

Yasunaga K, Glinsmann WH, Seo Y, Katsuragi Y, Kobayashi S, et al. 2004. Safety aspects regarding the consumption of high-dose dietary diacylglycerol oil in men and women in a double-blind controlled trial in comparison with consumption of a triacylglycerol control oil. *Food Chem. Toxicol.* 42:1419–29

Yoshioka M, Imanaga M, Ueyama H, Yamane M, Kubo Y, et al. 2004. Maximum tolerable dose of red pepper decreases fat intake independently of spicy sensation in the mouth. *Br. J. Nutr.* 91:991–95

Yoshioka M, St-Pierre S, Drapeau V, Dionne I, Doucet E, et al. 1999. Effects of red pepper on appetite and energy intake. *Br. J. Nutr.* 82:115–23

Zemel MB, Miller SL. 2004. Dietary calcium and dairy modulation of adiposity and obesity risk. *Nutr. Rev.* 62:125–31

Zemel MB, Richards J, Milstead A, Campbell P. 2005. Effects of calcium and dairy on body composition and weight loss in African-American adults. *Obes. Res.* 13:1218–25

Zemel MB, Sun X. 2008. Calcitriol and energy metabolism. *Nutr. Rev.* 66:S139–46

Zhang Y, Na X, Zhang Y, Li L, Zhao X, Cui H. 2009. Isoflavone reduces body weight by decreasing food intake in ovariectomized rats. *Ann. Nutr. Metab.* 54:163–70

Zhang Y, Proenca R, Maffei M, Barone M, Leopold L, Friedman JM. 1994. Positional cloning of the mouse obese gene and its human homologue. *Nature* 372:425–32

Rapid Detection and Limitations of Molecular Techniques

John J. Maurer[1,2]

[1]Department of Population Health, The University of Georgia, Athens, Georgia 30602

[2]Center for Food Safety, The University of Georgia, Griffin, Georgia 30223; email: jmaurer@uga.edu

Annu. Rev. Food Sci. Technol. 2011. 2:259–279

First published online as a Review in Advance on December 3, 2010

The *Annual Review of Food Science and Technology* is online at food.annualreviews.org

This article's doi: 10.1146/annurev.food.080708.100730

1941-1413/11/0410-0259$20.00

Keywords

PCR, sensitivity, specificity, inhibitors, pathogen detection

Abstract

Polymerase chain reaction (PCR) has become an important diagnostic tool in the detection of foodborne pathogens. Many PCR tests have been validated, harmonized, and commercialized to make PCR a standard tool used by food microbiology laboratories to detect pathogens in foods. Current PCR technology allows for rapid detection of pathogens in real time. Real-time PCR can provide qualitative as well as quantitative information. However, PCR does have its limitations because of false-negative and false-positive results that may be encountered with the daily running of PCR assays by a diagnostic laboratory. The intent of this review is to help the reader identify these problems as they occur, discuss the nature of this interference, and provide solutions. This review also discusses the future of molecular diagnostics, i.e., high throughput nucleic acid sequencing.

PCR: polymerase chain reaction

Pyrosequencing: new nucleic acid sequencing technology that measures incorporation of specific nucleotides by detecting photon emission produced by firefly luciferase

Anneal: hydrogen base-pair binding of oligonucleotide(s) or nucleic acid (DNA or RNA) to the complementary sequences present in the nucleic acid sample

DNA polymerase: an enzyme that is responsible for synthesizing DNA strands using the complementary strand as a template for its synthesis

Primer: an oligonucleotide, between 18–25 bp in length, that primes DNA synthesis of the complementary DNA strand

HISTORY OF PCR AND ITS EVOLUTION AS A DIAGNOSTIC TEST

The ability of any microbe to cause disease is dictated in part by its genetic composition. In some instances, its virulence rests in a single gene (Greenfield et al. 1983, Matsuda & Barsdale 1967). You detect the gene, you detect the pathogen (Mikhailovich et al. 1995). Molecular biology has transformed diagnostic microbiology since the early days of DNA:DNA hybridization technology (Southern 1975) through the advent of polymerase chain reaction (PCR) (Saiki et al. 1985), pyrosequencing (Ronaghi et al. 1996, Marguilies et al. 2005), single multitest microarrays (Schena et al. 1995), and fluorescent-microsphere technology (Fulton et al. 1997, McHugh et al. 1988), which may supplant today's PCR-based molecular tests. No one single molecular technique has transformed research and diagnostics more than PCR. The thermocycler has become not only the standard lab instrument of the research lab, but it is now commonplace in the diagnostic laboratory. PCR has gone from the theoretical to the practical. There are several commercial PCR kits available for *Salmonella*, *Campylobacter*, *Listeria monocytogenes*, *Escherichia coli* O157:H7, *Enterobacter sakazakii*, *Staphylococcus aureus*, and Norovirus detection (**Table 1**). Considerable resources have been put into designing, implementing, and validating PCR for detection of pathogens in food. Several of these PCR tests (e.g., *Salmonella* BAX PCR) (USDA Food Safety and Inspection Service 2007) are used by U.S. regulatory agencies involved in screening foods for pathogens (USDA Food Safety and Inspection Service 2007, 2008, 2009). However, PCR is a tool and like any tool it has its strengths and weaknesses. PCR may not be practical or economical, depending on the application. This review explores the current molecular tools available for rapid detection of pathogens in foods and their limitations. The emphasis here is placed on PCR, as it has the greatest application and use in detecting foodborne pathogens. Other future technologies are examined, but because of their experimental nature, the scope of their review is limited and introductory.

The PCR was borne out an understanding of the chemistry of DNA replication and requirements for synthesizing the complementary DNA strand: A single-stranded DNA template and a free, 3′ hydroxyl group is needed for the incorporation of the next nucleotide into the nascent, DNA strand. In the bacterial cell, the DNA gyrases and topoisomerases produce the single-stranded template, and the single-stranded binding proteins prevent the premature reannealing of the DNA strands before the complementary DNA can be synthesized by the DNA polymerase. The primase produces an RNA primer needed to synthesize the complementary DNA on the lagging DNA strand. This RNA primer provides the free 3′ hydroxyl group necessary in the nucleophilic attack

Table 1 Examples of commercially available PCR kits for pathogen detection in foods

Pathogen	PCR	Brand name	Manufacturer
Salmonella	TAQMAN	*Salmonella* BAX® PCR	DuPont Qualicon
	RT PCT with IAC	ADIAFOOD rapid pathogen detection system for *Salmonella* spp.	AES Chemunex Canada
	mPCR with IAC	Multipathogen PCR kit - *Salmonella* spp., *Listeria monocytogenes*, and *E. coli* O157	Diatheva
	RT PCR	AnDiaTec® *Salmonella* real time PCR Kit	AnDiaTec
Listeria monocytogenes	TAQMAN	*Listeria* BAX® PCR	DuPont Qualicon
	RT PCR with IAC	ADIAFOOD rapid pathogen detection system for *L. monocytogenes*	AES Chemunex Canada
Escherichia coli O157	TAQMAN	*E. coli* O157 BAX® PCR	DuPont Qualicon
	RT PCR with IAC	ADIAFOOD rapid pathogen detection system for *E. coli* O157 and *E. coli* O157:H7	AES Chemunex Canada

of the incoming nucleotide to the nascent DNA strand, producing the phosphodiester that strings the nucleotides together in the DNA strand (Kornberg 2000). In the test tube, these reactions and events can be recreated using heat (e.g., 94°C) to produce the single-stranded DNA template and an oligonucleotide primer to initiate synthesis of the complementary DNA strand. With the right salts, pH, and a supply of nucleotides, the purified DNA polymerase can synthesize both DNA strands, yielding double-stranded DNA product. The oligonucleotide primer determines if and where DNA synthesis can be initiated. Positioning of these priming oligonucleotides close to one another and oriented to produce overlapping, complementary DNA strands can over time and with repeated cycles of DNA replication produce a single DNA fragment. The size of this DNA fragment is a function of the distance between the two DNA priming oligonucleotides and its appearance dictated by the presence of DNA sequences complementary to both priming oligonucleotides (primers). To produce a new DNA strand in vitro requires three steps: (*a*) denaturation (94°C) to produce single-stranded DNA; (*b*) annealing at a lowered temperature optimal for the binding of the primers to their complementary, target sequence; and (*c*) extension at a temperature optimal for the DNA polymerase to synthesize the new DNA strand. These three steps can be repeated over and over, amplifying the DNA exponentially with each subsequent cycle.

The first PCR used *E. coli* DNA polymerase. Because of the heat denaturation step, new enzymes had to be added to each subsequent cycle (Saiki et al. 1985). The DNA polymerases of thermophilic bacteria such as *Thermophilus aquaticus* (*Taq*) are resistant to denaturation by boiling and enzymatically active when the temperature is reduced to 72°C. At present, a single application of the enzyme *Taq* DNA polymerase to the reaction mix allows repeated cycling of the denaturation, annealing, and extension steps (Saiki et al. 1988). With the development of the thermocycler, an instrument or heating block that could rapidly fluctuate temperatures from 94°C to 4°C (Saiki et al. 1988), PCR was born.

Extension: synthesis of the complementary DNA strand by the DNA polymerase in PCR, using the bound oligonucleotide as the primer for synthesis

***Thermophilus aqauticus* (*Taq*):** the thermophilic organism from which a key thermally stable DNA polymerase for PCR was obtained

Thermocycler: an instrument with a heating/refrigeration block that can be programmed for a wide range of temperatures

Amplicon: PCR product

Real time: detection of amplicon as it is produced with each cycle of PCR

GEL-BASED PCR DETECTION

Early PCR was a qualitative test that could assess presence or absence of a mutation (Saiki et al. 1985) or gene allele (Saiki et al. 1986). In fact, the earliest applications of PCR were for detecting inheritable metabolic disorders (Saiki et al. 1985). Later applications were turned to detection of infectious agents (Kwok et al. 1987, Olive 1989), reasoning that if the sequence targeted by PCR was present, so too was the pathogen. PCR amplified targeted sequences to sufficiently high levels (>25 ng DNA) to be observed in an ethidium-stained agarose gel. Using this gel-based format, PCR would remain a qualitative test until light/fluorescence detectors were incorporated into the thermocycler (Morrison et al. 1998) for detection of amplicons in real time. The thermocyclers have also evolved from the single heating block instruments (Saiki et al. 1988) to hot-air thermocyclers (Wittwer et al. 1989) to 96-well block thermocyclers (Murphy et al. 1993) and thermocyclers with programmable, individual wells (Raja et al. 2002). These advancements decreased the time it took to optimize PCR and later run these PCR tests. PCR reaction times that once took 90 minutes have been reduced to 10–15 minutes (Morrison et al. 1998, Wittwer et al. 1989) and decreased reaction volumes and cost associated with a single PCR test (Morrison et al. 1998, Wittwer et al. 1989).

REAL-TIME PCR ASSAY

With the birth of PCR came an explosion of diagnostic tests for detecting viruses, bacteria, and parasites in patient specimens, foods, and environmental samples. At the inception of PCR, detection was limited to a gel-based format, which required additional equipment (electrophoresis unit, camera, etc.) on top of the expensive thermocycler already needed for PCR. Also, the additional handling associated with gel detection opened potential sources for carryover contamination of PCR set-up area and reagents sometimes producing false-positive results (see section PCR Carryover Contamination). The greatest advancement in thermocycler technology came in the addition of a fluorometer/photometer for detection of fluorescent amplicons as they are produced in real time (Morrison et al. 1998). The earliest real-time PCR assay incorporated a sensitive fluorescent dye, SYBR-Green, that binds the double-stranded DNA as it is produced (Morrison et al. 1998). The advantage of this dye over ethidium bromide is that SYBR-Green is 1,000-fold more sensitive (Schneeberger et al. 1995). With the detector built into the thermocycler, the amplicon can now be detected once it reaches the threshold range for detection after x number of cycles. There is an inverse correlation between cycle number at which the amplicon is initially detected and target copy number, allowing one to estimate cell or viral numbers in positive samples (Richards et al. 2004, Wolffs et al. 2006). The fewer target cells present in a sample, the more cycles are needed before the amplicon is detected. The real-time PCR can therefore be standardized against a set of known target amounts (DNA concentration) or cell concentrations to transform this test from a qualitative test to a quantitative test (Morrison et al. 1998). The added utility of not only detecting pathogens in foods but also determining pathogen loads is an added benefit, as new regulatory decisions are now being developed based on both prevalence and pathogen load (e.g., *Campylobacter* and poultry) (New performance standards for *Salmonella* and *Campylobacter* in young chicken and turkey slaughter establishments; new compliance guides 2010).

Nonspecific amplicon: an erroneous PCR product of size or sequence composition different from that of the intended PCR target

Given that the PCR reaction and subsequent amplicon detection are self-contained, never requiring the reaction vessel to be opened following setup, the potential for carryover contamination is eliminated. However, the earlier real-time PCR tests were fraught with problems with false-positive results associated with sometime production of nonspecific amplicons (see What Is Considered a PCR Positive Result?).

TAQMAN PCR AND MOLECULAR BEACONS

The problems with false-positive results were later resolved with inclusion of internal probes in the real-time PCR assay (Livak et al. 1995, Tyagi & Kramer 1996). The internal probes central to 5′-nuclease PCR (also known as TAQMAN PCR) (Livak et al. 1995) and molecular beacons (Tyagi & Kramer 1996) reduced false-positive results by requiring annealing of these internal oligonucleotides to the true amplicon as it is produced. Rather than using the fluorescent dye SYBR-Green floating freely in the reaction mix, a fluorescent dye is physically incorporated into the internal probe along with a chemical quencher that interferes with fluorescence when the probe is unbound in solution (Livak et al. 1995). Only when the internal probe is bound to the true amplicon can the fluorescent marker be detected. In 5′-nuclease PCR, an exonuclease associated with the thermophilic DNA polymerase liberates the fluorescent chemical group from the chemical quencher, as the enzyme synthesizes the complementary DNA strand (Livak et al. 1995). For the molecular beacon, the internal probe consists of an internal nucleotide sequence complementary to the amplicon generated during PCR, flanked by sequences that are complementary to each other, allowing the 5′ and 3′ ends to anneal with one another and form a stem and loop structure. The fluorescent dye is situated on one end of the oligonucleotide probe and the chemical quencher is placed at the opposite end. The 3′ end of the probe also contains a dideoxy nucleotide, which prevents its incorporation into the nascent DNA strand or degradation by exonuclease activity of the DNA polymerase (Tyagi & Kramer 1996). When this internal probe is allowed to anneal with itself and form this stem and loop structure, the chemical quencher is now brought into close proximity with the fluorescent dye, blocking light emission when excited with ultraviolet (UV)

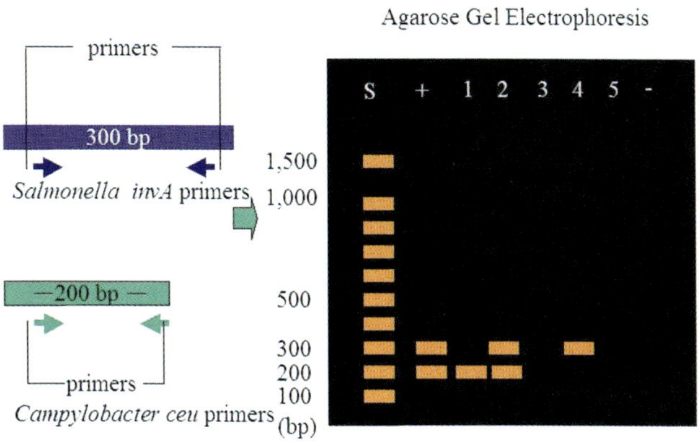

Figure 1

Multiplex PCR assay. PCR primers are designed to target sequences unique to pathogen *Salmonella* (*invA*) and *Campylobacter* (*ceu*) and also produce an amplicon with size that is unique for the pathogen being screened: *Salmonella*, 300-bp amplicon and *Campylobacter*, 200-bp amplicon. The primers are designed and PCR is optimized so that both primer pairs can work in the same reaction: a single test for two pathogens. PCRs for samples 1–5 are loaded into wells for gel electrophoresis. +, positive control and contains both *Salmonella* and *Campylobacter* template; −, negative control, water added in place of template; S, molecular weight standards for sizing PCR amplicons.

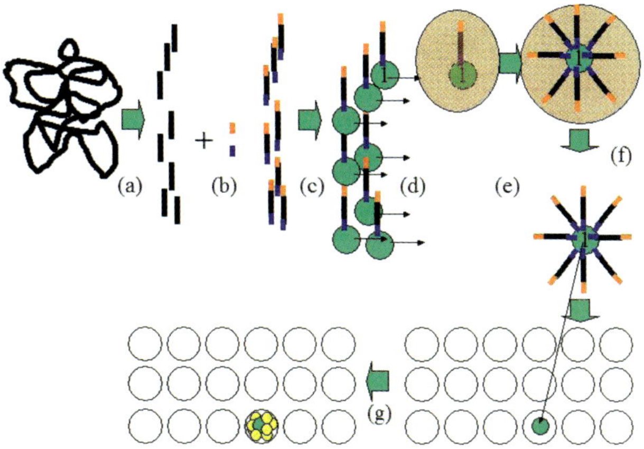

Figure 2

454 pyrosequencing. (*a*) DNA is sheared to produce smaller, 300–500-bp DNA fragments. (*b*) Oligonucleotide adapters are added to DNA fragments. (*c*) Through limiting dilution, individual DNA fragments are attached to a single bead. (*d*) The DNA-bound beads are placed in oil immersion–containing PCR reagents (primers, polymerase, etc.). A single oil droplet contains a single bead with a DNA fragment. (*e*) PCR amplifies the single DNA fragment into millions of copies now covering the surface of the bead. (*f*) Oil immersion is broken to free bead for its deposition into single well of a million-well slide. (*g*) Pyrosequencing reagents and enzymes are added to each well.

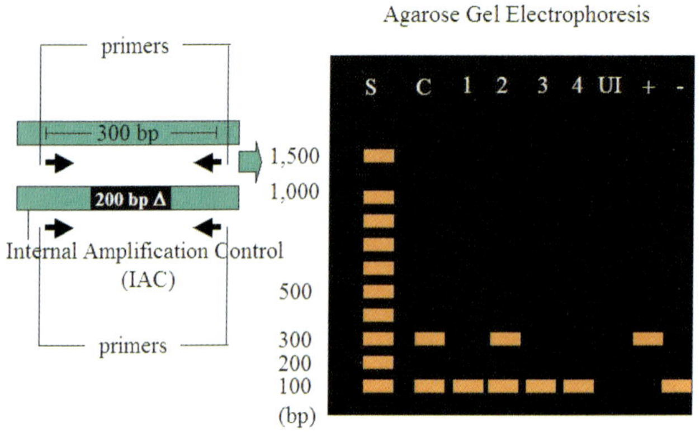

Figure 3

Internal amplification control (IAC). Primers are used to initially amplify targeted sequences. The amplicon is cloned and engineered to contain an internal 200-bp deletion. The plasmid containing the IAC is used to spike samples. Regardless of the pathogen's presence, all samples should be PCR assay-positive and produce the 100-bp amplicon for the IAC. If the pathogen is present, then two DNA fragments should be observed, the 300-bp amplicon for the pathogen and the 100-bp IAC amplicon. PCR reactions for samples 1–4 are loaded into wells for gel electrophoresis. C, positive control with IAC; UI, negative control: no IAC; -, IAC alone; S, molecular weight standards for sizing PCR amplicons.

radiation (Tyagi & Kramer 1996). If the true amplicon is present, the molecular beacon hybridizes or anneals to it, separating the fluorescent dye from the quencher and thus allowing the bound probe to fluoresce upon excitation with UV radiation. As a real-time PCR assay, 5′-nuclease PCR lends itself well as both a qualitative and quantitative test (Bassler et al. 1995). Several of today's commercially available PCR tests have been developed as a TAQMAN PCR (**Table 1**).

Multiplex PCR assay: a single PCR test for detecting multiple genes or pathogens, based on the detection of unique size amplicon

Genome: the complete genetic composition of an organism or virus. For a bacterium like *Escherichia coli* O157:H7, the genome includes plasmid, prophages, and chromosome

MULTIPLEX PCR ASSAY

The PCR assay was originally developed to detect a single target sequence or pathogen. As more unique target gene(s) or sequences were identified for detecting pathogens by PCR, the number of PCR tests a diagnostic laboratory could conduct quickly grew. Depending on the food tested, pathogen prevalence and cell numbers, and clientele's requirements, a laboratory may be required to run a minimum of three separate PCR tests. The natural progression in the evolution of the diagnostic PCR assay was toward a single test for the detection of multiple pathogens (Beuret 2004, O'Leary et al. 2009, Omiccioli et al. 2009), pathotypes (Lopez-Saucedo et al. 2003), serovars (Doumith et al. 2004, Hong et al. 2008, Paton & Paton 1998), phage types (Hu et al. 2002), and strain types (Cooke et al. 2007). Multiplex PCR assay was the logical next step, a single PCR assay that combines multiple primers for detecting multiple pathogens or strains (Beuret 2004, Cooke et al. 2007, Doumith et al. 2004, Hong et al. 2008, Hu et al. 2002, Lopez-Saucedo et al. 2003, O'Leary et al. 2009, Omiccioli et al. 2009, Paton & Paton 1998). Each primer set was designed to produce an amplicon with a defined signature size for the pathogen or strain being tested. The PCR primers were designed to produce a unique amplicon size specific to the gene or sequence being targeted (**Figure 1**, see color insert). Therefore, based on the size of the amplicon produced by PCR, one can identify the pathogen or strain present in sample x. This tool has become useful not only in detecting specific pathogens, but in typing bacterial (Doumith et al. 2004, Hong et al. 2008, Paton & Paton 1998) and viral (Iturriza-Gomara et al. 2004) isolates as well. The multiplex PCR assay has even been adapted to the real-time PCR assay, where in place of detecting specific-sized amplicons, the test is now developed to detect multiple-colored fluorescent dyes associated with the distinct, internal probes for pathogens X, Y, and Z (Woods et al. 2008).

PCR, PYROSEQUENCING, AND GENOMICS

Nucleic acid sequencing technology has made incredible leaps forward in the past five years with the development and commercialization of the open microfabricated high density picoliter sequencing reactors for rapid, high-throughput sequencing, also known as 454 pyrosequencing (Margulies et al. 2005). With the new high-throughput nucleic acid sequencing technologies, genomes can be completely sequenced in weeks rather than years because this methodology does not require DNA libraries and clones (Schloss 2008), only isolated nucleic acid. This new high-throughput sequencing has expanded the repertoire of bacterial genomes sequenced (Maze et al. 2010), including multiple pathogenic strains (Clawson et al. 2009, Gilmour et al. 2010, Hofreuter et al. 2006, Kotewicz et al. 2008, Poly et al. 2008). This powerful sequencing tool has helped identify potential bacterial or viral agents associated with diseases of previously unknown etiology (Coetzee et al. 2010, Cox-Foster et al. 2007, McKenna et al. 2008). As one-third of foodborne illnesses in the United States is of unknown etiology [Surveillance for foodborne disease outbreaks—United States, 2007. (2010)], 454 pyrosequencing and other high-throughput nucleic acid sequencing technologies (Schloss 2008) are likely to identify new bacterial, protozoal, or viral pathogens. The bottlenecks now for this new technology are data storage, processing, and analysis (Schloss 2008).

bp: base pair (or nucleotide)

PPi: pyrophosphate

CCD: charge-coupled device

454 pyrosequencing works as follows: The intact DNA ($\sim 4 \times 10^6$ bp; *E. coli* chromosome) is fractionated by sonication into smaller, 300–500-bp DNA fragments, to which oligonucleotide adapters are subsequently added for PCR amplification later in the procedure (**Figure 2**, see color insert). Using limiting dilution, a single DNA fragment is bound to a single bead. Millions of these beads, where each bead contains an individual DNA fragment, are immersed in an oil emulsion. In this emulsion, a single bead is present within an oil droplet. PCR is performed using primers that bind to the adaptors. That single DNA fragment is amplified to coat each bead with ten million copies of a unique template. The beads are subsequently removed from the emulsion, and bound DNA is denatured to produce a single-stranded template for sequencing and deposited into the wells of a fiber optic slide (**Figure 2**). A single slide contains a million wells, and each well contains a single bead with a unique template for sequencing. Sequencing enzymes are delivered to each well, bound to smaller beads that fill each chamber/well. Microfluidics administer to each well a cycle of dATP, dTTP, dCTP, and dGTP. Pyrophosphate (PPi) is produced upon incorporation of each nucleotide into the template DNA strand by the DNA polymerase and detected by luciferase, which produces a photon of light for every PPi molecule that is detected by a million pixel charge-coupled device (CCD) camera. Microfluids wash the wells of the unincorporated nucleotide and administer the next one to start the process anew. A single fiber optic slide can produce a million sequence reads, for which each read may have a 100–500-bp sequence.

Today, there is a plethora of PCR tests available for detecting the many viral, bacterial, and protozoal agents associated with foodborne illnesses. Several of these PCRs have been combined into a single test for detecting multiple pathogens (Beuret 2004, Cooke et al. 2007, Doumith et al. 2004, Hong et al. 2008, Hu et al. 2002, Lopez-Saucedo et al. 2003, O'Leary et al. 2009, Omiccioli et al. 2009, Paton & Paton 1998). It is tempting to abandon current standardized microbiological methods for these newer molecular tests. However, as with any diagnostic test, the PCR assay has its strengths and weaknesses. To bring this new technology into the diagnostic or food microbiology laboratory, one needs to become acquainted with nuances of PCR, including the details of sample preparation, interpretation of test results, the expense and practicality of using a PCR test, and identifying and troubleshooting problems as they arise.

INTERPRETATION OF PCR RESULTS

PCR Results, Statistics, and Validation

Research in the development of molecular diagnostic tests has made major advancements since their infancy, when reporting on the molecular specificity (differentiation of genus, species, serovar, or strain from evolutionarily/genetically related members) and sensitivity (the fewest cells detected) was sufficient for publication (Maurer et al. 1999, Thomas et al. 1991). Now, there are greater requirements placed on authors to validate their molecular test and demonstrate that the new test is comparable to, if not better than, the one currently adopted by diagnostic laboratories (Scope 2010). Authors must address the congruence of the new diagnostic test with an existing test(s), reporting on the statistical specificity (the proportion of true negative results) and sensitivity (the proportion of true positive results), compared with the currently used test that is considered the gold standard (Liu et al. 2002; Hong et al. 2003, 2008, 2009). With regards to validation of PCR tests for detecting foodborne bacterial pathogens, the gold standard is a culture method. A false-positive result occurs when the PCR assay indicates a positive result and the culture method fails to isolate and identify the pathogen of interest, and a false-negative result is the opposite, i.e., the failure of the PCR test to detect the pathogen of interest. What accounts for these false-positive and false-negative results, and what can be done to optimize the PCR test to improve the specificity and sensitivity of the test? These topics are the primary focus of this review and are discussed in the following sections.

Long PCR: specific PCR that refers to amplification of DNA fragments of 10–30 kb in size by PCR

Kb: kilobase (1 Kb = 1000 bp)

What Is Considered a PCR Positive Result?

In a PCR assay, the primers are important in setting the sensitivity and specificity of the test. The length of the individual oligonucleotide primer is important in setting the specificity as the inverse of the primer length (in bp) is equal to the probability that the primer sequence appears randomly within any given bacterial, protozoal, or viral genome. For example, any 10-bp oligonucleotide primer might appear in a four-million-bp bacterial genome [assume 50% guanocine/cytosine (GC) content] four times, whereas a primer twice that length is expected to appear within any bacterial genome 0.00004 times. Therefore, the length of most primers is set between 18–25 bp. The distance between the forward and reverse PCR primers dictates the size of the PCR product or amplicon. Most commercially available *Taq* DNA polymerases are best for amplifying DNA less than 5,000 bp. However, the newer thermophilic DNA polymerases, especially those with proofreading activity, can amplify larger DNA fragments in 5–25 Kb range (Ohler & Rose 1992). Referred to as "long PCR," this has become an important tool in closing sequencing gaps in bacterial genomes (Tettelin et al. 1999) and in characterizing variable gene(s) or sequences wedged between evolutionarily conserved genes in certain bacterial families, genera, species, serovars, or strains (Herbelin et al. 2000, Wang et al. 1998, Wang & Reeves 1998). However, with the targeted amplification of larger DNA fragments, one loses sensitivity with the PCR assay. Therefore, with conventional PCR and real-time PCR assays, the recommended spacing of primers is between 500–100 bp and 200–75 bp, respectively. Combined, both primers within the primer pair set the specificity for the PCR assay by their length and spacing between the forward and reverse primer. Although there may be some annealing of a primer to sequences other than the complementary target, it's the distance between it and the second primer that may preclude amplification of larger, nonspecific amplicons with *Taq* DNA polymerase.

A PCR result is considered positive if and only if it produces an amplicon of the expected size, based on the spacing of the forward and reverse primers. Most sequences targeted in the PCR assay are to genes, which are invariant in size within a bacterial population, species, or genera. Therefore, one expects to observe the same size amplicon produced for every individual within the population, species, or genera that is targeted for detection by that PCR assay. Any PCR assay that produces a product that does not correspond in size to the placement of the primers within the targeted genome is ignored and negative only if the expected size amplicon is not observed.

Amplicons produced in a PCR reaction, with size contrary to expected size for the primer pair used, are referred to as nonspecific amplicons. For PCRs where size is critical, % agarose and molecular weight standards selected are essential in providing the resolution, DNA separation, and molecular weight range needed to interpret a gel-based PCR test. Where gel electrophoresis is essential to PCR detection, it's important for the voltage used to allow sufficient time to elapse for adequate separation and resolution of DNA fragments within the size range of the molecular weight standard. Generally, one can use the dye front generated during electrophoresis as a guide to determine when to stop (dye front is approximately 1 cm from the bottom of the gel). Expediency (i.e., time) to generate results can impede accuracy in interpreting gel results and erroneously identify nonspecific amplicons as PCR-positive.

In real-time PCR, the dye SYBR-Green binds to the amplicons as they are synthesized and fluoresces once exposed to UV light. The signal intensifies with each successive round of the PCR until it plateaus, producing a sigmoidal curve for fluorescence versus PCR cycle number. The more target cells present, the sooner the PCR product is detected by the thermocyclers'

Viable but nonculturable (VBNC): a physiological state in which bacteria are still metabolically active but unable to grow using conventional culture methodology

fluorometer. If sample and reaction conditions should produce a nonspecific amplicon, this PCR cannot distinguish between the true versus nonspecific amplicons as they are detected in real time. However, one can distinguish nonspecific from true amplicons by the unique melting curve associated with targeted sequences versus the spurious amplification of unrelated gene sequences (Eyigor et al. 2002). Therefore, inclusion of melting curve analysis of each sample and amplicon obtained at the end of each PCR run is a necessary quality control measure for successfully running real-time PCR in the diagnostic laboratory. PCR-negative samples that produce these nonspecific amplicons are useful in further optimizing the PCR. The PCR reaction conditions can be tweaked by increasing the annealing temperature or decreasing the magnesium chloride concentration to eliminate these nonspecific amplicons. The newer, real-time PCR assays use oligonucleotide probes to sequences internal to the amplicon and therefore improve the specificity of the PCR as it eliminates the detection of nonspecific amplicons (Livak et al. 1995, Tyagi & Kramer 1996).

What Does a Positive PCR Result Mean?

The most conservative conclusion one can draw from any PCR test is that the targeted gene sequence is present in sample *x*, and by inference, the targeted pathogen as well. As DNA is often the template employed in most PCR reactions, this test cannot distinguish between live or dead cells or whether or not the agent present in sample *x* is infectious. Depending on the PCR test in question, one may not be able to infer more than the presence of a specific genus (*Salmonella* and *invA* PCR) (Rahn et al. 1992), species (*L. monocytogenes* and listeriolysin O PCR) (Thomas et al. 1991), or serovar (*E. coli* O157:H7 and *wba*/*fliC* PCR) (Paton & Paton 1998). Coupled with sample type, finding of generic *Salmonella*, for example, may or may not have any significance depending on whether one were examining the poultry house environment versus ready-to-eat deli turkey meat. Not being able to distinguish *Salmonella* further with the *invA* PCR, finding *Salmonella enterica* subspecies IIIa Arizona (0.0025% human cases for 2006) (CDC PHLIS Surveillance Data 2007) may not be as significant as *S. enterica* subspecies I Enteritidis (16.6% human cases for 2006) (CDC PHLIS Surveillance Data 2007) in, for example, a table egg-laying operation (Mumma et al. 2004). A few PCRs have been identified that can discern strain level differences directly (Hu et al. 2002) or with added sequencing of the amplicons (Grissa et al. 2008). However, until pyrosequencing becomes cost effective and significant advances are made in bioinformatics, epidemiologic investigations are going to continue to require a culture procedure and the isolation of suspect pathogen(s) from foods (Schloss 2008).

With any new test, one needs to be aware of the false-positive and false-negative results associated with it. Because of the sensitivity of the PCR assay and its ability to amplify millions of copies with time, the test can generate false-positive results from carryover PCR contamination of reagents, pipettors, etc. (Erlich et al. 1991). Also, most PCR assays cannot distinguish dead from live cells (Wolffs et al. 2005) and traditional culture may not be able to distinguish dead from damaged or viable but nonculturable (VBNC) cells (Oliver 2010, Reissbrodt et al. 2002).

Although there are many limitations and disadvantages associated with the PCR assay, which are discussed in more detail below, this assay does have the advantage over traditional culture-based approaches to pathogen detection as a qualitative and quantitative test. Real-time PCR can not only detect a specific pathogen but also determine its load in a sample (Richards et al. 2004, Wolffs et al. 2006) in less time than the most probable number (MPN) methods that have been developed to estimate pathogen cell numbers (Pavic et al. 2009, Wolffs et al. 2006). Being able to detect and quantify pathogen populations at different points within the food processing system can provide added validation information that inactivation treatments are working to reduce pathogen cell numbers.

Is a Negative PCR Result Really Negative?

A negative PCR result may be due to (*a*) absence of the targeted pathogen; (*b*) the pathogen is present at cell numbers below the threshold of detection; or (*c*) something in the sample is interfering with the PCR reaction, leading to an erroneous negative result. However, even with traditional culture-based testing, a negative result is not necessarily confirmatory of the pathogen's absence if its prevalence is less than the sample size needed for detection.

DIAGNOSTIC PCR CHALLENGES AND SOLUTIONS

False-Negative Results

Sometimes there is incongruence between PCR and culture, where the PCR is negative but culture yields a positive result. This is refered to as a false negative and has several causes, including (*a*) physical limits of detection associated with PCR and (*b*) sample inhibitors that interfere with PCR. Both topics are covered in the following sections.

Limits of PCR detection. The sensitivity of the PCR to detect the fewest target cells or virions possible varies depending on the food pathogen, food matrix, target sequence, and primers. Therefore, one may need to consider a number of factors in developing and optimizing a PCR method(s) for detecting the target organism in the food matrix in question. One starting point is to identify a procedure optimal for releasing total DNA or RNA from the microbial cell (Lalonde & Gajadhar 2008, Selma et al. 2008) or viral particle (Jean et al. 2004) in question. The physiochemical nature of the microbe, e.g., norovirus, can be exploited in the sample preparation, effectively concentrating and purifying the PCR template (Haramoto et al. 2004, Leggitt & Jaykus 2000). The PCR's sensitivity is also limited by volume constraints of the test. Most traditional culture-based tests involve processing gram and milliliter amounts and working with large culture volumes (e.g., *Salmonella* enrichment in tetrathionate: 100–250 ml), whereas most molecular-based methods involve final volumes that vary from 10 μl to at most 100 μl. The most sensitive PCR test detects a single cell or virion in 1-to 10-μl template samples. Therefore, for that one cell detected in a single μl, the limit of detection is 1000 cells ml^{-1}.

The sensitivity of the PCR assay can be improved by first concentrating the pathogen present in the food matrix (Comelli et al. 2008, Frazar & Orlandi 2007, Tian et al. 2008), capitalizing on the microbe's size and physiochemical properties, as is the case for noroviruses (Comelli et al. 2008), or using magnetic capture beads conjugated with the antibody (Frazar & Orlandi 2007, Tian & Mandrell 2006) or other substrate that specifically binds to the target pathogen (Tian et al. 2008). The magnetic capture beads have been adapted to the PCR detection of *E. coli* O157:H7 (Fu et al. 2005), *Campylobacter* spp. (Rudi et al. 2004), *L. monocytogenes* (Yang et al. 2007), *S. enterica* (Hagren et al. 2008), *Yersinia enterocolitica* (Kapperud et al. 1993), norovirus (Tian et al. 2008), hepatitis A virus (Jothikumar et al. 1998, Shan et al. 2005), and *Cryptosporidium parvum* (Frazar & Orlandi 2007) for samples where pathogen loads are at or below the threshold of PCR detection.

As alternatives to concentrating microbes present in a sample, several protocols have included an enrichment culture step to increase cell numbers to those above the threshold for PCR detection (Lund et al. 2004, Oberst et al. 1998, Stone et al. 1994). These enrichment cultures employ general, all-purpose media (Malorny et al. 2003a, Oberst et al. 1998) or media that are specific to the pathogen being screened (Lund et al. 2004, Oberst et al. 1998, Stone et al. 1994). Even enrichment cultures targeted to specific pathogens vary not only in their sensitivity and specificity in culture isolation of select pathogens (e.g., *Salmonella*) (Iveson & Kovacs 1967, Feder et al. 2001, Soumet et al. 1999) but interference with PCRs (Liu et al. 2002, Stone et al. 1994).

PCR inhibitors. A diagnostic microbiology laboratory may have to process a variety of food matrices. In addition to consideration of sample size, volumes, and processing steps needed to test foods, these foods can also contain natural PCR inhibitors (Wilson 1997). For example, unwashed produce may prove challenging to PCR tests because of the presence of soils. In several cases, these inhibitors have been identified (Al-Soud et al. 2000, Al-Soud & Radstrom 2001, Monteiro et al. 1997, Opel et al. 2010, Sutlovic et al. 2008) as well as the mechanism behind their inhibition (Al-Soud et al. 2000, Al-Soud & Radstrom 2001, Opel et al. 2010, Sutlovic et al. 2008). The humic acid present in soil interferes with PCRs by inhibiting *Taq* DNA polymerase (Sutlovic et al. 2008). The blood and fat present in meats can also interfere with PCR (Al-Soud et al. 2000, Al-Soud & Radstrom 2001). Hemoglobin, immunoglobulin, and lactoferrin present in blood inhibit the PCR reaction through their binding to single-stranded DNA or the DNA polymerase and preventing of DNA polymerization (Al-Soud et al. 2000, Al-Soud & Radstrom 2001). PCR inhibition can be circumvented through the addition of PCR facilitators/enhancers to the reaction (Al-Soud et al. 2000, Al-Soud & Radstrom 2001), selection of a thermophilic DNA polymerase that is resistant to PCR inhibitor(s) (Al-Soud & Radstrom 2001), or a template purification protocol that removes the inhibitor(s) (Cremonesi et al. 2006, Kim et al. 2008, Lelonde & Gajadhar 2008, Selma et al. 2008, Tian et al. 2008)

One approach to overcoming PCR inhibitors comes in sample and template preparation methodologies that remove PCR inhibitor(s) (Cremonesi et al. 2006, Kim et al. 2008, Lelonde & Gajadhar 2008, Selma et al. 2008, Tian et al. 2008). These methods have been developed in accordance to food matrices involved and the physiological nature of the pathogen being screened (Butot et al. 2007, Cremonesi et al. 2006, Kim et al. 2008, Lalonde & Gajadhar 2008, Selma et al. 2008, Tian et al. 2008, Wolffs et al. 2007). Adding magnetic capture beads can not only improve the sensitivity of the PCR detection (Frazar & Orlandi 2007, Fu et al. 2005, Hagren et al. 2008, Jothikumar et al. 1998, Kapperud et al. 1993, Shan et al. 2005, Tian et al. 2008), but also frees template of PCR inhibitors (Tian & Mandrell 2006). Several of these protocols have been developed to incorporate a nucleic acid purification step involving a solid support matrix with an affinity for nucleic acid (Hong et al. 2003) or an affinity for select nucleic acid species (polyadenylated mRNA) (Kim et al. 2008) or target sequences (Regan & Margolin 1997). Once bound, the nucleic acid can be washed free of the PCR inhibitors and eluted from the spin columns (Luan & Levin 2008) or beads (Hong et al. 2003, Kim et al. 2008) used to concentrate the PCR template. The physiochemical properties of foods can also be exploited by altering the temperature (Hong et al. 2003), using differential or density gradient centrifugation (Hong et al. 2003, Lindqvist 1997, Maurer et al. 1999, Wolffs et al. 2004, 2007), or using filtration (Butot et al. 2007, Wolffs et al. 2006) to remove fats (Hong et al. 2003, Maurer et al. 1999), colloids (Maurer et al. 1999), blood (Hong et al. 2003), or tissues (Butot et al. 2007). These procedures can effectively concentrate the template as well as remove PCR inhibitors. Density gradient centrifugation has the broadest application toward PCR detection of pathogens across diverse food matrices (Lindqvist 1997, Wolffs et al. 2004, 2007). However, some foods may necessitate extractions or digestions (Butot et al. 2007) to ultimately free the template of these inhibitors. Application of activated charcoal to samples has also proven effective in removing PCR inhibitors (Luan & Levin 2008).

Inclusion of additional reagents to the PCR reaction can counteract these inhibitors and facilitate or enhance PCR amplification of the target amplicon in the process (Al-Soud et al. 2000, Al-Soud & Radstrom 2001). The mechanism behind how these reagents facilitate or enhance these PCRs varies from physically removing the inhibitor to protecting the nucleic acid template from inactivation. In addition, facilitators such as DMSO help remove the secondary DNA structures in the primers, template, or product that interferes with DNA polymerase's ability to synthesize the complementary DNA strand (Choi et al. 1999). Target DNA or RNA sequences with high GC content, palindromes, or repetitive sequences are likely to form secondary structures, i.e., hairpins, that may interfere with initiation of the PCR or continued replication of the target amplicon (Choi et al. 1999). Also, dimer-pair formation between primers affects the PCR reaction and at least reduces the sensitivity of detection (Rychlik 1995). This is especially problematic for multiplex PCR assays in which multiple primer pairs are involved. DNA analysis programs can identify which primer pair combinations form potential dimers as well as secondary hairpins from the selected nucleotide sequence(s) (e.g., GeneRunner; **http://www.generunner.net/**). Depending on the percent GC content of targeted gene/sequence(s), there may not be any primers available that are free of secondary structures or dimer-pair formation. However, a facilitator such as DMSO melts these secondary structures (Varadaraj & Skinner 1994) and allows the primers to anneal to their complementary target with the specificity required of the PCR test.

IAC: internal amplification control

Internal amplification controls (IAC) have been developed to detect PCR inhibitors (Casas et al. 1997) and have become an important quality control measure for diagnostic PCR assays (Malorny et al. 2003b). Sample or processed templates are spiked with the control DNA (Malorny et al. 2003a). This control DNA or IAC is generally derived through an internal engineered deletion within the cloned amplicon (Abdulmawjood et al. 2002) (**Figure 3**, see color insert). Spiked with the IAC, the PCR primers would produce an amplicon with a size expected for the engineered deletion. A sample containing the targeted pathogen will produce two amplicons, one corresponding to the size expected for the pathogen and the other smaller amplicon expected for the IAC (Abdulmawjood et al. 2002). Inclusion of an IAC into the diagnostic PCR test has become an important part in harmonization of PCR-based detection protocols for foodborne pathogens (Malorny et al. 2003a). With the advance of real-time PCR, IAC have been adapted to these newer diagnostic tests as part of a TAQMAN PCR (Rodríguez-Lázaro et al. 2005). In this case, the internal oligonucleotide probe is directed to unique sequences obtained by the deletion of internal sequences present in the IAC. With inclusion of different colored fluorescent dyes in the labeling of pathogen-specific oligonucleotide probes and IAC probes, real-time thermocyclers can differentiate between the two signals obtained with either probe (Rodríguez-Lázaro et al. 2005).

False-positive PCR results. In the validation of the PCR assay, this molecular test is compared to another that is considered the standard in diagnostics. Depending on the pathogen, the gold standard for detection may be a culture, method, microscopy, or serology. The best PCR applications have significant congruence with culture-based methods for detecting pathogens, with few false-positive and false-negative results. Controlling for sample contamination or carryover contamination, to be discussed below, false-positive results may be attributed to (*a*) dead cells and a stable template (Wolffs et al. 2005); (*b*) damaged cells requiring resuscitation (Reissbrodt et al. 2002); (*c*) selectivity of the culture enrichment method (Iveson & Kovacs 1967); or (*d*) bacterial cells existing in a VBNC state (Oliver 2010).

LIMITATIONS TO CULTURE-BASED METHODS FOR PATHOGEN DETECTION

The broth enrichment cultures themselves vary in their uniformity in isolating a specific pathogen from a given sample type (Iveson & Kovacs 1967). For example, *Salmonella* isolation frequency varies depending on which enrichment media are used (Iveson & Kovacs 1967) or whether a delayed secondary enrichment is required (Waltman et al. 1991). However as a screen, the PCR assay has proven effective in identifying and improving pathogen isolation for samples requiring a delayed secondary enrichment (Liu et al. 2002). False-positive results may also be attributed to cells within the pathogen population that have an atypical biochemical profile (e.g., H_2S-negative

Salmonella) (Olsen et al. 1992), which is inadvertently missed in the enrichment culture, isolation, and identification process. Detection of pathogenic *E. coli* is especially challenging using culture-based methods for detection, as there are so few biochemical differences to set them apart from commensal *E. coli*. When a biochemical difference is identified (e.g., sorbitol fermentation and *E. coli* O157:H7), biochemically atypical isolates (Karch et al. 1993) may be missed but identified following a PCR-based assay. Even when reliable biochemical tests are available for detecting pathogenic *E. coli*, such as enterohemorrhagic *E. coli* O157, they are the minority relative to the majority of commensal *E. coli*, hence immunomagnetic separation is needed to enrich this minority population (Fu et al. 2005).

The choice of enrichment and differential culture media, additional modifications, and its application to a specific sample type need to be considered in the detection of pathogen *x* in sample *y*. Without confirmatory tests, the enrichment or differential medium may prove inappropriate for identifying pathogen *x* in sample *y* and thus erroneously report more culture-positive results than the PCR test (Blanco-Abad et al. 2009). Therefore, disagreement between culture and PCR methods may be due more to the inappropriateness of the culture method used and therefore obtain erroneous results for detecting the pathogen by culture method (Blanco-Abad et al. 2009).

PCR CARRYOVER CONTAMINATION

The PCR assay is a powerful, sensitive tool for detecting as few as one cell. Its sensitivity is attributed to multiple rounds of DNA replication that amplifies the DNA target exponentially to levels detectable with fluorescent dyes. In 30 cycles, the PCR can produce millions of amplicon molecules. While contained within its capped microfuge tube, simply opening the PCR tube can aerosolize the reaction mix, thereby contaminating surfaces that come in contact with the dispersed amplicon. The amplicon itself can now serve as a template rendering every subsequent PCR assay positive that comes in contact with contaminated pipettes, hands, or reagents.

The best way to address carryover PCR contamination is to introduce measures that avoid or lessen the likelihood of reagent contamination in the initial PCR setup. This can be accomplished by physically separating the three stages of any PCR protocol: (*a*) sample and template preparation; (*b*) PCR setup; and (*c*) analysis of PCR results (e.g., gel electrophoresis). A second, self-contained room for the PCR setup is critical. All reagents, materials, lab coats, disposable gloves, and pipettors should be kept here, including the –20°C freezer for storing templates, controls, primers, and other PCR reagents. Rather than having one tube of reagent (e.g., buffer), it is recommended to dispense aliquots into separate tubes. After finishing with PCR setup, it is best to dispose of the remaining reagent rather than return it to the freezer. This strategy is likely to reduce chances for PCR carryover contamination of reagents or at least help identify the likely reagent (e.g., *Taq* DNA polymerase) that became contaminated.

A set of micropipettors should be designated for this room, never to leave the PCR setup station. Barrier tips are also a necessity for performing PCR assays on a routine basis in the laboratory. These tips prevent backwash of fluids from contaminating the barrel or shaft of the pipettor. However, micropipettors can be disassembled and the component parts cleaned with bleach. Bleach is fairly effective in decontaminating PCR-contaminated surfaces. It is also recommended to set up all PCR reactions in a UV-illuminated PCR workstation or hood. Illuminating the workstation with UV light before and after each PCR setup is recommended for decontaminating surfaces within the hood. In the PCR setup room, it is recommended to have laboratory personnel wear designated lab coats and disposable gloves. A logical workflow is also recommended, with each stage physically separated or confined within specified areas in the laboratory, and assay activities should proceed in the direction from template preparation to PCR setup, thermocycler run, and final analysis (gel electrophoresis). One should limit back and forth movement especially at the later stages. The handling of PCR tubes and setting up of gel electrophoresis following the thermocycler run can introduce PCR carryover contamination by the technician. Going back into the PCR setup room increases the likelihood of contamination of reagents, especially if laboratory personnel do not change lab coats and dispose of gloves prior to entering the room. If these PCR stages cannot be physically separated due to room constraints, a UV PCR workstation/hood is essential.

In addition to the measures described above, substituting dTTP with dUTP and a pretreatment step with uracil *N*-glycosylase can eliminate carryover PCR contamination (Erlich et al. 1991). Uracil is incorporated into amplicons during the PCR assay, producing products that are susceptible to degradation with uracil *N*-glycosylase. Amplicons contaminating the PCR reaction mix are destroyed with initial preincubation at 37°C with uracil *N*-glycosylase. However, the DNA template itself is resistant to this enzymatic degradation. The initial DNA denaturation step at 94°C inactivates the uracil *N*-glycosylase and allows new amplicons to be produced during the PCR.

Real-time PCR, by design, reduces the likelihood of PCR carryover contamination. The amplicon is detected as it is synthesized in real time. Once the PCR reaction has been set up, the tube never needs to be opened again, as the fluorometer can detect fluorescence within the sealed tube. There is no need for additional handling of the PCR reaction tubes once the samples are set and placed in the real-time PCR thermocycler.

DIFFERENTIATING LIVE FROM DEAD CELLS

One of PCR's greatest weaknesses is its inability to distinguish dead from live cells. DNA serves as a template in most PCR tests. This molecule is quite stable as can be attested by the procedures developed for PCR assays that employ boiling (Madico et al. 1995) or ethanol treatment (Hilton et al. 1997) of cells in the template's preparation. At least two studies have revealed DNA stability following cell death (McKillip et al. 1999, Wolffs et al. 2005). The use of the DNA cross-linking agent ethidium monoazide (Soejima et al. 2008) can be exploited for detecting only live bacterial cells by PCR assay. This chemical agent permeates the cell membrane of dead cells and irreversibly cross-links DNA (Nogva et al. 2003). The cross-linked DNA cannot serve as a template in the PCR reaction. This application was successful in distinguishing between live and dead *L. monocytogenes* cells (Soejima et al. 2008), and dead versus live or VBNC *Campylobacter* (Josefsen et al. 2010).

Alternatively, RNA has been explored as a substitute template in PCR assays (Gonzalez-Escalona et al. 2009, McIngvale et al. 2002, McKillip et al. 1998, Werbrouck et al. 2007), as this molecule, depending on the treatment conditions, is quickly degraded upon death of the bacterial cell (McKillip et al. 1998). RNases are quite prevalent in the environment, requiring the inclusion of inhibitors (e.g., DEPC) (Permutt et al. 1976) to prevent the premature degradation of RNA. In the bacterial cell, mRNA generally has a short half-life. However, depending on the gene, the mRNA half-life can vary from 40 s to 20 min (Pedersen & Reeh 1978). Upon death, RNA is quickly degraded, undetectable by PCR within <2 h (McIngvale et al. 2002). Some RNA molecules within the cell exhibit greater stability and take longer to decay to below the level of PCR detection upon death of the cell (McKillip et al. 1998). Careful consideration, therefore, needs to be given in that the target primers need to be matched well with the nucleic acid template.

Another explanation in the reporting of PCR false-positive results may be attributed to bacteria in the VBNC state. The VBNC state may be attributed to the bacterial cell's adaptation to harsh environmental conditions, starvation, or physical injury to the cell (Oliver 2010) that may necessitate resuscitation (Reissbrodt et al. 2002). Several enrichment culture methods currently used in the isolation and detection of foodborne bacterial pathogens employ temperatures, chemicals (dyes, iodine, etc.), and antibiotics to suppress the unwanted growth of commensal bacteria and favor the growth of the pathogen. However, these same enrichment conditions may not favor growth of injured cells without a preenrichment culture (Liao & Fett 2003) or resuscitation of bacterial cells (Reissbordt et al. 2002) from the VBNC to a growth state. When *Campylobacter* enters the VBNC state, the normally helical bacterial cell rounds up into a cocci shape (Rollins & Colwell 1986). This type of profound change in cell shape is due to alterations in the cell wall (Costa et al. 1999, Spratt 1975). The media used to isolate *Campylobacter* includes cephalosporins, which are cell wall inhibitors (Bolton et al. 1983) that may prevent *Campylobacter* from exiting its VBNC state. *Campylobacter* and *Vibrio* are quite adept at transitioning into a VBNC state and persisting in the environment, especially an aquatic environment (Brayton et al. 1987, Rollins & Colwell 1986). The VBNC state is a limitation of the current culture methodology in detecting some pathogens.

FUTURE

The PCR has advanced considerably in the past twenty years, from conceptual (Saiki et al. 1988) to validation, harmonization (Malorny et al. 2003a,b), and use in the diagnostic laboratory setting (USDA Animal and Plant Health Inspection Service 2010; USDA Food Safety and Inspection Service 2007, 2008, 2009). In fact, the PCR assay is the only way some foodborne pathogens (e.g., noroviruses) can be detected in foods and the environment because of our current inability to cultivate them in the laboratory (Gentry et al. 2009). What will be the significant technological advances in the next 20 years? With the current rate of advances in high-throughput sequencing, the cost associated with this technology is expected to decrease at most to $1,000 per 1 billion bp genome(s) or one U.S. dollar per bacterial genome (1 million bp genome) (Schloss 2008). This means affordable high-throughput sequencing could replace some of the current antimicrobial susceptibility testing, serotyping, and strain-typing methods presently used by diagnostic laboratories. The new technology is expected to identify new pathogens associated with those 33% of foodborne outbreaks of unknown etiology [Surveillance for foodborne disease outbreaks—United States 2007. (2010)]. There will always be a need for standard culture and isolation of pathogens, except now it will be to assess the microbe's susceptibility to certain manufacturing processes developed to reduce or eliminate them from foods.

SUMMARY POINTS

1. The PCR has become an important diagnostic tool in the detection of foodborne pathogens.
2. Current PCR technology allows for rapid detection of pathogens in real time, because of fluorescence monitors built into the thermocycler. Real-time PCR assays can provide information regarding pathogen cell numbers in a sample.
3. False-negative results sometimes occur with any PCR test because (*a*) pathogen loads are below the limit of detection or (*b*) PCR inhibitors are present.
4. PCR false-negative results can be reduced by (*a*) using sample enrichment cultures, (*b*) adopting protocols that remove inhibitors or concentrate a pathogen template, (*c*) substituting *Taq* DNA polymerase with inhibitor-resistant polymerase, or (*d*) adding PCR enhancers and facilitators. Inclusion of an internal amplification control (IAC) can alert the user of problems with the PCR and template.

5. PCR false-positive results sometimes occur due to (*a*) nonspecific amplicons, (*b*) carryover contamination of PCR reagents or setup equipment, (*c*) presence of an atypical pathogen, (*d*) inability of the PCR assay to distinguish live from dead cells, or (*e*) presence of injured cells or cells existing in a VBNC state. Nonspecific amplicons and carryover contamination can be countered by adopting TAQMAN or molecular beacon real-time PCR assays. A preenrichment culture step may be useful in the recovery of injured cells. Using mRNA as target template or ethidium monoazide allows the user to detect only the viable cells present in the sample.

FUTURE ISSUES

1. As more PCR protocols become validated, harmonized, and commercialized, this molecular technique may become a standard tool of many food microbiology laboratories.
2. With recent advances in high-throughput sequencing, previously unrecognized viruses, bacteria, and protozoans associated with foodborne illnesses will be discovered, which in turn will lead to the development of new diagnostic tests for pathogens in foods.
3. High-throughput sequencing will become the prominent tool in epidemiologic investigations of foodborne outbreaks. With a decrease in cost, nucleic acid sequencing may supplant existing methods for determining antibiotic susceptibility, serotyping, and strain typing.

DISCLOSURE STATEMENT

The author is not aware of any affiliations, memberships, funding, or financial holdings that might be perceived as affecting the objectivity of this review.

LITERATURE CITED

Abdulmawjood A, Roth S, Bulte M. 2002. Two methods for construction of internal amplification controls for the detection of *Escherichia coli* O157 by polymerase chain reaction. *Mol. Cell. Probes* 16:335–39

Al-Soud WA, Jonsson LJ, Radstrom P. 2000. Identification and characterization of immunoglobulin G in blood as a major inhibitor of diagnostic PCR. *J. Clin. Microbiol.* 38:345–50

Al-Soud WA, Radstrom P. 2001. Purification and characterization of PCR-inhibitory components in blood cells. *J. Clin. Microbiol.* 39:485–93

Bassler HA, Flood SJ, Livak KJ, Marmaro J, Knorr R, Batt CA. 1995. Use of fluorogenic probe in a PCR-based assay for the detection of *Listeria monocytogenes*. *Appl. Environ. Microbiol.* 61:3724–28

Beuret C. 2004. Simultaneous detection of enteric viruses by multiplex real-time RT-PCR. *J. Virol. Methods* 115:1–8

Blanco-Abad V, Ansede-Bermejo J, Rodriguez-Castro A, Martinez-Urtaza J. 2009. Evaluation of different procedures for the optimized detection of *Vibrio parahaemolyticus* in mussels and environmental samples. *Int. J. Food Microbiol.* 129:229–36

Bolton FJ, Coates D, Hinchliffe PM, Robertson L. 1983. Comparison of selective media for isolation of *Campylobacter jejuni/coli*. *J. Clin. Pathol.* 36:78–83

Brayton PR, Tamplin ML, Huq A, Colwell RR. 1987. Enumeration of *Vibrio cholerae* O1 in Bangladesh waters by fluorescent-antibody direct viable count. *Appl. Environ. Microbiol.* 53:2862–65

Butot S, Putallaz T, Sanchez G. 2007. Procedure for rapid concentration and detection of enteric viruses from berries and vegetables. *Appl. Environ. Microbiol.* 73:186–92

Casas I, Tenorio A, Echevarría JM, Klapper PE, Cleator GM. 1997. Detection of enteroviral RNA and specific DNA of herpesviruses by multiplex genome amplification. *J. Virol. Methods* 66:39–50

CDC PHLIS Surveillance Data. 2007. *Salmonella* Annual Survey 2006. **http://www.cdc.gov/ncidod/dbmd/phlisdata/salmonella.htm#2006**

Choi JS, Kim JS, Joe CO, Kim S, Ha KS, Park YM. 1999. Improved cycle sequencing of GC-rich DNA template. *Exp. Mol. Med.* 31:20–24

Clawson ML, Keen JE, Smith TPL, Durso LM, McDaeld TG, et al. 2009. Phylogenetic classification of *Escherichia coli* O157:H7 strains of human and bovine origin using a novel set of nucleotide polymorphisms. *Genome Biol.* 10:R56

Coetzee B, Freeborough MJ, Maree HJ, Celton JM, Rees DJG, Burger JT. 2010. Deep sequencing analysis of viruses infecting grapevines: virome of a vineyard. *Virology* 400:157–63

Comelli HL, Rimstad E, Larsen S, Myrmel M. 2008. Detection of norovirus genotype I.3b and II.4 in bioaccumulated blue mussels using different virus recovery methods. *Int. J. Food Microbiol.* 127:53–59

Cooke FJ, Wain J, Fookes M, Ivens A, Thomson N, et al. 2007. Prophage sequences defining hot spots of genome variation in *Salmonella enterica* serovar Typhimurium can be used to discriminate between field isolates. *J. Clin. Microbiol.* 45:2590–98

Costa K, Bacher G, Allmaier G, Dominguez-Bello MG, Engstrand L, et al. 1999. The morphological transition of *Helicobacter pylori* cells from spiral to coccoid is preceded by a substantial modification of the cell wall. *J. Bacteriol.* 181:3710–15

Cox-Foster DL, Conlan S, Holmes EC, Palacios G, Evans JD, et al. 2007. A metagenomic survey of microbes in honey bee colony collapse disorder. *Science* 318:283–87

Cremonesi P, Castiglioni B, Malferrar G, Biunno I, Vimercati C, et al. 2006. Technical note: improved method for rapid DNA extraction of mastitis pathogens directly from milk. *J. Dairy Sci.* 89:163–69

Doumith M, Buchrieser C, Glaser P, Jacquet C, Martin P. 2004. Differentiation of the major *Listeria monocytogenes* serovars by multiplex PCR. *J. Clin. Microbiol.* 42:3819–22

Erlich HA, Gelfand D, Sninsky JJ. 1991. Recent advances in the polymerase chain reaction. *Science* 252:1643–51

Eyigor A, Carli KT, Unal CB. 2002. Implementation of real-time PCR to tetrathionate broth enrichment step of *Salmonella* detection in poultry. *Lett. Appl. Microbiol.* 34:37–41

Feder I, Nietfeld JC, Galland J, Yearly T, Sargeant JM, et al. 2001. Comparison of cultivation and PCR-hybridization for detection of *Salmonella* in porcine fecal and water samples. *J. Clin. Microbiol.* 39:2477–84

Frazar CD, Orlandi PA. 2007. Evaluation of two DNA template preparation methods for post-immunomagnetic separation detection of *Cryptosporidium parvum* in foods and beverages by PCR. *Appl. Environ. Microbiol.* 73:7474–76

Fu Z, Rogelj S, Kieft TL. 2005. Rapid detection of *Escherichia coli* O157:H7 by immunomagnetic separation and real-time PCR. *Int. J. Food Microbiol.* 99:47–57

Fulton RJ, McDade RL, Smith PL, Kienker LJ, Kettman JR Jr. 1997. Advanced multiplexed analysis with the FlorMetrix^{TM} system. *Clin. Chem.* 43:1749–56

Gentry J, Vinjé J, Lipp EK. 2009. A rapid and efficient method for quantitation of genogroups I and II norovirus from oysters and application in other complex environmental samples. *J. Virol. Methods* 156:59–65

Gilmour MW, Graham M, Van Domselaar G, Tyler S, Kent H, et al. 2010. High-throughput genome sequencing of two *Listeria monocytogenes* clinical isolates during a large foodborne outbreak. *BMC Genomics* 11:120

Gonzalez-Escalona N, Hammack TS, Russell M, Jacobson AP, De Jueus AJ, et al. 2009. Detection of live *Salmonella* sp. cells in produce by a TaqMan-based quantitative reverse transcriptase real-time PCR targeting *invA* mRNA. *Appl. Environ. Microbiol.* 75:3714–20

Greenfield L, Bjorn MJ, Horn G, Fong D, Buck GA, et al. 1983. Nucleotide sequence of the structural gene for diphtheria toxin carried by corynebacteriophage beta. *Proc. Natl. Acad. Sci. USA* 80:6853–57

Grissa I, Bouchon P, Pourcel C, Vergnaud G. 2008. On-line resources for bacterial micro-evolution studies using MLVA or CRISPR typing. *Biochimie* 90:660–68

Hagren V, von Lode P, Syrjala A, Korpimaki T, Tuomola M, et al. 2008. An 8-hour system for *Salmonella* detection with immunomagnetic separation and homogeneous time-resolved fluorescence PCR. *Int. J. Food Microbiol.* 125:158–61

Haramoto E, Katayama H, Ohgaki S. 2004. Detection of noroviruses in tap water in Japan by means of a new method for concentrating enteric viruses in large volumes of freshwater. *Appl. Environ. Microbiol.* 70:2154–60

Herbelin CJ, Chirillo S, Melnick KA, Whittam TS. 2000. Gene conservation and loss in the *mutS-rpoS* genomic regions of pathogenic *Escherichia coli*. *J. Bacteriol.* 182:5381–90

Hilton AC, Banks JG, Penn CW. 1997. Optimization of RAPD for fingerprinting *Salmonella*. *Lett. Appl. Microbiol.* 24:243–48

Hofreuter D, Tsai J, Watson RO, Novik V, Altman B, et al. 2006. Unique features of highly pathogenic *Campylobacter jejuni* strain. *Infect. Immun.* 74:4694–707

Hong Y, Berrang M, Liu T, Hofacre C, Sanchez S, et al. 2003. Rapid detection of *Campylobacter coli*, *C. jejuni* and *Salmonella enterica* on poultry carcasses using PCR-enzyme-linked immunosorbent assay. *Appl. Environ. Microbiol.* 69:3492–99

Hong Y, Liu T, Lee MD, Hofacre CL, Maier M, et al. 2008. Rapid screening of *Salmonella enterica* serovars Enteritidis, Hadar, Heidelberg and Typhimurium using a serologically-correlative allelotyping PCR targeting the O and H antigen alleles. *BMC Microbiol.* 8:178

Hong Y, Liu T, Lee MD, Hofacre CL, Maier M, et al. 2009. A rapid screen of broth enrichments for *Salmonella enterica* serovars Enteritidis, Hadar, Heidelberg, and Typhimurium using an allelotyping multiplex PCR that targets O and H antigen alleles. *J. Food Prot.* 72:2198–201

Hu H, Lan R, Reeves PR. 2002. Fluorescent amplified fragment length polymorphism analysis of *Salmonella enterica* serovar Typhimurium reveals phage-type-specific markers and potential for microarray typing. *J. Clin. Microbiol.* 40:3406–15

Iturriza-Gomara M, Kang G, Gray J. 2004. Rotavirus genotyping: keeping up with an evolving population of human rotaviruses. *J. Clin. Virol.* 31:259–65

Iveson JB, Kovacs N. 1967. A comparative trial of Rappaport enrichment medium for the isolation of salmonellae from faeces. *J. Clin. Pathol.* 20:290–93

Jean J, D'Souza DH, Jaykus LA. 2004. Multiplex nucleic acid sequence-based amplification for simultaneous detection of several enteric viruses in model ready-to-eat foods. *Appl. Environ. Microbiol.* 70:6603–10

Josefsen MH, Löfström C, Hansen TB, Christensen LS, Olsen JE, Hoorfar J. 2010. Rapid quantification of viable *Campylobacter* bacteria on chicken carcasses, using real-time PCR and propidium monoazide treatment, as a tool for quantitative risk assessment. *Appl. Environ. Microbiol.* 76:5097–104

Jothikumar N, Cliver DO, Mariam TW. 1998. Immunomagnetic capture PCR for rapid concentration and detection of hepatitis A virus from environmental samples. *Appl. Environ. Microbiol.* 64:504–8

Kapperud G, Vardund T, Skjerve E, Hornes E, Michaelsen TE. 1993. Detection of pathogenic *Yersinia enterocolitica* in foods and water by immunomagnetic separation, nested polymerase chain reactions, and colorimetric detection of amplified DNA. *Appl. Environ. Microbiol.* 59:2938–44

Karch H, Bohm H, Schmidt H, Gunzer F, Aleksic S, Heesemann J. 1993. Clonal structure and pathogenicity of Shiga-like toxin-producing, sorbitol-fermenting *Escherichia coli* O157:H-. *J. Clin. Microbiol.* 31:1200–5

Kim D, Kim SR, Kwon KS, Lee JW, Oh MJ. 2008. Detection of hepatitis A virus from oyster by nested PCR using efficient extraction and concentration method. *J. Microbiol.* 46:436–40

Kornberg A. 2000. Ten commandments: lessons from the enzymology of DNA replication. *J. Bacteriol.* 182:3613–18

Kotewicz ML, Mammel MK, LeClerc JE, Cebula TA. 2008. Optical mapping and 454 sequencing of *Escherichia coli* O157:H7 isolates linked to the US 2006 spinach-associated outbreak. *Microbiology* 154:3518–28

Kwok S, Mack DH, Mullis KB, Poiesz B, Ehrlich G, et al. 1987. Identification of human immunodeficiency virus sequences by using in vitro enzymatic amplification and oligomer cleavage detection. *J. Virol.* 61:1690–94

Lalonde LF, Gajadhar AA. 2008. Highly sensitive and specific PCR assay for reliable detection of *Cyclospora cayetanensis* oocysts. *Appl. Environ. Microbiol.* I74:4354–58

Leggitt PR, Jaykus LA. 2000. Detection methods for human enteric viruses in representative foods. *J. Food Prot.* 63:1738–44

Liao CH, Fett WF. 2003. Isolation of *Salmonella* from alfalfa seed and demonstration of impaired growth of heat-injured cells in seed homogenates. *Int. J. Food Microbiol.* 82:245–53

Lindqvist R. 1997. Preparation of PCR samples from food by a rapid and simple centrifugation technique evaluated by detection of *Escherichia coli* O157:H7. *Int. J. Food Microbiol.* 37:72–82

Liu T, Liljebjelke K, Bartlett E, Hofacre CL, Sanchez S, Maurer JJ. 2002. Application of nested PCR to detection of *Salmonella* in poultry environments. *J. Food Prot.* 65:1227–32

Livak KJ, Flood SJ, Marmaro J, Giusti W, Deetz K. 1995. Oligonucleotides with fluorescent dyes at opposite ends provide a quenched probe system useful for detecting PCR product and nucleic acid hybridization. *PCR Methods Appl.* 4:357–62

Lopez-Saucedo C, Cerna JF, Villegas-Sepulveda N, Thompson R, Velazquez FR, et al. 2003. Single multiplex polymerase chain reaction to detect diverse loci associated with diarrheagenic *Escherichia coli*. *Emerg. Infect. Dis.* 9:127–31

Luan C, Levin RE. 2008. Use of activated carbon coated with bentonite for increasing sensitivity of PCR detection of *Escherichia coli* O157:H7 in Canadian oyster (*Crassostrea gigas*) tissue. *J. Microbiol. Methods* 72:67–72

Lund M, Nordentoft S, Pedersen K, Madsen M. 2004. Detection of *Campylobacter spp.* in chicken fecal samples by real-time PCR. *J. Clin. Microbiol.* 42:5125–32

Madico G, Akopyants NS, Berg DE. 1995. Arbitrarily primed PCR DNA fingerprinting of *Escherichia coli* O157:H7 strains by using templates from boiled cultures. *J. Clin. Microbiol.* 33:1534–36

Malorny B, Hoorfar J, Hugas M, Heuvelink A, Fach P, et al. 2003a. Interlaboratory diagnostic accuracy of a *Salmonella* specific PCR-based method. *Int. J. Food Microbiol.* 89:241–49

Malorny B, Tassios PT, Rådström P, Cook N, Wagner M, Hoorfar J. 2003b. Standardization of diagnostic PCR for the detection of foodborne pathogens. *Int. J. Food Microbiol.* 83:39–48

Margulies M, Egholm M, Altman WE, Attiya S, Bader JS, et al. 2005. Genome sequencing in open microfabricated high density picoliter reactors. *Nature* 437:376–80

Matsuda M, Barsdale L. 1967. System for the investigation of the bacteriophage-directed synthesis of diphtheria toxin. *J. Bacteriol.* 93:722–30

Maurer JJ, Schmidt D, Petrosko P, Sanchez S, Bolton LF, Lee MD. 1999. Development of primers to O-antigen biosynthesis genes for specific detection of *Escherichia coli* O157 by PCR. *Appl. Environ. Microbiol.* 65:2954–60

Maze A, Boel G, Zuniga M, Bourand A, Loux V, et al. 2010. Complete genome sequence of the probiotic *Lactobacillus casei* strain BL23. *J. Bacteriol.* 192:2647–48

McHugh TM, Miner RC, Logan LH, Stites DP. 1988. Simultaneous detection of antibodies to cytomegalovirus and herpes simplex virus by using flow cytometry and a microsphere-based fluorescence immunoassay. *J. Clin. Microbiol.* 26:1957–61

McIngvale SC, Hlhanai D, Drake MA. 2002. Optimization of reverse transcriptase PCR to detect viable shiga-toxin-producing *Escherichia coli*. *Appl. Environ. Microbiol.* 68:799–806

McKenna P, Hoffmann C, Minkah N, Aye PP, Lackner A, et al. 2008. The macaque gut microbiome in health, lentiviral infection, and chronic enterocolitis. *PLoS Pathog.* 4:e20

McKillip JL, Jaykus L, Drake M. 1998. rRNA stability in heat-killed and UV-irradiated enterotoxigenic *Staphylococcus aureus* and *Escherichia coli* O157:H7. *Appl. Environ. Microbiol.* 64:4264–68

McKillip JL, Jaykus LA, Drake M. 1999. Nucleic acid persistence in heat-killed *Escherichia coli* O157:H7 from contaminated skim milk. *J. Food Prot.* 62:839–44

Mikhailovich VM, Melnikov VG, Mazurova IK, Wachsmuth IK, Wenger JD, et al. 1995. Application of PCR for detection of toxigenic *Corynebacterium diphtheriae* strains isolated during the Russian diphtheria epidemic, 1990 through 1994. *J. Clin. Microbiol.* 33:3061–63

Monteiro L, Bonnemaison D, Vekris A, Petry KG, Bonnet J, et al. 1997. Complex polysaccharides as PCR inhibitors in feces: *Helicobacter pylori* model. *J. Clin. Microbiol.* 35:995–98

Morrison TB, Weis JJ, Wittwer CT. 1998. Quantification of low-copy transcripts by continuous SYBR Green I monitoring during amplification. *Biotechniques* 24:954–58, 960, 962

Mumma GA, Griffin PM, Meltzer MI, Braden CR, Tauxe RV. 2004. Egg quality assurance programs and egg-associated *Salmonella enteritidis* infections, United States. *Emerg. Infect. Dis.* 10:1782–89

Murphy E, Hieny S, Sher A, O'Garra A. 1993. Detection of in vivo expression of interleukin-10 using a semi-quantitative polymerase chain reaction method in *Schistosoma mansoni* infected mice. *J. Immunol. Methods* 162:211–23

New performance standards for *Salmonella* and *Campylobacter* in young chicken and turkey slaughter establishments; new compliance guides. 2010. *Fed. Regist.* 75:27288–94

Nogva HK, Drømtorp SM, Nissen H, Rudi K. 2003. Ethidium monoazide for DNA-based differentiation of viable and dead bacteria by 5′-nuclease PCR. *Biotechniques* 34:804–8, 810, 812–13

O'Leary J, Corcoran D, Lucey B. 2009. Comparison of the EntericBio multiplex PCR system with routine culture for detection of bacterial enteric pathogens. *J. Clin. Microbiol.* 47:3449–53

Oberst RD, Hays MP, Bohra LK, Phebus RK, Yamashiro CT, et al. 1998. PCR-based DNA amplification and presumptive detection of *Escherichia coli* O157:H7 with an internal fluorogenic probe and the 5′ nuclease (TaqMan) assay. *Appl. Environ. Microbiol.* 64:3389–96

Ohler LD, Rose EA. 1992. Optimization of long-distance PCR using a transposon-based model system. *PCR Methods Appl.* 2:51–59

Olive DM. 1989. Detection of enterotoxigenic *Escherichia coli* after polymerase chain reaction amplification with a thermostable DNA polymerase. *J. Clin. Microbiol.* 27:261–65

Oliver JD. 2010. Recent finding on the viable but nonculturable state in pathogenic bacteria. *FEMS Microbiol. Lett.* 34:415–25

Olsen JE, Brown DJ, Baggesen DL, Bisgaard M. 1992. Biochemical and molecular characterization of *Salmonella enterica* serovar Berta, and comparison of methods for typing. *Epidemiol. Infect.* 108:243–60

Omiccioli E, Amagliani G, Brandi G, Magnani M. 2009. A new platform for real-time PCR detection of *Salmonella* spp., *Listeria monocytogenes* and *Escherichia coli* O157 in milk. *Food Microbiol.* 26:615–22

Opel KL, Chung D, McCord BR. 2010. A study of PCR inhibition mechanisms using real time PCR. *J. Foren. Sci.* 55:25–33

Paton AW, Paton JC. 1998. Detection and characterization of Shiga toxigenic *Escherichia coli* by using multiplex PCR assays for *stx1*, *stx2*, *eaeA*, enterohemorrhagic *E. coli hlyA*, *rfbO111*, and *rfbO157*. *J. Clin. Microbiol.* 36:598–602

Pavic A, Groves PJ, Bailey G, Cox JM. 2009. A validated miniaturized MPN method, based on ISO 6579:2002, for the enumeration of *Salmonella* from poultry matrices. *J. Appl. Microbiol.* 109:25–34

Pedersen S, Reeh S. 1978. Functional mRNA half lives in *E. coli*. *Mol. Gen. Genet.* 166:329–36

Permutt MA, Biesbroeck J, Chyn R, Boime I, Szczesna E, McWilliams D. 1976. Isolation of a biologically active messenger RNA: preparation from fish pancreatic islets by oligo(2′-deoxythymidylic acid) affinity chromatography. *Ciba Found. Symp.* 41:97–116

Poly F, Read TD, Chen YH, Monteiro MA, Serichantalergs O, et al. 2008. Characterization of two *Campylobacter jejuni* strains for use in volunteer experimental-infection studies. *Infect. Immun.* 76:5655–67

Rahn K, De Grandis SA, Clarke RC, McEwen SA, Galan JE, et al. 1992. Amplification of *invA* gene sequence of *Salmonella typhimurium* by polymerase chain reaction as a specific method of detection of *Salmonella*. *Mol. Cell. Probes* 6:271–79

Raja S, El-Hefnawy T, Kelly LA, Chestney ML, Luketich JD, Godfrey TE. 2002. Temperature-controlled primer limit for multiplexing of rapid, quantitative reverse transcription-PCR assays: application to intraoperative cancer diagnostics. *Clin. Chem.* 48:1329–37

Regan PM, Margolin AB. 1997. Development of a nucleic acid capture probe with reverse transcriptase-polymerase chain reaction to detect poliovirus in groundwater. *J. Virol. Methods* 64:65–72

Reissbrodt R, Rienaecker I, Romanova JM, Freestone PPE, Haigh RD, et al. 2002. Resuscitation of *Salmonella enterica* serovar Typhimurium and enterohemorrhagic *Escherichia coli* from the viable but nonculturable state by heat-stable enterobacterial autoinducer. *Appl. Environ. Microbiol.* 68:4788–94

Richards GP, Watson MA, Kingsley DH. 2004. A SYBR green, real-time RT-PCR method to detect and quantitate Norwalk virus in stools. *J. Virol. Methods* 116:63–70

Rodríguez-Lázaro D, Pla M, Scortti M, Monzó HJ, Vázquez-Boland JA. 2005. A novel real-time PCR for *Listeria monocytogenes* that monitors analytical performance via an internal amplification control. *Appl. Environ. Microbiol.* 71:9008–12

Rollins DM, Colwell RR. 1986. Viable but nonculturable stage of *Campylobacter jejuni* and its role in survival in the natural aquatic environment. *Appl. Environ. Microbiol.* 52:531–38

Ronaghi M, Karamohamed S, Pettersson B, Uhlen M, Nyren P. 1996. Real-time DNA sequencing using detection of pyrophosphate release. *Anal. Biochem.* 242:84–89

Rudi K, Høidal HK, Katla T, Johansen BK, Nordal J, Jakobsen KS. 2004. Direct real-time PCR quantification of *Campylobacter jejuni* in chicken fecal and cecal samples by integrated cell concentration and DNA purification. *Appl. Environ. Microbiol.* 70:790–97

Rychlik W. 1995. Selection of primers for polymerase chain reaction. *Mol. Biotechnol.* 3:129–34

Saiki RK, Bugawan TL, Horn GT, Mullis KB, Erlich HA. 1986. Analysis of enzymatically amplified beta-globin and HLA-DQ alpha DNA with allele-specific oligonucleotide probes. *Nature* 324:163–66

Saiki RK, Gelfand DH, Stoffel S, Scharf SJ, Higuchi R, et al. 1988. Primer-directed enzymatic amplification of DNA with a thermostable DNA polymerase. *Science* 239:487–91

Saiki RK, Scharf S, Faloona F, Mullis KB, Horn GT, et al. 1985. Enzymatic amplification of β-globin genomic sequences and restriction site analysis for diagnosis of sickle cell anemia. *Science* 230:1350–54

Schena M, Shalon D, Davis RW, Brown PO. 1995. Quantitative monitoring of gene expression patterns with a complementary DNA microarray. *Science* 270:467–70

Schloss JA. 2008. How to get genomes at one ten-thousandth the cost. *Nat. Biotechnol.* 26:1113–15

Schneeberger C, Speiser P, Kury F, Zellinger R. 1995. Quantitative detection of reverse transcriptase-PCR products by means of a novel and sensitive DNA stain. *PCR Methods Appl.* 4:234–38

Scope. 2010. *J. Clin. Microbiol.* **http://jcm.asm.org/misc/journal-ita_sco.dtl**

Selma MV, Martinez-Culebras PV, Aznar R. 2008. Real-time PCR based procedures for detection and quantification of *Aspergillus caronarius* in wine grapes. *Int. J. Food Microbiol.* 122:126–34

Shan XC, Wolffs P, Griffiths MW. 2005. Rapid and quantitative detection of hepatitis A virus from green onion and strawberry rinses by use of real-time reverse transcription PCR. *Appl. Environ. Microbiol.* 71:5624–26

Soejima T, Iida KI, Qin T, Taniai H, Seki M, Yoshida SI. 2008. Method to detect only live bacteria during PCR amplification. *J. Clin. Microbiol.* 46:2305–13

Soumet C, Ermel G, Rose V, Rose N, Drouin P, et al. 1999. Identification by a multiplex PCR-based assay of *Salmonella typhimurium* and *Salmonella enteritidis* strains from environmental swabs of poultry houses. *Lett. Appl. Microbiol.* 29:1–6

Southern EM. 1975. Detection of specific sequences among DNA fragments separated by gel electrophoresis. *J. Mol. Biol.* 98:503–17

Spratt BG. 1975. Distinct penicillin binding proteins involved in the division, elongation, and shape of *Escherichia coli* K12. *Proc. Natl. Acad. Sci. USA* 72:2999–3003

Stone GG, Oberst RD, Hays MP, McVey S, Chengappa MM. 1994. Detection of *Salmonella* serovars from clinical samples by enrichment broth cultivation-PCR procedure. *J. Clin. Microbiol.* 32:1742–49

Surveillance for foodborne disease outbreaks—United States, 2007. 2010. *MMWR* 59:973–79

Sutlovic D, Gamulin S, Definis-Gojanovic M, Gugic D, Adnjelinovic S. 2008. Interaction of humic acids with human DNA: proposed mechanisms and kinetics. *Electrophoresis* 29:1467–72

Tettelin H, Radune D, Kasif S, Khouri H, Salzberg SL. 1999. Optimized multiplex PCR: efficiently closing a whole-genome shotgun sequencing project. *Genomics* 62:500–7

Thomas EJ, King RK, Burchak J, Gannon VP. 1991. Sensitive and specific detection of *Listeria monocytogenes* in milk and ground beef with the polymerase chain reaction. *Appl. Environ. Microbiol.* 57:2576–80

Tian P, Engelbrekston, Mandrell R. 2008. Two-log increase in sensitivity for detection of norovirus in complex samples by concentration with procine gastric mucin conjubated to magnetic beads. *Appl. Environ. Microbiol.* 74:4271–76

Tian P, Mandrell R. 2006. Detection of norovirus capsid proteins in faecal and food samples by a real time immuno-PCR method. *J. Appl. Microbiol.* 100:564–74

Tyagi S, Kramer FR. 1996. Molecular beacons: probes that fluoresce upon hybridization. *Nat. Biotechnol.* 14:303–8

USDA Animal and Plant Health Inspection Service (APHIS). 2010. NPIP approved rapid assays for *Salmonella*. **http://www.aphis.usda.gov/animal_health/animal_dis_spec/poultry/**

USDA Food Safety and Inspection Service (FSIS). 2007. FSIS procedure for the use of a polymerase chain reaction (PCR) assay for screening *Salmonella* in raw meat, carcass sponge samples, whole bird rinses, ready-to-eat meat and poultry products and pasteurized egg products. **http://www.fsis.usda.gov/PDF/MLG_4C_02.pdf**

USDA Food Safety and Inspection Service (FSIS). 2008. FSIS procedure for the use of *Escherichia coli* O157:H7 screening tests. **http://www.fsis.usda.gov/PDF/Mlg_5A_01.pdf**

USDA Food Safety and Inspection Service (FSIS). 2009. FSIS procedure for the use of a *Listeria monocytogenes* polymerase chain reaction (PCR) screening test. **http://www.fsis.usda.gov/PDF/MLG_8A_04.pdf**

Varadaraj K, Skinner DM. 1994. Denaturants or cosolvents improve the specificity of PCR amplification of a G + C-rich DNA using genetically engineered DNA polymerases. *Gene* 140:1–5

Waltman WD, Horne A, Pirkle C, Dickson T. 1991. Use of delayed secondary enrichment for the isolation of *Salmonella* in poultry and poultry environments. *Avian Dis.* 35:88–92

Wang L, Curd H, Qu W, Reeves PR. 1998. Sequencing of *Escherichia coli* O111 O-antigen gene cluster and identification of O111-specific genes. *J. Clin. Microbiol.* 36:3182–87

Wang L, Reeves PR. 1998. Organization of *Escherichia coli* O157 O antigen gene cluster and identification of its specific genes. *Infect. Immun.* 66:3545–51

Werbrouck H, Botteldoorn N, Uyttendaele M, Herman L, Van Coillie E. 2007. Quantification of gene expression of *Listeria monocytogenes* by real-time reverse transcription PCR: optimization, evaluation and pitfalls. *J. Microbiol. Methods* 69:306–14

Wilson IG. 1997. Inhibition and facilitation of nucleic acid amplification. *Appl. Environ. Microbiol.* 63:3741–51

Wittwer CT, Fillmore GC, Hillyard DR. 1989. Automated polymerase chain reaction capillary tubes with hot air. *Nucleic Acid Res.* 17:4353–57

Wolffs PFG, Glencross K, Norling B, Griffiths MW. 2007. Simultaneous quantification of pathogenic *Campylobacter* and *Salmonella* in chicken rinse fluid by a flotation and real-time multiplex PCR procedure. *Int. J. Microbiol.* 117:50–54

Wolffs PF, Glencross K, Thibaudeau R, Griffiths MW. 2006. Direct quantitation and detection of salmonellae in biological samples without enrichment, using two-step filtration and real-time PCR. *Appl. Environ. Microbiol.* 72:3896–900

Wolffs P, Knutsson R, Norling B, Radstrom P. 2004. Rapid quantification of *Yersinia enterocolitica* in pork samples by a novel sample preparation method, flotation, prior to real-time PCR. *J. Clin. Microbiol.* 42:1042–47

Wolffs P, Norling B, Radstrom P. 2005. Risk assessment of false-positive quantitative real-time PCR results in food, due to detection of DNA originating from dead cells. *J. Microbiol. Methods* 60:315–23

Woods DF, Reen FJ, Gilroy D, Buckley J, Frye JG, Boyd EF. 2008. Rapid multiplex PCR and real-time TaqMan PCR assays for detection of *Salmonella enterica* and the highly virulent serovars Choleraesuis and Paratyphi C. *J. Clin. Microbiol.* 46:4018–22

Yang H, Qu L, Wimbrow AN, Jiang X, Sun Y. 2007. Rapid detection of *Listeria monocytogenes* by nanoparticle-based immunomagnetic separation and real-time PCR. *Int. J. Food Microbiol.* 118:132–38

Decontamination of Raw Foods Using Ozone-Based Sanitization Techniques

Jennifer J. Perry and Ahmed E. Yousef*

Department of Food Science and Technology, The Ohio State University, Columbus, Ohio; email: perry.1723@osu.edu, yousef.1@osu.edu

Annu. Rev. Food Sci. Technol. 2011. 2:281–298

First published online as a Review in Advance on December 3, 2010

The *Annual Review of Food Science and Technology* is online at food.annualreviews.org

This article's doi:
10.1146/annurev-food-022510-133637

1941-1413/11/0410-0281$20.00

*Corresponding author.

Keywords

food safety, pathogens, toxins, sanitizer, antimicrobial, fresh produce

Abstract

Popular foods such as fresh produce and dry nuts are increasingly implicated in outbreaks of food-transmitted diseases. These products are not amenable to conventional processing technologies; therefore, many alternative decontamination methods are actively investigated. Ozone is a versatile sanitizer with promising applications in some high-risk foods. This antimicrobial agent is active against a broad spectrum of microorganisms, and it can be used effectively in its gaseous or aqueous state. The flexibility afforded by ozone use makes it a viable option for application on easy-to-damage products like fresh produce. If process parameters are adequately controlled, ozone treatment can enhance safety and increase shelf life without adversely affecting product quality. Despite these advantages, ozone may not be suitable for some applications, including treatment of liquid foods and products rich in unsaturated fats and soluble proteins. Ozone, as a powerful oxidizer, must be carefully controlled at all times, and equipment must be rigorously maintained to ensure safety of workers.

OZONE AND OTHER ANTIMICROBIALS: DEFINING THE TERMS

The term antimicrobials is used in many writings in reference to chemicals with a lethal or inhibitory effect against microorganisms. The term also is used broadly to refer to physical, chemical, or biological processes that are lethal to microorganisms or suppressive to their growth. Therefore, antimicrobials, as broadly defined, include (*a*) physical agents, e.g., heat or irradiation, (*b*) chemical agents, e.g., sanitizers or preservatives, and (*c*) biological agents, e.g., bacteriophage preparations that are proposed to control pathogenic bacteria in food. Some antimicrobials are indispensable elements of food safety assurance, whereas others have many uses in other fields such as medicine. Food processors use the term antimicrobials synonymously with preservatives, whereas in the medical field, it is used to refer to antimicrobial drugs. The great interest in discovering and testing new antimicrobials is driven by their significant impact on human health and economy. Therefore, new chemicals with potent antimicrobial properties are continuously sought.

Chemical antimicrobials may be classified on the basis of structure (e.g., phenolics or halogens), mode of action (e.g., oxidants or alkylating agents), targeted organisms, efficacy, application, or combinations of these factors. When a target organism is the main consideration, these antimicrobials are classified into antibiotics, antifungals, antiprotozoals, and antivirals. Based on application, the antimicrobial may be described as a sanitizer, disinfectant, antiseptic, or sterilant. This last grouping is the most practical; however, it is applied mainly to the antimicrobials used in vitro. Chemical sterilants (e.g., hydrogen peroxide vapor) are used to destroy all viable organisms on an object (e.g., food packaging material). Disinfectants commonly refer to chemicals applied topically to kill or inhibit pathogenic organisms on objects where the use of sterilants is impractical (e.g., floors or tables). A disinfectant or an antiseptic is applied to accomplish similar goals except that the latter is used on living tissues (e.g., wounds) and thus should be sufficiently nontoxic.

Differences between sanitization and disinfection are sometimes subtle. However, disinfection implies that the treated matrix is expected to be infectious, where as sanitization may serve as a precautionary measure on matrices that are not often contaminated with infectious agents. Thus, disinfection is a higher level of sanitization. The term sanitizer traditionally refers to antimicrobial chemicals used to decontaminate food-contact surfaces. If selected and used properly, sanitizers destroy vegetative cells of microorganisms of public health significance and substantially inactivate other undesirable microorganisms without adversely affecting the quality of the product or the safety of the consumer (Code Fed. Regul. 2009). The United States Food and Drug Administration (FDA) makes a distinction between a sanitizer and a disinfectant on the basis of the need to rinse the antimicrobial off food-contact surfaces (US Food Drug Adm. 1993). Approved sanitizers in the United States are those that do not require a rinse after the sanitization step; these include household bleach and quaternary ammonium compounds.

A given antimicrobial agent, such as ozone, may belong to more than one group if it has diverse applications. The FDA approved ozone use in food as an antimicrobial additive (Code Fed. Regul. 2001). According to a United States Environmental Protection Agency (EPA) fact sheet, treatment of waste water with ozone gas is described as disinfection (US Env. Prot. Agency 1999). Furthermore, use of aqueous ozone to rinse food or food-contact surfaces may be considered sanitization. Some of these diverse applications are covered in this chapter, but most of the attention is given to ozone as a sanitizer in food processing.

GENERAL CHARACTERISTICS

Ozone is a triatomic oxygen molecule arranged to form an obtuse angle (Horvath et al. 1985). The compound is liquid above approximately 80 K (Brown et al. 1955, Jenkins & DiPaolo 1956) and boils at 161 K (Horvath et al. 1985). The reduction potential of ozone is 2.07 V, qualifying it as one of the strongest known oxidizers. In the gaseous state, ozone is denser than air (Horvath et al. 1985) and colorless at lower concentrations. It possesses a distinct odor described alternately as fresh or fishy, which is detectable by humans at concentrations as low as 0.02 ppm (Horvath et al. 1985). Under natural circumstances, small amounts of ozone are generated in the earth's atmosphere by the action of short-wave ultraviolet (UV) light (<300 nm) on molecular oxygen. It has been noted that the formation of stratospheric ozone confers a benefit to the biosphere by absorbing a considerable amount of UV light in the range that is most damaging to proteins and nucleic acids (Horvath et al. 1985). Ozone is extremely reactive, with a half life in the gaseous phase of approximately 12 hours (Horvath et al. 1985); in water, half life is reduced to only 20 to 30 minutes (depending on several factors, including water source, purity, temperature, etc.) (Kim et al. 2003). Because it is capable of reacting with a number of substances, including metals and organic compounds, the stability of ozone is greatly dependant on the materials used to contain it, the presence of organic contaminants, and other factors, including temperature and pH (with decreasing stability at increased temperatures and pH) (Kim 1998).

OZONE PRODUCTION

As a consequence of its reactivity, ozone cannot be stored for significant periods of time; therefore, it must be generated as needed. Ozone gas can be purposely generated using a number of methods. These include photochemical procedures, which employ UV light but generally result in low ozone concentrations, electrolysis of water to produce ozone and hydrogen gas, and corona discharge. Corona discharge is the most common method in use and is capable of producing relatively high concentrations of ozone. In this method, gas (air or dry oxygen) is passed between two electrodes separated by a dielectric material and a high energy discharge splits molecular oxygen into its atomic form. Atomic oxygen spontaneously combines with molecular oxygen to form triatomic ozone (Horvath et al. 1985). When oxygen is used as a feed gas, as opposed to air, higher levels of ozone are subsequently produced. Once produced, ozone can be used in the gaseous state or sparged into water to produce aqueous ozone for rinsing and washing applications.

OZONE DECOMPOSITION

The decomposition of ozone yields a number of oxidative radicals, including the superoxide anion radical and hydroperoxide radical, which subsequently gives rise to the hydroxyl radical. The hydroxyl radical is incredibly reactive, and much of the antimicrobial activity of ozone has been attributed to the subsequent reaction of its decomposition products. Radical reactions continuously self propagate until a quencher or inhibitor is encountered, at which point reaction ceases. Because radicals are known to react very quickly, efficacy of ozone diminishes when target microorganisms are surrounded with oxidizeable substrates.

OZONE MEASUREMENT

The high redox potential of ozone often allows for its use in small amounts and contributes to its rapid decomposition during application. The combination of these factors makes accurate measurement of ozone levels particularly difficult. As with its generation, there are several methods available for the determination of ozone concentration. Historically, the most reliable and widely used method for the determination of ozone in the aqueous phase has been the indigo method. This procedure is based on spectrophotometric determination of the decolorization of indigo trisulfonate upon its reaction with ozone (Bader & Hoigne 1981). Ozone acts by disrupting the sole carbon-carbon double bond of the indigo reagent. The indigo method is accurate within 2% (Grunwell et al. 1983) and is still often used to measure ozone in the aqueous phase. For quantification of gaseous ozone, the most common and trusted method is based on UV-light spectrometry. Absorbance of UV at 254 nm corresponds to ozone concentration in the gas sample (Dunlea et al. 2006). Many commercially available ozone monitors use this technology, which is appropriate for a wide range of ozone concentrations and allows continuous, near real-time quantification of ozone residuals.

SAFETY CONSIDERATIONS

Due to the strong oxidizing power of ozone, there are several considerations that must be taken into account to ensure its safe utilization. Human exposure to ozone above certain levels can lead to a number of negative health effects. At low concentrations, ozone is a respiratory irritant that can cause headaches, coughing, dizziness, and nausea. Exposure for long periods of time or to higher levels of ozone (6 ppm) can lead to pulmonary edema. In this case, inflammation causes obstruction to the entry of alveoli and/or reduction in alveolar volume, leading to diminished breathing capacity (Horvath et al. 1985). Repeated exposures to ozone can result in permanent lung damage (Scheel et al. 1959). The respiratory system is the primary site of action in humans, and other effects, including vision loss, have been reported as well (Lagerwerff 1963). Standards set forth by the Occupational Safety and Health Administration (OSHA) of the United States specify that workers may not be exposed to concentrations exceeding 0.1 ppm for extended periods of time, or 0.2 ppm for short term exposure (US Dep. Labor, Occup. Saf. Health Adm. 2004). In order to avoid inadvertent exposure, material selection and equipment maintenance are particularly important. Ozone reacts with several commonly used materials, including rubber and plastic. Surfaces exposed to ozone should consist only of compatible materials. This issue has been discussed previously in published literature (Kim et al. 2003).

Although the presence of ozone is expected in the Earth's stratosphere, it is considered a pollutant when found in the troposphere. Ozone is produced in the troposphere by the interaction of sunlight and volatile organic compounds or nitrogen oxides. Levels of tropospheric ozone vary depending on time of day, season, and location, with daily and annual peaks generally observed during the sunniest part of the day (Heagle 1989) and in the spring months (Vingarzan 2004). Common levels of tropospheric ozone have been reported to fall in the range of 20 to 250 ppb, depending upon the preceding factors (Heagle 1989, Sanderman 1996), representing an increase of at least 100% during the past century (Vingarzan 2004). The increase has been commonly attributed to the rising use of automobiles in this time period.

Rising levels of ozone in the troposphere have raised concerns for a number of reasons, particularly the implications of exposure to plant and human health. Elevated ozone levels have been demonstrated to reduce crop yield by more than ten percent (Heagle 1989), and to make plants more susceptible to subsequent stressors (Sanderman 1996). Ozone pollution has also been linked to damage of coniferous trees in the Northern Hemisphere. Deleterious effects on human health have long focused on the induction of respiratory distress, but elevated ozone levels can also precede vasoconstriction, causing a rise in blood pressure (Brook et al. 2002), and have been linked to increased risk of myocardial infarction (Ruidavets et al. 2005).

ANTIMICROBIAL ACTION

Ozone possesses a wide antimicrobial spectrum. Its efficacy has been demonstrated against both Gram-positive and Gram-negative bacteria (Ingram and Haines 1949, Guzel-Seydim et al. 2004), bacterial spores (Ishizaki et al. 1986, Khadre & Yousef 2001), fungi (Palou et al. 2001, Allen et al. 2003, Oztekin et al. 2006), viruses (Kim et al. 1980, Roy et al. 1981), and protozoa (Khalifa et al. 2001). Sensitivity of diverse microorganisms to ozone suggests that cells possess several sites for ozone action that leads to lethality. Early studies hypothesized that reaction of ozone with enzymatic systems interfered with cellular respiration (Ingram & Haines 1949). More recently, the focus has been on the interaction of ozone with the unsaturated lipids of the cell membrane (Victorin 1992, Thanomsub et al. 2002). Membrane damage induced by exposure to ozone has been demonstrated to result in leakage of cellular components followed by cell death (Scott & Lesher 1963). Membrane damage also allows ozone to penetrate into the cell, where it has been reported to cause DNA-strand breaks (Ishizaki et al. 1987). Damage to nucleic acids has been suggested to be a cause of viral inactivation by ozone (Kim et al. 1980, Roy et al. 1981). In bacterial spores, significant damage to spore coat has been observed (Khadre & Yousef 2001). A point of contention among researchers is whether the effects observed are attributable to the reactions of molecular ozone itself or to the decomposition products that are produced by its reversion to molecular oxygen. Among the products produced is the hydroxyl radical, the strongest known oxidizer, which leads many authors to believe that decomposition products are responsible for the antimicrobial effects (Block 2001). However, in a study conducted by Hunt & Marinas (1997), radical scavenging compounds were added to treatment media, and this addition did not have a significant effect on the reduction of *Escherichia coli* population by ozone treatment. This finding suggests that molecular ozone may play a significant role in bacterial inactivation. However, in a study conducted on *Bacillus subtilis* spores, hydroxyl radicals were found to be principally responsible for inactivation of these spores (Cho et al. 2002).

Several factors can alter the efficacy of ozone against microorganisms. The medium in which microorganisms are suspended or embedded plays a very important role in determining ozone's antimicrobial efficacy. Most significantly, the presence of organic material, especially proteins and fats, greatly reduces efficacy of ozone (Ingram & Haines 1949, Guzel-Seydim et al. 2004). As previously indicated, ozone stability decreases when medium pH increases. If molecular ozone reactions are necessary for inactivation, a low pH is desired; however, higher pH has been demonstrated to encourage formation of hydroxyl radicals, contributing to spore inactivation (Cho et al. 2002). Increased moisture also seems to enhance killing by gaseous ozone. This effect was observed in the treatment of barley grains to inactivate fungi (Allen et al. 2003). A similar study was conducted on wheat, wherein the authors concluded that increased water activity and increased treatment temperature (from 10°C to 40°C) led to greater inactivation of fungal spores (Wu et al. 2006). Increased relative humidity has been demonstrated to aid in bacterial spore inactivation (Ishizaki et al. 1986).

METHODS OF APPLYING ANTIMICROBIALS: GASEOUS VERSUS AQUEOUS STATE

Antimicrobial gases vary considerably in water solubility. Gases with low solubility may be mixed with water under pressure until being applied directly to the treated matrix (e.g., food). Gases that are readily soluble in water are well suited to aqueous applications. Food processors often contemplate the merits of applying antimicrobials as gaseous versus aqueous phases. In food processing, aqueous or gaseous sanitization should be a carefully designed unit operation. Aqueous sanitization is a standalone unit operation; however, this step is often combined, or directly preceded with a cleaning operation. Gaseous sanitization can be combined with many other unit operations such as transportation or refrigerated storage. This offers food processors a flexibility that is not attainable in aqueous sanitizing operations. Schematics and photographs of pilot-scale aqueous and gaseous ozone treatment setups are displayed in **Figures 1** and **2** (see color insert).

Regardless of water solubility, it may be preferable to apply antimicrobials in the gaseous rather than aqueous state. By their nature, gases diffuse faster than liquids and thus reach target microorganisms in the food more quickly, often within short treatment time. Additionally, applied gases are less likely to modify the composition of a treated matrix (e.g., its water and water-soluble contents). Simpler devices are generally used for treating a matrix with gases than with other forms of antimicrobials. However, antimicrobial gases are often toxic or explosive, and thus it is crucial to contain these gases during and after the treatment. Some antimicrobials, including ozone, have applications in both gaseous and aqueous states.

GASEOUS OZONE APPLICATIONS: EFFICACY AND CHALLENGES

Antimicrobial efficacy of gaseous treatments depends on the properties of the applied gas, properties of the treated matrix, and treatment conditions. Gases vary considerably in biocidal properties, which depend on the physical and chemical characteristics of the gas. A reactive gas with small molecular mass and good miscibility with water is likely more biocidal than gases with opposite characteristics. A matrix with a relatively smooth surface is likely less protective to exterior contaminants than one with a rough or porous surface. For example, it was easier to decontaminate an apple's smooth exterior surface than its rough surfaces at calyex and stem regions, when ozone gas was bubbled into wash water (Achen & Yousef 2001). Additionally, components of the food matrix may compete with contaminating microorganisms for applied gases.

Treatment conditions influence greatly the efficacy of biocidal gases. Concentration, time, temperature, and relative humidity are important parameters that should be watched carefully during treatment of food with antimicrobial gases (Vurma et al. 2009). Concentration of the antimicrobial gas in the treatment environment and time of exposure of the matrix to the gas define the treatment dosage. It is generally accepted that humidity is essential for reactivity of biocidal gases with treated microorganisms. Antimicrobials may have to pass from the gaseous to the aqueous phase to be effective against targeted microorganisms. Contribution of treatment temperature to the antimicrobial efficacy of biocidal gases is difficult to assess. Gases are more soluble in the aqueous phase of the food matrix at colder temperatures than at warmer temperatures, but reactivity of the gas with microorganisms should increase with temperature.

Treatment of food with antimicrobial gases has many challenges. Monitoring the sanitizer concentration is easier in aqueous than gaseous phases. In fact, there is no simple technique to compare the sanitizing efficacy of different gases (Hill 1905, Osipyan & Uspenskiy 1964). It is not surprising that aqueous sanitization is more developed and is applied more often, particularly in food, than are gaseous treatments. However, the recent increase in disease transmission by fresh produce is making it urgent to search for alternatives to conventional aqueous sanitization procedures. Gaseous decontamination of food, particularly fresh produce, is gaining interest in the food industry.

Ozone is applied as an antimicrobial agent in the gaseous or aqueous state. The gas has low water solubility; therefore, application of the agent in aqueous solution requires specialized equipment and well-trained operators. Low concentrations of ozone are used to decontaminate drinking water. Bottled water, for example, is treated so that residual ozone at the time of bottling does not exceed 0.4 mg liter^{-1} (Code Fed. Regul. 2006). Recently, moderate levels of gaseous ozone have been recommended in sanitization of fresh produce (Vurma et al. 2009). High ozone concentrations (~11% ozone in oxygen, wt/wt) have been tested successfully for decontamination of shell eggs (Rodriguez-Romo & Yousef 2005, Perry et al. 2008).

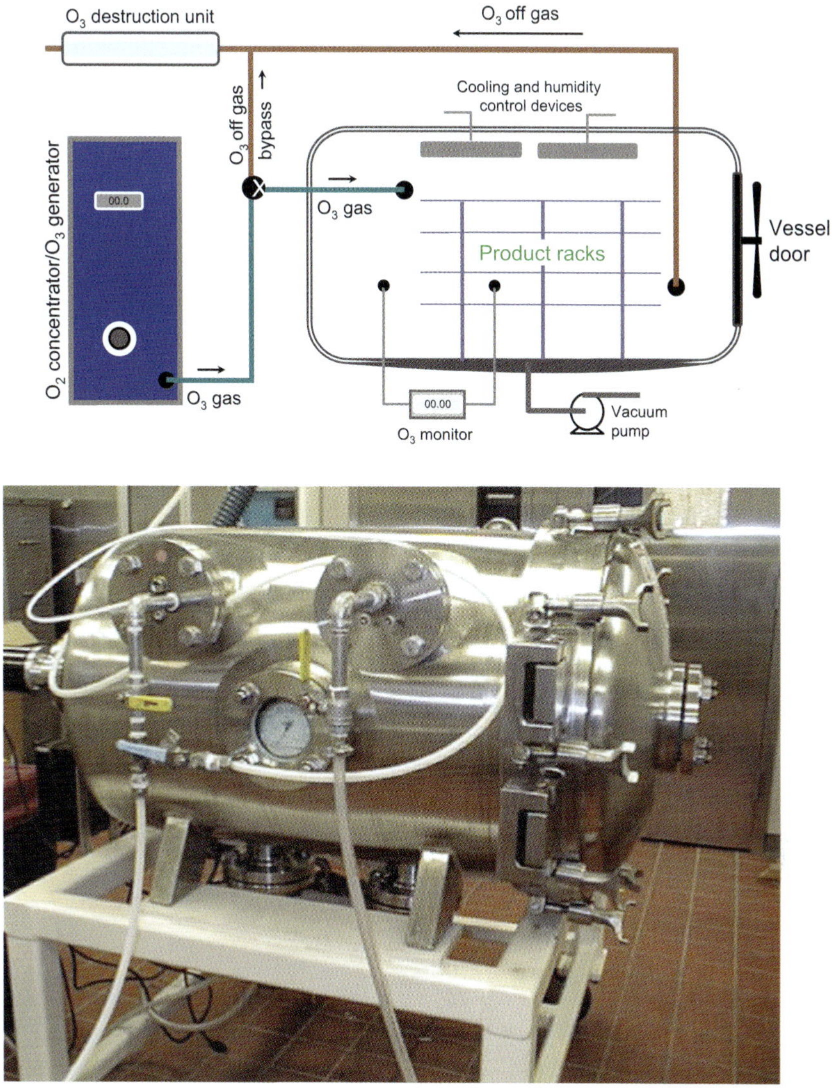

Figure 1

Prototype of a gaseous ozone system for decontaminating raw food products; equipment is set up and operational at the author's laboratory.

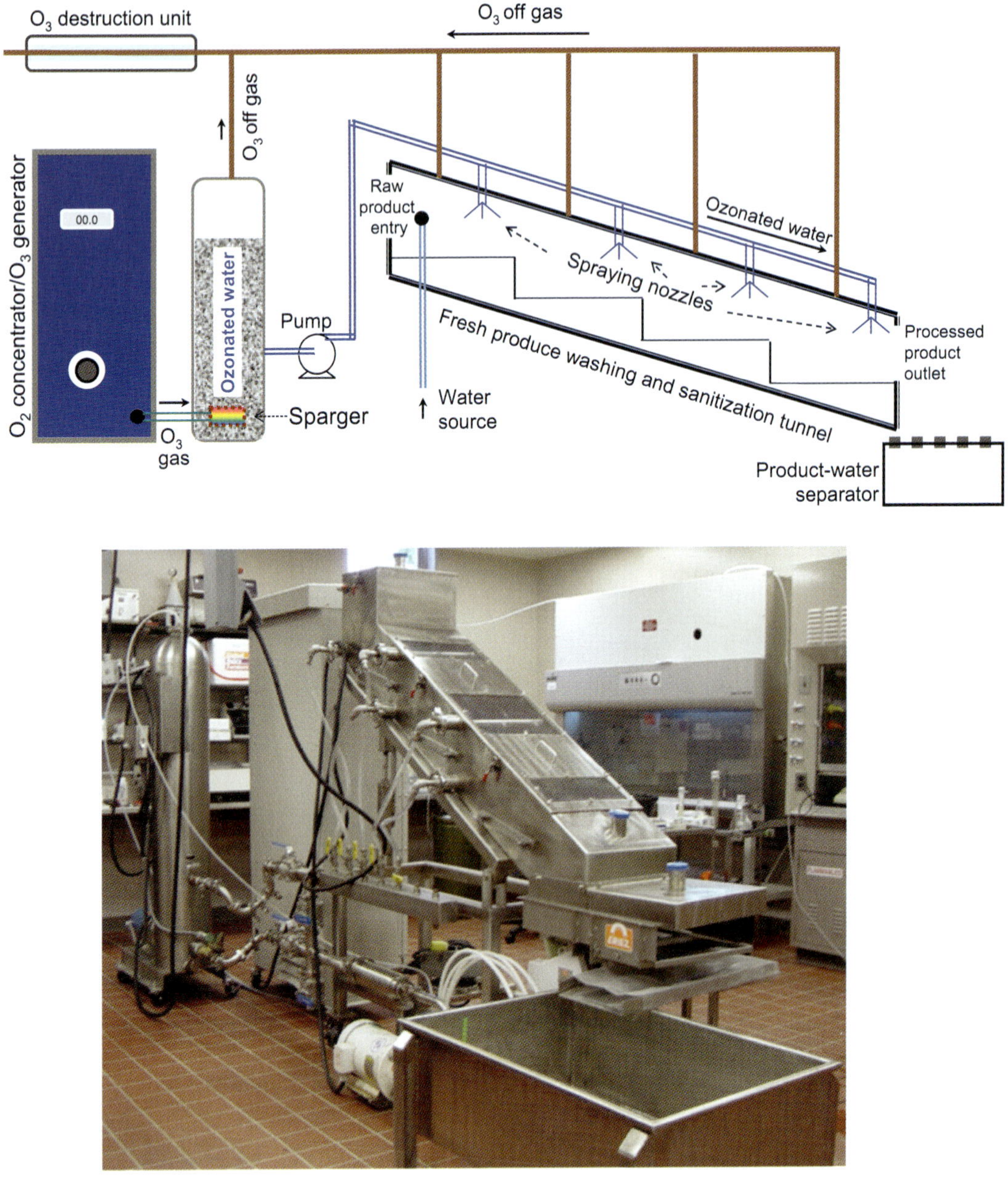

Figure 2

Prototype of an aqueous ozone system for application in fresh produce washing and sanitizing; equipment is set up and operational at the author's laboratory.

Figure 3

Baby spinach samples that were untreated or treated, during vacuum cooling, with gaseous ozone (1.5 g O_3 kg^{-1} gas mixture or 935 ppm v ozone/v gas mixture) followed by pressurization at 10 psig for different holding times to eliminate 1.8 log *Escherichia coli* O157:H7 (Vurma et al. 2009; pictures are courtesy of M. Vurma). (*a*) Untreated; (*b*) treated for 30 min, product quality comparable to the untreated control; (*c*) treated for 45 min, product quality deterioration is noticeable.

Figure 4

Strawberries that were untreated or treated with gaseous ozone/carbon dioxide mixture and held at 20°C for up to 3 days. Treatment involved subjecting the berries to an environment containing16 mg ozone kg^{-1} gas mixture (10 ppm v ozone/v gas mixture) for 4 hours (Vurma 2009). (*a*) Untreated at time zero; (*b*) untreated and stored for 3 days, mold was noticeable; (*c*) treated and stored for 3 days, berries remained mold-free.

SELECTED FOOD APPLICATIONS

Fresh Produce

Compared with other food industries, the fresh produce sector likely will benefit the most from the recent advances in ozone sanitization technology. Application of gaseous and aqueous ozone in fresh produce have been explored by several researchers and contemplated by some processors, but major implementations have not yet materialized. The following discussion covers emerging safety concerns about fresh produce and recent developments in ozone sanitization technology. This discussion may help processors reevaluate the feasibility of applying ozone in the decontamination of fresh produce.

Safety of fresh produce and the need for alternative sanitizers. The nature of fresh produce is such that this category of foods presents a unique challenge in terms of quality and safety. Fresh produce is expected to reach the consumer in the raw state, and many fruit and vegetable tissues are highly susceptible to damage. These factors limit rigorous processing of fresh produce; consequently, these products often have a short shelf life and a relatively poor microbial safety record. With the increased sales of fresh produce in recent years, disease outbreaks associated with this category of foods are on the rise.

To further complicate this situation, contaminants commonly associated with fresh produce include not only pathogenic bacteria, but also viruses, such as Norwalk and hepatitis A, and parasites, most notably *Cryptosporidium* and *Cyclospora*. In addition to pathogens, produce is also highly susceptible to fungal spoilage. Not only does this lead to significant monetary losses for producers, but the presence of some fungi is a potential health hazard due to the production of mycotoxins. Some *Penicillium* spp., commonly responsible for blue mold rot on the surface of various fruit crops, are known producers of the mycotoxin patulin. Chiefly associated with apple products, the toxicity of patulin to animals has been documented (Becci et al. 2006).

Opportunities for exposure to microbes are numerous in the fruit and vegetable production chains. Given that fruits and vegetables must be grown in soil, microbes from this source are plentiful on these products. The nature of the environment in which fresh produce is commonly grown precludes complete control over presence of animals, especially birds and rodents. Fecal contamination of fresh produce due to the presence of these animals is not uncommon. Fertilizers and irrigation water are other possible sources of microbial contaminants. The widely spread 2008 outbreak of salmonellosis was attributed to contaminated water used on tomatoes, peppers, and cilantro (Cent. Dis. Control Prev. 2008). The use of improperly composted manure has caused contamination of produce on more than one occasion. This is a particular concern in the production of organic produce, which prohibits the use of chemical fertilizers. Due to the sensitive nature of produce, many types are harvested by hand, presenting an additional opportunity for contamination due to the poor hygiene practiced by some pickers.

Conventional processing of fresh produce begins with removal of field heat. In its most basic incarnation, this is accomplished by moving harvested product quickly from the field to refrigerated storage, but the process may be sped up using forced-air cooling, immersion in ice water, or even application of a vacuum, depending on the particular commodity and facility capabilities. If possible, products are washed by spraying or immersion. This process is useful for the removal of soil and foreign contaminants, but with the addition of a sanitizing agent, most commonly chlorine, washing can be used to reduce levels of surface microbiota. Chlorine possesses a wide antimicrobial spectrum and has a long history of use; however, increasing attention is being given to the generation of potentially harmful byproducts of this sanitizer.

The use of ozone as a sanitizing agent presents numerous advantages over traditional methods. It has been demonstrated that ozone works well against pathogenic bacteria (including bacterial spores), viruses, parasites, and fungi at relatively low concentrations (Kim et al. 2003). The efficacy of ozone in both aqueous and gaseous phases allows it to be used on a wide variety of products. The antimicrobial efficacy of ozone may depend on the generation of reactive oxygen species (e.g., hydroxyl radicals), but these are short-lived byproducts that do not remain in treated food until the time of consumption. Therefore, the generation of toxic byproducts during sanitization is not a concern when using ozone, which decomposes to harmless molecular oxygen. Unlike chlorine, ozone has been defined as a suitable additive for organic products, making it one of few sanitizers available for use in this growing category of foods. The following sections provide a summary of current research regarding the use of ozone to enhance safety and quality of fresh produce.

Ozone in fresh produce processing. Ozone, applied in either the aqueous or gaseous states, has been investigated as a sanitizer for a number of produce commodities against several target pathogens. These treatments have been particularly successful on products with a smooth outer surface, where contaminants are easily accessible by the sanitizer. Das et al. (2006) reported complete inactivation of spot-inoculated *Salmonella* Enteritidis on cherry tomatoes treated with 20 mg liter^{-1} gaseous ozone for 15 min. Although this treatment resulted in color loss of treated product, lower levels of gaseous ozone (4 μl liter^{-1} for 30 min, repeated treatment) have been used successfully without producing this negative effect (Aguayo et al. 2006). Tomatoes subjected to this treatment displayed markedly slower softening of flesh (Aguayo et al. 2006), a finding that was also reported in kiwi fruits (Li et al. 2009) and has been attributed to inactivation of fruit pectin methylesterase, an enzyme involved in the degradation of pectin (Rodoni et al. 2010). Another possible fringe benefit of ozone treatment is increased accumulation of phenolic compounds. Enhanced production of these compounds has been demonstrated in tomatoes and grapes following ozone treatments (Artes-Hernandez et al. 2007, Rodoni et al. 2010). Treatment of apples with 23–30 mg liter^{-1} aqueous ozone resulted in a 3.7-log reduction of *E. coli* O157:H7, but reduction in the stem and calyx regions of the fruit was drastically less, not even one log (Achen & Yousef 2001). This difference aptly highlights the importance of the product's surface texture and accessibility of ozone to entrapped contaminants on sanitization efficacy.

Cantaloupe melons have repeatedly been the cause of outbreaks of salmonellosis due to the transfer of contaminants on the rind to cut fruit. In studies conducted by Selma et al. (2006, 2008a), whole melons were treated with ozone gas, hot water, or a combination of the two treatments. Immersion in 75°C water followed by treatment with 10,000-ppm gaseous ozone for 30 min resulted in a 3.8-log reduction of mesophilic bacteria and 2.1-log reduction of coliforms. In a study using precut melon cubes (2008b), this group reported a lack of adverse sensorial effects after treatment with 20,000-ppm gaseous ozone for 30 min, demonstrating the promise of ozone use to improve melon safety. Fruit juices have also been treated with ozone. Apple cider has previously been implicated in outbreaks of *E. coli* O157:H7 infections. In 2004, Williams and colleagues reported a 6-log reduction in this pathogen after 45 min of ozone addition (9 g h^{-1}) to apple cider held at 50°C. The same conditions produced a 4.8-log reduction of *Salmonella* in 30 minutes.

Many researchers have investigated the possibility of ozone use to sanitize leafy greens. Interest in leafy green safety has increased conspicuously since 2006, when baby spinach was linked to an outbreak in the United States of *E. coli* O157:H7, which sickened more than 200 people. In work with shredded lettuce, Kim et al. (1999) reported a 1.9-log reduction in total count after three minutes of treatment with 1.3 mM aqueous ozone. Treatment with 5-ppm aqueous ozone for five minutes was reported to decrease the counts of *Shigella sonnei* by 1.8 log (Selma et al. 2007).

Yuk et al. (2007) inoculated enoki mushroom with *E. coli* O157:H7 and *Listeria monocytogenes* and treated the inoculated product (without agitation) for 5 min with 3-ppm ozone solution. This treatment decreased the populations of these pathogens by only 0.94 and 0.34 log, respectively. Klockow & Keener (2009) developed a process that involves the generation of ozone within spinach packaging. Although this technique resulted in 3- to 5-log inactivation of *E. coli* O157:H7, the authors reported significant quality deterioration of the treated product. In a 2009 study, Vurma and colleagues addressed the possibility of integrating ozone into existing spinach processing. They applied gaseous ozone (1.5 g O_3 kg^{-1} gas mixture or 935 ppm v ozone/v gas mixture) during vacuum cooling to inactivate up to 1.8 log of *E. coli* O157:H7 without obvious quality loss (**Figure 3*a,b***, see color insert). Low-level ozone treatment (5 to 10 ppm) during simulated transportation resulted in a 1-log inactivation, and the combination of these procedures yielded $\geq$4-log reduction of this pathogen (Vurma et al. 2009). The processing of leafy greens, clearly a promising application for ozone technology, illustrates another commodity-based consideration. Because of the delicate nature of leaves, product damage must be avoided when designing a potential treatment. More intensive treatments were investigated in the research discussed earlier, but product damage was significant enough to preclude their use (**Figure 3*c***).

Concern regarding fungal spoilage prevents fresh berries from being washed between harvest and market. Gaseous ozone has been investigated for use in berries both to eliminate pathogens and to extend product shelf life. Treatment of blueberries with 5% (wt/wt) gaseous ozone for 64 min resulted in a 2.2-log reduction of *E. coli* O157:H7; similar conditions under pressure inactivated 3 log of *Salmonella* (Bialka et al. 2007). Despite the high levels of ozone and long treatment time utilized in this study, no color loss or other negative sensorial effects were reported. In an attempt to extend shelf life of strawberries, 0.35-ppm gaseous ozone was maintained during refrigerated storage for three days. Authors reported a slight decrease in incidence of gray mold after two days of storage, but no difference between treated and untreated strawberries was observed after four days (Perez et al. 1999). Experiments by another researcher involved storing strawberries at 25°C in an environment containing a mixture of ozone (10 ppm, v ozone/v gas mixture) and carbon dioxide (Vurma 2009). The author reported rapid quality deterioration of untreated strawberries, compared to ozone-treated product (**Figure 4**, see color insert). The ozone treatment provided up to an eight-day extension of shelf life when compared to untreated berries.

Delayed appearance of fungal growth has been observed in a number of ozone-treated commodities. Palou et al. (2001) reported a one-week extension of the shelf life of oranges stored under 0.3-ppm ozone for four weeks. Even after mold growth occurred, authors reported a significant decrease in sporulation of *Penicillium* spp. with continuous exposure to ozone, speculating that this effect may prevent the spread of fungal contamination on fruit during storage. In a study utilizing different types of produce, Tzortakis et al. (2008) reported suppression of fungal spore formation ranging from 20% (on plums) to 95% (on clementines) after storage in the presence of 0.1M ozone for 13 days. Fungal sporulation was prevented during four weeks of storage in the presence of 0.3-ppm ozone on peaches inoculated with *Monilinia fructicola*, *Botrytis cinerea*, *Mucor piriformis*, and *Penicillium expansum* (Palou et al. 2002). No injury to fruit was observed, and respiration and ethylene production were unaltered during subsequent ripening in ambient atmosphere.

Success in ozone treatment of fresh produce is not limited to laboratory and pilot-scale operations. A treatment involving 15- to 30-second exposure to 300-ppm gaseous ozone followed by extended storage in the presence of approximately 1-ppm ozone has been successful commercially in preventing the spread of fungal disease on onions and potatoes (Rice 2006). Producers implementing this system were able to increase yields of marketable product enough to recover the cost of equipment investment in the first growing season of use. A fresh produce processor in Tennessee integrated an ozone rinse into an existing production line and now uses ozone in conjunction with a subsequent application of lower concentrations of chlorine. This change has led to a nine-day increase in the shelf life of bagged salads and has significantly decreased water usage at the plant (Rice 2006).

The examples discussed earlier address a wide variety of commodities and treatments. The suitability of ozone treatment for a particular product depends largely on the product's susceptibility to damage during ozonation. Optimization of ozone concentration, treatment time, and phase of application can lead to favorable outcomes in the majority of commodities. There are however, several examples that illustrate the unsuitability of ozone for certain applications where ozone treatment does not achieve the desired reduction in microbial population or the expected improvement in product quality. Studies on alfalfa seeds and sprouts have demonstrated relatively low lethality toward pathogens inoculated on these products. A 64-min treatment consisting of constant sparging of ozone into water (initial concentration of 21 $\mu g\ ml^{-1}$) resulted in a 2.2-log reduction of *E. coli* O157:H7 on alfalfa seeds (Sharma et al. 2002). Similar treatments on alfalfa sprouts yielded a 2-log reduction of the same pathogen, and application of pressure did not increase lethality (Sharma et al. 2003). In treatments targeting *L. monocytogenes*, sparging of seeds in ozonated water (21.3 $\mu g\ ml^{-1}$) reduced pathogen population by less than 1.5 log and caused significant damage to seeds (Wade et al. 2003). Soaking of sprouts in ozonated water (20 $\mu g\ ml^{-1}$) for up to 20 min resulted in a 1.68-log reduction of aerobic microbes, but only 0.94-log reduction of *L. monocytogenes*, and significantly reduced the sensory quality of sprouts (Wade et al. 2003).

A series of studies conducted by Tiwari and associates investigated the effect of ozone treatment on anthocyanins and ascorbic acid in various fruit juices. Work performed on blackberry juice demonstrated significant decreases in ascorbic acid and anthocyanin content. Degradation of both compounds was correlated with both ozone concentration and treatment time (Tiwari et al. 2009a). Similar results were confirmed in strawberry and grape juices (Tiwari et al. 2009b, 2009c). On the contrary, treatments of fresh cut celery with up to 0.18-ppm aqueous ozone resulted in no appreciable difference in ascorbic acid content (Zhang et al. 2005), and treatment of whole blackberries with 0.3-ppm gaseous ozone did not elicit loss of either color or anthocyanins (Barth et al. 1995). Celery and blackberries did, however, display a significant decrease in activity of polyphenol oxidase and peroxidase, respectively, a positive outcome due to the quality deterioration associated with these enzymes.

Dried Foods

Dried foods are not generally susceptible to bacterial contamination due to their low water activity. This same characteristic, however, makes microbiota quite difficult to inactivate. Additionally, dry products are often heavily laden with fungal and bacterial spores. Many of these spores are resistant to heat, acid, and other antimicrobial treatments, making it extremely difficult to reduce these populations with minimal processing. Fumigation of such dried products has traditionally employed methyl bromide. However, owing to the fact that this chemical is an ozone layer–depleting substance, its use has been prohibited in recent years, leading to increased use of phosphine gas.

When Oztekin et al. (2006) treated dried figs with gaseous ozone (up to 10 ppm) for 5 h, they observed less than 1-log reduction of total aerobic and fungal counts. Coliform bacteria were more sensitive to this treatment; an initial population of 1.46 log g^{-1} was reduced to undetectable levels after three hours of exposure to 3-ppm ozone (Oztekin et al. 2006). A subsequent study compared gaseous and aqueous ozone treatments. Aqueous ozone (1.7 mg $liter^{-1}$) was more effective than the gaseous treatment (13.8 mg $liter^{-1}$) at reducing coliforms and yeast populations, but both treatments reduced native populations of *E. coli* and molds to below detection limit after 15 min of treatment (Zorlugenc et al. 2008). In a study on dates, coliforms and *Staphylococcus aureus* were both inactivated by more than 3 log after a 60-minute treatment with 5-ppm gaseous ozone (Habibi Najafi & Haddad Khodaparast 2009). Treatment of red pepper flakes with 9-ppm gaseous ozone for 360 min provided a 1.5-log reduction of *Bacillus cereus* spores but also reduced consumer scores for color and flavor (Akbas & Ozdemir 2008).

In 2003, Allen and colleagues reported that treatment of barley with gaseous ozone (0.16 mg g^{-1} min^{-1}, 5 min) resulted in greater than l-log reduction of fungal spores. The authors also reported that inactivation was positively correlated with increased water activity of the product and treatment temperature. Treatments of up to 0.98 mg g^{-1} min^{-1} ozone for 45 min had no detrimental effect on barley germination (Allen et al. 2003). Similar results were obtained in a subsequent study of stored wheat (Wu et al. 2006).

Insect infestation is a problem unique to stored products including grains. Reports of insect resistance to the most widely used grain fumigant, phosphine, have been widespread in recent years (Chaudhry 1997). In a study of stored maize, treatment with 50-ppm gaseous ozone for three days resulted in greater than 90% mortality of three common stored grain pests (Kells et al. 2001).

Animal Products

Animal products receive a great deal of attention among food safety specialists because of their association with well-known pathogens (i.e., enterohemorrhagic *E. coli* with beef and *Salmonella* with poultry). A recent large-scale outbreak of salmonellosis due to consumption of contaminated eggs (U.S. Cent. Dis. Cont. Prev. 2010) emphasizes the need for measures to control or eliminate pathogenic microorganisms in these products.

Meat. Undercooked meat is a common cause of foodborne illness, which makes it a high profile target for safety enhancing treatments. Unfortunately, success with ozone treatment of meat products has been limited. Reductions of target populations are typically low because ozone is consumed by reacting with organic compounds covering the surface of the meat, which, apart from decreasing antimicrobial activity, often also decreases the quality of the final product. This effect is illustrated well in a 1979 publication by Yang & Chen in which bacterial suspensions were made from spoiled poultry meat. Treatment with 19 mg $liter^{-1}$ aqueous ozone reduced an initial count of over 7 log per ml to undetectable levels, but addition of egg albumen significantly reduced the biocidal effect of ozone due to increased ozone demand of the medium (Yang & Chen 1979). In a study of beef prior to grinding, meat was treated with 1% aqueous ozone for up to 15 min. At the maximum treatment time, reductions in *E. coli*, *Salmonella* Typhimurium, coliforms, and aerobic plate count were all less than 1 log (Stivarius et al. 2002). A subsequent study utilizing 1% aqueous ozone for 15 min with successive treatments with either cetylpyridinium chloride or acetic acid produced slightly more inactivation, but all reductions were still less than 2 log. Additionally, treatments with ozone and either cetylpyridinium chloride or acetic acid decreased the red color of the meat, and the treatment utilizing acetic acid was reported to produce off odors (Pohlman et al. 2002). Gaseous ozone (0.03 ppm) was used to treat beef sides during dry aging, but treated samples displayed significantly more discoloration and shrinkage than controls, with no resulting shelf life increase of steaks (Greer & Jones 1989). Aqueous ozone (5 ppm) had limited lethality against *Clostridium perfringens* vegetative cells and spores on fabricated beef surfaces (Novak & Yuan 2004). Inactivation of the vegetative cells was enhanced when the ozone treatment was followed by heating at 45°C or 55°C for 30 min. Similarly, inactivation of *C. perfringens* spores increased when the ozone treatment was followed by a 30-min heating at 55°C or 75°C.

Chicken breasts were inoculated with *Salmonella* Infantis or *Pseudomonas aeruginosa* and treated with >2000 ppm gaseous ozone for up to 30 min. Reduction of these organisms was less than 2 log, and no reduction of native coliforms was detected (Al-Haddad et al. 2005).

Seafood. Multiple studies investigating the use of ozone in shrimp farming operations have shown the promise of this application. In these studies, ozone is introduced into hatchery tanks until a maximum residual ozone level is reached. Residual concentrations of 0.35 mg liter^{-1}, maintained for 30 min have been demonstrated to reduce levels of the pathogen *Vibrio harveyi* by approximately 3 log (Meunpol et al. 2003). Adolescent shrimp are not harmed by low-level ozone treatment, and the reduction in pathogens affected by these treatments results in greater survival of shrimp with reduced administration of antibiotics (Blogoslawski et al. 1992, Meunpol et al. 2003).

Ozone treatment (0.20 mg liter^{-1}) of water containing fish pathogens, including *Aeromonas*, *Yersinia*, and *Vibrio* spp., as well as infectious pancreatic necrosis virus, decreased their level by up to 4 log, regardless of water salinity (Liltved et al. 1995). However, modest results were observed when ozone was tested in aquaculture systems. Low-level ozone treatment (0.039 kg ozone kg^{-1} feed) reduced outbreaks of bacterial gill disease in rainbow trout, despite the observations that pathogen reduction in water was less than 1 log, and bacterial colonization of gills was not prevented (Bullock et al. 1997). Additionally, ozone toxicity to fish was an intermittent problem and has been observed in several species (Bullock et al. 1997, Summerfelt & Hochheimer 1997). Toxicity remains the main obstacle for the use of ozone in these applications.

Although use of ozone in fish farming is challenging, application of the sanitizer to extend the shelf life of whole or filleted fish seems promising. Low-level ozone treatment on fresh scad filets did not provide significant reductions in populations of inoculated microorganisms, but storage in the presence of ozone (0.25 mg liter^{-1}) increased the lag phase of several populations to five or more days (Da Silva et al. 1998). Treatment of oysters with 5 μg liter^{-1} ozonated water for 2 min resulted in a less than 1-log decrease of indigenous microbiota. A combination treatment utilizing ozone and chitosan provided a similar initial reduction, but extended the lag phase to ten days and increased the shelf life of the product from 8 to 20 days (Rong et al. 2010).

When whole fresh megrim were washed in 2-ppm aqueous ozone and subsequently stored for 12 days in ice made from ozonated water, total microbial counts on treated fish remained low enough for this product to be sold in the European Union, whereas untreated fish had to be discarded (Pastoriza et al. 2008). Additionally, sensory analysis indicated that ozone-treated fish stored for 3 to 11 days was preferred to untreated fish in both the raw and cooked states. In studies examining the storage of sardines in slurry ice (a mixture of salt water and ice crystals), the addition of ozone to the mixture (0.17 mg liter^{-1}) led to a shelf life increase of 3 to 4 days as well as improved sensory outcomes. The presence of ozone during storage in slurry ice (for up to 22 days) kept the levels of sardines' natural microbiota significantly lower than those in samples not subjected to ozone; ozone treatment was not associated with increased lipid oxidation (Losada et al. 2004, Campos et al. 2005). Similar results were obtained in a subsequent study on farmed turbot, with a shelf life extension of seven days (Campos et al. 2006). Despite the modest lethality reported in the previous studies, ozone delayed proliferation of microbial population during storage of these products. Treatments like these could minimize economic losses associated with spoilage of seafood.

Shell eggs. Several researchers have investigated the use of ozone to increase the safety of shell eggs. In the US, all liquid egg products are pasteurized, but no such treatment is required for shell eggs. It was estimated that 1 in 20,000 eggs produced in the United States is contaminated internally with *Salmonella* Enteritidis; however, many more may carry this pathogen on the shell (Musgrove et al. 2005; U.S. Dep. Agric., Food Safety Inspec. Serv. 2005). In a 2000 study, Koidis and associates dipped inoculated shell eggs into ozonated water (3.0 mg liter^{-1}) for 30 to 90 sec; this treatment decreased *Salmonella* Enteritidis population by less than 1.5 log per egg. Rodriguez-Romo & Yousef (2005) treated externally contaminated eggs with gaseous ozone, UV radiation, or a combination of the two steps. Treatment with gaseous ozone (5% by weight, 5 in lb^{-2} gauge) for 8 min decreased *Salmonella* Enteritidis by 2.6 log per gram of egg contents. Treatment with UV radiation (254 nm, 100 μw cm^{-2}) for 4 min resulted in a reduction of 3.8 log, but the combination of these technologies provided a reduction of 4.6 log in only 2 min of treatment time (Rodriguez-Romo & Yousef 2005). Subsequent investigation regarding the use of gaseous ozone against *Salmonella* Enteritidis inside shell eggs has led to the development of a process combining sequential application of mild heat and gaseous ozone under pressure to provide >6 log inactivation. This process is effective against *Salmonella* located in the egg yolk and produces eggs similar in quality to untreated eggs (Perry & Yousef 2010).

Potential Control of Toxins and Pesticide Residue

Presence of mold on grains, nuts, and some fruits is associated with the contamination of these products with mycotoxins. One of the mycotoxins is aflatoxin, a secondary metabolite of *Aspergillus* spp., occurring in four forms (B_1, B_2, G_1, and G_2). Presence of aflatoxin in food is heavily regulated due to the fact that this fungal metabolite is highly toxic. Aflatoxin B_1 is also a potent carcinogen. Due to these health risks, aflatoxin levels in foods are capped in the ppb range, varying slightly depending on the product. Contamination with aflatoxin leads to significant economic losses for producers of grains and nuts. Various experiments have been undertaken to assess the effect of ozone on aflatoxin. Short gaseous ozone treatments (2% by weight for 15 seconds) have reduced the toxicity of several mycotoxins, including aflatoxin, ochratoxin, and patulin suspended in liquid media (McKenzie et al. 1997). Although aflatoxins B_1 and G_1 were degraded by 2% ozone treatment for 5 min, aflatoxins B_2 and G_2 required treatment with 20% ozone. The relative susceptibility of toxins B_1 and G_1 has previously been reported in a study using peanut and cottonseed meal (Dwarakanath et al. 1968). More recently, corn kernels contaminated with aflatoxin were treated with gaseous ozone at 10% to 12% (wt/wt) for 96 hours. This treatment resulted in a 92% reduction of aflatoxin levels (Prudente & King 2002). When dried figs were spiked with aflatoxin B_1, treatment with gaseous ozone (13.8 mg liter^{-1}) for 180 min reduced the toxin level by more than 95% (Zorlugenc et al. 2008). In a 1997 study, it was reported that fifteen seconds of treatment with 10% ozone gas (wt/wt) reduced patulin in aqueous solution to undetectable levels and eliminated its toxicity (McKenzie et al. 1997). A more recent study reinforced the efficacy of ozone against patulin in diluted apple juice (Cataldo 2008).

In recent years, the presence of pesticide residue on fresh produce has become a source of alarm to many consumers. Consumers concern has contributed significantly to the increase in sales of organic products, especially in the fresh produce category, in the United States. Ozone can be used to sanitize organic products, and some researchers suggest the treatment can be useful in decreasing pesticide residue. Significant research has been conducted regarding the ability of ozone to reduce pesticide levels in drinking water (reviewed by Ikehata & El-Din 2005). Studies investigating degradation of pesticide residue on food products are few, but the results of such studies are promising. In a study utilizing pak choi spiked with different pesticides, degradation in aqueous solution was significantly greater than degradation on vegetable tissues (Wu et al. 2007). However, treatment with 2 mg liter^{-1} ozonated water for 30 min resulted in significantly greater removal of cypermethrin (61%), methyl-parathion (48%), parathion (54%), and diazinon (53%) than washing with tap water alone, which only resulted in 27% to 31% removal of these compounds (Wu et al. 2007). Washing apples with ozonated water (3 ppm) reduced commonly applied levels of mancozeb and ethylenethiourea to unquantifiable levels (Hwang et al. 2006). The ability of ozone to combat pathogens, mycotoxins, and chemical contaminants simultaneously is a benefit not offered by other treatments.

DISCLOSURE STATEMENT

The authors are not aware of any affiliations, memberships, funding, or financial holdings that might be perceived as affecting the objectivity of this review.

ACKNOWLEDGMENTS

This work is supported by grants from the National Institute of Food & Agriculture, USDA, under these programs: the Doctoral Training in Emerging Food Safety Issues and the National Integrated Food Safety Initiative. The authors would like to thank Dr. M. Vurma for providing the photographs included in this manuscript.

LITERATURE CITED

Achen M, Yousef AE. 2001. Efficacy of ozone against *Escherichia coli* O157:H7 on apples. *J. Food Sci.* 66:1380–84

Aguayo E, Escalona VH, Artes F. 2006. Effect of cyclic exposure to ozone gas on physiochemical, sensorial and microbial quality of whole and sliced tomatoes. *Postharvest Biol. Technol.* 39:169–77

Akbas MY, Ozdemir M. 2008. Effect of gaseous ozone on microbial inactivation and sensory of flaked red peppers. *Int. J. Food Microbiol.* 43:657–62

Al-Haddad KSH, Al-Qassemi RAS, Robinson RK. 2005. The use of gaseous ozone and gas packaging to control populations of *Salmonella infantis* and *Pseudomonas aeruginosa* on the skin of chicken portions. *Food Cont.* 16:405–10

Allen B, Wu J, Doan H. 2003. Inactivation of fungi associated with barley grain by gaseous ozone. *J. Environ. Sci. Health* 35:617–30

Artes-Hernandez F, Aguayo E, Artes F, Tomas-Barberan FA. 2007. Enriched ozone atmosphere enhances bioactive phenolics in seedless table grapes after prolonged shelf life. *J. Sci. Food Agric.* 87:824–31

Bader H, Hoigne J. 1981. Determination of ozone in water by the indigo method. *Water Res.* 15:449–56

Barth MM, Zhou C, Mercier J, Payne FA. 1995. Ozone storage effects on anthocyanin content and fungal growth in blackberries. *J. Food Sci.* 60:1286–88

Becci PJ, Hess FG, Johnson WD, Gallo MA, Babish JG, et al. 2006. Long-term carcinogenicity and toxicity studies of patulin in the rat. *J. App. Toxicol.* 1:256–61

Bialka KL, Demirci A. 2007. Decontamination of *Escherichia coli* O157:H7 and *Salmonella enterica* on blueberries using ozone and pulsed UV-light. *J. Food Sci.* 72:M391–96

Block SS. 2001. Peroxygen compounds. In *Disinfection, Sterilization, and Preservation*, 5th ed., ed. SS Block, 9:185–204. Philadelphia: Lippincott Williams & Wilkins

Blogoslawski WJ, Perez C, 1992. Ozone treatment of seawater to control vibriosis in mariculture of penaeid shrimp, *Penaeus vannameii*. In *Proc. Third Int. Symp. Use Ozone Aquat. Syst.*, ed. WJ Blogoslawski, pp. 123–33. Stamford, CT: Pan Am. Group Int. Ozone Assoc.

Brook RD, Brook JR, Urch B, Vincent R, Rajagopalan S, Silverman F. 2002. Inhalation of fine particulate air pollution and ozone causes acute arterial vasoconstriction in healthy adults. *Circulation* 105:1534–36

Brown D, Berger AW, Hersh CK. 1955. Phase diagram of liquid ozone-oxygen system. *J. Chem. Phys.* 23:1340–43

Bullock GL, Summerfelt ST, Noble AC, Weber AL, Durant MD, Hankins JA. 1997. Ozonation of a recirculating rainbow trout culture system I. Effects on bacterial gill disease and heterotrophic bacteria. *Aquaculture* 158:43–55

Campos CA, Losada V, Rodriguez O, Aubourg SP, Barros-Velazquez J. 2006. Evaluation of an ozone-slurry ice combined refrigeration system for the storage of farmed turbot (*Psetta maxima*). *Food Chem.* 97:223–30

Campos CA, Rodriguez O, Losada V, Aubourg SP, Barros-Velazquez J. 2005. Effects of storage in ozonised slurry ice on the sensory and microbial quality of sardine (*Sardina pilchardus*). *Int. J. Food Microbiol.* 103:121–30

Cataldo F. 2008. Ozone decomposition of patulin, a mycotoxin and food contaminant. *Ozone Sci.* 30:197–201

Cent. Dis. Control Prev. 2008. Outbreak of *Salmonella* serotype saintpaul infections associated with multiple raw produce items—United States, 2008. *MMWR* 57:929–34

Chaudhry MQ. 1997. A review of the mechanisms involved in the action of phosphine as an insecticide and phosphine resistance in stored-product insects. *Pestic. Sci.* 49:213–28

Cho M, Chung H, Yoon J. 2002. Effect of pH and importance of ozone initiated radical reactions in inactivating *Bacillus subtilis* spore. *Ozone Sci. Eng.* 24:145–50

Code Fed. Regul. 2001. *Secondary direct food additives permitted in food for human consumption: Title 21, Part 173.368.* **http://www.accessdata.fda.gov/scripts/cdrh/cfdocs/cfcfr/cfrsearch.cfm?fr=173.368**

Code Fed. Regul. 2006. *Direct food substances affirmed as generally recognized as safe: Title 21, Part 184.* **http://www.accessdata.fda.gov/scripts/cdrh/cfdocs/cfcfr/CFRSearch.cfm?CFRPart=184**

Code Fed. Regul. 2009. *Definitions: Title 21, Part 110.3.* **http://www.accessdata.fda.gov/scripts/cdrh/cfdocs/cfcfr/CFRSearch.cfm?fr=110.3**

Da Silva MV, Gibbs PA, Kirby RM. 1998. Sensorial and microbial effects of gaseous ozone on fresh scad (*Trachurus trachurus*). *J. App. Microbiol.* 84:802–10

Das E, Candan G, Alev B. 2006. Effect of controlled atmosphere storage, modified atmosphere packaging and gaseous ozone treatment on the survival of *Salmonella* Enteritidis on cherry tomatoes. *Food Microbiol.* 23:430–38

Dunlea EJ, Herndon SC, Nelson DD, Volkamer RM, Lamb BK, et al. 2006. Technical note: evaluation of standard UV absorption ozone monitors in a polluted urban environment. *Atmos. Chem. Phys.* 6:3163–80

Dwarakanth CT, Rayner ET, Mann GE, Dollear FG. 1968. Reduction of aflatoxin levels in cottonseed and peanut meals by ozonization. *J. Am. Oil Chem.* 45:93–95

Greer GG, Jones SDM. 1989. Effects of ozone on bacterial carcass shrinkage, muscle quality and bacterial spoilage. *Can. Inst. Food Sci. Technol. J.* 22:156–160

Grunwell J, Benga J, Cohen H, Gordon G. 1983. A detailed comparison of analytical methods for residual ozone measurement. *Ozone Sci.* 5:203–23

Guzel-Seydim Z, Bever PI Jr, Greene AK. 2004. Efficacy of ozone to reduce bacterial populations in the presence of food components. *Food Microbiol.* 21:475–79

Habibi Najafi MB, Haddad Khodaparast MH. 2009. Efficacy of ozone to reduce microbial populations in date fruits. *Food Cont.* 20:27–30

Heagle AS. 1989. Ozone and crop yield. *Annu. Rev. Phytopathol.* 27:397–423

Hill HW. 1905. A notable source of error in testing gaseous disinfectants. *Pub. Health Pap. Rep.* 31:210–13

Horvath M, Bilitzky L, Huttner J. 1985. *Ozone*. Budapest: Elsevier

Hunt NK, Marinas BJ. 1997. Kinetics of *Escherichia coli* inactivation with ozone. *Wat. Res.* 31:1355–62

Hwang H, Cash JN, Zabik MJ. 2006. Degradation of mancozeb and ethylenethiourea in apples due to postharvest treatments and processing. *J. Food Sci.* 67:3295–300

Ikehata K, El-Din MG. 2005. Aqueous pesticide degradation by ozonation and advanced oxidation processes: a review. *Ozone Sci. Eng.* 27:173–202

Ingram M, Haines RB. 1949. Inhibition of bacterial growth by pure ozone in the presence of nutrients. *J. Hyg.* 47:146–58

Ishizaki K, Sawadaishi K, Miura K, Shinriki N. 1987. Effect of ozone on plasmid DNA of *Escherichia coli* in situ. *Wat. Res.* 21:823–27

Ishizaki K, Shinriki N, Matsuyama H. 1986. Inactivation of *Bacillus* spores by gaseous ozone. *J. Appl. Bacteriol.* 60:67–72

Jenkins AC, DiPaolo FS. 1956. Some physical properties of pure liquid ozone and ozone-oxygen mixtures. *J. Chem. Phys.* 25:296–301

Kells SA, Mason LJ, Maier DE, Woloshuk CP. 2001. Efficacy and fumigation characteristics of ozone in stored maize. *J. Stored Prod. Res.* 37:371–82

Khadre MA, Yousef AE. 2001. Sporicidal action of ozone and hydrogen peroxide: a comparative study. *Int. J. Food Microbiol.* 71:131–38

Khalifa AM, El Temsahy MM, Abou El Naga IF. 2001. Effect of ozone on the viability of some protozoa in drinking water. *J. Egypt. Soc. Parasitol.* 31:603–16

Kim CK, Gentile DM, Sproul OJ. 1980. Mechanism of ozone inactivation of bacteriophage f2. *Appl. Environ. Microbiol.* 39:210–18

Kim JG. 1998. *Ozone as an antimicrobial agent in minimally processed foods.* PhD thesis. Ohio State Univ., Columbus. 243 pp.

Kim JG, Yousef AE, Chism GW. 1999. Use of ozone to inactivate microorganisms on lettuce. *J. Food Saf.* 19:17–34

Kim JG, Yousef AE, Khadre MA. 2003. Ozone and its current and future application in the food industry. *Adv. Food Nutr. Res.* 45:167–218

Klockow PA, Keener KM. 2009. Safety and quality assessment of packaged spinach treated with a novel ozone-generation system. *LWT—Food Sci. Technol.* 46:1047–53

Lagerwerff JM. 1963. Prolonged ozone inhalation and its effects on visual parameters. *Aerosp. Med.* 34:479–86

Li YJ, Sun XP, Guo KQ, Wang Y. 2009. Comparison of the storage effect on kiwi fruit between ozone and preservative. *Food Sci. Technol.* 34:45–48

Liltved H, Hektoen H, Efraimsen H. 1995. Inactivation of bacterial and viral fish pathogens by ozonation or UV irradiation in water of different salinity. *Aquacult. Eng.* 14:107–22

Losada V, Barros-Velazquez J, Gallardo JM, Aubourg SP. 2004. Effect of advanced chilling methods on lipid damage during sardine (*Sardina pilchardus*) storage. *Eur. J. Lipid Sci. Technol.* 106:844–50

McKenzie KS, Sarr AB, Mayura K, Bailey RH, Miller DR, et al. 1997. Oxidative degradation and detoxification of mycotoxins using a novel source of ozone. *Food Chem. Toxicol.* 35:807–20

Meunpol O, Lopinyosiri K, Menasveta P. 2003. The effects of ozone and probiotics on the survival of black tiger shrimp (*Penaeus monodon*). *Aquaculture* 220:437–48

Musgrove MT, Jones DR, Northcutt JK, Harrison MA, Ingram KD, Hinton AJ. 2005. Recovery of *Salmonella* from commercial shell eggs by rinse and shell crush methodologies. *Poult. Sci.* 84:1955–58

Novak JS, Yuan JTC. 2004. Increased inactivation of ozone-treated *Clostridium perfringens* vegetative cells and spores on fabricated beef surfaces using mild heat. *J. Food Prot.* 67:342–46

Osipyan VT, Uspenskiy ND. 1964. A method for determining the bactericidal activity of gaseous disinfectants. *J. Microbiol. Epidemiol. Immunobiol.* 8:8–12

Oztekin S, Zorlugenc B, Zorlugenc FK. 2006. Effects of ozone treatment on microflora of dried figs. *J. Food Eng.* 75:396–99

Palou L, Crisoto CH, Smilanick JL, Adaskaveg JE, Zoffoli JP. 2002. Effects of continuous 0.3 ppm ozone exposure on decay development and physiological responses of peaches and table grapes in cold storage. *Postharvest Biol. Technol.* 24:39–48

Palou L, Smilanick JL, Crisoto CH, Mansour M. 2001. Effect of gaseous ozone exposure on development of green and blue molds on cold stored citrus fruit. *Plant Dis.* 85:632–38

Pastoriza L, Bernardez M, Sampedro G, Cabo ML, Herrera JJR. 2008. The use of water and ice with bactericide to prevent onboard and onshore spoilage of refrigerated megrim (*Lepidorhombus whiffiagonis*). *Food Chem.* 110:31–38

Perez AG, Sanz C, Rios JJ, Olias R, Olias JM. 1999. Effects of ozone treatment on postharvest strawberry quality. *J. Agric. Food Chem.* 47:1652–56

Perry JJ, Rodriguez-Romo LA, Yousef AE. 2008. Inactivation of *Salmonella enterica* serovar Enteritidis in shell eggs by sequential application of heat and ozone. *Letters App. Microbiol.* 46:620–25

Perry JJ, Yousef AE. 2010. Pasteurization of shell eggs with sequential heat-ozone treatments, targeting *Salmonella* Enteritidis in the yolk. *Inst. Food Technol. Annu. Meet. 2010*, Chicago

Pohlman FW, Stivarius MR, McElyea KS, Johnson ZB, Johnson MG. 2002. The effects of ozone, chlorine dioxide, cetylpyridinium chloride and trisodium phosphate as multiple antimicrobial interventions on microbiological, instrumental color, and sensory color and odor characteristics of ground beef. *Meat Sci.* 61:307–13

Prudente ADJ, King JM. 2002. Efficacy and safety evaluation of ozonation to degrade aflatoxin in corn. *J. Food Sci.* 67:2866–72

Rice RG. 2006. IOA-PAG user success reports-commercial applications ozone in agri-foods. *Int. Water Technol. Ozone V Conf.*, Fresno

Rodoni L, Casadei N, Concellon A, Chaves Alicia AR, Vicente AR. 2010. Effect of short-term ozone treatments on tomato (*Solanum lycopersicum* L.) fruit quality and cell wall degradation. *J. Agric. Food Chem.* 58:594–99

Rodriguez-Romo LA, Yousef AE. 2005. Inactivation of *Salmonella enterica* serovar Enteritidis on shell eggs by ozone and UV radiation. *J. Food Prot.* 68:711–17

Rong C, Qi L, Bang-Zhong Y, Lan-Ian Z. 2010. Combined effect of ozonated water and chitosan on the shelf-life of Pacific oyster (*Crassostrea gigas*). *Innov. Food Sci. Emerg. Technol.* 11:108–12

Roy D, Wong PKY, Engelbrecht RS, Chian ESK. 1981. Mechanism of enteroviral inactivation by ozone. *App. Environ. Microbiol.* 41:718–23

Ruidavets JB, Cournot M, Cassadou S, Girou M, Maybeck M, Ferrieres J. 2005. Ozone air pollution is associated with acute myocardial infarction. *Circulation* 111:563–69

Sanderman H. 1996. Ozone and plant health. *Annu. Rev. Phytopathol.* 34:347–66

Scheel LD, Dobrogorski OJ, Mountain JT, Svirbely JL, Stokinger HE. 1959. Physiologic, biochemical, immunologic and pathologic changes following ozone exposure. *J. Appl. Physiol.* 14:67–80

Scott DBM, Lesher EC. 1963. Effect of ozone on survival and permeability of *Escherichia coli*. *J. Bacteriol.* 5:67–76

Selma MV, Beltran D, Allende A, Chacon-Vera E, Gil MI. 2007. Elimination by ozone of *Shigella sonnei* in shredded lettuce and water. *Food Microbiol.* 24:492–99

Selma MV, Beltran D, Chacon-Vera E, Gil MI. 2006. Effect of ozone on the inactivation of *Yersinia enterocolitica* and the reduction of natural flora on potatoes. *J. Food Prot.* 69:2357–63

Selma MV, Ibanez AM, Allende A, Cantwell M, Suslow T. 2008a. Effect of gaseous ozone and hot water on microbial and sensory quality of cantaloupe and potential transference of *Escherichia coli* O157:H7 during cutting. *Food Microbiol.* 25:162–68

Selma MV, Ibanez AM, Cantwell M, Suslow T. 2008b. Reduction by gaseous ozone of *Salmonella* and microbial flora associated with fresh-cut cantaloupe. *Food Microbiol.* 25:558–65

Sharma RR, Demirci A, Beuchat LR, Fett WF. 2002. Inactivation of *Escherichia coli* O157:H7 on inoculated alfalfa seeds with ozonated water and heat treatment. *J. Food Prot.* 65:447–51

Sharma RR, Demirci A, Beuhat L, Fett WF. 2003. Application of ozone for inactivation of *Escherichia coli* O157:H7 on inoculated alfalfa sprouts. *J. Food Proc. Pres. Res.* 27:52–64

Stivarius MR, Pohlman FW, McElyea KS, Apple JK. 2002. Microbial, instrumental color and sensory color and odor characteristics of ground beef produced from beef trimmings treated with ozone or chlorine dioxide. *Meat Sci.* 60:299–305

Summerfelt ST, Hochheimer JN. 1997. Review of ozone processes and applications as an oxidizing agent in aquaculture. *Prog. Fish Cult.* 59:94–105

Thanomsub B, Anupunpisit V, Chanphetch S, Watcharachaipong T, Poonkhum R, Srisukonth C. 2002. Effects of ozone treatment on cell growth and ultrastructural changes in bacteria. *J. Gen. Appl. Microbiol.* 48:193–99

Tiwari BK, O'Donnell CP, Muthukumarappan K, Cullen PJ. 2009a. Anthocyanin and color degradation in ozone treated blackberry juice. *Innov. Food Sci.* 10:70–75

Tiwari BK, O'Donnell CP, Patras A, Brunton N, Cullen PJ. 2009b. Anthocyanins and color degradation in ozonated grape juice. *Food Chem. Toxicol.* 47:2824–29

Tiwari BK, O'Donnell CP, Patras A, Brunton N, Cullen PJ. 2009c. Effect of ozone processing on anthocyanins and ascorbic acid degradation of strawberry juice. *Food Chem.* 113:1119–26

Tzortakis N, Singleton I, Barnes J. 2008. Impact of low-level atmospheric ozone-enrichment on black spot and antracnose rot of tomato fruit. *Postharvest Biol. Technol.* 47:1–9

U.S. Cent. Dis. Cont. Prev. 2010. *Investigation update: multistate outbreak of human* Salmonella *Enteritidis infections associated with shell eggs.* **http://www.cdc.gov/salmonella/enteritidis/**

U.S. Dep. Agric., Food Safety Inspec. Serv. 2005. *Risk assessment for* Salmonella *Enteritidis in shell eggs and Salmonella spp. in egg products, October 2005.* **http://www.fsis.usda.gov/Science/Risk_Assessments/index.asp#eggs**

U.S. Dep. Labor, Occup. Saf. Health Adm. 2004. *Chemical sampling information, ozone.* **http://www.osha.gov/dts/chemicalsampling/data/CH_259300.html**

U.S. Env. Prot. Agency. 1999. *Wastewater technology fact sheet: ozone disinfection*. Washington, DC: EPA

U.S. Food Drug Adm. 1993. *Sanitizing solutions: chemistry guidelines for food additive petitions*. Washington, DC: CFSAN, Off. Food Addit. Saf.

Victorin K. 1992. Review of the genotoxicity of ozone. *Mutat. Res.* 277:221–38

Vingarzan R. 2004. A review of surface ozone background levels and trends. *Atmos. Environ.* 38:3431–42

Vurma M. 2009. *Development of ozone based processes for decontamination of fresh produce to enhance safety and enhance shelflife*. PhD thesis. Ohio State Univ., Columbus. 227 pp.

Vurma M, Pandit RB, Sastry SK, Yousef AE. 2009. Inactivation of *Escherichia coli* O157:H7 and natural microbiota on spinach leaves using gaseous ozone during vacuum cooling and simulated transportation. *J. Food Prot.* 72:1538–46

Wade WN, Scouten AJ, McWatters KH, Wick RL, Demirci A, et al. 2003. Efficacy of ozone in killing *Listeria monocytogenes* on alfalfa seeds and sprouts and effects on sensory quality of sprouts. *J. Food Prot.* 66:44–51

Williams RC, Sumner SS, Golden DA. 2004. Survival of *Escherichia coli* O157:H7 and *Salmonella* in apple cider and orange juice as affected by ozone treatment temperature. *J. Food Prot.* 67:2381–86

Wu J, Doan H, Cuenca MA. 2006. Investigation of gaseous ozone as an antifungal fumigant for stored wheat. *J. Chem. Technol. Biotechnol.* 81:1288–93

Wu JG, Luan TG, Lan CY, Lo WH, Chan GYS. 2007. Efficacy evaluation of low-concentration of ozonated water in removal of residual diazinon, parathion, methyl-parathion and cypermethrin on vegetable. *J. Food Eng.* 79:803–9

Yang PPW, Chen TC. 1979. Stability of ozone and its germicidal properties on poultry meat microorganisms in liquid phase. *J. Food Sci.* 44:501–4

Yuk HG, Yoo MY, Yoon JW, Marshall DL, Oh DH. 2007. Effect of combined ozone and organic acid treatment for control of *Escherichia coli* O157:H7 and *Listeria monocytogenes* on enoki mushroom. *Food Cont.* 18:548–53.

Zhang L, Lu Z, Yu Z, Gao X. 2005. Preservation of fresh-cut celery by treatment of ozonated water. *Food Cont.* 16:279–83

Zorlugenc B, Zorlugenc FK, Oztekin S, Evliya IB. 2008. The influence of gaseous ozone and ozonated water on microbial flora degradation of aflatoxin B_1 in dried figs. *Food Chem. Toxicol.* 46:3593–97

New Developments and Applications of Bacteriocins and Peptides in Foods

S. Mills,[1] C. Stanton,[1,2,3] C. Hill,[1,3,4] and R.P. Ross[1,2,3]

[1]Food for Health Ireland, Moorepark Food Research Center, Fermoy, County Cork, Ireland; email: paul.ross@teagasc.ie

[2]Teagasc, Moorepark Food Research Center, Fermoy, County Cork, Ireland

[3]Alimentary Pharmabiotic Center, University College Cork, Cork, Ireland

[4]Department of Microbiology, University College Cork, Cork, Ireland

Annu. Rev. Food Sci. Technol. 2011. 2:299–329

The *Annual Review of Food Science and Technology* is online at food.annualreviews.org

This article's doi:
10.1146/annurev-food-022510-133721

1941-1413/11/0410-0299$20.00

Keywords

food safety, functional foods

Abstract

There is an increased desire for sophisticated foods, whereby consumers harbor higher expectations of health-promoting benefits above basic nutrition. Moreover, there is a move from the adulteration of foods with chemical preservatives toward biopreservation. Such expectations have led scientists to identify novel approaches to satisfy both demands, which utilize bacteriocin and peptide-based solutions. The best known examples of biopreservation involve bacteriocins. However, with the exception of nisin, bacteriocins have received limited use in the food industry. Peptides can be added to foods to improve consumer health. Some of the best known examples are angiotensin I–converting enzyme (ACE)-inhibitory peptides, which inhibit ACE, a key enzyme involved in blood pressure (BP) regulation. To be effective, these peptides must be bioavailable, but by their nature, peptides are degraded by digestion with proteolytic enzymes. This review critically discusses the use and potential of peptides and bacteriocins in food systems in terms of safety, quality, and improvement of human health.

INTRODUCTION

When considering new applications of bacteriocins and peptides in food systems, three criteria spring to mind, namely safety, quality, and nutrition/health, that are among the key issues driving continued efforts in food research and development. Remarkably, bacteriocins and peptides have the potential to affect all aspects of these three criteria from microbial quality and safety to taste perception and allerginicity, and even to health promotion through a range of biological activities that can be as diverse as drug-type effects on the central nervous system. Although bacteriocins and peptides are completely unrelated molecules in terms of functionalities, they are both composed of unique sequences of amino acids. Bacteriocins are ribosomally synthesized, heat-stable, antimicrobial peptides produced by one bacterium [which is immune to its own bacteriocin(s)] and are active against other bacteria, either in the same species (narrow spectrum of activity) or across genera (broad spectrum of activity) (Cotter et al. 2005). Bacteriocins generally act through depolarization of the target cell membrane or through inhibition of cell wall synthesis (Abee et al. 1995). They usually range from 30–60 amino acids in length and have been associated with numerous species of bacteria. However, the bacteriocins of lactic acid bacteria (LAB) have received much attention in terms of food safety due to their generally recognized as safe (GRAS) status (Settanni & Corsetti 2008). They can be readily introduced into fermented foods without prior purification or concentration (Cotter et al. 2005), and they exhibit activity against key Gram-positive pathogens such as *Listeria monocytogenes* and *Staphylococcus aureus* (Sobrino-López & Martín-Belloso 2008b). Although they generally don't target Gram-negative bacteria, bacteriocins may be effective at killing Gram-negatives if the outer membrane is destabilized (Stevens et al. 1991). However, despite a wealth of bacteriocins that have been investigated as potential biopreservatives for the food industry, to date only two LAB bacteriocins, namely nisin and pediocin PA-1, are commercially available. Nisin is available as a dried concentrated powder called Nisaplin (Danisco) and was admitted into the European food additive list in the early 1980s, where it was assigned the number E234 (EEC 1983). It has since received GRAS status by the Food and Drug Administration (FDA) (Federal Register 1988), and it is the only bacteriocin that has been approved by the World Health Organization for use as a food preservative (Sobrino-López & Martín-Belloso 2008b). Pediocin PA-1 is commercially exploited as a bacteriocin-containing fermentate powder, namely ALTA® 2351 (Kerry Bioscience).

Bioactive peptides have the potential to regulate a range of physiological functions of the body. They can be encrypted in the polypeptide chain of proteins and can be released via proteolysis, where they may interact with appropriate receptors, exhibiting hormone-like activity (Dziuba & Darewicz 2007). They generally contain between 3 and 20 amino acids (Pihlanto 2001), but may be larger in some cases. However, food-derived bioactive peptides generally contain two to nine amino acids (Möller et al. 2008). Their activity depends on their amino acid composition and sequence (Shahidi & Zhong 2008), and various bioactivities have been reported, including peptides that reduce blood pressure (BP) (antihypertensive peptides), antithrombotic peptides, opioid peptides, casein phospopeptides (CPP), antimicrobial peptides, cytomodulatory peptides, and immunomodulatory peptides (Hayes et al. 2007), although bioactive peptides have been recently cataloged into as many as 37 identified activities based on the BIOPEP database, an in silico application for processing bioactive peptide sequences (Minkiewicz et al. 2008).

The aim of this article is to critically discuss new developments and applications of both bacteriocins and peptides in food research and how these developments impact food safety, quality, and nutrition/health, and ultimately consider how scientific findings are shaping the perceptions and future uses of these types of molecules.

FOOD SAFETY APPLICATIONS OF BACTERIOCINS AND PEPTIDES

Food processors run the risk of significant economic losses annually due to food spoilage resulting from microbial contamination. Although chemical preservatives may provide a solution, the use of such preservatives is generally frowned upon, as many, such as nitrite, can have negative consequences for human health. Moreover, the extent of problems associated with food safety as a result of microbial contamination appears to be alarmingly high. Indeed, in industrialized countries the percentage of the population suffering from foodborne disease each year has been reported to be up to 30% (World Health Organization 2007). Interestingly, the application of bacteriocins and peptides in foods has enormous potential to prolong shelf-life and increase food safety, thus eliminating or dramatically reducing the need for undesirable preservatives. Bacteriocins can be incorporated into the food matrix through three different routes: They may be added directly to foods as purified or semipurified antimicrobial additives (such as nisin through Nisaplin), or as bacteriocin-based ingredients from fermented foods (as observed for pediocin PA-1 through ALTA® 2351), or through bacteriocin-producing starter cultures (Schillinger et al. 1996). The application of bacteriocins in foods using such methods has been the topic of several extensive reviews (Castellano et al. 2008; De Vuyst & Leroy 2007; Deegan et al. 2006; Gálvez et al. 2007, 2008, 2010; Settanni & Corsetti 2008; Sobrino-López & Martín-Belloso 2008b). However, application of a bacteriocin alone in a food is unlikely to provide sufficient protection against microbial contamination (Deegan et al. 2006), which may have influenced the lack of enthusiasm for using such molecules in food preservation. But many recent studies have investigated the efficacy of using bacteriocins in conjunction with other preservation methods or hurdles and demonstrated very promising results (**Table 1**). Moreover, bacteriocins have greater opportunity to target Gram-negative pathogens if the outer membrane has been destabilized by the presence of another hurdle such as a chelating agent (Deegan et al. 2006, Stevens et al. 1991). More than 60 potential hurdles for food preservation have already been described (Leistner 1999), and in this respect bacteriocins have received much attention (Chen & Hoover 2003, Deegan et al. 2006, Gálvez et al. 2007, Ross et al. 2003). Hurdle technology is especially attractive in exploiting bacteriocins, as some peptides have demonstrated additive or synergistic effects when used in conjunction with other compounds or physical treatments and could provide an attractive approach to minimize the development of resistant strains (Gálvez et al. 2008). Organic acids can work well with bacteriocins as the increase in net charge of bacteriocins at low pH may facilitate bacteriocin translocation through the cell wall. In addition, the solubility of some bacteriocins may also be improved at low pH, facilitating diffusion (Gálvez et al. 2007). Chelating agents permeate the outer membrane of Gram-negative bacteria, thus enabling bacteriocins to reach the cytoplasmic membrane (Helander et al. 1997, Schved et al. 1994). Combining two or more bacteriocins has also provided promising results, particularly if the bacteriocins belong to different grouping schemes targeting different cellular components (Luders et al. 2003). Physical treatments have also been shown to potentiate bacteriocin activity. For example, the nonthermal treatment of high intensity pulsed electric field (HIPEF) can lead to microbial inactivation by the application of high voltage pulses (Vega-Mercado et al. 1997), damaging the bacterial membrane and thus complementing the mode of action of bacteriocins. The observed synergy between bacteriocins and high hydrostatic pressure (HHP) has also been hypothesized to be a result of cumulative damage to the cytoplasmic membrane (Gálvez et al. 2007). The use of antimicrobial cocktails that target different bacteria may also enhance the efficacy of high pressure treatments based on studies using nisin with lysozyme, lactoferricin, and a synthetic lysozyme-derived peptide (Masschalck et al. 2003).

Antimicrobial peptides derived from edible proteins have also exhibited inhibitory activity against food spoilage and pathogenic microorganisms, including *Escherichia coli*, *Listeria*,

Table 1 Examples of the application of bacteriocins with other hurdles

Bacteriocin(s)	Natural antimicrobial(s)	Target microorganism	Background	Reference
Bacteriocin combined with NaCl				
Enterocin AS-48 (10 μg ml^{-1})	NaCl (6 or 7%) 4°C	*Staphylococcus aureus*	Culture media	(Ananou et al. 2004)
Bacteriocin combined with nitrite				
Nisin (450 mg l^{-1})	Nitrite (180 mg l^{-1})	*Leuconostoc mesenteroides*	Broth	(Gill & Holley 2003)
		Listeria monocytogenes		
Enterocin EJ97 (1 [a]AU ml^{-1})	Nitrite (25–100 μg ml^{-1})	*Bacillus macroides* *Bacillus maroccanus*	Broth	(García et al. 2004a)
Enterocin EJ97 (20 AU ml^{-1})	Nitrite (25–100 μg ml^{-1})	*Listeria monocytogenes*	Broth	(García et al. 2004b)
Enterocin AS-48 (5 μg ml^{-1})	Nitrite (150 ppm)	*Bacillus cereus*	Broth	(Abriouel et al. 2002)
Bacteriocin combined with organic acids				
Nisin (120–180 [b]IU g^{-1})	Sodium lactate (18 g kg^{-1})	*Listeria monocytogenes*	Cold smoked rainbow trout	(Nykanen et al. 2000)
Pediocin (6,000 AU ml^{-1})	Sodium diacetate (3%) and sodium lactate (6%)	*Listeria monocytogenes*	Beef franks	(Uhart et al. 2004)
Nisin (50 μg ml^{-1})	Sodium lactate (2%) or Potassium sorbate (0.02%)	*Salmonella*	Fresh cut cantaloupe	(Ukuku & Fett 2004)
Lacticin 3147 (2,500 AU ml^{-1})	Sodium citrate (2%) or Sodium lactate (2%)	*Clostridium perfringens*	Fresh pork sausage	(Scannell et al. 2000b)
Enterocin AS-48 (8 or 16 μg ml^{-1})	Sodium lactate (0.5%–3%)	*Bacillus cereus*	Rice gruel	(Grande et al. 2006)
Bacteriocin combined with chelating agents				
Nisin (300 IU ml^{-1})	EDTA (20 mM)	*Escherichia coli* *Salmonella* spp. *Listeria monocytogenes*	Apple cider	(Ukuku et al. 2009)
Enterocin AS-48 (50 or 100 μg ml^{-1})	Sodium tripolyphosphate (0.5%)	*Escherichia coli* O157:H7	Apple juice	(Ananou et al. 2005)
Nisin (450 mg l^{-1})	EDTA (900 mg/l)	*Listeria monocytogenes*	Broth	(Gill & Holley 2003)
Enterocin EJ97 (1 AU ml^{-1})	Sodium tripolyphosphate (0.3 or 0.5%)	*Bacillus macroides* *Bacillus maroccanus*	Broth	(García et al. 2004a)

Bacteriocin combined with essential oils				
Nisin (0.625 μg ml^{-1})	Carvacrol (0.0075%) or Thymol (0.01%) or Eugenol (0.02%) All with diglycerol fatty acid ester–$DGMC_{12}$ (0.0025%)	*Listeria monocytogenes*	Broth	(Yamazaki et al. 2004)
Nisin Z (40 IU ml^{-1})	Thymol (0.02%)	*Listeria monocytogenes*	Broth	(Ettayebi et al. 2000)
Nisin Z (75 IU ml^{-1})	Thymol (0.03%)	*Bacillus subtilis*		
Nisin (25–200 ppm)	Cinnamon (0.3%)	*Salmonella typhimurium* *Escherichia coli* O157: H7	Apple juice	(Yuste & Fung 2004)
Enterocin AS-48 (80 μg ml^{-1})	Hydrocinnamic acid (20 mM) or Carvacrol (126 mM)	*Staphylococcus aureus*	Carbonara sauce	(Grande et al. 2007)
Enterocin AS-48 (30 μg g^{-1})	Various essential oils at 1%	*Listeria monocytogenes*	Ready-to-eat salad	(Molinos et al. 2009)
Nisin (500 or 1,000 IU g^{-1})	Thyme (0.6%)	*Listeria monocytogenes*	Minced beef	(Solomakos et al. 2008)
Bactericins combined with other bacteriocins, peptides, and proteins				
Enterocin AS-48 (30 μg g^{-1})	Nisaplin (0.25% or 0.5%)	*Listeria monocytogenes*	Ready-to-eat salad	(Molinos et al. 2009)
Nisin (0.25 μM)	α_{s2}-casein f[c] (183–207)	*Listeria monocytogenes*	Broth	(Lopez-Exposito et al. 2008)
Nisin (50–1,000 [d]BU ml^{-1})	Pediocin (50–1,000 BU ml^{-1})	*Bacillus spores*	Sous vide products	(Cabo et al. 2009)
Nisin (10 or 100 IU ml^{-1})	Lactoperoxidase (0.2 or 0.8 U ml^{-1})	*Listeria monocytogenes*	UHT skim milk	(Zapico et al. 1998)
Nisin (50 IU ml^{-1})	Curvaticin 13 (160 AU ml^{-1})	*Listeria monocytogenes*	Broth	(Bouttefroy & Milliere 2000)
Nisin	Lysozyme	*Lactobacillus curvatus* *Staphylococcus aureus*	Broth or pork juice	(Chung & Hancock 2000)
Pediocin PA-1 or Sakacin P or (64–128 μg ml) Curvacin A	Eukaryotic antimicrobial peptide pleurocidin (16 μg ml^{-1})	*Escherichia coli*	Broth	(Luders et al. 2003)

(Continued)

Table 1 (*Continued*)

Bacteriocin(s)	Natural antimicrobial(s)	Target microorganism	Background	Reference
Bactericins combined with high pressure treatments				
Nisin (500 IU ml^{-1}) Nisin (500 IU ml^{-1}) Nisin (500 IU ml^{-1}) Nisin (500 IU ml^{-1})	500 MPa (5 min) 500 MPa (5 min) 400 MPa (5 min) 250 MPa (5 min	*Listeria innocua* *Lactobacillus viridescens* *Escherichia coli* *Pseudomonas fluorescens*	Milk	(Black et al. 2005)
Nisin (10 IU ml^{-1})	250 MPa	*Listeria innocua*	Apple juice Carrot juice	(Pathanibul et al. 2009)
Nisin (1%)	250 MPa (30 min)	*Salmonella enteriditis*	Saline	(Ogihara et al. 2009)
Lacticin 3147 (10,000 AU ml^{-1}) Lacticin 3147 (15,000 AU ml^{-1})	250 MPa (30 min) 275 MPa (30 min)	*Staphylococcus aureus* *Listeria innocua*	RSM Whey	(Morgan et al. 2000)
Bactericins combined with high-intensity pulsed-electric field (HIPEF)				
Nisin (20 IU ml^{-1}) & Enterocin AS-48 (28 arbitary units ml^{-1})	HIPEF (800 μs)	*Staphylococcus aureus*	Milk	(Sobrino-Lopez et al. 2009)
Enterocin AS-48 (2.0 μg ml^{-1})	HIPEF (1000 μs)	*Lactobacillus diolivorans*	Apple juice	(Martínez Viedma et al. 2009)
Nisin (300 IU ml^{-1})	HIPEF (1200 μs)	*Staphylococcus aureus*	Milk	(Sobrino-Lopez & Martin-Belloso 2008a)
Bactericins combined with other treatments				
Gassericin A (49 arbitary units ml^{-1})	Glycine (0.5%)	*Bacillus cereus* *Lactococcus lactis*	Custard	(Arakawa et al. 2009)
Nisin (25 mg ml^{-1})	Diacetyl (2.5 mm L^{-1})	*Enterobacter sakazakii*	Broth	(Lee & Jin 2008)
Nisin (100 IU ml^{-1})	Microgard^{TM} (5%)	*Listeria innocua*	Liquid cheese whey	(von Staszewski & Jagus 2008)
Nisaplin (0.5%)	Pulsed Light (10.1 J cm^{-2})	*Listeria innocua*	Ready-to-eat sausages	(Uesugi & Moraru 2009)
Divergicin M35 (0.125 mg ml^{-1})	Chitosan-2 kDa (1.25 mg ml^{-1}) Chitosan-20 kDa (1.25 mg ml^{-1}) Chitosan-100 kDa (0.3125 mg ml)	*Listeria monocytogenes*	Broth	(Benabbou et al. 2009)

[a]AU = activity units, [b]IU = international units, [c]f = fragment, [d]BU = bacteriocin units.

Salmonella, *S. aureus*, *Bacillus* species, yeasts, and filamentous fungi. Milk-derived antimicrobial peptides, including bovine-derived lactoferricins, human lactoferrin, and casein-derived antimicrobial peptides, have attracted the most attention in recent years (López-Expósito & Recio 2008). For example, enzymatic hydrolysis of bovine lactoferrin resulted in the generation of peptides able to inhibit the wine spoilage yeast *Dekkera bruxellenis* and LAB known to cause spoilage during the wine-making process (Enrique et al. 2008, 2009). Casein-derived antimicrobial peptides resulting after fermentation demonstrated antibacterial activity against the pathogenic strains *E. coli* and *Enterobacter sakazakii*, the latter of which can be problematic in milk-based infant formulas (Hayes et al. 2006). More recently, antimicrobial peptides were isolated from three commercial Cheddar cheese samples which exhibited activity against *Bacillus cereus* and *E. coli*. The most biologically active peptides were greater than 10 kDa in size (Pritchard et al. 2010). Interestingly, synergistic effects have also been reported for combinations of antimicrobial peptides and bacteriocins. Combining nisin with αs2-casein (f)(183–207) demonstrated synergistic antimicrobial activity against the food pathogen *L. monocytogenes* (López-Expósito et al. 2008). Moreover, combining any of three LAB bacteriocins, pediocin PA-1, sakacin P, and curvacin A, with 2 μg of the eukaryotic peptide pleurocidin resulted in complete inhibition of *E. coli* growth, which was not possible using any of the antimicrobial treatments alone (Luders et al. 2003).

Bacteriocin Bioengineering Strategies for Increased Efficacy

Bacteriocin bioengineering can be exploited to improve bacteriocin solubility and stability, increase the spectrum of bacteriocin inhibition, and enhance antimicrobial activity. The gene-encoded nature of bacteriocins renders these antimicrobial molecules ideal candidates for bioengineering strategies. Novel bacteriocins can be generated by either mutating bacteriocin-encoding genes or by fusing genes from different bacterial species (Gillor et al. 2005). For example, the solubility of nisin Z at neutral pH was markedly improved by replacing asparagine at position 27 and histidine at position 31 with lysine residues using site-directed mutagenesis (Rollema et al. 1995). Moreover, replacement of dehydroalanine at position 5 with dehydrobutyrine resulted in a mutant with lower activity but which was significantly more resistant to acid-catalyzed chemical degradation compared with the natural derivative. A more recent study demonstrated that various activities of nisin can be engineered independently (Rink et al. 2007). For example, mutation of ring A within the peptide results in variants with enhanced activity and a modulated spectrum of activity against target cells. C-terminally truncated nisin A mutants lacking rings D and E retain significant antimicrobial activity but are unable to permeabilize the target membrane, and the opening of ring B eliminates antimicrobial activity but retains autoinducing activity. Random mutagenesis was recently used to generate the largest bank of randomly mutated nisin derivatives reported to date (Field et al. 2008). This led to identification of a nisin-producing mutant with enhanced activity against the mastitic pathogen *Streptococcus agalactiae* as a result of an amino acid change in the hinge region. Based on this discovery, mutants were generated with enhanced antimicrobial activity against *L. monocytogenes* and *S. aureus* using site-directed and site-saturation mutagenesis of the hinge region residues of the peptide (**Figure 1**, see color insert).

Microcin J25 is produced by *E. coli* and is active against several human pathogens including *Salmonella* spp., *Shigella* spp., and *E. coli*, including *E. coli* 0157: H7 (Blond et al. 1999, Sable et al. 2000, Salomon & Farias 1992). Its resistance to proteolytic enzymes present in the stomach limits its potential use as a food biopreservative, as it can affect the normal intestinal microbiota of the host when ingested. Substitution of glycine at position 12 with tyrosine resulted in the generation of a chymotrypsin-sensitive microcin J25 derivative, which retained almost full activity and inhibited the growth of *Salmonella enterica* serovar Newport and *E. coli* 0157: H7 in skim milk and egg yolk, and this derivative was inactivated by digestive enzymes both in vitro and in vivo (Pomares et al. 2009). An improved version of the class IIa bacteriocin pediocin PA-1 was generated by fusing the C-terminal half of pediocin with the N-terminal half of enterocin A, which showed increased activity against a strain of *Leuconostoc lactis* isolated from sour-spoiled dairy product (Tominaga & Hatakeyama 2007). Moreover, shuffling four specific regions within the N-terminal half of pediocin PA-1 with the corresponding sequences from 10 other class IIa bacteriocins through a DNA-shuffling library resulted in active mutants with higher activity than the parental molecule, suggesting that DNA-shuffled bacteriocins could prove useful for inhibiting sour spoilage of dairy products (Tominaga & Hatakeyama 2007).

Although this type of technology has the potential to generate a limitless supply of potent naturally-derived food preservatives, consumer resistance to genetic engineering and restrictive legislation will undoubtedly limit its development and applications in the near future. However, as knowledge regarding genetically modified organisms expands beyond the scientific community and consumer demands for minimally processed foods increase, it is likely that engineered bacteriocins may enjoy a lucrative future in food safety.

Innovative Methods for Exploiting Food Safety Peptides and Bacteriocins in Foods

In many instances, peptides that exhibit effective antimicrobial activity in vitro fail to yield similar activities in vivo. For example, Enrique et al. (2007) observed that the efficacy of synthetic antimicrobial peptides was reduced when acting in wine, suggesting that the food matrix is an important consideration for the practical application of antimicrobial peptides. Many studies have demonstrated that food components can decrease the antimicrobial activity of nisin owing to proteolytic degradation (Bhatti et al. 2004, Chollet et al. 2008, Jung et al. 1992) or to binding of the peptide to fat or protein surfaces, resulting in reduced accessibility to bacterial cells (Laridi et al. 2003). Food packaging and peptide carrier systems offer innovative opportunities to exploit the full potential of antimicrobial peptides for food safety purposes. Although traditional food packaging provides mechanical support and protection from external influences and should have minimum interaction with food, antimicrobial/bioactive packaging deliberately interacts with the food or food environment (Dainelli et al. 2008), retarding microbial surface growth and extending shelf-life and promoting safety (Appendini & Hotchkiss 2002). The antimicrobial agents can be incorporated directly into polymers, can be coated or adsorbed onto polymer surfaces, or can be immobilized to polymers by ion or covalent linkages (Appendini & Hotchkiss 2002). However, the mode of activity of the antimicrobial agents is an important factor. Bacteriocins are ideal for incorporation into antimicrobial packaging because they interact with the external surface of the microorganism (cell wall and membrane) and do not have to be internalized to exhibit an effect. For example, immobilization of nisin onto polyethylene/polyamide pouches [at a concentration of 7,860 activity units (AU) cm^{-2}], which were used to package young Cheddar cheeses, deliberately inoculated on the surface with *Listeria innocua* reduced *L. innocua* levels by two logs when stored at 4°C over a 12-week period (Scannell et al. 2000a). Likewise, cellulose-based bioactive inserts impregnated with nisin (7,650 AU cm^{-2}) reduced levels of *Listeria* by $\geq$2 logs and *S. aureus* by $\sim$1.5 logs when interleaved between the slices of ham or cheese over a 24-day period at 4°C (Scannell et al. 2000a). Interestingly, lacticin 3147 did not adsorb to the plastic used in this study, which may be related to its two-component nature, requiring adsorption of both components for activity or interference with other proteins in the lacticin 3147 preparation (Scannell et al. 2000a). Nisin-coated polyethylene films (generated from a stock solution of nisin at a concentration of 6,400 AU ml^{-1}) were found to be effective at inhibiting *Micrococcus luteus* in broth and the bacterial flora in milk, resulting in a reduction of 0.9 logs in raw milk and a 1.3-log reduction in pasteurized milk stored at 4°C for seven days (Mauriello et al. 2005). Although nisin release from the films was unpredictable, it was favored by low pH and high temperature. Biodegradable polylactic acid polymer films incorporated with nisin (0.04 mg cm^{-2} of film) significantly inhibited *L. monocytogenes* in culture medium and liquid egg white, reduced the cell population of *E. coli* 0157:H7 in orange juice, and reduced *Salmonella enteriditis* levels in liquid egg white (Jin & Zhang 2008). Cellulose acetate films containing pediocin from ALTA® 2351 interleaved between slices of ham reduced *Listeria* numbers by 2 logs after 15 days of storage at 12°C (Santiago-Silva et al. 2009). Nisin incorporated into sorbitol-plasticized sodium caseinate films at 1,000 international units (IU) cm^{-2} resulted in a reduction of 1.1 log CFU g^{-1} in *L. innocua* counts on surface-inoculated cheese. However, the antimicrobial effectiveness was found to be dependent on the distance from the contact surface on the films containing nisin to the cheese matrix, as observed for deep *Listeria*-inoculated cheese (Cao-Hoang et al. 2010). Combining nisin with other compounds or treatments in antimicrobial films has also provided promising results. Edible films manufactured with malic acid and nisin exhibited higher antilisterial activity than using malic acid alone (Pintado et al. 2009). Edible soy protein isolate films containing grape fruit seed extract (1% w/w), nisin (10,000 IU g^{-1}), and ethylenediaminetetraacetic acid (EDTA) (0.16% w/w) were able to reduce populations of *E. coli* 0157: H7, *Salmonella typhimurium* and *L. monocytogenes* and may have applications in various food products (Sivarooban et al. 2008). Ionizing radiation in combination with pectin films containing 0.025% nisin provided promising results for reducing *L. monocytogenes* growth in ready-to-eat turkey meat samples after one week at 10°C (Jin et al. 2009). Enterocin-activated coatings have also demonstrated good antilisterial activity (Iseppi et al. 2008, Marcos et al. 2007). Moreover, EDTA was shown to enhance the activity of enterocin EJ97 in coated polyethylene films against *Bacillus coagulans* (Martínez Viedma et al. 2010). Controlled release of nisin was achieved using multilayer films with hydrophobic and hydrophilic layers composed of ethylcellulose/hydroxypropylmethylcellulose/ethylcellulose (EC/HPMC/EC) (Guiga et al. 2010). Indeed, nisin from two-layer films (EC/HPMC) totally desorbed within 0.5 h, whereas the three-layer films (EC/HPMC/EC) expanded the nisin release time over 20 h and showed significant antimicrobial activity. Controlled release of the antimicrobial agent could be highly advantageous, ensuring that a constant level of antimicrobial agent reaches the food surface. It can also eliminate the risk of inactivation of the preservative by food components or dilution below the active concentration due to migration into the bulk food matrix (Appendini & Hotchkiss 2002). Atomic force microscopy (AFM) has recently been used to study bacteriocin distribution on coated polyethylene films (La Storia et al. 2008). Interestingly, antimicrobial distribution differed between bacteriocins, whereby nisin displayed a sort of microtexturing giving the highest roughness values, whereas the bacteriocin Bac162W displayed the most homogenous distribution, suggesting that this is an area that could be further optimized by enhanced understanding of bacteriocin interactions with various films.

Although active packaging is already in use in the United States, Japan, and Australia, its use in Europe has been limited mainly because of legislative restrictions (de Kruijf & van Beest 2003). However, new rules and guidelines on the topic were introduced across Europe in 2009. Within these regulations substances not previously assessed by the European Food Safety Authority (EFSA) will likely require a migration study followed by a basic set of toxicology tests before acceptance for use in active packaging (Harrington 2010). Antimicrobials in food packaging that may migrate to food are considered food additives and must meet the food additives standards (Appendini & Hotchkiss 2002). Given that nisin is already recognized as a food additive, nisin-activated packaging is most likely to appear on European supermarket shelves in the near future.

Several studies have developed methods to protect the antimicrobials within the food matrix itself, thus enhancing stability and effectiveness. Liposomes are vesicles composed of one or more phospholipid bilayers encapsulating a volume of aqueous media (da Silva Malheiros et al. 2010a) and have gained much attention for their ability to encapsulate and protect nisin (da Silva Malheiros et al. 2010b). Manufacture of liposomes requires input of energy (e.g., in the form of sonication, homogenization, shaking, heating, etc.), resulting in the arrangement of the lipid molecules in the form of bilayered vesicles, achieving a thermodynamic equilibrium in the aqueous phase (Mozafari 2005). Production of such vesicles containing antimicrobials, however, requires selection of suitable lipid-antimicrobial combinations (Were et al. 2003). Laridi et al. (2003) encapsulated nisin Z (a natural variant of nisin A) in commercial preparations of proliposomes that were able to withstand the Cheddar cheese–making temperature cycle and did not appear to disturb the fermentation process. Encapsulated nisin in phosphatidylcholine (PC) and PC-cholesterol was shown to inhibit growth of *L. monocytogenes* growth by >2 logs compared with free nisin (Were et al. 2004). More recently, microencapsulated nisin in nanovesicles prepared from partially purified soy lecithin was shown to be as effective as free nisin at inhibiting *L. monocytogenes* growth in whole and skim milk at low temperatures over 14 days (da Silva Malheiros et al. 2010b). Encapsulation of a bacteriocin-like substance (BLS) from *Bacillus licheniformis* in phosphotadylcholine vesicles completely inhibited the growth of *L. monocytogenes* and the encapsulated BLS was stable for up to 30 days at 4°C compared to only 14 days for the free bacteriocin (Teixeira et al. 2008).

More recently, bacteriocin-silicate interactions were studied as an alternative method for bacteriocin purification and subsequent delivery into food (Ibarguren et al. 2010). Bacteriocin produced by *Enterococcus faecium* was adsorbed from a bacteriocin solution by the inert silicates zeosil (synthetic silicate) and expanded perlite (natural compound), which are authorized as food-grade anticaking, clarifying, or filtering agents. The adsorbed bacteriocin retained its antimicrobial activity, reducing *Listeria* growth by 2 logs (zeosil-adsorbed bacteriocin) and 6 logs (expanded perlite-adsorbed bacteriocin). Food-grade silicates could provide a viable solution for preparation and purification of bacteriocins for industrial-scale use.

FOOD QUALITY APPLICATIONS OF BACTERIOCINS AND PEPTIDES

An open-ended interview assessing consumers' perception of which factors are important for quality food products radiated around four major quality dimensions: taste, health, convenience, and process characteristics (Brunsø et al. 2002), with taste as the most influential factor determining consumer choice (Glanz et al. 1998). Humans are capable of sensing five basic tastes, namely, sweet, umami, bitter, sour, and salt. Interestingly, peptides play a significant role in food taste. For example, a chicken protein hydrolysate resulted in the production of six peptides (di- and tripeptides) that were found to enhance the umami taste of inosine monophosphate (Maehashi et al. 1999). A synthetic peptide previously found in meat, termed BMP, was shown to enhance the flavor of beef gravy very similar to monosodium glutamate (MSG), but did not present the salty taste associated with MSG (Spanier et al. 1995). Several acidic oligopeptides isolated from fish protein hydrolysate have also demonstrated MSG-like flavor qualities (Noguchi et al. 1975). Three peptides isolated from cooked pork loins were found to have a sourness-suppressing effect (Okumura et al. 2004). A Maillard-reaction peptide resulting from the enzymatic hydrolysis of soybean protein was found to produce an enhanced effect on flavor, including umami, continuity, and mouthfulness in consommé soup (Ogasawara et al. 2006).

Although the above examples represent peptides that exhibit savory and palatable tastes, partial degradation of protein due to abnormal proteolysis can generate bitter peptides and decrease the sensory quality of products (Maehashi & Huang 2009). Indeed, the formation of bitter peptides can be a major limitation in the exploitation of food protein hydrolysates (Saha & Hayashi 2001). Casein has been reported to produce the bitterest hydrolysates (Limieux & Suimard 1992, Minamiura et al. 1972), explaining the bitter taste associated with some cheese. Interestingly, significant correlations between increased angiotensin I–converting enzyme (ACE) inhibition and bitterness were also shown for casein-derived dipeptides based on experimental observations and quantitative structure-activity relationship (QSAR) models (Pripp & Ardo 2007). Both the peptide size and the presence of hydrophobic residues have been hypothesized as the main factors affecting the bitter taste of peptides (Maehashi & Huang 2009, Pripp et al. 2005). Of the 30 G protein–coupled taste receptors identified in humans, 25 are predicted to sense bitter tastes alone. Bitter molecules bind to the G protein–coupled receptor-type T2R on the apical membrane of the taste receptor cells located in the taste buds (Ley 2008). Most recently, the bitter taste receptor TR21 was shown to be activated by bitter-tasting dipeptides and tripeptides (Upadhyaya et al. 2010). Although several bitter-masking compounds have been identified, the majority have not been published in peer-reviewed journals but as patent applications (reviewed by Ley 2008). Interestingly, various acidic dipeptides containing asparaginic acid have demonstrated bitter-masking abilities (Fuller & Kurtz 1997, Harada & Kamada 2000).

Bacteriocins have also been used to improve the flavor and quality attributes of fermented foods. This has been achieved by using bacteriocin-producing LAB to control adventitious microbial populations, i.e., nonstarter lactic acid bacteria (NSLAB) (Ryan et al. 1996), and secondly by using bacteriocin-producing LAB as cell lysis–inducing agents to increase the rate of proteolysis in cheese (Morgan et al. 1997, O'Sullivan et al. 2002). NSLAB are responsible for defects such as the formation of calcium lactate crystals, slit formation, and off-flavor development, although they may also yield positive effects on flavor (Deegan et al. 2006). Based on such strategies, the NSLAB population of low-fat Cheddar cheese was successfully controlled during ripening using a lacticin 3147-producing transconjugant starter culture (Fenelon et al. 1999). A three-strain starter system consisting of a lactococcin A, B, and M producer (narrow-spectrum bacteriocins) resulted in the production of a cheese with decreased bitterness compared with cheese manufactured without the bacteriocin-producing adjunct as a result of bacteriocin-induced starter cell lysis during cheese manufacture and ripening (Morgan et al. 2002). A lacticin 481–producing adjunct culture was also shown to control NSLAB and accelerate starter cell lysis without compromising acid production of the starter (O'Sullivan et al. 2003). Enhanced lysis of adjunct cultures via a lacticin 3147–producing culture resulted in a concomitant increase in isoleucine transamination and about a twofold increase of the derived volatile compound 2-methylbutanal, resulting in an enhancement of the cheese aroma (Fernandez de Palencia et al. 2004). Using a similar concept, Danisco developed a freeze-dried culture of *Pediococcus acidilactici*, which is marketed as CHOOZIT™ Flav 43 and is suggested for use in Cheddar cheese and semihard cheeses as an adjunct that "accelerates and enhances strong and sweet flavour compounds, due to the production of bacteriocins." (**http://www.orchard-dairy.co.uk/downloads%5CChoozitFlavourAdjuncts_20022009102925.pdf**)

PEPTIDES IN NUTRITION AND HEALTH

Remarkably, through the years science has demonstrated that food can provide benefits to human health beyond just basic nutrition. Among the food constituents contributing to this effect are food-derived biologically active peptides that exhibit their effect through activity on eukaryotic cells. Indeed, several such peptides have been identified that are of plant and animal origin (**Table 2**). However, bovine milk, cheese, and dairy products have been reported to provide the greatest sources of bioactive proteins and peptides from food (Möller et al. 2008). These peptides may be

Table 2 Examples of food-derived sources of bioactive peptides

Source	Reference	Source	Reference
ACE inhibitory		**Antioxidant**	
Milk: β-casein, α_s1-casein, κ-casein, β-lactoglobulin, α-lactoglobulin	(FitzGerald et al. 2004) (Gobbetti et al. 2002) (Otte et al. 2007) (Hernández-Ledesma et al. 2007a) (Silva et al. 2006) (Hernández-Ledesma et al. 2007b) (Mao et al. 2007) (Chatterton et al. 2006)	Venison protein hydrolysate Wheat germ protein hydrolysate Milk Mackerel hydrolysate Soy hydrolysate Egg yolk hydrolysate Porcine collagen hydrolysate	(Kim et al. 2009) (Zhu et al. 2006) (Hogan et al. 2009) (Wu et al. 2003) (Gibbs et al. 2004) (Sakanaka et al. 2004) (Li et al. 2007)
Pork meat	(Escudero et al. 2010)	Canola protein hydrolysate	(Cumby et al. 2008)
Pacific hake fish hydrolysate	(Samaranayaka et al. 2010)	**Immunomodulatory**	
Sardine peptide	(Otani et al. 2009)	Whey protein hydrolysate	(Gauthier et al. 2006)
Antartic krill tail meat hydrolysate	(Hatanaka et al. 2009)	Salmon hydrolysate	(Yang et al. 2009)
Oat protein hydrolysate	(Cheung et al. 2009)	Soy hydrolysate	(Maruyama et al. 2003)
Corn gluten meal hydrolysate	(Yang et al. 2007)	Egg yolk peptides	(Nelson et al. 2007)
Royal jelly hydrolysate	(Takaki-Doi et al. 2009)	**Anticancer**	
Cooked eggs	(Majumder & Wu 2009)	Lunasin in soybean	(Hernández-Ledesma et al. 2009)
Egg white	(Miguel et al. 2007)	Soy proteins	(Kim et al. 2000)
Soybean	(Wu & Muir 2008)	Fish protein hydrolysate	(Picot et al. 2006)
Broccoli	(Lee et al. 2006)	Egg white hydrolysate	(Yi et al. 2003)
Chickpea legumin	(Yust et al. 2003)	Milk: lactoferricin	(Eliassen et al. 2002)
Sesame protein hydrolysate	(Nakano et al. 2006)	Ginseng	(Kim et al. 2003)
Buckwheat	(Ma et al. 2006)	Buckwheat	(Leung & Ng 2007)
Rice dreg hydrolysate	(He et al. 2005)	Chickpea protein hydrolysate	(Girón-Calle et al. 2010)
Hypocholesterolemic		**Antiobesity**	
Soy protein hydrolysates	(Zhong et al. 2007)	Soybean	(Nishi et al. 2003)
Milk: β-lactoglobulin	(Nagaoka et al. 2001)	Milk	(Aziz & Anderson 2003)
Fresh water clam hydrolysate	(Lin et al. 2010)	Fish protein hydrolysate	(Cudennec et al. 2008)
Anti-Thrombotic			
Milk: κ-casein	(Chabance et al. 1995)		
Pork	(Shimizu et al. 2009)		

released through the action of digestive enzymes in the intestine, chemical, or enzymatic hydrolysis in vitro, and via bacterial fermentation. Bioactive peptides may also be produced artificially via chemical synthesis, as well as through genetic engineering and biomanufacturing approaches (Shahidi & Zhong 2008).

Peptides offer huge potential in the development of functional food products by increasing their concentration in foods to a level that brings about a measureable biological effect or by introducing them into foods that are naturally free of them (De Leo et al. 2009). In this respect, bioactive peptides have become important constituents of several commercially available functional food products and ingredients (**Table 3**). In such products, the peptides are either added or enriched by modification of the usual manufacturing process (e.g., by changing the process parameters or

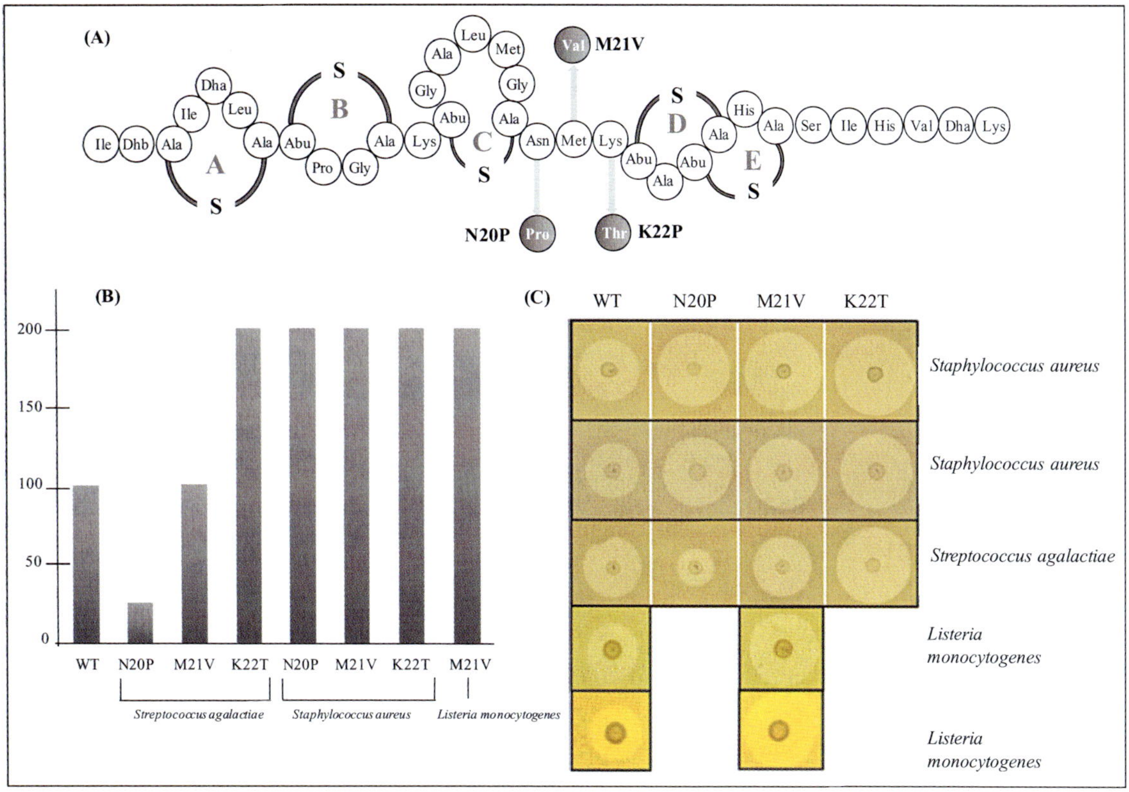

Figure 1

(*a*) Structure of nisin A; arrows indicate amino acid changes in mutant derivatives generated by genetic engineering. (*b*) Relative specific activity of purified nisin and nisin variants with wild-type (WT) nisin at 100%. (*c*) Growth inhibition of *Staphylococcus aureus* and *Streptococcus agalactiae* by N20P, M21V and K22T and of *Listeria monocytogenes* by M21V (from Field et al. 2008).

Table 3 Examples of commercially available functional foods or ingredients containing bioactive peptides[a]

Brand name	Product type	Health claim	Bioactive peptide	Manufacturer
Calpis	Sour milk	Reduction of blood pressure	VPP, IPP from β-casein and κ-casein	Calpis Co., Japan
Evolus	Fermented milk, calcium enriched	Reduction of blood pressure	VPP, IPP from β-casein and κ-casein	Valio, Finland
BioZate	Hydrolysed whey protein isolate	Reduction of blood pressure	Whey peptides	Davisco, USA
C12 Peption	Ingredient	Reduction of blood pressure	Casein-derived dodecapeptide FFVAPFPEVFGK	DMV, Netherlands
Peptide Soup	Soup	Reduction of blood pressure	Bonito-derived peptides	NIPPON, Japan
Casein DP Peptio Drink	Soft Drink	Reduction of blood pressure	Casein-derived dodecapeptide FFVAPFPEVFGK	Kanebo, Japan
BioPURE-GMP	Whey protein hydrolysate	Anticariogenic, Antimicrobial, Antithrombotic	Glycomacropeptide κ-casein f[b](106–169)	Davisco, USA
CholesteBlock	Drink powder	Hypocholesterolemic	Soy peptides bound to phospholipids	Kyowa Hakko, Japan
CSPHP ProDiet F200	Milk drink, confectionary	Reduce stress	α_{s1}-casein f(91–100) YLGYLEQLLR	Ingredia, France
Capolac	Ingredient	Helps mineral absorption	Caseinphosphopeptide	Arla Foods, Denmark
Tekkotsu Inryou	Soft drink	Helps mineral absorption	Caseinphosphopeptide	Suntory, Japan
Kotsu Kotsu calcium	Soft drink	Helps mineral absorption	Caseinphosphopeptide	Asahi, Japan
CE90CPP	Ingredient	Helps mineral absorption	Caseinphosphopeptide	DMV, Netherlands
Glutamine peptide	Dry milk protein hydrolysate	Immunomodulatory	Glutamine-rich peptides	DMV, Netherlands
Festivo	Fermented low-fat hard cheese	Reduction of blood pressure	α_{s1}-casein f(1–6) RPKHPI, f(1–7) RPKHPIK, f(1–9) RPKHPIKHQ	MTT Agrifood Research, Finland
Cysteine Peptide	Ingredient	Boost energy, improve sleep quality	Milk-derived peptide	DMV, Netherlands
PeptoPro	Ingredient	Improves athletic performance and muscle recovery	Casein-derived peptide	DSM, Netherlands
Vivinal Alpha	Ingredient	Aids relaxation and sleep	Whey-derived peptide	Borcula Domo Ingredients (BDI), Netherlands
Recaldent	Chewing gum	Anticariogenic	Caseinphosphopeptides	Cadbury Enterprises
Evolus Double Effect Spread	Margarine	Reduction of blood pressure	Milk-derived peptides	Valio, Finland

[a]Adapted and updated from Korhonen (2009), Korhonen & Pihlanto (2006), Hartmann & Meisel (2007).
[b]f = fragment.

the starter cultures used) (Hartmann & Meisel 2007). These peptides have the capacity to exert numerous health effects, as discussed below.

Peptides with Potential to Reduce the Risk of Cardiovascular Diseases

Cardiovascular diseases (CVDs) describe a group of disorders of the heart and blood vessels, and are the number one cause of death globally. Interestingly, several food-derived bioactive peptides have gained scientific interest as a result of their capacity to alleviate the risks associated with CVD. These include antihypertensive, antithrombotic, hypocholesterolemic, and antiobesity peptides (Erdmann et al. 2008).

Antihypertensive peptides. The antihypertensive peptides work by inhibiting a key enzyme involved in the regulation of BP, namely, ACE. These ACE inhibitors are thought to be competitive inhibitors of ACE by preventing ACE from synthesizing the potent vasoconstrictor, angiotensin II. In addition, ACE also hydrolyzes bradykinin, a vasodilator (Seppo et al. 2003). Peptides with ACE-inhibitory activity have been identified and studied from a range of food sources, including milk, egg, fish, soy, meat, sesame, broccoli, buckwheat, and rice (**Table 2**).

The ACE inhibitory peptides Val-Pro-Pro (Clare et al. 2003, Hamel et al. 1985, Juillard et al. 1995) and Ile-Pro-Pro (Chabance et al. 1995, Drouet et al. 1990) are derived from casein following bacterial fermentation and produced in the commercial fermented milk product, Calpis® (Calpis, Co. Ltd., Tokyo). Following oral consumption of 95 ml Calpis® over an 8-week period, a significant reduction in BP was obtained in mildly hypertensive patients (Hata et al. 1996). More recently, a spread containing Val-Pro-Pro and Ile-Pro-Pro and plant sterols was shown to have a beneficial effect on two major cardiovascular risk factors, BP and plasma lipids (Turpeinen et al. 2009). Remarkably, Val-Pro-Pro and Ile-Pro-Pro have the potential to inhibit ACE in a very similar fashion to the current synthetic ACE inhibitors Captopril, Enalaprilat, and Lisinopril by hydrogen bonding with similar residues in the ACE catalytic site (Pina & Roque 2008). Recombinant DNA technologies have now been exploited to produce antihypertensive peptides. Recombinant fusion proteins have been expressed in *E. coli* and are then purified and cleaved by proteinase from a selected strain of *Lactobacillus helveticus* (Losacco et al. 2007). This technology should enable scientists to generate designer peptides with stronger inhibitory activity and new therapeutic properties.

Antithrombotic peptides. Thrombosis is a pathological condition that results in clots or thrombus formation in arteries, veins, or the chambers in the heart. Interestingly, a significant amount of similarities exist between the mechanisms involved in milk clotting, defined by the interaction of κ-casein with chymosin and the mechanisms of blood clotting, defined by the interaction of fibrinogen with thrombin (Jolles 1975, Jolles & Henschen 1982, Rutherfurd & Gill 2000). Hence, some of the most antithrombotic peptides identified to date are derived from the enzymatic hydrolysis of bovine κ-casein. Indeed, having found structural similarities between bovine κ-casein and the human fibrinogen γ-chain, Jolles et al. (1978) hypothesized that both may have evolved from a common ancestor during the past 450 million years. The main antithrombotic peptide isolated from bovine κ-casein corresponding to f (106–116), with the amino acid sequence MAIPPKKNQDK termed casoplatelin, was also shown to inhibit ADP-induced platelet aggregation and fibrinogen binding in a concentration-dependant manner (Jolles et al. 1986). Interestingly, it is thought that milk protein–derived antithrombotic peptides are absorbed into the bloodstream. For example, two peptides from human and bovine κ-caseinoglycopeptide have been identified in the plasma of five-day-old newborns following ingestion of a cow milk–based formula (Chabance et al. 1995).

Hypocholesterolemic peptides. Positive correlations have been observed between the risk of developing CVD and hypercholesterolemia and/or hypertriglyceridemia (Hokanson & Austin 1996, Martin et al. 1986). Peptides derived from dietary soy protein, as well as whey-derived peptides, have reported hypocholesterolemic properties. The exact mechanisms responsible for these effects are unclear. However, the soy glycinin peptides with amino acid sequences LYPR and IAVPGEVA have demonstrated cholesterol-lowering effects by inhibiting 3-hydroxy-3-methylglutaryl coenzyme A reductase (HMGR), a key enzyme in cholesterol biosynthesis (Pak et al. 2005, Yoshikawa et al. 2000). The α'-subunit of soy β-conglycinin demonstrated plasma lipid–lowering properties and upregulation of liver β-very low density lipoprotein (VLDL) receptors in hypercholesterolemic rats following oral administration (Duranti et al. 2004). Various studies have demonstrated that milk whey protein has similar cholesterol-lowering effects to soy protein, which is more dramatic for the whey peptide fraction than the intact whey protein (Nagaoka 1996, Nagaoka et al. 1992). IIAEK (also called lactostatin) has been identified as the hypocholesterolemic peptide derived from β-lactoglobulin, which exhibited a greater cholesterol-lowering effect than β-sitosterol following oral administration in rats (Nagaoka et al. 2001). Recently, the activity of IIAEK was linked to the upregulation of a human cholesterol-metabolizing enzyme called cholesterol 7α-hydroxylase (CYP7A1) (Morikawa et al. 2007).

Peptides Associated With Satiety

Obesity is associated with numerous comorbidities, among which include CVD, type 2 diabetes, hypertension, certain cancers, and sleep apnea/sleep-disordered breathing (Poirier et al. 2006). Currently, weight loss programs have moved toward schedules favoring a decrease in energy intake while preserving the highest level of satiety possible (Tremblay et al. 2007). Many studies have speculated that peptides have the capacity to affect several satiety signals in the gut, with the result of preventing further food intake (Erdmann et al. 2008). Such satiety signals include opioid receptors, cholecystokinin (CCK)-A receptors, and the glucagon-like peptide (GLP)-1, whose roles in the regulation of appetite and food intake are well recognized (Druce & Bloom 2006). Peptides derived from soy and casein have been shown to induce satiety by the independent activation of both opioid and CCK-A receptors (Pupovac & Anderson 2002). The peptide VRIRLLQRFNKRS corresponding to f(51–63) of soy β-conglycinin was shown to be responsible for appetite suppression by stimulating CCK release in rats (Nishi et al. 2003). Opioid peptides called casomorphins released from casein via proteolysis have also been shown to slow gastric motility and prevent further food intake (Daniel et al. 1990). Peptides released from casein and whey have been linked to induction of satiety through the GLP-1 signaling pathway, resulting in suppression of food intake (Aziz & Anderson 2003, Hall et al. 2003). However, neither free amino acids nor intact proteins were capable of stimulating GLP-1 release (Cordier-Bussat et al. 1998).

Peptides and Immunomodulation

Peptides derived from various protein sources, including milk, egg, fish, and soy protein (**Table 2**), have demonstrated immunomodulatory effects ranging from the proliferation of lymphocytes, natural killer (NK) cell activity, antibody synthesis, and cytokine regulation (Gill et al. 2000, Horiguchi et al. 2005). For example, casein-derived immunopeptides have been shown to stimulate the phagocytic activities of both human and murine macrophages and to protect against *Klebsiella pneumoniae* infection in mice (Smacchi & Gobetti 2000). Immunomodulatory peptides derived from rice and soybean were shown to stimulate superoxide anions [reactive oxygen species (ROS)], which trigger nonspecific immune defences (Kitts & Weiler 2003). Recently, lunasin, a 43 amino acid peptide from soybean, and lunasin-like peptides were shown to inhibit inflammation by suppressing NF-κB pathway (Gonzalez de Mejia & Dia 2009). Korhonen & Pihlanto (2003) have suggested that immunomodulatory peptides may alleviate allergic reactions in humans and enhance mucosal immunity in the gastrointestinal tract. The release of such peptides from hydrolyzed milk protein preparations may be responsible for the antiallergenic effects observed for protein hydrolysate formulas also known as hypoallergenic formulas, which are used in many infant formulations for infants suffering from cow's milk allergy.

Mineral-Binding Peptides

Mineral-binding peptides such as the CPPs are negatively charged and can efficiently bind divalent cations such as Fe, Mn, Cu, and Se, thereby improving their bioavailability. Several studies have investigated whether CPPs in the diet can increase calcium absorption, but the results are contradictory between human and animal studies (Scholz-Ahrens & Schrezenmeir 2000). For example, 1.0 mg of CPPs administered extrinsically by gastric intubation to young male rats dramatically increased calcium absorption from calcium-fortified milk compared to the control (Tsuchita et al. 2001). Most recently, the addition of CPPs was also shown to have a beneficial effect on the absorption of calcium from calcium fortified bovine and caprine milks in growing rats (Mora-Gutierrez et al. 2007). It was also demonstrated that CPPs induce the influx of calcium into human HT-29 cells (Ferraretto et al. 2001). However, administration of one gram of CPPs did not affect calcium metabolism acutely in nine postmenopausal women following administration of either CPP-enriched milk or CPP-enriched fermented milk (Narva et al. 2003). Although the effect of high doses of two well-defined CPP-enriched preparations on 15 volunteers consuming calcium lactate drinks did indicate a positive effect of the CPPs on calcium absorption, it was concluded that the differences in calcium absorption were unlikely to have any biological significance (Teucher et al. 2006). CPPs have also demonstrated anticariogenic properties and can prevent enamel demineralization (Aimutis 2004, Grenby et al. 2001). Most recently, a highly diluted CPP-amorphous calcium phosphate (CPP-ACP) preparation showed potential as a tooth-transport medium by preserving the viability of an L929 fibtoblastic cell line (Cehreli et al. 2008). CPPs are currently being used in commercial products for dental care (Cross et al. 2007, Luo & Wong 2007) (**Table 2**).

Peptides Exhibiting Anticancer Activities

Numerous peptides with reported anticancer activities have been identified in a variety of proteins including fish, egg, milk, soy, buckwheat, and ginseng (**Table 2**). For example, lunasin has demonstrated anticancer activity in mammalian cells and was found to inhibit the activity of skin carcinogens in mice (Hernández-Ledesma & de Lumen 2008). It has been suggested that the peptide exhibits this effect by inhibiting core histone acetylation, which can have considerable influence on the organization of chromatin and on the control of gene expression and cell growth (Grunstein 1997, Kuo & Allis 1998). Waste whey peptides from Mozzarella di Bufala Campana cheese were recently shown to exert a significant antiproliferative effect on a Caco-2 cell line (De Simone et al. 2008).

Antioxidant Peptides

Peptides exhibiting antioxidant activity exert their effect by preventing the enzymatic and nonenzymatic peroxidation of essential fatty acids and have been found in a variety of sources including milk, soy, egg yolk, porcine skin, fish, and canola, among others (**Table 2**). The exact mechanism responsible for antioxidant activity is unclear. However, Erdmann et al. (2006) demonstrated that the biofunctional peptide MY derived from sardine muscle stimulated expression of the antioxidant defense proteins heme oxygenase (HO)-1 and ferritin in endothelial cells, resulting in a sustained cellular protection from oxidative stress. Casein and casein-derived peptides were found to inhibit the enzyme lipoxygenase, which catalyzes the peroxidation of unsaturated fatty acids such as linoleic (Rival et al. 2001). The antioxidant activities of whey-derived peptides have been linked to the presence of cysteine-rich proteins, which promote the synthesis of the intracellular antioxidant, glutathione (Meisel 2005). Such activities may help to alleviate the symptoms of CVD, as oxidative stress is another significant factor in the initiation and progression of several vascular diseases (Erdmann et al. 2008). Saito et al. (2003) constructed two tripeptide libraries based on an antioxidative peptide isolated from a soybean protein hydrolysate. One was a library of 108 peptides containing either His or Tyr residues, and the other was a library of 114 peptides related to Pro-His-His. Interestingly, two Tyr-containing tripeptides showed higher activities than those of two His-containing tripeptides in the peroxidation of linoleic acid, and cysteine-containing tripeptides demonstrated strong peroxynitrite scavenging activity. Recently, a fraction from a milk protein hydrolysate termed Val-F3 demonstrated significantly reduced meat lipid peroxidation at a level of 200 $\mu g\ g^{-1}$ in the meat (Hogan et al. 2009). Thus, as well as having a potential role to play in general health, antioxidant peptides may also be useful agents for maintaining the quality and freshness of meat products by preventing oxidative rancidity, which leads to rancid flavor and odors.

Peptides Involved in the Regulation of the Gastrointestinal Tract

The casein-derived peptide opioid β-casomorphin-7 and another milk-derived peptide termed mammary-associated serum amyloid A3 (M-SAA3) may have a role in maintaining homeostasis in the gastrointestinal tract. M-SAA3 is highly abundant in the colostrum of mammals (McDonald et al. 2001). A conserved amino acid motif in the M-SAA3 protein has been shown to enhance mRNA expression from human instestinal cells of a specific mucin, MUC3, which interferes with enteropathogen adherence to epithelial cells (Larson et al. 2003). In a similar fashion, β-casomorphin-7 was shown to significantly contribute to mucin production from both rat and human intestinal mucin-producing cells using real time–PCR and ELISA studies (Zoghbi et al. 2006). Because intestinal mucins play a protective role in the gut, consumption of products containing β-casomorphin-7 and M-SAA3 could help to improve intestinal health by retarding pathogen adherence to the intestinal surface and potentially reducing the onset of intestinal infections.

Increasing Peptide Bioavailability in Foods: Biopharming

One major goal of scientific research in functional foods is to increase the bioavailability of bioactive peptides by introducing amino acid sequences into food proteins through genetic engineering approaches, namely biopharming. Rice seed has recently been reviewed as a vehicle for oral delivery of high concentrations of bioactive peptide sequences (Yang et al. 2008). Soybean protein has also been reported as a good model for such approaches because the protein content among soybean is the highest among major crops (Prak et al. 2006). However, modified proteins must form the correct conformations; otherwise, misfolded proteins may be degraded by proteinases present in vacuoles and thus will not be able to accumulate as storage proteins (Prak et al. 2006). Matoba et al. (2001) introduced the potent antihypertensive peptide derived from ovalbumen, RPLKPW (novokinin), into β-conglycinin, one of the major storage proteins of soybean. β-conglycinin is composed of three subunits, α, α′, and β (Maruyama et al. 1998). Within the β-conglycin α′ subunit, three RPLKPW-like sequences (RPQHPE, RPRQPH, and RPHQPH) were changed to RPLKPW by site-directed mutagenesis and the modified protein was expressed in *E. coli*. After recovery and ion exchange chromatography, the RPLKPW peptide was released from the recombinant α′ subunit following trypsin and chymotrypsin digestion. The undigested RPLKPW-containing α′ subunit exerted a hypotensive effect on spontaneously hypertensive rats (SHRs) following oral administration of 10 mg kg^{-1} (Matoba et al. 2001). Optimizing the amino acid residues surrounding the three RPLKPW sites in the modified α′ subunit facilitated release by gastrointestinal proteases (Onishi et al. 2004). Moreover, introduction of a fourth RPLKPW, as well as an extension domain corresponding to residues 1–143 of the protein, resulted in a newly modified protein that had antihypertensive properties in SHRs at doses of 2.5 and 1.0 mg kg^{-1}, respectively, the latter of which is 1/2,000 that of ovalbumin (Onishi et al. 2004). More recently, the vector encoding the modified β-conglycin α′ subunit containing the four RPLKPW sequences was introduced into somatic embryos by whisker-mediated gene transformation to produce a transgenic soybean (Yamada et al. 2008). Protein extracted from the transgenic soybean reduced systolic BP after single oral administration in SHRs at a dose of 0.15 g kg^{-1}. Defatted flour from the transgenic soybean also reduced the systolic BP at a dose of 0.25 g kg^{-1}. Multiple repeats of the hypocholesterolemic peptide IIAEK, derived from bovine milk β-lactoglobulin, were introduced into the five variable regions of soybean proglycinin A1aB1b. When expressed in *E. coli*, large-scale production of a small peptide of fewer than 10 amino acids was accomplished (Prak et al. 2006, Prak & Utsumi 2009). LAB are also ideal candidates as carriers of bioactive peptide sequences, especially as these bacteria are food grade and inherent constituents of many fermented food products. Milk-derived bioactive peptides, namely the 11-residue antimicrobial peptide from bovine lactoferrin (BL-11) and the 12-residue hypotensive peptide from α_{s1}-casein, have been cloned in *Streptococcus thermophilus* using synthetic genes encoding each peptide (Renye & Somkuti 2008). Such strategies have the potential to augment the nutritional profile of crops, animal protein, and even food cultures. Given the vast range of health effects attributable to bioactive peptides, biopharming peptides could prove to be a worthwhile approach to promoting human health while keeping disease at bay through nutrition.

In Silico Methods for Identification of Bacteriocins and Peptides

Nowadays, the initial identification and analysis of bacteriocins and peptides are markedly more efficient thanks to computational tools and total genome sequencing, which together are providing a wealth of information regarding the global capabilities of living cells and biologically active molecules. Indeed, using conserved motifs through bioinformatic tools, scientists can rapidly mine genomes for specific genes and functional traits, or search within proteins for the presence of biologically active sequences. Searching for bacteriocins among the abundance of available microbial genomes has proven effective for the identification of novel bacteriocins and novel-producing strains with potential food safety applications. For example, complete genome sequencing and bioinformatic analysis of the alkaliphilic bacterium *Bacillus halodurans* C-125 revealed the presence of the genetic machinery involved in the production of a novel two-peptide lantibiotic designated haloduracin, which displayed antimicrobial activity against a wide range of Gram-positive bacteria (Lawton et al. 2007). Class II bacteriocins are generally synthesized as inactive prepeptides containing a conserved leader sequence called the double-glycine (GG) motif (Dirix et al. 2004a). The leader sequence is cleaved off the prepeptide by a transporter belonging to the peptidase C39 family domain, which contains two conserved motifs called the cysteine and histidine motifs (Havarstein et al. 1995). Dirix et al. (2004b) screened 45 fully sequenced Gram-positive genomes for peptides containing a GG motif and for the peptidease C39 domain at the nucleotide level. Interestingly, the screening resulted in a total of 48 candidate peptides, 15 of which were bacteriocins and 10 of which were bacteriocin homologs. More than 40% of the identified peptide genes were either unannotated or had not yet been recognized as secreted peptides in the genome-sequencing projects. Of the 29 hits for peptidase C39 domains, one or more possible GG peptides were found within the 10 kb limit of the in silico search. A similar search of 120 Gram-negative genomes identified peptides that show structural similarity to bacteriocin and peptide pheromones of Gram-positive bacteria (Dirix et al. 2004a). However, the limited sequence homology associated with bacteriocin structural genes prompted the development of the Web-based bacteriocin genome mining tool, BAGEL (**http://bioinformatics.biol.rug.nl/websoftware/bagel**) (de Jong et al. 2006). BAGEL combines information on sequence motifs, characteristics, and functions of the proteins involved in the biosynthesis of putative bacteriocins with the genetic context of the encoding genes. BAGEL enabled the identification of one additional potential bacteriocin in the genome sequence of *Streptococcus pneumoniae* TIGR4, which showed similarity to bacteriocin PlnB of *Lactobacillus plantarum*. Screening publicly available microbial genomes for genes encoding LanM proteins, which are required for posttranslational modification of type 2 lantibiotics, resulted in the identification of 89 LanM homologs, of which 61 were located in strains not known to be lantibiotic producers (Begley et al. 2009). This led to the identification of the novel two-peptide lantibiotic lichenicidin produced by *B. licheniformis*, which exhibited activity against *L. monocytogenes*, methicillan-resistant *S. aureus* (MRSA), and vancomycin-resistant *Enterococcus* strains.

Computational tools also exist that enable the identification of alternative sources of bioactive peptides, as well as insight into potential biological activities, a topic that has been recently reviewed (Minkiewicz et al. 2008). The four major peptide sequence databases include BIOPEP (Minkiewicz et al. 2008), EROP (Zamyatnin et al. 2006), SwePep (Falth et al. 2006), and PepBank (Shtatland et al. 2007). EROP, SwePep, and PepBank focus mainly on endogenous peptides, whereas BIOPEP concentrates mainly on peptides of food origin (Minkiewicz et al. 2008). QSAR, a computational approach that quantitatively derives the activity of a compound based on its chemical structure, has also been successfully applied to peptide science for predicting inhibitory properties of milk-derived and synthetic peptides (Pripp 2005, Wu et al. 2006a,b), peptides associated with bitterness (Kim & Li-Chan 2006), and antimicrobial peptides (Mikut 2010).

CONCLUSION: OUTLOOK FOR THE FUTURE

Today, the enormous challenges set for food manufacturers for fresh, nutritious, unadulterated foods, with the added benefit of reducing the risk of illness, have driven scientists to explore innovative means to fulfill safety, quality, and nutritional demands. In this respect, it is no coincidence that peptides, whether they are produced by bacteria as bacteriocins or are encrypted in protein sequences as bioactive peptides, are at the forefront of this food revolution. However, despite the wealth of examples provided in this review, certain issues must still be resolved before food manufacturers and consumers alike can fully appreciate the positive attributes of both sets of molecules. Bioactive peptides, which have the potential to protect the consumer from a myriad of health problems, are part of a lucrative food and drinks market that appears to be expanding globally. Yet, a major challenge to food scientists and manufacturers alike is the development of feasible, industrial-scale processes for the production of foods with physiologically significant concentrations of bioactive peptides to match their health claims. This bioavailability issue may be solved in the future through recombinant DNA approaches, which will result in the generation of designer foods with increased levels of bioactive sequences currently being studied in the laboratory. In addition, proteins and peptides in foods may be destroyed by gastrointestinal enzymes before they can even reach the site of activity. For example, Schmelzer et al. (2007) demonstrated that the release of known bioactive peptides is unlikely from β-casein following peptic digestion under simulated gastric conditions. Indeed, after 60 minutes of digestion only small proportions of the sequence were completely intact. Moreover, although the bioactivity of short-chain peptides may be preserved during the gastrointestinal transit, Roufik et al. (2006) demonstrated that long-chain bioactive peptides may require protection from gastrointestinal enzymes to prevent hydrolysis. One solution to this dilemma is to engineer peptides that are resistant to the action of gastrointestinal enzymes. Using just such an approach, O'Shea et al. (2010) engineered variants of the bacteriocin Salivaricin P, which were resistant to specific protease action but retained significant antimicrobial activity. Moreover, the biological activity of many of these peptides has only been proven in vitro or in animal models and must be proven in humans before they are deemed worthy of inclusion in foods.

The exploitation of bacteriocins in food systems, on the other hand, should follow a more direct route but is presumably hampered by a general lack of awareness regarding their potential role in food, and more significantly, restrictive food legislation for their approval and acceptance as food preservatives. Indeed, it is still surprising that despite the wealth of bacteriocins that have been explored in the laboratory for food safety applications, only nisin and pediocin PA-1 are commercially available. However, the unprecedented demands for organic and fresh produce sweeping the globe positions bacteriocins as forerunners in biopreservation technology.

Despite the hurdles that must yet be surmounted for the exploitation of bacteriocins and peptides in food systems, the innovations and developments discussed in this review provide a taste of future trends on supermarket shelves and suggest that the generation of sophisticated foods with an inherent intelligence for programming human health, as well as managing innate strategies for maintaining food safety and quality, is now closer to being a reality than ever before.

DISCLOSURE STATEMENT

The authors are not aware of any affiliations, memberships, funding, or financial holdings that might be perceived as affecting the objectivity of this review.

LITERATURE CITED

Abee T, Krockel L, Hill C. 1995. Bacteriocins: modes of action and potentials in food preservation and control of food poisoning. *Int. J. Food Microbiol.* 28:169–85

Abriouel H, Maqueda M, Gálvez A, Martínez-Bueno M, Valdivia E. 2002. Inhibition of bacterial growth, enterotoxin production, and spore outgrowth in strains of *Bacillus cereus* by bacteriocin AS-48. *Appl. Environ. Microbiol.* 68:1473–77

Aimutis WR. 2004. Bioactive properties of milk proteins with particular focus on anticariogenesis. *J. Nutr.* 134:S989–95

Ananou S, Galvez A, Martinez-Bueno M, Maqueda M, Valdivia E. 2005. Synergistic effect of enterocin AS-48 in combination with outer membrane permeabilizing treatments against *Escherichia coli* O157:H7. *J. Appl. Microbiol.* 99:1364–72

Ananou S, Valdivia E, Martínez Bueno M, Gálvez A, Maqueda M. 2004. Effect of combined physico-chemical preservatives on enterocin AS-48 activity against the enterotoxigenic *Staphylococcus aureus* CECT 976 strain. *J. Appl. Microbiol.* 97:48–56

Appendini P, Hotchkiss JH. 2002. Review of antimicrobial food packaging. *Innov. Food Sci. Emerg. Technol.* 3:113–26

Arakawa K, Kawai Y, Iioka H, Tanioka M, Nishimura J, et al. 2009. Effects of gassericins A and T, bacteriocins produced by *Lactobacillus gasseri*, with glycine on custard cream preservation. *J. Dairy Sci.* 92:2365–72

Aziz A, Anderson GH. 2003. Exendin-4, a GLP-1 receptor agonist, interacts with proteins and their products of digestion to suppress food intake in rats. *J. Nutr.* 133:2326–30

Begley M, Cotter PD, Hill C, Ross RP. 2009. Identification of a novel two-peptide lantibiotic, lichenicidin, following rational genome mining for LanM proteins. *Appl. Environ. Microbiol.* 75:5451–60

Benabbou R, Zihler A, Desbiens M, Kheadr E, Subirade M, Fliss I. 2009. Inhibition of *Listeria monocytogenes* by a combination of chitosan and divergicin M35. *Can. J. Microbiol.* 55:347–55

Bhatti M, Veeramachaneni A, Shelef LA. 2004. Factors affecting the antilisterial effects of nisin in milk. *Int. J. Food Microbiol.* 97:215–19

Black EP, Kelly AL, Fitzgerald GF. 2005. The combined effect of high pressure and nisin on inactivation of microorganisms in milk. *Innov. Food Sci. Emerg. Technol.* 6:286–92

Blond A, Peduzzi J, Goulard C, Chiuchiolo MJ, Barthelemy M, et al. 1999. The cyclic structure of microcin J25, a 21-residue peptide antibiotic from *Escherichia coli*. *Eur. J. Biochem.* 259:747–55

Bouttefroy A, Milliere JB. 2000. Nisin-curvaticin 13 combinations for avoiding the regrowth of bacteriocin resistant cells of *Listeria monocytogenes* ATCC 15313. *Int. J. Food Microbiol.* 62:65–75

Brunsø K, Fjord TA, Grunert KG. 2002. *Consumers' food choice and quality perception*. MAPP Work. Pap. 77. Aarhus, Den: Aarhus Sch. Bus.

Cabo ML, Torres B, Herrera JJ, Bernárdez M, Pastoriza L. 2009. Application of nisin and pediocin against resistance and germination of *Bacillus* spores in sous vide products. *J. Food Prot.* 72:515–23

Cao-Hoang L, Grégoire L, Chaine A, Waché Y. 2010. Importance and efficiency of in-depth antimicrobial activity for the control of *listeria* development with nisin-incorporated sodium caseinate films. *Food Control* 21:1227–33

Castellano P, Belfiore C, Fadda S, Vignolo G. 2008. A review of bacteriocinogenic lactic acid bacteria used as bioprotective cultures in fresh meat produced in Argentina. *Meat Sci.* 79:483–99

Cehreli SB, Gurpinar AO, Onur AM, Dagli FT. 2008. In vitro evaluation of casein phosphopeptide-amorphous calcium phosphate as a potential tooth transport medium: viability and apoptosis in L929 fibroblasts. *Dent. Traumatol.* 24:314–19

Chabance B, Jollès P, Izquierdo C, Mazoyer E, Francoual C, et al. 1995. Characterization of an antithrombotic peptide from kappa-casein in newborn plasma after milk ingestion. *Br. J. Nutr.* 73:583–90

Chatterton DEW, Smithers G, Roupas P, Brodkorb A. 2006. Bioactivity of β-lactoglobulin and α-lactalbumin—technological implications for processing. *Int. Dairy J.* 16:1229–40

Chen H, Hoover DG. 2003. Bacteriocins and their food applications. *Compr. Rev. Food Sci. Food Saf.* 2:82–100

Cheung IW, Nakayama S, Hsu MN, Samaranayaka AG, Li-Chan EC. 2009. Angiotensin I–converting enzyme inhibitory activity of hydrolysates from oat (*Avena sativa*) proteins by in silico and in vitro analyses. *J. Agric. Food Chem.* 57:9234–42

Chollet E, Sebti I, Martial-Gros A, Degraeve P. 2008. Nisin preliminary study as a potential preservative for sliced ripened cheese: NaCl, fat and enzymes influence on nisin concentration and its antimicrobial activity. *Food Control* 19:982–89

Chung W, Hancock REW. 2000. Action of lysozyme and nisin mixtures against lactic acid bacteria. *Int. J. Food Microbiol.* 60:25–32

Clare DA, Catignani GL, Swaisgood HE. 2003. Biodefense properties of milk: the role of antimicrobial proteins and peptides. *Curr. Pharm. Des.* 9:1239–55

Cordier-Bussat M, Bernard C, Levenez F, Klages N, Laser-Ritz B, et al. 1998. Peptones stimulate both the secretion of the incretin hormone glucagon-like peptide 1 and the transcription of the proglucagon gene. *Diabetes* 47:1038–45

Cotter PD, Hill C, Ross RP. 2005. Bacteriocins: developing innate immunity for food. *Nat. Rev. Microbiol.* 3:777–88

Cross KJ, Huq NL, Reynolds EC. 2007. Casein phosphopeptides in oral health—chemistry and clinical applications. *Curr. Pharm. Des.* 13:793–800

Cudennec B, Ravallec-Plé R, Courois E, Fouchereau-Peron M. 2008. Peptides from fish and crustacean by-products hydrolysates stimulate cholecystokinin release in STC-1 cells. *Food Chem.* 111:970–75
Cumby N, Zhong Y, Naczk M, Shahidi F. 2008. Antioxidant activity and water-holding capacity of canola protein hydrolysates. *Food Chem.* 109:144–48
Dainelli D, Gontard N, Spyropoulos D, Zondervan-van den Beuken E, Tobback P. 2008. Active and intelligent packaging: legal aspects and safety concerns. *Trends Food Sci. Technol.* 19:S103–12
Daniel H, Vohwinkel M, Rehner G. 1990. Effect of casein and beta-casomorphins on gastrointestinal motility in rats. *J. Nutr.* 120:252–57
da Silva Malheiros P, Daroit DJ, Brandelli A. 2010a. Food applications of liposome-encapsulated antimicrobial peptides. *Trends Food Sci. Technol.* 21:284–92
da Silva Malheiros P, Daroit DJ, da Silveira NP, Brandelli A. 2010b. Effect of nanovesicle-encapsulated nisin on growth of *Listeria monocytogenes* in milk. *Food Microbiol.* 27:175–78
Deegan LH, Cotter PD, Hill C, Ross P. 2006. Bacteriocins: biological tools for bio-preservation and shelf-life extension. *Int. Dairy J.* 16:1058–71
de Jong A, van Hijum SA, Bijlsma JJ, Kok J, Kuipers OP. 2006. BAGEL: a web-based bacteriocin genome mining tool. *Nucleic Acids Res.* 34:W273–79
de Kruijf N, van Beest MD. 2003. Active packaging. In *Encyclopedia of Agricultural, Food, and Biological Engineering*, ed. DR Heldman. London: Taylor & Francis
De Leo F, Panarese S, Gallerani R, Ceci LR. 2009. Angiotensin converting enzyme (ACE) inhibitory peptides: production and implementation of functional food. *Curr. Pharm. Des.* 15:3622–43
De Simone C, Picariello G, Mamone G, Stiuso P, Dicitore A, et al. 2008. Characterisation and cytomodulatory properties of peptides from Mozzarella di Bufala Campana cheese whey. *J. Pept. Sci.* 15:251–58
De Vuyst L, Leroy F. 2007. Bacteriocins from lactic acid bacteria: production, purification, and food applications. *J. Mol. Microbiol. Biotechnol.* 13:194–99
Dirix G, Monsieurs P, Dombrecht B, Daniels R, Marchal K, et al. 2004a. Peptide signal molecules and bacteriocins in Gram-negative bacteria: a genome-wide in silico screening for peptides containing a double-glycine leader sequence and their cognate transporters. *Peptides* 25:1425–40
Dirix G, Monsieurs P, Marchal K, Vanderleyden J, Michiels J. 2004b. Screening genomes of Gram-positive bacteria for double-glycine-motif-containing peptides. *Microbiology* 150:1121–26
Drouet L, Bal dit Sollier C, Cisse M, Pignaud G, Mazoyer E, et al. 1990. The antithrombotic effect of KRDS, a lactotransferrin peptide, compared with RGDS. *Nouv. Rev. Fr. Hematol.* 32:59–62
Druce M, Bloom SR. 2006. The regulation of appetite. *Arch. Dis. Child.* 91:183–87
Duranti M, Lovati MR, Dani V, Barbiroli A, Scarafoni A, et al. 2004. The α' subunit from soybean 7S globulin lowers plasma lipids and upregulates liver beta-VLDL receptors in rats fed a hypercholesterolemic diet. *J. Nutr.* 134:1334–39
Dziuba M, Darewicz M. 2007. Food proteins as precursors of bioactive peptides-classification into families. *Food Sci. Tech. Int.* 13:393–404
Eliassen LT, Berge G, Sveinbjørnsson B, Svendsen JS, Vorland LH, Rekdal Ø. 2002. Evidence for direct antitumor mechanism of action by bovine lactoferricin. *Anticancer Res.* 22:2703–10
Enrique M, Manzanares P, Yuste M, Martinez M, Vallés S, Marcos JF. 2009. Selectivity and antimicrobial action of bovine lactoferrin derived peptides against wine lactic acid bacteria. *Food Microbiol.* 26:340–46
Enrique M, Marcos JF, Yuste M, Martinez M, Vallés S, Manzanares P. 2007. Antimicrobial action of synthetic peptides towards wine spoilage yeasts. *Int. J. Food Microbiol.* 118:318–25
Enrique M, Marcos JF, Yuste M, Martinez M, Vallés S, Manzanares P. 2008. Inhibition of the wine spoilage yeast *Dekkera bruxellensis* by bovine lactoferrin-derived peptides. *Int. J. Food Microbiol.* 127:229–34
Erdmann K, Cheung BW, Schroder H. 2008. The possible roles of food-derived bioactive peptides in reducing the risk of cardiovascular disease. *J. Nutr. Biochem.* 19:643–54
Erdmann K, Grosser N, Schipporeit K, Schroder H. 2006. The ACE inhibitory dipeptide Met-Tyr diminishes free radical formation in human endothelial cells via induction of heme oxygenase-1 and ferritin. *J. Nutr.* 136:2148–52
Escudero E, Sentandreu MA, Arihara K, Toldra F. 2010. Angiotensin I–converting enzyme inhibitory peptides generated from in vitro gastrointestinal digestion of pork meat. *J. Agric. Food Chem.* 58:2895–901

Ettayebi K, El Yamani J, Rossi-Hassani B. 2000. Synergistic effects of nisin and thymol on antimicrobial activities in *Listeria monocytogenes* and *Bacillus subtilis*. *FEMS Microbiol. Lett.* 183:191–95

Eur. Comm. (EEC). 1983. Commission Directive 83/463/EEC 22 of July introducing temporary measures for the designation of certain ingredients in the labelling of foodstuffs for sale to the ultimate consumer. *Off. J. Eur. Comm.* L255, pp. 1–6

Falth M, Skold K, Norrman M, Svensson M, Fenyo D, Andren PE. 2006. SwePep, a database designed for endogenous peptides and mass spectrometry. *Mol. Cell Proteomics* 5:998–1005

Federal Register. 1988. Nisin preparation: affirmation of GRAS status as a direct human food ingredient. *Fed. Reg.* 53:11247–251

Fenelon MA, Ryan MP, Rea MC, Guinee TP, Ross RP, et al. 1999. Elevated temperature ripening of reduced fat Cheddar made with or without lacticin 3147-producing starter culture. *J. Dairy Sci.* 82:10–22

Fernández de Palencia P, de la Plaza M, Mohedano ML, Martínez-Cuesta MC, Requena T, et al. 2004. Enhancement of 2-methylbutanal formation in cheese by using a fluorescently tagged lacticin 3147 producing *Lactococcus lactis* strain. *Int. J. Food Microbiol.* 93:335–47

Ferraretto A, Signorile A, Gravaghi C, Fiorilli A, Tettamanti G. 2001. Casein phosphopeptides influence calcium uptake by cultured human intestinal HT-29 tumor cells. *J. Nutr.* 131:1655–61

Field D, Connor PM, Cotter PD, Hill C, Ross RP. 2008. The generation of nisin variants with enhanced activity against specific gram-positive pathogens. *Mol. Microbiol.* 69:218–30

FitzGerald RJ, Murray BA, Walsh DJ. 2004. Hypotensive peptides from milk proteins. *J. Nutr.* 134:S980–88

Fuller WD, Kurtz RJ. 1997. Specific eatable taste modifiers. *U.S. Patent No. 5643955*

Gálvez A, Abriouel H, Benomar N, Lucas R. 2010. Microbial antagonists to food-borne pathogens and biocontrol. *Curr. Opin. Biotechnol.* 21:142–48

Gálvez A, Abriouel H, López RL, Ben Omar N. 2007. Bacteriocin-based strategies for food biopreservation. *Int. J. Food Microbiol.* 120:51–70

Gálvez A, Lopez RL, Abriouel H, Valdivia E, Omar NB. 2008. Application of bacteriocins in the control of foodborne pathogenic and spoilage bacteria. *Crit. Rev. Biotechnol.* 28:125–52

García MT, Lucas R, Abriouel H, Omar NB, Pérez R, et al. 2004a. Antimicrobial activity of enterocin EJ97 against '*Bacillus macroides/Bacillus maroccanus*' isolated from zucchini puree. *J. Appl. Microbiol.* 97:731–37

García MT, Marínez Cañamero M, Lucas R, Ben Omar N, Pérez Pulido R, Gálvez A. 2004b. Inhibition of *Listeria monocytogenes* by enterocin EJ97 produced by *Enterococcus faecalis* EJ97. *Int. J. Food Microbiol.* 90:161–70

Gauthier SF, Pouliot Y, Saint-Sauveur D. 2006. Immunomodulatory peptides obtained by the enzymatic hydrolysis of whey proteins. *Int. Dairy J.* 16:1315–23

Gibbs BF, Zougman A, Masse R, Mulligan C. 2004. Production and characterization of bioactive peptides from soy hydrolysate and soy-fermented food. *Food Res. Int.* 37:123–31

Gill AO, Holley RA. 2003. Interactive inhibition of meat spoilage and pathogenic bacteria by lysozyme, nisin and EDTA in the presence of nitrite and sodium chloride at 24 degrees C. *Int. J. Food Microbiol.* 80:251–59

Gill HS, Doull F, Rutherfurd KJ, Cross ML. 2000. Immunoregulatory peptides in bovine milk. *Br. J. Nutr.* 84:S111–17

Gillor O, Nigro LM, Riley MA. 2005. Genetically engineered bacteriocins and their potential as the next generation of antimicrobials. *Curr. Pharm. Des.* 11:1067–75

Girón-Calle J, Alaiz M, Vioque J. 2010. Effect of chickpea protein hydrolysates on cell proliferation and in vitro bioavailability. *Food Res. Int.* 43:1365–70

Glanz K, Basil M, Maibach E, Goldberg J, Snyder D. 1998. Why Americans eat what they do: taste, nutrition, cost, convenience, and weight control concerns as influences on food consumption. *J. Am. Diet Assoc.* 98:1118–26

Gobbetti M, Stepaniak L, De Angelis M, Corsetti A, Di Cagno R. 2002. Latent bioactive peptides in milk proteins: proteolytic activation and significance in dairy processing. *Crit. Rev. Food Sci. Nutr.* 42:223–39

Gonzalez de Mejia E, Dia VP. 2009. Lunasin and lunasin-like peptides inhibit inflammation through suppression of NF-κB pathway in the macrophage. *Peptides* 30:2388–98

Grande MJ, López RL, Abriouel H, Valdivia E, Ben Omar N, et al. 2007. Treatment of vegetable sauces with enterocin AS-48 alone or in combination with phenolic compounds to inhibit proliferation of *Staphylococcus aureus*. *J. Food Prot.* 70:405–11

Grande MJ, Lucas R, Abriouel H, Valdivia E, Omar NB, et al. 2006. Inhibition of toxicogenic *Bacillus cereus* in rice-based foods by enterocin AS-48. *Int. J. Food Microbiol.* 106:185–94

Grenby TH, Andrews AT, Mistry M, Williams RJH. 2001. Dental caries-protective agents in milk products: investigations in vitro. *J. Dent.* 29:83–92

Grunstein M. 1997. Histone acetylation in chromatin structure and transcription. *Nature* 389:349–52

Guiga W, Swesi Y, Galland S, Peyrol E, Degraeve P, Sebti I. 2010. Innovative multilayer antimicrobial films made with nisaplin® or pure nisin and cellulosic ethers: physico-chemical characterization, bioactivity and nisin desorption kinetics. *Innov. Food Sci. Emerg. Technol.* 11:352–60

Hall WL, Millward DJ, Long SJ, Morgan LM. 2003. Casein and whey exert different effects on plasma amino acid profiles, gastrointestinal hormone secretion and appetite. *Br. J. Nutr.* 89:239–48

Hamel U, Kielwein G, Teschemacher H. 1985. beta-Casomorphin immunoreactive materials in cows' milk incubated with various bacterial species. *J. Dairy Res.* 52:139–48

Harada T, Kamada M. 2000. Taste-improving agent and a food having improved taste. *U.S. Patent No.* 6083549

Harrington R. 2010. *Active and intelligent packaging regs—evolution and innovation*. **http://www.meatprocess.com/content/view/print/281914**

Hartmann R, Meisel H. 2007. Food-derived peptides with biological activity: from research to food applications. *Curr. Opin. Biotechnol.* 18:163–69

Hata Y, Yamamoto M, Ohni M, Nakajima K, Nakamura Y, Takano T. 1996. A placebo-controlled study of the effect of sour milk on blood pressure in hypertensive subjects. *Am. J. Clin. Nutr.* 64:767–71

Hatanaka A, Miyahara H, Suzuki KI, Sato S. 2009. Isolation and identification of antihypertensive peptides from antarctic krill tail meat hydrolysate. *J. Food Sci.* 74:H116–20

Havarstein LS, Diep DB, Nes IF. 1995. A family of bacteriocin ABC transporters carry out proteolytic processing of their substrates concomitant with export. *Mol. Microbiol.* 16:229–40

Hayes M, Ross RP, Fitzgerald GF, Hill C, Stanton C. 2006. Casein-derived antimicrobial peptides generated by *Lactobacillus acidophilus* DPC6026. *Appl. Environ. Microbiol.* 72:2260–64

Hayes M, Stanton C, Fitzgerald GF, Ross RP. 2007. Putting microbes to work: dairy fermentation, cell factories and bioactive peptides. Part II: bioactive peptide functions. *Biotechnol. J.* 2:435–49

He G-Q, Xuan G-D, Ruan H, Chen Q-H, Xu Y. 2005. Optimization of angiotensin I-converting enzyme (ACE) inhibition by rice dregs hydrolysates using response surface methodology. *J. Zhejiang Univ. Sci. B* 6:508–13

Helander IM, von Wright A, Mattila-Sandholm T. 1997. Potential of lactic acid bacteria and novel antimicrobials against Gram-negtaive bacteria. *Trends Food Sci. Technol.* 8:146–50

Hernández-Ledesma B, Amigo L, Recio I, Bartolomé B. 2007a. ACE-inhibitory and radical-scavenging activity of peptides derived from beta-lactoglobulin f(19–25). Interactions with ascorbic acid. *J. Agric. Food Chem.* 55:3392–97

Hernández-Ledesma B, de Lumen BO. 2008. Lunasin: a novel cancer preventive seed Peptide. *Perspect. Med. Chem.* 2:75–80

Hernández-Ledesma B, Hsieh C-C, de Lumen BO. 2009. Lunasin, a novel seed peptide for cancer prevention. *Peptides* 30:426–30

Hernández-Ledesma B, Quiros A, Amigo L, Recio I. 2007b. Identification of bioactive peptides after digestion of human milk and infant formula with pepsin and pancreatin. *Int. Dairy J.* 17:42–49

Hogan S, Zhang L, Li J, Wang H, Zhou K. 2009. Development of antioxidant rich peptides from milk protein by microbial proteases and analysis of their effects on lipid peroxidation in cooked beef. *Food Chem.* 117:438–43

Hokanson JE, Austin MA. 1996. Plasma triglyceride level is a risk factor for cardiovascular disease independent of high-density lipoprotein cholesterol level: a meta-analysis of population-based prospective studies. *J. Cardiovasc. Risk* 3:213–19

Horiguchi N, Horiguchi H, Suzuki Y. 2005. Effect of wheat gluten hydrolysate on the immune system in healthy human subjects. *Biosci. Biotechnol. Biochem.* 69:2445–49

Ibarguren C, Audisio MC, Farfáan Torres EM, Apella MC. 2010. Silicates characterization as potential bacteriocin-carriers. *Innov. Food Sci. Emerg. Technol.* 11:197–202

Iseppi R, Pilati F, Marini M, Toselli M, de Niederhausern S, et al. 2008. Anti-listerial activity of a polymeric film coated with hybrid coatings doped with Enterocin 416K1 for use as bioactive food packaging. *Int. J. Food Microbiol.* 123:281–87
Jin T, Liu L, Sommers CH, Boyd G, Zhang H. 2009. Radiation sensitization and postirradiation proliferation of *Listeria monocytogenes* on ready-to-eat deli meat in the presence of pectin-nisin films. *J. Food Prot.* 72:644–49
Jin T, Zhang H. 2008. Biodegradable polylactic acid polymer with nisin for use in antimicrobial food packaging. *J. Food Sci.* 73:M127–34
Jolles P. 1975. Structural aspects of the milk clotting process. Comparative features with the blood clotting process. *Mol. Cell. Biochem.* 7:73–85
Jolles P, Henschen A. 1982. Comparison between the clotting of blood and milk. *Trends Biochem. Sci.* 7:325–28
Jolles P, Levy-Toledano S, Fiat AM, Soria C, Gillessen D, et al. 1986. Analogy between fibrinogen and casein. Effect of an undecapeptide isolated from kappa-casein on platelet function. *Eur. J. Biochem.* 158:379–82
Jolles P, Loucheux-Lefebvre MH, Henschen A. 1978. Structural relatedness of κ-casein and fibrinogen γ-chain. *J. Mol. Evol.* 11:271–77
Juillard V, Laan H, Kunji ER, Jeronimus-Stratingh CM, Bruins AP, Konings WN. 1995. The extracellular PI-type proteinase of *Lactococcus lactis* hydrolyzes beta-casein into more than one hundred different oligopeptides. *J. Bacteriol.* 177:3472–78
Jung DS, Bodyfelt FW, Daeschel MA. 1992. Influence of fat and emulsifiers on the efficacy of nisin in inhibiting *Listeria monocytogenes* in fluid milk. *J. Dairy Sci.* 75:387–93
Kim E-K, Lee S-J, Jeon B-T, Moon S-H, Kim B, et al. 2009. Purification and characterisation of antioxidative peptides from enzymatic hydrolysates of venison protein. *Food Chem.* 114:1365–70
Kim HO, Li-Chan EC. 2006. Quantitative structure-activity relationship study of bitter peptides. *J. Agric. Food Chem.* 54:10102–11
Kim SE, Kim HH, Kim JY, Kang YI, Woo HJ, Lee HJ. 2000. Anticancer activity of hydrophobic peptides from soy proteins. *Biofactors* 12:151–55
Kim SH, Kim JY, Park SW, Lee KW, Kim KH, Lee HJ. 2003. Isolation and purification of anticancer peptides from Korean ginseng. *Food Sci. Biotechnol.* 12:79–82
Kitts DD, Weiler K. 2003. Bioactive proteins and peptides from food sources. Applications of bioprocesses used in isolation and recovery. *Curr. Pharm. Des.* 9:1309–23
Korhonen H. 2009. Milk-derived bioactive peptides: from science to applications. *J. Funct. Foods* 1:177–87
Korhonen H, Pihlanto A. 2003. Food-derived bioactive peptides—opportunities for designing future foods. *Curr. Pharm. Des.* 9:1297–308
Korhonen H, Pihlanto A. 2006. Bioactive peptides: production and functionality. *Int. Dairy J.* 16:945–60
Kuo MH, Allis CD. 1998. Roles of histone acetyltransferases and deacetylases in gene regulation. *BioEssays* 20:615–26
Laridi R, Kheadr EE, Benech R-O, Vuillemard JC, Lacroix C, Fliss I. 2003. Liposome encapsulated nisin Z: optimisation, stability and release during milk fermentation. *Int. Dairy J.* 13:325–36
Larson MA, Wei SH, Weber A, Mack DR, McDonald TL. 2003. Human serum amyloid A3 peptide enhances intestinal MUC3 expression and inhibits EPEC adherence. *Biochem. Biophys. Res. Commun.* 300:531–40
La Storia A, Ercolini D, Marinello F, Mauriello G. 2008. Characterization of bacteriocin-coated antimicrobial polyethylene films by atomic force microscopy. *J. Food Sci.* 73:T48–54
Lawton EM, Cotter PD, Hill C, Ross RP. 2007. Identification of a novel two-peptide lantibiotic, haloduracin, produced by the alkaliphile *Bacillus halodurans* C-125. *FEMS Microbiol. Lett.* 267:64–71
Lee JE, Bae IY, Lee HG, Yang CB. 2006. Tyr-Pro-Lys, an angiotensin I–converting enzyme inhibitory peptide derived from broccoli (*Brassica oleracea Italica*). *Food Chem.* 99:143–48
Lee SY, Jin HH. 2008. Inhibitory activity of natural antimicrobial compounds alone or in combination with nisin against *Enterobacter sakazakii*. *Lett. Appl. Microbiol.* 47:315–21
Leistner L. 1999. Combined methods for food preservation. In *Handbook of Food Preservation*, ed. MS Rahman, pp. 457–85. New York: Marcel Dekker
Leung EHW, Ng TB. 2007. A relatively stable antifungal peptide from buckwheat seeds with antiproliferative activity toward cancer cells. *J. Pept. Sci.* 13:762–67

Ley JP. 2008. Masking bitter taste by molecules. *Chem. Percept.* 1:58–77
Li B, Chen F, Wang X, Ji B, Wu Y. 2007. Isolation and identification of antioxidative peptides from porcine collagen hydrolysate by consecutive chromatography and electrospray ionization-mass spectrometry. *Food Chem.* 102:1135–43
Limieux L, Suimard RE. 1992. Bitter flavour in dairy products. II. A review of bitter peptides from caseins: their formation, identification, structure masking and inhibition. *Lait* 72:335–82
Lin Y-H, Tsai J-S, Hung L-B, Sun Pan B. 2010. Hypocholesterolemic effect of compounded freshwater clam protein hydrolysate and *Gracilaria*. *Food Chem.* 123:395–99
López-Expósito I, Pellegrini A, Amigo L, Recio I. 2008. Synergistic effect between different milk-derived peptides and proteins. *J. Dairy Sci.* 91:2184–89
López-Expósito I, Recio I. 2008. Protective effect of milk peptides: antibacterial and antitumor properties. *Adv. Exp. Med. Biol.* 606:271–93
Losacco M, Gallerani R, Gobbetti M, Minervini F, De Leo F. 2007. Production of active angiotensin I–converting enzyme inhibitory peptides derived from bovine beta-casein by recombinant DNA technologies. *Biotechnol. J.* 2:1425–34
Luders T, Birkemo GA, Fimland G, Nissen-Meyer J, Nes IF. 2003. Strong synergy between a eukaryotic antimicrobial peptide and bacteriocins from lactic acid bacteria. *Appl. Environ. Microbiol.* 69:1797–99
Luo SJ, Wong LL. 2007. Oral care chewing gums and confections. *U.S. Patent No.* 20020071858
Ma MS, Bae IY, Lee HG, Yang CB. 2006. Purification and identification of angiotensin I–converting enzyme inhibitory peptide from buckwheat (*Fagopyrum esculentum Moench*). *Food Chem.* 96:36–42
Maehashi K, Huang L. 2009. Bitter peptides and bitter taste receptors. *Cell. Mol. Life Sci.* 66:1661–71
Maehashi K, Matsuzaki M, Yamamoto Y, Udaka S. 1999. Isolation of peptides from an enzymatic hydrolysate of food proteins and characterization of their taste properties. *Biosci. Biotechnol. Biochem.* 63:555–59
Majumder K, Wu J. 2009. Angiotensin I converting enzyme inhibitory peptides from simulated in vitro gastrointestinal digestion of cooked eggs. *J. Agric. Food Chem.* 57:471–77
Mao XY, Ni JR, Sun WL, Hao PP, Fan L. 2007. Value-added utilization of yak milk casein for the production of angiotensin-I-converting enzyme inhibitory peptides. *Food Chem.* 103:1282–87
Marcos B, Aymerich T, Monfort JM, Garriga M. 2007. Use of antimicrobial biodegradable packaging to control *Listeria monocytogenes* during storage of cooked ham. *Int. J. Food Microbiol.* 120:152–58
Martin MJ, Hulley SB, Browner WS, Kuller LH, Wentworth D. 1986. Serum cholesterol, blood pressure, and mortality: implications from a cohort of 361,662 men. *Lancet* 2:933–36
Martínez Viedma P, Abriouel H, Sobrino-López A, Omar NB, López RL, et al. 2009. Effect of enterocin AS-48 in combination with high-intensity pulsed-electric field treatment against the spoilage bacterium *Lactobacillus diolivorans* in apple juice. *Food Microbiol.* 26:491–96
Martínez Viedma P, Ercolini D, Ferrocino I, Abriouel H, Omar NB, et al. 2010. Effect of polythene film activated with enterocin EJ97 in combination with EDTA against *Bacillus coagulans*. *LWT—Food Sci. Technol.* 43:514–18
Maruyama N, Katsube T, Wada Y, Oh MH, Barba De La Rosa AP, et al. 1998. The roles of the N-linked glycans and extension regions of soybean beta-conglycinin in folding, assembly and structural features. *Eur. J. Biochem.* 258:854–62
Maruyama N, Maruyama Y, Tsuruki T, Okuda E, Yoshikawa M, Utsumi S. 2003. Creation of soybean beta-conglycinin beta with strong phagocytosis-stimulating activity. *Biochim. Biophys. Acta* 1648:99–104
Masschalck B, Deckers D, Michiels CW. 2003. Sensitization of outer-membrane mutants of *Salmonella typhimurium* and *Pseudomonas aeruginosa* to antimicrobial peptides under high pressure. *J. Food Prot.* 66:1360–67
Matoba N, Doyama N, Yamada Y, Maruyama N, Utsumi S, Yoshikawa M. 2001. Design and production of genetically modified soybean protein with anti-hypertensive activity by incorporating potent analogue of ovokinin(2–7). *FEBS Lett.* 497:50–54
Mauriello G, De Luca E, La Storia A, Villani F, Ercolini D. 2005. Antimicrobial activity of a nisin-activated plastic film for food packaging. *Lett. Appl. Microbiol.* 41:464–69
McDonald TL, Larson MA, Mack DR, Weber A. 2001. Elevated extrahepatic expression and secretion of mammary-associated serum amyloid A 3 (M-SAA3) into colostrum. *Vet. Immunol. Immunopathol.* 83:203–11

Meisel H. 2005. Biochemical properties of peptides encrypted in bovine milk proteins. *Curr. Med. Chem.* 12:1905–19
Miguel M, Manso M, Aleixandre A, Alonso MJ, Salaices M, López-Fandiño R. 2007. Vascular effects, angiotensin I–converting enzyme (ACE)-inhibitory activity, and antihypertensive properties of peptides derived from egg white. *J. Agric. Food Chem.* 55:10615–21
Mikut R. 2010. Computer-based analysis, visualization, and interpretation of antimicrobial peptide activities. *Methods Mol. Biol.* 618:287–99
Minamiura N, Matsumura Y, Yamamoto T. 1972. Bitter peptides in the casein digests with bacterial proteinase. II. A bitter peptide consisting of tryptophan and leucine. *J. Biochem.* 72:841–48
Minkiewicz P, Dziuba J, Iwaniak A, Dziuba M, Darewicz M. 2008. BIOPEP database and other programs for processing bioactive peptide sequences. *J. AOAC Int.* 91:965–80
Molinos AC, Abriouel H, López RL, Omar NB, Valdivia E, Gálvez A. 2009. Enhanced bactericidal activity of enterocin AS-48 in combination with essential oils, natural bioactive compounds and chemical preservatives against *Listeria monocytogenes* in ready-to-eat salad. *Food Chem. Toxicol.* 47:2216–23
Möller NP, Scholz-Ahrens KE, Roos N, Schrezenmeir J. 2008. Bioactive peptides and proteins from foods: indication for health effects. *Eur. J. Nutr.* 47:171–82
Mora-Gutierrez A, Farrell HM, Attaie R, McWhinney VJ, Wang C. 2007. Influence of bovine and caprine casein phosphopeptides differing in alphas 1-casein content in determining the absorption of calcium from bovine and caprine calcium-fortified milks in rats. *J. Dairy Res.* 74:356–66
Morgan S, Ross RP, Hill C. 1997. Increasing starter cell lysis in Cheddar cheese using a bacteriocin-producing adjunct. *J. Dairy Sci.* 80:1–10
Morgan SM, O'Sullivan L, Ross RP, Hill C. 2002. The design of a three starter system for Cheddar cheese manufacture exploiting bacteriocin-induced starter lysis. *Int. Dairy J.* 12:985–93
Morgan SM, Ross RP, Beresford T, Hill C. 2000. Combination of hydrostatic pressure and lacticin 3147 causes increased killing of *Staphylococcus* and *Listeria*. *J. Appl. Microbiol.* 88:414–20
Morikawa K, Kondo I, Kanamaru Y, Nagaoka S. 2007. A novel regulatory pathway for cholesterol degradation via lactostatin. *Biochem. Biophys. Res. Commun.* 352:697–702
Mozafari MR. 2005. Liposomes: an overview of manufacturing techniques. *Cell. Mol. Biol. Lett.* 10:711–19
Nagaoka S. 1996. Studies on regulation of cholesterol metabolism induced by dietary food constituents or xenobiotics. *J. Jpn. Soc. Nutr. Food Sci.* 49:303–13
Nagaoka S, Futamura Y, Miwa K, Awano T, Yamauchi K, et al. 2001. Identification of novel hypocholesterolemic peptides derived from bovine milk beta-lactoglobulin. *Biochem. Biophys. Res. Commun.* 281:11–17
Nagaoka S, Kanamaru Y, Kojima T, Kuwata T. 1992. Comparative studies on the serum cholesterol lowering action of whey protein and soybean protein in rats. *Biosci. Biotechnol. Biochem.* 56:1484–85
Nakano D, Ogura K, Miyakoshi M, Ishii F, Kawanishi H, et al. 2006. Antihypertensive effect of angiotensin I–converting enzyme inhibitory peptides from a sesame protein hydrolysate in spontaneously hypertensive rats. *Biosci. Biotechnol. Biochem.* 70:1118–26
Narva M, Karkkainen M, Poussa T, Lamberg-Allardt C, Korpela R. 2003. Caseinphosphopeptides in milk and fermented milk do not affect calcium metabolism acutely in postmenopausal women. *J. Am. Coll. Nutr.* 22:88–93
Nelson R, Katayama S, Mine Y, Duarte J, Matar C. 2007. Immunomodulating effects of egg yolk low lipid peptic digests in a murine model. *Food Agric. Immunol.* 18:1–15
Nishi T, Hara H, Asano K, Tomita F. 2003. The soybean beta-conglycinin beta 51–63 fragment suppresses appetite by stimulating cholecystokinin release in rats. *J. Nutr.* 133:2537–42
Noguchi M, Arai S, Yamashita M, Kato H, Fujimaki M. 1975. Isolation and identification of acidic oligopeptides occurring in a flavor potentiating fraction from a fish protein hydrolysate. *J. Agric. Food Chem.* 23:49–53
Nykanen A, Weckman K, Lapvetelainen A. 2000. Synergistic inhibition of *Listeria monocytogenes* on cold-smoked rainbow trout by nisin and sodium lactate. *Int. J. Food Microbiol.* 61:63–72
Ogasawara M, Katsumata T, Egi M. 2006. Taste properties of Maillard-reaction products prepared from 1,000 to 5,000 Da peptide. *Food Chem.* 99:600–4
Ogihara H, Yatuzuka M, Horie N, Furukawa S, Yamasaki M. 2009. Synergistic effect of high hydrostatic pressure treatment and food additives on the inactivation of *Salmonella enteriditis*. *Food Control* 20:963–66

Okumura T, Yamada R, Nishimura T. 2004. Sourness-suppressing peptides in cooked pork loins. *Biosci. Biotechnol. Biochem.* 68:1657–62

Onishi K, Matoba N, Yamada Y, Doyama N, Maruyama N, et al. 2004. Optimal designing of beta-conglycinin to genetically incorporate RPLKPW, a potent anti-hypertensive peptide. *Peptides* 25:37–43

O'Shea EF, O'Connor PM, Cotter PD, Ross RP, Hill C. 2010. Synthesis of trypsin-resistant variants of the *Listeria*-active bacteriocin salivaricin P. *Appl. Environ. Microbiol.* 76:5356–62

O'Sullivan L, Morgan SM, Ross RP, Hill C. 2002. Elevated enzyme release from lactococcal starter cultures on exposure to the lantibiotic lacticin 481, produced by *Lactococcus lactis* DPC5552. *J. Dairy Sci.* 85:2130–40

O'Sullivan L, Ryan MP, Ross RP, Hill C. 2003. Generation of food-grade lactococal starters which produce the lantibiotics lacticin 3147 and lacticin 481. *Appl. Environ. Microbiol.* 69:3681–85

Otani L, Ninomiya T, Murakami M, Osajima K, Kato H, Murakami T. 2009. Sardine peptide with angiotensin I–converting enzyme inhibitory activity improves glucose tolerance in stroke-prone spontaneously hypertensive rats. *Biosci. Biotechnol. Biochem.* 73:2203–9

Otte J, Shalaby SMA, Zakora M, Nielsen MS. 2007. Fractionation and identification of ACE-inhibitory peptides from α-lactalbumin and β-casein produced by thermolysin-catalysed hydrolysis. *Int. Dairy J.* 17:1460–72

Pak VV, Koo MS, Kasymova TD, Kwon DY. 2005. Isolation and identification of peptides from soy 11S-globulin with hypocholesterolemic activity. *Chem. Nat. Compd.* 41:710–14

Pathanibul P, Taylor TM, Davidson PM, Harte F. 2009. Inactivation of *Escherichia coli* and *Listeria innocua* in apple and carrot juices using high pressure homogenization and nisin. *Int. J. Food Microbiol.* 129:316–20

Picot L, Bordenave S, Didelot S, Fruitier-Arnaudin I, Sannier F, et al. 2006. Antiproliferative activity of fish protein hydrolysates on human breast cancer cell lines. *Process Biochem.* 41:1217–22

Pihlanto A. 2001. Bioactive peptides derived from bovine whey proteins: opioid and ace-inhibitory peptides. *Trends Food Sci. Technol.* 11:347–56

Pina AS, Roque AC. 2008. Studies on the molecular recognition between bioactive peptides and angiotensin-converting enzyme. *J. Mol. Recognit.* 22:162–68

Pintado CM, Ferreira MA, Sousa I. 2009. Properties of whey protein–based films containing organic acids and nisin to control *Listeria monocytogenes*. *J. Food Prot.* 72:1891–96

Poirier P, Giles TD, Bray GA, Hong Y, Stern JS, et al. 2006. Obesity and cardiovascular disease: pathophysiology, evaluation, and effect of weight loss: an update of the 1997 American Heart Association scientific statement on obesity and heart disease from the obesity committee of the council on nutrition, physical activity, and metabolism. *Circulation* 113:898–918

Pomares MF, Salomon RA, Pavlova O, Severinov K, Farias R, Vincent PA. 2009. Potential applicability of chymotrypsin-susceptible microcin J25 derivatives to food preservation. *Appl. Environ. Microbiol.* 75:5734–38

Prak K, Maruyama Y, Maruyama N, Utsumi S. 2006. Design of genetically modified soybean proglycinin A1aB1b with multiple copies of bioactive peptide sequences. *Peptides* 27:1179–86

Prak K, Utsumi S. 2009. Production of a bioactive peptide (IIAEK) in *Escherichia coli* using soybean proglycinin A1ab1b as a carrier. *J. Agric. Food Chem.* 57:3792–99

Pripp AH. 2005. Initial proteolysis of milk proteins and its effect on formation of ACE-inhibitory peptides during gastrointestinal proteolysis: a bioinformatic, in silico approach. *Eur. Food Res. Technol.* 221:712–16

Pripp AH, Ardo Y. 2007. Modelling relationship between angiotensin-(I)-converting enzyme inhibition and the bitter taste of peptides. *Food Chem.* 102:880–88

Pripp AH, Isaksson T, Stepaniak L, Sorhaug T, Ardo Y. 2005. Quantitative structure activity relationship modelling of peptides and proteins as a tool in food science. *Trends Food Sci. Technol.* 16:484–94

Pritchard SR, Phillips M, Kailasapathy K. 2010. Identification of bioactive peptides in commercial Cheddar cheese. *Food Res. Intern.* 43:1545–48

Pupovac J, Anderson GH. 2002. Dietary peptides induce satiety via cholecystokinin-A and peripheral opioid receptors in rats. *J. Nutr.* 132:2775–80

Renye JA Jr, Somkuti GA. 2008. Cloning of milk-derived bioactive peptides in *Streptococcus thermophilus*. *Biotechnol. Lett.* 30:723–30

Rink R, Wierenga J, Kuipers A, Kluskens LD, Driessen AJ, et al. 2007. Dissection and modulation of the four distinct activities of nisin by mutagenesis of rings A and B and by C-terminal truncation. *Appl. Environ. Microbiol.* 73:5809–16

Rival SG, Fornaroli S, Boeriu CG, Wichers HJ. 2001. Caseins and casein hydrolysates. 1. Lipoxygenase inhibitory properties. *J. Agric. Food Chem.* 49:287–94

Rollema HS, Kuipers OP, Both P, de Vos WM, Siezen RJ. 1995. Improvement of solubility and stability of the antimicrobial peptide nisin by protein engineering. *Appl. Environ. Microbiol.* 61:2873–78

Ross AI, Griffiths MW, Mittal GS, Deeth HC. 2003. Combining nonthermal technologies to control food-borne microorganisms. *Int. J. Food Microbiol.* 89:125–38

Roufik S, Gauthier SF, Turgeon SL. 2006. In vitro digestibility of bioactive peptides derived from bovine ß-lactoglobulin. *Int. Dairy J.* 16:294–302

Rutherfurd KJ, Gill HS. 2000. Peptides affecting coagulation. *Br. J. Nutr.* 84(Suppl. 1):S99–102

Ryan MP, Rea MC, Hill C, Ross RP. 1996. An application in cheddar cheese manufacture for a strain of *Lactococcus lactis* producing a novel broad-spectrum bacteriocin, lacticin 3147. *Appl. Environ. Microbiol.* 62:612–19

Sable S, Pons AM, Gendron-Gaillard S, Cottenceau G. 2000. Antibacterial activity evaluation of microcin J25 against diarrheagenic *Escherichia coli*. *Appl. Environ. Microbiol.* 66:4595–97

Saha BC, Hayashi K. 2001. Debittering of protein hydrolyzates. *Biotechnol. Adv.* 19:355–70

Saito K, Jin DH, Ogawa T, Muramoto K, Hatakeyama E, et al. 2003. Antioxidative properties of tripeptide libraries prepared by the combinatorial chemistry. *J. Agric. Food Chem.* 51:3668–74

Sakanaka S, Tachibana Y, Ishihara N, Juneja LR. 2004. Antioxidant activity of egg-yolk protein hydrolysates in a linoleic acid oxidation system. *Food Chem.* 86:99–103

Salomon RA, Farias RN. 1992. Microcin 25, a novel antimicrobial peptide produced by *Escherichia coli*. *J. Bacteriol.* 174:7428–35

Samaranayaka AG, Kitts DD, Li-Chan EC. 2010. Antioxidative and angiotensin-I-converting enzyme inhibitory potential of a Pacific hake (*Merluccius productus*) fish protein hydrolysate subjected to simulated gastrointestinal digestion and Caco-2 cell permeation. *J. Agric. Food Chem.* 58:1535–42

Santiago-Silva P, Soares NFF, Nobrega JE, Junior MAW, Barbosa KBF, et al. 2009. Antimicrobial efficacy of film incorporated with pediocin (ALTA® 2351) on preservation of sliced ham. *Food Control* 20:85–89

Scannell AG, Hill C, Ross RP, Marx S, Hartmeier W, et al. 2000a. Development of bioactive food packaging materials using immobilised bacteriocins lacticin 3147 and nisaplin. *Int. J. Food Microbiol.* 60:241–49

Scannell AG, Ross RP, Hill C, Arendt EK. 2000b. An effective lacticin biopreservative in fresh pork sausage. *J. Food Prot.* 63:370–75

Schillinger U, Guisen R, Holzapfel WH. 1996. Potential of antagonistic microorganisms and bacteriocins for the biological preservation of foods. *Trends Food Sci. Technol.* 7:158–64

Schmelzer CE, Schops R, Reynell L, Ulbrich-Hofmann R, Neubert RH, Raith K. 2007. Peptic digestion of beta-casein. Time course and fate of possible bioactive peptides. *J. Chromatogr. A* 1166:108–15

Scholz-Ahrens KE, Schrezenmeir J. 2000. Effects of bioactive substances in milk on mineral and trace element metabolism with special reference to casein phosphopeptides. *Br. J. Nutr.* 84(Suppl. 1):S147–53

Schved F, Henis Y, Juven BJ. 1994. Response of spheroplasts and chelator-permeabilized cells of gram-negative bacteria to the action of the bacteriocins pediocin SJ-1 and nisin. *Int. J. Food Microbiol.* 21:305–14

Seppo L, Jauhiainen T, Poussa T, Korpela R. 2003. A fermented milk high in bioactive peptides has a blood pressure–lowering effect in hypertensive subjects. *Am. J. Clin. Nutr.* 77:326–30

Settanni L, Corsetti A. 2008. Application of bacteriocins in vegetable food preservation. *Int. J. Food Microbiol.* 121:123–38

Shahidi F, Zhong Y. 2008. Bioactive peptides. *J. AOAC Int.* 91:914–31

Shimizu M, Sawashita N, Morimatsu F, Ichikawa J, Taguchi Y, et al. 2009. Antithrombotic papain-hydrolyzed peptides isolated from pork meat. *Thromb. Res.* 123:753–57

Shtatland T, Guettler D, Kossodo M, Pivovarov M, Weissleder R. 2007. PepBank–a database of peptides based on sequence text mining and public peptide data sources. *BMC Bioinform.* 8:280

Silva SV, Pihlanto A, Malcata FX. 2006. Bioactive peptides in ovine and caprine cheeselike systems prepared with proteases from *Cynara cardunculus*. *J. Dairy Sci.* 89:3336–44

Sivarooban T, Hettiarachchy NS, Johnson MG. 2008. Physical and antimicrobial properties of grape seed extract, nisin and EDTA incorporated soy protein edible films. *Food Res. Intern.* 41:781–85

Smacchi E, Gobetti M. 2000. Bioactive peptides in dairy products: synthesis and interaction with proteolytic enzyme. *Food Microbiol.* 17:129–41

Sobrino-López A, Martín-Belloso O. 2008a. Enhancing the lethal effect of high-intensity pulsed electric field in milk by antimicrobial compounds as combined hurdles. *J. Dairy Sci.* 91:1759–68

Sobrino-López A, Martín-Belloso O. 2008b. Use of nisin and other bacteriocins for preservation of dairy products. *Int. Dairy J.* 18:329–43

Sobrino-López A, Viedma-Martínez P, Abriouel H, Valdivia E, Gálvez A, Martin-Belloso O. 2009. The effect of adding antimicrobial peptides to milk inoculated with *Staphylococcus aureus* and processed by high-intensity pulsed-electric field. *J. Dairy Sci.* 92:2514–23

Solomakos N, Govaris A, Koidis P, Botsoglou N. 2008. The antimicrobial effect of thyme essential oil, nisin, and their combination against *Listeria monocytogenes* in minced beef during refrigerated storage. *Food Microbiol.* 25:120–27

Spanier AM, Bland JM, Miller JA, Glinka J, Wasz W, Duggins T. 1995. BMP: a flavour enhancing peptide found naturally in beef. Its chemical synthesis, descriptive sensory analysis, and some factors affecting its usefulness. *Dev. Food Sci.* 37:1365–78

Stevens KA, Sheldon BW, Klapes NA, Klaenhammer TR. 1991. Nisin treatment for inactivation of *Salmonella* species and other gram-negative bacteria. *Appl. Environ. Microbiol.* 57:3613–15.

Takaki-Doi S, Hashimoto K, Yamamura M, Kamei C. 2009. Antihypertensive activities of royal jelly protein hydrolysate and its fractions in spontaneously hypertensive rats. *Acta Med. Okayama* 63:57–64

Teixeira ML, dos Santos J, Silveira NP, Brandelli A. 2008. Phospholipid nanovesicles containing a bacteriocin-like substance for control of *Listeria monocytogenes*. *Innov. Food Sci. Emerg. Technol.* 9:49–53

Teucher B, Majsak-Newman G, Dainty JR, McDonagh D, FitzGerald RJ, Fairweather-Tait SJ. 2006. Calcium absorption is not increased by caseinophosphopeptides. *Am. J. Clin. Nutr.* 84:162–66

Tominaga T, Hatakeyama Y. 2007. Development of innovative pediocin PA-1 by DNA shuffling among class IIa bacteriocins. *Appl. Environ. Microbiol.* 73:5292–99

Tremblay A, Dumesnil JG, Després J-P. 2007. Diet, satiety and obesity treatment. *Br. J. Nutr.* 88:213–14

Tsuchita H, Suzuki T, Kuwata T. 2001. The effect of casein phosphopeptides on calcium absorption from calcium-fortified milk in growing rats. *Br. J. Nutr.* 85:5–10

Turpeinen AM, Kumpu M, Ronnback M, Seppo L, Kautiainen H, et al. 2009. Antihypertensive and cholesterol-lowering effects of a spread containing bioactive peptides IPP and VPP and plant sterols. *J. Funct. Foods* 1:260–65

Uesugi AR, Moraru CI. 2009. Reduction of *Listeria* on ready-to-eat sausages after exposure to a combination of pulsed light and nisin. *J. Food Prot.* 72:347–53

Uhart M, Ravishankar S, Maks ND. 2004. Control of *Listeria monocytogenes* with combined antimicrobials on beef franks stored at 4 degrees C. *J. Food Prot.* 67:2296–301

Ukuku DO, Fett WF. 2004. Effect of nisin in combination with EDTA, sodium lactate, and potassium sorbate for reducing *Salmonella* on whole and fresh-cut cantaloupet. *J. Food Prot.* 67:2143–50

Ukuku DO, Zhang H, Huang L. 2009. Growth parameters of *Escherichia coli* O157:H7, *Salmonella* spp., *Listeria monocytogenes*, and aerobic mesophilic bacteria of apple cider amended with nisin-EDTA. *Foodborne Pathog. Dis.* 6:487–94

Upadhyaya J, Pydi SP, Singh N, Aluko RE, Chelikani P. 2010. Bitter taste receptor T2R1 is activated by dipeptides and tripeptides. *Biochem. Biophys. Res. Commun.* 398:331–35

Vega-Mercado H, Martin-Belloso O, Qin BL, Chang FJ, Gongora-Nieto MM, et al. 1997. Non-thermal food preservation: pulsed electric fields. *Trends Food Sci. Technol.* 8:151–57

von Staszewski M, Jagus RJ. 2008. Natural antimicrobials: effect of Microgard^{TM} and nisin against *Listeria innocua* in liquid cheese whey. *Int. Dairy J.* 18:255–59

Were LM, Bruce B, Davidson PM, Weiss J. 2004. Encapsulation of nisin and lysozyme in liposomes enhances efficacy against *Listeria monocytogenes*. *J. Food Prot.* 67:922–27

Were LM, Bruce BD, Davidson PM, Weiss J. 2003. Size, stability, and entrapment efficiency of phospholipid nanocapsules containing polypeptide antimicrobials. *J. Agric. Food Chem.* 51:8073–79

World Health Organization (WHO). 2007. Food safety and foodborne illness. Fact Sheet Number 237. Geneva, Switzerland: World Health Organization

Wu H-C, Chen H-M, Shiau C-Y. 2003. Free amino acids and peptides as related to antioxidant properties in protein hydrolysates of mackerel (*Scomber austriasicus*). *Food Res. Int.* 36:949–57

Wu J, Aluko RE, Nakai S. 2006a. Structural requirements of angiotensin I-converting enzyme inhibitory peptides: quantitative structure-activity relationship modeling of peptides containing 4–10 amino acid residues. *QSAR Comb. Sci.* 25:873–80

Wu J, Aluko RE, Nakai S. 2006b. Structural requirements of angiotensin I-converting enzyme inhibitory peptides: quantitative structure-activity relationship study of di- and tripeptides. *J. Agric. Food Chem.* 54:732–38

Wu J, Muir AD. 2008. Isoflavone content and its potential contribution to the antihypertensive activity in soybean angiotensin I converting enzyme inhibitory peptides. *J. Agric. Food Chem.* 56:9899–904

Yamada Y, Nishizawa K, Yokoo M, Zhao H, Onishi K, et al. 2008. Anti-hypertensive activity of genetically modified soybean seeds accumulating novokinin. *Peptides* 29:331–37

Yamazaki K, Yamamoto T, Kawai Y, Inoue N. 2004. Enhancement of antilisterial activity of essential oil constituents by nisin and diglycerol fatty acid ester. *Food Microbiol.* 21:283–89

Yang L, Wakasa Y, Takaiwa F. 2008. Biopharming to increase bioactive peptides in rice seed. *J. AOAC Int.* 91:957–64

Yang R, Zhang Z, Pei X, Han X, Wang J, et al. 2009. Immunomodulatory effects of marine oligopeptide preparation from chum salmon (*Oncorhynchus keta*) in mice. *Food Chem.* 113:464–70

Yang Y, Tao G, Liu P, Liu J. 2007. Peptide with angiotensin I-converting enzyme inhibitory activity from hydrolyzed corn gluten meal. *J. Agric. Food Chem.* 55:7891–95

Yi HJ, Kim JY, Kim JH, Lee HJ, Lee HJ. 2003. Anticancer activity of peptide fractions from egg white hydrolysate against mouse lymphoma cells. *Food Sci. Biotechnol.* 12:224–27

Yoshikawa M, Fujita H, Matoba N, Takenaka Y, Yamamoto T, et al. 2000. Bioactive peptides derived from food proteins preventing lifestyle-related diseases. *Biofactors* 12:143–46

Yust MM, Pedroche J, Girón-Calle J, Alaiz M, Millán F, Vioque J. 2003. Production of ace inhibitory peptides by digestion of chickpea legumin with alcalase. *Food Chem.* 81:363–69

Yuste J, Fung DY. 2004. Inactivation of *Salmonella typhimurium* and *Escherichia coli* O157:H7 in apple juice by a combination of nisin and cinnamon. *J. Food Prot.* 67:371–77

Zamyatnin AA, Borchikov AS, Vladimirov MG, Voronina OL. 2006. The EROP-Moscow oligopeptide database. *Nucleic Acids Res.* 34:D261–66

Zapico P, Medina M, Gaya P, Nunez M. 1998. Synergistic effect of nisin and the lactoperoxidase system on *Listeria monocytogenes* in skim milk. *Int. J. Food Microbiol.* 40:35–42

Zhong F, Zhang X, Ma J, Shoemaker CF. 2007. Fractionation and identification of a novel hypocholesterolemic peptide derived from soy protein Alcalase hydrolysates. *Food Res. Intern.* 40:756–62

Zhu K, Zhou H, Qian H. 2006. Antioxidant and free radical–scavenging activities of wheat germ protein hydrolysates (WGPH) prepared with alcalase. *Process Biochem.* 41:1296–302

Zoghbi S, Trompette A, Claustre J, El Homsi M, Garzon J, et al. 2006. β-casomorphin-7 regulates the secretion and expression of gastrointestinal mucins through a mu-opioid pathway. *Am. J. Physiol. Gastrointest. Liver Physiol.* 290:G1105–13

The Influence of Milk Oligosaccharides on Microbiota of Infants: Opportunities for Formulas

Maciej Chichlowski,[1,2,6,7] J. Bruce German,[1,3,6,7] Carlito B. Lebrilla,[1,4,5,6] and David A. Mills[1,2,6,7,*]

[1]Foods for Health Institute, [2]Department of Viticulture and Enology, [3]Department of Food Science and Technology, [4]Department of Chemistry, [5]Department of Biochemistry and Molecular Medicine, [6]Functional Glycobiology Program, [7]Robert Mondavi Institute for Wine and Food Science, University of California, Davis, California 95616; email: damills@ucdavis.edu

Annu. Rev. Food Sci. Technol. 2011. 2:331–51

First published online as a Review in Advance on December 3, 2010

The *Annual Review of Food Science and Technology* is online at food.annualreviews.org

This article's doi:
10.1146/annurev-food-022510-133743

1941-1413/11/0410-0331$20.00

*Corresponding author.

Keywords

milk oligosaccharides, bifidobacteria, prebiotics

Abstract

In addition to a nutritive role, human milk also guides the development of a protective intestinal microbiota in the infant. Human milk possesses an overabundance of complex oligosaccharides that are indigestible by the infant yet are consumed by microbial populations in the developing intestine. These oligosaccharides are believed to facilitate enrichment of a healthy infant gastrointestinal microbiota, often associated with bifidobacteria. Advances in glycomics have enabled precise determination of milk glycan structures as well as identification of the specific glycans consumed by various gut microbes. Furthermore, genomic analysis of bifidobacteria from infants has revealed specific genetic loci related to milk oligosaccharide import and processing, suggesting coevolution between the human host, milk glycans, and the microbes they enrich. This review discusses the current understanding of how human milk oligosaccharides interact with the infant microbiota and examines the opportunities for translating this knowledge to improve the functionality of infant formulas.

INTRODUCTION

The process of bacterial colonization of the intestine begins naturally in a stepwise manner with three phases: delivery, breastfeeding, and weaning (Penders et al. 2006, Sherman et al. 2009). By the age of 18 months, the colonic bacterial microbiota is considered complete (Harmsen et al. 2000, Palmer et al. 2007, Rubaltelli et al. 1998). The gut microbiota of breastfed infants is modulated by human milk, the predominant diet of newborn infants. Milk is a truly unique food that has been shaped by mammalian evolution to provide both nutrition and protection to the developing infant, all at an energetic cost to the mother. As a result of this distinctive evolutionary tension, milk is unlikely to have retained superfluous contents that do not benefit the infant, as their presence comes at a cost to the mother. The benefits of breastfeeding in terms of infant development and protection have been well documented (Wu & Chen 2009). Various factors present in milk are known to modulate the developing microbiota within the infant gastrointestinal tract (GIT), including immunoglobulins, lactoferrin, lysozyme, bioactive lipids, leukocytes, and various milk glycans (glycolipids, glycoproteins, and free oligosaccahrides) among others (Newburg 2005). Although some of these bioactive components are known for their functionality in reducing pathogens in the infant GIT, others are believed to encourage specific bacterial populations, such as bifidobacteria—a genus first identified more than 100 years ago in the feces of breastfed infants (Moro 1900, Tissier 1900). Such a prebiotic function of human milk was originally described by Gyorgy and coworkers (1954), who first identified *N*-acetyl-glucosamine (GlcNAc)-containing oligosaccharides, generally termed human milk oligosaccharides (HMOs), as the bifidus factor responsible for enrichment of bifidobacteria (Gauche et al. 1954, German et al. 2008).

HMOs are believed to have many roles in a developing infant in addition to putative prebiotic functions. HMOs may possess antiadhesive effects that reduce the binding of pathogenic bacteria to colonocytes (Lane et al. 2010). HMOs have modulating effects on immunologic processes at the level of gut-associated lymphoid tissue (Guarner 2009) and may also decrease intestinal permeability in preterm infants in a dose-related manner in the first postnatal month (Taylor et al. 2009). Others have suggested that HMOs are an important source of *N*-acetyl-neuraminic acid (NeuAc; sialic acid), an essential monosaccharide during the period of neonate brain development and myelination (Wang et al. 2001).

The newborn infant gastrointestinal tract is initially colonized by aerobic and facultatively anaerobic bacteria, often species of enterobacteria, enterococci, and staphylococci (Adlerberth & Wold 2009). As these initial bacteria consume oxygen present in the intestine, anaerobic genera such as bifidobacteria, clostridia, and bacteroides are enriched. A number of studies have demonstrated that bifidobacteria are overrepresented in the gastrointestinal microbiota of breastfed infants by comparison with adults (Favier et al. 2003, Harmsen et al. 2000, Mariat et al. 2009, Penders et al. 2006). More recently, some studies have illustrated the sporadic and individualized nature of microbial colonization of infants (Koenig et al. 2010, Palmer et al. 2007). These recent approaches have also challenged the often-reported observation of bifidobacterial dominance of the breastfed infant GIT. Unfortunately, technical biases in these studies derived from sequencing V2 16S rDNA region amplicons may have led to an underestimation of the actinobacterial clade—as has been observed in studies comparing different 16S variable region amplicons (Turnbaugh et al. 2006) or by comparing to complementary metagenomic approaches (Koenig et al. 2010). Regardless, these new approaches hold significant promise in more comprehensively characterizing the influence of breast milk on the developing infant gut microbiota and its inherent metabolic capacity.

In a recent review of a number of studies undertaken in the past 20 years, Alderberth & Wold (2009) reported only minor differences in the levels of bifidobacteria present in formula-fed infant feces compared with breastfed infant feces, contrasting a commonly held perception of a low bifidobacterial presence in formula-fed infants. Certain microbial clades, such as clostridia, bacteroides, and *Enterobacteriaceae*, are more often observed in formula-fed than breastfed infants, resulting in a common description of formula-fed infants as having a more adult-like gastrointestinal microbiota (Adlerberth & Wold 2009). Moreover, a recent study noted that the specific bifidobacterial species diversity present in formula-fed infants is more adult-like (Haarman & Knol 2005).

The World Health Organization has clearly identified breastfeeding as providing the optimum nutrition and protection for developing infants (WHO 2009). In spite of this advice, there remains a great need for optimal infant formulas as a substitute for breastfeeding in cases where the latter is simply not possible. Recent advances in our understanding of the complex functions of human milk create a conceptual path for the design of more functional formulas. Such formulas would not only provide the complex nutritional needs for infants but also facilitate the microbial successions witnessed in breastfed infant GIT.

A variety of options are available for specific modification of microbial colonization in infants fed formula. Besides adding live bacteria, such as bifidobacteria and lactobacilli as probiotic additives, prebiotic oligosaccharides can be added as substrates that arrive undigested to the colon (Boehm & Moro 2008) and stimulate the growth and/or metabolic activity of beneficial bacterial species such as bifidobacteria (Manning & Gibson 2004). Interestingly, the structure of HMOs, compromising more than 200 different molecular structures (Bode 2006, Coppa et al. 2004, Ninonuevo et al. 2006), differs significantly from plant-derived fructooligosaccharides (FOS) or enzymatically synthesized galactooligosaccharides (GOS) (Fanaro et al. 2005a). To date, the variable oligosaccharide content of human milk cannot be successfully reproduced on a large scale for inclusion in infant formulas. (German et al. 2008, Guarner 2009, Manning & Gibson 2004, Sarney et al. 2000, Taylor et al. 2009, Wang et al. 2001). This manuscript focuses on the latest discoveries in the field of milk oligosaccharides as well their potential use in infant formula. In addition, structure and effects of bovine milk oligosaccharides (BMOs) and plant-derived oligosaccharides are briefly compared with those of HMOs.

HUMAN MILK OLIGOSACCHARIDES

HMOs are the third most abundant component of human milk (Kunz et al. 2000). Among all of the components, such as proteins, lactose, and nucleotides, the HMO is the only component that has been demonstrated to play a significant role in the stimulation of the growth of specific bacteria (Coppa et al. 2006). HMO-like structures are also found as components of glycolipids and glycoproteins (Newburg 1999). There are approximately 200 known compositions incorporating ≥ 3 carbohydrate monomers via 13 possible glycosidic linkages (Kunz et al. 2000, Ninonuevo et al. 2006). The molecular structure of these oligosaccharides is highly variable; additionally, the composition and concentration change significantly during lactation (described below) (Boehm & Moro 2008). After ingestion, HMOs pass mainly unabsorbed through the small intestine into the colon, where they are fermented to short-chain fatty acids (SCFA) and lactic acids, creating an acidic environment (Ogawa et al. 1992).

HMO Composition and Structure

The composition of milk oligosaccharides, as well as other milk components, differs among mammalian species and also during the course of lactation. Oligosaccharides in human milk are characterized by an enormous structural diversity (Chaturvedi et al. 2001). HMOs are formed by the attachment of a single glucose (Glc) molecule at the reducing end to galactose (Gal; bound to the Glc) to form a lactose core (Bode 2006). A linear chain is formed via β1–3 linkage attached to the core structure of GlcNAc, whereas a branched chain results when two GlcNAcs are added on both the β1–3 and β1–6 positions (Wu et al. 2010). After addition of the GlcNAc, another Gal is added either at β1–4 or β1–3. The resulting GlcNAc and Gal disaccharide may repeat multiple times. There are at least 12 different types of glycosidic bonds described in HMO (Newburg et al. 2005, Kobata 2003).). The smallest oligosaccharides are generated either when fucose (Fuc) is added to lactose, thus generating the trisaccharide fucosyllactose (2′FL; Fucα1–2, Galβ1–4Glc, and 3′FL; Gal β1–4[Fucα1–3]Glc), or when NeuAc is added to lactose, generating the sialyllactoses (3′SL; NeuAcα1–3Gal β1–4Glc and 6′SL; NeuAcα1–6Galβ1–4Glc) (Espinosa et al. 2007). However, these small oligosaccharides are generally less abundant than the larger, more complicated structures.

The synthesis of these oligosaccharides within the lactating mammary gland is catalyzed by a number of specific glycosyltransferases, including galactotransferases, *N*-acetylglucosaminyltransferases, fucosyltransferases, and sialyltransferases, whose expression is required for the synthesis of various glycoconjugates that are normally found in both lactating and nonlactating mammary tissue (Kelder et al. 2001). Because the human intestine does not express the luminal enzymes to cleave the α-glycosidic linkages of Fuc and sialic acid, as well as β glycosidic linkages in the core HMO molecule, these acids are resistant to enzymatic cleavages in the intestine (Engfer et al. 2000, Gnoth et al. 2000). As a result, HMOs can be detected in the feces of breastfed infants (Coppa et al. 2001). HMOs are also absorbed in vivo (Engfer et al. 2000, Gnoth et al. 2001, Kunz et al. 2000, Rudloff et al. 2006) through the intestinal wall in small amounts, possibly by receptor-mediated endocytosis (~1% of intake) and can be detected in urine (Coppa et al. 1990, Coppa et al. 2001). In this process, HMOs are taken unmodified up via trans- and para-cellular pathways (Gnoth et al. 2001).

HMOs are especially rich in the type 1 oligosaccharides. Lacto-*N*-biose (LNB; Galβ1–3GlcNAc) is a building unit of the three type 1 HMOs, such as lacto-*N*-tetraose (LNT; Galβ1–3GlcNAcβ1–3Galβ1–4Glc), lacto-*N*-fucopentaose I (LNFP; Fucα1–2Galβ1–3GlcNAcβ1–3Galβ1–4Glc), and lacto-*N*-difucohexaose I (Fucα1–2Galβ1–3[Fucα1–4]GlcNAcβ1–3Galβ1–4Glc)]. More detail on the structure and function of selected HMOs is available in a recent review by Bode (2006).

Although researchers began describing analytical methods for the isolation and characterizing of HMO over 40 years ago (Kobata & Ginsburg 1969), only recently has the technology advanced to precisely present and differentiate those complex glycans. Recently, Ninonuevo & Lebrilla (2009) discussed in detail the current methods for analysis of oligosaccharides in human milk. In recent years, more published data on the structure and function of HMOs allowed defining of the Lewis and Secretor blood groups corresponding to the specific HMOs produced by lactating mothers (Kunz & Rudloff 2008).

Lewis Blood Group and Secretor Status

Studies have shown that milk from different mothers may be qualitatively and quantitatively different with regards to its oligosaccharide content (Newburg 2000). A close relationship exists between HMO profiles, the structures of milk oligosaccharides, and the Lewis Blood Group and Secretor status (Kobata 1992, Thurl et al. 1997). The main criteria in the predicted variability of phenotypes seems to depend on the expression and activity of specific fucosyltransferases in the lactating mammary gland (Kunz & Rudloff 2008). Fucosyltransferase and fucosidase activities vary in milk specimens, both from different donors and from the same donors at different stages of lactation (Wiederschain & Newburg 1996). Additionally, these differences might also apply to other glycoconjugates (e.g., glycoproteins that are constructed via the same glycosyltransferases that synthesize HMOs). In human milk from individuals with blood type Le(a − b +) (~70% of the population), HMO with α1-2, α1-3, and α1-4-linked fucosyl residues occur (Kobata 1992). The second group, Le(a + b -) (20%) lacks compounds with α1-2-linked fucosyl compounds. Finally, in the remaining 10% of the population (Le(a − b -)), oligosaccharides with α1-4-linked fucose residues are missing. This system could potentially play a significant role in synchronizing select bacterial microbiota in infants with the mother's blood group. Population-based studies support this concept, and a high level of α1-2-linked Fuc relative to total HMOs has been shown to correlate with a lowered incidence of infant diarrhea (Morrow et al. 2005).

Variations in HMO Production

HMOs are solely produced in the lactating mammary gland and vary over the course of lactation (Chaturvedi et al. 2001). HMOs achieve a maximum concentration in the colostrum (above 20 g L^{-1}) with 5–14 g L^{-1} in mature milk (Kunz et al. 2000, Kunz et al. 1996). One limitation in the attempts to characterize HMO is a lack of availability in sufficient quantities and purity for in vitro and clinical studies. The majority of clinical studies using breast milk have to be interpreted carefully because assumed biological effects of HMO have also been credited to glycoproteins, glycolipids, and other milk constituents (Espinosa et al. 2007), and numerous other glycoconjugates might share the structural features with HMOs.

Given that various functions are associated with the diverse HMO structures, the details of variations in composition and differences of oligosaccharides among humans in remote populations need to be defined. Current analytical methods to characterize oligosaccharides in human milk include high-performance liquid chromatography (HPLC) (Chaturvedi et al. 1997, Leo et al. 2010), high pH anion exchange chromatography (HPAEC) (Thurl et al. 1996), capillary electrophoresis (CE) (Bao & Newburg 2008, Shen et al. 2000), and mass spectrometry (MS) (Albrecht et al. 2010, LoCascio et al. 2007, Marcobal et al. 2010, Niñonuevo & Lebrilla 2009). A method for precise quantification of consumption of individual HMOs named matrix-assisted laser desorption/ionization-Fourier transform ion cyclotron resonance mass spectrometry (MALDI-FTICR MS) allows detection of individual neutral oligosaccharides, which represent the majority of total HMOs (Ninonuevo et al. 2006).

Chaturvedi and coworkers have demonstrated that the ratio of fucosylated α1–2-linked oligosaccharide concentrations to oligosaccharides devoid of α1–2 linked Fuc changed during the first year of lactation from 5:1 to 1:1 (Chaturvedi et al. 2001). Furthermore, the concentrations of individual oligosaccharides varied substantially, both between the mothers and over the course of lactation. Those results suggest that the protective activities of HMOs might vary among the individuals and during the lactation. Interestingly, the attachment of Fuc was shown to be based on the Secretor status and Lewis blood group of the individual mother (Thurl et al. 1997). Another study analyzed the level of major neutral oligosaccharides for three consecutive days in human milk colostrums (Asakuma et al. 2007). Concentrations of 2′FL and lactodifucotetraose on day 1 were found to be substantially higher than those on day 2 and 3, whereas LNT concentration increased from day 1 to day 3.

Using HPLC-Chip/time-of-flight (TOF)-MS technology, Ninonuevo et al. (2008) reported significant variations in the oligosaccharide contents primarily with the minor HMO components, whereas there was a tendency to produce a single component in very large quantities among lactating mothers. In that study, the most abundant components were identified to be lacto-*N*-neotetraose (LNnT), LNT, and LNFP. These authors noted that LNnT,

LNT, and LNFP were also preferentially consumed by *Bifidobacterium longum* subsp. *infantis* (*B. infantis*), illustrating a unique correspondence between these most abundant oligosaccharides and the bacteria they enrich. Interestingly, adult-type bifidobacteria *Bifidobacterium adolescentis* and *Bifidobacterium animalis* do not degrade LNT (Xiao et al. 2010). It is generally accepted that the mother's diet, physiology, and feeding behavior may have an impact on the daily HMO production.

HMOs AS A DEFENSE MECHANISM

HMOs play a critical role in the infant's defense system, the development of a specific intestinal microbiota, and the inflammatory processes (Zopf & Roth 1996). Numerous local and systemic effects of HMOs have been described previously, including protective functions of HMOs against enteropathogens (Newburg et al. 2004a). Also, antipathogenic effects of fucosylated oligosaccharides, specifically those that contain the Fucα1–2 structural motif were elucidated (Newburg et al. 2004a, Newburg et al. 2004b, Ruiz-Palacios et al. 2003). For example, Ruiz-Palacios and coworkers have reported that infants fed with human milk having low concentrations of 2′FL may be more susceptible to diarrhea than babies fed the breast milk containing high concentrations of 2′FL (Ruiz-Palacios et al. 2003).

Prevention of Pathogen Adhesion

Other researchers reported that HMOs serve as soluble ligand analogs and block pathogen adhesion (Newburg et al. 2005). The chemical structures of HMO are homologous to the carbohydrate units of glycoconjugates, especially of glycolipids, on cell surfaces of mammalian epithelial cells. For example, binding of *Escherichia coli*, *Streptococcus pneumonia*, *Campylobacter jejuni*, *Helicobacter pylori*, and *Vibrio cholerae* was inhibited by the glycoconjugates present in HMOs (e.g., 2′fucosyllactosamine) (Bode 2009, Leach et al. 2005, Morrow et al. 2004, Newburg et al. 2005, Ruiz-Palacios et al. 2003). It is also possible that HMOs can have glycome-modifying effects through changing of the expression of intestinal epithelial cell surface glycans. Angeloni et al. (2005) demonstrated that Caco-2 cells change their surface glycan profile after the exposure to 3′SL, a constituent of HMOs. In that study, the expression of α2–3- and α2–6-linked sialic acid residues in Caco-2 cells was significantly downregulated. Thus, this particular HMO appears to modify the glycan content of the epithelial cell surface and the receptor sites for some pathogens. The same researchers further confirmed that the adhesion of enteropathogenic *E. coli* (EPEC) was reduced upon treatment with 3′SL. **Table 1** lists the HMOs that inhibit specific pathogens in vitro, ex vivo, or in vivo.

Role of Oligosaccharides in the Development of the Immune System

Previous research has demonstrated that HMOs directly affect the immune system (Eiwegger et al. 2004, Newburg 2009, Velupillai & Harn 1994). For example, HMOs have been shown to interact with selectins (Schumacher et al. 2006), integrins (Bode et al. 2004a), and toll-like receptors (Vos et al. 2007), as well as to affect leukocyte-endothelial cell and leukocyte-platelet interactions (Bode et al. 2004a, Bode et al. 2004b, Lasky 1995, McEver 1994, Schwertmann et al. 1996). Many sialylated and fucosylated HMOs may block the latter interactions by having significant effects on the progression of inflammatory responses (Kunz et al. 1999). A recent study has also shown that HMOs can inhibit transfer of HIV-1 virus to CD4+ lymphocytes (Hong et al. 2009). Furthermore, HMOs induce intracellular processes, including differentiation and apoptosis of intestinal epithelial cells. (Kuntz et al. 2009, Kuntz et al. 2008). Neutral HMO

Table 1 Pathogen inhibition by select HMOs in in vivo, ex vivo, and in vitro studies

Pathogen	HMO tested	Reference
Norwalk virus	Fucosylated oligosaccharides	(Ruvoën-clouet et al. 2006)
Campylobacter jejuni		(Morrow et al. 2004, Ruiz-Palacios et al. 2003)
Vibrio cholera		(Ruiz-Palacios et al. 2003)
Escherichia coli (heat-stable enterotoxin)		(Newburg et al. 1990, Newburg et al. 2004b)
Streptococcus pneumoniae	Sialyllactose	(Leach et al. 2005)
Cholera toxin		(Idota et al. 1995)
E. coli		(Virkola et al. 1993)
Pseudomonas aeruginosa		(Devaraj et al. 1994)
Aspergillus fumigates conidia		(Bouchara et al. 1997)
Influenza virus		(Gambaryan et al. 1997, Matrosovich et al. 1993)
Polymavirus		(Stehle et al. 1994)
Helicobacter pylori		(Mysore et al. 1999)
HIV-1	Oligosaccharides	(Hong et al. 2009)
Streptococcus pneumoniae		(Andersson et al. 1986, Idänpään-Heikkilä et al. 1997)
Enteropathogenic *E. coli* (EPEC)		(Cravioto et al. 1991)
Haemophilius influenzae		(Idänpään-Heikkilä et al. 1997)

structures, such as LNFP III and LNnT, affect murine IL-10 production (Velupillai and Harn 1994), suggesting that HMOs might be involved in the production of antiinflammatory mediators that suppress proinflammatory Th1 response in mice (Terrazas et al. 2001). In another study, HMOs affected Th1/Th2 skewing via production of cytokines as well as maturation and activation of human cord blood–derived T cells (Eiwegger et al. 2004). More recently, Eiwegger et al. (2010) demonstrated a novel, direct immunomodulatory effect of acidic fraction of HMO when compared with the same fraction from cow's milk. In this study, acidic HMOs stimulated production of IFN-γ and IL-10, directing the neonatal Th2-type T-cell phenotype toward a Th-0-type profile in cord blood–derived mononuclear cells. This effect also impacted Th-2-type immune response of allergen-specific T cells from peanut allergic individuals. Both results strongly suggest antiallergic properties of certain acidic HMOs.

HMOs AS GROWTH FACTORS FOR BIFIDOBACTERIA

A bifidobacterial presence in the feces of breastfed infants was described by Moro in 1900, who reported that human milk contains a growth factor for these bacteria (Moro 1900). Fifty years later, György identified the bifidus factor to be GlcNAc (previously named gynolactose) (Gyorgy 1953, Hoover et al. 1953) using growth of *Bifidobacterium bifidum* subsp. *Pennsylvanicum*. In vitro studies have demonstrated that GlcNAc-containing oligosaccharides are indeed able to enhance the growth of this bifidobacteria, while other sugars showed less growth-promoting activity (Petschow & Talbott 1991). The bifidogenic effect in infants is often associated with a reduction of stool pH and changes in SCFA pattern (Rinne et al. 2005). The ability of selected bifidobacteria to consume prebiotic oligosaccharides from human milk is likely an essential trait enabling this genera to be one of the most abundant colonizers of the breastfed infant gut (LoCascio et al. 2009, LoCascio et al. 2007).

Ward et al. (2006) first demonstrated vigorous growth of *B. infantis* on HMOs as a sole carbon, whereas *Lactobacillus gasseri*, a common inhabitant of the adult intestine, grew poorly. Further analysis revealed bifidobacterial species-specific differences in HMO growth, with *B. infantis* reaching a cell density threefold higher than *B. longum*, *Bifidobacterium breve*, *B. bifidum*, and *B. adolescentis*

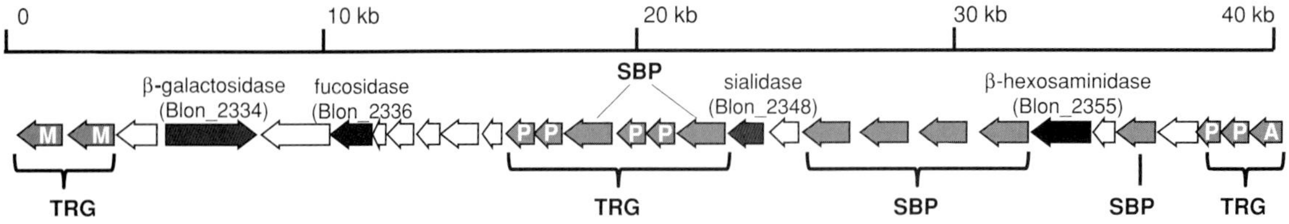

Figure 1

43 Kb gene cluster in *B. infantis* ATCC15697 containing glycosyl hydrolases and transport-related genes (TRG) required for importing and metabolizing HMOs. SBP: solute binding protein, M: major facilitator superfamily, P: ABC transporter permease component, and A: ABC transporter ATPase subunit. Adapted from Sela et al. (2008).

(Ward et al. 2007). Further work by LoCascio and colleagues (LoCascio et al. 2009, LoCascio et al. 2007) demonstrated preferential consumption by *B. infantis* of the smaller HMO species (degree of polymerization <7). These small HMO species represent the bulk of the HMOs present in pooled samples and are consistently presented over lactation (Ninonuevo et al. 2008). Tellingly, only *B. infantis* and *B. breve* could grow on the individual monosaccharide constituents of HMOs (Glc, Gal, GlcNAc, Fuc, NeuAc), suggesting another mechanism for these species to garner energy from these substrates within the intestine (Ward et al. 2007). Although growth of *B. bifidum* on HMO was less vigorous than *B. infantis*, direct consumption of HMO was observed (Ward et al. 2007). Interestingly, Fuc, GlcNAc, and NeuAc were not consumed by *B. bifidum* and remained in the media suggesting that this species is capable of deconstructing HMOs outside the cell to gain access to Glc and Gal constituents as growth substrates (Ward et al. 2007).

The recent genome sequence of *B. infantis* has enabled a more comprehensive analysis of the HMO growth phenotype by this species. Notably, Sela et al. (2008) described a 43 Kb gene HMO cluster containing the four glycosyl hydrolase activities needed to cleave HMO into its constituent monosaccharides (sialidase, fucosidase, galactosidase, and hexosaminidase) as well as an array of oligosaccharide transport-related genes (**Figure 1**). Proteomic analysis revealed that genes in this locus are induced upon growth on HMOs, suggesting that *B. infantis* imports the HMO, whereby the internalized oligosaccharides are catabolized by glycosidases prior to entry of the monosaccharides into the fructose-6-phosphate phosphoketolase central metabolic pathway (Sela et al. 2008). The transport proteins within the main HMO cluster contained six Family 1 extracellular solute binding proteins (SBP) predicted to bind oligosaccharides and to be a part of ABC transporters facilitating import and metabolism. A phylogenetic analysis of these six SBPs indicated a specific evolutionary divergence from other bifidobacterial SBP Family 1 proteins (Sela et al. 2008), suggesting a unique relationship to HMO metabolism. **Table 2** lists several bifidobacterial strains and corresponding genes related to HMO metabolism.

LoCascio et al. (2009) confirmed that the ability to consume HMOs is conserved in the entire *B. infantis* lineage, whereas other bifidobacteria isolated from infants reveal more strain-specific phenotypic variation. Recently, the same authors used comparative genomic hybridization to demonstrate a unique conservation of the HMO locus across the *B. infantis* subspecies. This work also revealed a mutant *B. infantis* strain (JCM1260) for which specific transporter genes within the main HMO cluster are absent (LoCascio et al. 2010). This mutant strain did not grow vigorously on HMOs unlike the other wild-type *B. infantis* strains (LoCascio et al. 2009), providing the first genetic evidence specifically linking the main HMO locus to the HMO growth phenotype. For a more detailed discussion of the phylogenomic aspects of HMO consumption in bifidobacteria, readers are referred to a recent review by Sela & Mills (2010).

Table 2 Presence of α-fucosidase, α-sialidase, and lacto-N-biose phosphorylase genes in sequenced bifidobacterial genomes

Sequenced bifidobacterial genomes	Fucosidases	Sialidases	Lacto-N-biose phosphorylases
Bifidobacterium adolescentis ATCC 15703; L2–32	–	–	–
Bifidobacterium animalis lactis AD011; HN019	–	–	–
Bifidobacterium animalis subsp. *lactis* BI-04; DSM 10140	–	–	–
Bifidobacterium bifidum NCIMB 41171	1	2	4
Bifidobacterium breve DSM 20213	–	1	2
Bifidobacterium catenulatum DSM 16992	–	–	–
Bifidobacterium dentium ATCC 27678	1	–	–
Bifidobacterium dentium Bd1	–	–	–
Bifidobacterium gallicum DSM 20093	–	–	–
Bifidobacterium longum DJO10A	–	–	2
Bifidobacterium longum NCC2705			1
Bifidobacterium longum subsp. *infantis* ATCC 15697	4	2	1
Bifidobacterium longum subsp. *infantis* ATCC 55813[a]	–	–	1
Bifidobacterium longum subsp. *infantis* CCUG 52486[a]	–	–	1
Bifidobacterium pseudocatenulatum DSM 20438	–	–	–

[a]LoCascio et al. (2010) indicated these strains to be *B. longum* subsp. *longum.*

Nishimoto & Kitaoka (2007a) identified the novel degradation pathway in bifidobacteria specific for LNB, an HMO building block. Wada et al. (2008) further described the pathway in bifidobacteria involving both LNB and galacto-*N*-biose (GNB; Galβ1–3GalNAc), a core structure of the mucin sugar that is present in the human intestine and milk (Lloyd et al. 1996). The latter pathway involves proteins and enzymes that are required for the uptake and degradation of disaccharides such as the GNB/LNB transporter (Suzuki et al. 2008, Wada et al. 2007), galacto-*N*-biose/lacto-*N*-biose I phosphorylase (GLNBP; LnpA) (Kitaoka et al. 2005, Nishimoto & Kitaoka 2007b), UDP-glucose-hexose 1-phosphate uridyltransferase (GalT), and UDP-galactose

Table 3 Specific monosaccharide linkages in HMO, BMO, and commercial oligosaccharides. Adapted from Kuntz et al. (2009)

Glycans	Monosaccharide linkages
HMO	
Lacto-N-tetraose/hexaose/octaose/decaose	β1–3, β1–4, β1–6
Fucosyllactose	α1–2, α1–3, α1–4, β1–3, β1–4
Sialyllactose	α2–3, α2–6, β1–4
Sialyl-lacto-N-tetraose	α2–3, α2–6, β1–3, β1–4
BMO	
Acetyllactosamine	β1–4
Galactosyllactose	β1–3, β1–4, β1–6
Acetylneuraminyllactose (Neu5Ac)	α2–3, α2–6, α2–8, β1–4
Glycolylneuraminyllactose (Neu5Gc)	α2–3, α2–6, β1–4
Galactooligosaccharides (GOS)	α1–2, α1–4, α1–6
Fructooligosaccharides (FOS)	β1–2

epimerase (GalE). Other researchers confirmed that several bifidobacteria strains, including *B. longum* subsp. *longum*, *B. infantis*, *B. breve*, *and B. bifidum* were able to grow on LNB (Groschwitz et al. 2009), whereas none of the strains for *B. adolescentis*, *B. catenulatum*, *B. dentium*, *B. angulatum*, *B. animalis* subsp. *lactis*, and *B. thermophilum* showed any growth. The presence of the LnpA gene coincided with the LNB utilization in that study. Furthermore, previous studies have shown that some bifidobacterial strains have a unique pathway for the degradation of HMO, specifically with a type 1 chain (β-linked LNB) involving lacto-*N*-biosidase (LnbB). It has been suggested that the presence of the LnbB and GNB/LNB pathways in some bifidobacterial strains could provide a nutritional advantage for these organisms, thereby increasing their populations within the ecosystem of the breastfed newborns (Wada et al. 2008). Among mammalian milk oligosaccharides, those of *Homo sapiens* are especially rich in the type 1 LNB structure (Asakuma et al. 2007) and LnbB activity was found in the strains of *B. longum* and *B. bifidum* but not in *B. animalis* and *B. pseudolongum* (Wada et al. 2008). Indeed, LoCascio et al. (2007) and Ward et al. (2006) suggested that the ability to assimilate type 1 HMO is limited to certain species of bifidobacteria, e.g., *B. bifidum* and *B. infantis*.

Using 2′FL as a substrate, Katayama et al. (2008) examined bifidobacterial strains for the occurrence of fucosidase. Those researchers reported that several bifidobacteria strains, including *B. bifidum* JCM1254 and *B. longum* JCM1217, produce 1,2-α-L-fucosidase; this enzyme cleaves α-L-fucosyl residue bound to Gal through the α-1–2 linkages found at the nonreducing termini of HMO (Podolsky 1985, Song et al. 2002). Beside 2′-FL, this enzyme readily hydrolyzed lacto-*N*-fucopentaose I; however, it showed a very limited activity for α-(1–3) -linked L-fucosyl residues of 3-fucosyllactose and lacto-*N*-fucopentaose V, and had no action on the α-1–4 linkage and α-1–6 linkage.

The various catabolic strategies for HMO observed among different infant-borne bifidobacteria suggest different evolutionary adaptations to the gain a growth advantage from the same complex substrate (Sela & Mills 2010). *B. infantis* appears to internalize small HMO species (LoCascio et al. 2009, LoCascio et al. 2007), whereas *B. bifidum* exports enzymes to selectively remove LNB from the HMO structure and processes LNB intracellularly (Katayama et al. 2004). *B. breve* and *B. longum* subsp. *longum* are able to consume free LNnT from the HMO pool (LoCascio et al. 2007, Ward et al. 2007). However, *B. breve* is also able to grow on the monosaccharide constituents of HMO (Ward et al. 2007). Given that these species are often isolated from the same infant feces, it is tempting to speculate that the various mechanisms may be linked to niche partitioning among bifidobacteria within the developing infant gastrointestinal tract.

ALTERNATIVE SOURCES FOR HMO-LIKE PREBIOTICS IN INFANT FORMULA: ANIMAL MILKS

Breastfed infants are better protected against several types of infections than formula-fed infants (Newburg 1997). Several researchers suggested supplementing infant formula with oligosaccharides similar to those found in human milk (McVeagh & Miller 1997, Motil 2000). Given that human milk is obviously not amenable to large-scale production, there is an urgent demand for alternative, yet functionally comparable, oligosaccharide sources from which to obtain sufficient amounts to perform clinical studies and examine the potential for use in infant nutrition. It was shown previously that the bioactivity of oligosaccharides from bovine and human milk is similar (Gopal & Gill 2000), and therefore BMOs could be used in milk products as bioactive components in human nutrition.

The oligosaccharides in milk of domestic animals, including bovine, differ in structure and have less complex structures with fewer isomers compared with HMOs, whereas the similarities include β-glycosidic linkage of Gal and *N*-acetylhexosamine to lactose (Urashima et al. 2001). The linkages to Fuc are rare, whereas linkages of Gal or *N*-acetylglucosamine are dominant. The human intestine lacks enzymes able to hydrolyze all β-glycosidic linkages except the one in lactose. Thus, β-glycosidically bound Gal is the structural element that protects these molecules from digestion during passage through the small intestine (Boehm and Stahl 2007). Sialic acid is a major structural element in the BMOs (Kunz & Rudloff 1993, Saito et al. 1984); however, in contrast to HMO, *N*-acetylneuraminic acid (Neu5Ac) and N-glycolylneuraminic acid (Neu5Gc) are present (Bode 2006). It is important because differences in the chemical structure of sialic acid in human versus cow's milk are likely to influence bioavailability. It was previously reported that sialylated oligosaccharides also have a role in the initial stage of inflammation and may be effective against the influenza virus and ulcers caused by *Helicobacter pylori* (Parente et al. 2003). Unique differences between BMOs and HMOs were reported previously in terms of the size, type, and relative amounts (Tao et al. 2008). Bovine colostrums contain sialyl *N*-acetyllactosamine (Gal(β1–4)GlcNAc) as well as 3′SL, whereas human milk contains only 3′SL (Martin-Sosa et al. 2003). Mature bovine milk also contains galactosyllactoses at concentrations of 40 to 60 mg L^{-1} (Davis et al. 1983). In a study by Tao et al. (2009), sialylated BMOs made up to 70% of colostrum and 50% of mature milk with the majority of the sialic acid Neu5Ac. Gopal & Gill (2000) reported 10 sialylated and eight neutral oligosaccharides in bovine milk and colostrums. Sialyllacto-*N*-tetraose c (LSTc), 6′SL, and disialyllacto-*N*-tetraose were the most representative constituents among sialyl-oligosaccharides (Coppa et al. 1999). Martin-Sosa et al. (2003) have shown that 3′SL was the most representative species in the bovine colostrums, although 6′SL remained at constantly high values during the lactation. The dominant neuramin lactose from human milk has the Neu5Ac acid linked to Gal via an α2-6 bond, whereas the dominant bovine neuramin lactose is linked α2–3.

It is possible that BMOs could have similar functions to HMOs in terms of pathgoen deflection. The free trisaccharide, Galα1–3Galβ1–4Glc, which is found in the bovine colostrum (Urashima et al. 1991), is thought to be an inhibitor of the binding of pathogenic organisms (e.g., *Clostridium difficile*) to the intestinal mucosa of newborn calves. Bovine colostrum also contains a potential prebiotic isoglobotriose (Galα1–3Galβ1–4Glc), which has not been described in human milk.

Tao et al. (2008) integrated the nanoflow liquid chromatography (nanoLC) with MS in a HPLC-Chip/TOF-MS instrument to profile HMO and BMO. In that study, 40 BMOs were identified, most of which were sialylated; fucosylation was not observed in any of the samples. The same researchers demonstrated that anionic oligosaccharides are minor components in HMOs (<20%) but represent about 70% of the total oligosaccharides in bovine colostrums. Also, sialylated BMOs decreased dramatically during the first 24 hours of lactation, whereas neutral oligosaccharides increased (Nakamura et al. 2003).

Among the other milks from domesticated mammals, goat milk is especially rich in complex lactose-derived oligosaccharides. Interestingly, goat milk oligosaccharides (GMOs) have been shown to contain higher levels of oligosaccharides than bovine milks and are also reported to contain fucosylated species (Nakamura & Urashima 2004). Lara-Villoslada (Lara-Villoslada et al. 2006) recently demonstrated that GMOs reduced the inflammation and body weight loss in rats exposed to dextran sodium sulfate, a common model of colitis and inflammatory bowel disease. Other effects of GMOs included less severe colonic lesions, more favorable intestinal microbiota, and increased intestinal function. Thus, goat milk is another potential source of GMOs for human nutrition applications, including infant formulas (Martinez-Ferez et al. 2006).

Future Opportunities with Animal Milks

The milk contents of each mammalian species are precisely customized to meet the specific needs of the cognate newborns. Although recent data indicate significant differences among milk from domestic animals (Martinez-Ferez et al. 2006), milk and colostrum of domestic animals uniformly contain large amounts of sialyl oligosaccharides as well as many kinds of neutral oligosaccharides (Nakamura & Urashima 2004). Clearly, of the highest priority for infant formula is the search for the structural elements of HMO that are considered crucial to their biological effect and would serve as scientific basis for the selection of oligosaccharides from sources other than human. BMOs are particularly attractive candidates because the large size of the existing bovine dairy industry positions them as a readily available source for significant amounts of oligosaccharides with biological functions close to HMO. Recently, Barile et al. (2009) determined the composition of a variety of neutral and sialylated oligosaccharides in whey permeate using a MALDI-FTICR technique. Seven of the 15 oligosaccharides identified in that study had the same composition as some HMO structures and contained NeuAc. Those results suggest that whey permeate, a common waste stream in cheesemaking, could be a source of oligosaccharides with compositions similar to those present in human milk.

It has been previously demonstrated that sialylated oligosaccharides are important in brain development and increased immunity in infants (Boehm & Stahl 2007, Montserrat & Alicia 2001, Wang & Brand-Miller 2003). Bovine mature milk, which is used currently to produce infant formulas, has a relatively low sialic acid content (Carlson 1985, Neeser et al. 1991, Sánchez-Díaz et al. 1997, Wang et al. 2001). In humans, the sialyloligosaccharides range from 1 g L^{-1} in colostrums to 90–450 mg L^{-1} in mature milk (Martin-Sosa et al. 2003, Martín-Sosa et al. 2004), whereas in bovine-based infant formulas the content of sialyloligosaccharides is as low as 15–35 mg L^{-1} (Martin-Sosa et al. 2003, Wang et al. 2001). The majority of sialic acid in infant formulas is bound to protein (70%), followed by free oligosaccharides, with only 1% in the free form (Wang et al. 2001). Thus, infants fed bovine-based formulas receive significantly less sialic acid compared with breastfed infants. Several researchers attempted to concentrate and isolate the milk sialyloligosaccharides naturally present in whey (described in Barile et al. 2009). However, the exact number and type of monosaccharide residues forming sialyloligosaccharides in whey currently is not well known.

As mentioned above, both fucosylation and sialylation play an important role in the prevention of pathogens binding to the intestinal epithelia and promotion of the growth of beneficial bacteria. However, although HMO are highly fucosylated (Ninonuevo et al. 2006), the BMOs examined to date are not (Tao et al. 2009). The lack of fucosylation in BMOs is interesting given that the recent analysis of the bovine genome clearly indicates that the genetic capacity for creation of fucosylated oligosaccharides is present (Elsik et al. 2009). Certainly, more research on the molecular basis for the observed lack of fucosylation in bovine milk is warranted.

CURRENT COMMERCIAL OLIGOSACCHARIDES USED IN INFANT FORMULA

Among the rather large array of currently available and emerging prebiotics (Crittenden & Playne 2009), relatively few have been examined for use in infant formulas. Stemming from the common observation of bifidobacteria in the feces of breastfed infants, attempts have been made to reproduce this bifidogenic aspect in formulas by adding commercial prebiotics, in particular FOS and GOS, which are known to be broadly bifidogenic (Crittenden & Playne 2009).

Although HMOs are complex glycans composed of five different monosaccharides, FOS and GOS are much simpler structures. FOS are linear fructose polymers, whereas the basic structure of GOS incorporates lactose at the reducing end that is typically elongated with up to six Gal residues, which can contain different branching ([Gal(β1–3/4/6)]1–6Gal(β1–4)Glc). FOS can be commercially produced through the reverse reaction of fructanases and sucrases or via enzymatic hydrolysis of inulin (Espinosa et al. 2007). FOS produced by the first method lacks a reducing end and contains one Glc residue and two or more fructose moieties [short chain (sc) FOS; degree of polymerization (DP) 2–6)] (Fanaro et al. 2005b), whereas hydrolysis of inulin produces free anomeric carbons and contains one fructose [long chain (lc) FOS; DP 7–60)] (Roberfroid 2005). Commercial GOS preparations are mostly produced by enzymatic treatment of lactose with β-galactosidases from different sources, such as fungi, yeast, or bacteria, which results in a mixture of oligomers with various chain lengths (Park & Oh 2010).

Previous work suggested that the upper limit for the DP for GOS is eight (Macfarlane et al. 2008). However, recent work by Barboza et al. (2009) clearly demonstrated that there were oligosaccharides with a DP of up to fifteen. The same researchers reported in vitro growth behavior of different bifidobacterial strains of disaccharide- and monosaccharide-free fractions of GOS (pGOS). MALDI-FTICR MS analysis demonstrated that although all the strains tested were able to grow on the pGOS substrate, there were strain- and DP-specific bifidobacterial preferences for pGOS utilization. In general, the infant borne–isolates (*B. infantis* and *B. breve*) were able to consume the GOS species with DP ranging from three to eight more efficiently, while *B. adolescentis* and *B. longum* subsp. *longum* exhibited more differential consumption of select DP. Previously, GOS consumption with specific DP preferences had been determined only for *B. adolescentis* DSM 20083 (Van Laere et al. 2000). The selective consumption of certain GOS structures by different bifidobacterial species hints at the intriguing possibility of targeting GOS prebiotics to enrich select bifidobacterial species.

Falony et al. (2009) investigated FOS and inulin degradation by a wide range of *Bifidobacterium* species, focusing in particular on the presence of a preferential FOS breakdown mechanism. That study revealed the existence of a limited number of phenotypically distinct clusters among the tested bifdiobacterial strains, however none of the species was able to degrade inulin or FOS completely. Noteworthy, common infant isolates *B. bifidum* and *B. breve* did not degrade inulin and FOS.

Perhaps the most studied prebiotic additive to infant formula is a GOS and FOS mixture, added at a 9:1 ratio (GOS:FOS) (Fanaro et al. 2005a). This particular ratio of prebiotics has been shown to increase bifidobacteria in infant feces (Boehm et al. 2002, Haarman & Knol 2005, Knol et al. 2005) and lower the incidence of pathogens (Knol et al. 2005). Other studies showed positive outcomes in terms of stool consistency and intestinal transit time with GOS/FOS (Mihatsch et al. 2006). Kapiki and colleagues showed that formula supplemented with FOS resulted in increased bifidobacteria and reduction in *E. coli* and enterococci (Kapiki et al. 2007). A recent study by Nakamura et al. (2009) demonstrated that fecal samples from infants fed formula supplemented with polydextrose, GOS, and lactulose (8 g L^{-1}) contained significantly less bifidobacteria (20.7%) than fecal samples from infants fed breast milk (83.5%). Interestingly, the same study also confirmed that the prebiotic blend may have a greater impact on infant fecal bacterial populations in younger than in older infants.

Future Opportunities with Commercial Prebiotics

Although the studies employing commercial prebiotic additions to infant formula look promising, at least in terms of enriching bifidobacteria, several questions remain. Growth on HMOs is restricted to select bifidobacteria, primarily *B. infantis* and *B. bifidum*, species that possess the requisite genetic capacity (in particular fucosidase and sialidase functions) to deconstruct the HMO polymer. In contrast, FOS and GOS are more broadly utilized across the genus and thus may more nonspecifically enrich from this clade. Assuming HMOs evolved in concert with both the human host and the cognate infant-borne bifidobacteria (as postulated in Sela & Mills 2010), is a nonspecific enrichment of any bifidobacterial species, perhaps as the result of a GOS or FOS treatment, inherently of value to an infant? In other words, is any bifidobacteria resulting from a bifidogenic prebiotic a good outcome? As described above, the functions of HMOs are multifold, and it is unlikely that FOS and GOS possess similar developmental, immunological, or antiadherence functions. A recent study by Shoaf et al. (2006) demonstrated the ability of GOS to reduce enteropathogenic *E. coli* adherence to tissue culture cells. However, these authors noted the high level of GOS required to witness a significant reduction in *E. coli* adherence, and they speculated that this antiadherence activity might be enhanced by fucosylation or sialyation of the GOS.

Thus, one clear opportunity is to decorate existing prebiotics to obtain more HMO-like structures and functions. The technology for chemoenzymatic construction of complex carbohydrates has advanced tremendously enabling both decoration of existing structures and wholesale construction of HMO-like structures (Muthana et al. 2009). Following such a path, the generation of specifically designed, individual HMO structures would greatly enhance our ability to link biological function to specific glycan structural motifs. Perhaps more importantly, this would also set the conceptual stage for the creation of tailored synbiotic partners—very specifically designed and constructed HMOs paired with specific cognate bifidobacteria—to achieve a regulatable colonization of either the infant, or adult, GIT.

DISCLOSURE STATEMENT

The authors are not aware of any affiliations, memberships, funding, or financial holdings that might be perceived as affecting the objectivity of this review.

ACKNOWLEDGMENTS

Authors thank David Sela and Daniel Garrido for their assistance in preparing this manuscript. This publication was made possible in part by grant support from the University of California Discovery Grant Program, the California Dairy Research Foundation, Dairy Management Inc., the Gates Foundation, USDA NRI-CSREES Award 2008-35200-18776, NIEHS Superfund P42 ES02710, the Charge study P01 ES11269, and by NIH-NICID awards 5R01HD059127 and 1R01HD061923.

LITERATURE CITED

Adlerberth I, Wold AE. 2009. Establishment of the gut microbiota in Western infants. *Acta Paediatr.* 98:229–38

Albrecht S, Schols HA, van den Heuvel EG, Voragen AG, Gruppen H. 2010. CE-LIF-MS n profiling of oligosaccharides in human milk and feces of breast-fed babies. *Electrophoresis.* 31(7):1264–73

Andersson B, Porras O, Hanson LA, Lagergård T, Svanborg-Edén C. 1986. Inhibition of attachment of *Streptococcus pneumoniae* and *Haemophilus influenzae* by human milk and receptor oligosaccharides. *J. Infect. Dis.* 153(2):232–37

Angeloni S, Ridet JL, Kusy N, Gao H, Crevoisier F, et al. 2005. Glycoprofiling with micro-arrays of glycoconjugates and lectins. *Glycobiology* 15:31–41

Asakuma S, Urashima T, Akahori M, Obayashi H, Nakamura T, et al. 2007. Variation of major neutral oligosaccharides levels in human colostrum. *Eur. J. Clin. Nutr.* 62:488–94

Bao Y, Newburg DS. 2008. Capillary electrophoresis of acidic oligosaccharides from human milk. *Electrophoresis* 29:2508–15

Barboza M, Sela DA, Pirim C, LoCascio RG, Freeman SL, et al. 2009. Glycoprofiling bifidobacterial consumption of galacto-oligosaccharides by mass spectrometry reveals strain specific, preferential consumption of glycans. *Appl. Environ. Microbiol.* 75(23):7319–25

Barile D, Tao N, Lebrilla CB, Coisson JD, Arlorio M, German JB. 2009. Permeate from cheese whey ultrafiltration is a source of milk oligosaccharides. *Int. Dairy J.* 19:524–30

Bode L. 2006. Recent advances on structure, metabolism, and function of human milk oligosaccharides. *J. Nutr.* 136:2127–30

Bode L. 2009. Human milk oligosaccharides: prebiotics and beyond. *Nutr. Rev.* 67:S183–S91

Bode L, Kunz C, Muhly-Reinholz M, Mayer K, Seeger W, Rudloff S. 2004a. Inhibition of monocyte, lymphocyte, and neutrophil adhesion to endothelial cells by human milk oligosaccharides. *Thromb. Haemost.* 92(6):1402–10

Bode L, Rudloff S, Kunz C, Strobel S, Klein N. 2004b. Human milk oligosaccharides reduce platelet-neutrophil complex formation leading to a decrease in neutrophil {beta} 2 integrin expression. *J. Leukoc Biol.* 76:820–26

Boehm G, Lidestri M, Casetta P, Jelinek J, Negretti F, et al. 2002. Supplementation of a bovine milk formula with an oligosaccharide mixture increases counts of faecal bifidobacteria in preterm infants. *Arch. Dis. Child. Fetal Neonatal Ed.* 86:F178–81

Boehm G, Moro G. 2008. Structural and functional aspects of prebiotics used in infant nutrition. *J. Nutr.* 138:1818S–28

Boehm G, Stahl B. 2007. Oligosaccharides from milk. *J. Nutr.* 137:847S–49

Bouchara J, Sanchez M, Chevailler A, Marot-Leblond A, Lissitzky J, et al. 1997. Sialic acid–dependent recognition of laminin and fibrinogen by *Aspergillus fumigatus* conidia. *Infect. Immun.* 65:2717–24

Carlson S. 1985. N-acetylneuraminic acid concentrations in human milk oligosaccharides and glycoproteins during lactation. *Am. J. Clin. Nutr.* 41:720–26

Chaturvedi P, Warren CD, Altaye M, Morrow AL, Ruiz-Palacios G, et al. 2001. Fucosylated human milk oligosaccharides vary between individuals and over the course of lactation. *Glycobiology* 11:365–72

Chaturvedi P, Warren CD, Ruiz-Palacios GM, Pickering LK, Newburg DS. 1997. Milk oligosaccharide profiles by reversed-phase HPLC of their perbenzoylated derivatives. *Anal. Biochem.* 251(1):89–97

Coppa GV, Bruni S, Morelli L, Soldi S, Gabrielli O. 2004. The first prebiotics in humans: human milk oligosaccharides. *J. Clin. Gastroenterol.* 38(6 Suppl):S80–83

Coppa GV, Gabrielli O, Giorgi P, Catassi C, Montanari MP, et al. 1990. Preliminary study of breastfeeding and bacterial adhesion to uroepithelial cells. *Lancet* 335:569–71

Coppa GV, Pierani P, Zampini L, Bruni S, Carloni I, Gabrielli O. 2001. Characterization of oligosaccharides in milk and feces of breast-fed infants by high-performance anion-exchange chromatography. *Adv. Exp. Med. Biol.* 501:307–14

Coppa GV, Pierani P, Zampini L, Carloni I, Carlucci A, Gabrielli O. 1999. Oligosaccharides in human milk during different phases of lactation. *Acta Paediatr. Suppl.* 88(430):89–94

Coppa GV, Zampini L, Galeazzi T, Gabrielli O. 2006. Prebiotics in human milk: a review. *Dig. Liver Dis.* 38:S291–S94

Cravioto A, Tello A, Villafán H, Ruiz J, del Vedovo S, Neeser JR. 1991. Inhibition of localized adhesion of enteropathogenic *Escherichia coli* to HEp-2 cells by immunoglobulin and oligosaccharide fractions of human colostrum and breast milk. *J. Infect. Dis.* 163(6):1247–55

Crittenden R, Playne MJ. 2009. Prebiotics. In *Handbook of Probiotics and Prebiotics*, ed. YK Lee, S Salminen, pp. 535–81. Hoboken, NJ: John Wiley Sons

Davis DT, Holt C, Christie WW. 1983. The Composition of Milk. In *Biochemistry of Lactation*, ed. TB Mepham, pp. 71–117. Amsterdam-New York: Elsevier

Devaraj N, Sheykhnazari M, Warren WS, Bhavanandan VP. 1994. Differential binding of *Pseudomonas aeruginosa* to normal and cystic fibrosis tracheobronchial mucins. *Glycobiology* 4:307–16

Eiwegger T, Stahl B, Haidl P, Schmitt J, Boehm G, et al. 2010. Prebiotic oligosaccharides: in vitro evidence for gastrointestinal epithelial transfer and immunomodulatory properties. *Pediatr. Allergy Immunol.* 21(8):1179–88

Eiwegger T, Stahl B, Schmitt J, Boehm G, Gerstmayr M, et al. 2004. Human milk–derived oligosaccharides and plant-derived oligosaccharides stimulate cytokine production of cord blood T-cells in vitro. *Pediatr. Res.* 56(4):536–40

Elsik CG, Tellam RL, Worley KC, Gibbs RA, Muzny DM, et al. 2009. The genome sequence of taurine cattle: a window to ruminant biology and evolution. *Science* 324:522–28

Engfer MB, Stahl B, Finke B, Sawatzki G, Daniel H. 2000. Human milk oligosaccharides are resistant to enzymatic hydrolysis in the upper gastrointestinal tract. *Am. J. Clin. Nutr.* 71:1589–96

Espinosa RM, Taméz M, Prieto P. 2007. Efforts to emulate human milk oligosaccharides. *Br. J. Nutr.* 98(Suppl 1):S74–79

Falony G, Lazidou K, Verschaeren A, Weckx S, Maes D, De Vuyst L. 2009. In vitro kinetic analysis of fermentation of prebiotic inulin-type fructans by bifidobacterium species reveals four different phenotypes. *Appl. Environ. Microbiol.* 75:454–61

Fanaro S, Boehm G, Garssen J, Knol J, Mosca F, et al. 2005a. Galacto-oligosaccharides and long-chain fructo-oligosaccharides as prebiotics in infant formulas: a review. *Acta Paediatr. Suppl.* 94(449):22–26

Fanaro S, Jelinek J, Stahl B, Boehm G, Kock R, Vigi V. 2005b. Acidic oligosaccharides from pectin hydrolysate as new component for infant formulae: effect on intestinal flora, stool characteristics, and pH. *J. Pediatr. Gastroenterol. Nutr.* 41:186–90

Favier CF, de Vos WM, Akkermans ADL. 2003. Development of bacterial and bifidobacterial communities in feces of newborn babies. *Anaerobe* 9:219–29

Gambaryan AS, Tuzikov AB, Piskarev VE, Yamnikova SS, Lvov DK, et al. 1997. Specification of receptor-binding phenotypes of influenza virus isolates from different hosts using synthetic sialylglycopolymers: non-egg-adapted human H1 and H3 influenza A and influenza B viruses share a common high binding affinity for 6′-sialyl(N-acetyllactosamine). *Virology* 232:345–50

Gauhe A, György P, Hoover JRE, Kuhn R, Rose CS, et al. 1954. Bifidus factor. IV. Preparations obtained from human milk. *Arch. Biochem. Biophys.* 48:214–24

German JB, Freeman SL, Lebrilla CB, Mills DA. 2008. Human milk oligosaccharides: evolution, structures and bioselectivity as substrates for intestinal bacteria. *Nestle Nutr. Workshop Ser. Pediatr. Program.* 62:205–18

Gnoth MJ, Kunz C, Kinne-Saffran E, Rudloff S. 2000. Human milk oligosaccharides are minimally digested in vitro. *J. Nutr.* 130:3014–20

Gnoth MJ, Rudloff S, Kunz C, Kinne RKH. 2001. Investigations of the in vitro transport of human milk oligosaccharides by a caco-2 monolayer using a novel high performance liquid chromatography-mass spectrometry technique. *J. Biol. Chem.* 276:34363–70

Gopal PK, Gill HS. 2000. Oligosaccharides and glycoconjugates in bovine milk and colostrum. *Br. J. Nutr.* 84(Suppl. 1):S69–74

Groschwitz KR, Ahrens R, Osterfeld H, Gurish MF, Han X, et al. 2009. Mast cells regulate homeostatic intestinal epithelial migration and barrier function by a chymase/Mcpt4-dependent mechanism. *Proc. Natl. Acad. Sci.* 106:22381–86

Guarner F. 2009. Prebiotics, probiotics and helminths: the "natural" solution? *Dig. Dis.* 27:412–17

Gyorgy P. 1953. A hitherto unrecognized biochemical difference between human milk and cow's milk. *Pediatrics* 11(2):98–108

Gyorgy P, Norris RF, Rose CS. 1954. Bifidus factor. I. A variant of *Lactobacillus bifidus* requiring a special growth factor. *Arch. Biochem. Biophys.* 48:193–201

Haarman M, Knol J. 2005. Quantitative real-time PCR assays to identify and quantify fecal bifidobacterium species in infants receiving a prebiotic infant formula. *Appl. Environ. Microbiol.* 71:2318–24

Harmsen HJM, Wildeboer-Veloo ACM, Raangs GC, Wagendorp AA, Klijn N, et al. 2000. Analysis of intestinal flora development in breast-fed and formula-fed infants by using molecular identification and detection methods. *J. Pediatr. Gastroenterol. Nutr.* 30:61–67

Hong P, Ninonuevo MR, Lee B, Lebrilla C, Bode L. 2009. Human milk oligosaccharides reduce HIV-1-gp120 binding to dendritic cell-specific ICAM3-grabbing nonintegrin (DC-SIGN). *Br. J. Nutr.* 101(4):482–86

Hoover JR, Braun GA, Gyorgy P. 1953. Neuraminic acid in mucopolysaccharides of human milk. *Arch. Biochem. Biophys.* 47(1):216–17

Idänpään-Heikkilä I, Simon PM, Zopf D, Vullo T, Cahill P, et al. 1997. Oligosaccharides interfere with the establishment and progression of experimental pneumococcal pneumonia. *J. Infect. Dis.* 176(3):704–12

Idota T, Kawakami H, Murakami Y, Sugawara M. 1995. Inhibition of cholera toxin by human milk fractions and sialyllactose. *Biosci. Biotechnol. Biochem.* 59(3):417–19

Kapiki A, Costalos C, Oikonomidou C, Triantafyllidou A, Loukatou E, Pertrohilou V. 2007. The effect of a fructo-oligosaccharide supplemented formula on gut flora of preterm infants. *Early Hum. Dev.* 83:335–39

Katayama T, Sakuma A, Kimura T, Makimura Y, Hiratake J, et al. 2004. Molecular cloning and characterization of *Bifidobacterium bifidum* 1,2-{alpha}-L-fucosidase (AfcA), a novel inverting glycosidase (glycoside hydrolase family 95). *J. Bacteriol.* 186:4885–93

Katayama T, Wada J, Fujita K, Kiyohara M, Ashida H, Yamamoto K. 2008. Functions of novel glycosidases isolated from bifidobacteria. *J. Appl. Glycosci.* 55:101–9

Kelder B, Erney R, Kopchick J, Cummings R, Prieto P. 2001. Glycoconjugates in human and transgenic animal milk. *Adv. Exp. Med. Biol.* 501:269–78

Kitaoka M, Tian J, Nishimoto M. 2005. Novel putative galactose operon involving lacto-N-biose phosphorylase in *Bifidobacterium longum*. *Appl. Environ. Microbiol.* 71:3158–62

Knol J, Boehm G, Lidestri M, Negretti F, Jelinek J, et al. 2005. Increase of faecal bifidobacteria due to dietary oligosaccharides induces a reduction of clinically relevant pathogen germs in the faeces of formula-fed preterm infants. *Acta Paediatr. Suppl.* 94(449):31–33

Kobata A. 1992. Structures and functions of the sugar chains of glycoproteins. *Eur. J. Biochem.* 209:483–501

Kobata A. 2003. Possible application of milk oligosaccharides for drug development. *Chang Gung Med J.* 26(9):621–36

Kobata A, Ginsburg V. 1969. Oligosaccharides of human milk. *J. Biol. Chem.* 244:5496–502

Koenig JE, Spor A, Scalfone N, Fricker AD, Stombaugh J, et al. 2010. Microbes and Health Sackler Colloquium: Succession of microbial consortia in the developing infant gut microbiome. *Proc. Natl. Acad. Sci. USA* In press.

Kuntz S, Kunz C, Rudloff S. 2009. Oligosaccharides from human milk induce growth arrest via G2/M by influencing growth-related cell cycle genes in intestinal epithelial cells. *Br. J. Nutr.* 101:1306–15

Kuntz S, Rudloff S, Kunz C. 2008. Oligosaccharides from human milk influence growth-related characteristics of intestinally transformed and non-transformed intestinal cells. *Br. J. Nutr.* 99:462–71

Kunz C, Rodriguez-Palmero M, Koletzko B, Jensen R. 1999. Nutritional and biochemical properties of human milk. Part I: general aspects, proteins, and carbohydrates. *Clin. Perinatol.* 26(2):307–33

Kunz C, Rudloff S. 1993. Biological functions of oligosaccharides in human milk. *Acta Paediatr.* 82(11):903–12

Kunz C, Rudloff S. 2008. Potential anti-inflammatory and anti-infectious effects of human milk oligosaccharides. *Adv. Exp. Med. Biol.* 606:455–66

Kunz C, Rudloff S, Baier W, Klein N, Strobel S. 2000. Oligosaccharides in human milk: structural, functional, and metabolic aspects. *Annu. Rev. Nutr.* 20:699–722

Kunz C, Rudloff S, Hintelmann A, Pohlentz G, Egge H. 1996. High-pH anion-exchange chromatography with pulsed amperometric detection and molar response factors of human milk oligosaccharides. *J. Chromatogr. B Biomed. Appl.* 685(2):211–21

Lane JA, Mehra RK, Carrington SD, Hickey RM. 2010. The food glycome: a source of protection against pathogen colonization in the gastrointestinal tract. *Int. J. Food Microbiol.* 142:1–13

Lara-Villoslada F, Debras E, Nieto A, Concha A, Gálvez J, et al. 2006. Oligosaccharides isolated from goat milk reduce intestinal inflammation in a rat model of dextran sodium sulfate-induced colitis. *Clin. Nutr.* 25:477–88

Lasky LA. 1995. Selectin-carbohydrate interactions and the initiation of the inflammatory response. *Annu. Rev. Biochem.* 64:113–40

Leach JL, Garber SA, Marcon AA, Prieto PA. 2005. In vitro and in vivo effects of soluble, monovalent globotriose on bacterial attachment and colonization. *Antimicrob. Agents Chemother.* 49:3842–46

Leo F, Asakuma S, Fukuda K, Senda A, Urashima T. 2010. Determination of sialyl and neutral oligosaccharide levels in transition and mature milks of Samoan women, using anthranilic derivatization followed by reverse phase high performance liquid chromatography. *Biosci. Biotechnol. Biochem.* 74(2):298–303

Lloyd KO, Burchell J, Kudryashov V, Yin BWT, Taylor-Papadimitriou J. 1996. Comparison of O-linked carbohydrate chains in MUC-1 mucin from normal breast epithelial cell lines and breast carcinoma cell lines. *J. Biol. Chem.* 271:33325–34

LoCascio RG, Desai P, Sela DA, Weimer B, Mills DA. 2010. Comparative genomic hybridization of Bifidobacterium longum strains reveals broad conservation of milk utilization genes in subsp. infantis. *Appl. Environ. Microbiol.* 76:7373–81

LoCascio RG, Ninonuevo M, Kronewitter S, Freeman SL, German JB, et al. 2009. A versatile and scalable strategy for glycoprofiling bifidobacterial consumption of human milk oligosaccharides. *Microb. Biotechnol.* 2333–42

LoCascio RG, Ninonuevo MR, Freeman SL, Sela DA, Grimm R, et al. 2007. Glycoprofiling of bifidobacterial consumption of human milk oligosaccharides demonstrates strain specific, preferential consumption of small chain glycans secreted in early human lactation. *J. Agric. Food Chem.* 55:8914–19

Macfarlane GT, Steed H, Macfarlane S. 2008. Bacterial metabolism and health-related effects of galacto-oligosaccharides and other prebiotics. *J. Appl. Microbiol.* 104:305–44

Manning TS, Gibson GR. 2004. Prebiotics. *Best Pract. Res. Clin. Gastroenterol.* 18:287–98

Marcobal A, Barboza M, Froehlich JW, Block DE, German JB, et al. 2010. Consumption of human milk oligosaccharides by gut-related microbes. *J. Agric. Food Chem.* 58:5334–40

Mariat D, Firmesse O, Levenez F, Guimaraes V, Sokol H, et al. 2009. The firmicutes/bacteroidetes ratio of the human microbiota changes with age. *BMC Microbiol.* 9:123

Martín-Sosa S, Martín M-J, García-Pardo L-A, Hueso P. 2003. Sialyloligosaccharides in human and bovine milk and in infant formulas: variations with the progression of lactation. *J. Dairy Sci.* 86:52–59

Martín-Sosa S, Martín M-J, García-Pardo LA, Hueso P. 2004. Distribution of sialic acids in the milk of Spanish mothers of full term infants during lactation. *J. Pediatr. Gastroenterol. Nutr.* 39:499–503

Martinez-Ferez A, Rudloff S, Guadix A, Henkel CA, Pohlentz G, et al. 2006. Goats' milk as a natural source of lactose-derived oligosaccharides: isolation by membrane technology. *Int. Dairy J.* 16:173–81

Matrosovich MN, Gambaryan AS, Tuzikov AB, Byramova NE, Mochalova LV, et al. 1993. Probing of the receptor-binding sites of the H1 and H3 influenza A and influenza B virus hemagglutinins by synthetic and natural sialosides. *Virology* 196:111–21

McEver RP. 1994. Role of selectins in leukocyte adhesion to platelets and endothelium. *Ann. N. Y. Acad. Sci.* 714:185–89

McVeagh P, Miller JB. 1997. Human milk oligosaccharides: only the breast. *J. Paediatr. Child Health* 33(4):281–86

Mihatsch WA, Hoegel J, Pohlandt F. 2006. Prebiotic oligosaccharides reduce stool viscosity and accelerate gastrointestinal transport in preterm infants. *Acta Paediatrica* 95:843–48

Montserrat R-U, Alicia S-O. 2001. Oligosaccharides: application in infant food. *Early Hum. Dev.* 65:S43–52

Moro E. 1900. Morphologische und bakterogische untersuchungen uber die Dambakterien des Sauglings: die bacterium flora des normalen frauenmilch stuhls. *Jahb Kinderheilkd* 61:686–734

Morrow AL, Ruiz-Palacios GM, Altaye M, Jiang X, Lourdes Guerrero M, et al. 2004. Human milk oligosaccharides are associated with protection against diarrhea in breast-fed infants. *J. Pediatr.* 145:297–303

Morrow AL, Ruiz-Palacios GM, Jiang X, Newburg DS. 2005. Human-milk glycans that inhibit pathogen binding protect breast-feeding infants against infectious diarrhea. *J. Nutr.* 135:1304–7

Motil KJ. 2000. Infant feeding: a critical look at infant formulas. *Curr. Opin. Pediatr.* 12:469–76

Muthana S, Cao H, Chen X. 2009. Recent progress in chemical and chemoenzymatic synthesis of carbohydrates. *Curr. Opin. Chem. Biol.* 13:573–81

Mysore JV, Wigginton T, Simon PM, Zopf D, Heman-Ackah LM, Dubois A. 1999. Treatment of *Helicobacter pylori* infection in rhesus monkeys using a novel antiadhesion compound. *Gastroenterology* 117(6):1316–25

Nakamura N, Gaskins HR, Collier CT, Nava GM, Rai D, et al. 2009. Molecular ecological analysis of fecal bacterial populations from term infants fed formula supplemented with selected blends of prebiotics. *Appl. Environ. Microbiol.* 75:1121–28

Nakamura T, Kawase H, Kimura K, Watanabe Y, Ohtani M, et al. 2003. Concentrations of sialyloligosaccharides in bovine colostrum and milk during the prepartum and early lactation. *J. Dairy Sci.* 86:1315–20

Nakamura T, Urashima T. 2004. The milk oligosaccharides of domestic farm animals. *Trends Glycosci. Glycotechnol.* 16:135–42

Neeser J-R, Golliard M, Del Vedovo S. 1991. Quantitative determination of complex carbohydrates in bovine milk and in milk-based infant formulas. *J. Dairy Sci.* 74:2860–71

Newburg DS. 1997. Do the binding properties of oligosaccharides in milk protect human infants from gastrointestinal bacteria? *J. Nutr.* 127:980S–84

Newburg DS. 1999. Human milk glycoconjugates that inhibit pathogens. *Curr. Med. Chem.* 6(2):117–27

Newburg DS. 2000. Are all human milks created equal? Variation in human milk oligosaccharides. *J. Pediatr. Gastroenterol. Nutr.* 30(2):131–33

Newburg DS. 2005. Innate immunity and human milk. *J. Nutr.* 135:1308–12

Newburg DS. 2009. Neonatal protection by an innate immune system of human milk consisting of oligosaccharides and glycans. *J. Anim. Sci.* 87:26–34

Newburg DS, Pickering LK, McCluer RH, Cleary TG. 1990. Fucosylated oligosaccharides of human milk protect suckling mice from heat-stabile enterotoxin of *Escherichia coli*. *J. Infect. Dis.* 162(5):1075–80

Newburg DS, Ruiz-Palacios GM, Altaye M, Chaturvedi P, Meinzen-Derr J, et al. 2004a. Innate protection conferred by fucosylated oligosaccharides of human milk against diarrhea in breastfed infants. *Glycobiology* 14:253–63

Newburg DS, Ruiz-Palacios GM, Altaye M, Chaturvedi P, Guerrero ML, et al. 2004b. Human milk alphal,2-linked fucosylated oligosaccharides decrease risk of diarrhea due to stable toxin of *E. coli* in breastfed infants. *Adv. Exp. Med. Biol.* 554:457–61

Newburg DS, Ruiz-Palacios GM, Morrow AL. 2005. Human milk glycans protect infants against enteric pathogens. *Annu. Rev. Nutr.* 25:37–58

Niñonuevo MR, Lebrilla CB. 2009. Mass spectrometric methods for analysis of oligosaccharides in human milk. *Nutr. Rev.* 67:S216–S26

Ninonuevo MR, Park Y, Yin H, Zhang J, Ward RE, et al. 2006. A strategy for annotating the human milk glycome. *J. Agric. Food Chem.* 54:7471–80

Ninonuevo MR, Perkins PD, Francis J, Lamotte LM, LoCascio RG, et al. 2008. Daily variations in oligosaccharides of human milk determined by microfluidic chips and mass spectrometry. *J. Agric. Food Chem.* 56:618–26

Nishimoto M, Kitaoka M. 2007a. Identification of N-acetylhexosamine 1-kinase in the complete lacto-N-biose I/galacto-N-biose metabolic pathway in *Bifidobacterium longum*. *Appl. Environ. Microbiol.* 73:6444–49

Nishimoto M, Kitaoka M. 2007b. Identification of the putative proton donor residue of lacto-N-biose phosphorylase (EC 2.4.1.211). *Biosci. Biotechnol. Biochem.* 71:1587–91

Ogawa K, Ben RA, Pons S, de Paulo MI, Bustos Fernández L. 1992. Volatile fatty acids, lactic acid, and pH in the stools of breast-fed and bottle-fed infants. *J. Pediatr. Gastroenterol. Nutr.* 15:248–52

Palmer C, Bik EM, DiGiulio DB, Relman DA, Brown PO. 2007. Development of the human infant intestinal microbiota. *PLoS Biol.* 5:e177

Parente F, Cucino C, Anderloni A, Grandinetti G, Porro GB. 2003. Treatment of *Helicobacter pylori* infection using a novel antiadhesion compound (3′sialyllactose sodium salt). A double blind, placebo-controlled clinical study. *Helicobacter* 8:252–56

Park A-R, Oh D-K. 2010. Galacto-oligosaccharide production using microbial β-galactosidase: current state and perspectives. *Appl. Microbiol. Biotechnol.* 85:1279–86

Penders J, Thijs C, Vink C, Stelma FF, Snijders B, et al. 2006. Factors influencing the composition of the intestinal microbiota in early infancy. *Pediatrics* 118:511–21

Petschow BW, Talbott RD. 1991. Response of bifidobacterium species to growth promoters in human and cow milk. *Pediatr. Res.* 29(2):208–13

Podolsky DK. 1985. Oligosaccharide structures of human colonic mucin. *J. Biol. Chem.* 260:8262–71

Rinne MM, Gueimonde M, Kalliomäki M, Hoppu U, Salminen SJ, Isolauri E. 2005. Similar bifidogenic effects of prebiotic-supplemented partially hydrolyzed infant formula and breastfeeding on infant gut microbiota. *FEMS Immunol. Med. Microbiol.* 43:59–65

Roberfroid MB. 2005. Introducing inulin-type fructans. *Br. J. Nutr.* 93(Suppl. 1):S13–25

Rubaltelli FF, Biadaioli R, Pecile P, Nicoletti P. 1998. Intestinal flora in breast- and bottle-fed infants. *J. Perinat. Med.* 26(3):186–91

Rudloff S, Obermeier S, Borsch C, Pohlentz G, Hartmann R, et al. 2006. Incorporation of orally applied 13C-galactose into milk lactose and oligosaccharides. *Glycobiology* 16:477–87

Ruiz-Palacios GM, Cervantes LE, Ramos P, Chavez-Munguia B, Newburg DS. 2003. *Campylobacter jejuni* binds intestinal H(O) antigen (Fucα1, 2Galβ1, 4GlcNAc), and fucosyloligosaccharides of human milk inhibit its binding and infection. *J. Biol. Chem.* 278:14112–20

Ruvoën-Clouet N, Mas E, Marionneau S, Guillon P, Lombardo D, Le Pendu J. 2006. Bile-salt-stimulated lipase and mucins from milk of "secretor" mothers inhibit the binding of Norwalk virus capsids to their carbohydrate ligands. *Biochem. J.* 393:627–34

Saito T, Itoh T, Adachi S. 1984. Presence of two neutral disaccharides containing N-acetylhexosamine in bovine colostrum as free forms. *Bioch. Biophys. Acta (BBA): Gen. Subj.* 801:147–50

Sánchez-Díaz A, Ruano M-J, Lorente F, Hueso P. 1997. A critical analysis of total sialic acid and sialoglycoconjugate contents of bovine milk–based infant formulas. *J. Pediatr. Gastroenterol. Nutr.* 24:405–10

Sarney DB, Hale C, Frankel G, Vulfson EN. 2000. A novel approach to the recovery of biologically active oligosaccharides from milk using a combination of enzymatic treatment and nanofiltration. *Biotechnol. Bioeng.* 69:461–67

Schumacher G, Bendas G, Stahl B, Beermann C. 2006. Human milk oligosaccharides affect P-selectin binding capacities: in vitro investigation. *Nutrition* 22:620–27

Schwertmann A, Rudloff S, Kunz C. 1996. Potential ligands for cell adhesion molecules in human milk. *Ann. Nutr. Metab.* 40(5):252–62

Sela DA, Chapman J, Adeuya A, Kim JH, Chen F, et al. 2008. The genome sequence of *Bifidobacterium longum* subsp. *infantis* reveals adaptations for milk utilization within the infant microbiome. *Proc. Natl. Acad. Sci. USA* 105:18964–69

Sela DA, Mills DA. 2010. Nursing our microbiota: molecular linkages between bifidobacteria and milk oligosaccharides. *Trends Microbiol.* 18:298–307

Shen Z, Warren CD, Newburg DS. 2000. High-performance capillary electrophoresis of sialylated oligosaccharides of human milk. *Anal. Biochem.* 279:37–45

Sherman PM, Cabana M, Gibson GR, Koletzko BV, Neu J, et al. 2009. Potential roles and clinical utility of prebiotics in newborns, infants, and children: proceedings from a global prebiotic summit meeting, New York City, June 27–28, 2008. *J. Pediatr.* 155:S61–70

Shoaf K, Mulvey GL, Armstrong GD, Hutkins RW. 2006. Prebiotic galactooligosaccharides reduce adherence of enteropathogenic *Escherichia coli* to tissue culture cells. *Infect. Immun.* 74:6920–28

Song J-F, Weng M-Q, Wu S-M, Xia Q-C. 2002. Analysis of neutral saccharides in human milk derivatized with 2-aminoacridone by capillary electrophoresis with laser-induced fluorescence detection. *Anal. Biochem.* 304:126–29

Stehle T, Yan Y, Benjamin TL, Harrison SC. 1994. Structure of murine polyomavirus complexed with an oligosaccharide receptor fragment. *Nature* 369(6476):160–63

Suzuki R, Wada J, Katayama T, Fushinobu S, Wakagi T, et al. 2008. Structural and thermodynamic analyses of solute-binding protein from *Bifidobacterium longum* specific for core 1 disaccharide and lacto-N-biose I. *J. Biol. Chem.* 283:13165–73

Tao N, DePeters EJ, Freeman S, German JB, Grimm R, Lebrilla CB. 2008. Bovine milk glycome. *J. Dairy Sci.* 91:3768–78

Tao N, DePeters EJ, German JB, Grimm R, Lebrilla CB. 2009. Variations in bovine milk oligosaccharides during early and middle lactation stages analyzed by high-performance liquid chromatography-chip/mass spectrometry. *J. Dairy Sci.* 92:2991–3001

Taylor SN, Basile LA, Ebeling M, Wagner CL. 2009. Intestinal permeability in preterm infants by feeding type: mother's milk versus formula. *Breastfeed. Med.* 4:11–15

Terrazas LI, Walsh KL, Piskorska D, McGuire E, Harn DA Jr. 2001. The schistosome oligosaccharide lacto-N-neotetraose expands Gr1+ cells that secrete anti-inflammatory cytokines and inhibit proliferation of naive CD4+ cells: a potential mechanism for immune polarization in helminth infections. *J. Immunol.* 167:5294–303

Thurl S, Henker J, Siegel M, Tovar K, Sawatzki G. 1997. Detection of four human milk groups with respect to Lewis blood group dependent oligosaccharides. *Glycoconj. J.* 14:795–99

Thurl S, Müller-Werner B, Sawatzki G. 1996. Quantification of individual oligosaccharide compounds from human milk using high-pH anion-exchange chromatography. *Anal. Biochem.* 235:202–6

Tissier H. 1900. *Recherches sur la Flore Intestinale des Nourrissons*. Paris: Univ. Paris

Turnbaugh PJ, Ley RE, Mahowald MA, Magrini V, Mardis ER, Gordon JI. 2006. An obesity-associated gut microbiome with increased capacity for energy harvest. *Nature* 444:1027–31

Urashima T, Saito T, Nakamura T, Messer M. 2001. Oligosaccharides of milk and colostrum in non-human mammals. *Glycoconj. J.* 18:357–71

Urashima T, Saito T, Ohmisya K, Shimazaki K. 1991. Structural determination of three neutral oligosaccharides in bovine (Holstein-Friesian) colostrum, including the novel trisaccharide; GalNAc alpha 1–3Gal beta 1–4Glc. *Biochim. Biophys. Acta* 1073(1):225–29

Van Laere KMJ, Abee T, Schols HA, Beldman G, Voragen AGJ. 2000. Characterization of a novel beta-galactosidase from *Bifidobacterium adolescentis* DSM 20083 active towards transgalactooligosaccharides. *Appl. Environ. Microbiol.* 66:1379–84

Velupillai P, Harn DA. 1994. Oligosaccharide-specific induction of interleukin 10 production by B220+ cells from schistosome-infected mice: a mechanism for regulation of CD4+ T-cell subsets. *Proc. Natl. Acad. Sci. USA* 91(1):18–22

Virkola R, Parkkinen J, Hacker J, Korhonen TK. 1993. Sialyloligosaccharide chains of laminin as an extracellular matrix target for S fimbriae of *Escherichia coli*. *Infect. Immun.* 61:4480–84

Vos AP, M'Rabet L, Stahl B, Boehm G, Garssen J. 2007. Immune-modulatory effects and potential working mechanisms of orally applied nondigestible carbohydrates. *Crit. Rev. Immunol.* 27(2):97–140

Wada J, Ando T, Kiyohara M, Ashida H, Kitaoka M, et al. 2008. *Bifidobacterium bifidum* lacto-N-biosidase, a critical enzyme for the degradation of human milk oligosaccharides with a type 1 structure. *Appl. Environ. Microbiol.* 74:3996–4004

Wada J, Suzuki R, Fushinobu S, Kitaoka M, Wakagi T, et al. 2007. Purification, crystallization and preliminary X-ray analysis of the galacto-N-biose-/lacto-N-biose I-binding protein (GL-BP) of the ABC transporter from *Bifidobacterium longum* JCM1217. *Acta Crystallogr. Sect. F Struct. Biol. Cryst. Commun.* 63(Pt 9):751–53

Wang B, Brand-Miller J. 2003. The role and potential of sialic acid in human nutrition. *Eur. J. Clin. Nutr.* 57:1351–69

Wang B, Brand-Miller J, McVeagh P, Petocz P. 2001. Concentration and distribution of sialic acid in human milk and infant formulas. *Am. J. Clin. Nutr.* 74:510–15

Ward RE, Ninonuevo M, Mills DA, Lebrilla CB, German JB. 2006. In vitro fermentation of breast milk oligosaccharides by *Bifidobacterium infantis* and *Lactobacillus gasseri*. *Appl. Environ. Microbiol.* 72:4497–99

Ward RE, Niñonuevo M, Mills DA, Lebrilla CB, German JB. 2007. In vitro fermentability of human milk oligosaccharides by several strains of bifidobacteria. *Mol. Nutr. Food Res.* 51:1398–405

WHO. 2009. Infant and young child feeding: model chapter for textbooks for medical students and allied health professionals. pp. 1–111

Wiederschain GY, Newburg DS. 1996. Compartmentalization of fucosyltransferase and alpha-L-fucosidase in human milk. *Biochem. Mol. Med.* 58:211–20

Wu S, Tao N, German JB, Grimm R, Lebrilla CB. 2010. Development of an annotated library of neutral human milk oligosaccharides. *J Proteome Res* 9:4138–51

Wu TC, Chen PH. 2009. Health consequences of nutrition in childhood and early infancy. *Pediatr. Neonatol.* 50:135–42

Xiao J-Z, Takahashi S, Nishimoto M, Odamaki T, Yaeshima T, et al. 2010. Distribution of in vitro fermentation ability of lacto-N-biose I, a major building block of human milk oligosaccharides, in bifidobacterial strains. *Appl. Environ. Microbiol.* 76:54–59

Zopf D, Roth S. 1996. Oligosaccharide anti-infective agents. *Lancet* 347(9007):1017–21

The Impact of Omic Technologies on the Study of Food Microbes

Sarah O'Flaherty[1] and Todd R. Klaenhammer[1,*]

[1]Department of Food, Bioprocessing and Nutrition Sciences, North Carolina State University, Raleigh, North Carolina 27695; email: klaenhammer@ncsu.edu

Annu. Rev. Food Sci. Technol. 2011. 2:353–71

First published online as a Review in Advance on December 3, 2010

The *Annual Review of Food Science and Technology* is online at food.annualreviews.org

This article's doi:
10.1146/annurev-food-030810-110338

1941-1413/11/0410-0353$20.00

*Corresponding author.

Keywords

sequencing, genome, probiotic, pathogen, microbiome, transcriptome

Abstract

The advent of the molecular biology era in the 1950s and the subsequent emergence of new technologies positively impacted on all areas of biology. New discoveries in molecular biology and experimental tools were developed over the next 60 years that have revolutionized the study of food microbiology. Previously, food microbiology relied on classic microbiology techniques, which had remained relatively unchanged since the discoveries of Louis Pasteur in the 1800s. More recently, new advances resulting in "omic" technologies have exploded the areas of genomics, transcriptomics, and proteomics and revealed many fundamental processes driven by both pathogens and commensals. This review outlines advances in omic technologies and how these have impacted food microbiology through providing examples of recently published landmark work.

INTRODUCTION

Superorganism: humans can be classed as superorganisms because of their symbiotic relationships with associated microbiota

Probiotic: live microorganisms that, when administered in adequate amounts, confer a health benefit on the host

More than thirty years after the introduction of Sanger DNA sequencing, omic technologies have accelerated our knowledge and understanding of food microbes. Over the past five years, there has been an explosive realization of the microbial world around and within us. In fact, the human is now considered a superorganism because of its intimate associations with its massive microbiota (Gill et al. 2006). Because foods provide both nutrients and often a favorable environment for growth, contamination by pathogenic and spoilage microbes continues to be a major concern. Many food groups, notably fermented foods including cheese, yogurt, sausage, beer, and wine, would not exist without the microbes that are responsible for their preservation. Other food microbes, such as probiotic bacteria, are intentionally added for their beneficial attributes. Additionally, the possibility of the delivery of therapeutics through food using beneficial microbes is an exciting development. These recent advances in particular have been due to the developments in omic technologies.

The discoveries of polymerase chain reaction (PCR) and DNA sequencing were pinnacle advancements that impacted biology and hence food microbiology (**Figure 1**). The importance and relevance of PCR in particular are in part due to subsequent improvements and modifications to adapt the method to important aspects of study, from whole genome sequencing to rapid detection of pathogens to unequivocal phylogenetic identification. Since the genome sequencing of the free living organism *Haemophilus influenzae* in 1995 (Fleischmann et al. 1995), the human genome has been sequenced numerous times as well as the genomes of other animals and thousands of microbes (**http://www.ncbi.nlm.nih.gov**). These advances in genome sequencing coupled with other omic technologies such as proteomics and transcriptomics have revolutionized food microbiology, helping us to understand our desirable and undesirable microbial worlds. Omic technologies have been reviewed extensively elsewhere, but herein we highlight recent developments that have exploited omic technologies to significantly advance our knowledge of food microbes.

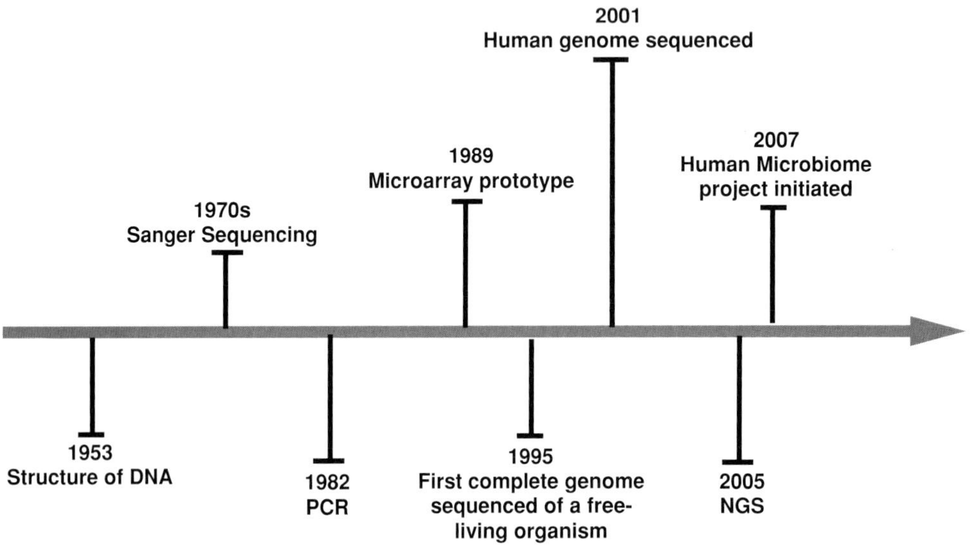

Figure 1

Timeline of important advances in omic-related technologies that impact food microbes.

IMPACT OF WHOLE GENOME AND NEXT GENERATION SEQUENCING TECHNOLOGIES ON FOOD MICROBES

Sanger sequencing, first described in the mid-1970s and long the method of choice for sequencing (Sanger et al. 1977), was improved by the emergence of new technologies that facilitated automated DNA sequencers (Edwards et al. 1990).

NGS: next generation sequencing

Less than 25 years after Sanger sequencing was introduced, the human genome was determined (Venter et al. 2001). Following the human genome sequencing project, it was evident that advances in sequencing technology were required to handle larger sequence output. This realization led to new novel sequencing techniques and ultimately the era of next generation sequencing (NGS). Presently, there are three main NGS technologies (**Table 1**; for details, see Ansorge 2009 and Pettersson et al. 2009). Unlike Sanger sequencing, NGS technologies do not require the cloning of template DNA into vectors but rather the DNA template is fragmented, amplified by PCR, and subsequently sequenced. Additionally, in some platforms millions of reactions take place simultaneously, thereby providing high throughput and large datasets. These large datasets, particularly of short reads, required the development of algorithms for sequence assembly. Sequencing both ends from the DNA fragment, termed pair-end sequencing, also aids in sequence assembly and is utilized by most of the commercial NSG technologies. The Roche 454 Genome Sequencer technology is based on sequencing by synthesis via pyrophosphate detection. Illumina acquired the Solexa sequencing technology in 2007, which is based on sequencing by synthesis chemistry with reversible terminator nucleotides each labeled with a different fluorescent dye. The third system is the ABI SOLiD sequencing platform, which is based on sequential ligation with dye-labeled oligonucleotides (Ansorge 2009, Pettersson et al. 2009). All three companies are constantly improving their technology to result in higher throughputs, longer read lengths, and lower costs.

More recently, advances in nanotechnology have enabled sequencing of a single molecule without the need for PCR amplification. Benefits of this system include reduction of reagents required and the omission of possible sequence bias introduced by PCR amplification. One such system is the Helicos platform, which does not require amplification of the DNA template but sequences single template molecules (Milos 2008). Additional technology in the pipeline is real-time DNA sequencing using single DNA polymerase molecules theoretically resulting in read lengths greater than 1,000 bp (Eid et al. 2009) and DNA nanoarray sequencing (Drmanac et al. 2010). These initiatives will further continue to benefit the study of food microbes, as they will allow for lower costs, larger datasets, and analyses that are not currently available.

Table 1 Details of current commercially available next generation sequencing (NGS) technologies

Manufacturer	Roche Applied Science	Illumina	Applied Biosystems
Next generation sequencer	454 GenomeSequencer	Genome Analyzer	ABI SOLiD System
Year of commercialization	2005	2006	2007
Platform	Pyrosequencing	Reversible terminator chemistry	Ligation chemistry
Latest model	Genome Sequencer FLX Titanium	Genome Analyzer IIx	5500xl SOLiD
Read length	~400–500 bp	~35–150 bp	~35–75 bp
Web site	**http://www.454.com**	**http://www.illumina.com**	**http://www.appliedbiosystems.com**

High-Throughput Sequencing of the 16S rRNA Gene and Metagenomics

IBD: inflammatory bowel disease

Sequencing the 16S ribosomal RNA (16S rRNA) gene as a means to distinguish between species is a powerful tool when coupled with the development of high-throughput sequencing methods. This allows for the assessment of bacterial diversity in a wide range of communities and environmental niches within a short period of time. In fact, omic technology, through high-throughput sequencing of 16S rRNA, has enabled the identification of new candidate beneficial microbes that, after further study and analysis, may be potential probiotic bacteria. One example is the description of *Faecalibacterium prausnitzii*, a member of the *Clostridium leptum* phylogenetic group. It was noted in the ileocolonic mucosa-associated microbiota of inflammatory bowel disease (IBD) patients by 16S rRNA sequencing (Frank et al. 2007, Manichanh et al. 2006) and PCR-denaturing gradient gel electrophoresis (PCR-DGGE) of 16S rRNA gene fragments that the numbers of *F. prausnitzii* were reduced in IBD patients (Martinez-Medina et al. 2006). Sokol et al. (2008) subsequently observed that the proportion of *F. prausnitzii* was lower in patients that showed endoscopic recurrence six months after surgical resection for active Crohns disease (CD). Following these observations, this group hypothesized that administrating this bacterium could be beneficial as a probiotic to ameliorate intestinal inflammation in CD. In vitro work demonstrated antiinflammatory effects by *F. prausnitzii* in peripheral blood mononuclear cells and *F. prausnitzii* supernatant-reduced secretion of the proinflammatory cytokine interleukin-8 (IL-8) by Caco-2 cells (Sokol et al. 2008). Additionally, both *F. prausnitzii* cells and culture supernatant-increased secretion of the antiinflammatory cytokine IL-10 decreased secretion of the proinflammatory tumor necrosis factor-alpha (TNF-α) and more importantly reduced the severity of trinitrobenzene sulfonic acid (TNBS)-induced colitis in mice (Sokol et al. 2008). The identification of this microbe as a candidate probiotic may not have been realized without high-throughput sequencing of the 16S rRNA gene of the mucosa-associated microbiota of Crohn's patients.

There is a growing body of evidence that probiotic bacteria may play a role in amelioration of inflammatory diseases (Grangette et al. 2005, Sartor 2005). The effects of probiotic and pathogenic bacteria on the gut microbiota can be facilitated by high-throughput sequencing. As a consequence of omic technologies and the ability to sequence vast amounts of 16S rRNA, a high density array termed the PhyloChip was created, which identifies approximately 8,500 bacterial taxa in a single experiment (Brodie et al. 2006). This chip has been utilized for numerous applications, such as the determination of bacterial diversity in air (Brodie et al. 2007) and within aspirates from intubated patients colonized by *Pseudomonas aeruginosa* (Flanagan et al. 2007). The technology was also applied to a recent study to analyze the effect of the probiotic bacterium *Lactobacillus casei* subsp. *rhamnosus* GG (LGG) on the composition of the infant microbiome (Cox et al. 2010). Previous studies with LGG administration during infancy of children at high risk of atopic disease resulted in reduced rates (Kalliomaki et al. 2001, 2003). This study determined bacterial diversity in infants at six months that had either high or low abundance of LGG (Cox et al. 2010). The infants were part of a larger study and had received LGG or a placebo daily from birth (Cabana et al. 2007). The results indicated that samples with a high LGG abundance demonstrated a distinct microbial community structure that included phylogenetically clustered and closely related taxa such as other probiotic bacteria (Cox et al. 2010). It was suggested that the beneficial effect of this probiotic bacterium was not only due to its presence in high numbers but also to the changes in the community structure when it was present in high abundance (Cox et al. 2010). In addition, high abundance of LGG supported the presence of other species like itself, which may also contribute toward beneficial effects of probiotic bacteria administered continuously at high numbers.

There are limits to 16S rRNA sequencing. The 16S rRNA gene is highly conserved, therefore it can be difficult to distinguish between closely related species and strains within species using 16S rRNA sequencing. Metagenomics is one method that overcomes this by sequencing all the nucleic acids directly from a sample and is, therefore, not restricted to the 16S rRNA gene. In addition to sequencing individual strains, one of the main outcomes of high-throughput sequencing has been the emergence of metagenomics. Although this technology was originally applied to environmental biology, in the past five years new information has been established in regard to our microbiome and relationship of the human microbiome and diet. By using NGS technology, the microbiome has been determined for humans from different ethnicities (Li et al. 2008), geographical areas (Kurokawa et al. 2007, Qin et al. 2010), and ages (Claesson et al. 2010). However, additional studies like those described above by Cox et al. (2010) relating to the effect of food microbes and food on the microbiome are needed.

Metagenomics: the global genetic content of microbes within a niche such as the soil or the gastrointestinal tract

Comparative genomics: comparison of the genetic repertoire of two or more genome sequences

Impact of Whole Genome Sequencing and Comparative Genomics

Sequencing technologies have had a profound effect on food microbiology from the detection of pathogens, identification of beneficial microbes, and whole genome sequencing. Advances in sequencing technology are evident by the number of strains that are currently sequenced or in progress (**Table 2**), demonstrating the lower cost and fast turnaround time of sequencing with current technologies. Interestingly, but not surprisingly, is the fact that the number of strains with sequencing "in progress" related to foodborne pathogens in particular outnumbers the amount of currently available finished genome sequences (**Figure 2**).

Comparison of one or more complete genomes termed comparative genomics has also revealed relationships between important industrial food microbes. It was known before genome sequencing of *Streptococcus thermophilus* and *Lactobacillus delbrueckii* subsp. *bulgaricus* that these microbes have a cooperative relationship termed protocooperation in milk fermentations. Whole genome sequencing of *S. thermophilus* and *L. bulgaricus* revealed insights into their cooperation in milk fermentation through in silico analysis of their genomes (Bolotin et al. 2004, van de Guchte et al. 2006). Analysis of the *L. bulgaricus* genome sequence revealed the gene for the extracellular cell wall–bound proteinase, PrtB, (which was known before whole genome sequencing) and genes for the biosynthesis of folate. *S. thermophilus* also encodes genes necessary for the biosynthesis of folate but additionally encodes the genes necessary for *p*-aminobenzoic acid, which feeds into the folate pathway. It is believed that when cocultured with *S. thermophilus* in yogurt fermentation, *L. bulgaricus* benefits from *p*-aminobenzoic acid synthesis (van de Guchte et al. 2006). A recent study using comparative genomics of both genomes predicted genes acquired by horizontal gene transfer for both species, which included the transfer of genes for the metabolism of sulfur-containing amino acids from *L. bulgaricus* (or *Lactobacillus helveticus*) to *S. thermophilus* and the transfer of an exopolysaccaride biosynthesis gene cassette from *S. thermophilus* to *L. bulgaricus* (Liu et al. 2009b). Analysis also indicated the evolution of *L. bulgaricus* from a plant-associated environment to the milk environment through protocooperation with *S. thermophilus* and loss of genes related to a plant-associated niche (Liu et al. 2009b).

Lactic acid bacteria in particular have evolved to nutritionally rich niches, e.g., milk and the gastrointestinal tract. Genome sequencing has revealed that the majority of sequenced lactobacilli isolated from nutrient-rich habitats have gained genes encoding transporters for acquisition of exogenous nutrient sources as they lack complete biosynthetic pathways (Makarova et al. 2006). Although many probiotic lactobacilli have lost certain biosynthetic capabilities, they encode for crucial features that allow transit through, and survival in, the gastrointestinal tract, such as acid and bile tolerance. Adaptation of probiotic lactobacilli to life in the gastrointestinal tract is further evident when genome sequences are compared between the probiotic species *Lactobacillus acidophilus* and the cheese starter species *L. helveticus*. Although *L. acidophilus* and *L. helveticus* share 75%

Table 2 Details of food microbes with complete or in progress genome sequencing projects (http://www.ncbi.nlm.nih.gov/genomes/lproks.cgi, compiled August 2010)

Bacteria	Source	Number of strains sequenced (in progress)
Industrial/beneficial food microbes		
Bifidobacterium animalis subsp. *lactis*	Probiotic	3 (1)
Bifidobacterium longum	Probiotic	2 (2)
Lactobacillus acidophilus	Probiotic	1 (1)
Lactobacillus brevis	Starter culture	1
Lactobacillus casei	Probiotic/dairy starter culture	3
Lactobacillus delbrueckii subsp. *bulgaricus*	Dairy starter culture	2 (1)
Lactobacillus fermentum	Probiotic	1 (2)
Lactobacillus gasseri	Probiotic	1 (4)
Lactobacillus helveticus	Dairy starter culture	1 (1)
Lactobacillus johnsonii	Probiotic	1 (1)
Lactobacillus plantarum	Probiotic/vegetable starter culture	2 (1)
Lactobacillus reuteri	Probiotic	2 (5)
Lactobacillus rhamnosus	Probiotic	2 (2)
Lactobacillus sakei subsp. *sakei*	Meat starter culture	1
Lactobacillus salivarius	Probiotic	1 (1)
Lactococcus lactis subsp. *cremoris*	Dairy starter culture	2
Lactococcus lactis subsp. *lactis*	Dairy starter culture	2
Leuconostoc mesenteroides subsp. *mesenteroides*	Vegetable fermentation	1 (1)
Oenococcus oeni	Wine fermentation	1 (2)
Streptococcus thermophilus	Dairy starter culture	3
Foodborne pathogens		
Bacillus cereus	Meats, milk, cheese, vegetables, fish	9 (35)
Campylobacter jejuni	Raw beef, poultry, raw milk, eggs	5 (10)
Clostridium botulinum	Meats, fish, canned foods	10 (5)
Clostridium perfringens	Meats	3 (6)
Escherichia coli O157:H7	Ground beef, raw milk, vegetables	4 (15)
Listeria monocytogenes	Meats, poultry, milk, cheese, vegetables	6 (20)
Salmonella enterica subsp. *enterica*	Meats, poultry, eggs, milk	16 (23)
Shigella spp.	Vegetables, meat, poultry, milk, water	8 (38)
Vibrio cholerae	Shellfish and fish	8 (24)

of their ORFeome, there are important differences reflecting their adaptation to different niches. *L. acidophilus* encodes for numerous mucin-binding proteins and bile salt hydrolases, whereas none are encoded by *L. helveticus*. *L. helveticus* has additional genes for fatty acid biosynthesis and specific amino acid metabolism but notably fewer cell surface factors and transporters for utilization of multiple sugars beyond lactose (Altermann et al. 2005, Callanan et al. 2008).

ORFeome: the total number of open reading frames predicted in a genome

Comparative genomics between the genome sequences of the probiotic bacteria LGG and the dairy starter culture *L. rhamnosus* LC705 showed important differences in genome content relating to their environmental niche. These differences were suggested to explain longer colonization properties of LGG compared with *L. rhamnosus* LC705 in the human gastrointestinal

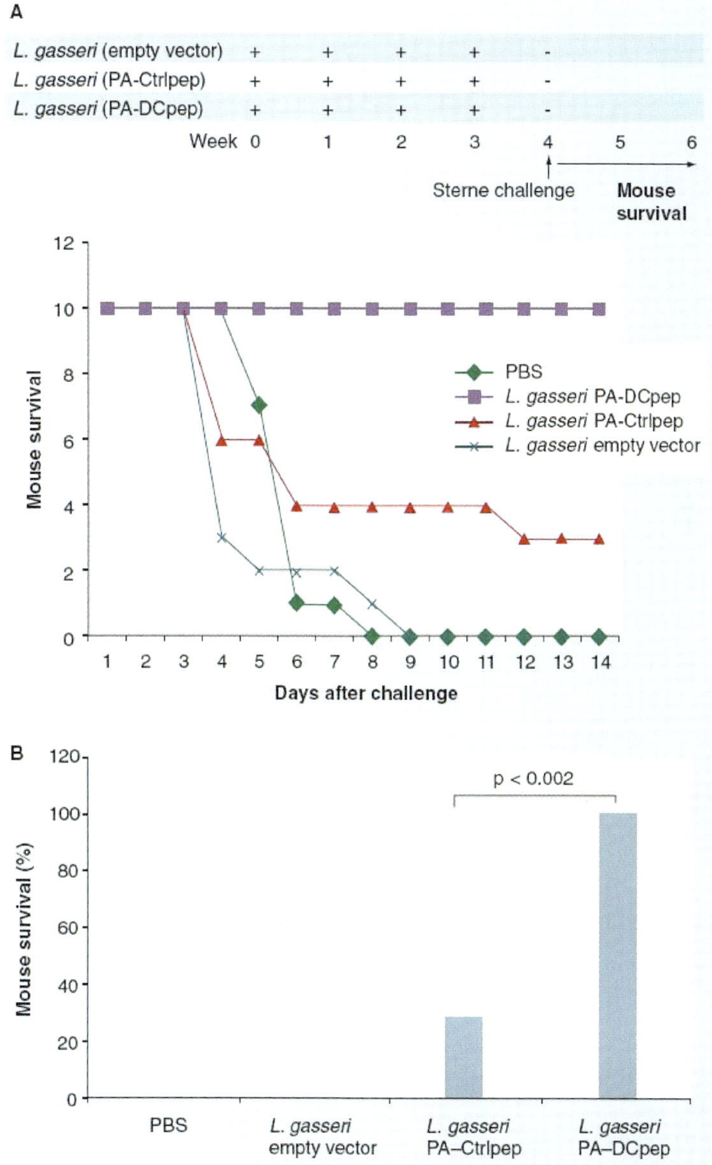

Figure 4

Induction of protective immunity against *Bacillus anthracis*. (*a*,*b*) Feeding and challenge regimen and mouse survival. Groups of mice (n = 10 per group) were orally vaccinated with *Lactobacillus gasseri* expressing PA–DCpep, PA–Ctrlpep, or empty vector (10^8 CFU/100 μl). Oral vaccination was repeated for four consecutive weeks. Seven days after the last vaccination, mice were challenged with Sterne, and mouse survival was monitored until day 14. Abbreviations: Ctrlpep, control peptide; DCpep, dendritic cell–targeting peptide; PA, protective antigen; PBS, phosphate buffered saline. Reproduced with permission from Mohamadzadeh et al. (2010).

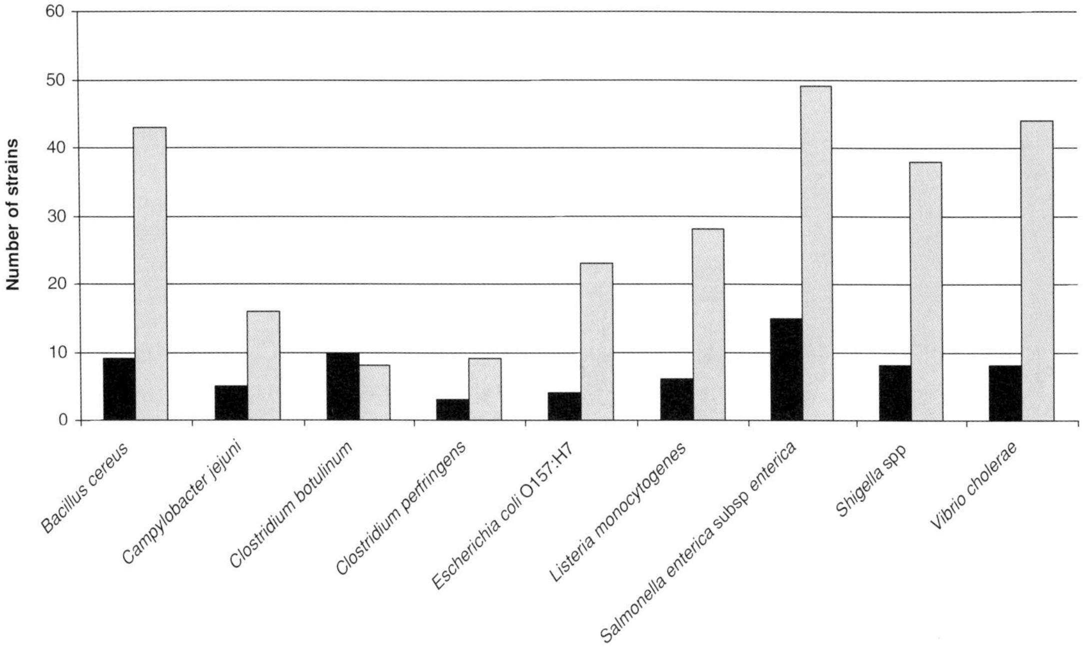

Figure 2

The impact of genome sequencing is demonstrated by the number of genome projects in progress (*gray bars*) and completed (*black bars*).

tract (Kankainen et al. 2009) and higher adherence rates to mucus (Tuomola et al. 2000) and epithelial cell lines (Jacobsen et al. 1999). These included the presence of pili on the cell wall of LGG and in silico analysis confirmed metabolic differences between the two strains that had been demonstrated experimentally. For example, compared with *L. rhamnosus* LC705, LGG is unable to ferment lactose, and in silico analysis revealed this was due to frameshifts in the antiterminator and 6-phospho-β-galactosidase genes (Kankainen et al. 2009). Sequencing of industrially important and beneficial food microbes has expanded our understanding of genome evolution and has also revealed the domestication of certain species toward specific environmental niches through genome reduction, gene decay, and acquisition of key capabilities through horizontal gene transfer (Douglas & Klaenhammer 2010).

Whole genome sequencing of food pathogens has revealed vital information on mechanisms of virulence and survival to better understand and ultimately control these microbes in food. New developments include the identification of virulence factors, mechanisms of survival in both foods and within host tissues, DNA sequences for rapid detection and identification, and antigenic and bacterial components that may serve as vaccines. For example, *Listeria monocytogenes* can survive and replicate in harsh environments such as low pH, high salt, and low temperature, which facilitates its survival in foods as these hurdles are often implemented to control food pathogens (Freitag et al. 2009). The first complete genome sequence of the foodborne pathogen *L. monocytogenes* was determined in 2001 (Glaser et al. 2001). Since then, five more strains have been sequenced and 28 more are in progress (**Table 2** and **Figure 2**). Comparative genomics of *L. monocytogenes* (Nelson et al. 2004) and the nonpathogenic *Listeria innocua* (Glaser et al. 2001), and four subsequently sequenced genomes of *L. monocytogenes* in 2004 revealed that genome organization is highly conserved among these strains. However, bile salt hydrolases, which contribute to survival of microbes in the gastrointestinal tract, were present in *L. monocytogenes*, but absent in *L. innocua* (Dussurget et al. 2002, Glaser et al. 2001). Genomic, proteomic, and transcriptomic comparisons of strains of different levels of pathogenicity will most certainly help determine the mechanisms by which pathogens survive in food and subsequently cause disease.

Pan genome: the total gene repertoire (core and dispensable genome) of a bacterial species

Genome sequencing and subsequent comparative genomics of pathogenic bacteria led to the description of the pan genome, which represents the total repertoire of genes for a bacterial species. The pan genome also encompasses accessory or dispensable genes unique to single strains and genes present in more than one strain (Medini et al. 2005). The pan genome is dynamic with the dispensable genome, in particular, increasing as more genomes are sequenced. Therefore, the pan genome can be orders of magnitude larger than the genome of a sequenced strain. The description of a pan genome has only become available through advances in omic technologies through sequencing of large numbers of genomes. Pan genomes are also described as open or closed (Medini et al. 2005). *Escherichia coli* and *Salmonella* are examples of food microbes with open pan genomes as they have opportunities for genetic exchange between species because of their environmental niche. The determination of pan genomes contributes to the genetic repertoire of a species or group and can identify important targets for vaccination, detection, and biotherapeutics.

MOLECULAR METHODS FOR IDENTIFYING FOOD MICROBES

As pathogens are undesirable food microbes, the ability to detect and identify them is an important area of research in food microbiology. Subsequently, with omic genetic techniques it is possible to rapidly detect strains and also determine evolutionary and virulence factors. In particular, the foodborne pathogens *L. monocytogenes*, *E. coli* O157:H7, and *Salmonella enterica* subsp. *enterica* have received much attention in this regard (Jasson et al. 2010). Molecular methods of bacterial identification have evolved over a relatively short period of time. DNA-DNA hybridization (Sibley & Ahlquist 1984) was initially used to differentiate between bacterial species. The introduction of PCR in the 1980s (Bartlett & Stirling 2003) revolutionized biology. Subsequently, numerous detection techniques have been developed that use PCR as a foundation, e.g., denaturing gradient gel electrophoresis, real-time PCR, terminal restriction fragment length polymorphism, and restriction fragment length polymorphism (described in Juste et al. 2008).

16S rRNA sequencing is one of the main methods of choice for species identification as the 16S RNA gene is ubiquitous in bacterial genomes and initial results correlated well with DNA-DNA hybridization (Keswani & Whitman 2001). Additionally, sequencing the 16S rRNA gene is a culture-independent method and can identify both live and dead cells. As 16S rRNA sequencing does not distinguish within species, multilocus enzyme electrophoresis (MLEE) was adapted from eukaryotic population genetics to distinguish subpopulations within species (Selander et al. 1986). Subsequently, multilocus sequence typing (MLST) was also utilized because of rapid advances in sequencing technologies (Maiden et al. 1998). Although sequencing large numbers of genomes within species revealed the limitations of these identification methods, they are still valued as a molecular tool in food microbiology.

Whole genome sequencing and microarrays have also been exploited for the identification of many food microbes. Large-scale whole genome sequencing through omic advances permitted the development of microarrays to detect 11 major foodborne pathogens based on probes that were identified through comparative genomics of sequenced genomes (Kim et al. 2008). The results demonstrated that pathogens hybridized to their respective probes, and the array could distinguish between nonpathogenic and pathogenic species. This combination of omic techniques and future advances will provide precise and fast identification of food pathogens, which is essential for their control.

A newer approach also adapted from use in humans and exploited as a consequence of advances in sequencing technology is examining single-nucleotide polymorphisms (SNPs) (Weissman et al. 2003). This method analyzes gene sequences for single nucleotide changes. In the case of *L. monocytogenes*, a successful SNP-based multilocus genotyping assay was developed for subtyping lineage I isolates, which are the main cause of listeriosis (Ducey et al. 2007). Recent studies demonstrated the power of SNP technology to identify clusters of *Salmonella enterica* subsp. *enterica* serovar Typhi, which causes typhoid in Nepalese children (Holt et al. 2010), and to differentiate closely related strains of bifidobacteria (Briczinski et al. 2009).

SNP: single-nucleotide polymorphism

Functional genomics: the determination of gene function using molecular methods

FUNCTIONAL GENOMICS AND BIOENGINEERING

The complete genome sequences of many food microbes classified as beneficial or harmful microbes have greatly facilitated functional genomic efforts to determine the function of one gene in a genome and the contribution of that gene product to the organism as a whole. In particular, methods are available to mutate, delete, or disrupt genes that potentially contribute to a particular attribute such as virulence (Sleator et al. 2005) or acid and bile tolerance (Begley et al. 2005, Klaenhammer et al. 2005). Additionally, once the sequence of a gene is known, it can be cloned and overexpressed in plasmid vectors, which is another method to confirm its phenotype.

Impact of Gene Inactivation and Deletion Systems on Food Microbes

Examples of gene deletions or insertions for food microbes have facilitated increased knowledge in a wide area of research, from pathogenesis to industrial microbes. For example, in the case of protocooperation between *S. thermophilus* and *L. bulgaricus*, deletion of the *prtS* gene from *S. thermophilus* demonstrated the necessity of this gene in cocultures and milk fermentations (Courtin et al. 2002). Functional genomics of probiotic bacteria have demonstrated the importance of numerous gene products in attributes such as bile tolerance, acid tolerance, adherence, and interactions with cells of the immune system, and in treatment of IBD (O'Flaherty & Klaenhammer 2010).

Functional genomics was instrumental in a study by Corr et al. (2007), which protected mice with the probiotic *Lactobacillus salivarius* UCC118 against infection with *L. monocytogenes*, in vivo. Protection was demonstrated as a result of a bacteroicin produced by *L. salivarius*. An isogenic mutant of *L. salivarius* UCC118 was constructed that could not produce the bacteriocin and failed to protect mice from *L. monocytogenes* infection (Corr et al. 2007). Notably, the bacteroicin-negative *L. salivarius* also protected mice from *Salmonella typhimurium*, indicating another mechanism of probiotic action for *L. salivarius* in addition to the production of a bacteriocin lethal to *L. monocytogenes*.

A recent example utilizing comparative and functional genomics was the discovery of a human mucus-binding pili protein in *L. rhamnosus* (Kankainen et al. 2009). Pili are found in many Gram-positive and Gram-negative pathogens (Kline et al. 2010), and their description in LGG indicated that probiotic and commensal microbes can employ shared strategies for survival in the gastrointestinal tract. A cluster of pilus-encoding genes (*spaCBA*) was discovered in LGG after comparative genomic analysis of the probiotic LGG genome and the closely related starter culture *L. rhamnosus* LC705 genome (Kankainen et al. 2009). Pilin proteins in Gram-positive bacteria contribute to adhesion to other bacteria and host cells (Kline et al. 2010). The presence of pili on the cell surface of LGG with the majority clustered at the cell poles was confirmed by immunogold electron microscopy (**Figure 3**). Subsequently, the *spaC* gene, which was predicted to encode for the large-sized minor pilin subunit, was inactivated using functional genomic methods. The *spaC*

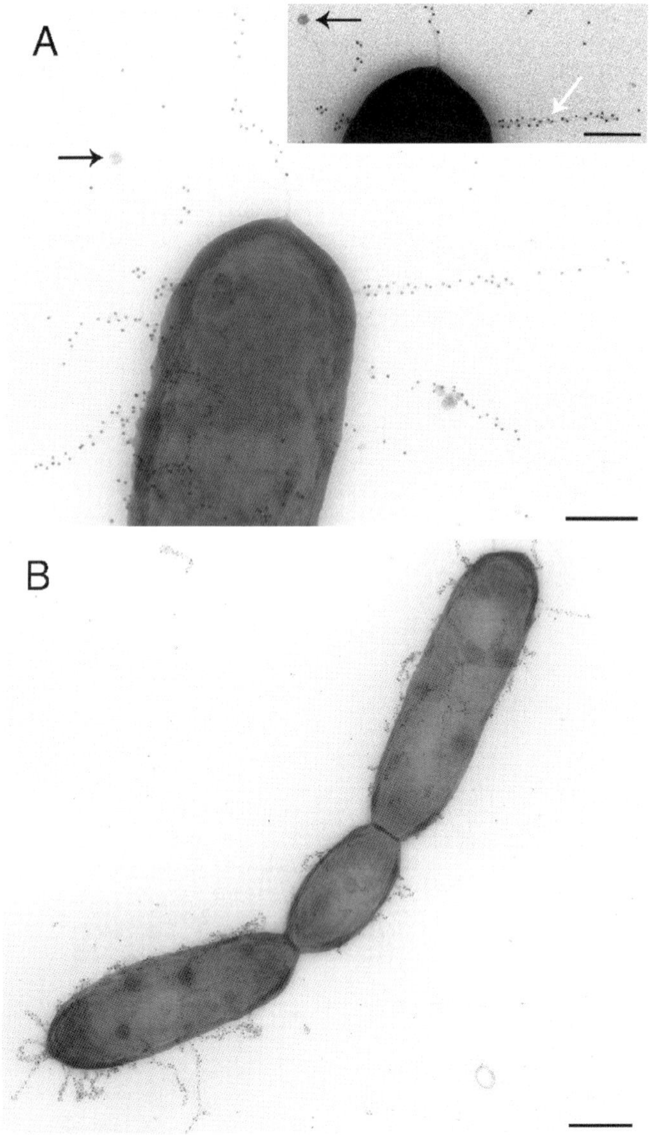

Figure 3

Identification of pili in *Lactobacillus rhamnosus* GG by immunogold electron microscopy. *L. rhamnosus* GG was grown to stationary phase, treated with anti-SpaC serum, labeled with protein A–conjugated gold particles (10 nm), negatively stained, and examined by transmission electron microscopy. (*a*) High-resolution electron micrograph showing multiple pili and an isometric bacteriophage (*black arrow*). Also included is a panel inset adjusted for heightened contrast and darkness to highlight the pilus ultrastructure (*white arrow*). (*b*) Electron micrograph showing pili clustered at the cell poles. (Bars: *a*, 200-nm; *b*, 500-nm.) Reproduced with permission from Kankainen et al. (2009).

mutant exhibited a significant reduction in binding to intestinal mucus (Kankainen et al. 2009). This study utilized comparative and functional genomics and proteomics to demonstrate the role of SpaC in mucin binding and potentially its importance to the survival of some lactobacilli in the gastrointestinal tract.

Using Food Microbes as Delivery Systems and Vaccines

Study of food pathogens such as *L. monocytogenes* has been used to investigate immune responses in antigen-presenting cells and T cells. Traditionally attenuated strains have been used for vaccination purposes. Both beneficial and pathogenic food-related bacteria are being harnessed as carriers of biotherapeutics and vaccines. *Salmonella* and *Listeria* are now being considered as candidates for delivery of antigens for cancer immunotherapy (Paterson et al. 2010). Moreover, the use of beneficial food microbes as delivery systems for different therapeutics and vaccine-type molecules was first pioneered by Wells & Mercenier (2008). One of the original systems employed for heterologous gene expression was the nisin-controlled gene expression system from *Lactococcus lactis* (Zhou et al. 2006). Numerous expression vectors were constructed for expression of the hepatitis B virus surface antigen (Zhang et al. 2010), the anti-*Listeria* agent pediocin (Renye & Somkuti 2010), and genes involved in stress tolerance (Abdullah Al et al. 2010).

The ability to express human IL-10 by *L. lactis* through omic techniques was a landmark development leading to a successful phase I clinical trial evaluating disease activity in CD patients (Braat et al. 2006). A genetically modified *L. lactis* strain was constructed that expressed the regulatory chemokine IL-10 in place of the thymidylate synthase gene *thyA* (Steidler et al. 2003). IL-10 is involved in suppressing inflammation at the gut mucosa by inhibiting proinflammatory cytokine synthesis and hence is a potential treatment for IBD (Li & He 2004). Thymidylate synthase catalyzes the conversion of deoxyuridylate to the nucleotide thymidylate. Replacing the *thyA* gene with *il10* removes the ability of the genetically modified *L. lactis* strain to synthesize thymidylate, thereby halting DNA synthesis and hence acting as an effective biological containment strategy. The use of *L. lactis* to administer therapeutic proteins termed ActoBiotics™ was developed and commercialized by the biopharmaceutical company ActoGeniX. A phase IIa clinical proof-of-concept in an ulcerative colitis model was recently completed (**http://www.actogenix.com**). Results showed that the product was safe, tolerable, and environmentally contained. However, there was not a statistically significant difference between the treatment and placebo in mucosal healing. Additional trials in humans are underway to assess a second product for the treatment of oral mucositis in cancer patients (**http://www.actogenix.com**).

More recently, oral vaccine delivery via *Lactobacillus*-based vectors has been markedly successful by fusion of a C-terminal (DC)-targeting peptide (12 mer) to the protective antigen (PA) for anthrax (Mohamadzadeh et al. 2009). Expression of this PA-DC cassette on a high-copy vector in *Lactobacillus gasseri* provided 100% protection of mice from challenge with anthrax (**Figure 4**, see color insert) (Mohamadzadeh et al. 2010). Omic technologies have facilitated the expression of DNA, enzymes, allergens, cytokines, antigens, and peptides by lactic acid bacteria (Wells & Mercenier 2008, Mohamadzadeh et al. 2008). The use of modified strains that can be safely ingested at high numbers as delivery agents for therapeutics, vaccines, and in the treatment of disease is an exciting prospect and a significant advancement in the study of food microbes.

TRANSCRIPTOMICS OF FOOD MICROBES

Microarrays have contributed significantly to our knowledge of food microbes, e.g., transcriptomics of food microbes during growth in stressful environments and various foods such as milk, cheese, and yogurt. Recently, gene expression studies from the duodenum of humans demonstrated that administration of *L. plantarum* can elicit immunomodulatory responses (van Baarlen et al. 2009). With regard to pathogens, transcriptomics has revealed important and invaluable insights into their pathogenicity, adaptation, and survival in food. Transcriptomics has been used to investigate intracellular expression of genes in *L. monocytogenes* (Chatterjee et al. 2006,

Joseph et al. 2006) during infection and host adaptation (Camejo et al. 2009) and those genes activated by the transcriptional regulars PrfA (Milohanic et al. 2003), VirR (Mandin et al. 2005), and the sigma B regulon (Hain et al. 2008, Raengpradub et al. 2008). Microarray technology has also expanded to include tiling arrays, which are designed to cover the complete genome and more than one genome (Mockler et al. 2005) rather than covering just the annotated ORFeome of a single genome. These arrays have facilitated a deeper view of transcription responses in food microbes such as *Bacillus subtilis* (Rasmussen et al. 2009), *L. monocytogenes* (Toledo-Arana et al. 2009), and *E. coli* O157:H7 (Jackson et al. 2007). Another technique that was originally applied to eukaryotes and has been adapted to prokaryotes is ChIP (chromatin immunoprecipitation), which in tandem with microarrays (termed ChIP-chip), studies protein-DNA interactions (Wade et al. 2007). ChIP-chip was first used in bacteria in 2002 and has since been utilized to study transcription factors in *B. subtilis*, *E. coli*, and *Helicobacter pylori* (Wade et al. 2007).

Next generation sequencing technologies are fast emerging as valuable tools in transcriptomics and in understanding regulatory processes. Recently, NGS technologies have been applied to sequencing of the transcriptome and are termed as RNA-seq or RNA deep sequencing (Wang et al. 2009). To date, NGS has mostly been utilized to sequence the transcriptome of eukaryotes, including eukaryotic microorganisms. This is in part due to the fact that unlike most bacterial mRNA, eukaryotic RNA contain a poly-A-tail, which is utilized in the amplification procedure to create cDNA. However, recently there have been some publications with food pathogens that have their transcriptome sequenced via RNA-seq (Liu et al. 2009a, Oliver et al. 2009, Perkins et al. 2009). Direct RNA sequencing for transcriptomics has the advantage over DNA microarrays, as transcripts are only detected on DNA microarrays if there is a corresponding probe on the array and DNA microarrays often do not cover the complete transcriptome but rather just annotated open reading frames. cDNA derived from RNA depleted of 16S and 23S rRNA from *S.* Typhi was sequenced using Illumina sequencing technology. The main outcome of this study from RNA-seq was the correction of the original genome annotation, the identification of transcriptionally active prophage genes, 40 new noncoding RNA sequences, and members of the OmpR regulon (Perkins et al. 2009). The OmpR regulon in *S.* Typhi regulates transcription of numerous genes, including those associated with Vi polysaccharide synthesis (Pickard et al. 1994), two component regulatory systems (Feng et al. 2003), and outer membrane porins (Fernandez-Mora et al. 2004). In the case of *Vibrio cholerae* sequencing of noncoding or small RNA (sRNA) was specifically targeted using 454 sequencing (Liu et al. 2009a). Twenty known *V. cholerae* sRNAs, 500 new putative intergenic sRNAs, and 127 putative antisense sRNAs from 407,039 sequence reads were identified. Additionally, a novel sRNA regulator of carbon metabolism was discovered. Illumina sequencing technology was also used to sequence the stationary phase stress response transcriptome of *Listeria* (Oliver et al. 2009). This study compared the transcriptomes of a *L. monocytogenes* strain with an isogenic mutant of the sigma B regulon, which was identified through microarray transcriptome studies as an important regulator of genes involved in virulence, stress response, transcriptional regulation, and carbohydrate metabolism and transport (Raengpradub et al. 2008). The study by Oliver et al. (2009) using RNA-seq demonstrated that 83% of all *L. monocytogenes* genes were transcribed in stationary phase and identified 96 genes with significantly higher transcript levels in the parent strain compared with the isogenic mutant indicating sigma B control of these genes. Importantly, RNA-seq also facilitated the identification of 67 (including 7 novel) noncoding RNA molecules (ncRNAs) transcribed in stationary phase *L. monocytogenes* and 65 putative sigma B promoters upstream of 82 of the 96 sigma B–regulated genes (Oliver et al. 2009). This latter study demonstrates the wealth of information obtained from RNA-seq, which can ultimately help the scientific community better understand the pathogenicity of *L. monocytogenes*. This technology will no doubt be applied to additional food microbes. DNA microarrays are still the method of choice due to the high cost of RNA-seq, but in the foreseeable future direct sequencing of RNA transcript will be commonplace with advances in technologies, improved bioinformatic software, and lower costs. Indeed, single molecule sequencing such as the Helicos system and other methods under development will also be applicable to RNA sequencing (Ozsolak et al. 2009). Direct RNA sequencing will bypass the need for cloning and/or amplification and reverse transcription of RNA to generate cDNA. Omission of these experimental steps will reduce time and cost and also omit experimental bias during the amplification of the original RNA template.

Metabolomics: global analysis of metabolites

ADVANCES IN PROTEOMICS

Proteomic tools allow the study of protein identification, expression, function, interaction, and structure. In particular, classical proteomic approaches have been used to study important food microbes used in dairy processing (Gagnaire et al. 2008). These techniques include two dimensional gel electrophoresis in which proteins are separated on a gel by their mass and isoelectric point. Protein spots are excised from the gel, proteins are digested within the spot, and then proteins are identified by mass spectrometry (MS). Different proteome profiles or reference maps are determined that allows the resolution of total protein abundance for many beneficial and pathogenic food microbes and also the comparison of protein expression under different stress or growth conditions such as in milk and synthetic media. However, this technique is limited to approximately one third of the ORFeome as not all proteins are represented on the electrophoresis gels, in part because of their hydrophobicity (Gagnaire et al. 2008).

Additional proteomic technologies are based on nuclear magnetic resonance (NMR) spectroscopy and MS, which allow the analysis of a large sample quantity and hundreds or more metabolites in a single run of samples. In MS, components within samples are separated using either gas or liquid chromatography (GC and LC, respectively). Fragmentation of samples isolated in the mass spectrometer and subsequent determination of these partial amino acid sequences, termed MS/MS, improved the system as related to available genetic information. However, current limitations include the low level of detailed molecular identification and the need for improved bioinformatic software suites to deal with the large dataset outputs. Examples of recent proteome studies that advanced our knowledge of food microbes include changes in the proteome of *E. coli* when grown in milk compared with synthetic media (Lippolis et al. 2009) and identification of cell surface–associated proteins from the probiotic bacteria *L. plantarum* (Beck et al. 2009). A major advancement in proteomics is the development of metabolomics, which has in particular been used to study gut microbe metabolites (Nicholson et al. 2005). Metabolomics aims to analyze all metabolites in a given sample or condition. This technology can be used to identify biomarkers that are related to a specific trait or disease, such as IBD. It is difficult to develop a metabolomic platform that could provide analyses of all microbial metabolites, as the number of metabolites varies depending on the type and number of bacterial species. Considering that the estimation of the gut microbiota is greater than one thousand taxa, the number of possible metabolites to be analyzed is a daunting task. However, proteomic techniques can establish a dataset or blueprint that can be linked to a specific trait, e.g., the identification of biomarkers that can be measured after administration of a probiotic bacterium to treat intestinal inflammation. The challenge is to determine those sets of metabolites or biomarkers relevant to the particular study.

CONCLUSIONS

The use of omic tools has unquestionably accelerated our knowledge and comprehension of the complexities of food microbes and their adaptation to specialized niches.

However, even with these advances, contamination of the food chain remains a problem that is a cost for the consumer in terms of health and disease. These costs also impact industry through recalls and lowered consumer confidence in their products. Although significant effort has traditionally been associated with the study of host-pathogen interactions, the use of omic technologies has driven our knowledge of beneficial microbes and how to better exploit them in industrial applications, fermentations, or as dietary probiotic supplements.

As omic technologies are further improved and applied to food microbes, there are a plethora of uses in food microbiology, from detection of pathogens, thereby improving food safety, to understanding the beneficial aspects of industrial strains. Food microbes can be modified by omic tools for production of vaccines and delivery of therapeutics. Omic technologies have advanced the prospect of personalized medicine, which impacts the food industry. Knowledge gained from genomics and proteomics of food microbes and their effects on the gut microbiota will contribute to the future study of personalized diets. Hence, the challenge for the food industry and scientific community is to determine the effect of food and food microbes on the gut microbiota and impact on human health, while ensuring food quality, nutrition, and pathogen-free products.

SUMMARY POINTS

1. Next generation sequencing technologies have greatly impacted the study of food microbes, including detection systems, construction of global microarry platforms, increased numbers of sequenced whole genomes, and identification of microbes with industrial potential.
2. Although there are a limited number of genome sequences currently available for food pathogens, advances in sequencing technology have rapidly increased whole genome sequencing, which will prompt better understanding of pathogen survival in food and pathogenesis in the host.
3. It is evident from omic technologies that studies are transitioning from the study of a single bacterium to groups of strains within a species or across species for a greater understanding of food microbe communities.
4. Functional genomics of beneficial food microbes have resulted in genetic engineering of specific species for the delivery of therapeutic molecules. Human clinical trials with these strains have been initiated, and there exists exciting possibilities in the near future in regard to delivery of therapeutic molecules and vaccines.
5. Advances in proteomics and metabolomics may establish metabolic blueprints that can be utilized as diagnostic tools, particularly for studying the effect of beneficial microbes used as delivery vehicles and in disease management.

FUTURE ISSUES

1. Advances in omic technologies have resulted in large datasets resulting in the requirement of giga- and terabytes of storage. A future issue is the open access and storage of these large datasets.
2. The constant development and improvement of bioinformatic tools are required to keep pace with advances in omic platforms.

3. Datasets from omic technologies must translate to biological meanings that are relevant for the scientific community and food industry, especially for control of pathogens and the treatment or prevention of disease.
4. As additional whole genome sequences become available, global tools will have to be updated to incorporate the new sequence information, e.g., expansion of the pan genome and modified microarray platforms.
5. Despite advances in omic technologies and knowledge on pathogens, food contamination remains a major issue. This is in part due to the rapid globalization of the food market and consumer requirements of the food industry. A challenge is harnessing knowledge from omic technologies for the control of food pathogens and ensuring safety throughout the food chain.

DISCLOSURE STATEMENT

The authors are not aware of any affiliations, memberships, funding, or financial holdings that might be perceived as affecting the objectivity of this review.

ACKNOWLEDGMENTS

The T.R.K. research program in probiotic lactobacilli and genomics is supported by the North Carolina Dairy Foundation, Danisco USA, Inc., and by the National Dairy Council, and is administered by the Dairy Research Institute. We would like to thank Dr. Yong Jun Goh for critical review of the manuscript.

LITERATURE CITED

Abdullah Al M, Sugimoto S, Higashi C, Matsumoto S, Sonomoto K. 2010. Improvement of multiple-stress tolerance and lactic acid production in *Lactococcus lactis* NZ9000 under conditions of thermal stress by heterologous expression of *Escherichia coli* dnaK. *Appl. Environ. Microbiol.* 76:4277–85

Altermann E, Russell WM, Azcarate-Peril MA, Barrangou R, Buck BL, et al. 2005. Complete genome sequence of the probiotic lactic acid bacterium *Lactobacillus acidophilus* NCFM. *Proc. Natl. Acad. Sci. USA* 102:3906–12

Ansorge WJ. 2009. Next-generation DNA sequencing techniques. *N. Biotechnol.* 25:195–203

Bartlett JM, Stirling D. 2003. A short history of the polymerase chain reaction. *Methods Mol. Biol.* 226:3–6

Beck HC, Madsen SM, Glenting J, Petersen J, Israelsen H, et al. 2009. Proteomic analysis of cell surface–associated proteins from probiotic *Lactobacillus plantarum*. *FEMS Microbiol. Lett.* 297:61–66

Begley M, Gahan CG, Hill C. 2005. The interaction between bacteria and bile. *FEMS Microbiol. Rev.* 29:625–51

Bolotin A, Quinquis B, Renault P, Sorokin A, Ehrlich SD, et al. 2004. Complete sequence and comparative genome analysis of the dairy bacterium *Streptococcus thermophilus*. *Nat. Biotechnol.* 22:1554–58

Braat H, Rottiers P, Hommes DW, Huyghebaert N, Remaut E, et al. 2006. A phase I trial with transgenic bacteria expressing interleukin-10 in Crohn's disease. *Clin. Gastroenterol. Hepatol.* 4:754–59

Briczinski EP, Loquasto JR, Barrangou R, Dudley EG, Roberts AM, Roberts RF. 2009. Strain-specific genotyping of *Bifidobacterium animalis* subsp. *lactis* by using single-nucleotide polymorphisms, insertions, and deletions. *Appl. Environ. Microbiol.* 75:7501–8

Brodie EL, Desantis TZ, Joyner DC, Baek SM, Larsen JT, et al. 2006. Application of a high-density oligonucleotide microarray approach to study bacterial population dynamics during uranium reduction and reoxidation. *Appl. Environ. Microbiol.* 72:6288–98

Brodie EL, DeSantis TZ, Parker JP, Zubietta IX, Piceno YM, Andersen GL. 2007. Urban aerosols harbor diverse and dynamic bacterial populations. *Proc. Natl. Acad. Sci. USA* 104:299–304

Cabana MD, McKean M, Wong AR, Chao C, Caughey AB. 2007. Examining the hygiene hypothesis: the trial of infant probiotic supplementation. *Paediatr. Perinat. Epidemiol.* 21(Suppl. 3):23–28

Callanan M, Kaleta P, O'Callaghan J, O'Sullivan O, Jordan K, et al. 2008. Genome sequence of *Lactobacillus helveticus*, an organism distinguished by selective gene loss and insertion sequence element expansion. *J. Bacteriol.* 190:727–35

Camejo A, Buchrieser C, Couve E, Carvalho F, Reis O, et al. 2009. In vivo transcriptional profiling of *Listeria monocytogenes* and mutagenesis identify new virulence factors involved in infection. *PLoS Pathog.* 5:e1000449

Chatterjee SS, Hossain H, Otten S, Kuenne C, Kuchmina K, et al. 2006. Intracellular gene expression profile of *Listeria monocytogenes*. *Infect. Immun.* 74:1323–38

Claesson MJ, Cusack S, O'Sullivan O, Greene-Diniz R, de Weerd H, et al. 2010. Microbes and health sackler colloquium: composition, variability, and temporal stability of the intestinal microbiota of the elderly. *Proc. Natl. Acad. Sci. USA.* doi: 10.1073/pnas.1000097107

Corr SC, Li Y, Riedel CU, O'Toole PW, Hill C, Gahan CG. 2007. Bacteriocin production as a mechanism for the antiinfective activity of *Lactobacillus salivarius* UCC118. *Proc. Natl. Acad. Sci. USA* 104:7617–21

Courtin P, Monnet V, Rul F. 2002. Cell-wall proteinases PrtS and PrtB have a different role in *Streptococcus thermophilus/Lactobacillus bulgaricus* mixed cultures in milk. *Microbiology* 148:3413–21

Cox MJ, Huang YJ, Fujimura KE, Liu JT, McKean M, et al. 2010. *Lactobacillus casei* abundance is associated with profound shifts in the infant gut microbiome. *PLoS One* 5:e8745

Douglas GL, Klaenhammer TR. 2010. Genomic evolution of domesticated microorganisms. *Annu. Rev. Food Sci. Technol.* 1:397–414

Drmanac R, Sparks AB, Callow MJ, Halpern AL, Burns NL, et al. 2010. Human genome sequencing using unchained base reads on self-assembling DNA nanoarrays. *Science* 327:78–81

Ducey TF, Page B, Usgaard T, Borucki MK, Pupedis K, Ward TJ. 2007. A single-nucleotide-polymorphism-based multilocus genotyping assay for subtyping lineage I isolates of *Listeria monocytogenes*. *Appl. Environ. Microbiol.* 73:133–47

Dussurget O, Cabanes D, Dehoux P, Lecuit M, Buchrieser C, et al. 2002. *Listeria monocytogenes* bile salt hydrolase is a PrfA-regulated virulence factor involved in the intestinal and hepatic phases of listeriosis. *Mol. Microbiol.* 45:1095–106

Edwards A, Voss H, Rice P, Civitello A, Stegemann J, et al. 1990. Automated DNA sequencing of the human HPRT locus. *Genomics* 6:593–608

Eid J, Fehr A, Gray J, Luong K, Lyle J, et al. 2009. Real-time DNA sequencing from single polymerase molecules. *Science* 323:133–38

Feng X, Oropeza R, Kenney LJ. 2003. Dual regulation by phospho-OmpR of ssrA/B gene expression in *Salmonella* pathogenicity island 2. *Mol. Microbiol.* 48:1131–43

Fernandez-Mora M, Puente JL, Calva E. 2004. OmpR and LeuO positively regulate the *Salmonella enterica* serovar Typhi ompS2 porin gene. *J. Bacteriol.* 186:2909–20

Flanagan JL, Brodie EL, Weng L, Lynch SV, Garcia O, et al. 2007. Loss of bacterial diversity during antibiotic treatment of intubated patients colonized with *Pseudomonas aeruginosa*. *J. Clin. Microbiol.* 45:1954–62

Fleischmann RD, Adams MD, White O, Clayton RA, Kirkness EF, et al. 1995. Whole-genome random sequencing and assembly of *Haemophilus influenzae* Rd. *Science* 269:496–512

Frank DN, St Amand AL, Feldman RA, Boedeker EC, Harpaz N, Pace NR. 2007. Molecular-phylogenetic characterization of microbial community imbalances in human inflammatory bowel diseases. *Proc. Natl. Acad. Sci. USA* 104:13780–85

Freitag NE, Port GC, Miner MD. 2009. *Listeria monocytogenes*—from saprophyte to intracellular pathogen. *Nat. Rev. Microbiol.* 7:623–28

Gagnaire V, Jardin J, Jan G, Lortal S. 2008. Invited review: proteomics of milk and bacteria used in fermented dairy products: from qualitative to quantitave to advances. *J. Dairy Sci.* 92:811–25

Gill SR, Pop M, Deboy RT, Eckburg PB, Turnbaugh PJ, et al. 2006. Metagenomic analysis of the human distal gut microbiome. *Science* 312:1355–59

Glaser P, Frangeul L, Buchrieser C, Rusniok C, Amend A, et al. 2001. Comparative genomics of *Listeria* species. *Science* 294:849–52

Grangette C, Nutten S, Palumbo E, Morath S, Hermann C, et al. 2005. Enhanced antiinflammatory capacity of a *Lactobacillus plantarum* mutant synthesizing modified teichoic acids. *Proc. Natl. Acad. Sci. USA* 102:10321–26

Hain T, Hossain H, Chatterjee SS, Machata S, Volk U, et al. 2008. Temporal transcriptomic analysis of the *Listeria monocytogenes* EGD-e sigmaB regulon. *BMC Microbiol.* 8:20

Holt KE, Baker S, Dongol S, Basnyat B, Adhikari N, et al. 2010. High-throughput bacterial SNP typing identifies distinct clusters of *Salmonella* Typhi causing typhoid in Nepalese children. *BMC Infect. Dis.* 10:144

Jackson SA, Mammel MK, Patel IR, Mays T, Albert TJ, et al. 2007. Interrogating genomic diversity of *E. coli* O157:H7 using DNA tiling arrays. *Forensic. Sci. Int.* 168:183–99

Jacobsen CN, Rosenfeldt Nielsen V, Hayford AE, Moller PL, Michaelsen KF, et al. 1999. Screening of probiotic activities of forty-seven strains of *Lactobacillus* spp. by in vitro techniques and evaluation of the colonization ability of five selected strains in humans. *Appl. Environ. Microbiol.* 65:4949–56

Jasson V, Jacxsens L, Luning P, Rajkovic A, Uyttendaele M. 2010. Alternative microbial methods: an overview and selection criteria. *Food Microbiol.* 27:710–30

Joseph B, Przybilla K, Stuhler C, Schauer K, Slaghuis J, et al. 2006. Identification of *Listeria monocytogenes* genes contributing to intracellular replication by expression profiling and mutant screening. *J. Bacteriol.* 188:556–68

Juste A, Thomma BP, Lievens B. 2008. Recent advances in molecular techniques to study microbial communities in food-associated matrices and processes. *Food Microbiol.* 25:745–61

Kalliomaki M, Salminen S, Arvilommi H, Kero P, Koskinen P, Isolauri E. 2001. Probiotics in primary prevention of atopic disease: a randomised placebo-controlled trial. *Lancet* 357:1076–79

Kalliomaki M, Salminen S, Poussa T, Arvilommi H, Isolauri E. 2003. Probiotics and prevention of atopic disease: 4-year follow-up of a randomised placebo-controlled trial. *Lancet* 361:1869–71

Kankainen M, Paulin L, Tynkkynen S, von Ossowski I, Reunanen J, et al. 2009. Comparative genomic analysis of *Lactobacillus rhamnosus* GG reveals pili containing a human-mucus binding protein. *Proc. Natl. Acad. Sci. USA* 106:17193–98

Keswani J, Whitman WB. 2001. Relationship of 16S rRNA sequence similarity to DNA hybridization in prokaryotes. *Int. J. Syst. Evol. Microbiol.* 51:667–78

Kim HJ, Park SH, Lee TH, Nahm BH, Kim YR, Kim HY. 2008. Microarray detection of food-borne pathogens using specific probes prepared by comparative genomics. *Biosens. Bioelectron.* 24:238–46

Klaenhammer TR, Barrangou R, Buck BL, Azcarate-Peril MA, Altermann E. 2005. Genomic features of lactic acid bacteria effecting bioprocessing and health. *FEMS Microbiol. Rev.* 29:393–409

Kline KA, Dodson KW, Caparon MG, Hultgren SJ. 2010. A tale of two pili: assembly and function of pili in bacteria. *Trends Microbiol.* 18:224–32

Kurokawa K, Itoh T, Kuwahara T, Oshima K, Toh H, et al. 2007. Comparative metagenomics revealed commonly enriched gene sets in human gut microbiomes. *DNA Res.* 14:169–81

Li MC, He SH. 2004. IL-10 and its related cytokines for treatment of inflammatory bowel disease. *World J. Gastroenterol.* 10:620–25

Li M, Wang B, Zhang M, Rantalainen M, Wang S, et al. 2008. Symbiotic gut microbes modulate human metabolic phenotypes. *Proc. Natl. Acad. Sci. USA* 105:2117–22

Lippolis JD, Bayles DO, Reinhardt TA. 2009. Proteomic changes in *Escherichia coli* when grown in fresh milk versus laboratory media. *J. Proteome Res.* 8:149–58

Liu JM, Livny J, Lawrence MS, Kimball MD, Waldor MK, Camilli A. 2009a. Experimental discovery of sRNAs in *Vibrio cholerae* by direct cloning, 5S/tRNA depletion and parallel sequencing. *Nucleic Acids Res.* 37:e46

Liu M, Siezen RJ, Nauta A. 2009b. In silico prediction of horizontal gene transfer events in *Lactobacillus bulgaricus* and *Streptococcus thermophilus* reveals protocooperation in yogurt manufacturing. *Appl. Environ. Microbiol.* 75:4120–29

Maiden MC, Bygraves JA, Feil E, Morelli G, Russell JE, et al. 1998. Multilocus sequence typing: a portable approach to the identification of clones within populations of pathogenic microorganisms. *Proc. Natl. Acad. Sci. USA* 95:3140–45

Makarova K, Slesarev A, Wolf Y, Sorokin A, Mirkin B, et al. 2006. Comparative genomics of the lactic acid bacteria. *Proc. Natl. Acad. Sci. USA* 103:15611–16

Mandin P, Fsihi H, Dussurget O, Vergassola M, Milohanic E, et al. 2005. VirR, a response regulator critical for *Listeria monocytogenes* virulence. *Mol. Microbiol.* 57:1367–80

Manichanh C, Rigottier-Gois L, Bonnaud E, Gloux K, Pelletier E, et al. 2006. Reduced diversity of faecal microbiota in Crohn's disease revealed by a metagenomic approach. *Gut* 55:205–11

Martinez-Medina M, Aldeguer X, Gonzalez-Huix F, Acero D, Garcia-Gil LJ. 2006. Abnormal microbiota composition in the ileocolonic mucosa of Crohn's disease patients as revealed by polymerase chain reaction–denaturing gradient gel electrophoresis. *Inflamm. Bowel. Dis.* 12:1136–45

Medini D, Donati C, Tettelin H, Masignani V, Rappuoli R. 2005. The microbial pan-genome. *Curr. Opin. Genet. Dev.* 15:589–94

Milohanic E, Glaser P, Coppee JY, Frangeul L, Vega Y, et al. 2003. Transcriptome analysis of *Listeria monocytogenes* identifies three groups of genes differently regulated by PrfA. *Mol. Microbiol.* 47:1613–25

Milos P. 2008. Helicos BioSciences. *Pharmacogenomics* 9:477–80

Mockler TC, Chan S, Sundaresan A, Chen H, Jacobsen SE, Ecker JR. 2005. Applications of DNA tiling arrays for whole-genome analysis. *Genomics* 85:1–15

Mohamadzadeh M, Duong T, Hoover T, Klaenhammer TR. 2008. Targeting mucosal dendritic cells with microbial antigens from probiotic lactic acid bacteria. *Expert Rev. Vaccines* 7:163–74

Mohamadzadeh M, Duong T, Sandwick SJ, Hoover T, Klaenhammer TR. 2009. Dendritic cell targeting of *Bacillus anthracis* protective antigen expressed by *Lactobacillus acidophilus* protects mice from lethal challenge. *Proc. Natl. Acad. Sci. USA* 106:4331–36

Mohamadzadeh M, Durmaz E, Zadeh M, Pakanati KC, Gramarossa M, et al. 2010. Targeted expression of anthrax protective antigen by *Lactobacillus gasseri* as an anthrax vaccine. *Future Microbiol.* 5:1289–96

Nelson KE, Fouts DE, Mongodin EF, Ravel J, DeBoy RT, et al. 2004. Whole genome comparisons of serotype 4b and 1/2a strains of the food-borne pathogen *Listeria monocytogenes* reveal new insights into the core genome components of this species. *Nucleic Acids Res.* 32:2386–95

Nicholson JK, Holmes E, Wilson ID. 2005. Gut microorganisms, mammalian metabolism and personalized health care. *Nat. Rev. Microbiol.* 3:431–38

O'Flaherty S, Klaenhammer TR. 2010. The role and potential of probiotic bacteria in the gut, and the communication between gut microflora and gut/host. *Int. Dairy J.* 20:262–68

Oliver HF, Orsi RH, Ponnala L, Keich U, Wang W, et al. 2009. Deep RNA sequencing of *L. monocytogenes* reveals overlapping and extensive stationary phase and sigma B-dependent transcriptomes, including multiple highly transcribed noncoding RNAs. *BMC Genomics* 10:641

Ozsolak F, Platt AR, Jones DR, Reifenberger JG, Sass LE, et al. 2009. Direct RNA sequencing. *Nature* 461:814–18

Paterson Y, Guirnalda PD, Wood LM. 2010. *Listeria* and *Salmonella* bacterial vectors of tumor-associated antigens for cancer immunotherapy. *Semin. Immunol.* 22:183–89

Perkins TT, Kingsley RA, Fookes MC, Gardner PP, James KD, et al. 2009. A strand-specific RNA-Seq analysis of the transcriptome of the typhoid bacillus *Salmonella typhi*. *PLoS Genet.* 5:e1000569

Pettersson E, Lundeberg J, Ahmadian A. 2009. Generations of sequencing technologies. *Genomics* 93:105–11

Pickard D, Li J, Roberts M, Maskell D, Hone D, et al. 1994. Characterization of defined ompR mutants of *Salmonella typhi*: ompR is involved in the regulation of Vi polysaccharide expression. *Infect. Immun.* 62:3984–93

Qin J, Li R, Raes J, Arumugam M, Burgdorf KS, et al. 2010. A human gut microbial gene catalogue established by metagenomic sequencing. *Nature* 464:59–65

Raengpradub S, Wiedmann M, Boor KJ. 2008. Comparative analysis of the sigma B-dependent stress responses in *Listeria monocytogenes* and *Listeria innocua* strains exposed to selected stress conditions. *Appl. Environ. Microbiol.* 74:158–71

Rasmussen S, Nielsen HB, Jarmer H. 2009. The transcriptionally active regions in the genome of *Bacillus subtilis*. *Mol. Microbiol.* 73:1043–57

Renye JA Jr, Somkuti GA. 2010. Nisin-induced expression of pediocin in dairy lactic acid bacteria. *J. Appl. Microbiol.* 108(6):2142–51

Sanger F, Nicklen S, Coulson AR. 1977. DNA sequencing with chain-terminating inhibitors. *Proc. Natl. Acad. Sci. USA* 74:5463–67

Sartor RB. 2005. Probiotic therapy of intestinal inflammation and infections. *Curr. Opin. Gastroenterol.* 21:44–50

Selander RK, Caugant DA, Ochman H, Musser JM, Gilmour MN, Whittam TS. 1986. Methods of multilocus enzyme electrophoresis for bacterial population genetics and systematics. *Appl. Environ. Microbiol.* 51:873–84

Sibley CG, Ahlquist JE. 1984. The phylogeny of the hominoid primates, as indicated by DNA-DNA hybridization. *J. Mol. Evol.* 20:2–15

Sleator RD, Wemekamp-Kamphuis HH, Gahan CG, Abee T, Hill C. 2005. A PrfA-regulated bile exclusion system (BilE) is a novel virulence factor in *Listeria monocytogenes*. *Mol. Microbiol.* 55:1183–95

Sokol H, Pigneur B, Watterlot L, Lakhdari O, Bermudez-Humaran LG, et al. 2008. *Faecalibacterium prausnitzii* is an anti-inflammatory commensal bacterium identified by gut microbiota analysis of Crohn disease patients. *Proc. Natl. Acad. Sci. USA* 105:16731–36

Steidler L, Neirynck S, Huyghebaert N, Snoeck V, Vermeire A, et al. 2003. Biological containment of genetically modified *Lactococcus lactis* for intestinal delivery of human interleukin 10. *Nat. Biotechnol.* 21:785–89

Toledo-Arana A, Dussurget O, Nikitas G, Sesto N, Guet-Revillet H, et al. 2009. The *Listeria* transcriptional landscape from saprophytism to virulence. *Nature* 459:950–56

Tuomola EM, Ouwehand AC, Salminen SJ. 2000. Chemical, physical and enzymatic pre-treatments of probiotic lactobacilli alter their adhesion to human intestinal mucus glycoproteins. *Int. J. Food Microbiol.* 60:75–81

van Baarlen P, Troost FJ, van Hemert S, van der Meer C, de Vos WM, et al. 2009. Differential NF-κB pathways induction by *Lactobacillus plantarum* in the duodenum of healthy humans correlating with immune tolerance. *Proc. Natl. Acad. Sci. USA* 106:2371–76

van de Guchte M, Penaud S, Grimaldi C, Barbe V, Bryson K, et al. 2006. The complete genome sequence of *Lactobacillus bulgaricus* reveals extensive and ongoing reductive evolution. *Proc. Natl. Acad. Sci. USA* 103:9274–79

Venter JC, Adams MD, Myers EW, Li PW, Mural RJ, et al. 2001. The sequence of the human genome. *Science* 291:1304–51

Wade JT, Struhl K, Busby SJ, Grainger DC. 2007. Genomic analysis of protein-DNA interactions in bacteria: insights into transcription and chromosome organization. *Mol. Microbiol.* 65:21–26

Wang Z, Gerstein M, Snyder M. 2009. RNA-Seq: a revolutionary tool for transcriptomics. *Nat. Rev. Genet.* 10:57–63

Weissman SJ, Moseley SL, Dykhuizen DE, Sokurenko EV. 2003. *Enterobacterial* adhesins and the case for studying SNPs in bacteria. *Trends Microbiol.* 11:115–17

Wells JM, Mercenier A. 2008. Mucosal delivery of therapeutic and prophylactic molecules using lactic acid bacteria. *Nat. Rev. Microbiol.* 6:349–62

Zhang Q, Zhong J, Huan L. 2010. Expression of hepatitis B virus surface antigen determinants in *Lactococcus lactis* for oral vaccination. *Microbiol. Res.* doi: 10.1016/j.micres.2010.02.002

Zhou XX, Li WF, Ma GX, Pan YJ. 2006. The nisin-controlled gene expression system: construction, application and improvements. *Biotechnol. Adv.* 24:285–95

Synbiotics in Health and Disease

Sofia Kolida and Glenn R. Gibson

Department of Food and Nutritional Sciences, The University of Reading, Reading RG6 6AP, United Kingdom; email: s.kolida@reading.ac.uk

Annu. Rev. Food Sci. Technol. 2011. 2:373–93

First published online as a Review in Advance on December 21, 2010

The *Annual Review of Food Science and Technology* is online at food.annualreviews.org

This article's doi:
10.1146/annurev-food-022510-133739

1941-1413/11/0410-0373$20.00

Keywords

prebiotic, probiotic, cancer, inflammatory bowel disease (IBD), irritable bowel syndrome (IBS), gut flora

Abstract

The synbiotic concept was first introduced, along with prebiotics, as "mixtures of probiotics and prebiotics that beneficially affect the host by improving the survival and implantation of live microbial dietary supplements in the gastrointestinal tract, by selectively stimulating the growth and/or by activating the metabolism of one or a limited number of health-promoting bacteria, thus improving host welfare" (Gibson & Roberfroid 1995). Since, there have been many in vitro and in vivo studies focusing on the application of prebiotics, firstly in health and gradually in disease states. Only recently have studies on synbiotics started to emerge with the main focus being on applications against disease. Here, we review the current literature, with the main focus on in vivo human studies.

INTRODUCTION

Only over the past 30 years has the intrinsic role of diet in the development of diseases such as cardiovascular disease and cancer been realized. In the same time frame, it has become apparent that the colon is one of the most metabolically active organs of the human body, harboring an extremely complex microbial ecosystem that does not only act as a barrier against infection but also plays an active role in salvaging energy from nondigestible food ingredients that human enzymes cannot affect. Studies have accumulated on the colonic microbiota, in particular with the use of newly developed molecular methodologies, and this has greatly aided the identification of targets that could improve human well being.

For the better part of the past three decades, two main avenues of gut microbiota manipulation have been used: probiotics and prebiotics. The concept of synbiotics was first defined in 1995 as "mixtures of probiotics and prebiotics that beneficially affect the host by improving the survival and implantation of live microbial dietary supplements in the gastrointestinal tract, by selectively stimulating the growth and/or by activating the metabolism of one or a limited number of health-promoting bacteria, thus improving host welfare" (Gibson & Roberfroid 1995). The definition is intrinsically bound to that of both prebiotics and probiotics.

Probiotics

The protective nature of certain microorganisms, in particular lactic acid bacteria, contained in fermented foods and drinks has a long history. Humans have been consuming live bacterial cultures for centuries in the form of fermented milk without any knowledge of the active ingredients or how they work. Probiotics are defined as "live microbial food supplements that beneficially affect the host by improving the intestinal microbial balance" (Fuller 1991).

It is difficult to identify with certainty the first time the term probiotic was used, but it is believed that one of the earliest citations was by Vergin (1954), suggesting that the intestinal microbial balance may be upset following antibiotic use and that it could be restored by a diet of probiotics, including fermented foods. The term was reintroduced in 1965 by Lilly & Stillwell who defined probiotics as "substances produced by microorganisms which promote the growth of other microorganisms," the antonym of antibiotics (Lilly & Stillwel 1965). The definition was further refined approximately 10 years later by Parker (1974), who defined probiotics as "organisms and substances which contribute to intestinal microbial balance," which is closer to the designation proposed by Fuller in 1991. In the past few years, several attempts have been made to improve on Fuller's definition of a probiotic to a more general form that includes beneficial effects of probiotic microorganisms in other sites apart from the colon, such as the urinary tract, or address the issue of adequate bacteria levels to mediate a specific health outcome. For example, Havenaar & Huis In't Veld (1992) defined probiotic as "a preparation or a product containing viable, defined microorganisms in sufficient numbers, which alter the microflora (by implantation or colonization) in a compartment of the host and by that exert beneficial health effects in this host." Salminen (1996) defined it as "a live microbial culture or cultured dairy product which beneficially influences the health and nutrition of the host." A current widely accepted definition is from WHO (2002): "Probiotics are live microorganisms which, when administered in adequate amounts, confer a health benefit to the host."

The main criteria to be met by a microorganism to be characterized as probiotic are (Dunne et al. 2001, Tannock 1998):

- Although certain commercially available probiotics are not of human origin, it is believed that if a probiotic is isolated from the human gastrointestinal (GI) tract it is safer for human consumption and may be more effective within the intestinal ecosystem.
- GRAS (generally regarded as safe) status is granted by the FDA to food/food components that have been proven to be safe for human consumption through scientific procedures or through experience based on common use in food, as based on a substantial history of consumption by a significant number of individuals. Bifidobacteria and lactobacilli have a long history of safe consumption without harmful effects on human health.
- Probiotics must be capable of being prepared on a large scale and in a viable manner. It is also very important to be viable and active in the specific delivery vehicle.
- Probiotics have to be resistant to gastric acidity and bile acid toxicity. A low gastric pH is one of the primary host defense mechanisms against ingested microorganisms, including probiotics.
- Probiotics must adhere to human intestinal cells and intestinal mucins. This improves persistence and multiplication in the intestine and may promote competitive exclusion of potential pathogens from mucosal surfaces.
- Probiotics must produce antimicrobial substances against gut pathogens for the restoration of a healthy microflora composition.
- Probiotics must be safe in food and during clinical use, even in immuno-compromised individuals.
- Probiotics must have their efficacy and safety proven in randomized, double-blind placebo-controlled human studies.

The idea of introducing microbial strains that will potentially benefit the host and improve well being is now widely accepted; however, ingested microorganisms must survive host physiological barriers that common pathogens encounter. As such, they have to survive passage though the stomach and small intestine and upon reaching the small intestine and colon, they must compete with well-established commensal flora.

Prebiotics

The concept of prebiotics is much more recent and was first introduced in 1995 by Gibson & Roberfroid as an alternative approach that would overcome the survivability issues of probiotics during storage, distribution, and GI passage. Prebiotics were defined "as nondigestible dietary ingredients that beneficially affect the host by selectively stimulating the growth and/or activity of one or a limited number of bacteria in the colon, thus improving host health" (Gibson & Roberfroid 1995).

Since they were first introduced, prebiotics have been heavily researched and constant attempts to redefine them include the following:

> In 2004, Gibson and coworkers proposed an updated definition that excludes nondigestibility and broadens the target organisms as the GI microflora: "A prebiotic is a selectively fermented ingredient that allows specific changes, both in the composition and/or activity in the GI microflora that confers benefits upon host well being and health."

In 2007, the new version of the definition focused again on the digestive ecosystem microbiota, but this time the focus was the formulation of the prebiotic ingredient to include whole foods and dietary supplements: "A prebiotic is a nonviable food component, ingredient, or supplement that selectively modulates the microbiota of the digestive ecosystem, thus conferring benefits upon host well being and health" (Roberfroid 2007).

In 2008, a further attempt was made to exclude the nondigestibility aspect and expand the target site being defined as the microbota to include skin, oral, and vaginal prebiotics: "A prebiotic is a nonviable food component that confers a health benefit on the host associated with modulation of the microbiota" (Pineiro et al. 2008).

The currently accepted definition remains closer to the 1995 concept. Mention is made on dietary prebiotics as opposed to other potential applications of vaginal or skin prebiotics, and the target organ is once again the GI microbiota: "A dietary prebiotic is a selectively fermented ingredient that results in specific changes in the composition and/or activity of the GI microbiota thus conferring benefit(s) upon host health" (Gibson et al. 2010).

Based on the current definition, criteria that have to be fulfilled for a dietary ingredient to be characterized as a prebiotic are as follows:

- Fermentability can be demonstrated in vitro in fecal batch culture experiments simulating the pH and temperature conditions of selected regions of the human colon. Substrates that stimulate bacterial growth can be further evaluated in more complex in vitro continuous culture models, established to simulate the transit of luminal contents through the proximal, transverse, and distal parts of the colon as well as varying pH and temperature conditions therein. Promising substrates should be further evaluated in double-blind, placebo-controlled randomized human studies to confirm the observed in vitro effect.
- The main attribute of a prebiotic is as a selective substrate for one or more beneficial bacteria commensal to the GI tract, which are stimulated to grow and/or are metabolically activated and consequently move the colonic microbiota of the host toward a healthier composition. In order to confirm selectivity of a prebiotic, it is of utmost importance to accurately monitor the changes in the fecal microbiota during prebiotic supplementation both in vitro and in vivo. Although both criteria are important for a dietary ingredient to be characterized as a prebiotic, selectivity is the most important and difficult to fulfill.

Nondigestibility of prebiotic ingredients has been excluded from later definitions. However, to elicit an effect on the target site, the prebiotic must be either nondigestible or partially digestible to reach targets that are lower in the GI tract.

Currently, only three dietary ingredients have achieved prebiotic status in the European Union and fulfill all the above-presented criteria: fructooligosaccharides (FOSs) (and inulin), galactooligosaccharides (GOSs), and lactulose. They have been studied extensively in vitro and in vivo in human studies, with the main drawback of this approach being selectivity. It is difficult to ensure that a nondigestible oligosaccharide will be fermented only by bacteria beneficial to the host and also that the products of fermentation will not be used to promote the growth and/or activity of potential pathogens.

SYNBIOTICS

Based on the evolution of the probiotic and prebiotic terms, a synbiotic should consist of probiotics, which are live microorganisms present in adequate amounts to confer a health benefit to the host, and prebiotics, nonviable food components, ingredients, or supplements that selectively modulate the microbiota of the digestive ecosystems, thus conferring benefits upon host well being and health as well as improving the survival and implantation of the probiotic in the GI tract by selectively stimulating the growth and/or by activating the metabolism of one or a limited number of health-promoting bacteria that improve host welfare.

In addition to the conditions for a product to be defined as a prebiotic and probiotic, a further condition must be fulfilled for synbiotics: The prebiotic selectively supports the growth of the probiotic component.

Since the first introduction of this concept in 1995, synbiotics have not been redefined. Although their definition has evolved as a result of the changes in the definitions of probiotics and prebiotics, a more rigorous framework is required for synbiotics as well.

The word synbiotic is derived from the Greek "$\sigma\upsilon\nu$" and "βίος," which literally translate to together and life. The use of the two words together also implies synergy.

Based on the current definition, two types of synbiotic approaches exist:

- Complementary, whereby the probiotic is chosen based on specific desired beneficial effects on the host, and the prebiotic is independently chosen to selectively increase concentrations of the beneficial microbiota components. The prebiotic may promote growth and activity of the probiotic, but only indirectly as part of its target range.
- Synergistic, whereby the probiotic is again chosen based on specific beneficial effects on the host, but the prebiotic is chosen to specifically stimulate growth and activity of the selected probiotic. Here, the prebiotic is selected to have a higher affinity for the probiotic and is chosen to improve its survival and growth in the host. It may also increase the levels of beneficial host GI microbiota, but the primary target is the ingested probiotic.

Both approaches may, directly or indirectly, comply with the synbiotic definition. However, it is the synergistic approach that is most relevant with the current synbiotic definition. The two approaches have different implications. For example, the complementary approach targets separately the host well being with a probiotic and a prebiotic. Because of this, each component must be administered in such a dose as to elicit a desirable effect via the vehicle of administration. The relatively high doses of prebiotic (commonly more than 6 g d^{-1} for adults) required to mediate an effect on the gut microflora will, in most cases, exclude the encapsulation option. With a synergistic approach, the synbiotic is perceived as a single product, whereby the primary role of the prebiotic is to improve the survivability and implantation of the probiotic. The implication is that the necessary dose of prebiotic may be limited to this effect alone, and as such a smaller dose of the probiotic is required.

By definition, synbiotics are mixtures of probiotics and prebiotics, implying that the efficacy of each component will be established for a synbiotic formulation. **Figure 1** (see color insert) summarizes suggested steps in establishing the efficacy of probiotic and prebiotic components and for a final synbiotic product. Briefly, each food ingredient/microorganism present in the synbiotic formula must be fully characterized using the latest available technologies. The criteria for each group will be established in conjunction with safety determinations for both the probiotic and prebiotic, as well as a combination of the two. The in vitro and in vivo efficacy will have to be examined. Specificity of the prebiotic for selective stimulation of the selected probiotic(s) should also established. Indications on the potential growth of a probiotic on a selected substrate can be obtained through a genomic scan of the glycosidase spectra of the microorganism, which may allow for a rational selection of the potential prebiotics. Growth curve experiments provide information on a prebiotic to achieve the highest growth rates and cell yields for the probiotic. However, such experiments are limited in the degree of information that they can provide, as they do not examine interactions with the commensal microbiota and cannot provide information on the affinity of other microbiota for the selected prebiotic. Further information on the behavior of the synbiotic and mechanism of its action may be provided via pH-controlled fecal batch culture experiments. This methodology allows running different combinations and controls on minimal media, with the test prebiotic as the sole growth substrate using the same fecal inoculum for all tests. The probiotic and prebiotic components of the formulation should be tested alone, as well as alongside the synbiotic. This type of experiment provides information on whether each of the components can mediate an effect on the fecal microbiota when used alone as well as on whether the synbiotic combination can mediate a superior effect. Using molecular-based methodologies, information on the survivability of the probiotic in a mixed fecal environment over the fermentation period, as well as to the mechanism of synbiotic activity, synergistic, or complementary can be obtained. Synbiotic efficacy must then be established in vivo in double-blind, placebo-controlled randomized human studies. Ideally, a crossover design should be followed, in that volunteers crossover from each probiotic, prebiotic, and synbiotic treatment, and the efficacy on health biomarkers is followed. For human studies, the synbiotic should preferably be administered in a formulation that it is going to be marketed in, as product formulations may influence not only shelf life but also probiotic survivability and potential impacts on the host.

With prebiotics, there has been a gradual progression from in vitro to in vivo studies in healthy human volunteers, followed by testing prebiotic efficacy against diseases such as inflammatory bowel disease (IBD), colon cancer, and irritable bowel syndrome (IBS). For synbiotics, however, a small number of preliminary in vivo studies have been performed to date, and the focus has been almost exclusively on disease management. The level to which studies fulfill the synbiotic criteria varies greatly. As yet, a study has not been published that has investigated all the necessary aspects of synbiotic development.

Healthy Adult Microbiota Manipulation

Tanaka et al. (1983) investigated the effect of GOS administration in combination with *Bifidobacterium breve* 4006 in sixteen healthy adult men. The selective fermentation of GOS by bifidobacteria and the ability of *B. breve* 4006 to utilize it were established in vitro, prior to the in vivo study. Volunteers were divided into three treatment groups, each being administered 3 g d^{-1} or 10 g d^{-1} GOS alone, 3×10^9 CFU d^{-1} *B. breve* 4006 alone, or a combination of the two treatments for a two-week period. The prebiotic and synbiotic treatments both resulted in an increase in commensal bifidobacterial levels, whereas the probiotic alone did not mediate the same effect. Although this was a very early study and gut microbiota changes were evaluated using only culture techniques, the selection of probiotic and its complementary prebiotic, as well as the inclusion of the proper probiotic and prebiotic controls, allows us to draw conclusions on the mechanism of synbiotic efficacy. As such, the prebiotic appeared to enhance numbers of the probiotic and the comensal bifidobacterial populations.

In a later study, the synbiotic efficacy of yogurt supplemented with lactulose (0.5 g 100 ml^{-1}) and *Bifidobacterium longum* (10^8 CFU g^{-1}) in 10 healthy adults was investigated (Tomoda et al. 1991). The test interventions were plain yogurt, lactulose supplemented yogurt, *B. longum* yogurt, lactulose/*B. breve* yogurt. Over a three-month intervention period, volunteers ingested over three to six-week periods, with each treatment in a sequential manner. No significant differences were observed in fecal microbiota between the three active treatments. All treatments increased bifidobacterium levels compared with plain yogurt. No mention was made as to whether the probiotic was prescreened for its ability to ferment lactulose prior to the study. Although the proper controls were included in this trial, the sequential administration of the different treatments and the absence of washout periods prohibited realistic conclusions.

It was not until the late 1990s that interest in synbiotics was reignited. The majority of recent studies in healthy adults utilized commercially available prebiotic and probiotic combinations without prescreening for utilization of the prebiotic by probiotic microbes.

The effect of 5×10^9 CFU *Lactobacillus paracasei* B21060 and B21070 0.5×10^9 CFU *Lactobacillus gasseri* B21090 (Flortec, Bracco SpA) combined with inulin/oligosaccharides (dose and product not specified by the authors), ingested three times daily for 15 days, was investigated in 12 healthy adults (Morelli et al. 2003). A combination of PCR-ARDRA (amplified ribosomal DNA restriction analysis) and microbial culture techniques was applied to follow changes in *L. paracasei* and total *Lactobacillus* and *Bifidobacterium* spp. in feces. Increases in overall bifidobacteria and lactobacilli populations were observed, and the probiotic strains could be detected in volunteer feces throughout the study and three days following treatment cessation. A small number of volunteers, an absence of placebo, and lack of proper controls did not allow for solid conclusions on the mechanisms of synbiotic action. Furthermore, the authors focused solely on bifidobacteria and lactobacilli detection, and no attempt was made to evaluate the effects on other members of the fecal microbiota. In a later study, Morelli and coworkers (2006) investigated the presence of *L. paracasei* B21060 in the colonic mucosa and feces. Seven volunteers scheduled for colonoscopy were administered a combination of 5×10^9 CFU *L. paracasei* B21060, 0.5 g xylooligoasaccherides (XOS), and 3 g inulin three times daily for a period of 15 days. Two days after completing the synbiotic treatment they underwent a colonoscopy, during which biopsies from different sites were obtained. With the exception of one volunteer, *L. paracasei* could be detected in the cecum, transverse, descending, and sigmoid colon biopsies, and in 74.7% of the colonic samples. With regard to the association of *L. paracasei* to different colonic regions, the results are interesting, but the absence of a probiotic-only control fails to provide insight on any role for the prebiotic components of the treatment.

A long-term placebo-controlled crossover study investigated the effect of lactulose (10 g) and *Saccharomyces boulardii* (2×10^9 viable cells) in 30 young healthy adults (Vanhoutte et al. 2006). This was a well-designed study in which volunteers were divided into three groups, each receiving different probiotic and prebiotic doses. Each group ingested the prebiotic, probiotic, synbiotic, and placebo treatments, followed by a final washout over an 18-week study period. Unfortunately, the washout between treatments was only four days, which may not have been sufficient to ensure that there was no treatment carry over. DGGE (denaturing gradient gel electrophoresis) of 16 rRNA gene amplicons was used to detect changes in the overall composition of the fecal microbiota as well as group specific subpopulation levels. The addition of *S. boulardii* in the study diet did not appear to exert any effect, whereas lactulose alone gave a significant increase in bifidobacterial levels. One main shortcoming of this study was that *S. boulardii* was not evaluated for its ability to ferment lactulose, perhaps explaining why no change was observed.

Casiraghi et al. (2007) investigated the effect of a synbiotic milk product containing 10^7 CFU ml^{-1} *Lactobacillus acidophilus* 74-2, 10^7 CFU ml^{-1} *Bifidobacterium lactis* 420, and 2% Raftiline (inulin, DP10, Orafti) in 26 healthy adults in a randomized, placebo-controlled, two-arm parallel study. Significant increases in fecal bifidobacteria and lactobacilli were observed upon synbiotic ingestion, as evaluated using microbial culture techniques. The effect of a synbiotic on colonic nitrogen-protein metabolism was investigated in a recent study of 20 healthy humans over a 16-week period (De Preter et al. 2007). Volunteers were randomly assigned into two groups, each testing a different probiotic combination: either *Lactobacillus casei* Shirota ($2 \times 6.5 \times 10^9$ CFU d^{-1}) or *B. breve* (2×10^9 CFU d^{-1}) (Yakult). During each four-week treatment period, volunteers ingested the prebiotic (2×10 g d^{-1} FOS Synergy 1), the probiotic, or the synbiotic. Each treatment was followed by a two-week washout. Fecal and urinary excretion of ammonia and *p*-cresol were analyzed as indicators of proteolytic colonic fermentation. Synergy 1 alone mediated significant increases in fecal bifidobacteria concentrations and decreases in urinary *p*-cresol and ammonia. There was no additive effect observed with either synbiotic formulation with regard to the proteolytic biomarkers. In a later study, the same group further investigated the effect on β-glucuronidase and β-glucosidase activities in a study of a similar design. Synergy 1 mediated a significant decrease in fecal β-glucuronidase activity, but when combined with probiotics this was not observed. Similarly, *B. breve* ingestion increased β-glucosidase activity, but this effect was not retained in the synbiotic. The results imply that there was neither synergy nor an additive effect between the probiotic and the prebiotic components of this synbiotic formulation.

Two recent studies investigated the effects on healthy elderly volunteers. Bartosch et al. (2005) investigated a synbiotic formula containing a total of approximately 3.5×10^{10} CFU *Bifidobacterium bifidum* BB-02 and 3.5×10^{10} CFU *B. lactis* BL-01(Rhodia) and 6 g Synergy 1 in a gelatin capsule in 18 healthy elderly volunteers in a double-blind, randomized, controlled study. The intervention mediated an increase in stool frequency and in fecal bifidobacteria and lactobacilli. At the end of the study, three weeks following treatment cessation, at least one of the probiotics was still detectable in feces. Ouwehand et al. (2009) investigated the effect of 2×10^9 CFU g^{-1} *L. acidophilus* NCFM (Danisco) in combination with 5 g Lactitol in a double-blind, placebo-controlled parallel study of 51 healthy elderly volunteers. They observed significant increases in fecal bifidobacteria and lactobacilli as evaluated by real time–polymerase chain reaction (RT-PCR) but no significant changes in immune markers IgA and PGE_2 compared to placebo.

Inflammatory Bowel Disease

IBD is a collective term describing three conditions: ulcerative colitis (UC), Crohn's disease (CD), and pouchitis. The disease is characterized by acute noninfectious inflammation of the intestinal mucosa and submucosa and is usually associated with diarrhea and rectal bleeding with an excess production of mucus. Geographically, there appears to be a higher incidence of ulcerative colitis in Westernized or industrialized countries (Maybery et al. 1991). The chronic nature of the disease and the need for constant medication pose a major financial burden on the health system. To date, there is no cure for IBD and treatment has been limited to maintenance of remission. Currently, drug therapy is mainly based on the administration of anti-inflammatory and immunomodulating drugs, nutritional support and in severe cases surgical resection. The disease etiology is as yet unknown. However, in germ-free rodents, intestinal inflammation cannot be induced, indicating that bacteria are necessary for the pathogenesis of chronic intestinal inflammation (Sartor 1997, Veltkamp et al. 2001). It has been suggested that IBD is at least partially due to a breakdown of tolerance to the normal commensal colonic flora (Macpherson et al. 1996) or disturbed colonic flora (Pathmakanthan et al. 1999). It is very likely that IBD is caused by a complex combination of genetics, environmental factors, and the immune system. Probiotic use against ulcerative colitis and pouchitis has been extensively investigated, and several studies report encouraging results. Thus far, single-strain bacterial products (Kuisma et al. 2003) have not been as successful as multi-strain bacterial products (Gionchetti et al. 2000, Gionchetti et al. 2003, Bibiloni et al. 2005, Mimura et al. 2004).

For synbiotics, Furrie et al. (2005) screened nineteen *Bifidobacterium* isolates, ten isolated from healthy colonic mucosae, five from healthy feces, and four obtained from culture collections, for their suitability as probiotics. The selected strains were tested for aerotolerance, acid tolerance, bile-salt resistance, adhesion to epithelial cells, and their ability to survive freeze drying and long-term storage. The ability to metabolize FOS as an energy source was also determined. Finally, the ability of the microbial strains to reduce production of proinflammatory cytokines (Interleukin 1α) was also investigated in the HT29 epithelial cell line. *B. longum* isolated from the healthy rectal mucosa was selected for further study. Eight volunteers ingested 2×10^{11} viable, freeze-dried *B. longum* in a gelatin capsule and 6 g Synergy 1(Orafti) twice daily for a four-week treatment period. The eight volunteers in the placebo group were given identical capsules containing starch and 6 g of maltodextrose (Orafti). Sigmoidoscopy scores were determined at the start and end of treatment for both groups, and tumor necrosis factor α (TNF α) and IL 1α were monitored. TNFα, IL 1α, and antimicrobial human β defensin peptides were all significantly decreased, and mucosal bifidobacteria increased in the active group. Although this was a double-blind, placebo-controlled, randomized pilot study in a small patient group, it is one of the few studies that followed a rational procedure for probiotic selection that would complement the selected prebiotic as well as target the disease. Not only were the probiotic technological characteristics fully determined, including fermentation of the selected prebiotic, but the strain was specifically selected for its ability to downregulate in vitro production of cytokines that have been involved in the active state UC. It would have been interesting to see what effect the probiotic and prebiotic alone would have over a longer treatment period.

Animal studies on a dextran sulfate sodium (DSS)-induced colitis rat model testing the effect of administration of *Bifidobacterium infantis* DSM 15158 or *B. infantis* DSM 15159, alone or in combination with Synergy 1 (Orafti), noted a significant reduction in disease activity indices [bacterial translocation, short-chain fatty acids (SCFAs), cytokine production, myeloperoxidase, and malondialdehyde] (Osman et al. 2006). Six groups of six Sprague-Dawley rats were pretreated for seven days with either one of the test probiotic strains alone or in combination with Synergy 1. Following the treatment, DSS colitis was induced. Rats continued the synbiotic or probiotic treatments for seven further days after colitis initiation. Although all treatments mediated a significant improvement in disease activity indices, there appeared to be an additive effect when Synergy 1 was used, as it mediated an increase in succinate production. There were clear differences between the efficacies of the two probiotic strains with *B. infantis* DSM 15,159 being superior in reducing malondialdehyde levels. This was a well-designed study comparing the effect of each of the synbiotic constituents alone and in combination and investigating the effect of strain specificity against the disease.

Studies on the effect of synbiotics against Crohn's disease are sparse. Fujimori et al. (2007) examined the effect of probiotic (3×10^{11} CFU *B. breve*, 3×10^{11} CFU *L. casei*, and 1.5×10^{10} CFU *B. longum* daily) and prebiotic (3.3 g psyllium three times daily) cotherapy in an open label study of 10 active CD patients. The study duration was 10 months, and seven patients reported improved symptom scores. In contrast to the above-reviewed study, psyllium is not an established prebiotic, and no attempt was made to determine if the ability of the test probiotic strains could utilize it. The absence of a control group and the small number of participants did not allow for the proper evaluation of the efficacy of this approach and of the selected synbiotic performance. A multicenter, randomized, placebo-controlled study investigating the efficacy of Synbiotic 2000 (10^{10} CFU of each of *Pediacoccus pentoseceus*, *Leuconostoc mesenteroides*, *L. casei* spp. *paracasei* F1977:1, *Lactobacillus plantarum* 2362, and 2.5 g each of β-glucans, resistant starch, inulin, and pectin; Medipharm) in 30 ileal resection CD patients over a period of 24 months failed to note an effect on remission or disease scores compared to placebo (Chermesh et al. 2007).

Research in inflammatory bowel disease using synbiotic treatments is still in its infancy. It is evident, however, that when an informed selection of the probiotic and complementary prebiotic is made, pilot studies have been successful. Evidence from animal studies indicates that efficacy may be strain dependent. The lack of studies on the efficacy of prebiotics against IBD does not allow us to speculate as to the mechanism of action against this group of diseases. This puts even more pressure toward the selection of complementary prebiotics, where their primary goal would be to enhance the survival and/or activity of the probiotic component of the synbiotic formulation. It is difficult to rationally design a synbiotic against a disease of unknown etiology. However, in the past decade research in this area has come a long way in identifying immune biomarkers that could be potential targets and could be considered during synbiotic development.

Irritable Bowel Syndrome

IBS is one of the most common GI disorders in primary and secondary care. It affects 9%–22% of the population in the United States and 3.5%–25% worldwide. It is estimated that only 10% of the people exhibiting IBS symptoms seek medical advice. Within this population, the ratio of females to males is 3:1 (Alaradi & Barkin 2002). Typical IBS symptoms include abdominal pain and discomfort, bloating, and changes in bowel habit. Three disease phenotypes have been identified: constipated predominant, diarrhea predominant, and alternating between the two. The disease etiology is as yet unknown, and although an involvement of the gut microbiota has long been suspected, there is no conclusive evidence. Sensorimotor dysfunction and abnormal brain-gut interaction have also been suspected without the presence of conclusive evidence, and increased stress also appears to be a factor. Some IBS patients respond very well to exclusion diets, which may indicate a degree of abnormal colonic fermentation. Although not always successful, there are recent studies reporting encouraging results on the alleviation of IBS symptoms upon the ingestion of various probiotic strains (O'Mahony et al. 2005, Kajander et al. 2005, Whorwell et al. 2006).

The efficacy of synbiotic formulations against IBS is far less well documented. To date, there are two published studies. Dughera et al. (2007) investigated the effect of a commercially available synbiotic product delivering a total daily dose of 5×10^9 CFU *B. longum* W11 and 2.5 g short chain FOS (Actilight) in an open label, prospective, uncontrolled multicenter study of 129 constipated IBS subjects. Patients were evaluated at the start of the trial, after one month, and at the end of the three-month intervention. A significant increase in stool frequency was reported as well as alleviation of pain and bloating as compared with baseline samples. However, this was an open label study in the absence of a placebo, and although the results are encouraging, further RCTs (randomized controlled trials) are required to confirm efficacy.

The task of designing a synbiotic against IBS is particularly difficult, as the disease etiology is not yet known. Improvement of IBS symptoms may be possible; however, owing to the lack of information on the colonic microbiota composition associated with this disease, informed choices on selection of potentially efficient probiotic strains and complementary prebiotics remains a difficult task.

Colon Cancer Risk

Colorectal cancer is one of the most common forms of malignancy in developed countries. Approximately 100 new cases of colorectal cancer are diagnosed daily in the United Kingdom. It is the third most common cancer, after breast and lung. The impact of colorectal cancer is even higher in terms of mortality, as it is the second most common cause of death from cancer in the United Kingdom, after lung cancer, with deaths exceeding 16,000 yearly (Cancer Research UK 2006). Although incidence is significantly lower in developing countries, worldwide it was the third most commonly diagnosed cancer and the fourth most common cause of death by cancer according to 2002 estimates (Cancer Research UK 2005). Large bowel cancer incidence is related to age with 83% of cases being diagnosed in people over 60-years-old. Lifestyle appears to have a central role in large bowel cancer risk, with diet being one of the most important factors identified to date. Bowel cancer incidence is higher in populations on Westernized diets, rich in red meat and fat. The EPIC study (European prospective investigation into cancer and nutrition)

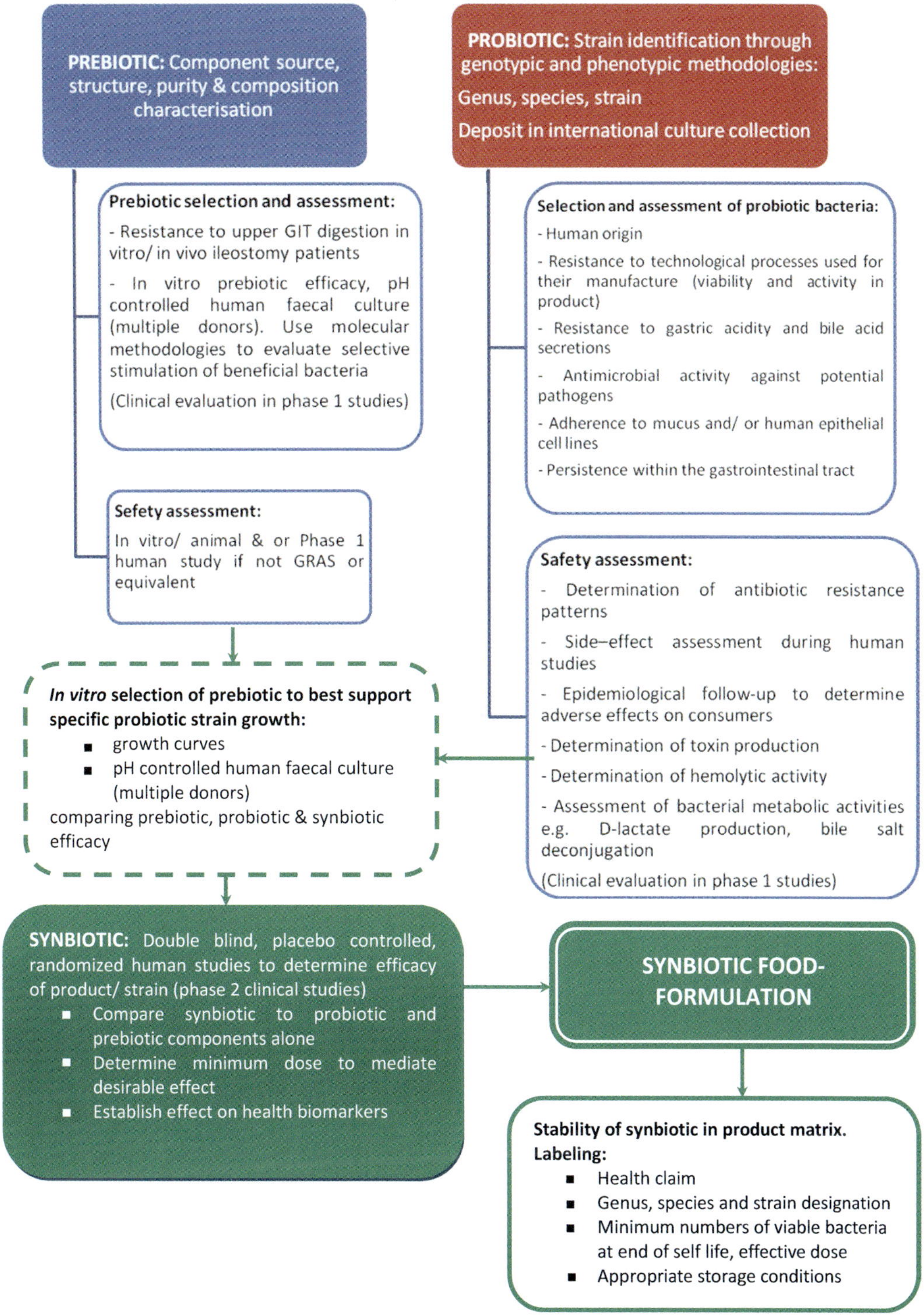
PREBIOTIC: Component source, structure, purity & composition characterisation
PROBIOTIC: Strain identification through genotypic and phenotypic methodologies:
Genus, species, strain
Deposit in international culture collection
Prebiotic selection and assessment:
- Resistance to upper GIT digestion in vitro/ in vivo ileostomy patients
- In vitro prebiotic efficacy, pH controlled human faecal culture (multiple donors). Use molecular methodologies to evaluate selective stimulation of beneficial bacteria
(Clinical evaluation in phase 1 studies)
Selection and assessment of probiotic bacteria:
- Human origin
- Resistance to technological processes used for their manufacture (viability and activity in product)
- Resistance to gastric acidity and bile acid secretions
- Antimicrobial activity against potential pathogens
- Adherence to mucus and/ or human epithelial cell lines
- Persistence within the gastrointestinal tract
Sefety assessment:
In vitro/ animal & or Phase 1 human study if not GRAS or equivalent
Safety assessment:
- Determination of antibiotic resistance patterns
- Side–effect assessment during human studies
- Epidemiological follow-up to determine adverse effects on consumers
- Determination of toxin production
- Determination of hemolytic activity
- Assessment of bacterial metabolic activities e.g. D-lactate production, bile salt deconjugation
(Clinical evaluation in phase 1 studies)
In vitro selection of prebiotic to best support specific probiotic strain growth:
growth curves
pH controlled human faecal culture (multiple donors)
comparing prebiotic, probiotic & synbiotic efficacy
SYNBIOTIC: Double blind, placebo controlled, randomized human studies to determine efficacy of product/ strain (phase 2 clinical studies)
Compare synbiotic to probiotic and prebiotic components alone
Determine minimum dose to mediate desirable effect
Establish effect on health biomarkers
SYNBIOTIC FOOD-FORMULATION
Stability of synbiotic in product matrix.
Labeling:
Health claim
Genus, species and strain designation
Minimum numbers of viable bacteria at end of self life, effective dose
Appropriate storage conditions

Figure 1

Suggested steps for establishing a synbiotic formulation.

suggested a significant increase (55%) in bowel cancer risk upon a 100 g d^{-1} increase in red and processed meat consumption, and a significant decrease with higher intake of fish (Norat et al. 2005). A lower cancer risk has been correlated with high dietary fiber intake (Park et al. 2005). Colon cancer risk increases by approximately 60% in men and 30% in women with a body mass index greater than 28.5. It is suggested that obese men have a 90% increased risk of dying from cancer, and the increased risk in obese women ranges between 23% and 37%. Central obesity has also been suggested as an indicator of colon cancer risk (Bianchini et al. 2002, Murphy et al. 2000, Moore et al. 2004). Studies indicate that fiber intake plays a role in colorectal cancer. Men and women in the highest quintile of fiber intake were at approximately 20% lower risk of bowel cancer manifestation compared to individuals in the lower quintile. More specifically, individuals with a high fiber intake were at 40% lower risk of developing left-sided colon cancer compared to those with low fiber intakes (Bingham et al. 2005). Dietary fiber increases fecal bulk and decreases transit time and as such reduces contact with fecal carcinogens.

The main body of evidence on the effect of synbiotics against colon cancer is either from studies on animal models of tumorigenesis, transgenic animals, and chemically induced models of mutagenesis, or from in vitro cell line models.

One of the first studies to investigate the potential application of synbiotics against colon cancer was by Rowland and coworkers (1998). They investigated the effect of 4×10^8 viable *B. longum* 25 cells g^{-1} diet combined with Raftiline HP at 5% (w/w) of diet in 60 three to four-weeks-of-age male Sprague-Dawley rats that were treated with azoxymethane so as to induce aberrant crypt foci (ACF) formation. The probiotic was prescreened for its in vitro ability to ferment Raftiline HP prior to the in vivo study. Rats ingested a control diet, probiotic only, prebiotic only, and the synbiotic diet. All animals ingested the control diet for a one-week period prior to azoxymethane dosing, following which, rats were divided in four groups of 15 each, ingesting one of the treatments for a two-week period. Cecal ammonia concentrations, β-glucuronidase, and β-glucosidase activities were measured along with ACF formation. *B. longum* 25 and Raftiline HP both reduced small ACF formation, cecal ammonia concentrations, and β-glucuronidase activity when tested individually compared to the control diet. When used in combination, they mediated a significantly higher inhibition of both small and large size ACF formation. Both Raftinline HP and the synbiotic caused significant increases in β-glucosidase activities; however, *B. longum* alone did not have an effect. The inclusion in this study of proper controls gives valuable insight into the behavior of this synbiotic. It is clear that the effect of the combination of the selected probiotic and prebiotic result in a superior formula that appears to be acting both synergistically (ACF inhibition) but also in an additive manner (reduced β-glucosidase production).

In a later study, using the same model of carcinogenesis, the effect of 10^{10} CFU g^{-1} *L. acidophilus* (LAFTI® L10), *B. lactis* (LAFTI B94, DSM Food Specialties) alone or in combination, and 10 g kg^{-1} diet resistant starch (Hi-maize958, National Starch) was investigated (Le Leu et al. 2005). The study end points included cecal bacteria enumeration, fecal and cecal SCFA levels, cell proliferation, and acute apoptotic response to a genotoxic carcinogen (AARGC). Probiotics and prebiotics were used either alone or in combination with resistant starch. When the synbiotic constituents were used in combination, no effect was observed on the response to the carcinogen. However, the combination of resistant starch and *B. lactis* increased the acute apoptotic response. The combination with *L. acidophilus* did not have the same effect, indicating a strain specific effect and synergy between *B. lactis* and resistant starch. Synbiotic ingestion resulted in lower fecal pH values and higher total and individual SCFA concentrations compared to the probiotics alone. The inclusion of resistant starch increased bifidobacteria and lactobacilli levels. The potential benefit of synbiotic ingestion against ACF in a male Wistar rat model employing 1,2 demethyhydrazine to initiate ACF formation was investigated in a later study (Gallaher & Khil 1999). An undefined *Bifidobacterium* culture (10^8 CFU g^{-1}) was combined with either oligofructose (GRC), soybean oligosaccharides (Ajinomoto), or wheat bran oligosaccahrides (Megazyme) at 2% (w/v) of the diet. The probiotic was tested alone or in combination with one of the test probiotics, and results were compared to a control diet group. Neither the probiotic nor the oligofructose treatment had an effect on ACF formation. However, when used in combination, they mediated a significant decrease as compared to the control group, which signifies a synergy between the components of the synbiotic. The other test prebiotics were only used in combination to the probiotic and not alone, and the results were not as consistent as with oligofructose.

Burns & Rowland (2004) used the Comet assay to evaluate the prophylactic potential of 10^8 *L. plantarum* (Rhodia), *Bifibobacterium* Bb12 (Chr. Hansen), *Enterococcus faecium* S13 (Danisco), *Bifidobacterium* sp. 420 (Danisco), *Streptococcus thermophilus*, and *Lactobacillus bulgaricus* against DNA damage of genotoxic fecal water on HT29 human adenocarcinoma cell lines (2004). The effect was strain specific with *L. plantarum* and *Bifidobacterium* Bb12 being the most effective. In a second experiment, the selected strains were preincubated with Raftiline HP, Raftilose, chicory inulin (Sigma), GOS (Borculo Domo), Actilight (Beghin Meiji), and Fibersol (maltodextrin; Matsutani), and the fermentation supernatants were incubated with the HT29 cells. The most pronounced effect was again observed with *L. plantarum* and *Bifidobacterium* Bb12 in combination with Inulin and Actilight. The degree of protection was even greater than when the bacteria were used alone in the absence of supernatants. Heat-killed bacteria did not have any effect. This suggested that cell viability was necessary to mediate the effect and that certain fermentation products enhanced the degree of protection. Two studies have investigated the tumor-preventative efficacy and fecal water genotixicity *Lactobacillus rhamnosus* and *B. lactis* each at 5×10^8 CFU g^{-1} diet either alone or in combination with 100 g kg^{-1} w/w Synergy 1 in 4 to 5-week-old male F344 rats (Femia et al. 2002, Klinder et al. 2004). Thirty-two rats were fed a control diet, 33 were fed Synergy 1, 32 were fed the probiotics, and 32 were fed the synbiotic. Ten days after being on the test diets, the rats were treated with AOM (azoxymethane) to induce cancer. Animals continued the dietary regime for a further 31 weeks, at which time their clinical condition was assessed. Rats fed the synbiotic and prebiotic diets presented significantly lower tumor numbers compared to rats not fed Synergy 1. Apoptosis was increased in the normal mucosa of the probiotic group; however, no variation was observed in the tumors. Colonic proliferation and SCFA levels were increased in the prebiotic and synbiotic groups. In the Synergy 1 ingesting groups, there was a reduced exposure to genotoxins in the feces, which correlated with tumor incidence in these animals. This implies that it is the fermentation of the prebiotic by the probiotic and the commensal flora that is central in the prophylactic effect. The results of this study indicate again the importance of bacterial fermentation products as protective agents against tumorigenesis.

One in vivo human study on the protective effect of synbiotics against colon cancer has been published (Rafter et al. 2007). The aim was to investigate the potential of a synbiotic preparation, 10^{10} CFU *L. rhamnosus* GG (Valio) and *B. lactis* Bb12 encapsulated in Eudragit L30-D55 (Chr. Hansen) combined with 12 g Synergy 1 in a 12-week randomized, double-blind, placebo-controlled study. Two groups were targeted: 43 polypectomized patients and 37 colon cancer patients. Following synbiotic ingestion, significant increases in fecal lactobacilli and bifidobacteria were observed, and a decrease in *Clostridium perfringens* evaluated using culture techniques. In polypectomized patients, the synbiotic improved the epithelial barrier function and reduced the ability of fecal water to induce colonic cell necrosis, and it prevented increases in Il2 by PBMCs. Analysis of biopsy samples at the end of the intervention indicated a reduced genotoxin exposure. In cancer patients, synbiotic ingestion increased the production of interferon γ. The results of this study are encouraging; however, they do not offer enough insight into the mechanism of synbiotic action. As our knowledge in this area is not very advanced and is mainly based on animal models, it is imperative that proper probiotic and prebiotic controls are used.

Surgical Patients

Morbidity and mortality among severely ill patients, such as transplant and postoperative patients, has remained at high levels despite medical advances in both surgical procedures and pharmacological treatments. Sepsis in intensive care units (ICUs) is unacceptably high and is the tenth most common cause of death in the United States (Bengmark 2004). Patients undergoing extensive surgery are under severe risk of contracting nosocomial bacterial infections, but there is also evidence that disruption of the gut barrier integrity in postoperative patients may greatly contribute towards the increased incidence of sepsis in the ICU (Marshall et al. 1993, MacFie 1997, MacFie et al. 1999). Synbiotic supplementation of the diet and enteral formulas of pre- and postoperative patients may be a promising route of manipulating the composition of the gut microbiota toward a more beneficial community, and the potential trophic effect of the prebiotic on the gut mucosa could preserve gut barrier function and suppress gut pathogen translocation.

In a double-blind, placebo-controlled study of 137 patients scheduled to undergo elective laparotomy, the efficacy of a synbiotic in preventing postoperative complications was evaluated (Anderson et al. 2004). Patients were divided into a synbiotic ($n = 72$) and a placebo ($n = 65$) treatment group. Patients in the synbiotic group received three times daily capsules delivering 4×10^9 CFU *L. acidophilus* La5, *L. bulgaricus*, *B. lactis* Bb12, and *S. thermophilus* (Trevis®, Christian Hansen) and twice daily 16 g of oligofructose. Patients in the placebo group received placebo capsules and sucrose. Treatment was intiated one to two weeks preoperatively and continued until patients were discharged from the hospital. No difference was observed between the active and placebo groups with regard to bacterial translocation and colonization, systemic inflammation, and septic complications.

In a double-blind study investigating the effect of Synbiotic 2000 in 66 patients scheduled for liver transplantation, a significant decrease in postoperative infections was observed (Rayes et al. 2005). The treatment was added in the enteral feed formula and was administered for 14 days starting on the day of the surgery. Patients were divided in two treatment groups, one receiving Synbiotic 2000 and the other receiving only the fiber components of Synbiotic 2000. Interestingly, in the group receiving the full synbiotic formula, postoperative infections were significantly lower (3%) compared to the fiber only group (48%). In the synbiotic group, the required antibiotic treatment duration was also significantly lower. In a later study, the same group evaluated the efficacy of Synbiotic 2000 against bacterial infection rates following pylorus-preserving pancreatoduodenectomy (Rayes et al. 2007). This time, the synbiotic treatment was administered one day preoperatively and was continued for eight days postoperatively. Eighty-nine adult patients were divided into two treatment groups, and they received identical treatments to the previous study. The results were in agreement with the liver transplantation study with bacterial infections being significantly lower in the synbiotic group (12.5%) compared with the fiber group (40%), despite the shorter postoperative treatment duration. Although these findings are very promising, one shortcoming of these studies was that it is not possible to determine whether it was the synbiotic or just the probiotic components of Synbiotic 2000 that mediated the effect. Also, no conventional treatment group was included in the study, and as such, results cannot be evaluated properly.

Synbiotic 2000 was also effective in reducing endotoxemia and blood ammonia levels and increasing fecal *Lactobacillus* concentrations in patients with cirrhosis suffering from minimal hepatic encephalopathy (MHE) (Liu et al. 2004). The same experimental approach was followed as described in the above Synbiotic 2000 studies, with 20 patients receiving the synbiotic and 20 receiving only the fiber components. However, a placebo group was also included that received a wheat-based, nonfermentable fiber (Medipharm). The gut microbiota of the MHE patients were characterized by an overgrowth of *Escherichia coli* and *Staphyloccocal* species. An increase in *Lactobacillus* upon ingestion of the synbiotic treatment normalized the flora. MHE reversal was observed in 50% of the synbiotic group patients with a significant reduction in endotoxemia. Treatment with the fiber components also had a beneficial effect in some of the volunteers.

As previously mentioned, timing of synbiotic intervention may be an important factor in preventing postoperative infection. This was investigated in 101 patients with biliary cancer undergoing scheduled high-risk hepatobiliary resection (Sugawara et al. 2006). Volunteers were divided into two groups, one receiving only postoperative treatment and one receiving both pre- and postoperative treatments two weeks prior and two weeks following surgery. The preoperative treatment of 4×10^{10} *L. casei* Shirota (80 ml Yakult 400), 10^{10} *B. breve* (100 ml Bifiel, Yakult), and 15 g GOS (Oligomate 55, Yakult) was administered orally and delivered daily. The postoperative treatment was delivered parenterally and delivered 15 g GOS, 10^8 CFU g^{-1} *L. casei*, and 10^8 CFU g^{-1} *B. breve*. Both probiotics were detected in patient feces in both patient groups; however, in the group receiving both pre- and postoperative synbiotic treatments, postoperative infections, white blood cell counts, and C-reactive protein were significantly lower compared to the group receiving only the postoperative treatment.

To date, all studies investigating the efficacy of synbiotic administration in surgical patients have used commercially available products. The results are indeed encouraging, and there seems to be scope for further studies and more widespread application of synbiotics in these patients. However, the lack of placebo and proper controls (e.g., prebiotic only, probiotic only) to elucidate the mechanism of the effects prevent the proper evaluation of the synbiotic effects. All studies to date have used multiprobiotic formulas, which limits insight into the actual functionally active ingredients mediating the observed effects.

PRODUCT FORMULATION

The concept of synbiotics offers a potential for increased efficacy to functional foods by exploiting the advantages that a combination of prebiotics with probiotics confers not only to health but also to product stability during storage. One of the main challenges that probiotic products have to meet is delivering an adequate concentration of live bacteria so as to mediate a desired health effect. Viability and stability during storage prior to ingestion have been two of the main issues that can greatly affect product efficacy and one of the challenges probiotic manufacturers must meet. The introduction of a prebiotic into the product should theoretically improve viability of the probiotic. However, fermentation of the prebiotic may have some undesirable effects on the food matrix, as lactate and SCFA production could mediate a decrease in the pH of the product and affect consistency. The synbiotic should be able to deliver a minimum dose of 10^8 CFU ml^{-1} product after storage at low temperature (Mattila-Sandholm et al. 2002).

The majority of probiotic or synbiotic foods available currently are either yogurts or dairy drinks, which, in addition to the traditional starter cultures, contain probiotic bacteria usually belonging to the genera *Bifidobacterium* and *Lactobacillus*. Any prebiotic introduced to the dairy product should be selective for growth of the probiotic. Prebiotic fermentation by the starter cultures should also be considered, as this may affect organoleptic properties of the product and reduce the amount of fermentable substrate available for the prebiotic. Several studies have investigated the effect on viability and palatability of dairy products when combined with a synbiotic. However, there are few well-designed studies that have followed a rational selection of the probiotic and the prebiotic and therefore arbitrarily use the term synbiotic.

One study to investigate the formulation of a synbiotic food product was by Crittenden et al. (2001). They screened 40 *Bifidobacterium* strains for their ability to ferment resistant starch (Hi-maize^{TM}) to be used in a synbiotic yogurt. Of the strains screened, *B. lactis* Lafti^{TM}B94 was selected for its ability to ferment resistant starch as well as a range of other potential prebiotics, including FOSs, GOSs, soybean oligosaccharides, and xylooligosaccharides. The authors tested extensively the probiotic isolates for their in vitro ability to survive simulated gastric conditions and bile secretions.

Desai et al. (2004) investigated the effect of commercially available oligosaccharides (Hi-maize^{TM}, Raftilose, lactulose, and chicory inulin; Sigma) on seven *Lactobacillus* strains (*L. casei* ASCC 1520, *L. rhamnosus* ASCC 1521, *L. casei* CSCC 2607, *L. zeae* ATCC 15820, *L. casei* ASCC 290, *L. paracasei* ASCC 292, and *L. casei* ASCC 279) in skimmed milk during refrigerated storage. Although the authors did not preselect the probiotic strains so as to ensure test prebiotic fermentation, their aim was to develop a synbiotic food whereby the prebiotics would enhance viability of the probiotics. It was observed that despite a decrease in viability in all test products, viability was in general improved as compared to the prebiotic negative control, and the most improved effect was observed with inulin. The growth, activity, and viability of the *Lactobacilllus* strains was both strain and prebiotic dependent, and prebiotic addition improved growth rates while decreasing fermentation time. A more novel approach of encapsulating the synbiotic to improve its stability both during storage in yogurt as well as during ingestion was investigated by Iyer & Kailasapathy (2005). Prebiotics were screened in vitro for their ability to support the growth of *L. acidophilus* CSCC 2400 or CSCC 2409. The efficacy of selected complementary prebiotics (Hi-maize^{TM} starch, Raftiline and Raftilose) in improving viability when coencapsulated with a probiotic was assessed under acidic conditions and during storage in yogurt. Hi-maize^{TM} at concentrations of up to 1% (w/v) significantly increased probiotic viability during incubation at pH 2 as compared with the fructans; however, further increases in prebiotic concentration did not further increase viability. The effect of coating was also investigated and chitosan encapsulation was proven to offer superior protection as compared with alginate and poly-L-lysine. In a similar study, Crittenden et al. (2006) investigated the effect of encapsulation within a film-forming-carbohydrate-oil emulsion on viability of *B. infantis* Bb-02 during nonrefrigerated storage and GI transit. Briefly, spray-dried *B. infantis* in FOS (Raftilose P95) capsules was stored in foil sachets at room temperature for a two-month period and their viability compared with that of nonencapsulated bacteria. Encapsulation significantly improved viability of *B. infantis* during storage but also during passage through an in vitro model of the human stomach and small intestine. FOS microencapsulation also improved probiotic viability under storage in an open container at 25°C and 50% humidity, which further indicates that this approach could improve product stability and shelf life. Although there is a synergy between the prebiotic and the probiotic and a superior formulation is achieved by combining the two, enhancement of viability during storage and passage through the GI tract is through the encapsulation process rather than fermentation of the prebiotic. Here the authors tested two different capsules; however, they both contained FOS, and they both offered the same levels of protection. It would have been interesting to see the effect of other potential prebiotics and prebiotic-free capsules to investigate if it was the synergy between the prebiotic and *B. infantis* that resulted in increased viability. Homayouni et al. (2008) investigated the survival of *L. casei* Lc-01 and *B. lactis* Bb-12 when encapsulated in alginate in the presence of 1% Hi-maize^{TM} in ice cream containing resistant starch. Viability was only compared with the nonencapsulated forms and not with capsules or ice cream in the absence of resistant starch. Although the product was characterized as a synbiotic, it is apparent that there was no added effect on viability due to the presence of the prebiotic. The superiority of the encapsulated formula was due to protection lent by the encapsulation.

Buriti et al. (2007) investigated the stability of fresh cream cheese supplemented with inulin (Raftiline) and *L. paracasei*. The probiotic was not prescreened so as to determine its ability to ferment inulin. The authors did not observe an improvement in the viability of *L. paracasei* during

Table 1 Emerging studies on synbiotic application in disease

Intervention (treatments per day)	Study design	Duration	Evidence of synbiotic efficacy	Reference
Refractory enterocolitis				
3 × daily: 10^9 *Bifidobacteriumbreve Yakult: B. breve and Lactobacillus casei Shirota: L. casei* 1 g galactooligosaccharide (GOS)-oligomate (Yakult)	Seven short bowel patients with refractory enterocolitis, 2–24 years	15–55 months	Improvement in intestinal bacterial flora composition (culture), increased short chain fatty acid (SCFA) production, accelerated body weight gain	Kanamori et al. 2004
***Helicobacter pylori*–colonization**				
Antibiotic triple therapy, 10^9 *Lactobacillus acidophilus* LB (lacteol forte), 250 g lyophilized *Saccharomyces boulardii* (Perenteryl, Merck) & 5 g inulin (Orafti)	254 *H. pylori*–positive children distributed in three treatment groups Randomized open study. Spontaneous clearance assessed in 81 positive untreated children	Group 1: eight days Groups 2 and 3: eight weeks	Synbiotic more efficient than *L. acidophilus* LB (12% eradication) but not as effective as antibiotic (66% eradication) based on C-Urea Breath Test	Gotteland et al. 2005
MRSA (methicillin resistant *Staphylococcus aureus*) enteritis				
3 g GOS (oligomate) 3 g *L. casei Shirota* & 120 mg vancomycin supplemented by 3 g *B. breve* (BBG-1)	Case study; three-month-old Down syndrome boy	*B. breve* introduced following 42 days on initial treatment	MRSA dominant flora eradicated by vancomycin treatment, anaerobic flora, SCFA levels, and stool appearance normalized by successive synbiotic treatment	Kanamori et al. 2003
Mineral bioavailability				
Folow-up infant formula plus: 5.5×10^7 CFU *Bifidobacterium bifidum and Bifidobacterium longum* 12, 50, 100 g kg^{-1} GOS (oligomate) -synbiotic combinations of the above	54 three-week-old weanling male Srague-Dawley rats Samples on days 8–10, 18–20, and 28–30	30 days	Increased Ca, Mg, P bioavailability with probiotic and prebiotic formulas, most efficient formulas tended to be the 50 g kg^{-1} and100 g kg^{-1} synbiotics; synbiotics significantly reduced lumen pH and increased crypt depth cell density in colon. Increased Ca and P in femur and tibia, Mg in tibia. Site of Ca absorption distal colon, Mg proximal and distal.	Pérez-Conesa et al. 2006; Pérez-Conesa et al. 2007

storage at low temperature, and they noted stability of inulin in the product, which indicates that the probiotic could not ferment it. The results in the product prior to ingestion strongly suggest that there will be no synergy in vivo. In a later study, the same group investigated the sensory quality, and prebiotic and probiotic stability in petit-suisse cheese (Cardarelli et al. 2008). Again, the same approach was followed as the probiotic strains (*B. animalis* subsp. *lactis* and *L. acidophilus*) were not preselected to ensure fermentation of the test prebiotics (Beneo ST and Beneo P95, Orafti). Their results suggested again that the test prebiotics were not fermented and as such were stable in the product. Similar results were reported for the combination of *L. paracasei* subsp. *paracasei* LCB82 and inulin (Raftiline GR, Orafti) in chocolate mousse. Probiotic viability and prebiotic levels were not affected during storage (Casale Aragon-Alegro et al. 2007).

CONCLUSIONS AND FUTURE PERSPECTIVES

Further evidence is emerging on the use of synbiotics on refractory entorocolitis, atopic dermatitis/immunomodulation, cholesterol profile improvement, *Helicobacter pylori* colonization, mineral bioavailability, and antipathogen activity. Study results are summarized in **Table 1**.

It is clear that the scope is broadening for the application of synbiotics in both health and disease. However, with few exceptions, the term synbiotic has been loosely used by the majority of published studies currently available. In most cases, there was no rational selection of the prebiotic-probiotic combinations, and some of the research lacked proper controls to confirm or deny the presence of a synergistic or additive effect. Furthermore, several studies used dietary fibers that are not recognized prebiotics. This combined with the fact that in most cases no attempt was made to confirm growth of the probiotic on the prebiotic implies that the nature of the effect is questionable.

The formulation of successful synbiotics is a particularly complex issue. Studies to date have not investigated the issue of minimum effective dose to mediate the desirable effect in the absence of side effects. In the future, it is imperative that both the probiotic and prebiotic components are rationally selected and the appropriate biomarkers are targeted during in vivo trials.

DISCLOSURE STATEMENT

The authors are not aware of any affiliations, memberships, funding, or financial holdings that might be perceived as affecting the objectivity of this review.

LITERATURE CITED

Alaradi O, Barkin JS. 2002. Irritable bowel syndrome: update on pathogenesis and management. *Med. Princ. Pract.* 11(1):2–17

Anderson AD, McNaught CE, Jain PK, MacFie J. 2004. Randomised clinical trial of synbiotic therapy in elective surgical patients. *Gut* 53(2):241–45

Aragon-Alegro LC, Alegro JHA, Cardarelli HR, Chiu MC, Saad SMI. 2007. Potentially probiotic and synbiotic chocolate mousse. *LWT* 40:669–75

Bartosch S, Woodmansey EJ, Paterson JC, McMurdo ME, Macfarlane GT. 2005. Microbiological effects of consuming a synbiotic containing *Bifidobacterium bifidum*, *Bifidobacterium lactis*, and oligofructose in elderly persons, determined by real-time polymerase chain reaction and counting of viable bacteria. *Clin. Infect. Dis.* 40(1):28–37

Bangmark S. 2004. Bio-ecological control of perioperative and ITU morbidity. *Langenbecks Arch Surg.* 389:145–154

Bianchini F, Kaaks R, Vainio H. 2002. Overweight, obesity, and cancer risk. *Lancet Oncol.* 3(9):565–74

Bibiloni R, Fedorak RN, Tannock GW, Madsen KL, Gionchetti P, et al. 2005. VSL#3 probiotic-mixture induces remission in patients with active ulcerative colitis. *Am. J. Gastroenterol.* 100:1539–46

Bingham SA, Norat T, Moskal A, Ferrari P, Slimani N, et al. 2005. Is the association with fibre from foods in colorectal cancer confounded by folate intake? *Cancer Epidemiol. Biomarkers Prev.* 14:1552–56

Buriti FCA, Cardarelli HR, Filisetti TMCC, Saad SMI. 2007. Synbiotic potential of fresh cream cheese supplemented with inulin and *Lactobacillus paracasei* in co-culture with *Streptococcus thermophilus*. *Food Chem.* 104:1605–10

Burns AJ, Rowland IR. 2004. Antigenotoxicity of probiotics and prebiotics on faecal water-induced DNA damage in human colon adenocarcinoma cells. *Mutat. Res.* 551(1–2):233–43

Cancer research UK. 2005. Cancer stats: Lifestyle and cancer. (**http://info.cancerresearchuk.org/cancerstats/**)

Cancer research UK. 2006. Cancer stats: Large bowel cancer—UK. (**http://info.cancerresearchuk.org/cancerstats/**)

Cardarelli HR, Buriti FCA, Castro IA, Saad AMI. 2008. Inulin and oligofructose improve sensory quality and increase the probiotic viable count in potentially synbiotic petit-suisse cheese. *Food Sci. Technol.* 41(6):1037–46

Casiraghi MC, Canzi E, Zanchi R, Donati E, Villa L. 2007. Effects of a synbiotic milk product on human intestinal ecosystem. *J. Appl. Microbiol.* 103(2):499–506

Chermesh I, Tamir A, Reshef R, Chowers Y, Suissa A, et al. 2007. Failure of synbiotic 2000 to prevent postoperative recurrence of Crohn's disease. *Dig. Dis. Sci.* 52:385–89

Crittenden R, Weerakkody R, Sanguansri L, Augustin M. 2006. Synbiotic microcapsules that enhance microbial viability during nonrefrigerated storage and gastrointestinal transit. *Appl. Environ. Microbiol.* 72(3):2280–82

Crittenden RG, Morris LF, Harvey ML, Tran LT, Mitchell HL, Playne MJ. 2001. Selection of a bifidobacterium strain to complement resistant starch in a synbiotic yoghurt. *J. Appl. Microbiol.* 90(2):268–78

De Preter V, Vanhoutte T, Huys G, Swings J, De Vuyst L, Rutgeerts P, Verbeke K. 2007. Effects of *Lactobacillus casei* Shirota, *Bifidobacterium breve*, and oligofructose-enriched inulin on colonic nitrogen-protein metabolism in healthy humans. *Am. J. Physiol. Gastrointest. Liver Physiol.* 292(1):G358–68

Desai AR, Powell IB, Shah NP. 2004. Survival and activity of probiotic lactobacilli in skim milk containing prebiotics. *J. Food Sci.* 69(3):M57–60

Dughera L, Elia C, Navino M, Cisarò F. 2007. Effects of synbiotic preparations on constipated irritable bowel syndrome symptoms. *Acta Biomed.* 78(2):111–16

Dunne C, O'Mahony L, Murphy L, Thornton G, Morrissey D, et al. 2001. In vitro selection criteria for probiotic bacteria of human origin: correlation with in vivo findings. *Am. J. Clin. Nutr.* 73(Suppl.):386S–92

Femia AP, Luceri C, Dolara P, Giannini A, Biggeri A, et al. 2002. Antitumorigenic activity of the prebiotic inulin enriched with oligofructose in combination with the probiotics *Lactobacillus rhamnosus* and *Bifidobacterium lactis* on azoxymethane-induced colon carcinogenesis in rats. *Carcinogenesis* 23(11):1953–60

Fujimori S, Tatsuguchi A, Gudis K, Kishida T, Mitsui K, et al. 2007. High dose probiotic and prebiotic cotherapy for remission induction of active Crohn's disease. *J. Gastroenterol. Hepatol.* 22(8):1199–204

Fuller R. 1991. Probiotics in human medicine. *Gut* 32:432–42

Furrie E, Macfarlane S, Kennedy A, Cummings JH, Walsh SV, et al. 2005. Synbiotic therapy (*Bifidobacterium longum*/Synergy 1) initiates resolution of inflammation in patients with active ulcerative colitis: a randomised controlled pilot trial. *Gut* 54:242–49

Gallaher DD, Khil J. 1999. The effect of synbiotics on colon carcinogenesis in rats. *J. Nutr.* 129(7 Suppl.):1483S–87

Gibson GR, Roberfroid MB. 1995. Dietary modulation of the human colonic microbiota: introducing the concept of prebiotics. *J. Nutr.* 125(6):1401–12

Gibson GR, Scott KP, Rastall RA, Tuohy KM, Hotchkiss A, et al. 2010. Dietary prebiotics: current status and new definition. *IFIS* 7(1):1–19

Gionchetti P, Rizzello F, Helwig U, Venturi A, Lammers KM, et al. 2003. Prophylaxis of pouchitis onset with probiotic therapy: a double-blind, placebo-controlled trial. *Gastroenterology* 124:1202–9

Gionchetti P, Rizzello F, Venturi A, Brigidi P, Matteuzzi D, et al. 2000. Oral bacteriotherapy as maintenance treatment in patients with chronic pouchitis: a double-blind, placebo-controlled trial. *Gastroenterology* 119:305–9

Gotteland M, Poliak L, Cruchet S, Brunser O. 2005. Effect of regular ingestion of *Saccharomyces boulardii* plus inulin or *Lactobacillus acidophilus* LB in children colonized by *Helicobacter pylori*. *Acta Paediatr.* 94(12):1747–51

Havenaar R, Huis In't Veld MJH. 1992. Probiotics, a general view. In *Lactic Acid Bacteria in Health and Disease.* Vol. 1, ed. BJ Wood, pp. 151–70. Amsterdam: Elsevier

Homayouni A, Azizi A, Ehsani MR, Yarmand MS, Razavi SH. 2008. Effect of microencapsulation and resistant starch on the probiotic survival and sensory properties of synbiotic ice cream. *Food Chem.* 111(1):50–55

Iyer C, Kailasapathy K. 2005. Effect of co-encapsulation of probiotics with prebiotics on increasing the viability of encapsulated bacteria under in vitro acidic and bile salt conditions and in yogurt. *J. Food Sci.* 70(1):M18–23

FAO/WHO. 2002. Joint FAO/WHO working group report on drafting guidelines for the evaluation of probiotics in food. London, Ontario, Can.: WHO

Kajander K, Hatakka K, Poussa T, Färkkilä M, Korpela R. 2005. A probiotic mixture alleviates symptoms in irritable bowel syndrome patients: a controlled 6-month intervention. *Aliment. Pharmacol. Ther.* 22(5):387–94

Kanamori Y, Hashizume K, Kitano Y, Tanaka Y, Morotomi M, et al. 2003. Anaerobic dominant flora was reconstructed by synbiotics in an infant with MRSA enteritis. *Pediatr. Int.* 45:359–62

Kanamori Y, Sugiyama M, Hashizume K, Yuki N, Morotomi M, et al. 2004. Experience of long-term synbiotic therapy in seven short bowel patients with refractory enterocolitis. *J. Ped. Surg.* 39:1686–92

Klinder A, Förster A, Caderni G, Femia AP, Pool-Zobel BL. 2004. Fecal water genotoxicity is predictive of tumor-preventive activities by inulin-like oligofructoses, probiotics (*Lactobacillus rhamnosus* and *Bifidobacterium lactis*), and their synbiotic combination. *Nutr. Cancer.* 49(2):144–55

Kuisma J, Mentula S, Jarvinen H, Kahri A, Saxelin M, Farkkila M. 2003. Effect of *Lactobacillus rhamnosus* GG on ileal pouch inflammation and microbial flora. *Aliment. Pharmacol. Ther.* 17:509–15

Le Leu RK, Brown IL, Hu Y, Bird AR, Jackson M, et al. 2005. A synbiotic combination of resistant starch and *Bifidobacterium lactis* facilitates apoptotic deletion of carcinogen-damaged cells in rat colon. *J. Nutr.* 135(5):996–1001

Lilly DM, Stillwell RH. 1965. Probiotics: growth promoting factors produced by microorganisms. *Science* 147:747–48

Liu Q, Duan ZP, Ha DK, Bengmark S, Kurtovic J, et al. 2004. Synbiotic modulation of gut flora: effect on minimal hepatic encephalopathy in patients with cirrhosis. *Hepatology* 39(5):1441–49

MacFie J. 1997. Bacterial translocation in surgical patients. *Ann. R. Coll. Surg. Engl.* 79(3):183–89

MacFie J, O'Boyle C, Mitchell CJ, Buckley PM, Johnstone D, et al. 1999. Gut origin of sepsis: a prospective study investigating associations between bacterial translocation, gastric microflora, and septic morbidity. *Gut* 45(2):223–28

Macpherson A, Khoo UY, Forgacs I, Philpott-Howard J, Bjarnason I. 1996. Mucosal antibodies in inflammatory bowel disease are directed against intestinal bacteria. *Gut* 38:365–75

Marshall JC, Christou NV, Meakins JL. 1993. The gastrointestinal tract. The "undrained abscess" of multiple organ failure. *Ann. Surg.* 218(2):111–19

Mattila-Sandholm T, Myllärinen P, Crittenden R, Mogensen G, Fondén R, Saarela M. 2002. Technological challenges for future probiotic foods. *Int. Dairy J.* 12:173–82

Maybery JF, Probert CSJ, Jayanthi V, Shivananda S. 1991. Epidemiology of inflammatory bowel disease: a European perspective. In *Inflammatory Bowel Disease*, ed. AA Anagnostides, HJF Hodgson, JB Kirsner, p. 163. London: Chapman and Hall

Mimura T, Rizzello F, Helwig U, Poggioli G, Schreiber S, et al. 2004. Once daily high dose probiotic therapy (VSL#3) for maintaining remission in recurrent or refractory pouchitis. *Gut* 53:108–14

Moore LL, Bradlee ML, Singer MR, Splansky GL, Proctor MH, et al. 2004. BMI and waist circumference as predictors of lifetime colon cancer risk in Framingham Study adults. *Int. J. Obes. Relat. Metab. Disord.* 28(4):559–67

Morelli L, Garbagna N, Rizzello F, Zonenschain D, Grossi E. 2006. In vivo association to human colon of *Lactobacillus paracasei* B21060: map from biopsies. *Dig. Liver Dis.* 38(12):894–98

Morelli L, Zonenschain D, Callegari ML, Grossi E, Maisano F, Fusillo M. 2003. Assessment of a new synbiotic preparation in healthy volunteers: survival, persistence of probiotic strains and its effect on the indigenous flora. *Nutr. J.* 9:2–11

Murphy TK, Calle EE, Rodriguez C, Kahn HS, Thun MJ. 2000. Body mass index and colon cancer mortality in a large prospective study. *Am. J. Epidemiol.* 152(9):847–54

Norat T, Bingham S, Ferrari P, Slimani N, Jenab M, et al. 2005. Meat, fish, and colorectal cancer risk: the European prospective investigation into cancer and nutrition. *J. Natl. Cancer Inst.* 97:906–16

O'Mahony L, McCarthy J, Kelly P, Hurley G, Luo F, et al. 2005. *Lactobacillus* and *Bifidobacterium* in irritable bowel syndrome: symptom responses and relationship to cytokine profiles. *Gastroenterology* 128:541–51

Osman N, Adawi D, Molin G, Ahrne S, Berggren A, Jeppsson B. 2006. *Bifidobacterium infantis* strains with and without a combination of oligofructose and inulin (OFI) attenuate inflammation in DSS-induced colitis in rats. *BMC Gastroenterol.* 28:6:31

Ouwehand AC, Tiihonen K, Saarinen M, Putaala H, Rautonen N. 2009. Influence of a combination of *Lactobacillus acidophilus* NCFM and lactitol on healthy elderly: intestinal and immune parameters. *Br. J. Nutr.* 101(3):367–75

Park Y, Hunter DJ, Spiegelman D, Bergkvist L, Berrino F, et al. 2005. Dietary fiber intake and risk of colorectal cancer: a pooled analysis of prospective cohort studies. *JAMA* 294(22):2849–57

Parker RB. 1974. Probiotics, the other half of the antibiotic story. *Anim. Nutr. Health* 29:4–8

Pathmakanthan S, Thornley JP, Hawkey CJ. 1999. Mucosally associated bacterial flora of the human colon and species-specific differences between normal and inflamed colonic biopsies. *Microb. Ecol. Health Dis.* 11:169–74

Pérez-Conesa D, López G, Abellán P, Ros G. 2006. Bioavailability of calcium, magnesium and phosphorus in rats fed probiotic, prebiotic and synbiotic powder follow-up infant formulas and their effect on physiological and nutritional parameters. *J. Sci. Food Agric.* 86:2327–36

Pérez-Conesa D, López G, Ros G. 2007. Effects of probiotic, prebiotic and synbiotic follow-up infant formulas on large intestine morphology and bone mineralisation in rats. *J. Sci. Food Agric.* 87(6):1059–68

Pineiro M, Asp NG, Reid G, Macfarlane S, Morelli L, et al. 2008. FAO technical meeting on prebiotics. *J. Clin. Gastroenterol.* 42(Suppl. 3)2:S156–59

Rafter J, Bennett M, Caderni G, Clune Y, Hughes R, et al. 2007. Dietary synbiotics reduce cancer risk factors in polypectomized and colon cancer patients. *Am. J. Clin. Nutr.* 85(2):488–96

Rayes N, Seehofer D, Theruvath T, Mogl M, Langrehr JM, et al. 2007. Effect of enteral nutrition and synbiotics on bacterial infection rates after pylorus-preserving pancreatoduodenectomy: a randomized, double-blind trial. *Ann. Surg.* 246(1):36–41

Rayes N, Seehofer D, Theruvath T, Schiller RA, Langrehr JM, et al. 2005. Supply of pre- and probiotics reduces bacterial infection rates after liver transplantation: a randomized, double-blind trial. *Am. J. Transplant.* 5(1):125–30

Roberfroid M. 2007. Prebiotics: the concept revisited. *J. Nutr.* 137(3 Suppl. 2):830S–37

Rowland IR, Rumney CJ, Coutts JT, Lievense LC. 1998. Effect of *Bifidobacterium longum* and inulin on gut bacterial metabolism and carcinogen-induced aberrant crypt foci in rats. *Carcinogenesis* 19:281–85

Salminen S. 1996. Uniqueness of probiotic strains. *IDF Nutr. News. Lett.* 5:16–18

Sartor RB. 1997. The influence of normal microbial flora on the development of chronic mucosal inflammation. *Res. Immunol.* 148:567–76

Sugawara G, Nagino M, Nishio H, Ebata T, Takagi K, et al. 2006. Perioperative synbiotic treatment to prevent postoperative infectious complications in biliary cancer surgery: a randomized controlled trial. *Ann. Surg.* 244(5):706–14

Tanaka R, Takayama H, Morotomi M, Kuroshima T, Ueyama S, et al. 1983. Effects of administration of TOS and *Bifidobacterium breve* 4006 on the human fecal flora. *Bifidobact. Microflora* 2:17–24

Tannock GW. 1998. Studies on the intestinal microflora: a prerequisite for the development of probiotics. *Int. Dairy J.* 8:527–33

Tomoda T, Nakano Y, Kageyama T. 1991. Effect of yogurt and yogurt supplemented with *Bifidobacterium* and/or lactulose in healthy persons: a comparative study. *Bifidobact. Microflora.* 10(2):123–30

Vanhoutte T, De Preter V, De Brandt E, Verbeke K, Swings J, Huys G. 2006. Molecular monitoring of the fecal microbiota of healthy human subjects during administration of lactulose and *Saccharomyces boulardii*. *Appl. Environ. Microbiol.* 72(9):5990–97

Veltkamp C, Tonkonogy SL, De Jong YP, Albright C, Grenther WB, et al. 2001. Continuous stimulation by normal bacteria is essential for the development and perpetuation of colitis in Tge26 mice. *Gastroenterology* 120:900–13

Vergin F. 1954. Anti- und probiotika. *Hippokrates* 25:16–119

Whorwell PJ, Altringer L, Morel J, Bond Y, Charbonneau D, et al. 2006. Efficacy of an encapsulated probiotic *Bifidobacterium infantis* 35624 in women with irritable bowel syndrome. *Am. J. Gastroenterol.* 101:1581–90

Application of Sensory and Instrumental Volatile Analyses to Dairy Products

A.E. Croissant, D.M. Watson, and M.A. Drake*

Department of Food, Bioprocessing, and Nutrition Sciences, Southeast Dairy Foods Research Center, North Carolina State University, Raleigh, North Carolina 27695;
email: maryanne_drake@ncsu.edu

Annu. Rev. Food Sci. Technol. 2011. 2:395–421

First published online as a Review in Advance on December 13, 2010

The *Annual Review of Food Science and Technology* is online at food.annualreviews.org

This article's doi:
10.1146/annurev-food-022510-133653

1941-1413/11/0410-0395$20.00

Keywords

descriptive sensory, flavor chemistry, instrumental analysis, sensory analysis, whey protein

Abstract

Comprehensive food flavor analysis requires a multidisciplinary approach. This article presents a comprehensive review of the relationship between sensory and instrumental analysis in the research of food flavor. Common practices for aroma flavor compound isolation, separation, and identification are discussed with strengths and weaknesses of the respective methodologies. A review of whey protein flavor research is presented to demonstrate the range of techniques available for the investigation of food flavors. These techniques are applicable to all food categories. The complexity introduced by food texture regarding flavor analysis is discussed using the attribute creaminess as an example.

FLAVOR IN FOOD

The sensory experience of a food (flavor and texture) is multimodal and encompasses psychological and physiological responses. In the most basic form, flavor represents perception of the basic tastes, aromas, and feeling factors of a product. Given that there are only five basic tastes and a limited number of trigeminal responses, most of what is considered flavor actually refers to aroma-active volatile compounds that are perceived ortho- or retronasally by the olfactory epithelium. Considerable effort has been recently made to relate taste and aroma perception, and to define flavor as a combination of sensory modalities. Auvray & Spence (2008) reviewed multimodal flavor analysis and argued that taste, aroma, feeling factors, the trigeminal system, and visual and auditory properties make up flavor perception, which defines flavor not by sensory modality but by perceptual modality brought together by the act of eating. However, because of the wide assortment of aromatic compounds and the hundreds of combinations of these compounds, a tremendous amount of work remains to be conducted to elucidate the role(s) of volatile compounds in foods. The current review focuses primarily on the analysis of volatile compound flavor contributions in foods. The majority of food flavor experience consists of aroma properties, but nonvolatile constituents should also be considered in the investigation of food flavor. Nonvolatiles and volatile compounds may present additive or reductive effects on perceived aroma and/or taste. Subthreshold concentrations of volatile compounds have been shown to amplify taste intensity and vice versa (Pfeiffer et al. 2005). Flavor perception is also a combination of physiological and memory responses. Previous consumer experience with aroma compounds has been demonstrated to play a role in flavor synergy (Nguyen et al. 2002, Pfeiffer et al. 2005, Stevenson et al. 1999). In addition to sensory methodology, psychophysical, neuroimaging, and neurophysiological studies contribute to the body of knowledge explaining flavor and flavor perception. An understanding of the chemical and physical factors responsible for the attributes of interest as well as panelist training can aid in reducing misinterpretation of results.

SENSORY TECHNIQUES AND APPLICATIONS

Sensory analysis was practiced in one form or another long before the application of quantitative sensory analysis techniques. When considering food systems, all consumers evoke their own form of sensory analysis, whether by the determination of foods with recognized terms or by their own nomenclature or perceived taste. Grading and judging established a preliminary methodology for quality evaluation (Bodyfelt et al. 1988). Such techniques are still widely employed throughout dairy, muscle, and produce food systems. However, these techniques are defect oriented and limited to the assessment of good or poor quality foods for consumption. When considering some food products, such as produce, companies may employ internal grading to separate premium stock for sale or as fresh versus stock destined for further processing. Often times, this grading is based on appearance and size, and may be subject to electronic monitoring and automation. Human judging and scoring protocols are subjective, nonlinear, and cannot be analyzed statistically or related to consumer likes and dislikes (Drake et al. 2001, Singh et al. 2003). Grading and judging are intended to be utilized as rapid-assessment tools and do not serve to capture the distinct flavor profiles of products or to quantitatively measure consumer acceptance.

Recently, descriptive sensory analysis has become the preferred method of analytical (objective) sensory evaluation (Drake 2007). These methods are intended to enable a group of individuals to perform as a single instrument in order to profile products on all sensory characteristics. This approach can be used to compare products, evaluate quality, and relate to instrumental or consumer responses (Murray et al. 2001, Singh et al. 2003). Each method requires the recruiting and training of a descriptive panel as well as the development or adoption of a sensory language (Drake & Civille 2003). Training is focused on use of the language with specific definitions and references. Terms are not defined as levels of good or bad but by intensities and attributes.

There are several approaches to the training and maintenance of a descriptive analysis panel. The flavor profile method and the texture profile method utilize panelists to form a group consensus (Lawless & Heymann 1999). Quantitative descriptive analysis® (QDA) and the Spectrum™ method are probably the two best-known approaches to descriptive panel training. QDA®, developed by Stone et al. (1974), uses nontechnical terms. Training is generally product or category specific, and references are used only to solve problems with terms. The panel leader does not participate with the 8–12 panelists but facilitates commentary. Data from QDA® is both quantitative and qualitative, but scaling is generally product specific (i.e., attribute intensities are only relatable to other products within the same category or product) (Lawless & Heymann 1999). The Spectrum™ method, developed by Civille of Sensory Spectrum (New Providence, NJ) (Lawless & Heymann 1999), relies on multiproduct, specialized training with references. Attributes are measured on a universal intensity scale and are thus not product specific; references are constant regardless of the product being evaluated. Training on this method is more time consuming, but a single panel can then readily evaluate multiple products or product categories and intensities from different products, and categories can be directly related to each other (i.e., a three in fruity flavor in cheese is the same as a three in fruity flavor of meal replacement beverages, etc.)

Lexicon development includes the designation of terms and references to describe the flavor attributes of a product or commodity. Drake & Civille (2003) reviewed the process for lexicon development as well as its application to understanding flavor. A good flavor lexicon is based on a diversity of products representing the range of flavors of the food product. A broad set of terms is developed then reduced to eliminate redundancies. Equally important is the variety and selection of food and/or chemical references to anchor the lexicon terms. The ideal lexicon maintains multiple references for each term, and is descriptive and discriminating (Drake & Civille 2003). A complete flavor lexicon coupled with a well-trained descriptive panel serves as the basis for flavor research. **Table 1** presents a compilation of sensory languages used to describe whey proteins and whey powders.

Civille & Lyons (1996) compiled a standardized definition and reference book of flavor descriptors that can be used to describe any product(s) or category. The dairy lexicons are applicable across all dairy products with requirements for addition and removal of some terms. Lexicons have been developed for numerous products and commodities, including but not limited to wine, cheese, peanuts and tree nuts, olive oil, fermented dairy products, distilled beverages and beer, chicken and meats, chocolate, rice, vanilla, and fruits (Drake & Civille 2003). Often with much overlap, lexicons have been developed to describe foods within the same category, such as different types of cheese (hard, semihard, soft; young versus aged; and specific types, such as regional cheeses) and different varietals of wine. Using specific and widely available references enables wider adoption of a flavor language.

Another type of sensory testing that generates quantitative data is affective testing. These tests involve consumers rather than trained panelists and are conducted in a manner that uses terms representative of the way consumers would describe a food rather than a developed lexicon used for descriptive sensory analysis. Affective tests measure intensity of a flavor attribute, degree of liking of a flavor attribute, and overall liking of a product. The overall preference between products can also be determined (Lawless & Heymann 1999). Data obtained from affective testing can be related to descriptive and/or instrumental data by external preference mapping.

Table 1 Sensory language for whey protein powders (SWP, WPC34–80, WPI)[a]

Descriptor	Definition	Reference/preparation
Aroma intensity	The overall orthonasal aroma impact of the rehydrated sample	Evaluated as the lid is removed from the cupped sample[c]
Sweet aromatic	Sweet aroma associated with dairy products	Colby Jack cheese shreds, mild Cheddar cheese[b]; 20 ppm vanillin in milk[c]; vanilla cake mix[e]; Quaker oatmeal (50 g soaked in 500 mL water)[e]
Milkfat	Aromatics associated with fresh whole milk	Heavy cream, δ-dodecalactone, 40 ppm[b]
Pasta	Aroma associated with water after pasta has been boiled in it[c]	Boil pasta in water for 30 min[c]; 2,4-decadienal, 20 ppm on filter paper in sniff jar[e]
Doughy/fatty	Aromatic associated with canned biscuit dough[c]	canned biscuit dough[c]; 1 ppm (*Z*)-4-heptenal in water[c]; (*E*,*E*)-2,4-decadienal (2 ppb in skim milk)[h]
Metallic/ meat serum	Aromatics associated with metals or with juices of raw or rare beef[e]	Raw beef steak or ground beef or juices from seared beef steak[e]
Cardboard/ wet brown paper	Aroma associated with cardboard and brown paper[e]	Cardboard in water[b]; cardboard paper[c]; 2 cm × 2 cm pieces of brown paper bag boiled in water for 30 min[e]; pentanal, heptanal, nonanal, 1-octen-3-one, & dimethyl trisulfide[f]
Animal/ wet dog	Aroma associated with wet dog hair[c]	Dissolve 1 bag of gelatin (28 g) in two cups of distilled water[c]
Brothy	Aromatics associated with vegetable stock or boiled potatoes[c]	1 ppm methional or freshly sliced potatoes[c]; drained broth from canned white potatoes[e]
Cooked	Aromatic associated with cooked milk[c]	Heated skim milk to 85°C for 30 min[b]
Musty	Aromatics associated with old books, decaying wood, or closed air spaces	Potting soil[b]
Buttery	Aromatics associated with fresh butterfat and sweet cream	Mild Cheddar[b]; 30 ppm diacetyl in water[d]
Cereal/grain	Aromatics associated with cereals and grains[e]	Cheerios, 50 g in 200 mL water[e]
Fruity	Aromatics associated with different fruits, particularly pineapple[e]	Ethyl hexanoate, 20 ppm on filter paper in sniff jar[e]
Catty	Aromatics associated with tomcat urine[e]	[2]-mercapto-[2]methyl-pentan-[4]-one, 200 ppm on filter paper in sniff jar[e]
Soapy	Aroma associated with medium-chain fatty acids and soap[c]	1 ppm lauric acid or shaved bar soap[c]; decanoic acid[h]
Fecal/dirty	Aromatics associated with animal excrement[e]	Skatole or indole, 20 ppm on filter paper in sniff jar[e]
Yeasty	Aromatics associated with fermenting yeast[e]	Freeze dried yeast packet, 7 g in 500 mL water[e]
Malty	Sweet fermented aromatic associated with dried sprouted grains[e]	Grape Nuts cereal, 20 g in 500 mL water[e]
Cabbage	Sulfurous aromatic associated with cooked cruciferous vegetables	Dimethyl trisulfide, boiled fresh cut cabbage[g]
Raisin/spicy	Aromatics associated with stewed raisins[h]	Boil 50 g dark raisins in 500 mL water[h]
Opacity	Visual term referring to the degree of opacity of the rehydrated protein solution[e]	Water = 0, whole fat fluid milk = 11[e]
Viscosity	Attribute evaluated in the mouth, place product in mouth (approximately 1 tsp), evaluate the rate of flow across the tongue[i]	Water = 1, heavy cream = 3, sweetened condensed milk = 12[d]
Cucumber	Aroma associated with freshly sliced cucumber[c]	1 ppm (*E*)-2-nonenal or freshly sliced cucumbers[c]

(Continued)

Table 1 (*Continued*)

Descriptor	Definition	Reference/preparation
Salty	Basic taste elicted by salts[i]	NaCl 2%[i]
Sour	Basic taste elicted by acids[i]	Citric acid, 1%[i]
Sweet	Basic taste elicited by sugars[i]	5% sucrose solution[i]
Astringent	Chemical feeling factor characterized by a drying or puckering of the oral tissues[i]	Soak six black tea bags in 500 mL water for 10 min; alum, 1% in water[c]
Bitter	Basic taste elicited by various compounds including caffeine and quinine[i]	Caffeine, 0.5% in water[i]

[a]Adapted from Carunchia Whetstine et al. (2005) & Russell et al. (2006).
[b]Karagul-Yuceer et al. 2003.
[c]Carunchia Whetstine et al. 2005.
[d]Mortenson et al. 2008.
[e]Russell et al. 2006.
[f]Whitson et al. 2010.
[g]Wright et al. 2006.
[h]Wright et al. 2009.
[i]Universal references in Meilgaard et al. 2007.

INSTRUMENTAL EVALUATION OF FLAVOR

The human nose is a more powerful tool for aroma evaluation than any machine to date. Flavor is, after all, a sensory experience. However, to understand flavor, sensory analysis techniques must be paired with instrumental techniques to identify specific compounds responsible for taste and aroma in foods. An understanding of the food matrix and the identification of flavor compounds of interest are required to determine the proper methods of extraction (McGorrin 2007, Reineccius 2006b). Factors for consideration include the physical state/composition of the product, sample size and availability, time, compound volatilities and stabilities, and resources. Each method of extraction has strengths and weaknesses in terms of sensitivity, time and resource commitment, and materials safety. Headspace analysis and solvent extraction remain the primary methods for volatile compound extraction. Some methods for direct analysis have been developed. It is important to note that because each extraction technique selects for certain compound classes, the most beneficial approach to flavor chemistry of foods combines more than one technique for analysis.

Aroma Extraction and Isolation Techniques

Although direct gas chromatography (GC) analysis of foods is theoretically possible, the resulting data may be inaccurate for a number of reasons: thermal degradation of nonvolatiles may result in false GC peaks; damage to the column and decreased separation efficiency (by water or other constituents); and column and sample contamination (Reineccius 2003). For these and other reasons, some form of sample extraction is required for a thorough and accurate analysis. Extraction techniques allow the researcher to preferentially solvate a class of compounds of interest (e.g., aroma volatiles) in an extracting solvent and then remove those compounds from the rest of the food matrix. However, extraction also picks up some unwanted organic material, so extraction is often carried out in tandem with purification or distillation of the extract. Researchers must understand that each method selects for some aroma compounds over others, so analysis and conclusions drawn must consider this bias (Reineccius 2006a).

DSE: direct solvent extraction

GC-O: gas chromatography-olfactometry

V-SDE: vacuum simultaneous distillation extraction

A-SDE: atmospheric simultaneous distillation extraction

Various methods exist for extracting the volatile components of foods into a form more easily analyzed. These methods include steam distillation, static and dynamic headspace sampling (DHS), direct solvent extraction (DSE), and vacuum distillation. Each method has distinct advantages and disadvantages, and each of these factors must be considered when choosing a method of extraction. In flavor chemistry, for example, high temperature extraction methods (e.g., steam distillation) often lead to artifact formation and ultimately inaccurate data (Reineccius 2006a). In the case of flavor chemistry, liquid solvent extractions are preferred; however, not all solvents extract organic compounds equally, some solvents are much more efficient than others (Prososki et al. 2007), and not all solvents may be used with gas chromatography-olfactometry (GC-O). Highly volatile compounds may also be masked by the solvent in GC analysis, so for these compounds headspace methods are preferred. Despite the drawbacks of using solvent extraction to recover aroma volatiles (can be time consuming, generates waste, nondiscriminatory, requires post-extraction purification and concentration steps that may lead to loss of volatile components), solvent extraction remains a preferred method of isolating aroma volatiles from food matrices.

Solvent extraction. DSE is generally performed by agitating solvent with crushed or ground analyte. A centrifugation step is often required to fully separate the solvent and sample layers. Diethyl ether (DE) is a very commonly used solvent for volatile extraction (Alewijn et al. 2003), although it has been shown to be less effective than other solvents, especially at extracting highly polar compounds (Prososki et al. 2007). Researchers noted that DE recovered only 35 compounds from sweet whey powder (SWP), as compared to 37 and 42 compounds recovered using methyl formate and methylene chloride, respectively. The study furthermore observed that DE recovered only 25%–50%, on average, of the volatile compounds known to be present across all classes of common food compounds. In a separate study, Alewijn et al. (2003) commented that despite its toxicity, acetonitrile was a superior solvent for the extraction of cheese volatiles, due to its ability to dissolve nearly all lipid-derived compounds. Despite these findings, however, DE remains a commonly used solvent for the extraction of aroma volatiles from food and is cited for use in numerous dairy and food flavor research papers (Drake et al. 2010, Song & Cadwallader 2008). DE is used because it is relatively safe to handle (Heath & Reineccius 1986), easily disposed, inexpensive, and most aroma compounds are readily soluble in organic solvents. DE extracts are considered safe for GC-O sniffing, unlike acetonitrile, methylene chloride, and to a lesser extent, methyl formate extracts. Supercritical fluid extraction offers the advantage of an evaporative solvent in CO_2. However, application to food products is limited by the high cost of equipment and the nonpolar nature of CO_2 (Zhang & Li 2010).

Another common solvent-extract technique is simultaneous distillation extraction (SDE), which simultaneously distills and solvent-extracts a sample (Chaintreau 2001). Samples are prepared for SDE by making a homogenous mixture of the sample with water. The sample and solvent are contained in separate flasks. Both flasks are boiled, vapors mix together, condense, and are separated into respective flasks by density. The extracting solvent is funneled into the solvent flask, and the process is repeated indefinitely. Historically, limitations to SDE were the relatively small sample size and the potential for artifact formation inherent to any extraction process that utilizes heat to drive the extraction (Majcher & Jelen 2009). Small sample size and solvent volume may be advantageous, resulting in an extract that requires no concentration step for analysis. SDE under vacuum has been utilized to reduce heat-generated artifact formation. Vacuum conditions reduce heating requirements by decreasing the boiling point of solvents and compounds. Higher boiling point solvents are required in V-SDE compared to A-SDE in order to reduce ice formation by increasing the condenser temperature and to condense the solvent at or near room temperature (Maignial et al 1992).

Solvent extracts must be concentrated prior to GC injection, ideally without any loss of solvated organic material, while also removing coextracted nonvolatile material. Concentration under vacuum and distillation are two of the more common methods for concentrating solvent extracts. High vacuum transfer (HVT) is a vacuum concentration technique and relies on a large temperature gradient to vaporize the sample volatiles, forcing the volatile fraction through a carrier tube into a collection flask (Engel et al. 1999). Solvent-assisted flavor evaporation (SAFE) is a relatively modern method of separating volatile from nonvolatile food components, typically used in conjunction with solvent extraction. However, the SAFE method has also gained popularity due to the ability to isolate volatiles from numerous food matrices without solvent extraction (Engel et al. 1999). HVT has been used with both solvent-extracted samples and whole food samples, but drawbacks include requiring a large amount of time and space to operate, as well as limitations to the type of food material and solvent that can be utilized (Engel et al. 1999). SAFE offers several other advantages over HVT, as described by Engel et al. (1999). When using DE to extract Cheddar cheese, for example, the highly nonpolar ether also solvates the lipid fraction of the cheese; SAFE distills the ether extract phase from the lipid phase, yielding a flavor volatile extract free of nonvolatile material that can be further concentrated and analyzed.

SAFE: solvent-assisted flavor evaporation

Distillate may also be phase separated to aid in compound detection by decreasing the number of compounds in a given GC-FID (flame ionization detector)/GC-O/MS (mass spectrometry) injection. Acidic (AC) and neutral-basic (NB) fractions are common (Evans et al. 2009, 2010; Milo & Reineccius 1997; Suriyaphan et al. 2001; Whetstine et al. 2003, 2005). The purpose of separating a sample into multiple fractions is purely algebraic. Some of the compounds end up in the NB fraction, and the rest end up in the AC fraction, making identification easier by reducing problems of coelution or peak masking. Coelution is of particular interest to control, because two or more compounds may elute simultaneously, although it is possible that only one of the compounds will have aroma activity. GC-O analysis of fresh goat cheese samples (Whetstine et al. 2003) revealed 29 AC fraction compounds and 53 NB fraction compounds. Phase separation also aids in the identification of different compound classes. Free fatty acids, for example, will remain in the AC fraction, while many aldehydes, ketones, and esters remain in the NB fraction.

Headspace sampling techniques. Headspace sampling methods are broadly lumped into one of two categories: static or dynamic (Wampler 1997). Static methods sample the headspace of a known volume or mass of sample in a closed chamber after the sample has equilibrated with the headspace. Static headspace sampling is especially useful when the analytes of interest are low molecular weight and low boiling point compounds, which tend to elute early on a GC column and are consequently easily masked by a solvent peak (Wampler 1997). DHS methods, unlike static methods, do not allow the establishment of headspace equilibrium within the sample vessel. Volatiles are removed from the headspace by the flow of carrier gas and concentrated in a trap by adsorption or cold trapping. Lack of established equilibrium results in greater volatile transfer from the sample to the headspace. Carrier gas may also be bubbled through the sample in the case of liquid matrices. DHS methods may increase the sensitivity of GC analysis compared with static headspace methods by increasing the actual amount of analyte sampled from a sample matrix. However, dynamic methods typically involve much more complex instrumentation and a greater number of steps in the process compared with static headspace methods, thus introducing more potential for error and inconsistency (Wampler 1997).

Solid phase microextraction (SPME) began as a method for analyzing air quality and pesticide residues in water (Arthur et al. 1992, Pawliszyn & Arthur 1990) but has since been widely adapted to use in food and flavor chemistry research. Readers are encouraged to study Marsili (1997, 2002) for reviews on SPME application and methodology and Spietleun et al. (2010) for a more recent discussion on SPME fiber coatings. With headspace SPME (HS-SPME), a coated silica fiber is injected into the sample headspace and analytes are partitioned between the vapor phase, the sample matrix, and the polymer coating of the fiber (Quach et al. 1999). Direct immersion SPME, whereby the fiber is immersed in the sample, is a technique more associated with semi- and nonvolatile compounds than volatile flavor compounds (Kataoka et al. 2000). Immersion has also been shown effective for extraction of nonpolar and higher molecular weight analytes (Shirey 2000a,b). The mass transfer of volatiles from the headspace to the fiber is limited by the slower diffusion of analytes from the matrix. This imbalance can be overcome by changes to the headspace volume, pH, sample size, agitation, and temperature, as well as the addition and concentration of salt (Lee et al. 2003; Quach et al. 1999; Werkhoff et al. 2002; D.M. Watson, unpublished data). As different matrices will affect the partitioning of analytes, optimization of SPME parameters with each product type is vital to ensure recovery of intended compounds.

HS-SPME: headspace solid phase microextraction

The SPME technique is applicable to gas and liquid chromatography analysis. An SPME unit consists of a fiber coated with a stationary phase, often dimethylsiloxane (nonpolar) or polyacrylate or divinylbenzene/Carboxen/poly(dimethylsiloxane) (polar) (Grosch 2007). The fiber coating is one of the most important factors for consideration, affecting compound selectivity, precision, and a representative volatile profile (Werkhoff et al. 2002). Some advantages of SPME are increased consistency and rapid measurement stemming from automation (Frank et al. 2004), equivalent methods for different phases, and heating of the sample is not required (dynamic SPME utilizes heat), reducing or eliminating the formation of artifacts (Harmon 2002). The greatest advantage of the SPME method over solvent extraction is the absence of solvents employed in the extraction. Lack of solvent and solvent disposal requirements makes SPME a less-costly volatile compound extraction method with reduced sample preparation time (Marshall 2003). Drawbacks to using SPME include linear range of the SPME fiber, competition between compounds for binding sites on the fiber can introduce inconsistency and error as well poor recovery of trace compounds, and reproducibility across multiple fibers with the same coating is questionable (e.g., in the event of fiber breakage) (Reineccius 2003).

Frank et al. (2004) utilized SPME-gas chromatography-mass spectrometry (GC-MS) and SPME-GC-O to analyze and identify aroma compounds in three types of cheeses, including Cheddar. Their basis for selecting SPME over solvent extraction methods was that important aroma compounds, especially those containing sulfur, were often present in foods below the limit of detection using conventional methods. A separate study, conducted by Bellesia et al. (2003), found that the recovery of volatiles by SPME was very comparable to the recovery of volatiles from the same samples by purge and trap headspace methodology. This finding is significant, as a prime factor slowing the widespread adoption of SPME was previous reliance on approved methods (Zhang & Yang 1994), such as purge and trap.

Gas chromatography. GC is used in flavor research to separate and identify unknown volatile compounds in food. GC analysis separates volatile compounds based primarily on polarity and volatility. Historically, columns were packed with a coated, granular material: The coating polarity was chosen to match the chemical properties of the compounds to be separated. As GC theory advanced, materials containing polar and nonpolar functional groups were introduced that allow for production of columns with a range of polarity (Reineccius 2003).

Careful column selection may make compound identification easier. Two commonly used columns are the DB-WAX (polar) and DB-5 (nonpolar) columns. Highly polar compounds, like free fatty acids, are well separated by polar columns (DB-WAX; also referred to as DB-FFAP). For this reason, polar columns are a good selection for any sample that is thought to contain a large constituency of acids (Reineccius 2003). Nonpolar compounds (e.g., lactones, esters, ketones, and aldehydes) are better separated by more nonpolar columns (e.g., DB-5MS). Because most foods contain some quantity of both polar and nonpolar compounds, samples are typically analyzed on at least one type of each column.

An additional driver for multiple column analysis is to increase the certainty of identification of an unknown compound. Although coelution of compounds may be common on a single column, the likelihood that the same compounds will coelute across multiple columns is exponentially less. Therefore, analyzing a sample with multiple columns helps nullify the effects of coelution and to positively identify unknown compounds. Compounds eluting from a GC column have a specific retention time (RT) for a given column (in reality, on a given column a compound will elute within a given range of RTs). Retention indices (RIs) are more stable and comparable across time, machine, and location than RT values. The RI, or Kováts index, normalizes retention times by comparison against an *n*-alkane series (van den Dool & Kratz 1963).

Compounds eluting from the column are analyzed at the detector. Although several types of detectors are available for use with GC, FID, the human nose (GC-O), and MS provide the most diverse detection capabilities and therefore provide a better overall picture of food flavor (Reineccius 2003). FIDs respond best to organic compounds (C–C or C–H bonds), have a good linear response and high dependability (Reineccius 2003), and are the most common GC detectors (Reineccius 2006a).

Mass spectrometry. MS first ionizes a molecule and then resolves the ionized molecule based on mass-to-charge (m/z) ratios in an electrostatic field (Smith & Thakur 2003). Detection and identification of analyte are based on the unique, predictable spectra created by the ionization of each compound. Mass spectra are compared to a computer database as well as spectra and retention index of an authentic standard for identification. Spectral retention indices are compared with GC-O or GC-FID retention indices for secondary affirmation that a compound is present in a sample. Researchers may also start with aroma properties and work their way back to confirmation by comparison to standards. MS detector function and types have been discussed (McMaster & McMaster 1998, Smith & Thakur 2003).

Quadrupole mass analyzers are the most common today, although ion trap analyzers are also commonly used (Smith & Thakur 2003). Sensitivity of both quadrupole and ion trap analyzers can be increased by selective ion monitoring (SIM) in which certain m/z ratios are detected and remaining ions are discarded (de Hoffmann & Stroobant 2002). This approach is useful when spectral information for compounds of interest is already known, providing greater resolution with less spectral information (Harmon 2002). Time of flight (TOF) analyzers contribute the ability to collect data in much shorter time frames at higher resolution compared with traditional scanning MS analyzers (Holland & Gardner 2002). Until recently, their contribution to flavor research was generally reserved for the analysis of large proteins, peptides, and polynucleotide molecules (McMaster & McMaster 1998). Two-dimensional (2D) GC × GC-TOFMS has been increasingly used in the investigation of volatile compounds and contaminants in food. Enhanced peak separation of GC × GC analysis compared with single GC allows for better characterization of compounds from complex matrices. 2D GC is generally paired with SPME and generally utilizes a polar and nonpolar column for each dimension. Application and advantages of GC-TOFMS in food analysis have been reviewed (Cajka & Hajslova 2006, Cajka et al. 2009, Williamson & Bartlett 2007).

High performance liquid chromatography (HPLC) and ion chromatography are widely used for the analysis of nonvolatile food components, i.e., taste components. Methods for analysis of taste compounds are generally well established. Additional techniques such as matrix-assisted laser desorption/ionization (MALDI) and electrospray ionization have seen increasing use in the investigation of nonvolatile food components that may influence flavor and flavor perception (Turnipseed 2006).

Gas chromatography-olfactometry. A final detector type commonly used with GC is neither FID nor MS: It is the human nose. GC-O is a method of evaluating odor-active compounds. This technique provides additional confirmation of compound identity and aids in the determination of the aroma quality of individual compounds and their significance to the flavor of a food. The procedure for GC-O combines GC with a human sniffer to determine what compounds are released from the column, aroma quality, and at what intensity the odor of the compound is found. The human sniffer records the aroma and intensity as compounds elute, while a chromatogram is established by the traditional detector, usually an FID. An additional injection is usually made separately on a GC-MS for comparison; GC effluent may also be split between the nose and an MS detector to obtain concurrent information and simplify analysis (Reineccius 2006a).

As with any analytical technique or methodology, GC-O has its advantages and its limitations. GC-O has high differentiating power, meaning the sniffer (if properly trained) is capable of detecting very subtle differences in column effluents. GC-O also affords the possibility to detect the aroma of compounds at a concentration below instrumental detection (Mistry et al. 1997). However, GC-O also has the distinct disadvantage of utilizing human responses to chemical stimuli, which are known to change over time, even with careful training (Mistry et al. 1997, Friedrich and Acree 2000). Human subjects must be carefully selected and calibrated by frequent lexicon and descriptive training. In addition, each sample should be sniffed on at least two different columns to account for poorly resolved compounds (Mistry et al. 1997). Because GC-O utilizes human response, this method is subject to inconsistencies. As demonstrated in **Table 2**, two sniffers may perceive the same compound differently. Sniffer training and experience with products of interest may help to alleviate such differences in recognition. GC-O should be used as a preliminary step in the investigation of aroma-active compounds. Compounds of interest are investigated further for positive identification, including comparison with chemical standards and sensory recombination techniques.

Table 2 Sensory descriptors of select compounds identified by two panelists in WPC80 by solvent extraction and gas chromatography-olfactometry[a]

RI (DB-5)	Compound	Sniffer 1 (female)	Sniffer 2 (female)
682	acetic acid	sour	vinegar
815	isopropyl butanoate	fruity/catty	tart fruit
862	butanoic acid	skunk(sulfur)/cheesy	sour milk
909	*Z*-4-heptanal	green/glue	plastic/waxy
947	2-acetyl-1-pyrroline	stale popcorn	brothy/meaty
965	dimethyl trisulfide	garlic/pungent	waxy/rancid/sulfur
1028	octanal	citrus	oranges/vitamin
1159	benzyl acetate	garlic	cabbage/potato
1188	(*E*)-2-nonenal	sweet/carpet/cucumber	carpet lingers
1202	dimethylsulfoxide	rubber	garlic
1292	phenylethyl acetate	cucumber/rosy	floral/plastic
1511	tridecanal	mothball	cinnamon

[a]Adapted from Evans et al. 2010, unpublished information.

Table 3 Summary of factors considered for different gas chromatography-olfactometry methods

	Dilution analysis?	Aroma	Intensity	Duration	# Responses
AEDA	Yes	+	−	−	−
CharmAnalysis	Yes	+	−	+	+
Osme	No	+	+	+	−
NIF/SNIF	No	+	−	+	+
Post Peak	No	+	+	−	−

(+) = positive response, (−) = negative response.

Just as the term extraction is limiting in its nonspecificity, the term GC-O is also limiting. GC-O describes a class of analysis methods, classified as detection frequency, dilution to threshold, or direct intensity (Delahunty et al. 2006). Those methods of olfactometry that are most common are postpeak sniffing, combined hedonic aroma response measurements (CharmAnalysis), Osme, aroma extract dilution analysis (AEDA), and nasal impact frequency/surface nasal impact frequency (NIF/SNIF). A summary of variables considered in GC-O methodology is presented in **Table 3**.

Postpeak sniffing is simply any method of olfactometry that splits the column effluent by some ratio (1:1 is most common) such that one direction of the split effluent is detected by FID or another detector, and the other half of the split effluent is evaluated by a human nose detector. CharmAnalysis is a dilution method developed at Cornell University to determine odor activity of compounds in a sample (Acree et al. 1984). CharmAnalysis is a combined hedonic aroma response measurement (Mistry et al. 1997, van Ruth 2001) based on a stepwise dilution of a sample, with randomized order of dilution presentation. This method notes both the sensory perception and intensity of an odor, as well as the duration of the perception. Charm values are calculated based on the number of panelists who perceived a particular odor and the dilution factor of the sample (Mistry et al. 1997, van Ruth 2001). An additional GC-O method is NIF/SNIF, a response frequency method. NIF/SNIF determines values based on the number of panelists who detect a certain aroma in an extract (Pollien et al. 1997).

AEDA, like CharmAnalysis, utilizes stepwise dilution of a sample extract to determine the most odor-active compounds in a sample. Unlike CharmAnalysis, AEDA does not take into account the time intensity of a particular odor or the number of coincident responses to an odor (van Ruth 2001). AEDA dilutions are carried out until no further odor is perceived. AEDA analysis assigns a flavor dilution (FD) value to a compound, which is the highest dilution at which a compound can still be detected by sniffing (Grosch 1993).

Osme was developed by McDaniel's group at Oregon State University for the aroma profile analysis of wine, hop oils, and beer (Miranda-Lopez et al. 1992). Osme, unlike AEDA and CharmAnalysis, is a nonserial dilution evaluation of aroma extracts and does not make any effort to determine odor activity values (OAVs) or odor importance to a sample. Osme is performed by four trained panelists using a 16-point scale (0 = none, 7 = moderate, 15 = extreme) to rank perceived odor intensity and the duration of the perceived odor (Miranda-Lopez et al. 1992, Mistry et al. 1997). An Osmegram is generated from the combined time-intensity averages for odors perceived by at least three of the four trained panelists.

Proponents of Osme support its use because it measures the odor intensity based on modern psychophysical theories (van Ruth 2001). AEDA and Charm have their limitations. They both assign an odor value to compounds and assume a linear relationship between compound concentration in a sample and its perceived intensity; both Fechner's and Steven's law disprove this assumption (van Ruth 2001). A second assumption inherent to AEDA and Charm that has

AEDA: aroma extract dilution analysis

received considerable discredit is that the same linear relationship (i.e., all slopes are the same) exists between all compounds and their perceived intensities. Many researchers have noted different linear relationships between concentration and perceived intensity for various compounds. Despite these criticisms and drawbacks, AEDA and Charm continue to be used for many aroma characterization and evaluation methods.

The electronic nose. The electronic nose (e-nose) or sensor array system was developed to mimic the discriminatory power of the mammalian olfactory system (Persaud & Dodd 1982). As is the case for all instrumental analysis, volatile and nonvolatile compounds are detected with e-nose systems, meaning that volatile compounds are detected by the machine. The presence of a volatile compound and its particular concentration in the food matrix do not necessarily relate to their role in flavor, as compounds may be present below sensory threshold and have no aroma activity and play little or no role in flavor. The application of e-nose systems to dairy products or any food product is thus limited by an understanding of the matrix, the compounds of interest, and their role in flavor (Ampuero & Bosset 2003). Dairy products have been analyzed by varied detector configurations but on a limited scope. E-nose holds suitable application for raw materials analysis and quality testing based on a strict set of parameters but does not hold as much power as human sensory analysis in terms of range of applicability to food products. As stated by Wilson & Baietto (2009) in a review of recent advances in e-nose technology, "A universal electronic nose capable of identifying or discriminating any gas sample type with high efficiency and for all possible applications has not as yet been built."

The application of the e-nose in food and beverage research has been focused on ingredient quality and origin, monitoring of manufacturing specifications, shelf life, and spoilage (Rock et al. 2008). Although numerous studies have been performed to assess the ability of the e-nose to differentiate food products, success is generally dependent on comprehensive descriptive sensory and/or instrumental analysis beforehand. For instance, Jonsdottir et al. (2004) related sensory attributes to GC-O and GC-MS to identify characteristic compounds of ripened roe. Sensory, GC, and e-nose data correlated well on the selected compounds of importance, but the e-nose by itself cannot determine quality unless a dataset is available for comparison. Given that dataset, any additional variation or off-flavor would require recalibration in order to differentiate samples in a meaningful manner.

LINKING SENSORY AND INSTRUMENTAL ANALYSIS

Identification of Flavor Attributes

Although instrumental analysis and descriptive sensory analysis are powerful tools on their own, they are even more powerful when used in combination. By relating instrumental data to descriptive sensory data, researchers are able to determine which compounds are responsible for specific flavors in food (Drake & Civille 2003). This goal is challenging because instruments may detect many compounds that are present at levels below the human threshold. Likewise, there are flavor active components that contribute to food flavor at concentrations below instrumental detection. Concurrently, compounds may exhibit distinct aroma and taste properties in the food matrix compared with isolated analysis and influence flavor at concentrations below human threshold. Differentiating the small number of aroma compounds that are present in foods above the human threshold from those that are not becomes challenging when there are so many volatile compounds in the product (Drake & Civille 2003). One such method that assists in linking instrumental data to the sensory perception of flavor is GC-O.

As a basic review of flavor research techniques, descriptive sensory analysis describes the flavor of a food product, MS techniques provide information on volatile (and semivolatile to nonvolatile) compounds, and GC-O techniques provide information on the aroma activity of volatile compounds. By utilization of these processes, compounds can be identified as important aroma impact compounds in a food product. A compound identified with high odor activity and high concentrations within a food product is not enough to conclusively state its importance to aroma. OAV, threshold values, and model systems play an important role in flavor perception by way of investigation of the effect of the food matrix.

Odor activity values are calculated as the ratio of the concentration of a compound in food to the perception threshold of that compound in air, water, or other specified matrix (Audouin et al. 2001, Karagül-Yüceer et al. 2004). Therefore, OAV values less than one are theoretically not detectable by a human. A high OAV suggests a high degree of contribution to a food's overall aroma by a given compound. Threshold information has been published for numerous compounds (Burdock 2010) in varied matrices (van Gemert 2003a,b). However, dairy systems contribute a complex matrix that cannot be substituted by simple water and oil systems. Threshold values of flavor compounds should be determined in a matrix comparable to the food product of interest. Upon identification of important flavor compounds, descriptive analysis of model systems is employed as a tool to evaluate the contribution of individual compounds to aroma. Models are compared to the real food product for similarity. In the case of off-flavor characterization, this process is straightforward. Addition of the suspect compound to the food matrix free of the off flavor should recreate the off flavor (Wright et al. 2006). In the case of flavor characterization (e.g., strawberry flavor), this process is more challenging. Mixtures with individual compounds added (model addition or $N + 1$) or removed from the complete model (model subtraction, omission studies or $N - 1$) are utilized to compare contributions of each compound to the overall aroma (Buettner & Schieberle 2001, Karagul Yuceer et al. 2004). This process is not exact because typically only the primary (high aroma impact) compounds are selected for model studies (owing to their expense and time consumption), and volatile compounds at low or subthreshold concentrations as well as nonvolatile compounds and the food structure itself can influence the flavor perception of a product.

Analysis of Flavor in Liquid Whey and Dried Whey Powders: From Processing Through Storage

In recent years, the popularity and value of whey protein products have grown. In response to a growing body of knowledge of functionality and flavor, in addition to advances in separation technologies, whey protein ingredient use and whey protein products on the market have increased tremendously. Competition and the requirement for bland-flavored whey protein powders continue to drive innovation and research of a cheese-production byproduct of little value and quality mere decades ago. As a food category, whey protein powders are manufactured in a diverse manner. Understanding the effects of processing and storage on flavor has been undertaken by researchers deploying numerous technologies.

Although whey protein is defined as and expected to be bland and similar in flavor to fresh fluid whey or milk, thereby suitable for a wide range of food applications, the reality is that whey protein flavor variability exists between and within manufacturing facilities (Carunchia Whetstine et al. 2005, Wright et al. 2009). In order to evaluate differences in flavor profiles, numerous steps are required. Following the establishment of a lexicon, baseline sensory and instrumental information are required. Compositional values and range of flavors determine acceptability within the product category. Once the basic flavor profile has been established, deviations from the standard may be investigated. The investigation of the flavor chemistry and sensory properties of liquid whey

WPC: whey protein concentrate

WPI: whey protein isolate

and whey protein powders is presented to demonstrate the range of techniques available to researchers investigating food flavors. Combining sensory science with instrumental tools provides the researcher opportunities to identify sources of variation and off-flavors between products. A summary of the techniques applied and conclusions of respective studies is presented in **Table 4**.

Flavor is influenced along the entire manufacturing scheme of food products from the starting material through storage and packaging. Whey protein flavor chemistry and off-flavor assessment have been studied for decades. However, until recently, research failed to link the two by quantitative sensory assessment and instrumental analysis. Carunchia Whetstine et al. (2005) investigated the flavor properties of whey protein concentrate (WPC) and whey protein isolate (WPI) from different U.S. manufacturers by relating descriptive sensory and instrumental analyses. A lexicon was adapted from dried dairy ingredients. The terms applied in this lexicon are contained within **Table 1**. Similar to other dried dairy proteins, flavors were differentiated as dairy and nondairy flavors. Both WPC and WPI exhibited a range of undesirable flavors. Researchers employed solvent extraction followed by HVT to isolate aroma compounds. Compounds were then analyzed by GC-MS as well as GC-O. Representative samples were further analyzed by AEDA. Baseline volatile compound profiles of whey protein were established with lipid oxidation, protein degradation, and heat-generated compounds of primary concern. These findings are in agreement with Mahajan et al. (2004), who determined important aroma compounds in whey powder to be derived from the milk and starter culture as well as processing. Differences noted in ratios of aroma-active compounds in WPCs and WPIs to whey powders were attributed to the compositional differences between the product classifications (e.g., lower protein/higher lactose versus higher protein/lower lactose).

The conversion of liquid whey into dried whey protein involves numerous processing steps, providing the source of a wide range of variation between manufacturers and the creation or loss of aroma compounds. Storage of liquid whey is common in commercial manufacturing of whey powders. Tomaino et al. (2004) used descriptive sensory analysis, SPME GC-FID free fatty acid analysis, and DHS GC-MS to determine that extended storage of liquid Cheddar whey resulted in increased levels of common lipid oxidation products, decreased free fatty acids, and the development of cardboard flavor. However, the storage time was much longer than current manufacturing practices. Researchers also determined that different starter cultures affect the oxidative stability of liquid whey and that oxidation begins during cheese production based on the presence of oxidation compounds and cardboard flavor in fresh whey.

Carunchia Whetstine et al. (2003) investigated the impact of 23 commercially produced liquid whey from different mesophilic start cultures using descriptive sensory analysis, SPME GC-FID free fatty acid analysis, and DHS GC-MS. All three methods differentiated Cheddar liquid whey samples. Liaw (2009) also investigated the role of starter culture on the oxidative stability of fresh and stored liquid whey. Sensory and instrumental analysis differentiated Mozzarella from Cheddar cheese as well as fresh versus stored liquid whey. Descriptive sensory analysis and HS-SPME were performed on fresh liquid whey and liquid whey stored at 4°C for three days.

In the processing of whey protein, it is quite common for liquid whey and concentrated whey, known as retentate, to be stored either for production efficiency reasons or for transport to another facility for further processing. The impact of liquid whey storage on flavor has been investigated (Tomaino et al. 2004, Liaw 2009). Both types of cheese whey resulted in increased cardboard aroma and lipid oxidation products with storage. However, Mozzarella cheese whey exhibited greater oxidative stability compared to Cheddar cheese whey. A maximum retentate storage time of 12 h has been suggested based on the results of a combination of descriptive sensory analysis, HS-SPME GC-MS, DSE SAFE GC-MS, and DSE SAFE GC-O and AEDA (Whitson 2010). This study analyzed Cheddar and Mozzarella WPC manufactured from retentate stored up to 48 h, an

Table 4 Summary of significant research studies of liquid whey and whey protein powders

Source	Sensory methods	Instrumental methods	Products analyzed	Research significance
Carunchia Whetstine et al. 2003	DSA	DHS GC-MS, SPME GC-FID FFA	Cheddar liquid whey	Milk source, Cheddar starter cultures, and processing parameters impact the flavor & aroma volatile compound profiles of commercially produced liquid whey Liquid whey flavor is variable between and within manufacturing facilities
Karagul-Yuceer et al. 2003	DSA	DSE HVT, GC-MS; DSE HVT, GC-O, AEDA	Cheddar liquid whey	Liquid whey flavor is impacted by starter culture, milk source, and processing Liquid whey flavor is variable between and within manufacturing facilities
Carunchia Whetstine et al. 2005	DSA	DSE HVT, GC-MS; DSE HVT, GC-O	Cheddar WPC80; Cheddar WPI; Mozzarella WPC80	Established a baseline flavor and aroma volatile compound profile for WPC80 and WPI Compounds of interest are products of lipid oxidation, protein degradation, and heat generated
Mahajan et al. 2004		DSE SAFE, GC-MS; DSE SAFE, GC-O	SWP	Sources of aroma compounds of interest in SWP can be from milk, cheese type, lipid oxidation, caramelization, and Maillard browning
Tomaino et al. 2004	DSA	SPME, GC-FID; Purge & trap GC-MS	Cheddar liquid whey	Oxidation reactions begin during cheesemake Different starter cultures affect the oxidative stability of liquid whey produced on a pilot scale Liquid whey storage results in increases in lipid oxidation, cardboard flavors, and loss of fresh flavors
Campbell et al. 2010	DSA	HS-SPME, GC-MS	Cheddar liquid whey; Mozzarella liquid whey	Cheddar liquid whey less oxidative stability compared to Mozzarella liquid whey Both Cheddar and Mozzarella liquid whey decrease dairy flavors and increase nondairy flavors with storage
I.W. Liaw, unpublished data	DSA	HS-SPME, GC-MS; DSE SAFE, GC-MS; DSE SAFE, GC-O, AEDA	Cheddar liquid whey; Mozzarella liquid whey	Both Cheddar and Mozzarella liquid whey increase in cardboard flavor and lipid oxidation products with storage Mozzarella liquid whey has greater oxidative stability compared with Cheddar liquid whey
M.E. Whitson, unpublished data	DSA	HS-SPME, GC-MS; DSE SAFE, GC-MS; DSE SAFE, GC-O, AEDA	Mozzarella WPC80 retentate; Cheddar WPI retentate; Cheddar WPI; Mozzarella WPC80	Lipid oxidation and protein degradation products are the main aroma compounds of interest in WPC80 and WPI Longer retentate storage time corresponds to increased lipid oxidation products, cardboard and serum flavors, and aroma intensity Maximum suggested retentate storage time prior to spray drying is 12 h to maximize shelf life
Mortenson et al. 2008	DSA	DSE SAFE, GC-MS DSE SAFE, GC-O	Cheddar WPC34, WPI; Mozzarella WPC34; WPI; agglom. Mozzarella WPC34, WPI	Benzoyl peroxide bleaching, agglomeration, and filtration method had no significant effect on flavor of WPC34 and WPI

(Continued)

Table 4 (*Continued*)

Source	Sensory methods	Instrumental methods	Products analyzed	Research significance
Javidipour & Qian 2008		HS-SPME, GC-MS	Cheddar & Mozzarella WPC80; agglom. Cheddar & Mozzarella WPC80	Lipid oxidation compounds increased with storage at elevated temperatures Instantized WPC80 had a higher off-flavor formation compared with nonagglomerated WPC80 Argon flushing decreased the formation of volatile compounds
Liaw et al. 2010	DSA	HS-SPME, GC-MS	Cheddar liquid whey; Mozzarella liquid whey; Cheddar WPC66;	Mozzarella liquid whey greater oxidative stability than Cheddar liquid whey during storage WPH and ascorbic acid as antioxidant treatments reduce cardboard flavor and lipid oxidation products WPH is more effective antioxidant compared to ascorbic acid but imparts potato/brothy flavor to WPC
Croissant et al. 2009	DSA	HS-SPME, GC-MS	Cheddar liquid whey; Cheddar WPC70	Liquid whey flavor is representative of WPC flavor; treatment effects can be measured in liquid whey, eliminating need to produce WPC for analysis Bleaching increases cardboard flavor and lipid oxidation products in liquid whey and WPC With equivalent bleaching efficacy, hydrogen peroxide bleaching produces less desirable WPC compared with benzoyl peroxide
Wright et al. 2009	DSA; Ingredient application; Consumer acceptance	HS-SPME, GC-MS	agglom. Cheddar WPC80, WPI; instant Cheddar WPC80, WPI; instant Mozzarella WPC80; nonagglom. Cheddar WPC80, WPI; nonagglom. Mozzarella WPC80	Whey powders developed cucumber, raisin, fatty, and brothy flavors with storage; cardboard flavor increased and sweet aromatic flavor decreased with storage Lipid oxidation volatile aroma products and flavors increased with storage of all samples, but to a greater extent in agglomerated and instantized whey powders Descriptive sensory with consumer acceptance suggests the shelf life of agglom. whey powders is 8–12 months, nonagglom. powder shelf life is 12–15 months
Whitson et al. 2010	DSA, n-1 model systems	HS-SPME, GC-MS	Cheddar WPI; cardboard	Cardboard flavor is of primary concern to whey protein products Aroma volatile compounds and concentrations responsible for cardboard flavor were determined using model system WPI Although hexanal is a primary indicator of lipid oxidation, it does not contribute to cardboard flavor in whey protein products
Wright et al. 2006	DSA, threshold, OAV, model systems	HS-SPME, GC-MS DSE SAFE, GC-O, AEDA	Cheddar WPI; Cabbage off-flavor Cheddar WPI	DMTS is a common volatile compound found in WPI Above threshold level, DMTS contributes cabbage flavor in WPI

Abbreviations: AEDA, aroma extract dilution analysis; agglom., agglomerated; DMTS, dimethyl trisulfide; DS, descriptive sensory analysis; DSE, direct solvent extraction; FID, flame ionization detector; FFA, free fatty acids; GC-MS, gas chromatography-mass spectrometry; GC-O, gas chromatography-olfactometry; HS-SPME, headspace solid phase microextraction; HVT, high vacuum transfer; nonagglom., nonagglomerated; OAV, odor activity values; SWP, sweet whey powder; WPC, whey protein concentrate, WPI, whey protein isolate.

industrially relevant holding timeframe. Retentate was spray dried at 0, 6, 12, 24, and 48 h intervals. WPCs were stored at room temperature and analyzed at intervals over 12 months. Sensory analysis of retentate and powders revealed decreased desirable dairy flavors and increased undesirable nondairy flavors with increasing retentate storage time. This trend was maintained in WPC and WPI throughout 12 months of storage. Although storage of all powders resulted in increasing undesirable flavors, shorter retentate storage time resulted in decreased undesirable flavors.

Given that lipid oxidation products are believed to be the most important compounds when considering whey protein, methods for control of oxidation are vital to the continued improvement of flavor. The application of antioxidants to liquid whey was investigated by Liaw et al. (2010) to determine their impact on the flavor of WPC. Ascorbic acid, nitrogen blanketing, and whey protein hydrolysate (WPH) were added separately to Cheddar and Mozzarella liquid whey following pasteurization and fat separation. Liquid whey and WPC were analyzed by descriptive sensory analysis and SPME GC-MS. Results were consistent with previous studies in that Mozzarella liquid whey was more stable in storage than Cheddar whey. Cheddar WPC was produced with a control, WPH, and ascorbic acid treatments. Both antioxidant treatments yielded lower cardboard intensities and lower relative abundance of lipid oxidation products in WPC compared with the control. However, ascorbic acid was a less effective antioxidant than WPH. The addition of WPH resulted in a potato/brothy aroma, an undesirable flavor in whey that is commonly associated with WPH.

An additional source of liquid whey oxidation is the bleaching step. Bleaching of liquid whey and concentrated liquid whey retentate is required for the production of yellow Cheddar cheese and resulting uncolored WPC and WPI. Cheddar cheese whey serves as the major source of liquid whey in the United States, and colored Cheddar is the primary type manufactured. Currently, peroxides (hydrogen and benzoyl) are utilized in the bleaching step with great manufacturer variability in bleaching conditions, including time, temperature, concentration, and total solids at time of bleaching (Kang et al. 2010). Croissant et al. (2009) performed descriptive sensory analysis and SPME GC-MS to quantify the impact of the two common, approved oxidative bleaching agents on WPC flavor. Both hydrogen peroxide (HP) and benzoyl peroxide (BP) treatments resulted in objectionable flavor compared with the unbleached control. With the same bleaching efficacy, HP was more detrimental to whey flavor than BP. Contrary to the findings of Croissant et al. (2009), Mortenson et al. (2008) concluded that bleaching did not significantly affect the flavor of WPC34 and WPI. However, different whey streams with different processing conditions, storage times, and starter cultures obtained from different manufacturers were compared. Lack of control of processing conditions beyond bleaching introduced variability, making a true comparison difficult in this instance.

Food ingredients may undergo postprocessing treatments in order to increase value by providing additional functional properties. Whey protein powders are often subjected to agglomeration—the addition of steam, whey, or lecithin—to aid in dispersion. Javidipour & Qian (2008) investigated selected compound formation by HS-SPME GC-MS in agglomerated and nonagglomerated WPC80 over 15 weeks of storage at elevated temperatures. Generally speaking, lipid oxidation products increased with temperature and storage time. Agglomerated WPC80 had higher off-flavor formation than nonagglomerated. Argon flushing reduced off-flavor formation with storage. Although researchers did not apply sensory analysis to their products, compounds were selected based on previous research combining instrumental and sensory analysis. Wright et al. (2009) identified the agglomeration step as a source of reduced storage stability through the application of sensory and instrumental analysis. The shelf life of agglomerated and nonagglomerated WPC80 and WPI was investigated by combining descriptive sensory analysis, SPME GC-MS, and consumer acceptance testing. Descriptive sensory analysis and instrumental analysis were performed at intervals throughout storage. Flavor carry-through in beverages was investigated to determine the consumer acceptance of flavored protein beverages made with fresh or stored whey proteins. Although numerous variables may be investigated within a given research project, prudence dictates that representative samples are chosen for ingredient application and subsequent consumer testing. Samples were chosen based on the data compiled by the trained sensory panel and volatile compound profiles. Shelf life was determined based on the consumer acceptance scores of flavored protein beverages made from fresh and stored WPC80 and WPI.

Cardboard flavor has been observed in many dried dairy products, specifically whey protein (Carunchia Whetstine et al. 2005, Evans et al. 2009, Russell et al. 2006, Wright et al. 2006). Cardboard flavor is commonly associated with whey proteins and has a negative effect on consumer liking in ingredient applications (Wright et al. 2009). Whitson et al. (2010) used a combination of sensory and analytical methods to determine the chemical compounds responsible for cardboard flavor in whey protein. The identification of specific lipid oxidation products as the source of cardboard flavor will aid in the ongoing effort to pinpoint the major factors associated with improving whey flavor by focusing instrumental detection methods. Sensory analysis was required to identify and compare representative WPI cardboard samples. Instrumental analysis was required to correlate volatile compounds with aroma. Numerous compounds have been detected in whey protein products (**Table 5**); determining which aroma compounds are of interest to a specific flavor requires preliminary investigation. Researchers evaluated samples of paper and cardboard soaked in water to identify the type of cardboard that represented the cardboard aroma found in whey protein. A WPI sample with high cardboard flavor was used as comparison for all testing. A stepwise approach to identify important aroma compounds is required. Often, one compound is not solely responsible for a flavor but rather a combination of compounds in varying concentrations (Carunchia Whetstine et al. 2006, Whetstine et al. 2005). Compounds were evaluated individually and in combination. Each compound was analyzed across a concentration range to account for changes in aroma (Avsar et al. 2004, Drake & Civille 2003, Karagul-Yuceer et al. 2004). Omission or subtraction models ($N - 1$) were used to identify the compounds that contributed most to cardboard aroma.

Through a combination of instrumental and sensory techniques applied to whey protein, researchers have developed a sensory language, identified sources of off-flavors, designated processing steps important to flavor, and determined compounds responsible for common aromas. Nonetheless, the whey protein flavor code has yet to be cracked. Numerous processing steps, conditions, and other variables require research in order to meet the lofty goal of a bland dairy protein ingredient with subtle dairy flavors.

LINKING LEXICONS AND FLAVOR CHEMISTRY TO THE CONSUMER

Preference Mapping

The ultimate goal of the sensory scientist and flavor chemist is to relate product attributes to the consumer. The determination of flavor attributes and the identification of compounds responsible for flavor serve the industry only when this data is converted to yield a better quality or higher-value food product. Descriptive sensory analysis yields a wealth of information but trained panelists function as part of an instrument rather than representing the consumer and determining product likes and dislikes. Through the use of preference mapping, volatile data and/or descriptive sensory data (aromatics, flavor, and/or texture attributes) can be modeled on consumer preference data. Preference mapping describes more than one technique, differentiated by the data used to locate products on the axes (Meilgaard et al. 2007, Drake 2007). Internal preference mapping places products by consumer acceptance values. External preference mapping places products using

Table 5 Volatile compounds identified in liquid whey and dried whey products[a]

Volatile compound	Whey type[b]	Volatile compound	Whey type[b]
(*E*)-2-hexenal	WPC80, agglom. WPC80, WPI, agglom. WPI	acetone	liquid
(*E*)-2-nonenal	liquid, SWP, WPC80, WPI	benzaldehyde	liquid, WPC80, agglom. WPC80, WPI, agglom. WPI
(*E*)-2-octenal	liquid, SWP, WPC80	butadiene	liquid, WPC80, WPI
(*E,E*)-2,4-decadienal	liquid, SWP, WPC80, WPI	butanoic acid	liquid, SWP, WPC80, WPI
(*E,E*)-2,4-nonadienal	SWP, WPI	butanol	liquid
(*E,E*)-2,4-octadienal	SWP	decanal	WPC80, WPI
(*E,Z*)-2,4-decadienal	SWP	decanoic acid	SWP, WPC, WPI
(*E,Z*)-2,4-nonadienal	SWP	delta-decalactone	liquid, SWP, WPC80, WPI
(*E-Z*)-2,6-nonadienal	liquid, SWP, WPC80, WPI	delta-dodecalactone	SWP, WPC80, WPI
(*Z*)-1,5-octadien-3-one	WPC66	delta-octalactone	SWP
(*Z*)-2-nonenal	liquid, SWP, WPI	delta-undecalactone	SWP
(*Z*)-4-heptanal	WPC80	diacetyl	liquid, SWP, WPC80, agglom. WPC80, WPI, agglom. WPI
(*Z*)-4-heptenal	SWP	dimethyl disulfide	SWP, WPC80, inst. WPC80, agglom. WPC80, WPI, agglom. WPI
1,2-propadiene; alkenyl	liquid	dimethyl sulfide	liquid, WPC80, WPI
1,5-octadienone	WPI	dimethyl trisulfide	liquid, SWP, WPC80, agglom. WCP80, WPI, agglom. WPI
1-dodecane	liquid	dimethylamine, allyl	liquid
1-hexen-3-one	WPC66	dodecanoic acid	SWP, WPC35, WPI
1-nonen-3-one	WPC66	ethanol	liquid
1-octen-3-ol	WPC80, agglom. WPC80, WPI, agglom. WPI	ethyl acetate	liquid
1-octen-3-one	liquid, SWP, WPC80, inst. WPC80, WPI	ethyl hexanoate	WPC66
1-pentanol	WPC66	formic acid	SWP
1-propanol	liquid	furfuryl alcohol	SWP
2,3-methylbutanal	WPC66	gamma-decalactone	SWP, WPC80
2,3-methylbutanol	liquid	gamma-dodecalactone	SWP
2,3,5-trimethylpyrazine	SWP	gamma-hexalactone	SWP
2,3-dimethylpyrazine	SWP	gamma-nonalactone	WPC80
2,3-methylbutanoic acid	liquid	gamma-octalactone	WPC66
2,3-pentanedione	WPC66	heptanal	liquid, SWP, WPC80, inst. WPC80, agglom. WPC80, WPI, agglom. WPI
2,5-dimethylpyrazine	SWP	heptanoic acid	SWP, WPC80, WPI
2,5-dimethyl-4-hydroxy-3-(2H) furanone (Furaneol)	SWP, WPC80, WPI	heptanone	liquid
2,5-octanedione	WPC66	hexanal	liquid, SWP, WPC80, inst. WPC80, agglom. WPC80, WPI, agglom. WPI

(Continued)

Table 5 (*Continued*)

Volatile compound	Whey type[b]	Volatile compound	Whey type[b]
2,6-dimethylpyrazine	SWP	hexanoic acid	liquid, SWP, WPC80, WPI
2-acetyl-1-pyrroline	liquid, SWP, WPC80, WPI	hydrocarboxyl	liquid
2-acetylpyridine	WPC66	isobutyric acid	liquid
2-acetylpyrrole	SWP	maltol	liquid, SWP, WPC35
2-acetylthiazole	SWP	methional	liquid, SWP, WPC80, WPI
2-butanol	liquid	methyl propanoic acid	liquid
2-butanone	liquid	nonanal	liquid, SWP, WPC80, agglom. WPC80, WPI, agglom. WPI
2-butanone	liquid	nonanoic acid	WPC80, WPI
2-ethylpyrazine	liquid, SWP	nonanol	WPC80, inst. WPC80
2-ethyl-1-hexanol	WPC80, agglom. WPC80, WPI, agglom. WPI	nonanone	liquid
2-furfural	liquid	*o*-aminoacetophenone	WPC80, WPI
2-heptanol	WPC80, inst. WPC80	octanal	liquid, WPC80, agglom. WPC80, WPI, agglom. WPI
2-heptanone	liquid, WPC80, agglom. WPC80, WPI, agglom. WPI	octanoic acid	liquid, SWP, WPC80, WPI
2-isobutyl-3-methoxypyrazine	liquid, WPC80, WPI	octanol	WPC80, inst. WPC80
2-isopropyl-3-methoxypyrazine	WPC66	*p*-cresol	SWP, WPC66
2-methoxyphenol (guiacol)	WPC80	pentanal	liquid
2-methoxy-3-isopropylpyrazine	liquid	pentanoic acid	liquid, SWP, WPC80, WPI
2-methyl propanoic acid	SWP	phenol	liquid
2-methyl-3-furanthiol	liquid, WPC66, WPI	phenyl ethyl acetate	WPC80
2-nonanol	WPC80, inst. WPC80	phenylacetaldehyde	SWP, WPC66, WPI
2-nonanone	liquid, WPC80, agglom. WPC80, WPI, agglom. WPI	propan-1-ol, alkyl	liquid
2-octanone	WPC80, inst. WPC80	propanoic acid	liquid, SWP, WPC66
2-pentylfuran	liquid, WPC80, agglom. WPC80, WPI, agglom. WPI	skatole	SWP, WPC66
2-phenethanol	WPC80, WPI	toluene	WPC80, agglom. WPC80, WPI, agglom. WPI
2-propanol	liquid	fatty acids	
2-propionyl-1-pyrroline	SWP	butyric	liquid
2-undecanone	WPC80, agglom. WPC80, WPI, agglom. WPI	caproic	liquid
3-hydroxy-4,5-dimethyl-2-(5H)-furanone (Sotolon)	liquid, SWP, WPC80, WPI	caprylic	liquid
3-methoxy-4-hydroxy benzaldehyde (vanillin)	WPC80	capric	liquid

(*Continued*)

Table 5 (*Continued*)

Volatile compound	Whey type[b]	Volatile compound	Whey type[b]
3-methyl butanoic acid	SWP	lauric	liquid
3-methyl furan	liquid	myristic	liquid
4-methyl octanoic acid	WPC80, WPI	palmitic	liquid
9-decanoic acid	SWP	palmitoleic	liquid
acetaldehyde	liquid	stearic	liquid
acetic acid	liquid, SWP, WPC80, WPI	oleic	liquid
acetoin	liquid	linoleic	liquid

[a]Adapted from Drake et al. 2009b.

[b]Cheese source. liquid: Cheddar, Gouda, Mozzarella, Paneer, Quarg, rennet casein, acid casein, lactic acid casein; SWP: Cheddar; WPC80: Cheddar, Mozzarella, Monterey Jack; inst. WPC80; Cheddar, Monterey Jack; agglom. WPC80; Cheddar, Mozzerella; WPI: Cheddar; agglom. WPI: Cheddar. Abbreviations: SWP, sweet whey powder; WPC80, whey protein concentrate 80% protein; inst. WPC80, instantized WPC80; agglom. WPC80, agglomerated WPC80; WPI, whey protein isolate >90% protein; agglom. WPI, agglomerated WPI.

Carunchia Whetstine et al. 2003, 2005; Croissant et al. 2009; Drake et al. 2003, 2009a; Gallardo-Escamilla et al. 2005; Javidipour & Qian 2008; Karagul-Yuceer et al. 2003; Mahajan et al. 2004; Russell et al. 2006; Tomaino et al. 2004; Wright et al. 2006, 2009.

descriptive sensory values or even instrumental values. Partial least-squares regression analysis is the most common type of modeling approach used with external mapping (Tenenhaus et al. 2005).

Given the proper line of consumer questioning, preference mapping provides consumer segment information and respective liking attributes. Murray & Delahunty (2000) investigated consumer preference for Cheddar cheese and cheese packaging. Demographic information allowed characterizations of consumer segments, and relationships between purchasing habits and liking were characterized. Preference mapping is equally suited for correlation of instrumental analysis with consumer liking. Pham et al. (2008) utilized HS-SPME GC-MS and GC-O to identify aroma impact compounds and descriptive sensory and consumer acceptance testing to determine drivers of liking of dry-cured hams. All products tested had similar volatile compound profiles but differed in relative concentrations. Consumer testing provided information on aroma compounds that may be responsible for higher and lower acceptability scores.

Check-all-that-apply (CATA) (Dooley et al. 2010) and open-ended questions (Ares et al. 2010) have been proposed as alternative approaches to gain additional product information from the consumer. Modeling of both approaches compared well with external preference mapping. Both methods provide additional information in the consumers' language rather than the trained panel. However, both methods results in data that is not comparable to descriptive language and intensities. Previous studies have also suggested that the use of open-ended questioning may influence consumer overall liking scores.

Texture

Barden et al. (2009) determined that flavor does not impact texture perception in WPI gels by consumers or trained panelists. Conversely, texture has been shown to influence the perception of flavor (Lubbers 2006) and overall consumer liking (Yates & Drake 2007). Although the relationship between texture, aroma release, and flavor perception is outside the scope of this review, the term creaminess is discussed briefly in order to highlight difficulties encountered when attempting to relate flavor chemistry to consumer response. "Texture is a sensory property" (Szczesniak 2002); as such, terms have been established for the sensory analysis of texture (Meilgaard et al. 2007). However, the term creaminess is a source of ambiguity in the sensory language, with applications in both texture and flavor, and probably implying different things with different foods. Representing texture, creaminess has been correlated with fat content (Richardson-Harman et al. 2000), particle size (Kilcast & Clegg 2002), viscosity or thickness (Daget et al. 1988, Frost & Danhoj 2007), and smoothness and consistency (Elmore et al. 1999, Frost & Danhoj 2007). From a flavor and consumer perspective, creaminess has been related to dairy and nondairy flavors (Frost & Danhoj 2007, Kirkmeyer & Tepper 2005, Richardson-Harman et al. 2000) and positively influencing overall liking (Kirkmeyer & Tepper 2005, Weenen et al. 2005). The term has been researched in numerous dairy products (Richardson-Harman et al. 2000) and is commonly used to describe appearance, texture, and flavor attributes (Elmore et al. 1999). Understanding the relationship between consumer perception and liking related to creaminess and texture/flavor profiles is important given the growing interest in low-fat foods, especially dairy products. The difficulty of quantifying this attribute is based on its lack of definition in descriptive sensory analysis and the inability of the consumer to differentiate flavor, texture, and liking. Generally, studies investigating the relationship between creaminess and consumer liking have shown positive correlation. However, differentiation between the physical and chemical properties of creaminess and the sensory perception of creaminess has not been achieved (Frost & Danhoj 2007). Frost & Danhoj (2007) concluded that texture properties correlated creaminess in liquid and semisolid dairy products, but the flavor properties correlated creaminess in weak gels (i.e., yogurts).

Creaminess perception includes both flavor and texture sensations (Tournier et al. 2007). Instrumental aroma analysis has also been utilized to investigate the role of volatile and semivolatile compounds on creaminess. Schlutt et al. (2007) identified several lactone compounds as contributors to creaminess flavor. These compounds, γ- and δ-octadecalactones and γ- and δ-eicosalactones, contribute to creaminess by influencing the melting behavior of cream in the oral cavity rather than having a direct influence on flavor. Only one compound when added to whipped cream above threshold, δ-tetradecalactone, was shown to affect creamy flavor. Creaminess in dairy products is a complex term involving compounds that elicit a creamy feeling factor, enhancing sensory attributes (e.g., cooked, milk fat), sensory attributes that decrease creamy perception (sour, bitter, e.g.,), and texture qualities (e.g., viscosity, particle size). A greater understanding of creaminess will only be accomplished by a complete approach utilizing sensory and instrumental techniques.

SUMMARY POINTS

1. Descriptive sensory analysis is a powerful analytical method to evaluate food products.
2. Sensory and instrumental analyses are complementary in the investigation of food flavor.
3. Sensory properties and flavor compound analysis can be related to consumer response to determine drivers of liking of food products.

FUTURE ISSUES

1. The effects of texture on flavor perception.
2. The relationship between the psychological and the physical consumer response.
3. Real-time measurement of flavor release and flavor perception by way of in-mouth analysis.

DISCLOSURE STATEMENT

The authors are not aware of any affiliations, memberships, funding, or financial holdings that might be perceived as affecting the objectivity of this review.

LITERATURE CITED

Acree TE, Barnard J, Cunningham DG. 1984. A procedure for the sensory analysis of gas chromatographic effluents. *Food Chem.* 14:273–86

Alewijn M, Sliwinski EL, Wouters JM. 2003. A fast and simple method for quantitative determination of fat-derived medium and low-volatile compounds in cheese. *Int. Dairy J.* 13:733–41

Ampuero S, Bosset JO. 2003. The electronic nose applied to dairy products: a review. *J. Sens. Actuators* 94:1–12

Ares G, Giménez A, Barreiro C, Gámbaro A. 2010. Use of an open-ended question to identify drivers of liking of milk desserts. Comparison with preference mapping techniques. *Food Qual. Prefer.* 21:286–94

Arthur CL, Killam LM, Motlagh S, Lim M, Potter DW, Pawliszyn J. 1992. Analysis of substituted benzene compounds in groundwater using solid-phase microextraction. *Environ. Sci. Technol.* 26:979–83

Audouin V, Bonnet F, Vickers ZM. 2001. Limitation in the use of odor activity values to determine important odorants in foods. In *Gas Chromatography-Olfactometry: The State of the Art*, ed. JV Leland, P Schieberle, A Buettner, pp. 156–71. Washington DC: Am. Chem. Soc.

Auvray M, Spence C. 2008. The multisensory perception of flavor. *Conscious. Cogn.* 17:1016–31

Avsar YK, Karagul-Yuceer Y, Drake MA, Singh TK, Yoon Y, Cadwaller KR. 2004. Characterization of nutty flavor in cheddar cheese. *J. Dairy Sci.* 87:1999–2010

Barden LM, Cakir E, Leksrisompong PN, Ryan KN, Foegeding EA, Drake MA. 2009. Effect of flavor on perceived texture of whey protein isolate gels. *J. Sens. Stud.* 1–16

Bellesia F, Pinetti A, Pagnoni UM, Rinaldi R. 2003. Volatile components of Grana Parmigiano-Reggiano type hard cheese. *Food Chem.* 83:55–61

Bodyfelt FW, Tobias J, Trout GM, eds. 1988. *The Sensory Evaluation of Dairy Products*. New York: Van Nostrand Reinhold

Buettner A, Schieberle P. 2001. Evaluation of differences between hand-squeezed juices from Valencis late and Navel oranges by quantitation of key odorants and flavor reconstitution experiments. *J. Agric. Food Chem.* 49:2387–94

Burdock GA. 2010. *Fenaroli's Handbook of Flavor Ingredients*. Boca Raton, FL: CRC Press. 2159 pp. 6th ed.

Campbell RE, Miracle RE, Gerard P, Drake MA. 2010. The effect of starter culture and storage on the flavor of fresh liquid whey. *J. Food Sci.* In press

Cajka T, Hajslova J. 2006. Gas chromatography-time-of-flight mass spectrometry in food analysis. *LCGC Europe.* 20:25–26, 28–31

Cajka T, Hajslova J, Mastovska K. 2009. Mass spectrometry and hyphenated instruments in food analysis. In *Handbook of Food Analysis Instruments*, ed. S Otles, pp. 197–228. Boca Raton, FL: CRC Press

Carunchia Whetstine ME, Parker JD, Drake MA, Larick DK. 2003. Determining flavor and flavor variability in commercially produced liquid cheddar whey. *J. Dairy Sci.* 86:439–48

Carunchia Whetstine ME, Croissant AE, Drake MA. 2005. Characterization of dried whey protein concentrate and isolate flavor. *J. Dairy Sci.* 88:3826–39

Carunchia Whetstine ME, Drake MA, Broadbent JR, McMahon D. 2006. Enhanced nutty flavor formation in Cheddar cheese made with a malty *Lactococcus lactis* adjunct culture. *J. Dairy Sci.* 89:3277–84

Chaintreau A. 2001. Simultaneous distillation-extraction: from birth to maturity: a review. *Flavour Fragr. J.* 16:136–48

Civille GV, Lyons BG. 1996. *Aroma and flavor lexicon for sensory evaluation: terms, definitions, references, and examples*. ASTM data series publication DS 66. West Conshohocken, PA: ASTM. 158 pp.

Croissant AE, Kang EJ, Campbell RE, Bastian E, Drake MA. 2009. The effect of bleaching agent on the flavor of liquid whey and whey protein concentrate. *J. Dairy Sci.* 92:5917–27

Daget N, Joerg M, Bourne M. 1988. Creamy perception 1 in model dessert creams. *J. Texture Stud.* 18:367–88

de Hoffmann E, Stroobant V. 2002. *Mass Spectrometry: Principles and Applications*. New York: Wiley

Delahunty CM, Eyres G, Dufour JP. 2006. Review: gas chromatography-olfactometry. *J. Sep. Sci.* 29:2107–25

Dooley L, Lee YS, Meullenet JL. 2010. The application of check-all-that-apply (CATA) consumer profiling to preference mapping of vanilla ice cream and its comparison to classical external preference mapping. *Food Qual. Prefer.* 21:394–401

Drake MA, McIngvale SC, Gerard PD, Cadwallader KR, Civille GV. 2001. Development of a descriptive language for Cheddar cheese. *J. Food Sci.* 66:1422–27

Drake MA, Civille GV. 2003. Flavor lexicons. *Compr. Rev. Food Sci. Food Saf.* 2:33–40

Drake MA, Karagul-Yuceer Y, Cadwallader KR, Civille GV, Tong PS. 2003. Determination of the sensory attributes of dried milk powders and dairy ingredients. *J. Sens. Stud.* 18:199–216

Drake MA. 2007. Sensory analysis of dairy foods. *J. Dairy Sci.* 90:4925–37

Drake MA, Miracle RE, Wright JM. 2009a. Sensory properties of dairy proteins. In *Milk Proteins: From Expression to Food*, ed. A Thompson, M Boland, H Singh, pp. 429–48. Amsterdam: Elsevier

Drake MA, Wright J, Whitson M, Lloyd M. 2009b. Impact of dairy ingredients on the flavor profiles of foods. In *Dairy-Derived Ingredients: Food and Nutraceutical Uses*, ed. M Corredig, pp 442–69. Boca Raton, FL: CRC Press

Drake MA, Miracle RE, McMahon DJ. 2010. Impact of fat reduction on flavor and flavor chemistry of Cheddar cheeses. *J. Dairy Sci.* 93:5069–81

Elmore JR, Heymann H, Johnson J, Hewett JE. 1999. Preference mapping: relating acceptance of "creaminess" to a descriptive sensory map of a semi-solid. *Food Qual. Prefer.* 10:465–75

Engel W, Bahr W, Schieberle P. 1999. Solvent assisted flavour evaporation: a new and versatile technique for the careful and direct isolation of aroma compounds from complex food matrices. *Eur. Food. Res. Technol.* 209:237–41

Evans J, Zulewska J, Newbold M, Drake MA, Barbano DM. 2009. Comparison of composition, sensory, and volatile components of thirty-four percent whey protein and milk serum protein concentrate. *J. Dairy Sci.* 92:4773–91

Evans J, Zulewska J, Newbold M, Drake MA, Barbano DM. 2010. Comparison of composition and sensory properties of 80% whey protein and milk serum protein concentrates. *J. Dairy Sci.* 93:1824–43

Frank DC, Owen CM, Patterson J. 2004. Solid phase microextraction (SPME) combined with gas-chromatography and olfactometry-mass spectrometry for characterization of cheese aroma compounds. *Lebensm.-Wiss. Technol.* 37:139–54

Friedrich JE, Acree TE. 2000. Issues in gas chromatography-olfactometry methodologies. In *Flavor Chemistry: Industrial and Academic Research*, ed. SJ Risch, C Ho, pp. 124–32. Washington, DC: Am. Chem. Soc.

Frost MB, Janhoj T. 2007. Understanding creaminess. *Int. Dairy J.* 17:1298–311

Gallardo-Escamilla FJ, Kelly AL, Delahunty CM. 2005. Sensory characteristics and related volatile flavor compound profiles of different types of whey. *J. Dairy Sci.* 88:2689–99

Grosch W. 1993. Detection of potent odorants in foods by aroma extract dilution analysis. *Trends Food Sci. Tech.* 4:68–73

Grosch W. 2007. Gas chromatography-olfactometry of aroma compounds. In *Flavours and Fragrances: Chemistry, Bioprocessing and Sustainability*, ed. RG Berger, pp. 363–78. Berlin, Germany: Springer/Heidelberg

Harmon AD. 2002. Solid-phase microextraction for the analysis of aromas and flavors. See Marsili 2002, pp. 75–106

Heath HB, Reineccius G. 1986. *Flavor Chemistry and Technology*. New York: Van Nostrand Reinhold

Holland JF, Gardner BD. 2002. The advantages of GC-TOFMS for flavor and fragrance analysis. See Marsili 2002, pp. 107–38.

Javidipour I, Qian M. 2008. Volatile component change in whey protein concentrate during storage investigated by solid-phase microextraction gas chromatography. *Dairy Sci. Technol.* 88:95–104

Jonsdottir R, Olafsdottir G, Martinsdottir E, Stefansson G. 2004. Flavor characterization of ripened cod roe by gas chromatography, sensory analysis, and electronic nose. *J. Agric. Food Chem.* 52:6250–56

Kang EJ, Campbell RE, Bastian E, Drake MA. 2010. Annatto usage and bleaching in dairy foods. *J. Dairy Sci.* 93:3891–901

Karagül-Yuceer Y, Drake MA, Cadwallader KR. 2003. Aroma-active components of liquid Cheddar whey. *J. Food Sci.* 68:1215–19

Karagül-Yuceer Y, Drake MA, Cadwallader KR. 2004. Evaluation of the character impact odorants in skim milk powder by sensory studies on model mixtures. *J. Sens. Stud.* 19:1–14

Kataoka H, Lord H, Pawliszyn J. 2000. Applications of solid-phase microextraction in food analysis. *J. Chromatogr A.* 880:35–62

Kilcast D, Clegg S. 2002. Sensory perception of creaminess and its relationship with food structure. *Food Qual. Prefer.* 13:609–23

Kirkmeyer SV, Tepper BJ. 2005. Consumer reactions to creaminess and genetic sensitivity to 6-n-propylthiouracil: a multidimensional study. *Food Qual. Prefer.* 16:545–56

Lawless HT, Heymann H. 1999. *Sensory Evaluation of Foods: Principles and Practices*. Gaithersburg, MD: Aspen Publishers, Inc.

Lee JH, Diono R, Kim GY, Min DB. 2003. Optimization of solid phase microextraction analysis for the headspace volatile compounds of Parmesan cheese. *J. Agric. Food Chem.* 51:1136–40

Liaw IW. 2009. *Flavor and flavor chemistry of liquid Mozzarella and Cheddar cheese whey*. MS thesis, North Carolina State Univ., Raleigh. 167 pp.

Liaw IW, Eshpari H, Tong PS, Drake MA. 2010. The impact of antioxidant addition on flavor stability of Cheddar and Mozzarella whey and Cheddar whey protein concentrate. *J. Dairy Sci.* In press

Lubbers S. 2006. Texture-aroma interactions. See Voilley 2006, pp. 327–44

Mahajan SS, Goddick L, Qian MC. 2004. Aroma compounds in sweet whey powder. *J. Dairy Sci.* 87:4057–63

Maignial L, Pibarot P, Bonetti G, Chaintreau A, Marion JP. 1992. Simultaneous-distillation extraction under static vacuum:isolation of volatile compounds at room temperature. *J. Chromatogr. A* 606:87–94

Majcher M, Jelen HH. 2009. Comparison of suitability of SPME, SAFE, SDE methods for the isolation of flavor compounds from extruded potato snacks. *J. Food Comp. Anal.* 22:606–12

Marshall WD. 2003. Analysis of pesticide, mycotoxin, and drug residues in foods. See Nielsen 2003, pp. 315–37

Marsili R. 1997. *Techniques for Analyzing Food Aroma*. New York: Marcel Decker

Marsili R. 2002. *Flavor, Fragrance, and Odor Analysis*. New York: Marcel Dekker

McGorrin RJ. 2007. Flavor analysis of dairy products. In *Flavor of Dairy Products*, ed. KR Cadwallader, MA Drake, RJ McGorrin, 2:23–49. Washington DC: Am. Chem. Soc.

McMaster M, McMaster C. 1998. *GC/MS: A Practical User's Guide*. New York: Wiley

Meilgaard MM, Civille GV, Carr BT. 2007. *Sensory Evaluation Techniques*. New York: CRC Press. 4th ed.

Milo C, Reineccius GA. 1997. Identification and quantification of potent odorants in regular-fat and low-fat mild cheddar cheese. *J. Agric. Food Chem.* 45:3590–94

Miranda-Lopez R, Libbey LM, Watson BT, McDaniel MR. 1992. Odor analysis of pinot noir wines from grapes of different maturities by a gas chromatography-olfactometry technique (Osme). *J. Food Sci.* 57:985–93

Mistry BS, Reineccius T, Olson LK. 1997. Gas chromatography-olfactometry for the determination of key odorants in foods. See Marsili 1997, pp. 265–92

Mortenson FE, Vickers ZM, Reineccius GA. 2008. Flavor of whey protein concentrates and isolates. *Int. Dairy J.* 18:649–57

Murray JM, Delahunty CM. 2000. Mapping consumer preference for the sensory and packaging attributes of Cheddar cheese. *Food Qual. Prefer.* 11:419–35

Murray JM, Delahunty CM, Baxter IA. 2001. Descriptive sensory analysis: past, present and future. *Food Res. Int.* 34:461–71

Nguyen DH, Valentin D, Ly MH, Chrea C, Sauvageot F. 2002. When does smell enhance taste? Effect of culture and odorant/tastant relationship. Presented at Eur. Chemorecept. Res. Organ. Conf., Erlangen, Germany

Nielsen SS. 2003. *Food Analysis*. New York: Plenum Publ.

Pawliszyn J, Arthur CL. 1990. Solid phase microextraction with thermal desorption using fused silica optical fibers. *Anal. Chem.* 62:2145–48

Persaud K, Dodd G. 1982. Analysis of discrimination mechanisms in the mammalian olfactory system using a model nose. *Nature* 299:352–55

Pfeiffer JC, Hollowood TA, Hort J, Taylor AJ. 2005. Temporal synchrony of sub-threshold taste and smell signals. *Chem. Senses* 30:539–45

Pham AJ, Schilling MW, Mikel WB, Williams JB, Martin JM, Coggins PC. 2008. Relationships between sensory descriptors, consumer acceptability and volatile flavor compounds of American dry-cured ham. *Meat Sci.* 80:728–37

Pollien P, Ott A, Montigon F, Baumgartner M. 1997. Hyphenated headspace-gas chromatography-sniffing technique: screening of impact odorants and quantitative aromagram comparisons. *J. Agric. Food Chem.* 45:2630–37

Prososki RA, Etzel MR, Rankin SA. 2007. Solvent type affects the number, distribution, and relative quantities of volatile compounds found in sweet whey powder. *J. Dairy Sci.* 90:523–31

Quach ML, Chen XD, Stevenson RJ. 1999. Headspace sampling of whey protein concentrate solutions using solid-phase microextraction. *Food Res. Int.* 31:371–79

Reineccius GA. 2003. Gas chromatography. See Nielsen 2003, pp. 479–99

Reineccius G. 2006a. Flavor analysis. In *Flavor Chemistry and Technology*, pp. 33–72. Boca Raton, FL: Taylor & Francis. 2nd ed.

Reineccius G. 2006b. Choosing the correct analytical technique in aroma analysis. See Voilley 2006. pp. 81–97

Richardson-Harman NJ, Stevens R, Walker S, Gamble J, Miller M, et al. 2000. Mapping consumer perceptions of creaminess and liking for dairy products. *Food Qual. Prefer.* 11:239–46

Rock F, Barsan N, Weimar U. 2008. Electronic nose: current status and future trends. *Chem. Rev.* 108:705–25

Russell TA, Drake MA, Gerard PD. 2006. Sensory properties of whey and soy proteins. *J. Food Sci.* 71:S447–55

Schlutt B, Moran N, Schieberle P, Hofmann T. Sensory-directed identification of creaminess-enhancing volatiles and semivolatiles in full-fat cream. *J. Agric. Food Chem.* 55:9634–45

Shirey RE. 2000a. Optimization of extraction conditions for low-molecular weight analytes using solid phase microextraction. *J. Chromatogr. Sci.* 38:109–16

Shirey RE. 2000b. Optimization of extraction conditions and fiber selection for semivolatile analytes using solid phase microextraction. *J. Chromatogr. Sci.* 38:279–88

Singh TK, Drake MA, Cadwallader KR. 2003. Flavor of Cheddar cheese: a chemical and sensory perspective. *Compr. Rev. Food Sci. Food Saf.* 2:166–89

Smith JS, Thakur RA. 2003. Mass spectrometry. See Nielsen 2003, pp. 423–33

Song H, Cadwallader KR. 2008. Aroma components of American country ham. *J. Food Sci.* 73:C29–35

Spietelun A, Pilarcyzk M, Kloskowski A, Namiesnik J. 2010. Current trends in solid-phase microextraction (SPME) fibre coatings. *Chem. Soc. Rev.* 39:4524–37

Stevenson RJ, Prescott J, Boakes RA. 1999. Confusing tastes and smell: how odours can influence the perception of sweet and sour tastes. *Chem. Senses* 24:627–635

Stone H, Siedel J, Oliver S, Woolsey A, Singleton RC. 1974. Sensory evaluation by quantitative descriptive analysis. *Food Technol.* 28:24

Suriyaphan O, Drake M, Chen XQ, Cadwallader KR. 2001. Characteristic aroma components of British farmhouse Cheddar. *J. Agric. Food Chem.* 49:1382–87

Szczesniak AS. 2002. Texture is a sensory property. *Food Qual. Prefer.* 13:215–25

Tenenhaus M, Pagés J, Ambroisine L, Guinot C. 2005. PLS methodology to study relationships between hedonic judgements and product characteristics. *Food Qual. Prefer.* 16:315–25

Tomaino RM, Turner LG, Larick DK. 2004. The effect of *Lactococcus lactis* starter cultures on the oxidative stability of liquid whey. *J. Dairy Sci.* 87:300–7

Tournier C, Martin C, Guichard E, Issanchou S, Sulmont-Rossé C. 2007. Contribution to the understanding of consumer's creaminess concept: a sensory and verbal approach. *Int. Dairy J.* 17:555–64

Turnipseed SB. 2006. The use of mass spectrometry in food analysis. In *Handbook of Food Science, Technology, and Engineering, Volume 1*, ed. YH Hui, pp. 48.1–48.9. Boca Raton, FL: Taylor and Francis

van den Dool H, Kratz PD. 1963. A generalization of the retention index system including linear temperature programmed gas-liquid partition chromatography. *J. Chromatog. A* 463–71

van Gemert LJ. 2003b. *Compilations of Flavour Threshold Values in Water & Other Media.* Utrecht, The Netherlands: Oliemans Punter & Partners BV

van Gemert LJ. 2003a. *Compilations of Odour Threshold Values in Air, Water & Other Media.* Utrecht, The Netherlands: Oliemans Punter & Partners BV

van Ruth SM. 2001. Methods for gas chromatography-olfactometry: a review. *Biomol. Eng.* 17:121–28

Voilley A, Etiévant P. 2006. *Flavour in Food.* Boca Raton, FL: CRC Press

Wampler TP. 1997. Analysis of food volatiles using headspace-gas chromatographic techniques. See Marsili 1997. pp. 27–58

Weenen H, Jellema RH, de Wijk RA. 2005. Sensory subattributes of creamy mouthfeel in commercial mayonnaises, custard desserts and sauces. *Food Qual. Prefer.* 16:163–70

Werkhoff P, Brennecke S, Bretschneider W, Bertram H. 2002. Modern methods for isolating and quantifying volatile flavor and fragrance compounds. See Marsili 2002, pp. 139–204

Whetstine MC, Karagul-Yuceer Y, Avsar YK, Drake M. 2003. Identification and quantification of character aroma components in fresh Chevre-style goat cheese. *J. Food Sci.* 68:2441–47

Whetstine MEC, Cadwallader K, Drake M. 2005. Characterization of aroma compounds responsible for the rosy/floral flavor in Cheddar cheese. *J. Agric. Food Chem.* 53:3126–32

Whitson ME. 2010. *Sources of flavor in whey proteins.* MS thesis, North Carolina State Univ., Raleigh. 173 pp.

Whitson ME, Miracle RE, Drake MA. 2010. Sensory characterization of chemical compounds responsible for cardboard flavor in whey protein. *J. Sens Stud.* In press

Williamson LN, Bartlett MG. 2007. Quantitative gas chromatography/time-of-flight mass spectrometry: a review. *Biomed. Chromatogr.* 21:664–69

Wilson AD, Baietto W. 2009. Applications and advances in electronic-nose technologies. *Sensors* 9:5099–148

Wright JM, Whetstine MEC, Miracle RE, Drake MA. 2006. Characterization of a cabbage off-flavor in whey protein isolate. *J. Food Sci.* 71:C86–90

Wright BJ, Zevchak SE, Wright JM, Drake MA. 2009. The impact of agglomeration and storage on flavor and flavor stability of whey protein concentrate 80% and whey protein isolate. *J. Food Sci.* 74:S17–29

Yates MD, Drake MA. 2007. Texture properties of Gouda cheese. *J. Sens. Stud.* 22:493–06

Zhang ZD, Yang MJ. 1994. Solid-phase microextraction: a solvent-free alternative for sample preparation. *Anal. Chem.* 66:844–53

Zhang Z, Li G. 2010. A review of advances and new developments in the analysis of biological volatile organic compounds. *Microchem. J.* 95:127–35

Mucosal Vaccination and Therapy with Genetically Modified Lactic Acid Bacteria

Jerry Wells

Host-Microbe-Interactomics, University of Wageningen, Animal Sciences Department, 6700 AH, Wageningen, The Netherlands; email: jerry.wells@wur.nl

Annu. Rev. Food Sci. Technol. 2011. 2:423–45

First published online as a Review in Advance on December 12, 2010

The *Annual Review of Food Science and Technology* is online at food.annualreviews.org

This article's doi:
10.1146/annurev-food-022510-133640

1941-1413/11/0410-0423$20.00

Keywords

lactic acid bacteria, mucosal vaccines, mucosal therapy, inflammatory bowel disease (IBD), allergy, autoimmune

Abstract

Lactic acid bacteria (LAB) have proved to be effective mucosal delivery vehicles that overcome the problem of delivering functional proteins to the mucosal tissues. By the intranasal route, both live and killed LAB vaccine strains have been shown to elicit mucosal and systemic immune responses that afford protection against infectious challenges. To be effective via oral administration, frequent dosing over several weeks is required but new targeting and adjuvant strategies have clearly demonstrated the potential to increase the immunogenicity and protective immunity of LAB vaccines. Oral administration of *Lactococcus lactis* has been shown to induce antigen-specific oral tolerance (OT) to secreted recombinant antigens. LAB delivery is more efficient at inducing OT than the purified antigen, thus avoiding the need for purification of large quantities of antigen. This approach holds promise for new therapeutic interventions in allergies and antigen-induced autoimmune diseases. Several clinical and research reports demonstrate considerable progress in the application of genetically modified *L. lactis* for the treatment of inflammatory bowel disease (IBD). New medical targets are on the horizon, and the approval by several health authorities and biosafety committees of a containment system for a genetically modified *L. lactis* that secretes Il-10 should pave the way for new LAB delivery applications in the future.

INTRODUCTION

Several species of lactic acid bacteria (LAB) have been explored as mucosal delivery vehicles for vaccines and therapeutic molecules. This includes *Streptococcus gordonii* and members of the dietary group of LAB, including *Lactobacillus plantarum*, *Lactobacillus casei*, *Lactobacillus acidophilus*, and *Lactococcus lactis*, which have a generally regarded as safe (GRAS) status owing to their longstanding use in human food fermentations and products. The LAB have limited biosynthetic abilities and require preformed amino acids, B vitamins, purines, pyrimidines, and (usually) a sugar as a carbon and energy source, which is fermented to produce lactic acid as a common end product. These nutritional requirements restrict their habitats to those in which the required compounds are abundant. Nevertheless, LAB occupy a variety of niches, including milk, plant surfaces, the oral cavity, the gastrointestinal (GI) tract, and the vagina of vertebrates. In the human ileum and jejunum, lactobacilli and streptococci are highly represented (10^3–10^5 organisms per gram of luminal contents). The more complex colonic microbiota comprises around 10^{11} bacteria per gram, with streptococci and lactobacilli present at relatively moderate densities (10^6–10^8 per gram) (Hayashi et al. 2005, Vaughan et al. 2002).

The mucosal delivery of vaccines for large-scale immunization programs is an explicit goal of the World Health Organization (WHO) for economical, logistical, and safety reasons. Additionally, oral (mucosal) vaccines have the potential to elicit antigen-specific secretory immunoglobulin A (sIgA) responses at mucosal surfaces, which can neutralize viruses or toxins and inhibit colonization by enteric microbes. It is now recognized that many of the existing vaccines could be improved by use of a mucosal delivery system that can elicit both antigen-specific sIgA and effective systemic immune responses (Lavelle & O'Hagan 2006, Mannam et al. 2004, Neutra & Kozlowski 2006). In reality, this objective is not easy to achieve via a single oral administration of a vaccine except in the case of an attenuated pathogen, thus the development of effective mucosal delivery systems remains an active area of research. The mucosal delivery of therapeutic molecules using LAB may also be a cost-effective approach for the treatment of mucosal-associated diseases, with the potential to lower the therapeutic dose and reduce or avoid possible side effects due to systemic administration.

To evoke mucosal responses, a delivery system is needed to avoid degradation of the antigen, promote uptake of the antigen in the GI tract, and stimulate adaptive rather than the tolerogenic immune responses seen in feeding studies with soluble antigens (Lavelle & O'Hagan 2006, Neutra & Kozlowski 2006). Another reason for using the dietary group of LAB as mucosal delivery vehicles stems from their long and safe association with humans and their food. This obviates the need to attenuate the bacterial vehicle to avoid reactogenicity (Tacket & Levine 2007) but nevertheless provides a vehicle that can potentially survive transit through the intestinal tract and produce recombinant vaccines or therapeutic molecules in situ. Another advantage of using LAB as mucosal delivery vehicles is that they can be engineered to express multiple proteins and other molecules, e.g., the expression of the type 3 capsule biosynthesis genes of *Streptococcus pneumoniae* in *L. lactis* produced an immunogenic serotype 3 capsular polysaccharide (Gilbert et al. 2000).

Over the past decade, this field of research has been the subject of several reviews. Thus, the aim of this article is not to extensively review the entire literature but to update progress and discuss major new developments and strategies. Ongoing challenges for the future goal of using LAB as mucosal delivery vehicles in human and veterinary medicine is also discussed.

FATE OF LACTIC ACID BACTERIA IN THE HOST AND IMPLICATIONS FOR MUCOSAL DELIVERY

Different species of LAB vary in their capacity to survive passage through the stomach and persist and replicate in the GI tract (Klijn et al. 1995, Vesa et al. 2000). The mucus layer secreted by goblet cells in the epithelium is a significant physical barrier between microbes and contact with the epithelium. Indeed, studies on human biopsy material indicated that most commensal bacteria were present either in suspension in the lumen or trapped in the mucus (van der Waaij et al. 2005). In the mouse, it was recently shown that the colonic mucus consists of two layers extending 150 μm above the epithelial surface with a similar protein composition (Johansson et al. 2008). Whereas the inner layer is densely packed and devoid of bacteria, the outer layer is less dense and colonized by bacteria (Johansson et al. 2008). In the small intestine, less is known about the composition and extent to which the secreted mucus layer covers the entire epithelium. However, in the small intestine the follicular epithelium covering the mucosal-associated lymphoid tissue of the Peyer's patches (PP) is considered to be more accessible to antigens and bacteria present in the luminal compartment. Here, specialized antigen sampling cells (M cells) in the follicular-associated epithelium (FAE) take up particulate antigens and specific binding proteins (e.g., cholera holotoxin or the pentameric binding domain) by endocytosis and transport them to the underlying immune cells. Dendritic cells (DCs) residing in the dome region of the lymphoid follicles are activated by contact with microbial antigens and then migrate to the draining lymph nodes, where they prime T cell responses. After being primed, naive T and B cells become memory/effector cells and migrate from the gut-associated lymphoid tissue (GALT) efferent lymph vessels to the draining lymph nodes and then via the thoracic duct to peripheral blood to other mucosal effector sites such as the lamina propria (LP). Homing of primed lymphocytes to distal mucosal sites is controlled by the profile of adhesion molecules and chemokines expressed on the endothelial cells of the gut microvasculature and is the basis for the compartmentalization of mucosal immune responses (Hanson 1959). M cell–mediated uptake of bacteria is also likely to occur in the isolated lymphoid follicles associated with the colonic epithelium.

In vitro coculture assays of human ileal tissue and Caco2 cell monolayers with nonpathogenic *Escherichia coli* has shown transcellular uptake of bacteria occurs in the FAE but also at lower levels in small intestinal enterocytes of the normal epithelium. Intestinal bacteria may also be sampled directly at the epithelial surface by laminar propia DCs and macrophages, which can extend protrusions through the epithelial tight junctions to the luminal compartment (Rescigno et al. 2001). This process is stimulated by infection with pathogens such as *Salmonella*, but it is not clear to what extent it contributes to the interaction of LAB with the host immune system. Definitive information on the sampling of LAB at mucosal surfaces is lacking, but uptake into the mucosal-associated lymphoid tissue is likely to be important in the induction of immune responses. This implies that the interaction of different LAB with dendritic cells will play a key role in determining the nature of the immune response.

DCs are the most important professional antigen-presenting cells (APC) and express up to 100-fold more major histocompatibility (MHC) antigen and are more effective at differentiating naive T cells than other APC (Inaba 1997, Levin et al. 1993). Microbial activation of DCs in the LP and PP is mediated via the binding of microbe-associated molecular patterns (MAMPs) to pattern recognition receptors (PRRs) expressed by mucosal dendritic cells. One such family of PRRs comprises the Toll-like receptors (TLRs), which are expressed by a variety of cells of the innate immune system, including immature DCs. Each TLR family member is endowed with the ability to recognize a distinct class of conserved MAMPs. Another class of PRRs are the nucleotide-binding and oligomerization domain (NOD)-like receptors NOD1 and NOD2, which recognize the synthetic peptidoglycan structures meso-diaminopimelic acid (meso-DAP) and muramyl dipeptide (MDP), respectively. The nature and combination of the different signals encountered by DC is known to shape the course of the immune response (Wells et al. 2010a). Several studies have shown that different LAB, and even different strains of the same species, have markedly different effects on DC maturation and cytokine production in vitro (Christensen et al.

2002, Meijerink et al. 2010). Additionally, there is evidence that the immune profile obtained in coculture assays with LAB in vitro (especially for Il-10 and Il-12) can be predictive of their in vivo immunomodulatory activities (Foligne et al. 2007, Kwon et al. 2010). This suggests that LAB strains for vaccine applications could be specifically selected on the basis of their ability to modulate DC function and prime T cells for a Th1, Th2, or mixed Th1/Th2 response.

FACTORS INFLUENCING THE IMMUNOGENICITY OF LAB VACCINES

Different LAB have been investigated as vaccine delivery vehicles using the non-toxic tetanus toxin fragment C (TTFC) as a model antigen including *L. lactis*, which passes only transiently through the GI tract and *L. plantarum*, which can persist in mice for several days (Grangette et al. 2004, Mercenier et al. 2000, Norton et al. 1996, Wells et al. 1996). All LAB vehicles induced protective responses but were not directly comparable because of differences in dosing, antigen expression level, and other methodologies (Grangette et al. 2002, Grangette et al. 2001, Norton et al. 1997, Robinson et al. 1997, Shaw et al. 2000, Wells & Mercenier 2008). The immune response to TTFC upon injection with alum adjuvant is dominated by a T helper 2 (T_H2) response and the production of IgG1 antibody, whereas mucosal delivery of TTFC-expressing *L. plantarum* and *L. lactis* promoted a mixed T_H-cell response (Grangette et al. 2002, Grangette et al. 2001, Norton et al. 1996, Robinson et al. 2004) (**Table 1**). This may in part be due to the use of a mucosal route of vaccination as a more pronounced Th1 response to TTFC is obtained when TTFC-expressing *L. lactis* was administered parenterally (Robinson et al. 2004) (**Table 1**).

Recently, *L. lactis* and *S. gordonii* (a non-food associated LAB) have been compared as vaccine delivery vehicles for a vaccine against *Giardia lamblia* (Lee et al. 2009). Both LAB were engineered to express recombinant *G. lamblia* cyst wall protein 2 (CWP2) on the bacterial cell surface as a fusion to the C terminal half of the M6 molecule. CWP2 was previously shown to reduce cyst excretion in infected animals following mucosal immunization with cholera toxin as an adjuvant (Larocque et al. 2003). Interruption of encystations is an attractive control measure against *Giardia* transmission, as the cysts allow parasite survival in the environment and thus transmission between susceptible hosts. Oral administration using different regimes for both vehicles increased CD4+ T helper and B cells in the mesenteric lymph nodes and PP of immunized mice and elicited an IgA response that was higher in mice immunized with *S. gordonii* than *L. lactis*. In challenge studies, mice vaccinated with the *L. lactis* and *S. gordonii* expressing rCWP2 showed significantly reduced cyst output by 71% and 90%, respectively. Additionally, the *S. gordonii*–vaccinated group shed 65% fewer cysts than the *L. lactis* counterparts. The differences in efficacy were not due to higher expression of rCWP2 in *S. gordonii*, as approximately four times more antigen was produced by the *L. lactis* vaccine strain. Analysis of the T cell responses to the vaccine strains revealed a balanced Th1/Th2 cytokine response to CWP2 delivered using *L. lactis* as reported previously for TTFC antigen (Robinson et al. 2004). In contrast, the *S. gordonii* vaccine strain induced a predominant Il-12 (Th1 cytokine response) to CWP2. Given the established role of Il-12 and CWP2-specific IgA in protection against *Giardia*, it seems likely that these factors were responsible for the superior performance of the *S. gordonii* vaccine. In contrast to *L. lactis*, which passes only transiently through the mouse GI tract, *S. gordonii* can persist for up to 30 days, and this may have contributed to the higher IgA response to CWP2 (Lee & Faubert 2006).

Several LAB vaccine studies have investigated the effect of antigen location (cytoplasmic, secreted, or anchored to the cell wall) on immunogenicity. Nevertheless, it has been difficult to conclude which location of the antigen provided optimal mucosal immunization because of strain differences in the amount of expressed antigen and the fact that a proportion of secreted antigen may remain cell associated depending on the construct and level of expression (reviewed by Wells & Mercenier 2008). More recently, the immunogenicity of recombinant strains of *L. casei* ATCC 393 either expressing infectious bursal disease virus (IBDV) capsid 2 antigen (VP2) anchored to the cell wall or secreting VP2 into the milieu was compared by oral immunization of mice (Yigang & Yijing 2008). Both strains elicited IgA in the intestinal lavages and serum IgG, which reacted with VP2 and neutralized virus in a plaque-forming assay on confluent cells in vitro. The highest levels of VP2-specific antibody and inhibition of viral plaque formation were obtained with the strain secreting VP2. This was somewhat surprising given that oral immunization with soluble antigens typically leads to oral tolerance (OT) and that a previous LAB vaccine study concluded that secreting the antigen was the least immunogenic (Bermudez-Humaran et al. 2004). One possibility is that a proportion of VP2 produced by the secretion vector remained cell associated and impacted on the immune response.

Expression of the OspA lipoprotein, a protective antigen against *Borrelia burgdorferi*, in *L. plantarum* was shown to elicit a protective antibody response in mice with Lyme disease (del Rio et al. 2008) (**Table 1**). More recently, the influence of lipidation on the immunogenicity of this antigen was investigated by del Rio et al. (2010). The *ospA* gene was mutated to change the cysteine at position 17 in the lipidation motif of OspA to aspartic acid, resulting in lack of lipid attachment. Assays with both forms of OspA showed that lipidation increased the immune responses of dendritic cells to purified OspA, presumably through binding of the diacyl groups to TLR2/6, resulting in immune activation. Higher amounts of cytokines were also induced in human peripheral blood mononuclear cells (PBMC) and DC coculture assays with *L. plantarum* expressing the lipidated form of OspA. Interestingly, recombinant strains of OspA-expressing *L. plantarum* or mutated OspA-expressing *L. plantarum* induced OspA-specific IgA in the bronchoalveolar lavage and stool suspensions as well as IgG1 and IgG2a serum antibodies to OspA. However, higher levels of OspA-specific IgG1 were elicited by the strain expressing the lipidated OspA, reflecting a shift from a Th2 to a Th1 response. These results confirm previous studies showing that the lipidation of OspA is a critical determinant of its immunogenicity (Erdile et al. 1993) and also highlight the potential to use OspA as a fusion partner for other antigens to enhance Th1 responses.

NOVEL STRATEGIES FOR ENHANCING LAB VACCINES

The fact that DCs play a key role in the induction of mucosal immunity to bacterial antigens was recently exploited to potentiate mucosal immune responses to the protective antigen (PA) of *Bacillus anthracis* (Mohamadzadeh et al. 2009). In this study, *L. acidophilus* was engineered to secrete the PA of *B. anthracis* fused to a 12 amino acid peptide (DCpep) that specifically binds to DCs and promotes endocytosis. The targeting peptide was selected from a phage display library screen and was fused to hepatitis C viral antigen and shown to elicit efficient antigen-specific responses without modulating the function of DCs (Mohamadzadeh et al. 2009). The efficiency of the strategy was tested by oral immunization of mice and challenge with a lethal dose of the *B. anthracis* Sterne strain. Oral vaccination with *L. acidophilus* expressing PA-DCpep induced anti-PA neutralizing antibodies and T cell immunity against *B. anthracis* (**Table 1**). The immune responses were comparable to those obtained with the current vaccine comprising recombinant PA and aluminum hydroxide given subcutaneously (s.c.). In comparison, *L. acidophilus* expressing PA fused to a control peptide showed only minor protection, and no protection was seen with *L. acidophilus* carrying the empty vector. The current recombinant PA vaccine is far from ideal, as it is administered in multiple s.c. injections and is reactogenic in some individuals. If the recombinant LAB (rLAB) vaccine for *B. anthracis* is further optimized and engineered to contain the transgene by an approach that is acceptable to the regulatory authorities, it

Table 1 Protection studies with lactic acid bacteria vaccines

Vaccine target	Vehicle	Antigen (mode)	Model (route)	Immune responses[a]	Protection model (outcome)	References
Helicobacter pylori	LP, LP *alr*	Urease B (cyt)	Mouse i.g.	Serum Ab	Colonization level (partial protection)	Corthesy et al. 2005
Helicobacter pylori	LL	Urease B (cyt)	Mouse i.g.	Not significant	Colonization level (no protection)	Lee 2003
Tetanus	LL	TTFC (cyt)	Mouse i.g., i.n., s.c.	Serum Ab, fecal IgA T cells, ELISPOT	Survival after tetanus toxin challenge (protection)	Norton et al. 1996, Robinson et al. 2004, Robinson et al. 1997, Wells et al. 1993
Tetanus	LP, LL, LP *alr*	TTFC (cyto)	Mouse i.g., i.n., intravaginal	Serum Ab, BALF, T cells, neutralizing Ab	Survival after tetanus toxin challenge (protection)	Grangette et al. 2002, Grangette et al. 2001, Grangette et al. 2004
Streptococcus pneumoniae	LL	PspA	Mouse i.n.	Serum Ab, BALF Ab	Infectious lethal challenge i.p. and i.n. (increased survival)	Hanniffy et al. 2007
Streptococcus pneumoniae	LP, LH	PsaA	Mouse i.n.	Ab in serum BALF, nasal wash	Nasal colonization (reduction in pneumococci)	Oliveira et al. 2006
Streptococcus pyogenes	LL	CRR of M protein serotype 6 (cwa)	Mouse i.n., s.c	Salivary IgA, serum Ab	Pharyngeal infection (i.n. route protective)	Mannam et al. 2004
HIV	LL	V2-V4 loop of gp120 (cwa)	Mouse i.g. with CT adjuvant	Serum Ab, fecal Ab, ICCS, tetramer assay, ELISPOT	Intraperitoneal challenge with HIV Env expressing vaccinia virus (viral load reduced)	Xin et al. 2003
Erysipelothrix rhusiopathiae	LL	SpaA (cwa)	Mouse i.n.	Serum Ab, fecal IgA	Challenge with *E. rhusiopathiae* (protection from death)	Cheun et al. 2004
Enterotoxigenic *Escherichia coli*	LA	K99 fimbriae	Pig intestinal brush border ex vivo	N/A	Inhibition of K99+ *E.coli* adhesion in porcine intestinal brush border	Chu et al. 2005
SARS-associated coronavirus	LC	Spike antigen segments (cm)	Mouse i.g., i.n.	Serum Ab, mucosal IgA	Viral neutralizing antibody elicited	Lee et al. 2006

Rotavirus	LL	VP7 (cyt, cwa, sec)	Mouse i.g.	Serum Ab	Virus neutralization assay (neutralizing Ab demonstrated for VP7 (cwa) vaccine)	Perez et al. 2005
IBDV	LL	VP2, VP3 (cyt, cwa, sec)	Chickens oral	No detectable immune response to antigens	Not performed, as no immune response detectable	Dieye et al. 2003
Group B *Streptococcus*	LL	Pilus (Island 1) (cwa)	Mouse s.c., i.p., i.n.	Serum Ab, Ab in nasal and vaginal washes	Survival of offspring from vaccinated mothers after infectious challenge	Buccato et al. 2006
Brucella abortus	LL	L7/L12 (cyt)	Mouse i.g.	Fecal IgA	Partial protection against i.p. inoculation of virulent *B. abortus*	Pontes et al. 2003
HPV-16-induced tumors	LL	E7 (cwa) plus IL-12 (sec)	Mouse i.g.	CTL, ELISPOT	Protection demonstrated against injection of E7-expressing tumor cell line	Bermudez-Humaran et al. 2005
HPV-16-induced tumors	LC	E7	Mouse i.g.	Serum Ab, mucosal IgA ELISPOT	Protection demonstrated against injection of E7-expressing tumor cell line	Poo et al. 2006
Plasmodium yoelii	LL	MSP-1 (cyt)	Mouse i.g.		Challenge with *P. yoelii* parasites (reduced parasitemia)	Zhang et al. 2005
Bacillus anthracis	LA	PA fused to DCpep	Mouse i.g.	Serum Ab, IgA staining of cells, PA neutralizing Ab, T cell responses	Increased mouse survival after challenge with *B. anthracis*. Protective immunity was equivalent to injected PA plus alum.	Mohamadzadeh et al. 2009
Enteropathogenic *E. coli* (EPEC)	LC	Intimin β	Mouse i.n.	IgA in nasal washes, serum Ab	Induction of serum antibodies that inhibit binding of EPEC to epithelial cells	Ferreira et al. 2008
Giardia lamblia	LL, SG	Cyst wall protein-2 (CWP-2)	Mouse i.g.	ELISA for intestinal IgG & IgA, cytokine ELISPOT mucosal leukocyte cultivation and analysis	Reduction in cyst output in infected mice. SG was superior to LL as a CWP-2 vaccine vehicle	Lee et al. 2009

(*Continued*)

Table 1 (*Continued*)

Vaccine target	Vehicle	Antigen (mode)	Model (route)	Immune responses[a]	Protection model (outcome)	References
Yersinia pseudotuberculosis	LL	Low calcium response antigen (LcrV)	Mouse i.n.	Serum Ab, ELISA of IgA in intestinal & BALF, cytokine assays on splenocytes	Protection against oral & systemic challenges with *Yersina*	Daniel et al. 2009
Enterotoxigenic *E.coli* (ETEC)	LC	F41 fimbrial antigen	Mouse i.g.	IgA in intestinal and BALF by ELISA, serum IgG	Post-infectious survival rates of mice after challenge with ETEC. LC vaccination increased survival	Liu et al. 2009
Borrelia burgdorferi	LP	OspA	Mouse i.g.	Fecal IgA, IgG	LP showed complete protection from challenge with *B. burgdorferi* infected ticks.	del Rio et al. 2008
Streptococcus pneumoniae	LC	PspA	Mouse i.n.	Serum IgG, IgA in nasal washes and saliva	Intraperitoneal challenge with virulent pneumococci. Increased survival shown for LC expressing PspA	Campos et al. 2008
S. pneumoniae	LC	PspA, PspC	Mouse i.n.	Serum and vaginal Ab, ELISPOT and ELISA for IFN-γ and Il-17 secretion in lung and spleen cells	Respiratory challenge with virulent pneumococci. Increased survival seen with LC expressing PspA and rPspA without adjuvant	Ferreira et al. 2009
Listeria monocytogenes	LL	Listeriolysin O	Mouse i.p., i.g	LLO-specific T cells by ELISPOT, serum Ab	Challenge with luminescent *Listeria*. Organ luminescence and *Listeria* counts showed partial protection with LL vaccine strain	Bahey-El-Din et al. 2008

[a]Responses detected using any of the indicated vaccination routes.

LP, *Lactobacillus plantarum*; LL, *Lactococcus lactis*; LC, *Lactobacillus casei*, LA, *Lactobacillus acidophilus*; LH, *Lactobacillus helveticus*; SG, *Streptococcus gordonii*; cyt, cytoplasmic; cwa, cell wall–associated; sec, secreted; i.g., intragastric; i.n., intranasal; s.c., subcutaneous; Ab, antibody; BALF, bronchoalveolar lavage fluid; IgG, immunoglobulin G; IgA, immunoglobulin A; PA, protective antigen; TTFC, tetanus fragment C; PspA, pneumococcal surface protein A; PspC, pneumococcal surface protein C; CT, cholera toxin; Ab, antibodies; CTL, cytotoxic lymphocytes; ELISA, enzyme-linked immunosorbent assay; ELISPOT, enzyme-linked immunosorbent spot assay; LLO, listeriolysin; IFN-γ, interferon gamma; ICCS, intracellular cytokine staining assay; CRR, C-repeat region; IBDV, infectious bursal disease virus (IBDV); VP2, virus capsid 2 antigen; VP7, virus outer-layer protein seven; MSP-1, merozoite specific protein 1; OspA, outer-membrane surface protein A; SpaA, surface protective antigen A.

would have considerable potential to be developed as a mucosal vaccine against this deadly pathogen.

Another targeting strategy employing the *E. coli* heat labile toxin B (LTB) subunit protein was recently evaluated as an approach to enhance immune responses to *L. casei* expressing a recombinant porcine rotavirus antigen VP4 (Qiao et al. 2009). Like *Vibrio cholera* toxin, LTB has been shown to be a mucosal adjuvant by virtue of the ADP-ribosylating activity of the A subunit and the GM1-gangliside binding activity of the pentameric B subunit. However, the holotoxins are too toxic for use in humans. As GM-1 is present on the follicular epithelium covering the PP, the nontoxic pentameric B subunits of both toxins have been explored as targeting molecules for recombinant and conjugated vaccine antigens (Yamamoto et al. 2001). *L. casei* expressing the major protective antigen VP4 of porcine rotavirus alone or as a fusion to VP4 were used to immunize mice. Both strains elicited a VP4-specific serum IgG response and VP4-specific IgA in the ophthalmic and vaginal washes after oral immunization (**Table 1**). The IgA titres were significantly higher in the mice immunized with the *L. casei* expressing recombinant VP4-LTB than in *L. casei* expressing only VP4 (Qiao et al. 2009). These authors concluded that LTB served as a mucosal adjuvant, but it is not clear whether the two vaccine strains expressed similar levels of amounts of antigen or whether the VP4-LTB protein could form pentamers on the cell surface of *L. casei*, which are capable of binding to GM-1.

Bacterial flagellin was recently explored as a fusion partner for vaccine antigens expressed in *L. casei* (Kajikawa et al. 2007, 2010). Flagellins can be protective antigens themselves but when expressed as a fusion protein with other antigens can also act as an adjuvant. This is most likely related to the ability of flagellin to bind to the innate TLR5 receptor and trigger host inflammatory responses. The SipC antigen of *Salmonella enterica* was expressed in *L. casei* alone and also as a fusion protein linked to the N or C terminus of flagellin in the pLP401 vector, which provided sequences for secretion and a cell wall anchoring of the recombinant protein. These strains all elicited similar responses to SipC, following intraperitoneal injection indicating that flagellin did not adjuvant the antibody responses to this antigen. The antibody titres to flagellin appeared to be influenced by the nature of the fusion protein, and highest titres were obtained with the strain that expressed SipC as a C-terminal fusion to flagellin. Further work is needed to conclusively determine whether flagellin could adjuvant immune responses to other antigens expressed in LAB, including an investigation into mucosal routes of administration and different modes of expression.

Another interesting development has exploited the recent discovery of pili in Gram-positive bacteria as antigen display systems (Quigley et al. 2010). As a proof of principle the maltose binding protein (MBP) of *E. coli* was fused to the C terminus of the tip protein from the T3 pilus of *Streptococcus pyogenes* and expressed in *L. lactis*. Intranasal immunization with this strain elicited mucosal IgA and serum IgG responses to MBP. This method of antigen presentation remains to be compared directly with other modes of expression (e.g., intracellular, cell wall anchored), but it seems to be a promising strategy for presentation of vaccine polypeptides in LAB.

Following the first demonstration that *L. lactis* could secrete biologically active Il-2 and Il-6 and stimulate mucosal and systemic responses to the model antigen TTFC (Steidler et al. 1995, 1998), several studies have sought to use the coexpression of cytokines to modulate LAB vaccine responses. Coadministration of an Il-12-secreting strain of *L. lactis* with another strain of *L. lactis* expressing a cell wall–anchored form of the E7 antigen from human papilloma virus (HPV)-16 increased protection in a mouse cancer model (Bermudez-Humaran et al. 2005). Recently, the adjuvant effects of *L. casei* secreting murine Il-1β were investigated in combination with a heat-killed *Salmonella enterica* serovar Entertidis (SE) vaccine. Biologically active murine IL-1β was secreted effectively at levels of up to 1 ug ml^{-1} in the culture supernatant. Intragastric immunization with LL-Il1-β elevated both serum IgG and mucosal IgA responses to the SE vaccine (Kajikawa et al. 2010).

The chemokines Mig and IP-10 have also been investigated as potential vaccine adjuvants owing to their pronounced chemotactic activities on mononuclear cells such as T cells, natural killer (NK) cells, and monocytes (Cortes-Perez et al. 2008). Intranasal administration of *L. lactis* producing a secreted Mig-IP-10 fusion protein and a cell wall–anchored form of the E7 antigen from HPV or *L. lactis* expressing E7 and control groups was used to investigate the potential adjuvant effect of Mig-IP-10. The humoral responses to E7 antigen were substantially higher in mice immunized with the strain expressing the Mig-IP-10 protein, suggesting that Mig-IP10 does indeed have immunostimulatory properties in vivo (Cortes-Perez et al. 2008) (**Table 1**).

PROTECTION STUDIES WITH LACTIC ACID BACTERIA VACCINES

Since the field was last extensively reviewed (Wells & Mercenier 2008), there have been several new publications describing the expression of different candidate vaccine antigens in LAB (Adachi et al. 2010, Cortes-Perez et al. 2009, Kim et al. 2009, Li et al. 2010, Liu et al. 2010, Qiao et al. 2009, Tang & Li 2009), some of which have been evaluated in protection models in vivo (Campos et al. 2008; Daniel et al. 2009; del Rio et al. 2008; Ferreira et al. 2008, 2009; Liu et al. 2009) (**Table 1**). The future development and implementation of LAB vaccines will depend on several factors, including relative cost, acceptability as contained genetically modified organisms (GMOs), and efficacy. A necessary step is to show that the subunit LAB vaccines confer an advantage over traditional routes of immunization and sufficient efficacy in protection models (e.g., compared to injected vaccines). To date, there are only a few LAB vaccine protection studies that directly compare immunogenicity and protection with administration of the antigen together with adjuvant (Corthesy et al. 2005, Hanniffy et al. 2007, Mohamadzadeh et al. 2009). Partial protection against *Helicobacter felis* was demonstrated in mice by the use of recombinant *L. plantarum* NCIMB8826 strains producing the urease B antigen, but this was not as effective as vaccination with the antigen plus cholera toxin as an adjuvant (Corthesy et al. 2005). Protective vaccination against *B. anthracis* was obtained by vaccination with *L. acidophilus* expressing the PA fused to a DC-targeting peptide (see above). The protective immunity induced by oral vaccination with rLAB was equivalent to that obtained by injection of PA with alum (Mohamadzadeh et al. 2009). Intranasal administration of *L. lactis* expressing pneumococcal surface protein A (PspA) afforded better protection against respiratory challenge with virulent pneumococci than intra-nasal (i.n.) PspA or PspA injected with alum Hanniffy et al. 2007. This important advance demonstrated that a LAB vaccine could be more effective than an injected vaccine in an in vivo challenge model. The higher protection afforded by *L. lactis* was attributed to a shift toward a T_H1 response compared to the injected antigen. Additionally, the lactococcal vaccine afforded protection on a par with that obtained with the injected vaccine in a sepsis model of pneumocccal disease. Decreased colonization of *S. pneumoniae* has also been observed in mice following nasal inoculation of different LAB expressing pneumococcal PspA (Oliveira et al. 2006). More recently, PspA-expressing *L. casei* was shown to induce cross-protective antibodies to both clade 1 and clade 2 variants of PspA and confer protection in a sepsis challenge model using a heterologous strain of pneumococcus (Campos et al. 2008). An independent study recently compared immune responses and protection from infectious challenge to different *L. casei* strains expressing the candidate vaccine antigens PspA and PspC, both of which have been shown to be protective protein antigens in challenge models. Immunization with the *L. casei* vaccine strains and PspC protein without adjuvant failed to elicit antigen-specific serum antibodies by the intranasal route. Via the s.c. route of immunization, only the purified protein elicited a specific humoral response. In contrast, PspA was found to be more immunogenic than PspC and i.n. immunization with purified PspA (clade5) and PspA5-expressing *L. casei* elicited anti-PspA serum antibodies and conferred protection against an i.n. challenge with virulent *S. pneumonia* (Ferreira et al. 2009). Humoral responses and mean survival time of challenged mice were higher in the group immunized with purified PspA5 without adjuvant. Cellular responses to the vaccines were also measured, and the highest levels of protection were characterized by increased levels of Il-17 and IFN-γ by lung and spleen cells, respectively, as well as low levels of TNF-β in the respiratory tract.

L. plantarum expressing OspA, a protective antigen against *B. burgdorferi*, in animals and humans has been evaluated as an experimental vaccine against Lyme disease in mice (del Rio et al. 2008). The mechanism of protection is somewhat unconvential for a vaccine, as it is aimed at blocking *B. burgdorferi* ticks in the midgut of the tick vector. OspA-expressing *L. plantarum* strains but not the control strain carrying the vector alone elicited mucosal sIgA and systemic IgG humoral responses following i.g. immunization. Furthermore, the OspA-expressing *L. plantarum* strains protected mice from challenge with *B. burgdorferi* infected ticks, which are the natural vectors of infection. One month after challenge, the immunized mice were shown to be free of *B. burgdorferi* by culture, polymerase chain reaction (PCR), and immunoblotting with serum raised against whole extracts of the pathogen. Interestingly, this study also showed that a mutant OspA lacking a potential autoantigenic epitope (Chen et al. 1999) was protective using *L. plantarum* as a delivery vehicle. This strain of *L. plantarum* did not colonize the gut, and higher numbers of *L. plantarum* (4×10^{10}) were used for intra-gastric (i.g.) vaccination than in many previous LAB vaccine studies. Furthermore the priming doses were given twice daily on days 1–4 and 8–11, and the booster immunizations twice on days 30–33 and days 52–55. The longer period of immunization and more frequent dosing may have contributed to the impressive protective capacity of the vaccine in mice.

DNA VACCINE DELIVERY

A recent development in the use of LAB as delivery vehicles has been in the field of DNA vaccination. The advantage of DNA vaccines lies in their ability to induce potent cellular immune responses in addition to antibodies and the flexibility to express multiple antigens or epitopes using one DNA vector. For viral antigens, the correct posttranslational modifications (e.g., glycosylation) should be carried out by the host cell machinery. Despite the successful use of DNA vaccination in small animals, its translation to primates, humans, and other large animals has been beset with problems (Jechlinger 2006).

Delivery of DNA into mammalian cells was demonstrated using native lactococci and a plasmid carrying the bovine β-lactoglobulin (BLG) gene under the control of the viral promoter P_{cmv}, which is not functional in *L. lactis* (Guimaraes et al. 2006). Expression of BLG was detected by PCR in Caco2 cells after incubation with *L. lactis* carrying the DNA vaccine vector expression plasmid, but not after incubation with the purified recombinant plasmid alone, or when the plasmid was mixed together with *L. lactis*. Although the efficiency of delivery was low this study showed clear potential to further optimize LAB as DNA vaccine delivery vehicles. Since then, recombinant *L. lactis* expressing internalin A, a cell wall–anchored protein and major invasin of *L. monocytogenes*, was shown to be internalized by epithelial Caco2 cells in vitro and enterocytes in vivo after administration to guinea pigs (Guimaraes et al. 2005). In vivo, the invasiveness of the internalin expressing strain was about 100-fold higher than for the *L. lactis* control strain. The ability of the strains to deliver a vaccine vector expressing green-fluorescent protein (GFP) under the control of the P_{cmv} promoter was also assessed in vitro. The bacterial strains were added at a ratio of 1000:1 bacteria per Caco2 cell, of which about 1% of the internalin-expressing lactococci were internalized by Caco2 cells (Guimaraes et al. 2005). Only 1.2% of the Caco2 cells expressed eGFP indicating that only some of the cells internalized several bacteria or that internalization does not always lead to plasmid transfer and expression. Recently, work by the same group showed that CFSE-labeled *L. lactis* were in fact not evenly distributed among the Caco2 cells and were predominantly located at the periphery of the cell clusters (Innocentin et al. 2009). Similar results were obtained with *L. lactis* expressing the fibronectin-binding protein A (FnBPA) of *Staphylococcus aureus* (Innocentin et al. 2009). These results are compatible with the basal lateral membrane localization of the host receptors for these bacterial invasion proteins. E-caderin, the receptor for internalin A, is not usually exposed at the surface of the intestinal epithelium, but it has been suggested that *Listeria* invade at the tip of the villi where apoptosis of enterocytes temporarily exposes the basolateral membrane and thus E-cadherin to the lumen.

One approach that may increase the efficiency of DNA vaccine delivery involves the use of listeriolysin (LLO) from pathogenic *L. monocytogenes*. Upon internalization into an endosome or phagosome, the acidification process activates LLO, allowing it to form pores in the membrane and permit escape of the bacteria. Although not yet utilized for DNA vaccine delivery, a strain of *L. lactis* expressing LLO has been tested for its ability to protect mice against live intraperitoneal challenge with *L. monocytogenes* (**Table 1**). The strain secreting LLO at the highest levels induced CD8+ T cell responses, indicating that LLO was presented via the cytosolic MHC class I pathway. This strain conferred protection against a *Listeria* challenge but only when administered by the intraperitoneal (i.p.) route but not the i.g. route (Bahey-El-Din et al. 2008). When the expression of LLO was combined with a truncated form of the *Listeria* P60 antigen, no significant improvement protection was observed over the *L. lactis* strain expressing only LLO. The expression of tP60 was relatively low and possibly insufficient for access to the cytoplasm (Bahey-El-Din et al. 2010).

An experimental DNA vaccine using *L. acidophilus* as a carrier for use against foot-and-mouth-disease virus was recently described (Li et al. 2007). Significant immune responses to the vaccine antigen were only measured or reported using the injected routes of administration, although it was indicated that mucosal administration could prime a specific immune response (Li et al. 2007). Clearly, there is some way to go before LAB can effectively deliver DNA vaccines via the oral route, but there is clear potential to optimize targeting strategies and combine this with LLO expression to facilitate release of the DNA vaccine into the cytoplasm. The next step will then be to demonstrate their immunogenicity and efficacy in animal models.

THERAPEUTIC APPLICATIONS IN INFLAMMATORY BOWEL DISEASE

Many species of LAB are members of the intestinal microbiota of humans and animals, and as such represent good vehicles for delivery of therapeutic biologicals to the GI tract. The mucosal immune system is faced with the difficult task of balancing opposing immune functions: immunological tolerance to harmless food or bacterial antigens and immunity to pathogenic organisms. Several important human intestinal disorders are associated with loss of homeostasis to harmless antigens, including food allergy, IBD, celiac disease, and autoimmune diseases. It is not surprising that the mechanisms supporting homeostasis of tolerance and immunity remain a highly active area of investigation (Wells et al. 2010b). Genetically modified LAB have the potential to produce and secrete therapeutic proteins in situ at different sites within the intestinal tract, thereby increasing availability of the therapeutic target cells. Consequently, the therapeutic dose is expected to be lower if delivered locally in the mucosa, thus avoiding the need for higher systemic concentrations and the risk of side effects. Furthermore, the production of biologicals is often difficult and costly.

The first therapeutic application of rLAB was based on the secretion of the inflammatory cytokine Il-10 by *L. lactis* and treatment of experimental colitis in mice as a model for IBD in humans (Steidler et al. 1998). IBD is a chronic inflammatory disorder with an average yearly incidence of 10–15 persons per 100,000 individuals in Western countries. The two major forms of IBD are Crohn's disease (CD) and ulcerative colitis (UC). The symptoms include bloody diarrhea or constipation, abdominal pain, fever, and weight loss. There is no cure, and therapy is focused on alleviation of the active disease and the accompanying symptoms.

In mice, the daily administration of Il-10-secreting *L. lactis* caused a 50% reduction in colitis induced by dextran sulfate sodium (DSS) at a dose that was 10,000-fold lower than that systemically administered. Treatment of of Il-$10^{-/-}$ Sv/Ev mice that spontaneously develop a severe colitis, with the Il-10-secreting *L. lactis* also prevented the onset of colitis (Steidler et al. 1998). This beneficial effect was dependent on secretion of Il-10 in situ by live lactococci. An environmentally contained version of the hIL-10-secreting strain (see section on Environmental Containment below) has also been evaluated in an open label Phase I trial in CD patients (Braat et al. 2006). The strain was formulated in capsules to optimize survival during passage through the stomach. During the trial, 8 out of 10 patients with moderate to severe disease showed significant clinical improvement, and five went into complete remission. In addition, the containment strategy was validated in humans, and no serious adverse effects were reported. A large Phase 2 trial is reported to be underway to further evaluate the safety, tolerability, and efficacy of the hIl-10-secreting *L. lactis* in UC patients (Rottiers et al. 2009).

In addition, there is potential to use the secretion of molecules, such as trefoil factors (TFF) or TNF blocking antibodies, by *L. lactis* to treat IBD. TFFs are a family of small peptides that promote mucosal protection and repair through the use of multiple mechanisms and also have effects on the immune system. TFFs are highly stable to acid denaturation and proteolytic degradation but are not effective as therapeutic agents when administered orally because they adhere to the mucus that is continuously removed from the intestine by peristalsis. However, i.g. administration of TFF-secreting *L. lactis* during or after DSS induction of colitis in mice resulted in the reduction of several disease parameters, including body weight and histological and inflammatory markers. Even rectal administration of 2,500-fold higher doses of TFF was not as effective as TFF-secreting *L. lactis*, suggesting that *L. lactis* is able to deliver TFF peptides in close proximity to the colonic epithelium (Vandenbroucke et al. 2004).

Monoclonal antibodies such as infliximab, which neutralize the proinflammatory cytokine TNF, are also being used as part of the therapeutic armamentarium of IBD. However, treatment requires periodic infusions of relatively large amounts of purified antibody. Other biologics include monoclonal antibodies that block leukocyte adhesion or T cell signaling via the Il-6 receptor as well as Il-12/23 cytokine blocking antibodies. Recently, *L. lactis* was engineered to secrete an anti-TNF single-domain antibody fragment derived from heavy chain camelid antibodies and shown to be effective in the treatment of DSS-induced colitis and established colitis in the Il-$10^{-/-}$ mouse model (Rottiers et al. 2009). In this study, anti-TNF antibodies were shown to be associated with the surface of cells of the lamina propia, where leukocyte infiltration was evident but was not measured in systemic circulation. This suggests that oral delivery would prevent the systemic side effects associated with injection of the antibodies in humans.

Another new strategy for treatment of colitis was reported based on secretion of low calcium response protein (LcrV), a protein produced by pathogenic *Yersinia*, to evade the host's immune response (Foligne et al. 2007). This protein induces and stimulates Il-10 production in the host mucosal tissues. The protective and therapeutic potential of LcrV-secreting *L. lactis* was demonstrated in the trinitrobenzene sulfonic (TNBS) acid and DSS mouse models of colitis. In the TNBS-induced colitis model the protective effect of *L. lactis* secreting LcrV was about 50% based on the macroscopic lesion score (Wallace score) and as efficient as the Il-10 secreting strain that was previously reported (Steidler et al. 2000). In summary, there is considerable potential for mucosal therapy of IBD in humans using rLAB.

PROPHYLAXIS AND THERAPY OF ALLERGIC DISEASE

Allergy is defined as a hypersensitivity reaction mediated by specific antibody-mediated or cell-mediated immunologic mechanisms, the clinical manifestation of which is called allergic disease. The progression of infant allergy to atopic diseases such as atopic eczema, allergic rhinoconjunctivitis, and ultimately asthma is becoming increasingly common and is now referred to as the pediatric allergic march. This is contributing to the so-called epidemic of allergic or atopic diseases that affect up to 30% of the European and U.S. population and are responsible for a substantial healthcare burden on society (Holgate 1999, Kalliomaki et al. 2010).

Recently, i.g. administration of Il-10-secreting *L. lactis* (described above) for three consecutive days before sensitization to BLG was shown to promote OT in young mice (Frossard et al. 2007). Administration of Il-10-secreting *L. lactis* reduced antigen-induced anaphylaxis and almost completely inhibited the production of IgE and IgG1 antibodies to BLG. Interestingly, these protective effects were partly attributable to *L. lactis* itself, as the wild-type strain also diminished the levels of BLG-specific IgE and IgG1. Moreover, the results of this study suggested that the recombinant *L. lactis* strain increased Il-10 levels in the mucosa and promoted the development of antigen-specific sIgA. In addition, the immunomodulatory effects of lactococcal-delivered Il-12 have been investigated in mouse models of OVA-induced asthma and BLG food hypersensitivity (Bermudez-Humaran et al. 2005, Wu et al. 2006). Cytokine-secreting LAB could be considered as a strategy to prevent food allergy, but the possibility of unexpected side effects of cytokines on the immune system is likely to be one of the safety concerns.

Mucosal delivery of allergen-expressing LAB have also been proposed for the immunotherapy of type I allergies. The rationale is based on the finding that some strains of LAB have been shown to modulate T-cell responses to an expressed or coadministered antigen towards a T_H1-type immune response (Chatel et al. 2003, Kruisselbrink et al. 2001, Murosaki et al. 1998, Repa et al. 2003), and the concept that mucosal vaccination against type I allergy may offer some advantages over the subcutaneous route for desensitization (Novak et al. 2004). However, the studies published to date have been focused on the prevention of allergic sensitization in mouse models. For example, oral pretreatment of mice with *L. lactis* strains producing the cow's milk allergen BLG was shown to cause a shift towards a Th1 immune response and decrease the levels of BLG-specific IgE (Adel-Patient et al. 2005). The most effective strains were those producing the highest amounts of BLG.

With respect to aero-allergens, oral administration of dust mite allergen Der p1–expressing *L. plantarum* and Der p5–expressing *L. acidophilus* were both shown to reduce local allergen-induced airway inflammation, hyperreactivity, and allergen-specific IgE production (Charng et al. 2006, Kruisselbrink et al. 2001). The modulation of allergic immune responses to the birch pollen allergen Bet v1 by rLAB has also been recently described (Daniel et al. 2007). Intranasalvaccination with *L. lactis* and *L. plantarum* strains producing substantial amounts of the Bet v1 allergen in two different cellular locations (intracellular, extracellular) enhanced allergen-specific mucosal IgA levels and induced a shift toward a Th1 response in a prophylactic mouse model of type I allergy to birch pollen. Via the intragastric route only recombinant *L. plantarum* was effective (Daniel et al. 2006). The *L. lactis* strain produced about fourfold less Bet v1 than the *L. plantarum* strains, so this may account for the lower efficacy of this strain. This is in agreement with previous observations that the reduction of BLG-specific IgE was most effective using *L. lactis* strains that produced the highest amount of allergen (Adel-Patient et al. 2005). However, differences in intrinsic immunomodulating capacities, gut persistence, or both, of these two strains cannot be ruled out as contributing factors.

The induction of OT to food antigens and autoantigens is an alternative approach to preventing allergic and autoimmune diseases, but several clinical trials attempting to induce OT have failed

(Faria & Weiner 2005, Kraus & Mayer 2005, Weiner 2004). In experimental models, high doses of antigen induced OT by clonal deletion or anergy of T cells recognizing the antigen, whereas low antigen doses led to antigen-specific regulatory T cells (Tregs) (Friedman & Weiner 1994, Yoshida et al. 1997). The capacity of chicken ovalbumin (OVA)-secreting *L. lactis* (LL-OVA) has been evaluated for its capacity to induce OT in transgenic DO11.10 mice, which express an ova-specific T cell receptor on CD4+ T cells (Huibregtse et al. 2007). The doses of OVA secreted in the gut by repeated feeding of *L. lactis* (up to 10 μg) were considerably lower than that typically used for effective low tolerance induction (5 mg) but nevertheless reduced delayed-type hypersensitivity (DTH) responses to OVA. Interestingly, *L. lactis* carrying the empty vector also suppressed ova-specific DTH responses but to a lesser extent than LL-OVA. The suppressive effect was associated with a TGF-β-dependent decrease in the proliferation of OVA-specific splenic T cells. Furthermore, the LL-OVA increased the Foxp3 and CTLA-4 positive cells in the CD4+ CD25-T cell population from 0.045% (control mice) to 4.11%, indicating that it induced Tregs. In contrast, Tregs induction was not detected in the mice fed ovalbumin (1 μg) or the *L. lactis* control strain. This raises the question: By what mechanism did the *L. lactis* control and ovalbumin-fed mice suppress the OVA-specific DTH response? Additionally, it would be interesting to know whether administration of *L. lactis* with low doses of soluble OVA also induces OT, as it may obviate the need to use GMOs.

The approach described above was recently used to investigate the induction of antigen-specific tolerance in an established genotypic celiac disease mouse model (Huibregtse et al. 2009). Celiac disease is caused by loss of tolerance to ingested gliadin and is associated with HLA-DQ2- or HLA-DQ8-restricted T cell responses to specific antigenic epitopes of gliadin. A transgenic NOD mouse expressing the human DQ8 MHC II gene (NOD ABo DQ8) develops autoimmune disease pathology in response to gliadin sensitization (Marietta et al. 2004). *L. lactis* secreting a modified epitope of DQ8 (LL-DQ8) mimicking the deaminated immunodominant epitope of β-gliadin (DQ8d) was administered i.g. on days 1–10 to mice presensitized with the same immunodominant gliadin peptide. As controls, *L. lactis* carrying the empty vector (LL-pT1Nx) and the inoculation buffer alone were administered to different groups of mice. The LL-DQ8 strain effectively suppressed the DTH response to DQ8 compared to the buffer control. Furthermore, treatment with LL-DQ8 also decreased the proliferative capacity of inguinal lymph nodes cells and lamina propria cells. LL-pTNX1, but the not the inoculation buffer control, somewhat reduced DTH response and the cellular proliferative response, but this was smaller than the effects measured in the LL-DQ8-treated mice. In agreement with previous studies using LL-OVA, the mechanism was attributed to an upregulation of Foxp3 Tregs secreting IL-10 and TGF-β, which were detected in the spleen and mucosal tissues of the LL-DQ8-treated mice. Taken together, these results indicate that in the future it might be possible to use rLAB to induce antigen-specific OT in humans as a therapy for autoimmune and allergic diseases.

ANTIINFECTIVE STRATEGIES

Over the past seven years, antiinfective agents have been expressed and tested in LAB with the ultimate aim of using recombinant strains to prevent infection by viral, fungal, or bacterial pathogens at the mucosal surfaces. Several approaches have utilized single chain variable fragments (ScFv) making up variable regions of the heavy and light chains of an immunoglobulin linked together via a linker peptide to neutralize (or immobilize) virions or bacteria before they reach a receptor site on a host cell. One striking example of this therapeutic approach is the protection against experimental vaginitis in rats using *S. gordonii* expressing a secreted or surface-displayed microbiocidal ScFv antibody against *Candida albicans* (Beninati et al. 2000). *Lactobacillus zeae* displaying a ScFv form of an antibody (Guy 13) directed against the major adhesion molecule of *Streptococcus* mutants was shown to protect against colonization on tooth enamel and dental caries by agglutination and clearance of this bacterium in the mouth (Kruger et al. 2002). In this study, the bacteria were administered daily, but a future aim would be to use a strain that persisted and continuously produced antibodies.

The intercellular adhesion molecule 1 (ICAM-1) receptor is involved in the binding of monocytes and activated CD4+ T lymphocytes to the epithelium, and antibody blocking of this receptor on the cervical epithelium would prevent cell-associated HIV-1 transmission. The expression of a ScFv specific for ICAM-1 in *L. casei* was shown to block monocyte-associated HIV-1 transmission across a cervical epithelial monolayer in vitro (Chancey et al. 2006). Other strategies to block HIV transmission at the mucosa include secretion of microbiocides, peptide inhibitors of viral-cell fusion, and receptors used by HIV to enter cells. For example, the two linked extracellular domains of the CD4 receptor (2D CD4) that binds HIV gp120 envelope protein have been successfully secreted from a vaginal colonizing strain of *Lactobacillus jensenii* at concentrations ranging from 100 ng ml^{-1} to 1 μg ml^{-1} in laboratory culture supernatants (Chang et al. 2003). Furthermore, the secreted 2D CD4 was able to inhibit HIV infection of cultured cells in a dose-dependent manner. Binding of gp120 to CD4 can also be inhibited by the high-affinity interaction of the microbicidal cyanovirin-N (CV-N) protein with the high-mannose structures present on gp120 (Boyd et al. 1997). A number of LAB have been used to express CV-N, including *S. gordonii* (Giomarelli et al. 2002), *L. lactis*, and *L. plantarum* (Pusch et al. 2005) and have been shown to neutralize the infectivity of both laboratory and primary isolates of HIV-1 in vitro (Pusch et al. 2005). More recently, a natural vaginal strain of *L. jensenii* was engineered to express CV-N from a stably integrated expression cassette recombined into the genome (Liu et al. 2006). This strain was capable of colonizing the vagina of mice and producing CV-N in situ, but no protection studies with this strain have yet been published. A different approach to inhibit cell-free HIV infection uses peptide-fusion inhibitors derived from the C-terminal heptad repeat of HIV gp41, as exemplified recently by the work of Rao et al. (2005) using the probiotic *E. coli* Nissle strain as a delivery vehicle. In a similar manner, lactobacilli expressing a HIV-1 fusion-inhibitor peptide have been experimentally evaluated as a potential bioshield (Pusch et al. 2006).

For this strategy to be successful, the colonizing LAB must be able to compete with the resident microbiota and secrete sufficient quantities of the inhibitory proteins to block infection in vivo. Some naturally occurring strains of *Lactobacillus* spp. that were introduced into the vagina to prevent vaginosis have been reported to persist for weeks or even months (Falagas et al. 2007). It is also encouraging to consider that cervico-vaginal transmission of HIV from men to women is an inefficient process (Chakraborty et al. 2001). Nevertheless, the lack of a containment system and thus the potential spread of the genetic trait will be a concern for such an approach in humans.

ENVIRONMENTAL CONTAINMENT

To address safety concerns over the use of Il-10-secreting *L. lactis* in humans, Steidler et al. replaced the chromosomal thymidylate synthase (*thyA*) with the Il10 transgene to generate a thymine auxotroph (Steidler 2002). The *thyA* gene is essential for the synthesis of thymine and thymidine and in the absence of these compounds the bacteria undergo thymineless death and lysis. Additionally, fragmentation of the genomic DNA occurs before lysis, reducing the risk of genetic transfer even further. Even in the unlikely event that *L. lactis* would acquire another lactococcal *thyA* gene by horizontal DNA transfer, recombination would lead to loss of the transgene. Viability of the *thyA* hIL10+ strain was reduced by several orders of magnitude in the absence of thymidine or thymine, and containment was validated in vivo in pigs (Steidler 2002). Currently, several health authorities and biosafety committees have positively evaluated this containment system for environmentally released, genetically modified *L. lactis* (Rottiers et al. 2009). As mentioned above a small pilot trial with the *thyA* hIL10^{+} strain in patients with Crohn's disease showed that the containment strategy was highly effective (Braat et al. 2006).

FUTURE PERSPECTIVES

Although there are several examples of successful vaccination and protection using rLAB in rodent models, the next challenge will be to demonstrate their efficacy and advantages over injected vaccines in animals or humans. For vaccine delivery, it is evident that it is easier to obtain immune responses by i.n. administration and that even killed LAB are effective by this route. The use of killed LAB would have distinct advantages over live organisms with respect to the regulatory issues for the clinical use of genetically modified organisms, but the safety of i.n. immunization with a bacterial carrier needs to be addressed. Oral (i.g.) immunization remains a very attractive alternative, but frequent dosing over a period of several weeks may be required to achieve solid protection. However, recent targeting strategies for LAB show that it is possible to enhance the immunogenicity and efficacy of LAB vaccines.

The delivery of DNA vaccines using LAB is attractive given the potential to use mucosal routes of administration, but to date the immune responses have been much less potent than those reported for injected DNA vaccines. Efforts are underway to enhance DNA vaccine delivery by expressing pathogen invasins such as internalin A and FnBPA in LAB. The receptors for these invasins are typically expressed on the basolateral membrane of intestinal epithelial cells and thus appear to be only partially accessible from the lumen in selected parts of the epithelium, such as the tips of the villus. Indeed, recent studies indicate that only a small percentage of epithelial cells in vitro and in vivo take up targeted *L. lactis*. DNA vaccine antigens synthesized in epithelial cells could also contribute to the nature and potency of the immune response, but to effectively prime T cell responses LAB vaccines will have to be endocytosed by dendritic cells or other antigen-presenting cells that can effectively present the expressed antigen. The successful expression of LLO in *L. lactis* and the ability of the strain to induce CD8+ T cell responses indicate potential for combining it with cell-targeting strategies to facilitate release of the DNA vaccine vector into the cytoplasm.

Several research publications and clinical reports demonstrate the considerable potential to use genetically modified LAB to deliver therapeutic peptides and proteins to the mucosa. A containment system for the genetically modified *L. lactis* based on replacement of lactococcal *thyA* gene with the Il-10 transgene has been positively evaluated by several health authorities and biosafety committees and should pave the way for other LAB delivery applications in the future. Most research has focused on the medical need for new therapeutic approaches for IBD, but new medical targets, such as oral mucositis, are on the horizon (Rottiers et al. 2009). A promising recent development has been the finding that oral administration of *L. lactis* can be used to induce antigen-specific OT to a secreted recombinant antigen. LAB delivery induces much more efficient responses than with purified antigen, thus avoiding the need for purification of large quantities of antigen. This approach holds promise for new therapeutic interventions in allergies and antigen-induced autoimmune diseases.

DISCLOSURE STATEMENT

The author is a named inventor on patents relating to the use of recombinant lactic acid bacteria as delivery vehicles and has financial interests in a biotechnology company.

LITERATURE CITED

Adachi K, Kawana K, Yokoyama T, Fujii T, Tomio A, et al. 2010. Oral immunization with a *Lactobacillus casei* vaccine expressing human papillomavirus (HPV) type 16 E7 is an effective strategy to induce mucosal cytotoxic lymphocytes against HPV16 E7. *Vaccine* 28:2810–17

Adel-Patient K, Ah-Leung S, Creminon C, Nouaille S, Chatel JM, et al. 2005. Oral administration of recombinant *Lactococcus lactis* expressing bovine beta-lactoglobulin partially prevents mice from sensitization. *Clin. Exp. Allergy* 35:539–46

Bahey-El-Din M, Casey PG, Griffin BT, Gahan CG. 2008. *Lactococcus lactis*–expressing listeriolysin O (LLO) provides protection and specific CD8(+) T cells against *Listeria* monocytogenes in the murine infection model. *Vaccine* 26:5304–14

Bahey-El-Din M, Casey PG, Griffin BT, Gahan CG. 2010. Expression of two *Listeria* monocytogenes antigens (P60 and LLO) in *Lactococcus lactis* and examination for use as live vaccine vectors. *J. Med. Microbiol.* 59:904–12

Beninati C, Oggioni MR, Boccanera M, Spinosa MR, Maggi T, et al. 2000. Therapy of mucosal candidiasis by expression of an anti-idiotype in human commensal bacteria. *Nat. Biotechnol.* 18:1060–64

Bermudez-Humaran LG, Cortes-Perez NG, Le Loir Y, Alcocer-Gonzalez JM, Tamez-Guerra RS, et al. 2004. An inducible surface presentation system improves cellular immunity against human papillomavirus type 16 E7 antigen in mice after nasal administration with recombinant lactococci. *J. Med. Microbiol.* 53:427–33

Bermudez-Humaran LG, Cortes-Perez NG, Lefevre F, Guimaraes V, Rabot S, et al. 2005. A novel mucosal vaccine based on live *Lactococci* expressing E7 antigen and IL-12 induces systemic and mucosal immune responses and protects mice against human papillomavirus type 16–induced tumors. *J. Immunol.* 175:7297–302

Boyd MR, Gustafson KR, McMahon JB, Shoemaker RH, O'Keefe BR, et al. 1997. Discovery of cyanovirin-N, a novel human immunodeficiency virus–inactivating protein that binds viral surface envelope glycoprotein gp120: potential applications to microbicide development. *Antimicrob. Agents Chemother.* 41:1521–30

Braat H, Rottiers P, Hommes DW, Huyghebaert N, Remaut E, et al. 2006. A phase I trial with transgenic bacteria expressing interleukin-10 in Crohn's disease. *Clin. Gastroenterol. Hepatol.* 4:754–59

Buccato S, Maione D, Rinaudo CD, Volpini G, Taddei AR, et al. 2006. Use of *Lactococcus lactis* expressing pili from group B *Streptococcus* as a broad-coverage vaccine against streptococcal disease. *J. Infect. Dis.* 194:331–40

Campos IB, Darrieux M, Ferreira DM, Miyaji EN, Silva DA, et al. 2008. Nasal immunization of mice with *Lactobacillus casei* expressing the pneumococcal surface protein A: induction of antibodies, complement deposition and partial protection against *Streptococcus pneumoniae* challenge. *Microbes Infect.* 10:481–88

Chakraborty H, Sen PK, Helms RW, Vernazza PL, Fiscus SA, et al. 2001. Viral burden in genital secretions determines male-to-female sexual transmission of HIV-1: a probabilistic empiric model. *Aids* 15:621–27

Chancey CJ, Khanna KV, Seegers JF, Zhang GW, Hildreth J, et al. 2006. Lactobacilli-expressed single-chain variable fragment (scFv) specific for intercellular adhesion molecule 1 (ICAM-1) blocks cell-associated HIV-1 transmission across a cervical epithelial monolayer. *J. Immunol.* 176:5627–36

Chang TL, Chang CH, Simpson DA, Xu Q, Martin PK, et al. 2003. Inhibition of HIV infectivity by a natural human isolate of *Lactobacillus jensenii* engineered to express functional two-domain CD4. *Proc. Natl. Acad. Sci. USA* 100:11672–77

Charng YC, Lin CC, Hsu CH. 2006. Inhibition of allergen-induced airway inflammation and hyperreactivity by recombinant lactic-acid bacteria. *Vaccine* 24:5931–36

Chatel JM, Nouaille S, Adel-Patient K, Le Loir Y, Boe H, et al. 2003. Characterization of a *Lactococcus lactis* strain that secretes a major epitope of bovine beta-lactoglobulin and evaluation of its immunogenicity in mice. *Appl. Environ. Microbiol.* 69:6620–77

Chen J, Field JA, Glickstein L, Molloy PJ, Huber BT, Steere AC. 1999. Association of antibiotic treatment–resistant Lyme arthritis with T cell responses to dominant epitopes of outer surface protein A of *Borrelia burgdorferi*. *Arthritis Rheum.* 42:1813–22

Cheun HI, Kawamoto K, Hiramatsu M, Tamaoki H, Shirahata T, et al. 2004. Protective immunity of SpaA-antigen producing *Lactococcus lactis* against *Erysipelothrix rhusiopathiae* infection. *J. Appl. Microbiol.* 96:1347–53

Christensen HR, Frokiaer H, Pestka JJ. 2002. Lactobacilli differentially modulate expression of cytokines and maturation surface markers in murine dendritic cells. *J. Immunol.* 168:171–78

Chu H, Kang S, Ha S, Cho K, Park SM, et al. 2005. *Lactobacillus acidophilus* expressing recombinant K99 adhesive fimbriae has an inhibitory effect on adhesion of enterotoxigenic *Escherichia coli*. *Microbiol. Immunol.* 49:941–48

Cortes-Perez NG, da Costa Medina LF, Lefevre F, Langella P, Bermudez-Humaran LG. 2008. Production of biologically active CXC chemokines by *Lactococcus lactis*: evaluation of its potential as a novel mucosal vaccine adjuvant. *Vaccine* 26:5778–83

Cortes-Perez NG, Kharrat P, Langella P, Bermudez-Humaran LG. 2009. Heterologous production of human papillomavirus type-16 L1 protein by a lactic acid bacterium. *BMC Res. Notes* 2:167

Corthesy B, Boris S, Isler P, Grangette C, Mercenier A. 2005. Oral immunization of mice with lactic acid bacteria producing *Helicobacter pylori* urease B subunit partially protects against challenge with *Helicobacter felis*. *J. Infect. Dis.* 192:1441–49

Daniel C, Repa A, Mercenier A, Wiedermann U, Wells J. 2007. The European LABDEL project and its relevance to the prevention and treatment of allergies. *Allergy* 62:1237–42

Daniel C, Repa A, Wild C, Pollak A, Pot B, et al. 2006. Modulation of allergic immune responses by mucosal application of recombinant lactic acid bacteria producing the major birch pollen allergen Bet v 1. *Allergy* 61:812–19

Daniel C, Sebbane F, Poiret S, Goudercourt D, Dewulf J, et al. 2009. Protection against *Yersinia* pseudotuberculosis infection conferred by a *Lactococcus lactis* mucosal delivery vector secreting LcrV. *Vaccine* 27:1141–44

del Rio B, Dattwyler RJ, Aroso M, Neves V, Meirelles L, et al. 2008. Oral immunization with recombinant *Lactobacillus plantarum* induces a protective immune response in mice with Lyme disease. *Clin. Vaccine Immunol.* 15:1429–35

del Rio B, Seegers JF, Gomes-Solecki M. 2010. Immune response to *Lactobacillus plantarum* expressing *Borrelia burgdorferi* OspA is modulated by the lipid modification of the antigen. *PLoS One* 5:e11199

Dieye Y, Hoekman AJ, Clier F, Juillard V, Boot HJ, Piard JC. 2003. Ability of *Lactococcus lactis* to export viral capsid antigens: a crucial step for development of live vaccines. *Appl. Environ. Microbiol.* 69:7281–88

Erdile LF, Brandt MA, Warakomski DJ, Westrack GJ, Sadziene A, et al. 1993. Role of attached lipid in immunogenicity of *Borrelia burgdorferi* OspA. *Infect. Immun.* 61:81–90

Falagas ME, Betsi GI, Athanasiou S. 2007. Probiotics for the treatment of women with bacterial vaginosis. *Clin. Microbiol. Infect.* 13:657–64

Faria AM, Weiner HL. 2005. Oral tolerance. *Immunol. Rev.* 206:232–59

Ferreira DM, Darrieux M, Silva DA, Leite LC, Ferreira JM Jr, et al. 2009. Characterization of protective mucosal and systemic immune responses elicited by pneumococcal surface protein PspA and PspC nasal vaccines against a respiratory pneumococcal challenge in mice. *Clin. Vaccine Immunol.* 16:636–45

Ferreira PC, Campos IB, Abe CM, Trabulsi LR, Elias WP, et al. 2008. Immunization of mice with *Lactobacillus casei* expressing intimin fragments produces antibodies able to inhibit the adhesion of enteropathogenic *Escherichia coli* to cultivated epithelial cells. *FEMS Immunol. Med. Microbiol.* 54:245–54

Foligne B, Dessein R, Marceau M, Poiret S, Chamaillard M, et al. 2007. Prevention and treatment of colitis with *Lactococcus lactis* secreting the immunomodulatory *Yersinia* LcrV protein. *Gastroenterology* 133:862–74

Friedman A, Weiner HL. 1994. Induction of anergy or active suppression following oral tolerance is determined by antigen dosage. *Proc. Natl. Acad. Sci. USA* 91:6688–92

Frossard CP, Steidler L, Eigenmann PA. 2007. Oral administration of an IL-10-secreting *Lactococcus lactis* strain prevents food-induced IgE sensitization. *J. Allergy Clin. Immunol.* 119:952–59

Gilbert C, Robinson K, Le Page RW, Wells JM. 2000. Heterologous expression of an immunogenic pneumococcal type 3 capsular polysaccharide in *Lactococcus lactis*. *Infect. Immun.* 68:3251–60

Giomarelli B, Provvedi R, Meacci F, Maggi T, Medaglini D, et al. 2002. The microbicide cyanovirin-N expressed on the surface of commensal bacterium *Streptococcus gordonii* captures HIV-1. *Aids* 16:1351–56

Grangette C, Muller-Alouf H, Geoffroy M, Goudercourt D, Turneer M, Mercenier A. 2002. Protection against tetanus toxin after intragastric administration of two recombinant lactic acid bacteria: impact of strain viability and in vivo persistence. *Vaccine* 20:3304–9

Grangette C, Muller-Alouf H, Goudercourt D, Geoffroy MC, Turneer M, Mercenier A. 2001. Mucosal immune responses and protection against tetanus toxin after intranasal immunization with recombinant *Lactobacillus plantarum*. *Infect. Immun.* 69:1547–53

Grangette C, Muller-Alouf H, Hols P, Goudercourt D, Delcour J, et al. 2004. Enhanced mucosal delivery of antigen with cell wall mutants of lactic acid bacteria. *Infect. Immun.* 72:2731–37

Guimaraes VD, Gabriel JE, Lefevre F, Cabanes D, Gruss A, et al. 2005. Internalin-expressing *Lactococcus lactis* is able to invade small intestine of guinea pigs and deliver DNA into mammalian epithelial cells. *Microbes Infect.* 7:836–44

Guimaraes VD, Innocentin S, Lefevre F, Azevedo V, Wal JM, et al. 2006. Use of native lactococci as vehicles for delivery of DNA into mammalian epithelial cells. *Appl. Environ. Microbiol.* 72:7091–97

Hanniffy SB, Carter AT, Hitchin E, Wells JM. 2007. Mucosal delivery of a pneumococcal vaccine using *Lactococcus lactis* affords protection against respiratory infection. *J. Infect. Dis.* 195:185–93

Hanson LA. 1959. Comparative analysis of human milk and human blood plasma by means of diffusion-in-gel methods. *Experientia* 15:473–74

Hayashi H, Takahashi R, Nishi T, Sakamoto M, Benno Y. 2005. Molecular analysis of jejunal, ileal, caecal and recto-sigmoidal human colonic microbiota using 16S rRNA gene libraries and terminal restriction fragment length polymorphism. *J. Med. Microbiol.* 54:1093–101

Holgate ST. 1999. The epidemic of allergy and asthma. *Nature* 402:B2–4

Huibregtse IL, Marietta EV, Rashtak S, Koning F, Rottiers P, et al. 2009. Induction of antigen-specific tolerance by oral administration of *Lactococcus lactis* delivered immunodominant DQ8-restricted gliadin peptide in sensitized nonobese diabetic Abo Dq8 transgenic mice. *J. Immunol.* 183:2390–96

Huibregtse IL, Snoeck V, de Creus A, Braat H, De Jong EC, et al. 2007. Induction of ovalbumin-specific tolerance by oral administration of *Lactococcus lactis* secreting ovalbumin. *Gastroenterology* 133:517–28

Inaba K. 1997. Dendritic cells as antigen-presenting cells in vivo. *Immunol. Cell Biol.* 75:206–8

Innocentin S, Guimaraes V, Miyoshi A, Azevedo V, Langella P, et al. 2009. *Lactococcus lactis* expressing either *Staphylococcus aureus* fibronectin-binding protein A or *Listeria monocytogenes* internalin A can efficiently internalize and deliver DNA in human epithelial cells. *Appl. Environ. Microbiol.* 75:4870–78

Jechlinger W. 2006. Optimization and delivery of plasmid DNA for vaccination. *Expert. Rev. Vaccines* 5:803–25

Johansson ME, Phillipson M, Petersson J, Velcich A, Holm L, Hansson GC. 2008. The inner of the two Muc2 mucin-dependent mucus layers in colon is devoid of bacteria. *Proc. Natl. Acad. Sci. USA* 105:15064–69

Kajikawa A, Masuda K, Katoh M, Igimi S. 2010. Adjuvant effects for oral immunization provided by recombinant *Lactobacillus casei* secreting biologically active murine interleukin-1{beta}. *Clin. Vaccine Immunol.* 17:43–48

Kajikawa A, Satoh E, Leer RJ, Yamamoto S, Igimi S. 2007. Intragastric immunization with recombinant *Lactobacillus casei* expressing flagellar antigen confers antibody-independent protective immunity against *Salmonella enterica* serovar Enteritidis. *Vaccine* 25:3599–605

Kalliomaki M, Antoine JM, Herz U, Rijkers GT, Wells JM, Mercenier A. 2010. Guidance for substantiating the evidence for beneficial effects of probiotics: prevention and management of allergic diseases by probiotics. *J. Nutr.* 140:713S–21

Kim SJ, Lee JY, Jun DY, Song JY, Lee WK, et al. 2009. Oral administration of *Lactococcus lactis* expressing *Helicobacter pylori* Cag7-ct383 protein induces systemic anti-Cag7 immune response in mice. *FEMS Immunol. Med. Microbiol.* 57:257–68

Klijn N, Weerkamp AH, de Vos WM. 1995. Genetic marking of *Lactococcus lactis* shows its survival in the human gastrointestinal tract. *Appl. Environ. Microbiol.* 61:2771–74

Kraus TA, Mayer L. 2005. Oral tolerance and inflammatory bowel disease. *Curr. Opin. Gastroenterol.* 21:692–96

Kruger C, Hu Y, Pan Q, Marcotte H, Hultberg A, et al. 2002. In situ delivery of passive immunity by lactobacilli producing single-chain antibodies. *Nat. Biotechnol.* 20:702–6

Kruisselbrink A, Heijne Den Bak-Glashouwer MJ, Havenith CE, Thole JE, Janssen R. 2001. Recombinant *Lactobacillus plantarum* inhibits house dust mite-specific T-cell responses. *Clin. Exp. Immunol.* 126:2–8

Kwon HK, Lee CG, So JS, Chae CS, Hwang JS, et al. 2010. Generation of regulatory dendritic cells and CD4+Foxp3+ T cells by probiotics administration suppresses immune disorders. *Proc. Natl. Acad. Sci. USA* 107:2159–64

Larocque R, Nakagaki K, Lee P, Abdul-Wahid A, Faubert GM. 2003. Oral immunization of BALB/c mice with *Giardia duodenalis* recombinant cyst wall protein inhibits shedding of cysts. *Infect. Immun.* 71:5662–69

Lavelle EC, O'Hagan DT. 2006. Delivery systems and adjuvants for oral vaccines. *Expert. Opin. Drug Deliv.* 3:747–62

Lee JS, Poo H, Han DP, Hong SP, Kim K, et al. 2006. Mucosal immunization with surface-displayed severe acute respiratory syndrome coronavirus spike protein on *Lactobacillus casei* induces neutralizing antibodies in mice. *J. Virol.* 80:4079–87

Lee P, Abdul-Wahid A, Faubert GM. 2009. Comparison of the local immune response against *Giardia lamblia* cyst wall protein 2 induced by recombinant *Lactococcus lactis* and *Streptococcus gordonii*. *Microbes Infect.* 11:20–28

Lee P, Faubert GM. 2006. Oral immunization of BALB/c mice by intragastric delivery of *Streptococcus gordonii*–expressing *Giardia* cyst wall protein 2 decreases cyst shedding in challenged mice. *FEMS Microbiol. Lett.* 265:225–36

Lee SF. 2003. Oral colonization and immune responses to *Streptococcus gordonii*: potential use as a vector to induce antibodies against respiratory pathogens. *Curr. Opin. Infect. Dis.* 16:231–35

Levin D, Constant S, Pasqualini T, Flavell R, Bottomly K. 1993. Role of dendritic cells in the priming of CD4+ T lymphocytes to peptide antigen in vivo. *J. Immunol.* 151:6742–50

Li YG, Tian FL, Gao FS, Tang XS, Xia C. 2007. Immune responses generated by *Lactobacillus* as a carrier in DNA immunization against foot-and-mouth disease virus. *Vaccine* 25:902–11

Li YJ, Ma GP, Li GW, Qiao XY, Ge JW, et al. 2010. Oral vaccination with the porcine rotavirus VP4 outer capsid protein expressed by *Lactococcus lactis* induces specific antibody production. *J. Biomed. Biotechnol.* 2010:708460

Liu JK, Hou XL, Wei CH, Yu LY, He XJ, et al. 2009. Induction of immune responses in mice after oral immunization with recombinant *Lactobacillus casei* strains expressing enterotoxigenic *Escherichia coli* F41 fimbrial protein. *Appl. Environ. Microbiol.* 75:4491–97

Liu S, Li Y, Xu Z, Wang Y. 2010. Immune responses elicited in mice with recombinant *Lactococcus lactis* expressing F4 fimbrial adhesin FaeG by oral immunization. *Vet. Res. Commun.* 34:491–502

Liu X, Lagenaur LA, Simpson DA, Essenmacher KP, Frazier-Parker CL, et al. 2006. Engineered vaginal lactobacillus strain for mucosal delivery of the human immunodeficiency virus inhibitor cyanovirin-N. *Antimicrob. Agents Chemother.* 50:3250–59

Mannam P, Jones KF, Geller BL. 2004. Mucosal vaccine made from live, recombinant *Lactococcus lactis* protects mice against pharyngeal infection with *Streptococcus pyogenes*. *Infect. Immun.* 72:3444–50

Marietta E, Black K, Camilleri M, Krause P, Rogers RS 3rd, et al. 2004. A new model for dermatitis herpetiformis that uses HLA-DQ8 transgenic NOD mice. *J. Clin. Invest.* 114:1090–97

Meijerink M, van Hemert S, Taverne N, Wels M, de Vos P, et al. 2010. Identification of genetic loci in *Lactobacillus plantarum* that modulate the immune response of dendritic cells using comparative genome hybridization. *PLoS ONE* 5:e10632

Mercenier A, Muller-Alouf H, Grangette C. 2000. Lactic acid bacteria as live vaccines. *Curr. Issues Mol. Biol.* 2:17–25

Mohamadzadeh M, Duong T, Sandwick SJ, Hoover T, Klaenhammer TR. 2009. Dendritic cell targeting of *Bacillus anthracis* protective antigen expressed by *Lactobacillus acidophilus* protects mice from lethal challenge. *Proc. Natl. Acad. Sci. USA* 106:4331–36

Murosaki S, Yamamoto Y, Ito K, Inokuchi T, Kusaka H, et al. 1998. Heat-killed *Lactobacillus* plantarum L-137 suppresses naturally fed antigen-specific IgE production by stimulation of IL-12 production in mice. *J. Allergy Clin. Immunol.* 102:57–64

Neutra MR, Kozlowski PA. 2006. Mucosal vaccines: the promise and the challenge. *Nat. Rev. Immunol.* 6:148–58

Norton PM, Brown HW, Wells JM, Macpherson AM, Wilson PW, Le Page RW. 1996. Factors affecting the immunogenicity of tetanus toxin fragment C expressed in *Lactococcus lactis*. *FEMS Immunol. Med. Microbiol.* 14:167–77

Norton PM, Wells JM, Brown HW, Macpherson AM, Le Page RW. 1997. Protection against tetanus toxin in mice nasally immunized with recombinant *Lactococcus lactis* expressing tetanus toxin fragment C. *Vaccine* 15:616–19

Novak N, Allam JP, Betten H, Haberstok J, Bieber T. 2004. The role of antigen presenting cells at distinct anatomic sites: they accelerate and they slow down allergies. *Allergy* 59:5–14

Oliveira ML, Areas AP, Campos IB, Monedero V, Perez-Martinez G, et al. 2006. Induction of systemic and mucosal immune response and decrease in *Streptococcus pneumoniae* colonization by nasal inoculation of mice with recombinant lactic acid bacteria expressing pneumococcal surface antigen A. *Microbes Infect.* 8:1016–24

Perez CA, Eichwald C, Burrone O, Mendoza D. 2005. Rotavirus vp7 antigen produced by *Lactococcus lactis* induces neutralizing antibodies in mice. *J. Appl. Microbiol.* 99:1158–64

Pontes DS, Dorella FA, Ribeiro LA, Miyoshi A, Le Loir Y, et al. 2003. Induction of partial protection in mice after oral administration of *Lactococcus lactis* producing *Brucella abortus* L7/L12 antigen. *J. Drug Target* 11:489–93

Poo H, Pyo HM, Lee TY, Yoon SW, Lee JS, et al. 2006. Oral administration of human papillomavirus type 16 E7 displayed on *Lactobacillus casei* induces E7-specific antitumor effects in C57/BL6 mice. *Int. J. Cancer* 119:1702–9

Pusch O, Boden D, Hannify S, Lee F, Tucker LD, et al. 2005. Bioengineering lactic acid bacteria to secrete the HIV-1 virucide cyanovirin. *J. Acquir. Immune Defic. Syndr.* 40:512–20

Pusch O, Kalyanaraman R, Tucker LD, Wells JM, Ramratnam B, Boden D. 2006. An anti-HIV microbicide engineered in commensal bacteria: secretion of HIV-1 fusion inhibitors by lactobacilli. *AIDS* 20:1917–22

Qiao X, Li G, Wang X, Li X, Liu M, Li Y. 2009. Recombinant porcine rotavirus VP4 and VP4-LTB expressed in *Lactobacillus casei* induced mucosal and systemic antibody responses in mice. *BMC Microbiol.* 9:249

Quigley BR, Hatkoff M, Thanassi DG, Ouattara M, Eichenbaum Z, Scott JR. 2010. A foreign protein incorporated on the Tip of T3 pili in *Lactococcus lactis* elicits systemic and mucosal immunity. *Infect. Immun.* 78:1294–303

Rao S, Hu S, McHugh L, Lueders K, Henry K, et al. 2005. Toward a live microbial microbicide for HIV: commensal bacteria secreting an HIV fusion inhibitor peptide. *Proc. Natl. Acad. Sci. USA* 102:11993–98

Repa A, Grangette C, Daniel C, Hochreiter R, Hoffmann-Sommergruber K, et al. 2003. Mucosal co-application of lactic acid bacteria and allergen induces counter-regulatory immune responses in a murine model of birch pollen allergy. *Vaccine* 22:87–95

Rescigno M, Rotta G, Valzasina B, Ricciardi-Castagnoli P. 2001. Dendritic cells shuttle microbes across gut epithelial monolayers. *Immunobiology* 204:572–81

Robinson K, Chamberlain LM, Lopez MC, Rush CM, Marcotte H, et al. 2004. Mucosal and cellular immune responses elicited by recombinant *Lactococcus lactis* strains expressing tetanus toxin fragment C. *Infect. Immun.* 72:2753–61

Robinson K, Chamberlain LM, Schofield KM, Wells JM, Le Page RW. 1997. Oral vaccination of mice against tetanus with recombinant *Lactococcus lactis*. *Nat. Biotechnol.* 15:653–57

Rottiers P, De Smedt T, Steidler L. 2009. Modulation of gut-associated lymphoid tissue functions with genetically modified *Lactococcus lactis*. *Int. Rev. Immunol.* 28:465–86

Shaw DM, Gaerthe B, Leer RJ, Van Der Stap JG, Smittenaar C, et al. 2000. Engineering the microflora to vaccinate the mucosa: serum immunoglobulin G responses and activated draining cervical lymph nodes following mucosal application of tetanus toxin fragment C-expressing lactobacilli. *Immunology* 100:510–18

Steidler L. 2002. In situ delivery of cytokines by genetically engineered *Lactococcus lactis*. *Antonie Van Leeuwenhoek* 82:323–31

Steidler L, Hans W, Schotte L, Neirynck S, Obermeier F, et al. 2000. Treatment of murine colitis by *Lactococcus lactis* secreting interleukin-10. *Science* 289:1352–55

Steidler L, Robinson K, Chamberlain L, Schofield KM, Remaut E, et al. 1998. Mucosal delivery of murine interleukin-2 (IL-2) and IL-6 by recombinant strains of *Lactococcus lactis* coexpressing antigen and cytokine. *Infect. Immun.* 66:3183–89

Steidler L, Wells JM, Raeymaekers A, Vandekerckhove J, Fiers W, Remaut E. 1995. Secretion of biologically active murine interleukin-2 by *Lactococcus lactis* subsp. *lactis*. *Appl. Environ. Microbiol.* 61:1627–29

Tacket CO, Levine MM. 2007. CVD 908, CVD 908-htrA, and CVD 909 live oral typhoid vaccines: a logical progression. *Clin. Infect. Dis.* 45(Suppl. 1):S20–23

Tang L, Li Y. 2009. Oral immunization of mice with recombinant *Lactococcus lactis* expressing porcine transmissible gastroenteritis virus spike glycoprotein. *Virus Genes* 39(2):238–45 van der Waaij LA, Harmsen HJ, Madjipour M, Kroese FG, Zwiers M, et al. 2005. Bacterial population analysis of human colon and terminal ileum biopsies with 16S rRNA-based fluorescent probes: commensal bacteria live in suspension and have no direct contact with epithelial cells. *Inflamm. Bowel Dis.* 11:865–71

Vandenbroucke K, Hans W, Van Huysse J, Neirynck S, Demetter P, et al. 2004. Active delivery of trefoil factors by genetically modified *Lactococcus lactis* prevents and heals acute colitis in mice. *Gastroenterology* 127:502–13

Vaughan EE, de Vries MC, Zoetendal EG, Ben-Amor KA, Akkermans ADL, de Vos WM. 2002. The intestinal LABs. *Ant. Leeuwenh.* 82:341–52

Vesa T, Pochart P, Marteau P. 2000. Pharmacokinetics of *Lactobacillus plantarum* NCIMB 8826, *Lactobacillus fermentum* KLD, and *Lactococcus lactis* MG 1363 in the human gastrointestinal tract. *Aliment. Pharmacol. Ther.* 14:823–28

Weiner HL. 2004. Current issues in the treatment of human diseases by mucosal tolerance. *Ann. N. Y. Acad. Sci.* 1029:211–24

Wells JM, Mercenier A. 2008. Mucosal delivery of therapeutic and prophylactic molecules using lactic acid bacteria. *Nat. Rev. Microbiol.* 6:349–62

Wells JM, Robinson K, Chamberlain LM, Schofield KM, Le Page RW. 1996. Lactic acid bacteria as vaccine delivery vehicles. *Antonie Van Leeuwenhoek* 70:317–30

Wells JM, Rossi O, Meijerink M, van Baarlen P. 2010a. Epithelial crosstalk at the microbiota-mucosal interface. *Proc. Natl. Acad. Sci. USA.* 2010 [Epub ahead of print]

Wells JM, Loonen LM, Karczewski JM. 2010b The role of innate signaling in the homeostasis of tolerance and immunity in the intestine. *Int. J. Med. Microbiol.* 300:41–48

Wells JM, Wilson PW, Le Page RW. 1993. Improved cloning vectors and transformation procedure for *Lactococcus lactis*. *J. Appl. Bacteriol.* 74:629–36

Wu C, Yang G, Bermudez-Humaran LG, Pang Q, Zeng Y, et al. 2006. Immunomodulatory effects of IL-12 secreted by *Lactococcus lactis* on Th1/Th2 balance in ovalbumin (OVA)-induced asthma model mice. *Int. Immunopharmacol.* 6:610–15

Xin KQ, Hoshino Y, Toda Y, Igimi S, Kojima Y, et al. 2003. Immunogenicity and protective efficacy of orally administered recombinant *Lactococcus lactis* expressing surface-bound HIV Env. *Blood* 102:223–28

Yamamoto M, McGhee JR, Hagiwara Y, Otake S, Kiyono H. 2001. Genetically manipulated bacterial toxin as a new generation mucosal adjuvant. *Scand. J. Immunol.* 53:211–17

Yigang XU, Yijing LI. 2008. Construction of recombinant *Lactobacillus casei* efficiently surface displayed and secreted porcine parvovirus VP2 protein and comparison of the immune responses induced by oral immunization. *Immunology* 124:68–75

Yoshida T, Hachimura S, Kaminogawa S. 1997. The oral administration of low-dose antigen induces activation followed by tolerization, while high-dose antigen induces tolerance without activation. *Clin. Immunol. Immunopathol.* 82:207–15

Zhang ZH, Jiang PH, Li NJ, Shi M, Huang W. 2005. Oral vaccination of mice against rodent malaria with recombinant *Lactococcus lactis* expressing MSP-1(19). *World J. Gastroenterol.* 11:6975–80

Hurdle Technology in Fruit Processing

Paula Luisina Gómez,[1] Jorge Welti-Chanes,[2] and Stella Maris Alzamora[3]

[1]CONICET-Universidad de Buenos Aires, Departamento de Industrias, Facultad de Ciencias Exactas y Naturales, Buenos Aires, Argentina; email: gzpaula@gmail.com

[2]Instituto Tecnológico y de Estudios Superiores de Monterrey, División de Biotecnología y Alimentos, Monterey, México; email: jwelti@itesm.mx

[3]Universidad de Buenos Aires, Departamento de Industrias, Facultad de Ciencias Exactas y Naturales, Buenos Aires, Argentina; email: smalzamora@gmail.com

Annu. Rev. Food Sci. Technol. 2011. 2:447–65

First published online as a Review in Advance on January 3, 2011

The *Annual Review of Food Science and Technology* is online at food.annualreviews.org

This article's doi:
10.1146/annurev-food-022510-133619

1941-1413/11/0410-0447$20.00

Keywords

combined methods, emerging factors, fruit, juice, minimally processed

Abstract

Conventional preservation technologies such as thermal processing ensure the safety and shelf life of fruit-derived products but can result in the loss of physicochemical and nutritional quality attributes. This review examines innovative hurdle techniques to obtain novel fruit products with fresh-like characteristics. The multifactorial processes were based on emerging preservation factors in combination or combining emerging factors with traditional ones. Selected practical examples of fruit processing using UV light, pulsed light (PL), ultrasound (US), and high hydrostatic pressure (HHP) are presented. Some issues of key importance for the design of combination processes are also addressed.

INTRODUCTION

MPF: minimally processed fruits

HHP: high hydrostatic pressure

PEFs: pulsed electric fields

US: ultrasound

PL: pulsed light

Hurdle: preservation factor or stress parameter

In response to consumer expectations, researchers in the food industry, the academy, and government institutions have explored in the past two decades milder fruit-preservation techniques with better retention of product flavor, texture, color, and nutrient content than comparable conventional treatments. Consumer trends toward fresh food on one side and convenience on the other side often conflict. In most cases, fresh quality is negatively affected by the processing procedure. The most crucial challenge is to retain the natural functional properties and the sensory and nutritional quality of fruits with the appropriate shelf life and safety. In addition, the potential for microbiological contamination of fresh fruits is high because of the wide variety of conditions to which produce is exposed during growth, harvest, and distribution. Over the past several years, the detection of outbreaks of foodborne illnesses associated with fresh fruits and fruit juices has increased, and produce has been identified as an area of food safety concern. Recent outbreaks of *Escherichia coli* 0157:H7 and *Salmonella* spp. in apple and orange juices have challenged the belief that high acid foods cannot harbor viable pathogenic bacteria. For this reason, raw fruits cannot be excluded from the application of any of the modern tools that prevail in today's food industry for ensuring safety of produce. Sanitation of whole fruit is conducted generally with an initial washing in tap water to eliminate pesticide residues, dirt, and plant debris, followed by a dip in chlorinated water to effectively reduce the microbial loads on the fruit surface. However, alternative decontamination methods are being investigated because of the association of chlorine with the formation of carcinogenic chlorinated compounds and its low effectiveness in reducing microorganism population in surface of fruits as well as the growing consumer refusal of chemical additives (Beuchat 2000).

The trends for minimally processed fruits (MPF) come with three approaches being investigated. The first one is the optimization of traditional preservation methods to enhance sensorial, nutritional, and microbiological quality of fruits, yield, and energy efficiency (i.e., radiofrequency heating, cryogenic freezing, vacuum dehydration). The second approach refers to the development of mild processes by novel combinations of traditional physical and chemical preservation factors, each one applied at low intensity, to obtain products with quality attributes reminiscent of the fresh or native state of a given fruit but with a longer shelf life (i.e., modified/controlled atmosphere packaging, active packaging techniques). Finally, the last approach places the interest on the development of innovative techniques to obtain novel fruit products with fresh-like quality attributes by using emerging preservation factors [e.g., nonthermal physical agents such as high hydrostatic pressure (HHP), pulsed electric fields (PEFs), ultrasound (US), pulsed light (PL), and UV light, and natural antimicrobials, among others] in combination or otherwise combining emerging factors with traditional ones, all of them applied at low doses. In fact, the novel alternative physical agents, intensely investigated in the past two decades, can cause inactivation of microorganisms at ambient or sublethal temperatures, avoiding the deleterious effects that severe heating has on quality.These approaches to obtaining fruit products of higher perceived quality face different limitations and possibilities for the design, optimization, and experimental assessment as well as for validation of process conditions. In particular, the classical hurdle concept introduced by Leitsner and colleagues (Leistner & Rödel 1976) and also deeply investigated by Gould (Gould & Jones 1989, Gould 1995, Gould et al. 1995) is the basis of the mild processes for fruit preservation found in the last two approaches. In the second group of techniques, an important sector of the MPF comprises chilled products that rely either exclusively or primarily on cold storage for preservation (i.e. raw fruits; low-risk raw and uncooked ingredients such as fruit salads). A major concern over the microbiological safety of these foods is improper refrigeration (accidental due to mechanical failure or intentional to save energy costs) during manufacture, distribution, retail sale, and at home. On the other side, many of the emerging inactivation agents are effective in destroying vegetative cells of bacteria, yeasts, and filamentous fungi, but spores of bacteria and molds are resistant to these factors. Thus, chilling and emerging preservation procedures have to be included as components or hurdles in combined preservation systems to assure food safety.

Microorganisms have evolved different mechanisms to resist the adverse effects of environmental stresses. As internal media stability (composition and volume of fluids) is vital for the survival and growth, these mechanisms, called homeostatic mechanisms, act to ensure that key physiological activities and parameters in the cells remain relatively unchanged, even when the environment around the cell is different and greatly perturbed (Leistner & Gould 2002, Gould 1995). For instance, when the water activity (a_w) of the medium is reduced, vegetative microorganisms lose water to come rapidly into osmotic equilibrium with the surroundings. Depending on water loss extent, metabolism is reduced or prevented and growth ceases. A universal and major response of vegetative cells to osmotic stress, often referred to as osmoregulation or osmoadaptation, is the accumulation, by synthesis and/or by active transport, of low molecular weight solutes in their cytoplasm at concentrations sufficient to just exceed the osmolality of the external medium. In this way, the cells regain water by osmosis and maintain the turgor in the membrane that is essential for its proper functioning. Reduced a_w causes an increase in maintenance metabolism and a reduction in yield and growth rate because of the energy input necessary for the accumulation process. If the osmoregulatory capacity of the cell is exceeded (by a severe reduction in a_w), the cell ceases growth. Another example is pH homeostasis. The maintenance of intracellular pH within a narrow range is essential for microorganism growth. Lowering the external pH by strong acids causes denaturation of enzymes present on the cell surface and lowering of the cytoplasmic pH due to proton permeation through membrane when the pH gradient is very large. When weak acids are used, undissociated acids act as proton ionophores and permeate through the membrane, increasing the rate at which protons enter the cytoplasm, but also the acid anion may have specific effects on metabolism, amplifying the action of the low pH. Major adaptive mechanisms to regulate the cytoplasmic pH are the energy-dependent proton extrusion, which acts to keep the cytoplasmic pH higher than that of the environment, and the extrusion of the organic acid (Booth & Kroll 1989, Leistner & Gould 2002). When the microorganisms' capacity for generating energy is not enough to prevent the net proton influx, the cytoplasmic pH falls, growth ceases, and the cells may die. Also, vegetative microorganisms react homeostatically to lowered and raised growth temperatures (by altering the composition of membrane lipids) and to ultraviolet (UV) radiation (by repairing the damaged DNA).

Homeostatic mechanisms that vegetative cells have evolved in order to survive extreme environmental stresses are energy dependent and allow microorganisms to continue functioning. In contrast, homeostasis in spores is passive, acting to keep the central protoplast in a constant low water–level environment, this being the prime reason for the extreme metabolic inertness or dormancy and resistance of these cells to high temperature, HHP, ultrasonication, and other hostile factors. Preservation procedures are effective when they overcome, temporarily or permanently, the various homeostatic reactions that microorganisms have evolved in order to resist stresses. The degree of change in environmental conditions will determine whether the microorganism is killed, ceases growth, or grows at a reduced rate. In foods preserved by combined methods, the active homeostasis of vegetative microorganisms and the passive refractory homeostasis of spores are disturbed by a combination of gentle antimicrobial factors at a number of sites (targets) or in a cooperative manner (Gould & Jones 1989). Low levels of different stresses are employed rather a single intensive stress. Moreover, a more effective preservation (i.e., synergistic effects of hurdles) is obtained if small stresses with different targets (multitarget preservation), instead of small

Stress: an applied state caused by deviation from normal conditions in the environment that generates changes in normal patterns of metabolism, imposing either reduced growth or survival potential

Homeostasis: tendency to uniformity or stability in the internal environment of the organisms

UV: ultraviolet

Multitarget preservation: disturbance of microorganism homeostasis by exposure to various sublethal stresses (simultaneous or sequential) that act on different cell targets

Metabolic exhaustion: autosterilization, the vegetative microorganisms completely use up their energy for repairing their homeostasis, become metabolically exhausted, and die

Sublethally damaged cells: surviving cells that have been injured by a mild (nonlethal) stress and show an increased sensibility to adverse environmental conditions

stresses with the same target (i.e., additive effect of hurdles), are selected to inhibit microorganisms' growth. For example, for vegetative cells (where homeostasis is energy dependent), the goal is to reduce the availability of energy (e.g., by limiting the amount of oxygen available for facultative organisms) and/or to increase the demand for energy (by imposing some other stresses). Placing a number of sublethal stresses (i.e., hurdles or preservation factors) and/or increasing the intensity of a particular sublethal hurdle on a microbial cell increases the expenditure of energy, and so more energy is diverted from the normal biosynthetic activities of growing cells, resulting in metabolic exhaustion and death (Leistner & Gould 2002). On the contrary, when preservation factors are used at high intensity, metabolic exhaustion does not occur because the initiation of homeostatic mechanisms is prevented, and survival of cells is actually enhanced. The metabolic exhaustion is of enormous practical significance in hurdle-preserved fruits because the microbiological status of such fruits improves with storage time. Examples of this phenomenon have been reported by Latin American researches in studies of autostable high-moisture fruit products preserved by a combination of factors (slight thermal treatment, pH, a_w, sorbate, sulphite): The population of bacteria, yeasts, and molds that survive the mild thermal treatment decreased quickly during unrefrigerated storage (Alzamora et al. 1995, Tapia de Daza et al. 1996). Sublethal treatment also results in an increased sensitivity to adverse environmental factors, such as the longer lag phase of sublethally damaged cells, when the cell resumes growth after treatment (Smelt et al. 2002). For spores (where homeostasis is nonenergetic and depends on the structures of the organism), the goal is to damage key structures (by chemical, enzymic, or physical attack on coats, cortex, etc.) or to release spores from dormancy (initiating germination with natural germinants or with false triggers, or applying high pressures) (Gould & Jones 1989).

In the past 20 years, the popularity of the hurdle concept has dramatically increased, and numerous publications have now indicated its potential for the development of MPF and/or the improvement of fresh fruit safety. Hurdle technology can be applied in many ways: (*a*) at various stages of the fruit distribution chain, in storage, in processing, and/or in packaging as a back-up measure in existing MPF products with short shelf lives, in order to diminish the risks and/or increase their shelf lives (26); (*b*) as an important tool for improving quality of long shelf life fruit products without sacrificing their microbiological stability; or (*c*) as a new preservation procedure deliberately intended for obtaining novel MPF.

The present review focuses on the application of combined technologies (already used industrially or still in development or testing) based on the third approach for obtaining MPF or improving the microbiological safety of fruit raw materials and final products. Examples of application involving inactivation of microorganisms by UV light, PL, US, and HHP are given. Some issues that should be addressed in setting criteria for a successful design of the MPF process are also reviewed.

This review does not pretend to cover the enormous amount of work conducted during the past few years in hurdle technologies for processing fruits and fruit juices (for further references, see Alzamora et al. 2000, Leistner & Gould 2002, Raso & Barbosa-Cánovas 2003, Ross et al. 2003, Raso et al. 2005, Allende et al. 2006, Rico et al. 2007, and Raybaudi-Massilia et al. 2009).

NONTHERMAL EMERGING PRESERVATION FACTORS AND HURDLE TECHNOLOGIES

Table 1 summarizes the mode of action, the critical parameters (variables of control) of the process, and the advantages and disadvantages of HHP, UV light, PL, and US, as well as their application for fruit preservation and some hurdles considered for the design of combined techniques.

Short-Wave UV Light

The maximum lethal effect of short-wave UV light (UV-C) has been reported in the range of 250–260 nm, inactivating bacteria, virus, protozoa, fungi, and algae (Shama 2006). Although UV-C radiation can be strongly absorbed by different cellular components, the most severe cell damage occurs when nucleic acids absorb UV-C light, crossing DNA pyrimidine bases of cytosine and thymine to form crosslinks and impairing formation of hydrogen bonds with a purine base pair on the complementary strand of DNA (Shama 2006). Cellular death occurs after the threshold of crosslinked DNA molecules is exceeded. The mutation can be reverted by dark and/or enzymatic mechanisms, and this depends on the repair systems of each microorganism. However, flow cytometry analysis demonstrated that targets other than DNA could account for UV-C inactivation. UV-C radiation also produces significant damage in the cytoplasmic membrane integrity and cellular enzyme activity (Schenk et al. 2011). Exposure to low doses of UV-C light has also been shown to elicit a range of chemical responses in fresh produce ranging from antifungal enzymes to phytoalexins (Shama 2007). This beneficial plant response of agricultural produce, called hormesis, results from the application of a low dose of a stressor (in this case UV-C irradiation). Hormetic effects to inhibit fungal pathogens and delay ripening occur after UV-C irradiation at periods of time ranging from hours to days. Hormesis is quite distinct from surface disinfection, occurs throughout the entire fruit, and may even be considered as an additive to it (Shama 2006). Direct inactivation by UV-C of surface-associated microorganisms is limited solely to the surface of the fruit, as UV-C has extremely low penetration into solids but inactivation of this kind can occur at the dose levels used to induce hormesis (0.5 to 9 kJ m^{-2} for optimal effects according to the type of fruit) (Shama & Alderson 2005). Both direct and induced inactivation effects are not easily distinguished in the literature.

UV-C: short-wave UV light

UV-C disinfection has been extensively studied as a postharvest treatment for reducing the number of microorganisms on the surface of fresh and cut fruits (Shama 2006, Allende & Artés 2003, Yaun et al. 2004, Fonseca & Rushing 2006) combined with posterior chilling or modified atmosphere packaging (MAP) to preserve quality.

Doses of UV-C radiation up to 6.9 kJ m^{-2} were a satisfactory sanitizing treatment ($\approx$1–1.5 log reduction) for fresh-cut watermelon without causing deterioration of quality in terms of juice leakage, flesh darkening, visual quality, and color values compared with controls after 7 d of storage at 3°C (Fonseca & Rushing 2006).

UV-C was investigated by Schenk et al. (2008) for its microbicidal effects on pear slices with and without peel. Semilogarithmic survival curves of inoculated *Listeria monocytogenes*, *Listeria innocua*, *Zygosaccharomyces bailii*, and *Debaryomices hansenii* showed upward concavity and pronounced tailing effect, indicating that the majority of the organisms were destroyed in a short time during UV-C exposure, whereas a fraction of the population survived after the treatment. Similar inactivation patterns were reported for other microorganisms inoculated on the surface of different fresh fruits and vegetables (e.g., tomatoes, apples, and lettuce) (Yaun et al. 2004, Gómez et al. 2010). This well-defined tail to the inactivation data was attributed to the heterogeneity in the resistances of the population to UV-C irradiation and the shielding or physical protection of microorganisms on the solid surface from incident UV-C (effect of surface topography).

Gómez et al. (2010) analyzed the effect of UV-C radiaton at different doses (with or without dipping into an antibrowning solution) followed by storage at 5°C on native flora of cut apple as well as of surface-inoculated microorganisms (*L. innocua, Escherichia coli, and Saccharomyces cerevisiae*). The log reduction ranges of inoculated population varied between 1.0 and 1.9 log cycles depending on the UV-C dose (5–14 kJ m^{-2}), the type of microorganism, and the apple pretreatment. During subsequent storage at 5°C, counts of inoculated bacteria maintained nearly

Table 1 Selected nonthermal emerging preservation factors

Factor and mechanism of inactivation	Critical parameters	Advantages	Limitations and drawbacks	Potential application/ products on the market	Hurdles investigated in combination
High hydrostatic pressure					
Application of 100–800 MPa, below 0°C to 100°C, from seconds to about 20 min, instantaneously and uniformly throughout food, independent of size, shape, and food composition. Mechanism: membrane damage, protein denaturation, leakage of cell contents, dissociation of ribosomes.	Temperature, pressure magnitude, rate of compression and decompression, holding time at pressure, time to achieve treatment pressure, composition, pH and a_w of the food, product initial temperature, and critical parameters of procedures used in combination.	Inactivation of some enzymes according to HHP dose. Little change on vitamins, pigments, flavor, and antioxidant activity, although effects depend on fruit matrix, pressure, and temperature.	High cost of equipment, increased metal fatigue, long cycle times. High resistance of browning enzymes and PME to HHP. Undesirable sensory changes at high doses (color, appearance, skin loss, structural/ texture changes).	Jam, jellies, fruit juices and purées, guacamole, fruit yogurts, dairy-based fruit smoothies, sauces (in use since 1990).	Low pH, natural and synthetic antimicrobials, temperatures below or above room temperature, vacuum packaging and refrigerated storage, mild heating.
Short-wave ultraviolet light					
Radiation from the short-wave ultraviolet region of the electromagnetic spectrum (200–280 nm). Mechanism: damage to DNA, membranes and enzyme activity induced by UV-C light absorption. Hormetic effects in agricultural produce	Transmissivity of the material, homogeneity of the flow pattern and the radiation field, UV wavelength, thickness of the radiation path through the food (geometric configuration of the system); product composition, solids content, and critical parameters of procedures used in combination.	Moderate to low cost of equipments. Little effect on color, vitamin C, and taste of fruit juices. Little changes in tissue darkening, color, texture and visual quality of cut fruits at low doses.	Low penetration into solids and opaque juices, long treatment times in solids. Enzymatic browning of cut fruit surfaces at high doses, more notorious as storage time increases.	Pasteurization of apple cider and clear juices (in use since 2000). Surface decontamination of whole and cut fruit surfaces. Reduction of fruit decay and softening.	Refrigerated storage, modified atmosphere packaging (MAP), mild thermal treatment, ultrasound (US).

Pulsed light					
Few flashes applied in a fraction of a second of intense pulses of broad spectrum light (ultraviolet to the near infrared region). Mechanism: damage to DNA and destruction of cellular components by the high peak power and the photothermal effects of visible and near-infrared portions of the flash spectrum.	Light characteristics (spectrum, intensity, duration, and number of pulses), homogeneity of the flow pattern and the radiation field, packaging and type, transparency and color of food, and critical parameters of procedures used in combination.	Very short treatment times ($\leq$60s). Little effect on color, texture, antioxidant, and sensory properties at low doses, although reports on the subject are few.	Low penetration into solids and opaque juices. Engineering solutions needed for juice treatment. Thermal damage of product at high doses. Browning and dehydration of cut fruit surfaces, more notorious as storage time and PL dose increase.	Reduction of microbial load on surfaces of whole and cut fruits and in clear juices.	Refrigerated storage, Ultraviolet (UV), Mild thermal treatment.
Ultrasound					
Energy generated by sound waves of 20 kHz or more. Mechanism: disruption of cellular structures (wall, membranes, organelles) and cell lysis attributed to cavitation.	Power and amplitude of ultrasonic waves, exposure time, volume, and composition of the food to be processed, temperature of treatment and critical parameters of procedures used in combination.	Inactivation of enzymes when US is combined with heat and pressure. Little change in color of juices and cut fruits.	High energy consumption, intensity of industrial-scale equipments limited, long treatment times. Heating of the product. Undesirable sensory changes and rupture of skin in berries at high doses.	No commercial fruit products; suggested for juice pasteurization. Actual applications limited to product modification and process efficiency improvements (enhancement of mass and heat transfer, degassing of liquids, cleaning of surfaces).	Moderate temperature, pressure, sanitizers, natural antimicrobials, UV, pulsed electric fields (PEFs).

constant levels in apples treated by UV-C, with or without dipping pretreatment, and were lower than those of untreated controls. Microflora counts were higher in UV-C untreated samples than in UV-C treated samples along the whole storage, meaning the shelf life of the product would be prolonged from the microbiological point of view.

Combination of UV-C with mild heat treatment (sequential hurdles) has also been suggested for controlling postharvest decay of berries (strawberries and sweet cherries) stored at room temperature (Marquenie et al. 2002, Pan et al. 2004). For instance, previous irradiation with UV-C (4.1kJ m^{-2}) enhanced the benefits of heat treatment (45°C, 3 h in air) and further reduced decay, softening, and reddening of the strawberry fruit (Pan et al. 2004).

UV-C illumination has also been focused on the treatment of liquid foods and beverages (Koutchma 2009) since the U.S. Food and Drug Administration (FDA) approved in 2000 the use of UV-C light as a novel technology for pasteurization of fruit juices. UV-C can be effectively used to reduce the number of spoilage and pathogenic bacteria, yeasts, and molds in different kinds of fruit juices, without affecting in a severe way color profiles, vitamin C content, and taste (Tran & Farid 2004, Keyser et al. 2008). The combination of UV-C treatment and low temperature storage allowed a shelf life extension from approximately two days to more than five days. However, the use of UV-C is still limited because of the low UV transmittance of fruit juices. The penetration of UV-C radiation depends on the type of liquid, its absorptivity, soluble solids, and suspended matter. Major researches efforts are now concentrated in UV-C reactor design to ensure effective radiation penetration (e.g., thin film, turbulent, laminar Taylor-Couette, Dean flow reactors) (Koutchma 2009).

Pulsed Light

PL involves the use of intense and short-duration (1 μs to 0.1 s) pulses of broad spectrum light of a wavelength ranging from UV to near-infrared (200 to 1,100 nm). The mechanisms responsible for microbial inactivation are still in debate. A major contribution to inactivation appears to be provided by the rich UV content from 220 to 290 nm in the UV spectrum. The primary mode of action is identical to that of UV-C radiation, but in addition to UV-C-induced photochemical changes, the high peak power and the photothermal effects caused by visible and near-infrared portions of PL spectrum seem to be involved (FDA 2000, Woodling and Moraru 2007, Gómez-López et al. 2007). Proteinaceous or fatty foods have been reported to be inappropriate for decontamination by PL because these components reduce the killing efficiency of PL. Foods poor in fats and proteins, such as fruits and vegetables, appear to be very suitable for it (Gómez-López et al. 2005).

The literature on hurdles in combination with PL is scarce. Combined methods have been devoted mainly to decontamination of fruit surfaces using PL alone or in combination with other inactivation factors, and then the produce was immediately packaged and stored in refrigeration to decrease/inhibit the growth rate of sublethally injured cells and other surviving microorganisms (simultaneous and sequential hurdles), focusing on an extension of shelf life and/or on increased fruit safety.

The application of PL (30 μs, 15 Hz, 40–250 s) alone or in combination with UV-C (0.5 or 1.0 kJ m^{-2}) or a thermal treatment (40 or 45°C, 3 or 15 min) to reduce the fungal development on strawberries inoculated with conidia of *Botrytis cinerea* and stored at 12°C for 10 d was investigated by Marquenie et al. (2003). When PL was used alone, no delay in fungal development was observed. Combining PL with UV-C illumination had no effect on fungal development at the end of the 10 d storage period, but the most severe conditions assayed (1.0 kJ m^{-2}, 120 s PL) delayed the appearance of mycelium on the fruit for one day. A combination of 120 s PL and 15 min-40°C thermal treatment resulted in a two day delay of fungal spoilage. The use of mild thermal treatments is important because external damage and softening of the fruit were found at 45°C.

Regarding fruit juices, Sauer & Moraru (2009) analyzed the effect of LP treatment (up to 12 pulses, 3 pulses per s, 360 μs, 0–13 J cm^{-2}) on the inactivation of *E. coli* inoculated in liquids with different levels of clarity [Buttersfield's phosphate buffer (BPB), tryptic soy broth (TSB) apple juice, and apple cider]. The different levels of PL effectiveness (for static treatment >8 log in BPB, ~3.5 log in TSB, ~2.6 log in apple juice, and 2.3–3.2 log in apple cider) were attributed to the absorption, reflection, and scattering of light by the substrate. However, it is possible to decrease the shading effects (reflection and scattering) caused by the particulates in the no-clear liquid substrates (TSB, apple juice, and apple cider) by performing the inactivation treatment under turbulence. Turbulent treatments resulted in 5.8- and 7.1-log reduction in cider and juice, respectively. This result is relevant for the potential commercial application of PL for pasteurization of apple juice or apple cider according to FDA requirements of a 5-log reduction in the numbers of the most resistant pathogen.

High-Power Ultrasound

Injury or disrupting microorganisms by high-energy US (i.e., intensities higher than 1 W cm^{-2} and frequencies between 18 and 100 kHz) is widely attributed to cavitation, i.e., the rupture of liquids when applying high-intensity US and the effects produced by the motion of the cavities or bubbles thus generated (Lauterborn et al. 1999). In the so-called stable cavitation, the bubbles can undergo relatively stable, low energy oscillations, provoking the liquid in the vicinity of the bubble flows or streams (microstreaming effect). This microstreaming could shear and disrupt cellular membranes or break cells. In the transient or inertial cavitation, small bubbles expand rapidly, often to many times their original size, and on the positive pressure half-cycle, collapse violently, breaking up into many smaller bubbles, resulting in shock waves with very high energy densities and short flashes of light that shear and break cell walls and membrane structures and also depolymerize large molecules. Recent transmission electron microscopy and flow cytometry studies of yeast, and Gram-negative and Gram-positive bacteria have demonstrated that (*a*) microbial cells contain several targets for the disruptive action of US (at least the cell wall, the cytoplasmic membrane, the DNA, the internal cell structure, and the outer membrane); (*b*) cytoplasmic membranes do not appear to be the primary target of US for *S. cerevisiae*, *E. coli*, and *Lactobacillus* spp.; and (*c*) the primary target depends on the specific microorganism (for instance, the outer membrane in *E. coli*) (Ananta et al. 2005, Alzamora et al. 2010).

Several reports have indicated that sonication applied alone (at room temperature and atmospheric pressure) is not very effective in inactivating microorganisms. However, the combination of US with other preservation factors and/or the selection of operative conditions that enhance the per se effect of high-power sonication shows considerable promise (Piyasena et al. 2003, Knorr et al. 2004). The efficiency of US has been demonstrated to be improved when applied in combination with heat and/or pressure, chemicals often used for sanitation and disinfection (e.g., synthetic or natural antimicrobials), and other physical preservation factors (e.g., UV-C light, PEFs) (Alzamora et al. 2010).

Thermo-ultrasonic treatment caused a higher killing effect than sonication treatment alone. If pressure changes that occur during cavitation are responsible for the inactivation effect of US, then raising the temperature and hence membrane fluidity (i.e., weakening the intermolecular forces) would enhance the disruption (Russell 2002). However, as temperature increases toward lethal values, the benefits of US application are reduced, probably as a result of an increased thermal effect and a reduced intensity of cavitation (López Malo et al. 1999). Inactivation studies with *L. monocytogenes* 10403S, an US resistant strain, were conducted at sublethal (20–40°C) and lethal (50–60°C) temperatures in apple cider (pH 3.4), with and without application of US (20 kHz,

TS: thermosonication

CIELAB: color space specified by the International Commission on Illumination

750 W, 99 ml sample) (Baumann et al. 2005). US increased the inactivation rate at both lethal and sublethal temperatures. The bactericidal effect of the combined process was additive. After a 5-min thermo-ultrasonic treatment at 60°C, cells of *L. monocytogenes* 10403S died during a 6-h period at room temperature. These treatment conditions could provide a solution for apple cider industries to achieve the required 5-log reduction in pathogenic populations.

Phenolic compounds have lipophilic nature and could accumulate in the lipid bilayer of the cell, disturbing and sensitizing the membrane to US (Brul & Coote 1999). In addition, ultrasonic waves improve the antimicrobial action by weakening the cell wall. Improved efficiency achieved by the combination of vanillin, citral, US, and moderate temperature was demonstrated by Ferrante et al. (2007). The addition of 1,000 ppm vanillin followed by sonication (600 W, 20kHz, 95 μm, 45°C) slightly improved *L. monocytogenes* inactivation observed in orange juice when single treatments were applied, achieving 1.8-log cycle reduction after 15-min exposure. The addition of a small proportion of citral (75 ppm) notoriously increased *L. monocytogenes* inactivation (>5 log reductions after 10-min treatment). Both vanillin and citral would alter microbial membrane permeability, facilitating the loss of specific ions from the interior affecting proton motive force and reducing the intracellular ATP content and the overall activity of microbial cells (Conner & Beuchat 1984). Ternary combination (citral plus vanillin plus sonication) at moderate temperature highly reduced times of exposure to US in order to reach a determined inactivation.

The effect of thermosonication (TS) followed by PEF on inactivation of *Staphylococcus aureus* and selected quality aspects in orange juice was investigated by Walkling-Ribeiro et al. (2009). TS for 10 min at 55°C with PEF at 40 kV cm^{-1} for 150 μs resulted in an overall bacterial reduction of 6.8 log cycles, similar to the cycle reduction obtained by conventional thermal pasteurization (94°C for 26 s). An additive effect on microbial inactivation between TS (1.8 log) and PEF (5.5 log) was detected. TS/PEF did not affect the pH, conductivity, or °Brix and had a milder impact on juice color than thermal treatment. Thermal treatment caused an overall darkening of orange juice. By contrast, when components of the CIELAB space were recorded,TS showed a significant increase in L^* (lightness or luminance), a minor decrease in a^* (chromaticity on a green (-) to red (+) axis), and increase in b^* (chromaticity on a blue (-) to yellow (+) axis). In conclusion, the TS/PEF hurdle approach showed great potential for improving the quality and the safety of orange juice.

Lopez-Malo et al. (2006) analyzed the response of *L. monocytogenes* and *S. cerevisiae* to the single and combined effects of high-intensity US (20 kHz, 400 W, 95.2 μm, T: 35°C) and UV-C light (continuous flow system; 90 cm long glass tube with a 100 W Hg lamp, 1100 μW cm^{-2}) in clarified apple juice. The inactivation pattern of individual and combined treatments was highly dependent on the type of microorganism. In spite of the presence of organic compounds and colored compounds that reduced the efficiency in UV-C disinfection, the effect of the US/UV-C combination was additive and led to sizeable inactivation (~4–5 log cycles reduction after 5-min treatment), with the majority of the population dead in the first minutes of treatment. The different survival patterns could be described in terms of Weibull distributions, considering that there was a spectrum of resistances to the treatments in the population (Peleg & Cole 1998). **Figure 1** illustrates survival data of *L. monocytogenes* and *S. cerevisiae* after having undergone US, UV-C, and US/UV-C treatments using the cumulative Weibull distribution function. The correspondent frequency distributions of resistances (not shown) show that the combined action of US/UV-C light not only increases the microbicidal effect of sonication but changes the distribution of inactivation times. When both physical inactivation agents were applied together, narrowest frequency shapes, skewed to the right with low dead time means and a very substantial decrease in its overall spread, were usually obtained.

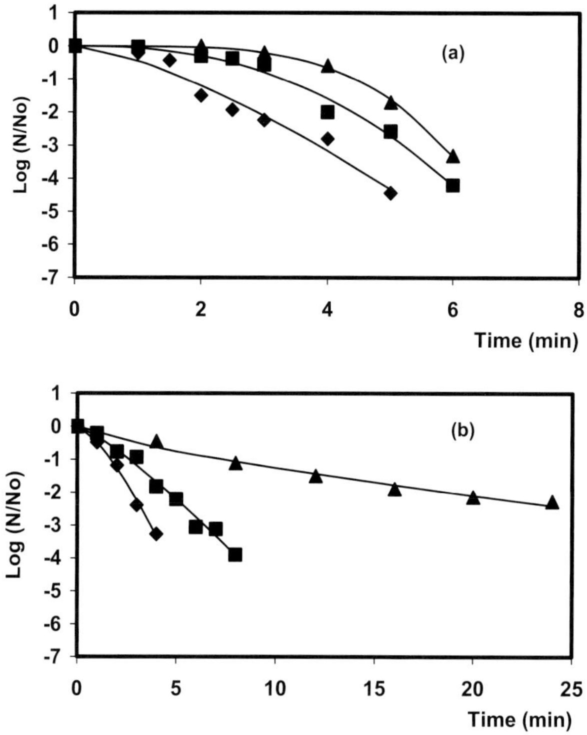

Figure 1

(*a*) Semilogarithmic survival curves of *Listeria monocytogenes* and (*b*) *Saccharomyces cerevisiae* in clarified apple juice. Experimental values: ▲, US treatment; ■, UV-C light treatment; ♦, combined UV-C/US treatment. Lines: fitted values by Weibullian model. No, initial number of microorganisms; N, number of microorganisms at time t, CFU ml^{-1}.

High Hydrostatic Pressure

The effects of pressure are multitargeted and depend on pressure level. HHP causes a perturbation of the membrane, inhibits the synthesis of some membrane proteins, dissociates ribosomes, and brings changes in the quaternary structure of proteins (Smelt et al. 2002). HHP affects enzymes, and there is an optimum temperature range at which proteins are more resistant to pressure. Yeasts, molds, and vegetative cells of bacteria can be inactivated by pressures in the range of 200–700 MPa near room temperature. Vegetative cells of bacteria become more susceptible to pressure at low pH, and bacteria surviving pressure treatment become more sensitive to suboptimal pH after processing. According to this mechanistic background, stress factors such as temperatures below or above room temperature during processing, natural and synthetic antimicrobials, and pH have been mainly considered in combined strategies.

HHP is gaining popularity in the fruit industry because of its ability to destroy microorganisms and to reduce significantly the enzymatic activity on acid fruit juices and fresh fruits without greatly affecting vitamins, pigments, and flavor and antioxidant activity, probably due to the stability of covalent unions to high pressure.

Because of inherent low pH, most fruits can be easily stabilized by HHP, but the presence of HHP-resistant browning enzymes requires an antibrowning treatment (Cano & de Anco 2005). As an example, best quality retention of strawberries was obtained when HHP was combined with vacuum packaging and refrigerated storage because polyphenol oxidase (PPO) is highly resistant to high-pressure inactivation (Terefe et al. 2009).

PPO: polyphenol oxidase

PME: pectinmethylesterase

The combination of HHP and plant essential oils had been suggested as an alternative control for fruit diseases. *Colletotrichum gloeosporioides* spores, which cause anthracnose in papaya, were efficiently inhibited by a 350 MPa-30 min treatment or 150 MPa-30 min and 0.75 mg ml^{-1} lemongrass oil. An explanation for the enhanced effect of pressure plus lemongrass essential oil is that pressure facilitates the uptake of the oil constituents into the spore, increasing the number of targets affected (Palhano et al. 2004).

In juice, control of pectinmethylesterase (PME) is crucial to assure cloud stability because demethylation of pectin results in the separation of a clear serum and a sediment constituted by complexes of low methoxyl pectin and calcium ions. In general, quality-related enzymes are pressure-stable and pressure treatments are usually combined with mild heating to obtain high quality juice or fruit (Balog et al. 2004). For example, a synergistic effect of HHP and temperature on orange PME inactivation was found by Polydera et al. (2004), except in the high temperature–low pressure region, where an antagonistic interaction was noted. Buckow et al. (2009) also reported a synergism between pressure and temperature on the inactivation of apple PPO above 300 MPa and antagonism at lower pressures.

Inactivation of enzymes was reported to be dependent on medium. Balog et al. (2004) studied the high-pressure inactivation of PME in carrot juice and carrot pieces. PME added to carrot juice at 700 MPa and 10°C was inactivated at a similar rate as in situ PME at 750 MPa and 40°C. This remarks on the importance of making resistance studies in whole cells and not in isolation.

ISSUES OF CONCERN FOR DESIGNING HURDLE PRESERVATION TECHNIQUES

Microbial Response

One important issue is the knowledge of the mode-of-action of the preservation factor(s) and the microorganisms' response. Microorganisms sometimes react or adapt to mild stress factors by evolving signal transduction systems, which in response to environmental stresses control the coordinated expression of genes involved in cellular defense mechanisms, repairing the damages and becoming even more resistant, surviving more severe homologous or heterologous stresses (global stress response) (Gould et al. 1995, Abee & Wouters 1999). After adaptation to mild stresses, cells behave differently from unadapted ones and can grow at values outside the traditionally known ranges of temperature, water activity, and pH determined under optimal conditions, or show greater resistance to inactivation agents. When developing hurdle technologies, it is crucial that resistance development is avoided. Microbiological challenge testing to assess the risk of food poisoning or to establish MP product stability needs careful design, and stressed known or potential pathogens would also be selected to validate the process.

To come to a knowledge-based rather than a mainly empirical combination of appropriate hurdles, modern tools in biology, such as genomics, protein expression data, and metabolic pattern recognition, can bring additional insights in mode-of-action of preservation factors (Brul & Coote 1999, Brul et al. 2002). The integration of these data can result in a clear understanding of the total response of cells toward their environment, allowing specific targets to be identified and collaborating in the development of extrapolable mechanistic models on microbial behavior. For example, construction of the *S. cerevisiae* cell wall is a tightly regulated process involving approximately 1,200 genes. The cell continually adapts its wall organization, as well as the proteins at the cell surface, to changing environmental stimuli. Thus, cell wall–assembling enzymes and enzymes involved in remodeling of cell wall polymers could be potential targets for new antifungal compounds (Klis et al. 2002).

Food preservation: temporary or permanent disturbance of microorganism homeostasis by preservation factor(s) or hurdle(s)

Characteristics of the Hurdle Interaction

The rational selection of hurdles in terms of type and intensity should result in synergistic or at least additive interaction. It is not easy to anticipate synergistic, additive, or antagonistic activity. When combining antimicrobials, for example, the effects had been reported to depend not only on the type of stress factors, but on the composition of the food matrix and the storage period (Alzamora et al. 2003). At pH 3.5, combinations of vanillin and potassium sorbate used to inhibit *Aspergillus flavus* growth initially appeared as synergistic and evolved to additive as incubation time increased. At pH 4.5, however, the interaction was antagonistic for all incubation times analyzed. Quantification of the interaction must be realized in the real fruit and should consider the desired shelf life.

Attached Versus Planktonic Cells

A biofilm is a community of microorganisms attached to a surface, biotic or abiotic, producing extracellular polymeric substance (EPS) and interacting with each other. Association of microorganisms with the surface is the prevailing microbial lifestyle, and planktonic cell studies constitute a biased view of microbial life (Lindsay & von Holy 2006). Biofilm cells in food surfaces or product contact surfaces are heterogeneous and much more resistant to preservation factors than the planktonic, freely suspended cells. Various mechanisms, such as the diffusion barrier to penetration of antimicrobial agents by the EPS, induction of resistant phenotypes, slow growth, and general stress response, have been proposed to account for this greater overall antimicrobial resistance.

Traditionally, physiology and kinetics studies to select preservation factors have focused on microbial cells in aqueous planktonic phase. However, such studies only have value as a preliminary screening, and experiments with attached cells should be carried out to evaluate the effectiveness of the combined techniques.

Quantification of Microbial Behavior

Kinetic data of inactivation and growth are essential to select preservation factors and levels with a statistical sense to develop food preservation processes that ensure safety (McMeekin & Ross 2002). Predictive microbiology provides the tools to compare the impact of different environmental stress factors/levels on reduction or growth inhibition of microbial population and is an aid to understanding biological system behavior. Thus, if we can predict with accuracy the decay or growth kinetics for an identified target microorganism under multiple factors in combination, the selection of such factors can be made on a sound basis, and the selected preservation factors can be kept at their minimum doses. Sensory selection of hurdles and their levels may be done between several safe equivalent combinations of interactive effects determined by the models. The experimental design for obtaining quantitative data must involve a wide range of the factors in combination to obtain a comprehensive picture of the microbial response to the dose.

As an example, Raffellini (2009) studied and modeled the influence of sanitizer concentration (0 to 3.00% w/v), pH (3.0–7.2), temperature (12.5–50°C), and exposure time on the antimicrobial activity of H_2O_2 against planktonic cells of *E. coli* ATCC 35218. In general, more *E. coli* was inactivated as the exposure temperature and the H_2O_2 concentration increased and the pH decreased. Traditionally, microbial inactivation has been considered a process that follows first-order kinetics. It has been implicitly assumed that all cells or spores have identical resistance to a lethal agent, and each microorganism has the same probability of dying. However, as in this case, the decrease of the population does not usually follow first-order kinetics (Peleg & Cole 1998). On the assumption that the individual microorganisms in a population do not have identical resistances and that microbial sensitivity to lethal agents is distributed, curvilinear (concave and convex), semilogarithmic survival curves can be modeled using the Weibull distribution. As microbial mortality is increased by lowering the organism's resistance to the treatment (e.g., when additive or synergistic combination of lethal agents are used and/or the severity of a lethal agent is increased), the mode and the mean of the distribution are lowered. From the point of view of preservation system design, the combinations of factors/levels to choose are those that also decrease the spread or variance of the distribution. **Figure 2*a,b*** illustrates the survival curves obtained at different

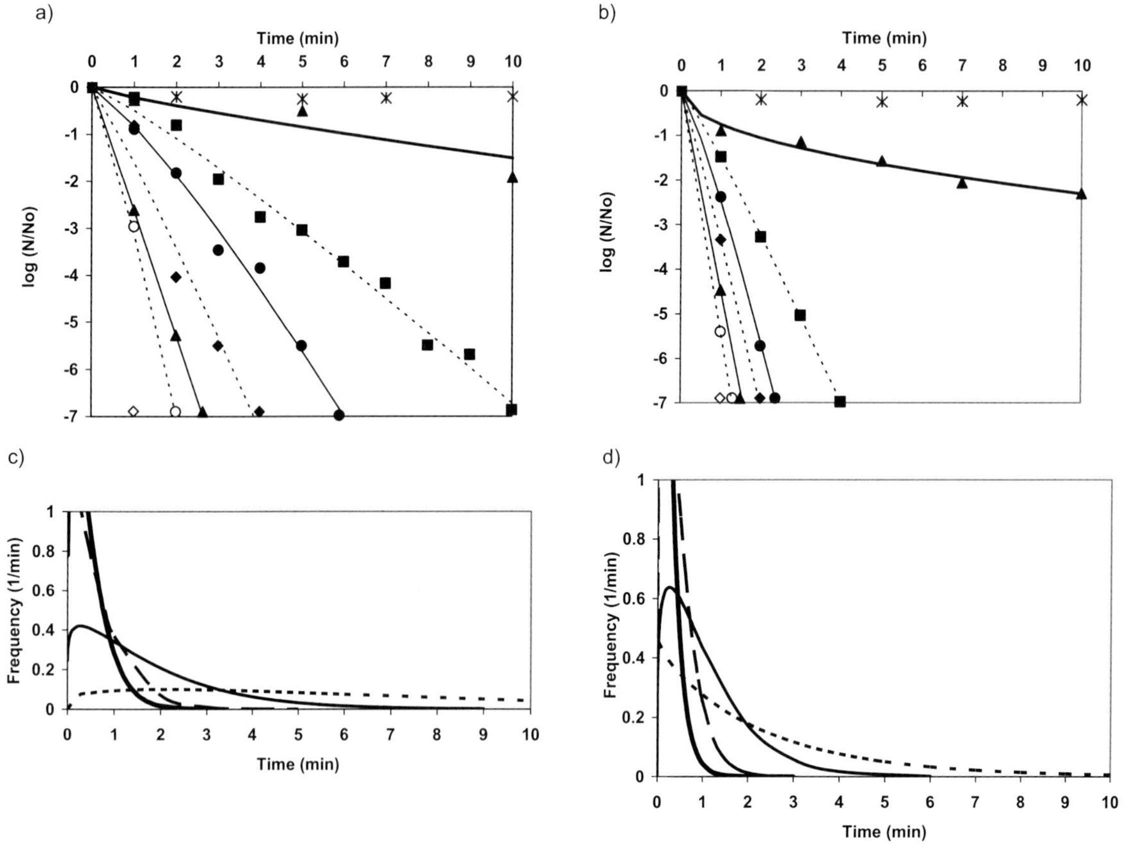

Figure 2

(*a,b*) Effect of H_2O_2 concentration and temperature on semilogarithmic survival curves of *Escherichia coli* at pH 5.8. Experimental (points) and fitted values derived from the Weibullian model (lines). Control (∗); 0.10% w/v H_2O_2 (▲); 0.50% w/v H_2O_2 (■);1.00% w/v H_2O_2 (•); 1.50% w/v H_2O_2 (♦); 2.00% w/v H_2O_2 (▲); 2.50% w/v H_2O_2 (O); 3.00% w/v H_2O_2 (◊); (*a*) 25.0°C; (*b*) 37.5°C. No, initial number of microorganisms; N, number of microorganisms at time t, CFU/ml). (*c,d*) Frequency distributions of resistances of *E. coli* obtained at different temperatures and H_2O_2 concentrations at pH 5.8: (- -) 12.5°C; (—) 25.0°C; (— — —) 37.5°C; (——) 50.0°C. (*c*) 0.50% w/v; (*d*) 1.00% w/v sanitizer concentrations and temperatures (25.0°C and 37.5°C) at pH 5.8, as well as the frequency distributions of resistances at the four temperatures assayed for 0.50% w/v and 1.00% w/v H_2O_2. Survival patterns and frequency distribution profiles markedly changed with H_2O_2 concentration and temperature. At the less drastic combinations, frequency shapes with a considerable spread of data, heavy tails, and large mode, mean, and variance values meant that an important fraction of the microorganism population survived after these treatments (**Figure 2*c*,*d***). The greater the H_2O_2 concentration and the greater the temperature, the narrower the distribution and the lower the mean, the mode, and the variance values. Population was not only more sensitive on average, but it had a more uniform sensitivity to the treatment.

Uniformity of the Process and Accessibility of the Preservation Agent to Microorganisms

The efficacy of a decontamination treatment is influenced by the accessibility of chemical and some physical agents to microorganisms. Many of the emerging techniques result in survival curves with a tailing effect. In surface decontamination, this shape of inactivation curves would indicate not only that a subpopulation of cells is more resistant to the treatment but probably irregularities of surface and internalization in fruit protect microorganisms from decontamination treatments (Gómez-López et al. 2008).

Process uniformity is another important factor that affects the effectiveness of the process and attempts with its successful commercialization (Heldman et al. 2008). For example, in continuous UV-C and PL processes, the distance and the relative position of the sample with respect to the Hg and Xe lamps influence significantly the received dose or fluence, as well as the increase in temperature with the PL dose (Gómez 2010).

Impact on Structure, Quality, and Functionality of the Product

Combinations of preservation factors should allow the required level of protection against pathogenic or spoilage microorganisms to be achieved while at the same time retaining organoleptic quality and functional and nutritive value. Systematic studies documenting the impact of combination techniques on structure and quality attributes of fruits are scarce. Because of this, it is crucial to investigate not only the effect of the preservation factors at different doses after processing but also the influence along storage. For instance, an increase in surface browning was observed in UV-C-irradiated cut apples over 7 d of storage at 5°C as compared with nonirradiated fruit or fruit just after irradiation, mainly at the greatest UV-C dose assayed (Gómez et al. 2010). This color modification was attributed to increased enzymatic activity caused by UV-C-induced membrane breakage, with consequent loss of compartmentalization. These results indicate that UV-C light must be combined with a suitable antibrowning pretreatment to be used as a tool by the minimally processed fruit industry to reduce surface microbial load and avoid color deterioration. Welti-Chanes et al. (2009) treated just-squeezed orange juice by high-pressure homogeneization (50 to 250 MPa) at three initial temperatures (22°C, 35°C, and 45°C) to inactivate PME to avoid the loss of cloudy appearance. The higher the pressure and the higher the initial temperature, the higher was the PME inactivation. However, the PME activity increased throughout 12 d storage at 4°C, probably due to the rise of isoenzymes. Lower PME activation was observed in orange juice previously heated at 45°C and treated at 250 MPa. This combination of temperature and high pressure maintained cloudy appearance for 12 d after refrigeration.

FUTURE ISSUES

1. Combining emerging technologies with conventional preservation technologies or with other novel techniques to interfere with the homeostatic mechanisms of microorganisms in fruits has been successfully explored in the last years. However, a more deep understanding of the combined techniques will be critical in obtaining safe and high quality fruit products.
2. New strategies and targets can arise from fundamental knowledge (e.g., physiological studies, omics research, multiparametric flow cytometry analysis) about the mechanisms of action of individual and combined factors and its integration with model development and process design. Relevant information is available in the scientific literature concerning factors/interaction of factors that influence microbial activities in foods, but it is seldom usable in formulating combined techniques and/or has low practical relevance.
3. Systematic studies documenting and modeling the dose response of native flora, inoculated microorganisms of concern, and quality attributes to single/combined factors need to be developed in the fruit matrix to support hurdles selection and their levels.

DISCLOSURE STATEMENT

The authors are not aware of any affiliations, memberships, funding, or financial holdings that might be perceived as affecting the objectivity of this review.

ACKNOWLEDGMENTS

The authors are grateful for the support from Universidad de Buenos Aires, CONICET and ANPCyT-BID from Argentina and from the Instituto Tecnológico y de Estudios Superiores de Monterrey and CONACyT from Mexico.

LITERATURE CITED

Abee T, Wouters JA. 1999. Microbial stress response in minimal processing. *Int. J. Food Microbiol.* 50:65–91

Allende A, Artes F. 2003. UV-C radiation as a novel technique for keeping quality of fresh processed "Lollo Rosso" lettuce. *Food Res. Int.* 36:739–46

Allende A, Tomás-Barberán FA, Gil MI. 2006. Minimal processing for healthy traditional foods. *Trends Food Sci.Technol.* 17:513–19

Alzamora SM, Cerrutti P, Guerrero S, López-Malo A. 1995. Minimally processed fruits by combined methods. In *Food Preservation by Moisture Control—Fundamentals and Applications*, ed. G Barbosa-Cánovas, J Welti-Chanes, pp. 463–92. Lancaster, PA: Technomic

Alzamora SM, Guerrero S, López-Malo A, Palou E. 2003. Plant antimicrobials combined with conventional preservatives for fruit products. In *Natural Antimicrobials for the Minimal Processing of Foods*, ed. S. Roller, pp. 235–49. Boca Raton, FL: CRC Press

Alzamora SM, Guerrero S, Schenk M, Raffellini S, López-Malo A. 2010. Inactivation of microorganisms. In *Ultrasound Technologies for Food and Bioprocessing*, ed. H Feng. New York: Springer

Alzamora SM, López-Malo A, Tapia MS. 2000. *Minimally Processed Fruits and Vegetables: Fundamentals and Applications*. Gaithersburg, MD: Aspen Publ.

Ananta E, Voigt D, Zenker M, Heinz V, Knorr D. 2005. Cellular injuries upon exposure of *Escherichia coli* and *Lactobacillus rhamnosus* to high-intensity ultrasound. *J. Appl. Microbiol.* 99:271–78

Balog T, Smout C, Nguyen BL, Van Loey AM, Hendrickx ME. 2004. Thermal and high-pressure inactivation kinetics of carrot pectinmethylesterase: from model system to real foods. *Innov. Food Sci. Emerg. Technol.* 5:429–36

Barbosa-Cánovas GV, Tapia MS, Cano MP, ed. 2005. *Novel Food Processing Technologies*. Boca Raton, FL: CRC Press

Baumann AR, Martín SE, Feng H. 2005. Power ultrasound treatment of *Listeria monocytogenes* in apple cider. *J. Food Prot.* 68:2333–40

Beuchat LR. 2000. Use of sanitizers in raw fruit and vegetable processing. See Alzamora 2000, pp. 63–78

Booth IR, Kroll RG. 1998. The preservation of foods by low pH. In *Mechanisms of Action of Food Preservation Procedures*, ed. GW Gould, pp. 119–60. London: Elsevier Appl. Sci.

Brul S, Coote P. 1999. Preservative agents in foods. Mode of action and microbial resistance mechanisms. *Int. J. Food Microbiol.* 50:1–17

Brul S, Klis FM, Oomes SJCM, Montijn RC, Schuren FHJ, et al. 2002. Detailed process design based on genomics of survivors of food preservation processes. *Trends Food Sci.Technol.* 13:325–33

Buckow R, Weiss U, Knorr D. 2009. Inactivation kinetics of apple polyphenol oxidase in different pressure-temperature domains. *Innov. Food Sci. Emerg. Technol.* 10:441–48

Cano MP, Ancos B. 2005. Advances in use of high pressure to processing and preservation of plant foods. See Barbosa-Cánovas 2005, pp. 283–309

Conner D, Beuchat LR. 1984. Effects of essential oils from plants on growth of food spoilage yeasts. *J. Food Sci.* 49:429–34

FDA. 2000. *Kinetics of microbial inactivation for alternative food processing technologies: ultraviolet light*. Rockville, MD: Center for Food Safety and Applied Nutrition. US Food and Drug Administration, **http://vm.cfsan.fda.gov/~comm/ift-uv.html**

Ferrante S, Guerrero S, Alzamora SM. 2007. Combined use of ultrasound and natural antimicrobials to inactivate *Listeria monocytogenes* in orange juice. *J. Food Prot.* 70:1850–57

Fonseca JM, Rushing JW. 2006. Effect of UV-C light on quality and microbial population of fresh-cut watermelon. *Postharvest Biol. Technol.* 40:256–61

Gómez P. 2010. *Procesamiento mínimo de manzana: efecto de la radiación UV-C y la luz pulsada de alta intensidad sobre la calidad*. PhD thesis. Univ. Buenos Aires, Argentina. 263 pp.

Gómez P, Castro MA, Salvatori DM, Alzamora SM. 2010. Effect of UV-C light dose on quality of cut-apple: microorganism, color and compression behavior. *J. Food Eng.* 98:60–70

Gómez-López VM, Devlieghere F, Bonduelle V, Debevere J. 2005. Intense light pulses decontamination of minimally processed vegetables and their shelf-life. *Int. J. Food Microbiol.* 103:79–89

Gómez-López VM, Ragaert P, Debevere J, Devlieghere F. 2007. Pulsed light for food decontamination: a review. *Trends Food Sci.Technol.* 18:464–73

Gómez-López VM, Ragaert P, Debevere J, Devlieghere F. 2008. Decontamination methods to prolong the shelf-life of minimally processed vegetables, state-of-the-art. *Crit. Rev. Food Sci. Nutr.* 48:487–95

Gould GW. 1995. *New Methods of Food Preservation*. Glasgow, Scotland: Blackie Acad. Prof.

Gould GW, Abee T, Granum PE, Jones MV. 1995. Physiology of food poisoning microorganisms and the major problems in food poisoning control. *Int. J. Food Microbiol.* 28:121–28

Gould GW, Jones MV. 1989. Combination and synergistic effect. In *Mechanisms of Action of Food Preservation Procedures*, ed. GW Gould, pp. 401–21. London: Elsevier Appl. Sci.

Heldman DR, Lund DB, Husain A. 2008. Cross-process issues impacting innovative food processing technologies. *Food Sci. Technol. Int.* 14:411–12

Keyser M, Müller IA, Cilliers FP, Nel W, Gouws PA. 2008. Ultraviolet radiation as a nonthermal treatment for the inactivation of microorganisms in fruit juice. *Innov. Food Sci. Emerg. Technol.* 9:348–54

Klis FM, Mol P, Hellingwerf K, Brul S. 2002. Dynamics of cell wall structure in *Saccharomyces cerevisiae*. *FEMS Microbiol. Rev.* 26:239–56

Knorr D, Zenker M, Heinz V, Lee DU. 2004. Applications and potential of ultrasonics in food processing. *Trends Food Sci.Technol.* 15:261–66

Koutchma T. 2009. Advances in UV light technology for non-thermal processing of liquid foods. *Food Bioprocess Technol.* 2:138–55

Lauterborn W, Kurz T, Mettin R, Ohl CD. 1999. Experimental and theoretical bubble dynamics. In *Advances in Chemical Physics*, ed. I Prigogine, SA Rice, pp. 295–380. New York: Wiley

Leistner L, Gould GW. 2002. *Hurdle Technologies. Combination Treatments for Food Stability, Safety and Quality*. New York: Kluwer Academic/Plenum Publ.

Leistner L, Rödel W. 1976. The stability of intermediate moisture foods with respect to microorganisms. In *Intermediate Moisture Foods*, ed. R Davies, GG Birch, KJ Parker, pp. 120–37. London: Appl. Sci. Publ., Ltd.

Lindsay D, von Holy A. 2006. What food safety professionals should know about bacterial biofilms. *Br. Food J.* 108:27–37

López-Malo A, Guerrero S, Alzamora SM. 1999. *Saccharomyces cerevisiae* thermal inactivation kinetics combined with ultrasound. *J. Food Prot.* 62:10–13

López-Malo A, Guerrero S, Santiesteban A, Alzamora SM. 2006. Inactivation kinetics of *Saccharomyces cerevisiae* and *Listeria monocytogenes* in apple juice processed by novel technologies. *ENPROMER 2005, August 14–18*, Rio das Pedras, Brazil

McMeekin TA, Ross T. 2002. Predictive microbiology: providing a knowledge-based framework for change management. *Int. J. Food Microbiol.* 78:133–53

Marquenie D, Lammertyn J, Geeraerd AH, Soontjens C, Van Impe JF, et al. 2002. Inactivation of conidia of *Botrytis cinerea* and *Monilinia fructigena* using UV-C and heat treatment. *Int. J. Food Microbiol.* 74:27–35

Marquenie D, Michiels CW, Van Impe JF, Schrevens E, Nicolaï BN. 2003. Pulsed white light in combination with UV-C and heat to reduce storage rot of strawberry. *Postharvest Biol. Technol.* 28:455–61

Palhano FL, Vilches TTB, Santos RB, Orlando MTD, Aires Ventura J, Fernandes PMB. 2004. Inactivation of *Colletotrichum gloeosporioides* spores by high hydrostatic pressure combined with citral or lemongrass essential oil. *Int. J. Food Microbiol.* 95:61–66

Pan J, Vicente AR, Martínez GA, Chaves AR, Civello PM. 2004. Combined use of UV-C irradiation and heat treatment to improve postharvest life of strawberry fruit. *J. Sci. Food Agric.* 84:1831–38

Peleg M, Cole MB. 1998. Reinterpretation of microbial survival curves. *Crit. Rev. Food Sci. Nutr.* 38:353–80

Piyasena P, Mohareb E, McKellar RC. 2003. Inactivation of microbes using ultrasound: a review. *Int. J. Food Microbiol.* 87:207–16

Polydera AC, Galanou E, Stoforos NG, Taoukis PS. 2004. Inactivation kinetics of pectin methylesterase of Greek Navel orange juice as a function of high hydrostatic pressure and temperature process conditions. *J. Food Eng.* 62:291–98

Raffellini S. 2009. *Inactivación de Escherichia coli en desarrollo planctónico y en biofilms mediante peróxido de hidrógeno: cuantificación del efecto de la concentración, el pH y la temperatura*. PhD thesis. Univ. Buenos Aires, Argentina. 211 pp.

Raso J, Barbosa-Cánovas GV. 2003. Nonthermal preservation of foods using combined processing techniques. *Crit. Rev. Food Sci. Nutr.* 43:265–85

Raso J, Pagán R, Condón S. 2005. Nonthermal technologies in combination with other preservation factors. See Barbosa-Cánovas 2005, pp. 453–75

Raybaudi-Massilia RM, Mosqueda-Melgar J, Soliva-Fortuny R, Martín-Belloso O. 2009. Control of pathogenic and spoilage microorganisms in fresh-cut fruits and fruit juices by traditional and alternative natural antimicrobials. *CRFSFS* 8:157–80

Rico D, Martín-Diana AB, Barat JM, Barry-Ryan C. 2007. Extending and measuring the quality of fresh-cut fruit and vegetables: a review. *Trends Food Sci. Technol.* 18:373–86

Ross AIV, Griffiths MW, Mittal GS, Deeth HC. 2003. Combining nonthermal technologies to control food-borne microorganisms. *Int. J. Food Microbiol.* 89:125–38

Russell NJ. 2002. Bacterial membranes: the effect of chill storage and food processing. An overview. *Int. J. Food Microbiol.* 79:27–34

Sauer A, Moraru CI. 2009. Inactivation of *Escherichia coli* ATCC 25922 and *Escherichia coli* O157:H7 in apple juice and apple cider, using pulsed light treatment. *J. Food Prot.* 72:937–44

Schenk M, Guerrero S, Alzamora SM. 2008. Response of some microorganisms to UV treatment on fresh-cut pear. *Food Bioprocess Technol.* 1:384–92

Schenk M, Raffellini S, Guerrero S, Blanco G, Alzamora SM. 2011. Inactivation of *Escherichia coli*, *Listeria innocua* and *Saccharomyces cerevisiae* by UV-C light: study of cell injury by flow cytometry. *LWT: Food Sci. Technol.* 44:191–198

Shama G. 2006. Ultraviolet light. In *Handbook of Food Science, Technology and Engineering*, ed. YH Hui, Vol. 3, 122-1–122-14. Boca Raton, FL: CRC/Taylor & Francis

Shama G. 2007. Process challenges in applying low doses of UV light to fresh produce for eliciting beneficial hormetic responses. *Postharvest Biol. Technol.* 44:1–8

Shama G, Alderson P. 2005. UV hormesis in fruits: a concept ripe for commercialisation. *Trends Food Sci.Technol.* 16:128–36

Smelt JPPM, Hellemons JC, Wouters PC, van Gerwen SJC. 2002. Physiological and mathematical aspects in setting criteria for decontamination of foods by physical means. *Int. J. Food Microbiol.* 78:57–77

Tapia de Daza MS, Alzamora SM, Welti-Chanes J. 1996. Combination of preservation factors applied to minimal processing of foods. *Crit. Rev. Food Sci. Nutr.* 36:629–59

Terefe NS, Matthies K, Simons L, Versteeg C. 2009. Combined high pressure-mild temperature processing for optimal retention of physical and nutritional quality of strawberries (*Fragaria* × *ananassa*). *Innov. Food Sci. Emerg. Technol.* 10:297–307

Tran MTT, Farid M. 2004. Ultraviolet treatment of orange juice. *Innov. Food Sci. Emerg. Technol.* 5:495–502

Walkling-Ribeiro M, Noci F, Riener J, Cronin DA, Lyng JG, Morgan DJ. 2009. The impact of thermosonication and pulsed electric fields on *Staphylococcus aureus* inactivation and selected quality parameters in orange juice. *Food Bioprocess Technol.* 2:422–30

Welti-Chanes J, Ochoa-Velasco CE, Guerrero-Beltrán JA. 2009. High pressure homogenization of orange juice to inactivate pectinmethylesterase. *Innov. Food Sci. Emerg. Technol.* 10:457–62

Woodling SE, Moraru CI. 2007. Effect of spectral range in surface inactivation of *Listeria innocua* using broad-spectrum pulsed light. *J. Food Prot.* 70:909–16

Yaun BR, Summer SS, Eifert JD, Marcy JE. 2004. Inhibition of pathogens on fresh produce by UV energy. *Int. J. Food Microbiol.* 90:1–8

Use of FTIR for Rapid Authentication and Detection of Adulteration of Food

L.E. Rodriguez-Saona and M.E. Allendorf

Food Science and Technology Department, The Ohio State University, Columbus, Ohio 43210; email: rodriguez-saona.1@osu.edu

Annu. Rev. Food Sci. Technol. 2011. 2:467–83

First published online as a Review in Advance on December 13, 2010

The *Annual Review of Food Science and Technology* is online at food.annualreviews.org

This article's doi:
10.1146/annurev-food-022510-133750

1941-1413/11/0410-0467$20.00

Keywords

spectroscopy, near infrared, mid-infrared, chemometrics, quantification

Abstract

Fourier transform infrared (FTIR) spectroscopy is an appealing technology for the food industry because simple, rapid, and nondestructive measurements of chemical and physical components can be obtained. Advances in FTIR instrumentation combined with the development of powerful multivariate data analysis methods make this technology ideal for large volume, rapid screening and characterization of minor food components down to parts per billion (ppb) levels. Because of the use of FTIR techniques in quality and process control applications, the food industry is already familiar with the technology and its potential to expand to monitoring for food adulteration. The aim of this review is to compile the current research on applications of near infrared (NIR) and mid-infrared (MIR) spectroscopy for rapid authentication and detection of adulteration in food.

INTRODUCTION

Fourier transform infrared (FTIR) spectroscopy has become an attractive alternative for traditional analytical methods because little sample preparation is needed, analysis is rapid, and the use of hazardous solvents is minimized. These advantages result in time and cost savings and an increase in the number of samples that can be analyzed. Numerous researchers have attempted to utilize these advantages by applying FTIR to food science. The scope of this review is to compile the current research on the applications of FTIR spectroscopy for authentication and detection of adulteration in food.

Knowledge of the basic principles behind spectroscopy facilitates the understanding of how the infrared (IR) technique can be applied to authenticate and detect adulteration in food. IR spectra are produced by recording changes in absorption of IR radiation by molecules, which undergo mechanical motions (vibrational and rotational modes) due to the absorption of energy (Diem 1993, Guillen & Cabo 1997). Within any molecule, a given functional group (i.e. carbonyl group or an amide group) gives characteristic IR absorption at specific, narrow frequency ranges regardless of their relationship with the rest of the molecule. Because of complex interactions of atoms within the molecule, each involved in its own vibrational transitions, the energy of a vibration and, thus, the position of the band in the IR spectrum are sometimes influenced by the atoms surrounding the vibrational group. Thus, the IR spectra can be used to identify or differentiate between samples and also give information about the quantity of functional groups (Diem 1993, Guillen & Cabo 1997). The IR region of the electromagnetic spectrum spans from 14,000–50 cm^{-1} and is divided into three areas: near IR (14,000–4,000 cm^{-1}), mid IR (4,000–400 cm^{-1}), and far IR (400–50 cm^{-1}). This review focuses on the first two regions. Near IR (NIR) and mid IR (MIR) techniques take advantage of the phenomenon occurring when electromagnetic radiation of a specific energy interacts with a molecule.

NIR spectra (**Figure 1*a***, see color insert) are the result of relatively weak and broad overtones and combination bands of fundamental vibrational transitions associated mainly with C-H, N-H, and O-H functional groups. NIR bands are the result of complex vibrational motion of chemical bonds that tend to deviate from harmonicity. These deviations (anharmonicity) result in bands arising from transitions over two (1st overtone), three (2nd overtone), or higher energy levels (12,500–4,000 cm^{-1}, 800–2,500 nm) of the frequency of fundamental vibrations, leading to a decreasing NIR absorption intensity with increasing rank of overtone. In addition, the NIR spectrum includes combination modes from the interaction of two or more vibrations taking place simultaneously from the absorption of a single photon (Osborne 2000, Barton 2002). Unfortunately, the superposition of many different overtone and combination bands in the NIR region causes a very low structural selectivity of NIR spectra compared to MIR spectra; however, lower NIR absorption intensity can be compensated by increasing the sample thickness for NIR measurements (from millimeters up to centimeters) compared to MIR (micrometers). NIR bands are 10 to 100 times less intense than their corresponding MIR fundamental bands. This can allow for the direct analysis of samples that are highly absorbing or strongly light scattering without dilution or extensive sample preparation (Hall et al. 1996, Shenk et al. 2001). FT-NIR instruments have found a niche in the food industry for chemical quality and process control because of their ruggedness and increased flexibility in handling, such as being able to analyze samples in glass vials. Furthermore, the relatively weak absorption due to water overtones enables high-moisture foods to be readily analyzed (Osborne 2000).

Spectra from the MIR region are commonly used for structural identification (fingerprinting) of organic compounds because the absorption bands are caused by fundamental vibrations of a specific functional group (Guillen & Cabo 1997). The fingerprint region, located within the

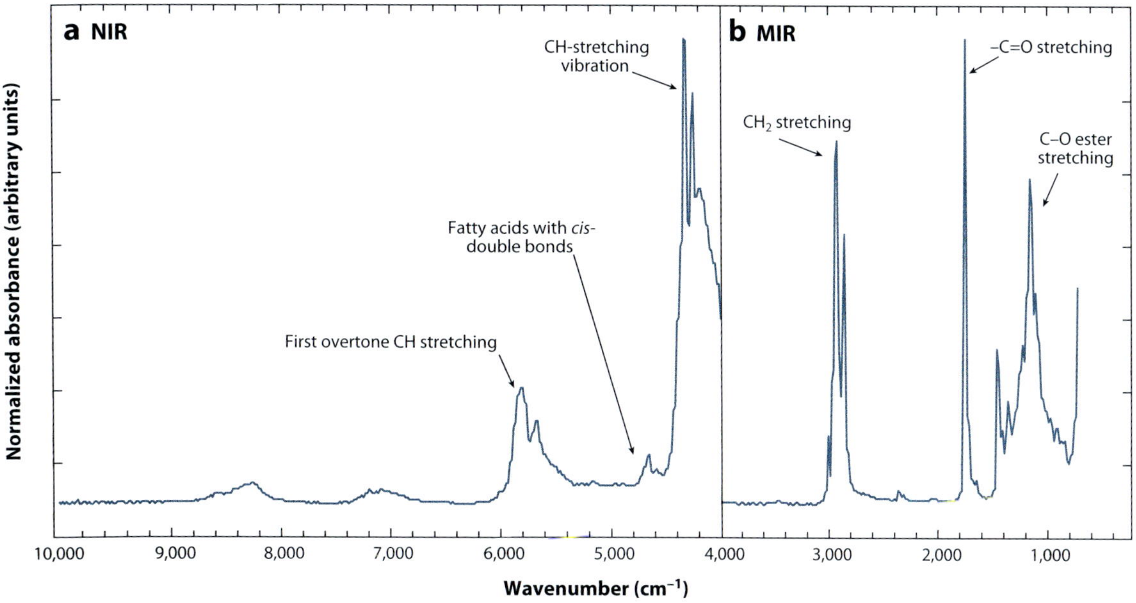

Figure 1

(*a*) Near-infrared (NIR) and (*b*) mid-infrared (MIR) raw spectra of grapeseed oil with peak identification.

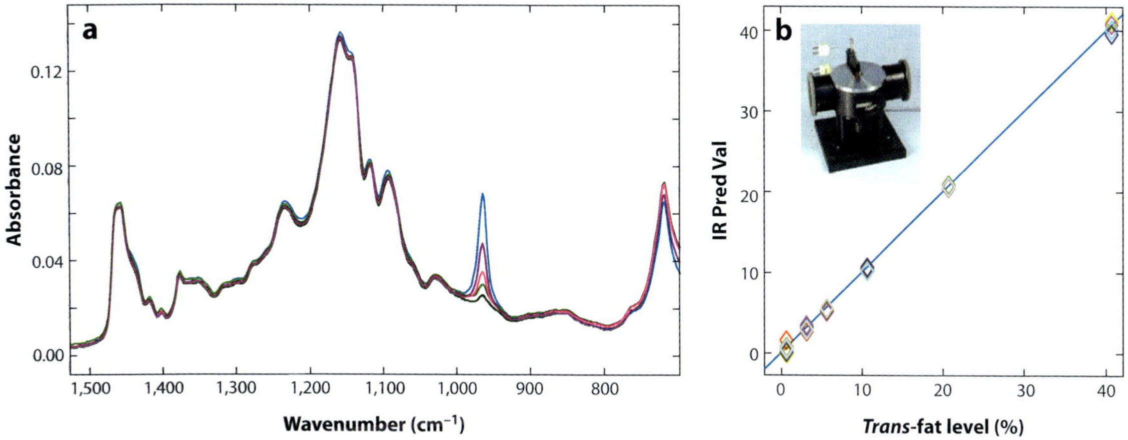

Figure 3

(*a*) Fourier transform infrared (FTIR) spectra of edible oil collected on a FatIR accessory highlighting the characteristic *trans* band at 966 cm^{-1}. (*b*) Partial least squares regression model of % *trans* fat using FTIR spectra.

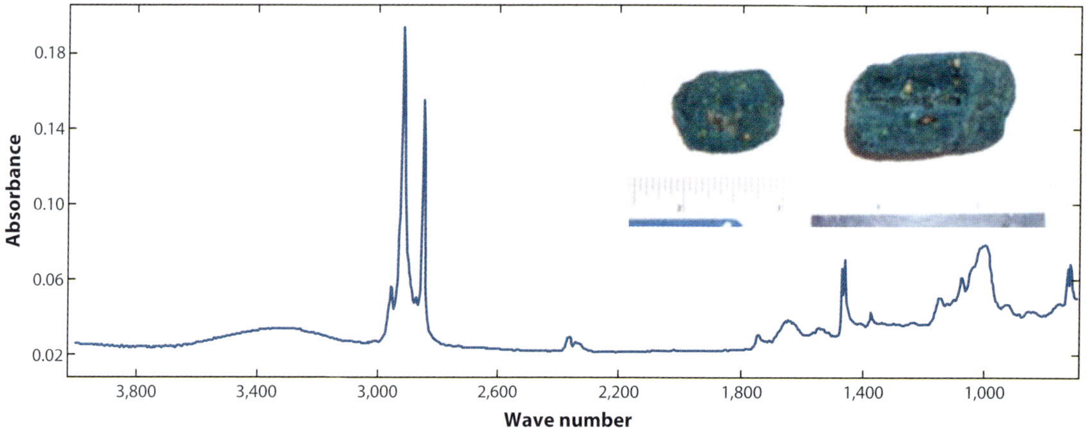

Figure 4

Attenuated total reflectance (ATR) spectra of the foreign material contaminant (block bait) found in the milk intake filter. Picture of the material is shown in the insert.

MIR region between 1,200 and 700 cm^{-1}, contains bands from lipids, proteins, carotenoids, and polysaccharides, and as a result is rich in structural information (Pare & Belanger 1997). Spectra from the MIR region (**Figure 1*b***) can be used for quantitative analysis applications because the intensities of the bands are proportional to the concentration of their respective functional group (Pare & Belanger 1997).

With the advent of FT instrumentation, the speed and accuracy of IR technology was increased by replacing the use of conventional prism and grating monochromators with an interferometer. FTIR utilizes interferometric modulation of radiation to measure multiple frequencies simultaneously, producing an interferogram that is recalculated using complex algorithms to give the original spectrum. Fourier deconvolution resolves overlapping IR bands, caused by complex samples, by reducing the bandwidth and increasing the peak height (Markovich 1991). Additional advantages of FTIR over traditional dispersive IR instruments include low mechanical wear on equipment because FTIR does not use moving grating parts; simultaneous acquisition of all the wave numbers of light, increasing the signal to noise (S/N) ratio; increased beam intensity going through the sample, leading to higher throughput; superior wavelength resolution; internal wavelength calibration; and advanced wavelength accuracy. Given that the wavelength of the laser is stable and very accurately known, the data can be precisely acquired, allowing for repetitive scans to be well aligned with respect to each other. In FT instrumentation, the resolution is not determined by the size of the beam, but by the stroke (travel) of the movable mirror and the number of data collected during a stroke. These optical advantages result in a significantly reduced data acquisition time compared with a spectrum obtained with similar resolution on a dispersive instrument (Diem 1993), making the technology an excellent tool for qualitative and quantitative analyses of food matrices.

The use of attenuated total reflectance (ATR) with FTIR allowed the spectral collection from solids, liquids, semisolids, and thin films. ATR IR spectroscopy provides a fast analytical tool as compared with traditional IR transmission spectroscopy, requiring less sample preparation, improving the sample-to-sample reproducibility, minimizing user-to-user spectral variation, and giving high throughput relative to the available energy in the FTIR sample compartment, which resulted in better quality data for more precise material verification and identification (Pike Technologies 2010). ATR is a reflection technique in which the IR light is reflected internally off the back surface of an internal reflection element with a high index refraction, which is in contact with the sample (PerkinElmer 2004). The IR beam travels inside the crystal and a standing wave of radiation, called the evanescent wave, is created (PerkinElmer 2004). A sample in contact with the crystal can interact with the evanescent wave, absorb IR radiation, and have its IR spectrum detected. The evanescent wave is attenuated by the sample's absorbance, which gives rise to the name ATR (PerkinElmer 2004). The high refractive index crystals typically are made of diamond, zinc selenide, KRS-5 (thallium iodide/thallium bromide), or germanium. The number of reflections at the surface of the crystal will vary depending on length and thickness of the crystal and the angle of incidence (PerkinElmer 2004). This provides the ATR with a multiple-fold increase in the sample's response compared with singe-reflection crystals (Pike Technologies 2010).

Several excellent books cover aspects of fundamental theory, instrumentation, chemometric methods, and applications of vibrational spectroscopy and should be referenced if more detailed information is desired (Chalmers & Griffiths 2001, Osborne 2000, Robinson 1991, Sielsler 2002, Williams & Norris 2001). Chemometrics is the science of extracting chemically relevant information from complex multidimensional data produced in chemical experiments by using multivariate analysis techniques to reduce the dimensionality of the data set.

APPLICATIONS OF FTIR FOR AUTHENTICATION AND DETECTION OF ADULTERANTS

Authentication of products by commodity, variety, and geographical origin is important for regulatory agencies, food processors, retailers, and consumers because expensive ingredients have the potential for adulteration and fraudulent or accidental mislabeling. There is a need for a rapid technique to validate these claims, and the potential application of FTIR has been explored in recent years. Combining FT-NIR and FT-MIR with multivariate statistical methods has been applied for authentication of herbal products, fruit juices, agricultural products, edible oils, dairy, and numerous other food products. These efforts have had varying degrees of success at classifying products as authentic or unauthentic depending on the region of the electromagnetic spectrum employed and chemometric techniques used on the spectra. Fingerprints of authentic commodities may be considered to represent their overall chemical composition and therefore have the potential to detect adulteration. This method of detection possesses various benefits as an authenticity screening tool; it is fast (tests can be carried out in 1–2 min) and simple to use. A large number of potential adulterants may be searched from a single spectrum, no sample preparation is required, and little waste material is generated. From a regulatory perspective, it has the additional benefit of not destroying the sample being tested (Kelly & Downey 2005). **Table 1** summarizes the applications of NIR spectroscopy in monitoring authentication of foods.

NIR reflectance spectroscopy has been used to develop a fast authentication system for herbal supplements. *Echinacea* species *E. purpurea* (L.) Moench, *E. angustifolia*, and *E. pallida* are widely used as immunostimulant herbal preparations, and commercial preparations are frequently adulterated or substituted with roots of *Parthenium integrifolium* L. or different *Echinacea* species that negatively affect the reliability and efficacy of *Echinacea* commercial products (Laasonen et al. 2002a). NIR spectroscopy has been reported for the fast identification of *E. purpurea* roots (Laasonen et al. 2002b) and the determination of echinacoside content (Schulz et al. 2002). The presence of other *Echinacea* species can be detected at a minimum of 10% adulteration by using FT-NIR spectroscopy (Laasonen et al. 2002b). Owing to the low content of echinacosides in the most valuable *E. purpurea* roots as compared with *E. pallida* and *E. angustifolia* (Laasonen et al. 2002b), partial least-squares (PLS) algorithms using NIR spectra produce robust models for the fast and reliable screening of *E. purpurea* in herbal preparations.

Adulteration of dietary supplement oils (DSOs) such as grapeseed oil, flax oil, burageseed oil, and evening primrose oil with cheaper and less beneficial oils has become a food quality/safety issue. Variations between different brands of the same oil due to plant origin, variety, and processing conditions, as well as oil types having very similar compositions, can result in possible misclassifications of authentic oils. A detection limit of 2% for DSOs adulterated (2%–20% v/v) with common foods oils has been reported (Ozen et al. 2003).

A noteworthy application of NIR spectroscopy has been for the detection of adulterants in juices, purees, and syrups. These products are often adulterated with cheaper juice concentrates, cane, corn, or beet sugars, and syrups for economic gain. Twomey et al. (1995) reported the use of NIR and factorial discriminant analysis for the detection of adulteration of orange juice with orange pulpwash, grapefruit juice, and synthetic sugar/acid mixture. Accurate classification rates >90% were determined for adulterated orange juice at 50 g kg^{-1} or higher levels, with no adulterated orange juice being predicted as authentic. Contal et al. (2002) showed that adulteration of strawberry or raspberry juice with apple juice could be detected at levels >10% by using PLS-NIR models. Transmittance NIR spectra can accurately and precisely predict the sugar levels in non-scattering juices (Rodriguez-Saona et al. 2001), whereas NIR transflectance data improve the prediction errors for scattering juice samples (Segtnan & Isaksson 2000). Furthermore, the

Table 1 Application of dispersive NIR for food authenticity

Sample	Method	Multivariate model	Results	Source
Echinacosides in Echinacea roots	Reflectance	PLSR	$R^2 = 0.94$, RMSECV = 0.23 g 100 g^{-1}	Schulz et al. 2002
Adulteration of orange juice	Reflectance	FDA	94% accuracy at levels >50 g kg^{-1} adulterants	Twomey et al. 1995
Cocoa procyanidins	Reflectance	PLSR	$R^2 = 0.98$, SECV = 6.20	Whitacre et al. 2003
Phenolic substances and alkaloids in green tea leaves	Reflectance	PLSR	Gallic acid, SECV: 0.2 g kg^{-1}, R^2: 0.89; epicatechin, SECV: 2.6 g kg^{-1}, R^2: 0.97; caffeine, SECV: 1.7 g kg^{-1}, R^2: 0.97	Schulz et al. 1999
Perseitol in avocado honey	Reflectance	PLSR, PCR	$R^2 = 0.87$, SEP = 0.13	Dvash et al. 2002
Citrus oils	Transflectance	PCA, PLSR	$R^2 = 0.79$–1.00, SEC = 0.03–1.09	Steuer et al. 2001
Apple adulteration in strawberry and raspberry purees	Reflectance	SIMCA, PLSR	Most accurate models produced prediction errors of 3.4% apple (in raspberry) and 5.5% (in strawberry)	Contal et al. 2002
Vegetable proteins in milk powder	Reflectance	MLR	$R^2 = 0.99$, SEP = 0.23	Maraboli et al. 2002
Authentication of green asparagus	Reflectance	PLSR	$R^2 = >0.96$, SEP = 0.07	Perez et al. 2001
Adulteration in alcoholic beverages	Transmittance	PCA, SIMCA	Correct classification of 100%	Pontes et al. 2006
(Online) acrylamide adulteration in chips	Reflectance	PLSR	$R^2 = 0.83$; prediction error 266.6 μg kg^{-1} (using low resolution equipment)	Pedreschi et al. 2010
Acrylamide adulteration in chips	Reflectance	PLSR	$R^2 = 0.95$, prediction error 256.6 μg kg^{-1}	Segtnan et al. 2006
Whey adulteration in cow milk	Reflectance	DPLS, SIMCA	$R^2 = 0.999$, RMSEP = 0.264	Kasemsumran et al. 2007

Abbreviations: PLSR, partial least squares regression; FDA, factorial discriminant analysis; PCA, principal component analysis; SIMCA, soft independent model class analogs; PCR, principal component regression; LDA, linear discriminant analysis; MLR, multiple linear regression.

interference from the strong and broad vibrational bands of water (Fischer et al. 1994) in NIR measurements of aqueous systems can be minimized by rapid solvent elimination and measurement of the dry extract by using diffuse reflectance spectroscopy (Alfaro et al. 1990, Li et al. 1996).

Table 2 summarizes the applications of MIR spectroscopy in monitoring authentication of foods. MIR has been used in juice authentication of high-value ingredients adulterated with inferior sources. Pomegranates have been praised for their antioxidant activity and for potential chemopreventative effects against prostate cancer (Vardin et al. 2008). MIR spectra have been used to differentiate pure pomegranate juice concentrate from juice adulterated with grape juice concentrate (2%–14% v/v) using principle component analysis (PCA) and the 1,780–1,685 cm^{-1} (C = O stretching) IR region (Vardin et al. 2008). Similarly, MIR has been successful in the differentiation of fruit varieties and geographical origins. An important parameter for monitoring authenticity in fruit purees, preps, and jams is the percent fruit content, and minimum requirements for each product type have been established. A partial least-squares regression (PLSR) correlating fruit content and FTIR spectra centered on a band at 1729 cm^{-1} and provided good calibration statistics ($R^2 = 0.94$) when applied to strawberry jam (Fugel et al. 2005). He et al. (2007) looked at cranberries, blueberries, concord grapes, plum nectar blend, and apple juices from

Table 2 Application of MIR for food authenticity

Sample	Multivariate model	Results	Source
Lard adulteration			
in cake	PLSR	R^2 = 0.9790; SEC = 1.75	Syahariza et al. 2005
in chocolate	PLSR	R^2 = 0.99; SE = 1.30	Che Man et al. 2005
Extra virgin olive oil			
Adulteration with vegatable oils		R^2 = 0.99; detection limit 6%	Vlachos et al. 2006
	PCA	Detection limit of 5% for binary mixture; error limit 1.04	Gurdeniz & Ozen 2009
Adulterated with palm oil	PLS and PCR	R^2 = 0.999; SECV = 0.285 (first derivation)	Rohman & Che Man 2010
Evaluating origin	PLS	Was able to correctly classify 80% (mean centered and first and second derivation)	Hennessy et al. 2009
Others			
Juice concentrate adulteration	PLSR	R^2 = 0.9751; could also predict total solids (R^2 = 0.9916) and titratable acidity (R^2 = 0.9114)	Vardin et al. 2008
Authentication of fruits	SIMCA	Extraction improved SIMCA; 100% correct classification at commodity level	He et al. 2007
Classifying honey adulterants as simple and complex sugars	LDA, PCA, LDS	100% classification of simple and complex sugars using PLS and LDA; combining honey varieties lowered it to 95.5%	Sivakesava & Irudayaraj 2002a
Artisianal honeys adulterated with sugar solutions	SIMCA, PLSR	Classification over 95% for beet sucrose and dextrose; could not unambiguously detect HFCS or invert beet	Kelly et al. 2006
Butter adulterated with margarine	PLSR	Using calibration models of selected ranges (0–5%, 0–25, 20–60, etc) R^2 = 0.99; SECV = 1.2% (second derivation)	Koca et al. 2010
Classifying wines as organic versus nonorganic	PCA, DPLS, LDA	DPLS correctly classified 85%; LDA correctly classified 75%	Cozzolino et al. 2009

Abbreviations: PLSR, partial least squares regression; SIMCA, soft independent model class analogy; PCA, principal component analysis; LDA, linear discriminant analysis; PCR, principal component regression.

various manufacturers. Spectral data collected after solid phase extraction of juices improved the pattern recognition [soft independent analysis of class analogy (SIMCA)] modeling power compared with using pure juice and allowed for differentiation of juices with varying origins. Solid phase extraction minimized the interference of sugar on the spectra and isolated the phenolic components that provided a unique fingerprint for juice authentication. The authors acknowledged the limitations of this method, including the extraction procedure and the need for a broader range of samples to improve the robustness of the model, but noted that this method was an improvement over previous attempts (He et al. 2007). Traditional methods for authenticating fruit juices include chromatography or carbon isotope ratio analysis, neither of which is very practical because they are time-consuming, not practical for quality control settings, use harmful solvents, and monitor only one parameter at a time.

Consumers are becoming more interested in organic products and are willing to pay a premium price for these items. The wine industry has acknowledged this trend, and vineyards around the world are currently producing many organic wines. As of 2009, there was no standardized wine-industry method that would enable organic wine composition and authenticity to be easily and efficiently determined (Cozzolino et al. 2009). Cozzolino et al. (2009) was the first to look at using the technology to classify commercial wines from organic versus nonorganic production systems. Nearly 200 samples of red and white wines from 13 regions in Australia were analyzed using MIR combined with PCA, discriminant PLS (DPLS) regression, and linear discriminant analysis (LDA). DPLS correctly classified 85% of organic wines, whereas LDA was able to classify 75%. In general, the PCA score plot separated the organic and nonorganic wine classes, but there was a slight overlap (Cozzolino et al. 2009). The authors reported that MIR combined with chemometric techniques allowed good discrimination between samples produced under organic and nonorganic production systems. Exploration of the PLS loadings did not show any particular individual chemical parameter that explained the separation between wines, rather that many chemical compounds, including phenolics and volatile or non-volatile compounds, could contribute to the discrimination between wines.

Maple syrup and honey products are also targets for unscrupulous manufacturers to make profit by adding cheaper cane and beet sugars. NIR and FTIR spectroscopy in combination with discriminant (LDA and canonical variate analysis) and quantitative (PLSR and principle component regression) analysis have been successfully applied for the classification of adulterants in maple syrup (Paradkar et al. 2003). Models developed with NIR measurements were suited for quantitative analysis of the presence of adulterants. Models developed from FTIR spectra using the fingerprint region resulted in models with superior quantitative and discriminative performances (**Table 3**, **Figure 2**) for detecting adulterants as compared with those obtained from dispersive NIR spectra. Similar results have been reported for the analysis of thyme, oregano, and chamomile essential oils by dispersive NIR and ATR-IR spectroscopy (Schulz et al. 2003).

Honey has been defined as a natural substance produced by honeybees and the addition of sugars voids this definition (Kelly et al. 2006). Diluting honey with simple and complex sugars is the most common way honey is adulterated. This is very difficult to detect because the adulterants mimic the natural sugar profile of honey (38.2% fructose and 31.2% glucose) (Sivakesava & Irudayaraj 2002a). Honey adulteration is also difficult to detect because of the large variability in the product due to flower and bee species, maturity, environment, and processing or storage conditions. Purity of honey is currently tested by carbon isotope ratio analysis, which is expensive and time consuming. In order to use MIR to authenticate honey, the spectra need to be corrected against a background of water to correct for water overlapping the signal from solutes. Analysis was focused on the region that corresponds to sugars (800–1,500 cm^{-1}). Pure honey was adulterated with 7%–25% glucose, fructose, sucrose, and invert sugar. LDA achieved 100% classification of simple sugars and PLS data compression achieved 100% classification for complex sugars. Combining varieties of honey required more factors and lowered the success rate to 95.5%. Further work must be conducted to include honey of many origins and with many adulterants (Sivakesava & Irudayaraj 2002a).

Another study looked at artisanal honey adulterated with different sugar syrups [invert beet syrup, high fructose corn syrup (HFCS), partial invert cane syrup, dextrose syrup, and beet sucrose]. Models were able to correctly classify 95% of authentic honey, beet sucrose, and dextrose samples but were not able to confidently detect adulteration with HFCS or invert beet syrup (Kelly et al. 2006). Iglasias (2006) used MIR to evaluate the botanical origin of honey when correlated with pollen analysis. As with many food products, honey produced in certain regions is prized for its outstanding sensory qualities and is sold for a high price. MIR could be used as a screening tool but would need to be combined with additional testing to confidently identify the origin of the product. Furthermore, MIR did not allow for a quantitative determination of hydroxymethyl furan (HMF) as an indicator of heat damage to the product (Iglasias 2006).

Table 3 Model validation of FT-NIR and FT-MIR methods for the determination of food components

Sample	Method	Factors	SECV	R^2	Source
Vitamin C in foods and pharmaceuticals	FTIR-attenuated total reflection	11	0.28%	0.998	Yang & Irudayaraj 2002
	NIR diffuse reflectance DRIFTS	9	1.93%	0.975	
	FTIR purged photoacustic detector	9	1.45%	0.985	
	NIR reflectance fiber optic probe	5	1.23%	0.973	
	FT-NIR reflectance	3	1.64%	0.980	
Cholesterol in dairy products	FT-NIR	2	1.44%	0.99	Paradkar & Irudayaraj 2002a
	FT-MIR; first derivative	1	0.68%	1.00	Paradkar & Irudayaraj 2002b
Tetracycline in milk (range 4–2000 ppb)	FT-NIR	4	450 ppb	0.72	Sivakesava & Irudayaraj 2002b
	FT-MIR	15	382 ppb	0.85	
Tetracycline in milk (range 4–520 ppb)	FT-NIR	4	110 ppb	0.87	
	FT-MIR	11	101 ppb	0.87	
Extra virgin olive oil adulteration	FT-NIR	13	3.48%	0.99	Yang & Irudayaraj 2001
	FT-MIR	11	4.74%	0.98	
Infant formula adulterated with melamine	FT-NIR	6	(RMSECV) 0.62	0.99	Mauer et al. 2009
	FT-MIR	10	(RMSECV) 1	0.95	
Maple syrup	FT-NIR	11	3.872	0.95	Paradkar et al. 2003
	FT-MIR (region 800–1200 cm^{-1})	6	2.091	0.97	

Abbreviations: SECV, standard error cross validation; FT, Fourier transform; IR, infrared; NIR, near-infrared; MIR, mid-infrared.

FTIR spectroscopic analysis has shown potential to determine lard adulteration. Syahariza et al. (2005) evaluated lard adulteration in shortening at levels of 0%–100% combined with PLSR models in the regions 1,117–1,097 cm^{-1} and 990–950 cm^{-1}, producing a model with an R^2 = 0.9790 and a standard error of calibration of 1.75. Also, ATR-IR combined with PLSR regression was able to detect cocoa butter spiked with lard (0%–15%) with an R^2 = 0.99 and a standard error of 1.305 (Che Man et al. 2005). Adulteration of olive oil dates back at least to the time of the Roman Empire (Ulberth & Buchgraber 2000). Applying spectroscopy for olive oil authentication emerged in the mid-1990s, and a considerable amount of work has been devoted to using the technique for detection of extra virgin olive oil (EVOO) adulteration, specifically for improving limits of detection. The band at 3,009 cm^{-1} has been identified for quantification of adulteration because the height of this band for EVOO is smaller than it is for other types of oils and changes according to the extent of adulteration. A high correlation coefficient (above 0.99) was established with a detection limit of approximately 6% (Vlachos et al. 2006). Wavelet compression prior to PCA produces a detection limit of 5% for binary oil mixtures (Gurdeniz & Ozen 2009). EVOO adulteration with palm oil can be detected using the first derivative of the FTIR spectra in the fingerprint region and PLSR (R^2 = 0.999, SECV = 0.285) (Rohman & Che Man 2010). FTIR spectra reflect different substitution patterns of triglycerides, differences in chain length of acyl moieties, and differing degrees of unsaturation (Guillen & Cabo 1997).

EVOO has also been the subject of studies to confirm geographical origin claims. The European Union supplies EVOO manufacturers with labels assigning protected designation of origin.

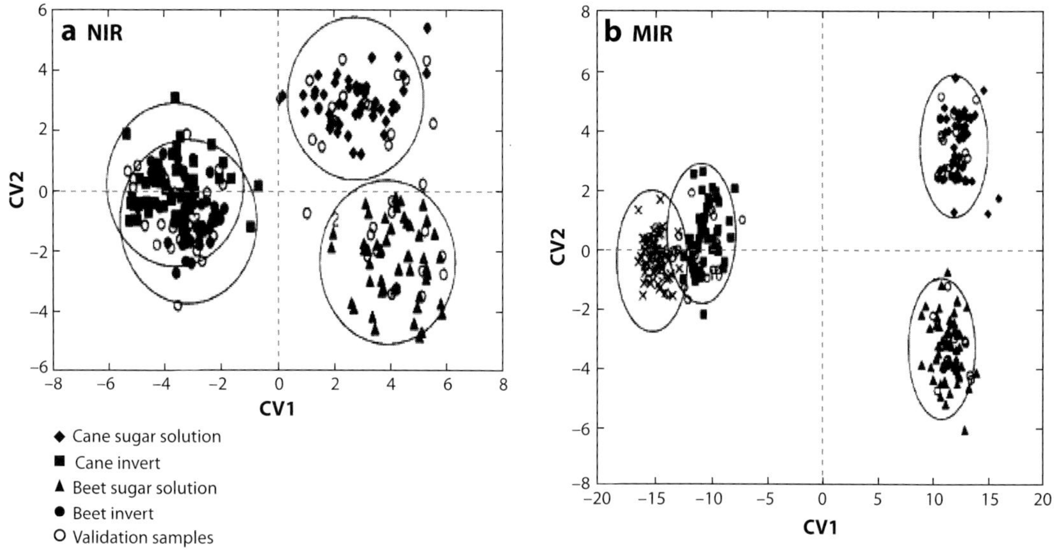

Figure 2

Classification of adulterants in maple syrup by (*a*) near-infrared (NIR) and (*b*) mid-infrared (MIR) using partial least squares (PLS)/canonical variate analysis (CVA) (Paradkar et al. 2003).

Nuclear magnetic resonance (NMR) has been used to classify samples with up to 90% success, but this method is expensive and time consuming. Mean-centered first and second derivative spectra combined with PLSR correctly classified 80% of samples on the basis of origin being ideal for screening because of the high throughput of the method (Hennessy et al. 2009).

Traditional methods for monitoring milk authenticity rely on wet chemistry to determine the amount of a marker compound in a suspect material and a subsequent comparison of values obtained with those from an equivalent material (Karoui & De Baerdemaeker 2007). Woodcock et al. (2008) reviewed the current state of development of both NIR and MIR in cheese authenticity with ATR-IR spectroscopy being widely employed. These techniques have the potential to assist food processors to adhere to increasingly stringent food authenticity legislation. Picque et al. (2002) reported the discrimination of Emmental cheeses from different regions by IR spectroscopy. Data from ATR-IR spectroscopy of a water-soluble fraction enabled the classification of the different types of Emmental cheeses with 78% accuracy, whereas 87% accuracy was obtained by using transmission spectra of dried extracts. The authors highlighted the ability of IR to discriminate according to the source of the milk used for the manufacturing process. In another study, Pillonel et al. (2002) reported the results of a broad screening test into the authenticity of Emmental cheese and its geographic traceability. NIR diffuse reflectance gave 100% discrimination by grouping into the six regions of cheese origin, whereas MIR transmittance achieved 100% correct classification when comparing Switzerland with the other regions pooled as one group.

The standard of identity of butter requires that the product contain no vegetable oil. Therefore, the addition of margarine violates this claim. Current techniques for authenticating butter include gas chromatography (GC), mass spectrometry (MS), NMR, and ultraviolet-visible (UV/Vis) spectroscopy. These methods have detection limits of 2%–5%, but they are expensive and time consuming. IR spectroscopy combined with PLSR-generated models that estimated adulteration of butter with levels of margarine ranging from 0% to 100% v/v with an $R^2 > 0.99$ and SECV < 1.2%. Development of chemometric models using smaller ranges of adulteration levels (0%–5%, 0%–25%, and 20%–60%) improved the robustness of the models (Koca et al. 2010).

APPLICATIONS OF FTIR FOR DETECTION OF POTENTIALLY HARMFUL ADULTERANTS

Food products are most commonly adulterated with materials that are of a lower quality and, as a result, are typically less expensive. A smaller segment of adulteration includes products contaminated with potentially harmful compounds. This includes compounds that unintentionally occur as a result of a production process (such as *trans* fats and acrylamide) and intentional chemical contaminants (e.g., melamine). Advances in FTIR spectroscopic instrumentation and multivariate data analysis techniques show significant potential for determining changes in food composition that may be indicative of the addition of harmful extraneous material.

The *trans*-fat content of food has recently been identified as a health concern for the public. Although small amounts of *trans* fats are found naturally in dairy and meat products, the major source is partially hydrogenated vegetable oils used in commercial food products (Mossoba et al. 2009). The hydrogenation process is beneficial in that it enables oils that are low in saturated fat to be used in place of saturated fats, but partial hydrogenation produces *trans* fats. *Trans*-fatty acids have been documented to increase low density lipoprotein (LDL) cholesterol and lower high density lipoprotein (HDL), increasing the risk for coronary heart disease (McCarthy et al. 2008). Beginning in 2006, the amount of *trans* fat present in food and dietary supplements is required on the nutrition label and is to be expressed as grams/serving (Mossoba et al. 2009). Amounts below 0.5 g are recorded as *trans* free. It is the FDA's policy that it is the manufacturer's responsibility to ensure the validity of a product's stated nutrition information. Further, they define a product as misbranded if the amount of *trans* fat found during FDA analysis is greater than 120% of what is presented on the nutrition label (Mossoba et al. 2009). The basic procedure for analysis via GC involves extracting the fat, preparing volatile fatty acid methyl ester (FAME) derivatives, resolving the mixture with a column that is capable of separating all the FAME components, summing all individual *trans* FAME, correcting the detector's response, and finally converting to triacylglycerol equivalents (Mossoba et al. 2009). Because each step needs to be quantitative or representative, these methods require highly trained technicians.

IR methods have been used since the 1950s to determine the amount of isolated *trans* double bonds in fats and oils. This method is based on the IR band at 966 cm^{-1} corresponding to CH-out-of-plane deformation (**Figure 3*a***, see color insert). This band is unique to isolated *trans* double bonds. The challenge with using this technique includes resolving the *trans* band from those due to conjugated double bonds or due to interferences attributed to other functional groups. It has been found that fats and oils with low levels of *trans*-fatty acids are affected the most by overlapping bands. The *trans* band is found on an elevated sloping baseline, decreasing the accuracy of area or height measurements as the level of *trans* fat decreases (Mossoba et al. 2009). Two ATR-FTIR official methods (AOCS Cd 14d-99 and AOAC method 2000.10) incorporate a background of *trans* fat–free oil to flatten the sloping baseline. Reference standards are created using trielaidin added to a *trans*-free reference oil. The standards are scanned on a 65°C single or multibounce ATR cell to generate a calibration curve. Using the curve, unknown *trans* levels, expressed as percent of total fat, can be calculated. It should be noted that using reference oil that differs considerably from the composition of the unknown sample can have an adverse affect on the accuracy of the model, especially below 5% total fat (Mossoba et al. 2009). A new negative second derivative ATR-FTIR method claims to improve accuracy and precision of quantitating levels of *trans* fat in a food sample and is currently being validated by an international study. This method measures the height of the negative second derivative of *trans* absorption relative to air (**Figure 3*b***). Reference standards are generated from *trans* monoene trielaidin diluted in tripalmitin. This rapid method is ideal for determining total *trans* content that is needed for current labeling requirements (Mossoba et al. 2009).

NIR spectroscopy can also be used to determine *trans* content in edible fats and oils. Li et al. (1999, 2000a,b) and Cox et al. (2000) have done extensive work on the use of FT-NIR for the rapid determination of important quality parameters of fats and oils such as peroxide value, iodine value, *cis* and *trans* content, and saponification number. Li et al. (2000c) developed a PLS calibration model from FT-NIR spectra for the rapid determination of *trans* fats and oils. The calibration model was correlated to *trans* values determined by using MIR with single-bounce IR horizontal attenuated total reflectance (IR-HATR) reference method (American Oil Chemist's Society official method). There was no discernible *trans* absorption band in the FT-NIR spectrum as compared with the strong *trans* signal at 966 cm^{-1} in the MIR spectrum. Nevertheless, the PLS-FT-NIR model was able to estimate the *trans* content of edible oils. By using a training set that included a wide variety of oil types, the calibration model predicted the *trans* content with an accuracy of $\pm 1.1\%$. It was possible to obtain more accurate and reproducible predictions ($\pm 0.5\%$) by calibrating a more limited training set that had specific characteristics. It is important to note that the reproducibility of the IR-HATR method is $\pm 0.4\%$. The product-specific calibration produced serious predictive errors when nonrepresentative samples were analyzed (Li et al. 2002b).

Acrylamide is a Maillard reaction product formed during baking, frying, and roasting foods such as potatoes and has been identified as a potential carcinogen. Standard procedures for acrylamide determination are based on chromatography and mass spectroscopy that are challenging to implement at manufacturing facilities for routine analysis. One acrylamide precursor, asparagine, is present in high levels in potatoes. High temperature/short time frying results in potato chips having one of the highest known levels of acrylamide (Segtnan et al. 2006). NIR spectral analysis has focused on the bands originating from carbohydrates, with a starch band at 1,934 nm found to be most significant. PLSR models using the spectra of ground chips in the region 400–2,498 nm correlated against predetermined quantities of acrylamide ($R^2 = 0.95$, prediction error of 256.6 $\mu g\ kg^{-1}$). NIR spectral models are accurate enough for screening of acrylamide contents in processed potato chips (Segtnan et al. 2006). However, the method needs to be tested and calibrated for each specific production process. Evaluation of the feasibility of using online monitoring of acrylamide in chips using NIR gave a model with a $R^2 = 0.83$ and prediction error of 266 μg kg^{-1}. The lower correlation was attributed to lower spectral resolution of the online instrument. Online NIR monitoring could be used to separate samples with very high levels of acrylamide from samples with average to low content (Pedreschi et al. 2010).

FT-NIR and multivariate analysis for the detection of food tampering with threat agents (Rodriguez-Saona et al. 2000) were developed and evaluated for the rapid detection of castor bean meal (CBM). The seeds of the castor plant (*Ricinus comunis*) contain the extremely toxic protein ricin that specifically and irreversibly inactivates eukaryotic ribosomes, promoting cell death by inhibiting protein synthesis. CBM is a byproduct of the production of castor oil and is readily available and could easily be used to deliberately contaminate the food supply, thus making it a potential threat (Wellner et al. 1995). Analysis of spiked food matrices (bleached flour, wheat flour, and blueberry pancake mix) with different CBM (0.5%–8% w/w) levels by diffuse reflectance FT-NIR predicted the CBM contamination with standard error of cross-validation (SECV) <0.6% and coefficient of correlation greater than 94%. Prediction of the CBM content by the calibration models was largely influenced by the spectral bands characteristic of amides

(4,880 and 4,555 cm^{-1}) and lipids (5,800, 5,685, 4,340, and 4,261 cm^{-1}). PLSR models accurately predicted the content of CBM in contaminated samples with no false positives for samples containing the placebo contaminants (egg white, soybean meal, tofu, and infant formula) (Rodriguez-Saona et al. 2000).

The rapid determination of tetracycline in milk was evaluated by FT-NIR spectroscopy (Sivakesava & Irudayaraj 2002b). Tetracycline antibiotics are widely used in animal husbandry for treatment of bacterial infections, suggesting a potential for tetracycline residues to be transferred to milk. The FDA has established a tolerance of 300 ppb for the sum of residues of tetracyclines in milk. The tetracycline concentration (ppb) range used in the calibration model drastically affected the performance of the chemometric models. Thus, by using separate ranges, the accuracy and predictive ability of the calibration model was significantly improved. Models developed by FT-MIR showed slightly better performance (lower SEP and higher R^2) than FT-NIR models but the repeatability of the FT-NIR was better than the FT-MIR procedure (Sivakesava & Irudayaraj 2002b). Similarly, Schulz et al. (2003) reported the reliable prediction of low concentrations of two carcinogenic compounds: methyleugenol (range 2–235 μg 100 g^{-1}) and estragole (range 34–138 μg 100 g^{-1}) in air-dried basil leaves by PLS calibration model based on NIR spectral data. The performance of the NIR calibration models gave values of SECV of 19.1 and 12.8 μg 100 g^{-1} and coefficient of correlation of 0.95 and 0.89 for methyleugenol and estragole, respectively.

Melamine (2,4,6-triamino-1,3,5-triazine) is used industrially in the production of plastics and glue, and also as a plant fertilizer. The compound's high nitrogen content increases the apparent protein content as measured by traditional protein analysis methods, which measure total nitrogen content as an indicator of protein levels. This makes melamine a potential adulterant in protein-rich foods such as milk and infant formula. Melamine adulteration has been reported in these products as well as in pet food, candy, coffee drinks, and others. Contaminated milk in China was likely the source of 300,000 cases of renal complications in children and at least six deaths (Mauer et al. 2009). Currently, the FDA uses an liquid chromatography–mass spectrometry (LC-MS)/MS method to detect melamine in infant formula. The detection limit for this method is 250 ppb, but it is time consuming and labor intensive. As a result, it is not efficient for screening large numbers of samples. Detection methods in other food products are also time consuming with varying levels of detection (Mauer et al. 2009).

NIR and MIR combined with multivariate statistical analysis has allowed classification of adulterated and unadulterated infant formulas with high confidence. FTIR-ATR analysis was done using the regions 3,330–2,993 cm^{-1} and 1,321–983 cm^{-1}, corresponding to the stretching vibration of amino groups and the fingerprint region generating a PLSR model with an $R^2 \geq 0.95$ and RMSECV ≤ 1. The NIR model (12,497–6,098 cm^{-1} and 5,450–4,248 cm^{-1}) performed slightly better based on a unique signal with an $R^2 = 0.999$ and RMSECV $= 0.62$ (Mauer et al. 2009). The FDA has established a threshold of 1 ppm for melamine in infant formula and 2.5 ppm in other foods. IR spectroscopy combined with chemometrics has been reported as a rapid method for detecting melamine in milk powder with detection limits of ~75–100 ppm (FOSS 2009). The technique has potential for use as a tool for screening adulteration in milk with unsuspected adulterants or contaminants at detection levels of 250–500 ppm (FOSS 2009). Factorization analyses of NIR and MIR spectra were able to distinguish between adulterated (1 ppm) and unadulterated infant formula samples (Mauer et al. 2009). NIR and FTIR methods for melamine detection are rapid and sensitive but are dependent on the food matrix, requiring new calibration models for different brands of infant formula or food products (Mauer et al. 2009).

A quality issue was identified by a dairy company regarding the safety of their products. Using a technique very similar to that used for melamine detection, a methodology was developed for the identification and quantitation of a foreign material found in the milk intake filter. The IR spectra of the foreign material was collected (**Figure 4**, see color insert) and matched with commercial block rodent bait TOM CAT®, providing identical IR absorption patterns. Once the foreign material had been identified, the concern shifted to the quality of the milk. The dairy company was interested in evaluating milk samples for possible contamination with the foreign material. A PLSR calibration model was developed by spiking uncontaminated milk with known levels of the bait (100–2,400 ppb), which gave performance statistics with $R^2 > 0.99$ and SECV of ~100 ppb (7 factors) in spiked milk samples at 850–1,500 cm^{-1}, showing potential for the estimation of the bait contaminant levels in few minutes (~2 min). Classification of potential contamination of the milk samples with the bait showed detection limits <1.2 ppm of the bait (L.E. Rodriguez-Saona, unpublished observations).

The development of IR microspectroscopy (IRMS) has allowed for the acquisition of spectra from a sample area measuring only a few microns (Baeten & Dardenne 2002). IRMS combines two analytical technologies for biological analysis by coupling an infinity-corrected microscope to a high-performance IR spectrometer equipped with a mercury-cadmium-telluride (MCT) detector that will produce a spectrum with a noise level 10 to 100 times lower than the noise from the commonly used deuterated triglycine sulfate (DTGS) detector. IRMS significantly improves the sensitivity, reproducibility, differentiation, and speed capabilities of IR spectroscopy and has permitted the acquisition of spectra from samples as small as 100 pg (10^{-10} g), promoting its application in the medical and biological fields (Ozen et al. 2003). IRMS provides capabilities for high-throughput screening of chemical contaminants and the ability to resolve spectral profiles within desired regions of the target. The new generation of powerful MIR spectroscopic chemical imaging techniques combines step-scan Fourier transform Michelson interferometry with indium antimonide focal-plane array (FPA) image detection. The IR focal-plane array detector provides an instrumental multiplex/multichannel advantage, enabling spectra at all pixels to be collected simultaneously, while the interferometer portion of the system allows all the spectral frequencies to be measured concurrently. This high-definition technique represents the future of IR chemical imaging analysis, which combines the capability of spectroscopy for molecular analysis with the power of visualization. IR imaging allows the precise characterization of the chemical composition, domain structure, and chemical architecture of a variety of substances, information often crucial to the understanding of complex samples (Diem 1993).

CONCLUSION

Vibrational spectroscopic methods such as FT-NIR and FT-MIR spectroscopy are emerging as powerful techniques in monitoring adulteration and authenticity of foods. In recent years, the food industry and consumers have experienced several new or unsuspected contamination problems such as acrylamide, organic pollutants, Sudan dyes, and recently melamine in dairy products. Analysis of chemical food contaminants and toxins requires the development and validation of analytical methods and their implementation as quality control programs and risk management systems by food producers and authorities. This review shows the ability of IR combined with chemometrics to achieve resolution of unique spectral markers for differentiation (unexpected agents) and quantitation (identified agent) of food contaminants. FTIR spectroscopy is a well-established analytical technique for rapid, high-throughput, nondestructive analysis of a wide range of sample types, providing a fingerprint characteristic of chemical or biochemical substances present in the sample. Advances in FTIR instrumentation and multivariate techniques have shown potential for analysis of complex multispectral information for the discrimination, classification, quantification, and identification of biological systems.

The ability of IR spectroscopy to reveal qualitative and quantitative characteristics about the nature of chemicals, their structure, interactions, and molecular environments provide unparalleled capabilities for detection of contaminants and adulterants in foods. Advantages of approaches based on vibrational spectroscopy include low operational cost, small size, compactness, robustness, high throughput, ease of use, and minimum background training to operate. Thus, FTIR spectroscopy can provide the food industry with rapid and specific tools for analysis of food chemical contaminants and for the reliable assessment of quality and safety. It will enable the food manufacturer to rapidly evaluate the quality of their food, allowing for timely correction measures during manufacture.

DISCLOSURE STATEMENT

The authors are not aware of any affiliations, memberships, funding, or financial holdings that might be perceived as affecting the objectivity of this review.

LITERATURE CITED

Alfaro G, Meurens M, Birth GS. 1990. Liquid analysis by dry extract near-infrared reflectance on fiberglass. *Appl. Spectrosc.* 44:979–86

Barton FE II. 2002. Theory and principles of near infrared spectroscopy. *NIR Spectrosc.* 14(1):2–18

Baeten V, Dardenne P. 2002. Spectroscopy: developments in instrumentation and analysis. *Grasas Aceites* 53:45–63

Chalmers JM, Griffiths PR. 2001. *Handbook of Vibrational Spectroscopy*. Chichester, UK: Wiley

Che Man YB, Syahariza ZA, Mirghani MES, Jinap S, Bakar J. 2005. Analysis of potential lard adulteration in chocolate and chocolate products using Fourier transform infrared spectroscopy. *Food Chem.* 90:815–19

Contal L, Leon V, Downey G. 2002. Detection and quantification of apple adulteration in strawberry and raspberry purees using visible and near infrared spectroscopy. *J. Near Infrared Spectrosc.* 10(4):289–99

Cox R, Lebrasseur J, Michiels E, Buijs H, Li H, et al. 2000. Determination of iodine value with a Fourier transform-near infrared based global calibration using disposable vials: an international collaborative study. *J. Am. Oil Chem. Soc.* 77(12):1229–34

Cozzolino D, Holdstock M, Dambergs RG, Cynkar WU, Smith PA. 2009. Mid infrared spectroscopy and multivariate analysis: a tool to discriminate between organic and nonorganic wines grown in Australia. *Food Chem.* 116:761–65

Diem M. 1993. *Introduction to Modern Vibrational Spectroscopy*. New York: Wiley

Dvash L, Afik O, Shafir S, Schaffer A, Yeselson Y, et al. 2002. Determination by near-infrared spectroscopy of perseitol used as a marker for the botanical origin of avocado (*Persea Americana* Mill.) honey. *J. Agric. Food. Chem.* 50:5283–87

Fischer WB, Eysel HH, Nielsen OF, Bertie JE. 1994. Corrections to the baseline distortions in the OH-stretch region of aqueous solutions. *Appl. Spectrosc.* 48:107–12

FOSS. 2009. *Abnormal spectrum screening module (ASM)*. **http://www.foss.dk/Solutions/ProductsDirect/MilkoScanftplus/asm.aspx**

Fugel R, Carle R, Schieber A. 2005. Quality and authenticity control of fruit purees, fruit preparations and jams: a review. *Trends Food Sci. Technol.* 16:433–41

Guillen M, Cabo N. 1997. Infrared spectroscopy in the study of edible oils and fats. *J. Sci. Food Agric.* 75(1):1–11

Gurdeniz G, Ozen B. 2009. Detection of adulteration of extra virgin olive oil by chemometric analysis of mid-infrared spectral data. *Food Chem.* 116:519–25

Hall JW, Valentine KG, Lefrant S, Mevellec JY, Mulazzi E. 1996. Spectroscopic properties of polyacetylenes synthesized via three modifications of Ziegler-Natta catalytic system. *Synth. Met.* 79:183–88

He J, Rodriguez-Saona LE, Giusti MM. 2007. Midinfrared spectroscopy for juice authentication- rapid differentiation of commercial juices. *J. Agric. Food Chem.* 55:4443–52

Hennessy S, Downey G, O'Donnell CP. 2009. Confirmation of food origin claims by Fourier transform infrared spectroscopy and chemometrics: extra virgin olive oil from Liguria. *J. Agric. Food Chem.* 57:1735–41

Iglesias MT. 2006. Quantitative analysis of physical and chemical measurands in honey by mid-infrared spectroscopy. *Eur. Food Res. Technol.* 223:22–35

Karoui R, De Baerdemaeker J. 2007. A review of the analytical methods coupled with chemometric tools for the determination of the quality and identity of dairy products. *Food Chem.* 102:621–40

Kasemsumran S, Thanapase W, Kiatsoonthon A. 2007. Feasability of near-infrared spectroscopy to detect and quantify adulterants in cow milk. *Anal. Sci.* 23:907–10

Kelly J, Downey G. 2005. Detection of sugar adulterants in apple juice using Fourier-transform infrared spectroscopy and chemometrics. *J. Agric. Food Chem.* 53(9):3281–86

Kelly J, Petisco C, Downey G. 2006. Application of Fourier transform midinfrared spectroscopy to the discrimination between Irish artisanal honey and such honey adulterated with various sugar syrups. *J. Agric. Food Chem.* 54:6166–71

Koca N, Kocaoglu-Vurma NA, Harper WJ, Rodriguez-Saona LE. 2010. Application of temperature-controlled attenuated total reflectance-mid-infared (ATR-MIR) spectroscopy for rapid estimation of butter adulteration. *Food Chem.* 121:778–82

Laasonen M, Harmia-Pulkkinen T, Simard CL, Michiels E, Rasanen M, Vuorela H. 2002a. Fast identification of *Echinacea purpurea* dried roots using near-infrared spectroscopy. *Anal. Chem.* 74:2493–99

Laasonen M, Wennberg T, Harmia-Pulkkinen T, Vuorela H. 2002b. Simultaneous analysis of alkamides and caffeic acid derivatives for the identification of *Echinacea purpurea*, *Echinacea angustifolia*, *Echinacea pallida* and *Parthenium integrifolium* roots. *Planta Med.* 68(6):572–74

Li H, van de Voort FR, Ismail AA, Cox R. 2000a. Determination of peroxide value by Fourier transform near infrared spectroscopy. *J. Am. Oil Chem. Soc.* 77(2):137–42

Li H, van de Voort FR, Sedman J, Ismail AA. 1999. Rapid determination of *cis* and *trans* content, iodine value, and saponification number of edible oils by Fourier transform near-infrared spectroscopy. *J. Am. Oil Chem. Soc.* 76(4):491–97

Li H, van de Voort FR, Sedman J, Ismail AA, Cox R, et al. 2000b. Discrimination of edible oil products and quantitative determination of their iodine value by Fourier transform near infrared spectroscopy. *J. Am. Oil Chem. Soc.* 77(1):29–36

Li H, van de Voort FR, Sedman J, Ismail AA, Cox R. 2000c. *Trans* determination of edible oils by Fourier transform near-infrared spectroscopy. *J. Am. Oil Chem. Soc.* 77(10):1061–67

Li W, Goovaerts P, Meurens MJ. 1996. Quantitative analysis of individual sugars and acids in orange juices by near-infrared spectroscopy of dry extract. *Agric. Food Chem.* 44(8):979–86

Maraboli A, Cattaneo P, Maria T, Giangiacomo R. 2002. Detection of vegetable proteins from soy, pea, and wheat isolates in milk powder by near infrared spectroscopy. *J. Near Infrared Spectrosc.* 10(1):63–69

Markovich RJ. 1991. Introduction to Fourier transform infrared spectroscopy and applications in the pharmaceutical sciences. *Pharm. Res.* 8(6):663–75

Mauer L, Chernyshova AA, Hiatt A, Deering A, Davis R. 2009. Melamine detection in infant formula powder using near- and mid-infrared spectroscopy. *J. Agric. Food Chem.* 57:3974–80

McCarthy J, Barr D, Sinclair A. 2008. Determination of *trans* fatty acid levels by FTIR in processed foods in Australia. *Asia Pac. J. Clin. Nutr.* 17(3):391–96

Mossoba MM, Moss J, Kramer JKG. 2009. Trans-fat labeling and levels in U.S. foods: assessment of chromatographic and infrared spectroscopic techniques for regulatory compliance. *J. Am. Oil Chem. Soc.* 92(5):1284–300

Osborne BG. 2000. *Near-Infrared Spectroscopy in Food Analysis*. Chichester, UK: Wiley

Ozen B, Weiss I, Mauer L. 2003. Dietary supplement oil classification and detection of adulteration using Fourier transform infrared spectroscopy. *J. Agric. Food Chem.* 51:5871–76

Paradkar MM, Irudayaraj J. 2002a. Determination of cholesterol in dairy products using infrared techniques 1. FTIR spectroscopy. *Int. J. Dairy Technol.* 55(3):127–32

Paradkar MM, Irudayaraj J. 2002b. Determination of cholesterol in dairy products using infrared techniques 2. FT-NIR method. *Int. J. Dairy Technol.* 55(3):133–38

Paradkar MM, Sivakesava S, Irudayaraj J. 2003. Discrimination and classification of adulterants in maple syrup with the use of infrared spectroscopic techniques. *J. Sci. Food Agric.* 83:714–21

Pare JRJ, Belanger JMR, eds. 1997. *Instrumental Methods in Food Analysis.* New York: Elsevier

Pedreschi F, Segtnan VH, Knutsen SH. 2010. On-line monitoring of fat, dry matter and acrylamide contents in potato chips using near infrared interactance and visual reflectance. *Food Chem.* 121:616–20

Perez DP, Sanchez MT, Cano G, Garrido A. 2001. Authentication of green asparagus varieties by near-infrared reflectance spectroscopy. *J. Food Sci.* 66(2):323–27

PerkinElmer. 2004. *ATR accessories. An overview.* **http://las.perkinelmer.com/Content/technicalinfo/tch_atraccessories.pdf**

Picque D, Cattenoz T, Corrieu G. 2002. Discrimination of Emmental cheeses by infrared spectroscopy. *Milchwiss. Milk Sci. Int.* 57:202–4

Pike Technol. 2010. *ATR theory and applications.* **http://www.piketech.com/technical/application-pdfs/ATR_Theory_andApplication.pdf#zoom=100%**

Pillonel L, Badertscher R, Butikofer U, Casey M, Dalla Torre M, et al. 2002. Analytical methods for the determination of the geographic origin of Emmentaler cheese. Main framework of the project; chemical, biochemical, microbiological, color and sensory analyses. *Eur. Food Res. Technol.* 215(3):260–70

Pontes MJC, Santos SRB, Araujo MCU, Almeida LF, Lima RAC, et al. 2006. Classification of distilled alcoholic beverages and verification of adulteration by near infrared spectrometry. *Food Res. Int.* 39:182–89

Robinson JW. 1991. *Practical Handbook of Spectroscopy.* Boca Raton, FL: CRC Press

Rodriguez-Saona LE, Fry FS, Calvey EM. 2000. Use of Fourier transform near-infrared reflectance spectroscopy for rapid quantification of castor bean meal in a selection of flour-based products. *J. Agric. Food. Chem.* 48:5169–77

Rodriguez-Saona LE, Fry FS, McLaughlin MA, Calvey EM. 2001. Rapid analysis of sugars in fruit juices by FT-NIR spectroscopy. *Carbohydr. Res.* 336:63–74

Rohman A, Che Man YB. 2010. FTIR spectroscopy combined with chemometrics for analysis of lard in the mixtures with body fats of lamb, cow, and chicken. *Int. Food Res. J.* 17:519–26

Schulz H, Engelhardt UH, Wegent A, Drews HH, Lapczynski SJ. 1999. Application of near-infrared reflectance spectroscopy to the simultaneous prediction of alkaloids and phenolic substances in green tea leaves. *J. Agric. Food Chem.* 47:5064–67

Schulz H, Schrader B, Quilitzsch R, Pfeffer S, Kruger H. 2003. Rapid classification of basil chemotypes by various vibrational spectroscopy methods. *J. Agric. Food. Chem.* 51:2475–81

Schulz H, Schrader B, Quilitzsch R, Steuer B. 2002. Quantitative analysis of various citrus oils by ATR/FT-IR and NIR-FT Raman spectroscopy. *Appl. Spectrosc.* 56:117–24

Segtnan VH, Isaksson T. 2000. Evaluating near infrared techniques for quantitative analysis of carbohydrates in fruit juice model systems. *J. Near Infrared Spectrosc.* 8:109–16

Segtnan VH, Kita A, Mielnik M, Jorgensen K, Knutsen SH. 2006. Screening of acrylamide contents in potato crisps using process variable settings and near infrared spectroscopy. *Mol. Nutr. Food Res.* 50:811–17

Shenk JS, Workman JJ, Weterhans MO. 2001. Application of NIRS to agricultural products. In *Handbook of Near-Infrared Analysis*, ed. DA Burns, EW Ciurczak, 16:419–74. New York: Marcel Dekker

Sielsler HW, Ozaki Y, Kawata S, Heise HM. 2002. *Near-Infrared Spectroscopy: Principles, Instruments, Applications.* New York: Wiley

Sivakesava S, Irudayaraj J. 2002a. Classification of simple and complex sugar adulterants in honey by mid-infrared spectroscopy. *Int. J. Food Sci. Technol.* 37:351–60

Sivakesava S, Irudayaraj J. 2002b. Rapid determination of tetracycline in milk by FT-MIR and FT-NIR spectroscopy. *J. Dairy Sci.* 85:487–93

Steuer B, Schulz H, Lager E. 2001. Classification and analysis of citrus oils by NIR spectroscopy. *Food Chem.* 72:113–17

Syahariza ZA, Che Man YB, Selamat J, Bakar J. 2005. Detection of lard adulteration in cake formulation by Fourier transform infared (FTIR) spectroscopy. *Food Chem.* 92:365–71

Twomey M, Downey G, McNulty PB. 1995. The potential of NIR spectroscopy for the detection of the adulteration of orange juice. *J. Sci. Food Agric.* 67:77–84

Ulberth F, Buchgraber M. 2000. Authenticity of fats and oils. *Eur. J. Lipid Sci. Technol.* 102:687–94

Vardin H, Tay A, Ozen B, Mauer L. 2008. Authentication of pomegranate juice concentrate using FTIR spectroscopy and chemometrics. *Food Chem.* 108:742–48

Vlachos N, Skopelitis Y, Psaroudaki M, Konstantinidou V, Chatzilazarou A, Tegou E. 2006. Applications of Fourier transform–infared spectroscopy to edible oils. *Anal. Chim. Acta* 573:549–65

Wellner RB, Hewetson JF, Ploi MA. 1995. Ricin: mechanism of action, detection, and intoxication. *J. Toxicol.-Toxin Rev.* 14(4):483–522

Whitacre E, Oliver J, van den Broek R, van Engelen P, Kremers B, et al. 2003. Predictive analysis of cocoa procyanidins using near-infrared spectroscopy techniques. *J. Food Sci.* 68(9):2618–22

Williams PC, Norris KH. 2001. *Near-Infrared Technology in the Agricultural and Food Industries*. St. Paul, MN: Am. Assoc. Cereal Chem.

Woodcock T, Fagan CC, O'Donnell CP, Downey G. 2008. Application of near and mid-infrared spectroscopy to determine cheese quality and authenticity. *Food Bioprocess Technol.* 1(2):117–19

Yang H, Irudayaraj J. 2001. Comparison of near-infrared, Fourier transform-infrared, and Fourier transform-Raman methods for determining olive pomace oil adulteration in extra virgin olive oil. *J. Am. Oil Chem Soc.* 78:889–95

Yang H, Irudayaraj J. 2002. Rapid determination of vitamin C by NIR, MIR and FT-Raman techniques. *J. Pharm. Pharmacol.* 54:1247–55